The Oxford Handbook of Behavioral Emergencies and Crises

OXFORD LIBRARY OF PSYCHOLOGY

Editor in Chief PETER E. NATHAN

The Oxford Handbook of Behavioral Emergencies and Crises

Edited by

Phillip M. Kleespies

OXFORD
UNIVERSITY PRESS

OXFORD
UNIVERSITY PRESS

Oxford University Press is a department of the University of Oxford. It furthers
the University's objective of excellence in research, scholarship, and education
by publishing worldwide. Oxford is a registered trade mark of Oxford University
Press in the UK and certain other countries.

Published in the United States of America by Oxford University Press
198 Madison Avenue, New York, NY 10016, United States of America.

© Oxford University Press 2017

Library of Congress Cataloging-in-Publication Data
Names: Kleespies, Phillip M., editor.
Title: The Oxford handbook of behavioral emergencies and crises / edited by
Phillip M. Kleespies.
Other titles: Handbook of behavioral emergencies and crises
Description: Oxford ; New York : Oxford University Press, [2017] | Series:
Oxford library of psychology | Includes bibliographical references and
index. | Description based on print version record and CIP data provided
by publisher; resource not viewed.
Identifiers: LCCN 2016020518 (print) | LCCN 2016018960 (ebook) |
ISBN 9780199352739 (ebook) | ISBN 9780199352722 (alk. paper)
Subjects: | MESH: Dangerous Behavior | Emergencies—psychology |
Psychotherapy—methods | Crisis Intervention—methods |
Suicide—prevention & control | Violence—prevention & control
Classification: LCC RC480.6 (print) | LCC RC480.6 (ebook) | NLM WM 401 | DDC
616.89/025—dc23
LC record available at https://lccn.loc.gov/2016020518

9 8 7 6 5 4 3 2 1

Printed by Sheridan Books, Inc., United States of America

SHORT CONTENTS

The *Oxford Library of Psychology*, a landmark series of handbooks, is published by Oxford University Press, one of the world's oldest and most highly respected publishers, with a tradition of publishing significant books in psychology. The ambitious goal of the *Oxford Library of Psychology* is nothing less than to span a vibrant, wide-ranging field and, in so doing, to fill a clear market need.

Encompassing a comprehensive set of handbooks, organized hierarchically, the *Library* incorporates volumes at different levels, each designed to meet a distinct need. At one level is a set of handbooks designed broadly to survey the major subfields of psychology; at another are numerous handbooks that cover important current focal research and scholarly areas of psychology in depth and detail. Planned as a reflection of the dynamism of psychology, the *Library* will grow and expand as psychology itself develops, thereby highlighting significant new research that will have an impact on the field. Adding to its accessibility and ease of use, the *Library* will be published in print and, later on, electronically.

The *Library* surveys psychology's principal subfields with a set of handbooks that capture the current status and future prospects of those major subdisciplines. This initial set includes handbooks of social and personality psychology, clinical psychology, counseling psychology, school psychology, educational psychology, industrial and organizational psychology, cognitive psychology, cognitive neuroscience, methods and measurements, history, neuropsychology, personality assessment, developmental psychology, and more. Each handbook undertakes to review one of psychology's major subdisciplines with breadth, comprehensiveness, and exemplary scholarship. In addition to these broadly conceived volumes, the *Library* also includes a large number of handbooks designed to explore in depth more specialized areas of scholarship and research, such as stress, health, and coping; anxiety and related disorders; cognitive development; or child and adolescent assessment. In contrast to the broad coverage of the subfield handbooks, each of these latter volumes focuses on an especially productive, more highly focused line of scholarship and research. Whether at the broadest or most specific level, however, all of the *Library* handbooks offer synthetic coverage that reviews and evaluates the relevant past and present research and anticipates research in the future. Each handbook in the *Library* includes introductory and concluding chapters written by its editor to provide a roadmap to the handbook's table of contents and to offer informed anticipations of significant future developments in that field.

An undertaking of this scope calls for handbook editors and chapter authors who are established scholars in the areas about which they write. Many of the nation's and world's most productive and best-respected psychologists have agreed to edit *Library* handbooks or write authoritative chapters in their areas of expertise.

For whom has the *Oxford Library of Psychology* been written? Because of its breadth, depth, and accessibility, the *Library* serves a diverse audience, including graduate students in psychology and their faculty mentors, scholars, researchers, and practitioners in psychology and related fields. Each will find in the *Library* the information they seek on the subfield or focal area of psychology in which they work or are interested.

Befitting its commitment to accessibility, each handbook includes a comprehensive index, as well as extensive references to help guide research. And because the *Library* was designed from its inception as an online as well as a print resource, its structure and contents will be readily and rationally searchable online. Furthermore, once the *Library* is released online, the handbooks will be regularly and thoroughly updated.

In summary, the *Oxford Library of Psychology* will grow organically to provide a thoroughly informed perspective on the field of psychology, one that reflects both psychology's dynamism and its increasing interdisciplinarity. Once published electronically, the *Library* is also destined to become a uniquely valuable interactive tool, with extended search and browsing capabilities. As you begin to consult this handbook, we sincerely hope you will share our enthusiasm for the more than 500-year tradition of Oxford University Press for excellence, innovation, and quality, as exemplified by the *Oxford Library of Psychology.*

Peter E. Nathan
Editor-in-Chief
Oxford Library of Psychology

ACKNOWLEDGMENTS

I would like to thank Oxford University Press for inviting me to edit this hand-book in their Oxford Library of Psychology series. It has been an opportunity to present the most comprehensive coverage, to date, of the area of psychological practice known as behavioral emergencies and crises.

As in all of my work in this area of practice, I am grateful to two groups in particular, the veterans who have sought emotional and mental assistance in the Department of Veterans Affairs Boston Healthcare System during times of great personal turmoil and the psychology interns and post-doctoral fellows whom I've had the privilege to train in emergency room and urgent care settings. As a clinical psychologist in public service, I have had the opportunity to work clinically with men and women in the VA Boston who have served their country, often at great cost to themselves, and who do not have the resources and support that many of us take for granted. I have learned to be a better clinician from observing and at-tempting to assist them in their struggles to obtain help, stabilize, and rehabilitate themselves. I have also learned a great deal from the questions and issues raised by the interns and fellows whom I have trained that became the impetus for my efforts to improve training in this area of practice.

I am, of course, indebted to the many authors and co-authors who have con-tributed chapters to this book. Evaluating and managing behavioral emergencies is a complicated and often anxiety-arousing area of service. It warrants having input from a range of mental health professionals who have specialized knowledge and skill in different facets of this work. I feel fortunate to have been able to as-semble an outstanding group of contributors with expertise in this field.

I am also grateful to the multidisciplinary staff from nursing, psychiatry, medi-cine, and social work who, over the years, have been good colleagues in emergency and urgent care services at VA Boston. Training interns and fellows in work with high-risk cases can put demands on the healthcare system. I wish to thank the staff for their patience and assistance in making this training possible.

Finally, I would like to thank my family, particularly my wife, Penelope, for her patience and support during the long hours required to write and edit this book; and thanks as well to my two grandsons, Declan and Otto, who lifted my spirits during times of stress.

ABOUT THE EDITOR

Phillip M. Kleespies

Phillip M. Kleespies, Ph.D., ABPP, has been a pioneer in developing the area of psychological practice known as behavioral emergencies. He was the founding president of the Section on Clinical Emergencies and Crises, a section of the APA Society of Clinical Psychology. His writings and teaching have emphasized acquiring a knowledge base as well as clinical skill in decision making with high-risk patients.

CONTRIBUTORS

Ron Acierno, Ph.D.
Medical University
of South Carolina
College of Nursing
Charleston, South Carolina

Christopher G. AhnAllen, Ph.D.
VA Boston Healthcare System
Harvard Medical School
Mental Health (Psychology) Service
Brockton, Massachusetts

Rebecca M. Ametrano, Ph.D.
VA Boston Healthcare System
Harvard Medical School
Mental Health (Psychology) Service
Boston, Massachusetts

Victoria Arango, Ph.D.
New York State Psychiatric Institute
Columbia University
Department of Psychiatry
New York, New York

Christal L. Badour, Ph.D.
Medical University
of South Carolina
Department of Psychiatry
and Behavioral Sciences
Charleston, South Carolina

Adam J. E. Blanchard, M.A.
Simon Fraser University
Department of Psychology
Burnaby, British Columbia
Canada

Bruce Bongar, Ph.D.
Palo Alto University
Dual Doctoral Program
in Psychology and Law
Palo Alto, California

Randy Borum, Psy.D.
University of South Florida
School of Information
Tampa, Florida

John C. Bradley, M.D.
VA Boston Healthcare System
Harvard Medical School
Department of Psychiatry
Boston, Massachusetts

Johann Brink, M.B., Ch.B., FRCPSC
University of British Columbia
Department of Psychiatry
Vancouver, British Columbia
Canada

Joyce Chu, Ph.D.
Palo Alto University
Clinical Psychology
Palo Alto, California

Emil F. Coccaro, M.D.
University of Chicago
Department of Psychiatry
and Behavioral Neuroscience
Chicago, Illinois

Glenn W. Currier, M.D., M.P.H.
University of South Florida
Morsani College of Medicine
Department of Psychiatry and Behavioral
Neurosciences
Tampa, Florida

Kevin S. Douglas, L.L.B., Ph.D.
Simon Fraser University
Department of Psychology
Burnaby, British Columbia
Canada

Paul R. Duberstein, Ph.D.
University of Rochester Medical Center
Departments of Psychiatry and Family
Medicine
Rochester, New York

Basak Efe, Ph.D.
Boston VA Health Care System
Harvard Medical School
Mental Health (Psychology) Service
Boston, Massachusetts

Eric B. Elbogen, Ph.D.
The University of North
    Carolina–Chapel Hill School
    of Medicine
Department of Psychiatry
Chapel Hill, North Carolina

Jennifer R. Fanning, Ph.D.
University of Chicago
Department of Psychiatry
    and Behavioral Neuroscience
Chicago, Illinois

Monica M. Fitzgerald, Ph.D.
University of Colorado at Boulder
Center for the Study and Prevention of
    Violence
Institute of Behavioral Science
Boulder, Colorado

Joseph Chad Franklin, Ph.D.
Harvard University
Psychology Department
Cambridge, Massachusetts

Karina S. Gilbert, Ph.D.
Boston VA Healthcare System
Boston University School of Medicine
Department of Psychiatry
Boston, Massachusetts

Peter Goldblum, Ph.D., M.P.H.
Palo Alto University
Sexual and Gender Identities Clinic
Palo Alto, California

Judelysse Gomez, Ph.D.
Alpert Medical School of Brown
    University
Department of Psychiatry and Human
    Behavior
Providence, Rhode Island

Robert Graziano, B.S.
The University of North
    Carolina–Chapel Hill
Department of Psychology and
    Neuroscience
Chapel Hill, North Carolina

Marnin J. Heisel, Ph.D., C.Psych.
The University of Western Ontario
Department of Psychiatry
London, Ontario
Canada

Melba A. Hernandez-Tejada, D.H.A.
Medical University of South Carolina
College of Nursing
Charleston, South Carolina

Marc Hillbrand, Ph.D.
Yale University School of Medicine
Department of Psychiatry
New Haven, Connecticut

Sharon Kelley, J.D., Ph.D.
University of Virginia
Institute of Law, Psychiatry, and
    Public Policy
Charlottesville, Virginia

Victoria Kendrick, M.S.
Palo Alto University
Department of Psychology
Palo Alto, California

Phillip M. Kleespies, Ph.D.
VA Boston Healthcare System
Boston University School
    of Medicine
Mental Health (Psychology) Service
Boston, Massachusetts

Reva B. Klein, M.D.
Boston University School
    of Medicine
Neurology Service
Boston, Massachusetts

Maxine H. Krengel, Ph.D.
Boston University School
    of Medicine
Department of Neurology
Boston, Massachusetts

Angela Kuemmel, Ph.D.
Louis Stokes VA Medical Center
Psychology Service/Spinal
    Cord Injury Service
Cleveland, Ohio

Adam D. LaMotte, B.A.
VA Boston Healthcare System
National Center for PTSD
Boston, Massachusetts

Tara L. Lauriat, Ph.D.
St. Elizabeth's Medical Center
Tufts University School
    of Medicine
Department of Psychiatry
Boston, Massachusetts

Dana Lockwood, J.D., M.S.
Palo Alto University
Dual Doctoral Program
  in Psychology and Law
Palo Alto, California

Sarah L. Logan, Ph.D., M.S., MSCR
Medical University of South Carolina
Department of Neurosciences
Charleston, South Carolina

Michael R. McCart, Ph.D.
Medical University
  of South Carolina
Department of Psychiatry
  and Behavioral Sciences
Charleston, South Carolina

Daniel C. Murrie, Ph.D.
University of Virginia
Institute of Law, Psychiatry, and
  Public Policy
Charlottesville, Virginia

Nyla Nasser, B.A.
University of Colorado
Department of Psychology
Boulder, Colorado

Tonia L. Nicholls, Ph.D.
University of British Columbia
Department of Psychiatry
Vancouver, British Columbia
Canada

Matthew K. Nock, Ph.D.
Harvard University
Department of Psychology
Cambridge, Massachusetts

Kimberly H. McManama O'Brien, Ph.D.
Simmons School of Social Work
Boston Children's Hospital/Harvard
  Medical School
Boston, Massachusetts

Wendy Packman, J.D., Ph.D.
Palo Alto University
Dual Doctoral Program in Psychology
  and Law
Palo Alto, California

Houri Parsi, J.D., Ph.D.
Palo Alto University
Dual Doctoral Program in Psychology
  and Law
Palo Alto, California

Samantha Pflum, M.S.
Palo Alto University
Clinical Psychology
Palo Alto, California

Megan L. Ranney, M.D., M.P.H.
Alpert Medical School of Brown University
Department of Emergency Medicine
Providence, Rhode Island

Heidi S. Resnick, Ph.D.
Medical University of South Carolina
National Crime Victims Research and
  Treatment Center
Department of Psychiatry and Behavioral
  Sciences
Charleston, South Carolina

Jacqueline A. Samson, Ph.D.
Harvard Medical School
Department of Psychiatry
Boston, Massachusetts

Catherine S. Shaffer, M.A.
Simon Fraser University
Department of Psychology
Burnaby, British Columbia
Canada

Anthony Spirito, Ph.D.
Alpert Medical School of Brown University
Department of Psychiatry and Human
  Behavior
Providence, Rhode Island

Stephen M. Strenges, M.A.
University of South Florida
Department of Psychiatry and Behavioral
  Neurosciences
Tampa, Florida

Glenn Sullivan, Ph.D.
Virginia Military Institute
Department of Psychology
Lexington, Virginia

Cynthia Cupit Swenson, Ph.D.
Medical University of South Carolina
Department of Psychiatry and Behavioral
  Sciences
Charleston, South Carolina

Casey T. Taft, Ph.D.
VA Boston Healthcare System
Boston University School of Medicine
National Center for PTSD
Boston, Massachusetts

Joseph Tomlins, M.S.
  Palo Alto University
  Department of Psychology
  Palo Alto, California
Mark D. Underwood, Ph.D.
  New York State Psychiatric Institute
  Columbia University
  Department of Psychiatry
  New York, New York
Kate L. Walsh, Ph.D.
  Columbia University
  Mailman School of Public Health
  Department of Epidemiology
  New York, New York
James L. Werth, Jr., Ph.D.
  Stone Mountain Health Services
  Jonesville, Virginia

Roberta F. White, Ph.D.
  Boston University School
    of Medicine
  Boston University School
    of Public Health
  Department of Environmental Health
  Boston, Massachusetts
Joah L. Williams, Ph.D.
  Medical University of South Carolina
  Department of Psychiatry
    and Behavioral Sciences
  Charleston, South Carolina
Kristyn Zajac, Ph.D.
  Medical University of South Carolina
  Department of Psychiatry
    and Behavioral Sciences
  Charleston, South Carolina

CONTENTS

A Framework for Practice and Training

Introduction

Phillip M. Kleespies

Abstract

This book is about behavioral emergencies and the association between interpersonal victimization and subsequent suicidality and/or risk for violence toward others. Section I focuses on the differences between behavioral crises and behavioral emergencies and presents an integrative approach to crisis intervention and emergency intervention. Section II discusses the evaluation of suicide risk, risk of violence, and risk of interpersonal victimization in children and adolescents. Sections III and IV explore behavioral emergencies with adults and the elderly, while Section V deals with certain conditions or behaviors that may either need to be differentiated from a behavioral emergency, or understood as relevant to possibly heightening risk. Section VI describes treatments for patients with recurrent or ongoing risks, and Section VII is devoted to legal, ethical, and psychological risks faced by clinicians who work with patients who might be at risk to themselves or others.

Key Words: behavioral emergencies, interpersonal victimization, suicidality, violence, behavioral crises, crisis intervention, emergency intervention, suicide risk, children, elderly

A 35-year-old man whom you have seen in therapy for depression and anxiety calls you and sounds very distraught. He reports that the preceding night he and his girlfriend had argued and he had grabbed her by the throat and pushed her against the wall. When she slumped to the floor, he came to his senses and felt remorseful about assaulting a woman, something that he had always said he would never do. Several weeks prior to this incident, the patient and his girlfriend had agreed that they would remain friends but that they would start dating other people. His girlfriend had become interested in another man and had started to see him. The patient, however, became intensely jealous. On a night when he knew that his girlfriend had been out with this other man, he had several drinks, took a handgun (which he had a license to carry), and went to her apartment to confront her. When she opened the door, the patient put the gun to his head and asked her if this was what she wanted; i.e., for

him to shoot himself. It was then that they argued and the incident noted above (in which he grabbed her) occurred. Although his girlfriend did not sustain any serious physical injury, he does not know if she will seek a restraining order. She told him that he needed to seek help. He fears that what he has done will result in the end of their relationship, and he doesn't know if he can tolerate that.[1]

If you are a mental health clinician, could an incident like this occur in your practice? For most active practitioners, it is probably not beyond belief, and they may have experienced incidents of their own that may have been equally or more intense. How you assess and respond to such a situation can have serious consequences for your patient, for others involved (such as the girlfriend in the case above), for you, and for your practice or clinic. What happens next between the clinician and the patient above could lead to what I have referred to as a *behavioral emergency* (Kleespies, 2009), a circumstance in which there is serious risk of harm to the patient and/or others, or it could lead to a de-escalation of these risks.

Historically, there has been a lack of agreement about how to define a mental health or behavioral emergency (Munizza et al., 1993). The term *emergency* itself can, of course, have different meanings. In a general sense, it may simply mean an unforeseen circumstance that calls for immediate action or intervention. For the purposes of this book, however, I consider it a *behavioral* emergency when a patient's or client's mental state is such that he or she is at imminent risk of behaving in a way that could result in serious harm or death to self or others.

We typically think of behavioral emergencies as intentional behaviors (as when someone attempts or commits suicide), but there can also be unintentional behavioral emergencies (as when someone's judgement is so impaired that he or she does not know to avoid oncoming traffic). Fortunately, there are only a few situations in clinical practice that meet the definition above. They include (1) suicidal states, (2) states of violence toward another person, (3) circumstances in which a relatively defenseless individual (such as a child or a person with a disability) is at risk of being victimized, and (4) conditions in which, as noted above, an individual's judgement is so impaired that he or she is unable to keep himself or herself safe from harm in the community.

In conceptualizing a *behavioral emergency* as I have above, it should be noted that there has been considerable discussion in the literature about the use of the term *imminent risk*. Typically, a situation of "imminent risk" has been taken to mean that there is risk that the patient will seriously harm or kill himself or herself or others "in the next few minutes, hours, or days" (Pokorny, 1983, p. 249). The discussion arises from the fact that, although there are many known risk factors for suicide, violence, and interpersonal victimization, there are no known *imminent* (or very short-term) risk factors. This state of affairs has resulted, in part, from the fact that patients or clients who are thought to be at imminent risk of harm to themselves or others must typically be excluded or removed from research studies for their own protection or the protection of others. Thus, Simon (2006) has maintained that the term *imminence* defies definition and that there are no validated short-term risk factors that can warn us about when or whether a patient will actually attempt or complete an act like suicide in the immediate future.

While Simon's argument has validity, there is also no doubt that behavioral emergencies occur. Sometimes patients attempt to commit suicide. Sometimes they become violent and attempt to kill others. Sometimes, in a manner of speaking, they "succeed." When, as a result of a mental disorder, a patient seems to be at some risk to self or others, the mental health clinician must attempt to estimate the risk and prevent the acts that appear to be imminent. He or she must decide if the situation is very likely an emergency that requires an emergency response. Ideally, such a decision is made after a thorough evaluation using the available empirical evidence to guide his or her judgement. It should be clear, however, that a statement that a patient is "at imminent risk of harm to self and/or others" is a clinical judgement and not a prediction. As discussed later in this book, the prediction of such low base-rate events as suicide or homicide eludes our current clinical capabilities.

Despite the fact that behavioral emergencies, cumulatively, occur with some frequency in mental health practice (see Chapter 34 of this volume for estimates of incidence), and despite the potentially serious consequences if these emergency situations are mismanaged, the training of most mental health practitioners in evaluating and managing patients or clients at risk continues to be limited. In terms of the assessment and management of suicidal patients, for example, the serious gaps in professional training have been clearly articulated in a report generated by a task force appointed by the American Association of Suicidology (Schmitz et al., 2012). There appear to be similar gaps in the training of psychologists for assessing and managing patients who are potentially violent (see, e.g., Gately & Stabb, 2005; and Guy, Brown, & Poelstra, 1990).

Given the need for improved training in dealing with behavioral emergencies, this book is intended as a handbook mental health clinicians can refer to when seeking information about the evaluation and management of such high-risk cases. In the section that follows, I will describe, for the interested reader, how this book is organized.

The Organizational Structure of This Handbook

There are four guiding ideas that have been influential in the writing and organization of this book. First, an emphasis has been placed on the interrelated aspects of the behavioral emergencies. By this I mean that, not only has there been an emphasis on risk factors that suicidal patients and patients who are potentially violent may simply have in common, but there has also been an emphasis on shared features or characteristics that may be more causatively related to both the potential for self-directed violence and that for other-directed violence. Moreover, there has also been an emphasis on the links between interpersonal victimization and subsequent suicidality and/or risk for violence toward others. Thus, for example, there is evidence that being physically or sexually abused in childhood contributes to one's risk of subsequent suicidal and/or violent behavior in adolescence and adulthood (Berliner & Elliott, 2002; Kolko, 2002).

Second, a lifespan orientation has been taken in this book. The risk of the behavioral emergencies can vary across the course of an individual's life. Van Dulmen et al. (2013) have provided evidence to that effect in their longitudinal study of associations between violence and suicidality from adolescence into young adulthood. This book, therefore, presents chapters on the evaluation and management of suicide risk, violence risk, and the risk of interpersonal victimization in youths, in adults, and in the elderly.

Third, as it is a handbook of behavioral emergencies and crises, a broad range of emergency and emergency-related topics and issues is presented. At its core, however, the book has been structured around a curriculum for acquiring a knowledge base in this area of practice, as described in previous publications (see, e.g., Kleespies, 2000).

Fourth, chapters in this book are evidence-based or evidence-informed. Statements about how to assess and manage behavioral emergencies have been grounded in the existing empirical evidence to the extent possible.

The book is divided into seven sections. In Section I, "A Framework for Practice and Training," there is this introductory chapter (Chapter 1) plus two other chapters. In Chapter 2, the author/editor examines the differences between behavioral crises and behavioral emergencies and presents an integrative approach to crisis intervention and emergency intervention. Such a perspective is one that can guide the clinician's thinking when attempting to evaluate and manage potential mental health emergencies. In this same chapter, he also presents evidence for viewing the behavioral emergencies (in particular, risk of suicide, risk of violence, and risk of interpersonal victimization) as, at least in certain respects, interrelated. From this perspective, he proposes that there are shared factors that contribute to the genesis of these high-risk behaviors or events. In Chapter 3

of this first section, the author/editor proposes that *naturalistic decision-making* models (as opposed to the *rational or normative* models typically used in scientific undertakings) are a better fit for the, at times, fast moving and dynamic decision-making necessitated by emergency conditions (Kleespies, 2014). He also advocates the use of a stress training model referred to as *Stress Exposure Training* (SET; Driskell & Johnston, 1998) as most appropriate for assisting clinicians in acquiring skill and competence in managing patients under the often stressful conditions that prevail when there is a risk of life-threatening behavior.

Section II, "Behavioral Emergencies with Youth," contains chapters that discuss the evaluation of suicide risk, risk of violence, and risk of interpersonal victimization in children and adolescents. Thus, Chapters 4 and 5, respectively, cover the evaluation of suicide risk and violence risk; while Chapter 6 is concerned with the assessment and prevention of child maltreatment and abuse. The remainder of this section addresses two special topics related to at-risk youth; namely, the problem of aggression and bullying in children and adolescents, and the evaluation and prevention of targeted violence in schools.

Sections III and IV address the topics "Behavioral Emergencies with Adults" and "Behavioral Emergencies with the Elderly," respectively. In the section on behavioral emergencies with adults, Chapters 9, 10, and 11 are chapters that discuss the evaluation and management of suicide risk, risk of violence, and interpersonal victimization in adult patients. The chapters that follow these three are chapters devoted to special emergency-related topics or particular adult populations that are at risk. Thus, Chapters 12 and 13 discuss the evaluation and management of suicide risk in military veterans and the risk of violence in combat veterans. After these chapters, there are chapters devoted to topics such as intimate partner violence (Chapter 14), homicide/suicide (Chapter 15), the assessment and management of victims of sexual violence (Chapter 16), and the assessment and prevention of abuse of persons with disabilities (Chapter 17). Chapter 18 examines the *structured professional judgement* approach to, and the development of, decision-support tools for evaluating the risk of violence; while Chapter 19 deals with interventions in cases of acute agitation. This section ends with chapters on the neurobiological factors in suicide (Chapter 20) and the neurobiological factors in aggression and violence (Chapter 21).

In the section on behavioral emergencies with the elderly (Section IV), Chapter 22 is concerned with the evaluation and management of suicide risk in the elderly; while Chapter 23 addresses the heightened risk of violence in the elderly who are suffering from cognitive and neurological impairments. Chapter 24 provides a discussion of the risks of elder abuse and what feasible measures may be used to try to prevent it. Finally, Chapter 25 discusses the burdens of medical illness as a risk factor for suicide in the elderly, as well as the psychological and ethical issues surrounding the assisted-death controversy.

Section V ("Crises and Conditions Associated with Behavioral Emergencies") is devoted to certain conditions or behaviors that, in clinical practice, may either need to be differentiated from a behavioral emergency, or understood as relevant to possibly heightening risk. Thus, non-suicidal self-injuries (NSSI) have frequently been mistaken for suicide attempts. Chapter 26 is about identifying self-injurious behaviors that the individual has engaged in without suicidal intent and how that person may need to be treated differently from someone who has engaged in suicidal behaviors. In addition, certain medical illnesses and conditions can present with psychological and/or behavioral symptomatology. The patient can appear to be in a behavioral crisis or emergency, and the clinician needs a resource to heighten his or her awareness that there may be an underlying medical condition. This section, therefore, includes chapters on neurological disorders associated with psychological/behavioral problems (Chapter 27) and endocrine disorders associated with psychological/behavioral problems (Chapter 28).

Patients who have a behavioral emergency such as discussed above are not necessarily without future risk once the emergency has passed. Follow-up treatment is frequently needed to reduce the risk of recurrence. In Section VI ("The Treatment of Patients with Recurrent or Ongoing Risk"), the clinician can find treatments that have been found to be effective at reducing such risks. Chapter 29 presents psychopharmacological treatments that have been effective in reducing the risk of recurrent suicidal behavior; while Chapter 30 discusses psychological or behavioral treatments that are empirically supported and have been found to reduce the risk of recurrent violent behavior. In addition, Chapter 31 presents treatments that have been found to be helpful with those who have been traumatized by interpersonal violence.

There are legal, ethical, and psychological risks for the clinician who works with patients who might be at risk of harming themselves or others. In Section VII ("Legal, Ethical, and Psychological Risk Management"), the book therefore includes a chapter on legal and ethical risk management for the clinician (Chapter 32) and a chapter on the clinician's obligations under the often cited "duty to protect" (Chapter 33). Given our limitations in predicting and preventing behavioral emergencies, there continue to be all-too-frequent instances in which patient suicide and/or violence occur. With this in mind, this section includes a chapter (Chapter 34) on the incidence and impact of negative events (i.e., patient suicide or patient violence) and offers suggestions for how clinicians might cope with the emotional aftermath.

In Section VIII, the editor offers his summarizing and concluding remarks about the book in Chapter 35.

Note

1. This case scenario is based on actual events, but changes have been made in the description of the people and of the circumstances to protect the identity of those involved.

References

Berliner, L., & Elliott, D. (2002). Sexual abuse of children. In J. Myers, L. Berliner, J. Briere, C. Hendrix, C. Jenny, & T. Reid (Eds.), *The APSAC handbook on child maltreatment* (2nd ed., pp. 55–78). Thousand Oaks, CA: Sage Publications.

Driskell, J., & Johnston, J. (1998). Stress exposure training. In J. Canon-Boweres & E. Salas (Eds.), *Making decisions under stress: Implications for individual and team training* (pp. 191–217). Washington, DC: American Psychological Association. doi: 10.1037/10278-007

Gately, L., & Stabb, S. (2005). Psychology students' training in the management of potentially violent clients. *Professional Psychology: Research and Practice, 36*, 681–687.

Guy, J., Brown, C., & Poelstra, P. (1990). Who gets attacked? A national survey of patient violence directed at psychologists in clinical practice. *Professional Psychology: Research and Practice, 21*, 493–495.

Kleespies, P. (2000). Behavioral emergencies and crises: An overview. *Journal of Clinical Psychology, 56*, 1103–1108.

Kleespies, P. (Ed.). (2009). *Behavioral emergencies: An evidence-based resource for evaluating and managing risk of suicide, violence, and victimization.* Washington, DC: APA Books.

Kleespies, P. (2014). *Decision making in behavioral emergencies: Acquiring skill in evaluating and managing high risk patients.* Washington, DC: APA Books.

Kolko, D. (2002). Child physical abuse. In J. Myers, L. Berliner, J. Briere, C. Hendrix, C. Jenny, & T. Reid (Eds.), *The APSAC handbook on child maltreatment* (2nd ed., pp. 21–54). Thousand Oaks, CA: Sage Publications.

Munizza, C., Furlan, P., d'Elia, A., D'Onofrio, M., Leggero, P., Punzo, F., ... Villari, V. (1993). Emergency psychiatry: A review of the literature. *Acta Psychiatrica Scandinavica, 88* (Suppl. 374), 1–51.

Pokorny, A. (1983). Prediction of suicide in psychiatric patients. *Archives of General Psychiatry, 40,* 249–259.

Schmitz, W., Jr., Allen, M., Feldman, B., Gutin, N., Jahn, D., Kleespies, P., Quinnett, P., & Simpson, S. (2012). Preventing suicide through improved training in suicide risk assessment and care: An American Association of Suicidology Task Force report addressing serious gaps in U.S. mental health training. *Suicide and Life-Threatening Behavior, 42,* 292–304.

Simon, R. (2006). Imminent suicide: The illusion of short-term prediction. *Suicide and Life-Threatening Behavior, 36,* 296–301.

Van Dulmen, M., Mata, A., Claxton, S., Klipfel, K., Schinka, K., Swahn, M., & Bossarte, R. (2013). Longitudinal associations between violence and suicidality from adolescence into adulthood. *Suicide and Life-Threatening Behavior, 43,* 523–531.

Integrative Perspectives on Behavioral Emergencies and Crises

Phillip M. Kleespies

Abstract

In this chapter, the author discusses two ways in which the area of behavioral emergencies can be viewed as integrative. First, evidence is presented demonstrating how the three major behavioral emergencies (i.e., risks of interpersonal victimization, suicide, and violence) overlap and are interrelated in certain respects. For example, data indicate that those who have been victims of violence have an increased risk of becoming perpetrators of violence and/or victims of suicidal behavior. Second, the author distinguishes between the concepts of crisis and emergency, and then discusses how crises often precede the development of behavioral emergencies, and how crisis intervention techniques can be used to avert a developing emergency. The chapter concludes with a discussion of the decision making involved in determining whether a patient at risk can be treated as an outpatient in crisis or needs to be hospitalized because of imminent risk of suicide or violence.

Key Words: behavioral emergency, crisis, behavioral crisis, suicide, violence, interpersonal victimization, victims of violence, emergency intervention, crisis intervention

As noted in the Introduction, the approach to behavioral emergencies in this volume is an integrative one. It is integrative in two respects. First, it places an emphasis on the linkages or associations among the three behavioral emergencies most frequently encountered by mental health clinicians—suicidality, a potential for violence, and vulnerability to interpersonal victimization. Second, although a distinction has been drawn between a behavioral emergency and a behavioral crisis in previous works by myself and others (see e.g., Callahan, 1998; Kleespies, 1998), it seems clear that human crises are often precipitants to or play a role in the development of an emergency situation. Under such circumstances, crisis intervention techniques can be useful in de-escalating a situation before emergency intervention becomes necessary. In this chapter, I will present a rationale for taking each of these perspectives.

The Interrelated Aspects of the Behavioral Emergencies

The interrelated aspects of the behavioral emergencies have not been a major focus of clinical or research attention until very recently. Rather, as Lutzger and Wyatt (2006) have pointed out, suicide research, violence research, and research on interpersonal victimization have generally been regarded as relatively independent areas of study. These authors have further noted that for more effective clinical service and research, it would be wise to see if one area might inform the other and thereby bring about more effective outcomes. Of course, it practically goes without saying that interpersonal violence leads to interpersonal victimization. It may be less obvious, however, that victimization may be a factor in contributing to a potential for violence, suicide, or revictimization, or that there may be an association between a potential for violence and a potential for suicide. In the sections that follow, I will summarize several studies that are part of the growing evidence that supports these contentions. Since other authors in this volume will discuss these issues in greater depth, I will only present a few representative studies here.

Interpersonal Victimization as a Factor in Risk of Violence

In a book chapter on child physical abuse, Kolko (2002, p. 32) noted that "one of the most extensively documented clinical consequences in child physical abuse victims is heightened aggression and related externalizing behaviors, including poor anger modulation." Not only does the experience of physical abuse as a child suggest that the individual is at greater risk of future aggression (in the broader sense of that term), but also that he or she is at greater risk of perpetrating intimate partner violence and other forms of domestic violence.

Ehrensaft et al. (2003), for example, conducted a longitudinal, prospective study using a community sample of 543 children. They investigated the relationship between childhood maltreatment, power-assertive punishment in childhood, and exposure to violence between parents on subsequent risk for adult partner violence. The study extended over a 20-year period, and, among other things, the investigators found that physical injury to a child by a caretaker significantly and directly increased the probability that similar violent tactics would be used in the participant's future intimate relationships. Although the development of a conduct disorder in adolescence mediated the effect of child abuse, exposure to violence between parents and power assertive punishment were additional, potent predictors of the perpetration of violence on partners in adolescence and young adulthood.

In a study of violence perpetrated by young adult children against their parents, Browne and Hamilton (1998) had a sample of 469 college students in England complete two questionnaires anonymously. One questionnaire assessed the tactics that they employed (including threats of violence and actual violence) during disagreements; the other examined incidents of violence or maltreatment toward or by the respondent during childhood and adolescence. Overall, the investigators found that 14.5% of the participants reported being violent with their mother and/or father, and 3.8% reported being severely violent with one or both parents. It was found that those who reported being abused or maltreated by their parents when they were children were significantly more likely to have reported that they were subsequently violent toward one or both parents. Moreover, participants who stated that they had been physically abused were significantly more likely to have been severely violent with one or both parents. The authors concluded that violence toward parents is associated with the experience of maltreatment during childhood and that violence toward parents is most often reciprocal to parental violence over time.

In a study of over 800 adults with severe mental illness (recruited from four different states), Swanson et al. (2002) collected self-report data on experiences of physical abuse or sexual abuse before age 16 (early life) and after age 16 (later life). The mean age of the sample was approximately 42 years. The investigators also collected data on social-environmental variables with a scale that measured exposure to community violence. Psychiatric diagnoses were obtained from chart review, and mental and emotional symptomatology, as well substance abuse, were assessed with established psychometric scales. Logistic regression analysis was used to examine the effects on risk of violent behavior associated with victimization and other variables. It was found that those individuals with serious mental disorders who were victimized as adults were significantly more likely to have engaged in violent behavior during the previous year even if they were not victimized as children. Participants who were victimized as both children and later as adults were even more likely to behave violently toward others in the previous year. The authors concluded that repeated abuse into adulthood had a cumulative association with violence. Like the experience of victimization, substance abuse and exposure to community violence were also found to be strongly associated with violent behavior.

Of course, there is the possibility that the potential for violence is genetically transmitted by violence-prone parents to their offspring. To test this hypothesis, Jaffee, Caspi, Moffitt, and Taylor (2004) conducted a longitudinal epidemiological study of 1,116 monozygotic (MZ) and dizygotic (DZ), same-sex, twin pairs. The genetic similarity of MZ twins is twice that of DZ twins; so, if nothing more than genetics influenced behavior, the MZ twins should be at least twice as similar in terms of heritable characteristics.

In this study by Jaffee et al., the twins were part of two consecutive birth cohorts (1994 and 1995), and the twins and their parents were interviewed at their homes when the children were 5 years old and 7 years old. Child maltreatment was assessed separately for each twin by interviewing the mothers with a standardized clinical interview protocol from a multisite child development project. The children's antisocial behavior was assessed at ages 5 and 7 with standardized aggression and delinquency scales. Compared with children who were not maltreated, physically maltreated children had significantly higher antisocial behavior scores at age 7. Thus, physical maltreatment prospectively predicted antisocial behavior. In addition, physical maltreatment had a dose-response relationship to antisocial outcome—the worse the physical maltreatment, the worse the subsequent antisocial behavior. More to the point, the effects of physical maltreatment remained significant after controlling for the parents' history of antisocial behavior; although genetic factors (with MZ twins compared to DZ twins) accounted for approximately half the association between physical maltreatment and childrens' antisocial behavior, the effect of physical maltreatment on subsequent antisocial behavior continued to be significant after controlling for any genetic transmission of this type of behavior. The authors concluded that approximately half the intergenerational transmission of antisocial behavior in their sample was environmentally transmitted.

Interpersonal Victimization as a Factor in Risk of Suicidal Behavior

Kilpatrick (2005) has suggested that interpersonal victimization can contribute to suicidality. In analyzing the data from a National Survey of Adolescents (Kilpatrick et al., 2003) that involved more than 4,000 interviewees ranging in age from 12 to 17, Kilpatrick (2005) reported that victimization increased the risk of suicide attempts after controlling for depression, posttraumatic stress disorder, and drug use disorders.

Joiner et al. (2007) drew upon a nationwide epidemiological study, the National Comorbidity Survey, to test whether violent physical and sexual abuse would be stronger predictors for the number of lifetime suicide attempts than would molestation and verbal abuse. While controlling for a number of covariates (e.g., age, gender, psychiatric history, etc.), they found that childhood physical and sexual abuse had significant and relatively pronounced associations with lifetime suicide attempts. Moreover, their effects exceeded those for molestation and verbal abuse in this regard. They concluded that childhood physical and violent sexual abuse should be seen as greater risk factors for future suicide attempts than childhood molestation and verbal abuse.

In a retrospective cohort study of over 17,000 adult members of a health maintenance organization (HMO) in California, Dube et al. (2001) examined the relationship between adverse childhood experiences (e.g., emotional, physical, and sexual abuse; household substance abuse, mental illness, and incarceration; parental domestic violence, separation, or divorce) and the risk of suicide attempts. Members of the HMO were mailed an Adverse Childhood Experiences study questionnaire that asked about experiences such as those noted above. The participants were also asked if they had ever attempted suicide, if they had ever been depressed, if they had ever considered themselves to be alcoholic, or if they had ever used street drugs. The investigators found that adverse childhood experiences in any category meant a twofold to fivefold increase in the risk of attempted suicide. As the number of such adverse experiences increased, the risk of attempted suicide during either childhood/adolescence or adulthood increased dramatically. They also noted that there was a strong relationship between adverse childhood experiences and alcohol or illicit substance abuse and depressive disorders, and these problems may partially mediate the relationship between these adverse experiences and suicide attempts.

Brown, Cohen, Johnson, and Smailes (1999) conducted a longitudinal study of the effects of childhood abuse and neglect with a random sample of 776 families over a 17-year period. The sample was drawn from two upstate New York counties in 1975, and the families were seen for follow-up interviews in 1983, 1986, and 1992. Data regarding child maltreatment were obtained from official abuse records (i.e., the New York State Central Registry for Child Abuse and Neglect). Self-reports of child abuse were also included in the study when obtained in the young-adult follow-up interview in 1992. Psychiatric disorders were assessed with the National Institute of Mental Health Diagnostic Interview Schedule for Children. Suicide attempts were reported by the children/adolescents and young adults with details of method, frequency, and associated treatment.

Using logistic regression analyses, the authors found that both dysthymia and major depressive disorder were significantly elevated in those with a history of abuse or neglect. They also found that suicidal behavior was strongly associated with a history of childhood maltreatment. Certainly, some of the effect of childhood abuse and neglect may have been mediated by depression. The rates of suicidal behavior, however, were without exception highest in those youths who had experienced sexual abuse. Physical abuse also carried an increased risk of suicidal behavior, but sexual abuse clearly carried the greatest risk of depression and suicidal behavior. It was estimated that between 16.5% and 19.5% of suicide attempts in young adults may be related to exposure to child sexual abuse.

Finally, in a study using data from a national youth risk behavior survey, Tomasula, Anderson, Littleton, and Riley-Tillman (2012) investigated the extent to which sexual assault predicted suicide attempts among adolescent students. After controlling for age and stratifying by gender, they found that adolescents with a history of sexual assault were approximately six times more likely to have attempted suicide in the past year when compared with adolescents who had no history of sexual assault. Although both male and female students with a sexual assault history were at greater risk for suicide attempts, male students appeared to be at a greater risk than might be expected. Thus, it was found that male students with a history of sexual assault were nearly 10 times more likely to have attempted suicide in the past year when compared to male students with no history of sexual assault. Moreover, male students with a sexual assault history who attempted suicide were nearly five times more likely to have made a medically serious attempt (defined as needing treatment by a doctor or nurse) when compared to male student suicide attempters who had no history of sexual assault.

Interpersonal Victimization as a Factor in Risk of Revictimization

There has been growing evidence that victims of childhood abuse are not only at greater risk of subsequent violence and/or suicidality, but that they may also be at greater risk of revictimization. Any given incident of victimization is likely to be distressing in itself, but there is also evidence that there can be a nearly linear increase in trauma symptoms with repeated victimizations (Turner, Finkelhor, & Ormrod, 2010).

In a study of lifetime revictimization, Widom, Czaja, and Dutton (2008) used a prospective cohort design of a group of physically and sexually abused and neglected children (with matched controls who had no documented history of abuse) and followed them into adulthood (approximately 40 years of age). The abuse and neglect was court-substantiated and the children were 11 years of age or younger at the time that they first entered the study (1967–1971). Of the original sample of 1575 children, 83% were located and 76% (or 1,196) were reinterviewed during 1989–1995. Of this group of 1,196 interviewees, 93% were located and 75% (or 896) were interviewed again in 2000–2002. A 30-item instrument known as the Lifetime Trauma and Victimization History (Widom, Dutton, Czaja, & DuMont, 2005) was used to gather data on lifetime trauma and victimization history in the context of a structured in-person interview.

In analyzing the data from the 2000–2002 interviewees (896), these investigators found that the individuals who had been abused and/or neglected as children reported a significantly higher number of lifetime victimization experiences. More specifically, the abuse and neglect group versus the control group differed in the number of victimization events in childhood and adulthood, but not in adolescence. The increased risk of revictimization was not across the board; it was associated with only certain types of traumas and victimizations—for example, physical assault and abuse, sexual assault and abuse, kidnapping/stalking, and having a family member or friend who was murdered or who committed suicide. Individuals with documented histories of multiple forms of abuse and neglect reported the highest prevalence of physical assault and abuse, and sexual assault and abuse. The investigators concluded that their results provided strong support for the hypothesis that childhood victimization leads to increased risk for lifetime revictimization. They also reported that the increased risk of revictimization did not apply to all categories of traumas or victimization experiences that they had assessed but rather to what they broadly considered instances involving *interpersonal* violence (physical assault/abuse, sexual assault/abuse, kidnapping/stalking, and murder or suicide of a family member or friend).

In a retrospective study of sexual revictimization, Merrill et al. (1999) surveyed 1887 female US Navy recruits. They selected only those recruits who reported childhood sexual abuse in which there was actual physical contact (but not with a peer) and a comparison sample of those recruits who reported no childhood sexual abuse. The final sample consisted of 1093 women. These women were assessed with the Sexual Events Questionnaire (Finkelhor, 1979) and with five items from the Sexual Experiences Survey (Koss, Koss, & Woodruff, 1991), as well as with a demographic questionnaire, a scale that assessed how their parents resolved parent–child conflicts, and a screening test for problems with alcohol.

Odds ratios indicated that women who had experienced childhood physical abuse (regardless of whether they had also experienced childhood sexual abuse) were 1.89 times more likely to have subsequently been raped; while women who had experienced childhood sexual abuse (regardless of whether they had experienced childhood physical abuse) were 5.12 times more likely to have subsequently been raped. A hierarchical logistic regression analysis was then used to derive estimates of the independent contributions of childhood physical abuse and childhood sexual abuse to adult rape. In this analysis, childhood sexual abuse remained a significant predictor of adult rape, but childhood physical abuse did not. The authors concluded that childhood sexual abuse was a much stronger predictor of adult rape than childhood physical abuse. Female Navy recruits with a history of childhood sexual abuse, or with a history of childhood sexual abuse and childhood physical abuse, reported prevalence rates of 56% and 65%, respectively. By contrast, female Navy recruits without a childhood history of abuse, or those with only a history of childhood physical abuse, reported a lower rape prevalence of 22% and 25%, respectively.

These investigators also considered whether problems with alcohol and multiple sexual partners might explain the likelihood of adult rape. It was found that women who had experienced childhood sexual abuse had a higher number of sexual partners and more problems with alcohol than did women who had not experienced childhood sexual abuse; however, when differences were controlled between sexually abused and non-abused women in regard to alcohol abuse and the number of sexual partners, the results did not eliminate the significant association between childhood sexual abuse and adult rape. The investigators concluded that, rather than mediating the relation between childhood sexual abuse and rape, alcohol problems and multiple sexual partners appeared to be largely independent risk factors for adult rape.

Violence as a Factor in Risk of Suicide and Vice Versa

For many years, Plutchik and colleagues (e.g., Plutchik, Botsis, & van Praag, 1995) have theorized that violence and suicide reflect an underlying aggressive impulse that is modified by variables that they have referred to as *amplifiers* and *attenuators*.

To support their theory, they have cited evidence of the overlap of suicidal and violent behavior in hospitalized psychotic adolescents, in incarcerated juvenile delinquents, and in adult psychiatric inpatients. Plutchik and van Praag (1990) have estimated that one-third of violent individuals have engaged in self-destructive behaviors, and that 10%–20% of self-destructive individuals have engaged in violent behavior.

Hillbrand (1995; 2001) also noted that there may be an overlap between aggression against self and aggression against others. In the study by Hillbrand (1995), he reviewed the records of over 100 male psychiatric patients hospitalized in a maximum security hospital on the basis of insanity acquittals, severe aggressive behavior in other psychiatric hospitals, and the like. These patients were divided into four groups: (1) those with no current or past suicidal behavior; (2) those with no current suicidal behavior but a history of past suicidal behavior; (3) those with current suicidal behavior but no history of past suicidal behavior; and (4) those with current suicidal behavior and a history of past suicidal behavior. The groupings were thought to reflect a continuum of severity or chronicity of suicidal behavior, and the patients' violent behaviors were monitored with a well-established scale completed after any incident of aggression over a three-year period. The findings indicated that group 4 (the group with the most severe or chronic suicidal behavior) engaged in significantly more aggressive acts. Hillbrand concluded that severe and chronic self-destructiveness identified a particularly violent group of individuals. He also noted that a substantial proportion of violent individuals seemed to alternate between aggression against self and aggression against others.

In a study on the relationship of violence to completed suicide, Conner et al. (2001) analyzed data from the 1993 National Mortality Followback Survey, a nationally representative telephone survey with decedents' next of kin. They compared data collected from the next of kin for victims of suicide and accident victims. Informants were asked to rate the decedents violent behavior in the last year of his or her life on a four-point scale from *often* to *never*. Data on alcohol use in the last year of life were also elicited. Multiple logistic regression was used to predict case status—for example, suicide victim versus accident victim. Violent behavior distinguished suicide victims from accident victims, and this finding was not attributable to alcohol use alone. In fact, the association of violence and suicide was stronger among individuals who did not have a history of alcohol abuse. It was also stronger among younger individuals and among women. The investigators noted that violence in women appeared to confer greater risk for suicide than violence in men. They commented on how intervention strategies that target women who display aggressive behavior are needed. They also were of the opinion that violence prevention and suicide prevention efforts can inform one another and could gain by the collaboration.

In a longitudinal study of associations between violence and suicidality, Van Dulmen et al. (2013) confirmed that violence is a risk factor for suicidal behavior but also found that a history of suicidal behavior is a risk factor for future violence. These investigators used data from the National Longitudinal Study of Adolescent Health in which the adolescents in the study were followed into adulthood. Data collection began in 1994 with an in-school survey of over 90,000 students in grades 7–12, and an in-home interview for a select sample (Wave I). One year later, there was a second wave of interviews (Wave II), followed by a third wave in 2001–2002 (Wave III), and a fourth in 2007–2008 (Wave IV). Interviewees were questioned about incidents of violent behavior and suicidal behavior. The study team then conducted a series of path analysis models with data from Waves II, III, and IV. One of the models included paths from suicidality predicting future (at the next time-point) violence, and another of the models included paths from violence predicting future (at the next time-point) suicidality.

In the first model, suicide attempts in adolescence and early adulthood significantly increased the risk of violence in early and young adulthood, respectively. Likewise, violent behavior in adolescence significantly increased the risk of suicide attempts in early adulthood. The investigators concluded that their study demonstrated that suicidality and violence mutually influence each other across time. Not only was violent behavior associated with increased risk for suicidality, but a history of suicidality increased the risk for future violence. They called for research efforts aimed at a better understanding of why and how suicidality and violence are associated across time.

An Integrated Approach to Crisis Intervention and Emergency Intervention

It is of heuristic value to initially differentiate behavioral emergencies from behavioral crises and then to consider the ways in which they are interrelated. Callahan (2009) has posited that understanding the distinction between *emergency* and *crisis* is often what drives our decision making when a clinical situation confronts us with the need to determine if emergency intervention or crisis intervention is the more appropriate response.

The Distinction Between Behavioral Emergencies and Crises

Mental health clinicians frequently use the terms crisis and emergency interchangeably. Each term also has a variety of meanings in common discourse. An emergency can be any unforeseen set of circumstances that calls for immediate action. You could, for example, have a housing emergency if you discovered that you had overdrawn your bank account, could not pay your rent, and were facing imminent eviction. Moreover, any serious or chronic problem can at times be referred to as a crisis. Someone might say that they are going through a midlife crisis or that their marriage was in a state of crisis.

In a mental health context, some have contended that the use of these terms in poorly defined ways or as synonyms only leads to confusion (Callahan, 2009; Kleespies & Hill, 2011). For the purposes of the current work, I have defined a behavioral emergency (in the *Introduction* to this volume) as meaning that an individual is at imminent risk of behaving in a way that could result in serious harm or death to self or others. Likewise, for the purposes of the current work, I would use the traditional definition of a behavioral crisis as noted in the preceding paragraph. In contrast to an emergency, a crisis does not necessarily imply risk of serious physical harm or life-threatening danger. Some have viewed a behavioral crisis as an emotionally significant event in which there may be a turning point for better or worse. If a crisis takes a turn for the worse, it may be a precipitant for a behavioral emergency. On the other hand, it should be noted that a crisis, in itself, is typically not a sufficient explanation for a behavioral emergency. Suicidal and/or violent states usually involve a number of contributing factors. If, for instance, an adolescent attempts suicide after he is rejected by his girlfriend, in addition to feeling overwhelmed by the loss it is likely that he also has engaged in all-or-nothing thinking about the relationship, has a history of depression and/or substance abuse, has a history of impulsivity, and so forth.

Confusion between the concepts of crisis and emergency is also present at the level of intervention. As Callahan (1998) has noted, many clinicians think that crisis intervention is the appropriate response to a patient who is at risk of suicide or violence. While resolving a crisis with crisis intervention techniques may decrease lower level risk, when the risk is high, the most appropriate response is an emergency intervention. An emergency intervention typically implies three things: (1) the need for an immediate response to a perceived imminent risk; (2) management to prevent serious harm or death; and (3) resolution of the immediate risk within a single encounter. Crisis intervention, on the other hand, typically implies (1) a response within 24–48 hours; (2) therapeutic intervention to develop or reestablish the ability to cope with the issues causing the crisis; and (3) achievement of a resolution within four to six sessions.

The Interrelated Aspects of Behavioral Emergencies and Crises

Now that we have differentiated crisis and emergency, as well as crisis intervention and emergency intervention, we can consider how they might be brought together in an integrated model such as that proposed by Callahan (2009). As mentioned earlier, a behavioral or emotional crisis is often a contributing (if not a precipitating) factor in the unfolding of a behavioral emergency. When a patient presents in an apparent state of crisis, it is usually wise to also screen the patient for risk of danger to self and/or others. If it appears that the risk is low, the clinician can proceed with evaluating the patient and determining whether he or she is in a crisis. As Callahan (2009) has pointed out, the work here is to be empathic, to engage in active listening, and, through questioning and interacting with the patient, to come to an understanding of how the patient perceives his or her condition and situation. A significant question is whether the patient's condition deviates from his or her baseline level of functioning and thus constitutes an acute episode of crisis. Some patients (e.g., those with borderline personality disorder) lead chaotic lives and are seemingly in a constant state of crisis at their baseline. What they present with is not an acute crisis but a chronic state of crisis, and intervention with them may require an approach such as Linehan's dialectical behavior therapy or DBT (Linehan, 1993).

In assessing a patient in crisis, it is clearly important to gain an understanding of the quality of the patient's preexisting baseline and what coping skills he or she typically has had available. This information will assist the clinician in determining what coping resources might be built upon or enhanced. It also helps in ascertaining what new skills might be encouraged or learned.

According to Aguilera (1998), there are three factors that determine a state of personal equilibrium—perception of events, situational supports, and coping mechanisms. In terms of perception of events, she states (in accord with Lazarus [1994]) that when confronted with a challenging or very demanding state of affairs, the individual engages in a process of appraisal of his or her condition or situation. If achieving the desired outcome is perceived as too difficult or overwhelming, he or she may resort to maladaptive efforts to cope and/or may become anxious and depressed. When feeling inadequate and/or facing a difficult or threatening situation, social support takes on great importance. If the individual can access significant others who can provide support and advice on solving the problem, it can make a big difference in terms of managing the crisis. If the person withdraws or does not have a support network, his or her stress is increased. At times, stress can seem so great that the person loses sight of how he or she has learned to cope with similar situations in the past. If the person can reinstate previous coping strategies or develop new ones, a resolution to the crisis may be at hand.

The clinician can aid the patient in these three areas by assisting the individual in making an accurate appraisal of his or her circumstances; encouraging the person to contact or reach out to potentially supportive people in his or her social environment; and reviewing the individual's past coping resources, working with him or her to develop new ones, and gently confronting maladaptive methods of coping. Work on these issues can continue throughout the course of crisis intervention. The primary goal is to resolve the crisis, but another goal is to promote growth and development so that the individual becomes a better crisis manager or problem solver in the future.

In the course of working with an individual in crisis, the clinician should always be alert to the possibility that the patient may become a risk to self or others. Stress from a variety of sources (e.g., interpersonal conflict/separation/loss, financial reversals, homelessness) can lead to a crisis, and such a crisis can become a risk factor or so-called accelerant for suicidal and/or violent behavior (see, e.g., chapters 9 and 10 of this volume). If it appears that a patient may be considering harm to self or others, an emergency assessment takes priority and emergency intervention may be necessary.

An emergency intervention typically takes place in an immediate, single-session interview.[1] In the course of this type of interview, the clinician must (1) if necessary, assist the patient in gaining sufficient control of his or her emotions to cooperate with the interview; (2) collaborate with the patient in defining the problem; (3) arrive at an estimate of the level of risk; and (4) provide for appropriate care and treatment. Even after defining the problem(s) and arriving at an estimated level of risk, however, it is not necessarily a black or white decision about how best to intervene. Some clinicians are disposed to hospitalize patients who are at risk because they feel that it is safer, and because they are concerned about liability issues if their judgment not to hospitalize is in error. Yet, many patients who have suicidal ideation or violent ideation can be (and are) managed successfully on an outpatient basis.

In working with patients who are at risk, clinicians need to be guided by a carefully considered estimate of the level of risk and by a weighing of the risks and benefits of each way of proceeding. The level of risk is often determined by a consideration of distal risk factors, proximal risk factors, and protective factors (Kleespies & Hill, 2011). Alternatively (or perhaps concurrently), the clinician might consider the level of risk from the perspective of static (or unchanging) risk factors and dynamic (or modifiable) risk factors. Static risk factors are typically dispositional or historical factors, such as gender, race/ethnicity, a past suicide attempt, or a history of violence. On the other hand, dynamic risk factors are typically clinical or situational factors such as hopelessness, acute depression, or the stress of a financial crisis. Static risk factors may always be there, but variations in the dynamic risk factors may lead the clinician to increase or decrease his or her estimate of risk.

Management of suicide risk on an outpatient basis. Outpatient management of patients considered to be at either mild or moderate risk of suicide has generally been found to be feasible and safe (Rudd, Joiner, & Rajab, 2001; chapter 9 of this volume). Stanley and Brown (2012) have recommended that the management of such patients include a Safety Planning Intervention (SPI). This type of intervention entails the development of a prioritized list of coping strategies and sources of support for use by the patient preceding or during a time when the risk of suicide increases. The listing is developed collaboratively by the clinician and the patient.

An SPI consists of six steps. The first step involves helping the patient to identify and pay attention to warning signs that occur when he or she begins to consider suicide. These warning signs may be thoughts, behaviors, or moods, and they are listed in the safety plan in the patient's own words. In the second step, the patient is asked to identify internal coping strategies that might be used to distract himself or herself from problems. Depending on the patient, activities such as walking, exercising, or reading might lead to a change of focus. If such internal strategies fail or are not feasible, the third step would be to have a list of social contacts, such as visits to a coffee shop or a preferred place of religion. Fourth on the SPI, the patient is to have a list of family and/or friends who could be contacted to talk with and inform that he or she is having thoughts of suicide. If none of the previous strategies are effective, a fifth step is for the patient to have a list of clinicians and/or professional agencies that could be contacted. This list should include contacts that can be reached during non-business hours, such as the National Crisis Hotline (1-800-273-TALK [8255]). Finally, the patient and the clinician should discuss what means the patient might use in a suicide attempt, and then work collaboratively on eliminating or limiting access to such means, particularly the more lethal means such as firearms.

As just described, Stanley and Brown (2012) focused on managing suicidal states by helping the patient to develop coping strategies. Rudd and Joiner (1998), on the other hand, have suggested that the clinician who is working with an outpatient who is at moderate risk might wish to consider the following adjustments: (a) an increase in the outpatient visits and/or the addition of telephone contacts, (b) frequent assessment of suicide risk, (c) recurrent evaluation for hospitalization while the risk continues, (d) 24-hour availability or coverage, (e) reevaluation of the treatment plan as needed, (f) consideration of a medication evaluation or change in regimen, and (g) use of professional consultation as warranted. For patients at mild risk, recurrent evaluation and monitoring of suicide potential may be sufficient.

The decision to hospitalize when suicide risk is high. An emergency intervention such as hospitalization is necessary when the level of risk is considered severe. This type of decision is often preceded by an effort to resolve or reduce a crisis that has precipitated an increase in suicidal intent. There are times when it is possible to achieve such a resolution and have the patient continue in outpatient treatment. Hospitalization is needed, however, when, as Comstock (1992) has pointed out, it is not possible to establish or reinstate a treatment alliance, when crisis intervention techniques fail, and/or when the patient continues to have intent to commit suicide in the immediate future. There is no evidence that hospitalization ultimately prevents suicide, but it does provide a relatively safer environment during a period of heightened risk. Typically, a one- or two-hour evaluation of a patient who continues to be considered at imminent risk of suicide is sufficient to convince clinicians to hospitalize the patient.

Many patients who require hospitalization for risk of suicide agree to a voluntary admission. They may do so because they have some ambivalence about taking such a final action as suicide. When patients assessed as at imminent risk refuse to be hospitalized, however, the clinician is faced with a decision about involuntary commitment. A decision to hospitalize someone against their will can be difficult because the estimation of suicide risk is not always reliable, and involuntary temporary commitment involves depriving patients of their freedom while possibly creating barriers to effective future treatment (i.e., alienating a patient and damaging the therapeutic alliance; Comstock, 1992). As Kleespies, Deleppo, Gallagher, and Niles (1999) have pointed out, however, it nonetheless remains the clinician's responsibility to decide whether hospitalization is needed to avert a serious risk that the patient will take his or her own life. In the final analysis, the decision to invoke an involuntary temporary commitment and hospitalize the patient should be based on evidence-based risk factors, the clinician's best judgment, and a consideration of the risk–benefit ratio. In making such decisions, it can be helpful to keep in mind that once hospitalization has occurred, resistant patients often gain perspective and begin to perceive the caring aspects and the necessity of the clinician's actions. The door is then open to repairing any damage to the therapeutic alliance that may have occurred.

Options for managing the risk of violence. In a classic paper, Monahan (1993) suggested three levels of intervention for working with the potentially violent patient: (a) intensifying treatment, (b) hardening the target, and (c) incapacitating the patient. When the patient is considered to be at mild-to-moderate risk and has some capacity to modulate or modify his or her behavior, it is possible to intensify treatment as a way of managing risk while the patient remains in the community.

Intensifying treatment could mean increasing the frequency of therapy sessions, having between-session telephone safety checks with the patient, having the patient enter a more structured outpatient or partial hospitalization program, developing a plan for 24-hour emergency coverage, and making frequent reassessments of the level of risk. Treatment sessions could be focused on ways to reduce the likelihood of violence—for example, increasing insight, teaching anger management techniques, increasing frustration tolerance, improving affect regulation, and so forth.

Hardening the target involves warning the intended victim(s) and/or alerting law enforcement. It makes it possible for the potential victim to take protective measures. Warning the intended victim became known to mental health clinicians as the *duty to warn* following the *Tarasoff* case in California (*Tarasoff v. Regents of University of California*, 1974). Many clinicians do not seem to realize, however, that the same California court reviewed the *Tarasoff* case two years later, vacated the so-called duty to warn ruling, and revised their opinion to what has subsequently been referred to as the *duty to protect* ruling (*Tarasoff v. Regents of University of California*, 1976; Welfel, Werth, & Benjamin, 2009; see chapter 33 of this volume). This revised opinion was that therapists have a broader duty to protect, rather than simply warning, the potential victims of patients or clients who are violent. Warning the individual in question may be one way to protect, but it is not necessarily the only way, and, depending on the circumstances, it may not necessarily be the best way.

Warning the intended victim can be frightening to the individual, or it can elicit retaliatory anger, and, as Borum (2009) has noted, it should be reserved for those times when other interventions have been rejected by the patient or are not feasible given the particular circumstances. If a warning is given, Borum's advice is that the clinician observe caution in reviewing the nature and seriousness of the threat with the intended victim and work with the individual to find sources of assistance as well as other protective measures.

Although Borum's cautionary note about warning the intended victim is well taken, the clinician must also be aware of his or her state's statutes that may regulate what actions a treatment provider is to take in managing a patient's or client's risk of violence (VandeCreek & Knapp, 2000). Some jurisdictions may require that the intended victim be warned.

In situations where the danger of serious harm is great and less restrictive means have failed or would be ineffective, the clinician may need to take steps to incapacitate the patient. *Incapacitating the patient* means using measures that directly decrease the person's ability to act in a violent manner. Such measures may include voluntary or involuntary hospitalization, sedating medication, and physical restraints or seclusion. The use of such means is typically regulated by law and institutional policy. Their use is sometimes necessary to avoid a worse alternative (i.e., the serious harm or death of an intended victim). These actions prevent immediate harm, but they are not a solution to the long-term risk of violence. They may allow, however, for a more complete evaluation and the initiation of treatment that may have longer lasting benefit.

The use of such restrictive measures can be a difficult decision because they are intrusive and involve depriving an individual of personal freedom. As with the suicidal patient, the use of involuntary hospitalization or the use of restraints with the potentially violent patient can damage the patient–clinician relationship. The individual may become angry with the clinician and/or feel betrayed. It may be possible to lessen the risk of such damage if the patient has been informed early in the treatment relationship that there are limits to confidentiality and that, if the patient is considered at imminent risk of seriously harming self or others, the clinician is ethically and often legally obligated to break confidentiality and initiate actions to protect the patient or others who may be at risk from the patient. Should such actions result in damage to the relationship, it can sometimes be repaired once the patient has become more stable.

Options for Managing the Risk of Interpersonal Victimization. If a mental health clinician believes that a patient or client is engaging in child abuse, elder abuse, or abuse of a person who is disabled, in most US jurisdictions the clinician is mandated to report the individual (or, if feasible, have the person report himself or herself) to the relevant state agency (see chapters 6, 17, and 24 of this volume). The laws governing mandated reporting typically do not require a presentation of extensive evidence. The protective services agency to which the clinician reports has the task of conducting a more complete investigation.

Although reporting may be mandated, it has been found that clinicians can have difficulty with these decisions. Zellman and Fair (2002), in a large survey of child abuse reporting behavior, noted that almost 40% of the respondents admitted that, at some point in their career, they had suspected childhood abuse or neglect, but they had decided not to report it. Those who did not report most frequently stated that they exercised discretion about reporting when they felt that there was insufficient evidence that abuse or maltreatment had occurred. What also distinguished them from others in the study was their negative opinion about the ability of the state's protective services staff, whom they saw as overburdened, to deal adequately with the situation. Most of these respondents were experienced in treating cases involving child maltreatment. They felt that reporting would risk termination of treatment and loss of the opportunity that they could provide to reduce the likelihood of further abuse.

In homes where there is child abuse, it has been found that there is an increased probability of partner abuse and vice versa. O'Leary, Slep, and O'Leary (2000) used data from two National Family Violence Surveys and found that when child abuse was present, the conditional probability of partner abuse was 31%. Moreover, when partner abuse was present, the conditional probability of child abuse was also 31%. Notably, arguments over child rearing have been found to be one of the most common precipitants of partner violence (O'Leary & Woodin, 2006).

Therapeutic work with a couple or with a member of a couple in which there is a risk of intimate partner violence can be trying (see chapter 14 of this volume). It is likely that at least one of the partners has problems with anger and aggression as well as issues with power and control. If therapy cannot resolve the problem, and one partner is being victimized, he or she may wish to separate. Unfortunately, there also can be heightened risk in attempting to end a relationship in which violence has been a factor. What may be a crisis in the relationship can quickly become an emergency in which there is a risk of serious harm to the partner who wishes to separate. Estranged wives or partners have been found to be at substantially higher risk of being killed by their partners than wives or partners in an intact relationship (Riggs, Caulfield, & Fair, 2009). Moreover, incidents in which a female partner was killed have been found to be approximately three times as likely as nonfatal assaults to be precipitated by the woman's leaving or attempting to leave a relationship.

During the tense times leading up to and during a separation or divorce, abused partners often seek the counsel of their therapists. The therapist may be involved in helping the patient or client come to decisions about how and when to terminate the relationship. If there is risk that the other partner may become violent, the patient and the therapist may need to formulate plans for how the potential victim might keep himself or herself safe. (The reader is referred to chapter 14 of this volume for a more detailed discussion of these issues.)

Concluding Remarks

In this chapter, evidence has been presented that supports the contention that there is an interplay among the major behavioral emergencies of suicide risk, risk of violence, and risk of interpersonal victimization. As described, there is research indicating that childhood physical abuse is a contributing or chronic/distal risk factor for the perpetration of intimate partner violence and, more broadly speaking, for the perpetration of violence in adolescence and adulthood. In addition, childhood abuse, but particularly childhood sexual abuse, appears to be a strong chronic/distal risk factor for suicidal behavior. Furthermore, childhood physical and/or sexual abuse seem to be chronic/distal risk factors for revictimization as an adolescent and/or an adult. Finally, there is evidence that violent behavior and suicidal behavior are chronic/distal risk factors for each other.

In my opinion, not only do clinicians need to assess for these risk factors when evaluating patients for either suicide risk or violence risk, but clinicians and researchers need to study these interactions in an effort to understand the possible meaning they may have in terms of the etiology of high-risk behaviors.

In our search for meaning in these findings, Joiner's interpersonal-psychological theory of suicide, for example, might posit that childhood victimization can lead to a sense of thwarted belongingness and/or perceived burdensomeness, as well as habituation to the pain and fear involved in self-harm. The latter can increase the individual's acquired capacity to engage in lethal self-injury (Joiner et al., 2007). Others might suggest that childhood victimization affects self-worth and self-esteem, and these issues mediate suicide risk. In terms of the interrelatedness of suicidality and potential for violence, Hillbrand (1995) has suggested that those who engage in violent behavior and those who engage in suicidal behavior may share such factors or characteristics as impulsivity, anger or hostility, depression, substance abuse, or, particularly in adolescents, modeling behavior. Still others, such as Beck (1999), might take

a cognitive perspective and view suicidal individuals and those who are potentially violent as sharing certain cognitive distortions—for example, dichotomous thinking, overgeneralization, catastrophizing, and personalization.

Most likely, there are many factors involved in and many paths that can lead to suicide and/or violence. The interactions between interpersonal victimization and suicidality or the potential for violence may eventually yield some additional insights into how an individual might move along such a pathway. Nonetheless, the findings noted suggest that a more integrated approach to suicide and violence risk-assessment and prevention may prove fruitful.

In this chapter, I have also distinguished between crises and behavioral emergencies (as well as between crisis intervention and emergency intervention). I have done so in an effort to reduce confusion about terminology and to demonstrate how the distinction between crisis and emergency frequently guides our thinking when we are confronted with patients in acute emotional distress. I have also discussed how crises can be precipitants for behavioral emergencies, and how, if a patient in crisis can have his or her state of equilibrium restored, an emergency situation may be avoided. In an integrated model of crisis intervention and emergency intervention, as just noted, if a crisis can be resolved, an emergency may be averted, but the clinician needs to remain alert to the possibility that a life-threatening situation may develop. If that occurs, he or she must be prepared to intervene on an emergency basis. I have further discussed the management of the levels of suicide risk, violence risk, and the risk of interpersonal victimization up to and including high or serious risk in which emergency measures are needed.

Note

1. For an example of an emergency interview, see Kleespies and Richmond (2009).

References

Aguilera, D. (1998). *Crisis intervention: Theory and methodology* (8th ed.). St. Louis, MO: Mosby.

Beck, A. (1999). *Prisoners of hate: The cognitive basis of anger, hostility, and violence.* New York, NY: HarperCollins Publishers, Inc.

Borum, R. (2009). Children and adolescents at risk of violence. In P. M. Kleespies (Ed.), *Behavioral emergencies: An evidence-based resource for evaluating and managing risk of suicide, violence, and victimization* (pp. 147–163). Washington, DC: APA Books.

Brown, J., Cohen, P., Johnson, J., & Smailes, E. (1999). Childhood abuse and neglect: Specificity of effects on adolescent and young adult depression and suicidality. *Journal of the American Academy of Child and Adolescent Psychiatry, 38,* 1490–1496.

Browne, K., & Hamilton, C. (1998). Physical violence between young adults and their parents: Associations with a history of child maltreatment. *Journal of Family Violence, 13,* 59–79.

Callahan, J. (1998). Crisis theory and crisis intervention in emergencies. In P. Kleespies (Ed.), *Emergencies in mental health practice: Evaluation and management* (pp. 22–40). New York, NY: Guilford Press.

Callahan, J. (2009). Emergency intervention and crisis intervention. In P. Kleespies (Ed.), *Behavioral emergencies: An evidence-based resource for evaluating and managing risk of suicide, violence, and victimization* (pp. 31–32), Washington, DC: APA Books.

Comstock, B. (1992). Decision to hospitalize and alternatives to hospitalization. In B. Bongar (Ed.), *Suicide guidelines for assessment, management, and treatment* (pp. 204–217). New York, NY: Oxford University Press.

Conner, K., Cox, C., Duberstein, P., Tian, L., Nisbet, P., & Conwell, Y. (2001). Violence, alcohol, and completed suicide: A case-control study. *The American Journal of Psychiatry, 158,* 1701–1705.

Dube, S., Anda, R., Felitti, V., Chapman, D., Williamson, D., & Giles, W. (2001). Childhood abuse, household dysfunction, and the risk of attempted suicide throughout the life span: Findings from the Adverse Childhood Experiences Study. *The Journal of the American Medical Association, 286,* 3089–3096.

Ehrensaft, M., Cohen, P., Brown, J., Smailes, E., Chen, H., & Johnson, J. (2003). Intergenerational transmission of partner violence: A 20-year prospective study. *Journal of Consulting and Clinical Psychology, 71,* 741–753.

Finkelhor, D. (1979). *Sexually victimized children.* New York, NY: Free Press.

Hillbrand, M. (1995). Aggression against self and aggression against others in violent psychiatric patients. *Journal of Consulting and Clinical Psychology, 63,* 668–671.

Hillbrand, M. (2001). Homicide-suicide and other forms of co-occurring aggression against self and against others. *Professional Psychology: Research and Practice, 32,* 626–635.

Jaffee, S., Caspi, A., Moffitt, T., & Taylor, A. (2004). Physical maltreatment victim to antisocial child: Evidence of an environmentally mediated process. *Journal of Abnormal Psychology, 113,* 44–55.

Joiner, T., Jr., Sachs-Ericsson, N., Wingate, L., Brown, J., Anestis, N., & Selby, E. (2007). Childhood physical and sexual abuse and lifetime number of suicide attempts: A persistent and theoretically important relationship. *Behavior Research and Therapy, 45,* 539–547.

Kilpatrick, D. (2005). The role of trauma in behavioral emergencies: Implications for policy and practice. Presidential address for Section VII of Division 12. Presented at 113th Annual Convention of the American Psychological Association. Washington, DC, August 19, 2005.

Kilpatrick, D., Ruggiero, K., Acierno, R., Saunders, B., Resnick, H., & Best, C. (2003). Violence and risk of PTSD, major depression, substance abuse/dependence, and comorbidity: Results from the National Survey of Adolescents. *Journal of Consulting and Clinical Psychology, 71,* 692–700.

Kleespies, P. (1998). The domain of psychological emergencies: An overview. In P. Kleespies (Ed.), *Emergencies in mental health practice: Evaluation and management* (pp. 9–21). New York, NY: Guilford Press.

Kleespies, P., & Hill, J. (2011). Behavioral emergencies and crises. In D. Barlow (Ed.), *The Oxford handbook of clinical psychology* (pp. 739–761). New York, NY: Oxford University Press.

Kleespies, P., & Richmond, J. (2009). Evaluating behavioral emergencies: The clinical interview. In P. M. Kleespies (Ed.), *Behavioral emergencies: An evidence-based resource for evaluating and managing risk of suicide, violence, and victimization* (pp. 33–55). Washington, DC: APA Books.

Kleespies, P., Deleppo, J., Gallagher, P., & Niles, B. (1999). Managing suicidal emergencies: Recommendations for the practitioner. *Professional Psychology: Research and Practice, 30,* 454–463.

Kolko, D. (2002). Child physical abuse. In J. Myers, L. Berliner, J. Briere, C. T. Hendrix, C. Jenny, & T. Reid (Eds.), *The APSAC handbook on child maltreatment* (2nd ed., pp. 21–54). Thousand Oaks, CA: Sage.

Koss, M., Koss, P., & Woodruff, W. (1991). Deleterious effects of criminal victimization on women's health and medical utilization. *Archives of Internal Medicine, 151,* 342–347.

Lazarus, R. (1994). *Emotion and adaptation.* New York: Oxford University Press.

Linehan, M. (1993). *Skills training manual for treating borderline personality disorder.* New York, NY: Guilford Press.

Lutzger, J., & Wyatt, J. (2006). Introduction. In J. Lutzger (Ed.), *Preventing violence: Research and evidence-based intervention strategies* (pp. 3–15). Washington, DC: APA Books.

Merrill, L., Newell, C., Thomsen, C., Gold, S., Milner, J., Koss, M., & Rosswork, S. (1999). Childhood abuse and sexual revictimization in a female Navy recruit sample. *Journal of Traumatic Stress, 12,* 211–225.

Monahan, J. (1993). Limiting therapist exposure to Tarasoff liability: Guidelines for risk containment. *American Psychologist, 48,* 242–250.

O'Leary, K., Slep, A., & O'Leary, S. (2000). Co-occurrence of partner and parent aggression: Research and treatment implications. *Behavior Therapy, 31,* 631–648.

O'Leary, K., & Woodin, E. (2006). Bringing the agendas together: Partner and child abuse. In J. Lutzker (Ed.), *Preventing violence: Research and evidence-based intervention strategies* (pp. 239–258). Washington, DC: American Psychological Association.

Plutchik, R., Botsis, A., & van Praag, H. (1995). Psychopathology, self-esteem, sexual and ego functions as correlates of suicide and violence risk. *Archives of Suicide Research, 1,* 27–38.

Plutchik, R., & van Praag, H. (1990). Psychosocial correlates of suicide and violence risk. In H. M. van Praag, R. Plutchik, & A. Apter (Eds.), *Violence and suicidality: Perspectives in clinical and psychobiological research* (pp. 37–65). New York, NY: Brunner/Mazel.

Riggs, D., Caulfield, M., & Fair, K. (2009). Risk for intimate partner violence: Factors associated with perpetration and victimization. In P. M. Kleespies (Ed.), *Behavioral emergencies: An evidence-based resource for evaluating and managing risk of suicide, violence, and victimization* (pp. 189–208). Washington, DC: APA Books.

Rudd, M. D., & Joiner, T. (1998). The assessment, management, and treatment of suicidality: Toward clinically informed and balanced standards of care. *Clinical Psychology: Science and Practice, 5,* 135–150.

Rudd, M. D., Joiner, T., & Rajab, M. H. (2001). *Treating suicidal behavior: An effective, time-limited approach.* New York, NY: Guilford Press.

Stanley, B., & Brown, G. (2012). Safety planning intervention: A brief intervention to mitigate suicide risk. *Cognitive and Behavioral Practice*, 19, 256–264.

Swanson, J., Swartz, M., Essock, S., Osher, F., Wagner, H. R., Goodman, L.,. . . Meador, K. (2002). The social-environmental context of violent behavior in persons treated for severe mental illness. *The American Journal of Public Health*, 92, 1523–1531.

Tarasoff v. Regents of University of California, 13 Cal. 3d 177 (1974).

Tarasoff v. Regents of University of California, 17 Cal. 3d 425 (1976).

Tomasula, J., Anderson, L., Littleton, H., & Riley-Tillman, T. C. (2012). The association between sexual assault and suicidal activity in a national sample. *School Psychology Quarterly*, 27, 109–119.

Turner, H., Finkelhor, D., & Ormrod, R. (2010). Polyvictimization in a national sample of children and youth. *American Journal of Preventive Medicine*, 38, 323–330.

VandeCreek, L., & Knapp, S. (2000). Risk management and life-threatening behaviors. *Journal of Clinical Psychology*, 56, 1335–1351.

Van Dulmen, M., Mata, A., Claxton, S., Klipfel, K., Schinka, K., Swahn, M., & Bossarte, R. (2013). Longitudinal associations between violence and suicidality from adolescence into adulthood. *Suicide and Life-Threatening Behavior*, 43, 523–531.

Welfel, E., Werth, J. Jr., & Benjamin, G. (2009). Introduction to the duty to protect. In J. Werth, Jr., E. Welfel, & G. Benjamin (Eds.), *The duty to protect: Ethical, legal, and professional considerations for mental health professionals* (pp. 3–8). Washington, DC: APA Books.

Widom, C., Czaja, S., & Dutton, M. (2008). Childhood victimization and lifetime revictimization. *Child Abuse and Neglect*, 32, 785–796.

Widom, C., Dutton, M., Czaja, S., & Dumont, K. (2005). Development and validation of a new instrument to assess lifetime trauma and victimization history. *Journal of Traumatic Stress*, 18, 519–531.

Zellman, G., & Fair, C. (2002). Preventing and reporting abuse. In J. Myers, L. Berliner, J. Briere, C. Hendrix, C. Jenny, & T. Reid (Eds.), *The APSAC handbook on child maltreatment* (2nd ed., pp. 449–475). Thousand Oaks, CA: Sage.

Training for Decision Making under the Stress of Emergency Conditions

Phillip M. Kleespies

Abstract

When under time or procedure pressure, people change their decision-making strategies. They may accelerate information processing and filter the information they will process. In this chapter, the author presents several models for decision making under pressure and compares them to more traditional models. The naturalistic decision-making models are proposed as more appropriate for decision making when working with high-risk patients under emergency conditions. Given that it is often stressful for clinicians to evaluate and manage patients or clients who are considered at acute risk to themselves or others, the author presents a model for training to reduce stress that is based on Meichenbaum's stress inoculation training. The chapter concludes with a discussion of the training for skill development and competence in dealing with behavioral emergencies that is consistent with the recommendations of the APA Task Force on the Assessment of Competence in Professional Psychology.

Key Words: decision making, decision making under stress, naturalistic decision-making models, behavioral emergencies, stress training, skill development with behavioral emergencies, competence with behavioral emergencies

As noted in the Introduction to this volume, this book is intended to be a handbook to which mental health clinicians can refer when they wish to acquire information about the evaluation and management of behavioral emergencies. In that sense, it is primarily devoted to the domain of knowledge, as in the knowledge, skill, and attitude (KSA) model that supports competency-based professional training (Baartman & Bruijn, 2011). Kleespies (2014) has addressed the issue of acquiring skill in this area of practice, and I will discuss that domain of the KSA model in this chapter. We will cover three major topics: (1) models for decision making under the stress of dealing with behavioral emergencies; (2) *stress* training, or a model for training to reduce the stress involved in managing behavioral emergencies; and (3) training for skill development and competence with *experience near* and actual behavioral emergencies.

Models for Decision Making under Stress

People change their decision-making strategies based on the task they are confronting. Payne, Bettman, and Johnson (1988) have shown that under increased time pressure, individuals will accelerate their information processing, filter what information they will process, and change the method that they use for decision making. Among the mental health disciplines, clinical and counseling psychologists have often been trained in the scientist-practitioner or Boulder model (Jones & Mehr, 2007). This model calls for an integration of science and practice such that the practitioner is directed by empirical data and scientific methods for the resolution of clinical issues. Through scientific inquiry, he or she is also to contribute to the development and enhancement of practice. In this model, Jones and Mehr have pointed out that the first role of the scientist-practitioner is that of a researcher.

The decision-making model of the scientist or researcher, however, is typically one in which the individual is very deliberative and analytical. Yet, this type of approach is not necessarily one that is best suited for the dynamic and fast-paced circumstances that can accompany the evaluation and management of behavioral emergencies, or even for the give-and-take of emotionally charged psychotherapy sessions. There is a need for a decision-making model for clinicians who must deal with patients or clients who are at high risk for harm to themselves or others, about whom information may be incomplete, whose emotional state may be highly charged, for whom the best course of action may be uncertain, and with whom there is time pressure to arrive at a decision. In this section, I will briefly discuss three broad categories of theoretical models for decision making (Polic, 2009; Shaban, 2005)—*rational* and *normative* models, *descriptive* models, and *naturalistic decision-making* models—with the intent of arriving at a model appropriate for dealing with behavioral emergency conditions.

Rational and Normative Models for Decision Making

In a rational model of decision making, the decision maker conducts a systematic, organized information search, considers all alternatives, generates a large set of options, compares the options, and selects the course of action that is most likely to lead to an optimal outcome (Driskell & Johnston, 1998). There is an assumption of a clearly defined problem and an impartial and fully rational decision maker.

Normative models are rational decision-making procedures that are based on probabilities. The Bayesian inference model (or Bayes theorem for judgments), perhaps the best known of these models, presents an analysis of all possible choices and their associated risks. The risks, however, are assigned weights and each choice is assigned a probability. By weighing risks and probabilities, the option with the highest utility for the decision maker can be determined (Shaban, 2005).

In the past, rational and normative models were considered ideal. They were the preferred models of the scientist or of those responsible for allocating financial resources. Deviations from the ideal were seen as a breakdown in the decision-making process (Janis & Mann, 1977). More recently, however, the limitations of these models for certain tasks has become evident. First, as it takes a relatively long time to elucidate all the options and come to a judgment, these models are best used for long-range planning rather than for the fast-paced decision making that may be needed in an emergency. Second, under dynamic and changing circumstances, when decisions must be made with incomplete knowledge, the requirements for complete quantification in a rational model cannot be adequately fulfilled. Finally, it has been demonstrated that in actual practice human decision making does not occur according to the processes described in rational models (Kahneman, Slovic, & Tversky, 1982). This latter point gave rise to interest in decision-making models that attempt to describe how people actually arrive at decisions.

Descriptive Models of Decision Making

Psychologists such as Simon (1957) and Tversky and Kahneman (1974) challenged the notion that people attempt to evaluate all available response choices as called for in rational models of decision making. Simon proposed a concept of *bounded* or limited rationality to describe typical human decision making. From this perspective, the individual considers only as many alternatives as needed to find one that satisfies him or her. From a somewhat different perspective, Tversky and Kahneman proposed that, under conditions of uncertainty, people frequently rely on a limited number of heuristic principles (or strategies) to reduce complex decision-making tasks to simpler judgmental operations. They provided empirical support for their proposal in numerous studies in which they demonstrated that when conditions were uncertain, not only relatively naïve subjects but also experienced researchers tended to abandon probabilities, such as the base rates of events or the sample size of groups, and they based their decisions on heuristics (or rules of thumb). An example of such a rule of thumb might be what they have referred to as *representativeness* (or having characteristics similar to those attributed to certain groups of people or things) (see Kahneman et al., 1982, for other examples).

In his book *Thinking, Fast and Slow*, Kahneman (2011) has placed the heuristics model within a larger, two-system framework for thinking and decision making. What he refers to as System 1 consists of thinking and perceiving that occurs automatically and quickly, without great effort. This is the system by which we recognize objects, perceive causality, and think intuitively. Heuristics, or rules of thumb, are a part of this system. On the other hand, System 2 consists of thinking that involves effortful mental activity and includes critical thought and analysis. Much of the time, System 2 runs in *low-effort mode*, but it is activated when tasks or events are encountered that require analytical and logical reasoning. The dominance of one or the other system, at any particular time, may be determined by the demands of the situation, by the preference of the individual, or by the degree of emotional involvement in the outcome of events.

Naturalistic Decision-Making Models

Although descriptive models approach the process of decision making in everyday life more closely than rational models, they nonetheless tend to be based on evidence from laboratory studies. As such, they fail to take into account the context that can accompany decision making in the real world where the decision maker may confront many different pressures. As a result, decision researchers and theorists began to question how experienced decision makers (i.e., those who worked in dynamic, uncertain, and fast-moving natural environments, and who were good at what they did) went about assessing situations and making decisions. This direction of theory and research is more consistent with the decision making that often occurs when evaluating and managing behavioral emergencies or situations in which a patient or client is at acute risk of suicide and/or violence. Several naturalistic decision-making (NDM) models have been proposed and I will briefly describe them here.

The recognition-primed decision model. Klein (2009) proposed the recognition-primed decision (RPD) model to explain how experienced decision makers can identify a situation and generate a course of action without needing to consider multiple options. He theorized that, in many situations, such a decision maker identifies the particular situation as similar to situations that he or she has experienced in the past and recognizes a typical course of action. When confronted with a situation for which he or she has no immediate match, the experienced decision maker searches for features of the situation whereby he or she might place it into a known category. If this *feature matching* effort fails, the decision maker tries to mentally synthesize relevant features into a new causal explanation of the situation. The more experienced the decision makers, the more likely they are able to have a mental match for the situation or be able to match features and have a feasible course of action.

The RPD model asserts that experience and expertise with a task can allow a decision maker to find a plausible option as one of the first (if not the first) considered. Time pressure need not have a negative effect on performance because the experienced decision maker uses pattern recognition, which can occur very quickly. Klein (2009) has cited various studies in support of his model. Two examples follow.

Randel, Pugh, Reed, Schuler, and Wyman (1994) studied electronic warfare technicians while they were performing a simulated task. They found that 93% of the decisions involved noncomparative deliberations in keeping with the RPD model. Only 2 of 38 decisions were found to involve comparisons between options. In a second study, Calderwood, Klein, and Crandall (1988) investigated the quality of chess moves by chess masters and Class B chess players under tournament conditions (2.6 minutes per move) and blitz conditions (6 seconds per move). Under the extreme stress of blitz chess, it was found that the rate of blunders increased for the Class B players (from 11% to 25%) but not for the chess masters, whose blunder rate remained essentially unchanged at 7% to 8%. The authors contended that the more experienced chess masters had a greater range of, and/or more easily accessible, matches to the chess board configurations.

The recognition/metacognition model. The recognition/metacognition (R/M) model (like the RPD model just discussed) posits that the experienced decision maker utilizes an initial level of pattern recognition, but it goes on to posit that pattern recognition activates schemas (or mental structures) related to past situations with similar elements (Cohen, Freeman, & Thompson, 2009). These schemas are said to be under metacognitive control and can be critiqued for problems with the recognitional schemas. Critiquing can identify problems such as missing key elements, contradictory elements, and faulty or doubtful assumptions. The critiquing process can lead to additional information retrieval and a reinterpretation of cues to bring about a more satisfactory situation model for decision making.

The R/M model attempts to include critical thinking in addition to recognition priming as part of the process utilized by experienced decision makers. It posits that proficient decision makers work with developing situation scenarios in which they go through a mental investigation of gaps and conflicts that may require modifications to the pattern that has been recognized. Cohen et al. have presented some evidence that these critiquing or critical thinking skills can be enhanced through training. In a small study, R/M trained participants considered significantly more factors in their evaluation of a battle scenario than a control group. They also placed greater value on the factors that more experienced senior officers valued.

The situation awareness model. Many errors that are said to be due to poor decision making are attributable to the situation awareness portion of the decision-making process. Given an individual's perception of the situation, he or she may make a correct decision, but there can be a problem with the perception. The situation awareness (SA) model of Endsley (2009) gives particular attention to accurate perception of the particular situation. It has three levels: (1) perceiving critical factors in the environment; (2) understanding what those factors mean; and (3) understanding what is likely to happen with a changing situation in the future.

Similar to the RPD and R/M models, the experienced decision maker in the SA model makes use of long-term memory stores of schemata or mental models (i.e., mental representations of similar situations or events) to aid in understanding the current situation and in making a decision about a course of action. In effect, they look for a best fit between characteristics of the situation and the characteristics of known categories of events. Of course, the decision maker needs to be careful not to become too automatic in responding because he or she could be susceptible to missing novel aspects of the situation.

The hypervigilant strategy. As previously noted, in many settings, decisions must be made under time pressure with incomplete, ambiguous, and/or conflicting information. Under these conditions, decision makers must conduct a less-than-exhaustive information search, do an accelerated evaluation of the data, consider a limited number of alternatives, and come to a rapid closure on a decision. Johnston, Driskell, and Salas (1997) referred to this type of decision-making process as a *hypervigilant* decision-making strategy. They contrasted it with a *vigilant* strategy by which they meant a rational-analytic approach, as described earlier. They contended that, in comparison to the vigilant approach, a hypervigilant strategy does not represent a defect in the decision-making process, but rather an adaptive response given the time-limited nature of the task.

Johnston et al. put their theory to the test with a naturalistic task. They had 90 US Navy enlisted personnel from a technical training school perform a computer-based simulation in which they had to monitor a radar screen for threats to their ship. Numerous unidentified contacts or potential threats popped up on the screen. The participants were initially trained in either a vigilant or a hypervigilant decision-making strategy. The task was to access three information fields or menus to classify the type of craft that had appeared, whether it was civilian or military, and whether its intentions were hostile or peaceful. They were told to work as quickly as they could so that they could identify the other ship and either engage it as hostile or clear it for safe contact with their ship. The researchers also manipulated stress levels with auditory distractions, task load, and time pressure.

The findings indicated that those who used a hypervigilant decision-making strategy made a significantly greater number of accurate target identifications. Performance was degraded under high-stress conditions for both types of strategies, but those using a vigilant strategy still performed significantly worse than those using a hypervigilant strategy. It was concluded that the *best-fit* pattern for decision making is likely to be dependent on the nature of the task demands. Under some conditions (e.g., time pressure, incomplete information), a hypervigilant approach can be the more effective strategy.

Naturalistic Decision Making in Behavioral Emergencies

Several of the NDM models for expert decision makers clearly have common ground. The RPD model, the R/M model, and the SA model all take experience and long-term memory storage as crucial to recognition in the present of similar patterns, situations, or events from the past. In most cases, this type of recognition enables the individual to make relatively quick decisions about a course of action when there is time pressure to do so. The R/M model stresses critiquing the fit of the pattern to a greater extent than either the RPD model or the SA model, while the SA model puts a greater emphasis on awareness of the current situation than the other two. The hypervigilant strategy describes how, in naturalistic task settings with time pressure, it is necessary to rapidly evaluate the limited information that can be gathered. It does not, however, invoke experience, long-term memory storage, and pattern recognition as important to the development of decision-making expertise.

I contend that the NDM models of decision making are crucial for understanding what must be learned to acquire the skills necessary to become competent in the evaluation and management of behavioral emergencies. When a clinician works with patients who may be at risk for suicide and/or violence, lives can be in the balance, and the time for evaluating and managing the situation can be very limited. It is important that the clinician have good situational awareness (e.g., be aware of the patient's demeanor and behavior, as well as the resources available to cope with the patient's behavior should problems escalate). He or she needs to rapidly gather and analyze the information that can be obtained in a limited period of time. Because time is limited, the focus must be on gathering information that is essential to the decision at hand, calling upon past experiences (or be recognition-primed) in evaluating the patient's condition and deciding if something preventive needs to be done. With recognition schema that seem to be a good fit, the clinician needs to be able to critique the schema to detect gaps or inconsistencies. In Kahneman's (2011) terms, the clinician needs to learn to recognize situations in which mistakes or biases are likely and try to avoid them, particularly when the stakes are high.

The Impact of Stress on Decision Making

Not only do we, as clinicians, need to have models for decision making under stress (as described earlier), but we also need to be able to cope with stress to minimize its potentially negative impact on our decision making. I should note that, when I speak of stress, I am referring to the cognitive-appraisal model of stress offered by Richard Lazarus (1994). In this model, stress is not something that is solely induced by events in the environment, nor is it solely a response in the individual. Rather, stress involves an interaction between the person or group and the environment, where the demands of the situation are appraised as taxing or exceeding the coping resources available to deal with them. The individual, therefore, feels distressed and under pressure to find a way to cope, meet the demands, and relieve the distress. In this model, it is the perception and assessment of his or her ability to manage the situation that can lead to stress, particularly if the person doubts that he or she has the resources to cope with or control the unfolding events.

I believe it is self-evident that dealing with behavioral emergencies can be stressful, but there is also evidence from various surveys that supports that opinion. Pope and Tabachnick (1993), in a national survey of psychologists, found that 97% of the respondents reported being afraid of losing a patient to suicide. In a survey of nearly 300 recently

graduated, former psychology interns, Kleespies, Penk, and Forsyth (1993) found that 97% of the sample had had a patient or patients with suicidal ideation or behavior during their training years, and that there was a dose-response increase in the emotional impact on the intern as a function of the increasing severity of the patient's suicidal behavior (i.e., from suicide ideation to suicide attempt to suicide completion). Rodolfa, Kraft, and Reilley (1988) surveyed staff and psychology trainees at 12 counseling centers and 14 VA medical centers. Participants rated 19 client behaviors and 24 therapist experiences in terms of how stressful they were. The two client behaviors that were ranked as most stressful were client–clinician violence and a suicide attempt by a client. In that national survey by Pope and Tabachnick (1993), 89% of the psychologists reported experiencing episodes in which they were afraid that a patient might attack a third party. There is also evidence in the literature indicating that clinicians who treat victims of interpersonal violence (e.g., victims of assault, rape, or torture) over a prolonged period of time may suffer negative effects that have been termed *vicarious trauma* (McCann & Pearlman, 1990) and *secondary traumatic stress* (Figley, 1995).

Of course, one can question whether stress can actually have a negative effect on decision making, and theorists such as Hammond (2000) have done so. As noted earlier, it has been found that people adapt and change their decision-making strategies to simpler operations depending on the intensity of the task and the time demands. These more abbreviated operations (e.g., the naturalistic decision-making strategies) have been found to be more effective under conditions of task and time pressure than lengthier, more complex rational strategies—at least with decision makers who are expert in their field. It seems feasible, therefore, that for some people (particularly those who are expert at what they do) performance might improve under stressful conditions rather than be degraded. The question remains, however, whether stress has a deleterious effect on the decision making of those who are not so expert or who are new at a particular task or in a particular field.

The study of chess players mentioned earlier in this chapter (Calderwood et al., 1988) has relevance in regard to this question. As noted in that study, the "blunder" rate of the more expert chess masters was essentially unchanged under the time pressure of "blitz" conditions (i.e., 6 seconds per move) as compared to tournament conditions (i.e., 2.6 minutes per move). The blunder rate of the less expert players, however, increased significantly under so-called blitz conditions.

In another laboratory study, LeBlanc, MacDonald, McArthur, King, and Lepine (2005) had flight paramedics from two levels of certification participate in either a low-stress or high-stress study condition. In the high-stress condition, the participants were in a simulated ambulance with an adult-sized mannequin on a stretcher. The mannequin was programmed to replicate many human physiologic functions, such as heart rate, pulse in limbs, breath sounds, and so forth. The paramedics had to diagnose and manage respiratory failure, including doing a tracheal intubation. They then completed an anxiety inventory and were required to complete a set of drug dosage problems. Those in the low-stress condition completed a study questionnaire and then completed the anxiety inventory and the set of drug dosage problems. Those in the high-stress condition reported a significantly higher level of anxiety and did significantly worse on solving the drug dosage problems. The investigators concluded that when paramedics had to calculate drug dosages after experiencing a highly stressful situation, their performance was impaired.

Several studies have examined issues pertinent to decision making under stressful, real-life conditions. In a case control study, Gawande, Studdert, Orav, Brennan, and Zinner (2003) investigated the occurrence of an adverse medical event (i.e., when a foreign body such as a gauze swab or an instrument is accidentally left in the body of a patient following surgery). Although such events are statistically rare, the investigators found that the probability of such an event was eight times more likely when the operation was performed under emergency conditions and three times more likely when the operation involved an unexpected change in procedure. They attributed these increased risks to the abandonment of routine procedures and to the time pressure that exists during an emergency operation.

In an example of the effects of *production pressure* on decision making, Gaba, Howard, and Jump (1994) conducted an anonymous survey of anesthesiologists in California. They defined production pressure as "overt and covert pressures and incentives on personnel to place production, not safety, as their primary priority" (p. 488). Survey respondents reported internal pressure to work agreeably with surgeons and to try to avoid delaying surgical cases. They also, however, reported overt pressure from surgeons and hospital administrators to proceed with cases instead of canceling them and to hasten anesthetic procedures. Nearly half (49%) of the respondents had observed an anesthesiologist pressured to administer anesthesia in what they considered an unsafe fashion; 31% had seen patients undergoing surgery with significant contraindications for either the surgery or the anesthesia; 34% had observed a colleague perform anesthesia on a patient for whom anesthesia had just been refused or canceled for safety reasons by another anesthesiologist. The authors concluded that production pressure from internal and external sources was perceived by survey participants as having resulted in, at least in some cases, decisions to proceed with anesthesia under unsafe conditions.

The Stress of Behavioral Emergencies and *Stress* Training

Evaluating and managing patients or clients who may be acutely suicidal or potentially violent, or at great risk of becoming a victim of violence, can be stress-inducing in and of itself; but, as we have seen earlier, it may not be the only source of stress for the clinician. It has been said that patients typically don't schedule a time to have an emergency or crisis. These events can, and often do, occur at very difficult times—for example, when the clinician has other distressed or agitated patients waiting to be seen, when other staff are being kept from their duties to see if their assistance may be needed, or when normal clinic activities are being disrupted to cope with such an emergency situation. Unfortunately, the mental health disciplines have generally not made training in this area of practice a routine and integrated part of their educational process (see, e.g., Schmitz et al., 2012), and they have clearly not made consistent efforts to assist clinicians in dealing with the stress that can accompany work with high-risk patients or clients (Kleespies & Ponce, 2009).

Although it might seem obvious, it is nonetheless reasonable to ask if training and/or experience with the evaluation of behavioral emergencies actually makes a difference in the management of patients. A recent study by Teo, Holly, Leary, and McNiel (2012) has provided some relevant information on this issue. As part of a larger study, these investigators examined whether unstructured violence risk assessments completed by experienced attending psychiatrists were more accurate than those completed by psychiatric residents. Using a retrospective case control design, the research team selected 151 patients from four locked psychiatric units of a county hospital who had physically assaulted staff during the years 2003–2008. They also selected an equal number of nonviolent patients matched for psychiatric inpatient unit and month of admission. On admission to these units, physicians rated each patient on a four-point assault precaution checklist that ranged from zero (no clinical indication for violence precautions) to three (strong intent is present or unable to control impulses). It was found that the clinical assessments by attending psychiatrists had a moderate degree of predictive validity, while those completed by residents were no better than chance. The violence risk assessments by the attending psychiatrists were significantly more accurate than the risk assessments by residents. The investigators concluded that less training and experience is associated with less accurate violence risk assessment.

There have been several recent efforts to provide models or programs for training in the behavioral emergencies or in a particular type of behavioral emergency. The books by Kleespies (1998, 2009) were organized as a proposed curriculum for teaching about behavioral emergencies and related topics. Two publications by McNiel and his colleagues (McNiel, Chamberlain, et al., 2008; McNiel, Fordwood, et al., 2008) have reported on a study in which they provided a 5-hour workshop for a group of psychiatry residents and psychology interns on evidence-based assessment and management of the risk of violence and risk of suicide. A comparison group attended a 3-hour workshop on the application of evidence-based medicine to psychiatry that was not focused on risk assessment for violence or suicide. The investigators found that, immediately after the training, the study group participants were able to identify the evidence-based variables that pertain to violence risk and suicide risk in a more systematic way. They were also able to be more explicit about the significance of risk and protective factors when they developed plans for intervention to reduce risk. In relation to the comparison group, the training group's improvements were described as substantial. Further, the risk assessment training was associated with increased confidence in risk assessment skill.

With a focus more exclusively on training in suicide risk assessment, Oordt, Jobes, Fonseca, and Schmidt (2009) also demonstrated that training in a workshop format with an empirically based assessment and treatment approach to suicidal patients could significantly impact the confidence, as well as a number of the suicide care practices, of US Air Force mental health professionals, both post-training and at the 6-month follow-up. Further, those who have been concerned with training in the evaluation and management of suicidal patients have developed what they consider to be core competencies needed to become clinicians capable of working with individuals at risk for suicide (Rudd, Cukrowicz, & Bryan, 2008; Suicide Prevention Resource center, 2006). There are eight sections that include competencies related to the clinician's attitude and approach to the suicidal patient, the clinician's understanding of suicide, the ability to collect accurate assessment information, the ability to formulate risk, the ability to develop a treatment and services plan, the ability to manage the care of a suicidal patient, the ability to document the assessment, formulation, plan, and so on, and the ability to understand legal and ethical issues related to suicidality.

There have been at least two workshop-type programs that have been developed for teaching content consistent with these core competencies. One is a 6-hour program titled *Assessing and Managing Suicide Risk: Core Competencies for Mental Health Professionals* (AMSR; Suicide Prevention Resource Center, 2011), and the other is a 16-hour program called *Recognizing and Responding to Suicide Risk* (RRSR; American Association of Suicidology, 2011).

Jacobson, Osteen, Jones, and Berman (2012) have published an outcome study using the RRSR. In this study, 452 participants in RRSR training workshops were assessed at three points (pretest, post-test, and at the 4-month follow-up). The assessments included a variety of measures related to attitudes toward suicide prevention, confidence in working with clients at risk of suicide, and changes in clinical practice behaviors. The results suggested that training in this workshop format could improve clinicians' attitudes toward working with suicidal patients, their confidence about doing so, and their clinical practice skills as measured by their response to suicidal client vignettes both post-test and at the 4-month follow-up. The practice skills assessed were the ability to identify risk and protective factors, the ability to make a formulation of risk, and the ability to make a management plan in response to the risk. One limitation of the study was the lack of opportunity to observe actual clinical practice and behavior in the assessment and management of actual suicidal patients.

These workshops appear to be informative, useful, and well constructed. Pisani, Cross, and Gould (2011), however, conducted a rather sobering review of the results of participating in workshops. The following three criteria were included in the review: (a) the target audience was primarily mental health professionals; (b) the program's educational objectives targeted clinical competence in the assessment and management of suicide risk; and (c) there was at least one peer-reviewed article that described or evaluated the training or explicated the clinical model. Twelve workshops met these criteria (including the AMSR and the RRSR). The investigators gave a cross-program description of the objectives and methods of the workshops. They also reviewed the training qualification and the feedback for the trainers who delivered the workshops, and they reviewed published studies about training outcomes (the study noted previously by Jacobson et al., 2012, was not available for this 2011 review). They found that research was very limited in terms of documenting real-world outcomes for those mental health clinicians who participated in these workshops. The available studies indicated that clinical knowledge and attitudes improved with the workshop training (at least during the relatively brief period of follow-up); and one study (McNiel, Fordwood, et al., 2008) found some evidence of improved clinical skill. Most importantly, however, the investigators found no evidence of improved real-life clinical care for suicidal patients.

Clearly, acquiring knowledge about suicide risk and violence risk, improving one's ability to do a formulation of the risk, and having practice in risk evaluation and management under the controlled conditions of a workshop can be a very valuable training experience. As I have contended earlier, however, it is only when the clinician confronts real-life conditions that he or she can ultimately learn to deal with the challenges of these high-stake situations in which there is risk of suicide or violence to others. Real-life emergencies are situations that are often stressful in themselves, but there can also be many other associated stressors (e.g., time pressure, other concurrent demands on the clinician, the needs of other patients). That is why it is important to have not only training but also what has been referred to as *stress training* (Driskell & Johnston, 1998).

Stress training has its roots in the stress inoculation training (SIT) of Donald Meichenbaum (1985, 2007). Meichenbaum's position is that the object of stress management training is not to eliminate stress "but to encourage clients to view stressful events as problems-to-be-solved rather than as personal threats. The goal is to make clients better problem solvers to deal with future stressful events as they might arise" (Meichenbaum, 1985, p. 30). In addition to helping people be better problem solvers, however, he has also emphasized learning techniques designed to relieve distress and foster emotion

regulation. As he has stated, "Rather than conceiving their stressors as being overwhelming, uncontrollable, unpredictable, debilitating, and hopeless, the SIT trainer helps clients develop a sense of 'learned resourcefulness'" (Meichenbaum, 2007, p. 513).

The SIT model has three phases: (1) a *conceptualization phase*; (2) a *skills acquisition and rehearsal phase*; and (3) an *application and follow-through phase*. In the conceptualization phase, the focus is on attaining a better understanding of the nature of stress, its effect on emotion and performance, and on re-conceptualizing it into transactional or cognitive-appraisal terms. The skills acquisition and rehearsal phase centers on developing and rehearsing a variety of coping skills, primarily through imaginal and behavioral rehearsal. Finally, the application and follow-through phase focuses on transitioning from the imaginal and behavioral rehearsal to graded in-vivo or real-life exposure to stressors.

Although it has been applied with some professional groups, the SIT model was originally developed as a clinical treatment program for individuals who had difficulty dealing with problems such as physical pain, anger, and phobic responses. It has retained an association with treatment for clinical conditions. In an effort to extend stress training beyond the clinical domain, Johnston and Cannon-Bowers (1996) have developed a modification of the SIT model (i.e., stress exposure training, or SET) to be used in training professionals who must perform tasks under high-stress conditions.

As presented by Driskell and Johnston (1998), the SET model has three objectives. The first is to convey knowledge of the stressful task and environment. This objective is based on the assumption that stress is reduced by giving an individual information about what to expect in performing under stressful conditions. The second objective is to emphasize skill development. This involves training people in the behavioral and cognitive skills needed to perform the task or tasks effectively under stress. The third objective is to build confidence in the ability to perform under stress. This can only be achieved when the person in training experiences success or task mastery under actual stressful conditions.

Consistent with these objectives, the SET approach has three stages: (1) an initial stage in which information is provided about the importance of stress training and what stressors are likely to be encountered; (2) a skills training phase in which cognitive and behavioral skills for performing the task or tasks under stress are acquired; and (3) a final stage of applying and practicing the acquired skills under conditions that increasingly approximate the potentially stressful environment or circumstances.

I have proposed that this three-phase model (with modifications) be used as a guide for training clinicians to deal with behavioral emergencies (Kleespies, 2014). Thus, there is a phase 1 in which information is provided about what stressors may be involved when a behavioral emergency arises; the clinician-in-training also learns, through lectures, readings, and/or workshops, about suicide risk, violence risk, and the risk of interpersonal victimization. Such preparatory information can begin to lessen the buildup of stress by clarifying misconceptions, reducing fear of the unknown, and increasing the clinician-in-training's understanding of this area of practice. It can provide a preview of the stressful events and make them less unfamiliar.

Phase 2 consists of cognitive and behavioral skills training through case conferences in which high-risk situations are discussed and/or through scenario-based training in which potentially stress-inducing clinical situations are presented and used for mental practice in making decisions about high-risk patients (see Kleespies, 2014, for some suggested scenarios). As noted by Meichenbaum (1985), it is in this phase that the clinician-in-training can rehearse attempts at how to cope and receive feedback on these exercises, as well as hear how others might have responded.

In phase 2, there are also certain stress training strategies that can begin to be integrated into the training process (Driskell & Johnston, 1998). *Mental practice* or *mental simulation* is most consistent with the scenario-based training previously noted. It refers to cognitive rehearsal without actually performing the task. It is a technique by which the mind creates a mental representation of a cognitive skill or a motor skill with the intent to mentally practice and enhance performance. In a meta-review of studies of mental simulation, van Meer and Theunissen (2009), concluded that "the general effectiveness of MS (mental simulation) for both motor and cognitive tasks has been established beyond reasonable doubt" (p. 104). Of course, it should not be used instead of actual practice, but it can be an excellent training adjunct. There is a debate in the literature about whether mental practice is as effective with *open skills* as with *closed skills,* where an open skill requires one to improvise and be reactive to changes while a closed skill is without much interference from external influences. With open skills, the investigators suggest reducing

complexity and practicing components of the task. Behavioral emergencies certainly require *open skills*. A clinician-in-training might think through and mentally practice how he or she would respond in a scenario in which a patient was feeling hopeless and expressing suicidal thoughts, or in a scenario in which a patient was feeling disrespected, angry, and having an urge to become violent to others.

In complex situations, where there are often competing demands, it can be crucial to learn *prioritization skills*. If there is time pressure and/or high stakes, the clinician may need to think through what is most important to deal with or accomplish first. Time and attention cannot be devoted to low priority tasks when one may lose the opportunity to deal with more critical issues. In scenario-based training with behavioral emergencies, he or she can mentally rehearse how multiple tasks or multiple patients might be prioritized in terms of the urgency of each person's condition.

Phase 3 involves applying and practicing skills under conditions that increasingly approximate the potentially stressful task or situation. With suicidal or potentially violent patients, applying and practicing evaluation and management skills is best initiated under close, on-site supervision. In fact, it can be an excellent learning experience if a more senior clinician or supervisor initially has the trainee or intern observe him or her doing an evaluation. On a subsequent case or two, they can switch and let the trainee or intern take the lead in the interview or evaluation while the supervisor is there to inquire further, if needed, or to assist in managing the case. In cases that follow, the trainee can do the evaluation more independently, with a supervisory consultation before the case is completed and before the management plan is decided on. In this way, the clinician-in-training can have a gradated experience leading to increasing mastery and autonomy.

This graduated approach allows the clinician-in-training to become more familiar with the stressors he or she may face with patients who are at risk without feeling overwhelmed. It also gradually builds confidence, and it is less likely than immediate exposure to an intensely stressful situation (without guidance or support) to interfere with learning and mastery of the task.

In this phase 3, the trainee or intern can practice additional stress training strategies. Thus, he or she can work on increasing his or her cognitive control while being involved with actual cases. Control can be improved by recognizing when thoughts irrelevant to the task or emotions occur, replacing them with task-focused cognitions. Attention can be consciously directed to task-relevant issues and away from distractions. The clinician can also employ physiological control strategies like relaxation through deep breathing exercises. The use of relaxation techniques is based on the premise that relaxation and stress are incompatible. If someone is relaxed, he or she is less likely to experience the negative reactions brought on by stress.

Overlearning has also been found to be a good training procedure for dealing with high-stress situations. The term refers to deliberate overtraining of a task beyond the level of proficiency. It is training to the point where aspects of the task become automatic and require less attention. Since stress can restrict attention in a negative way, making certain tasks automatic can compensate, to some degree, for the effects of stress. Of course, with overlearning and multiple experiences, the clinician-in-training also develops a store of memories or schemata of behavioral emergencies—for example, becoming more recognition-primed to understand a high-risk situation and quickly decide on a course of action to manage it.

Although this model for stress exposure training with behavioral emergencies has been presented in three phases, it should be noted that these phases are not intended to be strictly sequential. Clearly, the clinician-in-training can be acquiring a knowledge base in behavioral emergencies while simultaneously learning cognitive and behavioral skills through participation in case discussions and scenario-based training. Likewise, one can be learning cognitive and behavioral skills in simulated clinical scenarios while beginning to engage in the application of skills by doing evaluations with close supervisory monitoring. The model is presented in phases to emphasize the importance of taking a gradated approach to acquiring the skills needed to evaluate and arrive at decisions with high-risk patients under what are often stressful conditions. The three-phase model is also consistent with the position that a clinician-in-training is not fully competent until those skills learned in more controlled settings are put to the test in real-life situations with real-life consequences that can be life-threatening.

Training for Decision Making and Competence in Behavioral Emergencies

It is certainly possible that a clinician can know a great deal about risk and protective factors for suicide or violence, yet still lack skill in interacting and assisting patients who are suicidal or potentially violent. This possibility prompted Bongar, Lomax, and Harmatz (1992) to comment that "knowledge of risk factors and the capacity to respond in an effective way to those patients who present as an imminent risk of suicide may be independent areas of clinical competence" (pp. 262–263). This statement by Bongar et al. highlights my position (as noted previously) that making good decisions in high-stake situations in which a patient is at risk of suicide or violence to others, and in which there may be many associated stressors, is something that is only fully mastered under real-life conditions. As noted in the book by Kleespies (2014), this does not in any way negate the value of lectures, courses, workshops, discussions of past cases, or discussions of hypothetical case vignettes. These are all important methods by which mental health professionals learn about and, in some instances, practice the assessment and management of behavioral emergencies. They are methods that clearly help to prepare clinicians for actually dealing with patients or clients who are at acute risk of harm to themselves or others, and they do so under calm, controlled conditions that allow them to contemplate their decisions and actions without the stress of dealing with consequences if there is an error in judgment. However, these methods cannot provide the type of training that experience with actual patients in emergency situations can. Moreover, they are often discrete episodes of learning rather than extended experience that might be more likely to lead to recognition-priming and allow for greater mastery.

The APA Task Force on the Assessment of Competence in Professional Psychology (2006, October) has attempted to provide a conceptual framework for thinking about competence in the practice of psychology. They embrace a definition of professional competence that was proposed for the medical profession but which is felt to also be relevant for professional psychology. Within this definition, competence is "the habitual and judicious use of communication, knowledge, technical skills, clinical reasoning, emotions, values, and reflection in daily practice for the benefit of the individual and community being served" (Epstein & Hundert, 2002, p. 227). There is clearly an emphasis in this definition on *the habitual judicious use of knowledge, skills, and abilities in daily practice* as integral to achieving competence in professional functioning.

While recommending that there be a culture shift in psychology toward placing a high value on the assessment of competence, the APA Task Force also acknowledges that there have been many problems arriving at a consensus about what constitutes competence and how to assess competence and competencies. It emphasizes, however, that assessment should reflect fidelity to actual practice—for example, evaluating as closely as possible the actual behaviors that the clinician must perform in practice.

The Task Force goes on to state that there are *competencies* that are elements of *competence*. Competencies are conceptualized as clusters of integrated knowledge, skills, and abilities that enable an individual to fully perform a task. They are divided into foundational competencies and functional competencies. Foundational competencies have to do with scientific knowledge, scientific methods, knowledge of ethical and legal standards, and so forth. They form the building blocks of what psychologists do. Functional competencies, on the other hand, have to do with assessment, diagnosis, intervention, consultation, and so on. They reflect the knowledge, skills, and attitudes needed to actually perform the work of a professional psychologist. In my opinion, the assessment and management of behavioral emergencies is a functional competency, essential to the development of overall competence for practicing psychologists.

In assessing functional competencies, the Task Force has suggested the development of reliable methods that use case vignettes, video- or audio-tapes of patient–practitioner interactions, written work samples, and/or live patient–client situations. These methods are time intensive, labor intensive, and can be costly. Nonetheless, the Task Force's emphasis is on devising assessment methods that are *experience near*.

Experience near is a term used by the Task Force to describe the degree to which a task or measure reflects the actual behaviors the clinician must perform in practice. Thus, an assessment or training technique that involves the evaluation of a clinician while assessing a simulated patient is more experience near (i.e., closer to an actual experience with a patient) than having the clinician take a multiple-choice exam assessing his or her knowledge of a particular clinical condition. While a multiple-choice exam may be a good way to assess someone's knowledge base, evaluating a clinician while he or she assesses a simulated patient is a way to assess the individual's clinical skills.

In regard to becoming competent in the assessment and management of behavioral emergencies (i.e. assessing and managing patients/clients who are at high risk of suicide or violence or both),

I have contended that the training itself, let alone the assessment of competence, is best accomplished in real-life encounters with actual patients/clients at risk where the practitioner can have not only training, but the stress training discussed earlier in this chapter. In the pages that follow, I present a model for such a training program.

Training to evaluate and manage behavioral emergencies can be carried out using the three categories recommended in the APA Task Force (2006) report—knowledge, skill, and attitude. Such training also seems compatible with the stress exposure model (SET) for training.

A Knowledge Base for Behavioral Emergencies

In terms of a knowledge base, this volume can serve that purpose. The book starts with an overview of behavioral emergencies and then gives a framework for practice and training. These introductory chapters are followed by sections on (1) behavioral emergencies in youth (including chapters on the assessment and management of suicide risk, violence risk, and risk of victimization in children and adolescents); (2) behavioral emergencies in adults (including chapters on the assessment and management of suicide risk, violence risk, and risk of victimization in adults); and (3) behavioral emergencies in the elderly (including chapters on the assessment and management of suicide risk, violence risk, and risk of victimization in the elderly). These core sections are then followed by chapters covering (1) conditions that are either frequently associated with behavioral emergencies or need to be distinguished from behavioral emergencies (as, for example, non-suicidal self-injury, alcohol and drug-related issues, and neurological and endocrine disorders with behavioral manifestations); (2) the treatment of patients with ongoing or recurrent risk of suicide, violence, or interpersonal victimization (including psychological/behavioral treatment and psychopharmacological treatment); and (3) the legal, ethical, and psychological risks for the clinician who works with behavioral emergency cases.

A Supervisory Model for Teaching Skill and Attitude

As noted by Kleespies (1998, 2009), applying a knowledge base in practice with good supervision leads to skill development and clinical competency. When a patient or client is thought to be on the verge of suicide or violence, or of becoming a victim of violence, the situation can be stressful for the seasoned professional, let alone for those who are in training and less confident of their clinical abilities and status. When it comes to stressful clinical events, some working in the field have felt that clinicians-in-training have a protective advantage over professionals in that they work under the direction of a supervisor and can process events in an organized program (Brown, 1987). Rodolfa, Kraft, and Reilley (1988), however, found that patients' suicidal statements, patients' suicide attempts, and patients' attacks on the therapist were all rated as moderately to highly stressful by both professional psychologists and psychologists-in-training. Kleespies et al. (1993) also found evidence that the negative emotional impact of patients' suicidal behavior on psychologists-in-training may be as great or greater than that on professional psychologists. It seems clear that those who are first learning to cope with such difficult emergency situations need considerable instruction and support to reduce their level of stress.

A mentor model for learning under such conditions seems advisable. In this model, an experienced clinician and an intern or trainee are paired in settings where patients or clients at risk are evaluated. The intern or trainee has the opportunity to observe and work closely with the more seasoned professional who has been successfully engaged in this type of clinical work. The pressure of more complete clinical responsibility is only gradually assumed by the trainee, and anxiety is kept at manageable levels. In this model, it is important for the supervisor to be aware of the balance between support and intern responsibility, and to shift the balance appropriately over time to promote the more independent functioning of the clinician-in-training.

As recommended in the SET approach, the clinician-in-training, in working with a mentor, has the opportunity to begin applying and practicing the skills that he or she has acquired through lectures, workshops, mental practice with case vignettes, and observation. With this gradated approach, the stress inoculation discussed by Meichenbaum (2007) can begin to occur. As Meichenbaum noted, stress in these situations is never completely eliminated, but the objective of stress training is to assist the clinician in viewing these scenarios as problems that they have the skills to solve. Constructive attitudes develop from these experiences of mastery.

Clearly, there have been instances in which relatively inexperienced trainees have been placed in the front lines, so to speak, dealing with behavioral emergencies with little direct supervisory support. Under such circumstances, emergency and crisis work is often seen as trying and burdensome. Good support and supervision, however, can go a long way toward preventing a negative viewpoint and aiding in the development of a sense of competence in dealing with emotionally charged cases. Long ago, Barlow (1974) observed that psychology interns responded initially to emergency department duty with moderate to severe anxiety. He further observed that within about three months, a second response of increased clinical confidence began to emerge. This sense of competence was described by interns as one of the more important developments in their training.

A Model Program for Training in Emergency Psychological Services

Training in the evaluation and management of behavioral emergencies can occur in a number of different settings—an emergency room (ER), an urgent care clinic (UCC), a medical center that has a psychiatric consultation/liaison team, an acute inpatient psychiatry unit, or at a community-based walk-in clinic that occasionally sees patients who are suicidal or potentially violent. An ER is a very medical setting, but Covino (1989) found that the majority of psychiatric patients seen in a hospital ER had complaints that fell well within the competence of psychologists to evaluate and provide immediate management. Moreover, with good collaboration from the nursing and medical staff, complications can be minimized.

In the model program presented by Kleespies (2014) for psychology interns and/or postdoctoral fellows, the intern or fellow is on call to consult on cases in the ER or UCC on a morning or afternoon shift 1 day a week for 4–6 months. These consultations and evaluations take place under the supervision of a staff member (or mentor) who is experienced in this work and who coordinates the training experience. Interns may have three 4-month major rotations or two 6-month major rotations. During one of their major rotations (e.g., at a general mental health clinic or substance abuse treatment program) each intern in the internship program participates in consulting on cases in the ER or in a UCC where patients present with mental health or psychiatric problems or crises.

Given that it is important to prepare interns for the experience and to help them develop a knowledge base, the experience should have a lecture series that begins with a good orientation to the setting and to the types of patients and conditions that are likely to be encountered. The lecture series is one in which different staff or faculty with expertise on particular topics may be asked to provide lectures. The series might include topics such as the emergency interview, evaluating and managing suicide risk, evaluating and managing the risk of violence, alcohol and drug abuse problems, neurological disorders that may present as behavioral or psychological problems, and so forth.

Concurrent with the orientation and lectures, the participating interns can begin their experience in the ER or UCC by sitting in and observing the supervising psychologist as he or she does at least two evaluations. The patient is, of course, asked for verbal consent to allow the intern to observe for training purposes.[1] After two or three evaluations and the opportunity to read his or her mentor's written reports, the intern is usually ready to begin doing one or two evaluations, with the mentor observing and contributing as appropriate. Subsequently, the intern is typically ready to become more autonomous in doing evaluations, but the mentoring psychologist is always present in the ER, UCC, or walk-in clinic for consultation or assistance with difficult situations or decisions. Moreover, each case is discussed with the supervisor before a final decision is made about the disposition or plan for management and follow-up. Two to three days after the intern has been on-call, there is a wrap-up and supervision meeting where each of the cases seen that week are reviewed with the supervising psychologist. If two or three interns have been on-call, this supervision can be held in a group session. Through this process of close supervision and increasing autonomy, the intern develops a sense of being able to master the stresses and problems presented by work with patients who are at acute risk to themselves or others. They also begin to acquire a reservoir of experiences that they will be able to call upon in the future.

A Model for Assessing Competence in Evaluating and Managing Behavioral Emergencies

When a clinician-in-training has completed training in an area of practice such as behavioral emergencies, assessing whether the individual is competent to practice independently is not a simple matter. As the APA Task Force on the Assessment of Competence in Professional Psychology (2006, October) indicated, assessment models for competence should have validity, feasibility, and fidelity to actual practice. Validity, of course, refers to whether the assessment measures the competency it purports

to measure. Feasibility refers to practical issues such as the resources, cost, expertise, and the time needed to develop and maintain the assessment. Finally, as noted earlier in this chapter, fidelity refers to the degree to which the assessment reflects the actual behaviors that the clinician performs in practice.

If we are interested in measuring knowledge that a trainee has acquired, we typically look to multiple-choice, essay, and short-answer questions as measurements. If we are interested in measuring professional decision making, the APA Task Force seems to support the use of case-based oral examinations. This type of exam has been used extensively in specialty certification programs, such as with the American Board of Professional Psychology (ABPP) certification. Case materials are presented in the form of written vignettes, videotapes, audiotapes, the clinician's own reports, or live patient–clinician interactions. The clinician must explain his or her actions and decisions about assessment, diagnosis, treatment, and/or case management. Examiners then question the clinician about those decisions. This approach to assessment requires standardization of case materials (e.g., the video- or audiotape of an interaction that replicates a professional interaction), in addition to guidance for and training of the examiners to ensure inter-rater reliability.

In keeping with such a case-based model, McNiel and colleagues (McNiel, Hung, Cramer, Hall, & Binder, 2011) and Hung and colleagues (Hung et al., 2012) have made strides toward developing an approach to evaluating competence in assessing and managing risk of violence and/or suicide. Working within an OSCE framework, the investigators trained advanced psychiatry residents (third and fourth year residents) and psychology postdoctoral fellows to be standardized (simulated) patients and had them follow a script based on a clinical vignette of a young adult patient presenting to an emergency room. The script included the patient's chief complaint, history of present illness, psychiatric, medical, and psychosocial histories, and mental status examination findings. The subjects (or clinicians-in-training) were less advanced psychiatry residents (first and second year residents) and psychology predoctoral interns who initially had a 5-hour workshop on risk assessment for violence and suicide. Faculty members were trained as observers. Each OSCE team consisted of a clinician-in-training, a standardized patient, and a faculty member.

After receiving a brief description of the presenting problem, the clinician-in-training was asked to perform a violence risk assessment or a suicide risk assessment of the standardized patient. He or she interviewed the simulated patient and was asked to discuss what additional information he or she might seek if this were a real situation. The clinician-in-training was also asked to write a progress note and give an oral summary of the assessment and plan regarding the patient's risk.

To assess competence, the investigators developed two instruments: the Competency Assessment Instrument for Violence (CAI-V) and the Competency Assessment Instrument for Suicide Risk (CAI-S). These instruments were created based on literature reviews and input received from focus groups with mental health faculty at multiple sites in a large academic psychiatry department. The CAI-V and CAI-S consist of checklists of 31 and 30 components, respectively, on violence risk assessment and suicide risk assessment, including areas such as interviewing and data collection, case formulation and presentation, treatment planning, and documentation. In separate studies, the CAI-V and the CAI-S were found to have good internal consistency reliability (a = 0.93 and a = 0.94, respectively) and good inter-rater reliability (intra-class correlation coefficient [ICC] = 0.93 and ICC = 0.94, respectively).

After the clinician-in-training interviewed the standardized patient and discussed the case, the faculty observer rated the competence of the clinician's performance using CAI-V or CAI-S, as the case might be. For purposes of data analysis, the clinicians-in-training were divided into those at a senior level (second year residents who had 6 months of supervised inpatient psychiatry experience) and those at a junior level (first year residents). The mean scores on the CAI-V and on the CAI-S were significantly higher for the senior level clinicians-in-training. In addition, the global rating of the overall quality of the violence risk assessments and of the suicide risk assessments were significantly higher for the senior level learners. The risk assessments by senior learners were also significantly more likely to be rated as competent by the faculty examiners than the risk assessments by junior learners.

The investigators in these two studies noted that the CAI-V and the CAI-S had concurrent validity in that senior learners performed better than junior learners in the context of an OSCE. They further found that both learners and faculty expressed satisfaction with this method of assessment and that the CAI-V, CAI-S, and the OSCE provided helpful structure for feedback and supervision concerning violence risk and suicide risk assessment and management.

In terms of limitations of these assessment methods, the researchers have mentioned the cost of having faculty serve as examiners in an OSCE. In that regard, they suggest the possibility of having the simulated patient also be the person rating the clinician-in-training. They note that a second limitation is that simulated patients may not show the range of problems comparable to actual patients in high-risk, clinical situations. They comment that future research could investigate the applicability of these measures in clinical supervision with actual cases.

The author concurs that it is unlikely that simulated patients will show the range of problems that an actual patient in a state of crisis might present. The limitations of cost and of having a simulated patient mentioned by McNiel and his colleagues might be addressed in a setting such as an ER or a UCC using the mentor model of supervision discussed earlier in this chapter. The supervisor (again with the patient's permission) could be an observer of an actual evaluation with a patient who presents with a question of suicide risk or risk of violence. Immediately following the evaluation, he or she could evaluate the competence of the clinician-in-training by completing an instrument such as the CAI-S or the CAI-V. One drawback to assessing competence with actual patient interviews is that it is not possible to have a standardized patient.

Concluding Remarks

There is a great deal to be learned from naturalistic decision-making models regarding how best to approach the decision making-process when dealing with behavioral emergencies. In an acute clinical situation involving questions of risk to self or others, the task demands typically do not permit the painstaking approach of the rational and normative models of decision making. In fact, as we have seen, efforts to apply such models in time-limited, dynamic, and rapidly shifting circumstances can lead to poorer performance (Johnston et al., 1997). In some sense, we can take something from each of the NDM models that we have discussed in this chapter (recognition-primed model, recognition/metacognition model, situation awareness model, and the hypervigilant strategy) and find that it applies well to the evaluation and management of behavioral emergencies.

As I have also noted, we not only need models for decision making in behavioral emergencies, we also need to be able to cope with the attendant stress of emergency circumstances to minimize its potentially negative effect on decision making. Thus, I endorse a training model for this work (such as the stress exposure training model) that emphasizes the development of resources for coping with stress. In addition, and in accord with the APA Task Force on the Assessment of Competence in Professional Psychology, I contend that training for competence in behavioral emergencies (and competence itself) is ultimately achieved through a process that includes the development of a knowledge base, as well as through a gradated approach to acquiring skill, that culminates in well supervised, real-life encounters with actual patients who are at risk to themselves or others.

Note

1. In medical teaching facilities, when patients initially enter the health-care system, they are typically informed that teaching is an integral function of the particular health-care system and that care may be provided by clinicians-in-training under the supervision of a staff member. If they object to treatment or to involvement in treatment by a clinician in training, treatment is provided only by a fully credentialed staff member.

References

American Association of Suicidology. (2011). *Recognizing and responding to suicide risk.* Retrieved from http://suicidology.org/training-accreditation/rrsr

APA Task Force on the Assessment of Competence in Professional Psychology (2006, October). *APA Task Force on the Assessment of Competence in Professional Psychology: Final Report.* Washington, DC: American Psychological Association.

Baartman, L., & Bruijn, E. (2011). Integrating knowledge, skills, and attitudes: Conceptualizing learning processes towards vocational competence. *Educational Research Review, 6,* 125–134.

Barlow, D. (1974). Psychologists in the emergency room. *Professional Psychology, 5,* 251–256.

Bongar, B., Lomax, J., & Harmatz, M. (1992). Training and supervisory issues in the assessment and management of the suicidal patient. In B. Bongar (Ed.), *Suicide: Guidelines for assessment, management, and treatment* (pp. 253–267). New York: Oxford University Press.

Brown, H. (1987). Patient suicide during residency training: 1. Incidence, implications, and program response. *Journal of Psychiatric Education, 11,* 201–206.

Calderwood, R., Klein, G., & Crandall, B. (1988). Time pressure, skill, and move quality in chess. *The American Journal of Psychology, 101,* 481–493.

Cohen, M., Freeman, J., & Thompson, B. (2009). Training the naturalistic decision maker. In C. Zsambok & G. Klein (Eds.), *Naturalistic decision making* (pp. 257–268). New York, NY: Routledge.

Covino, N. (1989). The general hospital emergency ward as a training opportunity for clinical psychologists. *Journal of Training and Practice in Professional Psychology, 3,* 17–32.

Driskell, J., & Johnston, J. (1998). Stress exposure training. In J. Canon-Bowers & E. Salas (Eds.), *Making decisions under stress: Implications for individual and team training* (pp. 191–217). Washington, DC: American Psychological Association.

Endsley, M. (2009). The role of situation awareness in naturalistic decision making. In C. Zsambok & G. Klein (Eds.), *Naturalistic decision making* (pp. 269–283). New York, NY: Routledge.

Epstein, R., & Hundert, E. (2002). Defining and assessing professional competence. *Journal of the American Medical Association, 287,* 226–235.

Figley, C. (1995). Compassion fatigue as secondary traumatic stress: An overview. In C. Figley (Ed.), *Compassion fatigue: Coping with secondary traumatic stress disorder in those who treat the traumatized* (pp. 1–20). New York, NY: Brunner/Mazel.

Gaba, D., Howard, S., & Jump, B. (1994). Production pressure in the work environment: California anesthesiologists' attitudes and experiences. *Anesthesiology, 81,* 488–500.

Gawande, A., Studdert, D., Orav, E., Brennan, T., & Zinner, M. (2003). Risk factors for retained instruments and sponges after surgery. *The New England Journal of Medicine, 348,* 229–235.

Hammond, K. (2000). *Judgments under stress.* New York, NY: Oxford University Press.

Hung, E., Binder, R., Fordwood, S., Hall, S., Cramer, R., & McNiel, D. (2012). A method for evaluating competency in assessment and management of suicide risk. *Academic Psychiatry, 36,* 23–28.

Jacobson, J., Osteen, P., Jones, A., & Berman, A. (2012). Evaluation of the Recognizing and Responding to Suicide Risk training. *Suicide and Life-Threatening Behavior, 42,* 471–485.

Janis, I., & Mann, L. (1977). *Decision making: A psychological analysis of conflict, choice, and commitment.* New York, NY: Free Press.

Johnston, J., & Cannon-Bowers, J. (1996). Training for stress exposure. In J. Driskell & E. Salas (Eds.), *Stress and human performance* (pp. 223–256). Mahwah, NJ: Erlbaum.

Johnston, J., Driskell, J., & Salas, E. (1997). Vigilant and hypervigilant decision making. *Journal of Applied Psychology, 82,* 614–622.

Jones, J., & Mehr, S. (2007). Foundations and assumptions of the scientist-practitioner model. *American Behavioral Scientist, 50,* 766–771.

Kahneman, D. (2011). *Thinking, fast and slow.* New York, NY: Farrar, Strauss, and Giroux.

Kahneman, D., Slovic, P., & Tversky, A. (Eds.). (1982). *Judgment under uncertainty: Heuristics and biases.* New York, NY: Cambridge University Press.

Kleespies, P. (Ed.). (2009). *Behavioral emergencies: An evidence-based resource for evaluating and managing risk of suicide, violence, and victimization.* Washington, DC: APA books.

Kleespies, P. (2014). *Decision making in behavioral emergencies: Acquiring skill in evaluating and managing high risk patients.* Washington, DC: APA Books.

Kleespies, P. (Ed.). (1998). *Emergencies in mental health practice: Evaluation and management.* New York, NY: Guilford Press.

Kleespies, P., Penk, W., & Forsyth, J. (1993). The stress of patient suicidal behavior during clinical training: Incidence, impact, and recovery. *Professional Psychology: Research and Practice, 24,* 293–303.

Kleespies, P., & Ponce, A. (2009). The stress and emotional impact of clinical work with the patient at risk. In P. Kleespies (Ed.),

Behavioral emergencies: An evidence-based resource for evaluating and managing risk of suicide, violence, and victimization (pp. 431–448). Washington, DC: APA Books.

Klein, G. (2009). The recognition-primed decision (RPD) model: Looking back, looking forward. In C. Zsambok & G. Klein (Eds.), *Naturalistic decision making* (pp. 285–292). New York, NY: Routledge.

Lazarus, R. (1994). *Emotion and adaptation.* New York, NY: Oxford University Press.

LeBlanc, V., MacDonald, R., McArthur, B., King, K., & Lepine, T. (2005). Paramedic performance in calculating drug dosages following stressful scenarios in a human patient simulator. *Prehospital Emergency Care, 9,* 439–444.

McCann, I., & Pearlman, L. (1990). Vicarious traumatization: A framework for understanding the psychological effects of working with victims. *Journal of Traumatic Stress, 3,* 131–149.

McNiel, D., Chamberlain, J., Weaver, C., Hall, S., Fordwood, S., & Binder, R. (2008). Impact of clinical training on violence risk assessment. *American Journal of Psychiatry, 165,* 195–200.

McNiel, D., Fordwood, S., Weaver, C., Chamberlain, J., Hall, J., & Binder, R. (2008). Effects of training on suicide risk assessment. *Psychiatric Services, 59,* 1462–1465.

McNiel, D., Hung, E., Cramer, R., Hall, S., & Binder, R. (2011). An approach to evaluating competence in assessing and managing violence risk. *Psychiatric Services, 62,* 90–92.

Meichenbaum, D. (1985). *Stress inoculation training.* New York, NY: Pergamon Press.

Meichenbaum, D. (2007) Stress inoculation training: A preventative and treatment approach. In R. Lehrer, R. Woolfolk, & W. Sime (Eds.), *Principles and practice of stress management* (3rd ed.) (pp. 497–518). New York, NY: Guilford Press.

Oordt, M., Jobes, D., Fonseca, V., & Schmidt, S. (2009). Training mental health professionals to assess and manage suicidal behavior: Can provider confidence and practice behaviors be altered? *Suicide and Life-Threatening Behavior, 39,* 21–32.

Payne, J., Bettman, J., & Johnson, E. (1988). Adaptive strategy selection in decision making. *Journal of Experimental Psychology: Learning, Memory, and Cognition, 14,* 534–552.

Pisani, A., Cross, W., & Gould, M. (2011). The assessment and management of suicide risk: State of workshop education. *Suicide and Life-Threatening Behavior, 41,* 255–276.

Polic, M. (2009). Decision making: Between rationality and reality. *Interdisciplinary Description of Complex Systems, 7,* 78–89.

Pope, K., & Tabachnick, B. (1993). Therapists' anger, hate, fear, and sexual feelings: National survey of therapist responses, client characteristics, critical events, formal complaints, and training. *Professional Psychology: Research and Practice, 24,* 142–152.

Randel, J., Pugh, H., Reed, S., Schuler, J., & Wyman, B. (1994). *Methods for analyzing cognitive skills for a technical task.* San Diego, CA: Navy Personnel Research and Development Center.

Rodolfa, E., Kraft, W., & Reilley, R. (1988). Stressors of professionals and trainees at APA-approved counseling and VA medical center internship sites. *Professional Psychology: Research and Practice, 19,* 43–49.

Rudd, M. D., Cukrowicz, K., & Bryan, C. (2008). Core competencies in suicide risk assessment and management: Implications for supervision. *Training and Education in Professional Psychology, 2,* 219–228.

Schmitz, W., Jr., Allen, M., Feldman, B., Gutin, N., Jahn, D., Kleespies, P., ...Simpson, S. (2012). Preventing suicide through improved training in suicide risk assessment and care: An American Association of Suicidology Task Force report addressing serious gaps in U.S. mental health training. *Suicide and Life-Threatening Behavior, 42,* 292–304.

Shaban, R. (2005). Theories of clinical judgment and decision-making: A review of the theoretical literature. *Journal of Emergency Primary Health Care, 3,* 1–13.

Simon, H. (1957). *Models of man, social and rational: Mathematical essays on rational human behavior in a social setting.* New York, NY: Wiley.

Suicide Prevention Resource Center. (2006). *Core competencies in the assessment and management of suicidality.* Waltham, MA: Author.

Suicide Prevention Resource Center. (2011). *Assessing and managing suicide risk: Core competencies for mental health professionals.* Retrieved from http://sprc.org/bpr/section-lll/assessing-and-managing-suicide-risk-core-competencies-mental-health-professionals-am

Teo, A., Holly, S., Leary, M., & McNiel, D. (2012, November). The relationship between level of training and accuracy of violence risk assessment. *Psychiatric Services, 63,* 1089–1094.

Tversky, A., & Kahneman, D. (1974). Judgments under uncertainty: Heuristics and biases. *Science, 185,* 1124–1131.

van Meer, J., & Theunissen, N. (2009). Prospective educational applications of mental simulation: A meta-review. *Educational Psychology Review, 21,* 93–112.

Behavioral Emergencies with Youth

The Evaluation and Management of Suicide Risk in Adolescents in the Context of Interpersonal Violence

Anthony Spirito, Kimberly H. McManama O'Brien, Megan L. Ranney, *and* Judelysse Gomez

Abstract

In this chapter, risk factors for suicidal ideation and behavior are reviewed, including sociodemographics, prior suicidal behavior, nonsuicidal self-injury, depression, anxiety, substance use, family factors, physical and sexual abuse, sexual orientation, and access to firearms. Special emphasis is placed on the intersection of suicidality and interpersonal violence in terms of reciprocal risk. A review of the core areas to address in the acutely suicidal adolescent or the adolescent who has recently attempted suicide is also provided. Clinical questions regarding the adolescent's current emotional state, suicidal ideation/intent, reasons for suicidality, access to means, and capability of the environment to keep the adolescent safe are suggested. The chapter concludes with a discussion of safety planning.

Key Words: suicide, suicidal ideation, attempted suicide, interpersonal violence, adolescent

Suicide incidence increases markedly in the late teenage years and continues to rise until the early twenties. Suicide represents the third leading cause of death for 10- to 24-year-olds (National Center for Injury Prevention and Control [NCIPC], 2014) and is the second leading cause of death for 15- to 24-year-olds (McIntosh & Drapeau, 2014). Suicide attempts are defined as any intentional, nonfatal self-injury, regardless of medical lethality, if intent to die was indicated (O'Carroll et al., 1996). Nationally, the most recent results from the Youth Risk Behavior Surveillance Survey (YRBSS) of youth in Grades 9 through 12 found that 16% of students reported seriously considering suicide, 13% reported creating a plan to kill themselves, and 8% reported trying to kill themselves in the 12 months preceding the survey (Kann et al., 2014).

Interpersonal violence (assault or homicide), the third leading cause of death among 15- to 24-year-olds and fourth leading cause of death for 10- to 14-year-olds (McIntosh & Drapeau, 2014;

NCIPC, 2014), is defined as "the intentional use of physical force or power, threatened or actual, against another person or against a group or community that results in or has a high likelihood of resulting in injury, death, psychological harm, maldevelopment, or deprivation" (Krug, Dahlberg, Mercy, Zwi, & Lozano, 2002, p. 5). Interpersonal violence is divided into intimate partner violence (between current or former romantic partners), which is also referred to as dating violence (Centers for Disease Control and Prevention [CDC], 2012b), and peer nonpartner violence (e.g., fights at school, gang violence; CDC, 2012a). Many researchers and clinicians further differentiate bullying (which is defined as having a power differential) from other forms of peer violence. Nationally, 10.3% of adolescents endorse dating violence (being slapped, hit, or physically hurt on purpose) at the hands of a partner, with females (13%) endorsing higher rates of dating violence victimization than males (7.4%; Kann et al., 2014). Almost a quarter of adolescents surveyed endorse past-year peer physical fights (Kann et al., 2014), and 20% to 30% endorse past-year peer bullying (CDC, 2012c). Interpersonal violence, in all forms, is a significant risk factor for suicidality.

Accumulating evidence suggests strong links between dating violence and suicidality among adolescents. Adolescents who reported dating violence victimization had 3 times the odds of having attempted suicide within the timeframe of the abuse (CDC, 2006). Other studies (Silverman, Raj, Mucci, & Hathaway, 2001) suggest that adolescent female victims of dating violence are 6 to 8 times more likely to think about and attempt suicide than those who have not experienced dating violence. Among girls, experiencing dating violence at baseline was associated with suicidality at a one-year follow-up (Roberts, Klein, & Fisher, 2003), even after controlling for prior dating violence and other potential confounders. In a community sample of Latino youth 11 to 13 years of age, dating violence victimization among boys was associated with a history of suicidal ideation (Yan, Howard, Beck, Sattuck, & Hallmark-Kerr, 2010). Other studies show that both physical dating violence victimization and perpetration increased the odds of suicide ideation.

Peer violence is also strongly associated with risk of suicidality. For instance, adolescents reporting a past-year physical fight and weapon carriage have a higher likelihood of reporting past-year suicidal ideation and suicide attempts (Stack, 2014; van Geel, Vedder, & Tanilon, 2014). Studies suggest that there is a direct correlation between increasing frequency of physical peer victimization and rates of suicide ideation and suicide attempts (Kaminski & Fang, 2009; Turner et al., 2012). Interestingly, it is not just victimization that correlates with suicidality and suicide attempts. Mere exposure to violence—witnessing peer violence in the community—also correlates with higher rates of suicidal ideation (Lambert, Copeland-Linder, & Ialongo, 2008). Increased aggressiveness—for example, being a perpetrator of peer violence—predicts future suicidal behavior as well, particularly for girls (Juon & Ensminger, 1997; O'Donnell, Stueve, & Wilson-Simmons, 2005).

Reviews of the literature (e.g., Kim and Leventhal, 2008) suggest that adolescent perpetrators and victims of bullying are at increased risk for suicidal behavior. In a sample of 208 Swedish adolescents, any kind of bullying (victim, perpetrator, both) was associated with a history of suicide attempts (Ivarsson, Broberg, Arvidsson, & Gillberg,

2005). Likewise, Kim, Leventhal, Koh, and Boyce (2009) prospectively used a peer nomination design to study bullying and risk for suicide in a sample of 1,655 Korean seventh and eighth graders. Adolescent perpetrators and victims of bullying were at increased risk for suicidal ideation and attempts compared to adolescents not involved in any form of bullying. In addition, high school students who report being bullying victims *and* perpetrators are at higher risk of suicidal behavior than those who are only victimized or only bullied (Roland, 2002; Hepburn, Azrael, Molnar, & Miller, 2012).

Cyberbullying (i.e., bullying that takes place using electronic technology such as mobile phones and social media) is increasingly common. Confirming earlier single-site studies (e.g., Hinduja & Patchin, 2010), a recent meta analysis showed that cyberbullying is more highly correlated with both suicidal ideation and attempts than in-person bullying (van Geel et al., 2014). (See Chapter 7 of this volume by Samantha Pflum, Peter Goldblum, Joyce Chu, and Bruce Bongar for more information on bullying and suicide risk.)

Dating violence, peer violence, and suicidality tend to "cluster" in adolescents (Bossarte, Simon, & Swahn, 2008). Polyvictimization (e.g., experiencing a combination of peer and dating violence, sexual assault, and adverse childhood experiences such as child abuse) also predicts significantly higher rates of suicidal ideation (Turner, Finkelhor, Shattuck, & Hamby, 2012).

In this chapter, risk factors for suicidal ideation and behavior, including interpersonal violence, are reviewed. These background variables set the stage for the assessment of suicidal risk. Whenever possible, special emphasis is placed on the intersection of suicidality and interpersonal violence, both in terms of reciprocal risk as well as management.

Risk Factors for Suicidal Behavior

Sociodemographic factors related to suicidal behavior and their overlap with interpersonal violence are reviewed in the following.

Sex

Sex differences among 13- to 24-year-olds who die by suicide are pronounced (CDC NCIPC, 2013a). In 2011, more adolescent males (20.2 per 100,000) than females (5.4 per 100,000) died by suicide (McIntosh & Drapeau, 2014). Sex differences in the opposite direction exist with respect to suicide attempts. YRBSS (Kann et al., 2014) data indicate that female high school students (22.4%)

were more likely than males (11.6%) to have seriously considered suicide in the 12 months preceding the survey. Moreover, they were also more likely (16.9%) than males (10.3%) to report having a suicide plan. Similarly, female respondents (10.6%) were more likely than males (5.4%) to have attempted suicide in the year preceding the study and were more likely (3.6%) to have made an attempt requiring medical attention compared to males (1.8%). In one study, being female doubled the odds of reporting suicidal ideation, even after controlling for dating violence (Nahapetyan, Orpinas, Song, & Holland, 2014).

Sex differences in youth who die by suicide are related, in part, to the greater likelihood of males having multiple risk factors for suicide, including comorbid mood and alcohol abuse disorders and a higher likelihood of choosing more lethal suicide attempt methods (Gould, Fisher, Parides, Flory, & Shaffer, 1996; Shaffer & Pfeffer, 2001). Greater levels of aggressive behavior in males compared with females may also increase risk for eventual death by suicide (Brent, Baugher, Bridge, Chen, & Chiapetta, 1999).

Adolescent boys are more likely to be both victims and perpetrators of non-self-directed forms of violence as well, although sex differences in rates of peer violence are narrowing. Notably, between 19% and 27% of adolescent females participating in national surveys reported having been in a serious fight in the past year (Substance Abuse and Mental Health Services Administration, 2009), and 40% of assaulted adolescents seen in the emergency department in 2012 were female (CDC NCIPC 2013b); these rates parallel that of adolescent males. Like males, the majority of assaults among adolescent females are reported to be caused by peers, not dating partners (Mollen, Fein, Localio, & Durbin, 2004; Cheng et al., 2006; Walton et al., 2009).

Similarly, sex differences in dating violence are minimal, with mutual dating violence being commonplace among this age group (Chiodo et al., 2012). Most studies report comparable rates of dating victimization and perpetration among the two sexes (Archer, 2000; Foshee, Linder, MacDougall, & Bangdiwala, 2001; Jain, Buka, Subramanian, & Molnar, 2010; Rothman, Johnson, Azrael, Hall, & Weinberg, 2010; Foshee et al., 2011), although recent longitudinal study among high school students in the southeast region of the United States found that males were more likely to report dating violence victimization than girls, girls reported more perpetration than boys (Nahapetyan et al., 2014). A longitudinal dating prevention study

(Chiodo et al., 2012) found that 30% of 11th-grade adolescent girls endorsed being in a romantic relationship where they had experienced physical dating violence, of whom 26% reported being exclusively perpetrators and 53% reported being both perpetrators and victims. Severity of dating violence perpetration is also similar among adolescent females and males. One study (Rothman et al., 2010) conducted among a sample of adolescents with a history of alcohol use screened in a pediatric medical emergency department found that 55% of girls and 45% of boys endorsed at least one incident of dating violence perpetration; about a third (29%) of the girls endorsed severe dating violence perpetration compared to 15% of the boys. Severe dating violence included at least one incident of attempting to choke, causing an injury that necessitated medical attention, hitting with a fist or object, beating up, and/or assaulting with a knife or gun in the past six months (Rothman et al., 2010). Moreover, victimization and perpetration of this kind of violence was equally distributed among the girls (29% endorsed each), whereas 23% of the boys endorsed being victims of this kind of violence versus 15% perpetrators (Rothman et al., 2010). (See Chapter 4 of this volume by Randy Broum for more information about youth violence.)

Race/Ethnicity

In 2011, suicide rates among 15- to 24-year-olds were lower among Asian/Pacific Islanders (6.39 per 100,000), non-Latino Blacks (7.22 per 100,000), and Latino/as (7.04 per 100,000) than non-Latino Whites (13.52 per 100,000), according to National Vital Statistics data available from the CDC's NCIPC (2013b). American Indian/Alaska Natives (AI/AN) had the highest suicide deaths rates (29.33 per 100,000) among this age group. Among young adult females, AI/AN (12.02 per 100,000) had the highest suicide rates followed by non-Latino White females (4.83 per 100,000), Asian/Pacific Islander females (2.92 per 100,000), Latinas (2.91 per 100,000), and non-Latina Black females (2.36 per 100,000). Similarly, AI/AN males had the highest suicide rates among this age group (46.08 per 100,000), followed by non-Latino White males (21.85 per 100,000), non-Latino Black males (12.02 per 100,000), Latinos (10.81 Latino per 100,000), and Asian/Pacific Islander males (9.75 per 100,000).

In contrast to data regarding suicide deaths, YRBS (Kann et al., 2014) data shows higher rates of past-12-month suicide *attempts* among Latino/a (11.3%) and Black (8.8%) adolescents, as compared to White adolescents (6.3%). Latino/a (18.9%) students also reported higher rates of having seriously considered suicide than their White (16.2%) and Black counterparts (14.5%) and higher rates of having made a plan for how they would attempt suicide (Latino/a 15.7%, White 12.8%, Black 10.4%). Across race groups, females (22.4%) were more likely than males (11.6%) to report having seriously considered attempting suicide 12 months prior to the study and having made a suicide plan (16.9% vs. 10.3%; Kann et al., 2014).

Although recent YRBS race-based data reported by the CDC does not include comparisons for AI/AN students (due to small numbers), aggregate data (Rutman, Park, Castor, Taualii, & Forquera, 2008) suggests that AI/AN are at elevated risk for suicide. Aggregated YRBS data from 1997 to 2003 for AI/AN high school–age youth (1% of the aggregate sample) indicated (a) 27.9% of AI/AN youth endorsed seriously considering suicide in the year preceding the study compared to 18% of White students; (b) 25% of AI/AN compared to 14% of White students made a suicide plan; (c) 20.8% attempted suicide compared to 6.7% of their White counterparts; and (d) 10.9% of AI/AN youth compared to 1.9% of White youth made a suicide attempt that resulted in injury (Rutman et al., 2008). However, other studies have found that these rates vary considerably by tribe and by where these youth were raised (i.e., in urban areas vs. on a reservation; Freedenthal & Stiffman, 2004; Goldston et al., 2008).

Previous YRBS (CDC, 2012c) data indicate dating violence and peer violence disparities between adolescents of color and their White counterparts; White adolescents were less likely than their Black and Latino peers to have been the victims of dating or peer violence. Non-YRBS data sets show that Black and Latino youth are also more likely to witness peer violence than their White peers (e.g., Zimmerman & Messner, 2013). Although more Black students (34.7%), than Latino/a (28.4%) and White students (20.9%) reported being in a physical fight in the prior year (Kann et al., 2014), this relationship may be a function of poverty, exposure to violence, and exposure to delinquent peers (CDC, 2012a) rather than of race/ethnicity. Racial/ethnic disparities in prevalence of dating violence have decreased, with higher victimization rates among females across all race groups in the most recent YRBS data (Kann et al., 2014). Although there is no recent YRBS-based dating violence rates for AI/AN youth, analyses of prior YRBS years (Rutman et al., 2008; Pavkov, Travis, Fox, King, & Cross, 2010) show that AI/AN high school–age youth experience higher rates of both dating and peer physical violence.

Dating violence and peer violence have been strongly linked to suicidal behavior in ethnic minority adolescents. The 2004 Youth Violence Survey, which gathered data among mostly ethnic minority adolescent (45% Latino, 28% non-Latino Black, 23% non-Latino White) public high school students in a high-risk urban school district, found that a combination of victimization and perpetration—for either peer or dating violence—was the strongest correlate of reporting a past-year suicide attempt (Swahn et al., 2008). These findings did not vary by race/ethnicity, nor did researchers find an elevated association between suicide attempts and victimization or perpetration alone. Although studies cited did not find race differences in the relationship between dating or peer violence and suicidal behavior, most studies either do not report sociodemographics in their analyses (Klomek, Marrocco, Kleinman, Schonfeld, & Gould, 2008; Kaminski & Fang 2009; Chiodo et al., 2012), conflate heterogeneous ethnic minority groups into homogeneous groupings, or are not sufficiently powered to find these differences.

Age of Onset

Suicidal thoughts escalate significantly around age 12 and then continue to increase across adolescence (Nock et al., 2013). After puberty, rates of suicide increase with age until they stabilize in young adulthood (Heron et al., 2009). Psychological explanations for the onset of suicidality in early adolescence include the increase in psychopathology that emerges during adolescence, particularly mood disorder and substance abuse combinations (Shaffer, Gould, Fisher, & Trautman, 1996; Groholt, Ekeberg, Wichstrom, & Haldorsen, 1998; Brent et al., 1999). In addition, older adolescents have more autonomy and less parental supervision, which may make recognition of imminent risk from adults less likely.

With the development of cognitive skills, adolescents also become more capable of planning and executing a suicide attempt (Groholt et al., 1998; Brent et al., 1999). Indeed, the increase in suicidality and death by suicide across adolescence is likely a function of changes in the developing brain. Desmyter, Bijttebier, and van Heeringen (2013) conducted a review of studies that compared brains of individuals with and without suicidal behavior. Findings demonstrated differences in areas of the brain in the same network as decision-making processes for suicidal individuals, relative to non-suicidal individuals. This finding resonates with impulsivity research by Klonsky and May (2010) that found that adolescents and young adults who have attempted suicide demonstrate a diminished ability to think through their actions relative to those with suicidal ideation only. Another recent review by van Herringen and Mann (2014) found impairments of the serotonin neurotransmitter system and the hypothalamic-pituitary-adrenal axis stress-response system that manifest as deficits in mood regulation and problem solving, as well as a tendency toward aggressive traits, overreactivity to negative social signs, and heightened emotional distress, leading to suicidality. (See Chapter 20 of this volume by Victoria Arango and Mark Underwood for more information on neurobiological factors in suicide.)

The trajectory of youth violence is very similar to that of suicidality. Both peer and dating violence become fairly common during adolescence and has been shown to increase with age (CDC, 2012c). The highest rates are reported in midadolescence with this developmental period being a particularly vulnerable time when interpersonal violence is usually initiated (Smith, White, & Holland, 2003). This trajectory is thought to be due to the slow maturing of the frontal lobe, which is accompanied by an increase in impulsive and risky behaviors. Significant decreases in rates of both peer and partner violence occur by the late teens and early twenties.

Prior Suicidal Behavior

A prior suicide attempt is one of the best predictors of eventual death by suicide (Shaffer et al., 1996; Brent et al., 1999; Bridge, Goldstein, & Brent, 2006), as well as future suicide attempts (Prinstein et al., 2008; Goldston et al., 2009) among adolescents. Goldston et al. found the number of prior attempts was the strongest predictor of a post-hospitalization suicide attempt. A Scandinavian study (Groholt, Ekeberg, & Haldorsen, 2006) found that approximately two-thirds of adolescents who were hospitalized for a suicide attempt reported a repeat attempt within two years. The risk of a repeat attempt is estimated to range from 10% at six-month follow-up to 42% at 21-month follow-up, with a median recurrence rate range of 5% to 15% per year (Goldston et al., 1999; Hawton, Zahl, & Weatherall, 2003).

The rates of subsequent death by suicide are low, from 0.5% to 1% per year, but these rates are much higher than the general population (Hawton et al., 2003). In a sample of more than 5,000 adolescents and young adults treated in a hospital in the United Kingdom following an act of deliberate self-injury (with or without suicidal intent), the risk of death by suicide in the following year was 35 times the annual population risk in males and 75 times the annual population risk in females (Hawton et al., 2003).

Escalations in suicidal ideation, as well as the presence of suicide planning, are also important aspects of suicidal behavior that may increase the likelihood of an attempt. Longitudinal studies indicate that elevations in suicidal ideation (Prinstein et al., 2008) and/or frequent and long lasting suicidal ideation that is accompanied by the planning of a suicide attempt increases the likelihood of an eventual suicide attempt (Lewinsohn, Rohde, & Seeley, 1996), as well as increases risk for making another attempt among adolescents who have attempted suicide (Goldston et al., 1999).

Nonsuicidal Self-Injury

Nonsuicidal self-injury (NSSI), defined as self-harm without suicidal intent, is highly prevalent among adolescent suicide attempters and may differentiate repeat from first-time attempters (Nock, Joiner, Gordon, Lloyd-Richardson, & Prinstein, 2006; Prinstein et al., 2008; Hamza, Stewart, & Willoughby, 2012). Nock et al. found that 70% of psychiatrically hospitalized adolescents with a history of NSSI reported a lifetime history of a suicide attempt and 55% reported a history of multiple suicide attempts. Studies have also found that a longer history of NSSI is associated with a higher lifetime rate of suicide attempts (Nock et al., 2006; Asarnow et al., 2011).

Esposito, Spirito, Boergers, and Donaldson (2003) found greater severity of NSSI among multiple than first-time adolescent suicide attempters. Guan, Fox, and Prinstein (2012) found that a history of NSSI led to a seven-fold increase in risk for future suicide attempts, after controlling for past attempts, sex, and depressive symptoms among high school students. Further, Prinstein et al. (2008) found greater frequency of NSSI to be associated with slower remission of suicidal ideation among previously hospitalized adolescents, suggesting that NSSI may also be associated with a poor outcome among suicidal youth. (See Chapter 27 of this volume by Joseph Franklin and Matthew Nock for more information about the relationship of NSSI and suicidal behavior.)

Few studies have examined the role of interpersonal violence on NSSI or whether NSSI puts an adolescent at risk for dating or peer violence, or vice versa. However, one cross-sectional study

(Weismoore & Esposito-Smythers, 2010) conducted with a clinical sample of adolescents on an inpatient unit found that NSSI was associated with a history of assault in adolescence, including physical and sexual victimization at the hands of peers and dating partners, but not childhood abuse (physical or sexual) at the hands of caretakers. The authors also found that those adolescents with the most cognitive errors (i.e., overgeneralization, selective abstraction) and most negative self-views had higher odds of reporting NSSI.

Why do prior suicidal behavior, NSSI, and interpersonal violence increase risk for a repeat suicide attempt? It is possible that the underlying mechanism that drives an adolescent to attempt suicide is common to both types of intentional injury (i.e., self-directed vs. directed at others). Joiner (2005) emphasizes that a capacity to engage in lethal self-injury must be acquired over time and that people become capable of suicidal behavior only after they have habituated to dangerous behavior. Therefore, prior suicidal behavior lowers the threshold needed to precipitate future suicidal behavior. Both suicidal behavior as well as youth violence exposure may result in the experience of injury and pain over time, which may also lead individuals to lose their innate fear of pain, thus allowing them to engage in progressively more damaging and potentially lethal self-injurious acts and/or acts of violence against others (Joiner, 2005; Van Orden, Witte, Gordon, Bender, & Joiner, 2008).

Depressed Mood and Mood Disorders

There is a strong association between depressed mood and adolescent suicidal behavior in clinical and community samples (Evans, Hawton, & Rodham, 2004). Greater severity of depressed mood has been associated with slower remission of suicidal ideation (Prinstein et al., 2008). Goldston, Reboussin, and Daniel (2006) followed 180 adolescents discharged from a psychiatric inpatient unit for a median of 11 years and found that self-reported depressive symptoms predicted future suicide attempts. In a representative sample of 2,464 high school students, disturbed concentration, middle insomnia, and hopelessness, all symptoms of depression, were related to suicide attempts at baseline, but only worthlessness was prospectively found to predict suicide attempts between 15 and 20 years of age (Nrugham, Larsson, & Sund, 2008).

The relationship between severity of depressed mood and adolescent suicidality may vary by history of suicidality. Esposito, Spirito, Boergers, and

Donaldson (2003) found that adolescents with a history of more than one suicide attempt had more severe depressive symptoms than first-time attempters. In a similar study, repeat suicide attempters but not first-time attempters reported more severe depressive symptoms than adolescents with no suicide attempt history (Goldston, Daniel, Reboussin, & Kelley, 1996). Thus a severe depressed mood may be a particularly salient risk factor for a repeat attempt among adolescents with a prior attempt history.

Depressive disorders have consistently been reported in attempted suicide and death by suicide in adolescents (Gould, Greenberg, Velting, & Shaffer, 2003; Evans et al., 2004). A review of the literature suggests that rates of depressive disorders range from 49% to 64% among adolescent suicide victims (Gould et al., 2003). Further, the odds ratios of death by suicide among adolescents with mood disorders ranged from 11 to as high as 27.

A formal diagnosis of major depression disorder also is common in attempted suicide. In the Goldston et al. (2009) naturalistic, prospective study described previously, after controlling for demographic variables and prehospitalization suicide attempts, major depression disorder was associated with more than a five-fold increase in risk for suicide attempts, with this relationship increasing in strength with age. Major depression disorder and dysthymia were also found to be more common among repeat attempters than first-time attempters. An association between mood disorders and suicide attempts was found in a large community-based sample of 2,464 high school students (Nrugham et al., 2008), but only dysthymia diagnosed at age 15 was found to prospectively predict suicide attempts between 15 to 20 years of age, even after controlling for depressive symptoms. One study on pediatric bipolar disorder and suicide attempts in a clinical sample of 405 children and adolescents, ages 7 to 17 years, found approximately one-third of youth reported a history of suicide attempts (Goldstein et al., 2005).

The correlation between mood disorders and suicidal behavior may be explained, at least in part, through cognitive processes associated with depression, that is, cognitive errors (e.g., overgeneralization, catastrophizing, selective abstraction), the cognitive triad (i.e., negative views of self, world, and future), and depressive automatic thoughts (e.g., "I don't deserve to be loved"; Shirk, Boergers, Eason, & Van Horn, 1998; Jacobs, Reinecke, Gollan, & Kane, 2008). With repeated stressful events, these dysfunctional cognitions can become more stable and pervasive, especially if left untreated, and may result in suicidal ideation and an eventual attempt. Indeed, cognitive errors, hopelessness, and worthlessness have all been associated with suicidality among adolescents (Brent, Kolko, Allan, & Brown, 1990; Kingsbury, Hawton, Steinhardt, & James, 1999).

Depressive symptoms are also strongly associated with exposure to peer and partner violence (Kilpatrick et al., 2003; Robinson, Paxton, & Jonen, 2011; Ranney et al., 2013). Many correlates of depression—such as irritability, poor self-esteem, and poor self-regulation of emotions—are also commonly related to physical violence (Cyranowski, Frank, Young, & Shear, 2000; Goldsmith, Chesney, Heath, & Barlow, 2013). Violence may increase stress reactivity and reinforce maladaptive coping skills, thereby worsening depressive symptoms (Seiffge-Krenke, 2000). Whether sex mediates the interaction between violence and depression is undetermined. Some studies suggest that females are more likely than males to develop depression after violence exposure (Ranney et al., 2013), while other studies suggest that sex differences in depression are attenuated by violence exposure (Dunn, Gilman, Willett, Slopen, & Molnar, 2012; Javdani, Jaleel, Suarez, Nichols, & Farmer, 2014).

Anxiety Symptoms and Disorders

A large body of research suggests that adolescent suicide attempters report higher levels of anxiety and anxiety disorders than those without an attempt history, though results are not always consistent (Evans et al., 2004). Goldston et al. (1999, 2006) found that self-reported symptoms of anxiety, particularly trait anxiety, predicted future suicide attempts in adolescents over 5 to 11 years of follow-up. In a clinical sample, generalized anxiety disorder and panic disorder predicted future suicide attempts, though only panic disorder remained significant in a multivariate model. Generalized anxiety and panic disorder were also found to be more common among repeat attempters compared to first-time attempters (Goldston et al., 2009). Mazza (2000) found an association between posttraumatic stress symptomatology and suicidality (current ideation and attempt history) among a group of high school students. Students reporting higher posttraumatic stress symptom severity reported more suicide ideation and were more likely to have a suicide attempt history than those in the average severity group. Posttraumatic stress symptoms were positively and independently related to suicide ideation but not

attempt history, once depression and sex were controlled for (Mazza, 2000).

Similar to mood disorders, cognitive distortions in anxiety disorders are associated with suicidality. Adolescents with anxiety disorders have a lower threshold for perceived threat, expect negative outcomes in threatening situations, underestimate their competency in dealing with perceived threat, and experience higher levels of anxious automatic thoughts in comparison to children and adolescents without anxiety disorders (Barrett, Rapee, Dadds, & Ryan, 1996; Bögels & Zigterman, 2000). Because anxiety and depressive disorders often co-occur, if these cognitions are combined with depression-related cognitive distortions, such anxious thoughts may become overwhelming. Under such conditions, suicidal behavior may be considered as a means of escape.

There is also a strong link between violence exposure and anxiety disorders, particularly posttraumatic stress disorder (PTSD; Boccellari et al., 2007; Cisler et al., 2012; McLaughlin et al., 2013). This relationship is likely a dose–response relationship (Hedtke et al., 2008; Cougle, Resnick, & Kilpatrick, 2009). Adolescents who develop acute stress disorder immediately after an emergency department visit for a violent injury are likely to progress to full-blown PTSD (Fein et al., 2002; Pailler, Kassam-Adams, Datner, & Fein, 2007). Whether gender influences the risk of post-violence PTSD is under debate, with some authors suggesting different types of PTSD symptoms between the two genders (Langeland & Olff, 2008; McLaughlin et al., 2013; Steven Betts, Williams, Najman, & Alati, 2013; Javdani et al., 2014). The association between trauma experience, PTSD, depression, and suicidality is complicated, with some studies suggesting that PTSD may act as a mediating variable between violence and depression (Mazza & Reynolds, 1999; Kerig, Ward, Vanderzee, & Arnzen Moeddel, 2009) or that it may simply be a marker of general mental distress (Adams et al., 2013).

Anger, Impulsivity, Aggression, and Conduct Disorders

Disruptive behavior disorders are strongly associated with attempted suicide and death by suicide among adolescents, particularly in the presence of comorbid mood disorders (Gould et al., 2003; Evans et al., 2004). There is an especially strong association between disruptive behavior disorders and repeat suicide attempts (Esposito et al., 2003). Approximately one-third of males who died by suicide have been found to have had a conduct disorder diagnosis (Gould et al., 2003), and conduct disorder has been found to predict future suicide attempts among psychiatrically hospitalized adolescents (Goldston et al., 2009) but only in the presence of major depressive disorder. In a large epidemiologic sample of 1,420 children and adolescents (9 to 16 years old), disruptive behavior disorders were found to predict suicidality (ideation, plans, and/or attempts) over the course of three-month follow-up, even after adjusting for other disorders and covariates (Foley, Goldston, Costello, & Angold, 2006).

The association between anger and suicidality varies as a function of suicide history. In one study (Stein, Apter, Ratzoni, Har-Even, & Avidan, 1998), repeat attempters, first-time attempters, and non-suicidal inpatient controls reported more trait anger than community controls, but only repeat suicide attempters reported more anger than nonsuicidal inpatients. Esposito et al. (2003) found that repeat adolescent suicide attempters evaluated in a general hospital emergency department or pediatrics floor reported higher levels of trait anger than first-time attempters. In a third study (Goldston et al., 1996), higher levels of self-reported trait anger were found among adolescent inpatients with a previous suicide attempt compared to those who recently made a first attempt and those who never made a suicide attempt. No differences were found across groups on degree of state anger. Overall it appears that adolescents with more significant suicide histories report particularly high levels of trait anger. However, the work of Goldston et al. suggests that recent suicidal behavior may have a cathartic effect with respect to anger. A suicide attempt may also effectively reduce anger-related emotional arousal and/or temporarily remove adolescents from situations that promote intense anger. In another study that examined self-reported levels of anger before and after a suicidal crisis, anger was found to increase from the time of the precipitant stressor to the time of the suicidal crisis for all adolescents. However, those who carried through with an attempt during the suicidal crisis reported a greater decrease in anger than those who only reported suicidal ideation (Negron, Piacentini, Graae, Davies, & Shaffer, 1997). Thus it is possible that some adolescents may attempt suicide as a maladaptive means of coping with unresolved anger.

Impulsive aggression (i.e., quickly responding with heightened levels of hostility/anger to frustration or confrontation) may be more important than either impulsivity or aggression alone in contributing to suicidal behavior and may be genetically transmitted (Brent & Melhem, 2008; Bronisch & Lieb, 2008). A number of family studies suggest that impulsive aggression in adolescent offspring (Melhem et al., 2007) or both parent and adolescent offspring (Brent et al., 2002), increases risk for an adolescent suicide attempt. Brent et al. (2003) found that impulsive aggression among adolescent offspring was the most powerful predictor of the transmission of suicidal behavior from parent to child.

After controlling for depressive symptoms, impulsivity predicted suicidality for juvenile offenders but not for the psychiatrically hospitalized adolescents (Sanislow, Grilo, Fehon, Axelrod, & McGlashan, 2003). Thus the association between impulsivity and suicidality may vary as a function of the population under study with a stronger relationship found among adolescents with conduct/externalizing problems.

There is also a connection between aggressive and suicidal behaviors. O'Donnell et al. (2005) followed a community sample of 769 African American and Latino adolescents over the course of three years. Aggressive behaviors reported by adolescents in the eighth grade (i.e., fighting, carrying a weapon, use of a weapon) were found to predict suicidality (ideation, plan, and/or attempt) in the 11th grade for females but not for males. In a study of informant reports of aggressive behaviors in a sample of 55 child and adolescent suicide victims, compared to a community control sample of 55 nonsuicidal adolescents, history of aggressive behavior was found to be significantly greater among adolescents who died by suicide than community controls (Renaud, Berlim, McGirr, Tousignant, & Turecki, 2008). However, in a multivariate model controlling for psychiatric factors, the relation between aggression and suicide was reduced to non-significance. In a psychiatrically hospitalized sample of 270 adolescents, youth, but not parent, report of aggression was found to be associated with suicidal behavior among youth with internalizing symptoms (Kerr et al., 2007).

Substance Use Disorders

Substance use disorders (SUDs) have been associated with both attempted suicide and death by suicide among adolescents. In a review conducted by Esposito-Smythers and Spirito (2004), rates of any SUD among adolescents who died by suicide were found to range from 27% to 50%, alcohol use disorder ranged from 22% to 27%, and rates of illicit drug use disorders ranged from 13% to 25%. Among suicide attempters, rates of alcohol and/or cannabis use disorders were found to range from 27% to 50% in the Esposito-Smythers and Spirito review. Across studies reviewed, the presence of a SUD was associated with a three- to six-fold increase in likelihood of a suicide attempt. Additional research suggests that rates of alcohol and cannabis use disorders increase along with repetitive suicidal behavior (D'Eramo, Prinstein, Freeman, Grapentine, & Spirito, 2004).

In the Goldston et al. (2009) longitudinal study in which 180 adolescents were followed for up to 13 years post-psychiatric hospitalization, SUDs predicted future suicide attempts in univariate analyses and the relation between SUDs and suicidality strengthened as adolescents grew older. However, this association was nonsignificant in multivariate analyses, suggesting SUDs primarily confer risk for suicidal behavior in the presence of other mental health disorders. Similar results were found in a large epidemiologic sample of 1,420 children and adolescents ages 9 to 16. SUDs only predicted suicidality (ideation, plans, and/or attempts) in the presence of other mental health disorders, particularly depression, over the course of a three-month follow-up (Foley et al., 2006).

Bagge and Sher (2008) note that there are two dimensions of this association: directionality (alcohol leads to suicidal behavior, suicidal behavior leads to alcohol use, or a spurious relation) and temporality (proximal vs. distal effects of alcohol use and suicidal behavior). For example, Hufford (2001) suggests the acute effects of intoxication may heighten psychological distress, increase aggressiveness (toward self and others), enhance suicide-specific alcohol expectancies (e.g., "alcohol will give me the courage to make a suicide attempt"), and inhibit the generation and implementation of adaptive coping strategies. Among individuals contemplating suicide, this concurrent increase in psychological distress, aggressiveness, and cognitive distortion may be sufficient to propel suicidal thoughts into action. With respect to distal effects, alcohol use disorders may be associated with increases in stress and co-occurring psychopathology, which in turn increases risk for suicidal behavior. Over time, stress resulting from substance-related social, academic, and/or legal problems, when combined with depressive symptoms, may result in a suicide attempt.

Both peer and partner violence are associated with high rates of alcohol and other drug use (Yan et al., 2010; Cunningham et al., 2014). Substance use may increase the risk of violence, may co-occur due to clustering of risky behaviors, or may be a means of coping with post-violence consequences. For example, a longitudinal study of African American youth (Xue, Zimmerman, & Cunningham, 2009) found that early peer violence predicted later alcohol use; early alcohol use predicted later violent behavior; and decreases in alcohol use and violence were concurrent. This relationship was not modified by gender. Similarly, Yan et al. (2010) showed evidence for the link between alcohol and dating violence among a community sample of Latino youth. When compared to those who had not experienced dating violence, victims were more likely to experience adverse psychological outcomes like depression and suicidality and engage in alcohol related risk-behavior (heavy drinking). Specifically, girls who engaged in binge drinking were at about 27 times greater odds of experiencing dating violence victimization when compared to girls who did not report a binge-drinking history. For boys, those who reported dating violence victimization also reported high-risk behaviors, such as carrying a weapon, suicide ideation, and alcohol consumption.

Studies suggest that youth with a history of violence and alcohol and other drug use are at the highest risk of suicidality. For example, Silverman et al. (2001) found elevated odds of having a lifetime prevalence of sexual and physical dating violence among a nationally representative adolescent female sample when endorsing (a) past 30-day binge drinking (double the odds); (b) a history of cocaine use (triple the odds); (c) considering suicide in the 12 months prior to the study (six times the odds); and (d) suicide attempts (nine times the odds), independent of each other.

Comorbidity

Various combinations of comorbidity, within and between internalizing and externalizing disorders, increase risk for attempted suicide and death by suicide. The likelihood of adolescent suicide attempts increased greater than two-fold with each psychiatric disorder that was diagnosed in one study (Goldston et al., 2009). Mood disorders, in combination with disruptive behavior and/or SUDs, seems to greatly increase risk for suicidal behavior (Brent, Perper, Moritz, Baugher, Schweers, & Roth, 1993; Shaffer et al., 1996; Goldston et al, 2009). Foley et al. (2006) found that risk for suicidality (ideation, plans, and/or attempts) was greatest for adolescents when general anxiety disorder or oppositional-defiant disorder was diagnosed on top of a major depressive disorder. In a large epidemiologic sample of youth ages 9 to 16, anxiety disorders were found to predict suicidality (ideation, plans, and/or attempts) over the course of three-month follow-up, but this association was reduced to a trend level after adjusting for other disorders and covariates. Generalized anxiety disorder did predict suicidality when comorbid with major depressive disorder (Foley et al., 2006).

Among patients with a history of violence, exposure to multiple forms of violence also heightens risk. This finding may be explained in two ways. First, we see a high rate of overlap between perpetration and victimization, both for partner and nonpartner youth violence. Thus most perpetrators are also victims and vice versa. Second, for those youth who are exclusively victims or exclusively perpetrators, the relationship may be mediated by internalizing disorders (for victims) versus externalizing disorders (for perpetrators).

Familial Transmission of Suicidal Behavior and Abuse

Wagner, Silverman, and Martin (2003) published a comprehensive review of familial risk factors associated with adolescent suicidality. Low cohesion, high conflict, and unsatisfying parent–adolescent relationships, in particular, were more frequently observed in the families of adolescents who attempt and/or die by suicide than controls. Yet the relation between such family variables and adolescent suicidal behavior is often lessened or reduced to nonsignificance when other related factors, such as adolescent or parental psychopathology, are taken into account (Gould et al., 2003; Evans et al., 2004; Brent & Melhem, 2008). Here we focus on the relation between childhood physical and sexual abuse because it has been shown to be related to adolescent suicidal behavior as well as interpersonal violence.

A comprehensive review of studies examining the association between childhood abuse (sexual, physical, and/or neglect) and adolescent suicidality concluded that childhood abuse predicts suicidal thoughts and behavior among adolescents (King & Merchant, 2008). For example, in a large high school sample of 131,862 American adolescents, more than half with a history of sexual abuse reported a lifetime history of suicide attempt (Eisenberg, Ackard, & Resnick, 2007). Likewise, Fergusson, Beautrais, and Horwood (2003) examined the relationship between childhood sexual abuse and suicide attempts in 1,063 adolescents and young adults from New Zealand and found that adolescent victims of childhood sexual abuse had elevated rates of suicidal

ideation and attempts compared to nonvictims. In a study comparing a community sample of women with and without a childhood sexual abuse history (Briere & Runtz, 1986), women reporting childhood sexual abuse were more likely to have a suicide attempt history than those not endorsing such abuse. A higher percentage (87%) of women reporting having first attempted suicide in adolescence also reported a history of childhood sexual abuse; this was not the case for women whose first attempt was in adulthood. Results also suggested that number of previous attempts were associated with a combination of physical and sexual abuse (Briere & Runtz, 1986).

In an Australian sample of 2,485 high school students, sexually abused adolescents were more likely to report suicidal ideation, plans, threats, and attempts than nonabused adolescents (Martin, Bergen, Richardson, Roeger, & Allison, 2004). After controlling for depressive symptoms, hopelessness, and family functioning, sexual abuse did not predict suicide attempts for females, but for male adolescents the risk of suicide attempt was 15 times greater for victims of sexual abuse. Thus, the relationship between sexual abuse and suicidal behavior is likely moderated by factors such as sex, age at the time of detection, and number of perpetrators (Evans et al., 2004). In these distressed families, both the environment and genetic factors likely increase risk for offspring suicidal behavior.

With respect to physical abuse, one study found that Flemish adolescents who self-injured with the intent to die were more likely to have a physical abuse history than their counterparts who engaged in NSSI (Baetens, Claes, Muehlenkamp, Grietens, & Onghena 2011). There also is evidence that abuse may influence suicidal behavior through an association with impulsivity and aggression (Baud, 2005; Brodsky & Stanley, 2008), affect change (Bebbington et al., 2009), or by negatively impacting neurobiological development. These pathways may be similar in those exposed to peer violence.

Sexual Orientation and Gender Identity

Lesbian/gay/bisexual/transgender (LGBT) youth are at increased risk for suicide ideation and attempts as compared to their non-LGBT counterparts. According to the analysis by Silenzio, Pena, Duberstein, Cerel, and Knox (2007), National Longitudinal Study of Adolescent Health study data revealed elevated past-year ideation (17.2%) and attempt rates (4.9%) in LGB identified youth as compared to non-LGB identified youth (6.3%

ideation, 1.6% attempts) controlling for age, sex, and race. Although very few studies of suicidality have been conducted among transgender youth, the evidence that does exist suggests that they are at particularly high risk for suicide attempts and ideation (Grossman & D'Augelli, 2007). Specifically, Grossman and D'Augelli found that almost half (45%) of Transgender male and Transgender female adolescent participants sampled in their study had seriously thought about taking their lives in the year preceding the study, and a little over a quarter (26%) reported at least one lifetime suicide attempt. Moreover, 51% (8 of 14) of those with an attempt history agreed with the statement that their wish to be dead had to do with the difficulty associated with living as a transgender person. When comparing transgender attempters to nonattempters, those who attempted had more negative attitudes toward being LGBT, experienced more parental verbal and physical abuse, and reported lower body self-esteem (i.e., appearance and others disliking their bodies). (See Chapter 6 in this volume by Michael Hendricks for full discussion of LGBT youth and suicidal behavior).

LGBT youth also report almost double the incidence of peer violence and bullying compared with non-LGBT youth (Kann et al., 2011). The highest rates of peer violence are experienced by transgender youth (Kosciw, Greytak, Diaz, & Bartkiewicz, 2010). Multiple studies suggest a direct relationship between peer violence exposure and suicidality among LGBT youth (Savin-Williams, 1994; Kosciw et al., 2010; Nuttbrock et al., 2010; Toomey, Ryan, Card, & Russell, 2010). Interestingly, among LGBT youth with high levels of protective factors (e.g., supportive family relationships, absence of homophobic teasing), the rate of suicidal thoughts decreases to close to that of non-LGBT youth (Eisenberg & Resnick, 2006; Birkett, Espelage, & Koenig, 2009).

Exposure to Suicidal Behavior and Interpersonal Violence

A comprehensive review by Insel and Gould (2008) found that the majority of studies provide significant support for an association between exposure to the suicidal behavior of adolescent peers and an adolescent's subsequent suicide attempts. For example, one study of more than 5,000 high school students found that adolescents exposed to a peer who made a nonlethal suicide attempt were 3.5 times more likely to report suicidal ideation, 3.6 times more likely to report a suicide attempt, and 1.8 times more likely to inflict injuries requiring medical attention in the next year than adolescents

without this exposure history. Adolescents exposed to a peer who died by suicide were 5.4 times more likely to report suicidal ideation, 9.4 times more likely to report a suicide attempt, and 3.1 times more likely to inflict injuries requiring medical attention in the next year than adolescents who were not exposed to a peer who died by suicide (Cerel, Roberts, & Nilsen, 2005).

The media has a significant influence on suicidal behavior, more so for nonfictional descriptions of suicides (e.g., newspaper and television reports) than fictional portrayals of suicides on television or in movies (Insel & Gould, 2008). So-called cyber suicide pacts (suicide pacts among strangers who meet over the Internet) have also emerged in last decade (Insel & Gould, 2008). Although it is unclear why this cluster effect occurs, recent research by Gould, Kleinman, Lake, Forman, and Bassett Midle (2014) found that newspaper coverage of suicide that included specific story characteristics was significantly associated with the initiation of adolescent suicide clusters. Social modeling is another potential vehicle for transmission, but assertive pairing (i.e., youth with mental illness may be more likely to choose peers with similar problems) also may play a role in cluster suicides. Youth who are vulnerable to suicidality may belong to a group of like-minded peers prior to any suicidal acts.

The experience of violent, interpersonal stressors may increase risk in particular. For example, in a sample of 3,005 adolescents from Mexico City, the experience of any traumatic event, including a serious injury, being a victim of violence, and witnessing domestic violence, increased the likelihood of a making a suicide plan five-fold and making an attempt six-fold (Borges, Benjet, Medina-Mora, Orozco, Molnar, & Nock, 2008). Further, those who experienced three or more traumatic events were 13.7 times more likely to report a suicide attempt than those who did not experience any traumatic events.

Access to Firearms

The most recent data available indicate that firearms account for 38% of deaths by suicide for youth ages zero to 19 (CDC NCIPC, 2013a). Research demonstrates that youth who live in a home with a loaded gun are more than 30 times more likely to die by suicide than those who live in homes without a loaded gun (Brent et al., 1993). Additionally, suicide attempts using a firearm are more likely to be fatal (Wadman, Muellerman, Coto, & Kellermann, 2003). A recent observational study showed that

60% of youth with past-year suicidal ideation, past-year peer violence, and past-year alcohol use had immediate access to a firearm (Ranney et al., 2013). However, few psychiatrists, family physicians, internists, pediatricians, or emergency physicians currently query high-risk patients about firearm access (Grossman, Mang & Rivara, 1995; Price, Kinnison, Dake, Thompson, & Price, 2007; Betz, Barber, & Miller, 2010; Betz et al., 2013; Butkus & Weisman, 2014).

Assessment of Acutely Suicidal Adolescents and Adolescents Who Have Attempted Suicide

Suicidal adolescents and their parents should be interviewed separately and together when assessing for suicide risk. Even with their parents out of the room, eliciting suicidal intent, a key component of the risk evaluation, can be challenging. It is critical to ask both open-ended and detailed questions about the adolescent's suicidality, including the "who, what, when, where, why, and how." In general, the interview should result in a thorough description of the current problem and precipitants to the attempt including understanding current symptoms and their severity, specifically about the extent of hopelessness and irritability/anger as well as substance use, especially heavy drinking episodes.

A thorough discussion of recent suicidal thoughts and behaviors (as well as prior suicide attempts) is critical. The extent of suicidality should be determined by asking about ideation, method/plan, the presence of threats (e.g., suicide note), and actual behaviors. In an adolescent who endorses suicidal ideation, it is essential to assess the risk that the patient will move from low to higher risk. If an attempt has already occurred, it is critical to determine its nature and to assess future risk. The following lists the critical questions a clinician should consider when assessing a suicidal adolescent based on material coalesced from a variety of sources, including Brent, Poling, and Goldstein (2011), Rudd (2006), Shaffer and Pfeffer (2001), and Spirito and Overholser (2003).

Current Emotional State

Start by assessing the adolescent's mood and suicidality at the time of the interview.

CLINICAL QUESTIONS:
- What is your urge to harm yourself right now?
- Are you having thoughts of killing yourself right now?

- How often do you think about killing yourself?
- How well can you control your thinking about suicide right now?
- How well can you keep yourself from trying to kill yourself right now?

Were There Any Precipitating Events?

Precipitating events (e.g., bullying, fight with girl/boyfriend/parent, break-up) and stressors, and whether or not they are acute (e.g., recent humiliation) or chronic (e.g., school, illness, poverty, abuse/neglect), are important to assess.

CLINICAL QUESTIONS:
- Ask whether anything triggered the suicidal ideation (e.g., break up with significant other, death of a loved one, or fight with parent).
- Determine whether these circumstances still hold.
- If a conflict or fight with a partner or peer was the precipitant, consider addressing the underlying causes of conflict and violence and ensuring safety. If cyberbullying or cyberfighting was present, consider advising the adolescent on reducing involvement in social media, texting, and so on.

Does the Adolescent Give Any Specific Reasons for Attempting?

The Reasons for Overdose Scale (Hawton, O'Grady, Osborn, & Cole, 1982) can be administered for adolescents who have a difficult time articulating the reason for the attempt and may help to clarify for the adolescent the underlying motive.

What Does the Adolescent Say About the Frequency and Severity of His or Her Suicidal Ideation?

Current ideation should be assessed, as well as suicidal ideation at the time of a suicide attempt, for adolescents who have recently attempted suicide. Having changes in suicidal ideation frequency and severity is one of the best predictors of a suicide attempt (Prinstein et al., 2008). A number of measures are also available to assess suicidal ideation, such as the Suicidal Ideation Questionnaire (Reynolds, 1987).

CLINICAL QUESTIONS:
- How much of the day do you have suicidal thoughts?
- In a given hour, how much do you think about killing yourself?

- How well can you push away suicidal thoughts and think about something else (on a scale of 1 to 10)?
- How much do you think you can resist the urge to kill yourself (on a scale of 1 to 10)?

Does the Adolescent Endorse Suicidal Intent?

The intent of an adolescent suicide attempt has been found to be strongly related to the seriousness of a suicide attempt, often more so than the lethality of an attempt (Spirito, Sterling, Donaldson, & Arrigan, 1996). The Suicide Intent Scale (Beck, Schuyler, & Herman, 1974) is a useful tool to assess intent after a suicide attempt.

CLINICAL QUESTIONS:
- At the present moment, do you want to die?
- If yes: People have different reasons for wanting to die. What are the reasons you want to die?
- If the adolescent has trouble generating ideas: Other teens have mentioned things like they didn't particularly want to die but rather wanted to escape an intolerable situation or wanted to communicate something to someone like asking for help, getting attention, making someone feel sorry, or trying to get someone to change his or her mind.
- Is killing yourself something you think you might do?
- In an adolescent who has made a recent attempt, ask: Do you still feel the same way about wanting to die?

Was the Attempt Planned or Impulsive?

If the adolescent made an attempt, determine to what extent it was planned versus impulsive. Planned attempts have been found to be associated with greater depression and hopelessness than impulsive attempts (Brown, Overholser, Spirito, & Fritz, 1991).

CLINICAL QUESTIONS:
- How long have you been thinking about killing yourself?
- If the adolescent has attempted suicide before, ask how long the adolescent had been thinking about suicide before making the attempt.
- What have you done to prepare for suicide?
- Have you made any plans to kill yourself?
- Have you written a goodbye letter, a suicide note, or a letter of explanation?
- Have you thought about what you might say in such a note?

Does the Adolescent Have a Preferred Method and Access to Means? Is There Firearm Access?

As with the risk assessment, the parent(s) and child should be interviewed separately about access to lethal means. Although overdoses accounted for only 6% of youth suicide deaths in 4 (CDC NCIPIC, 2013a), ingestion represents one of the most common adolescent suicide attempt methods (O'Brien & Berzin, 2012), and therefore access to pills needs to be discussed. Due to the lethality of attempts with firearms, access to firearms should always be assessed, even if the adolescent does not endorse guns as a preferred method. If the adolescent reports one method initially, always ask *what other ways* he or she has considered—adolescents will often start by disclosing the least lethal method first.

CLINICAL QUESTIONS:
- Begin with an open-ended question but consider asking about hanging, jumping, drowning, stabbing, carbon monoxide, car crash, and cutting.
- Does the adolescent have a preferred plan or method he or she would use? Has he or she thought of more than one way to attempt suicide?
- Always ask about the availability of firearms and pills not only at home but also at relatives' and friends' houses. When asking about firearms or pills, ask specifically about type, how many, how stored (e.g., locked up or not), and, for firearms, how stored (e.g., locked up or not) and availability of ammunition.
- Assess for the youth's access to over-the-counter medications, household cleaning supplies, and even the youth's own prescription medications.
- Assess the parents' knowledge of the lethality of different means and provide psychoeducation whenever possible.
- For adolescents who have attempted suicide, assess the adolescent's perception of the lethality of the method.

What Is/Was the Potential for Discovery?

Inquire about the method and/or location/situation chosen to attempt suicide in order to determine if they would allow time for an intervention to reverse potentially lethal effects.

CLINICAL QUESTIONS:
- Are you doing anything to ensure that people don't find out about your suicide attempt?
- Would you take steps to save your life? Would you call a therapist, friend, and crisis line if you were feeling suicidal?

How Effective Is the Environment for Keeping the Adolescent Safe?

Can the adolescent and/or the parent/caregiver keep him or her safe in the current environment?

CLINICAL QUESTIONS:

- Consider availability of significant other, family, or caregiver to the adolescent, the quality of their relationship, whether abuse/neglect is present, and whether mental illness or substance abuse is present in a caregiver.

Can the Adolescent Give Any Reasons for Living?

Ask specifically what keeps the adolescent from killing him or herself, including reasons for living and adverse impact on other people.

The Reasons for Living Inventory for Adolescents (Osman et al., 1998) can also be administered to prompt adolescents on reasons they may have not considered.

CLINICAL QUESTIONS:

- Ask about what the adolescent thinks will happen after he or she dies.
- Ask about personal fate and impact of suicide on family and friends.
- Ask about the chances that the patient will make a suicide attempt: less than, equal to, or more than 50%.

Screening for Other Risk Factors Including Substance Use and Interpersonal Violence

As discussed previously, alcohol use and interpersonal violence increase risk for suicidal behavior.

CLINICAL QUESTIONS:

- Ask about future intent to use substances and their availability. Ask whether drugs or alcohol have been known to worsen mood or increase risk for impulsive actions.
- Assess exposure to peer/partner conflict; although there are no short, standardized screens for peer dating or nondating violence, modified versions of adult screens (e.g., "Has anyone hit, kicked, or punched you in the past year?") are clinically effective. It is important to assess the frequency and type of violence, as well as its simple presence. A pattern of recurrent fights, cyberbullying, or dating violence implies higher risk than a single episode.
- Discuss emotional responses to interpersonal violence; explicitly discuss the relationship between violence exposure and thoughts of self-harm.

- Assess safety (of self, of friends, and of the other party in the violent episode).
- Consider explicitly discussing fight-avoidance strategies and emotional self-regulation in the face of future violence exposure.

Determining Overall Suicide Risk

Rudd, Joiner, and Rajab (2001) recommend assigning patients levels of risk based on the following criteria:

1. *None to Mild* = infrequent, low-intensity ideation, no intent or plan; supportive environment; youth can be managed in the community; focus of treatment is on underlying concerns and not suicide risk.

2. *Moderate* = suicidal ideation, some intent, no plan; youth may or may not be able to be maintained in the community based on the balance of risk versus protective factors; presence of supportive and healthy home, school, and neighborhood environment; focus of treatment is the current suicidal crisis and efforts to minimize risk factors and enhance protective factors.

3. *High* = frequent and disruptive ideation, strong intent, and specific plan; youth cannot be maintained in the community and is admitted to an inpatient facility; focus of treatment is ensuring safety, identifying and gathering environmental supports, and developing a discharge plan to ensure continuity of care.

The Columbia Suicide Severity Rating Scale (Posner et al, 2011) also has an algorithm to classify suicide risk that may be useful to clinicians (http://www.cssrs.columbia.edu/scales_practice_cssrs.html).

Inpatient Psychiatric Hospitalization

If overall suicide risk is determined to be high, inpatient psychiatric hospitalization is frequently deemed necessary. Inpatient psychiatric hospitalization is needed when the adolescent demonstrates suicidal thoughts or behaviors that are so unstable and unpredictable that there is serious short-term risk (Shaffer & Pfeffer, 2001). It is not uncommon for a suicidal adolescent to be psychiatrically hospitalized. In one study, suicidal thoughts and behaviors were the most common reason youth were admitted to an inpatient psychiatric hospital (Wilson, Kelly, Morgan, Harley, & O'Sullivan, 2012). Inpatient psychiatric hospitalization represents the most restrictive level of care available to suicidal adolescents and is frequently used in cases where a decision needs to be made quickly to keep the adolescent safe. Ideally, adolescents who need hospitalization will be admitted voluntarily. However, there are situations in which adolescents are admitted involuntarily because their caregivers and/or clinicians feel that they are at imminent risk and the adolescent does not agree to admission.

One study compared the effectiveness of inpatient psychiatric hospitalization in reducing suicidality compared to outpatient multisystemic therapy for adolescents, primarily African American, presenting with a psychiatric emergency (Huey et al., 2004). Multisystemic therapy resulted in fewer suicide attempts at one-year follow-up compared to hospitalization, but because there was a higher rate of prior attempts in the multisystemic therapy group, this finding may have been related to regression to the mean. There is no data available for determining which adolescents who are at high risk for suicide would be better served in the community versus an inpatient psychiatric setting (Lamb, 2009). Nonetheless, because there is no evidence that psychiatric hospitalization prevents suicide, alternatives to inpatient care should be considered for adolescents who can be safely managed by a less restrictive level of care. In many cases, a crisis intervention that incorporates a safety plan can be used to stabilize the current suicidal crisis and serve as an alternative to hospitalization if it is accompanied by immediate participation in an intensive outpatient program or individual plus family treatment (Singer, 2005).

Safety Planning

After conducting a thorough suicide risk assessment and determining a return home is indicated, a safety plan should be developed with the adolescent and caregivers. Adolescents should be involved in the planning as much as possible in order to identify supports that are available at home, school, and through the therapist, as well as positive coping strategies. Parents/caregivers should be involved to limit access to means. The safety plan is not a "no-suicide" contract; it is designed to identify strategies to help adolescents cope with suicidal urges. No-suicide contracts are ineffective because they ask clients to promise to stay alive without providing a strategy on how to do so. No-suicide contracts provide clinicians with a false sense of security when in fact such contracts do not reduce the client's risk for suicide and do not reduce the clinician's risk for a lawsuit following a client's suicide (Wortzel, Matarazzo, & Homaifar, 2013).

Overview of the Safety Plan

The safety plan includes an agreement between the adolescent, parents/caregivers, and therapist that

should the adolescent have suicidal thoughts or impulses, he or she will inform a responsible adult and/or call the therapist or an emergency number. By agreeing to the plan, the adolescent is not promising he or she will never feel suicidal but rather that he or she will remain "safe" and not engage in further suicidal behavior without contacting someone. In addition, part of the plan is to collaboratively identify specific steps the adolescent and family would take if a suicidal crisis resurfaces. Specific steps should be written and easily available such as on a mobile phone for the adolescent to refer to in times of stress. Reaffirming the safety plan should be a part of every subsequent therapy visit until the crisis has passed.

Formulating the Safety Plan

The safety plan is developed and tailored to each adolescent and includes a hierarchically arranged list of coping strategies, developed collaboratively by the adolescent and the therapist. Whenever possible, the parent/caregiver should be informed of the coping strategies the adolescent reports are most effective, so that the parent/caregiver can help to coach the adolescent in those skills in a suicidal crisis. At a minimum, the safety plan should include the telephone numbers of social supports, the treating therapist, the on-call therapist, and the national suicide prevention lifeline (1-800-273-8255). The safety plan should also include an agreement between the adolescent, parents/caregivers, and therapist that, should the adolescent become suicidal, he or she will inform a responsible adult and/or call the therapist or emergency numbers. If partner/peer violence is a risk factor for suicidal ideation, the safety plan should include coping statements specific to this risk factor, as well as other alternative behaviors that might help in such situations (e.g., reporting the threat to a school guidance counselor).

Parents/caregivers are a party to the discussion of precipitants and motivations to the suicide attempt and to all aspects of the safety plan. The therapist must also obtain agreement for removal of firearms and lethal methods from the parents. Parents often are unwilling to remove knives and razors from the household, so the therapist should take particular care to discuss this aspect of safety planning, especially when the adolescent has also engaged in NSSI. In circumstances where the parent is one of the adolescent's triggers for suicidal ideation, the therapist facilitates a "truce" with adolescent and parent around hot topics/possible precipitants to future suicidality with the promise that these issues will be addressed in future therapy sessions.

Conclusions

There are a number of important risk factors to consider in evaluating adolescents with acute suicidality or those who have recently attempted suicide. Much of this information is obvious on presentation, including age, sex, and ethnic-minority status. Other information can be obtained in the interview of the adolescent and/or a collateral interview with a parent/caregiver, including history of self-injurious behavior (with and without suicidal intent) and its age of onset, history of mood and anxiety disorders, impulsivity, substance use, family history of suicidal behavior, sexual identity issues, and exposure to suicidal and violent behavior. Interpersonal violence is an equally if not more important area to assess given its close association with suicidality, especially with respect to its role as a potential trigger for suicidal behavior.

Once a history has been obtained, there are a series of important questions to ask with respect to the adolescent's current emotional state that need to be integrated with historical information in order to determine the appropriate disposition. These include the precipitating events/reasons for suicidal thoughts/behavior for the current suicidal crisis/attempt and their current status in the adolescent's life, the severity of the adolescent's suicidal ideation/suicidal intent, access to means, exposure to interpersonal violence at discharge, and the capacity of the family/social environment to keep the adolescent safe. All interviews must conclude with a comprehensive safety plan to ensure that both the adolescent and parent have a comprehensive, structured plan to manage the resurgence of suicidal thoughts.

References

Adams, Z. W., McCart, M. R., Zajac, K., Danielson, C. K., Sawyer, G. K., Saunders, B. E., & Kilpatrick, D. G. (2013). Psychiatric problems and trauma exposure in nondetained delinquent and nondelinquent adolescents. *Journal of Clinical Child and Adolescent Psychology*, 42, 323–331.

Archer, J. (2000). Sex differences in aggression between heterosexual partners: A meta-analytic review. *Psychological Bulletin*, 126(5), 651–680.

Asarnow, J. R., Porta, M. S., Spirito, A., Emslie, G., Clarke, G., Wagner, K. D., Vitiello, B., Keller, M., Birmaher, B., McCracken, J., Mayes, T., Berk, M., Brent, D. Suicide Attempts and Nonsuicidal Self-Injury in the Treatment of Resistant-Depression in Adolescents (TORDIA) Study (2011). *Journal of the American Academy of Child and Adolescent Psychiatry. 50*, 772-781.

Bagge, C. L., & Sher, K. J. (2008). Adolescent alcohol involvement and suicide attempts: Toward the development of a conceptual framework. *Clinical Psychology Review*, 28, 1283–1296.

Baetens, I., Claes, L., Muehlenkamp, J., Grietens, H., & Onghena, P. (2011). Non-suicidal and suicidal self-injurious behavior among Flemish adolescents: A web-survey. *Archives of Suicide Research*, 15, 56–67.

Barrett, P. M., Rapee, R. M., Dadds, M. M., & Ryan, S. M. (1996). Family enhancement of cognitive style in anxious and aggressive children. *Journal of Abnormal Child Psychology*, 24, 187–199.

Baud, P. (2005). Personality traits as intermediary phenotypes in suicidal behavior: Genetic issues. *American Journal of Medical Genetics Part C: Seminars in Medical Genetics*, 133C, 34–42.

Bebbington, P. E., Cooper, C., Minot, S., Brugha, T. S., Jenkins, R., Meltzer, H., & Dennis, M. (2009). Suicide attempts, gender, and sexual abuse: Data from the 2000 British Psychiatric Morbidity Survey. *American Journal of Psychiatry*, 166, 1135–1140.

Beck, A. T., Schuyler, D., & Herman, I. (1974). Development of suicidal intent scales. In A. T. Beck, H. L. P. Resnik, & D. J. Lettieri (Eds.), *The prediction of suicide* (pp. 45-56). Bowie, MD: Charles Press.

Betz, M. E., Barber, C. W., & Miller, M. (2010). Firearm restriction as suicide prevention: Variation in belief and practice among providers in an urban emergency department. *Injury Prevention*, 16(4), 278–281.

Betz, M. E., Miller, M., Barber, C., Miller, I., Sullivan, A. F., Camargo, C. A. Jr., ... ED-SAFE Investigators. (2013). Lethal means restriction for suicide prevention: Beliefs and behaviors of emergency department providers. *Depression and Anxiety*, 30(10), 1013–1020.

Birkett, M., Espelage, D. L., & Koenig, B. (2009). LGB and questioning students in schools: The moderating effects of homophobic bullying and school climate on negative outcomes. *Journal of Youth and Adolescence*, 38, 989–1000.

Boccellari, A., Alvidrez, J., Shumway, M., Kelly, V., Merrill, G. ... Okin, R. L. (2007). Characteristics and psychosocial needs of victims of violent crime identified at a public-sector hospital: Data from a large clinical trial. *General Hospital Psychiatry*, 29(3), 236–243.

Bögels, S. M., & Zigterman, D. (2000). Dysfunctional cognitions in children with social phobia, separation anxiety disorder, and generalized anxiety disorder. *Journal of Abnormal Child Psychology*, 28, 205–211.

Borges, B., Benjet, B., Medina-Mora, M., Orozco, R., Molnar, M., & Nock, M. (2008). Traumatic events and suicide-related outcomes among Mexico City adolescents. *Journal of Clinical Child Psychology and Psychiatry*, 49, 654–666.

Bossarte, R. M., Simon, T. R., & Swahn, M. H. (2008). Clustering of adolescent dating violence, peer violence, and suicidal behavior. *Journal of Interpersonal Violence*, 23(6), 815–833.

Brent, D. A., Baugher, M., Bridge, J., Chen, T., & Chiapetta, L. (1999). Age- and sex-related risk factors for adolescent suicide. *Journal of the American Academy of Child & Adolescent Psychiatry*, 38, 1497–1505.

Brent, D. A., Kolko, D. J., Allan, M. J., & Brown, R. V. (1990). Suicidality in affectively disordered adolescent inpatients. *Journal of the American Academy of Child & Adolescent Psychiatry*, 29, 586–593.

Brent, D. A., & Melhem, N. (2008). Familial transmission of suicidal behavior. *Psychiatric Clinics of North America*, 31, 157–177.

Brent, D. A., Oquendo, M., Birmaher, B., Greenhill, L., Kolko, D., Stanley, B., ... Mann, J. J. (2002). Familial pathways to early-onset suicide attempt: Risk for suicidal behavior in offspring of mood-disordered suicide attempters. *Archives of General Psychiatry*, 59, 801–807.

Brent, D. A., Oquendo, M. A., Birmaher, B., Greenhill, L., Kolko, D., Stanley, B., ... Mann, J. J. (2003). Peripubertal suicide attempts in offspring of suicide attempters with siblings concordant for suicidal behavior. *American Journal of Psychiatry*, 160, 1486–1493.

Brent, D. A., Perper, J. A., Moritz, G., Baugher, M., Schweers, J., & Roth, C. (1993). Firearms and adolescent suicide: A community case-control study. *American Journal of Diseases of Children*, 147(10), 1066–1071.

Brent, D., Poling, K., & Goldstein, T. (2011). *Treating depressed and suicidal adolescents: A clinician's guide*. New York: Guilford Press.

Bridge, J. A., Goldstein, T. R., & Brent, D. A. (2006). Adolescent suicide and suicidal behavior. *Journal of Child Psychology and Psychiatry*, 47, 372–394.

Briere, J., & Runtz, M. (1986). Suicidal thoughts and behaviours in former sexual abuse victims. *Canadian Journal of Behavioural Science/Revue Canadienne Des Sciences Du Comportement*, 18, 413–423.

Brodsky, B. S., & Stanley, B. (2008). Adverse childhood experiences and suicidal behavior. *Psychiatric Clinics of North America*, 31, 223–235.

Bronisch, T., & Lieb, R. L. (2008). Maternal suicidality and suicide risk in offspring. *Psychiatric Clinics of North America*, 31, 213–221.

Brown, L., Overholser, J., Spirito, A., & Fritz, G. (1991). The correlates of planning in adolescent suicide attempts. *Journal of the American Academy of Child & Adolescent Psychiatry*, 30(1), 95–99.

Butkus, R., & Weissman, A. (2014). Internists' attitudes toward prevention of firearm injury. *Annals of Internal Medicine*, 160, 821–827.

Centers for Disease Control and Prevention. (2006). Youth Risk Behavior Surveillance—United States, 2003. *Morbidity and Mortality Weekly Report Surveillance Summaries*, 55, 532–535. Retrieved from http://www.cdc.gov/mmwr/preview/mmwrhtml/mm5519a3.htm

Centers for Disease Control and Prevention. (2012a). Understanding youth violence: Fact Sheet 2012. Retrieved from http://www.cdc.gov/violenceprevention/pdf/yv_factsheet2012-a.pdf

Centers for Disease Control and Prevention. (2012b). What is teen dating violence? Retrieved from http://www.cdc.gov/violenceprevention/intimatepartnerviolence/teen_dating_violence.html

Centers for Disease Control and Prevention. (2012c). Youth Risk Behavior Surveillance—United States, 2011. *Morbidity and Mortality Weekly Report Surveillance Summaries*, 61(SS-4), 1–162.

Centers for Disease Control and Prevention, National Center for Injury Prevention and Control. (2013a). *Fatal Injury Reports, National and Regional, 1999–2011*. Retrieved from http://webappa.cdc.gov/sasweb/ncipc/mortrate10_us.html

Centers for Disease Control and Prevention, National Center for Injury Prevention and Control (2013b). *Web-Based Injury Statistics Query and Reporting System (WISQARS™)*. Retrieved from http://www.cdc.gov/injury/wisqars/nonfatal.html

Cerel, J., Roberts, T. A., & Nilsen, W. J. (2005). Peer suicidal behavior and adolescent risk. *Journal of Nervous and Mental Disease*, 193, 237–243.

Cheng, T. L., Johnson, S., Wright, J. L., Pearson-Fields, A. S., Brenner, R., Schwarz, D., ... Scheidt, P. C. (2006). Assault-injured adolescents presenting to the emergency department: Causes and circumstances. *Academic Emergency Medicine*, 13(6), 610–616.

Chiodo, D., Crooks, C. V., Wolfe, D. A., McIsaac, C., Hughes, R., & Jaffe, P. G. (2012). Longitudinal prediction and concurrent functioning of adolescent girls demonstrating various profiles of dating violence and victimization. *Prevention Science*, 13, 350–359.

Cisler, J. M., Begle, A. M., Amstadter, A. B., Resnick, H. S. Danielson, C. K., Saunders, B. E., & Kilpatrick, D. G. (2012). Exposure to interpersonal violence and risk for PTSD, depression, delinquency, and binge drinking among adolescents: Data from the NSA–R. *Journal of Traumatic Stress*, 25(1), 33–40.

Cougle, J. R., Resnick, H., & Kilpatrick, D. G. (2009). Does prior exposure to interpersonal violence increase risk of PTSD following subsequent exposure? *Behaviour and Research Therapy*, 47(12), 1012–1017.

Cunningham, R. M., Ranney M., Newton, M., Woodhull, W., Zimmerman, M., & Walton, M. A. (2014). Characteristics of youth seeking emergency care for assault injuries. *Pediatrics*, 133(1): e96–e105.

Cyranowski, J. M., Frank, E., Young, E., & Shear, M. K. (2000). Adolescent onset of the gender difference in lifetime rates of major depression: A theoretical model. *Archives of General Psychiatry*, 57, 21–27.

D'Eramo, K., Prinstein, M., Freeman, J., Grapentine, W., & Spirito, A. (2004). Psychiatric diagnoses and comorbidity in relation to suicidal behavior among psychiatrically hospitalized adolescents. *Child Psychiatry and Human Development*, 35, 35–41.

Desmyter, S., Bijttebier, S., & van Heeringen, K. (2013). The role of neuroimaging in our understanding of the suicidal brain. *CNS & Neurological Disorders—Drug Targets*, 12(7), 921–929.

Dunn, E. C., Gilman, S. E., Willett, J. B., Slopen, N. B., & Molnar, B. E. (2012). The impact of exposure to interpersonal violence on gender differences in adolescent-onset major depression: Results from the National Comorbidity Survey Replication (NCS–R). *Depression and Anxiety*, 29(5), 392–399.

Eisenberg, M.E., Ackard, D.M., & Resnick, M.D. (2007). Protective factors and suicide risk in adolescents with a history of sexual abuse. *Journal of Pediatrics*, 151, 482-487.

Eisenberg, M. E., & Resnick, M. D. (2006). Suicidality among gay, lesbian and bisexual youth: The role of protective factors. *Journal of Adolescent Health*, 39, 662–668.

Esposito, C., Spirito, A., Boergers, J., & Donaldson, D. (2003). Affective, behavioral, and cognitive functioning in adolescents with multiple suicide attempts. *Suicide and Life-Threatening Behavior*, 33, 389–399.

Esposito-Smythers, C., & Spirito, A. (2004). Adolescent suicidal behavior and substance use: A review with implications for treatment research. *Alcoholism: Clinical and Experimental Research*, 28(Suppl.), 77S–88S.

Evans, E., Hawton, K., & Rodham, K. (2004). Factors associated with suicidal phenomena in adolescents: A systematic review of population-based studies. *Clinical Psychology Review*, 24, 957–979.

Fein, J. A., Kassam-Adams, N., Gavin, M., Huang, R., Blanchard, D., & Datner, E. M. (2002). Persistence of posttraumatic stress in violently injured youth seen in the emergency department. *Archives of Pediatrics and Adolescent Medicine*, 156(8), 836–840.

Fergusson, D.M., Beautrais, A.L., & Horwood, L.J. (2003). Vulnerability and resiliency to suicidal behaviors among young people. *Psychological Medicine*, 33, 61-73.

Foley, D. L., Goldston, D. B., Costello, E. J., & Angold, A. (2006). Proximal psychiatric risk factors for suicidality in youth: The Great Smoky Mountains Study. *Archives of General Psychiatry*, 63, 1017–1024.

Foshee, V. A., Linder, F., MacDougall, J. E., & Bangdiwala, S. (2001). Gender differences in the longitudinal predictors of adolescent dating violence. *Preventive Medicine*, 32(2), 128–141.

Foshee, V. A., McNaughton Reyes, H. L., Ennett, S. T., Suchindran, C., Mathias, J. P., Karriker-Jaffe, K. J., ... Benefield, T. S. (2011). Risk and protective factors distinguishing profiles of adolescent peer and dating violence perpetration. *Journal of Adolescent Health*, 48(4), 344–350.

Freedenthal, S., & Stiffman, A (2004). Suicidal behavior in urban American Indian adolescents: A comparison with reservation youth in a southwestern state. *Suicide and Life-Threatening Behavior*, 34, 160–171.

Goldsmith, R. E., Chesney, S. A., Heath, N. M., & Barlow, M. R. (2013). Emotion regulation difficulties mediate associations between betrayal trauma and symptoms of posttraumatic stress, depression, and anxiety. *Journal of Traumatic Stress*, 26(3), 376–384.

Goldstein, T. R., Birmaher, B., Axelson, D., Ryan, N., Strober, M., Gill, M. K. ... Keller, M. (2005). History of suicide attempts in pediatric bipolar disorder: Factors associated with increased risk. *Bipolar Disorders*, 7, 525–535.

Goldston, D. B., Daniel, S. S., Erkanli, A., Reboussin, B. A., Mayfield, A., Frazier, P. H., & Treadway, S. L. (2009). Psychiatric diagnoses as contemporaneous risk factors for suicide attempts among adolescents and young adults: Developmental changes. *Journal of Consulting and Clinical Psychology*, 77, 281–290.

Goldston, D. B., Daniel, S., Reboussin, D. M., & Kelley, A. (1996). First-time suicide attempters, repeat attempters and previous attempters on an adolescent inpatient psychiatry unit. *Journal of the American Academy of Child & Adolescent Psychiatry*, 35, 631–639.

Goldston, D. B., Daniel, S. S., Reboussin, D. M., Reboussin, B. A., Frazier, P. H., & Kelley, A. E. (1999). Suicide attempts among formerly hospitalized adolescents: A prospective naturalistic study of risk during the first 5 years after discharge. *Journal of the American Academy of Child & Adolescent Psychiatry*, 38, 660–671.

Goldston, D. B., Molock, S., Whitbeck, L. B., Murakami, J. L., Zayas, L. H., & Hall, G. (2008). Cultural considerations in adolescent suicide prevention and psychosocial treatment. *American Psychologist*, 63, 14–31.

Goldston, D. B., Reboussin, B. A., & Daniel, S. S. (2006). Predictors of suicide attempts: State and trait components. *Journal of Abnormal Psychology*, 115, 842–849.

Gould MS, Fisher P, Parides M, Flory M, Shaffer D. (1996). Psychosocial risk factors of child and adolescent completed suicide. *Archives of General Psychiatry*. 53, 1155-62.

Gould, M. S., Greenberg, T., Velting, D. M., & Shaffer, D. (2003). Youth suicide risk and preventive interventions: A review of the past 10 years. *Journal of the American Academy of Child & Adolescent Psychiatry*, 42, 386–405.

Gould, M. S., Kleinman, M. H., Lake, A. M., Forman, J., & Bassett Midle, J. (2014). Newspaper coverage of suicide and initiation of suicide clusters in teenagers in the USA, 1988–96: A retrospective, population-based, case-control study. *The Lancet Psychiatry*, 1(1), 34–43.

Groholt B, Ekeberg Ø, Haldorsen T. (2006). Adolescent suicide attempters: what predicts future suicidal acts? *Suicide and Life Threatening Behavior*. 36, 638-50.

Groholt, B., Ekeberg, O., Wichstrom, L., & Haldorsen, T. (1998). Suicide among children and younger and older adolescents

in Norway: A comparative study. *Journal of the American Academy of Child & Adolescent Psychiatry*, 37, 473–481.

Grossman, A. H., & D'Augelli, A. R. (2007). Transgender youth and life-threatening behaviors. *Suicide and Life-Threatening Behavior*, 37, 527–537.

Grossman, D. C., Mang, K., & Rivara, F. P. (1995). Firearm injury prevention counseling by pediatricians and family physicians. Practices and beliefs. *Archives of Pediatrics and Adolescent Medicine*, 149(9), 973–977.

Guan, K., Fox, K. R., & Prinstein, M. J. (2012). Nonsuicidal self-injury longitudinally predicts adolescent suicide ideation and attempts in a diverse community sample. *Journal of Consulting and Clinical Psychology*, 80, 842–849.

Hamza, C. A., Stewart, S. L., & Willoughby, T. (2012). Examining the link between nonsuicidal self-injury and suicidal behavior: A review of the literature and an integrated model. *Clinical Psychology Review*, 32(6), 482–495.

Hawton, K., O'Grady, J., Osborn, M., & Cole, D. (1982). Adolescents who take overdoses: Their characteristics, problems and contacts with helping agencies. *British Journal of Psychiatry*, 140, 118–123.

Hawton, K., Zahl, D., & Weatherall, R. (2003). Suicide following deliberate self-harm: Long-term follow-up of patients who presented to a general hospital. *British Journal of Psychiatry*, 182, 537–542.

Hedtke, K. A., Ruggiero, K. J., Fitzgerald, M. M., Zinzow, H. M., Saunders, B. E., Resnick, H. S., & Kilpatrick, D. G. (2008). A longitudinal investigation of interpersonal violence in relation to mental health and substance use. *Journal of Consulting and Clinical Psychology*, 76(4), 633–647.

Hepburn, L., Azrael, D., Molnar, B., & Miller, M. (2012). Bullying and suicidal behaviors among urban high school youth. *Journal of Adolescent Health*, 51(1), 93–95.

Heron, M. P., Hoyert, D. L., Murphy, S. L., Xu, J. Q., Kochanek, K. D., & Tejada-Vera, B. (2009). *Deaths: Final data 2006*. National Vital Statistics Reports *57*(14). Hyattsville, MD: National Center for Health Statistics.

Hinduja, S., & Patchin, J. W. (2010). Bullying, cyberbullying, and suicide. *Archives of Suicide Research*, 14(3), 206–221.

Huey, S., Henggeler, S., Rowland, M., Halliday-Boykins, C., Cunningham, P., Pickrel, S., & Edwards, J. (2004). Multisystemic therapy effects on attempted suicide by youths presenting psychiatric emergencies. *Journal of the American Academy of Child & Adolescent Psychiatry*, 43, 183–190.

Hufford, M. R. (2001). Alcohol and suicidal behavior. *Clinical Psychology Review*, 21, 797–811.

Insel, B. J., & Gould, M. S. (2008). Impact of modeling on adolescent suicidal behavior. *Psychiatric Clinics of North America*, 31(2), 293–316.

Ivarsson, T., Broberg, A. G., Arvidsson, T., & Gillberg, C. (2005). Bullying in adolescence: Psychiatric problems in victims and bullies as measured by the Youth Self Report (YSR) the Depression Rating Scale (DSRS). *Nordic Journal of Psychiatry*, 59, 365–373.

Jacobs, R. H., Reinecke, M. A., Gollab, J. K., & Kane, P. (2008). Empirical evidence of cognitive vulnerability for depression among children and adolescents: A cognitive science and developmental perspective. *Clinical Psychology Review*, 28, 759–783.

Jain, S., Buka, S. L., Subramanian, S. V., & Molnar, B. E. (2010). Neighborhood predictors of dating violence victimization and perpetration in young adulthood: A multilevel study. *American Journal of Public Health*, 100(9), 1737–1744.

Javdani, S., Jaleel, A., Suarez, L., Nichols, S. R., & Farmer, A. D. (2014). Gender differences in the effects of community violence on mental health outcomes in a sample of low-income youth receiving psychiatric care. *American Journal of Community Psychology, 53*(3–4), 235–248.

Joiner, T. (2005). *Why people die by suicide.* Cambridge, MA: Harvard University Press.

Juon, H. S., & Ensminger, M. E. (1997). Childhood, adolescent, and young adult predictors of suicidal behaviors: A prospective study of African Americans. *Journal of Child Psychology and Psychiatry, 38*(5), 553–563.

Kaminski, J. W., & Fang, X. (2009). Victimization by peers and adolescent suicide in three US samples. *Journal of Pediatrics, 155*(5), 683–688.

Kann, L., Kinchen, S., Shanklin, S. L., Flint, K. H., Hawkins, J., Harris, W. A., … Zaza, S. (2014). Youth risk behavior surveillance—United States, 2013. *Morbidity and Mortality Weekly Report, 63*(4), 1–162.

Kann, L., Olsen, E. O., McManus, T., Kinchen, S., Chyen, D., Harris, W. A., … Centers for Disease Control and Prevention. (2011). Sexual identity, sex of sexual contacts, and health-risk behaviors among students in grades 9–12: Youth risk behavior surveillance, selected sites, United States, 2001–2009. *MMWR Surveillance Summary, 60*(7), 1–133.

Kerig, P. K., Ward, R. M., Vanderzee, K. L., & Arnzen Moeddel, M. (2009). Posttraumatic stress as a mediator of the relationship between trauma and mental health problems among juvenile delinquents. *Journal of Youth and Adolescence, 38*(9), 1214–1225.

Kerr, D. C., Washburn, J. J., Feingold, A., Kramer, A. C., Ivey, A. Z., & King, C. A. (2007). Sequelae of aggression in acutely suicidal adolescents. *Journal of Abnormal Child Psychology, 35*, 817–830.

Kilpatrick, D. G., Ruggiero, K. J., Acierno, R., Saunders, B. E., Resnick, H. S., & Best, C. L. (2003). Violence and risk of PTSD, major depression, substance abuse/dependence, and comorbidity: Results from the National Survey of Adolescents. *Journal of Consulting and Clinical Psychology, 71*, 692–700.

Kim, Y. S., & Leventhal, B. (2008). Bullying and suicide: A review. *International Journal of Adolescent Medicine and Health, 20*, 133–154.

Kim, Y. S., Leventhal, B. L., Koh, Y., & Boyce, W. T. (2009). Bullying increased suicide risk: Prospective study of Korean adolescents. *Archives of Suicide Research, 13*, 15–30.

King, C., & Merchant, C. (2008). Social and interpersonal factors relating to adolescent suicidality: A review of the literature. *Archives of Suicide Research, 12*, 181–196.

Kingsbury, S., Hawton, K., Steinhardt, K., & James, A. (1999). Do adolescents who take overdoses have specific psychological characteristics? A comparative study with psychiatric and community controls. *Journal of the American Academy of Child & Adolescent Psychiatry, 38*, 1125–1131.

Klomek, A. B., Marrocco, F., Kleinman, M., Schonfeld, I. S., & Gould, M. S. (2008). Peer victimization, depression, and suicidiality in adolescents. *Suicide and Life-Threatening Behavior, 38*(2), 166–180.

Klonsky, E. D., & May, A. (2010). Rethinking impulsivity in suicide. *Suicide and Life-Threatening Behavior, 40*(6), 612–619.

Kosciw, J. G., Greytak, E. A., Diaz, E. M., & Bartkiewicz, M. J. (2010). *The 2009 National School Climate Survey: The experiences of lesbian, gay, bisexual and transgender youth in our nation's schools.* New York: Gay, Lesbian and Straight Education Network.

Krug, E. G., Dahlberg, L. L., Mercy, J. A., Zwi, A. B., & Lozano, R. (Eds.). (2002). *World report on violence and health.* Geneva: World Health Organization.

Lamb, C. E. (2009). Alternatives to admission for children and adolescents: Providing intensive mental healthcare services at home and in communities: What works? *Current Opinion in Psychiatry, 22*(4), 345–350. doi: 10.1097/YCO.0b013e32832c9082

Lambert, S. F., Copeland-Linder, N., & Ialongo, N. (2008). Longitudinal associations between community violence exposure and suicidality. *Journal of Adolescent Health, 43*(4), 380–386.

Langeland, W., & Olff, M. (2008). Psychobiology of posttraumatic stress disorder in pediatric injury patients: A review of the literature. *Neuroscience and Biobehavioral Reviews, 32*(1), 161–174.

Lewinsohn, P. M., Rohde, P., & Seeley, J. R. (1996). Adolescent suicidal ideation and attempts: Prevalence, risk factors, and clinical implications. *Clinical Psychology: Science and Practice, 3*, 25–46.

Martin, G., Bergen, H.A., Richardson, A.S., Roeger, L., & Allison, S. (2004). Sexual abuse and suicidality: Gender differences in a large community sample of adolescents. *Child Abuse & Neglect, 28*, 491-503.

Mazza, J. J. (2000). The relationship between posttraumatic stress symptomatology and suicidal behavior in school-based adolescents. *Suicide and Life-Threatening Behavior, 30*, 91–103.

Mazza, J. J., & Reynolds, W. M. (1999). Exposure to violence in young inner-city adolescents: Relationships with suicidal ideation, depression, and PTSD symptomatology. *Journal of Abnormal Child Psychology, 27*(3), 203–213.

McIntosh, J. L., & Drapeau, C. W. (2014). U.S.A. suicide 2011: Official final data. Washington, DC: American Association of Suicidology. Retrieved from http://www.suicidology.org

McLaughlin, K. A., Koenen, K. C., Hill, E. D., Petukhova, M., Sampson, N. A., Zaslavsky, A. M., & Kessler, R. C. (2013). Trauma exposure and posttraumatic stress disorder in a national sample of adolescents. *Journal of the American Academy of Child & Adolescent Psychiatry, 52*(8), 815–830.

Melhem, N. M., Brent, D. A., Ziegler, M., Iyengar, S., Kolko, D. J., Oquendo, M., … Mann, J. J. (2007). Familial pathways to early-onset suicidal behavior: Familial and individual antecedents of suicidal behavior. *American Journal of Psychiatry, 164*, 1364–1370.

Mollen, C. J., Fein, J. A., Localio, A. R., & Durbin D. R. (2004). Characterization of interpersonal violence events involving young adolescent girls vs. events involving young adolescent boys. *Archives of Pediatrics and Adolescent Medicine, 158*(6), 545–550.

Nahapetyan, L., Orpinas, P., Song, X., & Holland, K. (2014). Longitudinal association of suicidal ideation and physical dating violence among high school students. *Journal of Youth and Adolescence, 43*, 629–640.

National Center for Injury Prevention and Control. (2014). Web-Based Injury Statistics Query and Reporting System (WISQARS): 10 leading causes of death by age group, United States—2010. Retrieved from http://www.cdc.gov/injury/wisqars

Negron, R., Piacentini, J., Graae, F., Davies, M., & Shaffer, D. (1997). Microanalysis of adolescent suicide attempters and ideators during the acute suicidal episode. *Journal of the American Academy of Child & Adolescent Psychiatry, 36*, 1512–1519.

Nock, M. K., Green, J. G., Hwang, I., McLaughlin, K. A., Sampson, N. A., Zaslavsky, A. M., & Kessler, R. C. (2013). Prevalence, correlates, and treatment of lifetime suicidal behavior among adolescents: Results from the National Comorbidity

Survey Replication Adolescent Supplement. *JAMA Psychiatry*, 70(3), 300–310. doi: 10.1001/2013.jamapsychiatry.55

Nock, M., Joiner, T., Gordon, K., Lloyd-Richardson, E., & Prinstein, M. (2006). Non-suicidal self-injury among adolescents: Diagnostic correlates and relation to suicide attempts. *Psychiatry Research*, 144, 65–72.

Nuttbrock, L., Hwahng, S., Bockting, W., Rosenblum, A., Mason, M., Macri, M., & Becker, J. (2010). Psychiatric impact of gender-related abuse across the life course of male-to-female transgender persons. *Journal of Sex Research*, 47, 12–23.

Nrugham, L., Larsson, B., & Sund, A. M. (2008). Specific depressive symptoms and disorders associates and predictors of suicidal acts across adolescence. *Journal of Affective Disorders*, 111, 83–93.

O'Brien, K., & Berzin, S. C. (2012). Examining the impact of psychiatric diagnosis andcomorbidity on the medical lethality of adolescent suicide attempts. *Suicide and Life-Threatening Behavior*, 42(4), 437–444.

O'Carroll, P. W., Berman, A. L., Maris, R. W., Moscicki, E. K., Tanney, B. L., & Silverman, M. M. (1996). Beyond the Tower of Babel: A nomenclature for suicidology. *Suicide and Life-Threatening Behavior*, 26, 237–252.

O'Donnell, L., Stueve, A., & Wilson-Simmons, R. (2005). Aggressive behaviors in early adolescence and subsequent suicidality among urban youths. *Journal of Adolescent Health*, 37(6), 517.

Osman, A., Downs, W. R., Kopper, B. A., Barrios, F. X., Baker, M. T., Osman, J. R., . . . Linehan, M. M. (1998). The Reasons for Living Inventory for Adolescents (RFL-A): Development and psychometric properties. *Journal of Clinical Psychology*, 54(8), 1063–1078.

Pailler, M. E., Kassam-Adams, N., Datner, E. M., & Fein, J. A. (2007). Depression, acute stress and behavioral risk factors in violently injured adolescents. *General Hospital Psychiatry*, 29(4), 357–363.

Pavkov, T. W., Travis, L., Fox, K. A., King, C. B., & Cross, T. L. (2010). Tribal youth victimization and delinquency: Analysis of youth risk behavior surveillance survey data. *Cultural Diversity and Ethnic Minority Psychology*, 16(2), 123–134.

Posner, K., Brown, G. K., Stanley, B., Brent, D. A., Yershova, K. V., Oquendo, M. A., . . . & Mann, J. J. (2011). The Columbia-Suicide Severity Rating Scale: Initial validity and internal consistency findings from three multisite studies with adolescents and adults. *American Journal of Psychiatry*, 168, 1266–1277.

Price, J. H., Kinnison, A., Dake, J. A., Thompson, A. J., & Price, J. A. (2007). Psychiatrists' practices and perceptions regarding anticipatory guidance on firearms. *American Journal of Preventive Medicine*, 33(5), 370–373.

Prinstein, M. J., Nock, M. K., Simon, V., Aikins, J. W., Cheah, C. S., & Spirito, A. (2008). Longitudinal trajectories and predictors of adolescent suicidal ideation and attempts following inpatient hospitalization. *Journal of Consulting and Clinical Psychology*, 76(1), 92–103.

Ranney, M. L., Walton, M., Whiteside, L., Epstein-Ngo, Q., Patton, R., Chermack, S., . . . Cunningham, R. (2013). Correlates of depressive symptoms among at-risk youth presenting to the emergency department. *General Hospital Psychiatry*, 35(5), 537–544.

Reynolds, W. M. (1987). *Suicidal Ideation Questionnaire (SIQ): Professional manual.* Odessa, FL: Psychological Assessment Resources.

Renaud, J., Berlim, M. T., McGirr, A., Tousignant, M., & Turecki, G. (2008). Current psychiatric morbidity, aggression/

impulsivity, and personality dimensions in child and adolescent suicide: A case control study. *Journal of Affective Disorders*, 105, 221–228.

Roberts T. A., Klein J. D., & Fisher, S. (2003). Longitudinal effect of intimate partner abuse on high-risk behavior among adolescents. *Archives Pediatric Adolescent Medicine*, 157, 875–881.

Robinson, W. L., Paxton, K. C., & Jonen, L. P. (2011). Pathways to aggression and violence among African American adolescent males: The influence of normative beliefs, neighborhood, and depressive symptomatology. *Journal of Prevention & Intervention in the Community*, 39(2), 132–148.

Roland, E. (2002). Bullying, depressive symptoms and suicidal thoughts. *Educational Research*, 44(1), 55–67.

Rothman, E. F., Johnson, R. M., Azrael, D., Hall, D. M., & Weinberg, J. (2010). Perpetration of physical assault against dating partners, peers, and siblings among a locally representative sample of high school students in Boston, Massachusetts. *Archives of Pediatric and Adolescent Medicine*, 164, 1118–1124.

Rudd, M. D. (2006). *The assessment and management of suicidality.* Sarasota, FL: Professional Resource Press.

Rudd, M. D., Joiner, T. E., & Rajab, M. H. (2001). *Treating suicidal behavior: An effective, time-limited approach.* New York: Guilford Press.

Rutman, S., Park, A., Castor, M., Taualii, M., & Forquera, R. (2008). Urban American Indian and Alaska Native youth: Youth risk behavior survey 1997–2003. *Maternal and Child Health Journal*, 12, S76–S81.

Sanislow, C. A., Grilo, C. M., Fehon, D. C., Axelrod, S. R., & McGlashan, T. H. (2003). Correlates of suicide risk in juvenile detainees and adolescent inpatients. *Journal of the American Academy of Child & Adolescent Psychiatry*, 42, 234–240.

Savin-Williams, R. C. (1994). Verbal and physical abuse as stressors in the lives of lesbian, gay male, and bisexual youths: Associations with school problems, running away, substance abuse, prostitution, and suicide. *Journal of Consulting and Clinical Psychology*, 62, 261–269.

Seiffge-Krenke, I. (2000). Causal links between stressful events, coping style, and adolescent symptomatology. *Journal of Adolescence*, 23, 675–691.

Shaffer, D., Gould, M. S., Fisher, P., & Trautman, P. (1996). Psychiatric diagnosis in child and adolescent suicide. *Archives of General Psychiatry*, 53, 339–348.

Shaffer, D., & Pfeffer, C. (2001). Practice parameters for the assessment and treatment of children and adolescents with suicidal behavior. *Journal of American Academy of Child & Adolescent Psychiatry*, 40 (7), 24–51.

Shirk, S. R., Boergers, J., Eason, A., & Van Horn, M. (1998). Dysphoric interpersonal schemata and preadolescents' sensitization to negative events. *Journal of Clinical Child Psychology*, 27, 54–68.

Silenzio, V. B., Pena, J. B., Duberstein, P. R., Cerel, J., & Knox, K. L. (2007). Sexual orientation and risk factors for suicidal ideation and suicide attempts among adolescents and young adults. *American Journal of Public Health*, 97, 2017–2019.

Silverman, J. G., Raj, A., Mucci, L. A., & Hathaway, J. E. (2001). Dating violence against adolescent girls and associated substance use, unhealthy weight control, sexual risk behavior, pregnancy, and suicidality. *Journal of the American Medical Association*, 286, 572–579.

Singer, J. B. (2005). Child and adolescent psychiatric emergencies: Mobile crisis response. In A. R. Roberts (Ed.), *Crisis* intervention handbook: Assessment, treatment, and research (3rd ed., pp. 319–361). Oxford: Oxford University Press.

Smith, P., White, J. W., & Holland, L. J. (2003). A longitudinal perspective on dating violence among adolescent and college-age women. *American Journal of Public Health*, 93, 1104–1109.

Spirito, A., & Overholser, J. (2003). *Evaluating and treating adolescent suicide attempters: From research to practice.* New York: Academic Press.

Spirito, A., Sterling, C., Donaldson, D., & Arrigan, M. (1996). Factor analysis of the Suicide Intent Scale with adolescent suicide attempters. *Journal of Personality Assessment*, 67, 90–101.

Stack, S. (2014). Differentiating suicide ideators from attempters: Violence—a research note. *Suicide and Life-Threatening Behavior*, 44(1), 46–57.

Stein, D., Apter, A., Ratzoni, G., Har-Even, D., & Avidan, G. (1998). Association between multiple suicide attempts and negative affects in adolescents. *Journal of the American Academy of Child & Adolescent Psychiatry*, 37, 488–494.

Steven Betts, K., Williams, G. M., Najman, J. M., & Alati, R. (2013). Exploring the female specific risk to partial and full PTSD following physical assault. *Journal of Traumatic Stress*, 26(1), 86–93.

Substance Abuse and Mental Health Services Administration, Office of Applied Studies. (2009). *The NSDUH report: Behaviors among adolescent females.* Rockville, MD: Author.

Swahn, M. H., Simon, T. R., Hertz, M. F., Arias, I., Bossarte, R. M., Ross, J.G., . . . Hamburger, M. E. (2008). Linking dating violence, peer violence, and suicidal behaviors among high-risk youth. *American Journal of Preventive Medicine*, 34, 30–38.

Toomey, R. B., Ryan, C., Card, N. A., & Russell, S. T. (2010). Gender non-conforming lesbian, gay, bisexual, and transgender youth: School victimization and young adult psychosocial adjustment. *Developmental Psychology*, 46, 1580–1589.

Turner, H. A., Finkelhor, D., Shattuck, A., & Hamby, S. (2012). Recent victimization exposure and suicidal ideation in adolescents. *Archives of Pediatrics and Adolescent Medicine*, 166(12), 1149–1154.

van Geel, M., Vedder, P., & Tanilon, J. (2014). Relationship between peer victimization, cyberbullying, and suicide in children and adolescents: A meta-analysis. *JAMA Pediatrics*, 168(5), 435–442.

van Heeringen, K., & Mann, J. (2014). The neurobiology of suicide. *The Lancet Psychiatry*, 1(1), 63–72.

Van Orden, K. A., Witte, T. K., Gordon, K. H., Bender, T. W., & Joiner, T. E. (2008). Suicidal desire and the capability for suicide: Tests of the interpersonal-psychological theory of suicidal behavior among adults. *Journal of Consulting and Clinical Psychology*, 76, 72–83.

Wadman, M. C., Muelleman, R. L., Coto, J. A., & Kellermann, A. L. (2003). The pyramid of injury: Using ecodes to accurately describe the burden of injury. *Annals of Emergency Medicine*, 42, 468–478.

Wagner, B. M., Silverman, M. A. C., & Martin, C. E. (2003). Family factors in youth suicidal behaviors. *American Behavioral Scientist: Suicide in Youth*, 46, 1171–1191.

Walton, M. A., Cunningham, R. M., Goldstein, A. L., Chermack, S. T., Zimmerman, M. A., Bingham, C. R., . . . Blow, F. C. (2009). Rates and correlates of violent behaviors among adolescents treated in an urban emergency department. *Journal of Adolescent Health*, 45(1), 77–83.

Weismoore, J. T., & Esposito-Smythers, C. (2010). The role of cognitive distortion in the relationship between abuse, assault, and non-suicidal self-injury. *Journal of Youth and Adolescence*, 39, 281–290.

Wilson, L. S., Kelly, B. D., Morgan, S., Harley, M., & O'Sullivan, M. (2012). Who gets admitted? Study of referrals and admissions to an adolescent psychiatry inpatient facility over a 6-month period. *Irish Journal of Medical Science*, 181(4), 555–560. doi: 10.1007/s11845-012-0817-6

Wortzel, H. S., Matarazzo, B., & Homaifar, B. (2013). A model for therapeutic risk management of the suicidal patient. *Journal of Psychiatric Practice*, 19(4), 323–326. doi: 10.1097/01.pra.0000432603.99211.e8

Xue, Y., Zimmerman, M. A., & Cunningham, R. M. (2009). Relationship between alcohol use and violent behavior among urban African American youths from adolescence to emerging adulthood: A longitudinal study. *American Journal of Public Health*, 99, 2041–2048.

Yan, F. A., Howard, D. E., Beck, K. H., Sattuck, T., & Hallmark-Kerr, M. (2010). Psychosocial correlates of physical dating violence victimization among Latino early adolescents. *Journal of Interpersonal Violence*, 25, 808–831.

Zimmerman, G. M., & Messner, S. F. (2013). Individual, family background, and contextual explanations of racial and ethnic disparities in youths' exposure to violence. *American Journal of Public Health*, 103(3), 435–442. doi: 10.2105/AJPH.2012.300931

Evaluating Violence Risk in Children and Adolescents

Randy Borum

Abstract

Emergency workers and behavioral health professionals who work in crisis or emergency settings should understand the fundamentals of assessing and managing violence risk in children and adolescents, but violence potential must be considered in its developmental context. This chapter presents an approach for assessing violence risk among youth in the context of behavioral emergencies. It begins with a brief discussion of the developmental context for risk assessment and how to think about violent outcomes among children and adolescents. Then, it covers the information an evaluator would need to collect, how to collect it, and how to reach a sound decision about a youth's risk level. It encourages evaluators in emergency or crisis settings to rely on evidence-based risk factors, while also applying individualized formulations to give texture to the assessments and to the subsequent forecasts about the nature and degree of risk for violence.

Key Words: youth violence, adolescents, juveniles, risk assessment, risk management

Although stories about violent youth continue to populate the headlines and stir public concern, actual rates of youth violence have been mostly declining for the past 20 years. In practice, however, clinicians working in emergency or crisis assessment settings commonly see children and adolescents who present because of a potential concern about violence (Borum & Verhaagen, 2006; Cheng et al., 2003; Dolan & Fein, 2011; Janssens, Hayen, Walraven, Leys, & Deboutte, 2013; Langan, 2010). A threatening statement or an outburst of angry, aggressive behavior may precipitate the visit, or a list of worrisome risk factors may incidentally emerge during history gathering. In some cases, evaluating violence risk may be the explicit reason for the assessment; in others, it may be an implicit part of the crisis evaluator's duty of care. In either case, it is useful to have a practical and systematic approach for gathering information and assessing the potential for violence in crisis settings. This chapter presents a methodology for assessing violence risk among youth in the context of behavioral emergencies. It

begins with a brief discussion of the developmental context for risk assessment and how to think about violent outcomes among children and adolescents. Then, it covers the information an evaluator would need to collect, how to collect it, and how to reach a sound decision about a youth's risk level.

Understanding Violence in Children and Adolescents
Developmental Considerations

During childhood and adolescence, young people experience profound changes in nearly all areas of functioning—physical, cognitive, and psychosocial (Borum, 2009; Cauffman & Steinberg, 2012; Herrenkohl, Maguin, Hill, Hawkins, Abbott, & Catalano, 2000). Developments in each domain often affect developments in one or more of the others. These changes are inextricably linked to behavior, including a propensity for aggression and violence. But developmental markers of maturity in physical, cognitive, and psychosocial domains often do not travel in a synchronous trajectory or at the same rate. Youth at the same age-level may be advanced in one area, but seriously delayed in another (Borum & Grisso, 2006; Compas, Hinden, & Gerhardt, 1995).

Complicating matters even further, developmental processes during adolescence often do not progress at a predictable pace, nor are behavioral patterns very stable or consistent. Development does not always move forward or progress over time, but rather is characterized by stops and starts, accelerations and regressions. Due in part to these vicissitudes of development, manifestations of personality traits and characteristic behavior in young people tend to vary considerably across situations and contexts. Patterns typically regarded as consistent and predictable in adults may fluctuate greatly among youth (Borum, 2003; Borum & Verhaagen, 2006; Cauffman & Steinberg, 2012; McCord, Widom, & Crowell, 2001; Griffin & Torbet, 2002; Mulvey, 2014; Piquero, Jennings, & Barnes, 2012).

Three aspects of psychosocial maturity, in particular, have been studied fairly extensively as they pertain to legally relevant decision making and behavior among children and adolescents:

• responsibility (the capacity to make decisions without undue influence from others);
• perspective-taking (the ability to appreciate other points of view and consider both short- and long-term implications of a decision); and
• temperance (the ability to exercise self-restraint and to control one's impulses).

All three of these capacities are still "under construction" through adolescence, as are the brain structures and pathways that regulate them (Cauffman & Steinberg, 2012; Cauffman, Steinberg, & Piquero, 2005; Steinberg & Cauffman, 1999).

The self-evident implication of this developmental evolution is that teens are different than adults. Understanding those differences is critical for behavioral health professionals who have to assess a young person's risk for future troublesome behavior. The US Supreme Court relied heavily on adolescent development research in *Roper v. Simmons*, in which they deemed it unconstitutional to impose the death penalty on a person who committed an offense before age 18, concluding that the "failings" of a minor could not be equated with those of an adult.

Prevalence Rates of Violence

Partly because of these developmental differences, the general rates of violence and criminal behavior among teens diverge substantially from the "norms" for adults. Adolescence is the highest developmental risk period for a first episode of serious violence (behavior approximating *aggravated assault*). Large scale research has found that nearly one in four girls and nearly 40% of boys in high school report being in a physical fight one or more times in the prior 12 months (Elliott, Ageton, Huizinga, Knowles, & Canter, 1983; Kann et al., 2002; US Department of Health and Human Services, 2001). Importantly, however, most young people who engage in violence during adolescence desist before they reach adulthood. That is, their adolescent episodes do not portend a future trajectory of violence and criminality, and the majority (about 80%) of those who engage in serious violence naturally stop before they reach age 21 (Elliott, 1994; US Department of Health & Human Services, 2001).

Subtypes of Aggression

Broad statistics on rates of violent behavior can conceal some important distinctions among different types of aggression. The most common characterization contrasts *reactive* and *proactive* forms of aggression (Babcock, Tharp, Sharp, Heppner, & Stanford, 2014; Crick & Dodge, 1996; Poulin & Boivin, 2000). Each type develops through different mechanisms, and each has different cognitive, affective, and behavioral features. *Reactive aggression* is usually characterized by an angry retaliatory response to a perceived provocation or threat (White & Turner, 2014). This is the most common type of aggression in youth. A contributing cognitive factor is often a hypersensitivity to—or even a tendency to misperceive—hostile or aggressive social cues from others (sometimes called a "hostile attribution bias") (Brugman et al., 2014). Reactive aggressors respond emotionally and physiologically to perceived hostile cues, and their own aggressive behaviors tend to be impulsive (Babcock et al., 2014).

Proactive aggression, by contrast, is more overtly instrumental (used as a tactic to gain a desired outcome). It is typically not retaliatory, nor is it done in an emotional outburst or response to perceived provocation. The contributing cognitive factors most often associated with proactive violence are a youth's attitudes and beliefs in the legitimacy of aggression to attain a goal, and his or her positive expectancies for success by using aggression (Brugman et al., 2014). The actor typically does not experience intense arousal or anger at the time, and the aggressive act tends to be more deliberate than impulsive. A young person being evaluated may have a history of both types, but when assessing violence history or forecasting possible scenarios in which aggressive behavior may be more or less likely, it is useful to distinguish between them (Babcock et al., 2014; Swogger, Walsh, Christie, Priddy, & Conner, 2015).

Subtypes of Juvenile Offenders

Across the range of aggressive behavior, most young people who engage in violence during their teen years are not violent in early childhood (before age 13) and do not persist in violence into adulthood. They are sometimes referred to as *adolescence-limited* (AL) offenders (Moffitt, 1993, 1997). AL offenders are largely responsible for the "peak" observed in the age-crime curve because they typically only manifest violent and delinquent behavior between the ages of 14 and 18. They are *less* likely to have (a) a history of childhood behavior problems; (b) a co-occurring disorder; (c) a consistent offending pattern; or (d) frequent episodes of proactive aggression; and they are *more* likely to form and maintain developmentally appropriate attachments to others (Jennings & Reingle, 2012; Moffitt, 1993, 2006; Piquero & Motffitt, 2005).

A much smaller subset of violent youth (approximately 5%–9%) start early (before age 13) and continue offending into adulthood. They tend to be the most troublesome. Known as *life-course-persistent* (LCP) offenders, they appear at both ends of the age-crime curve (Moffitt, 1997). LCP youth frequently have co-occurring behavioral disorders (e.g., oppositional defiant disorder, attention deficit hyperactivity disorder); they tend to have poor or superficial attachments to others; and some may characteristically engage in proactive violence.

Risk and Protective Factors for Youth Violence

A robust and extensive body of research has affirmed an array of factors that may increase the risk of violence and aggression (*risk factors*) or decrease that risk (*protective factors*) in children and adolescents (Bernat, Oakes, Pettingell, & Resnick, 2012; Cottle, Lee, & Heilbrun, 2001; Derzon, 2001; Hawkins et al., 1998; Henry, Tolan, Gorman-Smith, & Schoeny, 2012; Herrenkohl et al., 2000; Herrenkohl, Lee, & Hawkins, 2012; Howard & Jenson, 1999; Lipsey & Derzon, 1998; Loeber & Stouthamer-Loeber, 1998; O'Brien, Daffern, Chu, & Thomas, 2013; van der Merwe & Dawes, 2007). The term risk factor is borrowed from epidemiology to refer to a characteristic or condition that increases the

likelihood of a negative outcome. Risk factors may or may not *cause* an outcome, but they do statistically increase the likelihood of its occurrence.

The scientific literature on youth violence contains several excellent reviews and meta-analyses (Baglivio, Jackowski, Greenwald, & Howell, 2014; Cottle et al., 2001; Derzon, 2001; Hawkins et al., 1998; Herrenkohl et al, 2000; Howard & Jenson, 1999; Lipsey & Derzon, 1998; US Department of Health and Human Services, 2001; van der Merwe & Dawes, 2007). The details go well beyond the scope of this chapter, but what follows is a capsule summary of the factors that have a consistent foundation of empirical support. The reviews just cited can be referenced for lists of factor-specific studies. Risk factor differences between early childhood (ages 6–11) and later adolescence (ages 12–14) primarily reflect the diminishing effects of family influences and the ascending effects of peers over time (US Department of Health and Human Services, 2001).

Historical Factors

Historical factors tend to represent *static* characteristics known to be associated with subsequent violent behavior.

• *History of violence*: Having previously engaged in violent behavior generally increases the risk for subsequent violent behavior, though it does not necessarily predict violent offending into adulthood.

• *History of nonviolent offending*: This has one of the largest *effect sizes* based on meta-analytic reviews, sometimes even larger than a history of violent behavior, and the effect is particularly robust for adolescents (as opposed to children).

• *Early initiation of violence*: Initial episodes of serious violence (and delinquency) that emerge before age 13 tend to increase the likelihood, frequency and severity of subsequent violence.

• *Past supervision/intervention failures*: Engaging in transgressive behavior while under observation and supervision tends to indicate a greater propensity for later antisocial acts.

• *History of self-harm or suicide attempts*: Both intentional self-harm (even without suicidal intent) and suicidal gestures and attempts have been linked to violence potential in children and adolescents.

• *Exposure to violence in the home*: Children who are exposed to the use of violence in partner or parenting relationships tend to be at greater risk for engaging in violence themselves.

• *Childhood history of maltreatment*: Nearly all forms of childhood maltreatment—physical abuse as well as neglect—are linked to adolescent violence risk.

• *Parental or caregiver criminality*: Whether through genetic or social transmission, numerous studies have shown that having parents (including biological parents) and primary caregivers who have engaged in antisocial or illegal behavior increases a young person's own risk of offending.

• *Early caregiver disruption*: Being separated from one or more of a youth's primary caregivers (particularly those to whom they have formed an attachment) before age 16 has been associated with youth violence.

• *Poor school achievement*: While school performance itself is modifiable, numerous studies have shown that having a history of significant academic/achievement problems in school (e.g., failing courses, being held back) increases subsequent risk.

Social/Contextual Factors

• *Peer delinquency*: Young people whose primary peer group engages in violent and delinquent behavior tend to be more likely to engage in those behaviors themselves. This is especially true for any gang-like affiliations.

• *Peer rejection*: Rejected status is the condition of being liked by very few people in one's social sphere and actively disliked by most; this is associated with aggression and a range of other negative outcomes in children and adolescents.

• *Stress and poor coping*: Stressful life events can increase risk, particularly when the degree of impinging stress taxes or exceeds the young person's usual coping resources.

• *Poor parental management*: A range of poor parental management practices (e.g., overly strict, overly permissive, inadequate supervision) have been associated with delinquent and violent offending in children and adolescents.

• *Lack of personal or social support*: The absence of family or social support can increase the likelihood of negative outcomes including aggression and violent behavior.

• *Community disorganization*: Young people who live in neighborhoods with high levels of crime, disorder, and social disconnection may be more likely to engage in violence than those who do not.

Individual Factors

• *Negative attitudes*: Antisocial attitudes; beliefs that support violence; and hypersensitivity to hostile/negative cues have all been confirmed as risk factors for violence.

• *Risk taking/impulsivity*: While children and adolescents tend to be more impulsive than adults, those who are more extreme relative to developmental norms or who crave or engage in excessive risk taking may have a higher risk for aggression and violence.

• *Substance use difficulties*: Misuse of alcohol, drugs, or other psychoactive substances—especially with adolescents—is shown in nearly all studies to be a robust risk factor for youth violence.

• *Anger management problems*: Both under-control and over-control of anger, hostile impulses, and rage can potentiate violence risk.

• *Low empathy or remorse*: So-called "psychopathic traits" have been studied in children and adolescents, as they have been in adults, and tend to show some of the same behavioral correlates of criminal and violent behavior. Whether those traits are as stable as they are in adulthood and whether they truly represent *psychopathy* in children and adolescence is much less clear, based on currently available evidence.

• *Attention deficit or hyperactivity difficulties*: Both attention problems and hyperactivity have been associated with youth violence in numerous studies, though, of the two, hyperactivity tends to have a stronger and more robust effect.

• *Poor compliance*: As with supervision "failures," when the young person overtly defies intervention or does not believe that it is necessary or will be effective, he or she is less likely to follow guidelines designed to reduce his or her risk for violence.

• *Low interest or commitment to school*: School tends to be a prosocial anchor and influence for school-aged children and adolescents. Being disconnected and uncommitted tends to be associated with a higher risk for delinquency and violence.

Risk Factors for Females

Though historically, most research into youth violence and delinquency has focused on male offenders, in more recent years researchers have investigated gender differences in the frequency and valence of risk factors (Odgers, Moretti, & Reppucci, 2005). These studies primarily have shown that most risk factors derived from research on male juvenile offenders apply to females as well (Fagan, Van Horn, Hawkins, & Arthur, 2007; Schwalbe, 2008; Stephenson, Woodhams, & Cooke, 2013; Thompson & Morris, 2013; Vitopoulos, Peterson-Badali, & Skilling, 2012). Some studies show males to be exposed to more risk factors than their female counterparts, but this may depend on which kind of experiences are counted, and it is not true in all delinquent samples (Baglivio & Epps, 2015).

Evidence is beginning to converge, however, around the disproportionate influence of a small number of risk factors for female relative to male juveniles (Cauffman, Lexcen, Goldweber, Shulman, & Grisso, 2007; Daigle, Cullen, & Wright, 2007; Gammelgård, Weizmann-Henelius, Koivisto, Eronen, & Kaltiala-Heino, 2012; Hart, O'Toole, Price-Sharps, & Shaffer, 2007; Lovins, Schweitzer, & Sullivan, 2013; Moretti, Odgers, Reppucci, & Catherine, 2011; Thompson & Morris, 2013; see Shepherd, Luebbers, & Dolan, 2013, for a review). The three principal areas in which risk factors seem to have a greater salience for girls than boys are abuse victimization and trauma; behavioral health problems; and parental criminality or dysfunction (McCabe, Lansing, Garland, & Hough, 2002). Concerning the effects of trauma, prior research has shown that reported rates of child abuse (especially sexual abuse) are three times higher in female than in male offenders. While, among boys, sexual abuse victimization and traumatic sequelae have been inconsistent risk markers for future violence, the relationship does appear stronger and more consistent for girls (Ford, Elhai, Connor, & Freuh, 2010; Krischer & Sevecke, 2008; Wasserman & McReynolds, 2011). In at least one large-scale study of delinquents, however, adding a female "responsive" risk item pertaining to abuse and trauma did not improve the prediction or recidivism or offending (Baglivio & Jackowski, 2013).

A number of behavioral health concerns have also emerged as more substantial predictors of violence in female juveniles, relative to male offenders. In most studies, female offenders have significantly higher rates of mental health problems, but a number of those factors—including "emotional problems" (broadly), depression, low self-esteem, self-harm, and substance abuse—also appear to factor more prominently into the risk profiles of girls than they do for boys (Elkington, Teplin, Abram, Jakubowski, Dulcan, & Welty, 2015; Stephenson et al., 2013). Finally, indicators of parental criminality, including parents having a history of arrest and/or substance abuse problems may be more prevalent and more potent risk factors for girls than for boys (van der Put et al., 2011, 2014).

Protective Factors

In addition to the extensive literature on factors that increase risk, there is a smaller, nascent body of research investigating characteristics and conditions that may decrease risk (Bernat et al., 2012; de Vries

Robbé et al., 2012; de Ruiter & Nicholls, 2011; Fougere & Daffern, 2011; Henry et al., 2012). These are commonly referred to as protective factors. Lösel and Farrington (2012) have described a distinction among protective factors that is pertinent to *how* they might decrease risk. They refer to the types as *direct protective factors* and *buffering protective factors* and explain the difference in the following way.

> Direct protective factors predict a low probability of future problem behavior without taking other factors into account. They refer to the main effect of a variable. In contrast, the term buffering protective factors should be restricted to variables that predict a low probability of a negative outcome in the presence of risk factors. This terminology refers to the moderating or interaction effects of the factors. In other words, the buffering protective factor attenuates the impact of a risk. (p. s9)

While research on protective factors and resilience is growing, relatively few studies have focused specifically on serious violence as the outcome of interest. Lösel and Farrington (2012) provide a fairly comprehensive list of individual, family, peer, school, and neighborhood variables (and a review of supporting research) that are strong candidates for having protective effects against a range of negative outcomes such as youth violence, aggressive behavior, serious offending, delinquency, antisocial behavior, and gang involvement (see Table 5.1).

Risk Assessment

Emergency evaluators and behavioral health professionals use a range of approaches for assessing violence risk. One overarching best practice principle is to be systematic. That means the clinician should have a plan for what kinds of questions to ask, what information to collect, how to document the assessment, and how to make a decision about the nature, likelihood, and imminence of the juvenile's risk for violence. Research has firmly established that unstructured and purely clinical risk assessment approaches are not highly effective (Monahan, 1981; Monahan & Skeem, 2014; Skeem & Monahan, 2011).

The Structured Professional Judgment (SPJ) assessment approach has become a best practice, if not a standard of practice, for evidence-based risk assessments in a range of settings (Falzer, 2013; Guy, Packer, & Warnken, 2012; Neal & Grisso, 2014; Pedersen, Rasmussen, & Elsass, 2010). Using an SPJ

Table 5.1. Protective Factors Against Antisocial Behavior in Youth.

Individual factors
- Above-average intelligence
- Positive attitudes toward family and school
- Nonaggression-prone social cognitions and beliefs
- Low impulsivity and an easy temperament
- Low ADHD
- Enhanced anxiety and shyness
- High heart rate
- High MAO-A activity

Family factors
- Close relationship to at least one parent
- Intensive parental supervision
- Parental disapproval of aggressive behavior
- Low physical punishment
- Intensive involvement in family activities
- Above-average SES of the family
- Family models of constructive coping
- Positive parental attitudes toward the child's education

School factors
- Good school achievement
- Bonding to school
- Strong work motivation
- Reaching higher education
- Support and supervision by teachers
- Clear classroom rules
- Positive school climate

Peer factors
- Non-deviant good friends
- Peer groups that disapprove of aggression
- Involvement in religious groups
- Social isolation

Neighborhood factors
- Non-deprived neighbourhood
- Nonviolent neighbourhood
- Cohesion and informal social control

Adapted from Lösel and Farrington, 2012.

approach, the evaluator conducts a risk assessment by referring to an explicit list of factors that have been drawn from the existing professional literature, which are selected based on their demonstrated relationship to violence in the population of interest. Ideally, a definition and description is assigned to each item so the clinician can reliably rate its presence and severity. Having a systematic list helps the evaluator to gather and focus on information that has a demonstrated relationship to violent behavior in youth and to make a judgment about risk that is informed by a systematic analysis of those factors.

Several instruments or guides have been developed and used in different settings for structuring assessments of violence risk in children and adolescents, and a substantial number of empirical studies show that using them facilitates much more accurate risk judgments than unstructured approaches. The exigent nature of emergency assessments may limit the amount information available to an evaluator. It is useful, however, for evaluators to know that these instruments exist and can be employed to produce a more systematic assessment. What follows is not a review of these tools, but a brief description of some of the more commonly used instruments.

Risk Assessment Instruments

EARL-20B (Early Assessment Risk List for Boys) (Augimeri, Koegl, Webster, & Levene, 2001) was designed to aid evaluators in making judgments about future violence and antisocial behavior among boys under the age of 12—particularly those who exhibit behavioral problems and are considered to be at high risk. The 20 items are divided into three categories, including six *family items* (household circumstances; caregiver continuity; supports; stressors; parenting style; antisocial values and conduct); twelve *child items*: developmental problems; onset of behavioral difficulties; abuse/neglect/trauma; hyperactivity/impulsivity/attention deficits (HIA); likeability; peer socialization; academic performance; neighborhood; authority contact; antisocial attitudes; antisocial behavior; and coping ability; and two *responsivity items*: family responsivity and child responsivity. A complementary instrument for young girls is also available. The EARL-21G is a structured clinical risk assessment device that provides a comprehensive framework to evaluate 21 risk factors known to influence young girls' propensity to engage in future antisocial behavior. Items are organized under three broad sections: *child, family*, and *responsivity*. The device is research-based and informed by the clinical expertise of people with extensive experience treating girls under the age of 12 with conduct problems. The items are largely similar to those in the EARL-20B, with only a couple of girl-sensitive exceptions.

SAVRY (Structured Assessment of Violence Risk in Youth) (Borum, Bartel, & Forth, 2006) is designed to focus specifically on violence risk in adolescents (Vincent, Guy, Gershenson, & McCabe, 2012). The SAVRY protocol applies 24 evidence-based risk factors (and six protective factors), which are rationally clustered within three categories: *historical, individual*, and *social/contextual* (these are not intended as psychometric scales). In a systematic review of 68 studies (with more than 25,000 participants) evaluating violence risk assessment tools for youth and for adults, the SAVRY produced the highest rates of predictive validity among any of the instruments (Singh, Grann, & Fazel, 2011).

START:AV (Short-Term Assessment of Risk and Treatability: Adolescent Version) (Desmarais et al., 2012; Nicholls, Viljoen, Cruise, Desmarais, & Webster, 2010; Viljoen, Cruise, Nicholls, Desmarais, & Webster, 2012) is a clinical guide designed to assist in the assessment and management of adolescents' near-term risk for a broad range of adverse events, including but not limited to violence (e.g., general offending, suicide, victimization). It is composed of 23 dynamic items pertaining to the individual youth and his or her social context (e.g., social skills, emotional state, substance use, support from caregivers and other adults, support from peers, parenting, and home environment). It includes a balance of risk factors (which they call vulnerability) and protective factors (which they calls strength). Because the START:AV assesses short-term risks, each item is rated based on the past 3 months.

YLS/CMI (Hoge & Andrews, 2002) is a risk/needs assessment and case management tool based on the General Personality and Social Psychological Model of Criminal Conduct (Andrews & Bonta, 2010). It comprises 42 items assessing eight categories of criminogenic (risk) factors: prior and current offenses and dispositions, family circumstances and parenting, education and employment, peer relations, substance use, leisure and recreation, personality and behavior, and attitudes and orientation.

An unpublished short form exists, the Youth Level of Service, Screener Version, with items being rationally and theoretically selected to provide coverage across the eight original risk domains. A recent effort (Campbell et al., 2014), however, has developed a 10-item screening version, selecting items empirically based on their significance in predicting violence in an earlier study.[1] Using this approach, only four of the original eight domains are represented. In their study, the YLS/CMI screener interviews took between 12 and 15 minutes to administer.

Estimating Risk

After systematically gathering and assessing risk-related information, the evaluator must ultimately make a decision about violence potential. Even the structured assessment instruments, for the most part, are not designed to provide a numerical meter

of risk (e.g., score of 1–10 is low), because the facts of the case might make a simple tally of risk factors or scores relatively meaningless. For example, if a teen was known to have a gun in his possession, and he was expressing homicidal intent toward a particular target, and he talked about knowing where the target would be at any given point in the day, it would seem imprudent to conclude that the risk was *low* and that no action was necessary based solely on the absence of other significant risk factors in the case (e.g., past history of violence, substance abuse, childhood victimization, and so on).

The clinician should estimate risk based primarily on factors that have a strong relationship to adolescent violence based on known research studies, and cautiously titrate that estimate with information from dynamic and case-specific factors. The ultimate appraisal of risk should be individualized and developmentally informed. That is, the evaluator should consider risk factors derived from research, as well as from the youth's own history or recent behaviors.

All risk-related information should be weighed in light of the developmental issues discussed earlier. Different risk factors may operate based on the particular age of the youth (see US Department of Health and Human Services, 2001). For example, having delinquent peers in childhood (e.g., ages 6–11) does increase the risk for serious adolescent violence, but the effect of the increase is modest. However, with adolescents (e.g., age 12–14), having antisocial or delinquent peers is one of the strongest predictors of subsequent violence: its effect is approximately nine times greater at this stage than in the early stage. Indeed, most interventions for reducing violence in adolescents will be ineffective if the delinquent peer factor is not addressed and mitigated.

Figure 5.1 illustrates one approach for translating risk information into a risk-related judgment. This chart is a rationally derived heuristic, based roughly on the strength of the empirical relationship between the risk factor and violence, with more static factors considered in the first phase and more dynamic factors in the latter phase. This is not based on a specific actuarial or statistical formula or model. It is only a device for guiding a risk judgment.

In the first stage, because early onset of violent offending is strongly related to the likelihood and severity of future violence, the evaluator considers whether, during childhood (before age 13), the youth engaged in acts of serious violence (e.g., violence sufficiently severe to cause injury or that was committed with a weapon).

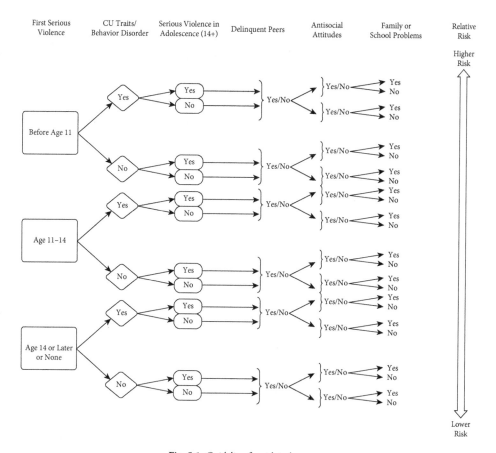

Fig. 5.1 Guideline for risk judgements.

In the second stage, the evaluator might consider whether the youth has a co-occurring disruptive behavior disorder (or serious problems related to such a disorder), such as conduct disorder or attention deficit hyperactivity disorder. A conduct disorder will reflect a history of multiple antisocial behaviors, and an attention problem or hyperactivity is a notable risk factor for violence in adolescents, creating a risk of arrest that is 5 to 25 times greater than if hyperactivity was not present.

In the third stage, consideration might be given to the recency of violent behavior, noting whether the youth has engaged in serious violence during adolescence (at or after age 14). More recent/proximate violent behavior may signal an increased risk for further violent incidents during the teen years (though not necessarily into adulthood).

The next phase of the flow chart is composed of three *dynamic* risk areas. The first of these considers the presence of delinquent peers or associates. For estimating risk in adolescents, this factor is weighted more heavily to account for the strong relationship between this factor and subsequent violence specifically found in the older age group. Subsequently,

the clinician may consider the presence of antisocial attitudes, particularly those that would condone or support the use of violence as a legitimate (or likely successful) strategy to solve problems or achieve a goal. Youth who possess more of these attitudes and beliefs and possess them more strongly would be considered to be at higher risk.

Finally, the evaluator might consider the presence of serious problems at home and/or at school. Prior reviews of risk factors for youth violence have highlighted how poor achievement, disregard for school, and school-related problem behaviors are associated with a risk for future violence. Similar research-based associations have been found for a range of home-based problems, including antisocial parents, poor parental management or supervision, and maltreatment. Again, youth with more problems and more serious problems have in past studies been found to be at higher risk for violence. Systematically considering these key factors can serve as an anchor-point for locating the youth's current risk level for violence.

An additional, or alternative approach to estimating risk is to use a theoretical framework to conceptualize the construct of risk. The General Personality and Social Psychological Model of Criminal Conduct (Andrews & Bonta, 2010), for example, identifies the following four key domains—referred to as the Big Four—that are useful for predicting and understanding antisocial behavior.

1. Antisocial cognitions (i.e., attitudes, values, beliefs, rationalizations and identities)
2. A history of antisocial behavior
3. Antisocial associates
4. An antisocial personality pattern

Although the precise nature, weight, and mechanism of each domain may vary somewhat between adults and adolescents and between general antisocial and specifically violent behavior, the fundamental importance of these four areas is relatively constant. The clinician can consider these four domains, along with the breadth, salience, and severity of problems (risk factors) that the youth might have in each. If serious problems are noted in all four areas, the clinician could approach the risk estimate by working backwards from a presumption of high risk. Not all cases with problems distributed across the Big Four domains are high risk. But this heuristic prompts the evaluator explicitly, in any given case, to assess and justify why not.

Screening Tools

Most of the SPJ tools are designed to support comprehensive risk assessments, but sometimes in emergency settings, access to information—and various sources of information—may be limited. A number of researchers have attempted to develop screening tools, decision trees, or heuristic algorithms to create a more systematic, and perhaps more valid, method of screening for cases that may warrant further risk evaluation in emergency departments.

One such screening tool is known as the Violence Prevention Emergency Tool-2 (VPET-2) (Rogers et al., 2012). The researchers borrowed 11 risk-related concepts from the SAVRY to create a 35-item screener (VPET-1). Through a Principal Components Analysis, they combined the VPET-1 with their 22-item Violence Exposure Scale (VEX) to create a 14-item second-generation screening tool, the VPET-2. An evaluator typically guides VPET-2 administration by asking the young person a series of questions about violence exposure, using a four-point Likert scale (i.e., never, one time, a few times, and lots of times). The authors administered

the VPET-2 to 200 patients (8–17 years old) in a pediatric emergency department and concluded that it may be a "feasible screening tool" for use in emergency departments to assess violence exposure. They also conducted another Principal Components Analysis to identify the best seven of those items, which collectively correspond to three key domains of violence.

> The first domain is witness of violence and is represented by questions such as seeing another person shot with a real gun. The second domain involves being the victim of violence and is represented by items asking about being injured or physically harmed by another person or being chased by an angry person. The final domain identifies perpetrators of violence and includes injuring another person, stealing, selling drugs, or destroying property. (p. S246)

Copelan, Messer, and Ashley (2006) took an alternative approach to emergency screening. Building on an instrument they had previously developed, they created a decision-tree or guideline called the Violence Ideation and Suicidality Treatment Algorithm (VISTA). If any of the following conditions are met, the VISTA suggests that the patient is at "intermediate to high risk for serious violent outcome requiring consultation/admission."

• At the time of triage, the patient has motor restlessness AND thoughts of self/other harm
• Recent history of stressful events illness or psych Rx (e.g., initiated changed, discontinued)
• History of violence to self or other violence; or a depressive or substance use disorder
• Interpersonal problems or threatened humiliation (e.g., romantic, legal, school, parent)
• Thoughts that are obsessive (e.g., death expectation), not logical, or the inability to listen to intercessions of others; or new behavioral changes by history of physical examination (e.g., pacing, rocking, stereotypic, repetitive movements)

If none of these conditions are met, the VISTA classifies the patient as being at "low risk for serious violent outcome requiring consultation/admission" (Copelan et al., 2006, p. 591).

Risk Management

One of the main functions of a thorough risk assessment is to inform interventions and strategies for violence prevention. Different youth may be at different levels of risk for different kinds of aggression toward different targets, in different contexts, and at different point in time. It is critical, therefore, to understand the nature of risk for the specific youth being evaluated and not just to tally or aggregate the risk factors (Yang & Mulvey, 2012).

Treatment and interventions can reduce risk and prevent violence, but not all interventions work equally well. Risk management interventions tend to work best when they respond to the specific needs of the young person. Andrews, Bonta, and Hoge (1990) developed a highly influential treatment/intervention model that has its foundation in three core principles: risk, needs, and responsivity (Luong & Wormith, 2011). These three principles can be an effective foundation for risk management in emergency settings as well.

• *The risk principle* guides *who* should be targeted for intervention, suggesting that the intensity of treatment/intervention efforts and resources should be aligned with the young person's level of risk. So, higher risk cases would be assigned to more intensive intervention/supervision.

• *The need principle* guides *what* should be targeted for intervention, suggesting that interventions should focus on "criminogenic needs," meaning those that are functionally related to the young person's violent behavior.

• *The responsivity principle* guides *how* interventions should be chosen and implemented, suggesting that they should match the young person's learning style, motivations, strengths, and abilities. In general, social learning-based approaches are some of the most effective, but the delivery can be tailored for the individual.

Finally, an intervention plan must be implemented and monitored for adjustments as needed. Lack of follow-up is where many failures occur. Even targeting criminogenic factors with evidence-based interventions will not be effective if those interventions are not properly implemented and monitored. Moreover, because adolescence can be a period of rapid change, it is particularly important to ensure that mechanisms are in place to ensure that treatment needs and risk factors are reassessed and that intervention plans are modified accordingly.

Conclusion

Understanding the fundamentals of violence risk and management for children and adolescents is essential for behavioral health professionals who work crisis or emergency settings (Copelan et al., 2006; Giggie, Olvera, & Joshi, 2007; Langan, 2010; Rogers et al., 2012). Behavioral risk must be considered in its developmental context. During childhood

and adolescence, personality is not fully developed; autonomy, self-control, and the ability to take different perspectives and anticipate consequences are evolving; and behaviors and responses are often inconsistent across different settings. All of these factors make the difficult task of anticipating future behavior even more challenging.

Evaluators in emergency or crisis settings should rely on evidence-based risk factors, while applying an individualized formulation to give texture to the assessment and to forecasts about the nature and degree of risk for violence. Having a systematic or even structured approach to identifying risk and protective factors and collecting a detailed history of violence helps to keep the examiner on track and facilitates a more complete evaluation. A methodical process also facilitates more transparent decisions and better informs risk reduction efforts. The guidelines provided in this chapter can support the emergency evaluator in applying an evidence-based approach to assessing violence risk in children and adolescence.

Note

1. The 10 items included in the screener version are disruptive behavior in the classroom; disruptive behavior on school grounds; low achievement in school; problems with peers in school; problems with teachers in school; some delinquent friends; limited organized activity; could make better use of free time; physical aggression; and short attention span.

References

Andrews, D. A., & Bonta, J. (2010). *The psychology of criminal conduct*. New York, NY: Routledge.

Andrews, D. A., Bonta, J., & Hoge, R. D. (1990). Classification for effective rehabilitation: Rediscovering psychology. *Criminal Justice and Behavior, 17*, 19–52.

Augimeri, L., Koegl, C., Webster, C., & Levene, K. (2001). *Early Assessment Risk List for Boys: EARL-20B, Version 2-Consultation Edition*. Toronto, Canada: Earlscourt Child and Family Centre.

Babcock, J. C., Tharp, A. L., Sharp, C., Heppner, W., & Stanford, M. S. (2014). Similarities and differences in impulsive/premeditated and reactive/proactive bimodal classifications of aggression. *Aggression and Violent Behavior, 19*(3), 251–262.

Baglivio, M. T., & Epps, N. (2015). The interrelatedness of adverse childhood experiences among high-risk juvenile offenders. *Youth Violence and Juvenile Justice*. doi:10.1177/1541204014566286

Baglivio, M. T., & Jackowski, K. (2013). Examining the validity of a juvenile offending risk assessment instrument across gender and race/ethnicity. *Youth Violence and Juvenile Justice, 11*(1), 26–43.

Baglivio, M. T., Jackowski, K., Greenwald, M. A., & Howell, J. C. (2014). Serious, violent, and chronic juvenile offenders. *Criminology & Public Policy, 13*(1), 83–116.

Bernat, D. H., Oakes, J. M., Pettingell, S. L., & Resnick, M. (2012). Risk and direct protective factors for youth violence: Results from the National Longitudinal Study of Adolescent Health. *American Journal of Preventive Medicine, 43*(2), S57–S66.

Borum, R. (2003). Managing at risk juvenile offenders in the community: Putting evidence based principles into practice. *Journal of Contemporary Criminal Justice, 19*, 114–137.

Borum, R. (2009). Children and adolescents at risk for violence. In P. M. Kleespies (Ed.), *Behavioral emergencies: An evidence-based resource for evaluating and managing risk of suicide, violence, and victimization* (pp. 147–163). Washington, DC: American Psychological Association.

Borum, R., Bartel, P., & Forth, A. (2006). *SAVRY: Structured Assessment of Violence Risk in Youth: Professional manual.* Odessa, FL: Psychological Assessment Resources.

Borum, R., & Grisso, T. (2006). Forensic assessment from a developmental perspective. In A. Goldstein (Ed.), *Forensic psychology: Emerging topics and expanding roles* (pp. 553–570). New York, NY: Wiley.

Borum, R., & Verhaagen, D. (2006). *Assessing and managing violence risk in juveniles.* New York, NY: Guilford.

Brugman, S., Lobbestael, J., Arntz, A., Cima, M., Schuhmann, T., Dambacher, F., & Sack, A. T. (2014). Identifying cognitive predictors of reactive and proactive aggression. *Aggressive Behavior, 9999*, 1–14. doi:10.1002/AB.21573

Campbell, C., Onifade, E., Barnes, A., Peterson, J., Anderson, V., Davidson, W., & Gordon, D. (2014). Screening offenders: The exploration of a Youth Level of Service/Case Management Inventory (YLS/CMI) Brief Screener. *Journal of Offender Rehabilitation, 53*(1), 19–34.

Cauffman, E., Lexcen, F. J., Goldweber, A., Shulman, E. P., & Grisso, T. (2007). Gender differences in mental health symptoms among delinquent and community youth. *Youth Violence and Juvenile Justice, 5*(3), 287–307.

Cauffman, E., & Steinberg, L. (2012). Emerging findings from research on adolescent development and juvenile justice. *Victims & Offenders, 7*(4), 428–449.

Cauffman, E., Steinberg, L., & Piquero, A. R. (2005). Psychological, neuropsychological, and physiological correlates of serious antisocial behavior in adolescence: The role of self-control. *Criminology, 43*, 133.

Cheng, T. L., Schwarz, D., Brenner, R. A., Wright, J. L., Fields, C. B., O'Donnell, R., . . . & Scheidt, P. C. (2003). Adolescent assault injury: Risk and protective factors and locations of contact for intervention. *Pediatrics, 112*(4), 931–938.

Compas, B. E., Hinden, B. R., & Gerhardt, C. A. (1995). Adolescent development: Pathways and processes of risk and resilience. *Annual Review of Psychology, 46*(1), 265–293.

Copelan, R. I., Messer, M. A., & Ashley, D. J. (2006). Adolescent violence screening in the ED. *The American Journal of Emergency Medicine, 24*(5), 582–594.

Cottle, C., Lee, R., & Heilbrun, K. (2001). The prediction of criminal recidivism in juveniles: A meta-analysis. *Criminal Justice and Behavior, 28*, 367–394.

Crick, N. R., & Dodge, K. A. (1996). Social information-processing mechanisms in reactive and proactive aggression. *Child Development, 67*(3), 993–1002.

Daigle, L. E., Cullen, F. T., & Wright, J. P. (2007). Gender differences in the predictors of juvenile delinquency assessing the generality-specificity debate. *Youth Violence and Juvenile Justice, 5*(3), 254–286.

de Ruiter, C., & Nicholls, T. L. (2011). Protective factors in forensic mental health: A new frontier. *International Journal of Forensic Mental Health, 10*, 160–170.

Derzon, J. (2001). Antisocial behavior and the prediction of violence: A meta-analysis. *Psychology in the Schools, 38*, 93–106.

Desmarais, S. L., Sellers, B. G., Viljoen, J. L., Cruise, K. R., Nicholls, T. L., & Dvoskin, J. A. (2012). Pilot implementation and preliminary evaluation of START: AV assessments in secure juvenile correctional facilities. *International Journal of Forensic Mental Health, 11*(3), 150–164.

de Vries Robbé, M., de Vogel, V., & Stam, J. (2012). Protective factors for violence risk: The value for clinical practice. *Psychology, 3*, 1259.

Dolan, M. A., & Fein, J. A. (2011). Pediatric and adolescent mental health emergencies in the emergency medical services system. *Pediatrics, 127*(5), e1356–e1366.

Elkington, K. S., Teplin, L. A., Abram, K. M., Jakubowski, J. A., Dulcan, M. K., & Welty, L. J. (2015). Psychiatric disorders and violence: a study of delinquent youth after detention. *Journal of the American Academy of Child & Adolescent Psychiatry, 54*(4), 302-312.

Elliott, D. S. (1994). Serious violent offenders: Onset, developmental course, and termination. The American Society of Criminology 1993 presidential address. *Criminology, 32*, 1–21.

Elliott, D., Ageton, S., Huizinga, D., Knowles, B., & Canter, R. (1983). *The prevalence and incidence of delinquent behavior: 1976–1980.* (The National Youth Survey Report No. 26.) Boulder, CO: Behavioral Research Institute.

Fagan, A. A., Van Horn, M. L., Hawkins, J. D., & Arthur, M. W. (2007). Gender similarities and differences in the association between risk and protective factors and self-reported serious delinquency. *Prevention Science, 8*(2), 115–124.

Falzer, P. R. (2013). Valuing structured professional judgment: Predictive validity, decision-making, and the clinical-actuarial conflict. *Behavioral Sciences & the Law, 31*(1), 40–54.

Ford, J. D., Elhai, J. D., Connor, D. F., & Frueh, B. C. (2010). Poly-victimization and risk of posttraumatic, depressive, and substance use disorders and involvement in delinquency. *Journal of Adolescent Health, 46*, 545–552. doi:10.1016/j.jado health.2009.11.212

Fougere, A., & Daffern, M. (2011). Resilience in youth offenders. *International Journal of Forensic Mental Health, 10*, 244–253.

Gammelgård, M., Weizmann-Henelius, G., Koivisto, A. M., Eronen, M., & Kaltiala-Heino, R. (2012). Gender differences in violence risk profiles. *Journal of Forensic Psychiatry & Psychology, 23*(1), 76–94.

Giggie, M. A., Olvera, R. L., & Joshi, M. N. (2007). Screening for risk factors associated with violence in pediatric patients presenting to a psychiatric emergency department. *Journal of Psychiatric Practice, 13*(4), 246–252.

Griffin, P., & Torbet, P. (2002). *Desktop guide to good juvenile probation practice.* Pittsburgh, PA: National Center for Juvenile Justice.

Guy, L. S., Packer, I. K., & Warnken, W. (2012). Assessing risk of violence using structured professional judgment guidelines. *Journal of Forensic Psychology Practice, 12*(3), 270–283.

Hart, J. L., O'Toole, S. K., Price-Sharps, J. L., & Shaffer, T. W. (2007). The risk and protective factors of violent juvenile offending: An examination of gender differences. *Youth Violence and Juvenile Justice, 5*(4), 367–384.

Hawkins, J., Herrenkohl, T., Farrington, D., Brewer, D., Catalano, R., & Harachi, T. (1998). A review of predictors of youth violence. In R. Loeber & D. Farrington (Eds.), *Serious and violent juvenile offenders: Risk factors and successful interventions* (pp. 106–146). Thousand Oaks, CA: Sage.

Henry, D. B., Tolan, P. H., Gorman-Smith, D., & Schoeny, M. E. (2012). Risk and direct protective factors for youth violence: Results from the Centers for Disease Control and Prevention's Multisite Violence Prevention Project. *American Journal of Preventive Medicine, 43*(2), S67–S75.

Herrenkohl, T. I., Farrington, D. P., Brewer, D., Catalano, R. F., Harachi, T. W., & Cothern, L. (2000). *Predictors of youth violence* (pp. 1–10). Washington, DC: US Department of Justice, Office of Justice Programs, Office of Juvenile Justice and Delinquency Prevention.

Herrenkohl, T. I., Lee, J., & Hawkins, J. D. (2012). Risk versus direct protective factors and youth violence: Seattle Social Development Project. *American Journal of Preventive Medicine, 43*(2), S41–S56.

Herrenkohl, T. I., Maguin, E., Hill, K. G., Hawkins, J. D., Abbott, R. D., & Catalano, R. F. (2000). Developmental risk factors for youth violence. *Journal of Adolescent Health, 26*(3), 176–186.

Hoge, R., & Andrews, D. (2002). *The Youth Level of Service/Case Management Inventory.* Toronto, Ontario, Canada: Multi-Health Systems.

Howard, M., & Jenson, J. (1999). Causes of youth violence. In J. Jenson & M. Howard (Eds.), *Youth violence: Current research and recent practice innovations,* pp. 19–42. Washington, DC: National Association of Social Workers Press.

Janssens, A., Hayen, S., Walraven, V., Leys, M., & Deboutte, D. (2013). Emergency psychiatric care for children and adolescents: A literature review. *Pediatric Emergency Care, 29*(9), 1041–1050.

Jennings, W. G., & Reingle, J. M. (2012). On the number and shape of developmental/life-course violence, aggression, and delinquency trajectories: A state-of-the-art review. *Journal of Criminal Justice, 40*(6), 472–489.

Kann, L., Kinchen, S. A., Williams, B., Ross, J. G., Lowry, R., & Kolbe, L. (2002). Youth Risk Behavior Surveillance—United States, 2001. *Morbidity and Mortality Weekly Report, 51,* 1–64.

Krischer, M. K., & Sevecke, K. (2008). Early traumatization and psychopathy in female and male juvenile offenders. *International Journal of Law and Psychiatry, 31,* 253–262. doi:10.1016/j.ijlp.2008.04.008

Langan, J. (2010). Challenging assumptions about risk factors and the role of screening for violence risk in the field of mental health. *Health, Risk & Society, 12*(2), 85–100.

Lipsey, M., & Derzon, J. (1998). Predictors of violent or serious delinquency in adolescence and early adulthood: A synthesis of longitudinal research. In R. Loeber & D. Farrington (Eds.), *Serious and violent juvenile offenders: Risk factors and successful interventions,* pp. 86–105. Thousand Oaks, CA: Sage.

Loeber, R., & Stouthamer-Loeber, M. (1998). Development of juvenile aggression and violence: Some common misconceptions and controversies. *American Psychologist, 53*(2), 242.

Lösel, F., & Farrington, D. P. (2012). Direct protective and buffering protective factors in the development of youth violence. *American Journal of Preventive Medicine, 43*(2), S8–S23.

Lovins, B., Schweitzer, M., & Sullivan, C. (2013). Gender neutral or gender specific predictors of recidivism: Should risk assessment incorporate separate scales for boys and girls? *Scientific Committee of Reviewers, 284.*

Luong, D., & Wormith, J. S. (2011). Applying risk/need assessment to probation practice and its impact on the recidivism of young offenders. *Criminal Justice and Behavior, 38*(12), 1177–1199.

McCabe, K. M., Lansing, A. E., Garland, A., & Hough, R. (2002). Gender differences in psychopathology, functional impairment, and familial risk factors among adjudicated delinquents. *Journal of American Academy of Child and Adolescent Psychiatry, 41,* 860–867.

McCord, J., Widom, C. S., & Crowell, N. A. (2001). *Juvenile crime, juvenile justice. Panel on juvenile crime: Prevention, treatment, and control.* Washington, DC: National Academy Press.

Moffitt, T. (1997). Adolescence-limited and life-course-persistent offending: A complementary pair of developmental theories. In T. Thornberry (Ed.), *Developmental theories of crime and delinquency* (pp. 11–54). New Brunswick, NJ: Transaction.

Moffitt, T. E. (1993). Adolescence-limited and life-course-persistent antisocial behavior: A developmental taxonomy. *Psychological Review, 100,* 674–701.

Moffitt, T. E. (2006). Life-course persistent versus adolescence-limited antisocial behavior. In D. Cicchetti & D. Cohen (Eds.), *Developmental psychopathology* (vol. 3, 2nd ed., pp. 570–598). New York, NY: Wiley.

Monahan, J. (1981). *Predicting violent behavior: An assessment of clinical techniques.* Beverly Hills, CA: Sage.

Monahan, J., & Skeem, J. L. (2014). The evolution of violence risk assessment. *CNS Spectrums, 19*(5), 419–424.

Moretti, M. M., Odgers, C., Reppucci, N. D., & Catherine, N. L. (2011). Serious conduct problems among girls at risk: Translating research into intervention. *International Journal of Child, Youth, and Family Studies, 2*(1/2), 142–161.

Mulvey, E. P. (2014). Using developmental science to reorient our thinking about criminal offending in adolescence. *Journal of Research in Crime and Delinquency, 51*(4), 467–479. doi:10.1177/0022427814522249

Neal, T. M., & Grisso, T. (2014). Assessment practices and expert judgment methods in forensic psychology and psychiatry: An international snapshot. *Criminal Justice and Behavior, 41,* 1406–1421. doi:0093854814548449

Nicholls, T. L., Viljoen, J. L., Cruise, K. R., Desmarais, S. L., & Webster, C. D. (2010). *Short-Term Assessment of Risk and Treatability: Adolescent Version (START: AV)* (Abbreviated Manual). Coquitlam, British Columbia, Canada: Mental Health and Addiction Services.

O'Brien, K., Daffern, M., Chu, C. M., & Thomas, S. D. (2013). Youth gang affiliation, violence, and criminal activities: A review of motivational, risk, and protective factors. *Aggression and Violent Behavior, 18*(4), 417–425.

Odgers, C. L., Moretti, M. M., & Reppucci, N. D. (2005). Examining the science and practice of violence risk assessment with female adolescents. *Law and Human Behavior, 29*(1), 7.

Pedersen, L., Rasmussen, K., & Elsass, P. (2010). Risk assessment: The value of structured professional judgments. *International Journal of Forensic Mental Health, 9*(2), 74–81.

Piquero, A. R., Jennings, W. G., & Barnes, J. C. (2012). Violence in criminal careers: A review of the literature from a developmental life-course perspective. *Aggression and Violent Behavior, 17*(3), 171–179.

Piquero, A. R., & Moffitt, T. E. (2005). Explaining the facts of crime: How the developmental taxonomy replies to Farrington's invitation. In D. P. Farrington (Ed.), *Integrated developmental and life-course theories of offending: Advances in criminological theory* (pp. 51–72). New Brunswick, NJ: Transaction.

Poulin, F., & Boivin, M. (2000). Reactive and proactive aggression: Evidence of a two-factor model. *Psychological Assessment, 12*(2), 115.

Rogers, S. C., Borrup, K., Parikh, C., Saleheen, H., Lapidus, G., & Smith, S. (2012). Can a youth violence screening tool be used in a pediatric emergency department setting? *Journal of Trauma and Acute Care Surgery, 73*(4), S243–S247.

Schwalbe, C. S. (2008). A meta-analysis of juvenile justice risk assessment instruments: Predictive validity by gender. *Criminal Justice and Behavior, 35,* 1367–1381.

Shepherd, S. M., Luebbers, S., & Dolan, M. (2013). Gender and ethnicity in juvenile risk assessment. *Criminal Justice and Behavior, 40*(4), 388–408.

Singh, J. P., Grann, M., & Fazel, S. (2011). A comparative study of violence risk assessment tools: A systematic review and metaregression analysis of 68 studies involving 25,980 participants. *Clinical Psychology Review, 31*(3), 499–513.

Skeem, J. L., & Monahan, J. (2011). Current directions in violence risk assessment. *Current Directions in Psychological Science, 20*(1), 38–42.

Steinberg, L., & Cauffman, E. (1999). Developmental perspective on serious juvenile crime: When should juveniles be treated as adults? *Federal Probation, 63,* 52.

Stephenson, Z., Woodhams, J., & Cooke, C. (2013). Sex differences in predictors of violent and non-violent juvenile offending. *Aggressive Behavior, 40*(2), 165–177.

Swogger, M. T., Walsh, Z., Christie, M., Priddy, B. M., & Conner, K. R. (2015). Impulsive versus premeditated aggression in the prediction of violent criminal recidivism. *Aggressive Behavior, 41*(4), 346–352.

Thompson, K. C., & Morris, R. J. (2013). Predicting recidivism among juvenile delinquents: Comparison of risk factors for male and female offenders. *Journal of Juvenile Justice, 3*(1): 36-47.

US Department of Health and Human Services. (2001). *Youth violence: A report of the Surgeon General.* Rockville, MD: US Department of Health and Human Services, Substance Abuse and Mental Health Services Administration, Center for Mental Health Services, National Institutes of Health, National Institute of Mental Health. Retrieved from http://www.surgeongeneral.gov/library/youthviolence

van der Merwe, A., & Dawes, A. (2007). Youth violence: A review of risk factors, causal pathways, and effective intervention. *Journal of Child and Adolescent Mental Health, 19*(2), 95-113.

van der Put, C. E., Deković, M., Hoeve, M., Stams, G. J. J., van der Laan, P. H., & Langewouters, F. E. (2014). Risk assessment of girls: Are there any sex differences in risk factors for re-offending and in risk profiles? *Crime & Delinquency, 60*(7), 1033–1056. doi:10.1177/0011128710384776

Van Der Put, C. E., Deković, M., Stams, G. J., Van Der Laan, P. H., Hoeve, M., & Van Amelsfort, L. (2011). Changes in risk factors during adolescence: Implications for risk assessment. *Criminal Justice and Behavior, 38*(3), 248–262.

Viljoen, J. L., Cruise, K. R., Nicholls, T. L., Desmarais, S. L., & Webster, C. D. (2012). Taking stock and taking steps: The case for an adolescent version of the Short-Term Assessment of Risk and Treatability. *International Journal of Forensic Mental Health, 11*(3), 135–149.

Vincent, G. M., Guy, L. S., Gershenson, B. G., & McCabe, P. (2012). Does risk assessment make a difference? Results of implementing the SAVRY in juvenile probation. *Behavioral Sciences & the Law, 30*(4), 384–405.

Vitopoulos, N. A., Peterson-Badali, M., & Skilling, T. A. (2012). The relationship between matching service to criminogenic need and recidivism in male and female youth examining the RNR principles in practice. *Criminal Justice and Behavior, 39*(8), 1025–1041.

Wasserman, G. A., & McReynolds, L. S. (2011). Contributors to traumatic exposure and posttraumatic stress disorder in juvenile justice youths. *Journal of Traumatic Stress, 24,* 422–429. doi:10.1002/jts.20664

White, B. A., & Turner, K. A. (2014). Anger rumination and effortful control: Mediation effects on reactive but not proactive aggression. *Personality and Individual Differences, 56,* 186–189.

Yang, S., & Mulvey, E. P. (2012). Violence risk: Re-defining variables from the first-person perspective. *Aggression and Violent Behavior, 17*(3), 198–207.

Children as Victims: Preventing and Reporting Child Maltreatment and Abuse

Cynthia Cupit Swenson *and* Sarah L. Logan

Abstract

Child maltreatment is a significant global public health problem that impacts children's health and mental health while young but also can follow them into adulthood, potentially carrying forward patterns of abusive parenting. To effectively manage and eliminate child maltreatment, a uniform definition of abuse and neglect must be developed for proper monitoring of prevalence. Reporting laws and protection of children should be followed with care, and evidence-based prevention strategies and interventions should be disseminated widely. At present, research on treatment of abuse and neglect has produced several models that are scientifically supported and rated as evidence based. Sufficient research has been conducted for the field to practice within the bounds of science. However, further research is needed on implementation of evidence-based treatments.

Key Words: child maltreatment, trauma, abuse, neglect, parenting

Child maltreatment is a significant global public health problem that impacts children's health and mental health while young but also can follow them into adulthood (United Nations Children's Fund, 2012). In the short term, maltreatment places children at risk of mental health difficulties such as anxiety, depression, and aggression (Cyr, Euser, Bakermans-Kranenburg, & Van Ijzendoorn, 2010; Kim, Cicchetti, Rogosch, & Manly, 2009). Children who experience maltreatment are 5 times more likely to attempt suicide (Dube et al., 2001) and are more likely to engage in criminal activity than nonmaltreated children (Gilbert et al., 2009). These difficulties may continue into adulthood and may even be transmitted across generations through parenting and family conflict (Sidebotham & Heron, 2006; Springer, Sheridan, Kuo, & Carnes, 2007). Adults who were maltreated as children are more likely to experience mental health difficulties such as depression, anxiety, posttraumatic stress

disorder (PTSD), substance abuse, and suicide attempts (Dube et al., 2001; Springer et al., 2007). A greater risk for physical health problems is also evident, especially severe obesity, ischemic heart disease, cancer, chronic lung disease, skeletal fractures, and liver disease (Chapman et al., 2004: Felitti et al., 1998). Child maltreatment also exacts a significant economic burden on families and society and has been estimated to cost $124 billion annually in the United States (Fang, Brown, Florence, & Mercy, 2012).

Eliminating the maltreatment of children will require a good understanding of (a) what constitutes maltreatment, (b) prevalence to monitor occurrence, (c) reporting laws and policies that must be followed to increase protection of children, (d) evidence-based primary prevention strategies, and (e) evidence-based treatments to prevent recurrence of maltreatment. In this chapter we review the current knowledge on each of these aspects of maltreatment.

Definition of Child Maltreatment

Maltreatment of children encompasses deliberate acts of commission (abuse) or omission (neglect) by a parent or caregiver that result in harm or the potential of harm to a child even when harm is not intended. Though forms of abuse and neglect may be defined differently from state to state in the United States and across countries of the world, the three major forms of abuse are generally recognized as physical, sexual, and psychological/emotional (Leeb, Paulozzi, Melanson, Simon, & Arias, 2008). In some countries emotional abuse may fall under a neglect category.

Physical abuse involves nonaccidental injury that can result in minor bruises to severe fractures or death. These injuries occur when a parent uses a hand, foot, stick, belt, or other object to hit, punch, beat, kick, choke, burn, bite, shake, throw, or stab a child. Physical discipline such as spanking is not considered abuse unless there is injury to the child such as marks. Sexual abuse involves sexual activity by a parent toward a child such as fondling, penetration, incest, rape, sodomy, exposure of oneself, or exploiting a child through prostitution or pornographic materials. Psychological or emotional abuse includes behaviors by a parent such as withholding love or affection, support, and guidance; ongoing constant criticism; threats; or rejection. Psychological abuse often co-occurs with other forms of abuse (Child Welfare Information Gateway, 2013).

Neglect refers to failure to meet a child's basic needs. Neglect can be seen in various forms such as physical (e.g., failure to provide food or supervision), medical (e.g., failure to provide medical or mental health treatment), educational (e.g., failure to educate a child or meet the child's special education needs), and emotional (e.g., failure to attend to the child's emotional needs). Many states in the United States have begun to define abandonment as a form of neglect. In addition, many states have come to define substance abuse-related situations (e.g., prenatal exposure, manufacturing methamphetamine in the presence of a child) as neglect in the United States (Child Welfare Information Gateway, 2013).

Prevalence of Child Maltreatment

Data on child maltreatment prevalence are commonly gathered through Child Protective Services (CPS) agencies, which record the number of reports of maltreatment and those that are founded or unfounded. In addition, national groups such as the National Center on Child Abuse and Neglect gather and maintain a composite of these data. Agency prevalence rates are thought to underestimate the number of children that experience maltreatment because of discrepancies in the definition of abuse across agencies, basing maltreatment rates on families rather than the number of children in the family, and basing prevalence only on cases reported to CPS (Cunningham, Swenson, & Henggeler, 1997). A recent study of confirmed reports in the United States that estimated the proportion of youth that would be maltreated by age 18 indicate that 12.5% of US children will have a confirmed case of maltreatment by age 18 (Wilderman et al., 2014). These figures amount to 1 in 8 US children. For Black children, the cumulative prevalence is 1 in 5 and for Native American children 1 in 7. It should be noted that nearly 80% of cases from this study in the National Child Abuse and Neglect Data System were neglect cases. From a more global perspective, in 2012 over one-fourth of children across the globe were victims of severe and repeated physical abuse. In addition, 1 in 5 females and 1 in 11 males were victims of sexual abuse (United Nations Children's Fund, 2012).

As can be seen, child maltreatment is a highly prevalent problem globally. One of the first critical steps in reducing maltreatment is to identify it and bring it into the open so that protection of children can be put in place.

Child Maltreatment Reporting

In many countries professionals that suspect abuse or neglect are required by law to report their concerns to CPS or law enforcement agencies. However, some countries do not at the present time have reporting laws. In the United States a report is mandated when an individual knows or has reasonable cause to believe or suspect that a child has been abused or neglected. Irrefutable evidence does not have to be present. It is the job of law enforcement or CPS to investigate and determine if there is sufficient evidence indicating that abuse or neglect has occurred and to put in place actions to protect the child. Generally reports are required to CPS if the person suspected of maltreating the child is in a parent or caregiver role. Individuals who are required to report maltreatment differ by state and country but typically are professionals who have contact with children such as teachers, school personnel, clergy, counselors, psychologists, physicians, and nurses. If they suspect maltreatment and do not report it, they are subject to legal sanctions that might even include arrest. The Child Welfare Information Gateway (2014) provides a list of maltreatment definitions, reporting laws, and mandated reporters for each state in the United States. It is imperative for professionals working with children to know the reporting laws of the place where they live.

Although there is a mandate to report suspected maltreatment, and although legal protection is extended to the reporter and failing to report maltreatment is associated with a greater risk of future maltreatment (Alvarez, Donohue, Kenny, Cavanagh, & Romero, 2005), many professionals are hesitant to make a report of suspected maltreatment (Hinson & Fossey, 2000). In a large-scale survey of child abuse reporting behavior, Zellman and Fair (2002) found that nearly 40% of respondents had suspected abuse of a child at some point in their career but did not report it. Likewise, in a survey of teachers, 73% had never made a report of maltreatment, and 11% made a conscious decision not to report when abuse was suspected (Kenny, 2001). Further, although the public schools report more cases of child maltreatment than any other institution (Sedlak & Broadhurst, 1996), research has shown that 84% of cases recognized in public schools are not reported (Zellman & Fair, 2002).

A number of barriers have been identified to reporting maltreatment. One of the most common reasons is fear of making an inaccurate report (Kenny, 2001). Especially when there is no visible physical injury, professionals worry they will be inaccurate. Other reasons for not reporting are a negative view of CPS and feeling they will not offer help to the children and instead the situation will possibly be made worse. Some mandated reporters do not report to avoid being involved in any potential legal proceedings. The failure to report suspected abuse is often due to lack of knowledge and skill in regard to the reporting process (Abrahams, Casey, & Daro, 1992).

Indeed, making a report can be quite complicated when a professional who has the role as mandated reporter suspects child maltreatment and is highly concerned that the report itself will place the child at risk. A concern of risk should not prevent mandated reporters from reporting maltreatment, but the reporting should be done with care, fully informing CPS or law enforcement of the concern about the child's safety. In some cases the mandated reporter is a therapist who has a relationship with the child and parent. The therapist, who has talked to the parent about the mandate to report suspected maltreatment as part of the intake interview, may be able to discuss the report with the parent and make that report together. In other cases, the parent may be angry over the report regardless of the legal mandate and may break engagement with the therapist. The therapeutic relationship can be repaired with careful work and a nonjudgmental view. If the mandated reporter is a teacher, it is critical to inform the school headmaster before making a report so that the teacher can be supported and advised. If the mandated reporter is a nurse or physician and the child is in a clinic or hospital, the medical professional will need to try to keep the child at the site until CPS can arrive to evaluate the safety risk. Making the mandated report can be complicated and must always be done with good clinical judgment and with a great attempt to be nonjudgmental toward the parent. All attempts should be made to avoid placing the child in a loyalty conflict between the parent and professional. The best-case scenario is for the report to be made and an immediate safety plan to be put in place without removal of the child from his or her family. Overall, mandated reporters would benefit from education on the reporting process, reporting procedures, child abuse signs and symptoms, and how to work collaboratively and effectively with CPS (Alvarez, Kenny, Donohue, & Carpin, 2004).

Significant research is being conducted to prevent maltreatment by working with families to reduce risk and increase the odds that maltreatment will never occur. We now turn to a review of the research-supported prevention programs that are being implemented.

Prevention of Child Maltreatment

Prevention programs are those that (a) are provided to a large portion of the population to reduce the risk of maltreatment or (b) target a clearly defined population of nonabusive families that are at risk of maltreatment. The Triple-P Positive Parenting Program (Sanders, 2008) is an example of a research supported universal prevention program that is supported by 30 years of development and research. Based on the premise that problematic parenting is more common than even child maltreatment, Triple-P has adopted a public health approach to reach large segments of the population and to remove the stigma of "an abuse program." Instead, Triple-P is disseminated as a parenting and family support program (Sanders, Prinz, & Shapiro, 2012).

The overarching goal of Triple-P is to prevent severe behavioral, emotional, and developmental problems in children and the maltreatment of children by enhancing the parent's knowledge, skills, and confidence (Sanders et al., 2012). The program, designed for parents of children and youth birth to age 16, includes five different levels of intervention. Level 1 involves media and communication in which parents are given information about parenting. Level 2 includes a one- to two-session intervention giving developmental information to parents of children with mild behavioral problems and 2-hour stand-alone large-group seminars on positive parenting. Level 3 targets parents of children with mild to moderate behavioral or emotional problems with a four-session skills training intervention. Level 4 is for parents with children who have severe behavioral and emotional difficulties and involves 8 to 10 sessions of individual or group parent training. Finally, Level 5 consists of behavioral family interventions for situations where parenting is complicated by other family issues such as marital conflict, stress, depression, or maltreatment.

Across a number of rigorous studies, Triple-P has been shown to reduce children's problem behavior and improve parenting skills (Nowak & Heinrichs, 2008; Sanders et al., 2008; Whittingham, Sofronoff, Sheffield, & Sanders, 2008). Most notably, a place randomization study was conducted across 18 counties in South Carolina. Nine of the counties received Triple-P and nine were comparison counties. Following 2.5 years of implementation, there were significantly fewer maltreatment cases, foster care placements, and hospital-treated maltreatment injuries in the intervention counties (Prinz, Sanders, Shapiro, Whitaker, & Lutzker, 2009).

The Nurse-Family Partnership (NFP; Olds, Henderson, Chamberlin, & Tatelbaum, 1986; Olds, Henderson, & Kitzman, 1994; Olds, 2006) is one of the best-known targeted preventions programs and is rated as well supported by research by the California Evidence-Based Clearinghouse for Child Welfare (www.cebc4cw.org). The program targets young mothers from a low socioeconomic level who are pregnant with their first child. Registered nurses make 60- to 90-minute home visits to mothers beginning during pregnancy (target is to start at 16 weeks) and continuing through the child's second birthday. Visits are weekly for the first month after intake and then every other week until the baby's birth. After the birth, visits are weekly for the first

six weeks of the baby's life and then every other week until the baby is 20 months of age. The last four visits occur monthly. The primary goals of the program are to improve pregnancy outcomes, improve child health, and enhance the parent's life-course development. Services are provided in the home and tap six domains: (a) personal health, (b) environmental health, (c) life-course development, (d) maternal role, (e) family and friends, and (f) health and human services. Nurses providing services participate in weekly clinical supervision with a senior nurse supervisor.

NFP has been subject to multiple randomized trials. Overall this program has shown favorable effects on health-care encounters for injuries or ingestions and substantiated abuse or neglect 15 years after program enrollment (Kitzman et al., 1997; Olds et al., 1997; Olds, Henderson, Tatelbaum, & Chamberlin, 1986; Zielinski, Eckenrode, & Olds, 2009).

Incredible Years (IY; Webster-Stratton & Reid, 2012) is a series of three separate, developmentally based curricula for parents, teachers, and children ages 4 to 8 years with the goal of promoting emotional and social competence and to prevent, reduce, and treat behavioral and emotional problems in young children. The program has been recognized by the California Evidence-Based Clearinghouse for Child Welfare (www.cebc4cw.org) as evidence-based for prevention of child maltreatment, but it is also relevant for helping parents who have already engaged in maltreatment. Adaptations have been developed for this population (Webster-Stratton & Reid, 2010).

IY is a group-based program that makes use of interactive discussion and video modeling. An emphasis is on the parent's strengths rather than deficits. The four versions of the Basic Parent Program are (a) infants (0–1 year), (b) toddlers (1–3 years), (c) preschoolers (3–5 years), and (d) school age (6–8 and 9–12). Topics covered in the 14- to 24-week program include strengthening the parent–child relationship, predictable routines, limit setting, nonpunitive discipline, and problem-solving. The 18- to 22-week Child Training Program (Dinosaur Social Skills and Problem-Solving) teaches management of emotions (e.g., emotion regulation and talking about feelings), social skills (e.g., cooperating with others and making friends), problem-solving, and classroom behavior (e.g., following rules; Webster-Stratton & Reid, 2012).

Multiple randomized controlled trials by the developer and independent researchers support the effectiveness of IY. IY parents showed improvements in parenting competencies (e.g., harsh parenting), and children showed improvements in social and emotional competence and child behavior problems (Webster-Stratton & Reid, 2010).

In summary, many programs are being implemented to prevent child maltreatment. Several of these programs (described here) have been rigorously evaluated and have proven effective. The program that is the best fit for providers looking to implement prevention depends on the population to be served and the age of the children. Triple-P, developed in Australia and tested in the United States and other countries, provides parent training to the general population and reduces risk for maltreatment. NFP targets young mothers having their first child and has been shown to reduce risk of maltreatment. IY also targets younger children and their parents and has been shown to improve parenting and child behavior. Noteworthy is an adaptation of this intervention for families who have already maltreated their child. The fact that the evidence base for prevention programs is growing is quite encouraging. Policymakers and funders should keep their attention closely focused on the research-supported programs. Next we move to a review of interventions for families that have already abused or neglected their child. In this section we follow the evidence base for treatments.

Interventions for Families That Have Maltreated Their Child

Families that come under CPS supervision due to abusing or neglecting a child generally must undergo some type of treatment. Their treatment needs and requirements will vary according to the severity and complexity of problems they are experiencing (i.e., whether they are a repeat family to CPS, what level of risk they are experiencing, and whether their children are removed from their home). In this section we begin by discussing the issue of engaging families who are not voluntarily entering treatment and as such are in the midst of an adversarial process. Engagement must occur for treatment to begin. Next, we review research-supported treatments for families who have already maltreated their child. The main goal is to prevent the recurrence of maltreatment and to reduce behavioral and mental health difficulties. There are many mental health treatments on the market, but only a few have been evaluated with rigorous research. These treatments are the focus of this section.

Engaging Families That Are in an Adversarial Position

Regardless of the type of treatment offered, the family must be engaged in the process to benefit.

Although the adversarial process that can happen between families and CPS has not been the subject of published empirical studies, it is quite common for families who come under the guidance of CPS to be unhappy with this turn of events. The unhappiness may be manifested through a number of behaviors that can lead to a crisis situation, such as refusal to answer the door or phone, running away from CPS (and sometimes the therapist) and hiding, verbal aggression, and physical aggression. Families that have been supervised by CPS in the past may have found that aggressive behaviors keep caseworkers and therapists at bay until enough time passes that the case is closed. For other families, behaviors that on the face are uncooperative can lead to removal of the child. The decision on managing the parent's reaction may be specific to a particular agency or social worker.

Through Multisystemic Therapy for Child Abuse and Neglect (MST-CAN; reviewed later), we have found that the therapist can play a significant role in facilitating a positive relationship between the family and CPS. At the start of the case it is critical to approach the family in a one-down, nonjudgmental way. In addition, making clear to the family that the therapist must earn their trust instead of expecting and assuming automatic trust is critical. Once the family is able to see that the therapist is there to help them with their relationship with CPS, it is possible to discuss "impression management" or how to interact with CPS so that the caseworker has a more positive feeling about the parent. On the other side of the coin, the therapist must keep a strengths-based stance about the family with CPS and never engage in any negative talk about one side or the other.

It should also be noted that once a family is engaged in treatment, this engagement may wax and wane depending on stressors or changes in a situation, especially if the family is dealing with very complicated mental health or clinical issues. A breach in engagement does not mean the family does not want help or that treatment is impossible. A breach in engagement can be a great learning and teaching opportunity. Parents can learn from the therapist or social worker ways to manage an interpersonal relationship without conflict by the way the professional handles the situation. In MST-CAN programs we have found that the majority of breaches in engagement are reparable and that families can resume their treatment rapidly and get back to work on their desired outcomes.

Interventions for Families with Young Children

PARENT–CHILD INTERACTION THERAPY

Parent–Child Interaction Therapy (PCIT), developed as a treatment for children ages 2 to 7 with emotional and behavioral disorders, targets improving the quality of the parent–child relationship and changing parent–child interaction patterns (Eyberg & Robinson, 1982). PCIT is rated as well supported by research by the California Evidence-Based Clearinghouse for Child Welfare. There are three parts to PCIT: (a) assessment of child functioning and parent interaction, (b) child-directed interaction (CDI), and (c) parent-directed interaction (PDI).

In the assessment phase, through interview and behavioral observation, the therapist works to identify the current salient problem the child is experiencing and the context surrounding this behavior. An understanding of parent behaviors that maintain or escalate the child's misbehavior and family strengths that can be enhanced are critical to developing focused treatment goals.

Once treatment goals are set, parents learn to follow their child's lead in play through CDI. Through active therapist coaching, the parent learns to give positive attention to desired behaviors and to avoid statements, commands, and questions that give attention to negative behaviors. Parents learn to ignore negative attention seeking behaviors such as whining or yelling and immediately reinforce when the child stops and is showing desired behavior. All of this learning takes place in the context of play activities. The CDI phase continues until parents have mastered the CDI skills (Niec, Eyberg, & Chase, 2012).

In the next phase, PDI, parents learn skills to lead and direct their child's behavior. These skills include giving direct, age-appropriate, positively stated commands and explaining a command before it is given or after it is obeyed. Parents are taught to give very specific praise when their child obeys. If the child does not obey, the parent is taught to implement a time-out sequence. The completion of PCIT relates to performance and meeting goals rather than the passage of a certain time period (Niec et al., 2012).

PCIT has been evaluated across 30 controlled trials and has shown more positive parental attitudes toward the child, reductions in child behavior problems, and parent self-report improvement in psychopathology and personal distress (Hembree-Kigin & McNeil, 1995). In recent years PCIT has been applied to families who have physically abused a child in the family (Urquiza & McNeil, 1996; also see http://pcit.ucdavis.edu). A preliminary study of pre- and post-treatment functioning indicated decreases in child behavior problems, parental stress, and abuse risk (Timmer, Urquiza, Zebell, & McGrath, 2005). Further work with more rigorous (random assignment) methodology and parents with multiple abuse reports showed at a median follow-up of 850 days, 19% of parents assigned to PCIT had a rereport for physical abuse compared with 49% of parents assigned to the standard community group (Chaffin et al., 2004).

SAFECARE

Rated as research supported by the California Evidence-Based Clearinghouse for Child Welfare, SafeCare is a treatment model for families of children ages zero to 5 where the parent is at risk of or has been reported for neglect. With services provided in the home, SafeCare focuses on child safety, health, parent–child interactions, and parenting skills modules. The approach is very structured and follows three steps in each module: (a) assessment, (b) four to five training sessions to teach new skills, and (c) posttraining assessment (Edwards-Gaura, Whitaker, Lutzker, Self-Brown, & Lewis, 2012).

The flagship study supporting SafeCare is a quasi-experimental study comparing habitually maltreating families referred by CPS to matched comparison families that were participating in a family preservation program. Three years after the intervention, SafeCare families had significantly lower recidivism rates, 15% versus 44% in the comparison group (Gershater-Molko, Lutzker, & Wesch, 2002). Recently, a randomized trial was completed in Oklahoma (Chaffin, Hecht, Bard, Silovsky, & Beasley, 2012). In this study, a statewide comparative effectiveness trial, the six service regions of Oklahoma were matched and randomized to SafeCare or Services As Usual, a six-month intensive family preservation program with a case management focus. Over 2,100 families were enrolled in the study and were followed for up to seven years postenrollment. SafeCare reduced child maltreatment recidivism by about 26% relative to Service as Usual.

Interventions for Families with School Age or Older Children

TRAUMA FOCUSED COGNITIVE BEHAVIORAL THERAPY

Trauma focused cognitive behavioral therapy (TFCBT; Cohen, Mannarino, & Deblinger, 2006) is recognized as the gold standard for treating traumatized children ages 3 to 18 and their nonoffending parents. The treatment is rated as well supported with research by the California Evidence-Based

Clearinghouse for Child Welfare. The major goal of TFCBT is to treat children who are experiencing emotional or behavioral difficulties related to a traumatic life event. Most of the studies evaluating TFCBT address PTSD, depression, shame, and behavioral difficulties that result from child sexual abuse. More recently the model has been extended to treat trauma symptoms of children who have experienced physical abuse or domestic violence (Rubin, 2012).

TFCBT is a very structured treatment that is administered across eight modules:

1. psychoeducation and parenting skills
2. relaxation (focused breathing, relaxation, thought stopping
3. affective expression and regulation (identifying and expressing emotions, self-soothing)
4. cognitive coping and processing (understanding the relationship between thoughts, feelings, behavior
5. trauma narrative development and processing (gradual exposure; i.e., child's version of imaginal exposure, identifying, challenging, and correcting unhelpful thinking)
6. in vivo gradual exposure (exposure to harmless trauma reminders in the child's environment)
7. conjoint child–parent sessions (psychoeducation, sharing the trauma narrative, anxiety management, and correction of unhelpful thinking)
8. enhancing safety and future development (personal safety skills and healthy sexuality/interpersonal relationships; encouraging the use of skills learned to manage future stressors and/or trauma reminders).

The treatment consists of 12 to 18 sessions each 30 to 45 minutes long and is meant to be conducted as a parallel process starting with individual sessions for children and nonoffending parents (or another supportive person). Although children are not engaging in directly processing memories about their traumatic event early in treatment, they are gradually being exposed to those memories. The early part of treatment helps children build a repertoire of skills for coping that can aid them in managing the direct processing of the event(s) they experienced. After much child and adult individual preparation, joint parent–child sessions occur in which the traumatic event is shared and processed. Treatment is concluded with planning for future safety and creating awareness of situations that might produce anxiety (i.e., trauma reminders) and how to manage such situations (Cohen et al., 2006).

TFCBT has been well supported for reducing posttraumatic symptoms with sexually abused children through multiple randomized trials (Cohen, Deblinger, Mannarino, & Steer, 2004; Cohen & Mannarino, 1996; Cohen, Mannarino, & Knudsen, 2005; Deblinger, Lippman, & Steer, 1996; Deblinger, Mannarino, Cohen, & Steer, 2006; Deblinger, Stauffer, & Steer, 2001; King et al., 2000). More recently a study with sexually exploited Congolese girls in a war context also supported the effectiveness of TFCBT in reducing PTSD symptoms (O'Callaghan, McMullen, Shannon, Rafferty, & Black, 2013). Finally, TFCBT has also been shown effective for reducing trauma symptoms among children exposed to intimate partner violence (Cohen, Mannarino, & Iyengar, 2011).

MULTISYSTEMIC THERAPY FOR CHILD ABUSE AND NEGLECT

Some families who come under the guidance of CPS are experiencing much more than child trauma symptoms or parenting issues. These multineed families are at high risk of their children being placed out of the home. If the complex issues across multiple systems are not addressed, these children will not be able to grow up in their family home.

Multisystemic Therapy for Child Abuse and Neglect (MST-CAN; Swenson, Schaeffer, Henggeler, Faldowski, & Mayhew, 2010) based on standard multisystemic therapy (Henggeler, Schoenwald, Borduin, Rowland, & Cunningham, 2009) was developed to meet the needs of families with very serious and complex needs. Rated as supported by research by the California Evidence-Based Clearinghouse for Child Welfare, the overarching goals of MST-CAN are to keep families together, assure that children are safe, prevent further abuse or neglect, reduce adult and child mental health difficulties, and increase natural social supports.

Families that qualify for MST-CAN programs are those with an indicated case for physical abuse or neglect no more than 180 days prior to referral and the children who experienced the maltreatment are in the age range of 6 to 17. Treatment is conducted in the home or community at times convenient to families, and a 24 hour a day, 7 days a week on-call service is in place to help manage crises. Treatment is provided by a clinical team of three therapists, a case manager, and supervisor. Each therapist carries a caseload of up to four families so that families can receive a minimum of three sessions per week.

MST-CAN follows an analytic process for intervention development and implementation. The purpose of assessment is to understand the factors driving a behavior of concern. For example, a therapist may discover that the driving factor for a mother disengaging from parenting is that when she tries to set rules the child makes statements that are trauma reminders of past domestic violence. This trauma cue leads her to shut down and not parent, which makes her appear to be neglecting her child. In such a case, the intervention would not be to teach parenting skills but to address the trauma symptoms to break the link between statements that remind her of trauma and anxiety. After completion of the initial intake, attaining desired outcomes from all in the ecology, and setting the treatment goals, the first step is to complete the "fit" assessment, the assessment of drivers of the target behavior. Once the drivers or fit factors are understood, evidence-based treatments are applied to those drivers. Treatment strategies used for all families in the MST-CAN model include

1. Safety planning—Each family completes a safety plan that is specific to the current risks early in treatment. Weekly safety assessments are conducted for the first month and as needed after that.

2. The MST-CAN team works closely with CPS, often including caseworkers in family sessions and considering them a valuable part of the team. Doing so demands a shared responsibility but also brings everyone together to implement consistent treatment strategies.

3. Each family completes a clarification process (Lipovsky, Swenson, Ralston, & Saunders, 1998) through which the parent addresses cognitions about the abuse or neglect incident and shows acceptance of responsibility and apology through development of a letter to the family and the reading of this letter in a family meeting.

Treatment strategies used on an as needed basis (i.e., when the focus of the treatment is a fit factor for the target behavior—e.g., anger management) include

1. Functional analysis for cases of physical abuse or ongoing family conflict to understand the sequences of events and where the interactions take a turn towards physical or verbal aggression. Interventions can be put in place when triggers for aggression are occurring to de-escalate the child or parents (Kolko & Swenson, 2002).

2. Cognitive behavioral treatment for anger management (e.g., Feindler, Ecton, Kingsley, & Dubey, 1986) is used when low skills in managing anger are evident for the child or parent.

3. Behavioral family treatment is used with families who have difficulty with communication and problem-solving (Robin, Bedway, & Gilroy, 1994).

4. Prolonged exposure (Foa & Rothbaum, 1998) is used to treat parents who are experiencing PTSD.

5. Reinforcement-based therapy (Tuten, Jones, Schaeffer, Wong, & Stitzer, 2012) is a behavioral treatment provided to parents for whom substance abuse is part of the child protection difficulty (Swenson & Schaeffer, 2012).

The structure of a team with low caseloads allows treatment of all family members and prevents families from having uncoordinated services brokered with many providers. Such a situation would place the family at risk of having their child removed as it is virtually impossible for a family to visit many providers weekly. In addition, low coordination and communication among service providers places caseworkers in a situation of not knowing how the family is doing yet they are solely responsible for making sure the child is safe. The MST-CAN therapist reports the family's progress on safety to the caseworker on at least a weekly basis, and joint sessions are held with the family as needed to emphasize the importance of adhering to interventions targeting safety concerns. The MST-CAN relationship with CPS can help a family manage and reduce safety risks rather than an automatic removal when safety risk is increased (Swenson & Schaeffer, 2012).

MST-CAN has been evaluated across two randomized trials with rigorous comparison groups (Brunk, Henggeler, & Whelan, 1987; Swenson et al., 2010). Findings support MST-CAN's effectiveness for reducing children's internalizing problems (dissociation, PTSD, internalizing and total symptoms of the Child Behavior Checklist), out-of-home placements, and, for those who were placed, changes in placement. With regard to caregivers, MST-CAN was more effective than enhanced outpatient treatment for reducing caregiver psychiatric distress and parenting associated with maltreatment (i.e., minor assault, severe assault, neglect, psychological aggression) and in reducing a decline in nonviolent discipline. MST-CAN was significantly more effective at increasing caregiver social support, and caregivers indicated greater treatment satisfaction. Fewer MST-CAN adolescents experienced an incident of re-abuse, but base rates were low and the difference was not statistically significant. Through these two randomized trials, MST-CAN has gathered support as an evidence-based treatment for families where child abuse and neglect occurs and where families are experiencing multiple and serious clinical needs.

MULTISYSTEMIC THERAPY—BUILDING STRONGER FAMILIES

Given that parental substance abuse is a leading determinant of child maltreatment, especially neglect (National Center on Addiction and Substance Abuse, 1999) and that substance abuse is involved in a growing number of CPS cases (Besinger, Garland, Litrownik, & Landsverk, 1999) yet parents rarely receive treatment (Child Welfare League of America, 1997), a special focus on substance abuse is sorely needed at this time. To address the gap in service for this co-occurring maltreatment and parental substance abuse, a model that includes MST-CAN and reinforcement-based therapy (RBT) called Multisystemic Therapy—Building Stronger Families (MST-BSF) was developed and piloted in the state of Connecticut for the last 10 years (Swenson et al., 2009; Schaeffer, Swenson, Tuerk, & Henggeler, 2013). At present this model is the subject of a randomized trial funded by the National Institute on Drug Abuse.

The MST-BSF model is implemented similarly to MST-CAN but is considered a special substance abuse program so all parents are those whose indicated case with Child Protection involves substance abuse. RBT interventions are provided in individual sessions with parents continuously and intensively throughout treatment with a primary goal of attaining sobriety and supporting activities to generalize and sustain the outcomes. In a recent study using a quasi-experimental design, mothers that received MST-BSF showed significant reductions in alcohol use, drug use, depression, and psychological aggression toward their child. Youth showed significant reductions in anxiety. Compared to families that received comprehensive community services, MST-BSF mothers were three times less likely to have another substantiated incident of maltreatment over a follow-up period of 24 months postreferral. The overall number of substantiated reabuse incidents in this same time frame were also significantly lower for MST-BSF families. Youth that received MST-BSF spent significantly fewer days placed out of the home (Schaeffer et al., 2013).

Summary and Conclusions

Despite significant progress on defining abuse, developing systems to protect children, and increasing the evidence base on prevention and intervention programs, annually child maltreatment continues to impact millions of children worldwide, leaving many with significant challenges in physical and mental health. Some areas in the field are not as advanced as others. For example, at this point in time we still lack uniform definitions of abuse or neglect that would allow us to monitor rates appropriately. With regard to actual child safety, some countries still have no reporting laws and no formal child protection system. Growth is still needed in the basic infrastructure for protecting children worldwide.

Much progress has been made over just the last 10 years in evaluating intervention and treatment programs to determine those that are judged to be effective from a scientific perspective. We now have a range of evidence-based interventions that meet the needs of people in a variety of situations. In the prevention area, Triple-P can be offered to families who have never been reported for abuse but who are in the general population with a likelihood that this program will prevent a future occurrence of maltreatment. For pregnant women who are experiencing risk factors or abuse potential, the work carried out through the Family Nurse Partnership may prevent that family from being one that comes through CPS for maltreatment. For families with young children who are at risk of abuse because of poor parenting and child behavior problems, the IY program is a go-to intervention to improve parenting and child behavior problems, decreasing the risk of maltreatment.

Once a family has been reported for abuse and comes under the guidance of CPS, several evidence-based programs can be used to solve the problems that are occurring and prevent a recurrence of abuse. The intervention to be recommended depends on the age of the child and the level of complexity of the case. PCIT has been proven effective with families who have young children who are experiencing physical abuse. SafeCare has proven effective for families with young children who are experiencing neglect. TFCBT is the gold standard for treating children across a large age range who have experienced sexual abuse or domestic violence and are suffering from trauma-related symptoms. In cases where families have children age 6 and above and also have very complex and long-term issues related to physical abuse and/or neglect and parent and child mental health, MST-CAN is a treatment that has proven effective for keeping families together, preventing re-abuse, and improving mental health functioning. For the complex multineed families that have co-occurring child maltreatment and parental substance abuse, MST-BSF has shown promise for effectively treating these special issues.

Given the current knowledge about what works, the obvious question is: Why are these prevention programs and treatments not so widespread that they blanket every state in the United States and every country in the world? Indeed, we have made progress in dissemination through efforts of agencies such as the Substance Abuse and Mental Health Services Administration in the United States that has helped disseminate TFCBT, but we still have much work to do. Policymakers have a grand task ahead to shift priorities to children, safety, and wellness, and agencies must develop funding for programs that work. Doing so may require shifting funds from nonworking programs. Perhaps the way to begin the change that needs to take place to eliminate child maltreatment and help aid the recovery of those who have already experienced maltreatment in their lives is for those very consumers to demand nothing less than the gold standard, nothing less than programs that are scientifically supported.

Disclosures

Cynthia Cupit Swenson is a consultant in the development of MST-CAN programs through MST Services, LLC, which has the exclusive licensing agreement through the Medical University of South Carolina for the dissemination of MST technology.

Acknowledgment

This publication was supported by grant funding through the National Institute on Drug Abuse, 5R01DA029726-05 and National Institute of Mental Health, RO1MH60663 (PI: Swenson) and the Annie E. Casey Foundation.

References

Abrahams, N., Casey, K., & Daro, D. (1992). Teachers' knowledge, attitudes and beliefs about child abuse and its prevention. *Child Abuse & Neglect*, 16, 229–238.

Alvarez, K. M., Donohue, B., Kenny, M. S., Cavanagh, N., & Romero, V. (2005). The process and consequences of reporting child maltreatment: A brief overview for professionals in the mental health field. *Aggression and Violent Behavior*, 10, 311–331. doi:10.1016/j.avb.2004.03.001

Alvarez, K. M., Kenny, M. C., Donohue, B., & Carpin, K. M. (2004). Why are professionals failing to initiate mandate reports of child maltreatment, and are there any empirically based training programs to assist professionals in the reporting process? *Aggression and Violent Behavior*, 9, 563–578.

Besinger, B. A., Garland, A. F., Litrownik, A. J., & Landsverk, J. A. (1999). Caregiver substance abuse among maltreated children placed in out-of-home care. *Child Welfare League of America*, 78, 221–239.

Brunk, M., Henggeler, S. W., & Whelan, J. P. (1987). Comparison of multisystemic therapy and parent training in the brief treatment of child abuse and neglect. *Journal of Consulting and Clinical Psychology*, 55, 171–178. doi:10.1037/0022–006X.55.2.171

Chaffin, M., Hecht, D., Bard, D., Silovsky, J. F., & Beasley, W. H. (2012). A statewide trial of the SafeCare home-based services model with parents in child protective services. *Pediatrics*, 129, 509–515.

Chaffin, M., Silovsky, J. F., Funderburk, B., Valle, L. A., Brestan, E. V., Balachova, T., ... Bonner, B.L. (2004). Parent–Child Interaction Therapy with physically abusive parents: Efficacy for reducing future abuse reports. *Journal of Consulting and Clinical Psychology*, 72, 500–510.

Chapman, D., Whitfield, C., Felitti, V., Dube, S., Edwards, V., & Anda, R. (2004). Adverse childhood experiences and the risk of depressive disorders in adulthood. *Journal of Affective Disorders*, 82, 217–225.

Child Welfare Information Gateway. (2013). *What is child abuse and neglect? Recognizing the signs and symptoms*. Washington, DC: US Department of Health and Human Services, Children's Bureau. www.childwelfare.gov/pubs/factsheets/whatiscan.cfm

Child Welfare Information Gateway. (2014). *Definitions of child abuse and neglect*. Washington, DC: US Department of Health and Human Services, Children's Bureau. https://www.childwelfare.gov/systemwide/laws_policies/statutes/define.cfm

Child Welfare League of America. (1997). *Alcohol and other drug survey of state child welfare agencies*. Washington, DC: Author.

Cohen, J. A., Deblinger, E., Mannarino, A. P., & Steer, R. (2004). A multi-site randomized controlled trial for children with sexual abuse-related PTSD symptoms. *Journal of the American Academy of Child & Adolescent Psychiatry*, 43, 393–402.

Cohen, J. A., & Mannarino, A. P. (1996). A treatment outcome study for sexually abused preschool children: Initial findings. *Journal of the American Academy of Child & Adolescent Psychiatry*, 35, 42–50.

Cohen, J. A., Mannarino, A. P., & Deblinger, E. (2006). *Treating trauma and traumatic grief in children and adolescents*. New York: Guilford Press.

Cohen, J. A., Mannarino, A. P., & Iyengar, S. (2011). Community treatment of posttraumatic stress disorder for children exposed to intimate partner violence. *Archives of Pediatrics & Adolescent Medicine*, 165(1), 16–21.

Cohen, J. A., Mannarino, A. P., & Knudsen K. (2005). Treating sexually abused children: One year follow-up of a randomized controlled trial. *Child Abuse & Neglect*, 29, 135–146.

Cunningham, P. B., Swenson, C. C., & Henggeler, S. W. (1997). Children and adolescents. In N. K. Worley (Ed.), *Mental health nursing in the community* (pp. 303-321). New York: Mosby.

Cyr, C., Euser, E. M., Bakermans-Kranenburg, M. J., & Van Ijzendoorn, M. H. (2010). Attachment security and disorganization in maltreating and high-risk families: A series of meta-analyses. *Development and Psychopathology*, 22, 87–108.

Deblinger, E., Lippmann, J., & Steer, R. (1996). Sexually abused children suffering posttraumatic stress symptoms: Initial treatment outcome findings. *Child Maltreatment*, 1, 310–321.

Deblinger, E., Mannarino, A. P., Cohen, J. A., & Steer, R. A. (2006). A follow-up study of a multi-site, randomized controlled trial for children with sexual abuse-related PTSD symptoms. *Journal of the American Academy of Child & Adolescent Psychiatry*, 45, 1474–1484.

Deblinger, E., Stauffer, L. B., & Steer, R. (2001). Comparative efficacies of supportive and cognitive behavioral group therapies for young children who have been sexually abused and their nonoffending mothers. *Child Maltreatment*, 6, 332–343.

Dube, S. R., Anda, R. F., Felitti, V. J., Chapman, D. F., Williamson, D. F., & Giles, W. H. (2001). Childhood abuse, household dysfunction, and the risk of attempted suicide throughout the lifespan: Findings from the Adverse Childhood Experiences Study. *Journal of the American Medical Association, 286,* 3089–3096.

Edwards-Gaura, A., Whitaker, D. J., Lutzker, J. R., Self-Brown, S., & Lewis, E. (2012). Application of an evidence-based program to prevent child maltreatment. In A. Rubin (Ed.), *Clinician's guide to evidence-based practice: Programs and interventions for maltreated children and families at risk* (pp. 259–272). Hoboken, NJ: John Wiley.

Eyberg, S. M., & Robinson, E. A. (1982). Parent–Child Interaction Training: Effect on family functioning. *Journal of Clinical Child Psychology, 11,* 130–137.

Fang, X., Brown, D. S., Florence, C. S., & Mercy, J. A. (2012). The economic burden of child maltreatment in the United States and implications for prevention. *Child Abuse & Neglect, 26,* 156–165.

Feindler, E. L., Ecton, R. B., Kingsley, D., & Dubey, D. R. (1986). Group anger-control training for institutionalized psychiatric male adolescents. *Behavior Therapy, 17,* 109–123. doi:10.1016/S0005-7894(86)80079-X

Felitti, V. J., Anda, R. F., Nordenberg, D., Williamson, D. F., Spitz, A. M., Edwards, V., . . . Marks, J. S. (1998). Relationships of childhood abuse and household dysfunction to many of the leading causes of death in adults: The Adverse Childhood Experiences (ACE) study. *American Journal of Preventive Medicine, 14,* 245–258.

Foa, E. B., & Rothbaum, B. O. (1998). *Treating the trauma of rape: Cognitive behavioral therapy for PTSD.* New York: Guilford Press.

Gershater-Molko, R., Lutzker, J., & Wesch, D. (2002). Using recidivism to evaluate project SafeCare: Teaching bonding, safety, and health care skills to parents. *Child Maltreatment, 7,* 277–285.

Gilbert, R., Widom, C. S., Browne, K., Fergusson, D., Webb, E., & Janson, S. (2009). Burden and consequences of child maltreatment in high-income countries. *Lancet, 373,* 68–81.

Hembree-Kigin, T., & McNeil, C. B. (1995). *Parent–Child Interaction Therapy.* New York: Plenum.

Henggeler, S. W., Schoenwald, S. K., Borduin, C. M., Rowland, M. D., & Cunningham, P. B. (2009). *Multisystemic therapy for antisocial behavior in children and Adolescents* (2nd ed.). New York: Guilford Press.

Hinson, J., & Fossey, R. (2000). Child abuse: What teachers in the '90s know, think, and do. *Journal of Education for Students Placed at Risk, 5,* 251–266.

Kenny, M. C. (2001). Child abuse reporting: Teachers' perceived deterrents. *Child Abuse & Neglect, 25,* 81–92.

Kim, J., Cicchetti, D., Rogosch, F. A., & Manly, J. T. (2009). Child maltreatment and trajectories of personality and behavioral functioning: Implications for the development of personality disorder. *Development and Psychopathology, 21,* 889–912.

King, N. J., Tonge, B. J., Mullen, P., Myerson, N., Heyne, D., Rollings, S., . . . Ollendick, T. H. (2000). Treating sexually abused children with posttraumatic stress symptoms: A randomized clinical trial. *Journal of the American Academy of Child & Adolescent Psychiatry, 39,* 1347–1355.

Kitzman, H., Olds, D. L., Henderson, C. R., Jr., Hanks, C., Cole, R., Tatelbaum, R., . . . Barnard, K. (1997). Effect of prenatal and infancy home visitation by nurses on pregnancy outcomes, childhood injuries, and repeated childbearing. A randomized controlled trial. *Journal of the American Medical Association, 278,* 644–652.

Kolko, D. J., & Swenson, C. C. (2002). *Assessing and treating physically abused children and their families: A cognitive-behavioral approach.* Thousand Oaks, CA: SAGE.

Leeb, R. T., Paulozzi, L., Melanson, C., Simon, T., & Arias, I. (2008). Child maltreatment surveillance: Uniform definitions for public health and recommended data elements, version 1.0. Atlanta: Centers for Disease Control and Prevention, National Center for Injury Prevention and Control. Available from: http://www.cdc.gov/violenceprevention/pdf/cm_surveillance-a.pdf

Lipovsky, J. A., Swenson, C. C., Ralston, M. E., & Saunders, B. E. (1998). The abuse clarification process in the treatment of intrafamilial child abuse. *Child Abuse & Neglect, 22,* 729–741. doi:10.1016/S0145-2134(98)00051-9

National Center on Addiction and Substance Abuse of Columbia University. (1999). *No safe haven: Children of substance abusing parents.* New York: Author.

Niec, L. N., Eyberg, S., & Chase, R. M. (2012). Parent–Child Interaction Therapy: Implementing and sustaining a treatment program for families of young children with disruptive behavior disorders. In A. Rubin (Ed.), *Clinician's guide to evidence-based practice: Programs and interventions for maltreated children and families at risk* (pp. 61–69). Hoboken, NJ: John Wiley.

Nowak, C., & Heinrichs, N. (2008). A comprehensive meta-analysis of Triple P—Positive Parenting Program using hierarchical linear modeling: Effectiveness and moderating variables. *Clinical Child and Family Psychology Review, 11,* 114–144.

O'Callaghan, P., McMullen, J., Shannon, C., Rafferty, H., & Black, A. (2013). A randomized controlled trial of Trauma-Focused Cognitive Behavioral Therapy for sexually exploited, war-affected Congolese girls. *Journal of the American Academy of Child & Adolescent Psychiatry, 52(4),* 359–369.

Olds, D. L. (2006). The nurse–family partnership: An evidence-based preventive intervention. *Infant Mental Health Journal, 27,* 5–25.

Olds, D. L., Eckenrode, J., Henderson, C. R., Jr., Kitzman, H., Powers, J., Cole, R., . . . Luckey, D. (1997). Long-term effects of home visitation on maternal life course and child abuse and neglect: Fifteen-year follow-up of a randomized trial. *Journal of the American Medical Association, 278,* 637–643.

Olds, D. L., Henderson, C. R., Jr., Chamberlin, R., & Tatelbaum, R. (1986). Preventing child abuse and neglect: A randomized trial of nurse home visitation. *Pediatrics, 78,* 65–78.

Olds, D. L., Henderson, C. R., Jr., & Kitzman, H. (1994). Does prenatal and infancy nurse home visitation have enduring effects on qualities of parental caregiving and child health at 25 to 50 months of life? *Pediatrics, 93,* 89–98.

Olds, D. L., Henderson, C. R., Jr., Tatelbaum, R., & Chamberlin, R. (1986). Improving the delivery of prenatal care and outcomes of pregnancy: A randomized trial of nurse home visitation. *Pediatrics, 77,* 16–28.

Prinz, R. J., Sanders, M. R., Shapiro, C. J., Whitaker, D. J., & Lutzker, J. R. (2009). Population-based prevention of child maltreatment: The U.S. Triple P system population trial. *Prevention Science, 10,* 1–12.

Robin, A. L., Bedway, M., & Gilroy, M. (1994). Problem solving communication training. In C. W. LeCroy (Ed.), *Handbook of child and adolescent treatment manuals* (pp. 92–125). New York: Lexington Books.

Rubin, A. (2012). Trauma-focused cognitive behavioral therapy for children. In A. Rubin (Ed.), *Clinician's guide to evidence-based practice: Programs and interventions for maltreated children and families at risk* (pp. 123–140). Hoboken, NJ: John Wiley.

Sanders, M. R. (2008). The Triple P—Positive Parenting Program as a public health approach to strengthening parenting. *Journal of Family Psychology*, 22, 506–517.

Sanders, M. R., Prinz, R. J., & Shapiro, C. (2012). Parenting and child maltreatment as public health issues: Implications from the Triple P system of intervention. In A. Rubin (Ed.), *Clinician's guide to evidence-based practice: Programs and interventions for maltreated children and families at risk* (pp. 297–312). Hoboken, NJ: John Wiley.

Sanders, M. R., Ralph, A., Sofronoff, K., Gardiner, P., Thompson, R., Dwyer, S., & Bidwell, K. (2008). Every family: A population approach to reducing behavioral and emotional problems in children making the transition to school. *Journal of Primary Prevention*, 29, 197–222.

Schaeffer, C., Swenson, C. C., Tuerk, E. H., & Henggeler, S. W. (2013). Comprehensive treatment for co-occurring child maltreatment and parental substance abuse: Outcomes from a 24-month pilot study of the MST-Building Stronger Families program. *Child Abuse & Neglect*, 37, 596–607. http://dx.doi.org/10.1016/j.chiabu.2013.04.004

Sedlak, A. J., & Broadhurst, D. D. (1996). *The Third National Incidence Study of Child Abuse and Neglect*. Washington, DC: US Department of Health and Human Services.

Sidebotham, P., & Heron, J. (2006). Child maltreatment in the children of the nineties: A cohort study of risk factors. *Child Abuse & Neglect*, 30, 497–522. doi:10.1016/j.chiabu.2005.1

Springer, K. W., Sheridan, J., Kuo, D., & Carnes, M. (2007). Long-term physical and mental health consequences of childhood physical abuse: Results from a large population-based sample of men and women, *Child Abuse & Neglect*, 31, 517–530. doi:10.1016/j.chiabu.2007.01.003

Swenson, C. C., & Schaeffer, C. (2012). Multisystemic therapy for child abuse and neglect. In A. Rubin (Ed.), *Clinician's guide to evidence-based practice: Programs and interventions for maltreated children and families at risk* (pp. 31–41). Hoboken, NJ: John Wiley.

Swenson, C. C., Schaeffer, C. M., Henggeler, S. W., Faldowski, R., & Mayhew, A. (2010). Multisystemic therapy for child abuse and neglect: A randomized effectiveness trial. *Journal of Family Psychology*, 24, 497–507.

Swenson, C. C., Schaeffer, C. M., Tuerk, E. H., Henggeler, S. W., Tuten, M., Panzarella, P., . . . Guillorn, A. (2009). Adapting multisystemic therapy for co-occurring child maltreatment and parental substance abuse: The Building Stronger Families project. *Emotional and Behavioral Disorders in Youth*, *17*, 3–8.

Timmer, S. G., Urquiza, A. J., Zebell, N. M., & McGrath, J. M. (2005). Parent–Child Interaction Therapy: Application to maltreating parent–child dyads. *Child Abuse & Neglect*, 29, 825–842.

Tuten, M., Jones, H. E., Schaeffer, C. M., Wong, C. J., & Stitzer, M. L. (2012). *Reinforcement-Based Treatment (RBT): A practical guide for the behavioral treatment of drug addiction*. Washington, DC: American Psychological Association.

United Nations Children's Fund. (2012). *Measuring and monitoring child protection systems: Proposed core indicators for the East Asia and Pacific Region*, Strengthening Child Protection Series 1. Bangkok: UNICEF East Asia and Pacific Regional Office.

Urquiza, A. J., & McNeil, C. B. (1996). Parent–Child Interaction Therapy: An intensive dyadic intervention for physically abusive families. *Child Maltreatment*, 1, 132–141.

Webster-Stratton, C., & Reid, M. J. (2010). The Incredible Years Program for children from infancy to preadolescence: Prevention and treatment of behavior problems. In R. Murrihy, A. Kidman, & T. Ollendick (Eds.), *Clinician's handbook for the assessment and treatment of conduct problems in youth* (pp. 117–138). Dordrecht: Springer Press.

Webster-Stratton, C., & Reid, M. J. (2012). The Incredible Years: Evidence-based parenting and child programs for families involved in the child welfare system. In A. Rubin (Ed.), *Clinician's guide to evidence-based practice: Programs and interventions for maltreated children and families at risk* (pp. 11–30). Hoboken, NJ: John Wiley.

Whittingham, K., Sofronoff, K., Sheffield, J., & Sanders, M. R. (2008). Stepping Stones Triple P: An RCT of a parenting program with parents of a child diagnosed with an autism spectrum disorder. *Journal of Abnormal Child Psychology*, 37(4), 469–480.

Wilderman, C., Emanuel, N., Leventhal, J. M., Putnam-Hornstein, E., Waldfogel, J., & Lee, H. (2014). The prevalence of confirmed maltreatment among US children, 2004 to 2011. *Journal of the American Medical Association Pediatrics*, *168*(8), 706–713.

Zellman, G. L., & Fair, C. C. (2002). *Preventing and reporting abuse*. In J. E. Myers, L. Berliner, J. Briere, C. T. Hendrix, C. Jenny, & T. A. Reid (Eds.), *The APSAC handbook on child maltreatment* (pp. 449–475). Thousand Oaks, CA: SAGE.

Zielinski, D. S., Eckenrode, J., & Olds, D. L. (2009). Nurse home visitation and the prevention of child maltreatment: Impact on the timing of official reports. *Developmental Psychopathology*, 21, 441–453.

CHAPTER 7

Bullying and Peer Aggression in Children and Adolescents: Implications for Suicide Management

Samantha Pflum, Peter Goldblum, Joyce Chu, *and* Bruce Bongar

Abstract

Crafting prevention and intervention strategies for peer bullying, aggression, and suicidality in youth is a complex, multifaceted task. Involvement in bullying and peer aggression is accompanied by numerous psychosocial consequences, including suicidal ideation and behavior. Care must be taken to examine this relationship in an objective, evidence-based manner, rather than overattributing or causally relating youth suicidality to bullying. Mental health professionals, medical providers, teachers, and school administrators are uniquely positioned to intervene in the risk factors that impact bullying and suicidality in youth. Taking an ecological systems perspective, this chapter will review extant efforts to ameliorate bullying, aggression, and suicidality in children and adolescents, with a focus on individual- and group-level protective factors that can facilitate positive health and academic outcomes. Recommendations for providers, educators, parents, policymakers, and researchers offer evidence-based guidance for future work in these domains.

Key Words: bullying, aggression, youth, suicidality, mental health, prevention, intervention

The prevalence and potential negative consequences of bullying have led to increased research on the correlates and consequences of bullying involvement. The pervasiveness of bullying among youth accentuates the significance of these problems. In considering the connection between bullying and suicidality, bullying can be both an overt and a covert influence on youth suicidal ideation and behavior. Severe bullying may be an immediate, overt precipitating factor in a psychiatric crisis, temporally preceding severe suicidal ideation, self-harm, and/or suicidal behavior. Bullying involvement may also be a covert or indirect factor in the development of internalizing or externalizing psychiatric symptoms.

Extant research indicates that an association with bullying in any capacity is associated with higher rates of suicidal ideation and behavior, with cross-sectional studies finding increased odds ratios of 1.4 to 10.0 (Kim & Leventhal, 2008). A nationally representative survey of US adolescents indicates that youth victimized by their peers were 2.4 times more likely to report suicidal ideation and 3.3 times more likely to report a suicide attempt than youth who denied bullying involvement (Kaminski & Fang, 2009). The relationship between bullying and suicidality is remarkably complex, involving numerous individual, interpersonal, community, and societal factors. Care must be taken neither to overattribute or underattribute youth suicidality to bullying involvement (Centers for Disease Control and Prevention [CDC], 2012; Goldblum et al., 2014).

This chapter will review the manifestation of aggression and bullying in youth and its multifaceted connection with suicidal ideation and behavior. This connection will be examined both in terms of present and long-term risk, incorporating the immediate and longitudinal consequences of bullying involvement. Protective factors and points of intervention for bullying and suicide among youth will also be reviewed, with a focus on extant research on suicide prevention/intervention strategies and school-based anti-bullying programs.

Bullying and Peer Aggression Among Youth
Bullying

Bullying describes repeated, purposeful, and hurtful actions directed toward another person who has difficulty defending him or herself (Olweus, 1993). A real or perceived imbalance of power is also involved in peer bullying. An imbalance of power exists when a bullying perpetrator or group of perpetrators have more physical, social, or intellectual power than the victim (Goldblum et al., 2014). Bullying can take many forms, including verbal harassment (e.g., name calling), physical aggression (e.g., kicking, pushing), spreading rumors, damaging personal property, and victimization based on cultural identity (e.g., race, ethnicity, sexual orientation, gender identity or expression). *Bullying* should not be used to describe repeated hurtful behavior that occurs between adults; the term *harassment* is more applicable to these adult relationships (Olweus & Limber, 2007; Arseneault, Bowes, & Shakoor, 2010).

Researchers commonly use the labels *victim, bully,* and *bully-victim* to refer to youth involved in bullying. Although these terms are used in the literature and when referencing research findings, they should not be used as labels for individual youth or in prevention work in schools or communities. These terms may incorrectly imply that aggressive behaviors or tendencies are fixed and unchangeable, and their use may be stigmatizing (Reiney & Limber, 2013). Additionally, using such labels implies that a youth's behavior does not change from one situation to the next and fails to capture the complexity of bullying involvement (Reiney & Limber, 2013).

Characteristics of bullies. Compared to uninvolved peers, bullies have been found to be more likely to exhibit symptoms of attention deficit hyperactivity disorder, oppositional defiant disorder, and conduct disorder (Kumpulainen, 2008; Copeland, Wolke, Angold, & Costello, 2013). Other research suggests bullies tend to be destructive, aggressive, impulsive, and physically strong, with low frustration tolerance and a strong dislike of school (Nansel et al., 2001; Copeland et al., 2013). In

regard to gender differences in bullying perpetration, the "gender paradox" proposes that females have lower overall rates of bullying and aggression but are at greater risk for negative psychosocial outcomes as a result of bullying involvement (Loeber & Keenan, 1994; Espelage, Mebane, & Swearer, 2004). Girls are often cited as using more relational aggression (e.g., excluding others from a peer group), although some studies report that girls who perpetrate bullying are also more angry, aggressive, impulsive, and dominating than their uninvolved female peers (Espelage et al., 2004). The presence of externalizing behaviors (e.g., temper tantrums, irritability, aggressiveness, disobedience) increases the likelihood of being a bully or a bully-victim among both girls and boys (Nansel et al., 2001; Kim, Leventhal, Koh, & Boyce, 2009; Luukkonen, Rasanen, Hakko, & Riala, 2010). Additionally, bullies are more likely to use alcohol and drugs, carry a weapon, demonstrate less empathy for others, and have a greater need for dominance as children (Copeland et al., 2013).

Characteristics of victims. Male and female victims of bullying have been identified as more quiet, insecure, tearful, physically weak, and submissive than their peers (Ball et al., 2008; Card & Hodges, 2008; Arseneault et al., 2010; Cooper, Clements, & Holt, 2012; Copeland et al., 2013). Most victimized children lack the social skills needed to establish peer group membership, such as humor, friendliness, and helpfulness (Crawford & Manassis, 2011). Cross-sectional studies suggest that children who are anxious, depressed, and/or learning disabled are at higher risk of being victims of bullying (Kumpulainen, Rasanen, & Puura, 2001; McCabe, Antony, Summerfeldt, Liss, & Swinson, 2003; Kumpulainen, 2008; Crawford & Manassis, 2011). As compared to male victims, girls who are victimized often endorse higher levels of depression (Espelage et al., 2004). Youth experiencing bullying report high levels of anxiety, and, conversely, anxious children report higher rates of peer victimization (Crawford & Manassis, 2011). Victims of bullying are three times more likely than nonvictims to have a formally diagnosed anxiety disorder. Bullying victimization is also significantly linked to generalized anxiety disorder and social phobia (Crawford & Manassis, 2011). Additionally, sexual and gender minority youth (lesbian, gay, bisexual, transgender, queer) are more likely than their heterosexual, cisgender, and gender-conforming peers to experience bullying and peer aggression. Victimization based on known or suspected sexual minority identity, in particular, is the most common form of bias-related violence (Herek, 1989; Pilkington & D'Augelli, 1995).

Characteristics of bully-victims. As a group, male and female bully-victims have been shown to exhibit more anxiety, as well as disobedient, hyperactive, impulsive, and aggressive behavior, and tend to be more psychologically troubled than their peers (Arseneault et al., 2010; Luukkonen et al., 2010; Copeland et al., 2013). Similar to bullies, bully-victims demonstrate greater symptoms of attention deficit hyperactivity disorder, oppositional defiant disorder, and conduct disorder than their uninvolved peers (Kumpulainen, 2008; Copeland et al., 2013). Bully-victim status in childhood has been found to predict both antisocial personality disorder and anxiety disorders in early adulthood (Kumpulainen, 2008; Copeland et al., 2013). Compared to uninvolved children, male bully-victims endorsing both bullying involvement and psychiatric symptoms had a five-fold risk for developing a psychiatric disorder in early adulthood (Kumpulainen, 2008). Additionally, bully-victims often endorse high rates of depression and behavioral disturbances (Kumpulainen, 2008). Those who are both bullies and victims are at highest risk for depression (Klomek, Marrocco, Kleinman, Schonfeld, & Gould, 2007), self-harm, suicidal ideation, and suicide attempts (Hepburn, Azrael, Molnar, & Miller, 2012). Longitudinally, bully-victims, as compared to victim-only youth, are significantly more likely to endorse symptoms of depression and agoraphobia in the later teenage years. Male bully-victims, in particular, are more likely than their victim-only or bully-only counterparts to endorse suicidality in adolescence (Copeland et al., 2013).

Bullying bystanders/witnesses. Witnessing the victimization of other students can account for elevated mental health risks above and beyond direct involvement as a bully, victim, or bully-victim (Rivers, Poteat, Noret, & Ashurst, 2009). Rivers and colleagues noted that observing peer bullying predicted greater mental health symptoms (i.e., substance use, depression, anxiety, obsessiveness, hostility), regardless of whether students were involved as victims. Among sexual minority (lesbian, gay, and bisexual [LGB]) youth, D'Augelli and colleagues (2002) suggested that those who observe fellow LGB students being victimized may experience many of the same psychological effects of direct victimization, particularly if they had been a victim in the past. As ethnic, sexual, and gender

minority youth often struggle to fit in with peers, observing the victimization of others can exacerbate anxiety related to their own perceived vulnerability. For some youth, observing the bullying of peers is a form of psychological re-victimization, which can increase mental health risk and substance use (Russell, Frantz, & Driscoll, 2001).

Peer Aggression

Peer aggression can be broadly defined as "acts intended or perceived as intended to cause harm" to another individual of the same age cohort (Finkelhor, Turner, & Hamby, 2012, p. 273). Most bullying involves peer aggression, be it through direct (e.g., pushing, hitting) or indirect (e. g., spreading rumors) means of harm. Research in this domain has typically defined acts of aggression in a broad manner, subsequently studying the contextual factors that make certain behaviors more or less harmful across various situations. Contextual features can include specific acts of aggression, peer status of the aggressors and victims, and the type of relationship in which the aggression takes place (Finkelhor et al., 2012).

The most serious forms of school-based peer aggression involve violence and crime. In 2011, students ages 12 to 18 were victims of over 1.2 million nonfatal victimizations at school, including physical assault, injury with a weapon, and property theft (Robers, Kemp, Truman, & Snyder, 2013). During this same year, about 7% of all US students in Grades 9 through 12 were threatened or injured with a weapon while on school property. Students may avoid school-related activities or certain areas of school campuses due to fear of violence and aggression; this avoidance is more common among female students, Black students, and Hispanic students. Rates of school-based violence and crime, as well as attacks by peers, significantly exceed rates outside of school, further reinforcing the fact that schools are not necessarily safe havens for instruction and learning (Robers et al., 2013).

Relational aggression is frequently observed among youth, particularly within friendships characterized by high levels of intimacy, self-disclosure, and interpersonal jealousy (Crick & Nelson, 2002; Holt & Espelage, 2007). This form of aggression is more covert, implicating "behavior which causes, or threatens to cause, damage to peer relationships, and particularly to friendship and acceptance" (Hawker & Boulton, 2000, p. 444; see also Crick et al., 1999; Crick & Nelson, 2002). Relational aggression may be more common among adolescent girls (Esplage et al., 2004; Holt & Espelage, 2007) and frequently extends to online methods of relational harm (Robers et al., 2013). In a report of indicators of school crime and safety, Robers and colleagues (2013) noted that more adolescent females than males (ages 12–18) were subjected to rumors, excluded from activities, and insulted by peers. Males, in contrast, were more likely to be both victims and perpetrators of physical aggression (i.e., being pushed, shoved, tripped, and spit on; Robers et al., 2013).

Epidemiology of Youth Suicide and Bullying

Suicide is the third leading cause of death among 15- to 24-year-olds in the United States and accounts for 20% of deaths among this age group each year (CDC, 2012). Recent findings indicate that nearly 16% of ninth to twelfth graders in US schools reported suicidal ideation, 12.8% had made a suicide plan, and 7.8% reported a suicide attempt in the past year (CDC, 2012; Murphy, Xu, & Kochanek, 2013). Among young adults ages 15 to 24, there are approximately 100 to 200 attempts for every completed suicide (CDC, 2012). Increases in rates of youth suicide, particularly beginning in 2003–2004 (the largest recent single-year change), have been attributed to the influence of social networking and pro-suicide websites, increased suicide rates of young US military members, and higher rates of untreated depression in the wake of "black box" warnings on antidepressants required by the FDA in 2004 (Cash & Bridge, 2009).

Bullying, like suicide, has been identified as a significant public health problem due to its pervasive detrimental effects (Hertz, Donato, & Wright, 2013). In 2011, 28% of students ages 12 to 18 reported that they had been bullied at school during the past year, and 9% had been cyberbullied via electronic communication (Robers et al., 2013). Among younger students in grades 3 through 12, 20% reported bullying involvement at least two to three times per month. More recent estimates of in-person bullying involvement among youth fall between 20% and 56%. Estimates of cyberbullying vary widely and are difficult to ascertain due to the diffuse and somewhat "anonymous" nature of online bullying (CDC, 2011; Borowsky, Taliaferro, & McMorris, 2013; Kowalski & Limber, 2013). Mapping these estimates onto a contemporary classroom of 30 students suggests that between 6 and 17 students are involved in bullying as a perpetrator, a victim, or a bully-victim at any given time (Hertz et al., 2013).

General Consequences of Bullying and Aggression Among Youth

One of the earliest examinations of the relationship between bullying and mental health symptoms in youth revealed that boys who had been bullied in middle school had significantly higher levels of depression and lower self-esteem at age 23 compared to boys who had not been bullied (Olweus, 1993). There appears to be a dose–response relationship between the frequency of childhood bullying and reported levels of psychiatric symptoms, with greater frequency of bullying being linked to exacerbations of psychiatric symptoms (Arseneault et al., 2010). Klomek and colleagues (2007) noted that more frequent involvement in bullying behavior (whether as a victim or a bully) is linked to increased rates of depression, suicidal ideation, and suicide attempts. Compared to uninvolved youth, adolescents who were "frequently" victims of bullying were seven times more likely to be depressed; infrequent victims of bullying were three times more likely to be depressed (Klomek et al. 2007, p. 43). A similar pattern has been noted for suicidal ideation and suicide attempts, with frequent bullying victims reporting the highest rates of suicidal ideation and attempts (Klomek et al., 2007). The strongest links between bullying, depression, and suicidality have been reported among bully-victims (Klomek et al., 2007; Hepburn et al., 2012).

In an examination of the psychological impact of bullying victimization, Hawker and Boulton (2000) conducted a meta-analysis of 23 cross-sectional studies published between 1978 and 1997. These studies included more than 5,000 youth and examined associations between peer victimization and psychosocial maladjustment. Victimization was classified into five categories (indirect, relational, physical, verbal, and generic), and psychosocial outcomes included depression, loneliness, generalized and social anxiety, and self-perceptions of global and social self-worth. Positive correlations were found between victimization, depression, loneliness, and anxiety. Negative correlations were found between victimization and self-perceptions of global and social self-worth. Out of all negative psychological outcomes, victimization was most strongly related to increases in depression and loneliness. Victims were consistently more likely than nonvictims to report symptoms of depression and suicidality. While bullying victims are generally anxious and have low self-esteem, they are even more likely to experience symptoms of dysphoria and loneliness that could place them at greater risk for suicidal ideation or behavior (Hawker & Boulton, 2000).

Bullying, Aggression, and Suicidality: Experiences of Diverse Youth
Ethnic Minorities

The study of youth suicide and bullying involves numerous cultural variations. Completed suicide currently occurs most frequently among White males, although rates are quickly growing among ethnic minority youth (Chu, Goldblum, Floyd, & Bongar, 2010; CDC, 2012). Among Native American and Alaskan Native youth, suicide is the second leading cause of death (CDC, 2012). Hispanic youth in the United States have higher rates of self-harm and suicide attempt than their non-Hispanic peers but are less likely to die by suicide than their White and Black counterparts (LeVasseur, Kelvin, & Grosskopf, 2013; Murphy et al., 2013). The intersection of bullying and suicide in ethnic minority populations is accompanied by distinctive risk factors and cultural themes, including cultural sanctions, idioms of distress, minority stress, and social discord (Chu et al., 2010). Chu and colleagues have articulated three theoretical principles into the Cultural Model for Suicide, a framework for enhancing understanding of culturally competent suicide assessment and prevention. These principles posit that "1) culture affects the types of stressors that lead to suicide; 2) cultural meanings associated with stressors and suicide affect the development of suicidal tendencies, one's threshold of tolerance for psychological pain, and subsequent suicidal acts; and 3) culture affects how suicidal thoughts, intent, plans, and attempts are expressed" (Chu et al., 2010, p. 25). Given the wide-reaching capacity of this model, it is reasonable to consider bullying involvement among ethnic minority youth a culturally relevant stressor.

Up to one-quarter of bullied youth are victimized due to their race or religion (Nansel et al., 2001). Some forms of bullying are directly related to societal-level stereotypes about particular group identities or intersectional identities, such as English proficiency or academic achievement (Tormala, Ivan, Floyd, & Beckum, 2014). Bullying has been found to be both intra- and interracial, and racial diversity of schools increases the overall prevalence of bullying among youth. Ethnic diversity, however, does not necessarily influence the occurrence of interracial bullying (Faris, 2006). While much depends on the specific contexts in which racial/ethnic bullying is measured, it appears that minorities tend to be involved in bullying more often than Whites (Faris, 2006). Ethnic-minority youth who bully others make larger gains in popularity than White students who perpetrate bullying (Faris, 2006). However, little consensus about the ethnic division of bullies, victims, and bully-victims exists, as differences in sampling and methodological approaches make direct comparisons of bullying across racial/ethnic groups difficult (Tormala et al., 2014).

Sexual Minorities

As a result of environmental stressors such as peer bullying, family rejection, poor health-care access, and community-based victimization, LGB youth are at particularly high risk for suicide. Despite variations in sampling approaches and definitions of constructs, several decades of research indicate that suicidal ideation, attempts, and completions are among the most concerning health disparities for the LGB population (Russell & Joyner, 2001; Poteat, Mereish, DiGiovanni, & Koenig, 2011; Cochran & Mays, 2013). Among LGB youth, the odds of attempting suicide are approximately two to seven times higher than the odds of suicide attempt among heterosexuals (King et al., 2008; Haas et al., 2010). There is an established correlation between discrimination, victimization, self-harm, suicidal ideation, and suicide attempts among LGB youth (Hershberger & D'Augelli, 1995; Poteat et al., 2011; Goldblum et al., 2012). Compared to victimization that is not bias based, homophobic victimization (based on sexual minority status) is associated with significantly higher levels of both suicidal ideation and attempts (Russell, Sinclair, Poteat, & Koenig, 2012). Although these results have been based primarily on cross-sectional studies, recent longitudinal findings offer prospective evidence of this relationship. Among diverse LGB youth, early reports of victimization predicted future suicidal ideation and deliberate self-harm (Liu & Mustanski, 2012). After suicide attempt history, victimization based on sexual minority status was the strongest predictor of self-injury (Liu & Mustanski, 2012).

School climate and overall school safety are strongly connected to the experience of peer victimization among sexual minority youth. Nationwide, 84.9% of LGB students in elementary, middle, and high schools have heard homophobic remarks from peers, teachers, and school staff (Kosciw, Greytak, Bartkiewicz, Boesen, & Palmer, 2012). In addition, 63.5% of sexual minority students felt unsafe and unwelcome at school, and 81.9% were verbally harassed because of their sexual orientation (Kosciw et al., 2012). Bias-based bullying and aggression significantly contributes to health disparities among LGB youth, contributing to adverse mental health, social, and educational outcomes. For more information regarding suicide risk among LGBT youth, please see Chapter 6 of this volume.

Transgender and Gender-Nonconforming Youth

Transgender and gender-nonconforming (TGNC) youth often experience peer harassment, discrimination, and abuse in school (Kosciw, Greytak, & Diaz, 2009). These negative events, including verbal assault, physical assault, sexual harassment, social exclusion, and interpersonal conflict, are often specifically linked to gender identity and expression (Kosciw et al., 2009). In the 2011 Gay, Lesbian and Straight Education Network (GLSEN) survey of middle and high school climate in the United States, Kosciw and colleagues (2012) discovered that over 61% of transgender and gender nonconforming students heard negative remarks about their gender expression from peers, and nearly 57% of these students heard similar negative remarks from teachers and/or school staff. Due to their gender expression, 64% of students were verbally harassed and over 27% of students were physically harassed (Kosciw et al., 2012). Also, 80% of transgender students reported that they felt unsafe at school due to their gender expression and were likely to miss entire days or weeks of school (Kosciw et al., 2012). The majority of students who were harassed or assaulted did not report such incidents to school staff, believing that the situation would stay the same or become worse if reported (Kosciw et al., 2012).

In-school bullying and peer aggression has been linked to negative psychological effects and health risk behaviors among TGNC adolescents, including depression, suicidality, low self-esteem, and substance use (Kosciw et al., 2009). TGNC students who experienced high levels of victimization based on their gender identity and/or expression had higher levels of depression than those who reported lower levels of such victimization. The experience of frequent victimization based on gender expression was also linked to low levels of self-esteem (Kosciw et al., 2012). Recent research has established that rates of suicidal ideation and attempted suicide within the transgender community significantly and consistently exceed those of the general population (Xavier et al., 2005; Clements-Nolle, Marx, & Katz, 2006; Goldblum et al., 2012; Haas et al., 2014; Testa & Hendricks, 2014). Between 38% and 83% of trans individuals have reported suicidal ideation at any point in time (Xavier et al., 2005; Grossman & D'Augelli, 2007; Goldblum et al., 2012; Testa et al., 2012; Haas et al., 2014), with approximately one-third of participants in any given study indicating a history of suicide attempts (Haas et al., 2010; Nemoto, Bodecker, & Iwamoto, 2011; Goldblum et al., 2012; Testa et al., 2012). These staggeringly high rates reinforce the connection between stressful discriminatory events and suicidality, particularly those experienced during the formative school years.

A Social-Ecological Perspective on Youth Bullying and Suicide

The social-ecological framework is particularly useful in understanding bullying and suicidality among youth (Bronfenbrenner, 1979; Swearer, Espelage, Vaillancourt, & Hymel, 2010; Goldblum et al., 2014). In this framework, youth behavior is shaped by individual characteristics and nested contextual factors, including schools, families, peer groups, neighborhoods, and overarching cultural/societal factors. Youth bullying, aggression, and suicidality must be understood as emerging from multiple ecological contexts that impact individual behavior and predispositions (Lee, Hong, & Espelage, 2010). A social-ecological perspective also helps to expand understanding of the factors impacting bullying involvement and suicidality, offering a more holistic view of peer victimization and its consequences and reinforcing the idea that individuals are consistently influenced by their surroundings (Swearer & Espelage, 2004; Swearer et al., 2010; Goldblum et al., 2014). A child's social ecology influences his or her engagement in peer bullying and aggression, reinforcing the idea that individuals are consistently influenced by their surroundings (Swearer & Espelage, 2004). The social-ecological framework indicates that prevention and intervention efforts within schools, health-care agencies, and communities need to address the complex interactions between these systemic levels. If a child or adolescent is identified as a perpetrator, victim, or bully-victim, there must be cooperative management of the impact of bullying involvement both within school and outside of school (e.g., mental health care, pediatrics). In order to successfully reduce youth bullying and suicide, prevention

Potential Immediate Effects of Bullying: When Bullying Becomes a Crisis

For students who have been bullied and also endorse other risk factors for suicidality (e.g., depression, family history of suicide, alcohol/drug use), they may express distress through a medium such as social networking. Once a student makes a direct threat to self or others, his or her speech is no longer protected. Effective intervention then relies upon identifying online threats, taking such threats seriously, and providing the young person with access to professional help. Pediatricians and mental health professionals, often on the forefront of identifying and assisting youth at risk for bullying involvement and suicidality, are responsible for recognizing the physical and psychological sequelae of bullying and suicidality. Health professionals are also uniquely poised to coordinate care between practitioners and schools, increasing the chance that distressed students receive the necessary support.

The Role of the Pediatrician

Early identification and intervention in bullying involvement is a crucial element of reducing potential mental health consequences of bullying. Pediatricians and other health-care professionals are often the first individuals to have contact with youth identified as bullies, victims, or bully-victims. Up to 90% of young people who commit suicide had visited their primary care doctors within the past year, affording pediatricians numerous opportunities to inquire about suicidal thoughts (Tingley, 2013). To recognize children who are involved in bullying, the American Academy of Pediatrics advises pediatricians to ask screening questions during wellness exams and patient visits (American Academy of Pediatrics, 2009; StopBullying.gov, 2013). Such questions include: Do you ever feel afraid to go to school? Do other kids ever bully you at school, in your neighborhood, or online? When and where does it happen? What do they say or do? What do you do if you see other kids being bullied? Who can you go to for help if you or someone you know is being bullied? Pediatricians should gently probe about bullying involvement when a young person suddenly presents with a school phobia, attention problems, or psychosomatic concerns (American Academy of Pediatrics, 2009; Stopbullying.gov, 2013). Violence-related assessment and screening should also incorporate inquiries into mental health history and disabilities, family stressors that could be linked to bullying involvement, disciplinary attitudes and practices of parents, appropriate supervision of youths' activities, exposure to violence in the home, contact with media violence (e.g., video games, television), and poor school performance (American Academy of Pediatrics, 1999). Pediatricians should incorporate preventative education and linkages to necessary intervention and follow-up services for youth at risk of or currently involved in peer bullying (American Academy of Pediatrics, 1999). Additionally, pediatricians who become involved with school administrators, teachers, and parent-teacher associations are able to foster a positive dialogue between multiple interrelated systems in a young person's life.

Involvement of Mental Health Professionals in Bully-Mediated Crises

The common cultural tendency to minimize peer bullying and mental health concerns among children and adolescents (i.e., "it's just part of being a kid," "you'll grow out of it") can significantly exacerbate the detrimental effects of bullying involvement. Mental health professionals are responsible for fostering greater understanding of mental illness among youth and are tasked with more advanced comprehension of the complex relationship between bullying and suicidality (Espelage et al., 2014; Slaby & Pflum, 2014). In working with youth who frequently present in "crisis mode" following bullying involvement, mental health professionals must be mindful of their own biases toward chronically victimized and/or suicidal youth, focusing on safety planning and reducing immediate risk (Corona, Jobes, & Berman, 2014). Providers should be patient and avoid labeling or promoting a pathological view of youth who engage in self-injury and/ or suicidal behaviors (Corona et al., 2014). Given the wide-reaching effects and persistent impact of bullying on mental health, early identification and treatment of problematic psychological symptoms (such as excessive worry, hopelessness, and thoughts of suicide) can help youth lead safe, healthy, and productive lives (Slaby & Pflum, 2014).

Potential Long-Term Effects of Bullying on Suicidality

Although contemporary research has established a strong connection between peer bullying and suicidal ideation and/or behavior (Hertz et al., 2013), less research on long-term consequences or causal relationships exists. To address this gap in the literature, Kim and colleagues (2009) examined the impact of bullying victimization on seventh- and eighth-grade students. Victims, bully-victims, and female students who had been bullied were found to be at increased risk for suicidal ideation 10 months later. This relationship remained robust after controlling for other suicide risk factors such as anxiety and depression (Kim et al., 2009).

Bullying is a strong risk factor for the later development of suicidal ideation and behavior (Kim et al., 2009; Klomek et al., 2013). Compared to uninvolved youth, bullies, victims, and bully-victims are at greater risk for suicidal ideation, intentional (but nonsuicidal) self-injury, and suicidal behavior, particularly in adolescence (Klomek et al., 2007; CDC, 2011; Cooper et al., 2012; Hepburn et al., 2012). This association holds even after taking race, ethnicity, gender, and immigration status into account (Hepburn et al., 2012). Among females, being bullied in childhood predicts suicide attempts up to 25 years after bullying has ceased (Klomek et al., 2007; Klomek, Sourander, & Gould, 2011). For all youth involved in bullying, the potential for suicidal ideation or behavior does not abate but continues into adulthood. As adults, bullying victims are more than twice as likely as uninvolved adults to attempt suicide later in life (Meltzer, Vostanis, Ford, Bebbington, & Dennis, 2011). Additionally, Copeland et al. (2013) found that after controlling for childhood psychiatric disorders and family stress, boys (ages 9–16) who were identified as bully-victims were at increased risk for suicidality (e.g., recurrent thoughts of wanting to die, suicidal plans, suicide attempts) in young adulthood, compared with uninvolved youth. The risk of self-directed violence subsequent to bullying appears to occur in a dose-related manner (Cooper et al., 2012), such that more frequent involvement in bullying exacerbates risk. The risk of suicide is greatest for bully-victims, who play multiple roles in bullying (Hepburn et al., 2012).

For youth at vulnerable developmental stages, suicidality can be exacerbated by involvement in bullying. Klomek and colleagues (2013) noted that adolescents who bullied others and demonstrated concurrent suicide risk were most likely to experience psychiatric problems at a two-year follow up. Suicide risk, as defined, included depression, substance use problems, suicidal ideation, and/or past suicide attempt(s), difficulties that were more frequently endorsed by bullying perpetrators. For a young person with a predisposition to developing mental health symptoms, "frequent bullying of others during high-school years increases the risk for later depression and suicidality above and beyond the other established risk factors of suicide" (Klomek et al., 2013, p. S41). Externalizing behavior, including bullying, is a significant correlate of depression and suicidality (Klomek et al., 2013). The complexity of the connection between bullying and psychiatric symptoms, particularly suicidality, underlies the importance of early psychological and programmatic intervention.

School-Based Anti-Bullying Efforts

Anti-bullying policies and legislation have become increasingly prevalent over the last decade. Although some research has found significant positive outcomes for school-based anti-bullying programs and prevention, successful implementation is not regularly reported (Espelage et al., 2014). Each state addresses bullying differently, making consistent policy execution nearly impossible due to lack of standardization. As of 2013, 41 states have both anti-bullying laws and policies (most of which cover cyberbullying); 8 states have laws only, and 1 state has a model policy only (StopBullying.gov, 2013). School-based anti-bullying programs often aim to increase awareness of bullying, to decrease bullying behaviors, and to improve peer relationships at school (Olweus, 1993; Swearer et al., 2010). Systematic bullying prevention programs, when implemented correctly, can be part of a comprehensive plan for suicide prevention (Limber, Riese, Snyder, & Olweus, 2014).

In a comprehensive meta-analysis of 44 program evaluations and randomized clinical trials, Ttofi and Farrington (2011) noted that the efficacy of prevention programs for school-based bullying and peer aggression varies across contexts. In their review, nearly two-thirds of the studies were conducted outside of the United States and Canada, making generalizations to US populations difficult. One-third of the programs were derived from the Olweus Bully Prevention Program (Olweus & Limber, 2007; Limber et al., 2014), limiting the diversity of approaches. Overall results indicated that prevention programs were associated with a 20% to 23% decrease in bullying perpetration and a 17% to 20% decrease in victimization (Ttofi & Farrington, 2011). Program elements associated with decreases in bullying perpetration included parent training/meetings, improved playground supervision, disciplinary methods, strong classroom management, teacher training, formal classroom rules, whole-school anti-bullying policies, school conferences, information for parents, and cooperative group work among teachers (Ttofi & Farrington, 2011; Espelage et al., 2014).

Steps to Respect

Steps to Respect (STR) is a bullying prevention program designed to help third through sixth graders build supportive interpersonal relationships (Committee for Children, 2001). STR utilizes an all-school approach to bullying prevention, addressing relational elements between staff, peer groups, and individual students. Content is developmentally adapted to be appropriate with the cognitive and emotional levels of each grade. STR is based on the social-ecological model, aiming to intervene at multiple levels of a young person's environment to address etiological aspects of bullying and their corresponding mental health consequences. The STR curriculum aims to improve students' social-emotional learning and endorsement of positive social values, including perspective taking, empathy, emotion regulation, healthy friendship, and fairness (Committee for Children, 2001; Espelage et al., 2014).

Empirical research has demonstrated that STR is associated with reductions in playground bullying, approval of bullying behavior, student argumentativeness, destructive bystander behavior, and physical aggression between peers. Additionally, STR is linked to increases in agreeable/positive peer interactions, perceived adult responsiveness to students, positive bystander behavior, and perceptions of a healthy school climate. These gains are most significant in schools with high engagement in the STR program (Low, Ryzin, Brown, Smith, & Haggerty, 2014). Adult involvement is essential to the success of the STR program; school staff participate in frequent trainings, deliver structured curriculum to students, and continually emphasize these lessons throughout the year. Administrators, teachers, or counselors who work directly with students who have been bullied or who are bullying others receive additional training (Committee for Children, 2001; Espelage et al., 2014).

Second Step: Student Success Through Prevention

Student Success Through Prevention (SSTP) is a social-emotional learning program for students in grades 6 through 8, designed specifically to address issues that manifest during the middle school years (Committee for Children, 2008; Espelage et al., 2014). This program incorporates bullying prevention, sexual harassment, aggression in dating relationships, and substance abuse prevention through lessons taught throughout the school year. SSTP addresses several risk factors, including inappropriate classroom behavior (e.g., aggression, impulsivity), favorable attitudes toward problem behavior (e.g., substance abuse, in-school violence), unhealthy friendships, peer rewards for aggressive/antisocial behavior, and peer rejection. This program capitalizes on protective factors such as social skills, empathy, school connectedness, perspective taking, and rejection of drug use to incite positive change. Lessons cater to the improved cognitive, social, and emotional development of the middle school years, incorporating structured group discussions and activities, dyadic exercises, whole-class instruction, and individual work. Students learn and practice positive bystander behaviors, including decreased support for bullying and providing direct aid to a victim. SSTP is designed to positively alter the peer context of schools, removing the social support necessary to sustain bullying and aggression.

Recent research indicates that SSTP is effective in reducing aggression, homophobic teasing, and sexual harassment in schools. A randomized clinical trial in 36 US middle schools noted that students who participated in the social-emotional learning components of SSTP were 42% less likely than students in control schools to engage in physical fights up to one year after receiving SSTP education (Espelage, Low, Polanin, & Brown, 2013). After two years of social-emotional learning curriculum, students in the SSTP schools were 56% less likely to report homophobic victimization and 39% less likely to report sexual violence perpetration than students in the control condition (Espelage et al., 2013). These findings are particularly important given the elevated risk of suicidal ideation and behaviors among youth who are targets of homophobic language, including LGB and gender nonconforming youth (D'Augelli et al., 2002).

Recognizing, Understanding, Labeling, Expressing, and Regulating Approach

The Recognizing, Understanding, Labeling, Expressing, and Regulating (RULER) approach is a multiyear program designed to improve the quality of classroom interactions for youth in kindergarten through eighth grade (Hagelskamp, Brackett, Rivers, & Salovey, 2013). Extensive professional development and structured classroom curricula are utilized to improve emotional literacy, foster emotional support, and improve social-emotional development among students. Emotional literacy is a social-emotional learning construct that incorporates recognizing, understanding, labeling, and expressing emotions appropriately (Hagelskamp et al., 2013; Espelage et al., 2014). A positive learning environment serves both teachers and students well, facilitating improved classroom management and student relationships. RULER also encompasses comprehensive professional development for teachers and administrators, a program element that is based on the idea that teachers who are skilled at understanding and regulating their own emotions are better able to maintain a regulated classroom and high quality instruction over time (Hagelskamp et al., 2013).

Extant research has established support for the distal outcomes of the RULER program. Following seven months of implementation, students in RULER-integrated classrooms demonstrated greater academic and social achievements compared to students in control classrooms. Two-year longitudinal research indicates that RULER has sustained positive impacts on social-emotional competency among students, instructional quality, and classroom organization (Hagelskamp et al., 2013). Use of the RULER curriculum can have beneficial impacts on both bullying and suicidality among youth; if students are better able to recognize and discuss their emotions, it stands to reason that they are better equipped to recognize signs of distress in themselves and their peers. Social-emotional learning programs can significantly improve the quality of learning environments by promoting healthy conflict resolution, improved empathy, and decreased tolerance of aggression (Hagelskamp et al., 2013; Espelage et al., 2014).

School-Based Suicide Prevention Programs
Signs of Suicide Prevention Program

The Signs of Suicide (SOS) program is a nationally recognized suicide prevention program designed for middle and high school students. The program is designed to teach students to identify signs of depression, self-injury, and suicidality in themselves and their classmates. SOS also encourages help-seeking and peer intervention, teaching students that suicidality is a result of multiple potential antecedents that can be ameliorated through professional help (Aseltine & DeMartino, 2004; Screening for Mental Health, 2010). Students are instructed to use three action steps to respond to signs of depression and suicidality: acknowledge, care, and tell (ACT). A randomized trial in five Georgia and Connecticut high schools demonstrated that SOS was correlated with significantly lower rates of suicide attempts, greater understanding of suicidality, and more

flexible attitudes about depression and suicide in the three months following program implementation (Aseltine & DeMartino, 2004). This program is one of few school-based intervention programs recognized by the Substance Abuse and Mental Health Services Administration's (SAMHSA) National Registry of Evidence-Based Programs and Practices that addresses suicide risk and depression (SAMHSA, 2013).

Lifelines Curriculum

Like SOS, Lifelines is a suicide-prevention program for middle and high school students (grades 8–12). Lifelines consists of three components—prevention, intervention, and postvention—that provide resources for preventing suicide, helping students at risk, and responding appropriately following a student suicide (Kalafat, O'Halloran, & Underwood, 2007). The goal of Lifelines is to promote a caring and sensitive school community that encourages and models help-seeking. The content of this program reflects research that most suicidal youth share their concerns more with peers rather than adults, and many youth are not adequately equipped to respond to distressed peers in patient and empathic ways. Students receive psychoeducation about suicide, and suicidal behavior is framed as an issue that should receive support rather than blame. Lifelines also seeks to increase the likelihood that staff and students will be able to identify at-risk youth, provide an appropriate response, and obtain professional help when necessary. Lifelines lessons are taught in conjunction with standard health curriculum, increasing their ease of implementation (Kalafat et al., 2007; SAMHSA, 2013). Efficacy research indicates that students receiving the Lifelines curriculum demonstrated significantly greater knowledge and compassionate attitudes about suicide, as well as increased willingness to seek adult help when feeling suicidal or learning of a friend's suicidal ideation (Kalafat et al., 2007; SAMHSA, 2013).

Protective Factors and Points of Intervention
Mental Health Professionals

Mental health professionals must keep abreast of the most recent literature on suicidality and bullying among youth. For those who work directly with youth, engaging in evidence-based practices for treating suicidal clients is both prudent and necessary. One important aspect of promoting youth safety is means restriction, or reducing risk in the home (i.e., securing firearms; restricting access to medications, alcohol, drugs, and toxic chemicals; securing razors and other sharp implements; Heilbron, Goldston, Walrath, Rodi, & McKeon, 2013). Clinicians should also provide explicit instruction to families regarding warning signs of increased suicide risk and resources in case of emergency (i.e., local emergency department, 911, crisis line; Heilbron et al., 2013; SAMHSA, 2013). Working with suicidal youth implicates the need for careful assessment with both the young person and collateral sources, particularly family members. Linkages to appropriate follow-up services, such as an intensive outpatient program, community-based parent support, and/or weekly therapy, are essential for reducing suicide risk in youth (Heilbron et al., 2013). Aftercare plans for youth who have made a suicide attempt should emphasize the importance of adequate communication with both the youth and his or her caregivers to ensure safety and to address any remaining risk factors (Heilbron et al., 2013). To advance the use of evidence-based practices in treating suicidal youth, SAMHSA provides a National Registry of Evidence-Based Programs and Practices that are available for reference by mental health professionals (http://www.nrepp.samhsa.gov). For more information regarding the assessment of suicide risk in children and adolescents, see Chapter 4 of this volume.

A retrospective study of youth health service utilization prior to death by suicide revealed that most youth have contact with the health-care system in the year prior to their death, but most are not seen for mental health reasons (Rhodes et al., 2013). Most health-care utilization occurred at an outpatient physician's office or at a hospital emergency department, indicating the need for suicide screenings and preventative interventions in these settings (Rhodes et al., 2013). The emergency department is an underused site for suicide prevention; high-risk groups (such as suicidal youth) may be more prevalent here and therefore more efficiently detected. Rhodes and colleagues (2013) revealed that 80% of suicidal youth were seen by an outpatient physician within the three months prior to their death, indicating the need for an integration of mental health care across different health settings.

Training for Educators and Administrators

For administrators, staff, and educators, training and ongoing education are crucial to the implementation of anti-bullying programs and suicide prevention efforts (Limber et al., 2014). During these trainings, all adults should be informed about the national and local prevalence rates of bullying, the populations of students most likely to be involved in bullying, and the connection between bullying and negative mental health outcomes (Limber et al., 2014). Teachers should be trained to actively work to prevent bullying in their classrooms, to focus on building community within classrooms and schools, to watch for signs of bullying and suicidality (particularly among stigmatized/minority groups), and to take quick action to stop bullying as it occurs. By implementing these steps, teachers, staff, and administrators can simultaneously address correlates of suicidal ideation and behavior among bullied youth (Limber et al., 2014).

Educators should also be informed that suicide prevention requires rapid identification of mental health resources for students struggling with depression or thoughts of suicide. This can involve training for administrators, teachers, and parents/guardians about behavioral indicators of suicide, effective crisis intervention (including utilizing the emergency department), and prompt referral for mental health services. Whenever possible, evidence-based suicide intervention strategies should be explored and implemented. Educators and staff should be cautioned against using role-plays or videos of bullying behaviors to depict the connection between bullying and suicide. Such presentations may be triggering to students who endorse mental health symptoms or who are seriously considering suicide (Limber et al., 2014).

Social Support Networks

Relevant to both bullying and suicidality among youth is the enhancement of student social support networks (Holt & Espelage, 2007). This may take the form of facilitating access to social support groups, helping youth develop skills to effectively use these networks, and identifying characteristics of healthy peers. Youth who have little social support and are also involved in bullying are significantly more likely than their uninvolved peers to report suicidal ideation (Rigby & Slee, 1999). In contrast, youth who seek peer support following peer victimization are less likely to continually be classified as victims, decreasing psychological consequences of continued bullying involvement (Holt & Espelage, 2007). Social support and school connectedness can protect against suicidality, both among ethnic/sexual minority students and nonminority students (Rigby & Slee, 1999; O'Donnell et al., 2004; Goodenow, Szalacha, & Westheimer, 2006).

For sexual minority adolescents, the presence of a gay–straight alliance (GSA) or similar group is significantly related to lower levels of peer victimization and suicide attempts (Goodenow et al., 2006). LGB youth are also positively influenced by the involvement of a supportive, nonjudgmental staff member; the presence of such an individual is significantly negatively correlated with multiple suicide attempts (Goodenow et al., 2006). Inclusive and comprehensive anti-bullying policies also have strong negative associations with suicide attempts, even after taking perceived support and peer victimization into account (Goodenow et al., 2006). Bolstering social support can potentially reduce both bullying and suicidality among youth, decreasing preexisting feelings of isolation and providing support in the wake of bullying involvement or a mental health crisis.

School Connectedness and Belongingness

Feelings of connection to the school environment can have a significant positive effect on students' emotional well-being (Nasir, Jones, & McLaughlin, 2011). Students' experiences of safety and connectedness at school have been linked to lower levels of depression, less emotional distress, less suicidal ideation, and fewer suicide attempts (Saewyc, 2011). Feelings of connection to one's academic environment can bolster mental health outcomes over and above the influence of parental attachment and support (Shochet, Homel, Cockshaw, & Montgomery, 2008). School connectedness can also have positive longitudinal impacts on mental health and well-being. Among young adolescents (12–14 years old), school connectedness was linked to fewer symptoms of anxiety among girls, fewer depressive symptoms for boys and girls, and fewer problems in general functioning (hyperactivity, emotional symptoms, conduct problems, and interpersonal problems) for boys at one-year follow-up (Shochet, Dadds, Ham, & Montague, 2006). Enhancing a student's feelings of perceived safety at school and connectedness to the academic environment can protect against suicide attempts among adolescents (Borowsky et al., 2013).

Youth who are involved in bullying, particularly as victims, are more likely than uninvolved students to feel ostracized at school. Connecting these youth with positive (nonparental) adults, such as relatives, counselors, and religious leaders, can contribute to a decrease in suicidal ideation and attempts (Borowsky et al., 2013). These adult connections are especially influential for bullies and victims, as well as for minority students (Goodenow et al., 2006). Additionally, academic achievement can enhance a young person's

self-efficacy and enjoyment of school, subsequently decreasing suicidality (Borowsky et al., 2013).

Parents and Families

Parental and familial relationships represent both risk and protective factors for youth. Warm and supportive family relationships are regarded as protective factors in the management of stressful life events (Bowes, Maughan, Caspi, Moffitt, & Arseneault, 2010; Lee et al., 2010); negative familial relationships can exacerbate suicidal ideation and leave youth vulnerable to peer bullying (Lee et al., 2010). Negative parenting strategies such as harsh discipline and physical abuse have been linked to increased suicidal ideation among Korean youth (Shon, 2005). Parental abuse, emotional abuse, and neglect have been found to significantly predict suicidal ideation among high school students (Park, 2005). In younger children, lack of parental support is associated with heightened risk of suicide among elementary school students (Lee & Heo, 2003).

As compared to families of children not involved in bullying, families of bullies, victims, and bully-victims demonstrate less functionality and internal support (Ball et al., 2008). Cross-sectional research indicates that, in such families, punishment from caregivers is frequently physical or overly emotional and is followed by a time in which the child is ignored (Smokowski & Kopasz, 2005). Perpetrators of bullying are more likely than their uninvolved peers to be victims of physical maltreatment by their parents. Additionally, children identified as bullies or peer aggressors are often taught that violence is an appropriate way to solve their problems (Smokowski & Kopasz, 2005, p. 103). Longitudinal research demonstrates that such youth receive less cognitive stimulation, less emotional support, and increased television exposure (Ball et al., 2008). Families of bully-victims are noted to be particularly inconsistent and abusive, often dictated by parents that are low in warmth, high in hostility and restrictive discipline, and lacking in parental management skills (Smokowski & Kopasz, 2005; Ball et al., 2008). These families are also less likely to be attuned to their children, making it difficult to recognize signs of bullying involvement and suicidality (i.e., bruises, torn clothing, missing property, and changes in mood and behavior).

Conversely, positive parent–child communication and secure attachment with parents have negative associations with suicidal ideation, bullying, and peer aggression among youth (Park, 2005). While the resilience developed in supportive families may not be a cure-all for bullying involvement, this resilience can alter the way a victim responds to his or her bully (Bowes et al., 2010). Youth with supportive families may also experience inoculation against the negative effects of bullying, such as self-deprecation, suicidal ideation, and suicidal behaviors (Rigby, Slee, & Martin, 2007; Kumpulainen, 2008; Bowes et al., 2010; Perkins, Craig & Perkins, 2011).

Parents and families are uniquely positioned to provide safe and supportive environments in which to minimize bullying and its effects on suicidality. These individuals are encouraged to educate themselves about the pernicious nature of bullying and suicidality; resources such as the American Foundation for Suicide Prevention and www.stopbullying.gov can provide extensive information and avenues for support.

Schools and Gatekeepers

Recommendations for working with suicidal youth in schools are fraught with inconsistencies, and intervening with at-risk youth often requires extensive planning and preparation. When peer bullying and aggression is also involved, school personnel may require additional support to handle high-risk circumstances. Mental health screening programs have therefore been implemented in schools, often including gatekeepers (individuals who are trained to recognize risk, inquire about suicidality, and help youth obtain support as needed). For instance, the Columbia Teen-Screen program (Shaffer et al., 2004) utilizes the Columbia Health Screen, an empirically supported instrument, to detect psychiatric symptoms among adolescents. If a teen endorses mental health symptoms, a school-based clinician conducts a short interview to determine whether additional assessment is warranted. To maintain youth safety, a parent/guardian is involved and provided with referrals for further assessment and treatment (Shaffer et al., 2004). Current research advises schools with screening programs to maintain an open dialogue with local mental health agencies to inform them about the screening program, to determine the potential volume of referrals, and to confirm the availability of crisis/emergency services (Heilbron et al., 2013).

School-based suicide prevention programs must be consistent with school mandates, culture, and available resources. Effective prevention programs must have a clear conceptual and empirical basis, use proven implementation and instructional strategies, and be systemic in nature. The social-ecological theory (Bronfenbrenner, 1979) posits that including relevant components of school and community can increase the efficacy of intervention programs for individual students (Kalafat, 2003). The main objective of suicide prevention curricula is to decrease barriers to help-seeking, particularly for nonsuicidal youth who wish to help their more distressed peers (Leenaars et al., 2001). Prevention programs therefore utilize psychoeducation about suicide warning signs, common precipitants, and myths about suicidality to elicit greater understanding and compassion for those struggling with thoughts of suicide (Leenaars et al., 2001).

Supporting Students and Schools After Suicide

Suicide in a school community is a tragic, often unexpected event that can leave students and staff feeling sad, confused, distracted, and angry. In 2011, the American Foundation for Suicide Prevention and Suicide Prevention Resource Center compiled a toolkit to help schools address and recover from a young person's suicide. The guidelines included in this toolkit are also applicable to the wider community, particularly mental health and medical professionals.

It is recommended that schools treat all student deaths in the same way. Different approaches reinforce the unfortunate stigma that surrounds suicide and can invalidate the pain felt by the deceased student's family and friends. Once a suicide death has been confirmed, the school should immediately initiate a coordinated crisis response in order to contain the situation, provide access to grief support, help students express and cope with their emotions about the student's death, and maintain a focus on typical educational activities. Memorializing the youth's death must be done appropriately, with a focus on objective circumstances rather than on subjective impressions of events that led to the student's suicide. Adolescents are vulnerable to suicide contagion, and it is essential to avoid simplifying, sensationalizing, or glamorizing the student's death. Despite being overused by some youth, social media (e.g., Facebook, Twitter, and Instagram) can be sensitively used to share prevention-oriented messaging, offer support to students who may be struggling, and disseminate resources (both online and in person) that can be utilized by students who need additional support (American Foundation for Suicide Prevention & American Foundation for Suicide Prevention and Suicide Prevention Resource Center, 2011).

As suicide is frequently connected to psychiatric symptoms, schools should emphasize that the student who died by suicide was likely struggling with mental health symptoms that may not have been apparent to others. This can be achieved by educating school staff and community members and can be facilitated by collaboration with mental health and medical professionals. Schools should also work with local mental health agencies to provide support to students struggling with a peer's suicide and/or their own mental health symptoms. School staff must remain attentive to their own limitations and may consider bringing in trained trauma responders and mental health professionals to provide enhanced support. Suicide awareness, education, and prevention should not end immediately after "resolving" a student's death but should extend into the months after a suicide (American Foundation for Suicide Prevention & American Foundation for Suicide Prevention and Suicide Prevention Resource Center, 2011).

In-School Bullying and Suicide Deaths

Schools are faced with an additional complication if in-school peer bullying was involved in a student's suicide. While research supports a connection between bullying involvement and suicidality (Kim & Leventhal, 2008), it is important to analyze this association within the broader social-ecological context and to recognize that bullying is one potential risk factor in a constellation of other risk and protective factors (Goldblum et al., 2014). In determining whether bullying was a factor in a student's suicide, it is essential to examine this relation in an objective manner, avoiding the proclamation of a one-to-one connection between bullying and suicide completion. Teachers and school administrators should attend carefully to signs of bullying within the student population, including less apparent forms of victimization such as cyberbullying and relational aggression. School personnel should subsequently work to implement components of evidence-based anti-bullying programs, such as those described earlier. It is also important for educators to remain aware of the connection between bullying involvement—be it as a bully, victim, or bully-victim—mental health symptoms, and suicidality. Compatible components of bullying prevention and suicide aftercare programs can be implemented simultaneously to address both bullying and suicidality with the educational environment.

Recommendations
For Mental Health
and Medical Professionals

• Remain up-to-date on emerging research and best practices in the fields of suicidology, bullying, and aggression. Evidence-based practices in these domains can be found in a comprehensive registry such as SAMHSA (http://www.nrepp.samhsa.gov).

• When working with diverse groups of youth, providers must be aware of their own biases and stereotypes; evaluate a student's experiences with bias and discrimination; understand initial apprehension regarding psychiatric care among ethnic, sexual, and gender minorities; and assess for family and community connections that have been disrupted due to mental health symptoms or suicidality (Tormala et al., 2014).

• Mental health and medical providers should consistently screen for exposure to bullying and aggression, as well as for thoughts of self-harm and suicide. Symptom checklists can facilitate the screening process and can be modified for use by students, parents, and teachers.

• Mental health services should be readily available in schools, and schools should be poised to connect youth at risk for suicidality and bullying involvement with community resources (i.e., mental health services, positive support groups). By continuing to dismantle the silos of health care, youth and their communities will receive more comprehensive, integrated, and productive care (Goldblum et al., 2014).

• Remain available to local schools following crises related to bullying and/or suicidality. Providing support and education to staff, students, and community members can help reduce the stigma associated with suicide and can reinforce the potential adverse consequences of bullying and peer aggression.

For Parents and Teachers

• Be attuned to signs that a child may be suffering from in-school bullying (excessive worry, hopelessness, physical injury, withdrawal, talking about "not wanting to be here").

• Talk with children about what happens in school. A positive, supportive, and structured home environment can foster the development of resilience in potentially vulnerable youth. Youth with supportive families are often protected from the negative effects of bullying, including suicidality (Rigby et al., 2007; Kumpulainen, 2008; Bowes et al., 2010; Perkins et al., 2011).

• Parents and teachers should be alert to the range of factors increasing risk for youth suicide, including not only bullying involvement but also factors such as depression and substance use.

• Parents, teachers, and school staff can be involved in implementing anti-bullying and suicide prevention programs and can serve as positive models for prosocial, support-seeking behavior.

• Social-emotional learning strategies are often components of structured bully prevention programs, but these skills can be developed and reinforced in numerous community settings, such as at family gatherings, on the playground, and at extracurricular activities (Espelage et al., 2014).

For Policymakers and Researchers

• Bullying and suicide should both be conceptualized as systemic problems that require intervention at multiple levels (individual, school, family, neighborhood, etc.).

• Prevention programs for bullying and suicide can have beneficial effects on student and teacher safety, educational outcomes, social-emotional intelligence, and overall school climate. Investing in and promoting these programs can aid in destigmatizing suicidality and can enhance the efficacy of prevention and intervention for peer bullying and aggression.

• As bullying, aggression, and suicide are multifaceted phenomena, future research should examine the relationships among bullying, homophobic and transphobic name-calling, sexual harassment, and suicidal behaviors in tandem to identify shared and unique influences, as well as to maximize the efficacy of interventions (Espelage et al., 2014).

References

American Academy of Pediatrics. (1999). The role of the pediatrician in youth violence prevention in clinical practice and at the community level. *Pediatrics, 103*(1), 173–181.

American Academy of Pediatrics. (2009). Role of the pediatrician in youth violence prevention. *Connected Kids: Safe, Strong, and Secure.* Retrieved from http://aappolicy.aappublications.org/cgi/reprint/pediatrics;124/1/393

American Foundation for Suicide Prevention, and Suicide Prevention Resource Center (2011). *After a Suicide: A Toolkit for Schools.* Newton, MA: Education Development Center, Inc.

Arseneault, L., Bowes, L., & Shakoor, S. (2010). Bullying victimization in youths and mental health problems: "Much ado about nothing"? *Psychological Medicine, 40,* 717–729. doi: 10.1017/S0033291709991383

Aseltine, R. H., & DeMartino, R. (2004). An outcome evaluation of the SOS suicide prevention program. *American Journal of Public Health, 94*(3), 446–451.

Ball, H. A., Arseneault, L., Taylor, A., Maughan, B., Caspi, A., & Moffitt, T. E. (2008). Genetic and environmental influences on victims, bullies and bully-victims in childhood. *Journal of Child Psychology and Psychiatry, 49*(1), 104–112. doi: 10.1111/j.1469-7610.2007.01821.x

Bowes, L., Maughan, B., Caspi, A., Moffitt, T. E., & Arseneault, L. (2010). Families promote emotional and behavioural resilience to bullying: Evidence of an environmental effect *Journal of Child Psychology and Psychiatry, 51*(7), 809–817. doi: 10.1111/j.1469-7610.2010.02216.x

Borowsky, I. W., Taliaferro, L. A., & McMorris, B. J. (2013). Suicidal thinking and behavior among youth involved in verbal and social bullying: Risk and protective factors. *Journal of Adolescent Health, 53*(1), S4–S12.

Bronfenbrenner, U. (1979). *The ecology of human development: Experiments by nature and design.* Cambridge, MA: Harvard University Press.

Card, N. A., & Hodges, E. V. E (2008). Peer victimization among schoolchildren: Correlations, causes, consequences, and considerations in assessment and intervention. *School Psychology Quarterly, 23*(4), 451–461. doi: 10.1037/a0012769

Cash, S. J., & Bridge, J. A. (2009). Epidemiology of youth suicide and suicidal behavior. *Current Opinion in Pediatrics, 21*(5), 613–619. doi: 10.1097/MOP.0b013e32833063e1

Centers for Disease Control and Prevention. (2011). Bullying among middle school and high school students—Massachusetts, 2009. *Morbidity and Mortality Weekly Report, 60,* 465–471.

Centers for Disease Control and Prevention. (2012). Youth risk behavior surveillance—United States, 2011. *Morbidity and Mortality Weekly Report Surveillance Summaries, 61*(SS4). Retrieved from http://www.cdc.gov/mmwr/preview/mmwrhtml/ss6104a1.htm

Clements-Nolle, C., Marx, R., & Katz, M. (2006). Attempted suicide among transgender persons: The influence of gender-based discrimination and victimization. *Journal of Homosexuality, 51*(3), 53-69. doi: 10.1300/J082v51n03_04

Chu, J., Goldblum, P., Floyd, R., & Bongar, B. (2010). The cultural theory and model of suicide. *Applied and Preventative Psychology, 14,* 25-40.

Cochran, S. D., & Mays, V. M. (2013). Sexual orientation and mental health. In J. C. Patterson and A. R. D'Augelli (Eds.), *Handbook of sexual orientation and mental health* (pp. 204–222). New York: Oxford University Press.

Committee for Children. (2001). *Steps to Respect: A Bullying Prevention Programme.* Seattle, WA: Author.

Committee for Children. (2008). *Second Step: Student Success through Prevention Program.* Seattle, WA: Author.

Cooper, G. D., Clements, P. T., & Holt, K. E. (2012). Examining childhood bullying and adolescent suicide: Implications for school nurses. *Journal of School Nursing, 28,* 275–283. doi: 10.1177/1059840512438617

Copeland, W. E., Wolke, D., Angold, A., & Costello, E. J. (2013). Adult psychiatric outcomes of bullying and being bullied by peers in childhood and adolescence. *JAMA Psychiatry, 70*(4), 419–426. doi: 10.1001/jamapsychiatry.2013.504

Corona, C. D., Jobes, D. A., & Berman, A. L. (2014). Social psychological model of adolescent suicide. In P. B. Goldblum, D. L. Espelage, J. Chu, & B. Bongar (Eds.), *Youth suicide and bullying: Challenges and strategies for prevention and intervention.* New York: Oxford University Press.

Crawford, A. M., & Manassis, K. (2011). Anxiety, social skills, friendship quality, and peer victimization: An integrated model. *Journal of Anxiety Disorders, 25,* 924–931. doi: 10.1016/j.janxdis.2011.05.005

Crick, N. R., & Nelson, D. A. (2002). Relational and physical aggression within friendships: Nobody told me there'd be friends like this. *Journal of Abnormal Child Psychology, 30,* 599–607.

Crick, N. R., Wellman, N. E., Casas, J. F., O'Brien, K. M., Nelson, D. A., Grotpeter, J. K., & Markon, K. (1999). Childhood aggression and gender: A new look at an old problem. In D.

Bernstein (Ed.), *Nebraska Symposium on Motivation, 45*, 75-141. Lincoln: University of Nebraska Press.

D'Augelli, A. R., Pilkington, N. W., & Hershberger, S. L. (2002). Incidence and mental health impact of sexual orientation victimization of lesbian, gay, and bisexual youths in high school. *School Psychology Quarterly, 17*, 148–167.

Espelage, D. L., De La Rue, L., & Low, S. (2014). School-wide bully prevention programs and social-emotional learning approaches to preventing bullying & peer victimization. In P. B. Goldblum, D. L. Espelage, J. Chu, & B. Bongar (Eds.), *Youth suicide and bullying: Challenges and strategies for prevention and intervention*. New York: Oxford University Press.

Espelage, D. L., Low, S., Polanin, J., & Brown, E. (2013). The impact of a middle school program to reduce aggression, victimization, and sexual violence. *Journal of Adolescent Health, 53*(2), 180–186. doi: 10.1016/j.jadohealth.2013.02.021

Espelage, D. L., Goldblum, P., Chu, J., Bongar, B., Pflum, S., & De La Rue, L. (2014). Developing an ecological approach to address challenges of youth bullying and suicide: Recommendations for research, practice, policy, and training. In P. B. Goldblum, D. L. Espelage, J. Chu, & B. Bongar (Eds.), *Youth suicide and bullying: Challenges and strategies for prevention and intervention*. New York: Oxford University Press.

Espelage, D. L., Mebane, S. E., & Swearer, S. M. (2004). Gender differences in bullying: Moving beyond mean level differences. In D. L. Espelage & S. M. Swearer (Eds.), *Bullying in American schools: A social-ecological perspective on prevention and intervention* (pp. 15–35). Mahwah, NJ: Lawrence Erlbaum.

Faris, R. (2006). Race, social networks, and school bullying. *Dissertation Abstracts International Section A: Humanities and Social Sciences, 68*(4-A), 1668.

Finkelhor, D., Turner, H. A, & Hamby, S. (2012). Let's prevent peer victimization, not just bullying. *Child Abuse and Neglect, 36*(4), 271–274. doi: 10.1016/j.chiabu.2011.12.001

Goldblum, P., Espelage, D., Chu, J., Bongar, B., Pflum, S., & De La Rue, L. (2014). Facing the challenges of preventing youth suicide and bullying. In P. B. Goldblum, D. L. Espelage, J. Chu, & B. Bongar (Eds.), *Youth suicide and bullying: Challenges and strategies for prevention and intervention*. New York: Oxford University Press.

Goldblum, P., Testa, R. J., Pflum, S., Hendricks, M. L., Bradford, J., & Bongar, B. (2012). The relationship between gender-based victimization and suicide attempts in transgender people. *Professional Psychology: Research and Practice, 43*(5), 468–475.

Goodenow, C., Szalacha, L., & Westheimer, K. (2006). School support groups, other school factors, and the safety of sexual minority adolescents. *Psychology in the Schools, 43*(5), doi: 10.1002/pits.20173

Grossman, A. H., & D'Augelli, A. R. (2007). Transgender youth and life-threatening behaviors. *Suicide and Life-Threatening Behavior, 37*(5), 527–537.

Haas, A. P., Eliason, M., Mays, V. M., Mathy, R. M., Cochran, S. D., D'Augelli, A. R., . . . Clayton, P. J. (2010). Suicide and suicide risk in lesbian, gay, bisexual, and transgender populations: Review and recommendations. *Journal of Homosexuality, 58*(1), 10–51. doi: 10.1080/00918369.2011.534038

Haas, A. P., Rodgers, P. L., & Herman, J. L. (2014). *Suicide attempts among transgender and gender non-conforming adults: Findings of the National Transgender Discrimination Survey*. Retrieved from http://williamsinstitute.law.ucla.edu/wp-content/uploads/AFSP-Williams-Suicide-Report-Final.pdf

Hagelskamp, C., Brackett, M. A., Rivers, S. E., & Salovey, P. (2013). Improving classroom quality with the RULER approach to social and emotional learning: Proximal and distal outcomes. *American Journal of Community Psychology, 51*, 530–543. doi: 10.1007/s10464-013-9570-x

Hawker, D. S. J., & Boulton, M. J. (2000). Twenty years' research on peer victimization and psychosocial maladjustment: A meta-analytic review of cross-sectional studies. *Journal of Child Psychology and Psychiatry, 41*(4), 441–455.

Heilbron, N., Goldston, D., Walrath, C., Rodi, M., & McKeon, R. (2013). Suicide risk protocols: Addressing the needs of high-risk youths identified through suicide prevention efforts in clinical settings. *Suicide and Life-Threatening Behavior 43*(2), 150–160. doi: 10.1111/sltb.12004

Hepburn, L., Azrael, D., Molnar, B., & Miller, M. (2012). Bullying and suicidal behaviors among urban high school youth. *Journal of Adolescent Health, 51*, 93–95.

Herek, G. M. (1989). Hate crimes against lesbians and gay men: Issues for research and social policy. *American Psychologist, 44*(6), 948–955.

Hershberger, S. L., & D'Augelli, A. R. (1995). The impact of victimization on the mental health and suicidality of lesbian, gay, and bisexual youths. *Developmental Psychology, 31*(1) 65–74.

Hertz, M., Donato, I., & Wright, J. (2013). Bullying and suicide: A public health approach. *Journal of Adolescent Health, 53*, S1–S3.

Holt, M. K., & Espelage, D. L. (2007). Perceived social support among bullies, victims, and bully-victims. *Journal of Youth & Adolescence, 36*, 984–994. doi: 10.1007/s10964-006-9153-3

Kalafat, J. (2003). School approaches to youth suicide prevention. *American Behavioral Scientist, 46*(9), 1211–1223. doi: 10.1177/0002764202250665

Kalafat, J., O'Halloran, S., & Underwood, M. (2007). *Lifelines: A school-based response to youth suicide*. Augusta: Maine Youth Suicide Prevention Program.

Kaminski, J. W., & Fang, X. (2009). Victimization by peers and adolescent suicide in three US samples. *Journal of Pediatrics, 155*(5), 683–688. doi: 10.1016/j.jpeds.2009.04.061

Kim, Y. S., & Leventhal, B. (2008). Bullying and suicide. A review. *International Journal of Adolescent Medicine and Health, 20*(2), 133–154. doi: 10.1515/IJAMH.2008.20.2.133

Kim, Y., Leventhal, B., Koh, Y., & Boyce, W. (2009). Bullying increased suicide risk: Prospective study of Korean adolescents. *Archives of Suicide Research, 13*(1), 15–30.

King, M., Semlyen, J., Tai, S. S., Killaspy, H., Osborn, D., Popelyuk, D., & Nazareth, I. (2008). A systematic review of mental disorder, suicide, and deliberate self harm in lesbian, gay and bisexual people. *BMC Psychiatry, 8*, 70. doi: 10.1186/1471-244X-8-70

Klomek, A. B., Kleinman, M., Altschuler, E., Marrocco, F., Amakawa, L., & Gould, M. S. (2013). Suicidal adolescents' experiences with bullying perpetration and victimization during high school as risk factors for later depression and suicidality. *Journal of Adolescent Health, 53*, S37–S42.

Klomek, A. B., Marrocco, F., Kleinman, M., Schonfeld, I. S., & Gould, M. S. (2007). Bullying, depression, and suicidality in adolescents. *Journal of the American Academy of Child & Adolescent Psychiatry, 46*(1), 40–49.

Klomek, A. B., Sourander, A., & Gould, M. S. (2011). Bullying and suicide: Detection and intervention. *Psychiatric Times, 29*(2), 1-6.

Kosciw, J. G., Greytak, E. A., Bartkiewicz, M. J., Boesen, M. J., & Palmer, N. A. (2012). *The 2011 National School Climate Survey: The experiences of lesbian, gay, bisexual and transgender* youth in our nation's schools. New York: Gay, Lesbian, and Straight Education Network.

Kosciw, J. G., Gretak, E. A., & Diaz, E. M. (2009). Who, what, where, when, and why: Demographic and ecological factors contributing to hostile school climate for lesbian, gay, bisexual, and transgender youth. *Journal of Youth and Adolescence*, *38*, 976–988. doi: 10.1007/s10964-009-9412-1

Kowalski, R. M., & Limber, S. P. (2013). Psychological, physical, and academic correlates of cyberbullying and traditional bullying. *Journal of Adolescent Health, 53*(1), S13–S20.

Kumpulainen, K. (2008). Psychiatric conditions associated with bullying. *International Journal of Adolescent Medical Health, 20*(2), 121–132.

Kumpulainen, K., Rasanen, E., & Puura, K. (2001). Psychiatric disorders and the use of mental health services among children involved in bullying. *Aggressive Behavior, 27*, 102–110.

Lee, J., & Heo, J. (2003). Family risk factors for child suicidal ideation. *The Korea Journal of Youth Counseling, 11*, 85–95.

Lee, S., Hong, J. S., & Espelage, D. L. (2010). An ecological understanding of youth suicide in South Korea. *School Psychology International, 31*(5), 531–546. doi: 10.1177/0143034310382724

Leenaars, A., Wenckstern, S., Appleby, M., Fiske, H., Grad, O., Kalafat, J., … Takahashi, Y. (2001). Current issues in dealing with suicide prevention in schools: Perspectives from some countries. *Journal of Educational and Psychological Consultation, 12*(4), 365–384.

LeVasseur, M. T., Kelvin, E. A., & Grosskopf, N. A. (2013). Intersecting identities and the association between bullying and suicide among New York City youths: Results from the 2009 New York City Youth Risk Behavior Survey. *American Journal of Public Health, 103*(6), 1082–1089.

Limber, S. P., Riese, J., Snyder, M. J., & Olweus, D. (2014). The Olweus Bullying Prevention Program: Efforts to address risks associated with suicide and suicide-related behaviors. In P. B. Goldblum, D. L. Espelage, J. Chu, & B. Bongar (Eds.), *Youth suicide and bullying: Challenges and strategies for prevention and intervention.* New York: Oxford University Press.

Liu, R. T., & Mustanski, B. (2012). Suicidal ideation and self-harm in lesbian, gay, bisexual, and transgender youth. *American Journal of Preventive Medicine, 42*(3), 221–228. doi: 10.1016/j.amepre.2011.10.023

Loeber, R., & Keenan, K. (1994). Interaction between conduct disorder and its comorbid conditions: Effects of age and gender. *Clinical Psychology Review, 14*, 497–523.

Low, S., Ryzin, M. J., Brown, E. C., Smith, B. H., & Haggerty, K. P. (2014). Engagement matters: Lessons from assessing classroom implementation of Steps to Respect: A bullying prevention program over a one-year period. *Prevention Science, 15*, 165–176. doi: 10.1007/s11121-012-0359-1

Luukkonen, A., Rasanen, P., Hakko, H., & Riala, K. (2010). Bullying behavior in relation to psychiatric disorders and physical health among adolescents: A clinical cohort of 508 underage inpatient adolescents in Northern Finland. *Psychiatry Research, 178*, 166–170. doi: 10.1016/j.psychres.2010.04.022

McCabe, R. E., Antony, M. M., Summerfeldt, L. J., Liss, A., & Swinson, R. P. (2003). Preliminary examination of the relationship between anxiety disorders in adults and self reported history of teasing or bullying experiences. *Cognitive Behaviour Therapy, 32*, 187–193.

Meltzer, H., Vostanis, P., Ford, T., Bebbington, P., & Dennis, M. S. (2011). Victims of bullying in childhood and suicide attempts in adulthood. *European Psychiatry, 26*, 498-503. doi: 10.1016/j.eurpsy.2010.11.006

Murphy, S. L., Xu, J., & Kochanek, K. D. (2013). Deaths: Final data for 2010. *National Vital Statistics Reports, 61*(4), 1–118.

Nansel, T. R., Overpeck, M., Pilla, R. S., Ruan, W. J., Simons-Morton, B., & Schiedt, P. (2001). Bullying behaviors among US youth: Prevalence and association with psychosocial adjustment. *Journal of the American Medical Association, 285*, 2094–2100.

Nasir, N. S., Jones, A., & McLaughlin, M. (2011). School connectedness for students in low-income urban high schools. *Teachers College Record, 113*, 1755—1793.

Nemoto, T., Bodecker, B., & Iwamoto, M. (2011). Social support, exposure to violence and transphobia, and correlates of depression among male-to-female transgender women with a history of sex work. *American Journal of Public Health, 101*(10), 1980–1988.

O'Donnell, L., O'Donnell, C., Merritt Wardlaw, D., & Stueve, A. (2004). Risk and resiliency factors influencing suicidality among urban African American and Latino youth. *American Journal of Community Psychology, 33*(1/2), 37-49.

Olweus, D. (1993). Victimization by peers: Antecedents and long-term outcomes. In K. H. Rubin & J. B. Asendorph (Eds.), *Social withdrawal, inhibition, and shyness in childhood* (pp. 315–341). Hillsdale, NJ: Lawrence Erlbaum.

Olweus, D., & Limber, S. P. (2007). *Olweus Bullying Prevention Program: Teacher guide.* Center City, MN: Hazelden.

Park, K. (2005). The moderating effects of problem-solving and social support on the relationship between child abuse and suicidal ideation. *The Korean Journal of School Psychology, 2*, 131–147.

Perkins, H. W., Craig, D. W., & Perkins, J. M. (2011). Using social norms to reduce bullying: A research intervention among adolescents in five middle schools. *Group Processes & Intergroup Relations, 14*(5), 703–722.

Pilkington, N. W., & D'Augelli, A. R. (1995). Victimization of lesbian, gay, and bisexual youth in community settings. *Journal of Community Psychology, 23*(1), 34–56.

Poteat, V. P., Mereish, E. H., DiGiovanni, C. D., & Koenig, B. W. (2011). The effects of general and homophobic victimization on adolescents' psychosocial and educational concerns: The importance of intersecting identities and parent support. *Journal of Counseling Psychology, 58*(4), 597–609. doi: 10.1037/a0025095

Reiney, E., & Limber, S. P. (2013). Why we don't use the word "bully" to label kids. Retrieved from http://www.stopbullying.gov/blog/2013/10/23/why-we-don%25E2%2580%2599t-use-word-%25E2%2580%259Cbully%25E2%2580%259D-label-kids

Rhodes, A. E., Kahn, S., Boyle, M. H., Tonmyr, L., Wekerle, C., Goodman, D., … Manion, I. (2013). Sex differences in suicides among children and youth: The potential impact of help-seeking behavior. *Canadian Journal of Psychiatry, 58*(5), 274–282.

Rigby, K., & Slee, P. (1999). Suicidal ideation among adolescent school children, involvement in bully-victim problems, and perceived social support. *Suicide and Life-Threatening Behavior, 29*(2), 119-130. doi: 10.1111/j.1943-278X.1999.tb01050.x

Rigby, K., Slee, P. T., & Martin, G. (2007). Implications of inadequate parental bonding and peer victimization for adolescent mental health. *Journal of Adolescence, 30*, 801–812. doi: 10.1016/j.adolescence.2006.09.008

Rivers, I., Poteat, V. P., Noret, N., & Ashurst, N. (2009). Observing bullying at school: The mental health implications of witness status. *School Psychology Quarterly, 24*(4), 211–223. doi: 10.1037/a0018164

Robers, S., Kemp, J., Truman, J., & Snyder, T. D. (2013). *Indicators of school crime and safety: 2012* (NCES 2013-036/NCJ 241446). National Center for Education Statistics, US Department of Education, and Bureau of Justice. Retrieved from http://nces.ed.gov/pubs2013/2013036.pdf

Russell, S. T., Frantz, B. T., & Driscoll, A. K. (2001). Same-sex romantic attraction and experiences of violence in adolescence. *American Journal of Public Health, 91*, 903–906.

Russell, S. T., & Joyner, K. (2001). Adolescent sexual orientation and suicide risk: Evidence from a national study. *American Journal of Public Health, 91*(8), 1276–1281.

Russell, S. T., Sinclair, K. O., Poteat, V. P., & Koenig, B. W. (2012). Adolescent health and harassment based on discriminatory bias. *American Journal of Public Health, 102*(3), 493–495. doi: 10.2105/AJPH.2011.300430

Saewyc, E. M. (2011). Research on adolescent sexual orientation: Development, health disparities, stigma, and resilience. *Journal of Research on Adolescence, 21*(1), 256-272. doi: 10.1111/j.1532-7795.2010.00727.x

Screening for Mental Health (2010). Youth programs. Retrieved from http://mentalhealthscreening.org/programs/youth

Shaffer, D., Scott, M., Wilcox, H., Ma-Slow, C., Hicks, R., & Lucas, C. P. (2004). The Columbia Suicide Screen: Validity and reliability of a screen for youth suicide and depression. *Journal of the American Academic of Child & Adolescent Psychiatry, 43*, 71–79.

Shochet, I. M., Dadds, M. R., Ham, D., & Montague, R. (2006). School connectedness is an underemphasized parameter in adolescent mental health: Results of a community prediction study. *Journal of Clinical Child and Adolescent Psychology, 35*, 170–179.

Shochet, I. M., Homel, R., Cockshaw, W. D., & Montgomery, D. T. (2008). How do school connectedness and attachment to parents interrelate in predicting adolescent depressive symptoms? *Journal of Clinical Child and Adolescent Psychology, 37*, 676–681.

Shon, B. D. (2005). Multivariate predictors on the depressed mood and suicidal risk among ordinary adolescents and adolescents with learning disabilities. *Korean Journal of Youth Studies, 12*, 207–228.

Slaby, A. E., & Pflum, S. (2014). Psychiatric models of bullying involvement: The impact of perceived psychiatric illness on victims, bullies, and bully-victims. In P. B. Goldblum, D. L. Espelage, J. Chu, & B. Bongar (Eds.), *Youth suicide and bullying: Challenges and strategies for prevention and intervention.* New York: Oxford University Press.

Smokowski, P. R., & Kopasz, K. H. (2005). Bullying in school: An overview of types, effects, family characteristics, and intervention strategies. *Children & Schools, 27*(2), 101–110.

StopBullying.gov (2013). *Policies and laws.* Retrieved from http://www.stopbullying.gov/laws/

Substance Abuse and Mental Health Services Administration. (2013). Lifelines curriculum. Retrieved from http://www.nrepp.samhsa.gov/ViewIntervention.aspx?id=37

Swearer, S. M., & Espelage, D. L. (2004). Introduction: A social-ecological framework of bullying among youth. In D. L. Espelage & S. M. Swearer (Eds.), *Bullying in American schools: A social-ecological perspective on prevention and intervention* (pp. 1–12). Mahwah, NJ: Lawrence Erlbaum Associates.

Swearer, S. M., Espelage, D. L., Vaillancourt, T., & Hymel, S. (2010). What can be done about school bullying? Linking research to educational practice. *Educational Researcher, 39*(1), 38–47. doi: 10.3102/0013189X09357622

Testa, R. J., & Hendricks, M. L. (2014). Suicide risk among transgender and gender nonconforming youth. In P. B. Goldblum, D. L. Espelage, J. Chu, & B. Bongar (Eds.), *Youth suicide and bullying: Challenges and strategies for prevention and intervention.* New York: Oxford University Press.

Testa, R. J., Sciacca, L. M., Wang, F., Hendricks, M., Goldblum, P., Bradford, J., & Bongar, B. (2012). Effects of violence on transgender people. *Professional Psychology: Research and Practice, 43*, 452–459.

Tingley, K. (2013, June 28). The suicide detective. *New York Times Magazine.* Retrieved from http://www.nytimes.com/2013/06/30/magazine/the-suicide-detective.html?pagewanted=all&module=Search&mabReward=relbias%3As&_r=0

Tormala, T. T., Ivan, I. I., Floyd, R., & Beckum, L. C. (2014). The connection between bullying and suicide in ethnic minority populations. In P. B. Goldblum, D. L. Espelage, J. Chu, & B. Bongar (Eds.), *Youth suicide and bullying: Challenges and strategies for prevention and intervention.* New York: Oxford University Press.

Ttofi, M. M., & Farrington, D. P. (2011). Effectiveness of school based programmes to reduce bullying: A systematic and meta-analytic review. *Journal of Experimental Criminology, 7*, 27–56. doi: 10.1007/s11292-010-9109-1

Xavier, J., Bobbin, M., Singer, B. & Budd, E. (2005). A needs assessment of transgendered people of color living in Washington, DC. *International Journal of Transgenderism, 8*(2-3), 31–47. doi: 10.1300/J485v08n02_04

Targeted Violence in Schools

Randy Borum

Abstract

Though targeted attacks at schools are rare events, educators and behavioral health professionals working in those settings must evaluate threats and threatening situations when they occur. Schools across the world have experimented with different methods over time, but the threat assessment approach—particularly executed by an interdisciplinary team—has emerged as a *best practice*. This chapter describes the results of the Safe School Initiative, an in-depth case analysis of 37 targeted school attacks involving 41 attackers over a 25-year period, and their implications for understanding the attackers, the situations, the settings, and the targets. It addresses the continuum of threats that schools may encounter and offers some heuristics for decision making, including recent research on key indicators of intent. It concludes by emphasizing the need for schools to have incident and post-incident response plans to mitigate harm if an attack does occur.

Key Words: school shooting, school violence, targeted violence, threat assessment, violence prevention

Over the past 15 years, a series of rare but tragic shooting events have disrupted America's view of schools as sanctuaries of safety for its children (Cornell, 2015; Flannery, Modzeleski, & Kretschmar, 2013; Nagy & Danitz, 2000). Though perceptions may have shifted abruptly, the objective risks have not. For a crisis and emergency management professional, understanding that distinction is critical. What are those objective risks? For that past decade, there have been about 21 homicides each year that have victimized one of the 60 million students attending one of America's 125,000 schools. Most school-associated homicide deaths involve only one victim and tend to be gang-related, drug-related, or otherwise linked to criminal activity or interpersonal disputes where the school is simply a site of opportunity for the attack (Cornell, 2015; Flannery et al., 2013). They are not the rare, targeted attacks that receive so much media attention. Targeted school-based attacks, where it was important to the attacker that

the shooting occur at the school—not simply those where an intended target just happened to be at the school—comprise a small minority of school-related deaths (Vossekuil, Fein, Reddy, Borum, & Modzeleski, 2002; Mayer & Furlong, 2010). The statistical risks are small, but the challenge of preventing these rare events is a reality for educators, administrators, and school systems (Borum, Cornell, Modzeleski, & Jimerson, 2010). Situations in schools where a student makes a threat or engages in some behavior or communication that causes someone to be concerned are not uncommon (Nekvasil & Cornell, 2012). Schools—or the behavioral health professionals working with them and in them—are responsible to assess the situation to determine how likely it may be that something bad is in the works (Rappaport, Pollack, Flaherty, Schwartz, & McMickens, 2014). This chapter intends to guide those prevention efforts by informing them with empirical evidence and best practices.

Threat Assessment as a Best Practice

School systems around the world have explored and experimented with a range of ways to assess and manage threatening situations (Böckler, Seeger, Sitzer, & Heitmeyer, 2013; Bondü, Scheithauer, Leuschner, & Cornell, 2013). Many of these methods have not been effective. Some have even created additional problems (Borum et al., 2010; Krauss, 2005). The idea of identifying potential school shooters by assessing students against a given *profile* has been discredited (Ferguson, Coulson, & Barnett, 2011). Research studies have failed to find any distinctive profile of young people who engage in school-based attacks. Even when a list of common characteristics is compiled, the overwhelming majority of students with those same traits do not ever plan or attempt a school shooting. Conversely, the threats posed by students whose behavior should signal the need for further attention are sometimes dismissed because they are deemed not to fit the profile.

Checklists of varying kinds have also proven to be largely unhelpful in assessing risk for school-based attacks. Although some checklists of warning signs and risk factors currently used by schools are derived from empirical research on youth violence and aggression, the relationship between these factors and the risk of targeted school violence is not yet known (Borum et al., 2010).

Expert consensus has emerged around the idea that multidisciplinary, team-based threat assessment is a *best practice* approach for assessing and managing threatening situations in schools (Borum et al., 2010; Meloy & Hoffmann, 2013). Threat assessment is a process for investigating situations in which a student makes a threat of violence, communicates intent, or otherwise engages in behavior suggesting plans or preparations for a school-based attack. The US Secret Service and the Department of Education outlined this process in, *Threat assessment in schools: A guide to managing threatening situations and to creating safe school climates* (Fein et al., 2002). The contours of the inquiry are based on a fundamental threat assessment principle, that "violence stems from an interaction among the potential attacker, past stressful events, a current situation, and the target," so each of these areas must be addressed.

• Attacker: An assessment of the attacker may consider relevant risk factors, the development and evolution of ideas concerning the attack, preparatory behaviors, and an appraisal of how the individual has dealt with unbearable stress in the past.

• Situation: Consideration of the current situation includes both an appraisal of the likelihood that past life events have triggered concern that self-destructive or violent behavior will reoccur (or are reoccurring) and an assessment of how others in the subject's environment are responding to his or her perceived stress and potential risk.

• Setting: Since others may act to prevent violence, it is useful to know whether people around the subject support, accept, or ignore the threat of violence or whether they express disapproval and communicate that violence is an impermissible and unacceptable solution to the problem.

• Target: The evaluation team must assess relevant factors about the intended target, including the subject's motives, degree of familiarity with the target's work and lifestyle patterns, the target's vulnerability, and the target's sophistication about the need for caution.

The US Department of Education and the US Secret Service's examination of attackers, situations, settings, and targets in the *Safe School Initiative* suggests that some future attacks may be preventable.

Understanding the Attackers

Despite popular stereotypes, there is no typical school shooter, nor is there any useful profile of these attackers (Heilbrun, Dvoskin, & Heilbrun, 2009; Langman, 2009; Vossekuil et al., 2002). It is clear, however, that they do not always mirror the characteristics of other seriously violent juvenile offenders. Students at risk for targeted violence may or may not possess many of the traditional risk factors associated with general violence recidivism and delinquency in youth; they may differ substantially not only from juveniles who engage in nonviolent delinquency but also from other juveniles who engage in different types of homicide. Studies of juvenile homicide have found that, relative to nonviolent delinquents, youth charged with homicide were *less* likely to have prior mental histories, *less* likely to have a history of prior arrests or placement in a juvenile facility, and *less* likely to have had problems with school adjustment. Youth convicted of homicide were also *less* likely to have histories of prior violent behavior than were juveniles convicted on assault charge (Cornell, 1990; Cornell, Benedek, & Benedek, 1987).

A number of case studies, anecdotal accounts, and secondary source evaluations of school shooters have been published over the past 15 years, but most draw from the same pool of cases and rely on the same data sources, so it is not surprising that there is general agreement among them (Bonanno & Levenson, 2014; Gerard, Whitfield, Porter, & Browne, 2015; Langman, 2009). The *Safe School Initiative* study conducted jointly by the US Secret Service and the US Department of Education (Vossekuil et al., 2002), using primary source material, has produced some of the most detailed findings to date on school-based attackers, examining 37 targeted school attacks involving 41 attackers over a 25-year period (Vossekuil et al., 2002). Nearly 85% of the attackers were males (primarily White) in their late teens (between the ages of 13 and 18) at the time of the attack. Almost two-thirds of the attackers came from two-parent families. A substantial proportion (41%) were doing well in school, generally receiving grades of As and Bs; very few were known to be failing. Many (41%) were considered mainstream students or were socialized with mainstream students and were often involved in organized social activities in or outside of school. Most had at least one close friend, but about one-third were characterized by others as "loners," or felt themselves to be loners. The attackers were rarely in trouble at school—only a quarter had ever been suspended. About one in four (28%) had a prior history of arrest, but fewer than one-third were known ever to have acted violently toward others at any point prior to the incident. More than half of the attackers (59%) demonstrated some interest in violence-related themes, through movies, video games, books, and other media, with many (37%) showing violence-related interests in their own writings, such as poems, essays, or journal entries.

Understanding the Situation

Understanding a pre-attack situation involves examining the events and stressors that are happening in a young person's life and how he or she may be coping. Indeed, among the school-based attackers studied, a large majority had experienced some major loss and appeared to have difficulty coping with losses, personal failures, or other difficult circumstances. Bullying is often cited as a central factor in narratives on school shootings (Klein, 2012; Leary, Kowalski, Smith, & Phillips, 2003). Not all of the attackers in the *Safe School Initiative* sample were bullied, however, nearly three-quarters had felt persecuted, bullied, threatened, attacked, or injured by others prior to the incident. Some—but not all—of those sentiments were related to bullying. In cases where bullying was evident, though, it was typically longstanding, severe, and a significant source of stress for the young person. Most of the attackers (81%) held some sort of grievance at the time of the attack, either against their target(s) or against someone else, and revenge was a motive for more than half (61%). Others were trying to solve a problem (34%) or were suicidal or desperate (27%).

Interestingly, in the period leading up to the attack, most of the young men showed no marked change in academic performance, friendship patterns, interest in school, or school disciplinary problems. Most of the attackers had not been formally diagnosed with a mental health or behavior disorder prior to the attack, but nearly two-thirds (61%) were known to be extremely depressed or desperate, and more than three-quarters of them (78%) had a history of suicide attempts or suicidal thoughts at some point prior to their attack. Though most did not show abrupt changes in school-related functioning, they did often show evidence of problems coping with stress and loss. Almost all of the attackers (93%) engaged in some behavior, prior to the incident, that caused others concern or indicated a need for help.

Understanding the Setting

An investigation of the setting surrounding a potential attack will account for interpersonal and environmental/contextual factors that might influence an attacker's decision-making and behavior. One pertinent consideration here is the culture or climate of safety in the school. The *National School Climate Center* (2015) defines school climate as characterizing "the quality and character of school life as it relates to norms and values, interpersonal relations and social interactions, and organizational processes and structures." Numerous studies have found that factors such as the presence of caring adults at the school and consistent enforcement of school rules and discipline not only increase students' perceptions of safety, but that less violence and harassment actually occurs at those schools (Klein, Cornell, & Konold, 2012; Osher, Bear, Sprague, & Doyle, 2010; Swearer, Espelage, Vallancourt, & Hymel, 2010; Thapa, Cohen, Guffey, & Higgins-D'Alessandro, 2013).

The interpersonal dimension of school climate is especially significant in light of the fact that, before the attack, most attackers showed evidence of needing help and that very often other people knew of the attacker's intent or plan prior to its execution. In most cases (76%), three or more people (often including at least one adult) were concerned by the attacker's behavior, which included actions related to the attack, such as efforts to get a gun, as well as other disturbing behaviors not related to the subsequent attack. A majority of the attackers (66%) also told other people about their grievances prior to their attacks.

Beyond these general concerns, prior to most incidents, other people actually knew about the attacker's idea and/or plan to attack (81%). Typically, the person who knew was a peer—a friend, schoolmate, or sibling who sometimes knew exactly what the attacker planned to do; others knew something "big" or "bad" was going to happen, and in several cases knew the time and date it was to occur. Studies have also noted the frequency with which attackers communicate their intent prior to an attack (Bondü & Scheithauer, 2014). The interpersonal "setting" for an attack is influenced by the attitudes and actions of people around the subject and whether they would support, accept, ignore, or discourage the threat of violence (Ajzen, 1985). Not only did most young people with information about a possible attack not come forward, some were even encouraging or complicit. Other people influenced the attacker decisions, dared or encouraged them to mount the attacks (or both) in almost half (44%) of the cases. Finally, just over two-thirds (68%) of the young attackers used weapons that were in their own home or that of a relative. The key point, as it pertains to the setting surrounding the attack, is not about family gun ownership, but about the importance of safe gun storage.

Finally, teachers and school administrators also affect the setting and can aid preventive efforts by creating an environment where students feel comfortable telling an adult whenever they hear about someone who is considering doing harm to another person, or even whether the person is considering harming him- or herself. Once such an environment is created, it will remain important that the adults in that environment listen to students and handle the information they receive in a fair and responsible manner.

Understanding the Target

In episodes of targeted violence, the attacker's motivation typically drives target selection. A prior study found that targeting certain individuals was a dominant theme in just over a quarter (27%) of the cases. The victims may be selected because of their symbolic significance to the offender or because they may have had a disagreement with the offender in the past (Harding, Fox, & Mehta, 2002). In school-based attacks, two other target-related considerations should be noted. First,

sometimes an attacker regards the school itself as a target. Feelings of pain, despair, and humiliation may be broadly attributed to the school experience, leading to animosity toward the school institution. This means that the ideas of who is targeted and who is at risk become more indiscriminate. Second, the actual victims of school shootings are often not the planned targets, and the intended targets are often not victimized. One cannot infer motivations after-the-fact based solely on who was injured or killed in the attack. The confluence of intent and opportunity often cause the intended targets and actual victims to be misaligned.

Applying a Continuum of Threat Assessment in Schools

All schools should have the authority, guidance, and capacity to conduct an inquiry into potentially threatening situations. Because *threats*, broadly conceived, may occur with some frequency, schools must screen to make an initial determination about whether further inquiry is warranted. The ultimate issue in any school-based threat assessment is whether the student *poses* a threat, not whether she or he *made* a threat. Accordingly, all threats should be taken seriously, but a communicated threat does not always indicate a high-risk situation, and the absence of a threat does not always indicate low-risk. So, schools should have a policy and a process for *triaging* threatening communications to separate those that require further inquiry from those that can be easily resolved.

Threat assessment should be a systematic assessment process. Threat assessment protocols should specify who should be notified, who should be involved in assessing the threat, what the criteria or guidelines are for making that assessment, who is responsible for documenting the assessment and recommendations, and who should monitor the plan's implementation.

Dr. Dewey Cornell and his team of researchers at the University of Virginia have developed a set of decision-tree guidelines for evaluating and responding to student threats involving potential violence (Cornell, 2003; Cornell & Sheras, 2006). These are often called the Virginia Threat Assessment Guidelines (VTAG). In the first stage of the process, the evaluator or assessment team gathers facts from the student, witnesses, and others to

• determine exactly what was said/communicated,
• understand the circumstances surrounding the statement, and
• gauge the student's capabilities and intent.

Based on this preliminary fact-finding process, the evaluator or assessment team initially categorizes the threat as either "transient" or "substantive." If the treat is transient, the guidelines recommend responses that might include reprimand, discipline, parental notification, or counseling/mediation. In prior studies, about 70% of threat referrals have been resolved as transient threats (Cornell et al., 2004). If the threat is substantive, the evaluators must assess whether it is *serious* (e.g. a threat to hit or assault) or *very serious* (e.g., a threat to kill or use a weapon). For serious threats, the school must first consider (a) whether immediate precautions and/or notifications might be needed to protect potential victims, and (b) whether law enforcement should be contacted. After addressing any immediate safety/notification issues, the threat assessment team can consider a range of options for further response, which might include discipline, counseling, or other intervention. After fully implementing VTAG, many schools have reported a reduction in long-term suspensions and reports of bullying, and an increase in students' willingness to seek help for bullying and threats, and in positive perceptions of the school climate. In none of the cases where VTAG has been studied have the threats been carried out.

For addressing serious threats, findings from the *Safe Schools Initiative* suggest that some future attacks may be preventable. Most incidents of targeted school violence are thought out and planned in advance. Before an incident occurs, the attacker's communication and behavior has provided clues that he or she was planning or preparing for an attack—regarded as *attack-related behavior*. As a result, prior to most incidents, the other people in the attacker's life (most often, the attacker's peers) knew or had strong reason to believe an attack was to occur. Moreover, the state of mind of most attackers was not *invisible*, but already was of concern to people in their lives (Vossekuil et al., 2002). Educators, law enforcement officials, and others with public safety responsibilities may be able to prevent some incidents of targeted school violence if they know what information to look for and what to do with such information when it is found. This requires the school to develop the capacity and authority to gather and analyze information regarding a student's behavior and communications.

School and law enforcement personnel might receive training concerning what information they should gather, how to collect and evaluate it, and how they might try to intervene in cases where the information collected suggests a student may be planning or preparing for a school-based attack. Because concerns about confidentiality and legal protection of student data often emerge, several states have enacted legislation that makes it easier for schools to share student information with law enforcement agencies and others who are trying to determine whether a student might be moving toward a school-based attack. Localities and states may wish to explore such options for supporting threat assessment components in schools and facilitating the sharing of information across school, law enforcement, and community systems participating in the threat assessment process. The ultimate objectives are twofold: to develop a school-based capacity to pick up on and evaluate available or knowable information that might indicate that there is a risk of a targeted school attack; and to employ findings from these risk evaluations or *threat assessments* to identify strategies for preventing potential school attacks from occurring.

Using the threat assessment approach, the person or team conducting the inquiry gathers information and answers key questions about the case to determine whether there is evidence to suggest the potential attacker is on a pathway (moving) toward violent action. In the threat assessment process, the primary objective is for the team to determine whether there is a reasonable basis for concern. This is a dynamic, behavioral, intent-based inquiry with a scope that differs from more general risk assessments of young people where the evaluators simply want to assess the likelihood that the subject will do harm to someone over a given period of time (see chapter 5 of this volume). The threat assessment focuses on ideas, behaviors, and situational influences that indicate intent, planning, or preparation for a violent act, rather than relying primarily on static, research-based correlates of violence.

A set of investigative questions guides that inquiry. Those questions focus on motivation for the behavior that brought the person being evaluated to official attention; communication about ideas and intentions; unusual interest in targeted violence; evidence of attack-related behaviors and planning; mental condition; level of cognitive sophistication or organization to formulate and execute an attack plan; recent losses (including loss of status); consistency between communications and behaviors; concern by others about the individual's potential for harm; and factors in the individual's life and/ or environment or situation that might increase or decrease the likelihood of an attack (see Table 8.1).

This multifaceted inquiry is designed to contextualize the original behavior or communication of concern and examine the available facts to determine not only whether a student has *made* a threat,

Table 8.1. Eleven Key Investigative Questions for Assessing Threats of Targeted Violence in Schools.

1. What is the student's motive(s) and goal(s)?
2. Has there been any communications suggesting ideas or intent to attack?
3. Has the student shown inappropriate interest in any of the following?
   a. School attacks or attackers
   b. Weapons (including recent acquisition of any relevant weapon)
   c. Incidents of mass violence (terrorism, workplace violence, mass murderers)
4. Has the student engaged in attack-related behaviors?
5. Does the student have the capacity to carry out an act of targeted violence?
6. Is the student experiencing hopelessness, desperation, and/or despair?
7. Does the student have a trusting relationship with at least one responsible adult?
8. Does the student see violence as acceptable or desirable or the only way to solve problems?
9. Is the student's conversation and "story" consistent with his or her actions?
10. Are other people concerned about the student's potential for violence?
11. What circumstances might affect the likelihood of an attack?

Adapted from Fein, Vossekuil, Pollack, Borum, Modzeleski, & Reddy (2002).

but also whether he or she *poses* a threat (Vossekuil et al., 2002). Posing a threat reflects a potential attacker's persistent violent intent, which drives the planning and preparation to carry out an attack. If careful consideration of the evidence suggests the student may *pose* a threat, the next step is to take action to prevent the threat from being carried out. Prevention efforts range from immediate security measures, such as notifying law enforcement and warning potential victims, to the development of an intervention plan designed to resolve the conflict or problem that precipitated the threat.

In addition to using the eleven key investigative questions from Table 8.1, another way to frame the areas of inquiry is to use the acronym ACTION to prompt examination of six key areas.

A: attitudes that support or facilitate violence
C: capacity
T: thresholds crossed
I: intent
O: other's reactions
N: noncompliance with risk reduction interventions

Borum and Reddy (2001) elaborated on each of these elements as follows.

• *Attitudes that support or facilitate violence*: What are the student's views on violence in general? What are the attitudes of others in the students *setting*? Does the student believe that the use of violence is justified under the circumstances? The youth's appraisal of his or her circumstances is the most critical factor because that perception, not the professional's perception, will most influence whether violence will occur. In general, people are more likely to engage in violence if they have assessed and affirmed its justification, both cognitively and affectively (Ajzen, 1985; Jemmott, Jemmott, Hines, & Fong, 2001).

• *Capacity*. What abilities and means does the student possess to carry out an attack, including physical and cognitive capabilities, access to means (i.e., weapons or materials necessary to effect the violent act), access to the target, and opportunity to commit the act?

• *Thresholds crossed*. What behavior, if any, has the student already undertaken in furtherance of a plan, particularly behaviors that require breaking laws and rules? In a threat assessment inquiry, it is helpful to think not only about the existence of a plan but also about the steps the student may have taken to further that plan, which may indicate commitment and proximity to action.

• *Intent*. Has the student simply entertained an idea of violence, or does he or she intend to commit the act? Attack-related behaviors may demonstrate a commitment to action in light of any anticipated consequences (Fein et al., 2002). Past school shooters have been known to feel desperate. Those who feel they have no available options or nothing to lose are sometimes more resolute in their commitment to a planned violent act.

One study compared actual school shooters with other "students of concern" to identify any behaviors that might distinguish between the two groups. The study was conducted on a German sample, but given the parallels with American sample, the authors believe their findings have implications across countries. Meloy, Hoffmann, Roshdi, and Guldimann (2014) found that pre-attack communications of intent were found in both groups, but they define and describe the factors that "distinguished the school shooters from those who showed no evidence of intent to act, and there were suggestive patterns for high risk cases," as follows (p. 204).

- *Pathway warning behavior*: any behavior that is part of research, planning, preparation, or implementation of an attack
- *Fixation warning behavior*: an increasingly pathological preoccupation with a person or a cause
- *Identification warning behavior*: a psychological desire to adopt an "attacker" identity or to identify with previous attackers or assassins, or identify oneself as an agent to advance a particular cause or belief system
- *Novel aggression warning behavior*: an act of violence, committed for the first time, that is functionally unrelated to pathway warning behaviors; these may involve self-harm or harm to others, but they test the potential attackers resolve and ability to follow through with a violent act
- *Last resort warning behavior*: evidence of "time imperative" in which the potential attacker feels desperate and devoid of options and has determined that violence is justified or necessary.
- *Others' reactions and responses*: How concerned are others who know the student that he/she might follow through with an attack? How does the student think others would respond to his plan of attack? If the young examinee has talked to anyone about his ideas or plans for violence, it may be helpful to know whether significant others have discouraged or condemned the ideas, offered no judgment, supported or escalated the violent ideas, or even facilitated the development of capacity or movement from idea to action? (Ajzen, 1985; Jemmott et al., 2001).
- *Noncompliance with risk reduction*: How motivated is the student to prevent or avoid a violent act? This might be affected by whether he or she thinks the risk mitigation plan (or recommended course of treatment) will be effective, whether the student has trust and alliance with the provider, the extent to which he or she understands and appreciates the severity of the potential for violence, and whether he or she has a history of adherence and willingness to comply with conditions of supervision or therapeutic regimens.

Threat Management in Schools

The primary objective for any school-based threat assessment is not to optimize prediction, but to prevent violence. To that end, managing risk becomes as important, if not more important, than merely assessing it. When a threat assessment evaluator or team determines that they have a reasonable basis for concern about violence, they must immediately begin to think about managing the situation and reducing

risk. Every risk management plan has three primary functions: containment, protection, and redirection. Containment's objective is to control the situation and prevent further forward movement toward an attack. Protection includes measures to alert a known target of a potential threat and to defend or reduce access to the target, including protecting and aiding the possible target. Redirection comprises efforts to move the would-be attacker away from a pathway toward violence and toward some alternative that is more hopeful and productive. Redirection activities include support and guidance to help the student deal successfully with his or her problems.

Risk management procedures should be outlined in a school's threat assessment protocol, and all actions should be carefully documented. Threat management plans should specify the components of the plan, and account for the roles and responsibilities of each person who has follow-up responsibilities for monitoring, reassessment, liaison, or direct intervention. This is especially important when the school is taking the lead. If the student remains in school, administrators might work with parents to impose and monitor the student's compliance with an approved supervision or management plan (Bonanno & Levenson, 2014; Rappaport et al., 2014).

Post-Shooting Crisis Response

Despite everyone's best efforts, sometimes a shooting or attack does occur at a school. Those incidents can be disruptive and sometimes traumatic for students, educators, staff, and the surrounding community (Daniels, Bradley, & Hays, 2007; Heath, Ryan, Dean, & Bingham, 2007). Efforts to mitigate the impact generally fall under the broader rubric of school crisis prevention and intervention. Interestingly, however, student-on-student physical assaults tend to be the most commonly reported crisis events in most schools (Nickerson & Zhe, 2004).

Schools vary considerably in the crisis response and support services they use, and very few of the approaches or programs have been systematically studied. Having a crisis response team (distinct from the threat assessment team) is the most common feature of school crisis responses, with one survey showing that 93% of schools used them, and most school psychologists find those teams to be among the most effective interventions. The preponderance of empirical evidence does not favor the effectiveness of one-time *debriefing* sessions (Bisson, 2003), but more comprehensive interventions or individual sessions, with the opportunity for referral to individual or family counseling, appear to have some support (Everly, Flannery, & Eyler, 2002).

One popular and widely used approach is the PREPaRE School Crisis Prevention and Intervention model promulgated by the National Association of School Psychologists (Brock et al., 2009). Attempting to promote a national standard, PREPaRE was designed to be consistent with guidance from the US Department of Education (2003, 2006) and the US Department of Homeland Security's National Incident Management System's Incident Command System (2004). The PREPaRE model addresses crisis response with a sequenced series of activities that correspond to phases of the post-event response.

- **P**reventing and preparing for psychological trauma
- **R**eaffirming physical health and perceptions of security and safety
- **E**valuating psychological trauma risk
- **P**roviding interventions
- **a**nd **R**esponding to psychological needs
- **E**xamining the effectiveness of crisis prevention and intervention.

Conclusion

School shootings are extremely rare events. Nevertheless, all schools must be prepared to assess and manage threatening situations when they occur. Effective management requires planning and preparation to avoid the confusing and inefficient scramble that can occur when a crisis emerges (Borum et al., 2010; Rappaport et al., 2014). Over the years schools have experimented with different approaches to assessing threats, but profiling students and relying on checklists have proven to be less than helpful. The Virginia Threat Assessment Guidelines (VTAG), developed by Dr. Dewey Cornell and colleagues have emerged as one of the few evidence-based protocols to address the continuum of student threats. The VTAG uses a decision-tree approach for evaluating (classifying as *transient* or *serious*) and responding to student threats involving potential violence (Cornell, 2003; Cornell & Sheras, 2006).

Multidisciplinary threat assessment teams have emerged as a *best practice* approach for assessing and managing threatening situations in schools. Teams apply a systematic, fact-based threat assessment process for investigating situations in which a student engages in threatening or otherwise concerning behavior that could indicate planning or an attack (Borum et al., 2010). The US Secret Service and the US Department of Education have conducted a detailed examination of past school shootings—the *Safe Schools Initiative*—and have determined that school-based attacks are driven by a confluence of factors pertaining to the potential attacker, past stressful events, the current situation, and the target. The findings from this study suggest that some future attacks may be preventable.

Using the threat assessment approach, the person or team conducting the inquiry gathers information and answers key questions about the case to determine whether there is evidence to suggest the potential attacker is on a pathway (moving) toward violent action. This is a dynamic, behavioral, intent-based inquiry with a scope that differs from more general risk assessments of young people where the evaluators simply want to assess the likelihood that the subject will do harm to someone, over a given period of time. The threat assessment focuses on ideas, behaviors, and situational influences that indicate intent, planning, or preparation for a violent act, rather than relying primarily on static, research-based correlates of violence. Details of the recommended process are outlined in *Threat Assessment in Schools: A Guide to Managing Threatening Situations and to Creating Safe School Climates* (Fein et al., 2002).

The threat assessment process is guided by a set of key questions designed to help the team determine whether there is a reasonable basis for concern that the student may be on a pathway toward a violent act. The inquiry does not focus on student characteristics, but on ideas, behaviors, and situational influences. The central issue in this assessment is whether the student *poses* a threat, and not just whether he or she *made* a threat. Relying on this kind of systematic process, based on evidence from program evaluations and studies of past school shootings, schools can responsibly manage concerning student behaviors and potentially prevent future school-based attacks.

References

Ajzen, I. (1985). *From intentions to actions: A theory of planned behavior* (pp. 11–39). Heidelberg, Germany: Springer Berlin.

Bisson, J. I. (2003). Single-session early psychological interventions following traumatic events. *Clinical Psychology Review, 23,* 481–499.

Böckler, N., Seeger, T., Sitzer, P., & Heitmeyer, W. (2013). School shootings: Conceptual framework and international empirical trends. In *School Shootings* (pp. 1–24). Springer New York.

Bonanno, C. M., & Levenson, R. L. (2014). School shooters history, current theoretical and empirical findings, and strategies for prevention. *SAGE Open, 4*(1), 1–11. doi:10.1177/2158244014525425

Bondü, R., & Scheithauer, H. (2014). Leaking and death-threats by students: A study in German schools. *School Psychology International*, *35*(6), 592–608. doi:10.1177/0143034314552346

Bondü, R., Scheithauer, H., Leuschner, V., & Cornell, D. G. (2013). International perspectives on prevention and intervention in school shootings. In *School Shootings* (pp. 343–362). Springer New York.

Borum, R., Cornell, D. G., Modzeleski, W., & Jimerson, S. R. (2010). What can be done about school shootings? A review of the evidence. *Educational Researcher*, *39*(1), 27–37.

Borum, R., & Reddy, M. (2001). Assessing violence risk in Tarasoff situations: A fact-based model of inquiry. *Behavioral Sciences & the Law*, *19*(3), 375–385.

Brock, S. E., Nickerson, A. B., Reeves, M. A., Jimerson, S. R., Lieberman, R., & Feinberg, T. (2009). *School crisis prevention and intervention: The PREPaRE model*. Bethesda, MD: National Association of School Psychologists.

Cornell, D. (2015). Our schools are safe: Challenging the misperception that schools are dangerous places. *American Journal of Orthopsychiatry*, *85*(3), 217–220.

Cornell, D. G. (2003). Guidelines for responding to student threats of violence. *Journal of Educational Administration*, *41*(6), 705–719.

Cornell, D. G. (1990). Prior adjustment of violent juvenile offenders. *Law and Human Behavior*, *14*(6), 569.

Cornell, D. G., Benedek, E. P., & Benedek, D. M. (1987). Juvenile homicide: Prior adjustment and a proposed typology. *American Journal of Orthopsychiatry*, *57*(3), 383.

Cornell, D., & Sheras, P. (2006). *Guidelines for responding to student threats of violence*. Longmont, CO: Sopris West.

Cornell, D., Sheras, P., Gregory, A., & Fan, X. (2009). A retrospective study of school safety conditions in high schools using the Virginia Threat Assessment Guidelines versus alternative approaches. *School Psychology Quarterly*, *24*, 119–129.

Cornell, D., Sheras, P., Kaplan, S., McConville, D., Douglass, J., Elkon, A., ... Cole, J. (2004). Guidelines for student threat assessment: Field-test findings. *School Psychology Review*, *33*, 527–546.

Daniels, J. A., Bradley, M. C., & Hays, M. (2007). The impact of school violence on school personnel: Implications for psychologists. *Professional Psychology: Research and Practice*, *38*(6), 652.

Everly, G. S., Flannery, R. B., & Eyler, V. A. (2002). Critical incident stress management (CISM): A statistical review of the literature. *Psychiatric Quarterly*, *73*, 171–182.

Fein, R., Vossekuil, B., Pollack, W., Borum, R., Modzeleski, W., & Reddy, M. (2002). *Threat assessment in schools: A guide to managing threatening situations and to creating safe school climates*. Washington, DC: US Secret Service and US Department of Education.

Flannery, D. J., Modzeleski, W., & Kretschmar, J. M. (2013). Violence and school shootings. *Current Psychiatry Reports*, *15*(1), 1–7.

Ferguson, C. J., Coulson, M., & Barnett, J. (2011). Psychological profiles of school shooters: Positive directions and one big wrong turn. *Journal of Police Crisis Negotiations*, *11*(2), 141–158.

Gerard, F. J., Whitfield, K. C., Porter, L. E., & Browne, K. D. (2015). Offender and offence characteristics of school shooting incidents. *Journal of Investigative Psychology and Offender Profiling*. doi:10.1002/jip.1439

Harding, D. J., Fox, C., & Mehta, J. D. (2002). Studying rare events through qualitative case studies lessons from a study of rampage school shootings. *Sociological Methods & Research*, *31*(2), 174–217.

Heath, M. A., Ryan, K., Dean, B., & Bingham, R. (2007). History of school safety and psychological first aid for children. *Brief Treatment and Crisis Intervention*, *7*(3), 206.

Heilbrun, K., Dvoskin, J., & Heilbrun, A. (2009). Toward preventing future tragedies: Mass killings on college campuses, public health, and threat/risk assessment. *Psychological Injury and Law*, *2*, 93–99.

Jemmott, J. B., III, Jemmott, L. S., Hines, P. M., & Fong, G. T. (2001). Testing the theory of planned behavior as a model of involvement in violence among African American and Latino adolescents. *Maternal Child Health Journal*, *5*, 253–263.

Klein, J. (2012). *The bully society: School shootings and the crisis of bullying in America's schools*. New York, NY: NYU Press.

Klein, J., Cornell, D., & Konold, T. (2012). Relationships between bullying, school climate, and student risk behaviors. *School Psychology Quarterly*, *27*(3), 154–169.

Krauss, D. A. (2005). Predicting school violence. In F. Denmark, H. Krauss, R. Wesner, E. Midlarsky, & U. Gielen, (Eds.),. *Violence in sSchools* (pp. 253–273). New York, NY: Springer US.

Langman, P. (2009). *Why kids kill: Inside the minds of school shooters*. New York, NY: Palgrave Macmillan.

Leary, M., Kowalski, R., Smith, L., & Phillips, S. (2003). Teasing, rejection, and violence: Case studies of the school shootings. *Aggressive Behavior*, *29*, 202–214.

Mayer, M. J., & Furlong, M. J. (2010). How safe are our schools? *Educational Researcher*, *39*(1), 16–26.

Meloy, J. R., & Hoffmann, J. (Eds.). (2013). *International handbook of threat assessment*. New York, NY: Oxford University Press.

Meloy, J. R., Hoffmann, J., Roshdi, K., & Guldimann, A. (2014). Some warning behaviors discriminate between school shooters and other students of concern. *Journal of Threat Assessment and Management*, *1*(3), 203.

Nagy, J., & Danitz, T. (2000). Parental fears heightened by Columbine, poll shows. Retrieved from http://www.stateline.org/live/ViewPage.action?siteNodeId=136&languageId=1&contentId=13994

National School Climate Center. (2015). *Facts about school climate*. Retrieved from http://www.schoolclimate.org/climate/faq.php

Nekvasil, E. K., & Cornell, D. G. (2012). Student reports of peer threats of violence: Prevalence and outcomes. *Journal of School Violence*, *11*(4), 357–375.

Nickerson, A. B., & Zhe, E. J. (2004). Crisis prevention and intervention: A survey of school psychologists. *Psychology in the Schools*, *41*(7), 777–788.

Osher, D., Bear, G. B., Sprague, J. R., & Doyle, W. (2010). How can we improve school discipline? *Educational Researcher*, *39*, 48–58.

Randazzo, M. R., Borum, R., Vossekuil, B., Fein, R., Modzeleski, W., & Pollack, W. (2006). Threat assessment in schools: Empirical support and comparison with other approaches. In S. R. Jimerson and M. J. Furlong (Eds.), *Handbook of school violence and school safety: From research to practice* (pp. 147–156). Mahwah, NJ: Erlbaum.

Rappaport, N., Pollack, W. S., Flaherty, L. T., Schwartz, S. E., & McMickens, C. (2014). Safety assessment in schools: Beyond risk—the role of child psychiatrists and other mental health professionals. *Child and Adolescent Psychiatric Clinics of North America*, *24*, 277–289.

Sewell, K. W., & Mendelsohn, M. (2000). Profiling potentially violent youth: Statistical and conceptual problems. *Children's Services: Social Policy, Research, and Practice*, *3*, 147–169.

Swearer, S. M., Espelage, D. L., Vallancourt, T., & Hymel, S. (2010). What can be done about school bullying? Linking research to educational practice. *Educational Researcher, 3*, 38–47.

Thapa, A., Cohen, J., Guffey, S., & Higgins-D'Alessandro, A. (2013). A review of school climate research. *Review of Educational Research, 83*(3), 357–385.

US Department of Education. (2006). *Emergency management for schools training.* Washington, DC: Author.

US Department of Education, Office of Safe and Drug-Free Schools. (2003). *Practical information on crisis planning: A guide for schools and communities.* Washington, DC: Author.

Retrieved from http://www.ed.gov/admins/lead/safety/emergencyplan/crisisplanning.pdf

US Department of Homeland Security. (2004). *National incident management system.* Washington, DC: Author. Retrieved from http://www.fema.gov/pdf/emergency/nims/NIMS_core.pdf

Vossekuil, B., Fein, R. A., Reddy, M., Borum, R., & Modzeleski, W. (2002). *The final report and findings of the Safe School Initiative: Implications for the prevention of school attacks in the United States.* Washington, DC: US Secret Service and US Department of Education.

Behavioral Emergencies with Adults

Evaluating and Managing Suicide Risk with the Adult Patient

Bruce Bongar, Glenn Sullivan, Victoria Kendrick, *and* Joseph Tomlins

Abstract

Suicide and suicidal behavior are major medical and social problems in many parts of the world, despite a growing understanding of how to adequately prevent suicide. Many health-care professionals do not have sufficient knowledge or training to provide adequate suicide assessment, nor do they have an understanding of the protocols necessary for the management of suicidal patients. Without validated predictive tools to use in cases of suspected suicidal ideation, it is usually left to the clinician to make a decision regarding risk and potential harm. In this chapter we describe how to identify a suicidal patient and the procedures necessary to adequately provide services.

Key Words: suicide, evaluation, patient, risk factors, attempters, completers, documentation, management, assessment

In 2010, suicide accounted for 38,000 deaths nationally and was the 10th leading cause of death in the United States (Centers for Disease Control, 2013). It continues to be a serious public health problem around the world, claiming approximately one million victims worldwide every year (Andriessen & Krysinska, 2012). It is vitally important for both mental health providers and primary care physicians to be vigilant in recognizing suicide risk and to be aware of factors that may contribute to an increased risk for suicide.

There are a number of terms used to differentiate the various types of thoughts, behaviors, and actions related to suicide, and it is important for clinicians to understand the differences so as to adequately distinguish high risk from low risk during assessment and inquiry. In recent literature, standardized definitions have emerged to ensure clear communication among clinicians, patients, and families (Gordon & Melvin, 2014). Suicidal ideation refers to passive thoughts about wanting to be dead or active thoughts about killing oneself. Suicidal ideation is not accompanied by preparatory behavior.

Non-suicidal self-injuries (NSSI) are behaviors associated with no intent to die, while suicidal behavior could potentially result in a fatal injury. A suicide attempt is defined as an act associated with at least some intent to die although injury may or may not occur. Finally suicide is defined as death caused by self-injurious behavior with intent to die (Crosby, Ortega, & Melanson, 2011).

Evaluation of the Suicidal Patient

There are a number of different factors that play important roles in the development of suicidal ideation and, later, the attempt or completion of suicidal behaviors. This chapter discusses how to identify the risk factors associated with adult suicidal patients as well as appropriate assessment tools that can provide insight into a patient's symptomatology. Management of a suicidal patient as well as appropriate documentation is imperative for clinicians. Understanding the necessary evaluation and management protocols requires flexibility. We discuss risk factors, differences between attempters and completers, as well as protective factors.

Appropriate practices, risk management guidelines, and standard of care are discussed, as well as the future direction of evaluation of a suicidal patient. (See chapter 4 of this volume for a discussion of suicide risk assessment and management with children and adolescents.)

Risk Factors

Clinicians working with suicidal patients should keep in mind the many risk and protective factors related to suicidal behavior. Knowledge surrounding these factors increases the likelihood that the clinician will successfully intervene in an appropriate manner. There are a number of important risk factors that are related to suicidal behavior, and some present as higher risk than others, including demographic, environmental, family, and clinical risk factors. Some of these risk factors are considered to be static, meaning they do not change over time (e.g., gender, past attempts, family history), while others are dynamic and can be modified by treatment (e.g., ideation, physical health, current stressors) (Gordon & Melvin, 2014).

The American Psychiatric Association Practice Guidelines list 56 factors, divided into 10 categories, which are linked to an increase in risk for suicide (Jacobs et al., 2003). These categories include suicidal thoughts and behaviors, which may comprise suicidal ideation, plans (both current and past), past attempts, lethality of plans and/or attempts, and suicidal intent. Other categories include psychiatric diagnoses with high-risk disorders such as major depressive disorder, bipolar disorder, schizophrenia, anorexia, and substance use disorders. Physical illnesses that are related to an increase in suicide risk include HIV/AIDS and diseases of the nervous system. Psychosocial features include recent lack of social support, unemployment, socioeconomic status, poor relationship with family, domestic partner violence, and recent stressful life events. Both sexual and physical abuse in childhood can increase the risk for suicide. Genetic familial effects including both a history of suicide and a history of mental illness increase the risk for suicide. Psychological features play an important role in risk assessment and it is important to determine if the patient shows signs and symptoms of hopelessness, panic attacks, shame or humiliation, decreased self-esteem, impulsiveness, aggression (including violence against others), or agitation. Cognitive features such as thought constriction, polarized thinking, closed-mindedness, and loss of executive function are also important risk factors that warrant attention. Demographic features such as being male, widowed, or Caucasian increase the risk for suicide. Clinicians should be aware that there are differences in high-risk factors for different population groups. Particularly close attention should be paid to the myriad demographic groups that patients might identify with and how these variables may alter their presentation of suicidal thoughts, behaviors, or plans.

For inpatient settings, three distinct factors predict a strong association with inpatient suicide, including depressed mood, psychomotor retardation, and loss of energy (Lin et al., 2014). This is vitally important for clinicians practicing in inpatient care because the suicide risk for psychiatric inpatients is about 50 times higher than for the general population (Ajdacic-Gross, Lauber, Baumgartner, Malti, & Rossler, 2009). The risk is also higher for clinicians practicing in outpatient settings because of the increased risk in the period immediately after admission to inpatient care as well as directly after discharge (Lin et al., 2014). Family and environmental factors should be specifically asked about during risk assessment, particularly the individual's access to lethal means to suicide. Removal and storage of lethal means has been shown to reduce suicide in suicidal patients (Gordon & Melvin, 2014). For adults in an outpatient setting, there are high correlations between suicidal behavior and mental illness as well as with previous attempts. Approximately 60% of suicides are associated with mood disorders (Molero et al., 2014), with 93.6% of suicide attempters and 85.9% of suicide completers found to have psychiatric diagnoses (Parra Uribe et al., 2013). A single past suicide attempt drastically increases an individual's risk for suicide. As a result, awareness of past suicide attempts is an integral facet of suicide prevention, although the absence of past attempts is not necessarily a reason to think that there is little or no risk.

Sexual Minorities. Rates of suicidal ideation and attempts among lesbian, gay, bisexual, and queer/questioning people (LGB) vary based on sampling approaches, definitions of constructs, geographical location, help-seeking, and other factors. However, several decades of research have consistently demonstrated that LGB individuals report higher levels of suicidal ideation and attempts when compared to their heterosexual peers (Cochran & Mays, 2013; Goodenow, Szalacha, & Westheimer, 2006; Mustanski, Garofalo, & Emerson, 2010; Russell & Joyner, 2001; Russell & Toomey, 2012). Among sexual minorities, the odds of attempting suicide are approximately two to seven times higher than the odds of suicide attempts among heterosexuals (King et al., 2008; Haas et al., 2010). A Rhode Island-based study demonstrated that 10% of sexual minorities, as compared to just over 3% of heterosexuals, reported suicide attempts severe enough to warrant medical attention (Jiang, Perry, & Hesser, 2010). It should be noted that sexual orientation itself does not lead to suicidality among LGB people; rather, environmental reactions to non-heterosexual orientations increase suicide risk in this population (Savin-Williams & Ream, 2003).

The minority stress model (Meyer, 2003) helps to elucidate some of the connections between sexual minority identity and suicidality. In most industrialized societies, individuals identifying as lesbian, gay, or bisexual are part of a stigmatized and disadvantaged cultural group. This disadvantaged social position leads to the experience of minority stress (Meyer, 2003). For LGB individuals, "stigma, prejudice, and discrimination create a hostile and stressful social environment that causes mental health problems" (Meyer, 2003, p. 674). These widespread experiences of stigma negatively impact self-perception and increase the expectation of social rejection (Hatzenbuehler, 2009; Meyer, 2003). Eventually, the elevated level of social adversity contributes to higher psychiatric morbidity (Hatzenbuehler, 2009; Meyer, 2003). (See chapter 6 of this volume for a more complete discussion of suicide risk in sexual minorities.)

Attempters versus Completers

There is a large body of research focused on the difference between individuals who are considered "attempters" and "completers" of suicide. This has been done in an effort to delineate the risk factors associated with each. Suicide attempts are between 10 and 40 times more common than completed suicides (Parra Uribe et al., 2013). Hall, Platt, and Hall (1999) found that patients who made serious suicide attempts but survived tended to be between 17 and 35 years old, and displayed depressive symptoms such as feelings of worthlessness, helplessness, hopelessness, global or partial insomnia, anxiety and panic episodes, anergia, and severe anhedonia. Parra Uribe et al. (2013) found that suicide completers were usually male, tended to be older, had precarious social situations, such as living alone, were in poor health, were depressed, and used more lethal methods

for attempts, while suicide attempters tended to be women, younger in age, and presented with less serious mental illnesses such as adjustment disorders.

A clinically relevant difference between attempters and completers centers on their contact with health-care services prior to their attempts. Few suicide completers had had contact with mental health services in the months prior to suicide, while a high proportion had been in contact with their primary care physician. On the other hand, suicide attempters tended to be in consistent contact with mental health services (Parra Uribe et al., 2013). This points to continued prevention tactics necessary within primary medical care facilities. Although there are distinct differences between these two groups, they do not negate the need for the clinician to conduct thorough risk assessment on patients that present as possible attempters compared to completers.

Violent Tendencies

Violent tendencies and the predisposition toward violence have been recent topics of interest in suicide research. Joiner (2005) suggested in the Interpersonal Theory of Suicide (IPTS) that past experiences with pain and violence can desensitize the individual to violence against oneself, leading to an increase in suicide risk. Consistent and continual victimization, bullying, domestic violence, and gang violence can all serve to make individuals more capable of suicidal behaviors. Violence involvement helped differentiate suicide attempters from suicide ideators, meaning that patients with violent tendencies tended to be at higher risk for suicide attempts (Stack, 2014).

Studies of psychiatric inpatient settings have demonstrated that higher levels of anger are uniquely associated with higher levels of suicide risk. Moreover, the experience of anger and its expression have predicted suicidal ideation, plans, and attempts (Hawkins et al., 2014). Anger, aggression, and hostility have all been linked to increased suicide risk. Additionally, these constructs are consistently associated with psychiatric disorders that play a role in suicide. It is important to note that the research on the connection between violence and suicidality is mixed, with some research showing strong predictors and others omitting violent tendencies as a predictor. More research is needed to specifically determine the connections between these two phenomena.

Protective Factors

Along with a wide range of factors that are related to an increased risk for suicide, there are a number of important protective factors that are equally important to pay attention to. Some of these protective factors, as determined by the APA Practice Guidelines (Jacobs et al., 2003), include, but are not limited to, positive coping skills such as meditation, physical activities, and socialization, positive social support, life satisfaction, religiosity, and positive problem-solving skills. Determining a patient's strengths from the initial session allows the clinician to provide the patient with adequate knowledge of where that person is successful in life. It also increases the therapeutic rapport and helps increase the patient's self-esteem in relationship to his or her abilities.

Assessment Tools

Assessment tools are vital to the continued appraisal of suicidal thoughts or behaviors. There are a number of tools that can be utilized including the clinical interview, screeners, and comprehensive evaluations. Screeners and fast assessment tools that can be used include specific questions on suicidal ideation and thoughts, which can be incorporated into the interview at appropriate intervals to monitor the patient's ideation and thoughts as well as changing risk levels.

When determining the type of assessment tool to utilize, it is important to consider the specific purpose of the instrument, the construct to be measured, and whether the instrument has been used previously in this setting and with this particular population (Goldston, 2003). Assessment tools that are used for the detection of suicidal ideation include the Beck Scale for Suicidal Ideation (BSS; Beck & Steer, 1991), which focuses on assessment of the severity of suicidal ideation, plans, and preparation in the past week; the Beck Depression Inventory (BDI), designed to assess the presence and severity of depressive symptoms during the past two weeks (Beck, Steer, & Brown, 1996); and the Acquired Capability for Suicide Scale (ACSS), designed to assess the patient's sense of fearlessness about death and an elevated pain tolerance (Van Orden, Witte, Gordon, Bender, & Joiner, 2008).

It is suggested that a high standard of care include a screening for suicide risk during the initial session and, moreover, continued attention must be paid throughout the course of treatment (Schmitz et al., 2012). Merely asking patients whether they are suicidal is an insufficient measure. If suicidal thoughts or ideation are identified during the clinical interview, a suicide risk assessment can be conducted with three goals: (1) identifying the specific factors that increase or decrease the risk for suicide, (2) addressing the immediate safety of the patient so that an appropriate treatment setting can be determined, and (3) identifying psychiatric illnesses that can be targeted in treatment (Frierson, 2007).

Management of the Suicidal Patient
Standards of Care

When working with a seriously suicidal individual, the mental health professional must continually assess the level of risk. The patient's demographic variables, the clinical interview, outcome measures, family members, and consultations can all be used to determine a patient's level of risk for suicide (Gutheil & Schetky, 1998). Concisely, the mental health professional's job is to determine whether the patient can continue to be seen in an outpatient setting. If the probability of imminent suicidal behavior is judged low enough to justify continued outpatient treatment, then treatment should continue on an intensified basis (e.g., twice weekly, with 24-hour telephone access to the therapist) (Bongar & Sullivan, 2013b). Slaby (1998) also identified the need to conduct recurring evaluations of suicidal ideation, in addition to providing the following: psychoeducation regarding suicide to the patient and his or her significant others; the arrangement of emergency coverage for evenings, weekends, and vacations; the development of a collaborative treatment plan with realistic goals; and the maintenance of detailed, accurate records.

After the patient is determined to be at a level of risk that does not warrant imminent threat, the therapist needs to be prepared to increase treatment options. Expanded care for suicidal patients includes increasing the number of sessions, allowing telephone access, scheduling regular consultations, and making appropriate referrals. Increasing the number of sessions is important because of the unreliable nature of long-term estimates of suicide risk when compared to short-term estimates—especially when considering that suicide attempts are often impulsive (i.e., attempters deciding to kill themselves less than 1 hour before their attempts; Simon et al., 2001). In essence, increased sessions limit the length between estimates, in addition to demonstrating the therapist's concern over the gravity of the situation.

Bongar and Sullivan (2013a) highlight the utility of electronic communication and encourage the use of telephones and email. Electronic communication can be used with the patient and with family members to check in with the therapist during pre-established times between sessions. It is important to ensure that the patient understands the limits to confidentiality when using electronic communication, despite the increasingly common nature of this form of communication. A specific consent form that includes those limits can be used. Bongar and Sullivan (2013a) outline a procedure to follow should a patient miss a preestablished check-in time. First, the procedure should be collaboratively determined in advance. Second, the therapist and patient should discuss a specific action plan, such as calling an emergency contact for a wellness check. Third, as standard practice, all psychotherapy outpatients should be provided with the national Suicide Prevention Lifeline Number: 1-800-273-TALK (8255). This is important to ensure that the patient is able to contact aid should the therapist become unavailable by the time the patient is able to access electronic communication again.

The Decision to Seek Inpatient Care

Although outpatient therapy is possible for persons at high suicidal risk, hospitalization is more usual in such cases because the opportunities to control and anticipate suicide are greater in an inpatient setting (Bongar & Sullivan, 2013b). Fremouw, de Perczel, and Ellis (1990) further noted that the determination of the level of danger in this decision is based on five considerations: (1) the imminence of the behavior and immediacy of the risk—whether the patient is a clear and imminent danger to self at the present time; (2) the target of the danger—whether the suicidal behaviors occur in the context of angry dyadic exchanges and whether there is a possibility of concurrent homicidal and suicidal thoughts and impulses; (3) the clarity of the danger—whether and to what degree the patient is specific in what he or she plans to do; the intensity of the impulses; whether the patient has selected the method, time, or place; (4) the intent of the behavior—whether there is a clear determination of both the patient's intention and his or her motive to die; and (5) the lethality or probability of death, which must be assessed on separate dimensions—risk–rescue ratio. Should it be determined that the therapist and other caretakers cannot reasonably ensure the safety of the patient, then the decision to seek inpatient care would likely be justified. Should the probability of imminent suicidal behavior be determined to be low enough to justify continued

outpatient treatment, then treatment should continue on an intensified basis (Ellis, Allen, Woodson, Frueh, & Jobes, 2009).

Suicide Prevention Contracts

The management of the suicidal patient is one of the most challenging, anxiety-provoking tasks facing mental health professionals. Suicide contracts have long been used as a means to both manage suicidal behavior and allay health-care provider disquiet (Drye, Goulding, & Goulding, 1973) and their use has increased in recent years (Lewis, 2007; Miller, Jacobs, & Gutheil, 1998). A suicide prevention contract is loosely defined as "an agreement in which the therapist elicits a promise from the patient that if the patient experiences suicidal ideas or impulses, the patient will inform a healthcare provider, family member or friend, rather than engage in self-injurious behavior" (Weiss, 2001, p. 414).

Although a suicide prevention contract appears to be a prudent response to suicide risk—and likely to increase the sense of control in the therapist—the contract itself may foster a false sense of security and thus lower the mental health professional's vigilance for future and lingering risk factors (Garvey, Penn, Campbell, Esposito-Smythers, & Spirito, 2009). In fact, postmortem examinations of individuals who completed suicide found that suicide prevention contracts were widely used (Miller et al., 1998). This suggests that although patients often agree to sign the contracts, they continue to be at risk.

Other concerns include the patient's ability to accurately understand the content of the contract—for example, that the patient is "only permitted to contact the clinician in the event of a suicidal crisis" (Bongar & Sullivan, 2013b, pp. 175–176). This is of particular concern given the suicidal patient's likely heightened cognitive rigidity, dichotomous thinking, impaired problem-solving ability, hopelessness, irrational beliefs, and dysfunctional attitudes (Handley et al., 2013; Weitz, Hollon, Kerkhof, & Cuijpers, 2014). Suicide prevention contracts should not substitute for suicide risk assessments (Bongar & Sullivan, 2013a). Suicide prevention contracts are widely used but they are not an effective means of managing ongoing suicidality.

A potentially useful form of suicide prevention contract is the Safety Plan Intervention (SPI), developed by the US Department of Veterans Affairs (Stanley & Brown, 2008). This intervention for suicidal veterans includes a comprehensive treatment plan and designed to manage risk. It is similar to the conventional suicide prevention contract in that it provides a structure for mental health professionals and patients to explicitly identify the goal of suicide prevention; however, the SPI also facilitates collaboration between clinician and patient, creates a hierarchical series of coping strategies, and helps the patient identify persons and agencies to contact to decrease an imminent risk for self-harm (Rings, Alexander, Silvers, & Gutierrez, 2012). The SPI is unique in that while other studies have examined suicide prevention contracts in the assessment and management of suicidal patients (e.g., Brown et al, 2005; Jobes, 2006; Linehan, 1993; Matarazzo, Homaifar, & Wortzel, 2014), none are considered "stand-alone" interventions as the SPI is. In sum, the SPI goes beyond a mere "contract" because it involves the patient in the collaboration of constructing a plan, fosters problem-solving, limits rigid thinking, develops coping skills, and creates alternatives to suicide.

Integrating Multiple Systems into Care

It is imperative that mental health professionals collaborate with the patient's multiple support systems (family members, significant others, and professionals involved in the patient's care). Berman (2006), for example, suggests that mental health professionals collaborate with family members by keeping them informed and involving them in treatment when the risk for suicide arises.

Bongar and Sullivan (2013a) strongly urge mental health professionals not to hesitate in calling family members and other social support because of the importance of enlisting them in the treatment plan. Family involvement is particularly important in suicide management because a breakdown in family relationships, unemployment, and a change in social roles can all be significant contributing factors to suicide (Berman, 2006; Goldney, 2002; Jobes, 2011; Pirkola, Suominen, & Isometsä, 2004; Richman, 1986). Clearly, interpersonal relationships play a huge role in the risk for suicide, particularly related to family issues. Jobes (2011) suggests that the range of relationships should be assessed to identify the patient's social support—from romantic to friendships, from lack of a support system to being overwhelmed by too many interpersonal obligations.

The strength of the relationship between family and suicide risk necessitates a systematic assessment of the patient's family and friends. Goldney (2002) suggested that mental health professionals be especially mindful when patients perceive themselves to be a burden on family and believe their family would be better off without them. In this case, the family should be engaged to address and hopefully correct this perception. Some researchers have found treatments that involve family to be the most efficacious in ameliorating suicidal behavior (Richman, 1986). In sum, it is the mental health professional's responsibility to ensure that the risk is made known to all concerned parties.

It is always preferred that the mental health professional attain consent from the patient before contacting family and/or important social support, however, any trepidation related to confidentiality must be subsumed within the overarching goal of patient safety. Breaking confidentiality in cases of imminent risk for suicide is supported by the beliefs and attitudes of family members who have had a loved one die from suicide. McAuliffe and Perry (2007) interviewed families about their experiences following the death of a family member to suicide. These families expressed their frustration that they were not sufficiently involved in the treatment and that there was a lack of recognition of the support they provided to their relative. They recommended that there be a formal policy to include family members in collecting initial information, in discharge planning, and in the development of a safety plan.

Lethality, Method, and Responsibility

Bryan, Stone, and Rudd (2011) posit, "to kill oneself, one must have the means for doing so." This statement speaks to the importance of means restriction as an integral facet of both the assessment and management of the suicidal patient. Means restriction is directly related to the lethality of a suicide attempt. Lethality can be described as an interaction between the lethality of method and the probability of rescue or successful medical intervention (Bongar & Sullivan, 2013a). Should the patient plan on committing suicide via a drug overdose, they would be at less risk of completion than should they have, instead, decided to attempt suicide via a firearm. Clearly, the lethality of an attempt is related to the patient's means of actually carrying out the plan. While an individual's intent to commit suicide only has a weak relationship to risk of completed suicide (Pirkola et al., 2004), having the means to commit suicide is strongly related to risk for completed suicide (Eddleston et al., 2006). This is likely due to the variation in the lethality of chosen methods for suicide. For example, the presence of firearms in the home significantly increases the risk for completed suicide (Brent & Bridge, 2003) and is associated with an 85% fatality rate (Vyrostek, Annest, & Ryan, 2004).

Impulsivity is paramount in suicidal behavior. Simon et al. (2001) reported that 70% of suicide attempters in their sample had decided to kill themselves less than 1 hour before their attempts. As a result of the integral role of impulsivity in suicidal behavior, steps must be taken to decrease the potential lethality of the patient's environment. It should be noted that all means for suicide cannot entirely be controlled. For instance, the patient will inevitably have access to the Internet, which contains myriad methods for committing suicide. Nonetheless, restricting means is imperative to the management of the suicidal patient. In the United States, death by firearm is the leading cause of completed suicide (Bryan et al., 2011). As a result, the amalgam of having firearms in the house coupled with impulsivity could potentially determine the outcome of a suicidal crisis and should consequently be limited, if possible.

Mental health professionals should assess for firearms as part of their standard practice. Should the patient have access to firearms, the weapons should be removed from the household, even if the patient's plan did not involve using them (Bongar & Sullivan, 2013a). After it is deemed that the patient has firearms in the household, a discussion about removing them should ensue. Bongar and Sullivan (2013a) warn mental health professionals not to be surprised by resistance to the idea of removing the firearms. It should be noted that a facet of the resistance is likely cultural (e.g., political, rural, military). One way to circumvent resistance is to introduce the notion that means-restriction is only a temporary precaution to ensure the patient's safety. Bryan et al. (2011) also suggest that temporary means-restriction can be particularly effective, because it provides the patient with a sense of control, reinforces the notion that the suicidal ideation is time-limited, and potentially instills hope for the future. Bryan et al. (2012) suggest the following options to instill autonomy in the patient: "Removing the means completely from the house (and other areas of access) by disposing of it; removing the means completely by giving it to a supportive other authorized to possess the means legally; locking the means up in a safe or another secured area with the combination or key secured by a supportive other (note that safes or locks designed with manual overrides in the event of lost or forgotten combinations or keys are inadequate)" (p. 341). In sum, restriction of means is an integral part of managing suicide. Although restriction for the most lethal means involves the restriction of access to firearms, the general approach can be applied to myriad other methods of suicide (e.g., pill restriction).

Practice and Risk Management Guidelines
Documentation

There are a number of important elements in the management of patients that present as suicidal. Documentation and consultation with colleagues play an integral role in a high standard of care. Documentation and, in particular, high-quality notes allow clinicians to focus their full attention on making sound clinical judgments. Thorough documentation can be the "cornerstone to the defense of a potential lawsuit resulting from a patient suicide" (Frierson, 2007). Good documentation does several things: in addition to recording the clinician's competence at identifying suicide risk factors and designing interventions, it makes a possible lawsuit surrounding the clinician's standard of care more difficult, and it also helps prevent future suicide by creating specific records to which the clinician can continually refer and review at future sessions (Frierson, 2007).

Meticulous progress notes give the clinician room to explain decision making in regard to patient care. If a clinician decides not to hospitalize a suicidal patient in an outpatient setting, it is important that the clinician document the reasons for making that specific treatment decision. These notes should include specific dates of incidents, the names of colleagues that the clinician consulted with before making the decision, as well as pertinent information discussed during that consultation (Frierson, 2007). It has been suggested by Simon and Shuman (2007) that when doubt arises regarding a clinical intervention, it is important for the clinician to write a risk–benefit progress note to provide documentation of the decision process, but also to ensure that all options were considered.

A risk–benefit note should include the following: the source of information (including clinical signs), acute and chronic risk factors, protective factors, an assessment of current level of suicide risk, the action under consideration, a clear statement of why the action was either taken or not taken, and a statement regarding the risks and benefits of the actions taken—and not taken (Simon & Shuman, 2007). Along with specific progress notes determining the psychologist's continued understanding of the patient and his or her symptoms, results of a formal suicide risk assessment should be organized and well documented, specifically in regard to the identified risk factors and protective factors (Frierson, 2007). Bongar and Sullivan (2013b) suggested that whenever a clinician writes a risk–benefit progress note relating to uncertainty in either assessment or management of a patient, the clinician should obtain a formal consultation.

Consultation

When faced with a high-risk patient, it is almost always important to consult with a professional colleague, preferably one that has past experience with high-risk patients. Consultation along with documentation of the decision-making process can serve as durable proof that the clinician has not been negligent (Stolberg & Bongar, 2009). The following guidelines, although not exhaustive, are important aspects when conducting a professional consultation in regard to a high-risk patient. A consultation should include a review of the overall management of the case, specific treatment issues, uncertainties in the assessment of elevated risk or in the diagnosis, and a discussion of the clinician's personal feelings about the progress of treatment, as well as feelings the clinician has toward the patient (both positive and negative). Furthermore, the consultation should discuss indications and contraindications for hospitalization, a review of available community crisis intervention resources, emergency and backup arrangements, family or group treatment options, and the psychologist's assessment criteria for evaluating dangerousness and imminence (Bongar & Sullivan, 2013b).

Knowledge of Community Resources

Knowledge of community resources is vital to the continued management of suicidal patients. Ready access to emergency teams, crisis centers, hotlines, as well as to day treatment programs, is essential so as to implement appropriate affirmative precautions (Bongar & Sullivan, 2013a). Furthermore, an understanding of community resources plays an important role in the development of safety planning but also allows clinicians to have a wide array of treatment opportunities for their patients that include both voluntary and involuntary hospital admissions.

Postvention

To ensure that clinicians are providing adequate and quality care to their patients, it is important that they are familiar with the current literature regarding risk factors, epidemiology, and management of a suicidal patient, and it is also vital that they are current and competent in the area of postvention. Postvention can be defined as "activities developed by, with or for suicide survivors, in order to facilitate recovery after suicide and to prevent adverse outcomes including suicidal behavior" (Andriessen, 2009). Suicide survivors often exhibit increased risk for suicide—between two and ten times that of the general population (Aguirre & Slater, 2010). There is a lack of consensus in the literature regarding the definition of a "suicide survivor," but most definitions share important commonalities. They focus on the fact that there exists a relationship between the deceased and the bereaved and that important measures need to be taken to ensure that those bereaved, be it close family members, distant relatives, friends, neighbors, or employers, have effective care—postvention (Andriessen & Krysinska, 2012; Jordan & McIntosh, 2011).

Gutheil (1999) determined that there are specific negative feelings that are associated with the consequence of suicide, including guilt, rage, grief, surprise, betrayal of trust, and psychological abandonment. Survivors may feel guilt that they should have or could have done something to stop the suicide at the same time as they feel that they have been left alone to deal with this terrible situation (Bongar & Sullivan, 2013b). While experiencing these feelings, many suicide survivors are also going through their own negative life events surrounding the loss of the loved one, including planning the funeral, settling of estates, and the stress of the actual suicide (Aguirre & Slater, 2010). It is vitally important that suicide survivors be able to manage these important feelings, specifically in relationship to their own risk of suicide.

A variety of psychosocial issues that suicide survivors experience have been identified to help postvention programs adequately serve this population. The issues include difficulties related to the disruption of family relations and routines, functional impairments in daily activities, difficulties with social and familial relationships, spiritual struggles, and financial and judicial problems (Andriessen & Krysinska, 2012). Postvention is not limited to the initial time following the shock of the loss; it should continue over a year or more to ensure continued care and safety of suicide survivors. As discussed by Bongar and Sullivan (2013b), there are general principles for postvention including postvention therapy. Postvention therapy shares many characteristics of psychotherapy, with the general principles and goals surrounding grief work and exploration into emotions (both negative and positive) as related to the deceased or to death itself (Graham et al., 2000).

There are a number of postvention efforts in effect in the United States as well as in other countries, although there are still considerable areas missing in regard to high quality care. A recent study of the Australian Standby Response Service, a community based outreach program providing support for people bereaved through suicide, found that the service reduced the negative impact of suicide bereavement on both physical and mental health. This includes lowering levels of suicidality and increasing levels of productivity (Jordan & McIntosh, 2011). The US Department of Health and Human Services (HHS) Office of the Surgeon General increased awareness for suicide prevention, which led to The National Strategy for Suicide Prevention. This program aims "to reduce the harmful after-effects associated with. . .the traumatic impact of suicide on family and friends" (Aguirre & Slater, 2010). Although the aim is specific to suicide survivors, there is little actual postvention in this program. A more comprehensive model is the Active Postvention Model (Campbell, Cataldie, McIntosh, & Miller, 2004) which is being implemented in a variety of countries including the United States. This program specifically "places a new first responder at the scene of suicides while the body is still present" with the sole purpose to come in contact with suicide survivors and intervene during the difficult time (Aguirre & Slater, 2010). With these interventions in mind, it is important for clinicians to be aware for themselves—as well as for the family members of their patients—how suicide affects them and how to access the best resources that are available for all.

Future Directions

Over the past several decades, there has been a widespread increase in information and knowledge surrounding suicide and self-harming behaviors, but there is always room for more knowledge and literature surrounding this important topic. Future directions should focus on a number of important areas that are lacking. Assessment tools used with high-risk patients tend to be inconsistent in their descriptions of suicidal behavior; as assessment tools and measures become a greater investment for clinicians, it is vital that these tools are measuring the same constructs. Furthermore, assessments that look at specific groups and specific behaviors (both passively and indirectly associated with suicide) will be an important step toward prevention and detection of suicidal thoughts and behaviors. In regard to postvention, it is important to

determine an operational definition of the term "suicide survivor," as well as to conduct studies to identify the specific experiences and needs of various subgroups of survivors based on age, gender, and circumstance of situation. This information will enable the introduction of specific postvention programs that can decrease the risk associated with suicide survivors.

Continued research on the correlation between anger and risk of suicide is an important and necessary direction for future research. More research is needed on the relationship between actual violence and suicidal behavior. The Interpersonal Theory of Suicide has had mixed results in explaining the link between violence and suicide, perhaps due to measurement issues (Stack, 2014). Unpacking the link between violence and suicide is likely to require more than a single psycho-theoretical framework.

References

Aguirre, R. T. P., & Slater, H. (2010). Suicide postvention as suicide prevention: Improvement and expansion in the United States. *Death Studies, 34*, 529–540.

Ajdacic-Gross, V., Lauber, C., Baumgartner, M., Malti, T., & Rossler, W. (2009). In-patient suicide—a 13-year assessment. *Acta Psychiatrica Scandinavica, 120*, 71–75.

Andriessen, K. (2009) Can postvention be prevention? *Crisis, 30*, 43–47.

Andriessen, K., & Krysinska, K. (2012). Essential questions on suicide bereavement and postvention. *International Journal of Environmental Research and Public Health, 9*, 24–32.

Beck, A. T., & Steer, R. A. (1991). *Manual for the Beck Scale for Suicide Ideation.* San Antonio, TX: Psychological Corporation.

Beck, A. T., Steer, R. A., & Brown, G. K. (1996). *Manual for Beck Depression Inventory-II.* San Antonio, TX: Psychological Corporation.

Berman, A. L. (2006). *Risk management with suicidal patients. Journal of Clinical Psychology, 62*(2), 171–184. doi:10.1002/jclp.20221

Bongar, B., & Sullivan, G. (2013a). Outpatient management and treatment of the suicidal patient. In B. Bongar and G. Sullivan (Eds.), *The suicidal patient: Clinical and legal standards of care* (3rd ed., pp. 157–199). Washington, DC: American Psychological Association. doi:10.1037/14184-005

Bongar, B., & Sullivan, G. (2013b) *The suicidal patient: Clinical and legal standards of care* (3rd ed.). Washington, DC: American Psychological Association.

Brent, D. A., & Bridge, J. (2003). Firearms availability and suicide: Evidence, interventions, and future directions. *American Behavioral Scientist, 46*, 1192–1210. doi:10.1177/0002764202250662

Brown, C. K., Have, T. T., Henriques, C. R., Xie, S. X., Hollander, J. E., & Beck, A. T. (2005). Cognitive therapy for the prevention of suicide attempts: A randomized controlled trial. *JAMA, 294*, 563–570. doi:10.1001/jama.294.5.563

Bryan, C. J., Corso, K. A., Corso, M. L., Kanzler, K. E., Ray-Sannerud, B., & Morrow, C. E. (2012). Therapeutic alliance and change in suicidal ideation during treatment in integrated primary care settings. *Archives of Suicide Research*, *16*(4), 316–323. doi:10.1080/13811118.2013.722055

Bryan, C. J., Stone, S. L., & Rudd, M. (2011). A practical, evidence-based approach for means-restriction counseling with suicidal patients. *Professional Psychology: Research and Practice*, *42*(5), 339–346. doi:10.1037/a0025051

Campbell, F., Cataldie, L., McIntosh, J., & Miller, K. (2004). An active postvention program. *Crisis, 25*, 30–32.

Centers for Disease Control. (2013). *Deaths: Leading Causes for 2010*. Retrieved from http://www.cdc.gov/nchs/data/nvsr/nvsr62/nvsr62_06.pdf

Cochran, S. D., & Mays, V. M. (2013). Sexual orientation and mental health. In J. C. Patterson and A. R. D'Augelli (Eds.), *Handbook of Sexual Orientation and Mental Health* (pp. 204–222). New York, NY: Oxford University Press.

Crosby, A. E., Ortega, L., & Melanson, C. (2011). Self-directed violence surveillance: Uniform definitions and recommended data elements. Atlanta: GA: Center for Disease Control and Prevention.

Drye, R. C., Goulding, R. L., & Goulding, M. E. (1973). No-suicide decisions: Patient monitoring of suicidal risk. *The American Journal of Psychiatry, 130*(2), 171–174.

Eddleston, M., Karunaratne, A., Weerakoon, M., Kumarasinghe, S., Rajapakshe, M., Sheriff, M. H. R.,... Gunnell, D. (2006). Choice of poison for intentional self-poisoning in rural Sri Lanka. *Clinical Toxicology, 44*, 283–286. doi:10.1080/15563650600584444

Ellis, T. E., Allen, J. G., Woodson, H., Frueh, B., & Jobes, D. A. (2009). Implementing an evidence-based approach to working with suicidal inpatients. *Bulletin of the Menninger Clinic, 73*(4), 339–354. doi:10.1521/bumc.2009.73.4.339

Frierson, R. L. (2007). The suicidal patient: Risk assessment, management, and documentation. *Psychiatric Times*. Retrieved from http://www.psychiatrictimes.com/articles/suicidal-patient-risk-assessment-management-and-documentation

Fremouw, W. J., de Perczel, M., & Ellis, T. E. (1990). *Suicide risk: Assessment and response guidelines*. Elmsford, NY: Pergamon Press.

Garvey, K. A., Penn, J. V., Campbell, A. L., Esposito-Smythers, C., & Spirito, A. (2009). Contracting for safety with patients: Clinical practice and forensic implications. *Journal of the American Academy of Psychiatry and the Law, 37*(3), 363–370.

Goldney, R. D. (2002). A global view of suicidal behavior. *Emergency Medicine, 14*(1), 24.

Goldston, D. B (2003). Summary, recommendations, and future directions. In D. B. Goldston, *Measuring suicidal behavior and risk in children and adolescents* (pp. 253–263). Washington, DC: American Psychological Association.

Goodenow, C., Szalacha, L., & Westheimer, K. (2006). School support groups, other school factors, and the safety of sexual minority adolescents. *Psychology in the Schools, 43*(5), 573–589. doi:10.1002/pits.20173

Gordon, M., & Melvin, G. (2014). Risk assessment and initial management of suicidal adolescents. *Australian Family Physician, 43*(6), 367–373.

Graham, A., Reser, J., Scuderi, C., Zubrick, S., Smith, M., & Turley, B. (2000). Suicide: An Australian Psychological Society discussion paper. *Australian Psychologist, 35*, 1–28.

Gutheil, T. G. (1999). Liability issues and liability prevention in suicide. In D. G. Jacobs (Ed.), *The Harvard Medical School guide to suicide assessment and intervention* (pp. 561–578). San Francisco, CA: Jossey-Bass.

Gutheil, T. G., & Schetky, D. (1998). A date with death: Management of time-based and contingent suicidal intent. *American Journal of Psychiatry, 155*(11), 1502.

Haas, A. P., Eliason, M., Mays, V. M., Mathy, R. M., Cochran, S. D., D'Augelli, A. R.,... & Clayton, P. J. (2010). Suicide and suicide risk in lesbian, gay, bisexual, and transgender populations: Review and recommendations. *Journal of Homosexuality, 58*(1), 10–51. doi:10.1080/00918369.2011.534038

Hall, R. C. W., Platt, D. E., & Hall, R. C. W (1999) Suicide risk assessment: A review of risk factors for suicide in 100 patients who made severe suicide attempts. *Psychosomatics, 40*(1), 18–27.

Handley, T. E., Kay-Lambkin, F. J., Baker, A. L., Lewin, T. J., Kelly, B. J., Inder, K. J., & Kavanagh, D. J. (2013). Incidental treatment effects of Cognitive Behavior Therapy on suicidal ideation and hopelessness. *Journal of Affective Disorders, 151*(1), 275–283. doi:10.1016/j.jad.2013.06.005

Hatzenbuehler, M. L. (2009). How does sexual minority stigma "get under the skin?": A psychological mediation framework. *Psychological Bulletin, 135*(5), 707–730. doi:10.1037/a0016441

Hawkins, K. A., Hames, J. L., Ribeiro, J. D., Silva, C., Joiner, T. E., & Cougle, J. R. (2014). An examination of the relationship between anger and suicide risk through the lens of the interpersonal theory of suicide. *Journal of Psychiatric Research, 50*, 59–65.

Jacobs, D., Baldessarini, R., Conwell, Y., Fawcett, J., Horton, L., Meltzer, H.,... Simon, R. (2003). Practice guidelines for the assessment and treatment of patients with suicidal behaviors. (Updated 2010). Washington, DC: American Psychiatric Association. Retrieved from http://psychiatryonline.org/pb/assets/raw/sitewide/practice_guidelines/guidelines/suicide.pdf

Jiang, Y., Perry, D. K., & Hesser, J. E. (2010). Adolescent suicide and health risk behaviors: Rhode Island's 2007 Youth Risk Behavior Survey. *American Journal of Preventative Medicine, 38*(5), 551–555. doi:10.1016/j.amepre.2010.01.019

Jobes, D. A. (2006). *Managing suicidal risk: A collaborative approach*. New York, NY: Guilford Press.

Jobes, D. A. (2011). Suicidal patients, the therapeutic alliance, and the collaborative assessment and management of suicidality. In K. Michel, D. A. Jobes (Eds.), *Building a therapeutic alliance with the suicidal patient* (pp. 205–229). Washington, DC: American Psychological Association. doi:10.1037/12303-012

Joiner, T. E. (2005). *Why people die by suicide*. Cambridge, MA: Harvard University Press.

Jordan, J. R., & McIntosh, J. L. (2011). A research agenda for suicide survivors. In J. R. Jordan & J. L. McIntosh (Eds.), *Grief after suicide* (pp. 507–522). New York, NY: Routledge.

King, M., Semlyen, J., Tai, S. S., Killaspy, H., Osborn, D., Popelyuk, D., & Nazareth, I. (2008). A systematic review of mental disorder, suicide, and deliberate self harm in lesbian, gay, and bisexual people. *BMC Psychiatry, 8*, 70. doi:10.1186/1471-244X-8-70

Lewis, L. (2007). No-harm contracts: A review of what we know. *Suicide and Life-Threatening Behavior, 37*(1), 50–57. doi:10.1521/suli.2007.37.1.50

Linehan, M. (1993). *Cognitive behavior therapy for borderline personality disorder*. New York, NY: Cuilford Press.

Lin, S. K., Hung, T. M., Liao, Y. T., Lee, W. C., Tsai, S. Y., Chen, C. C., & Kuo, C. J. (2014). Protective and risk factors for inpatient suicides: A nested case-control study. *Psychiatry Research, 217*, 54–59.

Matarazzo, B., Homaifar, B., & Wortzel, H. (2014). Therapeutic risk management of the suicidal patient: Safety planning. *Journal of Psychiatric Practice, 20*(3), 220–224. doi:10.1097/01.pra.0000450321.06612.7a

McAuliffe, N., & Perry, L. (2007). Making it safer: A health centre's strategy for suicide prevention. *Psychiatric Quarterly, 78*(4), 295–307. doi:10.1007/s11126-007-9047-x

Meyer, I. H. (2003). Prejudice, social stress, and mental health in lesbian, gay, and bisexual populations: Conceptual issues and research evidence. *Psychological Bulletin, 129*(5), 674–697. doi:10.1037/0033-2909.129.5.674

Miller, M., Jacobs, D. G., & Gutheil, T. G. (1998). Talisman or taboo: The controversy of the suicide-prevention contract. *Harvard Review of Psychiatry, 6*(2), 78–87. doi:10.3109/10673229809000314

Molero, P., Grunebaum, M. F., Galfalvy, H. C., Bongiovi, M. A., Lowenthal, D., Almedia, M. G.,... Oquendo, M. A. (2014). Past suicide attempts in depressed inpatient clinical versus research assessment. *Archives of Suicide Research, 18*, 50–57.

Mustanski, B. S., Garofalo, R., & Emerson, E. M. (2010). Mental health disorders, psychological distress, and suicidality in a diverse sample of lesbian, gay, bisexual, and transgender youths. *American Journal of Public Health, 100*, 2426–2432. doi:10.2105/AJPH.2009.178319

Parra Uribe, I., Blasco-Fontecilla, H., Garcia-Parés, G., Giro Batalla, M., Llorens Capdevial, M., Cebrià Meca, A.,... Palao Vidal, D. J. (2013). Attempted and completed suicide: Not what we expected? *Journal of Affective Disorders, 150*, 840–846.

Pirkola, S. P., Suominen, K., & Isometsä, E. T. (2004). Suicide in alcohol-dependent individuals: Epidemiology and management. *CNS Drugs, 18*(7), 423–436.

Richman, J. (1986). *Family Therapy for Suicidal People.* New York, NY: Springer Publishing Company.

Rings, J. A., Alexander, P. A., Silvers, V. N., & Gutierrez, P. M. (2012). Adapting the Safety Planning Intervention for use in a veterans psychiatric inpatient group setting. *Journal of Mental Health Counseling, 34*(2), 95–109.

Russell, S. T., & Joyner, K. (2001). Adolescent sexual orientation and suicide risk: Evidence from a national study. *American Journal of Public Health, 91*(8), 1276–1281.

Russell, S. T., & Toomey, R. B. (2012). Men's sexual orientation and suicide: Evidence for U. S. adolescent-specific risk. *Social Science and Medicine, 74*(4), 523–529. doi:10.1016/j.socscimed.2010.07.038

Savin-Williams, R. C., & Ream, G. L. (2003). Suicide attempts among sexual-minority male youth. *Journal of Clinical Child and Adolescent Psychology, 32*(4), 509–522.

Schmitz, W. M., Allen, M. H., Feldman, B. N., Gutin, N. J., Jahn, D. R., Kleespies, P. M.,... Simpson, S. (2012). Preventing suicide through improved training in suicide risk assessment and care: An American Association of Suicidology Task Force report addressing serious gaps in U. S. mental health training. *Suicide and Life-Threatening Behavior, 42*(3), 292–304. doi:10.1111/j.1943-278X.2012.00090.x

Simon, R. I., & Shuman, D. W. (2007). Clinical manual of psychiatry and law. Washington, DC: American Psychiatric Publishing.

Simon, T. R., Swann, A. C., Powell, K. E., Potter, L. B., Kresnow, M. J., & O'Carroll, P. W. (2001). Characteristics of impulsive suicide attempts and attempters. *Suicide and Life-Threatening Behavior, 32*, 49–59. doi:10.1521/suli.32.1.5.49.24212

Slaby, A. (1998). Outpatient management of suicidal patients. In B. Bongar, A. L. Berman, R. W. Maris, M. M. Silverman, E. A. Harris, & W. L. Packman (Eds.), *Risk management with suicidal patients* (pp. 34–64). New York, NY: Guilford Press.

Stack, S. (2014). Differentiating suicide ideators from attempters: Violence—a research note. *Suicide and Life-Threatening Behavior, 44*(1), 46–57.

Stanley, B., & Brown, C. K. (2008). *Safety plan treatment manual to reduce suicide risk: Veteran version.* Department of Veterans Affairs. Retrieved from http://www.mentalhealth.va.gov/docs/VA_Safety_planning_manual.pdf

Stolberg, R. A., & Bongar, B. (2009). Assessment of suicide risk. In J. Butcher (Ed.), *Oxford handbook of personality assessment.* New York, NY: Oxford University Press.

Van Orden, K. A., Witte, T. K., Gordon, K. H., Bender, T. W., & Joiner, T. E. (2008). Suicidal desire and the capability for suicide: Tests of the interpersonal-psychological theory of suicidal behavior among adults. *Journal of Consulting and Clinical Psychology, 76*, 72–83.

Vyrostek, S. B., Annest, J. L., & Ryan, G. W. (2004). Surveillance for fatal and nonfatal injuries—United States, 2001. *MMWR Surveillance Summaries, 53*, 1–57.

Weiss, A. (2001). The no-suicide contract: Possibilities and pitfalls. *American Journal of Psychotherapy, 55*(3), 414–419.

Weitz, E., Hollon, S., Kerkhof, A., & Cuijpers, P. (2014). Do depression treatments reduce suicidal ideation? The effects of CBT, IPT, pharmacotherapy, and placebo on suicidality. *Journal of Affective Disorders, 167*, 98–103.

Evaluating and Managing the Risk of Violence in Clinical Practice with Adults

Daniel C. Murrie *and* Sharon Kelley

Abstract

Although concerns about violence emerge regularly in routine clinical practice, many clinicians feel underprepared to assess and manage violence risk. One problem is that the rich knowledge base underlying violence risk assessment has largely remained in the specialties of forensic psychology and psychiatry, where it has been less familiar to clinicians in general practice. In this chapter we review the legal and ethical parameters that guide clinician appraisals of violence risk, and then we summarize the foundational knowledge and techniques—from both the forensic psychology approach and the emerging field of threat assessment. By integrating basic knowledge and practices from these specialized disciplines, clinicians can more comfortably incorporate violence risk assessment and management into their routine care for patients, better infuse risk assessment into the start of treatment, monitor risk over the course of treatment, and respond appropriately to any threats of violence that emerge.

Key Words: risk assessment, risk management, threat assessment, violence risk, *Tarasoff*, duty to warn, duty to protect

Concerns about violence risk routinely arise in clinical practice. Indeed, these concerns are common among mental health clinicians regardless of whether they practice in hospitals (e.g., emergency departments, psychiatric acute-care units, and psychiatric continuing care units; Binder & McNiel, 1999; Chu, Thomas, Ogloff, & Daffern, 2011), community clinics (Allnutt et al., 2013; Pabian, Welfel, & Beebe, 2009), or even schools and universities (Cornell et al., 2004; Halikias, 2004; Reddy et al., 2001). Decades ago, Shah (1978) documented at least 15 contexts in which clinicians must assess the risk of violence, most of which remain relevant today. Precisely because concerns about violence risk are ubiquitous across such diverse settings, violence risk assessment in clinical practice cannot be a competence that is limited to a highly specialized few. Rather, clinicians in *any* setting require at least some degree of basic competence in violence risk assessment. Consider, for example, the violence risk assessment and management duties

clinicians face in the following traditional practice scenarios: (1) identifying acutely ill patients at greatest risk for violence at an inpatient psychiatric unit; (2) considering when patients who have historically been violent can be safely discharged from a hospital setting; (3) determining whether an outpatient's threats of violence invoke the clinician's obligations to protect or warn potential victims; (4) considering whether an outpatient's risk of violence meets the threshold for civil commitment; and (5) assisting a school or university in handling a student's threatening statement or behavior.

As most clinicians know, identifying and managing patients who present a risk of violence involves navigating complex systems, balancing multiple interests, and honoring legal and ethical duties. The landscape of mental health service delivery in the United States has changed steadily over the past few decades, resulting in shorter inpatient stays, longer waiting lists for outpatient clinics, heavier caseloads for clinicians and increased burdens on providers to justify continuing treatment (Allnutt et al., 2013; Monahan et al., 2001). In this context, clinicians must delicately balance competing interests, such as providing care in the least restrictive setting, while also protecting patients from the potential harm they may inflict on themselves or others. Maintaining this balance in the course of violence risk assessment is one of the highest-stake tasks in clinical practice, along with the closely related task of suicide risk assessment (see chapter 9). Obviously, potential outcomes could be as severe as the loss of life or liberty. Furthermore, clinicians face the possibility of sanctions if their actions fall short of their legal and ethical responsibilities. Given these stakes, clinical responses to the possibility of violence may be shaped more by anxiety and liability concerns than by clear thinking or adherence to best practices (Pabian et al., 2009). Thus, the goal of this chapter is to help clinicians in routine practice more competently and confidently assess and manage violence risk among their adult patients. We begin with a review of the legal and ethical principles that shape clinicians' risk assessment responsibilities, then discuss well-established approaches to violence risk assessment, provide an overview of foundational knowledge, and present a framework for ongoing assessment and management of violence risk.

The Legal and Ethical Framework for Violence Risk Assessment and Management

For most clinicians in routine practice, concerns about violence risk are tightly intertwined with concerns about their legal and ethical duties. Conscientious clinicians struggle with questions such as,

- Should I report my increasing concerns about my patient's risk for violence?
- If so, at what point, and to whom?
- Does reporting these concerns violate patient confidentiality?
- How do I discuss with my patient my duty or decision to report these concerns?
- What happens if I am wrong about reporting (or failing to report) my concerns?

Indeed, because concerns about violence risk are so tightly intertwined with legal and ethical principles, it is helpful to review these duties before discussing violence-risk-assessment practice. Clinicians can more comfortably consider what they *should* do (i.e., best practices) once they understand what they

must do (i.e., laws and ethical standards). Generally, these laws and ethical standards can be summarized as those that cover *protecting* patient information and those that cover *divulging* patient information.

Ethical and Legal Obligations Regarding Privacy and Confidentiality

One cornerstone of therapeutic practice is protecting patient information. Disclosing patient information works against the therapeutic alliance and the overall efficacy of psychotherapy or assessment. It may also jeopardize privacy or violate confidentiality. To be clear, *privacy* is a legal concept that refers to limiting the access of others to personal information (e.g., medical or financial information, health-care decisions; Smith-Bell & Winslade, 1994). While the word "privacy" does not appear in the Constitution, the Supreme Court has recognized a constitutional right to privacy that extends to rights "deemed 'fundamental' or 'implicit in the concept of ordered liberty'" (*Roe v. Wade*, 1973, p. 152). A variety of federal and state laws protect individuals' privacy in specific areas (e.g., health or financial information). *Confidentiality* refers to the protection of private information that has been shared in a relationship—thus, confidentiality is primarily an ethical obligation.

Regarding privacy, clinicians have legal obligations to keep patient information private. At the federal level, the Health Insurance Portability and Accountability Act (HIPAA; 1996) created a Privacy Rule designed to protect individuals' medical records and other personal health information. Whereas HIPAA established the "floor," or minimum level of protection, many states also have more stringent privacy laws. In addition, all 50 states recognize a common law or statutory right to privacy, with many states offering specific remedies for public revelation of private facts (HIPAA, Privacy Rule, 2002). The most common penalty for violating privacy laws is a monetary fine, although certain HIPAA violations carry terms of imprisonment (HIPAA, Enforcement Rule, 2006). Regarding health-care providers specifically, many states also have laws creating civil liability, and sometimes criminal liability, for unauthorized disclosure of patient information (Bersoff, 2008).

As for confidentiality, guidance comes from relevant ethics codes. One of the aspirational principles in the American Psychological Association's (APA) Ethics Code (2002) is Respect for People's Rights and Dignity, which includes respecting "privacy and confidentiality" (p. 4). Standard 4, Privacy and Confidentiality, creates a set of professional obligations psychologists must satisfy in terms of protecting and disclosing patient information. Violating these or similar ethical obligations can have significant repercussions, including suspension or loss of a professional license or loss of membership in professional organizations (APA, 2002).

Therefore, ethical and legal obligations discourage disclosing patient information simply because *some* information related to violence risk arises. Rather, clinicians must consider their obligations to protect patient information from unnecessary disclosure, carefully weighing that against obligations to disclose, discussed next.

Legal and Ethical Obligations to Disclose Patient Information Regarding Violence Risk

Despite the importance of privacy and confidentiality in therapeutic practice, there are circumstances in which clinicians are permitted, or even required, to disclose patient information (see chapter 38 for a broader discussion). The current framework for understanding disclosures related to violence risk comes primarily from *Tarasoff v. Regents of the University of California* (1976). In this case, the California Supreme Court held that psychotherapists have a duty to protect intended victims of their patients' conduct if that conduct "presents a serious danger of violence to another" (p. 340). The court based this decision on the special relationship between a psychotherapist and patient. The nature of this relationship, the court held, created an obligation for the therapist to control the behavior of a third party—the patient. The court indicated that the duty could be fulfilled by a variety of methods, including "warn[ing] the intended victim or others likely to appraise the victim of the danger, notify[ing] the police, or tak[ing] whatever other steps are reasonably necessary under the circumstances" (p. 431).

However, several nuances further complicate this type of disclosure regarding a patient's risk of violence. First is the distinction between the *duty to protect* and the *duty to warn*. The former refers to a broad responsibility to take reasonable steps to protect a victim from harm. These steps might include warning (e.g., the potential victim or law enforcement), but they might also include providing treatment until the risk is reduced, pursuing hospitalization on a voluntary or involuntary basis, or otherwise preventing harm. The duty to warn is a much more narrow responsibility that requires the psychotherapist to actually *warn* the potential

victim, law enforcement, or both. Unfortunately, the duty to warn and duty to protect are often used synonymously when they actually confer different responsibilities. To complicate matters further, the language used to describe the duty to warn or protect and the actions necessary to fulfill that duty are often not perfectly aligned. For instance, although psychotherapists in California have a *duty to protect*, a California statute states, "The duty shall be discharged by the psychotherapist making reasonable efforts to communicate the threat to the victim or victims and to a law enforcement agency" (i.e., to *warn*; California Civil Code Section 43.92). So, while clinicians in California may choose to take other, reasonable steps to protect a potential victim from harm, they are protected from liability if they take steps consistent with a duty to warn.

A second nuance related to disclosing patient information is the breadth of circumstances that trigger a clinician's duty to protect or warn. *Tarasoff's* progeny include three cases that have broadened the potential for liability. The first, *Hedlund v. Superior Court of Orange County* (1983), involved a threat against a woman. The patient ultimately fired shotgun blasts into the woman's car while she was driving with her son. Although the son was not injured, the court allowed the mother to sue the therapist for negligent infliction of emotional distress based on the son's traumatization. Thus, the court extended a clinician's duty to foreseeable, innocent bystanders who may witness a patient's acts of violence. *Peck v. Counseling Services of Addison County* (1985) involved an adolescent who threatened to burn down his father's barn. The Vermont Supreme Court held that the clinician had a duty to warn in this case on the basis that the patient's father could have been in the barn. Therefore, it created the possibility of extending the *Tarasoff* duty to protecting property, at least in circumstances where there is some risk to human life. Finally, in *Ewing v. Goldstein* (2004), a patient's father relayed the patient's threat to his therapist. Although the threat was not received directly from the patient, the California court held that when a patient's immediate family member communicates a threat for the purpose of facilitating treatment, the *Tarasoff* duty is triggered.

A final nuance is the jurisdiction-specific nature of *Tarasoff* laws. The clinicians' duties to disclose are based on *state* law, either through case law or statutes. Thus, developments in one state do not impose obligations on clinicians in other states. The actual *Tarasoff* decision only created a duty for clinicians in California; the use of *Tarasoff* as shorthand for communicating duties to protect or warn was based on its impact on other jurisdictions throughout the country. A recent count indicates that 33 states have adopted the requirements of *Tarasoff*, 11 (including the District of Columbia) have made the duty discretionary, and 7 states have not addressed the issue (Bersoff, 2014). However, no two *"Tarasoff"* laws look alike and some states have specifically rejected the notion that clinicians have a duty to their patients' potential victims. For example:

- Texas clinicians *may* disclose a patient's threats to law enforcement or medical personnel (Tex. Code Ann. §611.004), but do not have a duty to warn potential victims (*Thapar v. Zezulka*, 1999). In fact, clinicians who make "good faith" disclosures to potential victims are *not* protected from civil liability.
- In Idaho, mental health professionals have a duty to warn if a patient communicates "an explicit threat of imminent serious physical harm or death to a clearly identified or identifiable victim or victims, and the patient has the apparent intent and ability to carry out such a threat" (Idaho Code § 6-1902).
- The North Carolina Court of Appeals declined to adopt a duty to warn or protect for clinicians in that state (*Gregory v. Kilbride*, 2002).

Despite the need for clinicians to know their state's laws regulating disclosure of patient information, a recent survey of psychologists revealed that most (76%) "were misinformed regarding their state laws, believing that they had a legal duty to warn when they did not, or assuming that warning was their only legal option when other protective actions less harmful to client privacy were allowed" (Pabian et al., 2009, p. 8). So, a first step for clinicians to competently and comfortably address violence risk is to *better learn their state laws governing any duty to warn*. These laws will influence some details of how clinicians integrate other best practices in risk management.

While there are significant legal responsibilities that guide disclosing patients' risk of violence, there are ethical guides as well. Although ethical guidelines primarily reference the patient, the APA Ethics Code's aspirational principle of Beneficence and Nonmaleficence takes a broader view when it states, "[P]sychologists seek to safeguard the welfare and rights of those with whom they interact professionally and other affected persons" (p. 3). Further, the principle of Fidelity and Responsibility states that

psychologists should be "aware of their professional and scientific responsibilities to society and to the specific communities in which they work" (p. 3). Of course, multiple ethical standards (i.e., 4.02, 9.03, 10.01) discuss the role of informed consent in making patients aware of the limits on confidentiality. Thus, most treatment relationships should begin with an explicit understanding that certain concerns about violence may require the clinician to disclose private information or otherwise intervene.

Well-Established Approaches to Violence Risk Assessment

Overall then, clinicians in routine practice often encounter concerns about violence risk, and they have professional, ethical, and legal duties to address these concerns in ways that promote safety. Indeed, assessment of violence risk is "a required professional ability for every clinical psychologist" (Grisso & Tomkins, 1996, p. 928). Nevertheless, violence risk assessment is not a standard component of most clinical training programs, and most clinicians in routine practice have had little, if any, formal training in violence risk assessment or risk management (Borum, 1996; Guy, Brown, & Poelstra, 1990; McNiel et al., 2008; Schwartz & Park, 1999). Rather, research and training that emphasize violence risk assessment have lingered primarily within the professional specialties of forensic psychology and forensic psychiatry. These fields have developed an extensive literature addressing base rates of violence and risk factors for violence, as well as tools and practices to assess the risk of violence (for summaries, see Conroy & Murrie, 2007; Heilbrun, 2009; Otto & Douglas, 2010). During recent years, another specialty known as *threat assessment* has emerged to address threats of targeted violence that arise in contexts other than traditional forensic practice with the courts. Both specialties—threat assessment and violence risk assessment—have much to offer mental health professionals who consider violence risk, regardless of their context. But contributions from these specialties have not yet been widely disseminated in routine clinical practice. Our premise in this chapter is that *clinicians in routine practice can benefit from a basic literacy in violence risk assessment and threat assessment*. Though clinicians in routine practice cannot always implement best practices from either specialty to the fullest extent, adopting some of the knowledge base and practices from each can help clinicians better address the concerns about violence that emerge in routine practice.

Overview of Forensic Approaches to Violence Risk Assessment

Over the past several decades, the field of forensic psychology has developed strategies for assessing violence risk in an effort to respond to legal questions and administrative procedures that consider an individual's risk for violence to others. Generally, these legal and administrative questions are broadly concerned with violence risk, including questions such as these: Can this forensic patient be safely released from the hospital to a community program? Can this criminal defendant safely serve a sentence of community probation rather than incarceration? Thus, most violence risk assessments are concerned with an individual's risk of violence against *any* potential victim for the foreseeable future. Given these types of referral questions, forensic assessments of violence risk make good use of empirical research, particularly research documenting the base rates of violence among particular populations (e.g., psychiatric patients, juvenile offenders, released prisoners, and so on), and the empirically supported risk factors for violence among these populations. Often, violence risk assessments rely on formal, structured violence-risk-assessment instruments to better incorporate base rate data and/or empirically supported risk factors (Monahan, 2008; Otto & Douglas, 2010; see also chapter 20). Empirical research consistently supports the validity of these violence-risk-assessment approaches, at least in terms of predicting violence with greater-than-chance levels of accuracy (Yang, Wong, & Coid, 2010).

Although violence risk assessments may vary across contexts, nearly every scientifically sound violence risk assessment must include certain key components (Conroy & Murrie, 2007):

• *Defining the question of risk:* Because violence risk is context specific, the "referral question" that guides a risk assessment must specify what risk behavior shall be assessed, over what time span, and across what settings.

• *Considering normative data and population base rates*: Evaluators form initial risk estimates by relying on empirically derived data. The field has long recognized that an assessment of violence risk must begin by considering bases rates—the known rate of violence among a particular population (Shah, 1978). Monahan (1981) emphasized, "knowledge of the appropriate base rate is the most important single piece of information necessary to make an accurate [violence] prediction" (p. 60). Base rates serve as a starting point for subsequent evaluation of probability (Borum, Otto, & Golding, 1993; Monahan, 1981). With the base rate as the anchor, evaluators can then cautiously adjust their appraisal of the risk of violence based on other assessment data, such as relevant violence risk factors.

• *Assessing empirically demonstrated risk and protective factors:* Over the past two decades, researchers have created a vast literature detailing factors that correspond with particular types of violence or offending among particular populations (for summaries, see Bonta, Law, & Hanson, 1998; Gendreau, Goggin, & Law, 1997; Gendreau, Little, & Goggin, 1996; Hanson & Morton-Bourgon, 2005). Evaluators consider whether the characteristics an examinee presents are empirically associated with violence. Indeed, the state of violence research has advanced to the point that any ethically or scientifically sound risk assessment should consider empirically demonstrated risk factors. Typically, evaluators use structured violence–risk-assessment instruments to guide their consideration of these factors (Monahan, 2008; Monahan & Skeem, 2014; Otto & Douglas, 2010; see also chapter 20).

• *Assessing idiographic or case-specific risk factors*: Though the empirically supported risk factors typically take primary focus, evaluators can and should consider the possibility of unique risk or protective factors that appear clear and compelling in the individual case.

• *Defining a risk management plan:* A well-conducted and empirically sound risk assessment is useless if does not inform a risk management plan. Assessments lay the groundwork for an individualized risk management plan.

Overview of Threat Assessment Approaches

Whereas forensic assessments of violence risk are usually prompted by legal or administrative proceedings and they address the risk of *general* violence, threat assessments are usually prompted, as the name suggests, by an individual's threat and, therefore, address *targeted* violence (Meloy, Hart, & Hoffman, 2014). Threats may be explicit or vague statements that convey intent to harm someone; indeed, some threats involve only behavior in the absence of a statement. Usually threats convey a specific, intended victim; but some threats are broader, such as the threat of a mass shooting in a particular location. Strictly defined, *threat assessment*, also known as "behavioral threat assessment," is a violence prevention strategy developed by the US Secret Service to protect federal officials (Borum, Fein, Vossekuil, & Berglund, 1999). But threat assessment is now more widely adopted as a best practice for preventing violence in the workplace (ASIS International, 2011) and in schools (American Psychological Association, 2013; Borum, Cornell, Modzeleski, & Jimerson, 2010; Cornell, 2014; Cornell & Allen, 2011; see chapter 8), contexts with which clinicians are much more familiar. Borum (2006) explained that the distinction between violence risk assessment and threat assessment

> becomes important because the factors considered and the assessment approach may differ (Borum & Reddy, 2001; Reddy et al., 2001) . . . These [threat] assessments should arguably rely on a fact-based assessment approach and may—for a variety of reasons—not rely primarily on base rates or a tally of empirically based risk factors for *general* violence. (p. 193)

Threat assessments therefore focus on behavioral indications that an individual is progressing toward violence (Borum et al., 1999; Reddy et al., 2001) and focus on a much shorter period than forensic violence risk assessments. Traditional risk assessments are often open-ended in determining whether someone is likely to commit *any* kind of violent act at *any* time in the future. In contrast, threat assessments are concerned with whether someone *currently* poses a risk of carrying out a specific attack in the *near future*. Threat assessments focus on the individual's readiness, motivation, and intention to commit a specific act of violence. They examine current behavior, such as whether the individual has engaged in planning or preparation to carry out an attack, and they place great emphasis on situational factors, such as an individual's support or stress that might increase the risk of violence.

Threat assessment approaches have evolved to include not only identifying and assessing threats, but also managing people who have made threats (Borum et al., 2010; Cornell, 2013, 2014). People tend to make threats because they are frustrated by a problem or conflict, so one effective violence prevention strategy is to resolve that frustration, thereby reducing the motivation for violence. Therefore, threat assessment approaches often expand from assessment to intervention; threat assessment is considered a problem-solving approach to violence prevention (Cornell, 2013, 2014; Meloy et al., 2014).

Applying Risk Assessment and Threat Assessment Approaches in Routine Practice

To what extent can clinicians apply the well-established best practices from forensic psychology and behavioral threat assessment to routine clinical contexts, such as psychiatric hospitals or outpatient therapy clinics? Substantially, we believe. Admittedly, neither approach can always be implemented to the fullest degree in routine clinical practice. Both prioritize collateral data sources, such as historical records and collateral interviews, that may be difficult for clinicians in some contexts to access. Yet both approaches have basic knowledge and techniques, summarized next, with which clinicians in *any* context should be familiar.

Foundational Knowledge for Violence Risk Assessment

The current literature on violence risk assessment is vast and increasingly nuanced, with a focus on narrow populations (e.g., juveniles, psychiatric patients, criminal offenders). Thus, keeping abreast of every development in this broad field is probably not feasible amid the demands of routine clinical practice. However, clinicians do need a *basic literacy* in the data underlying most violence risk assessment, particularly for the clinical population they serve. The most important basic knowledge for violence risk assessment involves (1) base rates of violence, and (2) empirically supported risk factors for violent behavior.

BASE RATES OF VIOLENCE

A base rate is simply the prevalence of a particular characteristic or behavior within a particular population (Arkes, 1989). Understanding base rates of violence is critical to assessing violence risk because it offers a starting point or context for the evaluation of other relevant data (Borum et al., 1993). Without first considering the frequency of a behavior (i.e., violent acts) in a relevant population, clinicians are prone to either underestimate or overestimate the likelihood of a particular patient engaging in violent behavior. In fact, Monahan (1981) emphasized that ignorance or neglect of base rates is one of the most significant errors clinicians make in violence risk assessment. Nevertheless, ample data from the field of cognitive psychology document the human tendency to disregard information about base rates in favor of vivid case-specific information (e.g., Ajzen, 1977; Kahneman & Tversky, 1973), and clinicians are no exception to this tendency (Shah, 1978).

Admittedly, analyzing base rates of violence involves conceptual and practical challenges. One important consideration reflects the population of interest (i.e., *who* is committing the act of violence). For instance, men and women have very different base rates of violence in most contexts, as do juveniles compared to adults. A second important consideration reflects how the "violence" is operationally defined in relevant studies (i.e., *what* behavior is considered "violent"). Imagine the distinctions between homicide, assault, and verbal threats—yet all may be considered "violent" in studies offering base rate data. A third, related issue is the different methods of detection used to identify violence (i.e., *how* are violent acts identified). Researchers have found dramatically different base rates of violence depending on whether they use arrest records, psychiatric records, self-report, collateral report, or some combination (Douglas & Ogloff, 2003; Steadman et al., 1998). While a more complete discussion of these issues (see Conroy & Murrie, 2007) is beyond the scope of this chapter, the underlying point is that clinicians must be thoughtful consumers of base rate information. The following is a brief summary of base rate information, organized according to relevant populations. Heilbrun (2009) identified four dimensions as particularly relevant when considering base rates of violence: age, gender, mental health status, and location.

Age. Age and violence have a robust relationship. Violent crime tends to peak in late adolescence or early adulthood, decline quickly thereafter, and continue to decline steadily throughout adulthood (Hirschi & Gottfredson, 1983; Sweeten, Piquero, & Steinberg, 2013). Therefore, older adults (i.e., > 30 years) commit acts of violence less frequently than younger adults.

Base rates of violence among juveniles tend to be much higher than the base rates of violence among adults. For example, in the Youth Risk Behavior Surveillance Survey conducted by the Centers for Disease Control and Prevention (2014), 25% of high school students reported engaging in a physical fight during the prior year. Similarly, a survey by the United States Department of Health and Human Services (2001) found that 30% of the sample (8th, 10th, and 12th grade students) committed a violent crime during the prior year. Among juveniles, base rate data are particularly enlightening because (1) delinquent behaviors, including some violent behaviors, are statistically normative among youth, but (2) most juveniles desist from delinquent or violent behavior by the time they reach adulthood (Moffitt, 1993, 2002). Clinicians can anticipate that violent behavior will be most common among juveniles, followed by young adults, with violence least common among adults who have reached middle age or beyond.

Gender. Base rates of violence also vary by gender. Generally, women commit violent acts far less frequently than men. Depending on the year and method of detection, women account for only 11%–20% of violent crime (Federal Bureau of Investigation [FBI], 2012; Greenfeld & Snell, 1999; Reiss & Roth, 1993). Base rates of violence by gender alone (without any other subdivisions) are relatively unhelpful given the sheer volume of the population and the relatively small proportion that commit violent crime. However, to provide one point of reference, using 2012 data from the United States Census Bureau and the FBI, the base rate of violence among women was approximately 0.05% and among men was approximately 0.2% (FBI, 2012; US Census Bureau, 2012).

There is, however, an important caveat to the general relationship between gender and violence. Among psychiatric populations, the base rates of violence among women are nearly equivalent to the base rates of violence among men. For instance, data from the MacArthur Violence Risk Assessment Study (discussed in greater detail later) revealed similar prevalence rates of violence among male (29.7%) and female (24.6%) psychiatric patients who were recently discharged at their 1-year follow-up (Robbins, Monahan, & Silver, 2003). However, significant differences emerged in the contextual nature of violence committed by men and women. The victims of women's violence were more likely to be family members, and the location of women's violence was more likely to be the home. Perhaps because women's violence tends to be less visible than men's, it is often underreported to law enforcement and underappreciated by clinicians. In fact, multiple studies reveal that *clinicians tend to underestimate their female patients' risk of violence* (e.g., Coontz, Lidz, & Mulvey, 1994; Elbogen, Williams, Kim, Tomkins, & Scalora, 2001; Skeem et al., 2005).

Psychiatric status. For nearly a century, researchers have attempted to identify and understand any meaningful relationship between mental illness and violence. Among hundreds of studies on this topic, perhaps the largest and most rigorous has been the MacArthur Violence Risk Assessment Study (Steadman et al., 1998), which followed 951 psychiatric patients ages 18–40 after discharge from psychiatric inpatient units in Kansas City, Missouri; Pittsburgh, Pennsylvania; and Worcester, Massachusetts. The most common diagnoses were depression (40%), schizophrenia (17%), and bipolar disorder (13%); approximately one-quarter of the sample (24%) were also diagnosed with substance use or dependence. Patients were interviewed before discharge and re-interviewed (along with a collateral informant) every 10 weeks for one year. Researchers compared the rates of violence among the discharged psychiatric patients to 519 people living in the same neighborhoods as the patients discharged in the Pittsburgh area. Results revealed that 27.5% of the sample had committed at least one act of violence in the 1-year follow-up period (i.e., an overall 27.5% base rate of violence), but the prevalence of violence differed greatly among those who had major mental disorders with co-occurring substance abuse (31.1%) versus those without substance abuse (17.9%). The effect of substance abuse was significant among comparisons with the community sample as well. Relative to the community sample, "the prevalence of violence among patients without symptoms of substance abuse is statistically indistinguishable from the prevalence of violence among others [i.e., non-patients] in their neighborhoods without symptoms of substance abuse" (Steadman et al., 1998, p. 400). Substance abuse was related to increased violence in both patient and community samples, although the patient sample was more likely to report symptoms of substance abuse.

Additional studies, whether from the MacArthur Violence Risk Assessment data or other elsewhere, have generally supported the premise that the relationship between mental illness and violence is mediated by a number of factors (Elbogen & Johnson, 2009; Steadman et al., 1998). Substance use and abuse is one of the most frequently cited variables that mediates the mental illness–violence relationship (e.g., Elbogen & Johnson, 2009; Fazel, Långström, Hjern, Grann, & Lichtenstein, 2009). Further, there are several *historical* (e.g., physical abuse, prior violence), *dispositional* (e.g., age, sex, education) and *contextual* (e.g., recent victimization, job loss) variables that are also associated with both mental illness and violence. Thus, base rates of violence among individuals with mental illness are affected by the fact that these individuals are often members of other subgroups with elevated base rates of violence (Elbogen & Johnson, 2009). For instance, individuals with severe mental illness often have co-occurring substance abuse or dependence, live in neighborhoods where violence is common, and experience environmental stressors (e.g., unemployment, victimization).

Location. Base rates of violence also vary by location, particularly between community and institutional settings. Base rates of violence in community mental health contexts are typically relatively low; one study estimated the prevalence of violent acts to be approximately 6% (Shergill & Szmukler, 1998). A survey of over 10,000 community residents found that approximately 8% of participants diagnosed with schizophrenia endorsed a violent act in the past year; rates increased to over 20% when substance abuse was present (Swanson, Holzer, Ganju, & Jono, 1990). In contrast, base rates of violence in psychiatric hospitals tend to be somewhat higher, ranging from 10%–44% depending on the study (e.g., Monahan et al., 2001; Newhill, Mulvey, & Lidz, 1995; Soliman & Reza, 2001). Factors such as the specific type of inpatient setting (e.g., acute vs. continuing care) and commitment status (e.g., civil vs. forensic) contribute to the wide range. In another inpatient setting, correctional facilities, base rates of violence are surprisingly low. Counterintuitively, rates of violence in prisons tend to be far lower than the public tends to expect, perhaps because prisons so effectively limit prisoners access to each other, to weapons, and to the drugs and alcohol that greatly contribute to violence in the community (DeMatteo, Murrie, Anumba, & Keesler, 2011). For example, the US Department of Justice reports that rates of homicide in prison (around .004%) are far lower than rates in the community, when demographics are held constant (Mumola, 2005).

EMPIRICALLY SUPPORTED RISK FACTORS

As with base rates, a working knowledge of empirically supported risk factors for violence is also critical for thorough violence risk assessment. But clinicians in routine practice underemphasize empirically supported risk factors and overemphasize factors that have little empirical support (at least according to the limited literature addressing risk-assessment approaches in routine practice; Elbogen, Calkins Mercado, Scalora, & Tomkins, 2002). The literature describes two basic domains of risk factors: *static risk factors*, which are historical and unlikely (or impossible) to change, and *dynamic risk factors*, which change over time and are potentially amenable to intervention.

Static Risk Factors

Past violence. One of the strongest predictors of future violence, not surprisingly, is past violence. Across meta-analyses and across various populations, criminal history variables consistently emerge as one of the strongest predictors of violent recidivism (e.g., Andrews, Bonta, & Wormwith, 2006; Bonta, Law, & Hanson, 1998). The predictive power of past violence holds true in essentially every group that has been studied in risk research, including adults with or without mental illnesses (Bonta et al., 1998; Elbogen & Johnson, 2009), sexual offenders (Boer, Wilson, Gauthier, & Hart, 1997), and juvenile offenders (Cottle, Lee, & Heilbrun, 2001). However, context matters: violence committed in one setting (e.g., the community) does not necessarily translate to risk of violence in a different setting (e.g., a structured environment such as a correctional facility or psychiatric hospital) (Conroy & Murrie, 2007).

Psychopathy. Having a well-established relationship with violent behavior, the construct of psychopathy broadly refers to a pattern of interpersonal (e.g., grandiose, manipulative, exploitative), affective (e.g., shallow or labile affect, unable to form enduring relationships, lacking in empathy), and behavioral (e.g., impulsive, tendency to violate social norms) qualities (Hare, 2003; and see chapter 18). Multiple meta-analyses indicate that psychopathy, as measured by the Hare Psychopathy Checklist-Revised (PCL-R; Hare, 2003) and related measures, predicts general antisocial behavior (Leistico, Salekin, DeCoster, & Rogers, 2008), violence (Hemphill, Hare, & Wong, 1998; Salekin, Rogers, & Sewell, 1996), and sexual offending (Hawes, Boccaccini, & Murrie, 2013). Psychopathy emerged as the strongest risk factor in the MacArthur Violence Risk Assessment Study (Skeem & Mulvey, 2001). The predictive validity of psychopathy with respect to violence is strong enough that the PCL-R is not only included in risk assessment instruments, but is often the *strongest* predictor in these risk measures (for discussion, see Douglas et al., 2006).

Though the construct of antisocial personality disorder (APD) is sometimes (inaccurately) used interchangeably with the more narrow construct of psychopathy, APD appears less clearly linked with violence. While associated with violence in certain studies (e.g., Bonta et al., 1998), the criteria for the diagnosis overlaps significantly with general crimes, and the prevalence of APD among offenders is so high that it does not necessarily identify the smaller subset prone to ongoing violence (Cunningham & Reidy, 1998). Therefore, the salience of APD as a risk factor may depend on context: In general clinical settings, consideration of APD is probably important, but in forensic or correctional settings, overreliance on APD as a risk factor for violence tends to lead to false positives (Conroy & Murrie, 2007).

Age. Age is typically considered a static risk factor for violence because, even though it invariably changes over time, it is not amenable to intervention. Age is relevant to violence in two distinct ways. First, earlier age at first offense predicts future offending (Steadman et al., 1994; Swanson, 1994). Second, as discussed earlier, rates of violence generally decline with age, particularly after age 30 (Hirschi & Gottfredson, 1983; Sweeten et al., 2013).

Prior supervision failure. With a tendency to be a risk factor for violent recidivism (e.g., Andrews et al., 2006; Bonta, Harman, Hann, & Cormier, 1996), prior supervision failure can take form in traditional correctional contexts, such as probation or parole violation, or violation of conditional release plans. Also relevant are prior *treatment* failures such as missing appointments, medication noncompliance, or faking treatment participation (Kindness et al., 2009; Swartz, Swanson, Hiday, Borum, & Burns, 1998).

Dynamic Risk Factors

Increasingly, the violence-risk-assessment literature has focused on dynamic risk factors. Though sometimes more challenging to assess, dynamic factors are often more predictive of violence in the short term and are promising targets for risk reduction efforts (Chu et al., 2011; Douglas & Skeem, 2005). Given the clinicians' role in risk management (discussed later), an understanding of dynamic risk factors is particularly important for mental health practitioners.

Substance abuse. Research consistently shows that substance use, abuse, and dependence are consistently related to violent behavior. Substance abuse, by itself, dramatically increases the odds of violence among individuals without mental disorders (Swanson, 1994), but also mediates the relationship between mental illness and violence (Elbogen & Johnson, 2009; Fazel et al., 2009). While substance abuse is often treated as a static risk factor, there is evidence that alcohol and drug use change over time and predict proximate acts of violence (Mulvey et al., 2006). The relationship between substance use and violence is multifaceted and likely includes direct (e.g., violence associated with illicit transactions) and indirect (e.g., disinhibition, instability in other life domains) pathways (Douglas & Skeem, 2005).

Impulsivity. Impulsivity refers to "the lack of control over affect, behavior, or cognition" (Douglas & Skeem, 2005, p. 359). Therefore, when confronted with frustration or provocation, impulsive individuals are less likely to inhibit or modulate their reaction, and more likely to respond without forethought or planning (Barratt, 1994). Empirically, impulsiveness predicts self-reported violent thoughts as well as violent behaviors (Grisso, Davis, Vesselinov, Appelbaum, & Monahan, 2000; Monahan et al, 2001).

Negative affect. The literature also documents a relationship between negative affect and violence. While "negative affect" is a broad term that refers to a range of problematic mood states, most research has focused on anger. Although anger has a dispositional component, it also has dynamic elements such as intensity and expression (Douglas & Skeem, 2005; Novaco, 1994). Studies have shown modest correlations between anger and violent behavior (Kay, Wolkenfeld, & Murrill, 1988; Novaco, 1994). Other types of negative affect, such as depression and anxiety, may also have a relationship with violent acts (Freese, Hiscoke, & Hodgins, 2002).

Psychosis. Research spanning decades has reached varied conclusions about the psychosis–violence relationship. Some studies have found that psychosis predicts violent behavior (e.g., Brennan, Mednick, & Hodgins, 2000; Swanson et al., 2002), while others have not (e.g., Monahan et al., 2001). Given the mixed results across research, scholars conducted a meta-analysis that now provides the best data regarding psychosis and violence (Douglas, Guy, & Hart, 2009). While psychosis was associated with a 49%–68% increased likelihood of violence across *all* studies, the authors noted, "Perhaps the most important finding to emerge from the present meta-analysis is the extent to which the strength of association between psychosis and violence differed as a function of moderator variables" (p. 693). Notably, the odds of violence for individuals with psychosis were *higher* when the comparison group was people with a nonpsychotic mental illnesses or no mental illness. However, the odds of violence associated with psychosis were *lower* when the comparison group was people with personality disorders (i.e., APD or psychopathy).

Admittedly, psychosis is a heterogeneous condition, and some facets of psychosis may be more relevant to violence risk than others. Coid and colleagues (2013) recently investigated the relationship between delusions and violence. Three types of delusions were significantly associated with violence: delusions of being spied on, of persecution, and of conspiracy. However, all three relationships were mediated by anger, indicating that the relationship between delusions and violence is indirect and attributable primarily to the experience of *anger* evoked by delusion. Regarding hallucinations, certain studies have found command hallucinations to perpetuate violence—specifically, they *did* predict violent behavior (McNiel, Eisner, & Binder, 2000; Monahan et al., 2001). However, studies of threat/control-override symptoms (i.e., symptoms that are threatening and remove one's sense of self-control) have produced mixed results (Appelbaum, Robbins, & Monahan, 2000; Swanson et al., 1996).

Treatment compliance. Finally, medication compliance and treatment participation have important but understudied implications for violence risk. Medication noncompliance, specifically, predicts violence among psychiatric patients (Bartels, Drake, Wallach, & Freeman, 1991; Monahan et al., 2001). Treatment participation and the therapeutic alliance are more complicated constructs that concern relationship quality and treatment effectiveness. On this topic, Elbogen and colleagues (2006) found that treatment engagement, indicated by patients' own perceptions of treatment need and treatment effectiveness, is associated with reduced odds of violence. Importantly, both medication compliance and treatment participation have been shown to fluctuate over time (e.g., Svedberg, Mesterton, & Cullberg, 2001), and both constructs have possible direct and indirect relationships with violence. Therefore, the clinician–patient relationship is an important factor to which clinicians should be attuned.

Ongoing Assessment of Violence Risk in Clinical Practice

Given this type of foundational knowledge, how best can clinicians use it? How should violence risk research inform routine practice? Because the clinician's goals involve violence *prevention* more than violence *prediction,* the aim is not only an overall risk estimate but, rather, ongoing identification and mitigation of any factors that may be conducive to violence or that may suggest a patient is progressing toward violence. One helpful framework for considering risk-relevant information is the distinction between *risk status* and *risk state* (Douglas & Skeem, 2005). The former is crucial to understanding an individual's risk relative to others, and the latter is crucial to understanding changes in risk over time.

Risk Status

Generally, risk status involves *a patient's risk of violent behavior relative to others in a particular population or context* (Douglas & Skeem, 2005). Some patients will always remain at higher risk status and warrant closer risk monitoring because of unalterable historical characteristics, such as past violence or substance abuse. Risk status is informed by the foundational knowledge from forensic assessment of violence risk—for example, the base rates of violence in the relevant population, and by well-known, empirically supported risk factors drawn from epidemiological research. These risk factors tend to be more enduring (i.e., fixed, historical, unchanging) characteristics such as a history of violence, early onset of violence, and a history of substance abuse.

Even before intake, clinicians can begin to form some impressions of a patient's risk status, or baseline risk compared to others in the same population. Upon referral, a clinician may receive information about a patient's psychiatric history, criminal history, and other personal data that allow the clinician to identify the patient's population or comparison group for purposes of considering base rates of violence. This referral information may include some basic static risk factors for violence. When such information is not already accessible, clinicians can replicate the practice of forensic evaluators, who place a high priority on seeking collateral information about violence risk (e.g., psychiatric, criminal, and social service records) immediately upon referral.

During any intake interview or procedure, clinicians can elicit more information about a patient's risk status. By inquiring about psychiatric history (including specific symptoms and patterns of behavior), substance abuse, and especially violence history, clinicians can more clearly assess risk status. We recommend all clinicians, regardless of context, include at least *some* degree of screening specific to violence history; clinicians in some contexts (e.g., inpatient versus outpatient) should probably include more in-depth inquiry than others.

Although asking explicitly about violence risk may seem self-evident, clinicians are often reluctant to do so. We urge all clinicians to *ask questions specific to past violence*. Such questions include a thorough review of all past instances of violence.

What was the nature, type, frequency, and severity? Who were past victims? What was the context or setting for the violence? What events preceded and followed the violence? How recent was last instance of violence, and is there any evidence of escalation? In short, try to elicit *all* information about past violence, because this is essential to understanding the contexts and situations in which the patient would most likely commit violence in the future. These details not only help inform risk status, they also plant the seeds of future risk management strategies. Finally, ask about instances in which the patient was nearly violent, but did *not* proceed with violence. This may provide clues to patient strengths and risk management strategies a clinician can use later.

When forming an initial impression of risk status, clinicians can also use one of the many well-researched and structured violence-risk-assessment instruments designed for the task (for reviews, see Monahan & Skeem, 2014; Murrie, 2016; Otto & Douglas, 2010; see also chapter 20). Clinicians typically form far more accurate assessments with these instruments, relative to their unstructured clinical judgment (Ægisdóttir et al., 2006; Grove et al., 2000; Hanson & Morton-Bourgon, 2009), so using these instruments is increasingly considered a best practice (Heilbrun, 2009; Lamberg, 2007). As one authority summarized, "The development of such specialized [violence risk assessment] tools has been one of the most important influences in promoting evidence-based practice in this area. Using such a specialized tool is clearly consistent with best practice" (Heilbrun, 2009, p. 123).

Another benefit of structured risk instruments is helping clinicians—who, by training, are prone to focus primarily on psychiatric symptoms—to avoid an overemphasis on psychiatric symptoms, and also to consider the much broader range of (non-psychiatric) risk factors for violence. As Monahan and Steadman (2012) emphasized, "A person with serious mental illness—*even one that bears a causal relationship to violence*—may have a high (or low) overall likelihood of violent recidivism for reasons independent of their illness" (p. 247). Clinicians should amass and consider all risk-relevant data to inform their initial opinion about risk status.

Finding that a new patient is at relatively high-risk status, relative to others in the clinician's clinical setting, should prompt the clinician to plan for more regular attention to violence risk, ongoing assessment, monitoring, and risk-reduction efforts. Although risk status can theoretically change (e.g., a patient who commits a first violent act is subsequently at a higher-risk status thereafter), risk status often remains unchanged over the course of treatment, despite ongoing fluctuations in *risk state*.

Risk State

In contrast to risk status, risk *state* refers to a person's *current* violence risk compared with his or her own risk at baseline or prior points in time. In other words, *risk state* involves the "individual's propensity to become involved in violence at a given time, based on particular changes in biological, psychological, and social variables in his or her life" (Douglas & Skeem, 2005, p. 349).

Therefore, assessing risk state involves a focus on the patient's current clinical status. Are there changes in the psychiatric symptoms that seem most relevant to violence risk? Is the patient increasingly abusing substances? Has his or her conflict with family escalated? In many ways, these are the types of tasks with which clinicians are already most comfortable—assessing improvement or decline in clinical functioning and intervening appropriately. But clinicians must be comfortable considering these clinical changes as they relate to violence potential, and explicitly discussing with patients the prospect of violence.

As when assessing risk status, monitoring risk state can be facilitated by well-researched risk assessment tools. A few tools that follow the Structured Professional Judgment model—such as the Historical, Clinical, Risk-20 (HCR-20; Douglas et al., 2013)—are particularly appropriate for ongoing monitoring (see chapters 20 and 33). These instruments help clinicians to monitor change on the risk factors most relevant to violence, and to consider whether changes in risk factors require changes in intervention strategies.

Again, assessment is an *ongoing* process that continues well beyond the initial assessment of risk status at intake. Optimal assessment involves not only addressing a patient's current risk state but also *anticipating* factors that would change that risk state. For example, is the patient's sobriety tenuous, with a potential for relapse to lead to violence? Is the patient involved in a volatile relationship that could escalate toward violence? Or conversely, is an otherwise high-risk patient in a stable and protective relationship such that—if he lost the relationship—he would likely resume violence without the stability

the relationship provides? We encourage clinicians, as they assess risk state, to also consider and anticipate potential changes or events that would rapidly alter risk state (see Pisani, Cross, Watts, & Conner, 2012, for a similar approach in suicide risk assessment).

Of course, clinicians may perceive a change in risk state because the patient conveys—whether to the clinician or to others—a *threat* of violence or a desire to harm a particular victim. Patients may convey threats in a manner that is overt and intentional, or inadvertent or accidental. In either scenario, authorities use the term "threat leakage" to describe situations in which an individual conveys to a third party an intent to harm a target (Meloy & O'Toole, 2011). Even absent threatening statements or articulated desires, threat leakage may include behaviors that leave a clinician concerned that the patient poses a threat to a particular victim(s). Indeed, threat assessment scholars consistently emphasize that an explicit threat is neither a necessary nor sufficient condition to prompt intervention; people may *pose* a threat even if they do not explicitly *make* a threat (Fein & Vossekuil, 1998; Meloy et al., 2014). For instance, a patient who loses a relationship or a job, increasingly ruminates on a grievance against the ex-partner or supervisor who caused the loss, and increasingly knows the whereabouts of that person may *pose* a threat even if the patient has not explicitly articulated a threat. Because of the potential for threats and other rapid changes in risk state to arise in routine practice, clinicians should maintain a basic command of threat assessment approaches (much like they maintain a basic command of the previously reviewed forensic approaches that inform assessment of risk status).

Although there are numerous ways to apply threat assessment practices to concerns that arise in routine clinical care, one of the simplest and most helpful illustrations comes from Borum and Reddy (2001), who provided a description of threat assessment approaches applied to *Tarasoff*-type situations that arise in psychotherapy and other mental health treatment. Generally, they emphasize that therapists should attempt to determine whether a patient is on a "pathway" to violence and how far along the pathway that patient has progressed. In other words, to what extent has the patient engaged in the types of behaviors (planning, preparation, rehearsal, and so on) that would likely precede an attack? Specifically, Borum and Reddy (2001) use the mnemonic acronym *ACTION* to encourage clinicians to consider:

• *Attitudes that support or facilitate violence*: Has the patient conveyed attitudes, beliefs, or expectations that support violence? Does the patient express thoughts about violence toward a particular person or group?

• *Capacity to carry out such violence*: Is the patient able to carry out the type of violence he or she seems to threaten? For example, does the patient have access to weapons and access to the potential victim?

• *Thresholds crossed*: Has the patient made a plan for violence and taken steps in that plan (particularly steps that involve sacrifice or consequences)?

• *Intent*: Does the patient's threatening statement or apparent threat reflect genuine intent, or just emotional distress? Similarly, authorities in school-based threat assessment suggest distinguishing a *substantive* threat from a passing comment or gesture (Cornell, 2013, 2014; Cornell & Sheras, 2006)

• *Other's reactions*: To the extent that the patient has conveyed violent intent, do others tend to support or discourage this potential violence? Does the patient expect positive reactions from others?

• *Noncompliance with risk-reduction interventions*: Is the patient willing to participate in an intervention to reduce risk? Those who do not intend harm others are usually eager to comply with risk-reduction efforts and convey there is no cause for concern; those who resist or thwart intervention efforts warrant greater concern.

Another factor that can suggest a threat is serious involves the patient's perception that there may be "nothing to lose" or "nothing left to live for." The risks for harm to self and harm to others are often tightly intertwined. These outcomes share many of the same risk factors (e.g., psychiatric illness, substance abuse, impulsivity) and may be facilitated by many of the same circumstances (e.g., loss or shame, access to weapons). Although the worst-case scenario of a homicide-followed-by-suicide is exceedingly rare (see Hillbrand, 2001; Liem, 2010; see chapter 21), any type of threat assessment should consider the possibility that a patient may harm himself, herself, or others. Thus, violence risk assessment and suicide risk assessment should occur together (Hillbrand, 2001; chapter 21).

As clinicians explore all of the issues described here, two practical strategies are important. The first is to *ask the patient directly*. Perhaps due to anxiety, or an untested assumption that patients will not be forthright, many clinicians are reluctant to explicitly ask about a patient's ideation, let alone plans, regarding violent acts. But this is crucial for threat assessment, and many patients are surprisingly open regarding their inclination toward violence. Indeed, many are ambivalent about committing violence and, at least to some extent, are open to discussing directly their violence risk. Of course, others are not inclined to discuss any propensity or plans for violence, which prompts a second recommendation: *pursue collateral data*. A core practice in violence risk assessment and threat assessment involves seeking collateral sources of data, such as interviews with treatment providers, family members, and others who know the examinee well. Admittedly, clinicians providing treatment may not have the same degree of access to collateral sources as those tasked specifically with risk or threat assessments. But, in general, clinicians utilize collateral data far less than they could and, in our view, should. As detailed next, risk assessment and risk management will require clear and consistent communication between everyone involved in a patient's care.

Management of Violence Risk: Risk Management as a Therapeutic Intervention

Ultimately, one of the clinician's primary goals is to help patients manage their risk for violence. Effective risk management efforts will always be informed by a thorough violence risk assessment, as described in the preceding sections. This section will provide an overview of risk management as a therapeutic intervention.

Overview of Risk Management

Risk management begins before concerns about violence arise. Thus, clinicians should begin assessing a patient's risk for violence during the intake session. This requires (1) conducting the type of intake assessment that provides risk-relevant information, and (2) obtaining access to important collateral sources that provide external perspectives on the patient's history, behavior, and functioning. A guiding theme through this process should be that the clinician's goal is violence *prevention*, not violence *prediction* (APA, 2013; Swanson, 2008). It is less important to predict *whether* a particular patient will be violent, and more important to identify the factors that contribute to a patient's likelihood of violence in the future and to develop plans to mitigate those risks.

Risk management can take many forms. The form familiar to most clinicians is *treatment*, whether it is psychotropic medication, psychotherapy, or both. Other forms of management include monitoring, supervision, and victim safety planning (Douglas, Hart, Webster, & Belfrage, 2013). *Monitoring*, or surveillance, evaluates changes in risk over time. This can take the form of contacting the client or relevant collaterals (e.g., family, treatment providers), visiting the client's home, initiating electronic surveillance, or drug testing. Thus, while individual clinicians may not oversee monitoring efforts, a patient's attendance at treatment appointments may be part of a larger monitoring plan. *Supervision* refers to forms of control or restrictions of liberty. This can take the form of incapacitation (e.g., involuntary commitment or incarceration) or restrictions in the community (e.g., mandated outpatient treatment, requirements to attend certain programming, restriction from alcohol/drug use, restriction from contacting certain individuals). Finally, *victim safety planning* involves bolstering a potential victim's ability to respond to violence if it occurs. While many aspects of this process may be outside the scope of conventional mental health treatment, clinicians may have a role if victims have historically been family members and the patient is willing to address risk management with them in treatment.

To effectively reduce a patient's risk for violence, management strategies should be aligned with risk factors. This principle is drawn from the Risk-Need-Responsivity (RNR) model (Andrews, Bonta, & Hoge, 1990), wherein higher-risk cases receive more intensive services, management efforts are targeted to address key dynamic risk factors, and services are delivered in a manner that is consistent with the learning style and motivation of those receiving them. Put simply, this requires that clinicians design treatment plans to address the factors that contribute to the patient's violence risk and implement the treatment plans in an empirically supported manner that matches the learning style of the particular patient. Generally, research supports the use of cognitive-behavioral and social learning approaches when designing and implementing interventions to reduce the likelihood of violent behavior (Andrews et al., 2006; Douglas et al., 2013).

Key treatment targets will likely be drawn from the set of dynamic risk factors that are salient for a particular patient. As discussed earlier, many of these factors will be symptoms or phenomena familiar to most clinicians, such as substance abuse, negative affect, impulsivity, or psychosis. There is a wealth of literature on research-supported treatments for many of these risk factors, including motivational interviewing for substance abuse (e.g., Hettema, Steele, & Miller, 2005), Acceptance and Commitment Therapy for depression (e.g., Forman, Herbert, Moitra, Yeomans, & Geller, 2007), and Cognitive-Behavioral Therapy for schizophrenia (e.g., Dickerson, 2004), to name a few. While there may not be established treatment packages for more isolated symptoms, such as anger or impulsivity, a thorough case conceptualization may identify the function of certain behaviors in a larger system. For example, anger and impulsivity may be part of a pattern resembling borderline personality disorder, which might lead a clinician to incorporate aspects of Dialectical Behavior Therapy (Linehan, Armstrong, Suarez, Allmon, & Heard, 1991) into the treatment program. Alternatively, the same symptoms might have emerged as part of post-traumatic stress disorder, in which case the patient might benefit from Cognitive Processing Therapy (Resick, Nishith, Weaver, Astin, & Feuer, 2002) or prolonged exposure (Foa et al., 2005).

Additionally, clinicians should consider treatment options for risk factors that are often seen as static. Literature on the RNR model provides guidance for how to conceptualize some historical behavior as dynamic criminogenic needs. For instance, a history of antisocial behavior can be translated into the dynamic need for developing noncriminal behavioral alternatives that the patient can implement in risky situations (Andrews et al., 2006). There are even arguments that psychopathic personality features can be addressed in treatment. Admittedly, much of the research on treating psychopathic patients has been characterized as bleak (for a review, see Hare, 2003). However, others have argued that this research is misleading, and evidence suggests certain psychopathic characteristics are amenable to change (Polascheck, 2014; Salekin, 2002; see chapter 19). Using data from the MacArthur Violence Risk Assessment Study, Skeem and colleagues (2002) found that "patients with psychopathic traits appeared as likely to benefit from *adequate* doses of treatment by becoming less violent as those without such traits" (p. 594). However, patients with psychopathic traits receiving *minimal* treatment did not see a reduction in violence potential, suggesting that the dose-response relationship is important.

Collaborating with Patients

The key collaborator in risk management should be the patient. To the greatest extent possible, patients should be involved in explicit conversations about their risk for future violence and in developing risk management plans. There is growing evidence that patients are able to predict their behavior in a number of domains, including the likelihood of engaging in violence (Skeem, Manchak, Lidz, & Mulvey, 2013). In fact, the results of a recent study showed that the self-perceptions of high-risk inpatients regarding their violence risk outperformed two brief, validated risk-assessment instruments in predicting acts of violence (Skeem et al., 2013). In eliciting self-perceptions about violence risk, the authors emphasized that interviewers first engaged participants in a discussion that was "meant to encourage patients to construe violence at less symbolic, more specific, and more contextualized levels" (p. 412). There is little empirical evidence on whether this type of "cognitive scaffolding" or rapport is necessary to gather accurate information about violence risk, but it seems that both scaffolding and rapport are likely related to a patient's willingness to engage in honest disclosure.

Collaborating with patients is also essential for treatment engagement. Multiple studies have found that treatment adherence reduces violence risk (Swanson, Swartz, & Elbogen, 2004; Swartz et al., 1998). Treatment *engagement* is often a necessary condition for treatment adherence, meaning that patient beliefs about the need for treatment, and treatment effectiveness, likely affect whether the individual attends appointments and follows clinician recommendations. As mentioned, Elbogen and colleagues (2006) found that both perceived treatment need and perceived treatment effectiveness were associated with reduced odds for violent behavior in the community. Conversely, a subsequent study found that individuals with severe mental illness who were either arrested, violent, or both in the past year were significantly more likely to deny needing treatment (Elbogen, Mustillo, Van Dorn. Swanson, & Swartz, 2007). Therefore, interventions based on Prochaska and DiClemente's (1983) transtheoretical model (e.g., Motivational Interviewing) may be a necessary first step in patient collaboration.

Research on the utility of patients' predictions of their own violence and the relationship between treatment engagement and violence underscore the principle that patients are essential collaborators if they are active participants in their own treatment. Again, the goal of violence risk assessment is prevention of violence. Therefore, clinicians should engage their patients in conversations about violence, not only to obtain a prediction of violence, but so that patients can elucidate relevant risk factors and

contextual variables that are related to violence. Patients can also contribute to discussions about the feasibility of plans and their willingness or ability to comply. Finally, patients will likely be more invested in risk management plans they have helped design, thereby increasing the likelihood that the plan will succeed (Heilbrun, 1997).

Collaborating with Other Providers and Systems in Risk Management

In some treatment contexts, such as large psychiatric facilities or court-ordered treatment arrangements, a clinician is part of a well-defined team from the start, and there are well-established protocols for sharing risk management plans. In other contexts, such as outpatient therapy in a community clinic, there may be a smaller, and less well-defined treatment team. Risk management plans are important in either type of context, but in the latter, clinicians may need to establish communication and collaboration with others involved in the patient's care. These may include professionals such as psychologists, psychiatrists, and case-managers but could also include other invested individuals such as the patient's family member, partner, friend, or supervisor. Clinicians may, at the start, seek the patient's assistance to identify and allow access to significant others. But regardless of who makes up the eventual team, open communication among all participants in a risk management plan is essential.

Unfortunately, a common error in risk management involves poor collaboration. One well-publicized, tragic example of a cross-system communication failure occurred with Seung Hui Cho, who ultimately shot 49 students and faculty (killing 32) at Virginia Tech before committing suicide. After the shooting, details about Cho's mental health history were revealed, including the fact that he had contact with the mental health system in December 2005, approximately 15 months before the shooting occurred (Flynn & Heitzmann, 2008). Cho had been hospitalized overnight after voicing suicidal ideation. He was released the following day with a court order to participate in outpatient treatment (Bonnie, Reinhard, Hamilton, & McGarvey, 2009). However, he never complied with the order, and his noncompliance apparently went unnoticed (Bonnie et al., 2009).

Communication failures can happen for a variety of reasons. One of the best ways to prevent a patient from "slipping through the cracks" is by identifying a centralized entity to monitor the risk management plan (Conroy & Murrie, 2007). Often, these plans will involve several different systems, such as mental health care, substance abuse programming, employment, and housing. If each agency is monitoring the patient individually, risk factors can accumulate without the other, relevant parties' knowledge. Further, having a centralized entity monitoring a patient's compliance with the risk management plan reduces the chances of particular system failing to report or losing track of obligations.

Additionally, clear channels of communication are crucial (Conroy & Murrie, 2007). This requires that all relevant parties know how often and to whom they are reporting, and that action plans are in place to accommodate a patient's deterioration in functioning. It is also wise to anticipate that communication will not necessarily occur in a static manner at regular intervals. Successful risk management plans will require, to a degree, a decision-tree in which certain procedures (e.g., monthly reporting to a centralized entity) are followed when the patient is stable, and alternate procedures are in place for emergent situations (e.g., immediate reporting to a centralized authority and other relevant agencies).

Conclusion

Nearly all mental health care demands some basic competence in violence risk assessment and risk management. Though violence-risk-assessment approaches have developed primarily in the forensic specialty niche, and few clinicians receive significant training in it, all could benefit from greater familiarity with risk and threat assessment approaches. We encourage clinicians to make use of the foundational knowledge from violence risk assessment by performing a thorough assessment of a patient's risk status at the outset of treatment, integrating a risk management plan with treatment, and monitoring closely a patient's risk state over the course of treatment. As acute concerns about violence emerge, clinicians can implement best practices from threat assessment to intervene. These steps not only comply with legal and ethical standards, but they contribute to high quality care and better outcomes for patients and their communities.

References

Ægisdóttir, S., White, M. J., Spengler, P. M., Maugherman, A. S., Anderson, L. A., Cook, R. S., ... Rush, J. D. (2006). The meta-analysis of clinical judgment project: Fifty-six years of accumulated research on clinical versus statistical prediction. *The Counseling Psychologist, 34*, 341–382. doi:10.1177/0011000005285875

Allnutt, S. H., Ogloff, J. R. P., Adams, J., O'Driscoll, C., Daffern, M., Carroll, A., ... Chaplow, D. (2013). Managing aggression and violence: The clinician's role in contemporary mental health care. *Australian and New Zealand Journal of Psychiatry, 47*, 728–736. doi:10.1177/0004867413484368

American Psychological Association (APA). (2002). *Ethical principles of psychologists and code of conduct.* Washington, DC: APA.

American Psychological Association (APA). (2013). *Gun violence: Prediction, prevention, and policy. APA panel of experts report.* Washington DC: Author.

Andrews, D. A., Bonta, J., & Hoge, R. D. (1990). Classification for effective rehabilitation: Rediscovering psychology. *Criminal Justice and Behavior, 17*, 19–52. doi:10.1177/0093854890017001004

Andrews, D. A., Bonta, J., & Wormith, J. S. (2006). The recent past and near future of risk and/or need assessment. *Crime and Delinquency, 52*, 7–27.

Appelbaum, P. S., Robbins, P. C., & Monahan, J. (2000). Violence and delusions: Data from the MacArthur Violence Risk Assessment Study. *American Journal of Psychiatry, 157*, 566–572.

Arkes, H. R. (1989). Principles in judgment/decision-making research pertinent to legal proceedings. *Behavioral Sciences and the Law, 7*, 429–456.

ASIS International and Society for Human Resources Management. (2011). *Workplace violence: Prevention and intervention.* Alexandria, VA: ASIS International.

Ajzen, I. (1977). Intuitive theories of events and the effects of base-rate information on prediction. *Journal of Personality and Social Psychology, 35*, 303–314. doi:10.1037/0022-3514.35.5.303

Barratt, E. (1994). Impulsiveness and aggression. In J. Monahan & H. J. Steadman (Eds.), *Violence and mental disorder: Developments in risk assessment* (pp. 61–79). Chicago, IL: University of Chicago Press.

Bartels, S. J., Drake, R. E., Wallach, M. A., & Freeman, D. H. (1991). Characteristic hostility in schizophrenic outpatients. *Schizophrenia Bulletin, 17*, 163–171. doi:10.1093/schbul/17.1.163

Bersoff, D. N. (2008). *Ethical Conflicts in Psychology* (4th ed.). Washington, DC: American Psychological Association.

Bersoff, D. N. (2014). Protecting victims of violent patients while protecting confidentiality. *American Psychologist, 69*, 461–467. doi:10.1037/a0037198

Binder, R. L., & McNiel, D. E. (1999). Contemporary practices in managing acutely violent patients in 20 psychiatric emergency rooms. *Emergency Psychiatry, 50*, 1553–1554. doi:10.1176/ps.50.12.1553

Boer, D. P., Wilson, R. J., Gauthier, C. M., & Hart, S. D. (1997). Assessing risk of sexual violence: Guidelines for clinical practice. In C. D. Webster & M. A. Jackson (Eds.), *Impulsivity: Theory, assessment, and treatment* (pp. 326–342). New York, NY: Guilford Press.

Bonnie, R. J., Reinhard, J. S., Hamilton, P., & McGarvey, E. L. (2009). Mental health system transformation after the Virginia Tech Tragedy. *Health Affairs, 28*, 793–804. doi:10.1377/hlthaff.28.3.793

Bonta, J., Harman, W. G., Hann, R. G., & Cormier, R. B. (1996). The prediction of recidivism among federally sentenced offenders: A re-validation of the SIR scale. *Canadian Journal of Criminology, 38*, 61–79.

Bonta, J., Law, M., &. Hanson, R. K. (1998). The prediction of criminal and violent recidivism among mentally disordered offenders: A meta-analysis. *Psychological Bulletin, 123*, 123–142.

Borum, R. (1996). Improving the clinical practice of violence risk assessment: Technology, guidelines, and training. *American Psychologist, 51*, 945–956.

Borum, R. (2006). Assessing risk for violence among juvenile offenders. In S. N. Sparta & G. P. Koocher (Eds.), *Forensic mental health assessment of children and adolescents* (pp. 190–202). Oxford, UK: Oxford University Press.

Borum, R., Cornell, D., Modzeleski, W., & Jimerson, S. R. (2010). What can be done about school shootings? A review of the evidence. *Educational Researcher, 39*, 27–37.

Borum, R., Fein, R., Vossekuil, B., & Berglund, J. (1999). Threat assessment: Defining an approach for evaluating risk of targeted violence. *Behavioral Sciences and the Law, 17*, 323–337.

Borum, R., Otto, R., & Golding, S. (1993). Improving clinical judgment and decision making in forensic evaluation. *Journal of Psychiatry & Law, 21*, 35–76.

Borum, R., & Reddy, M. (2001). Assessing violence risk in Tarasoff situations: A fact-based model of inquiry. *Behavioral Sciences and the Law, 19*, 375–385. doi:10.1002/bsl.447

Brennan, P. A., Mednick, S. A., & Hodgins, S. (2000). Major mental disorders and criminal violence. *Archives of General Psychiatry, 57*, 494–500. doi:10.1001/archpsyc.57.5.494.

California Civil Code Section 43.92.

Centers for Disease Control and Prevention. (2014, June). Morbidity and mortality weekly report. *Surveillance Summaries, 63*, no. 4.

Chu, C. M., Thomas, S. D. M., Ogloff, J. R. P., & Daffern, M. (2011). The short- to medium-term predictive accuracy of static and dynamic risk assessment measures in a secure forensic hospital. *Assessment, 20*, 230–241. doi:10.1177/1073191111418298

Coid, J. W., Ullrich, S., Kallis, C., Keers, R., Barker, D., Cowden, F., & Stamps, R. (2013). The relationship between delusions and violence: Findings from the East London First Episode Psychosis Study. *JAMA, 70*, 465–471. doi:10.1001/jamapsychiatry.2013.12

Conroy, M. A., & Murrie, D. C. (2007). *Forensic assessment of violence risk.* Hoboken, NJ: Wiley.

Coontz, P., Lidz, C., & Mulvey, E. (1994). Gender and the assessment of dangerousness in the psychiatric emergency room. *International Journal of Law and Psychiatry, 17*, 369–376.

Cornell, D. (2013). The Virginia Student Threat Assessment Guidelines: An empirically supported violence prevention strategy. In N. Böckler, T. Seeger, W. Heitmeyer, and P. Sitzer (Eds.), *School shootings: International research, case studies, and concepts for prevention* (pp. 379–400). New York, NY: Springer.

Cornell, D. (2014). Best practices in threat assessment in schools. In A. Thomas and P. Harrison (Eds.), *Best Practices in School Psychology*, 6th ed. (pp. 259–272). Bethesda, MD: National Association of School Psychologists.

Cornell, D., & Allen, K. (2011). Development, evaluation, and future directions of the Virginia Student Threat Assessment Guidelines. *Journal of School Violence, 10*, 88–106. doi:10.1080/15388220.2010.519432

Cornell, D., & Sheras, P. (2006). *Guidelines for responding to student threats of violence.* Longmont, CO: Sopris West.

Cornell, D., Sheras, P., Kaplan, S., McConville, D., Douglass, J., Elkon, A., . . . Cole, J. (2004). Guidelines for student threat assessment: Field-test findings. *School Psychology Review, 33*, 527–546.

Cottle, C. C., Lee, R. J., & Heilbrun, K. (2001). The prediction of criminal recidivism by juveniles: A meta-analysis. *Criminal Justice and Behavior, 28*, 367–394.

Cunningham, M. D., & Reidy, T. J. (1998). Antisocial personality disorder and psychopathy: Diagnostic dilemmas in classifying patterns of antisocial behavior in sentencing evaluations. *Behavioral Sciences and the Law, 16*, 331–351.

DeMatteo, D., Murrie, D. C., Anumba, N., & Keesler, M. (2011). *Forensic mental health assessments in death penalty cases.* New York, NY: Oxford University Press.

Dickerson, F. B. (2004). Update on cognitive behavioral psychotherapy for schizophrenia: Review of recent studies. *Journal of Cognitive Psychotherapy: An International Quarterly, 18*, 189–205. doi:10.1891/jcop.18.3.189.65654

Douglas, K. S., Guy, L. S., & Hart, S. D. (2009). Psychosis as a risk factor for violence to others: A meta-analysis. *Psychological Bulletin, 135*, 679–706. doi:10.1037/a0016311

Douglas, K. S., Hart, S. D., Webster, C. D., & Belfrage, H. (2013). *HCR-20V3: Assessing risk of violence–User guide.* Burnaby, Canada: Mental Health, Law, and Policy Institute, Simon Fraser University.

Douglas, K. S., & Ogloff, J. R. P. (2003). Multiple facets of risk for violence: The impact of judgmental specificity on structured decisions about violence risk. *International Journal of Forensic Mental Health, 2*, 19–34. doi:10.1080/14999013.2003.10471176

Douglas, K. S., & Skeem, J. L. (2005). Violence risk assessment: Getting specific about being dynamic. *Psychology, Public Policy, and Law, 11*, 347–383.

Douglas, K. S., Vincent, G., & Edens, J. F. (2006). Risk for criminal recidivism: The role of psychopathy. In C. Patrick (Ed.), *Handbook of Psychopathy.* New York, NY: Guilford.

Elbogen, E., & Johnson, S. C. (2009). The intricate link between violence and mental disorder: Results from the National Epidemiologic Survey on Alcohol and Related Conditions. *Archives of General Psychiatry, 66*, 152–161. doi:10.1001/archgenpsychiatry.2008.537

Elbogen, E. B., Mustillo, S., Van Dorn, R., Swanson, J. W., & Swartz, M. S. (2007). The impact of perceived need for treatment on risk of arrest and violence among people with severe mental illness. *Criminal Justice and Behavior, 34*, 197–210.

Elbogen, E. B., Mercado-Calkins, C., Scalora, M. J., & Tomkins, A. J. (2002). Perceived relevance of factors for violence risk assessment: A survey of clinicians. *International Journal of Forensic Mental Health, 1*, 37–47.

Elbogen, E., Van Dorn, R. A., Swanson, J. W., Swartz, M. S., & Monahan, J. (2006). Treatment engagement and violence risk in mental disorders. *British Journal of Psychiatry, 189*, 354–360. doi:10.1192/bjp.bp.105.017913

Elbogen, E., Williams, A., Kim, D., Tomkins, A., & Scalora, M. (2001). Gender and perceptions of dangerousness in civil psychiatric patients. *Law and Criminological Psychology, 6*, 215–228. doi:10.1348/135532501168299

Ewing v. Goldstein, 15 Cal. Rptr. 3d 864 (2004).

Fazel, S., Långström, N., Hjern, A., Grann, M., & Lichtenstein, P. (2009). Schizophrenia, substance abuse, and violent crime. *JAMA, 301*, 2016–2023. doi:10.1001/jama.2009.675

Federal Bureau of Investigation (2012). *Crime in the United States 2012.* Retrieved from http://www.fbi.gov/about-us/cjis/ucr/crime-in-the-u.s/2012/crime-in-the-u.s.-2012.

Fein, R. A., & Vossekuil, B. (1998). *Protective intelligence and threat assessment investigations: A guide for state and local law enforcement officials* (NIJ/OJP/DOJ Publication No. 170612). Washington, DC: US Department of Justice.

Flynn, C., & Heitzmann, D. (2008). Tragedy at Virginia Tech: Trauma and its aftermath. *The Counseling Psychologist, 36*, 479–489. doi:10.1177/0011000008314787

Foa, E. B., Hembree, E. A., Cahill, S. P., Rauch, S. A. M., Riggs, D. S., Feeny, N. C., & Yadin, E. (2005). Randomized trial of prolonged exposure for posttraumatic stress disorder with and without cognitive restructuring: Outcome at academic and community clinics. *Journal of Consulting and Clinical Psychology, 73*, 953–964. doi:10.1037/0022-006X.73.5.953

Forman, E. M., Herbert, J. D., Moitra, E., Yeomans, P. D., & Geller, P. A. (2007). A randomized controlled effectiveness trial of acceptance and commitment therapy and cognitive therapy for anxiety and depression. *Behavior Modification, 31*, 772–799. doi:10.1177/0145445507302202

Freese, R., Hiscoke, U., & Hodgins, S. (2002, September). *The treatment of mentally ill patients with a history of criminality or violence: What works and what doesn't work?* Paper presentation at 11th Congress of the Association of European Psychiatrists, Stockholm, Sweden.

Gendreau, P., Goggin, C., & Law, M. A. (1997). Predicting prison misconduct. *Criminal Justice and Behavior, 24*, 414–431.

Gendreau, P., Little, T., & Goggin, C. (1996). A meta-analysis of the predictors of adult recidivism: What works! *Criminology, 34*, 575–607.

Greenfeld L. A., & Snell, T. L. (1999, December). Women offenders. *Bureau of Justice Statistic Special Report*. Retrieved from http://www.bjs.gov/content/pub/pdf/wo.pdf.

Gregory v. Kilbride, 565 S.E.2d 685 (2002).

Grisso, T., Davis, J., Vesselinov, R., Appelbaum, P. S., & Monahan, J. (2000). Violent thoughts and violent behavior following hospitalization for mental disorder. *Journal of Consulting and Clinical Psychology, 68*, 388–398. doi:10.1037/0022-006X.68.3.388

Grisso, T., & Tomkins, A. J. (1996). Communicating violence risk assessments. *American Psychologist, 51*, 928–930.

Grove, W. M., Zald, D. H., Lebow, S., Snitz, B. E., & Nelson, C. (2000). Clinical versus mechanical prediction: A meta-analysis. *Psychological Assessment, 12*, 19–30. doi:10.1037//1040-3590.12.1.19

Guy, J. D., Brown, C. K., & Poelstra, P. L. (1990). Who gets attacked? A national survey of patient violence directed at psychologists in clinical practice. *Professional Psychology: Research and Practice, 21*, 493–495.

Halikias, W. (2004). School-based risk assessments: A conceptual framework and model for professional practice. *Professional Psychology: Research & Practice, 35*, 598–607.

Hanson, R. K., & Morton-Bourgon, K. (2005). The characteristics of persistent sexual offenders: A meta-analysis of recidivism studies. *Journal of Consulting and Clinical Psychology, 73*, 1154–1163.

Hanson, R. K., & Morton-Bourgon, K. E. (2009). The accuracy of recidivism risk assessments for sexual offenders: A meta-analysis. *Psychological Assessment, 21*, 1–21.

Hare, R. D. (2003). *Hare Psychopathy Checklist—Revised (PCL-R),* 2nd ed. Technical manual. Toronto: Multi-Health Systems.

Hawes, S. M., Boccaccini, M. T., & Murrie, D. C. (2013). Psychopathy and the combination of psychopathy and sexual deviance as predictors of sexual recidivism: Meta-analytic findings using the Psychopathy Checklist-Revised. *Psychological Assessment, 25*, 233–243. doi:10.1037/a0030391

Health Insurance Portability and Accountability Act (HIPAA) of 1996, Pub. L. No. 104–191, 100 Stat. 1936 (1996).

Health Insurance Portability and Accountability Act (HIPAA), Enforcement Rule, 45. C.F.R. § 160 (2006).

Health Insurance Portability and Accountability Act (HIPAA), Privacy Rule, 45 C.F.R. §§160 &164 (2002).

Hedlund v. Superior Court of Orange County, 669 P.2d 41 (1983).

Heilbrun, K. (1997). Prediction versus management models relevant to risk assessment: The importance of legal decision-making context. *Law and Human Behavior, 21*, 347–359. doi:10.1023/A:1024851017947

Heilbrun, K. (2009). *Evaluation for risk of violence in adults.* New York, NY: Oxford University Press.

Hemphill, J. F., Hare, R. D., & Wong, S. (1998). Psychopathy and recidivism: A review. *Legal and Criminological Psychology, 3*, 139–170.

Hettema, J., Steele, J., & Miller, W. R. (2005). Motivational interviewing. *Annual Review of Clinical Psychology, 1*, 91–111. doi:10.1146/annurev.clinpsy.1.102803.143833

Hillbrand, M. (2001). Homicide-suicide and other forms of co-occurring aggression against self and others. *Professional Psychology: Research and Practice, 32*, 626–635.

Hirschi, T., & Gottfredson, M. (1983). Age and the explanation of crime. *American Journal of Sociology, 89*, 552–584.

Idaho Code § 6-1902 (1991).

Kahneman, D., & Tversky, A. (1973). On the psychology of prediction. *Psychological Review, 80*, 237–251. doi:10.1037/h0034747

Kay, S. R., Wolkenfeld, F., & Murrill, L. M. (1988). Profiles of aggression among psychiatric patients: II. Covariates and predictors. *Journal of Nervous and Mental Disease, 176*, 547–557. doi:10.1097/00005053-198809000-00008

Kindness, A., Kim, H., Aider, S., Edwards, A., Parekh, A., & Olson, L M. (2009). Court compliance as a predictor of postadjudication recidivism for domestic violence offenders. *Journal of Interpersonal Violence, 24*, 1222–1238. doi: 10.1177/0886260508322197

Lamberg, L. (2007). New tools aid in violence risk assessment. *Journal of the American Medical Association, 298*, 499–501.

Leistico, A. R., Salekin, R. T., DeCoster, J., & Rogers, R. (2008). A large-scale meta-analysis related the Hare measures of psychopathy to antisocial conduct. *Law and Human Behavior, 32*, 28–45.

Liem, M. (2010). Homicide followed by suicide: A review. *Aggression and Violent Behavior, 15*, 153–161.

Linehan, M. M., Armstrong, H. E., Suarez, A., Allmon, D., & Heard, H. L. (1991). Cognitive-behavioral treatment of chronically parasuicidal borderline patients. *Archives of General Psychiatry, 48*, 1060–1064. doi:10.1001/archpsyc.1991.01810360024003

McNiel, D. E., Charmmberlain, J. R., Weaver, C. M., Hall, S. E., Fordwood, S. R., & Binder, R. L. (2008). Impact of clinical training on violence risk assessment. *American Journal of Psychiatry, 165*, 195–200.

McNiel, D. E., Eisner, J. P., & Binder, R. L. (2000). The relationship between command hallucinations and violence. *Psychiatric Services, 51*, 1288–1292. doi:10.1176/appi.ps.51.10.1288

Meloy, J. R., Hart, S. D., & Hoffman, J. (2014). Threat assessment and threat management. In J. R. Meloy and J. Hoffman (Eds.), *International handbook of threat assessment.* New York, NY. Oxford University Press.

Meloy, J. R., & O'Toole, M. E. (2011). The concept of leakage in threat assessment. *Behavioral Sciences and the Law, 29*, 513–527.

Moffitt, T. (1993). Adolescence-limited and life-course-persistent antisocial behavior: A developmental taxonomy. *Psychological Review, 100*, 674–701.

Moffitt, T. (2002). Males on the life-course-persistent and adolescence-limited antisocial pathways: Follow-up at age 26 years. *Development and Psychopathology, 14*, 179–207.

Monahan, J. (1981). *Predicting violent behavior: An assessment of clinical techniques*. Beverly Hills, CA: Sage.

Monahan, J. (2008). Structured risk assessment of violence. In R. Simon and K. Tardiff (Eds.), *Textbook of violence assessment and management* (pp. 17–33). Washington, DC: American Psychiatric.

Monahan, J., & Skeem, J. (2014). The evolution of violence risk assessment. *CNS spectrums, 19*, 419–424. doi:http://dx.doi.org/10.1017/S1092852914000145

Monahan, J., & Steadman, H. J. (2012). Extending violence risk reduction principles to justice-involved persons with mental illness. In J. A. Dvoskin, J. L. Skeem, R. W. Novaco, & K. S. Douglas (Eds.), *Using social science to reduce violent offending* (pp. 245–264). Oxford, UK: Oxford University Press.

Monahan, J., Steadman, H. J., Silver, E., Appelbaum, P. S., Robbins, P. C., Mulvey, E. P., ... Banks, S. (2001). *Rethinking risk assessment: The MacArthur study of mental disorder and violence*. Oxford, UK: Oxford University Press.

Mulvey, E. P., Odgers, C., Skeem, J., Gardner, W., Schubert, C., & Lidz, C. (2006). Substance use and community violence: A test of the relation at the daily level. *Journal of Consulting and Clinical Psychology, 74*, 743–754. doi:10.1037/0022-006X.74.4.743

Mumola, C. J. (2005, August). *Bureau of Justice Statistics special report: Suicide and homicide in state prisons and local jails*. Washington, DC: United States Department of Justice.

Murrie, D. C. (2016). Structured violence risk assessment: Implications for preventing gun violence. In L. Gold & R. Simon (Eds.), *Gun Violence and Mental Illness* (pp. 221–247). Arlington, VA. American Psychiatric.

Newhill, C., Mulvey, E., & Lidz, C. (1995). Characteristics of violence in the community by female patients seen in a psychiatric emergency service. *Psychiatric Services, 46*, 785–795. doi:10.1176/ps.46.8.785

Novaco, R. W. (1994). Anger as a risk factor for violence among the mentally disordered. In J. Monahan & H. J. Steadman (Eds.), *Violence and mental disorder: Developments in risk assessment* (pp. 21–59). Chicago, IL: University of Chicago Press.

Otto, R. K., & Douglas, K. S. (Eds.). (2010). *Handbook of violence risk assessment*. New York, NY: Routledge/Taylor &. Francis.

Pabian, Y. L., Welfel, E., & Beebe, R. S. (2009). Psychologists' knowledge of their states' laws pertaining to Tarasoff-type situations. *Professional Psychology: Research and Practice, 40*, 8–14. doi:10.1037/a0014784

Peck v. Counseling Services of Addison County, 499 A.2d 422 (1985).

Pisani, A. R., Cross, W. F., Watts, A., & Conner, K. (2012) Evaluation of the Commitment to Living (CTL) curriculum. *Crisis: The Journal of Crisis Intervention and Suicide Prevention, 33*, 30–38.

Polascheck, D. L. L. (2014). Adult criminals with psychopathy: Common beliefs about treatability and change have little empirical support. *Current Directions in Psychological Science, 23*, 296–301. doi:10.1177/0963721414535211

Prochaska, J. O., & DiClemente, C. C. (1983). Stages and processes of self-change of smoking: Toward an integrative model of change. *Journal of Consulting and Clinical Psychology, 51*, 390–395. doi:10.1037/0022-006X.51.3.390

Reddy, M., Borum, R., Berglund, J., Vossekuil, B., Fein, R., & Modzeleski, W. (2001). Evaluating risk for targeted violence in schools: Comparing risk assessment, threat assessment, and other approaches. *Psychology in the Schools, 38*, 157–172. doi:10.1002/pits.1007

Reiss, A. J. Jr., & Roth, J. A (1993). *Understanding and preventing violence*. Washington, DC: National Academy Press.

Resick, P. A., Nishith, P., Weaver, T. L., Astin, M. C., & Feuer, C. A. (2002). A comparison of cognitive-processing therapy with prolonged exposure and a waiting condition for the treatment of chronic posttraumatic stress disorder in female rape victims. *Journal of Consulting and Clinical Psychology, 70*, 867–879.

Robbins, P. C., Monahan, J., & Silver, E. (2003). Mental disorder, violence, and gender. *Law and Human Behavior, 27*, 561–571. doi:10.1023/B:LAHU.0000004886.13268.f2

Roe v. Wade, 410 U.S. 113 (1973).

Salekin, R. T. (2002). Psychopathy and therapeutic pessimism: Clinical lore or clinical reality? *Clinical Psychology Review, 22*, 79–112. doi:10.1016/S0272-7358(01)00083-6

Salekin, R. T., Rogers, R., & Sewell, K. W. (1996). A review and meta-analysis of the Psychopathy Checklist and Psychopathy Checklist—Revised: Predictive validity of dangerousness. *Clinical Psychology: Science and Practice, 3*, 203–215.

Schwartz, T. L., & Park, T. L. (1999). Assaults by patients on psychiatric residents: A survey and training recommendations. *Psychiatric Services, 50*, 381–383.

Shah, S. (1978). Dangerousness and mental illness: Some conceptual, prediction, and policy dilemmas. In C. Frederick (Ed.), *Dangerous behavior: A problem in law and mental health* (pp. 153–191). Washington, DC: Government Printing Office.

Skeem, J. L., Manchak, S. M., Lidz, C. W., & Mulvey, E. P. (2013). The utility of patients' self-perceptions of violence risk: Consider asking the person who may know best. *Psychiatric Services, 64*, 410–415. doi:10.1176/appi.ps.001312012

Skeem, J., Monahan, J., & Mulvey, E. (2002). Psychopathy, treatment involvement, and subsequent violence among civil psychiatric patients. *Law and Human Behavior, 26*, 577–603. doi:10.1023/A:1020993916404

Skeem, J. L., & Mulvey, E. (2001). Psychopathy and community violence among civil psychiatric patients: Results from the MacArthur Violence Risk Assessment Study. *Journal of Clinical and Consulting Psychology, 69*, 358–374. doi:10.1037//0022-006X.69.3.358

Skeem, J., Schubert, C., Stowman, S., Beeson, S., Mulvey, E., Gardner, W., & Lidz, C. (2005). Gender and risk assessment accuracy: Underestimating women's violent potential. *Law and Human Behavior, 29*, 173–186.

Shergill, S. S., & Szmukler, G. (1998). How predicable is violence and suicide in community psychiatric practice? *Journal of Mental Health, 7*, 393–401.

Smith-Bell, M., & Winslade, W. J. (1994). Privacy, confidentiality, and privilege in psychotherapeutic relationships. *American Journal of Orthopsychiatry, 64*, 180–193. doi:10.1037/h0079520

Soliman, A. E., & Reza, H. (2001). Risk factors and correlates of violence among acutely ill adult psychiatric inpatients. *Psychiatric Services, 52*, 75–80. doi:10.1176/appi.ps.52.1.75

Steadman, H. J., Monahan, J., Appelbaum, P. S., Grisso, T., Mulvey, E. P., Roth, L. H., ... Klassen, D. (1994). Designing a new generation of risk assessment research. In J. Monahan & H. J. Steadman (Eds.), *Violence and mental disorder: Developments in risk assessment* (pp. 297–318). Chicago, IL: University of Chicago Press.

Steadman, H. J., Mulvey, E. P., Monahan, J., Robbins, P. C., Appelbaum, P. S., Grisso, T., ... Silver, E. (1998). Violence by people discharged from acute psychiatric inpatient facilities and by others in the same neighborhoods. *Archives of General Psychiatry, 55*, 393–401.

Svedberg, B., Mesterton, A., & Cullberg, J. (2001). First-episode non-affective psychosis in a total urban population: A 5-year follow-up. *Social Psychiatry and Psychiatric Epidemiology*, *36*, 332–337.

Swanson, J. W. (1994). Mental disorder, substance abuse, and community violence: An epidemiological approach. In J. Monahan & H. J. Steadman (Eds.), *Violence and mental disorder: Developments in risk assessment* (pp. 101–136). Chicago, IL: University of Chicago Press.

Swanson, J. W. (2008). Preventing the unpredicted: Managing violence risk in mental health care. *Psychiatric Services*, *59*, 191–193.

Swanson, J. W., Holzer, C. E. III, Ganju, V. K., & Jono, R. T. (1990). Violence and psychiatric disorder in the community: Evidence from the epidemiological catchment area surveys. *Hospital and Community Psychiatry*, *41*, 761–770.

Swanson, J. W., Swartz, M. S., & Elbogen, E. (2004). Effectiveness of atypical antipsychotic medications in reducing violent behavior among persons with schizophrenia in community-based treatment. *Schizophrenia Bulletin*, *30*, 3–20. doi:10.1093/oxfordjournals.schbul.a007065

Swanson, J. W., Swartz, M. S., Essock, S. M., Wagner, H. R., Goodman, L. A., Rosenberg, S. D., & Meador, K. G. (2002). The social-environmental context of violent behavior in persons treated for severe mental illness. *American Journal of Public Health*, *92*, 1523–1531.

Swartz, M. S., Swanson, J. W., Hiday, V. A., Borum, R., Wagner, R., & Burns, B. J. (1998). Taking the wrong drugs: The role of substance abuse and medication noncompliance in violence among severely mentally ill individuals. *Social Psychiatry and Psychiatric Epidemiology*, *33* (Supp. 1). S75–S80. doi:10.1007/s001270050213

Sweeten, G., Piquero, A. R., & Steinberg, L. (2013) Age and the explanation of crime, revisited. *Journal of Youth and Adolescents*, *42*, 921–938. doi:10.1007/s10964-013-9926-4

Tarasoff v. Regents of the University of California, 551 P.2d 334 (1976).

Tex. Code Ann. §611.004.

Thapar v. Zezulka, 994 S.W.2d 635 (1999).

United States Census Bureau (2012). *The 2012 Statistical Abstract*. Retrieved from http://www.census.gov/compendia/statab/

United States Department of Health and Human Services (2001). *Youth Violence: A report of the Surgeon General*. Rockville, MD: US Department of Health and Human Services, Substance Abuse and Mental Health Services Administration, Center for Mental Health Services, National Institutes of Mental health, National Institutes of Health.

Yang, M., Wong, S. C., & Coid, J. (2010). The efficacy of violence prediction: A meta-analytic comparison of nine risk assessment tools. *Psychological Bulletin*, *136*, 740–767. doi:10.1037/a0020473

Victims of Violence: Evaluation and Management

Michael R. McCart *and* Kristyn Zajac

Abstract

This chapter provides a brief overview on the prevalence and common consequences of violent victimization among adults. It also summarizes practice guidelines for the evaluation and management of victims in the acute aftermath of an assault. Guidelines argue against delivery of debriefing interventions in the days following a traumatic event and advocate instead for the provision of Psychological First Aid or early, exposure-based protocols. Symptom-based assessments are recommended for tracking victims' distress levels over time. In addition, for individuals who continue to experience significant distress symptoms several weeks postincident, it may be advisable to deliver an evidence-based, early cognitive-behavioral intervention.

Key Words: victim, intervention, violent victimization, Psychological First Aid, cognitive-behavioral intervention, symptom-based assessments

Despite a trend toward decreased violent crime in the United States over the past two decades, adults continue to experience high levels of criminal victimization. Epidemiological data from the National Crime Victimization Survey indicated a violent crime rate (including incidents of rape, robbery, and physical assault) of 26.1 victimizations per 1,000 people among individuals 12 and older in 2012 (Truman, Langton, & Planty, 2013). Exposure to violent crime is associated with a number of potential psychosocial outcome trajectories. Fortunately, the most common is resilience, characterized by healthy and relatively stable levels of functioning in the aftermath of a traumatic event (Bonnano, Westphal, & Mancini, 2011). Specifically, though studies estimate that between 50% and 70% of adults in the United States have experienced at least one violent or life-threatening event during their lifetime, the large majority do not develop significant mental health problems as a result (Kessler, Sonnega, Bromet, Hughes, & Nelson, 1995). However, approximately 5% to 10% of victims will go on to develop

serious psychiatric disorders (Ozer, Best, Lipsey, & Weiss, 2003), such as posttraumatic stress disorder (PTSD; Hapke, Schumann, Rumpf, John, & Meyer, 2006; Scarpa, Haden, & Hurley, 2006), major depression (Boudreaux, Kilpatrick, Resnick, Best, & Saunders, 1998; Zlotnick, Johnson, & Kohn, 2006), and substance use disorders (Brady, Back, & Coffey, 2004; Kilpatrick, Acierno, Resnick, Saunders, & Best, 1997).

Many clinicians once believed that it was appropriate to provide psychological treatment to virtually all individuals exposed to trauma. This view led to the development of various "debriefing" interventions designed to be applied universally in the acute aftermath of a traumatic event. As mentioned earlier, a majority of individuals exposed to traumatic stressors do not experience psychological distress at a level that warrants formal clinical intervention (Bonanno et al., 2011). Further, though early studies of debriefing had positive findings, the results of more rigorous randomized controlled trials showed that it is, at best, not beneficial (Marchand et al., 2006; Mayou, Ehlers, & Hobbs, 2000; Rose, Brewin, Andrews, & Kirk, 1999) and, at worst, potentially harmful (Bisson, Jenkins, Alexander, & Bannister, 1997; Hobbs, Mayou, Harrison, & Worlock, 1996). In light of these findings, researchers have developed preliminary practice guidelines for psychological care immediately following a trauma (Bisson, Brayne, Ochberg, & Everly, 2007; Gray & Litz, 2005). Drawing heavily from the empirical literature, these guidelines advise against the use of debriefing procedures and advocate for the provision of Psychological First Aid (PFA). Furthermore, they emphasize timely assessments to identify individuals who may benefit from more intensive psychological interventions. In this chapter, we discuss how these guidelines inform clinical practice with adults who have recently experienced a violent crime. We also describe PFA in more detail as well as initial efforts to evaluate this model with victims of crime. First, however, we provide a brief overview of the prevalence and common consequences of violent victimization.

Prevalence of Violent Victimization

As noted previously, epidemiological studies have documented high rates of criminal victimization among adults in the United States. For example, in a nationally representative sample of 9,684 adults, 11% of women and 2% of men reported that they had been raped at some point during their lifetime (Basile, Chen, Black, & Saltzman, 2007). Similarly, in another sample of 5,877 adults, 7% of women and 11% of men reported a history of physical assault (Kessler, Chiu, Demler, & Walters, 2005). Finally, among a national sample of 4,008 women, 14% had experienced sexual molestation or attempted rape, 13% had experienced a completed rape, and 10% had a history of physical assault (Resnick, Kilpatrick, Dansky, Saunders, & Best, 1993).

The prevalence of criminal victimization varies by age, sex, and race. Data from the National Crime Victimization Survey indicate a steady decrease in the risk of victimization by violent crime after age 24 (Truman et al., 2013). Thus younger individuals are at increased risk for victimization. Victimization also varies by gender. Specifically, women are more likely than men to experience sexual assault, while incidents of robbery and physical assault are more common among men compared to women (Hapke et al., 2006; see Tolin & Foa, 2006, for a review). In addition, men are more likely to be physically assaulted by strangers, whereas women are more likely to be assaulted by an intimate partner (Lauritsen & Rezey, 2013).

There is also substantial variability in exposure to traumatic events by race and ethnicity (see Hatch & Dohrenwend, 2007, for a review). Data related to race from the 2012 National Crime Victimization Survey indicated that African American adults were victims of serious violence, including rape, robbery, and aggravated assault, at a higher rate (11.3/1,000 people) than were White adults (6.8/1,000 people; Truman et al., 2013). Rates among individuals of Hispanic/Latino descent fell between these two groups (9.3/1,000). In this report, victimization rates were considerably higher among American Indian/Alaskan Natives, though the authors cautioned that these estimates might be skewed due to the small sample size for this group.

One of the strongest predictors of future victimization is past victimization (see Arrata, 2002; Classen, Palesh, & Aggarwal, 2005; Noll & Grych, 2011, for reviews). For example, it is estimated that two out of three individuals who experience sexual assault will be revictimized in their lifetime (Classen et al., 2005). According to data from the National Violence Against Women Survey, male and female victims of childhood physical or sexual abuse are two to five times more likely to experience a subsequent physical or sexual assault in adulthood (Desai, Arias, Thompson, & Basile, 2002). Risk of repeat victimization among women appears to increase at a linear rate. That is, compared to women who had never been physically or sexually assaulted, the odds of experiencing a new assault over a two-year period are doubled for women with one assault, increase about 400% for women with two assaults, and increase about 1,000% for women with three or more prior victimizations (Kilpatrick et al., 1997). There are a few explanations for this phenomenon. First, several of the common consequences of trauma exposure, including symptoms of PTSD (e.g., Cougle, Resnick, & Kilpatrick, 2009; Messman-Moore, Brown, & Koelsch, 2005) and substance abuse problems (Ullman, Najdowski, & Filipas, 2009) have been found to put individuals at elevated risk for victimization. In addition, the inability to escape violent neighborhoods or the continued accessibility of an individual to the perpetrator (e.g., due to financial hardship, domestic violence) is likely to increase risk for revictimization (Hanson, Kilpatrick, Falsetti, & Resnick, 1995).

Impact of Victimization
Acute Medical Problems

Interpersonal violence is a common cause of injury and emergency department visits. In the National Violence Against Women Survey, approximately 42% of women and 20% of men who had been physically assaulted sustained injuries during their most recent victimization, though most injuries were minor, involving scratches, bruises, or welts (Tjaden & Thoennes, 2000a). More severe physical injuries often occur in the context of intimate partner violence (IPV), which is defined as physical assault, sexual assault, or stalking perpetrated by a current or former romantic partner or spouse. Approximately 35.6% of women and 28.5% of men in the United States have experienced IPV in their lifetime (Breiding, Chen, & Black, 2014). For women alone, IPV resulted in over 1,500 deaths in 2010 (Catalano, 2013) and is responsible for nearly 2 million emergency department visits each year (Centers for Disease Control and Prevention, 2003). Common IPV-related injuries include broken bones, contusions, vaginal tearing, knife wounds, traumatic brain injuries, and back pain (Black, 2011; Campbell et al., 2002; Plichta, 2004; Tjaden & Thoennes, 2000b).

Similarly, rape victims often sustain a variety of minor injuries, including scratches, bruises, or welts, while some sustain more serious injuries, including broken bones, sprained muscles, or broken teeth (Tjaden & Thoennes, 2006). In addition, women who are raped are at increased risk for a variety of gynecological problems. Prevalence estimates of sexually transmitted infections among rape victims range from 2% to 30% (Girardet et al., 2009; Goodman, Koss, & Russo, 1993; Reynolds, Peipert, & Collins, 2000). Other common complications include vaginal or urinary tract infections and pelvic pain (Campbell et al., 2002).

Acute Psychological Reactions

It is common for adults to experience symptoms of psychological distress in the acute aftermath of a violent event. Specifically, there are high rates of intrusive thoughts, dissociative symptoms (e.g., emotional numbing, derealization, depersonalization, dissociative amnesia), avoidant behaviors, hyperarousal, insomnia, concentration difficulties, irritability, and depressed affect observed among adults in the initial weeks following a trauma (Bryant, 2004). As mentioned earlier, most individuals will show a decrease in symptoms within a few weeks

or months of the traumatic event (Bonnano et al., 2011). A minority of trauma victims, however, will go on to develop chronic mental health problems, such as PTSD, depression, or substance abuse problems. Data from our ongoing clinical trial evaluating PFA for victims of crime (described in more detail later) have produced similar results. During the initial phase of that trial, we evaluated victims of violent crime (i.e., domestic violence, armed robbery, physical assault, or sexual assault) at baseline (within 10 days of the crime) and again at one-, two-, and four-months post baseline. At the baseline assessment, 46% of victims displayed symptoms consistent with a diagnosis of PTSD (with the exception of the one-month duration criterion); however, by the four-month follow-up assessment, only 10% met criteria for PTSD. Thus, although distress levels were elevated in the days following victimization, study participants demonstrated a relatively rapid rate of recovery over the subsequent 12 weeks.

Chronic Mental Health Problems

PTSD is one of the most commonly observed mental health problems following a violent crime. The essential features are reexperiencing the event through dreams and intrusive thoughts, avoiding reminders of the event, emotional numbing, and hyperarousal symptoms that persist for more than one month following a traumatic stressor (*Diagnostic and Statistical Manual of Mental Disorders* (fifth edition [*DSM–5*], American Psychiatric Association, 2013). Interpersonal victimization is associated with higher rates of PTSD than other types of traumatic events, including motor vehicle accidents and natural disasters (Breslau et al., 1998; Hapke et al., 2006; Pietrzak, Goldstein, Southwick, & Grant, 2011; Santiago et al., 2013). When left untreated, PTSD tends to follow a chronic, unremitting course. In fact, a review of the literature found that, among individuals who develop PTSD, only about one third no longer meet diagnostic criteria at a three-month follow-up, whereas almost 40% display a chronic course (Santiago et al., 2013).

Major depression is also relatively common among victims of crime and is highly comorbid with PTSD (Kessler et al., 2005). In a large national study of women, a lifetime occurrence of physical assault increased the odds of current depression by a factor of 3 (Kilpatrick, Edmunds, & Seymour, 1992). A study of female victims of interpersonal violence who had PTSD found that

52% of the sample also met diagnostic criteria for depression (Taft, Resick, Watkins, & Panuzio, 2009). Data from the National Violence Against Women Survey also reveal strong associations between a history of IPV and current depressive symptoms among both men and women (Coker et al., 2002). Not surprisingly, individuals with PTSD are also at elevated risk for panic disorder (Kessler et al., 2005).

Numerous clinical and epidemiological studies have also documented high rates of comorbidity between PTSD and substance use disorders (Kessler et al., 2005; Pietrzak et al., 2011; Swendsen et al., 2010). In a nationally representative sample of adults, over 50% of men and 28% of women with PTSD had comorbid alcohol abuse or dependence (Kessler et al., 1995). Other studies indicate that substance abuse is not only a common outcome of trauma but is also a risk factor for victimization (Messman-Moore, Ward, & Brown, 2009; Vaughn et al., 2010). Although directionality of the assault/substance abuse relationship remains somewhat ambiguous, the data clearly indicate that victims use substances at significantly higher rates than nonvictims do and that substance use appears to facilitate additional violence (Classen et al., 2005; Vaughn et al., 2010).

Risk Factors for Posttraumatic Stress Disorder

Considerable effort has been expended to identify factors that distinguish individuals who will experience transient distress from those who develop long-term mental health problems, particularly PTSD, following exposure to a traumatic stressor. As noted by Bryant (2003), acutely traumatized individuals who are at risk for developing poor outcomes may be good candidates for early intervention. The diagnosis of Acute Stress Disorder (ASD) was first introduced in the *Diagnostic and Statistical Manual of Mental Disorders* (fourth edition [*DSM–IV*], American Psychiatric Association, 2000) as a way to identify individuals who may be at risk for developing PTSD. The diagnostic criteria for ASD originally included three or more dissociative symptoms, one reexperiencing symptom, marked avoidance of stimuli that arouse recollections of the trauma, and symptoms of anxiety or increased arousal that occur within four weeks of a traumatic event. Ultimately, ASD has been shown to have limited predictive utility. A recent meta-analysis of 22 studies indicates that, while at least half of those with ASD go on to develop PTSD, the majority of individuals who eventually develop PTSD did not initially meet criteria for ASD (Bryant, 2011). Bryant concluded that there are likely to be multiple trajectories along which an individual will develop PTSD, and a diagnosis of ASD in the initial month following a trauma represents only one of these paths. Thus changes have been made to the ASD diagnostic criteria in the *DSM–5* to reflect the heterogeneity of acute responses, including less emphasis on dissociative features and allowing individuals to meet diagnostic criteria if they exhibit any 9 of the 14 symptoms regardless of symptom cluster (American Psychiatric Association, 2013).

There is also inconsistent evidence for a relationship between acute psychological symptoms (e.g., dissociation, hyperarousal, insomnia) and the development of PTSD (Bryant, 2003, 2011). For example, whereas some studies suggest that initial distress is associated with later psychopathology (Denson, Marshall, Schell, & Jaycox, 2007; King et al., 2000; Koopman, Classen, & Spiegel, 1994), others show no relationship between acute distress and subsequent adjustment (Harvey & Bryant, 1998; Yehuda, 2002). However, there is some evidence that early biological mechanisms and cognitive responses are powerful predictors of long-term psychological functioning among traumatized adults. For example, trauma survivors who evidence low cortisol levels, elevated resting heart or respiration rates, and panic attack symptoms shortly after a trauma appear to be at higher risk for developing PTSD (Bryant, 2006; Bryant, Creamer, O'Donnell, Silove, & McFarlane, 2008; Bryant, Harvey, Guthrie, & Moulds, 2000). Regarding acute cognitive responses, researchers have also noted strong relations between negative cognitive appraisals of the trauma or its sequelae and chronic PTSD (Andrews, Brewin, Rose, & Kirk, 2000; Ehring, Ehlers, & Glucksman, 2008; Engelhard, van den Hout, Arntz, & McNally, 2002).

Certain characteristics of either the individual or the traumatic event also influence the likelihood of mental health problems. For example, individuals are more likely to develop PTSD if they felt their life was in danger during the incident, if the event elicits extreme emotional responses or dissociation, or if they have a history of prior traumas or psychiatric problems (Ozer, Best, Lipsey, & Weiss, 2008). By contrast, stable sources of social support appear to buffer against development of trauma-related mental health problems (Norris et al., 2002; Ozer et al., 2008).

Links Between Violent Victimization, Offending, and Mental Health

It initially was assumed that victims of violence were distinct from those who perpetrate violent offenses. More recent research, however, has revealed considerable overlap between victims and offenders (Afifi, Henriksen, Asmundson, & Sareen, 2012; Caetano, Vaeth, & Ramisetty-Mikler, 2008; Daday, Broidy, Crandall, & Sklar, 2005; Jennings, Piquero, & Reingle, 2012; Menard, 2012). For example, Menard documented significant associations between victimization and offending in a representative sample of youth and adults residing in the United States. In a case control study of homicide victims, Dobrin (2001) reported that victims were two times more likely to have been previously arrested for a violent offense relative to nonvictims. Similarly, in the context of IPV, data indicate that mutual violence is more common than violence perpetrated by only one partner. For example, Caetano et al. (2008) examined patterns of violence in a nationally representative sample of married and cohabiting couples in the United States. Approximately 14% of couples reported a history of violence in their relationships. Of those couples, the majority (58%) reported bidirectional violence, 28% reported violence perpetrated by the male partner only, and 14% reported violence perpetrated by the female partner only. Several theories have been proposed to explain the link between victimization and offending. The most recognized is lifestyle-routine activities theory, which argues that when individuals come in regular contact with violence in their daily lives, they are more likely to engage in violence and interact with potential offenders (Schreck et al., 2008; Smith & Ecob, 2007). This theory is supported by data indicating that victims and offenders often exhibit similar offending histories and risky lifestyles and tend to live in similarly disorganized homes and communities (Daday et al., 2005).

Mental health problems also play a role in victimization and offending. Studies indicate that specific psychiatric diagnoses (e.g., psychotic, mood, and anxiety disorders) increase one's risk for engaging in violent acts and becoming a crime victim (Joyal, Dubreucq, Gendron, & Millard, 2007; Kirby et al., 2012; Lipsky, Caetano, & Roy-Byrne, 2011; Pandiani, Banks, Carroll, & Schlueter, 2007; Shorey, Febres, Brasfield, & Stuart, 2012; Silver, Arseneault, Langley, Caspi, & Moffitt, 2005). Others have documented elevated rates of suicidal ideation and suicide attempts among victims and perpetrators of violence (Cook, 2013; Lamis, Leenaars, Jahn, & Lester, 2013). Finally, there is substantial evidence linking substance use with victimization and offending (Afifi et al., 2012; Foran & O'Leary, 2008; Stalans & Ritchie, 2008; Stuart et al., 2013). For example, in a large representative sample of men and women residing in the United States, alcohol and cannabis use disorders were associated with a two-fold increase in the likelihood of victimization and offending, even after accounting for the effects of demographic characteristics and comorbid mental health problems (Afifi et al., 2012). Another study documented a temporal link between alcohol use and IPV among a sample of women participating in a batterer intervention program (Stuart et al., 2013). Specifically, women were 10 times more likely to have perpetrated IPV on days that they consumed alcohol relative to nondrinking days. Similarly, they were five times more likely to have been victimized by IPV on drinking relative to nondrinking days. It is important to acknowledge that, although the evidence supports a link between mental health problems, victimization, and offending, the vast majority of individuals with a mental illness will never experience violence or engage in violent acts (Joyal et al., 2007). Nevertheless, the literature clearly demonstrates that certain psychiatric disorders can increase risk for violent outcomes.

Acute Preventive Interventions for Victims of Violence

The risk for mental health problems among victims of violence underscores the importance of effective interventions for this population. As such, extensive work has advanced the development and validation of treatments for individuals who have already developed PTSD and related mental health difficulties. For example, prolonged exposure (Foa, Hembree, & Rothbaum, 2007), cognitive processing therapy (Resick & Schnicke, 1993), and eye movement desensitization and reprocessing (Shapiro, 2001) have all been studied extensively and are viewed as frontline treatments for PTSD (Bisson, Roberts, Andrew, Cooper, & Lewis, 2013; Bradley, Greene, Russ, Dutra, & Westen, 2005; Seidler & Wagner, 2006). Surprisingly, however, there has been much less research on acute preventive interventions for trauma victims (Roberts, Kitchiner, Kenardy, & Bisson, 2009). Acute preventive interventions are implemented in short temporal proximity to a traumatic event (i.e., within four weeks; National Institute of Mental Health, 2002), with the ultimate aim of reducing risk for PTSD and other difficulties.

Despite the limited research on acute preventive interventions for victims of trauma, leading experts have developed a set of preliminary practice guidelines based on the findings from existing research and the experiences of clinicians in the field (Gray & Litz, 2005; McNally, Bryant, & Ehlers, 2003). First, professionals are advised against delivering psychological debriefing (or similar protocols) to victims in the acute aftermath of a traumatic stressor. Second, although debriefing interventions are not recommended, the delivery of PFA is considered appropriate. In addition, emerging research has supported delivery of exposure-based interventions in the acute phase. Third, given that acute distress symptoms often dissipate with time, professionals are advised to wait at least one week before conducting comprehensive, symptom-based assessments with trauma-exposed adults. Fourth, for individuals who continue to experience distress symptoms two to four weeks following the traumatic event, early cognitive-behavioral protocols might be indicated. A more detailed description of each practice recommendation is provided next.

Psychological Debriefing

Critical Incident Stress Debriefing (CISD; Mitchell & Everly, 1996) represents one of the first acute interventions designed for victims of trauma. The initial targets of CISD were emergency service personnel who are regularly exposed to traumatic events, such as police officers, firefighters, and paramedics. Over time, however, this intervention was applied to a broader range of trauma-exposed adults, including victims of natural disasters (Everly & Mitchell, 1999) and victims of crime (Marchand et al., 2006). CISD is structured as follows. A single group meeting is held within 24 to 72 hours of the traumatic event. All exposed individuals are encouraged to attend the meeting and to discuss their acute emotional reactions. A group facilitator normalizes group members' symptoms and provides education regarding healthy and unhealthy coping techniques. The ultimate aims of CISD are to reduce participants' acute distress symptoms, prevent development of long term mental health problems, and identify individuals who might benefit from more formal treatment.

Professionals in the trauma field initially viewed CISD very favorably, and there was widespread dissemination of the model. Since that time, however, experts have raised several concerns about the CISD approach. The first concern pertains to the timing of intervention delivery. Specifically, experts have questioned the logic of implementing mental health services so soon after a traumatic event, before a victim's basic needs (e.g., shelter, safety, medical concerns) have been addressed (Gray & Litz, 2005). Second, in light of data indicating that most individuals are resilient in the aftermath of a traumatic stressor, the delivery of CISD to everyone exposed to a traumatic event is now viewed as unnecessary and potentially misguided (Bonanno et al., 2011; Litz, Gray, Bryant, & Adler, 2002). Third, researchers have raised questions about the potentially coercive nature of the CISD groups. For example, there is concern that participants might feel pressured to talk about their symptoms and reactions during the meetings, which might inadvertently cause discomfort and increased distress among group members (Gray & Litz, 2005).

Initial studies suggested that CISD was effective at reducing distress symptoms among acute trauma victims (Amir, Weil, Kaplan, Tocker, & Witztum, 1998; Chemtob, Tomas, Law, & Cremniter, 1997; Yule, 1992). However, these studies had significant methodological limitations (e.g., absence of a control group, lack of random assignment), which raised questions about the validity of the findings. Several more recent and well-designed trials have suggested that CISD is not beneficial (Adler et al., 2008; Deahl et al., 2000; Marchand et al., 2006; Mayou et al., 2000; Rose et al., 1999; Sijbrandij, Olff, Reitsma, Carlier, & Gersons, 2006) and potentially harmful (Bisson et al., 1997; Hobbs et al., 1996). Given these findings and the concerns noted earlier, CISD is now widely regarded as contraindicated for victims of trauma.

Psychological First Aid

In lieu of CISD, experts advocate for the delivery of PFA in the aftermath of a traumatic stressor. Unlike CISD, PFA does not assume that all trauma victims will develop chronic mental health problems, and it is limited to those who specifically request support following a traumatic event. As described in more detail subsequently, PFA was initially developed for victims of natural disaster or acts of terrorism. However, the model has broad applicability to other types of trauma victims, including victims of violence. Nevertheless, there have been no randomized trials of PFA with any trauma-exposed population, highlighting the critical need for more research on this promising acute intervention.

PFA (Brymer et al., 2006) was developed by trauma researchers at the National Child Traumatic Stress Network and the National Center for PTSD. The PFA model is comprised of eight core components (contact and engagement, stabilization, information gathering, safety and comfort, practical assistance, connection with social supports, information on coping, and linkage with collaborative services) that can be delivered by paraprofessionals within hours or days of a traumatic event. The tenets of PFA are based on research indicating that practical, social, and emotional support can reduce acute distress and buffer against the development of long term problems in trauma victims (Norris et al., 2002; Stapleton, Lating, Kirkhart, & Everly, 2006; Vernberg et al., 2008). Several public health agencies have adopted PFA, including the Centers for Disease Control and Prevention (2009), the American Red Cross (*Lessons from Katrina and Other Major Disasters,* 2009), and the World Health Organization (2003). To help facilitate broad dissemination of the model, the Centers for Disease Control and Prevention (2010) and the National Child Traumatic Stress Network (2010) have each developed online PFA training courses. In addition, the Red Cross provides PFA workshops for all members of its volunteer disaster response force (American Red Cross, 2011). Despite these dissemination efforts, however, PFA has not yet been empirically tested (Bisson & Lewis, 2009; Fox et al., 2012). The absence of any formal evaluation of PFA is likely due to the barriers to conducting intervention research in a postdisaster context (e.g., time spent waiting for an event to occur, need for researchers that can travel to an affected site quickly). Nevertheless, without any data on effectiveness, PFA currently represents only the "best guess" at what works.

Pertinent to the current chapter, many have noted that PFA has direct relevance to other trauma-exposed groups (Gray & Litz, 2005; McNally et al., 2003), including victims of crime (McCart, Fitzgerald, Acierno, Resnick, & Kilpatrick, 2009). Further, we argue that relative to victims of disaster or terrorism, crime victims represent a larger and much more readily accessible population with which to evaluate the model. Thus our team recently developed an adapted version of PFA for victims of crime (PFA-VC), which we are evaluating in the context of a pilot randomized controlled trial (Clinical Trials Identifier: NCT01934348). A complete description of PFA-VC is beyond the scope of this chapter. However, we briefly summarize key aspects of this acute intervention approach.

Psychological First Aid for Victims of Crime
MODEL OF SERVICE DELIVERY

PFA-VC is designed for delivery by bachelor's-level paraprofessionals who provide early assistance to victims of violent crime, such as victim advocates employed by police departments, domestic violence shelters, or rape crisis centers. The intervention can be flexibly implemented either via telephone or during in-person meetings. Due to the individualized nature of PFA-VC, the specific length of the intervention varies. However, the model is most commonly delivered over the course of two to three interactions with a victim occurring within one month of the crime.

INTERVENTION COMPONENTS

PFA-VC consists of the same eight core components used in standard PFA. The ordering and flow of the components are illustrated in Figure 11.1. As shown, victim engagement and stabilization are prioritized first. Subsequent areas are targeted based on the needs identified during the information-gathering component. Importantly, all skills are taught utilizing structured forms and handouts, and between-session practice is assigned to promote mastery. In addition, PFA-VC providers (a) proactively aid victims in identifying and problem solving barriers to the use of PFA-VC strategies, (b) adapt skills to meet victims' unique needs, and (c) help victims identify and address any discrepancies between their behaviors and goals to increase motivation.

CONTACT AND ENGAGEMENT

The goal of this component is to initiate contact with victims in a nonintrusive manner. Individuals exposed to traumatic events often experience a sense of disbelief and disorientation. Thus the initial contact by PFA-VC providers is designed to engage the victim in social contact that is compassionate and respectful. Specifically, PFA-VC providers calmly introduce themselves, ask for permission to speak with the victim, and explain their role. In addition, providers communicate that any information provided by the victim will remain strictly confidential, except in situations involving potential suicide/homicide or harm to a child. If the victim indicates that he or she is not able to speak with the provider at the point of contact, arrangements are made to call or meet with the victim at a more convenient time.

STABILIZATION

The primary focus of this component is to calm emotionally overwhelmed individuals. For a victim in extreme distress, the PFA-VC provider first normalizes the victim's acute reactions. Then, "grounding" techniques are used to orient the victim to the present and to promote a sense of calming. During a grounding

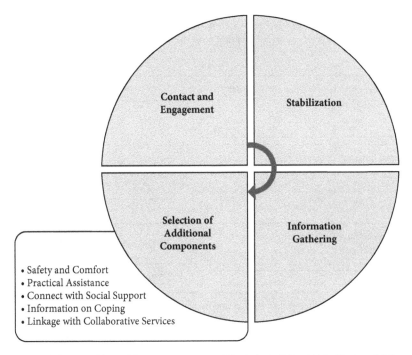

Fig. 11.1 Ordering and flow of the core components of Psychological First Aid for Victims of Crime.

exercise, the individual is asked to sit in a comfortable position, breathe slowly, and focus on nondistressing visual, auditory, and/or physical sensory cues. If a victim continues experiencing extreme distress, the provider will link the victim with more formal services from a medical or mental health professional.

INFORMATION GATHERING

This component focuses on gathering information about victims' immediate needs to tailor subsequent interventions. Questions are designed to gather basic information about the traumatic event and to assess victims' current concerns. Importantly, when querying victims about traumatic experiences and emotional reactions, PFA-VC providers avoid asking for in-depth descriptions, as this might provoke additional distress. That is, they follow each victim's lead in discussing what happened and never press for details of trauma or loss. When a victim expresses a willingness to talk about the incident, initial questions cover basic areas, such as when and where the assault occurred and the relationship of the perpetrator to the victim. In addition, PFA-VC providers query victims about any additional experiences with violence across their lifespan. This is particularly important because psychological responses and treatment needs might differ for individuals who have experienced only one assault versus multiple victimizations.

After gathering information about traumatic experiences, PFA-VC providers assess victims' current needs and concerns. This assessment is guided by a structured information-gathering form, which covers key problem areas common to victims of crime (see Table 11.1). For example, PFA-VC providers assess whether victims have concerns about their own or their family's safety. In addition, providers inquire about any unmet basic needs, such as lack of food or secure housing. Other areas assessed include concerns about physical health, financial/legal issues, emotional distress, substance use, lack of social support, and thoughts of harm to self or others. When screening for suicide and homicide, providers pay particular attention to factors that increase the likelihood of such events (e.g., ideation, threats, active preparation, past history of attempts). If an individual is deemed to be at elevated risk for suicide or homicide, efforts are immediately taken to reduce this risk (described later).

SAFETY AND COMFORT

This component covers techniques for enhancing the immediate and ongoing safety of victims. Specifically, PFA-VC providers work with crime victims to evaluate current safety and determine situations with high risk for future victimization. After potentially dangerous situations are identified, providers assist victims in developing

Table 11.1. Psychological First Aid for Victims of Crime Information Gathering Form
I'd like to ask a few questions to find out how I can best help you.

Concern		Relevant Module(s)
Safety: Do you have any concerns for your own or your family's safety? Describe: _____	☐ Yes ➡	Safety and Comfort
	☐ No	
Basic Needs: Do you have any concerns about your access to food or shelter? Describe: _____	☐ Yes ➡	Practical Assistance Linkage with Collaborative Services
	☐ No	
Physical Health: Do you have any concerns about your health or access to medication? Describe: _____	☐ Yes ➡	Linkage with Collaborative Services
	☐ No	
Financial/Legal: Do you have any financial or legal concerns? Describe: _____	☐ Yes ➡	Practical Assistance Linkage with Collaborative Services
	☐ No	
Emotional: Do you have any concerns about how you've been feeling since the incident? Describe: _____	☐ Yes ➡	Information on Coping Linkage with Collaborative Services
	☐ No	
Harm to Self/Others: Have you had thoughts about harming yourself or someone else? Describe: _____	☐ Yes ➡	Safety and Comfort
	☐ No	
Substance Use/Abuse: Do you have any concerns about your use of alcohol, drugs, or prescription medications? Describe: _____	☐ Yes ➡	Linkage with Collaborative Services
	☐ No	
Social Support: Are there family members, friends, or community agencies that you can rely on for support? Describe: _____	☐ Yes	
	☐ No ➡	Connection with Social Support
Other: Do you have any other concerns that you would like to share with me? Describe: _____	☐ Yes	
	☐ No	

individualized safety plans (see Table 11.2 for an example). Providers orally review these plans with victims and provide visual reminders (e.g., a reminder card to place in purse/wallet) to increase the probability that the plans will be implemented at the appropriate time. Providers also verify that crime victims have a safe place to reside in the immediate aftermath of an assault and make referrals to appropriate agencies (e.g., domestic violence shelters, other emergency housing facilities) as needed.

When indicated, safety planning also includes strategies to prevent suicidality and homicidality. If a crime victim is at high risk for suicide,

Table 11.2. Personalized Safety Plan.

Name: _____   Date: _____

The following are steps I can take to increase my safety and avoid further violence. Although I do not have control over other people's violent behavior, I do have a choice about how to keep my family and me safe.

Step 1: Safety in my home. There are many things that I can to do increase safety in my home. It may not be possible to do everything at once, but safety measures can be added step by step. Safety measures I can take:

A. I can change the locks on my doors and windows as soon as possible.
B. I can replace wooden doors with steel/metal doors.
C. I can install security systems, including additional locks, window bars, poles to wedge against doors, an electronic system, etc.
D. I can purchase rope ladders to be used to escape from second floor windows.
E. I can install smoke detectors and fire extinguishers for each floor of my house/apartment.
F. I can install an outside lighting system that activates when a person is close to the house.
G. I can provide a description of the perpetrator to my neighbors and ask them to call the police if they see him/her near my home. Neighbors that I can tell include

_____

H. I can consider staying temporarily with a friend or family member.

Step 2: Safety at work. If I am concerned about safety at work, I should consider each of the following carefully. Disclosing safety concerns to co-workers and bosses can be potentially helpful; however, it's up to me to decide if I am comfortable with this disclosure.

A. I can inform my boss, the security supervisor, and _____ at work about my safety concerns and provide them with a description of the perpetrator.
B. I can ask _____ to help me screen my telephone calls at work.
C. When leaving work, I can _____.
D. If I have a problem while driving home, I can _____.
E. If I use public transportation, I can _____.
F. I can carpool with another co-worker to ensure that I am never by myself.

Step 3: Safety in the community. A major part of community safety is to change my routine and travel with family and friends when possible. I might do any or all of the following:

A. I will go to different grocery stores and shopping malls to conduct my business and shop at different hours than I used to.
B. I will use a different bank/ATM than usual and go to the bank/ATM at different times than usual.
C. I will have trusted family members or friends accompany me on errands whenever possible.
D I will carry a cell phone and make sure it is charged before going out.

Step 4: Keeping my children safe (if applicable).

A. I will inform people about who has permission to pick my children up. The people I will inform about pick-up permission include:

_____ (name of babysitter/daycare provider)
_____ (name of teacher)
_____ (name[s] of others)

B. I will teach my children how to make collect calls and have them memorize my phone number.

Telephone numbers I need to know:
Police/sheriff's department (local)—911 or: _____
Police/sheriff's department (work):   _____
Prosecutor's office: _____
Victim advocate: _____

Form adapted from the Texas Advocacy Project's personal safety plan (Texas Advocacy Project, 2014) hospitalization may be necessary to ensure safety. Victims who acknowledge thoughts of self-harm but deny suicidal intent might still benefit from specific information regarding suicide hotlines, 24-hour crisis lines, social service referrals, and support groups. If victims express thoughts about retaliating against the perpetrator of their assault, it can be helpful to normalize their anger and to distinguish appropriate actions from thoughts and feelings. However, if the PFA-VC provider believes an individual is at high risk for committing an act of violence (i.e., he or she has the means and a plan for committing such an act), steps are taken to ensure the safety of the potential victim, including notifying local authorities.

PRACTICAL ASSISTANCE

This component provides practical support to address victims' basic needs. It is common for individuals to experience hopelessness in the aftermath of a traumatic event. However, the provision of practical assistance can help foster a sense of empowerment and optimism. Using the aforementioned information-gathering form, PFA-VC providers identify victims' most immediate needs and develop action plans to address those needs. For example, victims might benefit from information on legal advocacy and involvement in the criminal justice system. PFA-VC providers can also provide contact information for agencies that provide short-term housing, financial assistance, and/or mental health treatment. If relevant, PFA-VC providers link victims with local domestic violence shelters and rape crisis centers. In addition, victims of sexual assault are strongly encouraged to seek a medical exam for injuries, potential pregnancy, and/or sexually transmitted infection. If victims present within 72 hours of a sexual assault, forensic evidence also can be collected. Importantly, PFA-VC providers help victims apply for crime victim's compensation, which can help offset costs of medical and mental health treatment related to the crime.

SOCIAL SUPPORT

The goal of this component is to help victims establish ongoing contacts with primary support persons. This focus is based on research indicating that social support promotes symptom reduction following exposure to traumatic events (Litz et al., 2002; Norris et al., 2002). PFA-VC providers begin by educating victims about the benefits of social support (e.g., support networks can provide emotional comfort and assistance with basic needs). Providers then determine victims' preferred sources of support (e.g., spouse/partner, family members, coworkers) and assist them in developing a written plan for initiating and maintaining regular contact with those individuals. When developing a plan, providers help victims consider when and how they will contact their support persons and what they will say once contact is made. Importantly, providers explain to victims that they have complete control over how much information they provide to support persons about the traumatic event. For example, providers might say to a victim, "After a traumatic event, individuals sometimes find it helpful to talk with a support person about what they've been through. However, you can decide when and what to talk about. You don't have to talk about everything that occurred, only what you choose to share with each person." Victims are encouraged to implement their social support plan once it is finalized. Providers contact victims at a later date to determine the effectiveness of the plan, problem-solve potential barriers, and assist the victim in revising the plan as needed.

INFORMATION ON COPING

With this component, information is provided on normal stress reactions and positive coping techniques to reduce distress and promote adaptive functioning. For example, PFA-VC providers use a structured handout (see Table 11.3) to educate victims about symptoms that are common in the aftermath of a traumatic stressor, which can help validate their experiences, normalize reactions, and dispel faulty beliefs. In addition, suggestions are made on how victims might effectively cope with feelings of distress. Examples of recommended strategies include spending time with others, getting adequate rest, scheduling pleasant activities throughout the day, and engaging in relaxation techniques, such as diaphragmatic breathing. With diaphragmatic breathing, victims are taught to engage in slow, rhythmic abdominal breathing in anxiety-provoking situations. In addition, they are taught to pair cue words (e.g., *calm, peaceful*) with feelings of relaxation and to focus on those cues whenever they experience stress or tension. Finally, victims are discouraged from engaging in coping methods that are potentially harmful, such as use of alcohol or drugs, withdrawal from family or friends, over/undereating, and not getting enough rest.

LINKAGE WITH COLLABORATIVE SERVICES

When crime victims experience ongoing needs and concerns (e.g., persistent problems with coping,

Table 11.3. Common Reactions to Trauma and General Methods of Coping.

Individuals can experience a range of reactions during and immediately after a crime. These include:

Intrusive reactions
- Distressing thoughts or images of the event while awake or dreaming
- Upsetting emotional or physical reactions to reminders of the experience
- Feeling like the experience is happening all over again ("flashback")

Avoidance and withdrawal reactions
- Avoid talking, thinking, and having feelings about the traumatic event
- Avoid reminders of the event (places and people connected to what happened)
- Restricted emotions; feeling numb
- Feelings of detachment and estrangement from others; social withdrawal
- Loss of interest in usually pleasurable activities

Physical arousal reactions
- Constantly being "on the lookout" for danger, startling easily, or being jumpy
- Irritability or outbursts of anger, feeling "on edge"
- Difficulty falling or staying asleep, problems concentrating or paying attention

Grief reactions when a loved one has died
- Feelings of sadness, anger, guilt, or regret over the death
- Missing or longing for the deceased
- Dreams about seeing the person again

Depression reactions
- Sad or irritable mood
- Loss of appetite and/or energy
- Sleep disturbance
- Diminished interest or pleasure in life activities
- Feelings of worthlessness or guilt
- Thoughts about suicide

Physical reactions
- Headaches, stomach aches, muscle aches
- Dizziness
- Rapid heartbeat, tightness in the chest
- Hyperventilation

Positive changes in priorities, worldview, and expectations
- Enhanced appreciation that family and friends are precious and important
- Meeting the challenge of addressing difficulties by taking positive action steps and changing the focus of thoughts
- Shifting expectations about what to expect from day to day and about what is considered a "good day"
- Shifting priorities to focus more on quality time with family or friends
- Increased commitment to self, family, friends, and spiritual/religious faith

Individuals can cope with trauma reactions in various ways. Some coping strategies are helpful while others might make the problem worse.

Helpful coping strategies
- Talking to another person for support or spending time with others
- Getting adequate rest and eating healthy meals
- Engaging in positive distracting activities (sports, hobbies, reading)
- Trying to maintain a normal schedule
- Scheduling pleasant activities
- Using relaxation methods (breathing exercises, listening to soothing music)
- Participation in counseling or support groups

(continued)

Table 11.3. Continued.

Unhelpful coping strategies
- Using alcohol or drugs to cope
- Withdrawal from family or friends
- Withdrawal from work or other activities
- Working too much
- Taking things out on others (blaming, angry outbursts)
- Not taking care of yourself with regard to diet, sleep, and exercise

When individuals use helpful coping strategies, they often experience a gradual decrease in their feelings of distress. If distressing reactions persist for more than a month, however, consider contacting a local mental health provider for professional support.

Form adapted from the Psychological First Aid intervention manual (Brymer et al., 2006).

persistence of psychological symptoms for several weeks following the event), PFA-VC providers link victims with needed professional services. Providers take steps to ensure effective linkage with services by providing written referral information and assisting victims in making appointments.

In conclusion, PFA-VC takes a much different approach compared to CISD, with a focus on safety, social support, coping, and basic needs rather than forced emotional processing, and it has the potential to fill the void of acute trauma services. However, rigorous testing of such an intervention is crucial in determining its true safety and effectiveness.

Early Exposure-Based Treatment

Emerging research also has examined the potential value of delivering exposure-based treatment to victims of acute trauma. Specifically, Rothbaum and colleagues (2012) tested the efficacy of a brief, exposure therapy protocol with a sample of adults presenting to an emergency department within 72 hours of a traumatic injury. Participants were randomly assigned to either immediate intervention or assessment-only conditions. Trained mental health professionals delivered the exposure intervention across three individual therapy sessions. The first took place at the time of the emergency department visit, and two subsequent sessions occurred one week apart. At each session, therapists facilitated imaginal exposure exercises and provided instruction on self-care techniques. During imaginal exposure, patients provided repeated oral descriptions of their trauma in as much detail as possible, focusing on stimuli, thoughts, and feelings that were present during the event. For homework between sessions, patients were encouraged to confront feared objects, activities, and situations. Such imaginal and real-life exposures are thought to facilitate habituation, which refers to a gradual reduction in trauma-related fear

over time (Foa & Kozak, 1986). Trial results indicated that, relative to the control group, the exposure therapy group reported significantly lower levels of PTSD symptoms at 4 and 12 weeks postinjury and significantly lower levels of depression symptoms at 4 weeks postinjury. These findings suggest that an exposure-based protocol initiated soon after a traumatic event can yield improved mental health functioning in the short term. The authors point out the substantial differences between this approach and CISD. Specifically, this exposure-based approach uses individual rather than group delivery, specifically helps to develop coping skills (e.g., breathing retraining, self-care), and includes multiple sessions, which are likely more effective at promoting habituation than a single debriefing session (Rothbaum et al., 2012). Nevertheless, additional studies of this treatment are needed that ideally would include a longer follow-up period and consideration of additional outcomes (e.g., adaptive functioning).

Symptom-Based Assessment

Given the significant variability in responses following a violent crime, determining whether a victim's response is problematic can be difficult during the acute stage. Experts typically recommend waiting at least one week after the trauma before conducting symptom-based psychological assessments (Gray & Litz, 2005). Assessments conducted earlier will have limited clinical utility because the level of distress experienced immediately posttrauma is not a strong predictor of later psychological problems (Bryant, 2011). Indeed, it is common for many victims of crime to experience extreme distress in the acute aftermath of a traumatic event. Most of these individuals will go through a process of gradual recovery, involving a steady decrease in symptoms over time. Examining the individual's pattern of distress in the month following the crime can be helpful.

Bisson and colleagues (2007) suggest that a steady decline in distress is a sign of recovery, whereas persistent or increased symptoms may warrant a more comprehensive assessment. Thus, by monitoring crime victims' symptom levels from week to week, clinicians may be better able to identify individuals who will benefit from formal intervention.

Symptom-based assessment with a victim within one month of a violent crime should include measures of ASD. Two well-validated self-report measures that correspond to ASD symptom criteria are the Stanford Acute Stress Reaction Questionnaire (Cardena, Koopman, Classen, Waelde, & Spiegel, 2000) and the Acute Stress Disorder Scale (Bryant, Moulds, & Guthrie, 2000). The Acute Stress Disorder Interview (Bryant, Harvey, Dang, & Sackville, 1998) is a structured clinical interview frequently used to assess ASD among adults. It should be noted that these assessments were developed prior to the *DSM–5* changes to the ASD diagnostic criteria. However, as suggested by Bryant (2013), these measures are still useful, as the basic symptoms of ASD have remained the same. To adapt them for the *DSM–5* criteria, diagnoses should be based on the presence of 9 of the 14 ASD symptoms rather than the *DSM–IV* criteria of a certain number of symptoms from each cluster.

It can also be useful to assess for more general markers of distress in the month following a violent crime, including symptoms of anxiety, depression, and panic. Commonly used self-report measures of anxiety and depression include the Beck Anxiety Inventory (Beck & Steer, 1991) and the Beck Depression Inventory–II (Beck, Steer, & Brown, 1996), respectively. Another brief and widely available depression screening tool is the Patient Health Questionnaire–9 (Kroenke & Spitzer, 2002). Finally, a self-report inventory that can be used to assess symptoms of panic is the Physical Reactions Scale (Falsetti & Resnick, 1992). These scales have strong psychometric properties and relatively short administration times (i.e., 5 to 10 minutes each). Detailed reviews have been conducted for symptom-based assessment with victims of a recent trauma (e.g., Bryant, 2004; Orsillo, 2001; Ursano et al., 2004), and the reader is referred to these sources for more in-depth information on available measures.

Early Cognitive-Behavioral Therapy Protocols for Trauma Victims

Delivery of an evidence-based, early cognitive-behavioral therapy (CBT) protocol might be indicated for individuals whose distress symptoms persist for several weeks postincident. Several such protocols have been proven effective for victims of trauma (Agorastos, Marmar, & Otte, 2011; Forneris et al., 2013). These programs differ from CISD and PFA in that they are typically implemented two to four weeks after an incident (rather than within a few days), and they are limited to individuals presenting with significant, unremitting problems. For example, a five-session CBT intervention designed for treatment of ASD is delivered individually in four phases, including (a) psychoeducation, (b) relaxation training, (c) cognitive restructuring, and (d) exposure (Bryant, Harvey, Dang, Sackville, & Basten, 1998). During the psychoeducation phase, therapists provide information about the prevalence of interpersonal victimization and common psychological responses to traumatic events. During the relaxation phase, clients learn anxiety management techniques, such as diaphragmatic breathing and progressive muscle relaxation. Using cognitive restructuring, clients are taught to recognize and modify negative thoughts and dysfunctional beliefs stemming from the trauma (e.g., the world is unsafe). During the exposure phase, clients are instructed to engage in a repeated retelling of their trauma, including as much detail as possible. Several well-designed studies have demonstrated the effectiveness of this intervention in reducing symptoms of PTSD, general anxiety, and depression both immediately posttreatment (Bryant, Harvey, Dang, Sackville, & Basten, 1998; Bryant, Sackville, Dang, Moulds, & Guthrie, 1999; Bryant, Moulds, Guthrie, & Nixon, 2005) and at longer term follow-up (Bryant, Moulds, & Nixon, 2003; Bryant et al., 2006). Interestingly, a partial dismantling study has indicated that the exposure exercise is more effective than the cognitive restructuring techniques at achieving good clinical outcomes (Bryant et al., 2008).

Similarly, Foa, Hearst-Ikeda, and Perry (1995) developed a brief CBT protocol (B-CBT) for victims in the acute aftermath of an assault. Consistent with the intervention developed by Bryant and colleagues (1998), B-CBT consists of education, relaxation, cognitive restructuring, and exposure-based components. Results from an initial quasi-experimental study indicated that at posttreatment, B-CBT was more effective than an assessment-only condition at reducing PTSD symptom severity and diagnoses (Foa et al., 1995). In a subsequent randomized controlled trial, B-CBT was compared to supportive counseling and assessment-only control conditions (Foa, Zoellner, & Feeny, 2006). At both posttreatment and a three-month follow-up, B-CBT yielded greater reductions in distress symptoms relative to supportive counseling. However, B-CBT was not superior to the assessment-only condition at either time point. By the nine-month follow-up, all three interventions produced generally similar outcomes. Sijbrandij and colleagues (2006) conducted a separate, independent evaluation of B-CBT with individuals experiencing acute PTSD stemming from various types of trauma. Results indicated that at one-week postintervention, the B-CBT group had significantly fewer PTSD symptoms relative to a wait-list control group. However, by the four-month follow-up assessment, differences in PTSD symptoms between the B-CBT and comparison conditions were no longer significant. Taken together, these results suggest that B-CBT might accelerate recovery following a traumatic event, which is important for increasing quality of life and minimizing periods of functional impairment. However, the intervention does not appear to influence longer term clinical outcomes.

Conclusion and Clinical Resources

In this chapter, we summarized key practice recommendations for the evaluation and management of victims within the first few days or weeks of a violent crime. Research points to several promising acute interventions for these victims, although more controlled studies are clearly needed. As the traumatic stress field continues to rapidly advance, clinicians are advised to stay abreast of new research developments in this area. Fortunately, a number of websites provide up-to-date information regarding evidence-based acute interventions for trauma victims, and these can serve as useful resources for clinicians. Specifically, the website for the International Society for Trauma Stress Studies (www.istss.org) provides extensive information on empirically supported interventions for PTSD, fact sheets on the prevalence of different traumatic stressors, and information on training opportunities for clinicians. The National Center for PTSD's website (www.ptsd.va.gov/) is another helpful educational resource for mental health providers. This website provides a link to the complete PFA manual and to various measures for assessing trauma exposure and PTSD. Finally, the National Center for Victims of Crime represents the largest advocacy organization for crime victims in the United States. The organization's website (www.ncvc.org) provides crime victim statistics, links to training, and an extensive resource directory for service providers.

References

Adler, A. B., Litz, B. T., Castro, C. A., Suvak, M., Thomas, J. L., Burrell, L.,. ... Bliese, P. D. (2008). A group randomized trial of critical incident stress debriefing provided to U.S. peacekeepers. *Journal of Traumatic Stress*, 21, 253–263.

Afifi, T. O., Henriksen, C. A., Asmundson, G. J. G., & Sareen, J. (2012). Victimization and perpetration of intimate partner violence and substance use disorders in a nationally representative sample. *The Journal of Nervous and Mental Disease*, 200, 684–691.

Agorastos, A., Marmar, C. R., & Otte, C. (2011). Immediate and early behavioral interventions for the prevention of acute and posttraumatic stress disorder. *Current Opinions in Psychiatry*, 24, 526–532.

American Psychiatric Association. (2000). *Diagnostic and statistical manual of mental disorders* (4th ed., text rev.). Washington, DC: Author.

American Psychiatric Association. (2013). *Diagnostic and statistical manual of mental disorders* (5th ed.). Washington, DC: Author.

American Red Cross. (2011). *Psychological First Aid: Helping others in times of stress*. Retrieved from http://www.redcrossnca.org/

Amir, M., Weil, G., Kaplan, Z., Tocker, T., & Witztum, E. (1998). Debriefing with brief group therapy in a homogenous group of non-injured victims of a terrorist attack: A prospective study. *Acta Psychiatrica Scandinavica*, 98, 237–242.

Andrews, B., Brewin, C. R., Rose, S., & Kirk, M. (2000). Predicting PTSD in victims of violent crime: The role of shame, anger, and blame. *Journal of Abnormal Psychology*, 109, 69–73.

Arrata, C. M. (2002). Child sexual abuse and sexual revictimization. *Clinical Psychology: Science and Practice*, 9, 135–164.

Basile, K. C., Chen, J., Black, M. C., & Saltzman, L. E. (2007). Prevalence and characteristics of sexual violence victimization among U.S. adults, 2001–2003. *Violence and Victims*, 22, 437–448.

Beck, A. T., & Steer, R. A. (1991). Relationship between the Beck Anxiety Inventory and the Hamilton Anxiety Rating Scale with anxious outpatients. *Journal of Anxiety Disorders*, 5, 213–223.

Beck, A. T., Steer, R. A., & Brown, G. K. (1996). *Manual for the Beck Depression Inventory–II*. San Antonio, TX: Psychological Corporation.

Bisson, J. I., Brayne, M., Ochberg, F. M., & Everly, G. S. (2007). Early psychosocial interventions following traumatic events. *American Journal of Psychiatry*, 164, 1016–1019.

Bisson, J. L., Jenkins, P. L., Alexander, J., & Bannister, C. (1997). Randomised controlled trial of psychological debriefing for victims of acute burn trauma. *British Journal of Psychiatry*, 171, 78–81.

Bisson, J. I., & Lewis, C. (2009). *Systematic review of Psychological First Aid*. Geneva: World Health Organization.

Bisson, J. I., Roberts, N. P., Andrew, M., Cooper, R., & Lewis, C. (2013). Psychological therapies for chronic post-traumatic stress disorder (PTSD) in adults. *The Cochrane Database of Systematic Reviews*, 12, CD003388.

Black, M. C. (2011). Intimate partner violence and adverse health consequences: Implications for clinicians. *American Journal of Lifestyle Medicine*, 5, 428–439.

Bonanno, G. A., Westphal, M., & Mancini, A. D. (2011). Resilience to loss and potential trauma. *Annual Review of Clinical Psychology*, 7, 511–535.

Boudreaux, E., Kilpatrick, D. G., Resnick, H. S., Best, C. L., & Saunders, B. E. (1998). Criminal victimization, posttraumatic stress disorder, and comorbid psychopathology among a community sample of women. *Journal of Traumatic Stress*, 11, 665–678.

Bradley, R., Greene, J., Russ, E., Dutra, L., & Westen, D. (2005). A multidimensional meta-analysis of psychotherapy for PTSD. *American Journal of Psychiatry, 162,* 214–227.

Brady, K. T., Back, S. E., & Coffey, S. F. (2004). Substance abuse and posttraumatic stress disorder. *Current Directions in Psychological Science, 13,* 206–209.

Breslau, N., Kessler, R. C., Chilcoat, H. D., Schultz, L. R., Davis, G. C., & Andreski, P. (1998). Trauma and posttraumatic stress disorder in the community. *Archives of General Psychiatry, 55,* 626–632.

Breiding, M. J., Chen J., & Black, M. C. (2014). *Intimate partner violence in the United States—2010.* Atlanta, GA: National Center for Injury Prevention and Control, Centers for Disease Control and Prevention.

Bryant, R. A. (2003). Early predictors of posttraumatic stress disorder. *Biological Psychiatry, 53,* 789–795.

Bryant, R. A. (2004). Assessing acute stress disorder. In J. P. Wilson & T. M. Keane (Eds.), *Assessing psychological trauma and PTSD* (2nd ed., pp. 45–60). New York: Guilford Press.

Bryant, R. A. (2006). Longitudinal psychophysiological studies of heart rate: Mediating effects and implications for treatment. *Annals of the New York Academy of Sciences, 1071,* 19–26.

Bryant, R. A. (2011). Acute stress disorder as a predictor of posttraumatic stress disorder: A systematic review. *Journal of Clinical Psychiatry, 72,* 233–239.

Bryant, R. A. (2013). An update of acute stress disorder. *PTSD Research Quarterly, 24,* 1–7.

Bryant, R. A., Creamer, M., O'Donnell, M. Silove, D., & McFarlane, A. C. (2008). A multisite study of initial respiration rate and heart rate as predictors of posttraumatic stress disorder. *Journal of Clinical Psychiatry, 69,* 1694–1701.

Bryant, R. A., Harvey, A. G., Dang, S., & Sackville, T. (1998). Assessing acute stress disorder: Psychometric properties of a structured clinical interview. *Psychological Assessment, 10,* 215–220.

Bryant, R. A., Harvey, A. G., Dang, S. T., Sackville, T., & Basten, C. (1998). Treatment of acute stress disorder: A comparison of cognitive behavior therapy and supportive counseling. *Journal of Consulting and Clinical Psychology, 66,* 862–866.

Bryant, R. A., Harvey, A. G., Guthrie, R., & Moulds, M. (2000). A prospective study of acute psychophysiological arousal, acute stress disorder, and posttraumatic stress disorder. *Journal of Abnormal Psychology, 109,* 341–344.

Bryant, R. A., Moulds, M., & Guthrie, R. (2000). Acute Stress Disorder Scale: A self-report measure of acute stress disorder. *Psychological Assessment, 12,* 61–68.

Bryant, R. A., Moulds, M. L., Guthrie, R. M., & Nixon, R. D. V. (2005). The additive benefit of hypnotherapy and cognitive behavior therapy in treating acute stress disorder. *Journal of Consulting and Clinical Psychology, 73,* 334–340.

Bryant, R. A., Moulds, M. A., & Nixon, R. D. V. (2003). Cognitive behaviour therapy of acute stress disorder: A four-year follow-up. *Behaviour Research and Therapy, 41,* 489–494.

Bryant, R. A., Moulds, M. L., Nixon, R. D. V., Mastrodomenico, J., Felmingham, K., & Hopwood, S. (2006). Hypnotherapy and cognitive behaviour therapy of acute stress disorder: A 3-year follow-up. *Behaviour Research and Therapy, 44,* 1331–1335.

Bryant, R. A., Sackville, T., Dang, S. T., Moulds, M., & Guthrie, R. M. (1999). Treating acute stress disorder: An evaluation of cognitive behavior therapy and counseling techniques. *American Journal of Psychiatry, 156,* 1780–1786.

Brymer, M., Jacobs, A., Layne, C., Pynoos, R., Ruzek, J., Steinberg, A.,. . . . Watson, P. (2006). *Psychological first aid: Field operations guide, 2nd edition.* Retrieved from National Child Traumatic Stress Network & National Center for PTSD: http://www.nctsn.org/content/psychological-first-aid

Caetano, R., Vaeth, P. A. C., & Ramisetty-Mikler, S. (2008). Intimate partner violence victim and perpetrator characteristics among couples in the United States. *Journal of Family Violence, 23,* 507–518.

Campbell, J. C., Jones, A. S., Dienemann, J., Kub, J., Schollenberger, J., O'Campo, P.,. . . . Wynne, C. (2002). Intimate partner violence and physical health consequences. *Archives of Internal Medicine, 162,* 1157–1163.

Cardena, E., Koopman, C., Classen, C., Waelde, L. C., & Spiegel, D. (2000). Psychometric properties of the Stanford Acute Stress Reaction Questionnaire (SASRQ): A valid and reliable measure of acute stress. *Journal of Traumatic Stress, 13,* 719–734.

Catalano, S. M. (2013). *Intimate partner violence: Attributes of victimization, 1993–2011.* US Department of Justice Report NCJ 243300. Washington, DC: Office of Justice Programs.

Centers for Disease Control and Prevention. (2003). *Costs of intimate partner violence against women in the United States.* Retrieved from http://www.cdc.gov/violenceprevention/pdf/ipvbook-a.pdf

Centers for Disease Control and Prevention. (2009). *Virtual reality helps CDC staff deployed for outbreak response prepare for stress.* Retrieved from http://www.cdc.gov/news/2009/05/dsrt

Centers for Disease Control and Prevention. (2010, December 30). *Radiation emergency preparedness: Psychological First Aid [Audio podcast].* Retrieved from http://www2c.cdc.gov/podcasts/player.asp?f=4974866

Chemtob, C. M., Tomas, S., Law, W., & Cremniter, D. (1997). Postdisaster psychosocial intervention: A field study of the impact of debriefing on psychological distress. *American Journal of Psychiatry, 154,* 415–417.

Classen, C. C., Palesh, O. G., & Aggarwal, R. (2005). Sexual revictimization: A review of the empirical literature. *Trauma, Violence, and Abuse, 6,* 103–129.

Coker, A. L., Davis, K. E., Arias, I., Desai, S., Sanderson, M., Brandt, H. M., & Smith, P. (2002). Physical and mental health effects of intimate partner violence for men and women. *American Journal of Preventive Medicine, 23,* 260–268.

Cook, T. B. (2013). Recent criminal offending and suicide attempts: A national sample. *Social Psychiatry and Psychiatric Epidemiology, 48,* 767–774.

Cougle, J. R., Resnick, H., & Kilpatrick, D. G. (2009). PTSD, depression, and their comorbidity in relation to suicidality: Cross-sectional and prospective analyses of a national probability sample of women. *Depression and Anxiety, 26,* 1151–1157.

Daday, J. K., Broidy, L. M., Crandall, C. S., & Sklar, D. P. (2005). Individual, neighborhood, and situational factors associated with violent victimization and offending. *Criminal Justice Studies, 18,* 215–235.

Deahl, M., Srinivasan, M., Jones, N., Thomas, J., Neblett, C., & Jolly, A. (2000). Preventing psychological trauma in soldiers: The role of operational stress training and psychological debriefing. *British Journal of Medical Psychology, 73,* 77–85.

Denson, T. F., Marshall, G. N., Schell, T. L., & Jaycox, L. H. (2007). Predictors of posttraumatic distress 1 year after exposure to community violence: The importance of acute symptom severity. *Journal of Consulting and Clinical Psychology, 75,* 683–692.

Desai, S., Arias, I., Thompson, M. P., & Basile, K. C. (2002). Childhood victimization and subsequent adult revictimization assessed in a nationally representative sample of women and men. *Violence and Victims*, 17, 639–653.

Dobrin, A. (2001). The risk of offending on homicide victimization: A case control study. *Journal of Research in Crime and Delinquency*, 38, 154-173.

Ehring, T., Ehlers, A., & Glucksman, E. (2008). Do cognitive models help in predicting the severity of posttraumatic stress disorder, phobia, and depression after motor vehicle accidents? A prospective longitudinal study. *Journal of Consulting and Clinical Psychology*, 76, 219–230.

Engelhard, I. M., van den Hout, M. A., Arntz, A., & McNally, R. J. (2002). A longitudinal study of "intrusion-based reasoning" and posttraumatic stress disorder after exposure to a train disaster. *Behavior Research and Therapy*, 40, 1415–1424.

Everly, G. S., & Mitchell, J. T. (1999). *Critical Incident Stress Management (CISM): A new era and standard of care in crisis intervention* (2nd ed.). Ellicott City, MD: Chevron.

Falsetti, S. A., & Resnick, H. S. (1992). *The Physical Reactions Scale*. Charleston, SC: National Crime Victims Research and Treatment Center, Medical University of South Carolina.

Foa, E. B., Hearst-Ikeda, D., & Perry, K. J. (1995). Evaluation of a brief cognitive behavioral program for the prevention of chronic PTSD in recurrent assault victims. *Journal of Consulting and Clinical Psychology*, 63, 948–955.

Foa, E. B., Hembree, E. A., & Rothbaum, B. O. (2007). *Prolonged exposure therapy for PTSD: Therapist guide*. New York: Oxford University Press.

Foa, E. B., & Kozak, M. J. (1986). Emotional processing of fear: Exposure to corrective information. *Psychological Bulletin*, 99, 20.

Foa, E. B., Zoellner, L. A., & Feeny, N. C. (2006). An evaluation of three brief programs for facilitating recovery after assault. *Journal of Traumatic Stress*, 19, 29–43.

Foran, H. M., & O'Leary, K. D. (2008). Alcohol and intimate partner violence: A meta-analytic review. *Clinical Psychology Review*, 28, 1222–1234.

Forneris, C. A., Gartlehner, G., Brownley, K. A., Gaynes, B. N., Sonis, J., Coker-Schwimmer, E.,.... Lohr, K. N. (2013). Interventions to prevent post-traumatic stress disorder: A systematic review. *American Journal of Preventive Medicine*, 44, 635–650.

Fox, J. H., Burkle, F. M., Bass, J., Pia, F. A., Epstein, J. L., & Markenson, D. (2012). The effectiveness of psychological first aid as a disaster intervention tool: Research analysis of peer-reviewed literature from 1990–2010. *Disaster Medicine and Public Health Preparedness*, 6, 247–252.

Girardet, R. G., Lahoti, S., Howard, L. A., Fajman, N. N., Sawyer, M. K., Driebe, E. M.,.... Black, C. M. (2009). Epidemiology of sexually transmitted infections in suspected child victims of sexual assault. *Pediatrics*, 124, 79–84.

Goodman, L. A., Koss, M. P., & Russo, N. F. (1993). Violence against women: Physical and mental health effects: Part I. Research findings. *Applied and Preventive Psychology*, 2, 79–89.

Gray, M. J., & Litz, B. T. (2005). Behavioral interventions for recent trauma: Empirically informed practice guidelines. *Behavior Modification*, 29, 189–215.

Hanson, R. F., Kilpatrick, D. G., Falsetti, S. A., & Resnick, H. S. (1995). Violent crime and mental health. In J. R. Freedy & S. E. Hobfoll (Eds.), *Traumatic stress: From theory to practice* (pp. 129–161). New York: Plenum Press.

Hapke, U., Schumann, A., Rumpf, H. J., John, U., & Meyer, C. (2006). Posttraumatic stress disorder: The role of trauma, pre-existing psychiatric disorder, and gender. *European Archives of Psychiatry and Clinical Neuroscience*, 256, 299–306.

Harvey, A. G., & Bryant, R. A. (1998). Relationship of acute stress disorder and posttraumatic stress disorder following motor vehicle accidents. *Journal of Consulting and Clinical Psychology*, 66, 507–512.

Hatch, S. L., & Dohrenwend, B. P. (2007). Distribution of traumatic and other stressful life events by race/ethnicity, gender, SES and age: A review of the research. *American Journal of Community Psychology*, 40, 313–332.

Hobbs, M., Mayou, R., Harrison, B., & Worlock, P. (1996). A randomised controlled trial of psychological debriefing for victims of road traffic accidents. *British Medical Journal*, 313, 1438–1439.

Jennings, W. G., Piquero, A. R., & Reingle, J. M. (2012). On the overlap between victimization and offending: A review of the literature. *Aggression and Violent Behavior*, 17, 16–26.

Joyal, C. C., Dubreucq, J.-L., Gendron, C., & Millard, F. (2007). Major mental disorders and violence: A critical update. *Current Psychiatry Reviews*, 3, 33–50.

Kessler, R. C., Chiu, W. T., Demler, O., & Walters, E. E. (2005). Prevalence, severity, and comorbidity of 12-month *DSM–IV* disorders in the National Comorbidity Survey Replication. *Archives of General Psychiatry*, 62, 617–709.

Kessler, R. C., Sonnega, A., Bromet, E., Hughes, M., & Nelson, C. B. (1995). Posttraumatic stress disorder in the National Comorbidity Survey. *Archives of General Psychiatry*, 52, 1048–1060.

Kilpatrick, D. G., Acierno, R., Resnick, H. S., Saunders, B. E., & Best, C. L. (1997). A two year longitudinal analysis of the relationship between violent assault and alcohol and drug use in women. *Journal of Consulting and Clinical Psychology*, 65, 834–847.

Kilpatrick, D. G., Edmunds, C. N., & Seymour, A. K. (1992). *Rape in America: A report to the nation*. Arlington, VA: National Victim Center and Medical University of South Carolina.

King, D. W., King, L. A., Erickson, D. J., Huang, M. T., Sharkansky, E. J., & Wolfe, J. (2000). Posttraumatic stress disorder and retrospectively reported stressor exposure: A longitudinal prediction model. *Journal of Abnormal Psychology*, 109, 624–633.

Kirby, A. C., Beckham, J. C., Calhoun, P. S., Roberts, S. T., Taft, C. T., Elbogen, E. B., & Dennis, M. F. (2012). An examination of general aggression and intimate partner violence in women with posttraumatic stress disorder. *Violence and Victims*, 27, 777–792.

Koopman, C., Classen, C., & Spiegel, D. (1994). Predictors of posttraumatic stress symptoms among survivors of the Oakland/Berkeley, California, firestorm. *American Journal of Psychiatry*, 151, 888–894.

Kroenke, K., & Spitzer, R. L. (2002). The PHQ-9: A new depression diagnostic and severity measure. *Psychiatric Annals*, 32, 509–515.

Lamis, D. A., Leenaars, L. S., Jahn, D. R., & Lester, D. (2013). Intimate partner violence: Are perpetrators also victims and are they more likely to experience suicide ideation? *Journal of Interpersonal Violence*, 28, 3109–3128.

Lauritsen, J. L., & Rezey, M. L. (2013). Measuring the prevalence of crime with the National Crime Victimization Survey. US Department of Justice Report NCJ 241656. Washington, DC: Office of Justice Programs.

Lessons from Katrina and other major disasters. Hearing before the Subcommittee on Economic Development, Public Buildings and

Emergency Management of the House Committee on Transportation and Infrastructure, 111th Cong. (2009) (Testimony of Trevor Riggen, Senior Director, Disaster Services, American Red Cross).

Lipsky, S., Caetano, R., & Roy-Byrne, P. (2011). Triple jeopardy: Impact of partner violence perpetration, mental health and substance use on perceived unmet need for mental health care among men. *Social Psychiatry and Psychiatric Epidemiology, 46,* 843–852.

Litz, B. T., Gray, M. J., Bryant, R. A., & Adler, A. B. (2002). Early intervention for trauma: Current status and future directions. *Clinical Psychology: Science and Practice, 9,* 112–134.

Marchand, A., Guay, S., Boyer, R., Iucci, S., Martin, A., & St. Hilaire, M.-H. (2006). A randomized controlled trial of an adapted form of individual critical incident stress debriefing for victims of an armed robbery. *Brief Treatment and Crisis Intervention, 6,* 122–129.

Mayou, R., Ehlers, A., & Hobbs, M. (2000). Psychological debriefing for road traffic accident victims: Three-year follow-up of a randomized controlled trial. *British Journal of Psychiatry, 176,* 589–593.

McCart, M. R., Fitzgerald, M., Acierno, R., Resnick, H. S., & Kilpatrick, D. G. (2009). Evaluation and acute intervention with victims of violence. In. P. M. Kleespies (Ed.), *Behavioral emergencies: An evidence-based resource for evaluating and managing risk of suicide, violence, and victimization* (pp. 167–188). Washington, DC: American Psychological Association.

McNally, R. J., Bryant, R. A., & Ehlers, A. (2003). Does early psychological intervention promote recovery from posttraumatic stress? *Psychological Science in the Public Interest, 4,* 45–79.

Menard, S. (2012). Age, criminal victimization, and offending: Changing relationships from adolescence to middle adulthood. *Victims and Offenders, 7,* 227–254.

Messman-Moore, T. L., Brown, A. L., & Koelsch, L. E. (2005). Posttraumatic symptoms and self-dysfunction as consequences and predictors of sexual revictimization. *Journal of Traumatic Stress, 18,* 253–261.

Messman-Moore, T. L., Ward, R. M., & Brown, A. L. (2009). Substance use and PTSD symptoms impact the likelihood of rape and revictimization in college women. *Journal of Interpersonal Violence, 24,* 499–521.

Mitchell, J. T., & Everly, G. S. (1996). *Critical incident stress debriefing: An operations manual for the prevention of traumatic stress among emergency services and disaster workers* (2nd ed.). Ellicott, MD: Chevron.

National Child Traumatic Stress Network. (2010, Summer). *NCTSN IMPACT newsletter.* Retrieved from http://www.nctsn.org/resources/audiences/professionals/nctsn-newsletter

National Institute of Mental Health. (2002). *Mental health and mass violence: Evidence-based early psychological intervention for victims/survivors of mass violence. A workshop to reach consensus on best practices* (NIH Publication No. 02-5138). Washington, DC: US Government Printing Office.

Noll, J. G., & Grych, J. H. (2011). Read–react–respond: An integrative model for understanding sexual revictimization. *Psychology of Violence, 1,* 202–215.

Norris, F. H., Friedman, M. J., Watson, P. J., Byrne, C. M., Diaz, E., & Kaniasty, K. (2002). 60,000 disaster victims speak: Part I. An empirical review of the empirical literature, 1981–2001. *Psychiatry, 65,* 207–239.

Orsillo, S. (2001). Measures of acute stress disorder and posttraumatic stress disorder. In M. M. Antony, S. Orsillo, & L.

Roemer (Eds.), *Practitioner's guide to empirically based measures of anxiety* (pp. 255–307). New York: Kluwer Academic/Plenum Publishers.

Ozer, E. J., Best, S. R., Lipsey, T. L., & Weiss, D. S. (2003). Predictors of posttraumatic stress disorder and symptoms in adults: A metal-analysis. *Psychological Bulletin, 129,* 52–73.

Ozer, E. J., Best. S. R., Lipsey, T. L., & Weiss, D. S. (2008). Predictors of posttraumatic stress disorder and symptoms in adults: A meta-analysis. *Psychological Trauma: Theory, Research, Practice, and Policy,* (1), 3–36.

Pandiani, J. A., Banks, S., M., Carroll, B. B., & Schlueter, M. R. (2007). Crime victims and criminal offenders among adults with serious mental illness. *Psychiatric Services, 58,* 1483–1485.

Pietrzak, R. H., Goldstein, R. B., Southwick, S. M., & Grant, B. F. (2011). Prevalence and Axis I comorbidity of full and partial posttraumatic stress disorder in the United States: Results from Wave 2 of the National Epidemiological Survey on Alcohol and Related Conditions. *Journal of Anxiety Disorders, 25,* 456–465.

Plichta, S. B. (2004). Intimate partner violence and physical health consequences: Policy and practice implications. *Journal of Interpersonal Violence, 19,* 1296–1323.

Resick, P. A., & Schnike, M. K. (1993). *Cognitive processing therapy for rape victims: A treatment manual.* Newbury Park, CA: SAGE.

Resnick, H. S., Kilpatrick, D. G., Dansky, B. S., Saunders, B. E., & Best, C. L. (1993). Prevalence of civilian trauma and PTSD in a representative national sample of women. *Journal of Consulting and Clinical Psychology, 61,* 984–991.

Reynolds, M. W., Peipert, J. F., & Collins, B. (2000). Epidemiological issues of sexually transmitted diseases in sexual assault victims. *Obstetrical and Gynecological Survey, 55,* 51–57.

Roberts, N. P., Kitchiner, N. J., Kenardy, J., & Bisson, J. I. (2009). Systematic review and meta-analysis of multiple-session early interventions following traumatic events. *American Journal of Psychiatry, 166,* 293–301.

Rose, S., Brewin, C. R., Andrews, B., & Kirk, M. (1999). A randomized controlled trial of individual psychological debriefing for victims of violent crime. *Psychological Medicine, 29,* 793–799.

Rothbaum, B. O., Kearns, M. C., Price, M., Malcoun, E., Davis, M., Ressler, K. J., . . . Houry, D. (2012). Early intervention may prevent the development of posttraumatic stress disorder: A randomized pilot civilian study with modified prolonged exposure. *Biological Psychiatry, 72,* 957–963.

Santiago, P. N., Ursano, R. J., Gray, C. L., Pynoos, R. S., Spiegel, D., Lewis-Fernandez, R.,. . . . Fullerton, C. S. (2013). A systematic review of PTSD prevalence and trajectories in *DSM–5* defined trauma exposed populations: Intentional and non-intentional traumatic events. *PloS One, 8,* e59236.

Scarpa, A., Haden, S. C., & Hurley, J. (2006). Community violence victimization and symptoms of posttraumatic stress disorder: The moderating effects of coping and social support. *Journal of Interpersonal Violence, 21,* 446–469.

Schreck, C. J., Stewart, E. A., & Osgood, D. W. (2008). A reappraisal of the overlap of violent offenders and victims. *Criminology, 46,* 871–906.

Seidler, G., & Wagner, F. (2006). Comparing the efficacy of EMDR and trauma-focused cognitive-behavioral therapy in the treatment of PTSD: A meta-analytic study. *Psychological Medicine, 36,* 1515–1522.

Shapiro, F. (2001). *Eye movement and desensitization and reprocessing: Basic principles, protocols, and procedures.* New York: Guilford Press.

Shorey, R. C., Febres, J., Brasfield, H., & Stuart, G. L. (2012). The prevalence of mental health problems in men arrested for domestic violence. *Journal of Family Violence*, 27, 741–748.

Sijbrandij, M., Olff, M., Reitsma, J. B., Carlier, I. V. E., & Gersons, B. P. R. (2006). Emotional or educational debriefing after psychological trauma. *British Journal of Psychiatry*, 189, 150–155.

Silver, E., Arseneault, L., Langley, J., Caspi, A., & Moffitt, T. E. (2005). Mental disorder and violent victimization in a total birth cohort. *American Journal of Pubic Health*, 95, 2015–2021.

Smith, D. J., & Ecob, R. (2007). An investigation into causal links between victimization and offending in adolescents. *The British Journal of Sociology*, 58, 633–659.

Stalans, L. J., & Ritchie, J. (2008). Relationship of substance use/abuse with psychological and physical intimate partner violence: Variations across living situations. *Journal of Family Violence*, 23, 9–24.

Stapleton, A. B., Lating, J., Kirkhart, M., & Everly, G. S. (2006). Effect of medical crisis intervention on anxiety, depression, and posttraumatic stress symptoms: A meta-analysis. *Psychiatric Quarterly*, 77, 231–238.

Swendsen, J., Conway, K. P., Degenhardt, L., Glantz, M., Jin, R., Merikangas, K. R.,. . . . Kessler, R. C. (2010). Mental disorders as risk factors for substance use, abuse and dependence: Results from the 10-year follow-up of the National Comorbidity Survey. *Addiction*, 105, 1117–1128.

Stuart, G. L., Moore, T. M., Elkins, S. R., O'Farrell, T. J., Temple, J. R., Ramsey, S. E., & Shorey, R. C. (2013). The temporal association between substance use and intimate partner violence among women arrested for domestic violence. *Journal of Consulting and Clinical Psychology*, 81, 681–690.

Taft, C. T., Resick, P. A., Watkins, L. E., & Panuzio, J. (2009). An investigation of posttraumatic stress disorder and depressive symptomatology among female victims of interpersonal trauma. *Journal of Family Violence*, 24, 407–415.

Texas Advocacy Project. (2014). *Personal safety plan*. Retrieved from http://www.texasadvocacyproject.org/documents.php

Tjaden, P., & Thoennes N. (2000a). *Full report of the prevalence, incidence, and consequences of violence against women: Findings from the National Violence Against Women survey* (Publication No. NCJ 183781) Washington, DC: Department of Justice.

Tjaden, P., & Thoennes, N. (2000b). *Extent, nature, and consequences of intimate partner violence: Findings from the National Violence Against Women survey* (Publication No. NCJ 181867). Washington, DC: Department of Justice.

Tjaden, P., & Thoennes, N. (2006). *Extent, nature, and consequences of rape victimization: Findings from the National Violence against Women Survey*. Special Report. Washington, DC: National Institute of Justice and the Centers for Disease Control and Prevention.

Tolin, D. F., & Foa, E. B. (2006). Sex differences in trauma and posttraumatic stress disorder: A quantitative review of 25 years of research. *Psychological Bulletin*, 132, 959–992.

Truman, J., Langton, L., & Planty, M. (2013). *Criminal victimization, 2012*. US Department of Justice Report NCJ 243389. Washington, DC: Office of Justice Programs.

Ullman, S. E., Najdowski, C. J., & Filipas, H. H. (2009). Child sexual abuse, post-traumatic stress disorder, and substance use: Predictors of revictimization in adult sexual assault survivors. *Journal of Child Sexual Abuse*, 18, 367–385.

Ursano, R. J., Bell, C., Eth, S., Friedman, M., Norwood, A., Pfefferbaum, B.,. . . . Yager, J. (2004). Practice guideline for the treatment of patients with acute stress disorder and posttraumatic stress disorder. *American Journal of Psychiatry*, 161(Suppl. 11), 3–31.

Vaughn, M. G., Fu, Q., Delisi, M., Beaver, K. M., Perron, B. E., & Howard, M. O. (2010). Criminal victimization and co-morbid substance use and psychiatric disorders in the United States: Results from the NESARC. *Annals of Epidemiology*, 20, 281–288.

Vernberg, E. M., Steinberg, A. M., Jacobs, A. K., Brymer, M. J., Watson, P. J., Osofsky, J. D.,. . . . Ruzek, J. I. (2008). Innovations in disaster mental health: Psychological first aid. *Professional Psychology: Research and Practice*, 39, 381–388.

World Health Organization. (2003). *Mental health in emergencies: Mental and social aspects of health of populations exposed to extreme stressors*. Geneva: Author.

Yehuda, R. (2002). Posttraumatic stress disorder. *New England Journal of Medicine*, 346, 108–114.

Yule, W. (1992). Post-traumatic stress disorder in child survivors of shipping disasters: The sinking of the "Jupiter." *Psychotherapy and Psychosomatics*, 57, 200–205.

Zlotnick, C., Johnson, D. M., & Kohn, R. (2006). Intimate partner violence and long-term psychosocial functioning in a national sample of American women. *Journal of Interpersonal Violence*, 21, 262–275.

Evaluating and Managing Suicide Risk in Veterans

Phillip M. Kleespies *and* Christopher G. AhnAllen

Abstract

This chapter examines the findings on which populations of military veterans are known to be at risk of suicide. The impact of military culture on veterans as well as the impact of deployment, combat trauma, and sexual trauma are discussed, as well as the difficulties of readjusting to civilian life, particularly when the veteran has served in a combat zone. The chapter reviews some of the barriers that veterans must deal with when in need of mental health care. The limits of suicide prediction are discussed and a model for assessing suicide risk using risk factors within high risk diagnoses, including risk in combat-related posttraumatic stress disorder, is presented. Finally, suggestions for managing suicide risk in veterans are discussed. Since veterans are more likely to own firearms and commit suicide with a firearm than nonveterans, an emphasis is placed on employing means restriction counseling for veterans at risk.

Key Words: suicide, veterans, suicide risk, military culture, readjustment to civilian life, mental health care, assessing suicide risk, managing suicide risk, means restriction counseling

Amidst growing concern about suicides among veterans of the Iraq and Afghanistan Wars, Secretary of Veterans Affairs James B. Peake, MD, in 2008, appointed a Blue Ribbon Work Group on Suicide Prevention in the Veteran Population. The experts appointed to this work group found inconsistent reports of veteran suicide rates across large community-based studies examining whether or not veteran status per se (i.e., having served in the armed forces but not necessarily in combat) conferred an elevated risk of suicide. Some studies suggested that it did while others did not. The differences were intensely debated. (Gibbons, Brown, & Hur, 2012; Kaplan, McFarland, Huguet, & Newsom, 2012; Kaplan, Huguet, McFarland, & Newsom, 2007; Miller, Barber, Azrael, et al., 2009; Miller, Barber, Young, et al., 2012).

Similar controversies over veteran suicide rates are not entirely new. Following the Vietnam War, Hearst, Newman, and Hulley (1986) analyzed a randomized natural experiment, the military draft lottery of 1970–1972. Between the years 1974 and 1983, they found that their sample of men from Pennsylvania and California with birth dates that made them eligible for the draft had an increased rate of suicide relative to the group with birth dates that exempted them from the draft. They speculated about the emotional impact of potentially forced military service as a possible suicide risk factor. In a case control study, they then projected their results to apply to draft-eligible men who actually were drafted and served in the military. The estimated mortality risks for these men were elevated for suicide and motor vehicle accidents. They concluded that the most likely explanation for these findings was that military service during the Vietnam War caused an increase in subsequent deaths from suicide and motor-vehicle accidents.

In contrast, Breslin, Kang, Lee, Burt, and Shepard (1988) compared patterns of mortality among 24,235 randomly selected, deceased Army and Marine Corps Vietnam veterans and 26,685 randomly selected, deceased veterans who had not served in Southeast Asia. They found significant excess deaths for Army Vietnam War veterans for motor vehicle accidents, nonmotor vehicle accidents, and accidental poisonings, but risk of suicide itself was not elevated among these veterans. In addition, the Centers for Disease Control (1987) compared the post-service mortality (through 1983) of a cohort of 9324 US Army Vietnam War veterans with a cohort of 8989 Vietnam-era Army veterans who did not serve in a combat zone. Over the entire follow-up period, total mortality in Vietnam War veterans was 17% higher than for other veterans. The excess mortality, however, occurred mainly in the first five years after discharge from active duty and involved motor vehicle accidents, suicide, homicide, and accidental poisonings.

The results of these studies were inconclusive in terms of veteran status as a suicide risk factor, as well as in terms of military service in a combat zone as a suicide risk factor. It is possible, however, that some light may be shed on such veteran suicide controversies by recently published studies of suicide and suicidal behavior in active duty service members. The US Department of Defense (2010) in a task force report on the prevention of suicide by members of the armed forces, for example, noted that 40% or more of those dying by suicide had not yet been actually deployed to a combat area. As Rudd (in press) has pointed out, this finding has raised the question of whether there may be different paths to suicidality and suicide in military and veteran populations. Findings from the Army Study to Assess Risk and Resilience in Servicemembers (Army STARRS) have given further impetus to this question. While it was found that increased Army suicide rates were associated with being currently or previously deployed between the years 2004 and 2009, it was also found that soldiers who were never deployed during that time period also exhibited an increased suicide rate (Schoenbaum et al., 2014).

Despite the fact that Army regulations exclude the enlistment of applicants with a prior history of psychiatric or substance use problems, Kessler et al. (2014), in another of the STARRS studies, reported that significant numbers of soldiers with preenlistment psychiatric disorders were being accepted for military service. When such information is waived

to permit enlistment, it is referred to as an accession waiver.[1] In this regard, Nock et al., (2014) found that approximately one-third of post-enlistment suicide attempts were associated with preeenlistment mental disorders. Five mental disorders predicted post-enlistment first suicide attempts in multivariate analyses: pre-enlistment panic disorder, pre-enlistment post traumatic stress disorder, post-enlistment depression, and both pre-enlistment and post-enlistment intermittent explosive disorder. Further, nearly half of the soldiers with a history of lifetime suicide attempts reported that their first attempt occurred prior to enlistment.

Given the known association between mental disorders and suicide and between past suicide attempts and suicide, it seems plausible that receipt of an accession waiver might be associated with increased risk of suicide. Yet Schoenbaum et al. (2014) found that compositional changes in accession waivers over time explained little of the rise in Army suicides. These investigators, however, felt that the exploratory models that they used were of limited scope, and they reportedly plan to expand their set of predictors in future analyses.

Whether or not the use of accession waivers is found to be a factor in the increased suicide rate in the military, there is other recently reported evidence that suggests that pre-enlistment factors may contribute to an increased vulnerability to emotional disturbance and possible suicidality during enlistment and post-enlistment. Blosnich, Dichter, Cerulli, Batten, and Bossarte (2014) found that those service members from the all-volunteer service era (as compared with those from the draft era) had significantly greater odds of having had adverse childhood experiences (including physical abuse, sexual abuse, witnessing domestic violence, etc.). These results were viewed as lending preliminary support for the hypothesis that enlistment may serve as an escape from adversity for some individuals. Moreover, as noted in Chapter 2 of this volume, child maltreatment has been found to be strongly associated with suicidal behavior in adolescence and adulthood.

In this chapter, we first discuss military culture, the impact it may have had on those who are now in veteran status, and the barriers they may face when in need of mental health services. Then, we examine those groups of veterans who are or may be at increased risk of suicide, including veterans who seek or do not seek services in the Veterans

Administration (VA), and veterans who developed psychiatric disorders such as post traumatic stress disorder (PTSD), depression, substance use disorders, or comorbid psychiatric disorders. Finally, we discuss the process of assessing and managing suicide risk in veterans.

In still another register linkage study, Ilgen et al., (2012) linked all Operation Enduring Freedom (OEF)/Operation Iraqi Freedom (OIF) veterans who had a health-care encounter in the VA health-care system in the fiscal years 2007 and 2008 to the National Death Index. They found a significant interaction between psychiatric conditions and OEF/OIF status. More specifically, having a diagnosed mental health condition was associated with a greater risk of suicide among OEF/OIF veterans who sought care in the VA (hazard ratio = 4.41; 95% CI: 2.57–7.55, $p < .01$). In regard to mental health diagnoses, Ilgen et al., (2010) obtained diagnostic information from the VA National Patient Care Database on all individuals who used VA services in fiscal year 1999. They followed these patients through 2006 and linked their database to the National Death Index. Among the psychiatric disorders, bipolar disorder was found to have the strongest association with suicide followed closely by depression and then by substance use disorders, schizophrenia, anxiety disorders, and PTSD. These studies indicate that veterans who use the VA health-care system and have a mental health diagnosis, not surprisingly, have a heightened risk of suicide. The disorders found to be significantly associated with suicide among veterans who use the VA (as noted in the study by Ilgen et al., 2010) do not seem to differ markedly from those found to be associated with suicide in the general population (Kleespies & Dettmer, 2000).

In sum, the register linkage studies cited here suggest that veterans who use VA services have an elevated risk of suicide relative to the general population. In addition, veterans who are older than age 30 and utilize the VA seem to be at greater risk of suicide than veterans of that age range who do not use VA services. There appears to be a trend for those veterans under age 30, however, suggesting that those who use VA services have a decreased rate of suicide while those who do not use the VA have an increased rate. Finally, those veterans with particular mental disorders (i.e., affective disorders, substance use disorders, schizophrenia, and anxiety disorders including PTSD) are at heightened risk of suicide.

The Impact of Military Culture on Veterans
Joining the Military

Americans have elected to join the military service over the past four decades based on their own life decisions in a voluntary manner. This manner of military recruitment is in contrast to being informed of a required duty to join as was the case with the military draft that occurred during the Vietnam War. Therefore, persons who join the military today have a variety of reasons for seeking out military training and service, and these reasons are relevant to understanding their individualized experiences in integrating into military culture.

In terms of demographics, young adults are the modal group of service members with regard to age. Given that about 50% of the military service members are between the ages of 17 and 24, a significant portion of adults enter the military in a traditional manner after secondary school and during late adolescence/early adulthood (Kelty, Kleykamp, & Segal, 2010). This process of entering military service suggests a developmental process whereby Americans are seeking out military training during a period of increasing and emerging independence from family systems within American culture. The emphases noted within the military are uniquely suited to facilitating such a developmental process given the emphasis on personal responsibility, community building, physical fitness/health, and societal service as identified by Kelty et al. (2010). The military provides a developmental framework for personal growth that is similar to, but distinct from, higher education models that offer alternative learning, social, and duty roles. A few of the structured provisions within military service that are associated with supporting the increasing development of independence for young adults include rules and regulations, housing, meals, health care, and skills training.

In terms of why individuals volunteer to join the military, Americans are drawn to the military for a variety of reasons (Moore, 2011). Service members share a number of themes of why they seek out military service versus higher education or employment at this developmental juncture. Referred to as family tradition, some service members are drawn to the military because the military and veteran cultures have been represented within their extended family by previous generations. Of those who enlist in the military, there are more service members who come from families with a history of military service than those who do not (Gegax & Thomas, 2005). Other reasons may include economic improvement or the potential to improve socioeconomic status, as a call to patriotic duty, or to join a societal structure that is clearly defined and provides rules with which a person may identify.

Military Service as a Cultural Experience

Understanding military service as a cultural experience or exchange suggests that being in the military is associated with specific traditions, customs, and practices that are inherently integral to the cultural system. In the military, there are unique experiences that must be learned, understood, and practiced in order to develop acceptance by others within the system. These practices, to some degree, are relevant across individual branches of the military although each branch, type of unit, era of service, location of deployment, and specific shared duties may have their unique subcultures that are relevant to comprehend (Meyer, 2013). In fact, missions, mottos, core values, and language differ according to the branch of service. In the military, Hsu (2010) has pointed out the core values of honor, courage, loyalty, integrity, and commitment that are thought to translate across branches of service. Others cite other virtues that are less popularly discussed including peacefulness (preservation of harmony), restraint (judicious use of war), and obedience (obeying legitimate and moral orders; Coll et al., 2011). The military culture also includes emphases on discipline and hierarchy, prioritization of a collectivist approach compared with individualistic goals and needs, and culture-bound practices associated with rituals and symbols.

The military is structured on a unique hierarchical class system that is thought to be transparent in operation (Moore, 2011). In this system, military rank is divided into officers and enlisted service members. Officers are more highly educated and enter into leadership positions while enlisted service members are always under the direction of an officer and have their own unique class system. There is little socialization between these groups despite their need to operate together within the service professionally. The military includes members who are enlisted to perform specific duties, commissioned officers with specialized education and leadership roles, and warrant officers who are highly specialized in their duties.

An important construct within the military culture is cohesion, considered to be a "cardinal principle" (Coll et al., 2011). Cohesion, or the development of a trusted bond among group members, is cited as a necessity for military units to effectively operate in a collective fashion with the pursuit of shared goals and outcomes. Unit cohesion was previously cited as the reason why gay, lesbian, and bisexual service members should not be allowed to serve openly in the military, even though this rationale was questioned (Rand Corporation, 1993). Davenport (1987) has identified that unit cohesion is emphasized in a manner that may result in segregation from civilian society; yet civilian society is ultimately where the service member is most likely to return upon discharge from the service.

Military Stress: Deployment, Combat, and Sexual Trauma

Military service members are assigned to duties depending on the Military Occupational Speciality for which they are trained but also according to location with regard to serving stateside (within the United States) or overseas (which could include serving in a combat zone). Service members often do not have a choice as to where they are ordered to serve and therefore need to be accepting of receiving orders to conduct their duties in various assigned military zones, countries, and combat arenas.

Deployment overseas or to nations other than the United States can be a stressful experience for the service member. This can include a number of psychological difficulties for which it can take time to become accustomed (Vasterling et al., 2011). The service member may experience culture shock in adjusting to different lifestyles including new landscapes and weather, ethnicities of native persons, languages spoken, reduced access to American culturally-familiar items, and access to social supports. Additionally, service members often leave behind family supports including spouses and partners, children, and nonmilitary peers. In this regard the service members need to develop and maintain strong bonds with their fellow service members who are deployed as these persons become the available interpersonal supports for managing emotional distress, as well as other emotional experiences during deployment. Iverson et al. (2008) identify that military units defined by a high degree of cohesiveness among their members are less likely to experience negative consequences from exposure to stressful situations in combat environments. This social connectedness has been highlighted as a means to establish improved communication among service members and create a social identity (Cobb, 1976; Cohen & Willis, 1985).

Combat deployments are inherently associated with danger and potential for serious injury or death for service members. Deployment to regions in the recent wars in Iraq and Afghanistan could include exposure to events that are potentially traumatizing. For example, service members could be exposed to events such as surviving a surprise roadside bomb explosion; witnessing or participating in the wounding or killing of insurgents, civilians, or other service members; or hearing mortar explosions in close proximity. These are examples of events that may be associated with intense fear, helplessness, and/or horror and could serve as precipitating events for the development of PTSD. With regard to physical injury, combat exposure may increase risk for physical damage to the body. Moreover, service members in today's military are known to be surviving more serious injuries than in previous conflicts given advances in medicine and the integration of medics within military units (Pryce, Pryce, & Shackelford, 2012). Altogether, exposure to the psychological and physical traumas of combat put the service member at increased risk given that the combat theatre is inherently an unsafe environment.

Military sexual trauma (MST), defined by Title 38 U.S. Code 1720D, is "psychological trauma, which in the judgment of a VA mental health professional, resulted from a physical assault of a sexual nature, battery of a sexual nature, or sexual harassment which occurred while the Veteran was serving on active duty or training for active duty." The VA defines sexual harassment as "repeated, unsolicited verbal or physical contact of a sexual nature which is threatening in character." MST can occur for men and women, though the rates for women (1 in 4) are significantly greater than for male (1 in 100) service members self-reporting within a health-care-seeking population (July 2014 MST Fact Sheet, www.va.gov). MST aftereffects differ by person, but a number of negative outcomes are possible for the service member. These include distressing emotions, emotional numbness, sleep problems, cognitive problems, substance use disorders, relationship problems, physical health ailments, and PTSD.

The Veteran Identity

Termination of military service can occur for a few different reasons, and these are thought to have an impact on the identity of the veteran after military service. In general, a service member can be discharged under certain conditions that can significantly impact their accessibility to services after discharge. These conditions are referenced as honorable, general, other than honorable, and bad conduct. Discharge reasons may be due to, for example, the service member electing not to reenlist for a subsequent term of service, medical conditions (including psychiatric conditions), behavioral problems, and substance use problems.

Individuals who are discharged from the military re-enter the American culture that is devoid of the inherent structure and rules of the military. This can also be considered a culture shock given that the veteran must undergo significant readjustment during this time. Sloan and Friedman (2008) consider the shock of returning home to be more significant for veterans than the shock of going to combat. Coll et al. (2011) have noted that this readjustment is akin to the cultural shock of immigrants coming for the first time to the United States. They highlight that readjustment issues can include a loss of trust in the US government and American foreign policy and adjustment to physical or psychological problems. Additional issues can include reintegration into family systems including renegotiating family roles and responsibilities, reestablishing employment, and, for some, the difficulty with identifying missions in civilian life that are of comparable value to those learned or experienced within the military. James Munroe (2012) has highlighted the importance of understanding the transition from service member in a combat zone to civilian life in the American culture. This transition might need to include gaining an understanding and appreciation of transitioning out of a war-zone mindset or *battlemind*. Battlemind includes a set of skills that were necessary for survival in combat but need to be modified for successful transitioning into civilian life.

Issues Related to Homecoming

Discharge from military duties and, in some instances, returning "stateside" from overseas deployments including combat theaters is associated with a number of readjustment needs. Military personnel who are discharged, referred to as veterans, undergo a number of processes of readjusting to civilian life. This process of reintegration into American culture, even though it may be the culture from which they departed, can be endured with varying degrees of difficulty over varying amounts of time.

The challenges associated with readjustment and reintegration into American culture include issues related to family roles and responsibilities, employment, social role functioning, and adjustment to the loss of the established hierarchical order of military structure and routines (Lincoln, Swift, & Shorteno-Fraser, 2008). Veterans return to family systems that have operated in their absence and have adapted to such change but now need to readjust again in order to reincorporate the veteran into the family. This can include changes in partner relationships, child-rearing practices, household duties, and other family practices that have adapted to functioning without the veteran or have evolved over time. Veterans may find themselves unemployed or unable to relate to their civilian friends and partners whom they had been close with prior to military service or deployment on combat missions.

For some veterans the readjustment to civilian life can be associated with transitional emotional distress that can include irritability, nervousness, sleep problems, and poor concentration (Vasterling et al., 2011). These symptoms can be associated with symptoms of mental health problems including adjustment disorders, depression, anxiety, acute stress disorder, and PTSD. The psychological distress can therefore be considered an acute reaction to the "reverse culture shock" of reengaging into civilian life, or it may develop into a more prolonged mental health problem or set of problems that interrupt functioning in life (Koenig, Maguen, Monroy, Mayott, & Seal, 2014). In fact, veterans receive little cultural reintegration training following deployments or at discharge from the military (Westwood et al., 2002), and the process of transitioning from military culture to veteran or civilian lifestyles may involve resolution of competing social identities (Koenig et al., 2014). Veterans may also engage in excessive alcohol or drug use to manage their psychological distress including use of opiate-based drugs, which are thought to be a signature drug use problem of the recent OEF/OIF wars. Oliva, Trafton, Harris, and Gordon (2013) indicate that the number of veterans who are diagnosed with opiate use disorders in the VHA has increased by 45% between fiscal year 2004 to fiscal year 2010. Norman, Schmied, and Larson (2014) describe the associated negative psychosocial effects of the 42% of veterans who continue to exhibit problems with alcohol use beginning prior to and continuing

after the year following military separation. These include greater difficulties in adjusting to civilian life, greater rates of driving under the influence, and increased rates of aggression. Greater rates of PTSD symptoms are also noted as a predictor of continued problematic substance use during the year of separation. Data from the National Post-Deployment Adjustment Survey of Iraq and Afghanistan Veterans ($N = 1,388$) indicate that nearly half of these veterans (43%) experience serious psychological and substance use problems including PTSD, major depression, or alcohol abuse (Elbogen et al., 2013).

Barriers for Veterans Seeking Mental Health Care

The cultural identity of being a veteran, discussed earlier in this chapter, may contribute as a barrier to seeking mental health care. Embedded within the culture of the veteran, which is learned within the military as a core value, is an expectation of strength and endurance. Service members are trained to endure physical and psychological challenges to fulfill specified missions or support their fellow service members. Related to this concept, readjustment issues or mental illness may be conceptualized by the veteran as a source of weakness and vulnerability (Elbogen et al., 2013). In fact, service members who exhibit certain mental illnesses are at risk for discharge from the military, and thus there is already a culture established within the military to suggest that mental illness is associated with not being fit for duty or responsibilities.

Stigma about mental illness is an important barrier to mental health treatment access. According to a survey of OEF and OIF service members returning from combat, the perceptions about barriers to mental health treatment included the perception of being weak, as well as other notions of stigma by leadership and loss of confidence in them by others (Elbogen et al., 2013; Hoge et al., 2004). Others discuss the existence of a self-stigma, referred to as a negative evaluation of oneself associated with mental health treatment access, and public stigma, or the expectation of a negative evaluation within society for experiencing mental illness (Vogt, 2011). In fact, one study indicated that having a diagnosis of PTSD was most highly predictive of experiencing stigma and other barriers to care (Pietrzak et al., 2009). Stigma or negative attitudes toward treatment has also been noted as a specific barrier for OEF/OIF combat veterans (Garcia et al., 2014). Others suggest that stigma or beliefs about mental health services do not interfere with persistence in treatment for veterans seeking treatment for PTSD (Harpaz-Rotem et al., 2014).

Additional barriers to engagement in care are centered around issues associated with the veteran's return to life roles and duties. Veterans may expect that their experience of readjustment issues or mental illness will resolve without intervention by others or with support of family and friends (Drapalski et al., 2008). Veterans may be concerned about the need to reengage in duties within and outside the home including child-care or -rearing practices, household tasks, education, employment, socialization, and/or other needs (Garcia et al., 2014). There may also be practical issues interfering with mental health treatment access, including not knowing where to access care, uncertainty about trusting others who were not in the military or deployed on combat missions, as well as difficulties in scheduling care and prioritizing care over other needs.

Specific barriers for access to mental health treatment may exist for women veterans (Lehavot, Der-Martirosian, Simpson, Sadler, & Washington, 2013; Runnals et al., 2014). In a review of 32 articles published between January 2008 and July 2011 on women veteran's mental health within the VA, Runnals and colleagues (2014) indicate that women veterans are increasingly seeking out health care. Those who are younger, however, who have increased economic burdens, who are restricted by their ability to access care due to other duties (e.g., employment), and who have poorer health are less able to access mental health treatment. Friedman and colleagues (2011) note that the rate of women veterans accessing mental health treatment has increased significantly from 24% in 2003 to 40% in 2009. Across a survey of 3,608 women veterans, Washington, Bean-Mayberry, Riopelle, and Yano (2011) determined that being a racial minority, lacking health insurance, having low income, having a disability, having been diagnosed with a mental illness, and having a history of MST were notable barriers to engagement in health care. In addition, the authors note concern from the women veterans about the level of sensitivity within health-care settings to women veterans' needs.

While it is important to improve access to treatment services for veterans, initiation and retention within mental health treatment is an important subsequent issue that may follow. Identification of factors that facilitate or are associated with seeking out mental health treatment and then remaining in treatment are important to identify. In a survey of 137 treatment-referred and symptomatic veterans referred for PTSD treatment within the VA, severity of PTSD and unit support were identified as factors that increased the likelihood of initiating treatment for PTSD (Harpaz-Rotam et al., 2014). The factors that were linked to completing 12 sessions of treatment for PTSD included having greater levels of depressive and numbing symptoms of mental illness and post-high school education. Jakupcak and colleagues (2013) have identified that when veterans are ready to make changes in their lives, they utilize mental health services to a greater extent. Strategies to increase motivation to engage in treatment or make changes with regard to mental health or substance use may be fruitful in improving interest in treatment and might be expected to improve rates of access and initiation of care. Therefore, improving access, initiation, and retention in mental health treatment remain important goals for engagement of veterans in the future.

Veterans at Risk of Suicide

Veterans receive care both within and apart from the VA health-care system, and studies have attempted to examine the relationship of suicide risk with factors about veterans and where they receive care. In a large register linkage study that focused only on veterans who used the VA health-care system, it was found that there was an elevated standardized mortality ratio for suicide (SMR = 1.66, 95% confidence interval [CI]: 1.58–1.75) for veterans in the VA system when compared with age-matched individuals in the general population (McCarthy et al., 2009). In a study that investigated suicide rates among veterans who used VA health care and those who did not, Katz, McCarthey, Ignacio, and Kemp (2012) linked VA data from the Veterans Health Administration (VHA) to data in 16 states that fully participated in the National Violent Death Reporting System during the years 2005 to 2008. They found that approximately 17.9% of male veterans and approximately 21.8% of female veterans utilized VHA services. Further, they found that suicide rates for veterans ages 30 to 65 and older who used VA services were consistently higher than for veterans in the same age range who did not use VA services. For those veterans under

30 years of age (i.e., 18–29), however, there were dramatic reductions in suicide rates for those who used VA services during the time period of 2005 to 2008, while there were increased suicide rates among those of that age group who did not use VA services. The authors attributed the findings about decreasing suicide rates among those veterans under age 30 who utilized VA services to increased VA suicide prevention efforts through legislation such as the Joshua Omvig Veterans Suicide Prevention Act of 2007 (Cvetanovich & Reynolds, 2008).

Assessing Suicide Risk with Veterans

As noted earlier in this chapter, the Army STARRS study found that there was a heightened risk of suicide among both soldiers who were deployed and those who were never deployed in the Iraq and Afghanistan wars (Schoenbaum et al., 2014). In terms of assessing veterans from this war era, it would seem that one implication of this research is that mental health clinicians cannot assume that there is less risk of suicide among veterans who did not deploy to a combat zone and did not experience the stresses of combat. Rather, it might be advisable, as soldiers transition to veteran status, for clinicians to attend to both pre-enlistment and post-enlistment psychopathology as potentially heightening risk. As mentioned earlier, Nock et al. (2014) found that nearly half of those soldiers who had a history of suicide attempts reported that their first attempt occurred prior to enlistment. Moreover, they also found that five mental disorders predicted post-enlistment first suicide attempts; namely, pre-enlistment panic disorder, pre-enlistment PTSD, post-enlistment depression, and both pre-enlistment and post-enlistment intermittent explosive disorder.

Evaluating the Acute Risk of Suicide

We would be remiss when discussing the assessment of suicide risk in veterans (or in any population) if we did not mention the very definite limitations of such a task.

THE LIMITATIONS OF SUICIDE RISK ASSESSMENT

Suicide is a rare event. The Centers for Disease Control and Prevention (CDC, 2014) has reported that the age-adjusted suicide rate for the United States in 2014 (the latest year for which statistics are available) was 13.4/100,000 per year. Our clinical acumen as mental health practitioners and the existing assessment instruments at our disposal are simply not sensitive and specific enough to detect such low base rate events. We cannot know with any degree of certainty which individuals will actually commit suicide (Hillard, 1995; Kleespies & Dettmer, 2000; Nock et al., 2013).

To further illustrate the difficulties of estimating suicide risk, let us look at what is generally viewed as our best single predictor of suicide—that is, a past suicide attempt. The problem with this predictor is that only an estimated 10% to 15% of suicide attempters ever complete suicide, while an estimated 60% to 70% of those who complete suicide do so on the first known attempt (Maris, 1992). Thus although a history of a suicide attempt clearly heightens risk, the absence of such a history cannot be taken as diminishing it. Possibly making suicide prediction still more difficult, Maris (1992) has argued that those who commit suicide and those who engage in nonfatal suicide attempts may represent overlapping but to some degree separate populations as evidenced by the fact that the ratio of male-to-female individuals who commit suicide is approximately 4:1, but the ratio of male-to-female attempters is approximately 1:3 (CDC, 2014).

Given our inability to predict suicide on an individual level, our efforts as clinicians tend to be focused on improving our ability to estimate who may be at high risk for suicide or suicidal behavior. As Nock et al. (2013) have noted, in the absence of evidence to the contrary, and with the possible exception of factors associated with combat-related PTSD, it is plausible to assume that the factors that are likely to lead to suicide or suicidal behavior in the general population are just as likely to lead to suicide or suicidal behavior in soldiers, and we would argue in veterans as well.

USING RISK FACTORS WITHIN HIGH-RISK DIAGNOSES TO GUIDE ASSESSMENT

Nock et al. (2013) have noted that most models for assessing suicidal behavior in the literature have distinguished between distal (or vulnerability) risk factors, proximal (or dynamic) risk factors, and protective factors. We are of the opinion that there has been a promising model of this type that was proposed some 20 to 25 years ago but was apparently not more fully developed. This is the model that was offered by Clark and Fawcett (1992) as well as Hendin (1986) and that proposed the use of what they termed *diagnosis-specific risk factors* as a guide to improved risk estimation. (For alternative model for assessing suicide risk in adults, see Chapter 9 of this volume.) The approach was based on the results of a majority of the large community-based psychological autopsy studies (see, e.g., Rich, Young, & Fowler, 1986; Shaffer et al., 1996) in which it was found that more than 90% of adult and adolescent suicides suffered from a major mental or emotional disorder. As a result, it has long been known that mental or emotional disorders are factors in the majority of suicides. In fact, Tanney (1992), after an extensive review of studies on the relationship between mental disorders and suicide, concluded, "Among the heterogeneity of causes, mental disorders can lay claim to a position in the first rank of the matrix of causation" (pp. 309–310). In our opinion, such findings do not necessarily imply that all who commit suicide suffer from a mental illness or that there cannot be so-called *rational* suicides (as, e.g., among the terminally ill with intractable pain and suffering). In terms of estimating risk, however, it does indicate that one could focus on suicide risk in those with mental disorders and retain the vast majority of suicidal individuals within the field of study.

Only certain psychiatric diagnoses have been found to be associated with a risk of suicide that is significantly higher than that found in the general population. More than 30 years ago, Pokorny (1983) conducted a prospective study of suicide and suicidal behavior with 4,800 veterans who had been consecutively admitted to the psychiatric units at the Houston VA Medical Center. All of the veterans in the study were followed for four to six years. Using the primary admitting diagnosis, he found that the incidence of suicide by diagnosis was as follows: affective disorder (695/100,000/year), schizophrenia (456/100,000/year), drug abuse (194/100,000/year), alcoholism (187/100,000/year), and personality disorder (187/100,000/year). Although his method of determining diagnosis was not particularly rigorous, and he did not examine dual or comorbid diagnoses, his findings on high-risk diagnoses are very similar to what has been reported in the community-based psychological autopsy studies noted here; that is, the diagnoses with highly elevated suicide rates tend to be mood disorders, schizophrenia, and substance use disorders.

Within each high-risk diagnostic category, only a small percentage of patients actually commit suicide. Inskip, Harris, and Barraclough (1998) have estimated that the lifetime risk of suicide is 6% for affective disorders, 7% for alcohol dependence, and 4% for schizophrenia. The question becomes, however, whether there are risk factors related to a particular high-risk diagnosis (as Hendin [1986] and Fawcett et al. [1987] have hypothesized) that might help to differentiate the suicidal from the nonsuicidal. As Clark and Fawcett (1992) have noted, it would be significant if prototypical risk profiles could be developed for high-risk diagnoses that might assist clinicians in making a better estimate of which patients with a particular diagnosis are at greater risk of suicide. Fawcett et al. (1987) gave impetus to an association between certain risk factors and diagnosis with the publication of their prospective study of clinical predictors of suicide in patients with major affective disorders.

Despite the need for data on the evaluation of acute risk for suicide, most studies of suicide have investigated lifetime risk factors rather than acute or short-term risk factors. Very acute or imminent risk factors are very difficult to study. Acutely suicidal patients are either excluded from studies or, once an investigator is aware that a subject may be at grave risk of suicide, he or she is ethically obligated to institute preventive measures (Pokorny, 1983).

Nonetheless, there have been a number of studies in which researchers have been able to collect prospective data on risk within six months or a year of suicide. These studies have primarily been with patients diagnosed with affective disorder and patients diagnosed with schizophrenia. These two diagnostic categories have coincidentally been found in a large register linkage study to have the strongest population impact on the risk of suicide in people who have previously attempted suicide (Tidemalm, Langstrom, Lichtenstein, & Runeson, 2008). We initially summarize the findings in regard to these two diagnoses and suicide risk but then subsequently present what is known (often through retrospective studies) about acute risk of suicide in other high-risk diagnoses such as substance use disorders, combat-related PTSD, and personality disorders.

AFFECTIVE DISORDER AND ACUTE RISK OF SUICIDE

As noted previously, depression is the diagnosis most frequently associated with suicide. In a Swedish study, bipolar and unipolar mood disorder (as well as schizophrenia; Tidemalm et al., 2008) were found to have the greatest short-term risk (i.e., within a year) for suicide following a suicide attempt. In terms of acute, depression-related risk factors for suicide, the results of the large, multisite, prospective study by Fawcett et al. (1987, 1990) indicated that severe anhedonia, global insomnia, diminished concentration, severe anxiety, panic attacks, obsessive-compulsive symptoms, active use of alcohol, and a current episode of cycling affective illness (i.e., cycling between depression and hypomania or mania without intermittent recovery or stabilization) significantly heightened the risk of suicide within 6 to 12 months.[2] In addition, Pfeiffer, Ganoczy, Ilgen, Zivin, and Valenstein (2009) found that depression with co-morbid anxiety predicted greater risk of suicide than depression without anxiety. In Fawcett, et al., (1990), the distal risk factors of no children under 18 in the home and the depressive state being one of three or fewer lifetime episodes were also found to be associated with short-term risk. By implication, children under 18 in the home has been considered a protective factor for suicide.

Findings such as those of Fawcett et al. (1987, 1990) suggest that, among patients with a diagnosis of affective disorder (whether they be veterans or nonveterans) who have profound depression marked by severe anhedonia and insomnia combined with severe anxiety symptoms and/or comorbid alcohol abuse, or who have the emotional turmoil of rapidly cycling moods, are at greater short-term risk of suicide than other mood-disorder patients. Consistent with these findings, Oquendo et al. (2004), in a sample of patients presenting for treatment of a major depressive episode, reported that the patient's self-rating of the severity of depression on the Beck Depression Inventory was one of the most powerful predictors of future suicidal acts in a two-year follow-up period. In this prospective study, they also found that a history of suicide attempts, a pessimism factor, an aggression/impulsivity factor, and smoking or nicotine use were predictive of future suicidal acts. According to the study by Fawcett et al., 1987 the risk may be heightened when depressive episodes have not become chronically recurrent but are as yet relatively infrequent occurrences.

Oquendo et al. (2007), in a follow-up to Oquendo et al. (2004), investigated possible gender differences in clinical predictors of suicidal acts after a major depressive episode. It was found that, for both men and women in the sample, comorbid borderline personality disorder and cigarette smoking increased the risk of future suicidal acts. For men alone, a family history of suicidal acts, past drug use, and early parental separation each more than tripled the risk of future suicidal acts, while for women alone, suicidal ideation, the lethality of past suicide attempts, hostility, fewer reasons for living, and patient-rated severity of depressive symptoms significantly increased the risk.

SCHIZOPHRENIA AND ACUTE RISK OF SUICIDE

While the incidence of suicide in unipolar depression tends to reach a peak in older age (Conwell et al., 1996), the incidence of suicide in schizophrenia is thought to reach a peak in young adulthood, or relatively early in the course of the disorder. In a prospective study, Westermeyer, Harrow, and Marengo (1991) found that 60% of schizophrenic patients who committed suicide did so within six years of their first hospitalization, and, in a summary of eight demographic studies of suicide in patients with schizophrenia, Weiden and Roy (1992) reported a mean age at death of 32 years. In a more recent systematic review of studies on suicide in schizophrenia, however, Hor and Taylor (2010) reported some evidence that later age of onset of illness (age > 45) may also be associated with an increased risk of suicide.

Numerous studies have indicated that persons with schizophrenia who commit suicide (in the United States and the Western world) are predominantly White males who have never married (see, e.g., DeHert & Peuskens, 2000). Another frequent finding has been that suicide among persons with schizophrenia is associated with feelings of disappointment and frustration about the quality of their lives and the chronic nature of their disorder as well as fear of mental disintegration (Cohen, Test, & Brown, 1990; Drake, Gates, Whitaker, & Cotton, 1985; Hor & Taylor, 2010; Westermeyer et al., 1991). It is hypothesized that the lack of full recovery after the first few psychotic episodes can lead to hopelessness and despair in some patients, especially those who have a relatively higher level of intelligence, are better educated, and have greater expectations for themselves. Cohen et al. (1990) found that persons with schizophrenia who committed suicide had endorsed significantly more hopelessness, depression, obsessive-compulsive features, and paranoid ideation, as well as lower life satisfaction on standardized tests. In addition, Haas (1997) has characterized those with schizophrenia who committed suicide as having highly negative attitudes toward treatment. Previous suicide attempts have been found to lead to a significantly greater likelihood of subsequent suicide in persons with schizophrenia when compared to patients with other diagnoses who made previous nonfatal attempts (Tidemalm et al., 2008; Weiden & Roy, 1992). The implication seems to be that a history of suicide attempts should be taken very seriously as a suicide risk factor in those with schizophrenia.

In a comprehensive review, Caldwell & Gottesman (1990) characterized risk factors for suicide in schizophrenia as follows:

> being young and male, experiencing chronicity of illness with numerous acute exacerbations and remissions, postdischarge course with high levels of psychopathology and functional impairment, realistic awareness of the deteriorative effects of schizophrenia and a nondelusional assessment of the future (during a nonpsychotic phase), fear of further mental deterioration, excessive treatment dependence, or loss of faith in treatment. (p. 578)

One component of this characterization (i.e., that suicide for those with schizophrenia occurs in a nonpsychotic phase) has been called into question by a psychological autopsy study in Finland (Heila et al., 1997). The investigators in this study found that the majority of suicide victims in their sample were in the active phase of the disorder at the time of their deaths. There has been a similar finding in a study of suicide attempters versus nonattempters by Ran et al. (2005); that is, suicide attempters had a greater number of the positive symptoms of schizophrenia than nonattempters.

As this synopsis indicates, information about a risk profile in schizophrenia has increased; however, there has been little investigation of acute risk factors. Relative to acute risk, Peuskens et al. (1997) reported finding an increase in depression in suicide victims with schizophrenia immediately prior to death, as well as an increase in the number of attempts to treat the depression. Corroborating evidence has been reported by Heila et al. (1997), who found a depressive syndrome in nearly two-thirds of their patients who committed suicide. It would seem, then, that with young, male patients with schizophrenia who have relatively higher levels of intelligence, higher expectations of themselves, and higher awareness of the debilitating effects of their disorder, the presence of depression should be taken very seriously as a short-term risk factor for suicide.

SUBSTANCE USE DISORDERS AND ACUTE RISK OF SUICIDE

In a prospective study of alcohol intake and unnatural death, Klatsky and Armstrong (1993) found that, among those who drank six or more drinks daily, there was a six-fold increase in suicide risk relative to nondrinkers. This study illustrates the strong association between alcohol use disorders and suicide that was also found in comprehensive reviews by Pompili et al. (2010) and Wilcox, Conner, and Caine (2004). Although we know of the elevated suicide risk associated with alcoholism, it is not clear what the causal link(s) may be. In terms of psychological pathways to suicide, it is possible that alcohol abuse (a) lowers inhibitions about engaging in suicidal behavior; (b) increases aggressive behavior including self-aggression; (c) disrupts family and friendship relationships leading to loneliness, social isolation, and loss of support; (d) leads to substance-induced depression; (e) negatively affects judgment and decreases the cognitive ability to access coping strategies that would avoid suicidal behavior; or (f) some combination of these.

Jacobson et al. (2008), in the prospective Millennium Cohort Study of Iraq War and Afghanistan War service members, found that Reserve and National Guard personnel and younger active duty servicemembers who deployed with combat exposure were at increased risk of new-onset heavy weekly drinking, binge drinking, and alcohol-related problems after returning from deployment. These investigators have also noted that similar findings have been reported among Vietnam War and the 1991 Gulf War veterans. Regardless of the war era, however, these behaviors put veterans at increased risk of suicidal behavior and suicide.

The findings related to acute suicide risk factors for those who abuse alcohol have been primarily derived from retrospective, psychological autopsy studies. Murphy and Robins (1967), in a psychological autopsy study, found that interpersonal loss or disruption seemed to heighten vulnerability to suicide in alcoholics. Similar findings were also reported in studies by Murphy, Armstrong, Hermele, Fischer, and Clendenin (1979), Rich, Fowler, Fogarty, and Young (1988), and Duberstein, Conwell, and Caine (1993). Comorbid alcohol abuse and depression has also been found to heighten the risk of suicide in alcoholics (Barraclough, Bunch, Nelson, & Sainsbury, 1974; Conwell et al., 1996). Cornelius et al., (1995) found that more severe suicidal ideation on initial presentation to a psychiatric facility strongly distinguished depressed alcoholics from nonalcoholic (*pure*) depressives and nondepressed (*pure*) alcoholics. Since the depressed alcoholics in this study demonstrated a family history of depression similar to that of the *pure* depressives and a family history of alcoholism similar to that of *pure* alcoholics, the authors suggested that depressed alcoholics in their sample suffered the additive, or possibly synergistic, effect of two high-risk diagnoses resulting in a disproportionately high level of acute suicidal ideation. They felt that alcoholic patients with depressive symptoms should be carefully monitored for increased risk of suicide.

Increased risk of suicidal behavior and/or suicide has also been reported among inhalant users (Howard et al., 2010), heroin users (Darke & Ross, 2002), and cocaine users (Marzuk et al., 1992). Little is known about factors associated with the use of these substances that may increase risk. Borges, Walters, and Kessler (2000) found that the major risk of suicidal behavior was linked to the current use of these substances rather than to a history of use or abuse. They also found that polysubstance use was more important than a particular, single substance in predicting first suicide attempts. While alcoholic suicides are most likely to occur in middle age, polysubstance abuse and *pure* drug abuse suicides tend to occur earlier in the lifespan (Rich, Fowler, & Young, 1989). In the psychological autopsy data investigated by Porsteinsson et al. (1997), the mean age at suicide for polysubstance abusers was 30.7 years, while the mean age for alcoholics was 49.7 years. The reasons for this mean age difference are unclear, but hypotheses range from polysubstance abuse having a more negative influence on interpersonal relationships to polysubstance abuse having a more destructive effect on neurotransmitters like serotonin.

COMBAT-RELATED PTSD AND ACUTE RISK OF SUICIDE

There has been some controversy about whether combat-related PTSD is a risk factor for suicide. Krysinska and Lester (2010), for example, completed a review of 50 studies that examined the association between PTSD and suicidal behavior. They found evidence of a clear relationship of PTSD with suicidal behavior but felt that there was no evidence for an increased risk of completed suicide. Of the 50 studies reviewed, there were 4 studies of veteran suicide, 2 of which found an elevated rate of suicide for veterans with PTSD (Bullman & Kang, 1994; Drescher, Rosen, Burling, & Foy, 2003) and 2 that did not (Desai, Dausey, & Rosenheck, 2005; Zivin et al., 2007). The authors seem to have concluded that these studies nullified each other and that therefore there was no evidence of an elevated rate of suicide associated with combat-related PTSD.[3] Their findings, however, are in stark contrast to the more extensive review by Panagioti, Gooding, and Tarrier (2009), who not only found a strong relationship between combat-related PTSD and suicidal behavior but also found that the relationship was confirmed across studies examining completed suicides, suicide attempts, and suicidal ideation.

In a register linkage study of suicide among Vietnam veterans with PTSD, Bullman and Kang (1994) used the Agent Orange Registry (AOR) to follow 4,247 male veterans who had a diagnosis of PTSD and 12,010 randomly selected male veterans on the AOR who had no clinical diagnosis. They checked vital status by linking these two groups with the VA-maintained Beneficiary Identification and Record Locator Subsystem. Over a four- to five-year follow-up period, they found that those veterans with PTSD relative to those with no clinical diagnosis had a risk ratio of 3.97 (95% CI: 2.20–7.03) for suicide and a risk ratio of 2.89 (95% CI: 1.03–8.12) for death by accidental poisoning.

When compared to the US population rate of suicide, the veterans with PTSD in the Bullman and Kang (1994) study had an almost seven-fold increased risk for suicide (Standardized Mortality Ration [SMR] = 6.74, 95% CI: 4.40–9.87). The investigators also studied a subgroup of 1,001 veterans with PTSD who had comorbid diagnoses. Fifty-six percent had comorbid alcohol and drug dependency disorders, while 11% had comorbid neurotic disorder and 10% had comorbid depressive disorder. Among this group with comorbid disorders, there was almost a 10-fold increased risk for suicide (SMR = 9.81, 95% CI: 4.48–18.63). The study authors interpreted their findings as indicating that, for Vietnam veterans on the AOR, PTSD was associated with a significantly increased risk for death by suicide and accidental poisoning.

In the study noted previously by Drescher et al. (2003), the investigators studied death rates and causes of death among 1,866 veterans admitted for residential PTSD treatment between 1990 and 1998. Admissions to this program were clinician-referred veterans with military-related traumatic exposure and severe PTSD. Many also had comorbid diagnoses of mood disorder or substance use disorder. The investigators specifically focused on behavioral causes of death: that is, deaths associated with high-risk behaviors that are potentially amenable to psychosocial intervention. These deaths included deaths from vehicular accidents, accidental overdoses, suicide, encounters with the police, the chronic effects of substance use, and so forth.

One hundred ten veterans (or 5.9%) from the sample died during the study period. Of those who died, 62.4% were considered to have died from behavioral causes with many (37.6%) dying from the acute and/or chronic effects of alcohol or drug abuse. There was also a higher than expected number of intentional deaths, and deaths by suicide were significantly elevated (SMR = 4.0 [95% CI = 1.8–7.4]). The investigators noted that weaknesses of the study are that there was no comparison group of non-PTSD veterans and it was not possible to differentiate the relative contribution to mortality rates of PTSD alone from that associated with PTSD and comorbid disorders such as depression and substance dependence.

In a more recent study of suicide risk in veterans, Ilgen et al., (2010) obtained diagnostic information from the VA National Patient Care Database on all individuals who used VA services in fiscal year 1999. They followed these patients for seven years through 2006 and linked their database to the National Death Index. They reported that slightly less than half (46.8%) of those who died by suicide had at least one psychiatric condition at entry into the study. Among the psychiatric disorders, bipolar disorder was found to have the strongest association with suicide followed by depression, but several other disorders, including PTSD, were also found to have significant associations with completed suicide. The association of PTSD with suicide was not as robust as that of bipolar disorder or depression, but it was nonetheless significant.

Further, in a study that directly targeted OEF/OIF combat veterans, Rudd (in press) explored the relationship between severity of combat exposure, psychological symptoms, and suicide risk using an electronic survey that included measures such as the Combat Exposure Scale (Keane et al., 1989), the PTSD Checklist (military version) (PCL-M; Weathers, Litz, Herman, Huska, & Keane, 1993), and the Suicide Behaviors Questionnaire-Revised (SBQ-R; Osman et al., 2001). He found that those veterans who had heavy combat exposure (compared to all other categories of lesser combat exposure) had greater symptomatology across the board including general anxiety, depression, posttrauma symptoms, sleep disturbance, and suicide risk as assessed by the SBQ-R. Those with heavy combat exposure rated themselves as more likely to attempt suicide in the future than the other groups of combat veterans. Ninety percent of those reporting that a suicide attempt was likely in the future scored above the PCL-M cutoff for a diagnosis of PTSD. In addition, it was found that combat exposure per se did not provide any additional power in predicting suicidality or ratings of the likelihood of future suicide attempts once the variance attributed to post traumatic symptoms was allocated. Rudd (in press) concluded that these results suggest very high rates of posttraumatic symptoms and potential PTSD diagnoses among those with heavy combat experience. Moreover, he reported that a clinical trajectory for suicide risk is readily recognizable for OEF/OIF veterans with heavy combat experience and that posttraumatic symptoms appear to be prominent factors in that trajectory.

Although the weight of the evidence in the studies discussed here may not provide definitive evidence that combat-related PTSD per se is a risk factor for suicide, in sum they have led us to advise caution in regard to potential for suicide with combat veterans with severe PTSD and/or PTSD with comorbid disorders.

There have also been some studies that have been suggestive of potential risk factors for suicidal behavior that is specifically associated with PTSD. Hyer, McCranie, Woods, and Boudewyns (1990), for example, found that Vietnam veterans who reported higher levels of guilt and emotional liability and lower levels of psychological adjustment were most likely to engage in suicidal behavior. Similarly, Hendin and Haas (1991) found increased levels of guilt, depression, and anxiety to be associated with elevated risk of suicide attempts in veterans with PTSD. Both of these studies identified guilt as an important factor in discriminating veterans at risk of suicidal behavior. Hendin and Haas further described the guilt that veterans reported as either related to combat actions (e.g., killing or harming noncombatants) or to surviving when other service members died or were seriously injured. They indicated that most individuals who reported guilt related to combat actions also reported survival guilt and that the combination of the two was most strongly associated with suicidal behavior.

In studies with Vietnam veterans who had chronic PTSD, it has been found that having witnessed or participated in atrocities (e.g., torturing and killing prisoners of war, killing noncombatants, mutilating the bodies of enemies by cutting off ears or putting heads on sticks, and so forth) was associated with heightened levels of PTSD symptom severity, particularly reexperiencing or criterion B symptoms (Beckham, Feldman, & Kirby, 1998; Yehuda, Southwick, & Giller, 1992). Hiley-Young, Blake, Abueg, Rozynko, and Gusman (1995), in a study of Vietnam veterans with PTSD who had engaged in war-zone violence, found that participation in the mutilation of bodies predicted post-military suicide attempts. In still another study with Vietnam veterans, Bell and Nye (2007) assessed combat veterans for suicidal ideation and PTSD. They found that reexperiencing symptoms (criterion B; e.g., nightmares, intrusive thoughts, flashbacks) were significantly associated with suicide ideation while avoidance/numbing symptoms (criterion C) and arousal symptoms (now criterion E in the fifth edition of the *Diagnostic and Statistical Manual of Mental Disorders*) were not.

The studies cited here, of course, do not allow us to conclude that there is a causative link between participating in or witnessing atrocities, guilt, reexperiencing symptoms, and increased risk of suicidality. They do, however, raise questions of such linkage that can only be determined by further research.

PERSONALITY DISORDERS AND ACUTE RISK OF SUICIDE

Duberstein has coauthored two comprehensive reviews of the association of personality disorders and suicide (Duberstein & Conwell, 1997; Duberstein & Witte, 2009). He and his coauthors believe it could be beneficial to identify and intervene with at-risk patients with personality disorders well before they develop comorbid clinical disorders that, in combination with a personality disorder, move them in the direction of a suicidal crisis.

When Duberstein and Conwell (1997) reviewed postmortem (psychological autopsy) studies, they estimated that 30% to 40% of suicides met criteria for a personality disorder. Duberstein and Witte (2009) examined prospective cohort studies of personality disorders and suicide and estimated that 2.56% to 2.60% of personality disorder individuals died by suicide. In both reviews, it was found that people with borderline personality disorder and antisocial personality disorder were at elevated risk of suicide. Duberstein and Witte, based on the findings in postmortem studies, also concluded that those with avoidant personality disorders and schizoid personality disorders definitely had an elevated risk of suicide.

These same investigators have noted that cohort (prospective) studies of suicide have primarily focused on persons with borderline personality disorder. The suicide rate for those with borderline personality disorder was estimated as between 4.21% and 4.80%. Clearly, most individuals with borderline personality disorder (or any personality disorder) do not commit suicide. Although there is a need to try to differentiate those with borderline personality disorder who commit suicide from those who do not, Duberstein and Witte, in the 10 years of their review, could not find a single cohort study that attempted to make that differentiation. They caution, however, that, in regard to suicide risk, there may be reason for researchers and clinicians to focus intervention efforts on the treatment of mood-disordered patients with borderline personality disorder who have had a prior suicide attempt.

Managing Suicide Risk with Veterans
Means Restriction Counseling as a Suicide Risk Management Strategy

For a variety of reasons, veterans are more likely than those in the general population to own firearms or to live in homes in which there are firearms (Centers for Disease Control and Prevention, 2003). The presence of firearms in the home is a significant risk factor for suicide. Over 50% of suicides in the United States are by firearm (McIntosh & Drapeau, 2012), and the likelihood of death when a firearm is the method of choice for suicide has been estimated at 85% to 90% (Miller, Azrael, & Hemenway, 2004). Veterans are more likely to use a firearm for suicide than nonveterans (Kaplan et al., 2007; Miller et al., 2009). In working with a veteran who is suicidal, it is, therefore, important to ask about weapons in the home.

One method for talking with veterans (or nonveterans) about guns has been referred to as *means restriction counseling*. As noted by Bryan, Stone, and Rudd (2011), means restriction counseling is a process in which a clinician educates suicidal patients and supportive friends or family about the risks of having the means of suicide easily available. He or she then works collaboratively with the patient to develop a plan to make the means less available during a time of crisis or emotional instability. As noted by Bryan et al., means restriction has been shown to be effective as a suicide prevention strategy in a large number of studies (see review by Mann et al., 2005).

In means restriction counseling, the clinician might initially raise the issue by noting how the impulse to commit suicide can arise rapidly and at a time when the patient is in a very emotional state (Bryan et al., 2011). It has been found that having such a lethal means as a firearm available at such a time increases the risk of suicide greatly. Restricting access to weapons can reduce the risk of a regrettable, poorly considered decision before efforts to reduce the patient's emotional pain have had a chance to take effect. If the patient agrees with this line of reasoning, it may be possible to suggest the complete removal of all weapons. If that is not acceptable to the patient, however, the clinician can suggest options that limit access not permanently but during the time of crisis or instability. Such options might include dismantling a key component of the firearm(s), storing the firearm(s) in a safe or locker to which someone else holds the combination or key, or removing all ammunition.

Management of the Suicidal Patient on an Outpatient Basis

As noted by Kleespies and Hill (2011), as well as in Chapter 2 of this volume, there is no absolute rule for when a suicidal patient can be managed and treated on an outpatient basis or when one must make an emergency intervention and hospitalize the patient. The clinician needs to be guided by a carefully considered estimate of the level of risk as described earlier, and he or she must be particularly attuned to those risk factors (e.g., firearm ownership as mentioned earlier) that may be of particular risk for the patient.

Clinicians may be inclined to hospitalize patients with suicidal ideation because they feel it is safer and because they have a high index of concern about liability issues. There is little evidence, however, that hospitalization per se ultimately prevents suicide. It may help to reduce immediate risk, but the clinician should bear in mind that the two- to four-month period following hospital discharge is known to be a high-risk period for suicide (See Kleespies & Hill, 2011; Morgan & Stanton, 1997).

Again, as noted in Chapter 2 of this volume, many patients with suicidal ideation can be treated successfully on an outpatient basis, and, as suggested earlier in this chapter, the estimated level of risk is the key in making the decision to manage the patient as an outpatient or to hospitalize. Generally, outpatient management for patients assessed at mild or moderate risk has been found to be feasible and safe (Rudd, Joiner, & Rajab, 2001; Sullivan & Bongar, 2009). An example of a combat veteran at moderate risk might be a young ex-Marine with a few distal risk factors (e.g., chronic, moderate PTSD and chronic guilt about combat actions), several acute, proximal risk factors (e.g., combat-related nightmares, anger-control issues, and episodic suicidal ideation), and some protective factors that are beginning to weaken (e.g., a supportive spouse whose patience is being tried and an employer who is becoming frustrated with the patient about the number of days he has missed work).

For patients at a mild or moderate level of risk who are to be treated on an outpatient basis, Stanley and Brown (2008, 2011) have recommended that their management include a Safety Planning Intervention (SPI). An SPI consists of a prioritized written list of coping strategies and sources of support, developed collaboratively by the clinician and the patient, for use by the patient preceding or during a state of heightened suicidality. Stanley and Brown (2008) have developed a veteran version of the SPI as well as a more generic version for use with any suicidal patient (Stanley & Brown, 2011).

See Chapter 2 of this volume for a more complete description of Stanley and Brown's SPI as well as for a description of contingencies (suggested by Rudd & Joiner, 1998) that the clinician may wish to consider when working with a suicidal outpatient. We recommend that clinicians who work with suicidal veterans utilize the SPI proposed by Stanley and Brown while keeping in mind the contingencies recommended by Rudd and Joiner.

When Is Emergency Intervention Needed?

When, in the clinician's considered judgment, the suicide risk is high, emergency intervention to protect the patient is needed. In many cases, the patient presents in an emotional crisis and the clinician is involved in attempting to achieve a resolution that will enable the patient to continue in outpatient treatment. At times, the clinician and the patient, working collaboratively, can arrive at such a safe resolution. As Comstock (1992) has pointed out, however, hospitalization is indicated when it is not possible to establish or reinstate a treatment alliance, when crisis intervention techniques fail, and when the patient continues to voice suicidal intent in the near future. Although, as noted earlier, there is little evidence that hospitalization prevents suicide in the long run, it does provide a relatively safer environment during a period of heightened suicide risk. Typically, one or two hours with a patient who continues to seem to be at imminent suicide risk are sufficient to convince clinicians to hospitalize.

Most suicidal patients who are engaged with their therapist in an evaluation for heightened suicide risk have some ambivalence about such a final action as suicide and agree to voluntary hospital admission. When such patients refuse to be hospitalized, however, the clinician is faced with a decision about temporary involuntary commitment. In these situations, it is clearly important that the clinician know the law in his or her state or juris-diction that governs such actions. The decision to hospitalize a patient against his or her will can be difficult in itself because we know that the estima-tion of suicide risk is not always reliable, and, in ad-dition, involuntary hospitalization can damage the therapeutic relationship. Many high-risk patients who refuse voluntary hospitalization will none-theless comply with the process of being hospital-ized. Some, however, may physically resist. Under these circumstances, it may ultimately be necessary to have the patient restrained. Should the process of hospitalization require the use of restraints, it should be borne in mind that this type of procedure can be especially difficult for combat veterans who have been traumatized and who may be particularly concerned about being rendered defenseless. The clinical staff involved should remain sensitive to such issues and attempt to use the least restrictive means in trying to work safely with the veteran. In the final analysis, the decision to hospitalize invol-untarily must be based on sound, evidence-based judgment that considers the estimated seriousness of the suicide risk and the risk–benefit ratio of hos-pitalization versus outpatient management. For the clinician, it can be helpful to keep in mind that, once hospitalization has occurred, resistant patients often begin to perceive the caring nature of the cli-nician's actions and reestablish a treatment alliance.

Concluding Remarks

The increased rates of suicide among active-duty service members and certain groups of veterans of the wars in Afghanistan and Iraq have led to an un-precedented increase in support for research on this issue. As noted earlier in this chapter, the results of some large studies (such as the Army STARRS stud-ies) have yet to be reported. These are studies that may shift our thinking about suicide risk, the as-sessment of suicide risk, and approaches to suicide prevention among veterans. In this chapter, we have attempted to reflect the current status of the field in terms of the clinical assessment and management of suicide risk in veterans with the understanding that the field may yet be in a state of flux.

Notes

1. As Friedman (2014) has noted, a precedent for the use of ac-cession waivers occurred during the Vietnam War when the secretary of defense, Robert McNamara, lowered enlistment standards to increase recruitment. Friedman has cited at least one study at an Army hospital in Vietnam indicating that this cohort was referred for psychiatric treatment far more frequently than other troops.

2. It should be noted that Coryell and Young (2005) failed to replicate the study by Fawcett et al. (1990). They suggested that the differences between the studies had to do with the fact that they had fewer early suicides (i.e., fewer suicides in the first year of follow up) in their sample than Fawcett et al.
3. For a more detailed analysis of the review by Krysinska and Lester (2010), see Kleespies, Ahn Allen, and Adler (in press).

References

Barraclough, B., Bunch, J., Nelson, B., & Sainsbury, P. (1974). A hundred cases of suicide: Clinical aspects. *British Journal of Psychiatry, 125*, 355–373.

Beckham, J., Feldman, M., & Kirby, A. (1998). Atrocities ex-posure in Vietnam combat veterans with chronic posttrau-matic stress disorder: Relationship to combat exposure, symptom severity, guilt, and interpersonal violence. *Journal of Traumatic Stress, 11*, 777–785.

Bell, J., & Nye, E. (2007). Specific symptoms predict suicidal ideation in Vietnam combat veterans with chronic post-traumatic stress disorder. *Military Medicine, 172*, 1144–1147.

Blosnich, J., Dichter, M., Cerulli, C., Batten, S., & Bossarte, R. (2014). Disparities in adverse childhood experiences among individuals with a history of military service. *JAMA Psychiatry, 71*(9): 1041–1048. doi:10.1001/jamapsychiatry.2014.724

Blue Ribbon Work Group on Suicide Prevention in the Veteran Population. (2008). *Report to James B. Peake, MD, Secretary of Veterans Affairs.* Unpublished manuscript, Department of Veterans Affairs, Washington, DC.

Borges, G., Walters, E., & Kessler, R. (2000). Associations of sub-stance use, abuse, and dependence with subsequent suicidal behavior. *American Journal of Epidemiology, 151*, 781–789.

Breslin, P., Kang, H., Lee, Y., Burt, V., & Shepard, B. (1988). Proportionate mortality study of US Army and US Marine Corps veterans of the Vietnam War. *Journal of Occupational Medicine, 30*, 412–419.

Bryan, C., Stone, S., & Rudd, M. D. (2011). A practical, evidence-based approach for means-restriction counseling with suicidal patients. *Professional Psychology: Research and Practice, 42*, 339–346.

Bullman, T., & Kang, H. (1994). Posttraumatic stress disorder and the risk of traumatic deaths among Vietnam veterans. *The Journal of Nervous and Mental Disease, 182*, 604–610.

Bullman, T., & Kang, H. (1996). The risk of suicide among wounded Vietnam veterans. *American Journal of Public Health, 86*, 662–667.

Caldwell, C., & Gottesman, I. (1990). Schizophrenics kill them-selves too: A review of risk factors for suicide. *Schizophrenia Bulletin, 16*, 571–589.

Centers for Disease Control. (1987). Postservice mortality among Vietnam veterans: The Centers for Disease Control Vietnam Experience Study. *The Journal of the American Medical Association, 257*, 790–795.

Centers for Disease Control and Prevention. (2003). *Behavioral risk factor surveillance system survey data.* Atlanta, GA: Author.

Centers for Disease Control and Prevention. (2014). *Death rates for suicide, by sex, race, Hispanic origin, and age: United States, selected years 1950–2010.* Atlanta GA: Author.

Clark, D., & Fawcett, J. (1992). Review of empirical risk fac-tors for evaluation of the suicidal patient. In B. Bongar (Ed.): *Suicide: Guidelines for assessment, management, and treatment* (pp. 16–48). New York: Oxford University Press.

Cobb, S. (1976). Social support as a moderator of life stress. *Psychosomatic Medicine, 38*, 300–314.

Cohen, L., Test, M., & Brown, R. (1990). Suicide and schizophrenia: Data from a prospective community study. *American Journal of Psychiatry, 147,* 602–607.

Cohen, S., & Willis, T. A. (1985). Stress, social support, and the buffering hypothesis. *Psychological Bulletin, 98,* 310–357.

Coll, J. E., Weiss, E. L., & Yarvis, J. S. (2011). No one leaves unchanged: Insights for civilian mental health care professionals into the military experience and culture. *Social Work in Health Care, 50,* 487–500.

Conwell, Y., Duberstein, P., Cox, C., Herrmann, J., Forbes, N., & Caine, E. (1996). Relationships of age and Axis I diagnoses in victims of completed suicide: A psychological autopsy study. *American Journal of Psychiatry, 153,* 1001–1008.

Cornelius, J., Salloum, I., Mezzich, J., Cornelius, M., Fabrega, H., Ehler, J., ... Mann, J. (1995). Disproportionate suicidality in patients with comorbid major depression and alcoholism. *American Journal of Psychiatry, 152,* 358–364.

Coryell, W., & Young, E. (2005). Clinical predictors of suicide in primary major depressive disorder. *The Journal of Clinical Psychiatry, 66,* 412–417.

Cvetanovich, B., & Reynolds, L. (2008). Joshua Omvig Veterans Suicide Prevention Act of 2007. *Harvard Journal on Legislation, 45,* 619–640.

Darke, S., & Ross, J. (2002). Suicide among heroin users: Rates, risk factors, and methods. *Addiction, 97,* 1383–1394.

Davenport, M. (1987). Professionals or hired guns? Loyalties are the difference. In M. M. Watkin, K. Wenker, & J. Kempf (Eds.), *Military ethics: Reflections on principles—The profession of arms, military leadership, ethical practices, war and morality, educating the citizen soldier* (pp. 5–12). Washington, D.C.: National Defense University Press.

DeHert, M., & Peuskens, J. (2000). Psychiatric aspects of suicidal behavior: Schizophrenia. In K. Hawton & K. van Heeringen (Eds.), *The international handbook of suicide and attempted suicide* (pp. 121-134). Chichester, UK: John Wiley.

Desai, R., Dausey, D., & Rosenheck, R. (2005). Mental health service delivery and suicide risk: The role of individual patient and facility factors. *The American Journal of Psychiatry, 162,* 311–318.

Drake, R., Gates, C., Whitaker, A., & Cotton, P. (1985). Suicide among schizophrenics: A review. *Comprehensive Psychiatry, 26,* 90–100.

Drapalski, A. L., Milford, J., Goldberg, R. W., Brown, C. H., & Dixon, L. B. (2008). Perceived barriers to medical care and mental health care among veterans with serious mental illness. *Psychiatric Services, 59,* 921–924.

Drescher, K., Rosen, C., Burling, T., & Foy, D. (2003). Causes of death among male veterans who received residential treatment for PTSD. *Journal of Traumatic Stress, 16,* 535–543.

Duberstein, P., & Conwell, Y. (1997). Personality disorders and completed suicide: A methodological and conceptual review. *Clinical Psychology: Science and Practice, 4,* 359–376.

Duberstein, P., Conwell, Y., & Caine, E. (1993). Interpersonal stressors, substance abuse, and suicide. *Journal of Nervous and Mental Disease, 181,* 80–85.

Duberstein, P., & Witte, T. (2009). Suicide risk in personality disorders: An argument for a public health perspective. In P. Kleespies (Ed.), *Behavioral emergencies: An evidence-based resource for evaluating and managing risk of suicide, violence, and victimization* (pp. 257–286). Washington, DC: APA Books.

Elbogen, E. B., Wagner, H. R., Johnson, S. C., Kinneer, P., Kang, H., Vasterling, J. J., ... Beckham, J. C. (2013). Are Iraq and Afghanistan veterans using mental health services? New data from a national random-sample survey. *Psychiatric Services, 64,* 134–141.

Fawcett, J., Scheftner, W., Clark, D., Hedeker, D., Gibbons, R., & Coryell, W. (1987). Clinical predictors of suicide in patients with major affective disorders: A controlled prospective study. *The American Journal of Psychiatry, 144,* 35–40.

Fawcett, J., Scheftner, W., Fogg, L., Clark, D., Young, M., Hedeker, D., & Gibbons, R. (1990). Time-related predictors of suicide in major affective disorder. *The American Journal of Psychiatry, 147,* 1189–1194.

Friedman, M. (2014). Suicide risk among soldiers: Early findings from Army Study to Assess Risk and Resilience in Servicemembers (STARRS). *JAMA Psychiatry 71*(5):487–489. doi:10.1001/jamapsychiatry.2014.24

Friedman, S. A., Phibbs, C. S., Schmitt, S. K., Hayes, P. M., Herrera, L., & Frayne, S. M. (2011). New women veterans in the VA: A longitudinal profile. *Women's Health Issues, 21,* S103–S111.

Garcia, H. A., Finley, E. P., Ketchum, N., Jakupcak, M., Dassori, A., & Reyes, S. C. (2014). A survey of perceived barriers and attitudes toward mental health care among OEF/OIF veterans at VA outpatient mental health clinics. *Military Medicine, 179,* 273–278.

Gegax, T. T., & Thomas, E. (2005). The family business. *Newsweek, 145,* 24–31.

Gibbons, R., Brown, C. H., & Hur, K. (2012). Is the rate of suicide among veterans elevated? *American Journal of Public Health, 102*(Suppl. 1), S17–S19.

Haas, G. (1997). Suicidal behavior in schizophrenia. In R. Maris, M. Silverman, & S. Canetto (Eds.), *Review of Suicidology: 1997* (pp. 202–206). New York: Guilford Press.

Harpaz-Rotem, I., Rosenheck, R. A., Pietrzak, R. H., & Southwick, S. M. (2014). Determinants of prospective engagement in mental health treatment among symptomatic Iraq/Afghanistan veterans. *Journal of Nervous and Mental Disease, 202,* 97–104.

Hearst, N., Newman, T., & Hulley, S. (1986). Delayed effects of the military draft on mortality: A randomized natural experiment. *The New England Journal of Medicine, 314,* 620–624.

Heila, H., Isometsa, E., Henriksson, M., Heikkinen, M., Marttunen, M., & Lonnqvist, J. (1997). Suicide and schizophrenia: A nationwide psychological autopsy study on age- and sex-specific clinical characteristics of 92 suicide victims with schizophrenia. *The American Journal of Psychiatry, 154,* 1235–1242.

Hendin, H. (1986). Suicide: A review of new directions in research. *Hospital and Community Psychiatry, 37,* 148–154.

Hendin, H., & Haas, A. (1991). Suicide and guilt as manifestations of PTSD in Vietnam combat veterans. *The American Journal of Psychiatry, 148,* 586–591.

Hiley-Young, B., Blake, D., Abueg, F., Rozynko, V., & Gusman, F. (1995). Warzone violence in Vietnam: An examination of premilitary, military, and postmilitary factors in PTSD inpatients. *Journal of Traumatic Stress, 8,* 125–141.

Hillard, J. (1995). Predicting suicide. *Psychiatric Services, 46,* 223–225.

Hoge, C. W., Castro, C. A., Messer, S. C., McGurk, D., Cotting, D. L., & Koffman, R. L. (2004). Combat duty in Iraq and

Afghanistan, mental health problems, and barriers to care. *The New England Journal of Medicine, 351*, 13–22.

Hor, K., & Taylor, M. (2010). Suicide and schizophrenia: A systematic review of rates and risk factors. *Journal of Psychopharmacology, 24* (4 Suppl.), 81–90.

Howard, M., Perron, B., Sacco, P., Ilgen, M., Vaughn, M., Garland, E., & Freedentahl, S. (2010). Suicide ideation and attempts among inhalant users: Results from the National Epidemiologic Survey on Alcohol and Related Conditions. *Suicide and Life-Threatening Behavior, 40*, 276–286.

Hsu, J. (September, 2010). *Overview of military culture.* http://www.apa.org/about/gr/issues/military/military-culture.pdf

Hyer, L., McCranie, E., Woods, M., & Boudewyns, P. (1990). Suicidal behavior among chronic Vietnam theatre veterans with PTSD. *Journal of Clinical Psychology, 46*, 713–721.

Ilgen, M., Bohnert, A., Ignacio, R., McCarthy, J., Valenstein, M., Myra Kim, H., & Blow, F. (2010). Psychiatric diagnoses and risk of suicide in veterans. *Archives of General Psychiatry, 67*, 1152–1158.

Ilgen, M., McCarthy, J., Katz, I., Ignacio, R., Bohnert, A., Valenstein, M., & Blow, F. (2012). Psychopathology, Iraq and Afghanistan service, and suicide among Veterans Health Administration patients. *Journal of Consulting and Clinical Psychology, 80*, 323–330.

Inskip, H., Harris, E. C., & Barraclough, B. (1998). Lifetime risk of suicide for affective disorder, alcoholism, and schizophrenia. *British Journal of Psychiatry, 172*, 35–37.

Iverson, A. C., Fear, N. T., Ehler, A., Hacker Hughes, J., Hull, L., Earnshaw, M., . . . Hotopf, M. (2008). Risk factors for post-traumatic stress disorder among UK Armed Forces personnel. *Psychological Medicine, 38*, 511–522.

Jacobson, I., Ryan, M., Hooper, T., Smith, T., Amoroso, P., Boyko, E., || Bell, N. (2008). Alcohol use and alcohol-related problems before and after military combat deployment. *The Journal of the American Medical Association, 300*, 663–675.

Jakupcak, M., Hoerster, K. D., Blais, R. K., Malte, C. A., Hunt, S., & Seal, K. (2013). Readiness for change predicts VA mental healthcare utilization among Iraq and Afghanistan war veterans. *Journal of Traumatic Stress, 26*, 165–168.

Kaplan, M., Huguet, N., McFarland, B., & Newsom, J. (2007). Suicide among male veterans: A prospective population-based study. *Journal of Epidemiology and Community Health, 61*, 619–624.

Kaplan, M., McFarland, B., Huguet, N., & Newsom, J. (2012). Estimating the risk of suicide among U.S. veterans: How should we proceed from here? *American Journal of Public Health, 102* (Suppl. 1), S21 & S23.

Katz, I., McCarthy, J., Ignacio, R., & Kemp, J. (2012). Suicide among veterans in 16 states, 2005 to 2008: Comparisons between utilizers and nonutilizers of Veterans Health Administration (VHA) services based on data from the National Death Index, the National Violent Death Reporting System, and VHA administrative records. *American Journal of Public Health, 102* (Suppl. 1), S105–S110.

Keane, T., Fairbank, J., Caddell, J., Zimering, R., Taylor, K., & Mora, C. (1989). Clinical evaluation of a measure to assess combat exposure. *Psychological Assessment: A Journal of Consulting and Clinical Psychology, 1*, 53–55.

Kelty, R., Kleykamp, M., & Segal, D. R. (2010). The military and the transition to adulthood. *Future of Our Children, 20*, 181–207.

Kessler, R., Heeringa, S., Stein, M., Colpe, L., Fullerton, C., Hwang, I., . . . Ursano, R. (2014). Thirty-day prevalence of DSM-IV mental disorders among nondeployed soldiers in the U.S. Army: Results from the Army Study to Assess Risk and Resilience in Servicemembers (Army STARRS). *JAMA Psychiatry, 71*(5):504–513. doi:10.1001/jamapsychiatry.2014.28

Koenig, C. J., Maguen, S., Monroy, J. D., Mayott, L., & Seal, K. H. (2014). Facilitating culture-centered communication between health care providers and veterans transitioning from military deployment to civilian life. *Patient Education and Counseling, 95*, 414–420.

Klatsky, A., & Armstrong, M. (1993). Alcohol use, other traits, and risk of unnatural death: A prospective study. *Alcoholism: Clinical and Experimental Research, 17*, 1156–1162.

Kleespies, P., AhnAllen, C., & Adler, A. (in press). Suicide risk assessment with combat veterans. In G. Sullivan, L. James, & B. Bongar (Eds.), *The Oxford handbook of suicide in military and veteran populations.* New York: Oxford University Press.

Kleespies, P., & Dettmer, E. (2000). An evidence-based approach to evaluating and managing suicidal emergencies. *Journal of Clinical Psychology, 56*, 1109–1130.

Kleespies, P., & Hill, J. (2011). Behavioral emergencies and crises. In D. Barlow (Ed.), *The Oxford handbook of clinical psychology* (pp. 739–751). New York: Oxford University Press.

Krysinska, K., & Lester, D. (2010). Post-traumatic stress disorder and suicide risk: A systematic review. *Archives of Suicide Research, 14*, 1–23.

Lehavot, K., Der-Martirosian, C., Simpson, T. L., Sadler, A. G., & Washington, D. L. (2013). Barriers to care for women veterans with posttraumatic stress disorder and depressive symptoms. *Psychological Services, 10*, 203–212.

Lincoln, A., Swift, E., & Shorteno-Fraser, M. (2008). Psychological adjustment and treatment of children and families wit parents deployed in military combat. *Journal of Clinical Psychology, 64*, 984–992.

Mann, J., Apter, A., Bertolote, J., Beautrais, A., Currier, D., Haas, A., . . . Hendin, H. (2005). Suicide prevention strategies: A systematic review. *The Journal of the American Medical Association, 294*, 2064–2074.

Maris, R. (1992). The relationship of non-fatal suicide attempts to completed suicides. In R. Maris, A. Berman, J. Maltsberger, & R. Yufit (Eds.), *Assessment and prediction of suicide* (pp. 362–380). New York: Guilford Press.

Marzuk, P., Tardiff, K., Leon, A., Stajic, M., Morgan, E., & Mann, J. (1992). Prevalence of cocaine use among residents of New York City who committed suicide during a one-year period. *The American Journal of Psychiatry, 149*, 371–375.

McCarthy, J., Valenstein, M., Myra Kim, H., Ilgen, M., Zivin, K., & Blow, F. (2009). Suicide mortality among patients receiving care in the Veterans Health Administration Health System. *American Journal of Epidemiology, 169*, 1033–1038.

McIntosh, J., & Drapeau, C. (2012). U.S.A. Suicide 2010: Official final data. Washington, DC: American Association of Suicidology, September 20. http://www.suicidology.org

Miller, M., Azrael, D., & Hemenway, D. (2004). The epidemiology of case fatality rates for suicide in the Northeast. *Annals of Emergency Medicine, 43*, 723–730.

Miller, M., Barber, C., Azrael, D., Calle, E., Lawler, E., & Mukamal, K. (2009). Suicide among US veterans: A prospective study of 500,000 middle-aged and elderly men. *American Journal of Epidemiology, 170*, 494–500.

Miller, M., Barber, C., Young, M., Azrael, D., Mukamel, K., & Lawler, E. (2012). Veterans and suicide: A re-examination of the National Death Index-linked National Health Interview survey. *American Journal of Public Health, 102* (Suppl. 1), S154–S159.

Moore, B. (2011). Understanding and working within military culture. In B. Moore & W. Penk (Eds.), *Treating PTSD in military personnel: A clinical handbook* (pp. 9–22). New York: Guilford Press.

Morgan, H., & Stanton, R. (1997). Suicide among psychiatric inpatients in a changing clinical scene. *British Journal of Psychiatry, 171*, 561–563.

Munroe, J. F. (2012). *Transitioning war zone skills: Information for veterans and those who care.* Unpublished manuscript.

Murphy, G., Armstrong, J., Hermele, S., Fischer, J., & Clendenin, W. (1979). Suicide and alcoholism: Interpersonal loss confirmed as a predictor. *Archives of General Psychiatry, 36*, 65–69.

Murphy, G., & Robins, E. (1967). Social factors in suicide. *The Journal of the American Medical Association, 199*, 81–86.

Meyer, E. (2013). Case report: Military subcultural competency. *Military Medicine, 178*, e848.

Nock, M., Deming, C., Fullerton, C., Gilman, S., Goldenberg, M. Kessler, R, ... Ursano, R. (2013). Suicide among soldiers: A review of psychosocial risk and protective factors. *Psychiatry, 76*, 97–125.

Nock, M., Stein, M., Heeringa, S., Ursano, R., Colpe, L., Fullerton, C., ... Kessler, R. (2014). Prevalence and correlates of suicidal behavior among soldiers: Results from the Army Study to Assess Risk and Resilience in Servicemembers (Army STARRS). *JAMA Psychiatry, 71*(5), 514–522. doi:10.1001/jamapsychiatry.2014.30

Norman, S. B., Schmied, E., & Larson, G. E. (2014). Predictors of continued problem drinking and substance use following military discharge. *Journal of Studies on Alcohol and Drugs, 75*, 557–566.

Oliva, E. M., Trafton, J. A., Harris, A. H. S., & Gordon, A. J. (2013). Trends in opioid agonist therapy in the Veterans Health Administration: Is supply keeping up with demand? *The American Journal of Drug and Alcohol Abuse, 39*, 103–107.

Oquendo, M., Bongiovi-Garcia, M., Galfalvy, H., Goldberg, P., Grunebaum, M., Burke, A., & Mann, J. J. (2007). Sex differences in clinical predictors of suicidal acts after major depression: A prospective study. *The American Journal of Psychiatry, 164*, 134–141.

Oquendo, M., Galfalvy, H., Russo, S., Ellis, S., Grunebaum, M., Burke, A., & Mann, J. J. (2004). Prospective study of clinical predictors of suicidal acts after a major depressive episode in patients with major depressive disorder or bipolar disorder. *The American Journal of Psychiatry, 161*, 1433–1441.

Osman, A., Bagge, C., Gutierrez, P., Konick, L., Kopper, B., & Barrios, F. (2001). The Suicidal Behaviors Questionnaire—Revised (SBQ-R): Validation with clinical and nonclinical samples. *Assessment, 8*, 443–454.

Panagioti, M., Gooding, P., & Tarrier, N. (2009). Post-traumatic stress disorder and suicidal behavior: A narrative review. *Clinical Psychology Review, 29*, 471–482.

Peuskens, J., DeHert, M., Cosyns, P., Pieters, G, Theys, P., & Vermote, R. (1997). Suicide in young schizophrenic patients during and after inpatient treatment. *International Journal of Mental Health, 25*, 39–44.

Pfeiffer, P., Ganoczy, D., Ilgen, M., Zivin, K., & Valenstein, M. (2009). Comorbid anxiety as a suicide risk factor among depressed veterans. *Depression and Anxiety, 26*, 752–757.

Pietrzak, R. H., Johnson, D. C., Goldstein, M. B., Malley, J. C., & Southwick, S. M. (2009). Perceived stigma and barriers to mental health care utilization among OEF-OIF veterans. *Psychiatric Services, 60*, 1118–1122.

Pokorny, A. (1983). Prediction of suicide in psychiatric patients: Report of a prospective study. *Archives of General Psychiatry, 40*, 249–257.

Pompili, M., Serafini, G., Innamorati, M., Dominici, G., Ferracuti, S., Kotzalidis, G., ... & Lester, D. (2010). Suicidal behavior and alcohol abuse. *International Journal of Environmental Research and Public Health, 7*, 1392–1431.

Porsteinsson, A., Duberstein, P., Conwell, Y., Cox, C., Forbes, N., & Caine, E. (1997). Suicide and alcoholism: Distinguishing alcoholic patients with and without comorbid drug use. *The American Journal of Addictions, 6*, 304–310.

Pryce, J. G., Pryce, D. H. & Shackelford, K. K. (2012). *The costs of courage: Combat stress, warriors and family survival.* Chicago: Lyceum Books.

Ran, M., Xiang, M., Mao, W., Hou, Z., Tang, M., Chen, E. Y., ... Conwell, Y. (2005). Characteristics of suicide attempters and nonattempters with schizophrenia in a rural community. *Suicide and Life-Threatening Behavior, 35*, 694–701.

RAND Corporation. (1993). *Sexual orientation and U.S. military personnel policy: Options and assessment.* Santa Monica, CA: Author.

Rich, C., Fowler, R., Fogarty, L., & Young, D. (1988). San Diego Suicide Study: III. Relationships between diagnoses and stressors. *Archives of General Psychiatry, 45*, 589–592.

Rich, C., Fowler, R., & Young, D. (1989). Substance abuse and suicide: The San Diego Study. *Annals of Clinical Psychiatry, 1*, 79–85.

Rich, C., Young, D., & Fowler, R. (1986). San Diego suicide study: I. Young vs. old subjects. *Archives of General Psychiatry, 43*, 577–582.

Rudd, M. D. (in press). Severity of combat exposure, psychological symptoms, social support, and suicide risk in OEF/OIF veterans. *Journal of Consulting and Clinical Psychology.*

Rudd, M. D., & Joiner, T. (1998). The assessment, management, and treatment of suicidality: Toward clinically informed and balanced standards of care. *Clinical Psychology: Science and Practice, 5*, 135–150.

Rudd, M. D., Joiner, T., & Rajab, M. H. (2001). *Treating suicidal behavior: An effective, time-limited approach.* New York: Guilford Press.

Runnals, J. J., Garovoy, N., McCutcheon, S. J., Robbins, A. T., Mann-Wrobel, M. C., Elliott, A., ... Strauss, J. L. (2014). Systematic review of women veterans' mental health. *Women's Health Issues, 24*(5), 485–502.

Schoenbaum, M., Kessler, R., Gilman, S., Colpe, L., Heeringa, S., Stein, M., ... and Cox, K. (2014). Predictors of suicide and accident death in the Army Study to Assess Risk and Resilience in Servicemembers (Army STARRS): Results from the Army Study to Assess Risk and Resilience in Servicemembers (Army STARRS). *JAMA Psychiatry, 71*(5), 493–503. doi:10.1001/jamapsychiatry.2013.4417

Shaffer, D., Gould, M., Fisher, P., Trautman, M., Moreau, D., Kleinman, M., & Flory, M. (1996). Psychiatric diagnosis in child and adolescent suicide. *Archives of General Psychiatry, 53*, 339–348.

Sloan, L. B., & Friedman, M. J. (2008). *After the war zone: A practical guide for returning veterans.* Philadelphia, PA: De Capo Press.

Stanley, B., & Brown, G. (2008). *Safety plan treatment manual to reduce suicide risk: Veteran version.* Washington, DC: US Department of Veterans Affairs.

Stanley, B., & Brown, G. (2011). Safety planning intervention: A brief intervention to mitigate suicide risk. *Cognitive and Behavioral Practice, 19*(2), 256–264. doi:10.1016/j.cbpra.2011.01.001

Sullivan, G., & Bongar, B. (2009). Assessing suicide risk in the adult patient. In P. Kleespies (Ed.): *Behavioral emergencies: An evidence-based resource for evaluating and managing risk of suicide, violence, and victimization* (pp. 59–78). Washington, DC: APA Books.

Tanney, B. (1992). Mental disorders, psychiatric patients, and suicide. In R. Maris, A. Berman, J. Maltsberger, & R. Yufit (Eds.), *Assessment and prediction of suicide* (pp. 277–320). New York: Guilford Press.

Tidemalm, D., Langstrom, N., Lichtenstein, P., & Runeson, B. (2008). Risk of suicide after suicide attempt according to co-existing psychiatric disorder: Swedish cohort study with long term follow up. *British Medical Journal, 337*, a2205. doi:10.1136/bmi.a2205

US Department of Defense, Task Force on the Prevention of Suicide by Members of the Armed Forces. (2010). *The challenge and the promise: Strengthening the force, preventing suicide, and saving lives: Final report of the Department of Defense task force on the prevention of suicide by members of the armed forces.* Washington, DC: Author.

Vasterling, J. J., Daly, E. S., & Friedman, M. J. (2011). Posttraumatic stress reactions over time: The battlefield, homecoming, and long-term course. In J. I. Ruzek, P. P. Schnurr, J. J. Vasterling, & M. J. Friedman (Eds.), *Caring for veterans with deployment-related stress disorders: Iraq, Afghanistan and beyond*

(pp. 35–55). Washington, DC: American Psychological Association.

Vogt, D. (2011). Mental health-related beliefs as a barrier to service use for military personnel and veterans: A review. *Psychiatric Services, 62*, 135–142.

Washington, D. L., Bean-Mayberry, B., Riopelle, D., & Yano, E. M. (2011). Access to care for women veterans: Delayed healthcare and ummet needs. *Journal of General Internal Medicine, 26*, 655–661.

Weathers, F., Litz, B., Herman, D., Huska, J., & Keane, T. (1993, October). *The PTSD Checklist (PCL): Reliability, validity, and diagnostic utility.* Paper presented at the Annual Meeting of the International Society for Traumatic Stress Studies, San Antonio, TX.

Weiden, P., & Roy, A. (1992). General versus specific risk factors for suicide in schizophrenia. In D. Jacobs (Ed.), *Suicide and clinical practice* (pp. 75–100). Washington, DC: American Psychiatric Press.

Westermeyer, J., Harrow, M., & Marengo, J. (1991). Risk for suicide in schizophrenia and other psychotic and nonpsychotic disorders. *The Journal of Nervous and Mental Disease, 179*, 259–266.

Westwood, M. J., Black, T. G., & McLean, H. B. (2002). A re-entry program for peacekeeping soldiers: Promoting personal and career transition. *Canadian Journal of Counseling, 36*, 221–232.

Wilcox, H., Conner, K., & Caine, E. (2004). Association of alcohol and drug use disorders and completed suicide: An empirical review of cohort studies. *Drug and Alcohol Dependence, 76*(Suppl.), S11–S19.

Yehuda, R., Southwick, S., & Giller, E., Jr.(1992). Exposure to atrocities and severity of chronic posttraumatic stress disorder in Vietnam combat veterans. *The American Journal of Psychiatry, 149*, 333–336.

Zivin, K., Kim, M., McCarthy, J., Austin, K., Hoggatt, K., Walters, H., & Valenstein, M. (2007). Suicide mortality among individuals receiving treatment for depression in the Veterans Affairs Health System: Associations with patient and treatment setting characteristics. *American Journal of Public Health, 97*(12), 2193–2198.

Assessing Acute Risk of Violence in Military Veterans

Eric B. Elbogen *and* Robert Graziano

Abstract

Research has shown aggression toward others is a problem in a subset of military veterans. Evaluating this kind of aggression would be helpful in clinical settings. To our knowledge, there currently are no risk assessment tools or screens that have been validated to specifically evaluate acute violence among veterans. This chapter reviews what we do and do not know about violence in veterans so that clinicians who are making decisions about acute violence can be informed by the existing scientific knowledge base. Examining these empirically supported risk and protective factors using a systematic approach may optimize clinical decision making when assessing acute violence in veterans.

Key Words: veterans, violence, aggression, posttraumatic stress disorder, combat exposure

Although a subset of military veterans has been shown to have difficulties with violent or aggressive behavior toward others, there is relatively little research available on risk assessment for acute violence in veteran populations. To our knowledge, there are no risk assessment tools or screens that have been validated to evaluate acute violence among veterans in crisis in emergency rooms or inpatient/outpatient mental health treatment settings. For these reasons, health professionals have relatively little guidance from empirical studies on how to optimally assess for acute violence risk in veterans in these clinical contexts.

Despite this, we can draw from a number of studies that have identified risk and protective factors related to aggression and violence in veteran populations. This chapter reviews what we do and do not currently know about violence in veterans so that decision making about acute violence can, at the very least, be informed by existing empirical knowledge.

We will first examine the characteristics related to aggression in military veterans, dividing the review into static (unchanging) and dynamic (malleable)

risk factors—the former useful for gauging the level of risk and the latter for targeting interventions to reduce risk. Careful examination of the literature reveals that most risk factors related to violence in veterans are similar to those found in civilian populations, which has important implications for assessment of acute risk.

We will also examine to what extent military-specific characteristics relate to community violence in veterans. Overall, the research finds mixed evidence of a direct link between combat exposure and violence. While it does indicate a consistent, though intricate, link between posttraumatic stress disorder (PTSD) and violence, the majority of veterans with PTSD do not report problems with violence; the relationship between PTSD and violence is complicated by co-occurring conditions (e.g., alcohol abuse) and specific symptoms (e.g., anger) that are difficult to disentangle from the diagnosis.

Most research has examined factors related to increased violence in veterans, but a few studies have begun to explore protective factors associated with reduced violence. This could assist clinicians in developing risk management plans—particularly relevant for veterans assessed as being at higher risk. Moreover, recent research has offered structured decision-making tools to improve the screening of longer-term violence in veterans, which might be of use in a variety of clinical settings. We will conclude by describing how the use of a systematic method for combining risk and protective factors may help optimize clinical decision making when assessing acute violence in veterans.

Static Risk Factors for Violence in Veteran Populations

As in the general population, research indicates that *younger age* is related to higher incidence of aggression (Beckham, Feldman, & Kirby, 1998; Elbogen, Johnson, Wagner, et al., 2014; Ganzini, Edwards, Surkan, & Drummond, 1995; Jakupcak et al., 2007; Renshaw & Kiddie, 2012; Taft, Kaloupek, et al., 2007) and to intimate partner violence (Fonseca et al., 2006; Forgey & Badger, 2006; McCarroll et al., 1999; McCarroll et al., 2000; McCarroll et al., 2003; Petrik, Rosenberg, & Watson, 1983; Rumm, Cummings, Krauss, Bell, & Rivara, 2000) in Vietnam-era veterans, as well as in Iraq and Afghanistan vets. Of note, age may have an effect on aggression through PTSD hyperarousal symptoms, which were found in one study to be more prominent in younger veterans (Taft, Kaloupek, et al., 2007). *Lower educational attainment* has also been related to aggressive behavior in veterans (Begic & Jokic-Begic, 2001).

Personality traits have been examined—in particular, the *trait of anger* has been linked to aggression in veterans with PTSD (Taft, Street, Marshall, Dowdall, & Riggs, 2007). Further, as with civilians, a personality disorder elevates the risk of violence in veterans, including borderline (Windle & Windle, 1995), narcissistic (Rothschild, Dimson, Storaasli, & Clapp, 1997), and antisocial (Taft et al., 2005) personality disorders.

A *history of violence* has been linked to future violence in veterans. Perpetrating violent behavior before deployment has been shown to increase the likelihood of perpetrating violence after deployment (Begic & Jokic-Begic, 2001; Elbogen, Johnson, Wagner, et al., 2014; Hartl, Rosen, Drescher, Lee, & Gusman, 2005; Yesavage, 1984). Parallel findings have shown that domestic violence prior to military deployment portends future domestic violence military service members (McCarroll et al., 2003; White, Merrill, & Koss, 2001). A *history of criminal arrest* also predicts domestic (Gondolf & Foster, 1991) and community violence (Elbogen, Johnson,

Wagner, et al., 2014) in veterans, as well. *Childhood antisocial behavior* has been found to relate to intimate partner violence among veterans who had combat exposure or who perceived a fear of safety in the war zone and had associated PTSD symptoms (Orcutt, King, & King, 2003).

A *history of childhood abuse* (Begic & Jokic-Begic, 2001) is another risk factor for aggression in veterans. Physical abuse, maltreatment, or neglect as a child has been linked to adult perpetration of intimate partner violence in military service members (Merrill, Hervig, & Milner, 1996; Rosen, Kaminski, Parmley, Knudson, & Fancher, 2003; Wasileski, Callaghan-Chaffee, & Chaffee, 1982; Zoricic, Buljan, Thaller, & Karlovic, 2003; Zoricic, Karlovic, Buljan, & Marusic, 2003), with only one study of veterans having contrasting findings (Taft et al., 2005). *Witnessing parental violence* as a child has been shown to be correlated with aggression in veterans from different eras of service (Elbogen, Beckham, Butterfield, Swartz, & Swanson, 2008; Taft et al., 2005) and *exposure to violence* (Chapin, 1999) or to violent death (Pardeck & Nolden, 1983) before enlisting in the military has been related to higher incidence of post-military violent behavior among veterans and military service members. Experiencing *post-military traumatic events* has also been shown to be associated with aggression (Lenhardt, Howard, Taft, Kaloupek, & Keane, 2012).

Dynamic Risk Factors for Violence in Veteran Populations

Several clinical risk factors have been found to relate to aggression in veterans as they have in civilians. *Substance abuse* is associated with violent and aggressive behavior in veterans (Elbogen et al., 2012; Ganzini et al., 1995; Jakupcak et al., 2007; Lehmann, McCormick, & Kizer, 1999; Moss, 1989; Owens et al., 2014; Pasternack, 1971; Windle & Windle, 1995). *Alcohol problems* (Fonseca et al., 2006; Hurlbert, Whittaker, & Munoz, 1991; Gallaway, Fink, Millikan, & Bell, 2012; Merrill, Crouch, Thomsen, & Guimond, 2004; Merrill et al., 1996; Rosen et al., 2003; Shin, Rosen, Greenbaum, & Jain, 2012; Wright, Foran, Wood, Eckford, & McGurk, 2012), particularly higher quantity drinking (Savarese, Suvak, King, & King, 2001), relate to aggression in veterans. *Drug abuse* also has been related to criminal behavior, intimate partner violence, and sexual aggression in veterans and military service members from different eras of service (Millikan et al., 2012; Taft et al., 2005; Weaver, Trafton, Kimerling, Timko, & Moos, 2013).

Other psychiatric symptoms and diagnoses have been associated with violence in veterans particularly *depression* (Hartl et al., 2005; Taft, Vogt, Marshall, Panuzio, & Niles, 2007; Windle & Windle, 1995; Wright et al., 2012). Both depressive symptoms and major depressive episodes among veterans (Sherman, Sautter, Jackson, Lyons, & Han, 2006; Taft et al., 2005; Teten, Sherman, & Han, 2009) seem to be particularly related to episodes of violence and may also exacerbate the relationship between PTSD and physical aggression (O'Donnell, Cook, Thompson, Riley, & Neria, 2006).

Several studies examine the role of affect, anger, and emotion in perpetration of violence in veterans. *State anger* has been related to violence in a number of studies (Finley, Baker, Pugh, & Peterson, 2010; Hellmuth, Stappenbeck, Hoerster, & Jakupcak, 2012; Renshaw & Kiddie, 2012). *Difficulties regulating affect* related to intimate partner violence (Merrill et al., 2004) and high levels of experiential avoidance (attempts to avoid unwanted emotions) have been linked to higher levels of physical aggression (Reddy, Meis, Erbes, Polusny, & Compton, 2011). In one study, veterans who had been impulsively aggressive demonstrated *alexithymia*, or difficulty understanding others' emotions, through both language and emotion (Teten, Miller, Bailey, Dunn, & Kent, 2008).

Research on the connection between *traumatic brain injury* and violence in veterans is limited. Two studies have shown higher levels of violence among veterans with traumatic brain injury (Elbogen et al., 2008; Grafman et al., 1996), whereas some research suggests the relationship between the two might be indirect and weak (Elbogen, Wagner, et al., 2010; Taft et al., 2012).

There have been some studies examining situational risk factors in veteran populations. Financial status contributes to violence in several ways. *Lower income* relates to interpersonal violence (Beckham, Feldman, Kirby, Hertzberg, & Moore, 1997) and aggression (Begic & Jokic-Begic, 2001) in military veterans. *Living instability* and *homelessness* have been shown to be statistically associated with violence in veterans in two separate datasets (Elbogen et al., 2012; Elbogen et al., 2008). *Unemployment* increases the odds of family violence (McCarroll et al., 2003) and of community violence (Elbogen et al., 2012) in veterans and service members. For example, there is increased risk for couples in which both partners are violent and the husband is unemployed

(Forgey & Badger, 2006). Another study has shown that female service members are more likely to inflict violence on their civilian husbands if their husbands are unemployed (McCarroll et al., 2003). *Poor social environment* as a whole—including work conflicts, perceptions of stigma, barriers to care and to organizational support—has been related to an increase in overall aggression in veterans of Iraq and Afghanistan (Wright et al., 2012).

As a result, it is not surprising that *poor marital adjustment* (Byrne & Riggs, 1996; Rosen et al., 2003; Taft et al., 2005) is also a predictor of domestic violence in veterans and service members. One study has shown that females in a relationship are much more likely to perpetrate physical violence if their male partner is also physically violent (Dutra, de Blank, Scheiderer, & Taft, 2012), while another suggests that many men who perpetrate aggression may be in a mutually violent relationship (Teten et al., 2010). Being a *current victim of family violence* relates to perpetration of violence and aggression in several studies of veterans and military service members (Forgey & Badger, 2006; Jordan & et al., 1992; Merrill et al., 1996; Teten et al., 2009; White et al., 2001).

Combat Exposure, PTSD, and Violence in Veterans

As already illustrated, a wide array of static and dynamic factors that are not unique to military experience relate to the risk of violence in military and veteran populations. What role, if any, do military-specific factors play? Although there are studies that have shown *combat exposure* to be related to veteran violence, there are others that have not. Some studies find that combat exposure has been linked to an increased risk of violence among veterans of different combat arenas (Beckham et al., 1998; Beckham et al., 1997; Elbogen et al., 2012; Gallaway et al., 2012; Lenhardt et al., 2012; MacManus et al., 2012; Stappenbeck, Hellmuth, Simpson, & Jakupcak, 2013; Yesavage, 1983). Others studies have found that combat exposure itself does not predict violent behavior post-deployment (Hiley-Young, Blake, Abueg, & Rozynko, 1995; Jakupcak et al., 2007) or that combat exposure is related to violence but only in the presence of PTSD (Taft, Kaloupek, et al., 2007; Taft, Vogt, et al., 2007).

In studies examining this phenomenon in more detail, specific experiences in the theater of combat have been shown to predict post-deployment violence. These include events that "left a strong impact" on the veteran, events in which the veteran felt that he or she had suffered psychological distress (Yesavage, 1983)—for example, being exposed to a high frequency of violent combat, surviving a close call, witnessing high levels of human trauma (Killgore et al., 2008), killing someone or seeing killings (Killgore et al., 2008; Van Winkle & Safer, 2011; Yesavage, 1983), and engaging in war zone violence (Hiley-Young et al., 1995). Overt aggressive physical violence has also been predicted by the intensity of the combat in veterans of Iraq and Afghanistan—the more intense the combat, the more aggressive the behavior (Gallaway et al., 2012).

Combat experience has been related to an increased incidence of antisocial behavior, such as intimate partner violence, particularly when veterans are diagnosed with PTSD (Gimbel & Booth, 1994). Other studies suggest that exposure to atrocities (Taft et al., 2005) and perceived threat during war service (Orcutt et al., 2003), rather than general combat exposure, are the variables that relate to post-deployment violence. Still, two studies found no significant difference in perpetration of domestic violence between veterans with and without combat experience (Bradley, 2007; Petrik et al., 1983), though it should be noted that these articles did not delve into details surrounding the veterans' combat experience. In one study of former prisoners of war, the severity of trauma during captivity predicted physical aggression against romantic partners later when returned to the community (O'Donnell et al., 2006).

Taken together, the data do not conclusively show that the mere presence or absence of combat exposure is enough to place a veteran at higher risk of violence. Rather, specific aspects of the combat experience appear to be relevant. In contrasts, research has shown more consistently that *PTSD* does link to a higher incidence of violence and aggressive behavior in veterans and military service members (Beckham et al., 1998; Begic & Jokic-Begic, 2001; Calhoun et al., 2002; Carlson, Lauderdale, Hawkins, & Sheikh, 2008; Elbogen et al., 2008; Freeman & Roca, 2001; Hartl et al., 2005; Jakupcak et al., 2007; Kulka et al., 1990; Lasko, Gurvits, Kuhne, Orr, & Pitman, 1994; McFall, Fontana, Raskind, & Rosenheck, 1999; Renshaw & Kiddie, 2012; Silver & Iacono, 1984; Taft, Vogt, et al., 2007; Teten et al., 2010; Zatzick et al., 1997). Further, more severe PTSD symptoms are related to a higher frequency of violent behavior in veterans of Vietnam, Iraq, and Afghanistan (Orcutt et al., 2003; Shin et al., 2012; Stappenbeck et al., 2013).

Despite this research, understanding the link between PTSD and violence is challenging for a number of reasons. First, there have been only a few large scale studies to explicitly compare the prevalence of violent behavior, and each of the efforts arguably had at least some methodological limitations. In one landmark study on the topic, a large national cohort sample of United Kingdom military personnel linked clinical data to criminal records (MacManus et al., 2013). Among those meeting criteria for PTSD, 7.2% had been criminally arrested for violent offenses, whereas among those *not* meeting criteria for PTSD, 3% had been criminally arrested for violent offenses. However, only a small proportion of violent behavior results in criminal arrest, so although this association between PTSD and violent crime was found, a specific number determining the prevalence of violence itself is not clearly determined.

In the United States, the National Vietnam Veterans Readjustment Study (NVVRS) reported that 33% of male Vietnam veterans with PTSD endorsed intimate partner violence (IPV) during the previous year whereas only 13.5% without PTSD endorsed intimate partner violence (IPV) during the previous year (Kulka et al., 1990). The NVVRS surveyed a representative sample of Vietnam veterans; however, these reports are based upon a somewhat broad measure of IPV, the definition of which ranges from threatening to throw something to sexual and physical assault. Also, because of the cross-sectional design, interpreting the numbers is limited as it is unknown if participants had PTSD at the time of violence (i.e., the study asked about current PTSD symptoms and past violence).

A national longitudinal survey of a random sample of post-9/11 veterans in the United States found that approximately 20% of veterans with PTSD and 6.4% without PTSD reported severe violence in the a one-year time frame (Elbogen, Johnson, Wagner, et al., 2014). Whether these results generalize to other cohorts of veterans is unknown; in particular, the survey had a 56% corrected response rate so it was not perfectly representative of military veterans. This study also utilized a self-report measure, which is known to have led to inaccuracy.

Despite these limitations, this research does suggest at least two things about the link between PTSD and violence in veterans: (1) veterans with PTSD have a higher prevalence of violence than those without PTSD; and (2) the majority of veterans with PTSD were not found to be violent.

There is another complicating factor in understanding the link between PTSD and violence: PTSD is correlated with several risk factors known to increase the potential for violence. *Co-occurring alcohol misuse and PTSD* has been shown in a number of studies to be associated with a marked increase in violence in veterans of Iraq and Afghanistan (Elbogen, Johnson, Wagner, et al., 2014; Gallaway et al., 2012; McCauley, Killeen, Gros, Brady, & Back, 2012; Stappenbeck et al., 2013). To illustrate, in the Elbogen, Johnson, et al. (2014) study, it was found that "veterans with both PTSD and alcohol misuse had a substantially higher rate of subsequent severe violence (35.9%) compared with veterans with alcohol misuse without PTSD (10.6%), PTSD without alcohol misuse (10.0%), or neither PTSD nor alcohol misuse (5.3%)." Of note, two-thirds of those meeting the criteria for PTSD did not meet criteria for misusing alcohol; thus, the majority of veterans with PTSD fell into the lower risk group.

Thus, the link between PTSD and violence among veterans may be due to its association with alcohol abuse, as well as other risk factors listed in previous sections of this chapter, including depression (O'Donnell et al., 2006; Taft et al., 2005), lack of communication (Carroll, Rueger, Foy, & Donahoe, 1985), poor marital adjustment, high levels of exposure to atrocities (Taft et al., 2005), heightened anger reactivity (Renshaw & Kiddie, 2012; Taft, Street, et al., 2007), and shame (Hundt & Holohan, 2012). Other research has highlighted even more nuances in the relationship between PTSD and violence in veterans, which may be less pronounced among older veterans (Ganzini et al., 1995). One study revealed that co-occurring PTSD and psychotic symptoms correlated with increased violent thoughts and behavior (Sautter et al., 1999).

Finally, research suggests that *specific symptoms of PTSD*, rather than a PTSD diagnosis, increase the risk of violence in veterans. Perhaps the most consistent finding is that hyperarousal/physiological arousal portend higher risk of aggression and problems with violence in veterans (Elbogen, Wagner, et al., 2010; McFall et al., 1999; Taft, Kaloupek, et al., 2007). Avoidance/numbing symptoms of PTSD have been shown to predict violence in some research with Vietnam veterans (McFall et al., 1999), but not all (Taft, Kaloupek, et al., 2007). More recent studies of Iraq and Afghanistan veterans show both hyperarousal and numbing symptoms to be related to an increase in aggression through trait anger (Hellmuth et al., 2012;

Makin-Byrd, Bonn-Miller, Drescher, & Timko, 2012). Reexperiencing symptoms have also been connected to an increase in violence in veterans of Iraq and Afghanistan (Hellmuth et al., 2012; Makin-Byrd et al., 2012). One study examining types of violence found that flashbacks predicted future aggression toward strangers whereas PTSD anger symptoms predicted aggression toward family members (Sullivan & Elbogen, 2013). Additionally, rumination has been found as a mediator between PTSD and risky behaviors in general (Borders, McAndrew, Quigley, & Chandler, 2012).

Taken together, this research shows that although most veterans with PTSD are not severely violent, PTSD is associated with higher risk, meaning that a veteran with PTSD has statistically higher odds of violent behavior compared to a veteran without PTSD. At the same time, the research reveals that this link between PTSD and violence is not straightforward. Much of the link can be attributed to the co-occurrence of PTSD with other risk factors, like alcohol abuse, and because of specific PTSD symptoms, like anger, rather than just the diagnosis of PTSD.

Enhancing Protective Factors

A few studies have begun to explore possible protective factors for violence in military veterans. A cross-sectional study of veterans found protective effects in stable living, working, and social environments (Elbogen et al., 2012) consistent with research on violence risk among civilians, which has shown that situational factors that increase stress and vulnerability are significantly linked to violence (Silver & Teasdale, 2005; Steadman, 1982; Swanson et al., 2002; Ullrich & Coid, 2011). Specifically, researchers demonstrated that lower violence was associated with a veteran's overall psychosocial health, defined as his or her level of *socioeconomic functioning* (e.g., living, work, and financial stability) and *psychosocial well-being* (e.g., social support, spirituality, and resilience). This finding was maintained even after statistically controlling for robust risk factors for violence. In multivariate analyses, veterans with high scores on measures of psychosocial health were substantially less likely to report violence and aggression compared to veterans with low scores.

It is important to note that many of these protective factors (e.g., living stability, employment, social support, self-direction, basic needs) may not be present when service members separate from the military and transition to civilian life. As such, if a veteran is assessed as high risk, helping them find employment, maintain stable living, manage finances, strengthen resilience, and build a social support network may reduce the risk of violence in the community. From the perspective of psychosocial rehabilitation, management of violence risk may thus include efforts to address issues such as homelessness, retraining veterans for civilian work, improving financial literacy, and improving social support (Cattelani, Zettin, & Zoccolotti, 2010; Goldberg & Resnick, 2010; LePage et al., 2006; Manderscheid, 2007; Martz, Bodner, & Livneh, 2009; Penk et al., 2010; Schutt et al., 2003).

The finding that greater *perceived self-determination* was related to lower odds of violence was noteworthy from a clinical perspective. One could hypothesize that veterans who perceive that they have greater control over their future and who have higher psychological resilience would have greater internal motivation to refrain from violence and acting on aggressive impulses. This finding is relevant to assessing for acute violence, as scholarship has long advocated for greater client participation in the process of violence risk assessment (Douglas & Skeem, 2005; Elbogen, Van Dorn, Swanson, Swartz, & Monahan, 2006; Heilbrun, 1997). Engaging veterans in the risk assessment process as well as in developing a collaborative safety plan may be an important consideration for clinicians evaluating acute violence.

A recent longitudinal study found psychosocial as well as physical protective factors were associated with decreased violence in veterans (Elbogen, Johnson, Newton, et al., 2014). Specifically, the study found that protective factors in the following domains predicted decreased aggression and violence one year later: *socioeconomic* (money to cover basic needs, stable employment), *psychosocial* (resilience, perceiving control over one's life, social support), and *physical* (healthy sleep, no physical pain). This association held especially among veterans at higher risk of violence. This study suggests that rehabilitation aimed at improving socioeconomic, psychosocial, and physical well-being has the potential to reduce aggression and violence among veterans after returning home from military service.

These findings support the notion that management of medical and physical symptoms may be integrally related to risk reduction in veterans. Veterans with poor physical health, inadequate sleep, and chronic pain may be likely to experience more physiological stress and increased levels of anger and irritability. As a result, clinical consideration of comorbid medical and psychiatric symptoms should be made when assessing violence in veterans, and physical rehabilitation or medical intervention could also help reduce violence risk.

Structuring Assessment of Acute Violence Risk in Veterans

Certainly, it is important for clinicians assessing risk of acute violence in veterans to be aware of this research on risk and protective factors. At the same time, it is also important to recognize the empirical literature has study limitations. Many studies described here enrolled male-only samples of veterans from different eras of military service, whereas women veterans comprise an increasing proportion of the military. Studies also vary in how they measure violence (e.g., some include verbal aggression; few examine acute violence), which needs to be considered when interpreting results. Finally, the majority of studies are retrospective, and only a few are longitudinal, restricting causal interpretation of the link between risk factors and violence.

Keeping these limitations in mind, research still recommends that clinicians consider empirically supported variables in their risk assessments. This is, in large part, because clinical judgments of whether an individual will be violent have been found to be only modestly better than chance (Monahan, 2001; Mossman, 1994) in both civilian and veteran samples (Elbogen, Fuller, et al., 2010). How clinicians frame the task of violence risk assessment determines which risk factors are used and which are most heavily weighted in decision making (Grisso & Tomkins, 1996; Heilbrun, 1997); and there are different types of decision-making errors (Tversky & Kahneman, 1981) for which clinicians are vulnerable when assessing violence in veterans. For example, clinicians may make a "fundamental attribution error" (Ross, 1977) by focusing on an individual's characteristics rather than on how the person's environment and situation (e.g., living in a neighborhood with a high rate of violence) influences the risk of engaging in violent behavior. Other biases have been hypothesized, including focusing too heavily on readily accessible, highly salient, or unusual characteristics of the case, which may not be related or even inversely related to violent behavior (Quinsey, 1995). Empirical research has found clinicians conducting violence risk assessments often rely on readily observed variables with little empirical basis and they underrate the relevance of environmental and situational risk and protective factors factors (Douglas & Ogloff, 2003; Elbogen, 2002; Elbogen, Huss, Tomkins, & Scalora, 2005; Elbogen, Mercado, Scalora, & Tomkins, 2002).

To improve clinical decision-making accuracy and reliability in the context of violence risk assessment, it is generally accepted that clinicians need to make their decision making more structured and systematic by using screening tools, decision-aides or checklists, and risk assessment instruments (Skeem & Monahan, 2011). This way, clinicians can ensure that all critical information is gathered in clinical practice (Elbogen, Fuller, et al., 2010; Gawande, 2009). At the same time, it is important that data not only be examined in a systematic way, but also that the risk and protective factors examined actually have at least some empirical support (Douglas, Cox, & Webster, 1999; Heilbrun, 2009; Otto & Douglas, 2009). For these reasons, there have been a number of structured violence risk assessment instruments developed in civilian populations in the past two decades that have shown promise to improve the accuracy of violence risk assessment (Douglas et al., 2014; Monahan, 2010).

To our knowledge, there have been no instruments developed to assess the risk of acute violence in veteran populations. A brief violence screening tool designed for a military veteran population was recently validated (Elbogen, Cueva, et al., 2014). The Violence Screening and Assessment of Needs (VIO-SCAN) queries veterans about five items—financial instability, combat experience, alcohol misuse, history of violence and arrests, and PTSD plus frequent anger symptoms—and offers several potential benefits to help clinicians improve decision making by (1) systematically gauging the level of concern about veterans' risk; (2) considering not just individual factors but a combination of factors; 93) recognizing that PTSD alone does not lead to a high risk of violence in veterans; to elevate risk dramatically, it must combine with other risk factors; and (4) developing risk management plans, as several items are dynamic (e.g., anger and PTSD, alcohol misuse, having money to cover basic needs).

However, there are important limitations to VIO-SCAN in the context of the current chapter. First, and most importantly, it was validated for long-term violence risk, one year after the screen. As such, future research is needed to determine its utility for acute violence prediction. Related, and importantly, the VIO-SCAN should not be relied upon for any civil commitment decisions. Second, the VIO-SCAN is not the same as a comprehensive assessment covering a host of the aforementioned risk and protective factors and does not replace informed clinical decision making, which is necessary for properly interpreting results. Instead, what is perhaps most useful about the VIO-SCAN is that it encourages clinicians to conduct the risk assessment in a structured and systematic way. As such, the VIO-SCAN tool involves a rapid approach that prompts clinicians to evaluate five (at a minimum) important risk factors for violence in veterans, which could be especially useful in settings where acute violence risk is being assessed, with, again, the caveat of limited validation for acute violence.

Concluding Remarks

This chapter provides clinicians with a review of risk and protective factors found in the empirical literature to be statistically associated with violence in veteran populations. Given that research has long shown that human beings are prone to decision-making errors, clinicians can improve the assessment process by examining these types of risk and protective factors with empirical support in a structured way. Research shows that while military-specific variables like PTSD are relevant to assessing violence risk in veterans, it is critical to recognize that nonmilitary variables must be considered as well. Thus, it is important for clinicians to "go beyond PTSD" when trying to understand violence in veterans. Clinicians should continue to stay up to date on scholarship, as well as understand study limitations regarding the current literature on risk and protective factors for violence.

As there are likely time pressures in many of the clinical settings in which acute violence will be assessed in veterans, employing decision-making support tools, as well as making sure to review the empirically supported risk and protective factors described in this chapter, should, at the very least, help provide some guidance on how to assess veterans in these contexts. Although clinicians do not have a crystal ball for predicting acute or chronic violence (Monahan & Steadman, 2001), decisions can be based on what we currently know from the scientific literature regarding both the content and process of risk assessment and, in this way, clinicians can optimize their decision making in practice.

References

Beckham, J. C., Feldman, M. E., & Kirby, A C. (1998). Atrocities exposure in Vietnam combat veterans with chronic posttraumatic stress disorder: Relationship to combat exposure, symptom severity, guilt, and interpersonal violence. *Journal of Traumatic Stress, 11*(4), 777–785.

Beckham, J. C., Feldman, M. E., Kirby, A. C., Hertzberg, M. A., & Moore, S. D. (1997). Interpersonal violence and its correlates in Vietnam veterans with chronic posttraumatic stress disorder. *Journal of Clinical Psychology, 53*(8), 859–869.

Begic, D., & Jokic-Begic, N. (2001). Aggressive behavior in combat veterans with post-traumatic stress disorder. *Military Medicine, 166*(8), 671–676.

Borders, A., McAndrew, L. M., Quigley, K. S., & Chandler, H. K. (2012). Rumination moderates the associations between PTSD and depressive symptoms and risky behaviors in U. S. veterans. *Journal of Traumatic Stress, 25*(5), 583–586. doi: 10.1002/jts.21733

Bradley, C. (2007). Veteran status and marital aggression: Does military service make a difference? *Journal of Family Violence, 22*(4), 197–209.

Byrne, C. A., & Riggs, D. S. (1996). The cycle of trauma: Relationship aggression in male Vietnam veterans with symptoms of posttraumatic stress disorder. *Violence and Victims, 11*(3), 213–225.

Calhoun, P. S., Beckham, J. C., Feldman, M. E., Barefoot, J. C., Haney, T., & Bosworth, H. B. (2002). Partners' ratings of combat veterans' anger. *Journal of Traumatic Stress, 15*(2), 133–136.

Carlson, E. B., Lauderdale, S., Hawkins, J., & Sheikh, J. I. (2008). Posttraumatic stress and aggression among veterans in long-term care. *Journal of Geriatric Psychiatry and Neurology, 21*(1), 61–71.

Carroll, E. M., Rueger, D. B., Foy, D. W., & Donahoe, C. P. (1985). Vietnam combat veterans with posttraumatic stress disorder: Analysis of marital and cohabitating adjustment. *Journal of Abnormal Psychology, 94*(3), 329–337.

Cattelani, R., Zettin, M., & Zoccolotti, P. (2010). Rehabilitation treatments for adults with behavioral and psychosocial disorders following acquired brain injury: A systematic review. *Neuropsychology Review, 20*(1), 52–85.

Chapin, M. G. (1999). A comparison of violence exposure and perpetration in recruits and high school students. *Military Medicine, 164*(4), 264–268.

Douglas, K. S., Cox, D. N., & Webster, C. D. (1999). Violence risk assessment: Science and practice. *Legal and Criminological Psychology, 4*(Part 2), 149–184.

Douglas, K. S., Hart, S. D., Webster, C. D., Belfrage, H., Guy, L. S., & Wilson, C. M. (2014). Historical-Clinical-Risk Management-20, Version 3 (HCR-20V3): Development and overview. *The International Journal of Forensic Mental Health, 13*(2), 93–108.

Douglas, K. S., & Ogloff, J. R. (2003). Multiple facets of risk for violence: The impact of judgmental specificity on structured decisions about violence risk. *International Journal of Forensic Mental Health, 2*(1), 19–34.

Douglas, K. S., & Skeem, J. L. (2005). Violence risk assessment: Getting specific about being dynamic. *Psychology, Public Policy, and Law, 11*(3), 347–383.

Dutra, L., de Blank, G., Scheiderer, E., & Taft, C. (2012). Correlates of female veterans' perpetration of relationship aggression. *Psychological Trauma: Theory, Research, Practice, and Policy, 4*(3), 323–329. doi: 10.1037/a0026849

Elbogen, E. B. (2002). The process of violence risk assessment: A review of descriptive research. *Aggression and Violent Behavior, 7*(6), 591–604.

Elbogen, E. B., Beckham, J. C., Butterfield, M. I., Swartz, M., & Swanson, J. (2008). Assessing risk of violent behavior among veterans with severe mental illness. *Journal of Traumatic Stress, 21*(1), 113–117. doi: 10.1002/jts.20283

Elbogen, E. B., Cueva, M., Wagner, H. R., Sreenivasan, S., Brancu, M., Beckham, J. C., & Van Male, L. (2014). Screening for violence risk in military veterans: Predictive validity of a brief clinical tool. *American Journal of Psychiatry, 171*(7), 749–757. doi: 10.1176/appi.ajp.2014.13101316

Elbogen, E. B., Fuller, S., Johnson, S. C., Brooks, S., Kinneer, P., Calhoun, P. S., & Beckham, J. C. (2010). Improving risk assessment of violence among military veterans: An evidence-based approach for clinical decision-making. *Clinical Psychology Review, 30*(6), 595–607. doi: 10.1016/j.cpr.2010.03.009

Elbogen, E. B., Huss, M. T., Tomkins, A. J., & Scalora, M. J. (2005). Clinical decision making about psychopathy and violence risk assessment in public sector mental health settings. *Psychological Services, 2*(2), 133–141.

Elbogen, E. B., Johnson, S. C., Newton, V. M., Timko, C., Vasterling, J. J., Van Male, L. M.,... Beckham, J. C. (2014). Protective mechanisms and prevention of violence and aggression in veterans. *Psychological Services.* doi: 10.1037/a0035088

Elbogen, E. B., Johnson, S. C., Wagner, H. R., Newton, V. M., Timko, C., Vasterling, J. J., & Beckham, J. C. (2012). Protective factors and risk modification of violence in Iraq and Afghanistan war veterans. *Journal of Clinical Psychiatry, 73*(6), e767–e773. doi: 10.4088/JCP.11m07593

Elbogen, E. B., Johnson, S. C., Wagner, H. R., Sullivan, C., Taft, C. T., & Beckham, J. C. (2014). Violent behaviour and posttraumatic stress disorder in US Iraq and Afghanistan veterans. *British Journal of Psychiatry.* doi: 10.1192/bjp.bp.113.134627

Elbogen, E. B., Mercado, C. C., Scalora, M. J., & Tomkins, A. J. (2002). Perceived relevance of factors for violence risk assessment: A survey of clinicians. *International Journal of Forensic Mental Health, 1*(1), 37–47.

Elbogen, E. B., Van Dorn, R., Swanson, J. W., Swartz, M. S., & Monahan, J. (2006). Treatment engagement and violence risk in mental disorders. *British Journal of Psychiatry, 189,* 354–360.

Elbogen, E. B., Wagner, H. R., Fuller, S. R., Calhoun, P. S., Kinneer, P. M., & Beckham, J. C. (2010). Correlates of anger and hostility in Iraq and Afghanistan war veterans. *American Journal of Psychiatry, 167*(9), 1051–1058. doi: 10.1176/appi.ajp.2010.09050739

Finley, E. P., Baker, M., Pugh, M. J., & Peterson, A. (2010). Patterns and perceptions of intimate partner violence committed by returning veterans with post-traumatic stress disorder. *Journal of Family Violence, 25*(8), 737–743. doi: 10.1007/s10896-010-9331-7

Fonseca, C. A., Schmaling, K. B., Stoever, C., Gutierrez, C., Blume, A. W., & Russell, M. L. (2006). Variables associated with intimate partner violence in a deploying military sample. *Military Medicine, 171*(7), 627–631.

Forgey, M. A., & Badger, L. (2006). Patterns of intimate partner violence among married women in the military: Type, level, directionality, and consequences. *Journal of Family Violence, 21*(6), 369–380.

Freeman, T. W., & Roca, V. (2001). Gun use, attitudes toward violence, and aggression among combat veterans with chronic posttraumatic stress disorder. *Journal of Nervous and Mental Disease, 189*(5), 317–320.

Gallaway, M. S., Fink, D. S., Millikan, A. M., & Bell, M. R. (2012). Factors associated with physical aggression among US Army soldiers. *Aggressive Behavior, 38*(5), 357–367. doi: 10.1002/ab.21436

Ganzini, L., Edwards, P., Surkan, P. J., & Drummond, D. J. (1995). Characteristics of violent elderly in the emergency department. *International Journal of Geriatric Psychiatry, 10*(11), 945–950.

Gawande, A. (2009). *The Checklist Manifesto: How to Get Things Right*. New York, NY: Henry Holt.

Gimbel, C., & Booth, A. (1994). Why does military combat experience adversely affect marital relations? *Journal of Marriage and the Family*, 56(3), 691–703.

Goldberg, R. W., & Resnick, S. G. (2010). US Department of Veterans Affairs (VA) efforts to promote psychosocial rehabilitation and recovery. *Psychiatric Rehabilitation Journal*, 33(4), 255–258.

Gondolf, E. W., & Foster, R. A. (1991). Wife assault among VA alcohol rehabilitation patients. *Hospital & Community Psychiatry*, 42(1), 74–79.

Grafman, J., Schwab, K., Warden, D., Pridgen, A., Brown, H. R., & Salazar, A. M. (1996). Frontal lobe injuries, violence, and aggression: A report of the Vietnam head injury study. *Neurology*, 46(5), 1231–1238.

Grisso, T., & Tomkins, A. J. (1996). Communicating violence risk assessments. *American Psychologist*, 51(9), 928–930.

Hartl, T. L., Rosen, C., Drescher, K., Lee, T. T., & Gusman, F. (2005). Predicting high-risk behaviors in veterans with posttraumatic stress disorder. *Journal of Nervous and Mental Disease*, 193(7), 464–472.

Heilbrun, K. (1997). Prediction versus management models relevant to risk assessment: The importance of legal decision-making context. *Law and Human Behavior*, 21(4), 347–359.

Heilbrun, K. (Ed.). (2009). *Evaluation for Risk of Violence in Adults*. New York, NY: Oxford University Press.

Hellmuth, J. C., Stappenbeck, C. A., Hoerster, K. D., & Jakupcak, M. (2012). Modeling PTSD symptom clusters, alcohol misuse, anger, and depression as they relate to aggression and suicidality in returning U. S. veterans. *Journal of Traumatic Stress*, 25(5), 527–534. doi: 10.1002/jts.21732

Hiley-Young, B., Blake, D. D., Abueg, F. R., & Rozynko, V. (1995). Warzone violence in Vietnam: An examination of premilitary, military, and postmilitary factors in PTSD inpatients. *Journal of Traumatic Stress*, 8(1), 125–141.

Hundt, N. E., & Holohan, D. R. (2012). The role of shame in distinguishing perpetrators of intimate partner violence in U.S. veterans. *Journal of Traumatic Stress*, 25(2), 191–197. doi: 10.1002/jts.21688

Hurlbert, D. F., Whittaker, K. E., & Munoz, C. J. (1991). Etiological characteristics of abusive husbands. *Military Medicine*, 156(12), 670–675.

Jakupcak, M., Conybeare, D., Phelps, L., Hunt, S., Holmes, H. A., Felker, B.,... McFall, M. E. (2007). Anger, hostility, and aggression among Iraq and Afghanistan war veterans reporting PTSD and subthreshold PTSD. *Journal of Traumatic Stress*, 20(6), 945–954.

Jordan, B., Marmar, C. R., Fairbank, J. A., Schlenger, W. E., Kulka, R. A., Hough, R. L., & Weiss, D. S. (1992). Problems in families of male Vietnam veterans with posttraumatic stress disorder. *Journal of Consulting and Clinical Psychology*, 60(6), 916–926.

Killgore, W. D. S., Cotting, D. I., Thomas, J. L., Cox, A. L., McGurk, D., Vo, A. H.,... Hoge, C. W. (2008). Postcombat invincibility: Violent combat experiences are associated with increased risk-taking propensity following deployment. *Journal of Psychiatric Research*, 42(13), 1112–1121.

Kulka, R. A., Schlenger, W. E., Fairbank, J. A., Hough, R. L., Jordan, B. K., Marmar, C. R., & Weiss, D. S. (1990). *Trauma and the Vietnam War generation: Report of findings from the National Vietnam Veterans Readjustment Study*. New York, NY: Brunner/Mazel.

Lasko, N. B., Gurvits, T. V., Kuhne, A. A., Orr, S. P., & Pitman, R. K. (1994). Aggression and its correlates in Vietnam veterans with and without chronic posttraumatic stress disorder. *Comprehensive Psychiatry*, 35(5), 373–381.

Lehmann, L. S., McCormick, R. A., & Kizer, K. W. (1999). A survey of assaultive behavior in Veterans Health Administration facilities. *Psychiatric Services*, 50(3), 384–389.

Lenhardt, J. M., Howard, J. M., Taft, C. T., Kaloupek, D. G., & Keane, T. M. (2012). Examining aggression in male Vietnam veterans who receive VA services: The role of traumatic events and combat exposure. *Journal of Traumatic Stress*, 25(4), 461–464. doi: 10.1002/jts.21717

LePage, J. P., Bluitt, M., McAdams, H., Merrell, C., House-Hatfield, T., & Garcia-Rea, E. (2006). Effects of increased social support and lifestyle behaviors in a domiciliary for homeless veterans. *Psychological Services*, 3(1), 16–24.

MacManus, D., Dean, K., Al Bakir, M., Iversen, A. C., Hull, L., Fahy, T.,... Fear, N. T. (2012). Violent behaviour in UK military personnel returning home after deployment. *Psychological Medicine*, 42(8), 1663–1673. doi: 10.1017/s0033291711002327

MacManus, D., Dean, K., Jones, M., Rona, R. J., Greenberg, N., Hull, L.,... Fear, N. T. (2013). Violent offending by UK military personnel deployed to Iraq and Afghanistan: A data linkage cohort study. *Lancet*, 381(9870), 907–917. doi: 10.1016/S0140–6736(13)60354–2

Makin-Byrd, K., Bonn-Miller, M. O., Drescher, K., & Timko, C. (2012). Posttraumatic stress disorder symptom severity predicts aggression after treatment. *Journal of Anxiety Disorders*, 26(2), 337–342. doi: 10.1016/j.janxdis.2011.11.012

Manderscheid, R. W. (2007). Helping veterans return: Community, family, and job. *Archives of Psychiatric Nursing*, 21(2), 122–124.

Martz, E., Bodner, T., & Livneh, H. (2009). Coping as a moderator of disability and psychosocial adaptation among Vietnam theater veterans. *Journal of Clinical Psychology*, 65(1), 94–112.

McCarroll, J. E., Newby, J. H., Thayer, L. E., Norwood, A. E., Fullerton, C. S., & Ursano, R. J. (1999). Reports of spouse abuse in the U. S. Army Central Registry (1989–1997). *Military Medicine*, 164(2), 77–84.

McCarroll, J. E., Ursano, R. J., Liu, X., Thayer, L. E., Newby, J. H., Norwood, A. E., & Fullerton, C. S. (2000). Deployment and the probability of spousal aggression by U.S. Army soldiers. *Military Medicine*, 165(1), 41–44.

McCarroll, J. E., Ursano, R. J., Newby, J. H., Liu, X., Fullerton, C. S., Norwood, A. E., & Osuch, E. A. (2003). Domestic violence and deployment in US Army soldiers. *Journal of Nervous and Mental Disease*, 191(1), 3–9.

McCauley, J. L., Killeen, T., Gros, D. F., Brady, K. T., & Back, S. E. (2012). Posttraumatic stress disorder and co-occurring substance use disorders: Advances in assessment and treatment. *Clinical Psychology: Science and Practice*, 19(3), 283–304. doi: 10.1111/cpsp.12006

McFall, M., Fontana, A., Raskind, M., & Rosenheck, R. (1999). Analysis of violent behavior in Vietnam combat veteran psychiatric inpatients with posttraumatic stress disorder. *Journal of Traumatic Stress*, 12(3), 501–517.

Merrill, L. L., Crouch, J. L., Thomsen, C. J., & Guimond, J. M. (2004). Risk for intimate partner violence and child physical abuse: Psychosocial characteristics of multirisk male and female Navy recruits. *Child Maltreatment*, 9(1), 18–29.

Merrill, L. L., Hervig, L. K., & Milner, J. S. (1996). Childhood parenting experiences, intimate partner conflict resolution, and adult risk for child physical abuse. *Child Abuse & Neglect, 20*(11), 1049–1065.

Millikan, A. M., Bell, M. R., Gallaway, M. S., Lagana, M. T., Cox, A. L., & Sweda, M. G. (2012). An epidemiologic investigation of homicides at Fort Carson, Colorado: Summary of findings. *Military Medicine, 177*(4), 404–411.

Monahan, J. (2001). *Major mental disorder and violence: Epidemiology and risk assessment.* In G.-F. Pinard & L. Pagani (Eds.), *Clinical assessment of dangerousness: Empirical contributions* (pp. 89–102). New York, NY: Cambridge University Press.

Monahan, J. (2010). The Classification of Violence Risk. In R. K. Otto & K. S. Douglas (Eds.), *Handbook of violence risk assessment.* (pp. 187–198). New York, NY: Routledge/Taylor & Francis.

Monahan, J., & Steadman, H. J. (2001). *Violence risk assessment: A quarter century of research.* In L. Frost, & R. J. Bonnie (Eds.), *The evolution of mental health law* (pp. 195–211). Washington, DC: American Psychological Association.

Moss, H. B. (1989). Psychopathy, aggression, and family history in male veteran substance abuse patients: A factor analytic study. *Addictive Behaviors, 14*(5), 565–570.

Mossman, D. (1994). Assessing predictions of violence: Being accurate about accuracy. *Journal of Consulting and Clinical Psychology, 62*(4), 783–792.

O'Donnell, C., Cook, J. M., Thompson, R., Riley, K., & Neria, Y. (2006). Verbal and physical aggression in World War II former prisoners of war: Role of posttraumatic stress disorder and depression. *Journal of Traumatic Stress, 19*(6), 859–866.

Orcutt, H. K., King, L. A., & King, D. W. (2003). Male-perpetrated violence among Vietnam veteran couples: Relationships with veteran's early life characteristics, trauma history, and PTSD symptomatology. *Journal of Traumatic Stress, 16*(4), 381–390.

Otto, R., & Douglas, K. (Eds.). (2009). *Handbook of violence risk assessment tools.* Milton Park, UK: Routledge.

Owens, G. P., Held, P., Blackburn, L., Auerbach, J. S., Clark, A. A., Herrera, C. J.,. . . Stuart, G. L. (2014). Differences in relationship conflict, attachment, and depression in treatment-seeking veterans with hazardous substance use, PTSD, or PTSD and hazardous substance use. *Journal of Interpersonal Violence, 29*(7), 1318–1337. doi: 10.1177/0886260513506274

Pardeck, J. T., & Nolden, W. L. (1983). Aggression levels in college students after exposure or non-exposure to an aggressive life experience. *Adolescence, 18*(72), 845–850.

Pasternack, S. A. (1971). Evaluation of dangerous behavior of active duty servicemen. *Military Medicine, 136*(2), 110–113.

Penk, W., Drebing, C. E., Rosenheck, R. A., Krebs, C., Van Ormer, A., & Mueller, L. (2010). Veterans Health Administration transitional work experience vs. job placement in veterans with co-morbid substance use and non-psychotic psychiatric disorders. *Psychiatric Rehabilitation Journal, 33*(4), 297–307.

Petrik, N. D., Rosenberg, A. M., & Watson, C. G. (1983). Combat experience and youth: Influences on reported violence against women. *Professional Psychology: Research & Practice, 14*(6), 895–899.

Quinsey, V. L. (1995). The prediction and explanation of criminal violence. *International Journal of Law and Psychiatry, 18,* 117–127.

Reddy, M. K., Meis, L. A., Erbes, C. R., Polusny, M. A., & Compton, J. S. (2011). Associations among experiential avoidance, couple adjustment, and interpersonal aggression in returning Iraqi war veterans and their partners. *Journal of Consulting and Clinical Psychology, 79*(4), 515–520. doi: 10.1037/a0023929

Renshaw, K. D., & Kiddie, N. S. (2012). Internal anger and external expressions of aggression in OEF/OIF veterans. *Military Psychology, 24*(3), 221–235. doi: 10.1080/08995605.2012.678197

Rosen, L. N., Kaminski, R. J., Parmley, A. M., Knudson, K. H., & Fancher, P. (2003). The effects of peer group climate on intimate partner violence among married male U.S. Army soldiers. *Violence Against Women, 9*(9), 1045–1071.

Ross, L. (1977). The intuitive psychologist and his shortcomings: Distortions in the attribution process. In L. Berkowitz (Ed.), *Advances in experimental social psychology* (Vol. 10, pp. 173–220). New York: Academic Press.

Rothschild, B., Dimson, C., Storaasli, R., & Clapp, L. (1997). Personality profiles of veterans entering treatment for domestic violence. *Journal of Family Violence, 12*(3), 259–274.

Rumm, P. D., Cummings, P., Krauss, M. R., Bell, M. A., & Rivara, F. P. (2000). Identified spouse abuse as a risk factor for child abuse. *Child Abuse & Neglect, 24*(11), 1375–1381.

Sautter, F. J., Brailey, K., Uddo, M. M., Hamilton, M. F., Beard, M. G., & Borges, A. H. (1999). PTSD and comorbid psychotic disorder: Comparison with veterans diagnosed with PTSD or psychotic disorder. *Journal of Traumatic Stress, 12*(1), 73–88.

Savarese, V. W., Suvak, M. K., King, L. A., & King, D. W. (2001). Relationships among alcohol use, hyperarousal, and marital abuse and violence in Vietnam veterans. *Journal of Traumatic Stress, 14*(4), 717–732.

Schutt, R. K., Cournoyer, B., Penk, W. E., Drebing, C. E., van Ormer, E. A., Krebs, C., & Losardo, M. O. (2003). Building the future: Psychosocial rehabilitation with a veterans construction team. *Psychiatric Rehabilitation Journal, 27*(2), 186–189.

Sherman, M. D., Sautter, F., Jackson, M. H., Lyons, J. A., & Han, X. (2006). Domestic violence in veterans with posttraumatic stress disorder who seek couples therapy. *Journal of Marital & Family Therapy, 32*(4), 479–490.

Shin, H. J., Rosen, C. S., Greenbaum, M. A., & Jain, S. (2012). Longitudinal correlates of aggressive behavior in help-seeking U.S. veterans with PTSD. *Journal of Traumatic Stress, 25*(6), 649–656. doi: 10.1002/jts.21761

Silver, E., & Teasdale, B. (2005). Mental disorder and violence: An examination of stressful life events and impaired social support. *Social Problems, 52*(1), 62–78.

Silver, S. M., & Iacono, C. (1984). Factor-analytic support for DSM-III's post-traumatic stress disorder for Vietnam veterans. *Journal of Clinical Psychology, 40*(1), 5–14.

Skeem, J. L., & Monahan, J. (2011). Current directions in violence risk assessment. *Current Directions in Psychological Science, 20*(1), 38–42. doi: 10.1177/0963721410397271

Stappenbeck, C. A., Hellmuth, J. C., Simpson, T., & Jakupcak, M. (2013). The effects of alcohol problems, PTSD, and combat exposure on nonphysical and physical aggression among Iraq and Afghanistan war veterans. *Psychological Trauma: Theory, Research, Practice, and Policy, 6*(1), 65–72. doi: 10.1037/a0031468

Steadman, H. J. (1982). A situational approach to violence. *International Journal of Law & Psychiatry, 5*(2), 171–186.

Sullivan, C. P., & Elbogen, E. B. (2013). PTSD symptoms and family versus stranger violence in Iraq and Afghanistan veterans. *Law and Human Behavior, 38*(1), 1–9. doi: 10.1037/lhb0000035

Swanson, J. W., Swartz, M. S., Essock, S. M., Osher, F. C., Wagner, H., Goodman, L. A.,. . . Meador, K. G. (2002). The social-environmental context of violent behavior in persons treated for severe mental illness. *American Journal of Public Health*, *92*(9), 1523–1531.

Taft, C. T., Kachadourian, L. K., Suvak, M. K., Pinto, L. A., Miller, M. M., Knight, J. A., & Marx, B. P. (2012). Examining impelling and disinhibiting factors for intimate partner violence in veterans. *Journal of Family Psychology*, *26*(2), 285–289. doi: 10.1037/a0027424

Taft, C. T., Kaloupek, D. G., Schumm, J. A., Marshall, A. D., Panuzio, J., King, D. W., & Keane, T. M. (2007). Posttraumatic stress disorder symptoms, physiological reactivity, alcohol problems, and aggression among military veterans. *Journal of Abnormal Psychology*, *116*(3), 498–507.

Taft, C. T., Pless, A. P., Stalans, L. J., Koenen, K. C., King, L. A., & King, D. W. (2005). Risk factors for partner violence among a national sample of combat veterans. *Journal of Consulting and Clinical Psychology*, *73*(1), 151–159.

Taft, C. T., Street, A. E., Marshall, A. D., Dowdall, D. J., & Riggs, D. S. (2007). Posttraumatic stress disorder, anger, and partner abuse among Vietnam combat veterans. *Journal of Family Psychology*, *21*(2), 270–277.

Taft, C. T., Vogt, D. S., Marshall, A. D., Panuzio, J., & Niles, B. L. (2007). Aggression among combat veterans: Relationships with combat exposure and symptoms of posttraumatic stress disorder, dysphoria, and anxiety. *Journal of Traumatic Stress*, *20*(2), 135–145.

Teten, A. L., Miller, L. A., Bailey, S. D., Dunn, N. J., & Kent, T. A. (2008). Empathic deficits and alexithymia in trauma-related impulsive aggression. *Behavioral Sciences & the Law*, *26*(6), 823–832.

Teten, A. L., Miller, L. A., Stanford, M. S., Petersen, N. J., Bailey, S. D., Collins, R. L.,. . . Kent, T. A. (2010). Characterizing aggression and its association to anger and hostility among male veterans with post-traumatic stress disorder. *Military Medicine*, *175*(6), 405–410.

Teten, A. L., Sherman, M. D., & Han, X. (2009). Violence between therapy-seeking veterans and their partners: Prevalence and characteristics of nonviolent, mutually violent, and one-sided violent couples. *Journal of Interpersonal Violence*, *24*(1), 111–127.

Tversky, A., & Kahneman, D. (1981). The framing of decisions and the psychology of choice. *Science*, *211*, 453–458.

Ullrich, S., & Coid, J. (2011). Protective factors for violence among released prisoners: Effects over time and interactions with static risk. *Journal of Consulting and Clinical Psychology*, *79*(3), 381–390.

Van Winkle, E. P., & Safer, M. A. (2011). Killing versus witnessing in combat trauma and reports of PTSD symptoms and domestic violence. *Journal of Traumatic Stress*, *24*(1), 107–110. doi: 10.1002/jts.20614

Wasileski, M., Callaghan-Chaffee, M. E., & Chaffee, R. B. (1982). Spousal violence in military homes: An initial survey. *Military Medicine*, *147*(9), 761–765.

Weaver, C. M., Trafton, J. A., Kimerling, R., Timko, C., & Moos, R. (2013). Prevalence and nature of criminal offending in a national sample of veterans in VA substance use treatment prior to the Operation Enduring Freedom/Operation Iraqi Freedom conflicts. *Psychological Services*, *10*(1), 54–65. doi: 10.1037/a0030504

White, J. W., Merrill, L. L., & Koss, M. P. (2001). Predictors of premilitary courtship violence in a Navy recruit sample. *Journal of Interpersonal Violence*, *16*(9), 910–927.

Windle, R. C., & Windle, M. (1995). Longitudinal patterns of physical aggression: Associations with adult social, psychiatric, and personality functioning and testosterone levels. *Development and Psychopathology*, *7*(3), 563–585.

Wright, K. M., Foran, H. M., Wood, M. D., Eckford, R. D., & McGurk, D. (2012). Alcohol problems, aggression, and other externalizing behaviors after return from deployment: Understanding the role of combat exposure, internalizing symptoms, and social environment. *Journal of Clinical Psychology*, *68*(7), 782–800. doi: 10.1002/jclp.21864

Yesavage, J. A. (1983). Differential effects of Vietnam combat experiences vs. criminality on dangerous behavior by Vietnam veterans with schizophrenia. *Journal of Nervous and Mental Disease*, *171*(6), 382–384.

Yesavage, J. A. (1984). Correlates of dangerous behavior by schizophrenics in hospital. *Journal of Psychiatric Research*, *18*(3), 225–231.

Zatzick, D. F., Marmar, C. R., Weiss, D. S., Browner, W. S., Metzler, T. J., Golding, J. M.,. . . Wells, K. B. (1997). Posttraumatic stress disorder and functioning and quality of life outcomes in a nationally representative sample of male Vietnam veterans. *American Journal of Psychiatry*, *154*(12), 1690–1695.

Zoricic, Z., Buljan, D., Thaller, V., & Karlovic, D. (2003). Aggression in posttraumatic stress disorder comorbid with alcohol dependence. *European Journal of Psychiatry*, *17*(4), 243–247.

Zoricic, Z., Karlovic, D., Buljan, D., & Marusic, S. (2003). Comorbid alcohol addiction increases aggression level in soldiers with combat-related post-traumatic stress disorder. *Nordic Journal of Psychiatry*, *57*(3), 199–202.

Intimate Partner Violence: Evaluation of Victims and Perpetrators

Casey T. Taft, Adam D. LaMotte, *and* Karina S. Gilbert

Abstract

Intimate partner violence (IPV) remains a significant public health concern. Research has demonstrated that IPV can hold numerous and severe consequences for those victimized, and thus IPV necessitates effective evidence-based assessment, prevention, and treatment approaches. This chapter provides an overview of several different aspects of this phenomenon, starting with the definitions of distinct forms of IPV. Next, rates and consequences of IPV victimization are investigated. Additionally, four prominent theories of IPV perpetration are examined in conjunction with relevant research: feminist theory, social learning theory, I^3 theory, and social information processing theory. Following, the chapter reviews different instruments developed to assess risk of IPV perpetration and victimization as well as the efficacy of existing interventions designed to treat and prevent IPV. Finally, important areas for future directions are discussed.

Key Words: IPV, intimate partner violence, risk, feminist theory, social learning theory, I^3 theory, social information processing theory

Intimate partner violence (IPV) represents a serious public health problem, as it can have severe physical and psychological consequences for those victimized (Catalano, 2013; Golding, 1999). Researchers have endeavored to learn more about the nature and etiology of IPV in the interest of aiding assessment, prevention, and treatment approaches. In this chapter, we present a broad overview of this literature in order to provide a better understanding of the diverse aspects of this phenomenon. We begin by defining and distinguishing between different forms of IPV. Next, we examine rates of IPV and discuss the many effects that IPV has on those victimized. Then we review several prominent theories about the etiology of IPV perpetration and assess the research pertinent to these theories. Following, we outline different instruments that have been developed to assess one's risk for IPV perpetration and victimization and review studies that have examined the efficacy of existing IPV interventions. Finally, we discuss future directions for the IPV field.

Forms of IPV

Acts of IPV are typically categorized into one of four distinct types, as outlined by the US Centers for Disease Control and Prevention (CDC; Saltzman, Fanslow, McMahon, & Shelly, 1999): (a) physical violence, (b) sexual violence, (c) threats of physical or sexual violence, and (d) psychological/emotional abuse. The standardized definition of physical violence presented by the CDC is

> The intentional use of physical force with the potential for causing death, disability, injury, or harm. Physical violence includes, but is not limited to: scratching, pushing, shoving, throwing, grabbing, biting, choking, shaking, poking, hairpulling, slapping, punching, hitting, burning, use of a weapon (gun, knife, or other object), and use of restraints or one's body, size, or strength against another person. (Saltzman et al., 1999, pp. 10–11)

The CDC delineates three types of sexually violence acts, including (a) the "use of physical force to compel a person to engage in a sexual act against his or her will," (b) a "sex act involving a person who is unable to understand the nature or condition of the act, to decline participation, or to communicate unwillingness to engage in the sexual act," and (c) abusive sexual conduct, which involves the intentional touching of private areas of any person against his or her will, or of any person who does not have the ability to provide consent (Saltzman et al., 1999, p. 43). Threats of physical or sexual violence involve the use of words, gestures, or weapons to indicate intent to commit physical violence or to compel someone to engage in sexual acts or abusive sexual conduct (Saltzman et al., 1999).

The definition of psychological/emotional abuse is somewhat more imprecise, as it includes behaviors on the following list that are sometimes but not always perceived as abusive by the victims:

> Humiliating the victim, controlling what the victim can and cannot do, withholding information from the victim, getting annoyed if the victim disagrees, deliberately doing something to make the victim feel diminished [. . .] or embarrassed, using money that is the victim's, taking advantage of the victim, disregarding what the victim wants, isolating the victim from friends or family, prohibiting access to transportation or telephone, getting the victim to engage in illegal activities, using the victim's children to control victim's behavior, threatening loss of custody of children, smashing objects or destroying property, denying the victim access to money or other basic resources, [and] disclosing information that would tarnish the victim's reputation. (Saltzman et al., 1999, p. 13)

Another form of psychological/emotional abuse that is receiving more attention is stalking, defined as "harassing or threatening behavior that an individual engages in repeatedly, such as following a person, appearing at a person's home or place of business, making harassing phone calls, leaving written messages or objects, or vandalizing a person's property" (Tjaden & Thoennes, 1998, p. 1). It is important to note the CDC's recommendation that psychological/emotional abuse only be considered a type of violence in the context of prior acts or threats of physical or sexual violence (Saltzman et al., 1999).

Alongside the difficulties in defining psychological/emotional abuse, which is inherently more open to interpretation than a physical act of violence, there is considerable variability in the measures designed to capture the construct. For instance, the psychological aggression subscale of the Revised Conflict Tactics Scales (Straus, Hamby, Boney, McCoy, & Sugarman, 1996), the most widely used measure of IPV, assesses strategies that may be used occasionally during even low levels of interpartner conflict in well-adjusted relationships (e.g., "*I shouted or yelled at my partner,*" "*I stomped out of the room or house or yard during a disagreement*"). In contrast, the Multidimensional Measure of Emotional Abuse (Murphy & Hoover, 1999) was designed to assess four distinct forms of emotional abuse, including *dominance/intimidation* (i.e., aggressive behaviors intended to produce fear or submission), *restrictive engulfment* (i.e., behaviors intended to restrict the partner from social contacts and activities to increase the partner's dependency), *denigration* (i.e., behaviors intended to humiliate and degrade the partner), and *hostile withdrawal* (i.e., withholding emotional contact and withdrawing from the partner in a hostile fashion). The different problematic patterns captured by these measures highlight the large scope of behaviors that fall under the umbrella of psychological/emotional abuse.

Researchers have also categorized IPV based on its motives within the context of the relationship. For example, Johnson (2006; Johnson & Ferraro, 2000) developed a typology of violent relationships, distinguishing between four different types of IPV. The first type, originally called *common couple violence*, was renamed *situational couple violence*. This type "is not connected to a general pattern of control. It arises in the context of a specific argument in which one or both of the partners lash out physically at the other" (Johnson & Ferraro, 2000, p. 949). *Situational couple violence* is hypothesized to be the most prominent form of IPV, as it occurs when common arguments between partners escalate into aggression. The next type, called *intimate terrorism*, involves one partner using IPV as a tactic in an overall pattern of trying to control his or her partner. This type is more likely to lead to serious injury, less likely to be mutual, and more likely to escalate over time than is *situation couple violence* (Johnson & Ferraro, 2000). The third type, called *violent resistance*, consists of violence that is used to resist or protect oneself against *intimate terrorism*. Finally, the fourth type, *mutual violent control*, describes a pattern in which both partners use IPV in an effort to control the other and is thought to be the least common pattern of violence (Johnson & Ferraro,

2000). Johnson contends that making distinctions between types of IPV on the basis of its motivation is crucial, as findings of one type may not necessarily generalize to another. Thus IPV has been defined and categorized in a number of different ways, all of which are important to consider when examining the research on the phenomenon.

Rates of IPV

Rates of IPV in the United States indicate the severity of this national public health problem. The CDC and National Center for Injury Prevention and Control's National Intimate Partner and Sexual Violence Survey (Black et al., 2011), consisting of 16,507 completed phone interviews with respondents from across the country, estimated that approximately 4.7 million women and 5.4 million men had experienced physical IPV victimization over the past 12 months. The statistics become even more disheartening when examining lifetime prevalence: Estimates suggest that one in three women (39.2 million) and over one in four men (31.9 million) in the United States had experienced physical IPV victimization over the course of their lifetime. Additionally, the survey projected that approximately 11.2 million women had been raped by an intimate partner and that 12.8 million women had been stalked by an intimate partner at least once in their lifetime (Black et al., 2011). Lifetime prevalence of rape was not estimated for men in the survey, but approximately 2.4 million men reported being stalked by an intimate partner at least once in their lifetime (Black et al., 2011). Rates in the United States are even higher for psychological IPV, as defined as either expressive aggression (e.g., partner acted angry in a way that seemed dangerous) or coercive control (e.g., partner tried to keep from seeing or talking to family or friends). Nearly one in seven (16.6 million) women had experienced psychological IPV in the past 12 months, and nearly half (57.6 million) of women had experienced it over their lifetimes (Black et al., 2011). Rates of psychological IPV victimization were similarly high for men, with nearly one in five (20.5 million) reporting its occurrence within the past 12 months and nearly half (55.2 million) reporting its lifetime occurrence (Black et al., 2011).

Compared to prior national surveys (Baum, Catalano, Rand, & Rose, 2009; Tjaden & Thoennes, 2000), the National Intimate Partner and Sexual Violence Survey estimated a higher prevalence of stalking as well as a higher prevalence of physical IPV victimization among women and men. Black and colleagues (2011) suggest that the greater estimate of stalking prevalence may be due to the assessment of stalking tactics related to newer technologies, which have provided greater ease of communication and access to personal information. With regard to the greater estimate of physical IPV, they point out distinctions in the survey's phrasing, which was intended to focus the respondents on violent acts specifically perpetrated by a romantic or sexual partner and which may have promoted more honest reporting of IPV.

Not only does IPV occur at alarming rates in the United States, but it is also a significant public health problem globally. The World Health Organization (2013) calculated worldwide and regional prevalence estimates of IPV against women by compiling data from existing studies. Calculations indicated that, globally, approximately 30% of women who had ever had an intimate partner had experienced physical or sexual IPV during their lifetime. Lifetime IPV prevalence was highest among regions of Africa, the Eastern Mediterranean, and Southeast Asia at approximately 37% of ever-partnered women. However, this report did not assess global prevalence of IPV against men, and to our knowledge no researchers or organizations have yet estimated global prevalence of IPV against men. Such research is needed, considering data largely from the United States that indicates even greater rates of men's physical IPV victimization than women's (Archer, 2000; Black et al., 2011; Desmarais, Reeves, Nicholls, Telford, & Fiebert, 2012).

Consequences of IPV

There is a large body of research showing the severe toll that IPV can take on the victims of the abuse. One explicit consequence of physical IPV is the injury resulting from the violence. Between 2002 and 2011 in the United States, an estimated 50% of females and 44% of males victimized by an intimate partner suffered a resulting injury (Catalano, 2013). Furthermore, 13% of female IPV victimizations and 5% of male IPV victimizations resulted in severe physical injury, including internal injuries, unconsciousness, broken bones, sexual violence injuries, as well as gunshot and knife wounds (Catalano, 2013). As a result, IPV-related injuries comprise a substantial portion of emergency room visits for women (Abbott, Johnson, Koziol-McLain, & Lowenstein, 1995; Rand & Strom, 1997), although data from the Bureau of Justice Statistics suggest that the majority of injured victims do not seek professional health care for their injuries (Rennison & Welchans, 2000).

However, the physical health sequelae of IPV extend far beyond the immediate injury. Victims of physical IPV, particularly when the abuse recurs over time, may sustain traumatic brain injuries and experience related cognitive deficits (Jackson, Philp, Nuttall, & Diller, 2002; Kwako et al., 2011). The injuries and stress involved in IPV victimization can also lead to chronic health conditions via their effects on the immune, gastrointestinal, cardiovascular, and endocrine systems (Campbell, 2002; Crofford, 2007; Leserman & Drossman, 2007). The consequences of physical IPV also take the form of missed workdays and related compensation (National Center for Injury Prevention and Control, 2003), and the estimates of financial burden on the healthcare system for women within the first 12 months of IPV victimization span from $2.3 billion to $7.0 billion, depending on the estimation approach used (Brown, Finkelstein, & Mercy, 2008).

Outside of physical injuries and health conditions, IPV victimization has been shown to contribute to severe psychological distress. Golding's (1999) review of studies on the mental health consequences of IPV victimization found that women exposed to IPV were 3.8 times more likely to experience depression, 3.6 times more likely to experience suicidality, 3.7 times more likely to experience posttraumatic stress disorder (PTSD), and 5.6 times more likely to experience alcohol and drug abuse or dependence. A number of studies have also found IPV to be related to poorer mental health for men, including PTSD symptoms (Hines, 2007; Hines & Douglas, 2011) and depressive symptoms (Reid et al., 2008; Simonelli & Ingram, 1998). Research has demonstrated a dose–response relationship between IPV and mental health outcomes, such that the more severe and the more types of IPV experienced, the more severe the PTSD symptoms (Astin, Lawrence, & Foy, 1993; Basile, Arias, Desai, & Thompson, 2004) and depressive symptoms (Campbell, Kub, Belknap, & Templin, 1997; Houry, Kemball, Rhodes, & Kaslow, 2006).

Several studies have also compared how different types of IPV uniquely contribute to PTSD and depression symptoms. Using data from the National Violence Against Women Survey, Basile and colleagues (2004) entered physical, sexual, psychological, and stalking victimization into a regression and found that physical, psychological, and stalking victimization each uniquely predicted PTSD symptoms. Mechanic, Weaver, and Resick (2008) found that, when controlling for the effects of physical violence, sexual violence, injuries, and sexual coercion, psychological abuse and stalking uniquely predicted PTSD and depression symptoms. Other studies have highlighted the importance of psychological IPV in PTSD symptoms. For example, Norwood and Murphy (2012) found among partners of men in treatment for IPV perpetration that psychological aggression was the only form of IPV to uniquely contribute to all three symptom clusters of PTSD. When comparing the four types of psychological abuse conceptualized in the Multidimensional Measure of Emotional Abuse (Murphy & Hoover, 1999), this and a prior study (Taft, Murphy, King, Dedeyn, & Musser, 2005) found denigration to be a significant, unique predictor of PTSD symptoms. These findings highlight the potential importance of psychological/emotional IPV in contributing to psychological distress, particularly in relationships characterized by other forms of abuse, as incidents of psychological/emotional IPV may serve as triggering reminders of the traumatic violence. However, this is not to diminish the detrimental psychological impact of physical and sexual IPV, especially considering that the predictive power of psychological IPV in these studies may be artificially inflated due to its overall greater frequency and higher measurement reliability (Norwood & Murphy, 2012).

A study by Matlow and DePrince (2013) suggests that the relationship between IPV and PTSD is moderated by factors outside the type of IPV experienced. The researchers found that IPV victimization by multiple perpetrators was associated with a different PTSD symptom pattern than was repeated IPV victimization by the same perpetrator. Specifically, victimization by multiple perpetrators was uniquely predictive of several emotional numbing and hyperarousal symptoms of PTSD, while repeated victimization by the same perpetrator was uniquely predictive of an avoidance symptom. Much more research is needed on the factors that exacerbate and mitigate the psychological impact of IPV. Overall, evidence of the physical and mental health sequelae of IPV speaks to the clear need for a better understanding of the causes of this phenomenon with the aim of being better equipped to prevent it.

Theories of IPV

Many theories have been proposed to explain the nature and etiology of IPV. These theories have been used as guiding frameworks for the research of IPV perpetration and the design of interventions to treat it. In the following sections we present an overview of several prominent theories of IPV perpetration with the goal of providing a better understanding of the differing perspectives on the phenomenon.

Feminist Theory

Developed in the 1970s, the feminist perspective of IPV was very influential, as it was largely responsible for directing mass attention to the problem of male-perpetrated IPV, setting up shelters for female victims of abuse, and establishing violence against women as a criminal offense in the criminal justice system (Ali & Naylor, 2013; McPhail, Busch, Kulkarni, & Rice, 2007). Additionally, the majority of IPV intervention programs today are based in the feminist perspective (Eckhardt et al., 2013; Pence & Peymar, 1993). The feminist view contends that IPV is an outgrowth of patriarchal society that maintains men's oppression over women, such that men use IPV as an instrument of power and control over their partners and as a means to uphold male privilege (Dobash & Dobash, 1979; Walker, 1979). Inherent to this view is a primary focus on male-perpetrated IPV, and female perpetration of IPV is most often interpreted as an act of self-defense (Barnett, Lee, & Thelen, 1997; Dobash & Dobash, 2004).

Some support for the feminist theory comes from cross-cultural evidence. For example, Archer's (2006) meta-analysis of sex differences in physical IPV across nations found that, among community samples, as gender equality decreased, female victimization increased relative to male victimization. This supported prior findings tying women's empowerment to a decrease in women's victimization rates (Levinson, 1989; Straus, 1994; Vandello & Cohen, 2005). However, this finding was not replicated with samples of college students, which Archer attributed to the idea that the behavior of college students of different nations may not be representative of those nations (Williams & Best, 1990). Overall, these studies suggest the feminist theory of IPV may have relevance at the societal level.

Conversely, when investigating feminist theory at the level of the individual or the couple, it has not received strong support. For example, a meta-analysis by Sugarman and Frankel (1996) summarizes the early research on patriarchal ideology and male-perpetrated IPV. Patriarchal ideology was assessed in terms of (a) attitudes toward violence, (b) gender attitudes (i.e., expectations about gender roles, such as the expectation that women be deferent to men), and (c) gender schema (i.e., the extent to which one's self-description embodies culturally defined gender attributes). Contrary to expectations, the researchers did not find martially violent men to report significantly more traditional gender attitudes than nonviolent men, although there were significant findings when obtaining the partners' reports of their husbands' gender attitudes. With regard to gender schema, Sugarman and Frankel (1996) reviewed studies that assessed masculinity (includes traits such as assertiveness, strength, and dominance) and femininity (includes traits such as emotional expressiveness, compassion, and understanding). The researchers also unexpectedly found that maritally violent men scored lower on masculinity than nonviolent men and fit more into the "undifferentiated" gender orientation category characterized by low masculinity and low femininity. The only of Sugarman and Frankel's predictions to receive strong support was that martially violent men would exhibit more positive attitudes toward the use of violence than would nonviolent men. However, using attitudes toward violence as an indication of patriarchal ideology in this context seems tautological because such attitudes are already intimately tied to violent behavior (e.g., Schumacher, Feldbau-Kohn, Slep, & Heyman, 2001).

Another important construct in the feminist theory of IPV is that of power and control. The theory holds that men use IPV tactics to threaten and intimidate their partners and thus maintain power and control in their relationships. Research on this idea has provided mixed support. As noted by Malik and Lindahl (1998) in their review, early studies on power and control in IPV were plagued by methodological limitations, most notable among them being the failure to empirically validate relationship power as a construct. A study by Babcock, Waltz, Jacobson, and Gottman (1993) implemented several methodological improvements over earlier studies by operationalizing the three power domains: power bases, power processes, and power outcomes. They found no association between power base discrepancies (i.e., differences between husbands' and wives' education and income) and husbands' IPV, but they did find power outcomes to be related to IPV, such that husbands were more violent when their partners had more control over decision making in the relationship. This finding suggests that men exhibit more acts of IPV when their partners hold greater power in their relationships, and their IPV may be an attempt to regain power over their partners. With regard to power processes, maritally violent men were more likely than nonviolent men to report an interactional style in which they demanded and their wives withdrew. In Babcock and colleagues' interpretation of this pattern, the person withdrawing is considered to hold more power than the person demanding, because the person withdrawing wishes to maintain the status quo and the person demanding seeks change (Christensen & Heavey, 1990). However, another potential interpretation is that the wives withdrew out of the fear or intimidation that resulted from their husbands' IPV perpetration, rather than out of an effort to hold onto relationship power.

Several more recent studies have found a relationship between controlling behaviors (e.g., insisting on knowing where one's partner is at all times, trying to limit his or her contact with family and friends) and IPV in relationships (e.g., Kershaw et al., 2006; Tjaden, & Thoennes, 2000; Whitaker, 2013), yet research has not supported the gender-related motivations that are a central component of the feminist theory of IPV. For instance, a recent review by Archer (2013) reported that among studies of sex differences in controlling relationship behaviors, only 2 of 17 found men to be more controlling, whereas 5 found women to be more controlling and 10 found no sex differences. Additionally, six studies that assessed the relationship between controlling behaviors and physical aggression found that the two were associated for both men and women (Archer, 2013). This literature clearly contradicts the notion that men are unique in using IPV to control their partners.

One of the most frequent critiques of the feminist theory of IPV is that it holds a narrow focus on men's IPV while largely ignoring the issue of women's IPV. This singular focus becomes problematic for several reasons. First, it classifies IPV by the gender of the perpetrator rather than the severity or implications of the abuse and, in doing so, places an unnecessary qualifier on the issue of IPV as a public health problem. Additionally, this viewpoint stands in opposition to a wealth of research that suggests that women perpetrate physical IPV at rates equal to or higher than men (Archer, 2000; Black et al., 2011; Capaldi, Kim, & Shortt, 2007; O'Leary et al., 1989; Straus & Gelles, 1986). Research does suggest that men perpetrate severe physical IPV (e.g., hit with a fist, beat up, slam against something) at higher rates than women (Black et al., 2011), and men's IPV

perpetration is more likely to lead to injury than women's IPV perpetration (Archer, 2000; Catalano, 2013; Tjaden & Thoennes, 2000). However, IPV can lead to serious injury regardless of the gender of the perpetrator (Archer, 2000; Felson & Cares, 2005). The feminist theory's focus on male-to-female IPV has also been criticized for not being germane to the occurrence of IPV in same-sex relationships (Baker, Buick, Kim, Moniz, & Nava, 2013; Nowinski & Bowen, 2012; Ofreneo & Montiel, 2010). Furthermore, while the constructs of power and control are highly relevant to IPV, viewing them as the singular etiological factors for IPV has been regarded as overly simplistic (Murphy & Eckhardt, 2005), particularly as it does not account for other important risk factors such as psychopathology (Crane, Hawes, Devine, & Easton, 2014; Kessler, Molnar, Feurer, & Appelbaum, 2001). Overall, the impact of the feminist perspective on the field of IPV is undeniable, but its primary emphasis on males' perpetration, patriarchy, and power has made it a controversial viewpoint.

Social Learning Theory

Social learning theory has been another prominent framework for explaining IPV. Bandura (1973) contends that people model behavior that they have been exposed to in childhood, and thus, aggression and violence are learned through observation of others. These behaviors are then reinforced throughout childhood and adulthood as an appropriate way of resolving conflict and as an appropriate reaction to stress (Bandura, 1973; Mihalic & Elliott, 1997). Social learning theory also proposes that violence victimization can be learned through violence exposure, as the exposure instills the acceptance of violence between partners (Bandura, 1973; Gelles, 1972). In addition to direct reinforcement of one's own behavior, violence may be reinforced indirectly by witnessing the consequences of others' violence (Riggs & O'Leary, 1989). Social learning theory also suggests that learning violent behavior is more likely when one sees the model of the behavior as competent, powerful, respected, or admired (Akers, 2000; Sims, Dodd, & Tehada, 2008). Therefore, parents' behaviors are often the focus of social learning theory because of parents' immense influence as role models. Additionally, social learning theory has also been used to explain the effects of violence in television and other media (Anderson & Dill, 2000; Friedrich-Cofer & Huston, 1986).

Social learning theory for IPV has been supported by extensive evidence of the intergenerational transmission of violence. That is, when children witness their parents' IPV or experience parent-to-child violence, they have a higher likelihood of IPV perpetration and victimization in their adult relationships. Numerous studies have observed this finding (Desai, Arias, Thompson, & Basile, 2002; Ehrensaft et al., 2003; Fritz, Slep, & O'Leary, 2012; Magdol, Moffitt, Caspi, & Silva, 1998; Mihalic & Elliott, 1997; Stith et al., 2000), including the National Family Violence Surveys (Straus, 1990; Straus, Gelles, & Steinmetz, 1980). A review by Delsol and Margolin (2004) indicated that, across studies, between 34% and 54% of men reporting family-of-origin violence engaged in marital violence, compared with between 8% and 27% of men not reporting family-of-origin violence. These studies strongly suggest that exposure to violence in the household puts one at greater risk for perpetrating and experiencing IPV later in life.

Fewer studies have specifically tested social learning theory's proposed mechanisms of this association, but some have provided support. For example, O'Hearn and Margolin (2000) found in a sample of men that attitudes condoning violence moderated the link between family-of-origin violence and IPV perpetration. In men who condoned violence toward a spouse, there was a strong connection between their family-of-origin violence and IPV, while there was no connection in men who did not condone violence toward a spouse. Similarly, among male college students, Simons, Burt, and Simons (2008) found using structural equation modeling that beliefs about the legitimacy of violence in relationships partially mediated the association between abusive parenting and IPV perpetration. Other studies have reported similar findings (Reitzel-Jaffe & Wolfe, 2001; Stith & Farley, 1993). These studies suggest that family-of-origin violence may influence subsequent IPV perpetration in part by inculcating the belief that IPV can be justified or is a normal aspect of relationships.

Additionally, limited evidence suggests that family-of-origin violence is associated with diminished skills in nonviolent conflict resolution. With data from the National Family Violence Survey, Straus and Yodanis (1996) found that corporal punishment in adolescence was associated with greater levels of unresolved disagreements in current relationships, which was then associated with physical IPV perpetration. Another study by Burnett and Daniels (1985) compared male undergraduates from violent and nonviolent families on constructive conflict resolution and found that those from nonviolent families were able to resolve significantly more conflict situations than those from violent families. These findings are in line with the idea that children exposed to family violence may have less opportunity to learn nonviolent conflict-resolution skills. However, these studies have notable methodological limitations, as Straus and Yodanis used unresolved relationship disagreements as a proxy variable for deficits in conflict-resolution skills, and Burnett and Daniels had a small sample size ($N = 32$).

Certain predictions of social learning theory for IPV have not received strong support. For example, the effects of sex-linked modeling that have been demonstrated outside the context of violence (Bussey & Bandura, 1984) have received only limited support when applied to IPV. The theory of sex-linked modeling suggests that, as children have a tendency to emulate same-sex models over opposite-sex models (Bussey & Bandura, 1984), witnessing IPV perpetrated by the same-sex parent would be associated with subsequent IPV perpetration and witnessing IPV victimization of the same-sex parent would be associated with subsequent IPV victimization. A number of studies that have examined sex-specific intergenerational transmission of violence have found mixed results. Some studies have found some of the predicted sex-specific associations but not others (Fritz, Slep, & O'Leary, 2012; Hendy et al., 2003; Jankowski, Leitenberg, Henning, & Coffey, 1999), and some studies have not found evidence of sex-specific effects (Kwong, Bartholomew, Henderson, & Trinke, 2003; Langhinrichsen-Rohling, Neidig, & Thorn, 1995). Moreover, some research has demonstrated the influence of the opposite-sex parent (Dejonghe, 2008; Moretti, Obsuth, Odgers, & Reebye, 2006). Thus while the sex of the parent may play a role in modeling violence, it is clear that learning violence from one's parent is not contingent on being a member of the same sex. One potential complication in this literature is the commonality of mutual IPV perpetration among violent relationships (Whitaker, Haileyesus, Swahn, & Saltzman, 2007), which may make it difficult to find effects of violence transmission from one parent over the other.

A number of critiques have been raised against social learning theory for IPV. One primary critique is that not all people exposed to family-of-origin violence grow up to perpetrate or experience IPV, and not all people who perpetrate and experience IPV have been exposed to family-of-origin violence (Delsol & Margolin, 2004). Therefore, family-of-origin violence is clearly an important risk factor for

IPV but does not constitute the sole explanation for it. Another criticism of social learning theory for IPV is that the majority of its research has utilized retrospective self-reports about family-of-origin violence, which are subject to bias and have not matched up well with previous reports taken around the time of the violence (Henry, Moffitt, Caspi, Langley, & Silva, 1994). Additionally, there have been inconsistencies in how different studies have conceptualized family-of-origin violence, ranging from mild forms of corporal punishment to severe parent-to-child violence (Ali & Naylor, 2013; Delsol & Margolin, 2004). Finally, while many studies have found an influence of family-of-origin violence, there remains a paucity of research specifically examining the mechanisms proposed by social learning theory (Ali & Naylor, 2013). Overall, social learning theory has identified family-of-origin violence as a significant risk factor for IPV, but many aspects of the theory have yet to be corroborated empirically.

I^3 Theory

Although the early theories of IPV propose only a few central mechanisms, the literature on IPV has expanded to include many diverse risk factors, including financial stress (Neff, Holamon, & Schluter, 1995), socioeconomic status (Cunradi, Caetano, & Schafter, 2002), relationship distress and conflict (Murphy & O'Leary, 1989; Slep, Foran, Heyman, & Snarr, 2010), alcohol and drug use (Feingold, Kerr, & Capaldi, 2008), and various psychopathologies (Huesmann, Dubow, & Boxer, 2009; Kim & Capaldi, 2004). More recent frameworks for understanding IPV have attempted to incorporate and organize these different factors rather than suggest a single reason for IPV. One such framework is Finkel's (2007) I^3 theory (pronounced "I-cubed theory"), which classifies all IPV-related factors into three categories: violence-instigating triggers, violence-impelling forces, and violence-inhibiting forces. Violence-instigating triggers are described as "discrete situational events or circumstances that induce rudimentary action tendencies toward physical aggression" (Slotter & Finkel, 2011, p. 37). Examples of violence-instigating triggers include perceived provocation from one's partner, witnessing or learning of infidelity, being cut-off in traffic, and being fired from one's job. By definition, some form of violence-instigating trigger must be an antecedent to one's violence.

However, whether or not one becomes violent in the face of an instigating trigger is determined by violence-impelling and violence-inhibiting forces.

Violence-impelling forces are factors that increase the likelihood of experiencing aggressive impulses when triggered, and violence-inhibiting forces are factors that increase the likelihood of overriding aggressive impulses rather than acting on them (Slotter & Finkel, 2011). Finkel (2007) gives the example of the partner who picks up a lamp in rage and prepares to throw it at the other partner, but moments later, this impulse is overridden, and the partner places the lamp back on the table, deciding instead to storm out of the house. According to I^3 theory, people have different thresholds for the intensity of the instigating trigger needed to produce an aggressive response, which is determined by the strength of their impelling and inhibiting forces. One is particularly likely to perpetrate IPV when he or she is influenced by strong impelling forces and weak inhibiting forces and is presented with a strong instigating trigger.

Early evidence for I^3 theory comes from Finkel and his colleagues. Across five studies, Finkel, DeWall, Slotter, Oaten, and Foshee (2009) examined self-regulatory processes in determining whether or not partner-violent impulses were acted on. In Study 1, they asked undergraduate participants to describe the most serious argument or fight they had experienced with a romantic partner and report the degree to which they were tempted to engage in different violent behaviors and the degree to which they enacted the behaviors. Results indicated that participants were 2.4 times more likely to experience a violent impulse that they did not act upon than experience a violent impulse that they did act upon, establishing that many violent impulses do get overridden. Study 2 showed that adolescents high in dispositional self-control perpetrated significantly fewer acts of IPV than those low in dispositional self-control, in both cross-sectional and longitudinal analyses. These results suggest that the ability to self-regulate is associated with the degree of IPV that is enacted.

Studies 3, 4, and 5 used in vivo measures of IPV and experimentally manipulated the ability to self-regulate. Study 3 found that participants who responded immediately to a partner provocation scenario were significantly more likely to verbalize a tendency toward IPV than those who responded after a 10-second delay. The extra time given may have provided participants with the cognitive resources necessary to override their initial violent impulses. Study 4 tested the effects of self-control depletion before measuring aggressive behavior toward one's partner in both provoked and unprovoked conditions. Results showed that depleted self-control was associated with greater aggressive behavior but only when provoked, indicating the important interaction between the instigating trigger and the self-regulation needed to inhibit a violent response. Finally, Study 5 found that participants who completed a 2-week self-regulation bolstering regimen showed reduced inclination to perpetrate IPV in response to provocation, which was not found for participants in the control condition. Overall, Finkel and colleagues' (2009) findings demonstrate the significance of self-regulation processes in IPV, as well as show that self-regulation may be influenced by other variables.

Another series of studies has further bolstered predictions made by I[3] theory (Finkel et al., 2012). The researchers found that dispositional aggressiveness, a violence-impelling force, was particularly associated with IPV perpetration when violence-inhibiting forces were weak and violence-instigating triggers were strong. Findings were consistent across different samples, using cross-sectional and longitudinal designs and utilizing different operationalizations of the constructs. These studies offer strong initial support for the applicability of I[3] theory.

Researchers have increasingly used the I[3] framework to understand how particular factors may instigate, impel, and inhibit IPV perpetration (Maldonado, DiLillo, & Hoffman, 2014; Rasmussen & Boon, 2014; Sinclair, Ladny, & Lyindon, 2011; Taft et al., 2012). One advantageous feature of I[3] theory is that, because it does not propose a singular cause of IPV, it can be used across many different variables in which IPV researchers are interested. However, it is important to note that some risk factors may fit into multiple categories. For example, relationship distress may be considered a weak violence-inhibiting force because holding negative views of one's partner may make one less likely to inhibit a violent behavior toward him or her. Relationship distress may also be considered a violence-instigating trigger because it may promote greater frequency of negative interactions that elicit a violent response. Thus I[3] theory has the potential to expand the IPV literature by prompting researchers to take broader risk factors and investigate how they may influence IPV specifically at the level of dyadic interaction. One limitation that has been noted of I[3] theory is that its focus on self-regulatory processes is better suited to explain situational couple violence than it is to explain intimate terrorism (Johnson & Ferraro, 2000), which is guided by more instrumental goals such as controlling one's partner (Finkel et

al., 2009). While in its early stages, I[3] theory has clearly demonstrated its utility as a framework for understanding the etiology of IPV.

Social Information Processing Theory

Another framework that has been used to integrate a number of distinct risk factors for IPV is social information processing (SIP) theory, which considers interpersonal aggression within the broader context of social competence. Developed by McFall (1982), the original SIP model proposed that socially competent behavior is the outcome of a series of sequential stages that occur during social interaction. The first stage, *decoding*, involves the reception, perception, and interpretation of social stimuli. Several factors may interfere with this stage. For instance, one may not attend to or may misinterpret the stimuli as a result of his or her own faulty attributions or irrational beliefs (Bradbury & Fincham, 1990; Eidelson & Epstein, 1982; Holtzworth-Munroe, 1992). The second stage, *decision making*, consists of a set of skills used to select an appropriate response to the social stimuli. This involves producing a range of possible responses, matching these responses to the task demands, choosing the optimal response, searching one's behavioral repertoire for the ability to carry out the response, and finally weighing the costs against the benefits of executing the response. For example, one may show a tendency toward violence when he or she is not able to generate nonviolent response options or when he or she overestimates the benefits and underestimates the costs of selecting a violent response (Holtzworth-Munroe, 1992). The third and final stage, *enactment*, involves executing the chosen response and monitoring the impact of the action to assess the congruence between the intended and observed effects. Just as one may misinterpret incoming social stimuli, one may lack the ability to accurately assess the negative impact of his or her violent actions.

Crick and Dodge (1994) created a reformulated SIP model, expanding it to include six stages: (1) encoding of social cues, (2) interpretation of social cues, (3) clarification of goals, (4) response access or construction, (5) response decision, and (6) behavioral enactment. One major distinction from McFall's (1982) model is that Crick and Dodge's model does not follow a strict sequential structure. Instead, they suggest that different stages of SIP may occur simultaneously (e.g., interpretation of social cues while encoding) and that each stage has a bidirectional link to a central database of social information, including rules, social schemas, and social knowledge. This central database of social information is updated constantly based on the outcomes of one's social interactions and other factors. Additionally, the reformulated model conceptualizes the stages as part of a circular feedback loop where the assessment of one's behavioral enactment can then affect subsequent interpretation of social cues (e.g., following one's own aggression, one may view his or her partner's response as retaliatory; Murphy, 2013). Thus Crick and Dodge's reformulated model reflects that the processing of and response to social stimuli is dynamic, both within a single interpersonal interaction and over time.

Researchers have had great success in applying these SIP concepts to IPV perpetration. With regard to encoding and interpreting social cues, evidence suggests that men who perpetrate physical IPV make different cognitive interpretations of wife behavior than men who do not perpetrate physical IPV. For instance, Margolin, John, and Gleberman (1988) found that physically violent husbands were more likely than were verbally aggressive and withdrawing husbands to report feeling attacked during discussions with their wives. Holtzworth-Munroe and Hutchinson (1993) assessed cognitive interpretations of marital situations more directly. They found that, when listening to a series of marital situation vignettes, husbands who had perpetrated physical IPV were more likely than nonperpetrating husbands to rate the vignette wife's intentions as negative. In other words, husbands who had perpetrated IPV showed a cognitive bias toward attributing negative wife behaviors to negative wife intentions.

Men who perpetrate IPV have also evidenced difficulties with the decision-making stage of SIP. A study by Holtzworth-Munroe and Anglin (1991) compared to men who had and had not perpetrated physical IPV on the social competency of their responses to problematic marital situation vignettes. Following each vignette, participants were first asked what they would say or do in that situation. Later, they listened to a subset of the vignettes again and were asked what they thought would be the best thing to say or do in that situation. These answers were then rated for level of social competency by independent coders who were blind to participant condition. Results indicated that the men who had perpetrated physical IPV offered less competent responses than did the men who had not perpetrated physical IPV, both when asked what they would say or do and when asked what the best thing to say or do would be. This study suggests that men who perpetrate IPV have difficulty with generating socially competent responses, regardless of whether they think they would enact the responses.

Additionally, in both male and female samples, physical IPV perpetrators report greater expectations of positive consequences of using relationship aggression (e.g., getting one's way and winning an argument) than do non-IPV perpetrators (Leisring, 2009; Riggs & Caulfield, 1997). Furthermore, a study using the Implicit Association Test found that men in treatment for IPV perpetration showed more positive implicit attitudes toward violence than did nonviolent men (Eckhardt, Samper, Suhr, & Holtzworth-Munroe, 2012), suggesting that the tendency to view violence positively may operate automatically and without much conscious awareness. These findings indicate that those who perpetrate IPV may weigh the costs and benefits of a violent response differently than do non-IPV perpetrators as part of the decision-making stage of SIP.

Research has also shown SIP to be a valuable framework for understanding the mechanisms through which several risk factors may lead to IPV. One such risk factor is alcohol intoxication. For example, Eckhardt (2007) administered alcohol, a placebo drink, or no drink to maritally violent and nonviolent men before having them complete the Articulated Thoughts in Simulated Situations procedure (Davison, Vogel, & Coffman, 1997). This procedure asked participants to imagine themselves in different audiotaped scenarios (one neutral scenario and two anger-arousing scenarios) and then to talk out loud about their thoughts and feelings into a voice recorder. Results indicated that the alcohol manipulation had no impact on aggressive verbalizations among the maritally nonviolent men but increased the number of aggressive verbalizations among the maritally violent men. There may be an interaction between alcohol intoxication and previously existing SIP deficits, such that intoxication potentiates the selection of an aggressive response among those who have a tendency to generate aggressive response options.

Another IPV risk factor that may have effects via SIP deficits is trauma. Among a community sample, Taft, Schumm, Marshall, Panuzio, and Holtzworth-Munroe (2008) used structural equation modeling to examine the potential pathways through which family-of-origin maltreatment led to IPV perpetration. Results indicated that the effects of childhood parental rejection and adulthood trauma exposure on IPV perpetration were indirect through PTSD symptom severity and SIP deficits. The effects of

PTSD symptom severity on psychological IPV were indirect through SIP deficits, and the effects of PTSD symptom severity on physical IPV were both direct and indirect through SIP deficits. When someone is exposed to trauma and develops PTSD, he or she may be more hypervigilant to trauma cues and perceptions of threat, which may bias his or her interpretation of others' behavior as being more hostile or threatening (Constans, 2005). A study by Taft and colleagues (2015) examined the relationship between PTSD symptom severity and SIP variables using the Articulated Thoughts in Simulated Situations procedure. They found that cognitive biases (e.g., making assumptions in the absence of evidence, suspiciousness of the motivation of others) elicited during the general anger scenario mediated the relationship between PTSD symptom severity and anger expression, although PTSD symptom severity was not associated with hostile attribution biases, offering partial support. Another study by Sippel and Marshall (2011) found that implicit processing of shame cues assessed via an emotional Stroop task mediated the relationship between PTSD symptom severity and IPV perpetration. Shame is thought to instigate hostility toward the source of expected rejection in order to defend one's self-image (Lewis, 1971), and so a PTSD-related automatic bias in the processing of shame cues may constitute an early-stage SIP deficit that leads to IPV perpetration.

These studies indicate the clear utility of the SIP framework in organizing the literature on risk factors for IPV. Similar to I³ theory, SIP theory prompts researchers to consider the impact of different risk factors at the level of the dyadic interaction. For example, overall dissatisfaction with one's relationship may become a lens through which individual actions of one's partner are interpreted. A nice gesture from one's partner may be attributed to ulterior motives (e.g., "you only did me a favor because you wanted something in return"), and one may place less weight on the costs of harming one's partner when that partner is viewed negatively. However, the literature on SIP in regard to IPV has much more room for development. Many known IPV risk factors have yet to be explored through this framework, and many aspects of the framework itself need to be bolstered with empirical studies. For instance, several aspects of Crick and Dodge's (1994) reformulated model, such as the central database of social knowledge, require further investigation. Additionally, it has not yet been shown that changes in SIP account for reductions in IPV perpetration

following treatment (Murphy, 2013). Thus SIP theory needs more thorough study but represents a promising direction for future IPV research.

IPV Risk Assessment

Along with gaining a better understanding of the etiology of violence in relationships, it is a crucial necessity in the field of IPV to develop methods that more accurately assess one's risk for IPV perpetration and victimization. Traditionally, clinicians have relied on their professional judgment to assess IPV risk, but such unstructured clinical judgment has been widely criticized for its limited accuracy and vulnerability to personal bias (Nicholls, Pritchard, Reeves, & Hilterman, 2013). In response to the problems with relying on unstructured clinical judgment, groups of researchers have developed different actuarial risk assessments for IPV. Actuarial risk assessments utilize statistical models that integrate different risk factors in order to compute the probability that a future event, such as IPV, will occur.

One such risk assessment measure is the Ontario Domestic Assault Risk Assessment (Hilton et al., 2004), which is designed for use by police officers and other frontline personnel on the scene of an IPV-related call. It contains 13 items that assess information on the perpetrator's criminal background, substance abuse, and IPV history in order to predict IPV recidivism. Studies have shown moderate to high predictive accuracy of the Ontario Domestic Assault Risk Assessment (for a review, see Nicholls et al., 2013), although recidivism in these studies was determined using only official records of subsequent IPV episodes, which are likely to underrepresent the actual number of IPV episodes. Another measure designed for use by police officers is the Domestic Violence Supplementary Report (Ontario Ministry of the Solicitor General, 2000). A validation study found this report to be significantly predictive of recidivism, but it did not perform as well as the Ontario Domestic Assault Risk Assessment (Hilton et al., 2004). Another risk assessment measure, the Domestic Violence Evaluation (Ellis & Stuckless, 2006a) was intended to assess the risk of IPV during divorce mediation proceedings, as the termination of a relationship is a considered a high-risk time for IPV (Wilson & Daly, 1993). The divorce mediator administers the measure to both members of the couple privately, which then produces a rating of risk that the mediator uses to determine the need for offering risk management tactics and assisting with safety planning (Ellis & Stuckless, 2006a; Nicholls et al.,

2013). Only one empirical study to date has been conducted with the Domestic Violence Evaluation (Ellis & Stuckless, 2006b), and it does not report the predictive validity of the total instrument score.

Several other actuarial risk assessments for IPV bear note. The Domestic Violence Screening Instrument (Williams & Houghton, 2004) was created for use by probation officers as a screening measure that indicates the need for a more detailed assessment of IPV. Research suggests that the Domestic Violence Screening Instrument has moderate predictive accuracy for more severe threatening behavior and physical IPV but is low for reoffending behaviors that are not as severe (Williams & Houghton, 2004). The Propensity for Abusiveness Scale (Dutton, 1995) was designed to assess one's inclination to be abusive without directly asking about abusive behaviors in order to reduce potential social desirability bias that results in misrepresentation. The Propensity for Abusiveness Scale assesses personality traits, anger, trauma symptoms, parental warmth and rejection, and attachment (Dutton, 1995). The measure has shown strong associations with partner reports of emotional and physical abuse but has not been used to look at recidivism (Dutton, Landolt, Starzomski, & Bodnarchuk, 2001; Nicholls et al., 2013). The Partner Abuse Prognostic Scale (PAPS; Murphy, Morrel, Elliot, & Neavins, 2003) is an actuarial risk assessment comprised of three primary subscales (relationship violence problem severity, substance use, and aggression history) and includes two additional indicators (unemployment and cohabitation status). The PAPS incorporates information from both the perpetrator and the victim. Data on the predictive accuracy of the PAPS comes from a single study (Murphy et al., 2003). The total PAPS score significantly predicted all IPV outcomes, but two of its subscales did not predict IPV as expected (aggression history did not significantly predict IPV outcomes, and substance abuse was negatively associated with physical IPV at six months following IPV treatment).

One unique actuarial risk assessment instrument is the Danger Assessment Scale (DA; Campbell, 1986; Campbell, Webster, & Glass, 2009), which was specifically designed to assess the risk of femicide among women experiencing IPV from a current or ex-partner. In the revised version of the DA (Campbell et al., 2009), the person being assessed first indicates incidents of IPV victimization on a past year calendar and then answers 20 yes/no questions designed to assess future femicide risk. These answers yield a placement in one of four risk categories: *variable danger, increased danger, severe danger,* and *extreme danger.* A study with data across 11 US cities examined the ability of the revised DA to predict attempted femicide cases ($n = 194$) over female abuse cases ($n = 324$), finding strong support for the predictive accuracy of the measure. For example, only 1.3% of attempted femicide victims fell within the *variable danger* category, while 53.1% of abuse victim controls fell within that category. Conversely, 54.5% of attempted femicide victims and only 3.5% of abuse victim controls fell within the *extreme danger* category. However, a limitation of this study is that attempted femicide victims were administered the DA after the attempt had taken place, which may have biased their reports. The low base rate of attempted femicide limits the practicality of prospective study designs with the DA. However, such a study would provide stronger support for the instrument's ability to identify femicide risk.

While an improvement over unstructured clinical judgment, actuarial risk assessments for IPV hold certain limitations (e.g., they do not account for more case-specific risk variables, actuarial models created with a certain sample often decline in accuracy upon cross-validation), and structured professional judgment instruments have been developed in order to capture the strengths and minimize the weaknesses of both actuarial risk and unstructured clinical judgment approaches (Nicholls et al., 2013). One notable structured professional judgment instrument is the Spousal Assault Risk Assessment Guide (SARA; Kropp, Hart, Webster, & Eaves, 2008). The SARA includes 20 items evaluating known IPV risk factors, and the assessor makes a judgment of total risk based on these items. However, the developers of the measure advocate that a person does not need to obtain high score on the SARA in order to be determined as high risk, because particular combinations of individual risk factors may indicate risk, even in the absence of others (Kropp, Hart, Webster, & Eaves, 1999). Research has established convergent validity with other IPV risk assessment instruments and suggests moderate predictive validity across a number of distinct samples (for a review, see Nicholls et al., 2013). A shorter version of the SARA, called the Brief Spousal Assault Form for the Evaluation of Risk (B-SAFER; Kropp, Hart, & Belfrage, 2005), has been developed for use by police officers and other criminal justice professionals. Though this form has not been as extensively researched as the SARA, emerging evidence suggests that it is predictive of recidivism (Storey, Kropp, Hart, Belfrage,

& Strand, 2014). Despite the proposed enhancements of structured professional judgment over actuarial risk assessments, studies comparing the two approaches have not demonstrated strong support for one over the other (Dahle, 2006; Douglas & Yeomans, & Boer, 2005; Heilbrun, Yasuhara, & Shah, 2010).

Intervention Programs for IPV Perpetration

When conducting research to gain a better understanding of the nature and etiology of IPV, the ultimate goal is to translate this knowledge into effective treatment and prevention of IPV perpetration. Currently, the vast majority of intervention programs for IPV perpetrators fall within one of two approaches. The first and more widespread approach is based in the feminist theory of IPV (e.g., the Duluth model; Pence & Peymar, 1993). With this approach, the primary method of treatment is educating male IPV perpetrators about their patriarchal attitudes and use of IPV as an instrument of power and control over their partners, in addition to encouraging them to take personal responsibility for their IPV perpetration. The second approach is rooted in a cognitive-behavioral therapy (CBT) framework and is focused on emotion regulation and relationship skills training, as well as challenging cognitive distortions.

Recently, Eckhardt and colleagues (2013) reviewed the existing research assessing the effectiveness of these intervention programs. Of the 14 identified studies that compared a feminist-based intervention program to a no-treatment control group or matched dropout comparisons, only 7 showed a statistically significant difference in IPV recidivism, and of the 4 identified studies that compared a CBT-based intervention program to a control group, only 2 showed a significant difference. Thus of the two major approaches to IPV intervention, researchers are as likely to find an effect of the intervention as they are to find no effect of the intervention. Furthermore, Eckhardt and colleagues note that of the nine studies to show a significant effect of the IPV intervention program, three involve considerable methodological flaws, such as providing limited information about sample selection and follow-up procedures (Dobash, Dobash, Cavanagh, & Lewis, 1996), using only official records as follow-up data (Palmer, Brown, & Barrera, 1992), and allowing the possibility that the effects were due to criminal justice supervision rather than the intervention itself (Taylor, Davis, & Maxwell, 2001). Additionally, only one (Taylor et al., 2001)

of the nine studies showing a treatment effect used a randomized design. Clearly, existing studies of the two major types of intervention programs for IPV perpetrators have not shown strong support for the efficacy of these programs.

Eckhardt and colleagues (2013) also reviewed studies examining the efficacy of alternative IPV intervention programs and identified four that compared an active treatment group to a control group. Three investigated the effects of a brief motivational enhancement intervention, either on its own (Mbilinyi et al., 2011; Woodin & O'Leary, 2010) or as an antecedent to a CBT-based IPV intervention (Musser, Semiatin, Taft, & Murphy, 2008). Of these, two (Mbilinyi et al., 2011; Woodin & O'Leary, 2010) found a significant difference such that participants who received the motivational enhancement intervention evidenced greater reductions in physical IPV perpetration than those who did not. The study by Musser and colleagues found a marginally significant difference, with lower rates of IPV perpetration among participants who received motivational enhancement before the IPV intervention. The fourth study examined the effects of a couples' treatment for IPV informed by both feminist and CBT approaches (Stith, Rosen, McCollum, & Thomsen, 2004) and found significantly lower rates of male IPV recidivism in the multicouple therapy group than in the comparison group. However, the comparison group in this study consisted of only nine couples who had failed to attend treatment and thus likely differed from the other group in ways beyond the receipt of treatment.

Another avenue that has been explored to address IPV perpetration is primary prevention. Whitaker, Murphy, Eckhardt, Hodges, and Cowart (2013) conducted a systematic review of studies examining the effectiveness of primary prevention interventions and identified nine methodologically strong studies that measured IPV behaviors as the outcome variables. Primary prevention efforts for IPV have largely targeted middle or high school age teenagers, as IPV can only occur within the context of intimate relationships and this is the age at which intimate relationships are first acknowledged (Whitaker et al., 2013). Four of the studies examined school-based IPV interventions. Of these, one found an unqualified positive effect of the intervention (Foshee et al., 2005), one found a positive effect qualified by gender (i.e., effect found for boys only; Wolfe et al., 2009), one found no effect of the intervention on behavior (Jaycox et al., 2006), and one found both positive and negative effects of the interventions (i.e., one intervention group showed greater reductions in sexual violence victimization, but the other intervention group showed increases in sexual violence perpetration, and both intervention groups showed increases in physical IPV perpetration relative to controls; Taylor, Stein, & Burden, 2010).

The remaining five methodologically rigorous studies assessed the effects of non-school-based interventions. These included an IPV intervention for youth involved in child protective services (Wolfe et al., 2003), an intervention for adult women living in Limpopo, Kenya (Pronyk et al., 2006), an intervention for families with teenagers (Foshee et al., 2012), an intervention for pregnant teens and their partners (Florsheim, McArthur, Hudak, Heavin, & Burrow-Sanchez, 2011), and an intervention for couples planning to get married (Markman & Floyd, 1980). All of these studies found beneficial effects of the interventions on IPV behaviors, albeit one of these studies only found marginally significant differences between groups (Florsheim et al., 2011).

Whitaker and colleagues (2013) make a few important observations about the overall literature on primary prevention for IPV. First, it is notable that most primary prevention efforts have been for teenagers in general, rather than a specific set of teenagers at increased IPV risk. Exceptions to this are an intervention for pregnant teens and their partners (Florsheim et al., 2011), as IPV can be common during pregnancy (Silverman, Decker, Reed, & Raj, 2006), and an intervention for young males adjudicated for violent offenses (Salazar & Cook, 2006). A particular challenge for primary prevention efforts trying to target teenagers at increased risk for IPV is finding teenagers that are at heightened risk but have not yet perpetrated IPV. Another limitation of this literature is that, although several studies show the efficacy of different IPV prevention interventions, no studies have been done to replicate the findings for each intervention. Additionally, while several of the interventions include the same elements, it is unclear from the existing research what the active ingredients are of each intervention. Thus much more research is needed before any one IPV primary prevention intervention can be disseminated on a large scale.

Conclusions and Future Directions

Clearly, IPV is a complex and serious public health problem with myriad causes and harmful consequences. Having an understanding of different theoretical conceptualizations of and risk factors for IPV is necessary if one is to effectively assess and work with individuals using or experiencing IPV since each perspective offers a useful clinical perspective that may explain abusive events within an individual or dyad. As the field continues to move forward, it is hoped that researchers and theorists will work to integrate these different perspectives to offer a more comprehensive understanding. For example, interactions among different risk factors highlighted by feminist, social learning, and SIP theories could and perhaps should be examined consistent with the I[3] framework. Such work would be useful not only in gaining a fuller picture of IPV that occurs in real-world settings but also in bringing together those who intervene with respect to this problem, combining efforts and energies to determine the most effective strategies for ending IPV and bringing about true, sustainable change.

Not surprisingly, it is difficult to adequately capture the complexity of IPV using standard questionnaire- and interview-based methods. No single assessment method is able to provide complete confidence that the reports are an accurate reflection of abusive episodes. Available methods generally do not assess the context in which IPV occurs, including the antecedents and dynamics contributing to the episode, and partners evidence only modest concordance between their reports of IPV. Thus it is especially important to gather as many points of data as possible, including self- and collateral reports, criminal justice reports if available, hospital charts, and so on to facilitate the most accurate and clinically useful assessment possible.

Great advancements have been made in the United States for identifying IPV and for codifying into the law statutes that assist those who experience abuse, but much more work needs to be done. Beyond improving awareness and assessment methods, universal IPV screening of both women and men who experience and use IPV across medical settings would have a huge impact on addressing this problem since service providers are often the patient's most trusted potential helper. Further development of mental health and psychoeducational interventions will also prove key in continuing our advancement on this issue and ultimately ending abuse.

References

Abbott, J., Johnson, R., Koziol-McLain, J., & Lowenstein, S. R. (1995). Domestic violence against women: Incidence and prevalence in an emergency department population. *JAMA: Journal of the American Medical Association, 273*(22), 1763–1767.

Akers, R. L. (2000). *Criminological theories: Introduction, evaluation, and application* (3rd ed.). Los Angeles, CA: Roxbury.

Ali, P., & Naylor, P. B. (2013). Intimate partner violence: A narrative review of the feminist, social and ecological explanations for its causation. *Aggression and Violent Behavior, 18*(6), 611–619.

Anderson, C. A., & Dill, K. E. (2000). Video games and aggressive thoughts, feelings, and behavior in the laboratory and in life. *Journal of Personality and Social Psychology, 78*(4), 772–790.

Archer, J. (2000). Sex differences in aggression between heterosexual partners: A meta-analytic review. *Psychological Bulletin, 126*(5), 651–680.

Archer, J. (2006). Cross-cultural differences in physical aggression between partners: A social-role analysis. *Personality and Social Psychology Review, 10*(2), 133–153.

Archer, J. (2013). Can evolutionary principles explain patterns of family violence? *Psychological Bulletin, 139*(2), 403–440.

Astin, M. C., Lawrence, K. J., & Foy, D. W. (1993). Posttraumatic stress disorder among battered women: Risk and resiliency factors. *Violence and Victims, 8*(1), 17–28.

Babcock, J. C., Waltz, J., Jacobson, N. S., & Gottman, J. M. (1993). Power and violence: The relation between communication patterns, power discrepancies, and domestic violence. *Journal of Consulting and Clinical Psychology, 61*(1), 40–50.

Baker, N. L., Buick, J. D., Kim, S. R., Moniz, S., & Nava, K. L. (2013). Lessons from examining same-sex intimate partner violence. *Sex Roles, 69*(3–4), 182–192.

Bandura, A. (1973). *Aggression: A social learning analysis.* Englewood Cliffs, NJ: Prentice Hall.

Barnett, O. W., Lee, C. Y., & Thelen, R. E. (1997). Gender differences in attributions of self-defense and control in interpartner aggression. *Violence Against Women, 3*(5), 462–481.

Basile, K. C., Arias, I., Desai, S., & Thompson, M. P. (2004). The differential association of intimate partner physical, sexual, psychological, and stalking violence and posttraumatic stress symptoms in a nationally representative sample of women. *Journal of Traumatic Stress, 17*(5), 413–421.

Baum, K., Catalano, S., Rand, M., & Rose, K. (2009). Stalking victimization in the United States. Special Report (NCJ-224527). Washington, DC: US Department of Justice, Bureau of Justice Statistics.

Black, M.C., Basile, K. C., Breiding, M. J., Smith, S. G., Walters, M.L., Merrick, M. T., ... Stevens, M. R. (2011). *The National Intimate Partner and Sexual Violence Survey (NISVS): 2010 summary report.* Atlanta, GA: National Center for Injury Prevention and Control, Centers for Disease Control and Prevention.

Bradbury, T. N., & Fincham, F. D. (1990). Attributions in marriage: Review and critique. *Psychological Bulletin, 107*(1), 3–33.

Brown, D. S., Finkelstein, E. A., & Mercy, J. A. (2008). Methods for estimating medical expenditures attributable to intimate partner violence. *Journal of Interpersonal Violence, 23*(12), 1747–1766.

Burnett, E. C., & Daniels, J. (1985). The impact of family of origin and stress on interpersonal conflict resolution skills in young adult men. *American Mental Health Counselors Association Journal, 7*(4), 162–171.

Bussey, K., & Bandura, A. (1984). Influence of gender constancy and social power on sex-linked modeling. *Journal of Personality and Social Psychology, 47*(6), 1292–1302.

Campbell, J. C. (1986). Nursing assessment for risk of homicide with battered women. *Advances in Nursing Science, 8*(4), 36–51.

Campbell, J. C. (2002). Health consequences of intimate partner violence. *Lancet, 359*(9314), 1331–1336.

Campbell, J. C., Kub, J., Belknap, R., & Templin, T. N. (1997). Predictors of depression in battered women. *Violence Against Women, 3*(3), 271–293.

Campbell, J. C., Webster, D., & Glass, N. (2009). The Danger Assessment: Validation of a lethality risk assessment instrument for intimate partner femicide. *Journal of Interpersonal Violence, 24*(4), 653–674.

Capaldi, D. M., Kim, H. K., & Shortt, J. (2007). Observed initiation and reciprocity of physical aggression in young, at-risk couples. *Journal of Family Violence, 22*(2), 101–111.

Catalano, S. (2013). Intimate partner violence: Attributes of victimization, 1993–2011. Special Report (NCJ-243300). Washington, DC: US Department of Justice, Bureau of Justice Statistics.

Christensen, A., & Heavey, C. L. (1990). Gender and social structure in the demand/withdraw pattern of marital conflict. *Journal of Personality and Social Psychology, 59*(1), 73–81.

Constans, J. I. (2005). Information-processing biases in PTSD. In J. J. Vasterling & C. R. Brewin (Eds.), *Neuropsychology of PTSD: Biological, cognitive, and clinical perspectives* (pp. 105–130). New York: Guilford Press.

Crane, C. A., Hawes, S. W., Devine, S., & Easton, C. J. (2014). Axis I psychopathology and the perpetration of intimate partner violence. *Journal of Clinical Psychology, 70*(3), 238–247.

Crick, N. R., & Dodge, K. A. (1994). A review and reformulation of social information-processing mechanisms in children's social adjustment. *Psychological Bulletin, 115*(1), 74–101.

Crofford, L. J. (2007). Violence, stress, and somatic syndromes. *Trauma, Violence, & Abuse, 8*(3), 299–313.

Cunradi, C. B., Caetano, R., & Schafer, J. (2002). Socioeconomic predictors of intimate partner violence among White, Black, and Hispanic couples in the United States. *Journal of Family Violence, 17*(4), 377–389.

Dahle, K. P. (2006). Strengths and limitations of actuarial prediction of criminal reoffence in a German prison sample: A comparative study of LSI-R, HCR-20 and PCL-R. *International Journal of Law and Psychiatry, 29*, 341–442.

Davison, G. C., Vogel, R. S., & Coffman, S. G. (1997). Think-aloud approaches to cognitive assessment and the articulated thoughts in simulated situations paradigm. *Journal of Consulting and Clinical Psychology, 65*, 950–958.

Dejonghe, E. S. (2008). *Genderized vs. gender-specific intimate partner violence: Childhood exposure and adult perpetration* (Doctoral dissertation). Retrieved from ProQuest Dissertations and Theses database. (UMI No. 3298034).

Delsol, C., & Margolin, G. (2004). The role of family-of-origin violence in men's marital violence perpetration. *Clinical Psychology Review, 24*(1), 99–122.

Desai, S., Arias, I., Thompson, M. P., & Basile, K. C. (2002). Childhood victimization and subsequent adult revictimization assessed in a nationally representative sample of women and men. *Violence and Victims, 17*(6), 639–653.

Desmarais, S. L., Reeves, K. A., Nicholls, T. L., Telford, R. P., & Fiebert, M. S. (2012). Prevalence of physical violence in intimate relationships, part 2: Rates of male and female perpetration. *Partner Abuse, 3*(2), 170–198.

Dobash, R. E., & Dobash, R. P. (1979). *Violence against wives: A case against the patriarchy.* New York: Free Press.

Dobash, R. P., & Dobash, R. (2004). Women's violence to men in intimate relationships: Working on a Puzzle. *British Journal of Criminology, 44*(3), 324–349.

Dobash, R., Dobash, R. E., Cavanagh, K., & Lewis, R. (1996). Re-education programmes for violent men—An evaluation. *Research Findings, 46*, 1–4.

Douglas, K. P., Yeomans, M., & Boer, D. P. (2005). Comparative validity analysis of multiple measures of violence risk in a sample of criminal offenders. *Criminal Justice and Behaviour, 32*(5), 479–510.

Dutton, D. G. (1995). A scale for measuring propensity for abusiveness. *Journal of Family Violence, 10*, 203–221.

Dutton, D. M., Landolt, M. A., Starzomski, A., & Bodnarchuk, M. (2001). Validation of the propensity for abusiveness scale in diverse male populations. *Journal of Family Violence, 16*(1), 59–73.

Eckhardt, C. I. (2007). Effects of alcohol intoxication on anger experience and expression among partner assaultive men. *Journal of Consulting and Clinical Psychology, 75*(1), 61–71.

Eckhardt, C. I., Murphy, C. M., Whitaker, D. J., Sprunger, J., Dykstra, R., & Woodard, K. (2013). The effectiveness of intervention programs for perpetrators and victims of intimate partner violence. *Partner Abuse, 4*(2), 196–231.

Eckhardt, C. I., Samper, R., Suhr, L., & Holtzworth-Munroe, A. (2012). Implicit attitudes toward violence among male perpetrators of intimate partner violence: A preliminary investigation. *Journal of Interpersonal Violence, 27*(3), 471–491.

Ehrensaft, M. K., Cohen, P., Brown, J., Smailes, E., Chen, H., & Johnson, J. G. (2003). Intergenerational transmission of partner violence: A 20-year prospective study. *Journal of Consulting and Clinical Psychology, 71*(4), 741–753.

Eidelson, R. J., & Epstein, N. (1982). Cognition and relationship maladjustment: Development of a measure of dysfunctional relationship beliefs. *Journal of Consulting and Clinical Psychology, 50*(5), 715–720.

Ellis, D. N., & Stuckless, N. (2006a). Domestic violence, DOVE, and divorce mediation. *Family Court Review, 44*(4), 658–671.

Ellis, D. N., & Stuckless, N. (2006b). Separation, domestic violence, and divorce mediation. *Conflict Resolution Quarterly, 23*(4), 461–485.

Feingold, A., Kerr, D. R., & Capaldi, D. M. (2008). Associations of substance use problems with intimate partner violence for at-risk men in long-term relationships. *Journal of Family Psychology, 22*(3), 429–438.

Felson, R. B., & Cares, A. C. (2005). Gender and the seriousness of assaults on intimate partners and other victims. *Journal of Marriage and Family, 67*(5), 1182–1195.

Finkel, E. J. (2007). Impelling and inhibiting forces in the perpetration of intimate partner violence. *Review of General Psychology, 11*(2), 193–207.

Finkel, E. J., DeWall, C. N., Slotter, E. B., McNulty, J. K., Pond, R. S., & Atkins, D. C. (2012). Using I³ theory to clarify when dispositional aggressiveness predicts intimate partner violence perpetration. *Journal of Personality and Social Psychology, 102*(3), 533–549.

Finkel, E. J., DeWall, C., Slotter, E. B., Oaten, M., & Foshee, V. A. (2009). Self-regulatory failure and intimate partner violence perpetration. *Journal of Personality and Social Psychology, 97*(3), 483–499.

Florsheim, P., McArthur, L., Hudak, C., Heavin, S., & Burrow-Sanchez, J. (2011). The Young Parenthood Program: Preventing intimate partner violence between adolescent mothers and young fathers. *Journal of Couple & Relationship Therapy, 10*(2), 117–134.

Foshee, V. A., Bauman, K. E., Ennett, S. T., Suchindran, C., Benefield, T., & Linder, G. F. (2005). Assessing the effects of the dating violence prevention program "Safe Dates" using random coefficient regression modeling. *Prevention Science, 6*(3), 245–258.

Foshee, V. A., Reyes, H. L. M., Ennett, S. T., Cance, J. D., Bauman, K. E., & Bowling, J. M. (2012). Assessing the effects of Families for Safe Dates, a family-based teen dating abuse prevention. *Journal of Adolescent Health, 51*(4), 349–356.

Friedrich-Cofer, L., & Huston, A. C. (1986). Television violence and aggression: The debate continues. *Psychological Bulletin, 100*(3), 364–371.

Fritz, P., Slep, A., & O'Leary, K. (2012). Couple-level analysis of the relation between family-of-origin aggression and intimate partner violence. *Psychology of Violence, 2*(2), 139–153.

Gelles, R. J. (1972). *The violent home: A study of physical aggression between husbands and wives.* Newbury Park, CA: SAGE.

Golding, J. M. (1999). Intimate partner violence as a risk factor for mental disorders: A meta-analysis. *Journal of Family Violence, 14*(2), 99–132.

Heilbrun, K., Yasuhara, K., & Shah, S. (2010). Violence risk assessment tools: Overview and critical analysis. In R. K. Otto & K. S. Doublas (Eds.), *Handbook of violence risk assessment* (pp. 1–17). New York: Routledge/Taylor & Francis.

Hendy, H. M., Weiner, K., Bakerofskie, J., Eggen, D., Gustitus, C., & McLeod, K. C. (2003). Comparison of six models for violent romantic relationships in college men and women. *Journal of Interpersonal Violence, 18*(6), 645–665.

Henry, B., Moffitt, T. E., Caspi, A., Langley, J., & Silva, P. A. (1994). On the "remembrance of things past": A longitudinal evaluation of the retrospective method. *Psychological Assessment, 6*(2), 92–101.

Hilton, N. Z., Harris, G. T., Rice, M. E., Lang, C., Cormier, C. A., & Lines, K. J. (2004). A brief actuarial assessment for the prediction of wife assault recidivism: The Ontario Domestic Assault Risk Assessment. *Psychological Assessment, 16*, 267–275.

Hines, D. A. (2007). Posttraumatic stress symptoms among men who sustain partner violence: An international multisite study of university students. *Psychology of Men & Masculinity, 8*(4), 225–239.

Hines, D. A., & Douglas, E. M. (2011). Symptoms of posttraumatic stress disorder in men who sustain intimate partner violence: A study of helpseeking and community samples. *Psychology of Men & Masculinity, 12*(2), 112–127.

Holtzworth-Munroe, A. (1992). Social skill deficits in maritally violent men: Interpreting the data using a social information processing model. *Clinical Psychology Review, 12*, 605–618.

Holtzworth-Munroe, A., & Anglin, K. (1991). The competency of responses given by maritally violent versus nonviolent men to problematic marital situations. *Violence and Victims, 6*(4), 257–269.

Holtzworth-Munroe, A., & Hutchinson, G. (1993). Attributing negative intent to wife behavior: The attributions of maritally violent versus nonviolent men. *Journal of Abnormal Psychology, 102*(2), 206–211.

Houry, D. J., Kemball R., Rhodes, K. V., & Kaslow N. J. (2006). Intimate partner violence and mental health symptoms in African American female ED patients. *American Journal of Emergency Medicine, 24*, 444–450.

Huesmann, L., Dubow, E. F., & Boxer, P. (2009). Continuity of aggression from childhood to early adulthood as a predictor of life outcomes: Implications for the adolescent-limited and life-course-persistent models. *Aggressive Behavior, 35*(2), 136–149.

Jackson, H., Philp, E., Nuttall, R. L., & Diller, L. (2002). Traumatic brain injury: A hidden consequence for battered women. *Professional Psychology: Research and Practice, 33*(1), 39–45.

Jankowski, M., Leitenberg, H., Henning, K., & Coffey, P. (1999). Intergenerational transmission of dating aggression as a function of witnessing only same sex parents vs. opposite sex parents vs. both parents as perpetrators of domestic violence. *Journal of Family Violence, 14*(3), 267–279.

Jaycox, L. H., McCaffrey, D., Eiseman, B., Aronoff, J., Shelley, G. A., Collins, R. L., & Marshall, G. N. (2006). Impact of a school-based dating violence prevention program among Latino Teens: Randomized controlled effectiveness trial. *Journal of Adolescent Health, 39*(5), 694–704.

Johnson, M. P. (2006). Conflict and control: Gender symmetry and asymmetry in domestic violence. *Violence Against Women, 12*(11), 1003–1018.

Johnson, M. P., & Ferraro, K. J. (2000). Research on domestic violence in the 1990s: Making distinctions. *Journal of Marriage and the Family, 62*(4), 948–963.

Kershaw, T. S., Small, M., Joseph, G., Theodore, M., Bateau, R., & Frederic, R. (2006). The influence of power on HIV risk among pregnant women in rural Haiti. *AIDS and Behavior, 10*(3), 309–318.

Kessler, R. C., Molnar, B. E., Feurer, I. D., & Appelbaum, M. (2001). Patterns and mental health predictors of domestic violence in the United States: Results from the National Comorbidity Survey. *International Journal of Law and Psychiatry, 24*(4–5), 487–508.

Kim, H. K., & Capaldi, D. M. (2004). The association of antisocial behavior and depressive symptoms between partners and risk for aggression in romantic relationships. *Journal of Family Psychology, 18*(1), 82–96.

Kropp, P. R., Hart, S. D., & Belfrage, H. (2005). *Brief Spousal Assault Form for the Evaluation of Risk (B-SAFER): User manual*. Vancouver: Proactive Resolutions.

Kropp, P. R., Hart, S. D., Webster, C. D., & Eaves, D. (1999). *Spousal Assault Risk Assessment: User's guide*. Toronto: Multi-Health Systems.

Kropp, P. R., Hart, S. D., Webster, C. D., & Eaves, D. (2008). *Spousal Assault Risk Assessment: User's guide* (2nd ed.). Vancouver: British Columbia Institute Against Family Violence.

Kwako, L. E., Glass, N., Campbell, J., Melvin, K. C., Barr, T., & Gill, J. M. (2011). Traumatic brain injury in intimate partner violence: A critical review of outcomes and mechanisms. *Trauma, Violence, & Abuse, 12*(3), 115–126.

Kwong, M. J., Bartholomew, K., Henderson, A. Z., & Trinke, S. J. (2003). The intergenerational transmission of relationship violence. *Journal of Family Psychology, 17*(3), 288–301.

Langhinrichsen-Rohling, J., Neidig, P., & Thorn, G. (1995). Violent marriages: Gender differences in levels of current violence and past abuse. *Journal of Family Violence, 10*(2), 159–176.

Leisring, P. A. (2009). What will happen if I punch him? Expected consequences of female violence against male dating partners. *Journal of Aggression, Maltreatment & Trauma, 18*(7), 739–751.

Leserman, J., & Drossman, D. A. (2007). Relationship of abuse history to functional gastrointestinal disorders and symptoms: Some possible mediating mechanisms. *Trauma, Violence, & Abuse, 8*(3), 331–343.

Levinson. D. (1989). *Family violence in cross-cultural perspective*. Newbury Park, CA: SAGE.

Lewis, H. B. (1971). *Shame and guilt in neurosis*. Oxford: International Universities Press.

Magdol, L., Moffitt, T. E., Caspi, A., & Silva, P. A. (1998). Developmental antecedents of partner abuse: A prospective-longitudinal study. *Journal of Abnormal Psychology, 107*(3), 375–389.

Maldonado, R. C., DiLillo, D., & Hoffman, L. (2014). Can college students use emotion regulation strategies to alter intimate partner aggression-risk behaviors? An examination using I3 theory. *Psychology of Violence*. doi: 10.1037/a0035454

Malik, N. M., & Lindahl, K. M. (1998). Aggression and dominance: The roles of power and culture in domestic violence. *Clinical Psychology: Science and Practice, 5*(4), 409–423.

Margolin, G., John, R. S., & Gleberman, L. (1988). Affective responses to conflictual discussions in violent and nonviolent couples. *Journal of Consulting and Clinical Psychology, 56*(1), 24–33.

Markman, H. J., & Floyd, F. (1980). Possibilities for the prevention of marital discord: A behavioral perspective. *American Journal of Family Therapy, 8*(2), 29–48.

Matlow, R. B., & DePrince, A. P. (2013). The influence of victimization history on PTSD symptom expression in women exposed to intimate partner violence. *Psychological Trauma: Theory, Research, Practice, and Policy, 5*(3), 241–250.

Mbilinyi, L. F., Neighbors, C., Walker, D. D., Roffman, R. A., Zegree, J., Edleson, J., & O'Rourke, A. (2011). A telephone intervention for substance-using adult male perpetrators of intimate partner violence. *Research on Social Work Practice, 21*(1), 43–56.

McFall, R. M. (1982). A review and reformulation of the concept of social skills. *Behavioral Assessment, 4*, 1–33.

McPhail, B. A., Busch, N., Kulkarni, S., & Rice, G. (2007). An integrative feminist model: The evolving feminist perspective on intimate partner violence. *Violence Against Women, 13*(8), 817–841.

Mechanic, M. B., Weaver, T. L., & Resick, P. A. (2008). Mental health consequences of intimate partner abuse: A multidimensional assessment of four different forms of abuse. *Violence Against Women, 14*(6), 634–654.

Mihalic, S., & Elliott, D. (1997). A social learning theory model of marital violence. *Journal of Family Violence, 12*(1), 21–47.

Moretti, M. M., Obsuth, I., Odgers, C. L., & Reebye, P. (2006). Exposure to maternal vs. paternal partner violence, PTSD, and aggression in adolescent girls and boys. *Aggressive Behavior, 32*(4), 385–395.

Murphy, C. M. (2013). Social information processing and the perpetration of intimate partner violence: It is (and isn't) what you think. *Psychology of Violence, 3*(3), 212–217.

Murphy, C. M., & Eckhardt, C. I. (2005). Clinically relevant characteristics of perpetrators. In C. M. Murphy & C. I. Eckhardt (Eds.), *Treating the abusive partner: An individualized cognitive-behavioral approach* (pp. 19–49). New York: Guilford Press.

Murphy, C. M., & Hoover, S. A. (1999). Measuring emotional abuse in dating relationships as a multifactorial construct. *Violence and Victims, 14*(1), 39–53.

Murphy, C. M., Morrel, T. M., Elliott, J. D., & Neavins, T. M. (2003). A prognostic indicator scale for the treatment of partner abuse perpetrators. *Journal of Interpersonal Violence, 18*(9), 1087–1105.

Murphy, C. M., & O'Leary, K. (1989). Psychological aggression predicts physical aggression in early marriage. *Journal of Consulting and Clinical Psychology, 57*(5), 579–582.

Musser, P. H., Semiatin, J. N., Taft, C. T., & Murphy, C. M. (2008). Motivational interviewing as a pregroup intervention for partner-violent men. *Violence and Victims, 23*(5), 539–557.

National Center for Injury Prevention and Control. (2003). Costs of intimate partner violence against women in the United States. Atlanta: Centers for Disease Control and Prevention.

Neff, J., Holamon, B., & Schluter, T. (1995). Spousal violence among Anglos, Blacks, and Mexican Americans: The role of demographic variables, psychosocial predictors, and alcohol consumption. *Journal of Family Violence, 10*(1), 1–21.

Nicholls, T. L., Pritchard, M. M., Reeves, K. A., & Hilterman, E. (2013). Risk assessment in intimate partner violence: A systematic review of contemporary approaches. *Partner Abuse, 4*(1), 76–168.

Norwood, A., & Murphy, C. (2012). What forms of abuse correlate with PTSD symptoms in partners of men being treated for intimate partner violence? *Psychological Trauma: Theory, Research, Practice, and Policy, 4*(6), 596–604.

Nowinski, S. N., & Bowen, E. (2012). Partner violence against heterosexual and gay men: Prevalence and correlates. *Aggression and Violent Behavior, 17*(1), 36–52.

Ofreneo, M. P., & Montiel, C. (2010). Positioning theory as a discursive approach to understanding same-sex intimate violence. *Asian Journal of Social Psychology, 13*(4), 247–259.

O'Hearn, H., & Margolin, G. (2000). Men's attitudes condoning marital aggression: A moderator between family of origin abuse and aggression against female partners. *Cognitive Therapy and Research, 24*(2), 159–174.

O'Leary, K., Barling, J., Arias, I., Rosenbaum, A., Malone, J., & Tyree, A. (1989). Prevalence and stability of physical aggression between spouses: A longitudinal analysis. *Journal of Consulting and Clinical Psychology, 57*(2), 263–268.

Ontario Ministry of the Solicitor. (2000). A guide to the domestic Violence Supplementary Report Form. Toronto: Police Services Division.

Palmer, S. E., Brown, R. A., & Barrera, M. E. (1992). Group treatment program for abusive husbands: Long-term evaluation. *American Journal of Orthopsychiatry, 62*(2), 276–283.

Pence, E., & Peymar, M. (1993). *Education groups for men who batter: The Duluth Model.* New York: Springer.

Pronyk, P. M., Hargreaves, J. R., Kim, J. C., Morison, L. A., Phetla, G., Watts, C., ... Porter, J. D. H. (2006). Effect of a structural intervention for the prevention of intimate-partner violence and HIV in rural South Africa: A cluster randomised trial. *Lancet, 368*(9551), 1973–1983.

Rand, M., & Strom, K. (1997). Violence-related injuries treated in hospital emergency departments. Special Report (NCJ-156921). Washington, DC: US Department of Justice.

Rasmussen, K. R., & Boon, S. D. (2014). Prevalence and stability of physical aggression between spouses: A longitudinal analysis. *Personality and Individual Differences, 56*, 51–56.

Reid, R. J., Bonomi, A. E., Rivara, F. P., Anderson, M. L., Fishman, P. A., Carrell, D. S., & Thompson, R. S. (2008). Intimate partner violence among men: Prevalence, chronicity, and health effects. *American Journal of Preventive Medicine, 34*(6), 478–485.

Reitzel-Jaffe, D., & Wolfe, D. A. (2001). Predictors of relationship abuse among young men. *Journal of Interpersonal Violence, 16*(2), 99–115.

Rennison, C., & Welchans, S. (2000). Intimate partner violence. Bureau of Justice Statistics Report (NCJ 178247). Washington, DC: US Department of Justice.

Riggs, D. S., & Caulfield, M. B. (1997). Expected consequences of male violence against their female dating partners. *Journal of Interpersonal Violence, 12*(2), 229–240.

Riggs, D. S., & O'Leary, K. D. (1989). A theoretical model of courtship aggression. In M. A. Pirog-Good & J. E. Stets (Eds.), *Violence in dating relationships: Emerging social issues* (pp. 53–71). New York: Praeger.

Salazar, L. F., & Cook, S. L. (2006). Preliminary findings from an outcome evaluation of an intimate partner violence prevention program for adjudicated, African American, adolescent males. *Youth Violence and Juvenile Justice, 4*(4), 368–385.

Saltzman, L. E., Fanslow, J. L., McMahon, P. M., & Shelley G. A. (1999). *Intimate partner violence surveillance: Uniform definitions and recommended data elements, Version 1.0.* Atlanta: National Center for Injury Prevention and Control, Centers for Disease Control and Prevention.

Schumacher, J. A., Feldbau-Kohn, S., Slep, A., & Heyman, R. E. (2001). Risk factors for male-to-female partner physical abuse. *Aggression and Violent Behavior, 6*(2–3), 281–352.

Silverman, J. G., Decker, M. R., Reed, E., & Raj, A. (2006). Intimate partner violence victimization prior to and during pregnancy among women residing in 26 US states: Associations with maternal and neonatal health. *American Journal of Obstetrics and Gynecology, 195*(1), 140–148.

Simonelli, C. J., & Ingram, K. M. (1998). Psychological distress among men experiencing physical and emotional abuse in heterosexual dating relationships. *Journal of Interpersonal Violence, 13*(6), 667–681.

Simons, L., Burt, C., & Simons, R. L. (2008). A test of explanations for the effect of harsh parenting on the perpetration of dating violence and sexual coercion among college males. *Violence and Victims, 23*(1), 66–82.

Sims, E., Dodd, V., & Tejeda, M. J. (2008). The relationship between severity of violence in the home and dating violence. *Journal of Forensic Nursing, 4*(4), 166–173.

Sinclair, H., Ladny, R. T., & Lyndon, A. E. (2011). Adding insult to injury: Effects of interpersonal rejection types, rejection sensitivity, and self-regulation on obsessive relational intrusion. *Aggressive Behavior, 37*(6), 503–520.

Sippel, L. M., & Marshall, A. D. (2011). Posttraumatic stress disorder symptoms, intimate partner violence perpetration, and the mediating role of shame processing bias. *Journal of Anxiety Disorders, 25*(7), 903–910.

Slep, A., Foran, H. M., Heyman, R. E., & Snarr, J. D. (2010). Unique risk and protective factors for partner aggression in a large scale air force survey. *Journal of Community Health, 35*(4), 375–383.

Slotter, E. B., & Finkel, E. J. (2011). I³ theory: Instigating, impelling, and inhibiting factors in aggression. In P. R. Shaver & M. Mikulincer (Eds.), *Human aggression and violence: Causes, manifestations, and consequences* (pp. 35–52). Washington, DC: American Psychological Association.

Stith, S. M., & Farley, S. C. (1993). A predictive model of male spousal violence. *Journal of Family Violence, 8*(2), 183–201.

Stith, S. M., Rosen, K. H., McCollum, E. E., & Thomsen, C. J. (2004). Treating intimate partner violence within intact couple relationships: Outcomes of multi-couple versus individual couple therapy. *Journal of Marital and Family Therapy, 30*(3), 305–318.

Stith, S. M., Rosen, K. H., Middleton, K. A., Busch, A. L., Lundeberg, K., & Carlton, R. P. (2000). The intergenerational transmission of spouse abuse: A meta-analysis. *Journal of Marriage and the Family, 62*(3), 640–654.

Storey, J. E., Kropp, P., Hart, S. D., Belfrage, H., & Strand, S. (2014). Assessment and management of risk for intimate partner violence by police officers using the brief spousal assault form for the evaluation of risk. *Criminal Justice and Behavior, 41*(2), 256–271.

Straus, M. A. (1990). Ordinary violence, child abuse, and wife beating: What they have in common? In M. A. Straus &

R. J. Gelles (Eds.), *Physical violence in American families: Risk factors and adaptations to violence in 8,145 families* (pp. 403–421). New Brunswick, NJ: Transaction.

Straus. M. A. (1994). State-to-state differences in social inequality and social bonds in relation to assaults on wives in the United States. *Journal of Comparative Family Studies, 25,* 7–24.

Straus, M. A., & Gelles, R. J. (1986). Societal change and change in family violence from 1975 to 1985 as revealed by two national surveys. *Journal of Marriage and the Family, 48*(3), 465–479.

Straus M. A., Gelles, R. J., & Steinmetz, S. K. (1980). *Behind closed doors: Violence in the American family.* Garden City, NY: Anchor Press/Doubleday.

Straus, M. A., Hamby, S. L., Boney-McCoy, S., & Sugarman, D. B. (1996). The revised Conflict Tactics Scales (CTS2): Development and preliminary psychometric data. *Journal of Family Issues, 17*(3), 283–316.

Straus, M. A., & Yodanis, C. L. (1996). Corporal punishment in adolescence and physical assaults on spouses in later life: What accounts for the link? *Journal of Marriage and the Family, 58*(4), 825–841.

Sugarman, D. B., & Frankel, S. L. (1996). Patriarchal ideology and wife-assault: A meta-analytic review. *Journal of Family Violence, 11*(1), 13–40.

Taft, C. T., Kachadourian, L. K., Suvak, M. K., Pinto, L. A., Miller, M. W., Knight, J. A., & Marx, B. P. (2012). Examining impelling and disinhibiting factors for intimate partner violence in veterans. *Journal of Family Psychology, 26*(2), 285–289.

Taft, C. T., Murphy, C. M., King, L. A., Dedeyn, J. M., & Musser, P. H. (2005). Posttraumatic stress disorder symptomatology among partners of men in treatment for relationship abuse. *Journal of Abnormal Psychology, 114*(2), 259–268.

Taft, C. T., Schumm, J. A., Marshall, A. D., Panuzio, J., & Holtzworth-Munroe, A. (2008). Family-of-origin maltreatment, posttraumatic stress disorder symptoms, social information processing deficits, and relationship abuse perpetration. *Journal of Abnormal Psychology, 117*(3), 637–646.

Taft, C. T., Weatherill, R. P., Scott, J. P., Thomas, S. A., Kang, H. K., & Eckhardt, C. I. (2015). Social information processing in anger expression and partner violence in returning veterans. *Journal of Traumatic Stress, 28*(4), 314–321. doi: 10.1002/jts.22017

Taylor, B. G., Davis, R. C., & Maxwell, C. D. (2001). The effects of a group batterer treatment program: A randomized experiment in Brooklyn. *Justice Quarterly, 18*(1), 171–201.

Taylor, B., Stein, N., & Burden, F. (2010). The effects of gender violence/harassment prevention programming in middle schools: A randomized experimental evaluation. *Violence and Victims, 25*(2), 202–223.

Tjaden, P., & Thoennes, N. (1998). Stalking in America: Findings from the National Violence Against Women Survey. (NCJ 169592). Washington, DC: US Department of Justice, National Institute of Justice.

Tjaden, P., & Thoennes, N. (2000). Full report of the prevalence, incidence, and consequences of violence against women: Findings from the national violence against women survey. (NIJ Publication No. 183781). Washington, DC: US Department of Justice, National Institute of Justice.

Vandello. J. A., & Cohen. D. (2005). *Cultural themes associated with domestic violence against women: A cross cultural analysis.* Unpublished manuscript.

Walker, L. E. (1979). *The battered woman.* New York: Harper & Row.

Whitaker, D. J., Haileyesus, T., Swahn, M., & Saltzman, L. S. (2007). Differences in frequency of violence and reported injury between relationships with reciprocal and nonreciprocal intimate partner violence. *American Journal of Public Health, 97*(5), 941–947.

Whitaker, D. J., Murphy, C. M., Eckhardt, C. I., Hodges, A. E., & Cowart, M. (2013). Effectiveness of primary prevention efforts for intimate partner violence. *Partner Abuse, 4*(2), 175–195.

Whitaker, M. (2013). Centrality of control-seeking in men's intimate partner violence perpetration. *Prevention Science, 14*(5), 513–523.

Williams, J. E., & Best. D. L. (1990). Sex and psyche: Gender and self viewed cross-culturally. Beverly Hills. CA: SAGE.

Williams, K. B., & Houghton, A. B. (2004). Assessing the risk of domestic violence reoffending: A validation study. *Law & Human Behavior, 28*(4), 437–455.

Wilson, M., & Daly, M. (1993). Spousal homicide risk and estrangement. *Violence and Victims, 8*(1), 3–16.

Wolfe, D. A., Crooks, C., Jaffe, P., Chiodo, D., Hughes, R., Ellis, W., … Donner, A. (2009). A school-based program to prevent adolescent dating violence: A cluster randomized trial. *Archives of Pediatrics & Adolescent Medicine, 163*(8), 692–699.

Wolfe, D. A., Wekerle, C., Scott, K., Straatman, A. L., Grasley, C. C., & Reitzel-Jaffe, D. (2003). Dating violence prevention with at-risk youth: A controlled outcome evaluation. *Journal of Consulting and Clinical Psychology, 71*(2), 279–291.

Woodin, E. M., & O'Leary, K. D. (2010). A brief motivational intervention for physically aggressive dating couples. *Prevention Science, 11,* 371–383.

World Health Organization. (2013). *Global and regional estimates of violence against women: Prevalence and health effects of intimate partner violence and non-partner sexual violence.* Geneva: Author.

Homicide-Suicide

Marc Hillbrand

Abstract

Homicide-suicide entails a homicide followed by the perpetrator's suicide within one week. The incidence of homicide-suicide in the US was 0.23% per 100,000 in 2013 (about 5% of all US homicides). In Western Europe and other low violence countries, such as Japan, homicide-suicides make up a much higher proportion of all homicides. Subtypes are filicidal, spousal (including jealous and declining health subtypes), familial, and extrafamilial homicide-suicide. Spousal homicide-suicides are the most common, yet extrafamilial homicide-suicides receive the most media attention, despite their rarity. Related phenomena include mass murder, victim-precipitated suicide ("suicide by cop"), politically motivated homicide-suicide, and suicide in violent offenders. We review several conceptual models of the etiology of homicide-suicide, namely developmental, dynamic, biological, and cognitive models, and draw implications from the current state of knowledge about homicide-suicide.

Key Words: homicide, suicide, homicide-suicide, murder-suicide, interpersonal violence, aggression

Homicide is defined as the intentional, unlawful killing of a person by another person (United Nations Office on Drugs and Crime [UNODC], 2013; National Violent Death Reporting System [NVDRS], 2014). More than 16,000 individuals annually are victims of homicide in the United States (NVDRS, 2014). A very conservative estimate of global deaths attributable to homicide is half a million (UNODC, 2013). Suicide is defined as death caused by self-directed injurious behavior with any intent to die as a result of the behavior (Crosby, Ortega, & Melanson, 2011). More than 38,000 individuals annually die by suicide in the country (NVDRS, 2014). Global deaths attributable to suicide have been estimated to be about one million annually (Murray & Lopez, 1997). Homicide-suicide (HS) is defined as a homicide or a series of homicides followed by the perpetrator's suicide within one week (Marzuk, Tardiff, Hirsch, 1992). The term homicide-suicide is preferable to the commonly used term of murder-suicide because the term *murder* is a legal, not a scientific term (Hillbrand, 2001). Until recently, it was only possible to *estimate* the number of victims of homicide-suicide in the United States each year (Eliason, 2009). These estimates were in the 500–1,000 range (Marzuk et al., 1992). Global annual deaths attributable to homicide-suicide have been estimated to be about 100,000 (Marzuk et al., 1992; Eliason, 2009).

The recently developed National Violent Death Reporting System (NVDRS) reveals that 216 deaths were attributable to homicide-suicides in the reporting states in 2011, the most recent year for which data are available. Seventeen US states currently participate in the NVDRS, with a total population of 95 million. These 216 deaths yield a rate of 0.23% per 100,00 (NVDRS, 2014). Extrapolating from these data, we estimate that 700–800 deaths annually in the United States are attributable to homicide-suicide.

The incidence of homicide-suicide in other countries is similar to that in the United States, between 0.2% and 0.3% per 100,000 per year (Carcach & Grabosky, 1998; Coid, 1983; Milroy, 1993; Travis, Johnson, & Milroy, 2007), with some exceptions, such as 0.02%–0.07% in the Netherlands (Liem, Postulart, & Nieuwbeerta, 2009). This similarity stands in stark contrast with the dramatic discrepancies in homicide rates by country. The United States, a country with a high incidence of homicides, has about 10 times more homicides than countries with low incidence, such as Japan or Austria (Fingerhut & Kleinman, 1990; UNODC, 2013). This has been shown to be a function of a number of factors, such as high rates of firearm ownership in the United States (Hemenway & Miller, 2000; Miller, Azrael, & Hemenway, 2002, 2007). Homicide-suicides are thus a much greater proportion of all homicides in countries that have low rates of homicidal violence (Hillbrand, 2001). Milroy (1993), for instance, found that in parts of the United Kingdom, one-third of all homicides were followed by suicide. The common belief that homicide-suicide is a rare subtype of homicide may be a fairly unique US perception, one that is shared with other countries with high incidence of homicidal violence (Hillbrand, 2014).

Characteristics of Homicide-Suicides

Perpetrators of homicide-suicide tend to be male. Among 21 studies reviewed by Travis and colleagues (2007), the majority reported that more than 90% of the perpetrators in their samples were males. Most victims of homicide-suicide are female (Marzuk et al., 1992; Eliason, 2009), which is attributable to the fact that the majority of homicide-suicides are of the spousal/consortial category, in which an individual kills a current or prior intimate partner and then completes suicide (see section 4). Most studies report 80%–90% female victims.

Many characteristics associated with homicide-suicides distinguish homicide-suicide perpetrators from homicide perpetrators who do not complete suicide (Eliason, 2009; Hillbrand, 2014). The modal age range of perpetrators is 40–50, considerably older than homicide perpetrators who do not complete suicide (Eliason, 2009). Victims vary widely in age, covering the entire life span (Eliason, 2009; Marzuk et al., 1992). Substance abuse is present in a much smaller proportion of homicide-suicides than in homicides not followed by suicide, with a range of estimates of 15%–35% (Eliason, 2009). Prior criminality is relatively rare among perpetrators of homicide-suicide,

in the 10%–25% estimated range (Eliason, 2009). A lifelong pattern of impulsivity is usually absent among perpetrators (Marzuk et al., 1992). Studies that mention employment status report that most perpetrators are employed (Eliason, 2009).

Homicide-suicides are predominantly perpetrated with firearms. Estimates range between 85% and 95% (Eliason, 2009), considerably higher than for homicide overall. From 2002 to 2011, the majority (95%) of US homicide incidents involved a single victim. In 2011, 66% of homicides with a single victim involved a firearm, compared to 79% of homicides involving multiple victims (Cooper & Smith, 2013).

Mood disorder is the most common diagnosis among perpetrators, and major losses, such as marital separation or dismissal from a job, are common precipitants (Eliason, 2009; Roma et al., 2012). The predominance of mood disorder diagnoses may help explain the relatively similar incidence of homicide-suicide rates across the globe (Hillbrand, 2001). Mood disorders have a considerable genetic loading (Craddock & Forty, 2006). Disorders with high genetic loadings, such as schizophrenia or autism, have similar cross-cultural prevalence (Torrey, 2013). By contrast, disorders with low genetic loadings have variable cross-cultural prevalence. For example, US and UK suicide rates (a phenomenon strongly associated with mood disorders) are similar, namely 12.3 per 100,000 and 11.8 per 100,000, respectively; but US and UK homicide rates (a phenomenon with a low association with mood disorders or any other genetic factor) are greatly disparate, 4.8 per 100,000 and 1.0 per 100,000, respectively (Hillbrand, 2014).

This review of characteristics of homicide-suicides reveals that homicide-suicide perpetrators are dissimilar from individuals who kill but do not go on to suicide, but are quite similar to individuals who die by suicide. Indeed, they are mostly older males with mood disorders who have suffered a loss or multiple losses. They have cognitive myopia and see "no way out." They are different from individuals who only kill themselves in that they have an overvalued idea that they have been harmed by another (or other) individual(s) against whom they seek revenge.

Subtypes of Homicide-Suicides

Marzuk and his colleagues (1992) have proposed a typology of homicide-suicide that many researchers have adopted. They distinguish between filicide-suicide, familicide-suicide, spousal/consortial homicide-suicide, and extrafamilial homicide-suicide.

Filicide-Suicide

In this type of homicide-suicide, a parent kills a child and then commits suicide. It should be noted that in a majority of cases of child homicide, a parent or stepparent is the perpetrator (Cooper & Smith, 2011). Suicide immediately after the homicide is frequent in child homicide by a parent. It occurs in about 50% of the cases in which the father is the perpetrator, and in about a third of cases in which the mother is the perpetrator. Filicide-suicide is the second most common type of intra-familial violence (Eliason, 2009; Dabby, Patel, & Poore, 2010). It is noteworthy that the first year of life is a dangerous year for all US children (Palladino, Singh, Campbell, Flynn, & Gold, 2011). The age distribution of female homicide victims peaks in the first year of life. For males, the distribution is bimodal, with peaks in the 1st and the 25th year of life (Cooper & Smith, 2011, 2013).

An early typology of filicide-homicide was proposed by Phillip Resnick (1969). He proposed distinguishing between altruistic filicide, filicide in the context of acute psychosis, accidental filicide (fatal child abuse), filicide of an unwanted child, and filicide motivated by revenge against the spouse.

Altruistic filicide is motivated by parental love and aims to relieve the imagined or occasionally real suffering of the child. An example of this may involve a mother who is suicidal but unwilling to leave her child motherless in what she views as a "cruel world." This may occur in the context of an *extended suicide*, a concept first proposed by Näcke (Näcke, 1908; cited in Meszaros, & Fischer-Danzinger, 2000). Filicide in the context of acute psychosis involves a parent responding to psychotic thought processes such as command hallucinations to kill his or her child. Accidental filicide results from child neglect or abuse, including Münchausen syndrome by proxy. Parents who commit spouse revenge filicide kill children to cause pain to their spouse or ex-spouse.

Resnick (1969) described a phenomenon that he labels *relief of tension* that occurs in some filicides. He speculated that this relief of tension could exert either a facilitating or a deterring effect on the probability of the perpetrator's suicide. It can cause a sort of psychic exhaustion after the child's death that leads some perpetrators to abandon their original plan to complete filicide-suicide. Alternatively, it can lead other perpetrators to attempt suicide impulsively once they grasp the gravity of their act.

Mood disorder is the modal diagnosis among filicidal parents (Eliason, 2009). Major depressive disorder with psychotic features may be particularly associated with filicidal behavior (Meszaros, & Fischer-Danzinger, 2000).

Spousal/Consortial Homicide-Suicide

The victim of this type of homicide-suicide is the perpetrator's current or past spouse or intimate partner. This phenomenon has also been dubbed *femicide-suicide*, a neologism that has not been adopted widely except in the feminist literature (PATH, 2009). This type makes up the most homicide-suicides in the United States (Logan, et al., 2008), in part, a function of the prominent use of firearms in these crimes. In one state (Kentucky), for instance, fewer than 7% of all firearm homicides were followed by a firearm suicide, but in two-thirds of the cases in which a women was shot in an intimate partner-related homicide, the male perpetrator then killed himself with the firearm (Walsh & Hemenway, 2005). More than half of all men who kill their intimate partner go on to kill themselves (Barber et al., 2008). Relational distance between victim and perpetrator is thus an important variable. It is defined as the amount and intensity of interaction between two people. Relational distance is strongly associated with the probability of post-homicide suicide: the closer the distance, the more likely the perpetrator is to suicide (Liem, Postulart, & Nieuwbeerta, 2009).

There are two subtypes of spousal/consortial homicide-suicides.

Jealous type. The jealous type represents more than half of all homicide-suicides in the United States, where a woman is killed by an intimate partner every 6 hours (PATH, 2009). The jealous type of homicide-suicide involves a jealous male who kills his sexual partner, often following a phase of stalking, and then kills himself (Meloy, 2013). He is usually motivated by pathological jealousy that may be of psychotic proportion. In some instances, it also involves the killing of a third party, such as the current intimate partner of the victim. In a 12-city case-control study of 220 US homicides of women, Koziol-McLain (2006) found the following factors to be predictive of spousal/consortial homicide-suicide: being married (as opposed to unmarried cohabitation), firearm ownership, prior threat to victim with firearm, prior threat to kill the victim, presence of a stepchild in the household, and prior suicide threat by the perpetrator.

Declining health type. In the declining health type of spousal homicide-suicide, an older male kills his physically incapacitated spouse and then himself. The perpetrator is usually motivated by factors such as depression with prominent hopelessness in despair. The records of 65% of cases in one study indicated the presence of depression, in most cases untreated: antidepressants had not been prescribed, though benzodiazepines had (Malphurs & Cohen, 2005). Unlike the jealous type, it typically does not involve psychotic depression.

Familicide-Suicide

Familicide-suicide involves an individual who kills a spouse and children and occasionally also other relatives, bystanders, and pets. It constitutes an overlap between the categories of filicide-suicide and spousal/consortial homicide-suicide. The perpetrator is typically an older male who is depressed and paranoid, and who may abuse alcohol. Websdale has distinguished between "suicide by proxy" and "murder by proxy" subtypes of familicide-suicide (Websdale, 2010). In suicide by proxy, a despondent father seeks to die and kills the family to "protect" them from an adverse outcome. In "murder by proxy," the children are chosen as victims because the father identifies them with the primary object of his murderous wrath, his consort.

Extrafamilial Homicide-Suicide

This type of homicide-suicide involves an individual who seeks revenge for real or imagined slights by killing those considered responsible and then himself. Extra-familial homicide-suicide is the type that receives the most media coverage, yet it is the least common of the four types. Several researchers have pointed out the theme of retaliation as the prominent motivation of the perpetrators who may use the expression "payback time" to communicate this. Rejection, failure, and loss of autonomy create frustration and anger that at some point overwhelm the individual and turn into the need to retaliate (Dietz, 1986; Mullen, 2004).

Attempted Homicide-Suicide

In some instances, the intent to complete homicide-suicide coupled with the means to complete homicide-suicide exists (and may be documented in a suicide note), but does not result in the death of the perpetrator. This is a function of factors that are not under the control of the perpetrator: help summoned by a witness, prompt

emergency medical response, weapon malfunction, and so on. Examples include a man with schizophrenia who had carefully planned a patricide-suicide, killed his father, but survived a drug overdose that is usually lethal; and a woman with a psychotic depression who killed all her children and hanged herself, but survived. Studies of individuals who have made near-lethal suicide attempts have limitations (Tennant, Bebbington, & Hurry, 1980), yet such studies have played an important role in our understanding of the role of hopelessness and extreme psychic pain in suicide (Beck, Steer, Beck, & Newman, 1993). Cases of attempted homicide-suicide thus yield the possibility to learn about the mental processes of the perpetrator. The only study of attempted homicide-suicide that a literature review yielded was that of Meszaros and Fischer-Danzinger (2000). In their small sample, the altruistic motive was prominent among individuals with a mood disorder. Interviews with perpetrators/survivors of attempted homicide-suicide have been underused as an investigational tool to study homicide-suicide. The discoverability of interview data from perpetrators/survivors, which could possibly incriminate the participant, is one of the challenges that future research will need to overcome.

Related Phenomena
Mass Murder

Most homicide-suicides involve two deaths, that of the perpetrator and of his or her victim (Marzuk et al., 1992). Some homicide-suicides involve multiple homicides followed by the suicide of the perpetrator and fall under the heading of *mass murder*. This term is used to describe *the willful injuring of five or more persons of whom three or more are killed by a single offender in a single incident* (Dietz, 1986). Suicide is a common conclusion of these killing sprees, occurring in about half the mass murders (Dietz, 1986; Hempel, Meloy, & Richards, 1999). Individuals who commit mass murder are often loners preoccupied with (real or imagined) past harm done to them—for example, rejected ex-intimate partners or disgruntled employees. They tend to view the world through the lens of their severe paranoia, be severely socially isolated, and live with chronic, extreme anger. They often feel hopeless and want to die, though not until they have exacted revenge from their "victimizer."

One subtype has been dubbed "pseudo commando" mass murder (Dietz, 1986; Knoll, 2010). The event occurs in public places during the daytime, according to a well-planned method of killing, and involves an extensive arsenal of weapons and munitions. The perpetrator has no escape plan and fully expects to be killed during the incident. He is driven by strong feelings of anger and resentment for being persecuted.

Most such murderous rampages involve a phenomenon that may be conceptualized as the *exhaustion of the murderous drive*. The killings typically end after about a dozen killings, as if the perpetrator, maybe exhausted by the psychic cost of the havoc he or she has caused, runs out of the desire to kill. Of 45 school shootings in the 2000–2010 period, only one had more than 10 victims. For example, Robert Steinhäuser, a teenager who shot and killed 16 people at his high-school in Erfurt, Germany, in 2002, was overheard saying, "That's enough" ("Für heute reicht's"), after shooting his last victim. He killed himself soon thereafter. Kip Kinkel shot 25 people at Thurston High School, Oregon, in 1998, killing 2. After his killing spree, he encouraged police to shoot him ("Shoot me, kill me!").

There are a few notable exceptions to the phenomenon of *exhaustion of the murderous intent*. One is Adam Lanza, the man who broke into a Connecticut school and killed 26 students and teachers in 2012. It is conceivable that his psychiatric condition on the autism spectrum may account for this exception. His lack of understanding of, empathy for, and ability to put himself in the shoes of others may explain the scope of his murderous rage. His violent spree ended in self-inflicted death. Though suicide is not the inevitable conclusion of mass murder, occurring about half the time, it is conceivable that just as some individuals appear to run out of murderous rage, they may also run out of the desire to kill themselves.

Suicide by Victim-Precipitated Homicide

In victim-precipitated homicides, an individual uses real or simulated lethal force with the intent to cause someone to kill him or her, either law enforcement personnel or the apparent victim. The suicidal intent of the individual only becomes apparent after the event, either from a suicide note written before the incident or from crime investigation data (Kennedy, Homant, & Hupp, 1998; Van Zandt, 1993). The most common manifestation of this phenomenon involves the deliberate attempt by an individual to fool law enforcement personnel into believing that he or she poses a lethal threat, leading the officer(s) to kill the individual. These incidents are often labeled "suicide by cop."

A Connecticut incident illustrates this: A substance-addicted individual decided to end his life, which he had come to experience as unbearable and hopeless. He wrote a suicide note documenting his motivation and intent, which included first killing his beloved therapist for reasons that the suicide note did not make clear. He went to the therapist's clinic early, awaiting her arrival, armed with a hunting knife and a handgun. He used the knife to kill the therapist, and then calmly sat on the sidewalk awaiting the arrival of the police. When they arrived, he aimed the handgun at them, causing them to draw their weapons and fire, killing him. Police later discovered that the gun was unloaded and they concluded that he had planned the entire course of events.

In the United States, such homicides by law enforcement personnel fall in the legal category of *justifiable* or *legal* homicides, akin to homicides on the battlefield or legal executions. Law enforcement officers are now trained to detect such situations and prevent harm, if possible, possibly resulting in a decrease in the incidence of such events (Parent, 1998; Van Zandt, 1993). A recent example involves a man with a severe psychiatric disability who attempted to elicit the police to shoot him by brandishing what appeared to be a handgun at a busy highway access ramp at dusk. The officers did not shoot, maybe detecting the implausibility of the situation, and safely seized him. He was eventually returned to the hospital where he explained that he "did not have the guts" to kill himself and thought this would be an "easy" way to die.

Politically Motivated Homicide-Suicide

Incidents fall under this heading that are commonly referred to as "suicide-bombing" or "suicide-terrorism" (Hiss & Kahana, 1988; Townsend, 2007, 2014). A sadly common type of politically motivated homicide-suicide is exemplified by a terrorist who straps on a concealed explosive vest that is detonated in enemy territory. Such events typically occur in crowded settings. Victims are usually civilians, but also include security and military personnel. Circumstances often indicate the intent to inflict as many casualties as possible—for instance, by packing explosives with nails and shrapnel. These attacks usually, although not always, cause the death of the perpetrator (Taylor & Ryan, 1988; Townsend, 2007).

The label *politically motivated homicide-suicide* is more accurate than the more commonly used terms of *suicide-bombing* or *suicide-terrorism*, which suggest that suicide plays an important role in the phenomenon. In fact, all evidence converges to indicate that the death of the perpetrators of politically motivated homicide-suicides are epiphenomena or unavoidable "by-products" (Townsend, 2007). These perpetrators are principally motivated to kill others, and placidly accept death as the price for accomplishing the homicidal goal (Townsend, 2007, 2014).

The extant knowledge about the phenomenon of politically motivated homicide-suicides comes from a variety of sources, namely psychological autopsies, surveys of at-risk individuals, crime reconstructions, and interviews of "unsuccessful" bombers who survived the attacks (Merari, 1998; 2005; 2008). Politically motivated homicide-suicides are different from other homicide-suicides, including mass-murders, for four main reasons. Typically motivated by the triad of murderous intent against members of a group perceived as oppressors, for religious beliefs, and with the desire to seek vengeance for perceived harm, they are not instigated by real suicidal intent (Townsend, 2014). The primary motivation is to kill and instill terror, with the ultimate goal to elicit political change. The killing is typically to avenge *global* harm allegedly committed by the community to which the victims of the attacks belong (e.g., the United States) against the community to which the perpetrator belongs (e.g., the Arab Middle-East, in the case of the 9/11 attacks). In some instances, the vengeance is in part retribution for *specific* harm to the perpetrator of the attack. Several studies have shown that a disproportionate number of perpetrators of politically motivated homicide-suicides had a relative or friend who died at the hands of the "oppressor" group (Townsend, 2014).

Religious beliefs play a crucial role in many politically motivated homicide-suicides. Several unsuccessful perpetrators have emphatically denied that suicide was intended. Suicide is indeed explicitly forbidden in the Koran (Abdel-Khalek, 2004). These unsuccessful perpetrators stressed their intent of committing martyrdom or *istishad*, which means *sacrifice in the name of Allah* (Abdel-Khalek, 2004; Hazani, 1993; Post et al., 2009). They equate their efforts with the attacks led by the prophet Muhammad and his early followers in the seventh century to proselytize among Meccan tribes and spread his religious doctrine (Esposito, 2002). Other psychological factors relevant to politically motivated homicide-suicides include the presence of a sense of hope (in contrast to the hopelessness experienced by most suicide completers), the careful manipulation of perpetrators by politically motivated leaders who exploit the perpetrators' religious and social beliefs, and the absence of psychopathology (Townsend, 2014).

Etiology of Homicide-Suicide: Conceptual Models
Developmental Models

These models are relevant to understanding the developmental trajectory leading to aggression against other and against self. The developmental paths leading to aggression against others have been studied extensively (Dahlberg & Potter, 2001; Granic & Patterson, 2006; Loeber & Stouthamer-Loeber, 1998; Patterson & Yoerger, 2002). Loeber and Stouthamer-Loeber, for instance, suggested that several developmental pathways associated with significant interpersonal problems exist beginning in early childhood, and these can lead to aggression. The overt pathway is characterized by bullying, followed by fighting, and later to severe violence. The early pathway starts with stubbornness, followed by defiance and authority avoidance. The covert pathway begins with minor covert disruptive behavior and property damage, leading to moderate delinquency and, ultimately, to serious crime.

The developmental path to aggression against self has been studied less extensively, yet it is slowly becoming understood. Social support throughout the lifespan is among the strongest protective factor for suicide; conversely, the absence of social support is among the strongest risk factors for suicide, in particular when combined with hopelessness (McLean, Maxwell, Platt, Harris, & Jepson, 2008). Séguin and colleagues (2014) have identified two pathways to suicide, one associated with a high burden of adversity, leading to suicide in the early 20s, the other associated with a more moderate burden of adversity, leading to later suicide. The former is characterized by conduct and behavioral problems, social isolation, and conflicts mediated by school-related difficulties, the end of a love relationship, and previous suicide attempts.

Although no clear understanding of the developmental trajectory leading to homicide-suicide has yet emerged, a number of relevant contributions have been made toward the goal of developing this understanding. Shaffer (1974; 1982) for instance described a common pathway to aggression against oneself and others in a group of violent individuals who completed suicide. The pathway included impulsivity leading to interpersonal difficulties, depression, and interpersonal violence, aggravated by alcohol and drug abuse. Future research will determine whether this is the typical pathway leading to homicide-suicide.

Dynamic

Plutchik and van Praag (1990 1994) have proposed a two-stage model of countervailing forces influenced by ethological-evolutionary theories. They posit that when an individual experiences losses, threats, challenges, and status changes, aggressive impulses are activated. For instance, criticism or rejection by a spouse activates aggressive urges. These urges can lead to overt aggressive behavior as a function of two sets of factors, labeled *amplifiers* and *attenuators*. Amplifiers increase the probability of aggressive behavior. They include, among many other factors, poor socialization, lack of trust, access to weapons, and a tolerant attitude toward the expression of aggression. Attenuators diminish the likelihood of aggressive behavior and involve factors such as empathy, timidity, close family ties, and appeasement from others. The complex interaction among amplifiers and attenuators determines the probability of aggressive behavior and constitutes the first stage of the model. The second stage refers to the object of the aggression, self or other(s). The choice of the object of aggression is determined by other factors. Factors that increase the probability that the aggression will be directed against self include the presence of psychopathology, in particular depression and its component of hopelessness. Factors that increase the probability that the aggression will be directed toward others include paranoid thinking, impulsivity, conduct disorder, and psychopathy. According to this model, an individual in whom both sets of factors are present (e.g., both hopelessness and paranoid thinking) has an increased risk of harming others *and* self.

Biological

The serotonin-aggression hypothesis is a biological model potentially relevant to understanding the etiology of homicide-suicide (Coccaro et al., 1989; Coccaro, 1995). According to this model, serotonergic dysfunction results in poor behavioral inhibition and aggressive behavior, which manifest itself as increased sensitivity to stimuli that elicit aggression and diminished sensitivity to cues that signal punishment. It should be noted that the model makes no prediction with regard to homicide-suicide. Support for the serotonin-aggression hypothesis has come

from correlational as well as experimental studies of rodents, nonhuman primates, and humans (Moffitt et al., 1998; see chapters 21 and 22 in this volume for more information about neurobiological factors in suicide and homicide).

Cognitive Models

Beck (1999) has proposed a cognitive theory of violence. He argues that the cognitive distortions that account for the genesis of depression and suicidality (egocentric bias, automatic thoughts, catastrophizing, dichotomous thinking, personalization, and various other attributional biases) also account for the genesis of anger, hostility and violence. Anger is primarily an emotional construct, yet it has cognitive, physiological, motivational, and behavioral components (Berkowitz, 1993; 1999). The cognitive component of anger entails the perception that one or more individuals illegitimately interfere with important personal goals. The motivational component of anger consists of hostile and aggressive impulses. Hostility is primarily an attitudinal construct. It is the predisposition to dislike and mistrust others and to interpret their behavior as egoistic and hurtful (Miller, Smith, Turner, Guijarro, & Hallet, 1996). Anger and hostility are fueled by cognitive distortions and activate each other and motivate aggressive behavior against others.

Beck argues that loss and fear cause distress that, in some individuals predisposed to hostility, lead to a focus on the individual viewed as responsible for the loss and fear, who is perceived as the *offender*. This process results in feelings of anger and in mobilization for attack. Interpersonal losses, fears, and threats activate thoughts and then feelings that lead to aggression. An important contribution of this theory is the emphasis on the role played by the cognitive change of focus from the self onto the *offender* (the one perceived to be causing the distress) in the genesis of aggression against another person. Beck argues that by contrast, in self-directed aggression, this cognitive change of focus usually does not occur. The motivation to kill others and then oneself may thus be viewed as resulting from cognitive distortions that include this change of focus onto future victim(s) that coexist with distortions that lead to self-destruction.

In recent years the association between posttraumatic stress disorder (PTSD) and anger has become clearer. Earlier studies primarily focused on the role of fear in the etiology of PTSD. Several meta-analyses have now shown that anger and hostility are substantially associated with PTSD among trauma-exposed adults and that effect sizes are comparable between anger and hostility in their link with PTSD (Novaco & Chemtob, 2002; Orth & Wieland, 2006). Two theories have been proposed to account for the relation between anger and PTSD. Chemtob, Novaco, and colleagues have proposed a *survival mode theory* that stresses the fact that individuals with PTSD have a lowered threshold to perceiving situations as threatening (Chemtob, Hamada, Roitblat, & Muraoka, 1994; Chemtob, Novaco, Hamada, & Gross, 1997; Chemtob, Novaco, Hamada, Gross, & Smith, 1997; Novaco & Chemtob, 2002). The perception of threat activates a biological survival mode that includes fear, anger, and fight or flight reactions. In individuals with PTSD, a *fear avoidance theory* has been proposed that stresses the propensity to avoid trauma-related feelings of fear activated by posttraumatic intrusions (Feeny, Zoellner, & Foa, 2000; Foa, Riggs, Masie, & Yarczower, 1995; Riggs et al., 1992). In this view, trauma-related anger provides an alternate focus of attention, and one that is preferable because anger has a more positive emotional valence than fear.

A number of other cognitive factors have been shown to contribute to violence. Numerous studies have for instance identified the role of narcissistic injury and threatened egotism in the etiology of violence, including those demonstrating that threatened egotism is an important normally distributed personality dimension predictive of aggressiveness in nonclinical samples (Baumeister, Smart, & Boden, 1995; Baumeister, 2001; Baumeister, 1999; Bushman & Baumeister, 1998; Nestor, 2002). Operating from a psychoanalytic perspective, Bateman and Fonagy (2004, 2006, 2008) have implicated the role of faulty attachment experiences in the etiology of violence and, in particular, the deficient mentalization ability of the violent individual. They define mentalization as the ability to reflect on one's mental states and distinguish them from those of others. They speculate that children become increasingly aware of their own mental processes through their growing awareness of the mental processes of their mothers. This requires that the mother demonstrates that she thinks of the child as separate. If this does not occur, aggression arises as a response to defend the fragile emerging self. The child then internalizes the image of the caregiver as bad. Once adult, the person is then forced to develop an identity around an alien persecutory internal object that has to be defended against by violent means. Bateman and Fonagy (2008) called this discontinuity within the self *the alien self*. Future

research should clarify the role of these factors in homicide-suicide.

The Relatedness of Homicide and Suicide

In homicide-suicide, the suicide promptly follows the homicide(s). Homicidal offenders have also been shown to be at an elevated lifetime risk of suicide. Jokinen and colleagues (2009) have, for instance, shown an increased lifetime suicide risk among homicide perpetrators in Sweden, with the first two years post-homicide as the highest suicide risk. About 30% of the total mortality in their cohort was caused by suicide. In a nested case-control study comparing 27,000 adult suicides in Denmark from 1981 to 2006 and more than half a million age- and gender-matched living comparison individuals, Webb and colleagues (2012) found an elevated rate of death by suicide among sex offenders, a higher rate of death by suicide among (non-homicidal) violent offenders, and the highest rate of death by suicide among homicidal violent offenders. The pattern was even more pronounced among females (female OR = 30.9, 95% CI: [11.9, 80.6] versus male OR = 12.0, 95% CI: [8.3, 17.3]). The elevated rate of suicide among offenders has been noted extensively in studies from North America, Australia, and Western Europe, with the female suicide rate much higher than the male rate (Binswanger et al., 2007; Jokinen et al., 2009; Joukamaa, 1998; Pratt, Piper, Appleby, Webb, & Shaw, 2006, 2010; Stewart, Henderson, Hobbs, Ridout, & Knuiman, 2004; Webb et al., 2012). A related phenomenon is the elevated all-cause mortality of released prisoners (Zlodre, & Fazel, 2012).

Implications

A single homicide-suicide has a dramatic impact beyond the deaths of the perpetrator and victim(s). Their friends and relatives, along with direct witnesses of the homicide-suicide, experience the traumatic impact of the killings. They become indirect victims and experience mental health sequelae of the event (Anderson et al., 2001; Linton, 1995). They join the amazingly large segment of the population that has experienced the homicide or suicide of a friend or loved one. Linton (1995) conducted a survey of a representative sample of 505 US adults that revealed that 43% had witnessed interpersonal violence and 5% had a friend or relative die from homicide or suicide.

In the Littleton High School massacre, for instance, there were 15 deaths (including the two shooters), but there were also physical injuries to 23 students, including some causing permanent disabilities; in addition, friends, relatives, witnesses, emergency personnel, school personnel, and indeed the community at large experienced severe emotional trauma. Beyond increasing the climate of fear for the safety of schoolchildren, the school massacre also resulted in additional deaths, including the deaths by suicide of one Columbine High School student and the mother of one of the victims, both severely distraught over the killings, and of two students killed under unresolved circumstances in the year following the massacre (DeAngelis, 2000). A single homicide-suicide has enormous costs to society.

Hillbrand (2001, 2014) has proposed that homicide-suicide should be viewed as the most severe form of a much larger problem. It lies at the upper end of a spectrum of coexisting violence against others and against self, of which it constitutes only a small noticeable part. This spectrum includes attempted homicide-suicides, mass murders, suicides by victim-precipitated homicides, suicides of homicidal offenders while incarcerated, and many other clinical phenomena that have been described in isolation but have not been conceptualized as part of a spectrum of coexisting violence against others and against oneself. This includes suicidal behavior in violent offenders (Fruehwald, Matschnig, Koenig, Bauer, & Frottier, 2004; Shaw, Baker, Hunt, Moloney, & Appleby, 2004; Webb et al., 2012, 2013), violence and suicidality in individuals with severe psychiatric disabilities (Apter et al., 1989, 1991; Hillbrand, 1995), suicidality in children and adolescents with conduct disorder (Apter, Bleich, Plutchik, Mendelsohn, & Tyano, 1988; Cohen-Sandler, Berman, & King, 1982a, 1982b; Pfeffer, Plutchik, & Mizruchi, 1983; Shaffer, 1982), violence among suicidally depressed individuals (Stringer et al., 2013), suicidality among spouse batterers (Bossarte, Simon, & Barker, 2006; Bossarte, Simon, & Swahn, 2008; Swahn, Bossarte, Palmier, Yao, & Van Dulmen, 2013), and many other areas of research.

All these studies note the strong association between self-directed and other-directed aggression. The study of Swahn and colleagues (2013) illustrates this. They re-analyzed data from the 2009 Youth Risk Behavior Survey (n = 16,410 high school students) and looked at the relationship between fighting and suicidal behavior. Youths who fought frequently (12 or more times a year) were 6 times more likely to have attempted suicide in the past year (adjusted OR = 6.16; 95% CI = 3.70–10.28).

Concluding Remarks

Homicide-suicides are such rare events that prediction is not possible. Preventive efforts should be global and take the form of integrated risk assessment in all clinical situations. Clinicians are thus encouraged to always conduct a risk assessment of a new patient, or of an ongoing patient if his or her status changes, and this assessment should examine both the risk of harm to self and harm to others (Hillbrand, 2001, 2014; Kleespies, Deleppo, Gallagher, & Niles, 1999; Kleespies & Richmond, 2009). Some risk assessment tools address the coexisting risk of harm to self and harm to others, such as the Short-Term Assessment of Risk and Treatability (START; Nicholls, Brink, Desmarais, Webster, & Martin, 2006).

The literature reviewed in these pages has implications for homicide in general. It demonstrates that individuals who kill another human being are at a considerably increased risk of killing themselves, either immediately after the homicide or months or years later. This is particularly true if the relational distance to the victim is small (e.g., Hillbrand, Alexandre, Young, & Spitz, 1999). The pattern of suicide after homicide characterizes males, and it is even stronger in women; women who have killed are more likely than men to go on to kill themselves. This raises the possibility that suicidal intent underlies many homicides. In some cases, homicide may, in part, be a function of a profound sense of hopelessness, the desperate solution of a hopeless individual. If supported by future research, this view of the etiology of homicides, including homicide-suicides, has profound implications for prevention and for health policy. Of particular interest is the question of the interrelationship between trauma, depression, and posttraumatic stress disorder in the lives of individuals who go on to kill (Beckham et al., 1996; 2002).

References

Abdel-Khalek, A. (2004). Neither altruistic suicide, nor terrorism but martyrdom: A Muslim perspective. *Archives of Suicide Research*, 8, 99–113.

Anderson, M., Kaufman, J., Simon, T. R., Barrios, L., Paulozzi, L., Ryan, G., Hammond, R., Modzeleski, W., Feucht, T., Potter, L., & the School-Associated Violent Deaths Study Group. (2001). School-associated violent deaths in the United States, 1994–1999. *Journal of the American Medical Association*, 286, 2695–2702.

Apter, A., Bleich, A., Plutchik, R., Mendelsohn, S., & Tyano, S. (1988). Suicidal behavior, depression, and conduct disorder in hospitalized adolescents. *Journal of the American Academy of Child & Adolescent Psychiatry*, 27, 696–699.

Apter, A., Kotler, M., Sevy, S., Plutchik, R., Brown, S. L., Foster, H., Hillbrand, M., Kora, M. L., & van Praag, H. M. (1991).

Correlates of risk of suicide in violent and nonviolent patients. *American Journal of Psychiatry, 148,* 883–887.

Apter, A., Plutchik, R., Sevy, S., Korn, M., Brown, S., & van Praag, H. (1989). Defense mechanisms in risk of suicide and risk of violence. *American Journal of Psychiatry, 146,* 1027–1031.

Barber, C. W., Azrael, D., Hemenway, D., Olson, L. M., Nie, C., Schaechter, J., & Walsh, S. (2008). Suicides and suicide attempts following homicide: Victim-suspect relationship, weapon type, and presence of antidepressants. *Homicide Studies, 12,* 285–297.

Bateman, A., & Fonagy, P. (2004). *Psychotherapy for borderline personality disorder: Mentalization-based treatment.* Oxford, UK: Oxford University Press.

Bateman, A., & Fonagy, P. (2006). *Mentalization-based treatment for borderline personality disorder: A practical guide.* Oxford, UK: Oxford University Press.

Bateman, A., & Fonagy, P. (2008). Co-morbid antisocial and borderline personality disorders: Mentalization-based treatment. *Journal of Clinical Psychology: In Session, 64,* 181–194.

Baumeister, R. F. (1999). *Evil: Inside human violence and cruelty.* San Francisco: W. H. Freeman.

Baumeister, R. F. (2001) Violent pride. *Scientific American, 284,* 96–101.

Baumeister, R. F., Smart, L., & Boden, T. (1995). Relation of threatened egotism to violence and aggression: The dark side of high self-esteem. *Psychological Review, 103,* 5–33.

Beck, A. T. (1999). *Prisoners of hate: The cognitive basis of anger, hostility, and violence.* New York, NY: HarperCollins.

Beck, A. T., Steer, R. A., Beck, J. S., & Newman, C. F. (1993). Hopelessness, depression, suicidal ideation, and clinical diagnosis of depression. *Suicide and Life-Threatening Behavior, 23,* 139–145.

Beckham, J. C., Roodman, A. A., Barefoot, J. C., Haney, T. L., Helms, M. J., Fairbank, J. A.,... Kudler H. S. (1996). Interpersonal and self-reported hostility among combat veterans with and without posttraumatic stress disorder. *Journal of Traumatic Stress, 9,* 335–342.

Beckham, J. C., Vrana, S. R., Barefoot, J. C., Feldman, M. E., Fairbank, J., & Moore, S. D. (2002). Magnitude and duration of cardiovascular responses to anger in Vietnam veterans with and without posttraumatic stress disorder. *Journal of Consulting and Clinical Psychology, 70,* 228–234.

Berkowitz, L. (1999). Anger. In T. Dalgleish & M. J. Power (Eds.), *Handbook of cognition and emotion* (pp. 411–428). Chichester, UK: Wiley.

Berkowitz, N. (1993). *Aggression: Its causes, consequences, and control.* New York, NY: McGraw-Hill.

Binswanger, I. A., Stern, M. F., Deyo, R. A., Heagerty, P. J., Cheadle, A., Elmore, J. G., & Koepsell, T. D. (2007). Release from prison—a high risk of death for former inmates. *New England Journal of Medicine, 356,* 157–165.

Bossarte, R. M., Simon, T. R., & Barker, L. (2006). Characteristics of homicide followed by suicide incidents in multiple states, 2003–2004. *Injury Prevention, 12,* 33–38.

Bossarte, R. M., Simon, T. R., & Swahn, M. H. (2008). Clustering of adolescent dating violence, peer violence, and suicidal behavior. *Journal of Interpersonal Violence, 23,* 815–833.

Bushman, B. J., & Baumeister, R. F. (1998). Threatened egotism, narcissism, self-esteem, and direct and displaced aggression. *Journal of Personality and Social Psychology, 75,* 219–229.

Carcach, C., & Grabosky, P. N. (1998). Murder-suicide in Australia. *Australian Institute of Criminology Trends and Issues in Crime and Criminal Justice Series, 82,* 1–6.

Chemtob, C. M., Hamada, R. S., Roitblat, H. L., & Muraoka, M. Y. (1994). Anger, impulsivity, and anger control in combat-related post-traumatic stress disorder. *Journal of Consulting and Clinical Psychology, 62,* 827–832.

Chemtob, C. M., Novaco, R. W., Hamada, R. S., & Gross, D. M. (1997). Cognitive–behavioral treatment for severe anger in posttraumatic stress disorder. *Journal of Consulting and Clinical Psychology, 65,* 184–189.

Chemtob, C. M., Novaco, R. W., Hamada, R. S., Gross, D. M., & Smith, G. (1997). Anger regulation deficits in combat-related posttraumatic stress disorder. *Journal of Traumatic Stress, 10,* 17–36.

Coccaro, E. F. (1995). The biology of aggression. *Scientific American* (January–February), 38–47.

Coccaro, E. F., Siever, L. J., Klar, H. M., Maurer, G., Cochrane, K., Cooper, T. B., Mohs, R. C., & Davis, K. L. (1989). Serotonergic studies in patients with affective and personality disorders. *Archives of General Psychiatry, 46,* 587–599.

Cohen-Sandler, R., Berman, A. L., & King, R. A. (1982a). Life stress and symptomatology; Determinants of suicidal behavior in children. *Journal of the American Academy of Child Psychiatry, 21,* 178–186.

Cohen-Sandler, R., Berman, A. L., & King, R. A. (1982b). A follow-up study of hospitalized suicidal children. *Journal of the American Academy of Child Psychiatry, 21,* 398–403.

Coid, J. (1983). The epidemiology of abnormal homicide and murder followed by suicide. *Psychological Medicine, 13,* 855–860.

Cooper, A., & Smith, E. L. (2011). Homicide trends in the United States, 1980–2008. *U.S. Department of Justice Office of Justice Programs Bureau of Justice Statistics.* Washington, DC. Retrieved June 1, 2014 from http://www.bjs.gov/content/pub/ascii/htus8008.txt

Cooper, A., & Smith, E. L. (2013). Homicide in the U.S. known to law enforcement, 2011. *U.S. Department of Justice Office of Justice Programs Bureau of Justice Statistics.* Washington, DC. Retrieved June 1, 2014 from http://www.bjs.gov/index.cfm?ty=pbdetail&iid=4863

Craddock, N., & Forty, L. (2006). Genetics of affective (mood) disorders. *European Journal of Human Genetics, 14,* 660–668.

Crosby, A., Ortega, L., & Melanson, C. (2011). *Self-directed violence: Uniform definitions and recommended data elements* (Version 1.0). Atlanta, GA: Centers for Disease Control and Prevention.

Dabby, C., Patel, H., & Poore, G. (2010). Shattered lives: Homicides, domestic violence and Asian families. *Asian and Pacific-Islander Institute on Family Violence.* San Francisco, CA.: Asian and Pacific Islander American. http://www.apiidv.org/files/Homicides.DV.AsianFamilies-APIIDV-2010.pdf

Dahlberg, L. L., & Potter, L. B. (2001). Youth violence developmental pathways and prevention challenges. *American Journal of Preventive Medicine, 20,* 3–14.

DeAngelis, T. (2000). In the aftermath of Columbine. *APA Monitor* (September), *33.*

Dietz, P. E. (1986). Mass, serial, and sensational homicides. *Bulletin of the New York Academy of Medicine, 62,* 477–491.

Eliason, S. (2009). Murder-suicide: A review of the recent literature. *Journal of the American Academy of Psychiatry and Law, 37,* 371–376.

Esposito, J. (2002). *What everyone needs to know about Islam.* Oxford, UK: Oxford University Press.

Feeny, N. C., Zoellner, L. A., & Foa, E. B. (2000). Anger, dissociation, and posttraumatic stress disorder among female assault victims. *Journal of Traumatic Stress, 13,* 89–100.

Fingerhut, L. A., & Kleinman, J. C. (1990). International and interstate comparisons of homicide among young males. *The Journal of the American Medical Association, 263*, 3292–3295.

Foa, E. B., Riggs, D. S., Masie, E. D., & Yarczower, M. (1995). The impact of fear activation and anger on the efficacy of exposure treatment for posttraumatic stress disorder. *Behavior Therapy, 26*, 487–499.

Fruehwald, S., Matschnig, T., Koenig, F., Bauer, P., & Frottier, P. (2004). Suicide in custody: A case-control study. *British Journal of Psychiatry, 185*, 494–498.

Granic, I., & Patterson, G. R. (2006). Toward a comprehensive model of antisocial development: A systems dynamic systems approach. *Psychological Review, 113*, 101–131.

Hazani, M. (1993). Sacrificial immortality: Towards a theory of suicidal terrorism and related phenomena. *Psychoanalytic Study of Society, 19*, 441–442.

Hemenway, D., & Miller, M. (2000). Firearm availability and homicide rates across 26 high income countries. *Journal of Trauma, 49*, 985–988.

Hempel, A. G., Meloy, J. R., & Richards, T.C. (1999). Offender and offense characteristics of a nonrandom sample of mass murderers. *Journal of the American Academy of Psychiatry and Law, 27*, 213–225.

Hillbrand, M. (1995). Aggression against self and aggression against others in violent psychiatric patients. *Journal of Consulting and Clinical Psychology, 63*, 668–671.

Hillbrand, M. (2001). Homicide-suicide and other forms of co-occurring aggression against self and against others. *Professional Psychology: Research and Practice, 32*, 626–635.

Hillbrand, M. (2014). Overlap between suicidal behavior and interpersonal violence. In M. K. Nock (Ed.), *The Oxford handbook of suicide and self-injury* (pp. 431–443). New York, NY: Oxford University Press.

Hillbrand, M., Alexandre, J. W., Young, J. L., & Spitz, R. T. (1999). Parricides: Characteristics of offenders and victims, legal factors, and treatment issues. *Aggression and Violent Behavior, 4*, 179–190.

Hiss, J., & Kahana, T. (1988). Suicide bombers in Israel. *American Journal of Forensic Medicine and Pathology, 19*, 63–66.

Jokinen, J., Forslund, K., Nordström, A. L., Lindqvist, P., & Nordström, P. (2009). Suicide risk after homicide in Sweden. *Archives of Suicide Research, 13*, 297–301.

Joukamaa, M. (1998). The mortality of released Finnish prisoners: A 7-year follow-Up study of the WATTU project. *Forensic Sciences International, 96*, 11–19.

Kennedy, D. B., Homant, R. J., & Hupp, R. T. (1998). Suicide by cop. *Federal Bureau of Investigation Law Enforcement Bulletin, 67*, 21–27.

Kleespies, P. M., Deleppo, J. D., Gallagher, P. L., & Niles, B. L. (1999). Managing suicidal emergencies: Recommendations for the practitioner. *Professional Psychology: Research and Practice, 30*, 454–463.

Kleespies, P. M., & Richmond, J. S. (2009). Evaluating behavioral emergencies: The clinical Interview. In P. M. Kleespies (Ed.), *Behavioral emergencies: An evidence-based resource for evaluating and managing risk of suicide, violence, and victimization.* Washington, DC: APA Press.

Knoll, J. L. (2010). The "pseudocommando" mass murderer: Part I, the psychology of revenge and obliteration. *Journal of the American Academy of Psychiatry and Law, 38*, 87–94.

Koziol-McLain, J. (2006). Risk factors for femicide-suicide in abusive relationships: Results from a multisite case control study. *Violence and Victims, 21*, 3–21.

Liem, M., Postulart, M., & Nieuwbeerta, P. (2009). Homicide-suicide in the Netherlands: An epidemiology. *Homicide Studies, 13*, 91–92.

Linton, J. C. (1995). Acute stress management with public safety personnel: Opportunities for clinical training and pro bono community service. *Professional Psychology: Research and Practice, 26*, 566–573.

Loeber, R., & Stouthamer-Loeber, M. (1998). Development of juvenile aggression and violence: Some common misconceptions and controversies. *American Psychologist, 53*, 242–259.

Logan, J., Hill, H. A., Lynberg Black, M., Crosby, A. E., Karch, D. L., Barnes, J. D., & Lubell, K. M. (2008). Characteristics of perpetrators in homicide-followed-by-suicide incidents: National Violent Death Reporting System—17 US States, 2003–2005. *American Journal of Epidemiology, 168*, 1056–1064.

Malphurs, J. E., & Cohen, D. (2005). A statewide case-control study of spousal homicide-suicide in older persons. *American Journal of Geriatric Psychiatry, 13*, 211–217.

Marzuk, P. M., Tardiff, K., Hirsch, C. S. (1992). The epidemiology of murder-suicide. *Journal of the American Medical Association, 267*, 3179–3183.

McLean, J., Maxwell, M., Platt, S., Harris, F., & Jepson, R. (2008). *Risk and protective factors for suicide and suicidal behaviour: A literature review.* Edinborough, UK.: Scottish Government Social Research.

Meloy, J.R. (2013). Stalking. In J. A. Siegel & P. J. Saukko (Eds.), *Encyclopedia of Forensic Sciences* (2nd ed., pp. 202–205). Waltham, MA: Academic Press.

Merari, A. (1998). The readiness to kill and die: Suicidal terrorism in the Middle-East. In W. Reich (Ed.), *Origins of terrorism: Psychologies, ideologies, theologies, states of mind* (pp. 192–207). Washington, DC: Woodrow Wilson Center Press.

Merari, A. (2005). Suicide terrorism. In R. Yuffit & D. Lester (Eds.), *Assessment, prevention, and treatment of suicidal behavior* (pp. 431–453). New York, NY: Wiley.

Merari, A. (2008, August). *The psychology of suicide terrorism.* Paper presented at the annual convention of the American Psychological Association, Boston, MA.

Meszaros, K., & Fischer-Danzinger, D. (2000). Extended suicide attempt: Psychopathology, personality, and risk factors. *Psychopathology, 33*, 5–10.

Miller, M., Azrael, D., & Hemenway, D. (2002). Household firearm ownership levels and homicide rates across U.S. regions and states, 1988–1997. *American Journal of Public Health, 92*, 1988–1993.

Miller, M., Azrael, D., & Hemenway, D. (2007). State-level homicide victimization rates in the U.S. in relation to survey measures of household firearm ownership, 2001–2003. *Social Science and Medicine, 64*, 656–664.

Miller, T. Q., Smith, T. W., Turner, C. W., Guijarro, M. L., & Hallet, A. J. (1996). A meta-analytic review of research on hostility and physical health. *Psychological Bulletin, 119*, 322–348.

Milroy, C. M. (1993). Homicide followed by suicide (dyadic death) in Yorkshire and Humberside. *Medical Science and Law, 33*, 167–171.

Moffitt, T. E., Brammer, G. L., Caspi, A., Fawcett, J. P., Raleigh, M., Yuwiler, A., & Silva, P. (1998). Whole blood serotonin relates to violence in an epidemiological study. *Biological Psychiatry, 43*, 446–457.

Mullen, O. (2004). The autogenic (self-generated) massacre. *Behavioral Sciences and The Law, 22*, 311–323.

Murray, C. J., & Lopez, A. D. (1997). Mortality by cause for eight regions of the world: Global Burden of Disease Study. *Lancet*, 349, 1269–1276.

Näcke, P. (1908). Der Familienmord in gerichtlich-psychiatrischer Beziehung. *Zeitung Gerichtliche Medizin*, 35, 137–157.

National Violent Death Reporting System (2014). *Injury Prevention and Control*. Centers for Disease Control and Prevention.

Nestor, P. G. (2002). Mental disorders and violence: Personality dimensions and clinical features. *American Journal of Psychiatry*, 159, 1973–1978.

Nicholls, T. L., Brink, J., Desmarais, S. L., Webster, C. D., & Martin, M. L. (2006). The Short-Term Assessment of Risk and Treatability (START): A prospective validation study in a forensic psychiatric sample. *Assessment*, 13, 313–327.

Novaco, R. W., & Chemtob, C. M. (2002). Anger and combat-related posttraumatic stress disorder. *Journal of Traumatic Stress*, 15, 123–132.

Orth, U., & Wieland, E. (2006). Anger, hostility, and post-traumatic stress disorder in trauma-exposed adults: A meta-analysis. *Journal of Consulting and Clinical Psychology*, 74, 698–706.

Palladino, C. L., Singh, V., Campbell, J., Flynn, H., & Gold, K. (2011). Homicide and suicide during the perinatal period: Findings from the National Violent Death Reporting System. *Obstetrics and Gynecology*, 118, 1056–1063.

Parent, R. B. (1998). Suicide by cop: Victim-precipitated homicide. *The Police Chief*, 65, 111–114.

PATH (2009). Strengthening understanding femicide: Using research to galvanize action and accountability. Washington, DC: Author. Retrieved 22JAN15 at http://www.path.org/publications/files/GVR_femicide_rpt.pdf

Patterson, G. R., & Yoerger, K. (2002). A developmental model for early- and late-onset antisocial behavior. In J. B. Reid, J. Snyder, & G. R. Patterson (Eds.), *Antisocial behavior in children and adolescents: A developmental analysis and model for intervention*, (pp. 147–172). Washington, DC: American Psychological Association.

Pfeffer, C. R., Plutchik, R., & Mizruchi, S. (1983). Suicidal and assaultive behavior in children, classification, measurement, and interrelation. *American Journal of Psychiatry*, 140, 154–157.

Plutchik, R., & van Praag, H. M. (1990). Psychosocial correlates of suicide and violence risk. In H. M. van Praag, R. Plutchik, & A. Apter (Eds.), *Violence and suicidality: Perspectives in clinical and psychobiological research* (pp. 37–65). New York, NY: Brunner/Mazel.

Plutchik, R., & van Praag, H. M. (1994). Suicide risk: Amplifiers and attenuators. In M. Hillbrand & N. J. Pallone (Eds.), *The psychobiology of aggression* (pp. 173–186). Binghamton, NY: Haworth Press.

Pratt, D., Appleby, L., Piper, M., Webb, R., & Shaw, J. (2010). Suicide in recently released prisoners: A case-control study. *Psychological Medicine*, 40, 827–835.

Pratt, D., Piper, M., Appleby, L., Webb, R., & Shaw, J. (2006). Suicide in recently released prisoners: A population-based cohort study. *Lancet*, 368, 119–123.

Post, J. M., Ali, F., Henderson, S. W., Shanfield, S., Victoroff, J., & Weine, S. (2009). The psychology of suicide terrorism. *Psychiatry*, 72, 13–31.

Resnick, P. J. (1969). Child murder by parents: A psychiatric review of filicide. *American Journal of Psychiatry*, 126, 73–82.

Riggs, D. S., Dancu, C. V., Gershuny, B. S., Greenberg, D., & Foa, E. B. (1992). Anger and post-traumatic stress disorder in female crime victims. *Journal of Traumatic Stress*, 5, 613–625.

Roma, P., Pazzelli, F., Pompili, M., Lester, D., Girardi, P., & Ferracuti, S. (2012). Mental illness in homicide-suicide: A review. *Journal of the American Academy of Psychiatry and Law*, 40, 462–468.

Séguin, M., Beauchamp, G., Robert, M., Dimambro, M., & Turecki, G. (2014). Developmental model of suicide trajectories. *British Journal of Psychiatry*, 205, 120–126.

Shaffer, D. (1974). Suicide in childhood and early adolescence. *Journal of Child Psychology and Psychiatry*, 15, 275–291.

Shaffer, D. (1982). Diagnostic considerations in suicidal behavior in children and adolescents. *Journal of the American Academy of Child Psychiatry*, 21, 414–416.

Shaw, J., Baker, D., Hunt, I. M., Moloney, A., & Appleby, L. (2004). Suicide by prisoners: National clinical survey. *British Journal of Psychiatry*, 184, 263–267.

Stewart, L. M., Henderson, C. J., Hobbs, M. S., Ridout, S. C., & Knuiman, M. W. (2004). Risk of death in prisoners after release from jail. *Australian and New Zealand Journal of Public Health*, 28, 32–36.

Stringer, B., van Meijel, B., Eikelenboom, M., Koekkoek, B., Licht, C. M., Kerkhof, A. J., Penninx, B. W., & Beekman, A. T. (2013). Recurrent suicide attempts in patients with depressive and anxiety disorders: The role of borderline personality traits. *Journal of Affective Disorders*, 151, 23–30.

Swahn, M. H., Bossarte, R. M., Palmier, J. B., Yao, H., & Van Dulmen, M.H. (2013). Psychosocial characteristics associated with frequent physical fighting: Findings from the 2009 National Youth Risk Behavior Survey. *Injury Prevention*, 19, 143–146.

Taylor, M., & Ryan, H. (1988). Fanaticism, political suicide, and terrorism. *Terrorism*, 11, 91–111.

Tennant, C., Bebbington, P., & Hurry, J. (1980). Parental death in child-hood and risk of adult depressive disorders: A review. *Psychological Medicine*, 10, 289–299.

Torrey, E. F. (2013). *Surviving schizophrenia* (6th ed.). New York, NY: HarperCollins.

Townsend, E. (2007). Suicide terrorists: Are they suicidal? *Suicide and Life-Threatening Behaviors*, 37, 35–49.

Townsend, E. (2014). Suicide terrorism. In M. K. Nock (Ed.), *The Oxford handbook of suicide and self-injury* (pp. 444–459). New York, NY: Oxford University Press.

Travis, A., Johnson, L., & Milroy, C. (2007). Homicide-suicide (dyadic death), homicide and firearms use in England and Wales. *American Journal of Forensic Medicine and Pathology*, 28, 314–318.

United Nations Office on Drugs and Crime (2013). *2013 global study on homicide*. Retrieved June 19, 2014 from http://www.unodc.org/documents/gsh/pdfs/2014_GLOBAL_HOMICIDE_BOOK_web.pdf

Van Zandt, C. R. (1993). Suicide by cop. *The Police Chief*, 7, 24–30.

Walsh, S., & Hemenway, D. (2005). Intimate partner violence: Homicides followed by suicides in Kentucky. *Journal of the Kentucky Medical Association*, 103, 667–670.

Webb, R. T., Qin, P., Stevens, H., Shaw, J., Appleby, L., Mortensen, P. B. (2013). National study of suicide method in violent criminal offenders. *Journal of Affective Disorder*, 150, 237–244.

Webb, R. T., Shaw, J., Stevens, H., Mortensen, P. B., Appleby, L., & Qin, P. (2012). Suicide risk among violent and sexual criminal offenders. *Journal of Interpersonal Violence*, 27, 405–424.

Websdale, N. (2010). *Familicidal hearts: The emotional style of 211 killers*. New York, NY: Oxford University Press.

Zlodre, J., & Fazel, S. (2012). All-cause and external mortality in released prisoners: Systematic review and meta-analysis. *American Journal of Public Health*, 102, 67–75.

Victims of Sexual Assault: Evaluation and Management

Heidi S. Resnick, Kate L. Walsh, *and* Christal L. Badour

Abstract

Given the high prevalence of sexual assault within both the general population and among college student samples, professionals working in a wide range of medical and mental health care settings should be prepared to address the acute and long-term physical and psychological consequences of sexual assault. It is also important to be aware of the prevalence and service needs among victims of sexual assault who seek acute medical care. This chapter reviews data regarding the prevalence and characteristics of rape and sexual assault, approaches to assessing sexual assault history, acute and long-term victim concerns and consequences associated with rape, access to and utilization of post-assault medical care and other agency services, and prevention and early intervention approaches that may be implemented in the medical setting.

Key Words: rape, sexual assault, post-rape medical care, PTSD, substance abuse

The purpose of this chapter is to address emergent behavioral, mental, and physical health concerns among victims of sexual assault within the United States with primary emphasis on rape victimization among adult women in the general population and college women, as well as those seen acutely for post-rape medical care in emergency department (ED) or other agency settings. Multiple victimization risk (revictimization as well as prior history of sexual assault or other violence exposure), including overlap with intimate partner physical assault is also addressed in this context. The chapter focuses primarily on women, given greatest identified prevalence and extant literature. Some information is however provided regarding prevalence of sexual victimization of men. We also emphasize current medical services and options available to recent rape victims within the United States and findings related to service access. Military sexual trauma is not addressed here; however, comparable or higher prevalence of sexual violence and associated mental health problems have been observed (Kimerling et al., 2010; Maguen et al., 2012; Zinzow, Grubaugh, Monnier, Suffoletta-Maierle, & Frueh, 2007).

It is important to understand the types of events that comprise sexual assault; the prevalence, characteristics, and contexts of sexual assault; measurement approaches; emergent medical issues; suicide and other health risk behaviors; other mental health correlates; service settings in which victims may be seen; and strategies to reduce the negative impact of rape. Particular emphasis is placed on medical concerns about the human immunodeficiency virus (HIV), other sexually transmitted diseases, or pregnancy that may result from rape; substance-related rape as a type of assault; increased risk of suicide, revictimization, and substance use disorder; and mental health problems, including posttraumatic stress disorder (PTSD) and depression in particular, as potential mediators of associations between rape victimization and emergent or health risk behaviors. Other potential emergent issues may include basic resource, safety, and criminal justice options. Throughout the chapter we provide definitions, findings about prevalence, and characteristics based on extant literature, as well as findings from a study by Kilpatrick, Resnick, Ruggiero, Conoscenti, and McCauley (2007) that included unique information about forcible and substance-related rape prevalence and mental health correlates within both a national telephone household sample and a separate college sample of women.

Definitions, Prevalence, and Characteristics of Rape
Definitions

As summarized by Kruttschnitt and colleagues in a recent National Research Council report (National Research Council, 2014), based on review of legal definitions, rape may include penile, digital, tongue or other object-vaginal, oral, or anal penetration incidents, occurs in the presence of force or threat of force against the victim or another person, without the victim's consent or when he or she is unable to consent (e.g., under legal age of consent, due to loss of consciousness or significant impairment, operationalized in some jurisdictions as inability to control conduct as a result of substance intoxication or other reasons). Forms of sexual assault other than rape can involve any unwanted sexual contact (e.g., touching of breasts or genitals) that does not include penetration. In addition, as reviewed by Basile and Smith (2011), the Centers for Disease Control and Prevention (CDC) includes noncontact verbal harassment, unwanted visual exposure, and being forced to view sexual content as part of a broader definition of sexual violence. Basile and Smith also emphasize coercion (e.g., threats of negative consequences related to an ongoing relationship, job, or resources) as a sexual assault tactic that may occur in the context of intimate partner relationships or as part of misuse of authority. They also make note of *inability to refuse* due to threats of violence or actual physical violence as an important element of sexual assault related to consent (e.g., apart from overt nonconsent and inability to consent). Other types of sexual violence briefly noted include rapes that may occur during war and human trafficking (Basile & Smith, 2011). Sexual violence and harassment associated with use of social media is also an important developing area of research (Thompson, 2014).

SUBSTANCE-RELATED RAPE

Substance-related rape includes drug- or alcohol-facilitated or incapacitated rape, with the former comprising incidents in which an assailant administers a substance or attempts to get the victim intoxicated, resulting in loss of consciousness or inability to control her own behavior and the latter indicating incidents in which alcohol or drugs are voluntarily used by the victim leading to loss of consciousness or inability to control her behavior (e.g., see Kilpatrick

et al., 2007). Hereafter, we use the term drug or alcohol facilitated or incapacitated rape (DAFR) to refer to incidents involving *either* voluntary use or substance facilitation that leads to loss of consciousness or significant impairment. DAFR is considered a rape tactic as force or threat are rape tactics, and it is important that there be greater understanding that DAFR constitutes rape (e.g., see National Research Council, 2014). DAFR itself may be considered a behavioral emergency that poses potential physical health risk due to level of impairment due to substances, along with being a rape tactic in which the victim is unable to consent or resist in cases of sexual assault. In addition, a higher prevalence of substance abuse has been observed among those experiencing DAFR type incidents (Kilpatrick et al., 2007).

Approaches to Defining Rape and Sexual Assault

The review of prevalence and characteristics of rape described here is based on relatively large and representative telephone household or general population sample studies and college samples that used behavioral definitions to specify component behaviors that comprise rape or other sexual assault. These studies typically included multiple screening items to assess rape as described previously. This is in contrast to definitions based on legal terms or those derived from criminal justice sources providing information about crimes reported to police. This distinction is critical, as it is estimated that 65% of rapes in the United States between 2006 and 2010 were not reported to police, making rape the most underreported crime in the country (Langton, Berzofsky, Krebs, & Smiley-McDonald, 2012). Sexual assaults occurring among college students are even more rarely reported to police or campus authorities (Fisher, Daigle, Cullen, & Turner, 2003). Rapes that are reported to police appear to be subject to biases about what rape victimization entails and other factors that may increase or decrease likelihood of making a formal report, and thus data on reported cases yields a much lower prevalence of rape and less representative rape characteristics than approaches asking about all incidents, regardless of whether or not they were reported to police (e.g., see Wolitzky-Taylor et al., 2011). Similarly, survey methods that use legal terms such as "rape" or "sexual assault" yield lower prevalence as victims may not understand what is meant by such terms if they are inconsistent with held biases about more stereotypic rape characteristics (e.g., forcible or violent assaults perpetrated by strangers). For detailed recent reviews of assessment approaches and factors related to underestimates of rape across different types of studies or government reports such as the National Crime Victimization Survey, see Cook, Gidycz, Koss, and Murphy (2011), Kilpatrick and McCauley (2009), and the National Research Council report (2014).

BEHAVIORALLY SPECIFIC QUESTIONS USED TO ASSESS RAPE

The National Research Council report by Kruttschnitt and colleagues (2014) provides verbatim questions used to assess rape across key US national and college women studies that include the National Women's Study (NWS), National Women's Study–Replication (NWS-R), National Violence Against Women Survey (NVAW), and others. Cook and colleagues (2011) also review rape measurement issues. Initial screening questions used to assess rape in the NWS-R (Kilpatrick et al., 2007) are provided here to illustrate the inclusion of an orienting preface and behaviorally specific questions as opposed to legal terms. These screening questions were then followed by additional structured questions to determine presence of forcible and drug or alcohol facilitation or incapacitation tactics involved in specific index incidents.

The opening preface used by Kilpatrick and colleagues (2007) is presented here, with phrasing used for the college sample noted in parentheses followed by an initial set of screening questions used to determine history of rape that included forcible rape and or DAFR tactics:

Many (college) women tell us they have experienced unwanted sexual advances at some point during their lives. Women do not always report such experiences to police or discuss them with family or friends. Such experiences can happen anytime in a woman's life— even as a child. (Some of these experiences happen when women are in college.) The person making these unwanted advances can be friends, boyfriends, (professors,) co-workers, teaching assistants, supervisors, family members, strangers, or someone they just met. The person making the unwanted sexual advances can be male or female . . .

Regardless of how long ago it happened

1. Has a man or boy ever made you have sex by using force or threatening to harm you or someone close to you? Just so there is no mistake, by having sex, we mean putting a penis in your vagina.

2. Has anyone, male or female, ever made you have oral sex by force or threatening to harm you? So there is no mistake, by oral sex, we mean that a man or boy put his penis in your mouth or someone penetrated your vagina or anus with their mouth or tongue?

3. Has anyone ever made you have anal sex by force or threatening to harm you? By anal sex, we mean putting their penis in your anus or rectum.

4. Has anyone ever put fingers or objects in your vagina or anus against your will by using force or threatening to harm you?

Some women tell us they have had sex when they didn't want to because they were very high, intoxicated, or even passed out because of alcohol or drugs. We would like to ask you about these types of experiences you might have had. Again, we are interested in these experiences regardless of how long ago it happened, who did it, or whether or not it was reported to police.

5. Has anyone ever had sex with you when you didn't want to after you drank so much alcohol that you were very high, drunk, or passed out? By having sex, we mean that a man or boy put his penis in your vagina, your anus, or your mouth?

6. Has anyone ever had sex with you when you didn't want to after they gave you, or you had taken enough drugs to make you very high, intoxicated, or passed out? By having sex we mean that a man or boy put his penis in your vagina, your anus, or your mouth? (p. 16)

Follow-up questions were asked about up to two lifetime incidents (a most recent incident and a first incident if a women reported the experience of more than one rape) and included asking about whether the incident involved physical force; presence of threats of harm to self or others; relationship to the assailant; use of drugs, alcohol, or both; whether substance use was voluntary; whether another person tried to get them drunk or gave them drugs or both; if substance use was reported, whether the participant passed out or was too drunk or high to know what they were doing or to control their behavior; presence of no, minor, or serious injuries as a result of the incident; and whether the incident involved penile-oral, vaginal, or anal penetration. For classification purposes, unwanted penetrative sexual incidents that included substance use and that led to the victim being passed out or unable to control behavior were considered DAFR incidents. Cases in which the victim reported physical force, verbal threats, or sustained injuries were considered to include forcible rape tactics. An orientation regarding the relevance of a history of sexual assault as related to physical and mental health functioning and the purpose of asking such behaviorally specific questions may also be useful for screening conducted in primary care, mental health, or other agency settings (e.g., see Acierno, Resnick, & Kilpatrick, 1997).

Prevalence and Characteristics

FORCIBLE RAPE IN THE GENERAL POPULATION

The NWS examined prevalence of rape, other types of violence, substance abuse, PTSD, and other mental health correlates within a household probability sample of 4,008 US adult women assessed via structured telephone interview initially in 1989 with two subsequent yearly follow-up interviews (Kilpatrick et al., 1992; Resnick, Kilpatrick, Dansky, Saunders, & Best, 1993). Behaviorally specific questions were used to assess forcible rape incidents that included unwanted penile, digital, or object vaginal, anal, or oral penetration in situations that involved physical force or threat of force. Women were provided with an initial preface stating that they were being asked about incidents involving unwanted sexual experiences whether or not those incidents were reported to police and that such incidents may have occurred at any age and have involved strangers, friends, relatives, or husbands/partners. Lifetime prevalence of rape was 12.7%, with past-year prevalence of 0.71%. The NVAW (Tjaden & Thoennes, 2000) included structured telephone interviews with a representative US sample of 8,000 men and 8,000 women. Using behaviorally specific questions as described here to ask about forcible rape, the researchers found that 17.6% of women and 3.0% of men reported a lifetime history of completed or attempted rape. A total of 9.6% of women and 0.8% of men reported a rape incident occurring since age 18. Additionally, 0.3% of women and 0.1% of men reported that they had been raped in the preceding 12 months.

FORCIBLE RAPE IN COLLEGE SAMPLES

College students appear to be a high-risk group for rape victimization. This may relate to ages of typical college students, social interactions among predominantly single young adults, and high prevalence of alcohol use. The National College Women's Sexual Violence Survey assessed experiences of forcible rape occurring within a school year (Fisher, Cullen, & Turner, 2003). Results of interviews with a nationally representative sample of 4,446 college women who were interviewed using behaviorally specific questions similar to those used within the NWS to identify experiences of forcible rape indicated a prevalence of 1.7% among women for

completed rape with a corresponding annual estimate of 3% accounting for the limited seven-month study time frame.

FORCIBLE AND SUBSTANCE-RELATED RAPE

Studies of national and college student samples have varied in terms of whether only forcible rape was assessed, with more recent studies including measurement of DAFR. First, findings from a community sample of 1,014 women between the ages of 18 to 30 (Testa, Livingston, Vanzile-Tamsen, & Frone, 2003) indicated that a total of 17.2% of women reported either type of rape since the age of 14, with 10.7% experiencing at least one forcible rape and 9.4% experiencing at least one instance of DAFR. Similarly, data from a national sample within the NWS-R (Kilpatrick et al., 2007) indicated that 16.1% or an estimated 18 million women had experienced a forcible rape in their lifetime (whether or not any DAFR elements were present) and 5%, or an estimated 5.6 million, had experienced a DAFR type rape. In total, 18% or an estimated 20.2 million women had experienced either forcible rape or DAFR. Past 7-month prevalence of either forcible or DAFR victimization was .60%, with projected annual (12-month) prevalence of .94% or 940 per 100,000 women. Finally, Kilpatrick and colleagues looked at overlap of forcible and DAFR tactics across all rape incidents studied. Approximately 50% of all DAFR incidents also included forcible rape tactics. Most recently, findings from the National Intimate Partner and Sexual Violence Survey within the United States (Breiding, Smith et al., 2014) indicated that 19.3% of adult women, estimated at over 23 million, had experienced a lifetime completed or attempted rape that included forcible or substance facilitated or incapacitated rape, with a 12 month prevalence of 1.6%. A total of 1.7% of men were reported to have experienced a lifetime rape incident.

Kilpatrick and colleagues (2007) further assessed forcible and substance-related rape within a sample of 2,000 college women representing a subsample of women included in the American Student List as part of the aforementioned NWS-R study. Using the same behaviorally specific questions to assess forcible and DAFR incidents as in the general population sample, 11.5% reported lifetime history of any type of completed rape, with 6.4% (roughly half) meeting criteria for DAFR. Prevalence of forcible or DAFR rape was 2.95% within the 7-month period assessed within the study with a projected annual

(12-month) prevalence of 5.15%. Again, slightly fewer than half of all incidents of DAFR studied included forcible elements plus DAFR as opposed to DAFR tactics alone. In an earlier nationally representative sample of female college students, Koss, Gidycz, and Wisniewski (1987) reported that 15.4% of women experienced a history of rape since the age of 14, while 207 of 3,187 women indicated that they had experienced one or more DAFR or forcible rapes in the preceding academic year. Finally, a web-based study of 5,446 undergraduate women randomly selected from two large public universities (Krebs et al., 2009) reported that 5% experienced a forcible sexual assault and 11% experienced a sexual assault while incapacitated due to substances since college entry. Thus studies of college women indicate that lifetime prevalence of rape is high, as is recent incidence, and proportionally DAFR type rapes represent a greater percentage of all rapes.

A major finding of the NWS-R (Kilpatrick et al., 2007), which is consistent with a growing body of literature (e.g., Abbey, 2002; Krebs, Lindquist, Warner, Fisher, & Martin, 2009; Mohler-Kuo, Dowdall, Koss, & Wechsler, 2004; Testa et al., 2003), is that alcohol was the most commonly reported substance, and incapacitated rape following *voluntary* use is most typical with regard to substance-related rape. In almost all cases of facilitated or incapacitated rape within the study by Kilpatrick and colleagues, alcohol was used either alone (national sample: 71%; college sample: 79%) or along with another substance (national sample: 27%; college sample: 17%) The use of drugs alone was significantly less common (national sample: 2%; college sample: 4%). The most commonly ingested drug was marijuana (used in 58% [national sample] or 72% [college sample] of DAFR cases involving drugs), followed by smaller percentages reporting a sedative type drug, a stimulant, and Rohypnol, or other unknown drug. The finding that alcohol and marijuana were most commonly reported substances is consistent with findings from laboratory studies of samples in cases in which substance use or administration was suspected (e.g., Hindmarch, ElSohly, Gambles, & Salamone, 2001; Scott-Ham & Burton, 2005; Slaughter, 2000).

AGE AT TIME OF ASSAULT

Findings across studies consistently indicate that rape often first occurs when victims are young. Results of the aforementioned NWS (Kilpatrick, Edmunds, & Seymour, 1992) indicated that of all cases, 29.3% reportedly occurred when women were less than 11 years old; 32.3% occurred when women were ages 11 to 17; 22.2% occurred between ages 18 to 24; and 13.2% at age 25 or older. Similar findings were observed in the NVAW (Tjaden & Thoennes, 2000). Specifically, of those positive for lifetime history of rape, 54% of women and 71% of men were younger than 18 when first assaulted. Adult rape victimization was also twice as prevalent among women who had been victims of childhood rape (for further information on issues related to child abuse, see Chapter 6 of this volume).

Kilpatrick and colleagues (2007) provided separate characteristic data on forcible and DAFR among incidents reported in the US telephone household sample of the NWS-R. Among those reporting forcible rape without DAFR tactics, age at time of incident distribution was similar to that reported in the NWS and NVAW, with 28% of incidents occurring prior to age 12; 27% between ages 12 to 17; and 42% at age 18 or above. In contrast, 30% of DAFR incidents (rapes that included DAFR tactics regardless of forcible elements) occurred between ages 12 to 17; with 67% occurring at age 18 or older. Findings from a national sample of adolescents were also consistent with this pattern. Within the National Survey of Adolescents Replication study subsample of 1,763 adolescent girls between the ages of 12 and 17, 11.8% reported a sexual assault (9.7% forcible and 2.1% DAFR), and DAFR was significantly more likely to occur among older adolescents between ages 15 and 17 (McCauley et al., 2009). Finally, with regard to age of occurrence patterns among college students, Kilpatrick and colleagues found that among total forcible rape incidents, 23% occurred prior to age 12; 41% between ages 12 and 17; and 34% age 18 or older. Among incidents that involved DAFR, 31% occurred between ages 12 to 17 and 68% occurred at age 18 or older.

RELATIONSHIP TO ASSAILANT

Across studies, assailants known to the victim are the most commonly reported perpetrators of rape (Kilpatrick et al., 1992, 2007; Tjaden & Thoennes, 2000). Kilpatrick, Resnick, Saunders, and Best (1998) described characteristics of lifetime and recent incidents among women participating in the NWS. Approximately one-fifth (22%) of incidents were perpetrated by strangers. Similarly, new rape incidents that occurred between Years 1 and 3 of the longitudinal study were more likely to be committed by someone known to the victim, with 24% indicating assault by strangers, 22% by husbands/ex-husbands, 20% by boyfriends/ex-boyfriends, 10% by relatives, 25%

by friends, or other nonrelatives. Findings from the NWS-R about all *lifetime* rape incidents assessed in the national telephone household sample (Kilpatrick et al., 2007) indicated that only 11% of forcible and 19% of DAFR cases were perpetrated by strangers (never seen before or seen before but not known well), while 24% of forcible and 16% of DAFR cases were perpetrated by an intimate or ex-intimate partner, 29% of lifetime forcible incidents were perpetrated by some type of relative versus 5% of DAFR, 12% of forcible and 31% of DAFR were perpetrated by a friend, and 24% of forcible and 27% of DAFR incidents were perpetrated by another nonrelative.

As with findings from general population samples, most perpetrators of rape in college samples are known to the victim, with intimate partners and friends being among the most frequent categories (Kilpatrick et al., 2007). Specifically, Kilpatrick et al. found that in 6% of lifetime forcible and 17% of DAFR the perpetrator was a stranger; in 29% of forcible and 9% of DAFR it was an intimate or ex-intimate; in 19% of forcible and 3% of DAFR the perpetrator was a relative of the victim; in 29% of forcible and 61% of DAFR it was a friend or classmate; in 15% of forcible and 11% of DAFR it was some other nonrelative. Littleton, Grills-Taquechel, and Axom (2009) described relationship to rape perpetrator among 340 victims of adolescent or adult forcible or DAFR rape. Victim status related to substance use during assault was classified as either not impaired due to substances, impaired but not unconscious due to substances, and unconscious due to substances at time of assault. Findings indicated similar low prevalence of stranger or familial assailants across the three groups and higher percentage of romantic partners among nonimpaired as compared to impaired or incapacitated. Findings reviewed here in both general population and college samples may be seen as partially consistent with a study by Testa, VanZile-Tamsen, and Livingston (2007) that found that heavy alcohol use was a predictor of sexual assaults by nonintimate partners in a study of community women whereas drug use was a positive predictor of intimate partner sexual assault. In addition, number of sexual partners was a predictor of nonintimate partner violence whereas prior intimate partner violence and low refusal assertiveness were additional predictors of intimate partner sexual assault (Testa et al., 2007).

Rape in the Context of Intimate Partner Violence

Key information about prevalence of rape in the context of intimate partner violence and overlap with other types of intimate partner violence is provided from the NVAW and National Intimate Partner and Sexual Violence Survey (NISVS) studies. The NVAW survey (Tjaden & Thoennes, 2000) found that 7.7% of 8,000 women reported a lifetime rape incident by an intimate or ex-intimate partner and 0.2% reported being raped by an intimate or ex-intimate in the preceding 12 months. Furthermore, 64% of women victimized in adulthood by rape, physical assault, or stalking had experienced violence by an intimate or ex-intimate partner. Results of the NISVS survey of 9,086 US women regarding experiences of intimate partner violence indicated that a total of 9.4% reported any type of completed or attempted rape by an intimate partner, including 3.4% who reported a DAFR incident (Breiding, Chen, & Black, 2014). Past year prevalence of forced rape or attempted rape by an intimate partner was 0.4% among women.

Reviews of the literature indicate that marital rape occurs in the context of other forms of violence within intimate relationships (Martin, Taft, & Resick, 2007) and may be associated with relatively more severe patterns of physical violence as compared to intimate partner violence relationships that do not include rape (Resnick, Cahill, & Falsetti, 2000). Breiding and colleagues (2014) found that 14.4% of women reported both physical violence and stalking; 8.7% rape and physical violence; and 12.5% rape, physical violence, and stalking. In addition, a subgroup of women who have sexual violence histories have also had exposure to multiple rape incidents (Walsh et al., 2012) and/or multiple forms of violence by various perpetrators (Pimlott-Kubiak & Cortina, 2003). Given the high prevalence of intimate partner sexual assault and the possibility that a woman may be at risk for experiencing other forms of violence in the context of an ongoing relationship, it may be critical to a woman's safety to conduct a screen for all forms of intimate partner violence if she is seen (or screened) in primary or emergency care for health concerns related to either rape or physical assault regardless of relationship to assailant in the "presenting" incident. Thus, among women seeking post-rape sexual assault medical care, regardless of relationship to the assailant, it would be important to evaluate possible ongoing risk of intimate partner sexual and physical violence, level of risk, related safety issues and planning, options within the criminal justice system, and provision of referral resources including domestic violence services as indicated (Campbell, 2004; Dutton & Kropp, 2000; Monnier, Resnick, Kilpatrick, Seals, & Holmes, 2002).

The NVAW study (Tjaden & Thoennes, 2000) found that American Indian/Alaska Native women were more likely to report history of rape than women who said that they were White, African American, or of mixed race. Conversely, women of Hispanic ethnicity were less likely to report a history of rape than non-Hispanic women. Additionally, while men were most often perpetrators of intimate partner violence, women or men who had ever lived with a same-sex intimate partner were significantly more likely to have a history of rape as an adult or as a child and to have a history of physical assault. The NISVS (Breiding, Chen, & Black, 2014) found that women who were Black and non-Hispanic and multiracial women were more likely to report a history of rape or other violence by an intimate than White non-Hispanic women who in turn were more at risk than Asian non-Hispanic women. The NISVS also found that women who said they were bisexual had a higher prevalence of any type of intimate partner violence. Finally, women who had financial concerns related to food or housing in the preceding 12 months were more likely to have experienced intimate partner violence (Breiding et al., 2014). Similarly, Byrne, Resnick, Kilpatrick, Best, and Saunders (1999), using longitudinal data from the NWS found that income below poverty level and becoming divorced were associated with exposure to physical assault or rape while, conversely, victimization was associated with risk of unemployment, reduced income, and divorce. Those providing mental health or medical services to victims of sexual assault or intimate partner violence should be familiar with local community resources including housing, food, educational, and training opportunities in order to provide clients with linkages to such services if needed. Addressing such needs may be seen as consistent with an approach termed "psychological first aid" (Vernberg et al., 2008) which was developed to guide assistance responses following disaster incidents. Psychological first aid includes guidelines for addressing practical needs, facilitation of social support, engagement with collaborative agencies or services, and provision of information about coping (Vernberg et al., 2008). See Chapter 11 in this volume regarding specific adaptation of psychological first aid strategies with victims of crime.

Acute Concerns among Rape Victims
Assault-Related Physical Injuries

As reviewed by Koss and Heslet (1992), rape may be associated with nongenital physical injuries including abrasions, lacerations, and bruising in 40% of cases with higher prevalence noted for head, neck, and face or extremities. However, an estimated 50% may experience microscopic or more significant genital injuries. Descriptive data from a national household sample of forcible rape cases indicated that 40% of women reported receipt of either serious (16%) or minor (34%) injuries (Kilpatrick et al., 2007). Thirty percent of DAFR incidents within the NWS-R general population study involved either serious (5%) or minor (23%) injuries (Kilpatrick et al., 2007). Fairly similar patterns of injury were reported by college women as compared to telephone household sample women with regard to lifetime cases of forcible rape, with 6% reporting serious and 40% reporting minor injury. Similarly, relatively lower percentages of all DAFR cases included serious (1%) or minor (19%) injury (Kilpatrick et al., 2007). Examination records of victims presenting for a rape-related medical exam indicate that 52% to 67% of victims have general body physical trauma and 20% to 53% have genital trauma (Riggs, Houry, Long, Markovchick, & Feldhaus, 2000; Sugar, Fine & Eckert, 2004). In terms of specific genital injuries, a case series of female adolescents age 14 to 19 who presented for a rape-related medical exam revealed that 36% had vaginal tearing and 18% to 32% had genital swelling or redness; victims who were seen sooner after the rape had more severe genital trauma (Adams, Girardin, & Faugno, 2001). Evidence suggests that vaginal tears or injuries may pose increased risk of HIV transmission and thus rape, with frequently observed microscopic or other injuries, may be associated with increased risk of sexual transmission if an assailant is HIV positive (CDC, 2005). Despite this factor, there is limited data on actual transmission risk following rape among women (CDC, 2005). As described further in the later section "Access to Acute Medical Care or Other Agency Services," specialized sexual assault medical forensic exam (SAMFE) services are provided to rape victims who seek services within days of assault that may be provided by physicians or sexual assault nurse examiner (SANE) specialists (Campbell, Patterson, & Lichty, 2005; Ledray, 1999; Logan, Cole, & Capillo, 2007). Individuals who receive acute care receive counseling and services to prevent pregnancy due to rape and sexually transmitted diseases. Counseling specifically related to HIV risk and/or related prophylactic treatment varies, as described later. Forensic aspects of the SAMFE, psychological reactions to rape, provision of support, and information including referral resources are also addressed by multidisciplinary teams at the time of the rape exam (Campbell et al., 2005). In addition to medical personnel, these teams often include rape crisis advocates (Campbell et al., 2006).

Pregnancy

Data indicate that rape victims are concerned about pregnancy due to rape. The report by Kilpatrick and colleagues (2007) indicated that there was some or extreme concern about pregnancy following 37% of forcible and 54% of DAFR cases in the telephone household sample and 52% of forcible and 43% of DAFR cases in the college sample without regard to age at time of assault. In national samples, the prevalence of rape-related pregnancy is approximately 5% among victims of reproductive age (Goodman, Koss, & Russo, 1993; Holmes, Resnick, Kilpatrick, & Best, 1996). The prevalence of rape-related pregnancy is reportedly even higher among particular subgroups of women. For example, among women seeking protection orders from abusive partners, 20% reported a rape-related pregnancy (McFarlane et al., 2005). Although rape-related pregnancies commonly occur among women who do not report their rapes to police (Holmes et al., 1996), concern about pregnancy may motivate rape victims to seek medical care following rape (Zinzow et al., 2012).

Human Immunodeficiency Virus and Other Sexually Transmitted Infections

Regardless of actual risk, many women report concern about HIV due to rape (e.g., Baker, Burgess, Brickman, & Davis, 1990; Kilpatrick et al., 1992; Resnick et al., 2002). Specifically, among women in the national telephone sample, women in 24% of forcible and 43% of DAFR cases reported being somewhat or extremely concerned about getting HIV following the incident (Kilpatrick et al., 2007). Among incidents assessed in the college sample, women expressed concern about HIV following rape in 24% of forcible and 35% of DAFR incidents. Resnick and colleagues (2002) found that almost all women (91.9%) reported concern about HIV due to rape in a sample of 62 women who had recently sought medical care post-assault. Concerns about HIV post-rape are understandable, as HIV status of the assailant is likely to be unknown, rape typically involves penile-vaginal, oral, or anal penetration with possible transmission of semen, and, as noted, rape may include microscopic tears or other injuries. The CDC has published guidelines regarding HIV post-exposure prophylaxis in cases of sexual assault or other nonoccupational exposures (CDC, 2005) that recommend assessment at the time of medical care of factors that may indicate increased risk of exposure and potential benefit from prophylactic medication. Factors associated with recommended post-exposure prophylaxis generally include the person being seen less than 72 hours versus beyond 72 hours post-assault; vaginal, oral, anal, or other mucous membrane exposure to semen or other specified body fluids (e.g., blood); and knowledge that the source is HIV positive. When the source patient status is unknown, prophylactic treatment that includes medication taken over the course of approximately one month is recommended to be determined on a case-by-case basis (CDC, 2005). Thus while several risk indicators are present in cases of sexual assault, given that the status of the assailant is most typically unknown, there is likely a lack of consistency across sexual assault services in terms of consideration of prophylactic medication treatment.

Sexual assault nurse examiner programs in the United States and Canada that provide care to victims seeking acute medical forensic exams have been found to vary with regard to existence of policies for addressing HIV concerns, including provision of testing and prophylaxis and conditions under which prophylaxis is offered (Draughon, Anderson, Hansen, & Sheridan, 2014). Draughon et al. found that Canadian programs studied were more likely to have a protocol for decision-making about prophylactic treatment and offer HIV testing and prophylaxis than US programs studied. Specifically, 96% of responding Canadian programs versus 58% of responding US programs said they provided prophylactic treatment routinely or at the victim's request. In general, programs that provided HIV testing were also more likely to provide prophylaxis. In a recent review and meta-analysis of US, Canadian, and other international studies, the observed rate of adherence (completing a course of treatment over 28 days) ranged from 40.3% to 48.1% of sexual assault patients administered the treatment (Chacko, Ford, Sbaiti, & Siddqui, 2012). The latter finding indicates that interventions targeting adherence could be beneficial in cases in which prophylaxis is available to victims of sexual assault. Overall, findings indicate that it would be important to address rape victims' concerns about HIV more consistently and comprehensively as part of SAMFE services. In addition, rape victims who have not sought immediate medical care may still have concerns about HIV or other sexually transmitted diseases that could be inquired about and addressed among women seeking primary care or other services. In such cases, women could receive counseling regarding risk and be informed about testing and other services. Although the prevalence of HIV infection as a result of rape is thought to be relatively low for vaginal rapes, rape nonetheless represents a possible means of HIV acquisition.

Rape victims also reported concerns about other sexually transmitted infections (STIs) in the study by Kilpatrick and colleagues (2007). Of all forcible rape cases assessed, concern about sexually transmitted diseases other than HIV was reported following 28% of forcible and 50% of DAFR incidents in the telephone household and 34% of forcible and 55% of DAFR incidents in the college sample. Other STIs as a result of rape are far more common. For example, in a community sample of women in high drug use neighborhoods, 38.7% of women who experienced a rape in the previous year had at least one STI compared to 18.7% of women without a recent rape (Irwin et al., 1995). However, studies examining acquisition of HIV and STIs are scarce, and those that do exist may not be representative of the broader population of rape victims given the low levels of reporting and service seeking.

Social and Other Concerns

Many rape victims do express concerns about reactions of family members or friends that surpass levels of concern regarding potential health consequences (Kilpatrick et al., 2007). Thus reports of being somewhat or extremely concerned about one's family knowing about the incident (61% forcible and 54% DAFR in the telephone household sample; 71% forcible and 51% DAFR in the college sample) surpassed concerns about HIV, other STIs, or pregnancy due to rape. Concern about individuals other than family members knowing about the assault was comparable to concerns about family. Concern about being blamed by others was reported in 62% of forcible and 65% of DAFR incidents in the telephone household and 72% of forcible and 67% of DAFR incidents in the college sample (Kilpatrick et al., 2007). Again, these levels of concern surpassed health-related concerns.

As reviewed by Campbell, Wasco, Ahrens, Sefl, and Barnes (2001), rape survivors may experience negative reactions from agencies they seek services from and as a result experience further traumatization and/or fail to receive services, both of which might negatively impact health. Rape victims may also experience negative reactions from others in the community to whom they disclose a rape experience (Ullman, 1996). Ullman found that negative reactions by others was a significant predictor of negative psychological adjustment, and this effect appeared to be mediated by avoidance coping. Some data indicate that contact with rape crisis advocates is associated with reduced distress surrounding police and medical system interactions and improved treatment (Campbell, 2006). Campbell, Patterson, and Lichty (2005) also reviewed the effectives of SANE programs specifically and suggested preliminary support for these specialized nurse examiner programs in improving attention to psychological responses, effectiveness of medical and forensic aspects of the exam, and legal outcomes. Social concerns and potential barriers to reporting to police and medical service seeking are discussed further later in the section "Rape Acknowledgement and Barriers to Service Seeking."

Physical and Mental Health Problems
PHYSICAL HEALTH CONSEQUENCES

Sexual assault has been associated with numerous longer term physical health problems. Gynecologic problems are the most prevalent health problems reported by women with a history of sexual assault when compared to women without a sexual assault history. Population studies have demonstrated that sexual assault is associated with a higher prevalence of STIs; vaginal pain, bleeding, or infection; pelvic pain; urinary-tract infections; and inflammatory disease (Campbell et al., 2002; Latthe, Migini, Gray, Hills, & Khan, 2006; Plichta, 1996; Weinbaum et al., 2001). Similar findings have been documented among samples of patients presenting to EDs (Brokaw et al., 2002; Muelleman, Lenaghan, & Pakieser, 1998), primary care (Coker, Smith, Bethea, King, & McKeown, 2000), and other specialty care settings (King, Britt, McFarlane, & Hawkins, 2000; Letourneau, Holmes, & Chasedunn-Roark, 1999). Relatedly, sexual assault has been linked to subsequent problems with sexual functioning. For example, adolescent sexual assault victims were more likely than nonvictimized controls to report sexual dysfunction, including lubrication problems, pain, and pelvic floor dysfunction, when assessed three years after the rape (Postma, Bicanic, van der Vaart, & Laan, 2013). In adult women, lifetime or adult experience of rape more than doubles the odds of developing sexual problems (Letourneau, Resnick, Kilpatrick, Saunders, & Best, 1996; Lutfey, Link, Litman, Rosen, & McKinlay, 2008).

Population-based samples of adult women have also linked sexual assault to perceptions of poor health, functional limitations, several chronic diseases, and both medically explained and unexplained somatic symptoms (Golding, 1994). In a population-based sample of older adult women, a dose-response effect was observed between number of sexual assaults and risk for arthritis and breast cancer (Stein & Barrett-Connor, 2000). Among female veterans, the experience of military sexual assault has been linked with poor physical health across a variety of domains including gastrointestinal, genitourinary, musculoskeletal, and neurological functioning (Smith et al., 2011). Among civilian women, sexual assault by intimate partners has been associated with substantially lower self-reported physical health compared to women without intimate partner violence (Bonomi, Anderson, Rivara, & Thompson, 2007).

MENTAL HEALTH CONSEQUENCES

The mental health consequences of sexual assault, including PTSD and major depressive disorder (MDD), can also be longer term. Approximately 26.6% to 45.2% of sexual assault victims from representative samples of adolescent, college, and adult household-residing women meet lifetime criteria for PTSD (Walsh et al., 2012). Similarly, among representative samples of college and adult community-residing women, 40% of sexual violence victims report a lifetime diagnosis of MDD (Kilpatrick et al., 2007). The development of PTSD or MDD also may explain associations between sexual violence exposure and physical health problems, as data from female veterans indicate that PTSD symptoms mediate associations between military-related sexual assault and gastrointestinal, genitourinary, musculoskeletal, and neurological symptoms measured after deployment (Smith et al., 2011). Factors that predict the development and severity of PTSD following sexual assault include less education, a more severe history of sexual assault, greater perceived life threat during the sexual assault, and emotional detachment during the assault (Dunmore, Clark, & Ehlers, 1999; Ullman & Filipas, 2001; Ullman, Filipas, Townsend, & Starzynski, 2007). Factors that predict the chronicity of PTSD following sexual assault include number of reexperiencing symptoms, rape history, and childhood assault history (Cougle, Resnick, & Kilpatrick, 2013).

SUBSTANCE USE

Substance use and disorders are also common longer term outcomes associated with sexual assault. Nationally representative data indicate that girls and women with a lifetime history of sexual assault report significantly more past-year binge drinking, marijuana use, illicit drug use, and nonmedical prescription drug use when compared to nonvictims (Walsh et al., 2014). Furthermore, in a national sample of young adult women, lifetime exposure to incapacitated rape was associated with increased odds of past-year binge drinking, marijuana use, and illicit drug use; while lifetime history of forcible and drug-facilitated rape was associated with past-year marijuana and illicit drug use (McCauley, Ruggiero, Resnick, & Kilpatrick, 2010). Similarly, in a national sample of college women, lifetime exposure to drug- or alcohol-facilitated or incapacitated rape, but not forcible rape, was associated with more than 2.5 times the odds of past-year substance abuse (defined as binge drinking or other substance abuse; McCauley et al., 2009). Among women in a national sample who reported seeking medical services, approximately 25% reported past-year drug use, 15% met past-year criteria for substance abuse, and 8% reported monthly binge drinking (McCauley, Kilpatrick, Walsh, & Resnick, 2013). In a study of women recruited at the time of a rape-related medical exam, those who reported substance use at the time of the assault or in the six weeks prior to the assault were more likely to meet criteria for alcohol or marijuana abuse and reported more days of alcohol and marijuana use approximately six weeks after the rape (Resnick et al., 2012). Finally, in a longitudinal study of women, sexual or physical assault experienced since the baseline interview was associated with a 2.5-fold increase in the odds of substance use or abuse at follow-up two years later after controlling for assault and substance use and abuse at baseline (Kilpatrick, Acierno, Resnick, Saunders, & Best, 1997).

SUICIDAL IDEATION AND BEHAVIOR

Over the past several decades, an extensive literature has emerged documenting associations between childhood sexual abuse (CSA) and both increased suicidal ideation and suicidal behavior in adulthood (for reviews see Colquhoun, 2009; Fondacaro & Butler, 1995; Santa Mina & Gallop, 1998; Ullman, 2004). Of particular relevance to treating providers within acute care settings, CSA appears to be a consistent predictor of recent suicide attempts among patients admitted to EDs and psychiatric inpatient units (Brodsky et al., 2001; Coll, Law, Tobias, & Hawton, 1998; Kaslow, Thompson, Brooks, & Twomey, 2000; Kingree, Thompson, & Kaslow, 1999; Law, Coll, Tobias, & Hawton, 1998; Manetta, 1999; Thompson, Kaslow, & Kingree, 2000).

Although much of the research on sexual victimization and suicide has focused on CSA as a risk factor for ideation and attempts among adults, several national probability samples have also identified a specific link between lifetime sexual assault history at various ages among adults and an increased prevalence of both suicidal ideation and suicide attempts (Burnam et al., 1988; Davidson, Hughes, George, & Blazer, 1996; Kilpatrick et al., 1985; Ullman & Brecklin, 2002). For example, Kilpatrick and colleagues found that 44% of female rape victims report suicidal ideation, while 19% report having made a suicide attempt. In one such study involving a reanalysis of data from the National Comorbidity Survey, Ullman and Brecklin (2002) found that age at which sexual victimization occurred was unrelated to suicidal ideation or attempts. However, 35% of women with a lifetime history of sexual assault or sexual abuse reported significant suicidal ideation, while 17% endorsed at least one suicide attempt. Women with a history of victimization occurring both in childhood and adulthood (i.e., revictimization) were three times more likely than those with victimization occurring only in childhood or adulthood to have attempted suicide. Suicidal ideation and suicide attempts were also more than three times more likely to follow sexual assault than to occur prior to or within the same year as a sexual assault. Those reporting either ideation or attempts endorsed more stressful events during the past year, had a history involving a greater number of traumatic events, identified less current social support, and were more likely to have had one or more alcohol dependence symptoms or diagnoses of PTSD or MDD. Suicidal ideation was also associated with being unmarried and being unemployed, while suicide attempts were linked to being younger, having never attended college, and reporting more current social conflict.

Suicidal ideation and behavior are also shown to be frequent correlates of adult sexual assault within community and college student samples. For example, Koss, Dinero, and Seibel (1988) estimated that 28% of women sexually assaulted in college (including rape) contemplated suicide after their assault to the degree that they considered a method. No differences emerged as a function of whether the perpetrator was a stranger or an acquaintance in this study. In relation to intimate partner assault, McFarlane and colleagues (2005) found that among women presenting to a special family violence unit within the District Attorney's office, those reporting being sexually assaulted by an intimate partner were 5.3 times more likely to have threatened or attempted suicide within the past 90 days compared to women who were only physically abused.

To date, there have only been a few studies that have begun to examine specific mechanisms through which sexual assault in adulthood may lead to increased suicidal ideation or behavior. Consistent with findings from population samples, mental health disorders including PTSD, depression, and substance use appear to be potential mediators of the association between sexual assault and subsequent suicidal ideation and attempts (Ullman & Najdowski, 2009; Vaszari, Bradford, O'Leary, Abdallah, & Cottler, 2011). Findings suggest that sexual revictimization or a history of other nonsexual traumatic events may also serve as an important moderator of suicidal ideation or behavior among sexually victimized adults (Bryan, McNaughton-Cassill, Osman, & Hernandez, 2013), although other studies have not supported this hypothesis (Nilsen & Conner, 2002). Increased suicidal ideation has also been linked to demographic characteristics (e.g., younger age, minority status, bisexuality), rape characteristics (e.g., having multiple offenders), and maladaptive coping methods (e.g., using substances to cope, self-blame; Ullman & Najdowski, 2009). Suicide attempts have been linked to the experience of completed rape/penetrative rape (Stepakoff, 1998; Ullman & Najdowski, 2009) and formal disclosure of an assault (Ullman & Najdowski, 2009). Compared to CSA, adult sexual assault has been linked to increased hopelessness and suicidal ideation among undergraduate women (Stepakoff, 1998), and one study found that sexually victimized college women reported fewer reasons for living, fewer coping beliefs, and fewer moral objections to suicide (Segal, 2009). Preliminary evidence suggests greater perceived control over recovery following sexual assault and aid/support when disclosing an assault may serve as protective factors against suicidality (Ullman & Najdowski, 2009).

Despite the extensive literature documenting increased risk of suicidality associated with both CSA and adult sexual assault, there is limited research examining acute risk for suicide in the immediate aftermath of a sexual assault (e.g., assessment of suicide risk as part of post-rape medical care). This is surprising, as in addition to acute distress associated with sexual assault, many patients presenting to the ED following a sexual assault may have preexisting risk factors for suicide. For example, severe anxiety; panic attacks; depressed mood; recent abuse of drugs or alcohol; feelings of hopelessness, helplessness, worthlessness; insomnia; recent interpersonal loss or unemployment; and recent impulsive behavior have all been identified as acute predictors of suicide attempts among patients hospitalized following an attempt (Hall, Platt, & Hall, 1999). As highlighted earlier, it may also be important to consider characteristics of the recent assault, historical stressors and trauma exposure (including CSA), and current resources/support to aid in coping with the assault when assessing level of risk among recently assaulted women. It may be particularly important to conduct a thorough psychological or psychiatric evaluation and consider suicide risk within safety planning/follow-up care as research suggests that psychiatric evaluations within an ED setting can decrease subsequent deliberate self-harm among patients at high risk for suicide (Hickey, Hawton, Fagg, & Weitzel, 2001). For further information on the assessment and management of suicide risk in adolescents and adults, see Chapters 3 and 9 of this volume.

Revictimization Risk

Women with sexual assault histories are at substantially increased risk for later sexual assault, a phenomenon termed "revictimization." More than 50% of rape victims in national samples of adolescent girls, adult college women, and adult community-residing women report revictimization (Walsh et al., 2012). In self-selecting convenience samples, women with childhood sexual assault histories have been shown to be between 3 and 11 times more likely to experience a sexual assault later in life when compared to women without early life sexual assault experiences (Classen, Palesh, & Aggarwal, 2005). High rates of revictimization also have been observed in emergency room samples. Specifically, among rape victims seeking rape-related medical treatment, 59% had a prior history of physical or sexual assault (Resnick et al., 2012). The high prevalence of revictimization highlights a strong need to provide effective secondary prevention programming to women with a history of sexual assault.

Access to Acute Medical Care or Other Agency Services

As previously noted, rape is an underreported crime. For example, between the years 1992 and 2000, 36% of rapes of female victims age 12 or older were not reported to police (Rennison, 2002). Findings from the NWS-R indicated that among a national telephone household sample asked about their most recent rape only, only 17.5% of forcible rapes and 15.8% of DAFR incidents were reported to police (Wolitzky-Taylor et al., 2011). In addition, Rennison (2002) found that victims of rapes who reported to police were more likely to receive medical care for assault-related injuries than nonreporters to police (59% vs. 17%), and this pattern is consistent with findings from other studies of post-rape medical care access (Resnick et al., 2000; Zinzow et al., 2012). Of all lifetime incidents among college women, 16% of forcible and 7% of DAFR were reported to police (Kilpatrick et al., 2007).

Victims of rape may represent a medically underserved population as only 20% of rape victims seek any rape-related medical services (Zinzow et al., 2012). Medical services provided as part of the SAMFE may be provided by physicians or SANE specialists who receive intensive training in the conduct of the medical and forensic aspects of the exam (Campbell et al., 2005; Ledray, 1999; Logan et al., 2007). Such programs provide 24-hour response for provision of care that includes medical and preventive services (e.g., sexually transmitted diseases, unwanted pregnancy due to rape), as well as gathering of evidence that may aid in case investigation and prosecution. As noted, rape crisis advocates who typically volunteer are often key members of the response team along with sexual assault examiners (Campbell et al., 2006). Advocates are unique in their role of focusing on the emotional and informational needs of the victim, and rape crisis advocates or staff may also serve as support during subsequent criminal justice proceedings (Campbell et al., 2006).

Whereas in the past, provision of state-funded SAMFE services was typically restricted to those who reported the incident to police, the 2005 reauthorization of the Violence Against Women Act (VAWA, 2005) mandated that states receiving VAWA funds provide medical exams at no cost to the victim while allowing her to choose whether or not to report the incident to the police (Violence Against Women and Department of Justice Reauthorization Act, 2005). For rape victims who choose initially to not report to police, this approach includes provision of medical care and storing of evidence not identified by name that is destroyed after a set period of time (e.g., one year), if a victim does not decide to report within a specified time frame (Price, 2010). It is possible that this change in policy will result in increased numbers of women receiving medical care, including those experiencing less stereotypic rape incidents that are more likely to be reported to police (e.g., Wolitzky-Taylor et al., 2011). Typically, sexual assault medical forensic exams are provided to victims who seek services within days (e.g., 120 hours) of an assault (Logan et al., 2007). Thus it is important for service providers (medical personnel, police, rape crisis advocates, mental health and medical care professionals) to inform rape victims and clients seeking other post-rape services of the availability of such exams and the fact that they can receive such an exam whether or not they choose to report to the police. In addition to the need for frontline providers to give this information to recent victims of rape who they encounter directly, it may be crucial to provide this information to women in the general population that such services are available should they experience a rape. Mandatory reporting of *adult* rape incidents is required only in cases in which the victim is elderly or disabled (Linden, 2011). Finally, regardless of whether an incident was initially reported to police or whether the individual sought medical care, individual states vary in terms of the statute of limitations for pressing criminal charges following a rape. Thus those working with victims of rape should be aware of laws within their state in order to provide basic information and provide referral information to those with expertise regarding the law.

Characteristics of Rape Victims Seeking Post-Assault Medical Care

As described earlier, victims accessing medical care for a rape occurring as an adult or older adolescent are more likely to have rape-related health concerns and to have reported to the police (Resnick et al., 2000; Zinzow et al., 2012). Rape victims who report to police or victim service agencies appear to be at higher risk for PTSD (e.g., Rothbaum, Foa, Riggs, Murdock, & Walsh, 1992) than those with history of rape assessed in general population studies (e.g., Resnick et al., 1993). Resnick and colleagues (2000) found that among adult rape victims from the NWS study, 26.2% said they had received medical care following a most recent incident, with reporting to police and concern about STIs being the primary predictors. Findings from the NWS-R among women who experienced rape victimization at age 14 or older indicated that 21% received post-assault medical care following a most recent incident (Zinzow et al., 2012), with Black racial identification, rape-related health concerns, and reporting to police remaining significant predictors after controlling for other variables. Finally, prevalence of DAFR or substance-related rape also appears to be greater

in samples seeking acute ED-based post-rape medical care, with 50% reporting use of alcohol or drugs proximal to the incident (Avegno, Mills, & Mills, 2009; Resnick et al., 2012). Within the national telephone household NWS-R, McCauley and colleagues (2013) found that 33% of victims receiving postrape medical care that may have included ED or other settings said they were using substances at the time of incident. In addition, the vast majority of this group reported loss of consciousness or inability to control behavior due to the substance use.

Rape Acknowledgment and Barriers to Service Seeking

Reasons for not reporting rape to police include embarrassment or shame at the idea of others knowing what happened; concerns about being treated poorly by police, lawyers, or other parts of the criminal justice system; and failure to acknowledge the incident as rape (Cohn, Zinzow, Resnick, & Kilpatrick, 2013). Reasons for not seeking medical services include lack of access to or knowledge of available medical and mental health services (Logan, Evans, Stevenson, & Jordan, 2005) and concern about others knowing what happened (Kilpatrick et al., 2007; Thompson, Sitterle, Clay, & Kingree, 2007; Wolitzky-Taylor et al., 2011; Zinzow & Thompson, 2011). One especially important factor in both reporting and service seeking is acknowledgement of the incident as rape (Cohn et al., 2013). Specifically, women who have experienced more stereotypical rapes, including those that involve force and those that are perpetrated by strangers, are more likely to acknowledge their experiences as rape (Littleton, Axsom, Breitkopf, & Berenson, 2006). Women who have experienced DAFR, in contrast, are less likely to acknowledge their experiences as rape, and diminished acknowledgment partially explains associations between rape type (forcible vs. substance-related) and disparities in service seeking (Walsh, Zinzow, Badour, Kilpatrick, & Resnick, 2015).

Rape reporting and service seeking do not consistently overlap (i.e., individuals who utilize one service do not necessarily seek other services). In a national sample of rape victims who sought any medical, crisis, or police services, 65% sought medical attention, 62% sought crisis help, and 42% reported their rape to the police (Walsh et al., 2015). Thus, police, medical, and crisis service providers would benefit from knowledge and understanding of other service options and their availability to rape victims. However, reporting to police has been a significant predictor of receipt of medical care (Resnick et al., 2000; Zinzow et al., 2012). To the extent that the new VAWA (2005) provision stipulates that exams may be obtained free of charge even if not formally reported to police may reduce barriers related to the need to report, more women may obtain medical services. However, it will be important for women to be made aware that such services are available.

RESPONSES OF OTHERS TO RAPE DISCLOSURE

Although victims may not seek formal services for the reasons cited earlier, the majority of victims (~80%) will disclose their assault informally to at least one other person (Ahrens, Cabral, & Abeling, 2009; Starzynski, Ullman, Filipas, & Townsend, 2005; Ullman & Filipas, 2001). Responses of others to disclosure can have an important impact on victims of rape. For example, although most victims who disclose report positive disclosure experiences, a portion of women report distressing disclosure experiences (Ahrens & Campbell, 2000; Banyard, Moynihan, Walsh, Cohn, & Ward, 2010). Recipients of disclosure are in a unique position to facilitate formal reporting of sexual assault and medical care seeking (Ahrens, Campbell, Ternier-Thames, Wasoc, & Selfl, 2007; Patterson & Campbell, 2010; Paul, Zinzow, McCauley, Kilpatrick, & Resnick, 2013). In national samples of women who report receiving a rape disclosure from another woman, more than two-thirds of recipients indicate that they encouraged victims to formally report their rapes (Paul et al., 2014; Paul, Walsh, et al., 2013), and victims who received this encouragement were more likely to formally report to police (Paul, Zinzow, et al., 2013). Thus training in how to respond to disclosures and to encourage seeking services that may include formal reporting to police or access to medical care with or without reporting to police in a supportive manner may increase overall levels of formal reporting or medical services access among victims. However, trainings should be sensitive to the fact that disclosure recipients often have their own histories of sexual assault and mental health problems including PTSD, depression, and substance use, and they are more likely to report seeking help for emotional distress in the past (Paul et al., 2014; Paul, Walsh, et al., 2013).

Prevention and Early Intervention Following Rape

As noted earlier, there is some support for improved SAMFE services for rape victims, particularly as evaluated with specialized nurse examiner-led programs (Campbell et al., 2005). In addition, Campbell and colleagues demonstrated improved services and reduced distress associated with rape crisis advocacy services that are typically integrated with the SAMFE (Campbell et al., 2006). The past several decades have also fostered development of a number of promising prevention and early intervention programs aimed at reducing risk for post-assault concerns including PTSD, depression, and problematic substance use. The ED or other acute medical settings in which recent rape victims are seen might provide an opportunity to implement screening, brief intervention, and referral for additional mental health or substance abuse treatment as needed. This approach has been implemented successfully with other ED and primary care populations (e.g., see Madras et al., 2009). Indeed, Zatzick and colleagues (2004) found that acutely injured trauma victims benefited from implementation of a stepped care intervention beginning at an initial hospital contact that involved continuous case management, motivational interviewing (Miller, Rollnick, & Moyers, 1998), targeting problematic alcohol use, and pharmacotherapy and/or cognitive behavioral therapy for patients who had developed PTSD at three months post-trauma. A more recently reported study by this group found that a collaborative stepped care approach involving coordinated care management, pharmacotherapy, and cognitive behavioral therapy initially delivered in a surgical inpatient ward and transitioned into outpatient clinics, over the telephone, and finally into primary care and community rehabilitation centers reduced PTSD symptoms and resulted in improved physical function as compared to a usual care condition one year after severe traumatic injury requiring surgical hospitalization (Zatzick et al., 2013).

Drawing from knowledge regarding the efficacy and effectiveness of Prolonged Exposure Therapy (Foa & Rothbaum, 1998) as an empirically supported cognitive behavioral treatment for PTSD subsequent to rape and other traumatic events (Powers, Halpern, Ferenschak, Gillihan, & Foa, 2010), Rothbaum and colleagues (2012) developed a modified and abbreviated protocol for rape victims (and individuals experiencing other traumatic events) to be delivered in the ED as a PTSD prevention program. The intervention involves three hour-long weekly sessions comprised of psychoeducation, relaxation training, in-session imaginal exposure, and homework instructions for imaginal and in vivo exposure. Compared to an assessment-only control group, victims receiving this intervention reported significantly reduced PTSD symptoms at 4- and 12-week follow-up.

Another potentially promising cognitive behavioral prevention program for PTSD included two sessions with both the patient and a significant other presenting to the ED following any type of life-threatening traumatic event (Brunet, Des Groseilliers, Cordova, & Ruzek, 2013). The treatment content included psychoeducation and other cognitive behavioral strategies aimed at facilitating supportive disclosure and coping with support of the significant other. Acute symptoms of PTSD reported by the patient were significantly lower in the intervention condition as compared to controls at the end of the two sessions. Although this study did not include a follow-up assessment, it does draw on a growing literature supporting the importance of incorporating partners and other family members into PTSD-related interventions (for a review, see Monson, Macdonald, & Brown-Bowers, 2012).

Despite preliminary support for the efficacy of these prevention/early intervention approaches, other studies in this domain have found mixed evidence for the usefulness of similar interventions. For example, Kilpatrick and Veronen (1983) reported no differences between rape victims who were within one month post assault who received a brief cognitive behavioral intervention versus assessment. Foa, Zoellner, and Feeny (2006) and Foa, Hearst-Ikeda, and Perry (1995) implemented a multisession brief cognitive behavioral therapy with assault victims, including sexual assault less than one month post-incident who otherwise met PTSD symptom criteria. Results indicated significantly reduced PTSD symptoms at posttreatment in the cognitive behavioral relative to comparison groups but no differences in PTSD at longer term follow-up. This highlights the need for additional research in this area.

In an effort to target the unique concerns faced by rape victims, our research group developed a brief video intervention to be delivered at the time of the post-rape medical exam that includes separate components aimed at (a) preparation for and understanding of medical exam procedures and (b) psychoeducation and instruction in coping strategies that might facilitate recovery post-rape (Resnick, Acierno, Amstadter, et al., 2007; Resnick, Acierno, Waldrop, et al., 2007). Both components included modeling of individuals participating in the exam and using coping strategies including in vivo exposure to approach realistically nondangerous cues. Modeling of engagement in activities such as work or spending time with family and not using substances as a coping strategy were also included. Health-care providers and advocates depicted in the video provided supportive information regarding seeking medical care and statements regarding the assailant being to blame for assault and the individual herself being responsible for recovery. Findings of a first report indicated that among women with a prior history of rape, those in the intervention condition reported reduced frequency of PTSD and reduced intensity of depression symptoms at approximately six weeks post-assault but there were no differences with the standard care condition at six months post-rape (Resnick, Acierno, Waldrop, et al., 2007). The second report described findings related to substance use and abuse, with results indicating lower frequency of marijuana use through the six-month follow-up time frame among pre-rape marijuana users who were shown the video (Resnick, Acierno, Amstadter, et al., 2007). These results are particularly promising given that this protocol involved only a single session and can be delivered with minimal drain on ED resources.

In sum, data regarding prevention and early intervention efficacy indicate that multiple-session (and possibly some types of single-session) approaches that incorporate evidence-based cognitive behavioral strategies are supported, particularly for those at risk for PTSD based on initial symptom profile or persistence of symptoms (Ehlers & Clark, 2003; Litz, Gray, Bryant, & Adler, 2002). Very brief interventions targeting substance abuse in ED or primary care settings have received stronger support (e.g., Madras et al., 2009). Additional research is needed to develop a systematic understanding of how such interventions targeting PTSD and comorbid problems that may include substance use disorders may be best delivered in the ED setting either alone or as an adjunct/component of a more intensive or multisession approach. Barriers to implementation may include time limitations in the post-assault exam setting. Another potential barrier includes fear of perceived blame on the part of victims should screening related to substance use or abuse be conducted in that setting (see Cole & Logan, 2008; Ledray, 2008).

For rape victims, additional elements may be key to deliver at the time of the exam, including information regarding options to report the assault to police immediately or to have an anonymous exam (e.g., see Price, 2010); education about HIV/STIs, pregnancy, or other health concerns; and discussion of concerns surrounding assault disclosure. Additionally, more information could be usefully provided about revictimization, risk-reduction strategies, and DAFR as a type of assault. Further, screening for suicide risk might be beneficial as is recommended for ED settings (Ting et al., 2012). This information could be combined with implementation of screening, brief intervention, and referral to additional treatment, as this approach has demonstrated efficacy targeting substance use and abuse within single-session implementation (e.g., see Madras et al., 2009). In addition to this approach, it may also be important to consider developing methods to begin broader outreach to women who do not seek post-rape services and/ or traditional mental health services. This might include web-based self-help with (e.g., Littleton, Buck, Rossman, & Grills-Taquechel, 2012) or without (e.g., Ruggiero et al., 2006) therapist facilitation or interaction.

Concluding Remarks

Findings across samples indicate that a history of rape or sexual assault is highly prevalent among adult women, with at least 1 in 6 women experiencing rape (including forcible, DAFR, combined DAFR/forcible, or attempted rape) across the lifespan. The vast majority of rapes are not reported to police, and screening is optimally done using a series of behaviorally specific questions to define key elements of assault. Rape typically occurs when women are children, adolescents, and young adults, with first incidents often happening to girls. Men who have experienced rape or attempted rape are also most often first victimized as children. DAFR incidents occur typically during older adolescence and adulthood. Most rapes are perpetrated by those known to the victim, with intimate or ex-intimate partners representing a large percentage.

Those exposed to rape are also at risk of other sexual and physical violence, including intimate partner physical assault, across the life span. History of cohabitation, lower economic resources or social support, and in some cases minority race and nonheterosexual sexual orientation have been associated in some studies with increased risk of rape and/or intimate partner violence including rape. Rape poses risk of health consequences requiring emergent care or prevention in the case of potential exposure to STIs and unwanted pregnancy, as well as any physical injuries that may have been sustained. Many rape victims report both health concerns, as well as concerns about how others may react. More consistent information and services regarding HIV testing and prophylaxis should be provided. The post-rape sexual assault medical forensic exam constitutes a setting in which health concerns, mental health needs, and resource needs might be addressed. However, as noted, the majority of rape victims do not access such care. We suggest that it would be helpful to provide information about services available to victims of rape, including post-assault medical care that may be received regardless of whether an incident is reported to police. Successful communication about this issue likely will also require education about the types of incidents that constitute rape, including DAFR, to counter biases about what qualifies as rape. Finally, emerging evidence suggests that brief prevention/early intervention programs delivered within ED settings either as stand-alone protocols or in combination with stepped care approaches or referrals to more intensive treatment options may offer benefit in preventing and/or ameliorating PTSD, as well as additional problems prevalent among victims of rape including substance use disorders, depression, revictimization risk, and suicide behaviors.

Author's Note

Manuscript preparation was supported by grant numbers: DA023099, MH018869, and DA031099.

Views expressed do not necessarily represent those of the agencies supporting this research.

References

Abbey, A. (2002). Alcohol-related sexual assault: A common problem among college students. *Journal of Studies on Alcohol*, 14, 118–128.

Acierno, R., Resnick, H. S., & Kilpatrick, D. G. (1997). Health impact of interpersonal violence: 1. Prevalence rates, case identification, and risk factors for sexual assault, physical assault, and domestic violence in men and women. *Behavioral Medicine*, 23, 53–64.

Adams, J. A., Girardin, B., & Faugno, D. (2001). Adolescent sexual assault: documentation of acute injuries using photocolposcopy. *Journal of Pediatric and Adolescent Gynecology*, 1\4), 175–180.

Ahrens, C. E., Cabral, G., & Abe, S. (2009). Healing or hurtful: Sexual assault survivors' interpretations of social reactions from support providers. *Psychology of Women Quarterly*, 33, 81–94.

Ahrens, C. E., Campbell, R., Ternier-Thames, N. K., Wasco, S. M., & Sefl, T. (2007). Deciding whom to tell: Expectations and outcomes of rape survivors' first disclosures. *Psychology of Women Quarterly*, 31(1), 38–49.

Ahrens, C., & Campbell, R. (2000). Assisting rape victims as they recover from rape: The impact on friends. *Journal of Interpersonal Violence*, 15, 959–986.

Avegno, J., Mills, T. J., & Mills, L. D. (2009). Sexual assault victims in the emergency department: Analysis by demographic and event characteristics. *Journal of Emergency Medicine*, 37, 328–334.

Baker, T. C., Burgess, A. W., Brickman, E., & Davis, R. C. (1990). Rape victims' concerns about possible exposure to HIV infection. *Journal of Interpersonal Violence*, 5, 49–60.

Banyard, V. L., Moynihan, M. M., Walsh, W. A., Cohn, E. S., & Ward, S. (2010). Friends of survivors: The community impact of unwanted sexual experiences. *Journal of Interpersonal Violence*, 25, 242–256.

Basile, K. C., & Smith, S. G. (2011). Sexual violence victimization of women: Prevalence, characteristics, and the role of public health and prevention. *American Journal of Lifestyle Medicine*, 5, 407–417.

Bonomi, A. E., Anderson, M. L., Rivara, F. P., & Thompson, R. S. (2007). Health outcomes in women with physical and sexual intimate partner violence exposure. *Journal of Women's Health*, 16(7), 987–997.

Breiding, M. J., Chen, J., & Black, M. C. (2014). *Intimate partner violence in the United States—2010*. Atlanta, GA: National Center for Injury Prevention and Control, Centers for Disease Control and Prevention.

Breiding M, Smith S, Basile K, Walters M, Chen J, Merrick M. Prevalence and characteristics of sexual violence, stalking, and intimate partner violence victimization—National intimate partner and sexual violence survey, United States, 2011. *MMWR: Morbidity and Mortality Weekly Report*, 63, 1–17. Retrieved from http://www.cdc.gov/mmwr/pdf/ss/ss6308.pdf. 2014.

Brodsky, B. S., Oquendo, M., Ellis, S. P., Haas, G. L., Malone, K. M., & Mann, J. J. (2001). The relationship of childhood abuse to impulsivity and suicidal behavior in adults with major depression. *American Journal of Psychiatry*, 158, 1871–1877.

Brokaw, J., Fullerton-Gleason, L., Olson, L., Crandall, C., McLaughlin, S., & Skylar, D. (2002). Health status and intimate partner violence: A cross-sectional study. *Annals of Emergency Medicine*, 39, 31–38.

Brunet, A., Des Groseilliers, I B., Cordova, M. J., & Ruzek, J. I. (2013). Randomized controlled trial of a brief dyadic cognitive-behavioral intervention designed to prevent PTSD. *European Journal of Psychotraumatology*, 4. http://dx.doi.org/10.3402/ejpt.v4i0.21572

Bryan, C. J., McNaughton-Cassill, Osman, A., & Hernandez, A. M. (2013). The associations of physical and sexual assault with suicide risk in nonmilitary and undergraduate samples. *Suicide and Life-Threatening Behavior*, 43, 223–234.

Burnam, M. A., Stein, J. A., Golding, J. M., Siegel, J. M., Sorenson, S. B., Forsythe, A. B., & Telles, C. A. (1988). Sexual assault and mental disorders in a community population. *Journal of Consulting and Clinical Psychology*, 56, 843–850.

Byrne, C. A., Resnick, H. S., Kilpatrick, D. G., Best, C. L., & Saunders, B. E. (1999). The socioeconomic impact of interpersonal violence on women. *Journal of Consulting and Clinical Psychology*, 67, 362–366.

Campbell, J. C. (2004). Helping women understand their risk in situations of intimate partner violence. *Journal of Interpersonal Violence*, 19, 1464–1477.

Campbell, J., Jones, A. S., Dienemann, J., Kub, J., Schollenberger, J., O'Campo, P., . . . Wynne, C. (2002). Intimate partner violence and physical health consequences. *Archives of Internal Medicine*, 162, 1157–1163.

Campbell, R. (2006). Rape survivors' experiences with the legal and medical systems. Do rape victim advocates make a difference? *Violence Against Women*, 12, 30–45.

Campbell, R., Patterson, D., & Lichty, L. F. (2005). The effectiveness of sexual assault nurse examiner (SANE) programs: A review of psychological, medical, legal, and community outcomes. *Trauma, Violence, & Abuse*, 6, 313–329.

Campbell, R., Townsend, S. M., Long, S. M., Kinnison, K. E., Pulley, E. M., Adames, S. B., & Wasco, S. M. (2006). Responding to sexual assault victims' medical and emotional needs: A national study of the services provided by SANE programs. *Research in Nursing & Health*, 29, 384–398.

Campbell, R., Wasco, S. M., Ahrens, C. E., Sefl, T., & Barnes, H. E. (2001). Preventing the "second rape": Rape survivors' experiences with community service providers. *Journal of Interpersonal Violence*, 16, 1239–1259.

Centers for Disease Control and Prevention. (2005). Antiretroviral postexposure prophylaxis after sexual, injection-drug use, or other nonoccupational exposure to HIV in the United States: recommendations from the U.S. Department of Health and Human Services. *MMWR*, 54(RR-2), 1–20.

Chacko, L., Ford, N., Sbaiti, M., & Siddqui, R. (2012). Adherence to HIV post-exposure prophylaxis in victims of sexual assault: A systematic review and meta-analysis. *Sexually Transmitted Infections*, 88(5), 335–341. doi:10.1136/sextrans-2011–050371

Classen, C. C., Palesh, O. G., & Aggarwal, R. (2005). Sexual revictimization: A review of the empirical literature. *Trauma, Violence, & Abuse*, 6, 103–129.

Cohn, A. M., Zinzow, H. M., Resnick, H. S., & Kilpatrick, D. G. (2013). Correlates of reasons for not reporting rape to police: Results from a national telephone household probability sample of women with forcible or drug-or-alcohol facilitated/incapacitated rape. *Journal of Interpersonal Violence*, 28, 455–473.

Coker, A. L., Smith, P. H., Bethea, L., King, M. R., & McKeown, R. E. (2000). Physical health consequences of physical and psychological intimate partner violence. *Archives of Family Medicine*, 37, 451–457.

Cole, J., & Logan, T. K. (2008). Sexual assault response teams' responses to alcohol-using victims. *Journal of Forensic Nursing*, 4, 174–181.

Coll, X., Law, F., Tobias, A., & Hawton, K. (1998). Child sexual abuse in women who take overdoses: I. A study of prevalence and severity. *Archives of Suicide Research*, 4, 291–306.

Colquhoun, F. (2009). *The relationship between child maltreatment, sexual abuse and subsequent suicide attempts*. London: National Society for the Prevention of Cruelty to Children.

Cook, S. L., Gidycz, C. A., Koss, M. P., & Murphy, M. (2011). Emerging issues in the measurement of rape victimization. *Violence Against Women*, 17, 201–218.

Cougle, J. R., Resnick, H., & Kilpatrick, D. G. (2013). Factors associated with chronicity in posttraumatic stress disorder: A prospective analysis of a national sample of women. *Psychological Trauma: Theory, Research, Practice, and Policy*, 5, 43–49.

Davidson, J. R., Hughes, D. C., George, L. K., & Blazer, D. G. (1996). The association of sexual assault and attempted suicide within the community. *Archives of General Psychiatry*, 53, 550–555.

Draughon, J. E., Anderson, J. C., Hansen, B. R., & Sheridan, D. J. (2014). Nonoccupational postexposure HIV prophylaxis in sexual assault programs: A survey of SANE and FNE program coordinators. *Journal of the Association of Nurses in AIDS Care*, 25, S90–S100.

Dunmore, E., Clark, D. M., & Ehlers, A. (1999). Cognitive factors involved in the onset and maintenance of posttraumatic stress disorder (PTSD) after physical or sexual assault. *Behaviour Research and Therapy*, 37, 809–829.

Dutton, D. D., & Kropp, P. R. (2000). A review of domestic violence risk instruments. *Trauma, Violence, & Abuse*, 1, 171–181.

Ehlers, A., & Clark, D. (2003). Early psychological interventions for adult survivors of trauma: A review. *Biological Psychiatry*, 53, 817–826.

Fisher, B.S., Daigle, L.E., Cullen, F.T., & Turner, M.G. (2003). Reporting sexual victimization to police and others: Results from a national-level study of college women. *Criminal Justice and Behavior*, 30, 6–38.

Foa, E. B., Zoellner, L. A., & Feeny, N. C. (2006). An evaluation of three brief programs for facilitating recovery after assault. *Journal of Traumatic Stress*, 19, 29–43.

Foa, E. B., Hearst-Ikeda, D., & Perry, K. (1995). Evaluation of a brief cognitive-behavioral program for the prevention of chronic PTSD in recent assault victims. *Journal of Consulting and Clinical Psychology*, 63, 948–955.

Foa, E., & Rothbaum, B. (1998). *Treating the trauma of rape: Cognitive behavioral therapy for PTSD*. New York: Guilford Press.

Fondacaro, K. M., & Butler, W. M. (1995). Suicidality in female survivors of childhood sexual abuse. In S. S. Canetto, & D. Lester (Eds.), *Women and suicidal behavior* (pp. 192–204). New York: Springer.

Golding, J. M. (1994). Sexual assault history and physical health in randomly selected Los Angeles women. *Health Psychology*, 13, 130–138.

Goodman, L. A., Koss, M. P., & Russo, N. F. (1993). Violence against women: Physical and mental health effects. Part I: Research findings. *Applied and Preventive Psychology*, 2, 79–89.

Hall, R. C., Platt, D. E., & Hall, R. C. W. (1999). Suicide risk assessment: A review of risk factors for suicide in 100 patients who made severe suicide attempts: Evaluation of suicide risk in a time of managed care. *Psychosomatics*, 40, 17–27.

Hickey, L., Hawton, K., Fagg, J., & Weitzel, H. (2001). Deliberate self-harm patients who leave the accident and emergency department without a psychiatric assessment: Neglected population at risk of suicide. *Journal of Psychosomatic Research*, 50, 87–93.

Hindmarch, I., ElSohly, M., Gambles, J., & Salamone, S. (2001). Forensic urinalysis of drug use in cases of alleged sexual assault. *Journal of Clinical Forensic Medicine*, 8, 197–205.

Holmes, M. M., Resnick, H. S., Kilpatrick, D. G., & Best, C. L. (1996). Rape-related pregnancy: Estimates and descriptive characteristics from a national sample of women. *American Journal of Obstetrics and Gynecology*, 2, 320–325.

Irwin, K. L., Edlin, B. R., Wong, L., Faruque, S., McCoy, H. V., Word, C., ... Holmberg, S. D. (1995). Urban rape survivors: Characteristics and prevalence of human immunodeficiency virus and other sexually transmitted infections. *Obstetrics & Gynecology*, 85(3), 330–336.

Kaslow, N. J., Thompson, M. P., Brooks, A. E., & Twomey, H. B. (2000). Ratings of family functioning of suicidal and nonsuicidal African American women. *Journal of Family Psychology*, 14, 585–599.

Kilpatrick, D. G., & Veronen, L. J. (1983). Treatment for rape-related problems: Crisis intervention is not enough, pp. 165–185. In L. Cohen, W. Claiborn, & G. Specter (Eds.), *Crisis intervention* (2nd ed.). New York: Human Services Press.

Kilpatrick, D. G., Acierno, R., Resnick, H. S., Saunders, B. E., & Best, C. L. (1997). A two year longitudinal analysis of the relationship between violent assault and alcohol and drug use in women. *Journal of Consulting and Clinical Psychology*, 65, 834–847.

Kilpatrick, D. G., Best, C. L., Veronen, L. J., Amick, A. E., Villeponteaux, L. A., & Ruff, G. A. (1985). Mental health correlates of criminal victimization: A random community survey. *Journal of Consulting and Clinical Psychology*, 53, 866–873.

Kilpatrick, D. G., Edmunds, C. N., & Seymour, A. K. (1992). *Rape in America: A report to the nation*. Arlington, VA: National Victim Center.

Kilpatrick, D. G., Resnick, H. S., Ruggiero, K. J., Conoscenti, L. M., & McCauley, J. (2007). Drug-facilitated, incapacitated, and forcible rape: A national study. Final report submitted to the National Institute of Justice. Grant number 2005-WG-BX-0006. Charleston, SC: Medical University of South Carolina, National Crime Victims Research & Treatment Center.

Kilpatrick, D. G., Resnick, H. S., Saunders, B. E., & Best, C. L. (1998). Victimization, posttraumatic stress disorder, and substance use and abuse among women. In C. L. Wetherington & A. B. Roman (Eds.), *Drug addiction research and the health of women* (pp. 285–307). Rockville, MD: US Department of Health and Human Services.

Kilpatrick, D., & McCauley, J. (2009). Understanding National Rape Statistics. National Online Resource Center on Violence against Women. http://new.vawnet

Kimerling, R., Street, A. E., Pavao, J., Smith, M. W., Cronkite, R.C., Holmes, T. H., & Frayne, S. M. (2010). Military-related sexual trauma among Veterans Health Administration patients returning from Afghanistan and Iraq. *American Journal of Public Health*, 100, 1409–1412.

King, E., Britt, R., McFarlane, J., & Hawkins, C. (2000). Bacterial vaginosis and Chlamydia trachomatis among pregnant abused and nonabused Hispanic women. *Journal of Obstetric, Gynecologic, and Neonatal Nursing*, 29, 606–612.

Kingree, J. B., Thompson, M. P., & Kaslow, N. J. (1999). Risk factors for suicide attempts among low-income women with a history of alcohol problems. *Addictive Behaviors*, 24, 583–587.

Koss, M. P., & Heslet, L. (1992). Somatic consequences of violence against women. *Archives of Family Medicine*, 1, 53–59.

Koss, M. P., Dinero, T. E., & Seibel, C. A. (1988). Stranger and acquaintance rape. *Psychology of Women Quarterly*, 12, 1–24.

Koss, M. P., Gidycz, C. A., & Wisniewski, N. (1987). The scope of rape: Incidence and prevalence of sexual aggression and victimization in a national sample of higher education students. *Journal of Consulting and Clinical Psychology*, 55, 162–170.

Krebs, C. P., Lindquist, C. H., Warner, T. D., Fisher, B. S., & Martin, S. L. (2009). College women's experiences with physically forced, alcohol- or other drug-enabled, and drug-facilitated sexual assault before and since entering college. *Journal of American College Health*, 57, 639–647.

Langton, L., Berzofsky, M., Krebs, C. P., & Smiley-McDonald, H. (2012). Victimizations not reported to police, 2006–2010. Washington, DC: US Department of Justice, Office of Justice Programs, Bureau of Justice Statistics.

Latthe, P., Mignini, L., Gray, R., Hills, R., & Khan, K. (2006). Factors predisposing women to chronic pelvic pain: Systematic review. *British Medical Journal*, 332, 749–755.

Latthe, P., Migini, L., Gray, R., Hills, R., & Khan, K. (2006). Factors predisposing women to chronic pelvic pain: Systematic review. *British Medical Journal*, 1, 749–755.

Law, F., Coll, X., Tobias, A., & Hawton, K. (1998). Child sexual abuse in women who take overdoses: II. Risk factors and associations. *Archives of Suicide Research*, 4, 307–327.

Ledray, L. E. (1999). *Sexual assault nurse examiner (SANE) development and operations guide*. Washington, DC: Office for Victims of Crime, US Department of Justice.

Ledray, L. E. (2008). Alcohol and sexual assault: What can/should we do in the emergency department. *Journal of Forensic Nursing, 4*, 91–93.

Letourneau, E. J., Holmes, M., & Chasedunn-Roark, J. (1999). Gynecologic health consequences to victims of interpersonal violence. *Women's Health Issues, 9*, 115–120.

Letourneau, E. J., Resnick, H. S., Kilpatrick, D. G., Saunders, B. E., & Best, C. L. (1996). Comorbidity of sexual problems and posttraumatic stress disorder in female crime victims. *Behavior Therapy, 27*, 321–336.

Linden, J. A. (2011). Care of the adult patient after sexual assault. *New England Journal of Medicine, 365*, 834–841.

Littleton, H. L., Axsom, D., Breitkopf, C. R., & Berenson, A. (2006). Rape acknowledgment and postassault experiences: How acknowledgment status relates to disclosure, coping, worldview, and reactions received from others. *Violence and Victims, 21*, 761–778.

Littleton, H., Buck, K., Rossman, L., & Grills-Taquechel, A. (2012). From survivor to thriver: A pilot study of an on-line program for rape victims. *Cognitive and Behavioral Practice, 19*, 315–327.

Littleton, H., Grills-Taquechel, A., & Axom, D. (2009). Impaired and incapacitated rape victims: Assault characteristics and post-assault experiences. *Violence and Victims, 24*, 439–457.

Litz, B. T., Gray, M. J., Bryant, R. A., & Adler, A. B. (2002). Early intervention for trauma: Current status and future directions. *Clinical Psychology: Science and Practice, 9*, 112–134.

Logan, T. K., Cole, J., & Capillo, A. (2007). Sexual assault nurse examiner program characteristics, barriers, and lessons learned. *Journal of Forensic Nursing, 3*, 24–34.

Logan, T. K., Evans, L., Stevenson, E., & Jordan, C. E. (2005). Barriers to services for rural and urban survivors of rape. *Journal of Interpersonal Violence, 20*, 591–616.

Lutfey, K. E., Link, C. L., Litman, H. J., Rosen, R. C., & McKinlay, J. B. (2008). An examination of the association of abuse (physical, sexual, or emotional) and female sexual dysfunction: Results from the Boston Area Community Health Survey. *Fertility and Sterility, 90*, 957–964.

Madras, B. K. Compton, W. M., Avula, D., Stegbauer, T., Stein, J. B., & Clark, H. W. (2009). Screening, brief intervention, referral to treatment (SBIRT) for illicit drug and alcohol use at multiple healthcare sites: Comparison at intake and 6 months later. *Drug and Alcohol Dependence, 99*, 280–295.

Maguen, S., Cohen, B., Ren, L., Bosch, J., Kimerling, R., & Seal, K. (2012). Gender differences in military sexual trauma and mental health diagnoses among Iraq and Afghanistan veterans with posttraumatic stress disorder. *Women's Health Issues, 22*, e61–e66.

Manetta, A. A. (1999). Interpersonal violence and suicidal behavior in midlife African American women. *Journal of Black Studies, 29*, 510–522.

Martin, E. K., Taft, C. T., & Resick, P. A. (2007). A review of marital rape. *Aggression and Violent Behavior, 12*, 329–347.

McCauley, J. L., Conoscenti, L. M., Ruggiero, K. J., Resnick, H. S., Saunders, B. E., & Kilpatrick, D. G. (2009). Prevalence and correlates of drug/alcohol-facilitated and incapacitated sexual assault in a nationally representative sample of adolescent girls. *Journal of Clinical Child & Adolescent Psychology, 38*, 295–300.

McCauley, J. L., Kilpatrick, D. G., Walsh, K., & Resnick, H. S. (2013). Substance use among women receiving post-rape medical care, associated post-assault concerns and current substance abuse: Results from a national telephone household probability sample. *Addictive Behaviors, 38*, 1952–1957.

McCauley, J. L., Ruggiero, K. J., Resnick, H. S., & Kilpatrick, D. G. (2010). Incapacitated, forcible, and drug/alcohol-facilitated rape in relation to binge drinking, marijuana use, and illicit drug use: A national survey. *Journal of Traumatic Stress, 23*, 132–140.

McFarlane, J., Malecha, A., Gist, J., Watson, K., Batten, E., Hall, I., & Smith, S. (2005). Intimate partner sexual assault against women and associated victim substance use, suicidality, and risk factors for femicide. *Issues in Mental Health Nursing, 26*, 953–967.

McFarlane, J., Malecha, A., Watson, K., Gist, J., Batten, E., Hall, I., & Smith, S. (2005). Intimate partner sexual assault against women: frequency, health consequences, and treatment outcomes. *Obstetrics & Gynecology, 105*(1), 99–108.

Miller, W. R., Rollnick, S., & Moyers, T. B. (1998). *Motivational interviewing*. Albuquerque: University of New Mexico.

Mohler-Kuo, M., Dowdall, G. W., Koss, M. P., & Wechsler, H. (2004). Correlates of rape while intoxicated in a national sample of college women. *Journal of Studies on Alcohol, 65*, 37–45.

Monnier, J., Resnick, H. S., Kilpatrick, D. G., Seals, B., & Holmes, M. (2002). Patterns of assault in a sample of recent rape victims. *Violence Against Women, 8*, 585–596.

Monson, C. M., Macdonald, A., & Brown-Bowers, A. (2012). Couple/family therapy for posttraumatic stress disorder: Review to facilitate interpretation of VA/DOD Clinical Practice Guideline. *Journal of Rehabilitation Research and Development, 49*, 717–728.

Muellemann, R. L., Lenaghan, P.A., & Pakieser, R. A. (1998). Nonbattering presentations to the ED of women in physically abusive relationships. *American Journal of Emergency Medicine, 16*, 128–131.

National Research Council. (2014). *Estimating the incidence of rape and sexual assault*. Panel on Measuring Rape and Sexual Assault in Bureau of Justice Statistics Household Surveys, C. Kruttschnitt, W. D. Kalsbeek, & C. C. House (Eds.). Committee on National Statistics, Division of Behavioral and Social Sciences and Education. Washington, DC: National Academies Press.

Nilsen, W., & Conner, K. B. (2002). The association between suicidal ideation and childhood and adult victimization. *Journal of Child Sexual Abuse, 11*, 49–53. org/Assoc_Files_VAWnet/AR_RapeStatistics.pdf

Patterson, D., & Campbell, R. (2010). Why rape survivors participate in the criminal justice system. *Journal of Community Psychology, 38*, 191–205.

Paul, L. A., Walsh, K., McCauley, J. L., Ruggiero, K. J., Resnick, H. S., & Kilpatrick, D. G. (2013). College women's experiences with rape disclosure: A national study. *Violence Against Women, 19*(4), 486–502. doi:10.1177/1077801213487746

Paul, L. A., Walsh, K., McCauley, J. L., Ruggiero, K. J., Resnick, H. S., & Kilpatrick, D. G. (2014). Characteristics and life experiences associated with receiving a rape disclosure within a national telephone household probability sample of women. *Journal of Community Psychology, 42*, 583–592.

Paul, L. A., Zinzow, H. M., McCauley, J. L., Kilpatrick, D. G., & Resnick, H. S. (2013). Does encouragement by others increase rape reporting? Findings from a national sample of women. *Psychology of Women Quarterly, 38*(2), 222–232. doi:10.1177/0361684313501999

Pimlott-Kubiak, S., & Cortina, L. M. (2003). Gender, victimization, and outcomes: Reconceptualization risk. *Journal of Consulting and Clinical Psychology*, 71, 528–539.

Plichta, S. B. (1996). Violence and abuse: Implications for women's health. In M. F. Falik & K. S. Collins (Eds.), *Women's health: Results from the Commonwealth Fund Survey* (pp. 237–270). Baltimore: Johns Hopkins University Press.

Postma, R., Bicanic, I., van der Vaart, H., & Laan, E. (2013). Pelvic floor muscle problems mediate sexual problems in young adult rape victims. *Journal of Sexual Medicine*, 10, 1979–1987.

Powers, M. B., Halpern, J. M., Ferenschak, M. P., Gillihan, S. J., & Foa, E. B. (2010). A meta-analytic review of prolonged exposure for posttraumatic stress disorder. *Clinical Psychology Review*, 30, 635–641.

Price, B. (2010). Receiving a forensic medical exam without participating in the criminal justice process: What will it mean? *Journal of Forensic Nursing*, 6, 74–87.

Rennison, C. M. (2002). Rape and sexual assault: Reporting to police and medical attention, 1992–2000. NCJ 194530. Washington, DC: US Department of Justice, Office of Justice Programs, Bureau of Justice Statistics.

Resnick, H. S., Falsetti, S. A., & Cahill, S. P. (2000). Marital rape. In R. T. Ammerman & M. Hersen (Eds.), *Case studies in family violence* (2nd ed., pp. 375–414). New York: Kluwer Academic/Plenum.

Resnick, H. S., Holmes, M. M., Kilpatrick, D. G., Clum, G., Acierno, R., Best, C. L., & Saunders, B. E. (2000). Predictors of post-rape medical care in a national sample of women. *American Journal of Preventive Medicine*, 19, 214–219.

Resnick, H. S., Kilpatrick, D. G., Dansky, B. S., Saunders, B. E., & Best, C. L. (1993). Prevalence of civilian trauma and posttraumatic stress disorder in a representative national sample of women. *Journal of Consulting and Clinical Psychology*, 61, 984–991.

Resnick, H. S., Walsh, K., McCauley, J. L., Schumacher, J. A., Kilpatrick, D. G., & Acierno, R. (2012). Assault related substance use as a predictor of substance use over time within a sample of recent victims of sexual assault. *Addictive Behaviors*, 37, 914–921.

Resnick, H., Acierno, R., Waldrop, A. E., King, L., King, D., Danielson, C., . . . Kilpatrick, D. (2007). Randomized controlled evaluation of an early intervention to prevent postrape psychopathology. *Behaviour Research and Therapy*, 45, 2432–2447.

Resnick, H., Monnier, J., Seals, B., Holmes, M., Nayak, M., Walsh, J., . . . Kilpatrick, D. G. (2002). Rape-related HIV risk concerns among recent rape victims. *Journal of Interpersonal Violence*, 17, 746–759.

Resnick, H. S., Acierno, R., Amstadter, A. B., Self-Brown, S., & Kilpatrick, D. G. (2007). An acute post-sexual assault intervention to prevent drug abuse: Updated findings. *Addictive Behaviors*, 32, 2032–2045.

Riggs, N., Houry, D., Long, G., Markovchick, V., & Feldhaus, K. M. (2000). Analysis of 1,076 cases of sexual assault. *Annals of Emergency Medicine*, 35, 358–362.

Rothbaum, B. O., Kearns, M. C., Price, M., Malcoun, E., Davis, M., Ressler, K. J., . . . Houry, D. (2012). Early intervention may prevent the development of posttraumatic stress disorder: A randomized pilot civilian study with modified prolonged exposure. *Biological Psychiatry*, 72, 957–963.

Rothbaum, B.O., Foa, E.B., Riggs, D.S., Murdock, T., & Walsh, W. (1992). A prospective evaluation of post-traumatic stress disorder in rape victims. *Journal of Traumatic Stress*, 5, 455–475.

Ruggiero, K. J., Resnick, H. S., Acierno, R., Carpenter, M. J., Kilpatrick, D. G., Coffey, S. F., . . . Galea, S. (2006). Internet-based intervention for mental health and substance use problems in disaster-affected populations: A pilot feasibility study. *Behavior Therapy*, 37, 190–205.

Santa Mina, E. E., & Gallop, R. M. (1998). Childhood sexual and physical abuse and adult self-harm and suicidal behaviour: A literature review. *Canadian Journal of Psychiatry*, 43, 793–800.

Scott-Ham, M., & Burton, F. C. (2005). Toxicological findings in cases of alleged drug-facilitated sexual assault in the United Kingdom over a 3-year period. *Journal of Clinical Forensic Medicine*, 12(4), 175–186.

Segal, D. L. (2009). Self-reported history of sexual coercion and rape negatively impacts resilience to suicide among women students. *Death Studies*, 33, 848–855.

Slaughter, L. (2000). Involvement of drugs in sexual assault. *The Journal of Reproductive Medicine*, 45, 425–430.

Smith, B. N., Shiherd, J. C., Schuster, J. L., Vogt, D. S., King, L. A., & King, D. W. (2011). Posttraumatic stress symptomatology as a mediator of the association between military sexual trauma and post-deployment physical health in women. *Journal of Trauma & Dissociation*, 12, 275–289.

Starzynski, L. L., Ullman, S. E., Filipas, H. H., & Townsend, S. M. (2005). Correlates of women's sexual assault disclosure to informal and formal support sources. *Violence and Victims*, 20, 417–432.

Stein, M. B., & Barrett-Connor, E. (2000). Sexual assault and physical health: Findings from a population-based study of older adults. *Psychosomatic Medicine*, 62, 838–843.

Stepakoff, S. (1998). Effects of sexual victimization on suicidal ideation and behavior in U.S. college women. *Suicide and Life-Threatening Behavior*, 28, 107–126.

Sugar, N. F., Fine, D. N., & Eckert, L. O. (2004). Physical injury after sexual assault: findings of a large case series. *American Journal of Obstetrics and Gynecology*, 190, 71–76.

Testa, M., Livingston, J. A., Vanzile-Tamsen, C., & Frone, M. R. (2003). The role of women's substance use in vulnerability to forcible and incapacitated rape. *Journal of Studies on Alcohol*, 64, 756–764.

Testa, M., VanZile-Tamsen, C., & Livingston, J. A. (2007). Prospective prediction of women's sexual victimization by intimate and nonintimate male partners. *Journal of Consulting and Clinical Psychology*, 75, 52–60.

Thompson, M. P. (2014). Risk and protective factors for sexual aggression and dating violence: Common themes and future directions. *Trauma, Violence, & Abuse*, 15(4), 304–309. doi:10.1177/1524838014521025

Thompson, M. P., Kaslow, N. J., & Kingree, J. B. (2000). Childhood maltreatment, PTSD, and suicidal behavior among African American females. *Journal of Interpersonal Violence*, 15, 3–15.

Thompson, M., Sitterle, D., Clay, G., & Kingree, J. (2007). Reasons for not reporting victimizations to the police: Do they vary for physical and sexual incidents? *Journal of American College Health*, 55, 277–282.

Ting, S. A., Sullivan, A. F., Miller, I., Espinola, J. A., Allen, M. H., Camargo, C. A., & Bourdreaux, E. D. (2012). Multicenter study of predictors of suicide screening in emergency departments. *Academic Emergency Medicine*, 19, 239–243.

Tjaden, P., & Thoennes, N. (2000). Full report of the prevalence, incidence, and consequences of violence against women. Findings from the National Violence Against Women Survey. Grant number 93-IJ-CX-0012. Washington, DC: National Institute of Justice, Office of Justice Programs, US

Department of Justice, and the Centers for Disease Control and Prevention.

Ullman, S. E. (1996). Social reactions, coping strategies, and self-blame attributions in adjustment to sexual assault. *Psychology of Women Quarterly*, 20, 505–526.

Ullman, S. E. (2004). Sexual assault victimization and suicidal behavior in women: A review of the literature. *Aggression and Violent Behavior*, 9, 331–351.

Ullman, S. E., & Brecklin, L. R. (2002). Sexual assault history and suicidal behavior in a national sample of women. *Suicide and Life-Threatening Behavior*, 32, 117–130.

Ullman, S. E., & Filipas, H. H. (2001). Predictors of PTSD symptom severity and social reactions in sexual assault victims. *Journal of Traumatic Stress*, 14, 369–389.

Ullman, S. E., Filipas, H. H., Townsend, S. M., & Starzynski, L. L. (2007). Psychosocial correlates of PTSD symptom severity in sexual assault survivors. *Journal of Traumatic Stress*, 20, 821–831.

Ullman, S. E., & Najdowski, C. J. (2009). Correlates of serious suicidal ideation and attempts in female adult sexual assault survivors. *Suicide and Life-Threatening Behavior*, 39, 47–57.

Vaszari, J. M., Bradford, S., O'Leary, C. C., Abdallah, A. B., & Cottler, L. B. (2011). Risk factors for suicidal ideation in a population of community-recruited female cocaine users. *Comprehensive Psychiatry*, 52, 238–246.

Vernberg, E. M., Steinberg, A. L., Jacobs, A. K., Brymer, M. J., Watson, P. J., Osofsky, J. D., . . . Ruzek, J. I. (2008). Innovations in disaster mental health: Psychological first aid. *Professional Psychology: Research and Practice*, 39, 381–388.

Violence Against Women and Department of Justice Reauthorization Act of 2005. H.R. 3402, 109th Cong. (2005–2006).

Walsh, K., Danielson, C. K., McCauley, J. L., Saunders, B. E., Kilpatrick, D. G., & Resnick, H. S. (2012). National prevalence of posttraumatic stress disorder among sexually revictimized adolescent, college, and adult household-residing women. *Archives of General Psychiatry*, 69, 935–942.

Walsh, K., Resnick, H. S., Danielson, C. K., McCauley, J. L., Saunders, B. E., & Kilpatrick, D. G. (2014). Patterns of drug and alcohol use associated with lifetime sexual revictimization and current posttraumatic stress disorder among three national samples of adolescent, college, and household-residing women. *Addictive Behaviors*, 39, 684–689.

Walsh, K., Zinzow, H. M., Badour, C. L., Kilpatrick, D. G., & Resnick, H. S. (2015). Understanding disparities in service seeking following forcible versus drug or alcohol facilitated/incapacitated rape. *Journal of Interpersonal Violence*. Advance online publication. doi:10.1177/0886260515576968

Weinbaum, Z., Stratton, T. L., Chavez, G., Motylewski-Link, C., Barrera, N., & Courtney, J. G. (2001). Female victims of intimate partner physical domestic violence (IPP-DV), California 1998. *American Journal of Preventive Medicine*, 21, 313–319.

Wolitzky-Taylor, K. B., Resnick, H. S., McCauley, J. L., Amstadter, A. B., Kilpatrick, D. G., & Ruggiero, K. J. (2011). Is reporting of rape on the rise? A comparison of women with reported versus unreported rape experiences in the National Women's Study-Replication. *Journal of Interpersonal Violence*, 26, 809–832.

Zatzick, D., Jurkovich, G., Rivara, F. P., Russo, J., Wagner, A., Wang, J., . . . Katon, W. (2013). A randomized stepped care intervention trial targeting posttraumatic stress disorder for surgically hospitalized injury survivors. *Annals of Surgery*, 257, 390–399.

Zatzick, D., Roy-Byrne, P., Russo, J., Rivara, F., Droesch, R., Wagner, A., . . . Katon, W. (2004). A randomized effectiveness trial of stepped collaborative care for acutely injured trauma survivors. *Archives of General Psychiatry*, 61, 498–506.

Zinzow, H. M., & Thompson, M. (2011). Barriers to reporting sexual victimization: Prevalence and correlates among undergraduate women. *Journal of Aggression, Maltreatment & Trauma*, 20, 711–725.

Zinzow, H. M., Resnick, H. S., Barr, S. C., Danielson, C. K., & Kilpatrick, D. G. (2012). Receipt of post-rape medical care in a national sample of female victims. *American Journal of Preventive Medicine*, 43, 183–187.

Zinzow, H.M., Grubaugh, A.L., Monnier, J., Suffoletta-Maierle, S., & Frueh, C.B. (2007). Trauma among female veterans. A critical review. *Trauma, Violence, & Abuse*, 8, 384–400.

Abuse of Persons with Disabilities: Prevention and Reporting

Angela Kuemmel

Abstract

Abuse of people with disabilities is a substantial problem because of the particular physical, emotional, and sexual vulnerabilities that people with disabilities have, in addition to being vulnerable to the abuse associated with their disabilities. The problem of abuse for the disabled population is complicated by a lack of knowledge in health-care professionals, lack of awareness in people with disabilities themselves, and limited resources for, and barriers to, intervention. In this chapter I will examine the nature of the problem, the types of abuse related to disability, and the vulnerability factors that increase risk. We will look at how to assess for abuse in people with disabilities, the consequences often faced in reporting abuse, and the best practices for assessment. I will also review the limited research on different cognitive, behavioral, or psycho-educational intervention approaches. Given the challenges to successfully evaluating and addressing this problem, mental health providers must have a thorough understanding of this issue.

Key Words: disability, abuse, vulnerability factors, abuse assessment, abuse intervention

According to the Americans with Disabilities Act of 1990, a person with a disability is defined as one with "a physical or mental impairment that substantially limits one or more of the major life activities of the individual" (Curry, Hassouneh-Phillips, & Johnston-Silverberg, 2001, p. 63). There are approximately 56.7 million Americans with disabilities (US Census Bureau, 2012), which include physical and sensory disabilities such as spinal cord injury, blindness, hearing loss, cerebral palsy, and cognitive disabilities such as brain injuries, autism, and mental retardation. This means that people with disabilities represent approximately 18.7% of the general US population (2012) and constitute the largest minority in the country.

People with disabilities face vulnerabilities for physical, emotional, and sexual abuse, as well as abuse associated with their disabilities. The first studies on people with disabilities and abuse focused only on the experiences of abuse of children and adults with intellectual and other developmental disabilities (Sobsey & Doe, 1991; Sobsey, 1994), because it was assumed at the time that only those with developmental and/or cognitive disabilities were at risk for abuse. In 2001, the landmark National Study of Women with Physical Disabilities shed light on the topic of abuse of people with disabilities, despite its main goal being to examine the experience of sexuality and relationships in the lives of women with disabilities (Nosek, Howland, Rintala, Young, & Chanpong, 2001). The major finding of the study, which included over 1,000 women with and without physical disabilities, was that the same percentage (62%) of women with disabilities as without disabilities had experienced emotional, physical, or sexual abuse, but women with disabilities experienced abuse for longer periods of time (Nosek, Howland, et al., 2001). These results contested popular beliefs that women with disabilities were not at risk for abuse. In years following this study, the problem of abuse of people with physical disabilities received a greater amount of attention from researchers who now recognize abuse as a significant problem for the disabled population.

In this chapter, I will initially discuss the experience of abuse in the context of disability, the types of abuse related to disability, and the stages of the cycle of abuse for people with disabilities. I will then present the role of caregivers in the abuse of people with disabilities and disability-related vulnerability factors. Finally, I will conclude with descriptions of assessment and intervention approaches.

The Experience of Abuse and Disability

To understand the relationship between physical disabilities and abuse, researchers have examined abuse issues in the context of disabilities, as well as the abuse experiences of people with and without physical disabilities. Nosek, Foley, Hughes, and Howland (2001) conducted a survey of 860 women, 439 with disabilities and 421 without. Of these, 181 women with disabilities reported that they had experienced emotional, physical, or sexual abuse. The participants' experiences of disability-related emotional abuse included blaming, rejection, intolerance, and abandonment because of their disabilities. Disability-related physical abuse included rough handling by personal care assistants and confinement in an inaccessible location or physical restraint. Disability-related sexual abuse occurred as fondling by personal care assistants or forced sexual activity in return for receiving help. Women with disabilities were also exposed to many disability-related settings, such as residential facilities, hospitals, clinics, and para-transit services, which foster isolation. Experiences of abuse related to those involved in helping the participants with disabilities included threats of withholding assistance, inappropriate touching during care, and stealing. The authors noted that this was exacerbated by difficulty finding and retaining qualified help, which increases the tolerance of people with disabilities for abusive behaviors. The researchers determined that although the abuse revolved around power and control similar to abuse experienced by able-bodied people, the disability itself or a disability-related setting or relationship allows for different manifestations of these dynamics that able-bodied people do not experience.

Cycle of Abuse in People with Disabilities

Copel (2006) examined the abuse experiences of people with disabilities by focusing on frequent themes involved in the cycle of abuse, including an accumulation of stressors, stress exceeding the ability to cope, abuse episodes, separation and distraction periods, and a return to a superficial normal. The theme of an accumulation of stressors included health problems, financial problems, unmet emotional and sexual needs, and the disabled woman's inability to fulfill certain roles. Stress exceeding the ability to cope was described as reaching a point where the increased stressors decreased the male partner's ability to cope, resulting in abusive language and hurtful comments. Several participants noted that they realized right before the abusive episode that the situation had gone beyond the point of being effectively managed. The next theme, the onset of abuse episodes, starts off with meanness, nastiness, and, finally, an episode of violence. The abuse episodes involved verbal name-calling, rape, property damage, physical battering, and confiscation of medicine or assistive devices. The reports of separation and distraction periods included the male partner going out or to an inaccessible place in the house. For some participants, the experience was comparable to a time-out. The final theme participants reported was a return to a superficial normal, which included strange interactions and acting as though nothing had happened, as well as being ignored by the male partner. These themes form the cycle of intimate partner violence experienced by women with physical disabilities. Copel then compared her model of intimate partner violence of women with disabilities to Walker's Cycle of Violence (Walker, 1979, 2000), which was developed from the experiences of able-bodied women. The main difference was the lack of a loving contrition or honeymoon-like phase in the experiences of women with disabilities.

Role of Caregivers in Abuse of People with Disabilities

Approximately 4.5 million women use personal caregivers, which is defined as one or more persons assisting another person with tasks that the individual would do if they did not have a disability (Litvak, Zukas, & Heumann, 1987). An estimate of how many men with disabilities use personal caregivers has not been reported in the literature, but the study by Litvak et al., 1987) stated that 10 million people use personal attendant services.

The use of caregivers or personal assistant services is a key concept of abuse among people with disabilities. There are five hallmark studies that shaped the understanding of the complex relationships in which people with disabilities are abused by their caregivers.

Saxton et al. (2001) and Powers et al. (2002) studied the relationships of women with physical disabilities and their personal assistant service (PAS) providers. Saxton et al. (2001) did qualitative research to solely determine the experience of abuse of women with disabilities by PAS providers, while Powers et al. (2002) used survey methodology to build upon the knowledge of the Saxton et al. (2001) study, with continued examination of the experience of abuse, as well as of the most harmful abusive behaviors, the barriers to ending abuse, and which intervention strategies were most helpful. Similarly, Ulincy, White, Bradford, and Matthews (1990); Saxton et al. (2006); and Powers et al. (2008) studied the relationships of men with physical disabilities and their PAS providers. The focus of Ulincy et al. (1990) was to determine the incidence of financial exploitation of men with disabilities by personal assistance services, but the researchers also looked at the incidence of physical abuse. The purpose of Saxton et al. (2006) was to investigate the abuse of men with disabilities by PAS providers using qualitative methodology. Similar to Powers et al. (2002), Powers et al. (2008) built on the qualitative finding by using a survey to determine the experience of abuse by PAS providers, as well as the most hurtful abusive behaviors, the challenges that hinder men's handling of abuse, and which intervention strategies were most helpful to prevent or stop abuse.

Saxton et al. (2001) examined how women with physical and cognitive disabilities describe the personal and social barriers to coping with abuse, how they define personal assistant abuse, how they respond to abusive situations, and what strategies they recommend to prevent abuse from occurring. The themes that emerged included social and personal boundary confusions and power dynamics, difficulties of recognizing, defining, and describing abuse in the PAS relationship, the complexity of using family and friends as providers, barriers to responding to abuse, and the strategies used to prevent and manage abuse. Study participants revealed that social and personal boundaries are blurred by complicated issues of privacy, autonomy, and the fine line between business relationships and friendships with caregivers, who take on multiple roles, one of which may take on a dimension of sexual intimacy.

Participants reported experiencing a wide range of abuse, including physical, sexual, emotional, and financial abuse, as well as medication manipulation, equipment disablement, and the neglect to provide needed services. The complexities of using family and friends as PAS providers included the difficulty of being the boss of someone you know and the tendency to minimize their needs for fear of being a burden. One participant captured the difficulty of asserting her independence in the caregiving relationship she had with her husband when she commented "I'm going to do whatever I can to change this marriage. And by the way, can you bring my scooter so I can leave you?" (Saxton et al., 2001, p. 402). The women identified a number of barriers to addressing abuse, such as their own difficulty in recognizing abuse and having their experiences validated, a lack of personal care providers and emergency backup services, the fear of having to admit themselves into a nursing home for care, the fear of loss of custody of their children, a lack of access to abuse resources, and a lack of help from law enforcement. The strategies that participants suggested for preventing abuse included learning about domestic violence resources, developing skills such as assertiveness to manage PAS providers more effectively, rigorously interviewing and conducting background screening when hiring new caregivers, and establishing reliable backup care providers.

The purpose of the Powers et al. (2002) study was to gather more information regarding the experience of abuse, including the most harmful abusive behaviors, barriers to ending abuse, and which intervention strategies were most helpful. Descriptive statistics were used to determine the prevalence of abuse by caregivers (20%) and the prevalence of physical (67%) and sexual (53%) abuse by any perpetrator. The results of the second part of the survey regarding hurtful behaviors found that all the behaviors listed were rated in the "quite hurtful" to "a lot hurtful" range and that the "most hurtful behaviors" had an incidence rate of 20% or higher. These behaviors included physical abuse, abuse of children, theft of money or other items, and forced sexual activity. The results of the third part of the survey demonstrated that all barriers were rated in the "medium" to "big" range. The barriers identified as the greatest to overcome included a shortage of qualified caregivers and low wages for providers. The most helpful behaviors included accessing resources and setting limits on relationships with caregivers.

Saxton et al. (2006) is similar to Saxton et al. (2001), except the former focuses solely on the abuse of males with disabilities by personal assistance services. The research studies on abuse of men with disabilities are relatively fewer than on abuse of women with disabilities. This may be because of cultural beliefs that view men as the perpetrators of domestic violence and abuse rather than the victims. Research that has examined data of adult protective services indicates that men with disabilities are less likely to be abused than women with disabilities (Allington, 1992; Turk & Brown, 1993). Saxton et al. (2001) focused specifically on the nature of abuse perpetrated by formal and informal PAS providers, perceptions of abuse, disclosure of abuse, and the barriers and strategies for men in identifying and addressing abuse. The themes that emerged included how people with disabilities define and describe abuse from paid and unpaid providers, how they perceive the personal and social barriers they face in handling the abuse, how they respond to abusive situations, and the strategies they recommend for preventing or stopping PAS abuse in their lives. Study participants commonly defined abuse as personal assistant behaviors such as not showing up for work, rough handling, being rushed to eat, or forced to go to bed early, but also mistreatment by the social services system.

The men with disabilities named personal and societal barriers they faced in handling abuse, such as the negative attitudes demonstrated by PAS providers, a lack of adequate PAS services, the fear of institutionalization, a lack of individual knowledge about abuse resources, feelings of being a burden, and fear of retaliation by the provider. The participants also named the culture of male ethics that prevents them from complaining about abuse, the difficulty others have in believing the men were abused by a female PAS, and societal expectations to take abuse as just another obstacle. In regard to responding to abuse, the participants mentioned reducing their expectations, reducing their standards for care, passively accepting their fate, and learning to live with the abuse. The strategies they reported using to respond and cope with abuse involved taking protective steps, such as criminal background checks, using good communication, using a contract, and implementing careful supervision.

Powers et al. (2008) and Powers et al. (2002), are similar in their goals to gather more information regarding the experience of abuse, including the most harmful abusive behaviors, barriers to ending abuse, and which intervention strategies were most helpful. However, Powers et al. (2008) focused on males rather than females. They found 65% of the participants reported experiencing physical abuse in their lifetime, which is similar to women with disabilities (Powers et al., 2002), and 24% experienced sexual abuse in their lifetime, half the rate endorsed by women with disabilities (Powers et al., 2002).

The second part of the survey focused on hurtful behaviors. The five most hurtful behaviors reported were theft of money, valuables, or equipment; forgery of checks or credit cards; being hit, kicked, slapped, or physically hurt; threats to hurt, withhold care, or leave them unattended; and intentionally being left in a dangerous situation. These behaviors were endorsed by over 90% of the participants. The results of the third part of the survey identified the following barriers to participants' handling of PAS abuse: low wages and benefits for providers, reporting abuse may lead to losing independence, a shortage of qualified providers, provider burnout, and the fact that people don't believe that men can be abused. The most important strategies to stop or prevent abuse by personal assistants were reported as the ability to choose who provides personal assistant services, having backup emergency care providers lined up, and having access to emergency transportation.

These six studies highlight several important concepts essential to understanding abuse in the context of a disability. Nosek, Foley, et al. (2001) helped differentiate abuse that people with disabilities suffer from abuse that able-bodied people suffer. Copel (2006) developed a model of the cycle of abuse experienced by people with disabilities and then compared it to Walker's Cycle of Abuse, based on the abuse experiences of able-bodied people. Copel found the main difference to be the lack of a loving contrition or honeymoon-like phase in the experiences of women with disabilities. Saxton et al. (2001) identified key issues essential to understanding the abuse of people with disabilities in the context of PAS providers, such as boundary confusion, power dynamics, the complication of caregivers with dual relationships, as well as underscoring the importance of having strong management skills to direct caregivers. Saxon et al. (2006) helped compare and contrast how abuse is experienced between males and females by focusing on males with disabilities. Powers et al. (2002) and (2008) demonstrated that abuse by personal caregivers takes many different forms and presents significant barriers for people with disabilities to live independently and achieve good health, as well as highlighting the importance of strategies to stop abuse. While these studies provide important findings for the overall picture, they leave out key concepts such as why a disability is a risk factor for abuse.

Disability-Related Vulnerability Factors for Abuse

The current body of research demonstrates that a physical disability is a risk factor for abuse. Very few studies, such as Nosek, Foley, et al. (2001), have specifically addressed disability-related vulnerability factors. Perpetrators of abuse do not choose their victims by sexual appearance. Abuse is about power and control, and people with disabilities have many vulnerability factors to consider, several of which increase the chances that physical, emotional, sexual, or disability abuse will occur and continue. Research not only demonstrates that a disability is an increased risk factor for abuse, but also that it is the reason the abuse continues for long periods of time (Nosek, Howland, et al., 2001). The disability-related factors that impact this trend are an increased need for personal care assistance, increased exposure to institutions, environmental barriers, social isolation, low resources, increased disability-related stress to families, devaluation by society, and health status (Andrews & Veronen, 1993; Hassouneh-Phillips, 2005; Nosek, Foley, et al., 2001). These very same reasons, along with the fact that women with disabilities have few options to escape abuse, contribute to its continuation.

One of the most significant risk factors for abuse of people with disabilities is the need for personal care assistance. Many of those with disabilities are unable to complete their activities of daily living independently. They may need help showering, using the bathroom, or getting dressed. They may require assistance being transferred from their bed to wheelchairs. Many rely on friends and family for assistance. Others are able to receive professional help from home health caregiver agencies. The majority of community-based personal caregiver services are provided by unpaid informal providers (79%), with 11% of users receiving a combination of paid formal services and informal services, and 10% getting exclusively paid services (Rutgers University, Bureau of Economic Research, 1990).

Access to reliable caregivers is essential for people with disabilities to live independently. They must rely on help with very intimate tasks. Prime examples of sexual abuse in these situations include inappropriate touching during a shower, demanding a kiss before agreeing to transfer someone, or forcing vaginal penetration of a woman stranded on her bed who is unable to get up without assistance. Another factor complicating this problem is the shortage of available caregivers. Many women with disabilities are trapped in abusive caregiver relationships, especially if the perpetrator is a family member or friend, because they do not have anyone else to turn to for help. There have not been any studies specifically on the exploitation of females with disabilities by their hired attendants. However, in one study that focused on the exploitation of both men and women with disabilities by their hired attendants (Ulincy et al., 1990), 44% of the participants reported being robbed of money, jewelry, prescription medications, televisions, stereos, clothing, and having checks forged by attendants. Physical abuse by attendants, as well as robbery, was reported by 10%—in this category, with the reports solely by men. Of the respondents who reported theft, 25% said they refused to confront the caregiver for fear of retribution, and 19% overlooked the exploitation to avoid having to find a new care provider who might be worse.

This problem may be caused by the absence of a system for registering or monitoring caregivers. In attempt to meet the high demand for care with a limited supply of caregivers, agencies cannot afford to be selective. Some do not even require a criminal background check. Adding to this problem is the lack of formal training for caregivers, lack of sanctions for caregiver abuse, and the absence of emergency backup systems for caregivers. As a result, people with disabilities who rely on some form of caregiver assistance often encounter the dilemma of deciding how much abuse they will tolerate to have their basic needs met (Curry et al., 2001). In Hassouneh-Phillips's (2005) research on the Abuse Pathways Model, study participants listed substance abuse by caregivers or intimate partners as another problem related to abuse. People with disabilities reported that their caregivers or intimate partners who abused substances tended to be "lower functioning, more violent, more likely to steal, and more likely to neglect their caregiving duties than those who did not abuse substances" (Hassouneh-Phillips, 2005, p. 78).

Another risk factor that increases the vulnerability of women with disabilities is their increased exposure to institutionalized care and medical settings. Many women who are unable to care for themselves and whose families are unable to meet their personal care needs must resort to living in a group home, nursing home, or other medical facility. These people are at an exceptional risk, because their disabilities may be more severe and there are fewer situational safeguards in place to protect them from potential harm (Andrews et al., 1993). These institutions have been described as "self retaining microcosms of disempowerment" (Crossmaker, 1991, p. 211). They are "not only oppressive but are unsafe environments that pose a serious risk of sexual abuse and repeated victimization that extends beyond discharge" (Curry et al., 2001, p. 71). Research has found that physical and sexual abuse is at least twice as common in institutions as they are in community settings (Blatt & Brown, 1986). Previously described risks associated with home health caregivers are also potential risks in institutions. Though institutions are viewed as agencies that help people, given their distinct characteristics, they have historically been viewed as potential sources of abuse. The workers are permitted to intrude deeply into the residents' lives. They have extreme control over them through bribes for things such as grounds privileges or threats of seclusion, restriction, or delayed release (Andrews & Veronen, 1993), all of which leave residents feeling powerless and depersonalized.

People with disabilities also face increased exposure to medical settings and encounter more health-care professionals. Many people with disabilities experience more medical problems than people who are not disabled. Medical settings pose a threat because people with disabilities must depend on health-care workers to assist them in undressing or transferring to an examining table, which may put them at risk for abuse. Many of the participants in Saxton et al. (2001) described abuse by health providers, including nurses, physicians, occupational therapists, and physical therapists. They spoke of providers "'pushing them beyond their limits' such as forcing them to stand for intolerable amounts of time or to do things that were painful" (p. 405). Additionally, medical professionals, such as physicians, may contribute to the problem of abuse through the lack of informational resources in their offices to educate disabled patients about sexuality and their vulnerabilities for abuse.

This lack of education on disability and sexuality on the part of physicians may be caused by a lack of disability competency in their training, as "there are few medical or nursing schools that offer any training on the reproductive health of people with disabilities" (Saxton, 1995, p. 290). The 2005 Surgeon General's Call to Action to Improve the Health and Wellness of Persons with Disabilities emphasizes the insufficient knowledge and awareness arising from health service providers and community attitudes and behaviors, as well as the inadequacy of health services for people with disabilities. In the National Study of Women with Physical Disabilities, the researchers found that only 59% of the sample reported that they received adequate information about how their disability affects their sexual functioning (Nosek, Howland, et al., 2001). The study participants also reported that the professionals they went to for information on sexuality were, first, their gynecologists, second, family physicians, and third, psychologists.

Even worse than practitioners who lack information or education on the topics of disability, sexuality, and abuse, "many medical practitioners and health care facilities do not even consider offering reproductive health care services to their patients who have disabilities," which may be caused by the stereotype that people with disabilities are asexual (Saxton, 1995, p. 290). The inference here is that if reproductive health services are not offered by physicians because of a lack of education or the perception of asexuality among disabled patients, discussions between physician and patient regarding sexual abuse are possibly not taking place either. Disabled women are dependent on their caregivers, nurses, and doctors for assistance and medical advice. Health professionals provide women with disabilities with little assistance to identify, manage, and prevent abuse. Research has found that women with disabilities identified a lack of support from professionals as a barrier to stopping abuse by personal assistance providers, and these women would reportedly welcome being asked about their experiences and offered assistance to access intervention resources (Powers et al., 2002).

Environmental barriers can also foster situations that leave women with disabilities exposed to or at risk for abuse. They may live in housing that is not wheelchair accessible, greatly diminishing their access to the outside world. Within their homes, they may not have access to a bathroom or be unable to exit the house because they cannot open the door. Their living quarters may not be designed to offer independence, which forces them to be more dependent on caregivers. They may not be able to use the phone by themselves, or they may lack access to other forms of communication. Another huge environmental barrier is transportation. As Beck-Massey (1999) found, "frequently accessible transportation is hard to come by, forcing the women to depend on their abuser to leave home" (p. 271). Many forms of accessible transportation, such as a special van or even a car, require assistance from another person, which in many cases is the perpetrator of abuse or their caregiver. This gives the victim no way to escape and the perpetrator more control. Public transportation is not always reliable and many women cannot afford to use it. If women are able to overcome these environmental barriers and escape abuse, they may not have anywhere to go. Battered women's shelters may not be wheelchair accessible or may not able to provide for personal care needs.

Few research studies have addressed the challenges that domestic violence programs face in assisting clients with disabilities. Chang et al. (2003) examined how domestic violence shelters in North Carolina met the needs of their clients with disabilities. The programs reported the main challenges they faced to help clients with disabilities were lack of funding to ensure adequate and educated staff and equipment and structural limitations in program facilities. Another feasible option for escaping abuse may be family or friends, however, even if they are willing to take the individual in, they may not have an accessible place to stay. These factors not only contribute to the increased risk factor, but also to the prolonged abuse that people with disabilities face.

Many people with disabilities must battle social isolation and the effects of discrimination from social affairs. Rokach, Lechcier-Kimel, and Safarov (2006) examined the relationship between loneliness, social isolation, and physical disability by having participants complete the Loneliness Questionnaire (Rokach & Brock, 1997). People with disabilities scored higher on the emotional distress, social alienation, self-alienation subscales than those without disabilities. These three subscales addressed inner pain, intense turmoil, social alienation, self-depreciation, and a lack of close and intimate relationships, which frequently negatively affect the support systems of people with disabilities (Rokach et al., 2006). These characteristics, associated with loneliness, cause an increased vulnerability for abuse. Social isolation also increases the risk of being manipulated (Andrews & Veronen, 1993), and the individual may have trouble establishing friendships and relating to people.

People who live in institutions or hospitals might not be able to talk with anyone. They rarely interact or communicate with people outside the institution (Sobsey, 1994). Discrimination may also contribute to social isolation. Disabled people may be denied opportunities in areas of employment and education (Nosek, Foley, et al., 2001). For disabled women this adds an increased risk for abuse. They may not have anyone that they can talk to about the abuse. The perpetrator may be their sole human connection. Womendez and Schneiderman (1991), two women with disabilities who experienced abuse and researched it, wrote that girls with disabilities may not be welcome at social events, which leads to less exposure to social interaction. As girls with disabilities grow up, this social discrimination decreases the opportunities they have for healthy sexual activities, and they may lack the ability to define personal boundaries (Womendez & Schneiderman, 1991). The social isolation that people with disabilities experience may prevent them from opportunities to learn about self-defense, safety planning, and community resources that could help them overcome barriers caused by their physical limitations and living situations (Nosek, Foley, et al., 2001).

People with disabilities are also at risk because of a lack of financial resources. Among working age women, only 30% of disabled women work, while 75% of women without disabilities are employed (LaPlante, Miller, & Miller, 1992). In comparison to able-bodied women and men with disabilities, economic disadvantage is greater for women with disabilities, which in turn increases their inclination to enter into and stay in abusive relationships (Nosek, Foley, et al., 2001). Women with disabilities face challenges to obtain employment because of a lower education levels than able-bodied women. However, even disabled women with college degrees are less successful in achieving employment than college educated men with disabilities or able-bodied women without college degrees (Fine & Asch, 1988). Along with a lack of adequate education, unemployment is also attributed to a lack of transportation, forcing many to depend on government financial aid. According to the US Social Security Administration (2012), women received an average of $993 in monthly social security disability payments in 2012, much less than the average of $1,253 that disabled men received every month. Thus women with disabilities are more likely to live in low-income neighborhoods with higher rates of crime, further increasing their vulnerability to victimization (Nosek, Foley, et al., 2001).

Abuse is more likely to occur in families that experience a high level of stress, and research has shown that families in which a member has a disability experience higher levels of stress because of the needs of the disabled person. Adults must manage the roles of both parent and caregiver to the family member with a disability. Copel (2006) reported the presence of "continual stress from primary and secondary problems related to the disability and their health issues; such as the change of roles or not being able to fulfill a role adequately" (p. 118). This leads to discomfort for the disabled individual and frustration for the family, which triggers explosive communication or physical abuse. Thus, Copel (2006) emphasized the themes of an accumulation of stressors and stress exceeding the ability to cope as important parts of the cycle of abuse for people with disabilities. It has also been found that disruption in attachments between children and their parents leads to an increase in abuse (Youngblade & Belsky, 1989). Parents of children with disabilities are often less attached to their children for disability-related reasons (Wasserman, Lennon, Allen, & Shilansky, 1987). These reasons include rejection and refusal to accept their disabled children, as well as the additional roles which they may be forced into, such as therapy assistant or nurse's aide. These conditions may put the disabled child at risk for abuse.

People with disabilities, especially women, are devalued by society. They are seen as dependent and helpless and unable to fill the traditional roles of caretaker and nurturer. Having a disability is seen as a disadvantage. Society leads women with disabilities to believe that they are undesirable and that "they should be grateful that any man wants to marry, date or have sex with them" (Beck-Massey, 1999, p. 270). After studying people with disabilities, their dating habits, and the likelihood for abuse, Gill (1996) noted the following.

> The need to demonstrate and prove our essential womanhood can be dangerous pressure to enter into relationships and stay in them, regardless of abusive treatment. Because she has fewer options for meeting potential partners due to both her social devaluation and environmental access problems, a woman with a disability may view it as her only opportunity to experience sexuality, marriage, childbearing, and other rites of womanhood. She may also have internalized her social devaluation to the point that she feels too inferior as a woman to merit a better relationship. (p. 185).

Hassouneh-Phillips & McNeff (2005) found that societal devaluation influenced the inclination of women with disabilities toward low self-esteem (both bodily and sexually), as well as their perceived need to be partnered, and their preference for being with able-bodied men. Social devaluation also limits women's options for forming and maintaining intimate partner relationships by influencing

and turning off potential partners. The pervasive influence of social devaluation affects women's decision making as they enter into and stay in abusive relationships. Moreover, women with disabilities often lower their standards for relationships and, once in relationships, they are more likely to tolerate a certain level of abuse rather than face being alone (Hassouneh-Phillips & McNeff, 2005).

Little is known about the effects of abuse on the health of people with disabilities and the role it plays in increasing vulnerability for further abuse. Although the harmful effects have been well-documented in able-bodied women, only one study has examined the detrimental effects of abuse on the health of women with disabilities (Hassouneh-Phillips, 2005). In researching an Abuse Pathways Model, Hassouneh-Phillips found that when people with disabilities encounter abuse, the narrow margins of health and physical ability of this population are further compromised by injuries and other effects. For example, one participant with a spinal cord injury reported that her rotator cuff was injured in a physical assault, giving her limited use of her upper extremities. The injury reduced her independence and mobility so considerably that she could no longer use a manual wheelchair and likely required more assistance from a caregiver. Other physical effects experienced and reported by participants were worsening bowel and bladder control, poor nutrition, skin breakdown, and impaired mobility as a result of physical injury. The psychological effects of abuse most commonly reported included stress, depression, anxiety, and suicidal ideation. Hassouneh-Phillips considers the detrimental effects of abuse on physical and mental health one of the key findings of her research. Research conducted on able-bodied women who suffered abuse found that domestic violence increases by 10-fold the risk of physical injury and triples women's hospitalization rates for mental health disorders, substance abuse, and suicidality (Kernic, Wolf, & Holt, 2000). Given that women with disabilities have less physical ability than able-bodied women, it is likely that this is an even greater problem with serious consequences for the disabled population.

Research demonstrates that having a disability is a risk factor for abuse because of the increased need for personal care assistance, increased exposure to institutions, the environmental barriers, social isolation, low resources, increased disability-related stress to families, devaluation by society, and health status. One risk factor that research has neglected, however, is the lack of knowledge and awareness of abuse. Despite the overwhelming amount of research that demonstrates how a physical disability serves as a risk factor for abuse, Nosek, Foley, et al. (2001) suggest that the general public, medical professionals, disability–related caregivers, and women with disabilities react to information about abuse with shock and disbelief, because they consider a physical disability a method of protection against sexual abuse and other types of abuse. Kuemmel, Fins, Somoza, and Marker (2014) examined three different groups—college students, caregivers for people with physical disabilities, and people with physical disabilities—to see how they perceived the likelihood of abuse and risk factors for abuse of people with and without disabilities. They presented participants with descriptions of males and females with disabilities of varying severity and asked them to rate their perceived vulnerability for different types of abuse. Kuemmel et al. found that participants did not consistently attribute a high degree of vulnerability to the scenario of the individual with the most severe disability, which supports existing literature indicating that people do not completely understand the phenomena of disability and abuse (Nosek, Howland, & Young, 1997; Nosek, Foley, et al., 2001; Saxton et al., 2001).

Abuse Assessment of People with Disabilities

The screening and assessment of abuse in patients with disabilities by mental health providers is very important. Even if patients do not disclose that they are being abused when assessed for it, they may decide to seek help or improve their safety (Scholle et al., 2003). However, the assessment must be done in a specific way to detect abuse among patients with disabilities.

As previously mentioned, people with disabilities may face grave consequences if they report they are currently being abused, including loss of independence and increased violence and retaliation, especially if they are dependent on their abuser for personal care. Given that mental health providers are mandated reporters of abuse, it is essential to explain the limits of confidentiality regarding disability and abuse with specific examples during informed consent in clinical settings. Using specific examples is vital because of the difficulty that people with disabilities have in recognizing and identifying abuse, as documented in the literature (Curry et al., 2011). It is also important to explain reporting procedures during the informed consent, with consideration for institutional and legal policies. It

would be ideal to conduct an abuse assessment or screening alone with the patient in a private space. However, a personal care attendant, family member, or friend who accompanies a patient may become suspicious or angry if asked to leave the room. It is essential to utilize good clinical judgment to make this decision. It may also be helpful to normalize that during an individual psychological evaluation it is important to eliminate observer bias of the assessment by asking the person or persons accompanying the patient to leave the room.

Fortunately, researchers have developed screening questions that clinicians could easily include in a clinical interview. The most commonly used assessment to screen for abuse in those without disabilities is Soekan, McFarlane, Parker and Campbell's Abuse Assessment Screen (AAS) (as cited in McFarlane et al., 2001), which consists of two questions that inquire about the frequency, severity, site of injury, and perpetrator of physical and sexual abuse suffered in the past year. Abuse assessment instruments, such as the AAS, that only address physical and sexual abuse are not sensitive to the different ways people with disabilities experience abuse and the vulnerabilities they face.

In response to the need for an abuse assessment that addresses disability-related vulnerabilities, two screening tools were created. The first, the Abuse Assessment Screen–Disability (AAS-D), was developed by McFarlane et al. (2001). The AAS-D contains two questions regarding disability-related abuse in addition to questions on physical and sexual abuse found on the AAS. If the patient admits experiencing abuse, they are given a list of perpetrators, including a care provider. When this was administered to 511 women with physical disabilities, 9.8% of the women with disabilities reported experiencing abuse. Using the first two questions on physical and sexual abuse, 7.8% of participants reported abuse. After hearing questions the next two questions on disability abuse, an additional 2% of the participants reported abuse. The goal of McFarlane et al. was not to validate this tool, but to demonstrate that solely assessing for physical and sexual abuse was not sufficient for the complex types of abuse experienced by women with disabilities.

The second screening instrument has eight questions and was developed by a systematic approach (Curry, Powers, & Oschwald, 2003). The first two questions are modified versions of the physical and sexual abuse questions on the AAS and the third question asks about safety. The remaining five questions address abusive behaviors that are disability-specific, such as restricting use of an assistive mobility device, withholding medication, stealing money or valuables, refusing care, neglecting personal needs, and yelling hurtful remarks. Of the 47 women with physical and/or cognitive disabilities who completed the abuse screening by telephone, 70% of the participants (n = 33) reported that they experienced physical, sexual, or disability-specific abuse in the past year. The increased prevalence rates detected by Curry et al., as opposed to MacFarlane et al., may have been due to the modifications made to the questions, which provided more defining information to the concept of abuse, or it may have been a result of the more comprehensive, systematic approach used to develop the screening tool.

These tools were developed with the rationale that screening for abuse was best done by a self-report questionnaire or interview questions. Later research, however, showed that computer interviews consistently found higher rates of disclosure of sensitive information, such as domestic violence, than did paper questionnaires or face to face interviews (Davis, Hoffman, Morse, & Luehr, 1992; Gerbert et al., 1999; Rhodes, Lauderdale, He, Howes, & Levinson, 2002). Oschwald et al. (2009) developed an audio computer-assisted self-interview designed to address barriers to disclosure about abuse, while at the same time giving women with disabilities an accessible and anonymous way to identify abusive situations and learn safety planning skills, which could not be offered in face-to-face interviews. In their evaluation of this program, 69% of the 305 women participants with physical or mental disabilities endorsed that they would prefer answering personal questions about violence using a computer rather than telling friends or family, and 62% endorsed that they prefer using a computer over professionals such as case managers or health-care providers. Finally, 51% of the sample endorsed that their decision to answer questions honestly was influenced by the fact that their answers would not be reported to Adult Protective Services (APS) or the police. Although computer technology is not meant to replace clinicians, it may serve as an additional resource should it become readily available to healthcare providers and consumers.

Clinicians and researchers could also consider using the specific assessment approach used in the computer interview (Oschwald et al., 2009), which included 17 dichotomous yes-or-no questions about the experience of abuse and 12 yes-or-no questions regarding perpetrator risk characteristics

(Curry et al., 2009). These items were also found to be a valid and reliable method to assess abuse and perpetrator risk characteristics among women with disabilities. Although these items were used in a computer interview, they could easily be given as a self-report questionnaire or worked into a clinical interview. Curry and colleagues also recommend giving the items in the same order that the researchers did, asking about safety and emotional abuse before physical and sexual abuse, because it allows for a less threatening approach. Administering the perpetrator items can offer clinicians key information essential for intervention and safety planning.

Curry et al. (2003) and Curry et al. (2009) found prevalence rates of abuse in their study samples (70 and 68, respectively) consistent with previous abuse prevalence rates (Nosek, Howland, et al., 2001). This is likely due to them including an emotional abuse item, having more items sensitive to the various types of abuse experienced by women with disabilities, and using a systematic approach to develop the items. However, all three assessments were studied with a method that gave women anonymity and freedom from mandated reporting, which may not be possible if used in a clinical setting.

Beyond utilizing an assessment approach that will detect abuse in people with disabilities, mental health providers must be aware and knowledgeable of facilitators and the barriers to disclosing abuse, as well as to patient preferences regarding whom they disclose to. Only 21% of women with disabilities reported that they had ever been screened for abuse by a health provider (Powers et al., 2002), and only 15% reported that a health provider had ever discussed abuse and personal safety with them (Curry et al., 2011). When Powers et al. (2002) asked 200 women with disabilities which professionals they prefer to perform the abuse screens, the women selected counselors first, followed by religious clergy and case managers over doctors, nurses, and therapists. In an interdisciplinary team setting, several different providers may ask about abuse. However, when Powers et al. (2008) asked 342 men with disabilities the same question, they preferred doctors, counselors, and religious clergy over case managers, therapists, and nurses. The researchers hypothesized that this may be an indication of the comfort level that men with disabilities have in talking with someone who is more likely to be another man.

In the inpatient rehabilitation hospital setting, the nursing, psychology, and social work staff routinely ask about abuse and safety. The highest rated reasons for reporting their abuse, according to 276 women with disabilities who have a history of abuse, were protection for loved ones, receipt of emotional support and services (transportation, shelter, and support group), and to be respected and believed. These were followed by a respect for privacy, safety, and personal needs and wishes (Curry et al., 2011). Given that respect and feeling believed are facilitators of abuse disclosure, the interdisciplinary team could consider having the team member with the best relationship with the patient, regardless of discipline, follow up when a concern for abuse is received. The barriers to reporting abuse for these women included difficulty discerning if they were being abused, fear of retaliation, fear of making a police report, shame, embarrassment, loss of personal care or a loved one, loss of independence, bad experiences stemming from past reports, fear of further harm or injury, and the belief that nothing can be done (Curry et al., 2011).

Best practices for abuse assessment in patients with disabilities include informed consent of mandated reporting, conducting the session in a private space, understanding potential relationship dynamics between patient and perpetrator, giving specific examples of various types of abuse in the questions, and communicating that you respect and believe the patient. Regardless of how abuse is screened for or assessed in the disabled population, merely asking about the topic can validate the abuse experience of people with disabilities and provide an opportunity to offer information, support, and resources, whether the patients disclose abuse or not.

Intervention Programs for People with Disabilities

Given that people with disabilities have difficulty in recognizing abuse and that this is one of the main barriers to disclosure, as well as it being a vulnerability risk factor, one would think there would be a considerable emphasis on prevention and intervention programs. Unfortunately, this area has received the least amount of attention from researchers, although it is growing. People with disabilities face transportation, architectural, and programmatic barriers to access community resources for those who suffer domestic violence. Even if these barriers are overcome, domestic violence services may not be equipped to address the complex issues that must be considered in safety planning for people with disabilities. Thus, it is essential to develop and evaluate intervention programs. According to Hughes (2005, p. 29) programs should include information on recognizing abuse, protecting oneself in abusive situations, and removing oneself from potentially abusive relationships and situations. Lund (2011) completed a recent literature review on violence intervention and prevention programs for adults with disabilities and found 10 articles on skills-based prevention programs for people with disabilities. Only two of them (Robinson-Whelen et al., 2010; Hughes et al., 2010) focused on all disability types, while the other eight were strictly for those with intellectual disabilities.

Most disability-focused abuse prevention programs have been based on behavioral, cognitive, or psycho-education interventions (Lund, 2011). Robinson-Whelen et al. (2010) utilized a randomized control group design to evaluate the effects of a brief computerized, disability-specific, abuse assessment on abuse awareness, safety self-efficacy, and safety-promoting behaviors. The Safer and Stronger Program (SSP) is a 1–1.5 hour computer program in which women with disabilities are asked about their abuse experiences, the characteristics of the perpetrators, and their safety-promoting behaviors. The SSP also features four interpersonal violence (IPV) survivors of varying races and disabilities in video vignettes, sharing their experiences with abuse and survival. The IPV survivors also provide education on the warning signs of abuse, safety strategies, and community resources, and they offer support and encouragement. The development of the SSP is explained in detail in Oschwald et al. (2009). With a sample of 305 women, including women with and without exposure to physical, sexual, or multiple types of abuse in the past year, the SSP had a significant effect on abuse awareness but no measurable effect on safety self-efficacy or safety-promoting behaviors. The participants who made the most gains in abuse awareness from this intervention were those with little or no abuse in the past year. However, there were significant differences in safety self-efficacy according to abuse status.

Lund et al. (2014) recently developed a similar program, The Safer and Stronger Program for men with disabilities. The SSP for men includes eight distinct sections: introduction, financial abuse, neglect, emotional abuse, physical abuse and threats of physical abuse, sexual abuse and threats of sexual abuse, types of abusers and warning signs, and things you can do. The 31 men who participated in the pilot study completed the program in 1.5–2.5 hours. The focus of the pilot was to determine the participants' satisfaction with the program and receive input to improve the program. Most of the pilot participants regarded the program as helpful and easy to use. The men gave positive feedback, stating they could relate to the males with disabilities who survived abuse and who told their stories in the videos. Given the stigma associated with men disclosing abuse, this program may diminish the initial shame and anxiety related to sharing abuse experiences with other people. In addition, the majority of the participants endorsed "a lot" (41.9%) and "quite a bit" (29%) as their preference to use an Internet program to learn about abuse reporting rather than disclosing to a health-care professional. While clinical outcomes have not been published, this intervention offers promise for males with diverse disabilities and emphasizes the importance of addressing the impact of both gender and disability on abuse for this population.

Hughes et al. (2010) developed an intervention program titled A Safety Awareness Program for Women with Disabilities, which consisted of eight 2.5 hour interactive didactic sessions. The topics covered in the eight-session curriculum included self-care, assertiveness, boundaries, and action planning; healthy relationships and relaxation; definition, types, and signs of abuse; disability-related abuse, coping, and social support; cycle of violence, safety in hiring, and managing personal care assistants; safety and safety planning, with exercise; sexuality and disability; and the disability bill of rights. The program's goals were to improve safety self-efficacy, safety skills, social relationships, and safety-promoting behaviors, and the seven women in the pilot program yielded significant improvement in self-efficacy and safety skills. Hughes et al. also saw non-significant improvement in safety-promoting behavior. In addition, the study highlighted the benefits of group treatment, and one of the greatest benefits reported by multiple participants was learning that they were not alone.

Robinson-Whelen et al. (2014) expanded the findings of Hughes et al. with a randomized, controlled trial using a national sample of women with diverse disabilities to examine the effectiveness of A Safety Awareness Program (ASAP) for Women with Disabilities. Their sample of 213 women with diverse disabilities from varied geographical locations was recruited through 10 centers for independent living (CILs). The intervention group participated in eight 2.5-hours sessions and the control group received the usual CIL services with pre-, post-, and six month follow-up measures. The two groups scored similarly at the pre-test on safety awareness, abuse, and safety knowledge, safety skills, safety self-efficacy, social support, and safety-promoting behaviors, At both the post-test and follow-up, however, the intervention group scored significantly better on all protective factors measured. Two additional findings were particularly encouraging. First, women who reported the most abuse experienced the greatest gains in safety self-efficacy. Second, women with cognitive or learning disabilities experienced treatment benefits comparable to those without cognitive disabilities. These results offer hope that ASAP for Women can increase safety protective factors for women with varying disabilities.

Concluding Remarks

People with disabilities face great vulnerability for physical, emotional, and sexual abuse, as well as for abuse associated with their disabilities. They may also be abused by a wide variety of perpetrators including caregivers, family, friends, and partners. For people with disabilities, exposure to, or the experience of abuse, especially if it is severe and ongoing, can be a behavioral emergency that impacts their safety, health, and mental well-being. Mental health practitioners need to understand the different types of abuse associated with disability, so they can recognize, assess, and offer intervention to their patients, especially since the patients themselves may not identify that they are in abusive situations. Mental health professionals need to include the intersectionality of gender and disability in their understanding of abuse for the disabled population. They must also appreciate the consequences that people with disabilities could face if they report abuse and the disability-related barriers that their patients can face in leaving abusive situations, including the fear of losing independence, fear of not being believed, and dependence on the abuser for assistance with activities of daily living. They need to be ready to provide their patients with education resources that are accessible to those with diverse disabilities. While this important topic has not gotten the attention from researchers it deserves, the more recent work, especially the intervention programs, offer hope that people with disabilities can learn to recognize abuse and improve their safety skills and overall functioning. Consider this your call to action to gain knowledge and demonstrate competence in the best practices of assessment and provision of intervention resources—it can certainly make a difference in preventing and decreasing the vulnerability for abuse of people with disabilities.

References

Allington, C. L. J. (1992). Sexual abuse within services for people with learning disabilities: Staffs' perceptions, understandings of and contact with the problems of sexual abuse. *Mental Handicap*, 20, 59–63.

Andrews, A. B., & Veronen, L. J. (1993). Sexual assault and people with disabilities. *Journal of Social Work and Human Sexuality*, 8, 137–159.

Beck-Massey, D. (1999). Sanctioned war: Women, violence, and disabilities. *Sexuality and Disability*, 17, 269–276.

Blatt, E. R., & Brown, S. W. (1986). Environmental influences on incidents of alleged child abuse and neglect in New York State psychiatric facilities: Toward an etiology of institutional child maltreatment. *Child Abuse and Neglect*, *10*, 171–180. In D. Sobsey (Eds.), *Violence and abuse in the lives of people with disabilities: The end of silent acceptance?* Baltimore, MD: Paul H. Brookes.

Chang, J. C., Martin, S. L., Moracco, K. E., Dulli, L., Scandlin, D., Loucks-Sorrel, M. B.,. . . Bou-Saada, I. (2003). Helping women with disabilities and domestic violence: Strategies, limitations, and challenges of domestic violence programs and services. *Journal of Women's Health*, *12*, 699–708.

Copel, L. C. (2006). Partner abuse in physically disabled women: A proposed model for understanding intimate partner violence. *Perspectives in Psychiatric Care*, 42, 114–129.

Crossmaker, M. (1991). Behind locked doors: Institutional sexual abuse. *Sexuality and Disability*, 7, 201–219.

Curry, M. A., Hassouneh-Phillips, D., & Johnston-Silverberg, A. (2001). Abuse of women with disabilities: An ecological model and review. *Violence Against Women*, 7, 60–79.

Curry, M. A., Powers, L. E., & Oscwald, M. (2003). Development of an abuse screening tool for women with disabilities. *Journal of Aggression, Maltreatment & Trauma*, 8, 123–141.

Curry, M. A., Reneker, P., Hughes, R. B., Robinson-Whelen, S. Oschwald, M., Swank, P. R., & Powers, L. E. (2009). Development of measures of abuse among women with disabilities and the characteristics of their perpetrators. *Violence Against Women*, 15, 1001–1025.

Curry, M. A., Renker, P., Robinson-Whelen, S., Hughes, R. B., Swank, P., Oschwald, M., & Powers, L. E. (2011). Facilitators and barriers to disclosing abuse among women with disabilities. *Violence and Victims*, *26*, 430–444.

Davis, L., Hoffman, N., Morse, R., & Luehr, J. (1992). Substance use disorder diagnostic schedule (SUDDS): The equivalence and validity of a computer-administered and an interview administered format. *Alcoholism: Clinical and Experimental Research*, *16*, 250–254.

Fine, M., & Asch, A. (Eds.). (1988). *Women with disabilities: Essays in psychology, culture, and politics*. Philadelphia, PA: Temple University Press.

Gerbert, B., Bronstone, A., Pantilat, S., McPhee, S., Allerton, M., & Moe, J. (1999). When asked, patients tell: Disclosure of sensitive health risk behaviors. *Medical Care*, 37, 104–111.

Gill, Carol J. (1996). Dating and relationship issues. *Sexuality and Disability*, 14, 183–190.

Hassouneh-Phillips, D. (2005). Understanding abuse of women with physical disabilities: An overview of the abuse pathways model. *Advances in Nursing Science*, 28, 70–80.

Hassouneh-Phillips, D., & McNeff, E. (2005). "I thought I was less worthy": Low sexual and body esteem and increased vulnerability to intimate partner abuse in women with physical disabilities. *Sexuality and Disability*, 23, 227–240.

Hughes, R. B. (2005). Violence against women with disabilities: Urgent call for action. *The Community Psychologist*, 38, 28–30.

Hughes, R. B., Robinson-Whelen, S., Pepper, A. C., Gabrielli, J., Lund, E. M., & Legerski, J. (2010). Development of a safety awareness group intervention for women with diverse disabilities: A pilot study. *Rehabilitation Psychology*, 55, 263–271.

Kernic, M., Wolf, M., & Holt, V. (2000). Rates and relative risk of hospital admission among women in violent intimate partner relationships. *American Journal of Public Health*, 90, 1416–1420.

Kuemmel, A. M., Fins, A. I., Somoza, M. P., & Marker, C. (2014). Vulnerabilities for abuse in the physically disabled: Perceptions of people with disabilities, caregivers, and college students. [Manuscript in preparation.]

LaPlante, M., Miller, S., & Miller, K. (1992). People with work disability in the U.S. *Disabilities Statistics Abstract Number 4*. Washington DC: National Institute on Disability and Rehabilitation Research.

Litvak, S., Zukas, H., & Heumann, J. E. (1987). *Attending to America: Personal assistance for independent living: A survey of attendant service programs in the United States for people of all ages with disabilities*. Berkeley, CA: World Institute on Disability.

Lund, E. M. (2011). Community-based services and interventions for adults with disabilities who have experienced intrapersonal violence: A review of the literature. *Trauma, Violence, & Abuse*, 12, 171–182.

Lund, E. M., Oschwald, M., Latorre, A., Hughes, R. B., Liston, B., Shelton, R.,. . . Powers, L. E. (2014). Development of the Internet-based safer and stronger program for men with disabilities. *Rehabilitation Counseling Bulletin*, 1–15.

McFarlane, J., Hughes, R., Nosek, M., Groff, J., Swedland, N., & Mullens, P. (2001). Abuse assessment screen disability (AAS-D): Measuring frequency, type and perpetrator of abuse toward women with physical disabilities. *Journal of Women's Health & Gender-Based Medicine*, 10, 861–866.

Nosek, M. A., Foley, C. C., Hughes, R. B., & Howland C. A. (2001). Vulnerabilities for abuse among women with disabilities. *Sexuality and Disability*, 19, 177–188.

Nosek, M. A., Howland, C. A., Rintala, D. H., Young, E. M., & Chanpong, G. F. (2001). National study of women with disabilities: Final report. *Sexuality and Disability*, 19, 5–39.

Nosek, M. A., Howland, C. A., & Young, M. E. (1997). Abuse of women with disabilities: Policy implications. *Journal of Disability Policy Studies*, 8, 157–175.

Oschwald, M., Renker, P., Hughes, R. B., Arthur, A., Powers, L. E., & Curry, M. A. (2009). Development of an accessible audio computer assisted self-interview (A-CASI) to screen for abuse and provide safety strategies for women with disabilities. *Journal of Interpersonal Violence*, 24, 795–818.

Powers, L. E., Curry, M. A., Oschwald, M., Maley, S., Eckels, K., & Saxton, M. (2002). Barriers and strategies in addressing abuse within personal assistance relationships: A survey of disabled women's experiences. *Journal of Rehabilitation*, 68, 4–13.

Powers, L. E., Saxton, M., Curry, M. A., Powers, J. L., McNeff, E., & Oschwald, M. (2008). End the silence: A survey of abuse against men with disabilities. *Journal of Rehabilitation*, *74*, 41–53.

Rhodes, K. V., Lauderdale, D. S., He, T., Howes, D. S., & Levinson, W. (2002). "Between me and the computer": Increased detection of intimate partner violence using a computer questionnaire. *Annals of Emergency Medicine*, 40, 476–484.

Robinson-Whelen, S., Hughes, R. B., Gabrielli, J., Lund, E. M., Abramson, W., & Swank, P. R. (2014). A safety awareness program for women with diverse disabilities: A randomized controlled trial. *Violence Against Women*, 20, 1–23.

Robinson-Whelen, S., Hughes, R. B., Powers, L. E., Oschwald, M., Renker, P., Swank, P. R., & Curry, M. A. (2010). Efficacy of a computerized abuse and safety assessment intervention for women with disabilities: A randomized controlled trial. *Rehabilitation Psychology*, 55, 97–107.

Rokach, A. & Brock, H. (1997). Loneliness: A multidimensional experience. *Psychology: A Journal of Human Behavior*, 34, 1–9.

Rokach, A., Lechcier-Kimel, R., & Safarov, A. (2006). Loneliness of people with physical disabilities. *Social Behavior and Personality*, 34, 681–700.

Rutgers University, Bureau of Economic Research, and The World Institute on Disability. (1990). *Towards an understanding of the demand for personal assistance*. New Brunswick, NJ: Rutgers.

Saxton, M. (1995). Reproductive rights: A disability rights issue. In E. Disch (Ed.), *Reconstructing Gender: A Multicultural Anthology*. New York, NY: McGraw Hill.

Saxton, M., Curry, M. A., Powers, L. E., Maley, S., Eckels, K., & Gross, J. (2001). "Bring my scooter so I can leave you": A study of disabled women handling abuse by personal assistance providers. *Violence Against Women*, 7, 393–417.

Saxton, M., McNeff, E., Powers, L., Curry, M. A., Limont, M., & Benson, J. (2006). We're all little John Waynes: A study of disabled men's experience of abuse by personal assistants. *Journal of Rehabilitation*, 72, 3–13.

Scholle, S. H., Buranosky, R., Hanusa, B. H., Ranieri, L., Dowd, K., & Valappil, B. (2003). Routine screening for intimate partner violence in an obstetrics and gynecology clinic. *American Journal of Public Health*, 93, 1070–1072.

Sobsey, D. (1994). *Violence and abuse in the lives of people with disabilities: The end of silent acceptance*. Baltimore, MD: Paul H. Brooks.

Sobsey, D. & Doe, T. (1991). Patterns on sexual abuse and assault. *Journal of Sexuality and Disability*, 9, 243–259.

Surgeon General's Call to Action (2005). http://www.cdc.gov/ncbddd/disabilityandhealth/pdf/whatitmeanstoyou508.pdf

Turk, V., & Brown, H. (1993). The sexual abuse of adults with learning disabilities: Results of a two-year incidence survey. *Mental Handicap Research,* 6 (3), 193–216.

Ulincy, G. R., White, G. W., Bradford, B., & Matthews, R. M. (1990). Consumer exploitation by attendants: How often does it happen and can anything be done about it? *Rehabilitation Counseling Bulletin*, 33, 240–246.

US Census Bureau. (2012). Facts for Features: Americans with Disabilities Act. *U.S. Census Bureau News*. Washington DC: US Department of Commerce.

US Social Security Administration. (2012). Disability statistics. Retrieved from http://www.disabilitycanhappen.org/chances_disability/disability_stats.asp

Walker, L. E. (1979). *The battered woman*. New York, NY: Harper & Row.

Walker, L. E. A. (2000). *The battered woman syndrome* (2nd ed.). New York, NY: Springer.

Wasserman, G. A., Lennon, M. C., Allen, R., & Shilansky, M. (1987). Contributors to attachment in normal and physically handicapped infants. *Journal of the American Academy of Child and Adolescent Psychiatry*, 26, 9–15. In D. Sobsey (Eds.), *Violence and abuse in the lives of people with disabilities: The end of silent acceptance?* Baltimore, MD: Paul H. Brooke.

Womendez, C. & Schneiderman, K. (1991). Escaping from abuse: Unique issues for women with disabilities. *Sexuality and Disability*, 9, 273–280.

Youngblade, L. M., & Belsky, J. (1989). Child maltreatment, infant–parent attachment security, and dysfunctional peer relationships in toddlerhood. *Topics in Early Childhood Special Education*, 9, 1–15. In D. Sobsey (Eds.), *Violence and abuse in the lives of people with disabilities: The end of silent acceptance?* Baltimore, MD: Paul H. Brookes.

Decision Support Tools in the Evaluation of Risk for Violence

Adam J. E. Blanchard, Catherine S. Shaffer, *and* Kevin S. Douglas

Abstract

Professionals often utilize some form of structured approach (i.e., decision support tool or risk assessment instrument) when evaluating the risk of future violence and associated management needs. This chapter presents an overview of decision support tools that are used to assist professionals when conducting a violence risk assessment and that have received considerable empirical evaluation and professional uptake. The relative strengths and weaknesses of the two main approaches to evaluations of risk (actuarial and structured professional judgment) are discussed, including a review of empirical findings regarding their predictive validity. Following a summary of commonalities among the tools, this chapter provides a brief description of 10 decision support tools focusing on their applicability and purpose, content and characteristics, and available empirical research. Finally, the chapter concludes with a discussion of several critical considerations regarding the appropriate use and selection of tools.

Key Words: decision support tools, violence risk assessment, structured professional judgment, actuarial, sexual violence, spousal violence, stalking

It was not long ago that court challenges on the ability of mental health professionals to evaluate the risk for violence—or, as it often was called, dangerousness—were commonplace (*Barefoot v. Estelle*, 1983; *Kansas v. Hendricks*, 1997; *United States v. Salerno*, 1987). Legal and professional condemnations painted a picture of unreliable judgments that had no demonstrable connection to actual future violence (Ennis & Litwack, 1974; Kozol, Boucher, & Garofalo, 1972; Steadman & Cocozza, 1974). Persons subjected to "dangerousness assessments" could and often did have restrictions of liberty forced upon them—through increased supervision, hospitalization, lengthy prison sentences, or even the death penalty—in part on the basis of these assessments.

Indeed, early research suggested that the task of dangerousness assessment vastly overestimated actual risk. Steadman and Cocozza's (1974) seminal work on a cohort of so-called "mentally disordered dangerous accused" revealed a stunningly low violent recidivism rate of 11% among a group of offenders and patients who had all been deemed "dangerous," but who later were released or transferred to less secure facilities because of a court decision that found the legal mechanism responsible for their post-sentence confinement illegal (*Baxstrom v. Herald*, 1966). Monahan's (1981) oft-cited monograph concluded that two-thirds of positive predictions of violence were simply incorrect. Although he also provided caveats to this dire conclusion (see also Monahan, 1984)—for instance, that short-term predictions based on empirically validated risk factors might be more promising—the take-home message was clear: the field was struggling with this important task. As Ennis and Litwack (1974) sardonically subtitled their article, we were essentially "flipping coins in the courtroom."

Monahan's (1981, 1984) classic summary of "first generation" risk assessment research was limited to the five available studies at the time. Of course, this is a very small number of studies, but they did reveal poor validity. Others have criticized the methodology of those studies (Litwack, 1996, 2001) and also adroitly pointed out that the clinical methods that were used to evaluate risk were, quite simply, unsophisticated and inappropriate for such a complex task. For instance, the assessments of dangerousness studied in Steadman's early work with the Baxstrom patients were essentially administrative in nature and based on a few sparse considerations (Litwack, 1996, 2001).

Despite their methodological and clinical shortcomings, these early studies were invaluable to later generations of risk assessment researchers and professionals. They caused concern. They spurred action, both legal and empirical. As previously reviewed, mental health testimony on violence was often challenged, but courts generally upheld it. In fact, they often demanded it (*Addington v. Texas*, 1979). Most readers will be familiar with the duty to protect placed upon mental health professionals by the Tarasoff case in California (*Tarasoff v. Regents of the University of California*, 1976). Although the duty to protect has evolved to take different forms in different jurisdictions over the years, most mental health professionals are under some form of duty to protect others from clients, patients, or offenders whom they could reasonably foresee hurting others.

Legislation has evolved worldwide that requires violence risk assessments in many legal settings. As reviewed by Wilson and Douglas (2009), decisions about the risk for violence are legally required in a host of settings and situations: involuntary civil commitment; conditional release of insanity acquitees; occupational health and safety complaints; sexually violent predator cases; criminal sentencing, including the death penalty; parole hearings; immigration rulings; and juvenile raise cases. Moreover, professionals at civil and forensic hospitals, prisons, jails, and youth facilities must assess and manage the risk of those individuals admitted to their institutions, and their risk in the community if discharged.

There is a massive difference between the risk assessment landscape today and that of several decades ago. Today, there are many hundreds, if not thousands, of research studies on violence risk assessment, in particular on the predictive validity of violence risk assessment instruments or measures. And there are many thousands of studies on violence risk factors that these various risk assessment instruments attempt to capture.

Our focus in the present chapter is to review violence risk assessment instruments that have received considerable empirical evaluation and professional uptake. It is with some degree of irony that we note that today there may be *too many* risk assessment instruments, whereas only two or three decades ago there were not enough, or indeed any. As described by Singh et al. (2014), in a sample of 2,135 clinicians across 44 countries, over 200 violence risk assessment instruments were reported to be used. The vast majority of these, however, are used infrequently, and most have not been subjected to much, if any, evaluation; hence we will not consider them in this chapter. We will focus mainly on instruments developed using the structured professional judgment approach to violence risk assessment and management, although we also will describe the actuarial approach to risk assessment.

Approaches to Violence Risk Assessment

Various approaches to the assessment of violence risk have been described in the literature (e.g., Boer, Hart, Kropp, & Webster, 1997; Hanson, 1998; Meehl, 1954/1996; Melton, Petrila, Poythress, & Slobogin, 1997; Monahan, 2006). In the following section we describe the two most common structured approaches used to reach opinions about violence risk: *actuarial* and *structured professional judgment*. The descriptions provided are brief, as a more in-depth discussion of the different approaches and their merits are provided elsewhere (e.g., Douglas, Hart, Groscup, & Litwack, 2014; Hart & Logan, 2011). For each approach, the main features, strengths, and, in the case of actuarial approach, limitations are provided. This section concludes with comparative research on the predictive validity of instruments developed under the actuarial and SPJ models.

Initially, clinical assessment of an individual's potential for violence was determined largely through the use of unguided (Hanson, 1998) or unstructured clinical judgment (Hart, 2001; Hart et al., 2003). Evaluators would reach conclusions about violence risk based on their clinical training, experience, theoretical orientation, or intuition (Monahan et al., 2005). Unstructured clinical judgment has broad applicability across a number of practice settings; it allows for clinical flexibility, the consideration of case-specific factors, and it can, in principle, connect violence risk assessment to intervention and management strategies (Hart, 1998). However, predictions made using unstructured judgment were found to be limited with respect to objectivity, transparency, inter-rater reliability, and predictive validity (Grove & Meehl, 1996; Kemshall, 1996; Lidz, Mulvey, & Gardner, 1993). Moreover, it could not be determined through this approach the extent to which the evaluator's unaided judgment has been sufficiently informed or guided by the empirical literature and best practice in the field (Hart & Logan, 2011).

Criticisms of unstructured clinical judgment led to the development of two evidence-based approaches that were empirically grounded, transparent, and systematic: the actuarial approach (Hanson, 1997; Harris, Rice, & Quinsey, 1993) and the structured professional judgment model (Douglas, Cox, & Webster, 1999; Hart, 1998; Kropp & Hart, 2000; Webster, Douglas, Eaves, & Hart, 1997). In contrast to unstructured clinical judgment, these approaches emphasize the use of structured protocols or decision tools to help determine violence risk. Although these approaches share several similar features (e.g., structure, transparency), they differ with respect to how risk factors are combined, how final risk estimates are produced, and the degree of clinical discretion required when using the tool to arrive at a decision about risk for violence (Monahan, 2008).

Actuarial Approach. The primary purpose of the approach known as actuarial (e.g., algorithmic, statistic, mechanical) is to predict an individual's likelihood for future violence (Heilbrun, 1997). The actuarial approach was developed to provide a priori guidelines and explicit rules to weigh and combine information regarding violence risk (Grove & Meehl, 1996; Meehl, 1954/1996). Rather than allowing clinicians to determine (a) the relevant risk factors, (b) the weight of these risk factors, and (c) the ultimate degree of risk posed by the client, the actuarial approach grounded the decision making in statistical relationships. Decision tools developed under this framework—for example, the Violence Risk Appraisal Guide (VRAG; Quinsey, Harris, Rice, & Cormier, 1998, 2006; Static-99, Hanson & Thornton, 1999)—have three distinct features. First, items are identified on the basis of theory, experience, or their ability to empirically discriminate between violent and nonviolent individuals. Second, items are assigned a corresponding numerical weight based on their association with violent outcomes and ability to differentiate between those who were and were not violent. Third, scores on these items are combined using a statistical or mechanical algorithm (usually additive) to assign an individual a probabilistic estimate that

he or she will engage in violence over a fixed time period, based on data from a norm-based reference group (Hanson, 1998). Put another way, the likelihood that an individual would engage in violence is determined using analogical reasoning (e.g., Jones resembles group Y, 52% of group Y was violent, and therefore Jones has a 52% risk for future violence; Hart, Michie, & Cooke, 2007).

One advantage of the actuarial approach is that it is more reliable and valid than unstructured clinical judgment (Grove & Meehl, 1996; Litwack, 2001; Quinsey et al., 1998). This approach provides an objective and consistent method to determine the level of risk: by using fixed guidelines each individual is evaluated using the same criteria and can be directly compared to other individuals who have the same tool administered. Further, this approach can inform the overall level of risk management required (i.e., an individual at greater risk should receive a greater level of management and resources).

Actuarial tools are also easy to administer and time-efficient. Aside from basic training on the tool, all that is required is the accurate gathering of relevant information to be entered into the risk assessment algorithm (Andrews, Bonta, & Wormith, 2006; Monahan et al., 2007). The final risk score produced allows for a quick examination of an individual's putative level of risk (Hanson, 2009).

Despite advantages of actuarial risk assessments over unstructured clinical judgment, there are at least six potential problems with actuarial tools that limit their utility in clinical and psycho-legal contexts. First, actuarial tools consider only a small subset of risk factors from the empirical literature and ignore case-specific variables (i.e., unique, unusual, or context-specific) that might play a disproportionate role in increasing (or decreasing) an individual's level of risk (Grubin, 1997; Hart, 1998, Monahan et al., 2001). Second, actuarial approaches address risk at an aggregate level; however, it is difficult to apply violence rates from group data onto individual cases (Cooke & Michie, 2010; see also Hájek & Hall, 2002). Further, the final risk estimates, often in the form of probability statements, communicate little practical information regarding the frequency, pattern, severity, or imminence of violence that an individual will engage in (Hart, 1998). Third, the actuarial approach often emphasizes static (i.e., historical) indicators of violence (e.g., history of noncompliance), while ignoring dynamic factors (e.g., active psychotic symptoms) that could be targeted through intervention to mitigate an individual's risk for violence (Hart, 1998). This makes it difficult to use actuarial tools to formulate treatment and prevention strategies. Fourth, actuarial tools can have poor external validity; risk factors that are optimized in one setting may not be predictive in other settings (McDermott, Quanbeck, Busse, Yastro, & Scott, 2008; Thomson, Davidson, Brett, Steele, & Darjee, 2008), and even if used with an individual from the test-development population, patient groups and settings can change over time causing the predictive validity of the tools to shrink between calibration and validation samples (e.g., Blair, Marcus, & Boccaccini, 2008; Wollert, 2002). Fifth, by shifting the locus of decision making from the professional onto the actuarial tool, important clinical information that might contribute to the prediction of violence and assist with the development of treatment plans is ignored (Buchanan, 1999). Finally, and most importantly, actuarial tools are solely *predictive*; they are not intended to identify specific interventions that may be useful for managing or reducing violence risk. As such, actuarial tools are incongruent with most clinical practice (Douglas & Kropp, 2002; Hart, 1998; Litwack, 2001).

Structured Professional Judgment Model. Because of the limitations of the actuarial approach and unstructured clinical judgment, several scholars suggested that clinical discretion might be improved when combined with a well-defined structure to guide decision making (Webster et al., 1997). The model known as structured professional judgment (SPJ; i.e., structured clinical judgment, structured discretion, empirically-guided clinical judgment) was developed to minimize the weakness of its predecessors. Like the actuarial approach, the SPJ model was grounded in empirical evidence and the structured identification of risk factors, but it diverged from the actuarial approach by allowing for clinical flexibility and a focus on case-specific influences (Doyle & Dolan, 2002). Further, in contrast to the actuarial approach, the main goal of the SPJ approach was to reduce and manage violence (Douglas & Kropp, 2002).

A defining feature of tools developed under the SPJ framework, such as the Historical-Clinical-Risk Management-20 (HCR-20; Douglas, Hart, Webster, & Belfrage, 2013; Webster et al., 1997) or Spousal Assault Risk Assessment Guide (SARA; Kropp & Hart, 2000) is that information is gathered, weighted, and combined according to the evaluator's judgment, assisted by guidelines, or an *aide-memoire*, that reflect current scientific knowledge and professional practice (Hart et al., 2003). These guidelines typically include the following features: (1) a checklist of historical and dynamic risk factors to be considered, (2) coding rules for these factors, (3) recommendations for collecting information, (4) instructions for determining final decisions, and (5) recommendations for communicating opinions about violence risk. Although a number of predetermined risk factors (e.g., 20–30) must be considered in every case, the evaluator is encouraged to incorporate additional case-specific risk factors. Evaluators are also allowed to exercise discretion regarding the weight to be given each risk factor, the relevance of each risk factor to the case, and risk management strategies that are required to mitigate the individual's risk (Hart, 2009). Final judgments are not determined numerically but rather are communicated in a categorical manner (e.g., low, moderate, high risk) (Davis & Ogloff, 2008). In addition to offering an opinion about future violence risk, the evaluator is also required to identify and describe scenarios of future violence, including the nature, likelihood, seriousness, and imminence of violent behavior. Following the assessment, the evaluator provides a road map of how the final decision was reached (including important risk factors, treatment plans, and scenarios for future violence) to provide transparency and facilitate communication among professionals.

Tools developed under the SPJ framework have many of the same advantages as actuarial tools: reliability, validity, and transparency (e.g., Belfrage, Fransson, & Strand, 2000; Douglas & Webster, 1999). The SPJ approach is also advantageous because of its synchronicity with routine clinical and legal practice. By identifying case-specific risk factors and allowing the evaluator to determine the relevance of risk factors for the given individual, SPJ instruments are unique to every individual instead of being group-based (Webster et al., 1997). SPJ instruments also recognize that violence risk is not necessarily a linear function of the number of risk factors that are present; an individual can be high-risk even in the presence of a single risk factor (e.g., preoccupation with violence). By emphasizing dynamic factors, SPJ tools provide identifiable treatment targets and can be reused to appraise an individual's risk and monitor treatment effectiveness (Maden, 2007; Webster, Haque, & Hucker, 2007). Most importantly, rather than abrogating the professional discretion of the evaluator, the SPJ framework acknowledges that the clinician can offer key insight into the personal circumstances and motivations of their patients, which could be related to violence risk.

Comparative Research. More than 100 actuarial and SPJ tools are currently available in mental health and criminal justice settings. A central question is whether future violence outcomes are most accurately predicted by tools developed under an actuarial or SPJ approach (Heilbrun, Yashuhara, & Shah, 2010). Proponents of the actuarial approach have argued that the SPJ method allows clinical discretion and is therefore vulnerable to the same limitations of unstructured clinical judgment (see e.g., Quinsey et al., 1998, 2006). Conversely, supporters of the SPJ model have argued that structured professional judgment has comparable predictive validity to actuarial tools but is the more appropriate form of risk assessment because it allows for the consideration of case-specific factors and provides guidance on mitigating violence risk (Hart & Logan, 2011; Sreenivasan, Weinberger, Frances, & Cusworth-Walker, 2010).

At least eight meta-analyses have directly examined SPJ tools versus actuarial tools. Three reported that the SPJ approach was more predictive than the actuarial (Fazel, Singh, Doll, & Grann, 2012; Guy, 2008; Singh, Grann, & Fazel, 2011). Other meta-analyses, however, reported that actuarial tools were more predictive than SPJ (Hanson & Morton-Bourgon, 2009) or that there was comparable predictive accuracy across both approaches (Campbell, French, & Gendreau, 2009; Campbell, Glass, Sharps, Laughon, & Bloom, 2007; Singh & Fazel, 2010; Yang, Wong & Coid, 2010). For example, in a meta-analysis of 28 studies in six countries, Yang, Wong, and Coid (2010) found the predictive validity of nine actuarial and SPJ tools (including the HCR-20 and the VRAG) did not significantly differ (i.e., they had overlapping 95% confidence intervals). Similarly, in a review of 126 actuarial and SPJ risk assessment measures (including violence risk assessment tools for youth), Singh and Fazel (2010) found that no single measure consistently provided any advantages with respect to predictive validity. One possible explanation for why actuarial and SPJ tools have comparable predictive validity is that, even though they have varied items, formats, and scoring procedures, actuarial and SPJ tools measure common risk factors that have been collected and coded in a similar manner (Skeem & Monahan, 2011; see also Kroner, Mills, & Reddon, 2005).

Although these findings suggest that tools developed under the two approaches may be able to predict violence with the same relative accuracy and, therefore, they can be used interchangeably to assess risk for violence, when the purpose of the assessment is to identify pertinent risk factors for a given individual, develop risk management plans, and mitigate violence risk, the SPJ approach may offer advantages over actuarial approaches (Borum, 1996; Douglas et al., 2014). At least 10 studies have investigated whether final risk judgments (i.e., low, moderate, or high) add incremental predictive validity to the numerical use of SPJ tools or other actuarial instruments for violence risk. In all but two (Schmidt, Campbell, & Houlding, 2011; Vincent, Chapman, & Cook, 2011), the final risk judgments were found to add incrementally to the predictive validity of the numerical scores on the same measure (Arbach-Lucioni, Andres-Pueyo, Pomarol-Clotet, & Gomar-Sones, 2011; de Vogel & de Ruiter, 2006; Desmarais, Nicholls, Wilson, & Brink, 2012; Douglas, Ogloff, & Hart, 2003; Douglas, Yeomans, & Boer, 2005; Enebrink, Långström, & Gumpert, 2006; Kropp & Hart, 2000; Neves, Goncalves, & Palma-Oliveira, 2011; van den Brink, Hooijschuur, van Os, Savenije, & Wiersma, 2010) and other actuarial instruments (de Vogel & de Ruiter, 2006; Douglas et al., 2003, 2005; Desmarais, Nicholls, Wilson, & Brink, 2012; Kropp & Hart, 2000). Given that the construction of accurate risk management plans is a core function of mental health practitioners, front-line workers, police officers, and victim support personnel, the remainder of this chapter will mainly focus on decision support tools developed under the SPJ model that should be used to inform decisions about the risk for violence, except when no SPJ instruments are available for a specific type of violence.

Decision Support Tools

Decision support tools used in the evaluation of the risk for violence can be separated based on the type of violence (e.g., general violence, sexual violence, or stalking), the time frame of violence (e.g., imminent or distant), or the intended victim (e.g., intimate partner or stranger). The following sections provide brief introductions to various decision support tools that have considerable empirical support or considerable clinical promise in the evaluation of different types of violence. Each of these sections highlights the main features of the decision support tools, including the criterion it is meant to assess, the target populations, intended applications, content, and other unique features, as well as an overview of the empirical evidence supporting its reliability and validity (with a focus on inter-rater reliability and predictive validity). As these tools are complex in nature, features common to SPJ tools will be discussed at the outset, followed by descriptions of the individual tools. Subsequently, two actuarial tools for the evaluation of imminent violence are described, as no reliable or valid SPJ tools for this type of violence are available. Table 18.1 provides a quick reference guide to the tools discussed in this chapter.

Common Features of Structured Professional Judgment Tools

Development. In general, the SPJ tools described in this chapter were developed through similar means. As previously mentioned, the model and tools developed under SPJ attempt to retain the strengths of both the unstructured clinical and actuarial approaches to decision making, while at the same time reducing or eliminating their weaknesses. Each of these tools was developed through a systematic review of the available scientific literature (e.g., Boer et al., 1997; de Vogel, de Ruiter, Bouman, & de Vries Robbé, 2012; Douglas et al., 2013; Hart et al., 2003; Kropp, Hart, & Belfrage, 2005, 2010; Kropp, Hart, & Lyon, 2008; Kropp, Hart, Webster, & Eaves, 1994, 1995, 1999; Webster et al., 1997; Webster, Martin, Brink, Nicholls, & Desmarais, 2009). Items were selected for inclusion based on logical or rational item selection, in contrast to the empirical item selection used in most actuarial measures. This approach involves the selection of items that have shown a relationship with the outcome of interest across a number of samples and settings, or that have a considerable clinical or theoretical foundation for inclusion. This approach was used to foster the generalizability of the risk factors across settings and populations. Thus, items are ultimately selected that are (a) supported by the existing empirical literature, (b) consistent with clinical and professional recommendations, and (c) legally acceptable (i.e., consistent with civil and human rights legislation). These tools also were meant to ensure that the set of items were not unduly long but reasonably comprehensive and that they were described in language consistent with practitioners in the field. In addition, relevant standards of practice, ethical codes, and laws were taken into consideration. Any deviations from this general developmental framework or additional steps in the process for particular tools are now described in the following for each particular tool.

Evaluation Steps. The SPJ tools about to be described are also generally consistent with regard to the steps involved in the evaluation process. That is, the manner in which the tool is used to support clinical decision making is consistent across the tools. Outlined next are the seven main steps in the process of utilizing an SPJ tool to assist in an evaluation for risk of (some form of) violence (Douglas et al., 2013). Notably, the respective manuals for these individual tools do not always discuss each step in detail, and sometimes certain steps are grouped together; nevertheless, each of the following steps should at least be considered, if not fully undertaken and documented, when utilizing such tools.

The SPJ tools described herein are at a minimum meant to assist in the evaluation of the risk factors that are present in a given individual, the relevance of those risk factors for the individual, and the determination of which risk management strategies should be employed to mitigate the individual's risk of violence (e.g., Boer et al., 1997; Douglas et al., 2013; Kropp et al., 1994, 1995, 1999, 2005, 2008, 2010; Webster et al., 1997, 2009). Specifically, an evaluation using these tools should consist of the following steps (Douglas et al., 2013):

(1) *Gather all the necessary information.* Typically, information from up to five general categories is used: an interview with the individual being evaluated; interview(s) with collateral informants, including interview(s) with the victims; review of collateral file information; psychiatric, diagnostic, personality or other psychological test data; and direct observation.

(2) *Determine the presence of risk factors.* Each risk factor is coded on a three-point scale (e.g., not present, possibly or partially present, definitely present, or 0, 1, 2). A rating of 0 indicates that the item does not apply or is absent. A rating of 1 indicates that the item is possibly present or present only to a limited degree. A rating of 2 indicates that the item is definitely present. All the SPJ tools allow the evaluator to include case specific risk factors (e.g., access to weapons) that may be important to consider in a given case but are not included on the given tool.

(3) *Determine the relevance of these risk factors.* The relevance of risk factors should at a minimum be considered, but it can also be coded using a similar three-point scale as the presence of risk factors (e.g., low, moderate, or high relevance). Relevance is generally considered in terms of the functional (i.e., causal) relationship between the given item and violence for the given individual.

Table 18.1. Quick Reference Guide to Decision Support Tools in the Evaluation of Risk for Violence.

	Approach		User Qualifications			Item Content				Time Frame		
	Actuarial	SPJ	Violence[a]	Assessment	Health[b]	Static	Dynamic	Protective	Victim[c]	Hours	Weeks	Months
General Violence												
START		✓	✓	✓	✓		✓	✓			✓	
HCR-20		✓	✓	✓		✓	✓					✓
SAPROF		✓	✓	✓		✓	✓	✓				✓
BVC	✓		✓		✓		✓			✓		
DASA	✓		✓		✓		✓			✓		
Sexual Violence												
SVR-20		✓	✓	✓		✓	✓					✓
RSVP		✓	✓	✓	✓	✓	✓					✓
Spousal Violence												
SARA		✓	✓	✓		✓	✓					✓
B-SAFER		✓	✓	✓		✓	✓		✓			✓
Stalking												
SAM		✓	✓	✓		✓	✓		✓			✓

Note. B-SAFER = Brief Spousal Assault Form for the Evaluation of Risk; BVC = Broset Violence Checklist; DASA = Dynamic Appraisal of Situational Aggression; HCR-20 = Historical-Clinical-Risk Management-20; RSVP = Risk for Sexual Violence Protocol; SAM = Guidelines for Stalking Assessment and Management; SAPROF = Structured Assessment of Protective Factors for Violence Risk; SARA = Spousal Assault Risk Assessment Guide; START = Short-Term Assessment of Risk and Treatability; SVR-20 = Sexual Violence Risk-20.

[a] Knowledge of the specific type of violence under consideration.

[b] Evaluator should be a qualified health professional, or be knowledgeable of mental health assessment, disorders, and diagnoses.

[c] Victim vulnerability factors.

(4) *Develop a risk formulation.* The risk formulation is intended to integrate all the information obtained in steps 1, 2, and 3 into a coherent understanding of the individual's risk for violence—essentially answering the question, "Why has this person been violent in the past?" or "Why might this person be violent in the future?"

(5) *Develop risk scenarios.* Risk scenarios are meant to identify the most likely circumstances under which the individual will perpetrate violence in the future—essentially answering the question, "What is this person likely to do in the future?"

(6) *Develop risk management strategies.* This step is often considered the most critical, as the ultimate purpose of the assessment is the prevention of violence. It involves making recommendations for intervention, treatment, or other services based on all the previous steps to mitigate the risk posed.

(7) *Determine the conclusory opinions.* The conclusory opinions (i.e., final risk judgments or summary risk judgments) are also made on a three-point scale (low/routine, moderate/elevated, high/urgent). The number and type of conclusory opinions differ by tool, but always include a general case prioritization (or general risk for some type of violence) opinion.

User Qualifications. Each of the SPJ tools described contains at least two general user qualifications (e.g., Boer et al., 1997; Kropp et al., 1994, 1995, 1999, 2005, 2008, 2010; Webster et al., 1997, 2009). First, evaluators must have expertise in individual assessment. This should involve some formal education (e.g., university courses, specialized educational training, supervised work experience), as well as the requisite professional credentials for the given settings (e.g., licensed, registered, certified). Second, evaluators must have expertise in (the relevant type of) violence. That is, evaluators should have knowledge of the scientific and professional literature regarding the nature, causes, and management of (the relevant type of) violence.

Decision Support Tools for the Evaluation of General Violence

SHORT-TERM ASSESSMENT OF RISK AND TREATABILITY

Description and use of tool. The Short-Term Assessment of Risk and Treatability (START; Webster et al., 2009) is a decision support tool developed under the SPJ model that is meant to facilitate assessments of multiple risk domains: risk to others, suicide, self-harm, victimization, substance use, unauthorized absences, and self-neglect. Although a relatively new tool, START has received considerable international uptake (Viljoen, Cruise, Nicholls, Desmarais, & Webster, 2012). It has been translated into four languages, with several additional translations underway (Nicholls, Petersen, Brink, & Webster, 2011), and it is currently in use in at least 10 different countries (Desmarais et al., 2012).

START is meant to be used with individuals aged 18 years or older that have a history of mental illness. It is intended for inpatient and outpatient general mental health settings, as well as specialized forensic psychiatric, correctional, and probationary settings. In addition to the general user qualifications described, the START tool requires that the evaluator be a qualified mental health professional (e.g., nurse, psychiatrist, psychologist, and the like).

START was developed to address several specific limitations inherent to other decision support tools (Nicholls, Brink, Desmarais, Webster, & Martin, 2006; Webster, Nicholls, Martin, Desmarais, & Brink, 2006; Webster et al., 2009). Specifically, many other tools focus either exclusively or predominately on static risk factors that can have limited clinical utility in providing treatment; as such, START consists entirely of dynamic risk factors. Furthermore, individuals with mental illnesses are at increased risk for a variety of adverse outcomes in addition to violence (e.g., suicide, victimization). That is, patients often present with multiple risks and management challenges that intersect and interact, and the risk factors for these various domains often overlap considerably. Finally, most other tools contain only risk factors and ignore protective factors or strengths.

START includes 20 dynamic items that are rated as both risk factors (labeled as *vulnerabilities*) and protective factors (labeled as *strengths*). In addition, evaluators are encouraged to consider *historical* or *static* risk factors known to be associated with the relevant risks, such as the Historical Scale of the HCR-20 (Webster et al., 2006; Wilson, Desmarais, Nicholls, & Brink, 2010). Notably, the rating of strengths and vulnerabilities are independent in that a person may have any combination of strength and vulnerability ratings on a single given risk factor. Although formal ratings of an item's relevance are not required, after rating the presence of the characteristic, evaluators are encouraged to designate which ones are "critical" risks or "key" strengths, essentially the most important risk and strength factors influencing the individual. Evaluators are also required to consider any "signature risk signs"—a set of case specific symptoms, beliefs, or behaviors that are early, reliable, and unique signs of an impending increase in risk. Evaluators then make their conclusory opinions (i.e., final risk judgments) across each of the seven risk domains. The opinions are meant to focus on the short-term future (i.e., weeks to months), and re-evaluations should be conducted every three months or sooner.

Empirical research. Although a relatively new tool, several examinations of START have been conducted that support its reliability and validity for assessing risk for violence and other risk domains. That is, previous research has found START to have good[1] predictive validity and inter-rater reliability (e.g., Braithwaite, Charette, Crocker, & Reyes, 2010; Chu, Thomas, Ogloff, & Daffern, 2011; Desmarais et al., 2012; Gray et al., 2011; Nicholls et al., 2006; Nonstad et al., 2010; Wilson, Desmarais, Nicholls, Hart, & Brink, 2013). At least seven studies have investigated the inter-rater reliability of START ratings, generally finding reliability coefficients in the good to excellent range. O'Shea and Dickens (2014) report mean intraclass correlation coefficients (ICC) across these studies with the vulnerability scale yielding the largest coefficient (mean ICC = 0.86), while the strength scale (mean ICC = 0.78) and the final risk judgments (mean ICC = 0.82) yielded slightly lower coefficients.

Additionally, previous research has found that START Vulnerability scores and final risk judgments are predictive of violence toward others, verbal aggression, aggression toward objects, and sexually inappropriate behavior (e.g., Braithwaite et al., 2010; Chu et al., 2011; Desmarais et al., 2012; Gray et al., 2011; Nonstad et al., 2010; Nicholls et al., 2006; Wilson et al., 2010). START scores and final risk judgments have also been found to predict other adverse outcomes, including substance use (Braithwaite et al., 2010), victimization (Gray et al., 2011), self-neglect (Gray et al., 2011), self-harm (Gray et al., 2011; Nicholls et al., 2006), and unauthorized absence (Braithwaite et al., 2010). Notably, START strength scores have also been found to be inversely related to future violence (e.g., Braithwaite et al., 2010; Chu et al., 2011; Desmarais et al., 2012; Gray et al., 2011; Wilson et al., 2010), as well as to other adverse outcomes including self-neglect (Gray et al., 2011), unauthorized leave (Braithwaite et al., 2010), and substance use (Braithwaite et al., 2010).

These findings have been confirmed by a recent meta-analysis conducted by O'Shea and Dickens (2014), who report weighted AUC values for the various scales across a number of outcomes. Of note, the vulnerability scale (AUCw = 0.74 across eight studies and 493 participants), strength scale (AUCw = 0.71 across eight studies and 477 participants), and final risk judgments (AUCw = 0.73 across five studies and 282 participants) were predictive of aggression.

HISTORICAL-CLINICAL-RISK MANAGEMENT-20

Description and use of tool. The Historical-Clinical-Risk Management-20 (HCR-20; Webster et al., 1997; Douglas et al., 2013) was one of the first violence risk assessment protocols developed under the SPJ model. Currently, the HCR-20 has been translated into over 20 languages and is used in a variety of correctional, forensic, and psychiatric systems throughout North American, Europe, South America, Asia, and Australia.

The HCR-20 is meant to assist in the evaluation of risk for general violence, defined as the "actual, attempted, or threatened harm to a person or persons" (Webster et al., 1997, p. 24), and more recently as the "actual, attempted, or threatened infliction of bodily harm on another person" (Douglas et al., 2013, p. 36). This definition coincides with most legal systems in that any action that is deemed of a serious enough nature that it could result in criminal or civil litigation should be considered violent for the purposes of using the HCR-20 in an evaluation.

The HCR-20 was developed for use with men or women ages 18 and over; under certain circumstances it may be appropriate to use with an individual who is slightly younger (if they have been living independently for some time) or to not use with someone who is slightly older (if they are still largely dependent on their parents). It is intended to be used to facilitate assessments of risk for interpersonal violence in civil psychiatric patients, forensic psychiatric patients, and criminal offenders both mentally disordered and not, and it is meant to be a flexible tool that is capable of meeting the needs of various settings and populations. Specific settings and contexts in which the HCR-20 is used include admission and release decision making, as well as monitoring the risk of incarcerated, institutionalized, or community supervised individuals (Douglas & Reeves, 2010).

The HCR-20 consists of 20 risk factors grouped into three domains: *historical, clinical,* and *risk management.* They are meant to cover the past, present, and future functioning of the individual, respectively. The historical scale consists of 10 mostly static risk factors pertaining to the individual's lifetime history. The clinical scale comprises five dynamic risk factors related to current functioning. The risk management scale consists of five dynamic risk factors related to future considerations. In general, decisions made using the HCR-20 should concern the upcoming six months to a year, and reassessments should be conducted within this same time frame.

Empirical research. More than 150 examinations of this protocol's reliability and validity have been conducted (e.g., Douglas, Shaffer, et al., 2014; Guy, 2008). Over 215 unique disseminations, involving research with over 33,000 participants in over 20 countries, have contributed reports on the psychometric properties of the HCR-20. Previous research has generally found the HCR-20 to have good to excellent predictive validity and inter-rater reliability. Both narrative (Douglas, Shaffer, et al., 2014) and meta-analytic (Guy, 2008) reviews of the instrument have confirmed these findings.

The majority of studies regarding inter-rater reliability have found the intraclass correlation coefficients (ICC) to be greater than 0.80 (Douglas & Reeves, 2010). Across 36 studies, Douglas and Reeves (2010) report the inter-rater reliability to be in the good to excellent range (ICC = 0.67 to 0.95), with a median reliability coefficient of 0.85. Previous research had found higher inter-rater reliability for the historical scale (median IRR value of 0.86) compared to the clinical (median IRR value of 0.74) and risk management scales (median IRR value of 0.68). Much fewer studies have investigated the reliability of the final risk judgments, finding a median IRR value of 0.65.

In terms of predictive validity, the majority of studies have found that the association between the HCR-20 and violence is in the moderate to large magnitude. A comprehensive meta-analysis found that the HCR-20 summary risk ratings were predictive of violence with an average AUC of 0.76, compared to an AUC of 0.73 for the total score (Guy, 2008). Additional meta-analyses have found that the HCR-20, on average, across all studies, produces some of the largest effect sizes compared to other structured risk assessment instruments (e.g., Campbell, French, & Gendreau, 2009; Yang et al., 2010). Once again, fewer studies have investigated the final risk judgments compared to the numerical scores on the HCR-20. These studies have found that the final risk judgments generally outperform the numerical ratings by a slight margin and have been shown to add incrementally to the predictive validity of the numerical scores (e.g., for a review, see Douglas, Shaffer, et al., 2014).

STRUCTURED ASSESSMENT OF PROTECTIVE FACTORS FOR VIOLENCE RISK

Description and use of tool. The Structured Assessment of Protective Factors for Violence Risk (SAPROF; de Vogel et al., 2012) is a decision support tool consisting solely of protective factors intended to be used in conjunction with a structured professional judgment risk assessment tool, such as the HCR-20. A protective factor is defined as "any characteristic of a person, his/her environment or situation which reduces the risk of future violent behaviour" (p. 23). It has currently been translated into 10 languages (de Vries Robbé, de Vogel, & Douglas, 2013).

The SAPROF was developed to complement the assessment of risk for general violence or sexually violent behavior. The exact definition of the relevant outcome depends on the risk being evaluated (i.e., the ultimate purpose of the evaluation and the tool that is used in conjunction with the SAPROF). It is intended for use with individuals aged 18 years or older with a history of violence or sexual violence who suffer from a mental illness or personality disorder. Its main applications include forensic and civil psychiatric settings, as well as correctional and probationary services. The SAPROF was developed to counterbalance the fact that almost all other decision support tools focus exclusively on risk factors (de Vries Robbé, de Vogel, & de Spa, 2011).

The SAPROF consists of 17 protective factors grouped in three domains: five *internal items* (referring to individual characteristics), seven *motivational items* (referring to the motivation to be a positive member of society), and five *external items* (referring to beneficial environmental factors that offer protection from outside the individual). Of the 17 items, 15 are considered dynamic and two are primarily static.

Unique features of using the SAPROF include the rating of "key" and "goal" items. A key item is one in which "a high score (1 or 2) on the item is considered essential for the prevention of violent behaviour by the individual" (de Vogel et al., 2012, p. 26), a similar rating to critical items on START. A goal item is one in which "an item with a score of 0 or 1 can be labelled a goal because it is considered important as a treatment goal, as improvement on this item is thought to have a protective effect" (p. 26). Subsequent to rating the individual items, a final protection judgment is also made regarding the extent to which "the factors have a reducing effect on the risk for future violent behaviour" (p. 27). Subsequent to this stage, the evaluator combines the information gleaned from the SAPROF with information collected from another SPJ tool to make the final risk judgments. The time frames for decision are generally consistent with the HCR-20 in that opinions should concern the upcoming six months to a year, and re-evaluations should take place in a similar time frame.

Empirical research. As a relatively new tool, the SAPROF has not been subjected to an extensive array of empirical investigations as compared to some other tools. Nevertheless, several studies have found support for the inter-rater reliability, concurrent validity, and predictive validity of the SAPROF (e.g., Abidin et al., 2013; de Vries Robbé et al., 2011, 2013; Yoon, Spehr, & Briken, 2011). With regard to inter-rater reliability, the SAPROF total scores and final protection judgments have yielded excellent reliability coefficients in samples of violent forensic psychiatric patients (ICC = 0.88 and 0.85, respectively), and sexually violent forensic psychiatric patients (ICC = 0.85 and 0.73, respectively) (de Vogel et al., 2012; de Vries Robbé et al., 2011, 2013). All the individual items have also shown fair to excellent inter-rater reliability (ICC = 0.42 to 0.94; de Vries Robbé et al., 2011).

With regard to predictive validity, Abidin and colleagues (2013) found the SAPROF total scores were predictive of an absence of violence (AUC = 0.85) and an absence of self-harm (AUC = 0.77) after a six-month follow-up in 100 forensic psychiatric patients. At the item level, 12 of the 17 items were predictive of the absence of violence. In addition, in a sample of 188 forensic psychiatric patients, the SAPROF has been found to be predictive of non-recidivism at the 1-year (AUC = 0.85), 3-year (AUC = 0.75), and 11-year (AUC = 0.73) follow-up. The final protection judgments were also predictive of all three follow-up times (AUC = 0.80, 0.72, and 0.66, respectively). There has also been mixed findings with regard to the incremental validity of the SAPROF when combined with the HCR-20, with some findings indicating the SAPROF adds incrementally to the predictive validity of the HCR-20, and others finding no such effect (de Vries Robbé et al., 2011, 2013).

Decision Support Tools for the Evaluation of Risk for Sexual Violence
SEXUAL VIOLENCE RISK-20

Description and use of tool. The Sexual Violence Risk-20 (SVR-20; Boer et al., 1997) is an SPJ instrument designed to assist in the evaluation of the risk for sexual violence. Sexual violence is defined as the "actual, attempted, or threatened sexual contact with another person that is non-consensual" (Boer et al., 1997, p. 9). This definition is meant to be inclusive in the sense that a large variety of acts that would be considered violations of criminal law in most countries would be included under this definition.

The SVR-20 is intended for use with males aged 18 years or older who have a known or suspected history of sexual violence, but it may also be used with younger males (i.e., 16 or 17) who are beginning to display sexually violent behavior, as well as with adult females who have a history of sexual violence. Moreover, the SVR-20 is intended for use by a wide range of professionals in a broad array of criminal justice and civil settings, including but not limited to "pre-trial and sentencing evaluations; correctional intake and discharge evaluations; post-sentence civil commitment or 'sexually violent predator' evaluations; duty to protect, community notification, and sex offender registration evaluations; and child protection or custody/access evaluations" (Hart & Boer, 2010, p. 270).

The SVR-20 contains 20 risk factors grouped in three domains. The *psychosocial adjustment scale* consists of 11 items related to the perpetrators psychological and social functioning. The *history of sexual offenses scale* consists of seven items related to the perpetrators history of sexual offenses. Finally, two items are related to *future plans*. In addition to the typical steps involved in using an SPJ tool, when the future violence is likely to be targeted at a specific (i.e., known) potential victim, evaluators are strongly encouraged to consider victim vulnerability factors, such as those found in two tools we will discuss later, the Guidelines for Stalking Assessment and Management (SAM; Kropp et al., 2008) and the Brief Spousal Assault Form for the Evaluation of Risk (B-SAFER; Kropp et al., 2005, 2010). Subsequent to coding the presence of risk factors, the evaluator must also determine whether there has been any recent change in the presence of the risk factor, coded on a three-point scale (exacerbation, no change, amelioration). The determination of "recent" is up to the evaluator and must be documented. The SVR-20 is meant to assist with decisions concerning the coming months and up to a year, and re-evaluations should also conform to this time frame.

Empirical research. Numerous studies have found support for the inter-rater reliability of ratings made using the SVR-20. Specifically, over nine studies across five different countries have examined the inter-rater reliability of the SVR-20. Excluding two studies that found reliability coefficients in the poor to fair range (Hildebrand, de Ruiter, & de Vogel, 2004; Sjöstedt & Långström, 2002), the other seven studies have generally found reliability coefficients in the excellent range (Barbaree, Langton, Blanchard, & Boer, 2008; de Vogel, de Ruiter, van Beck, & Mead, 2004; Hill, Habermann, Klusman, Berner, & Briken, 2008; Rettenberger & Eher, 2007; Watt & Jackson, 2008; Zanatta, 2005). Generally, studies have found excellent inter-rater reliability for the total scores (ICC = 0.75 to 0.93), as well as the scale scores (ICC = 0.74 to 0.89). Good to excellent reliability has also been found at the item level (ICC = 0.62 to 0.96; M = 0.83; Watt & Jackson, 2008).

At present, at least eight studies have examined the predictive validity of the SVR-20 (e.g., Barbaree et al., 2008; Craig, Browne, Beech, & Stringer, 2006; de Vogel et al., 2004; Dempster, 1998; Rettenberger, Boer, & Eher, 2011; Rettenberger, Matthes, Boer, & Eher, 2010; Sjöstedt & Långström, 2002; Stadtland et al., 2005). Generally, these studies have found support for the predictive validity of the total scores (AUC = 0.48 to 0.83) and final risk judgments (AUC = 0.56 to 0.83). Additionally, a meta-analysis of 68 studies involving 25,980 participants found the highest predictive validity coefficients (AUC = 0.78 across three studies and 380 participants) for the SVR-20 compared to eight other risk assessment instruments (Singh et al., 2011).

Another meta-analysis (Hanson & Morton-Bourgon, 2009), reporting on 536 effect sizes from 118 unique samples, including over 45,000 participants from 16 countries, reported the average effect sizes (indexed using Cohen's *d*) for the SVR-20 across a number of outcomes. For sexual recidivism, the SVR-20 total scores yielded an average effect of 0.68 (median = 0.60) based on 10 studies and 1,699 participants, while the final risk judgments yielded an average effect of 1.11 (median = 1.23) across three studies and 245 participants. For general violent recidivism, the SVR-20 total scores yielded an average effect of 0.39 (median = 0.27) based on four studies and 760 participants.

RISK FOR SEXUAL VIOLENCE PROTOCOL

Description and use of tool. The Risk for Sexual Violence Protocol (RSVP; Hart et al., 2003) is another SPJ tool designed for the evaluation of risk for sexual violence. In fact, the RSVP and SVR-20 "may be considered equivalent or parallel forms of the same guidelines" (Hart & Boer, 2010, p. 269). The RSVP, however, places more emphasis on the psychological functioning of the perpetrator and the development of management strategies.

The RSVP defines sexual violence as the "actual, attempted, or threatened sexual contact with another person that is non-consensual" (Hart et al., 2003, p. 2). This tool is meant for use with males aged 18 years or older who have a known or suspected history of sexual violence, but it may also be used with younger males (i.e., 16 or 17) who are beginning to display sexually violent behavior, as with adult females who have a history of sexual violence. Compared to the SVR-20, the RSVP is intended for use primarily by "sex offender specialists in management- and treatment-oriented evaluations" (Hart & Boer, 2010, p. 273). Accordingly, in addition to the general user qualifications, evaluators using the RSVP must have expertise in the assessment and diagnosis of mental disorders.

The RSVP is comprised of 22 risk factors grouped in five domains: five items related to the perpetrator's *history of sexual violence*, five related to *psychological adjustment*, five to *mental disorder*, four to *social adjustment*, and three items related to *manageability*. As with the SVR-20, the evaluator should consider victim vulnerability factors when the future violence is likely to be targeted at a specific potential victim. A unique feature of the RSVP is that the presence of each item is coded both for past (more than one year prior to the evaluation) and recent (within a year of the current evaluation) time frames. The RSVP is meant to assist with decisions concerning the coming months and up to a year, and re-evaluations should also conform to this time frame.

Empirical research. The RSVP has been the subject of a number of empirical investigations. The inter-rater reliability of the RSVP has been investigated in at least four studies (Hart, 2003; Sutherland et al., 2012; Watt, Hart, Wilson, Guy, & Douglas, 2006; Watt & Jackson, 2008). Generally, these studies have found good to excellent inter-rater reliability for the presence-past total score (ICC = 0.95 to 0.99) and scale scores (ICC = 0.75 to 0.98). Similar results were found for the presence-recent total scores (ICC = 0.85 to 0.96) and scale scores (ICC = 0.68 to 0.96), as well as for the relevance ratings at the total score level (ICC = 0.91 to 0.98) and the scale score level (ICC = 0.72 to 0.95). The inter-rater reliability of the conclusory opinions was also excellent for the case prioritization rating (ICC = 0.75), the risk for serious harm rating (ICC = 0.85), and the immediate action required rating (ICC = 0.81). Sutherland and colleagues (2012) conducted a comprehensive analysis of the inter-rater reliability of the RSVP, finding that at the item level inter-rater reliability was generally fair, and the reliability coefficients were higher for the conclusory opinions.

Fewer studies have examined the predictive validity of the RSVP. Kropp (2001), using a sample of 53 offenders in Canada, found that the final risk judgments (i.e., case prioritization) were predictive of sexual recidivism ($r = 0.40$); however, the total scores were not ($r = 0.23$). In addition, Hart and Jackson (2008) investigated the predictive validity of the RSVP in a sample of 90 adult male sex offenders based in Canada. The final risk judgments were found to be predictive of future sexual recidivism ($r = 0.31$). The odds of recidivism were 1.90 times higher in the moderate risk group compared to the low risk group and 9.50 times higher in the high-risk group compared to the low risk group. The final risk judgments were also found to add incrementally to the predictive validity of the numerical total scores.

Decision Support Tools for the Evaluation of Risk for Spousal Violence

SPOUSAL ASSAULT RISK ASSESSMENT GUIDE

Description and use of tool. The Spousal Assault Risk Assessment Guide (SARA; Kropp et al., 1994, 1995, 1999) is one of the first tools developed under the SPJ model. It has been translated into at least 10 different languages and is used internationally on five continents, including at least 15 countries (Kropp & Gibas, 2010). The SARA is meant to assist in evaluations of spousal assault, defined as "any actual, attempted, or threatened physical harm perpetrated by a man or woman against someone with whom he or she has, or has had, an intimate, sexual relationship" (Kropp et al., 1995, p. 1). This is a broad, inclusive definition, including acts that may not result in physical injury, regardless of the legal status or genders of those involved. The SARA is intended for use with individuals aged 18 or over with a known

or suspected history of spousal assault, regardless of gender, sexual orientation, or marital status. It is meant for use in a variety of assessments of spousal assault in criminal justice settings, such as pretrial or pre-sentence assessments and correctional intake or discharge, as well as in civil justice matters and any other instance in which a professional may need to take action because of a concern of imminent risk.

The SARA contains 20 risk factors grouped into four domains: three items related to the *criminal history*, seven related to *psychosocial adjustment*, seven related to the *spousal assault history*, and three related to the *current or most recent incident*. The first two domains (i.e., criminal history, psychosocial adjustment; part 1) are relevant to both general and spousal violence, whereas the last two domains (i.e., spousal assault history, current or most recent incident; part 2) are specific to spousal violence. Eleven of the items are primarily static, whereas the other nine are at least potentially dynamic. As with most other SPJ tools, evaluations are meant to focus on the immediate months ahead, up to one year, and re-evaluations should also conform to this time frame.

Empirical research. To date, at least three studies have examined the inter-rater reliability of the SARA (e.g., Grann & Wedin, 2002; Kropp & Hart, 2000; Mowat-Léger, 2001), and the findings showed support for the inter-rater reliability of SARA total scores (ICC = 0.84 to 0.99), as well as for part 1 (ICC = 0.63 to 0.98) and part 2 (ICC = 0.74 to 0.93) scores. In only one of these studies was the inter-rater reliability of the final risk judgments examined (ICC = 0.63), and those researchers reported item level reliability coefficients (ICC = 0.45 to 0.86; median = 0.65; Kropp & Hart, 2000).

Additionally, researchers in at least 12 studies have reported findings regarding the predictive validity of the SARA (Andrés-Pueyo, López, & Álvarez, 2008; Belfrage et al., 2012; Gibas, Kropp, Hart, & Stewart, 2008; Glackman, 2004; Grann & Wedin, 2002; Heckert & Gondolf, 2004; Hilton, Grant, Rice, Houghton, & Eke, 2008; Kropp, 2003; Kropp & Hart, 2000; Reeves, Kropp, & Cairns, 2008; Williams & Houghton, 2004; Wong & Hisashima, 2008). Helmus and Bourgon (2011) summarized the findings from 11 of these studies (excluding Belfrage et al., 2012, which was published later). Authors in eight of the studies reported on the predictive validity of SARA total scores (N = 2,072), finding an average weighted AUC of 0.63 (AUC = 0.57 to 0.77). Five reported findings regarding the final risk judgments with an average AUC of 0.67 (AUC = 0.56 to 0.87). The results of Belfrage and colleagues (2012) are consistent with these findings (AUC = 0.63 for the total scores; AUC = 0.57 for the final risk judgments). Several researchers have also found the SARA to be predictive of general violence (e.g., Gibas et al., 2008; Glackman, 2004; Wong & Hisashima, 2008). Finally, Messing and Thaller (2013) report results from a meta-analysis of 10 prospective studies that examined the predictive validity of spousal assault risk assessment instruments. They found that the SARA yielded an average AUC of 0.63 (range = 0.59 to 0.65) across six studies (N = 2,656). The SARA yielded the second largest weighted effect size of the five instruments included in the meta-analysis.

BRIEF SPOUSAL ASSAULT FORM FOR THE EVALUATION OF RISK

Description and use of tool. The Brief Spousal Assault Form for the Evaluation of Risk (B-SAFER; Kropp et al., 2005, 2010) is a decision support tool meant to assist in the evaluation of risk for spousal assault. It has been translated into a number of different languages and is used internationally by a number of law enforcement agencies. Spousal assault "also referred to as intimate partner violence, wife assault, spousal violence, and domestic violence—is the actual, attempted, or threatened physical harm of a current or former intimate partner" (Kropp et al., 2010, p. 1). This includes violence in any form of intimate (e.g., romantic, sexual) relationship, "regardless of its legal status or the gender of the people involved" (p. 1). The B-SAFER is intended for use with individuals aged 18 or over with a known or suspected history of spousal assault, regardless of gender, sexual orientation, or marital status. It may also be used with caution with younger people who have a history of intimate partner violence.

Notably, the development of the B-SAFER differed slightly from other SPJ instruments in that it was created out of the SARA for use specifically with law enforcement. As such, in addition to the typical review of the scientific literature, the development of the B-SAFER also involved statistical analysis of the SARA for item redundancy and pilot testing of the SARA and B-SAFER with various police agencies.

The B-SAFER contains 15 factors divided into three domains. The first domain consists of five risk factors related to the perpetrator's *history of intimate partner violence*. The second domain comprises five risk factors related to the perpetrator's *history of psychosocial adjustment*. The third section has five *victim vulnerability factors*, related to the victim's willingness, ability, and opportunity to engage in self-protective behaviors. A unique feature of the B-SAFER when coding the presence of risk factors is the requirement to code the factor both in the past and recent (i.e., the last four weeks) time frames. As with many SPJ instruments, the B-SAFER is meant to assist with decisions concerning the upcoming six months to a year, and formal re-evaluations should take place within this same time frame.

Empirical research. The B-SAFER has relatively less empirical support compared to some other SPJ instruments. According to Storey, Kropp, Hart, Belfrage, and Strand (2013), "at present, the primary evidence supporting the validity of the B-SAFER is indirect, that is, its content was based on a systematic literature review derived from the SARA, which has been empirically validated" (p. 260). The authors go on to state that at least eight examinations of the tool have taken place and "indicate that the B-SAFER can be used to make ratings of individual risk factors and global ratings of risk with good inter-rater reliability, concurrent validity (especially with respect to the SARA), and predictive validity" (p. 260).

In particular, Au and colleagues (2008) found that the B-SAFER was able to correctly differentiate between a group of known spousal assaulters and a control group, with spousal assaulters scoring higher on all scales and ratings. Belfrage and Strand (2012) found that the final risk judgments were predictive of the amount of management strategies implemented by the police, but were not predictive of subsequent violence. This was attributed to the fact that police were only implementing management strategies in the high-risk group; these results may, thus, be interpreted as the effective prevention of violence and may support the utility of the B-SAFER. Additionally, Loinaz (2014), using a sample of 100 spousal assaulters in Spain, found the SARA was predictive of spousal assault (AUC = 0.76). Finally, Storey and colleagues (2013), examining a sample of 249 cases of spousal violence in Sweden found that B-SAFER total scores (AUC = 0.70) and final risk judgments (AUC = 0.65) were predictive of recidivism.

Decision Support Tools for the Evaluation of Risk for Stalking

GUIDELINES FOR STALKING ASSESSMENT AND MANAGEMENT

Description and use of tool. The Guidelines for Stalking Assessment and Management (SAM; Kropp et al., 2008) is an SPJ tool designed to assist in an evaluation for stalking risk—one of the first tools specifically created for this task. Stalking is defined as the "unwanted and repeated communication, contact, or other conduct that deliberately or recklessly causes people to experience reasonable fear or concern for their safety or the safety of others known to them" (p. 1). It is intended for use with individuals aged 18 years or older with a known or suspected history of stalking, regardless of the perpetrator's gender or sexual orientation. It may also be used with caution on younger perpetrators. The tool is most appropriate for stalking cases in which there is a single perpetrator and a single victim, but it can accommodate other stalking situations (e.g., multiple perpetrators, multiple victims). The SAM was developed for use in a variety of settings in which stalking may arise, including law enforcement, forensic settings, correctional settings, and victim-safety planning. It is meant to be used by criminal justice, security, and mental health professionals.

The SAM contains 30 items grouped in three domains. The *nature of stalking* domain consists of 10 items related to the pattern of stalking and this is meant to characterize the severity of the stalking behavior. The *perpetrator risk* factors consist of 10 items concerning the adjustment and background of the perpetrator, which address the perpetrators decision to engage in stalking. The *victim vulnerability* factors consist of 10 items reflecting the adjustment and background of the victim, which are associated with decisions to engage in self-protective behavior. A unique feature of the SAM is the need to determine when the current or most recent pattern of stalking began and separate this current pattern from any previous stalking behavior. Items are then coded both for their current and previous status. That is, current refers to from the beginning of the current pattern of stalking and previous refers to anything prior to this point in time. As with many other SPJ instruments, the SAM is mean to assist with decisions concerning the upcoming six to 12 months, and formal re-evaluations coincide with this time frame.

Empirical research. The SAM underwent "extensive pilot testing in Canada and Sweden in law enforcement and forensic mental health settings" (Storey, Hart, Meloy, & Reavis, 2009, p. 240; see also Kropp et al., 2008). Subsequently, at least three studies have reported on the reliably, predictive validity, and utility of the SAM (e.g., Belfrage & Strand, 2008; Kropp, Hart, Lyon, & Storey, 2011; Storey et al., 2009). Belfrage and Strand (2008) examined 230 stalking assessments using the SAM conducted by law enforcement in Sweden. They found that police officers were able to easily code the SAM, and they also found a positive correlation between the number of risk factors present and the final risk judgments. Overall, they concluded that the SAM is a viable tool for use by law enforcement agencies.

Storey and colleagues (2009) examined the SAM in a sample of 62 male offenders with a history of stalking offenses. They found good to excellent levels of inter-rater reliability for the three scales scores (ICC = 0.77 for nature of stalking; ICC = 0.68 for perpetrator risk factors; ICC = 0.63 for victim vulnerability factors). Concurrent validity was also demonstrated with correlations of all three scales scores, and many individual items, with psychopathic personality traits.

Finally, Kropp and colleagues (2011), using a sample of 109 offenders with a history of stalking related offenses in Canada, found excellent inter-rater reliability for the total scores (ICC= 0.82), but lower reliability coefficients for the scale scores (ICC = 0.77 for nature of stalking; ICC = 0.76 for perpetrator risk factors; ICC = 0.44 for victim vulnerability factors). They also found evidence for concurrent validity, as the SAM total score, scale scores, and final risk judgments were correlated with levels of psychopathy; however, mixed findings were presented between the SAM and the VRAG.

Decision Support Tools for the Evaluation of Imminent Violence

BRØSET VIOLENCE CHECKLIST

Description and use of tool. The Brøset Violence Checklist (BVC; Almvik & Woods, 1998, 1999, 2003; Almvik, Woods, & Rasmussen, 2000; Woods & Almvik, 2002) is an actuarial tool that is currently in widespread use in mental health and other healthcare settings (e.g., Abderhalden et al., 2006, 2008; Björkdahl, Olsson, & Palmstierna, 2006; Clarke, Brown, & Griffith, 2010; Vaaler, Morken, Fløvig, Iversen, & Linaker, 2006; Woods, Ashley, Kayto, & Heusdens, 2008). The BVC is meant to assess risk for imminent violence, typically defined as violence within the upcoming 24-hour period. It is intended to be used with health-care patients in a variety of inpatient settings. Specifically, the BCV is used in acute inpatient mental health settings, but also in geriatric and other health-care settings. Typically, the BVC is administered by health-care professionals (e.g., nurses).

The BVC was developed from the work of Linaker and Busch-Iversen (1995). They examined the nursing records from all patients ($N = 92$) admitted to the Brøset Regional Secure Unit in Trondheim, Norway, between 1988 and 1993. In particular, the authors studied the behaviors that were recorded in the 24-hour period prior to a violent incident on the forensic psychiatric ward. They found 55 different factors were reported in this period. The most common six factors present during the time immediately preceding a violent incident were selected and the combination of these six items was found to be predictive of violent incidents in a logistic regression analysis.

The BVC consists of these six items. Three of the items are characteristics of the patient (*confused, irritable*, and *boisterous*) and three items are patient behaviors (*physically threatening, verbally threatening*, and *attacking objects*). The BVC is meant to be coded by any staff member who has had contact with or observed the patient. The evaluator codes the presence of each of the six items. Each of the items is dichotomous [Yes (1)/No (0)] and the number of items present is totaled. A total score of zero indicates the risk is small; a score of one or two indicates there is moderate or elevated risk and preventative measures may be required; and a score over two indicates the risk is high or urgent and preventative measures should be taken. Evaluations are made regarding the upcoming hours to a maximum of 24 hours, and re-evaluations should occur within this time frame. Generally, re-evaluations should occur whenever shift changes occur.

Empirical research. The BVC has been extensively tested on various acute wards, geriatric wards, and nursing homes in Norway, as well as in various settings internationally (e.g., Woods et al., 2008). A number of disseminations have been published reporting on the BVC (e.g., Abderhalden et al., 2004; Almvik & Woods, 1998, 1999, 2003; Almvik et al., 2000, 2007; Björkdahl et al., 2006; Clarke et al., 2010; Vaaler et al., 2011; van de Sande et al., 2011, 2013; Woods & Almvik, 2002; Woods et al., 2008). Inter-rater reliability has been reported in at least two studies. Abderhalden and colleagues (2004) investigated the reliability of the BVC across four nurses who independently rated 16 cases. They

found reliability coefficients ranged from good to excellent ($r = 0.64$ to $r = 1.00$). Almvik and colleagues (2000) reported the inter-rater reliability across 39 cases finding reliability coefficients ranging from fair to excellent ($\kappa = 0.48$ to $\kappa = 1.00$) for the individual items, as well as fair for the total score ($\kappa = 0.44$).

With regard to predictive validity, Abderhalden and colleagues (2004), using a sample of 219 patients from three psychiatric hospitals in Switzerland, found that the BVC was predictive of violent incidents in the subsequent 12-hour period (AUC = 0.88, OR = 2.3). Almvik and colleagues (2000; see also Almvik & Woods, 1998, 1999, 2003; Woods & Almvik, 2002) found similar results (AUC = 0.82) in a sample of 109 psychiatric inpatients admitted to four psychiatric wards in Norway. As well, Almvik and colleagues (2007), examining 8,835 BVC assessments, found it was predictive of violence in the following 24-hour period (AUC = 0.69), as well as violence occurring on the same shift as the assessment (AUC = 0.92).

Björkdahl and colleagues (2006), using a sample of 73 patients admitted to a psychiatric care unit in Sweden, found that the BVC was predictive of subsequent violence in the following 24-hour period. They reported that a score of one or more on the BVC increased the hazard of a violent incident by 5.99, whereas a score of two or more increased the hazard by 4.35. Of the six items, they also found that four individually increased the hazard of a violent incident (hazard ratios of 3.0 to 6.3). Moreover, Vaaler and colleagues (2011) found the BVC was predictive of violence in the following 72-hour period. In a multivariate analysis, they reported the BVC to be predictive of violent incidents after controlling for segregation and for diagnoses of substance use and schizophrenia.

Several researchers also found that the daily use of the BVC has led to the reduction in seclusion time on the ward (Abderhalden et al. 2006, 2008; Clarke et al., 2010; van de Sande et al., 2011), as well as a reduction in the number of violent incidents on the ward (Abderhalden et al. 2006, 2008; van de Sande et al., 2011, 2013).

DYNAMIC APPRAISAL OF SITUATIONAL AGGRESSION

Description and use of tool. The Dynamic Appraisal of Situational Aggression (DASA; Ogloff & Daffern 2006) is meant to assist in evaluations of risk for imminent aggression in inpatients settings. Imminent aggression is defined as the occurrence of any behavior included on the Overt Aggression Scale (OAS; Yudofsky, Silver, Jackson, Endicott, & Williams, 1986). The OAS categorizes aggressive behaviors into verbal aggression, physical aggression against objects, and physical aggression against other people, with each category containing a number of behaviors arranged by severity. The DASA is intended for use with hospitalized patients with mental illnesses. That is, the primary applications are inpatient psychiatric settings, including both forensic and civil psychiatric settings. It is meant to be used by a qualified health-care professional (e.g., nurse).

The DASA was developed because of a lack of tools for assisting in evaluations for the risk of imminent violence and for the ongoing monitoring of risk for imminent violence. Moreover, the main existing tool, the BVC, lacked a focus on dynamic factors that were amenable to treatment. The DASA was developed empirically by testing items from the BVC and the HCR-20, as well as several novel items drawn from a systematic review of the scientific literature in three secure acute inpatient psychiatric wards in a psychiatric hospital in Australia. All the potential items were assessed over a period of six months. Items were chosen based on combinations that yielded the highest predictive power (i.e., the strength of their ability to predict subsequent violence in this development sample); each item was chosen based on its unique ability to predict aggression and distinguish between those patients who were and were not aggressive.

The DASA is comprised of seven dynamic risk factors: *negative attitudes, impulsivity, irritability, verbal threats, sensitivity to perceived provocation, easily angered when requests are denied,* and *unwillingness to follow directions.* The presence of the seven items is coded dichotomously [Yes (1)/No (0)], and the number of items present is then totaled. A score of zero indicates low risk, a score of one to three indicates moderate risk and suggests that preventative measures should be taken, and a score over three indicates a high risk. DASA assessments should focus on the preceding 24-hour period to rate the items, and predictions should concern the upcoming 24-hour period.

Empirical research. DASA has been the subject of numerous empirical investigations in a number of different countries (e.g., Barry-Walsh, Daffern, Duncan, & Ogloff, 2009; Chu, Hoo, Daffern, & Tan, 2012; Chu, Thomas, Daffern, & Ogloff, 2012; Daffern & Howells, 2007; Daffern et al., 2009; Ogloff & Daffern, 2006; Vojt, Marshall, & Thomson, 2010).

However, no published study to date has reported on the inter-rater reliability of the DASA. With regard to predictive validity, in the development sample (Ogloff & Daffern, 2006), the DASA was predictive of violence in the upcoming 24 hours (AUC = 0.82).

In a sample of high secure forensic psychiatric patients, Daffern and Howells (2007) found that the DASA was predictive of aggression (AUC = 0.65) and self-harm (AUC = 0.67) in the upcoming 24-hour period. Daffern and colleagues (2009) found similar results (AUC = 0.65), in a sample of 51 personality-disordered offenders in England. Griffith, Daffern, and Godber (2013), examining 482 DASA assessments carried out in two inpatient mental health units in Australia, also found the DASA scores were predictive of aggression in the next 24 hours (AUC = 0.71). Moreover, actuarial assessments completed with the DASA were more accurate than unstructured clinical predictions and structured clinical predictions.

Vojt and colleagues (2010) found the DASA was predictive of aggressive incidents (AUC = 0.74), verbal aggression (AUC = 0.71), and physical aggression (AUC = 0.78). Barry-Walsh and colleagues (2009), examining 10,013 DASA assessments, found it was predictive of aggression (AUC = 0.69), with the strongest predictive validity for physical aggression toward staff (AUC = 0.80). Dumais, Larue, Michaud, and Goulet (2012) examined the French version of the DASA in an intensive care psychiatric unit. They found that DASA total scores were predictive of a number of indexes of aggression, including aggression against objects (AUC = 0.66), others (AUC = 0.73), and staff members (AUC = 0.72). Furthermore, Chu, Thomas, and colleagues (2012) examined the performance of 1,054 DASA ratings on 60 forensic psychiatric inpatients. They found that DASA mean scores (for individual patients), peak scores, and most recent ratings were predictive of interpersonal violence, verbal threats, and overall aggression.

Emerging and Other Risk Assessment Tools

Currently, there are a number of additional tools that have not received the same empirical and/or clinical attention as those we have reviewed, but they nevertheless show considerable promise for the future. The following are likely to emerge as reliable and valid tools to assist in the evaluation of risk for various forms of violence:

• The Stalking Risk Profile (SRP; MacKenzie et al., 2009) is an SPJ tool developed to assist in evaluations of risk for stalking;

• The Multi-Level Guidelines (MLG; Cook, Hart, & Kropp, 2013) is an SPJ tool designed to assist in evaluations of risk for group-based violence, defined as "the actual, attempted, or threatened physical injury of other people that is deliberate and nonconsensual, perpetrated by individuals whose decisions and behavior are influenced by a group to which they currently belong or with which they are affiliated" (Cook, 2014, p. 1–2; see also, Cook et al., 2013);

• The Assessment of Risk for Honour Based Violence (PATRIARCH; Kropp, Belfrage, Hart, 2013) is an SPJ tool designed to assist in evaluations for risk of honor-based violence, defined as "the actual, attempted, or threatened physical harm that is motivated, at least in part, by beliefs about honour";

• The Elder Abuse Risk Assessment Guide (EARA; Storey, Hart, & Kropp, 2011) is an SPJ tool designed to assist in evaluations of violence directed toward the elderly.

Critical Considerations
Dynamic Risk and Risk Reduction

As described earlier, one of the core assumptions of the SPJ model is that management strategies should be designed to address changeable risk factors. The basis for this assumption is that if these factors worsen, risk will increase, and if they improve, risk will decrease. Although this assumption has not been evaluated as frequently as has the basic predictive validity of instruments, numerous studies support it. Within the broad mental health and treatment fields, numerous risk-relevant constructs (i.e., anger; stress; psychotic symptoms; substance use problems) have been shown to change over time, either through intervention or spontaneously (see Douglas & Skeem, 2005, for a review). Many studies have tested whether ostensibly dynamic risk factors, or their summation on various risk instruments, predict violence. There are hundreds of studies to support such predictive validity (for reviews, see Douglas, Shaffer, et al., 2014; Douglas & Skeem, 2005). However, most such studies only measure the risk factors or indices once, and hence, while they do test the validity of these risk factors, they do no test whether their dynamic nature (i.e., changes on the risk factors) are associated with violence.

Several studies have tested the basic assumption that the HCR-20 clinical (C) and risk management (R) factors are sensitive to change. Belfrage and Douglas (2002), in a sample of 150 forensic psychiatric patients, reported decreases on several C and R items, as well as their overall item sums, over the course of forensic treatment. Douglas and Belfrage (2001) found that C scale items dropped by an average of three points (out of ten, when summed for research purposes) between admission to and discharge from a psychiatric hospital.

A number of studies have tested whether changes on risk factors predict violence. Michel and colleagues (2013) tested whether changes on the HCR-20 C and R scale items were related to violence. They followed 248 civil and forensic psychiatric patients for two years, re-evaluating the C and R items every four months. They tested whether changes between time periods predicted increases or decreases in violence in the subsequent time period. For six of the ten individual items, change on the item ratings predicted subsequent violence. Violence increased after increases on the risk factors, and decreased after decreases on the risk factors. Similarly, Douglas, Strand, and Belfrage (2011) reported that changes on the HCR-20 C scale scores predicted later changes in violence within a sample of 174 forensic psychiatric inpatients who were re-evaluated every six months across two years.

Wilson, Desmarais, Nicholls, Hart, and Brink (2013) studied whether changes in the HCR-20 and START dynamic factors predicted violence among forensic psychiatric inpatients. To do so, they followed 30 patients for one year, coding the instruments every three months, and measuring violence within these time frames as well. Importantly, the authors held historical factors constant, and observed using event history analysis that fluctuations in the C and R items added incremental validity to the historical factors of the HCR-20 in terms of predicting subsequent violence. The same pattern of findings was reported for the START vulnerability ratings (i.e., risk factors) but not for the START strength ratings. For the HCR-20 C and R ratings, and the START vulnerability ratings, the historical scale of the HCR-20 was no longer a significant contributor to the model once all ratings were included in the model. That is, changes in dynamic factors had incremental validity over historical factors, and contributed the only unique predictive effects when historical factors were controlled.

Blanchard (2013; see also Blanchard & Douglas, 2014) used generalized estimating equations to test whether changes in the C and R scale over six measurement periods, roughly four to six weeks apart, among civil psychiatric patients and offenders were predictive of community violence. He found that fluctuations on the C and R scales predicted later violence, both in terms of any aggression, as well as physical violence. START strength scores predicted decreased physical violence. For every one unit change (increase) on the C scale, there was a 25%–33% increase in the likelihood of violence. For the R scale, there was a 21%–23% increase, and for the START strength scale, there was a 6% decrease.

Several studies have evaluated more specifically the role of changes across treatment vis-à-vis violence. For instance, in a sample of 108 forensic psychiatric patients, de Vries Robbé, de Vogel, Douglas, and Nijman (2014) tested whether changes on the HCR-20 across a period of forensic psychiatric treatment within the hospital, as well as changes on a measure of protective factors (the SAPROF), predicted post-discharge violence. They reported that pre-post changes on the HCR-20 C and R scales, and the SAPROF, were associated with violence up to 11 years post-discharge. Patients who showed decreases on risk factors, and increases on protective factors, controlling for baseline risk (HCR-20 total scores), were less likely to be violent in the community after discharge.

Olver and Wong (2011) similarly reported that pre-post changes on the Violence Risk Scale—Sex Offender (VRS-SO) version were predictive of violence post-release in a sample of sex offenders. In addition, they found that high-risk offenders (as determined by an actuarial measure of risk) who showed greater change on the VRS-SO dynamic factors recidivated at a lower rate than higher-risk offenders who showed less change on the VRS-SO. Lewis, Olver, and Wong (2013) demonstrated a similar finding for high-risk (nonsexual) offenders using the VRS. That is, controlling for baseline risk, pre-post change on the VRS predicted later violent recidivism in that greater reductions on VRS dynamic factors were associated with reduced violent offending post-release.

Belfrage and colleagues (2012) tested whether use of the SARA could reduce rates of violence. Although this study did not evaluate dynamic risk, it tested whether offenders who classified as high risk using SPJ procedures would have lower recidivism if they received high- (versus low) intensity case management. In a Swedish sample of 429 domestic violence cases, police officers completed the SARA for all offenders, providing ratings of low, moderate, and high risk. Belfrage et al. (2012) then coded whether the case management strategies of the police were of high or low intensity. The authors reported that subsequent intimate partner violence among the high-risk group was lower when there was high-intensity case management, compared to when there was low-intensity case management. In low-risk cases, there was actually a higher level of risk when high-intensity management was used.

Taken together, the research reviewed in this section provides support for the position that changes in risk are capable of being captured by SPJ instruments, and that such changes also tend to predict higher or lower violence in the future. Moreover, changes specifically demonstrated within the context of treatment, even when controlling for historical risk, have been linked to changes in future violence. Offenders deemed to be high risk who also receive high-intensity case management have been shown to have lowered recidivism relative to high-risk offenders who receive less-intensive case management.

Future Directions and Research

Despite enormous growth in the risk assessment field over the past two decades, there is more work to do. Specifically, we would urge continued work in terms of (a) linking assessment with treatment and (b) evaluating recent conceptual developments in risk assessment. These research topics are clearly more difficult to tackle compared with traditional (though fundamentally important) predictive validity studies, which could explain why such studies are less common.

In terms of treatment, there is a fairly large literature on "what works" in the reduction of general criminality, and, to a somewhat lesser extent, in a reduction of violence (for review, see Andrews, 2012; Douglas, Nicholls, & Brink, 2009, this volume). Research cited earlier (i.e., Belfrage et al., 2012; Blanchard, 2013; de Vries Robbé et al., 2014; Lewis et al., 2013; Olver & Wong, 2011) has started to bridge the assessment and treatment literature and to demonstrate that use of structured risk assessment protocols can forecast and reduce violence.

Conducting randomized clinical trials in the risk assessment field is close to impossible. Ethically, one cannot assign high-risk individuals to receive no or low supervision, monitoring, or intervention. As such, the field must rely upon evidence of decreased risk and violence as associated with decreases in risk factors and quasi-experimental or correlational studies of treatment programs, both of which support decreased violence achieved through targeting and reduction of dynamic risk factors (as reviewed earlier). Additional research such as that conducted by Belfrage et al. (2012), in which offenders or patients are classified as low, moderate, or high risk through the use of a structured assessment procedure and then are linked with varying levels of intensity of intervention or case management are critically needed.

In addition, studies that test whether treatment intensity moderates predictive validity are needed. In essence, such studies can address the question of whether predictive validity is lowered because of effective use of management. Olver and Wong's (2011) work addresses this to some extent in that the predictive strength of an actuarial instrument was lowered among those who showed the largest reductions on their dynamic risk factors across the course of treatment. Ideally, the field should aim to show that effective intervention can prevent subsequent violence, hence rendering initial assessments of high risk less predictive, because the outcome that was predicted ultimately was prevented.

In terms of conceptual developments, recent approaches to risk assessment have emphasized the importance of tasks such as formulation and scenario planning (Douglas et al., 2013; Douglas, Hart, Groscup & Litwack, 2014; Hart et al., 2003; Hart, Sturmey, Logan, & McMurran, 2011). Formulation is an important clinical task. However, to date, it has rarely been evaluated empirically within the risk assessment field. Researchers should aim to test whether professionals can agree upon formulations and scenarios (i.e., reliability) and also test whether such formulations or scenarios are borne out in any subsequent violence that unfolds. Of course, ethically, such research would have to be done in a quasi-experimental or retrospective follow-up design, most likely by coding past files of offenders or patients. Some initial research shows that professionals are able to come to reasonable agreement about formulations (Wilson et al., 2013).

Finally, there are a host of interesting questions within the risk assessment field that await further exploration. In terms of dynamic risk, it would be of benefit to explore the time frames over which dynamic risk factors change, whether this differs depending on the type of dynamic risk factors, whether such change is linear or nonlinear, and the extent to which change is affected by or interacts with situational or contextual variables. Evaluating how dynamic risk factors might influence or interact with each other will also be important. Finally, testing the extent to which dynamic risk factors, and risk assessment instruments more broadly, might be influenced by indices of diversity such as gender and ethnicity requires further work.

Despite these areas for future growth, the field is far more advanced than it was two decades ago.

Clinicians in a variety of settings have well validated the risk assessment measures at their disposal—there really is no convincing reason not to use such instruments, as they have been shown to increase the ability to identify who poses greater or lesser risk. Further, although there is more work to do, converging lines of evidence also indicate that such instruments can be used to track changes in risk over time, and that the use of such instruments can reduce violence.

Note

1. Cicchetti and Sparrow (1981; see also Cicchetti, 2001), referring to kappa, weighted kappa, and ICC values, defined reliability indices below 0.40 as poor, 0.40 to 0.59 as fair, 0.60 to 0.74 as good, and above 0.75 as excellent. These categories are fairly consistent with those proposed by Landis and Koch (1977), defining coefficients below 0.00 as poor, 0.00 to 0.20 as slight, 0.21 to 0.40 as fair, 0.41 to 0.60 as moderate, 0.61 to 0.80 as substantial, and 0.81 to 1.00 as almost perfect.

References

Abderhalden, C., Needham, I., Dassen, T., Halfens, R., Haug, H. J., & Fischer, J. (2006). Predicting inpatient violence using an extended version of the Brøset-Violence-Checklist: Instrument development and clinical application. *BMC Psychiatry, 6*, 17–25. doi:10.1186/1471-244X-6-17

Abderhalden, C., Needham, I., Dassen, T., Halfens, R., Haug, H. J., & Fischer, J. E. (2008). Structured risk assessment and violence in acute psychiatric wards: Randomised controlled trial. *The British Journal of Psychiatry, 193*, 44–50. doi:10.1192/bjp.bp.107.045534

Abderhalden, C., Needham, I., Miserez, B., Almvik, R., Dassen, T., Haug, H. J., & Fischer, J. E. (2004). Predicting inpatient violence in acute psychiatric wards using the Brøset-Violence-Checklist: A multicentre prospective cohort study. *Journal of Psychiatric and Mental Health Nursing, 11*, 422–427. doi:10.1111/j.1365-2850.2004.00733.x

Abidin, Z., Davoren, M., Naughton, L., Gibbons, O., Nulty, A., & Kennedy, H. G. (2013). Susceptibility (risk and protective) factors for in-patient violence and self-harm: Prospective study of structured professional judgement instruments START and SAPROF, DUNDRUM-3, and DUNDRUM-4 in forensic mental health services. *BMC Psychiatry, 13*, 197–214. doi:10.1186/1471-244X-13-197

Addington v. Texas, 441 U.S. 418 (1979).

Almvik, R., & Woods, P. (1998). The Brøset Violence Checklist (BVC) and the prediction of inpatient violence: Some preliminary results. *Psychiatric Care, 5*(6), 208–211.

Almvik, R., & Woods, P. (1999). Predicting inpatient violence using the Brøset Violence Checklist (BVC). *International Journal of Psychiatric Nursing Research, 4*(3), 498–505.

Almvik, R., & Woods, P. (2003). Short-term risk prediction: The Brøset Violence Checklist—Research in Brief. *Journal of Psychiatric and Mental Health Nursing, 10*(2), 236–238. doi:10.1046/j.1365-2850.2003.00563.x

Almvik, R., Woods, P., & Rasmussen, K. (2000). The Brøset Violence Checklist (BVC): Sensitivity, specificity and interrater reliability. *Journal of Interpersonal Violence, 15*, 1284–1296. doi:10.1177/088626000015012003

Almvik, R., Woods, P., & Rasmussen, K. (2007). Assessing risk for imminent violence in the elderly: The Brøset Violence Checklist. *International Journal of Geriatric Psychiatry, 22*, 862–867. doi:10.1002/gps.1753

Andrés-Pueyo, A., López, S., & Álvarez, E. (2008). Valoración del riesgo de violencia contra la pareja por medio de la SARA. [Assessment of the risk of intimate partner violence and the SARA.] *Papeles del Psicólogo, 29*, 107–122. Retrieved from http://www.papelesdelpsicologo.es/english/1543.pdf

Andrews, D. A. (2012). The risk-need-responsivity (RNR) model of correctional assessment and treatment. In J. A. Dvoskin, J. L. Skeem, R. W. Novaco, & K. S. Douglas (Eds.), *Using social science to reduce violent offending* (pp. 127–156). New York, NY: Oxford University Press.

Andrews, D. A., Bonta, J., & Wormith, S. J. (2006). The recent past and near future of risk and/or need assessment. *Crime & Delinquency, 52*, 7–27. doi:10.1177/0011128705281756

Arbach-Lucioni, K., Andres-Pueyo, A., Pomarol-Clotet, E., & Gomar-Sones, J. (2011). Predicting violence in psychiatric in-patients: A prospective study with the HCR-20 violence risk assessment scheme. *Journal of Forensic Psychiatry & Psychology, 22*, 203–222. doi:10.1080/14789949.2010.530290

Au, A., Cheung, G., Kropp, R., Yuk-Chung, C., Lam, G. L., & Sung, P. (2008). A preliminary validation of the Brief Spousal Assault Form for the Evaluation of Risk (B-SAFER) in Hong Kong. *Journal of Family Violence, 23*, 727–735. doi:10.1007/s10896-008-9198-z

Barbaree, H. E., Langton, C. M., Blanchard, R., & Boer, D. P. (2008). Predicting recidivism in sex offenders using the SVR-20: The contribution of age-at-release. *International Journal of Forensic Mental Health, 7*(1), 47–64. doi:10.1080/14999013.2008.9914403

Barefoot v. Estelle, 463 U.S. 880 (1983).

Barry-Walsh, J., Daffern, M., Duncan, S., & Ogloff, J. (2009). The prediction of imminent aggression in patients with mental illness and/or intellectual disability using the Dynamic Appraisal of Situational Aggression instrument. *Australasian Psychiatry, 17*(6), 493–496. doi:10.1080/10398560903289975

Baxstrom v. Herald, 383 U.S. 107 (1966).

Belfrage, H., & Douglas, K. S. (2002). Treatment effects on forensic psychiatric patients measured with the HCR-20 violence risk assessment scheme. *International Journal of Forensic Mental Health, 1*, 25–36. doi:10.1080/14999013.2002.10471158

Belfrage, H., Fransson, R., & Strand, S. (2000). Prediction of violence using the HCR-20: A prospective study in two maximum-security correctional institutions. *The Journal of Forensic Psychiatry, 11*, 167–175. doi:10.1080/095851800362445

Belfrage, H., & Strand, S. (2008). Structured spousal violence risk assessment: Combining risk factors and victim vulnerability factors. *International Journal of Forensic Mental Health, 7*(1), 39–46. doi:10.1080/14999013.2008.9914402

Belfrage, H., & Strand, S. (2012). Measuring the outcome of structured spousal violence risk assessments using the B-SAFER: Risk in relation to recidivism and intervention. *Behavioral Sciences & the Law, 30*, 420–430. doi:10.1002/bsl.2019

Belfrage, H., Strand, S., Storey, J. E., Gibas, A. L., Kropp, P. R., & Hart, S. D. (2012). Assessment and management of risk for intimate partner violence by police officers using the Spousal Assault Risk Assessment Guide. *Law and Human Behavior, 36*, 60–67. doi:10.1007/s10979-011-9278-0

Björkdahl, A., Olsson, D., & Palmstierna, T. (2006). Nurses' short-term prediction of violence in acute psychiatric intensive care. *Acta Psychiatrica Scandinavica, 113*(3), 224–229. doi:10.1111/j.1600-0447.2005.00679.x

Blair, P. R., Marcus, D. K., & Boccaccini, M. T. (2008). Is there an allegiance effect for assessment instruments? Actuarial risk assessment as an exemplar. *Clinical Psychology: Science and Practice, 15*, 346–360. doi:10.1111/j.1468-2850.2008.00147.x

Blanchard, A. J. E. (2013). *Dynamic risk factors in violence risk assessment: A multiple time-point evaluation of the HCR-20 and START* (Unpublished master's thesis, Simon Fraser University, Burnaby, BC, Canada). Retrieved from http://summit.sfu.ca/item/13752

Blanchard, A. J. E., & Douglas, K. S. (2014, March). *Dynamic risk: A prospective repeated measures examination of the HCR-20 and START.* Paper presented at the annual convention of the American Psychology-Law Society, New Orleans, LA.

Boer, D. P., Hart, S. D., Kropp, P. R., & Webster, C. D. (1997). *Manual for the Sexual Violence Risk-20 (SVR-20): Professional guidelines for assessing risk of sexual violence.* Vancouver, BC, Canada: BC Institute Against Family Violence and the Mental Health, Law, and Policy Institute, Simon Fraser University.

Borum, R. (1996). Improving the clinical practice of violence risk assessment: Technology, guidelines, and training. *American Psychologist, 51*, 945–956. doi:10.1037//0003-066x.51.9.945

Braithwaite, E., Charette, Y., Crocker, A. G., & Reyes, A. (2010). The predictive validity of clinical ratings of the Short-Term Assessment of Risk and Treatability (START). *International Journal of Forensic Mental Health, 9*(4), 271–281. doi:10.1080/14999013.2010.534378

Buchanan, A. (1999). Risk and dangerousness. *Psychological Medicine, 29*, 465–473. doi:10.1017/s0033291798008101

Campbell, J. C., Glass, N., Sharps, P. W., Laughon, K., & Bloom, T. (2007). Intimate partner homicide review and implications of research and policy. *Trauma, Violence & Abuse, 8*, 246–269. doi:10.1177/1524838007303505

Campbell, M. A., French, S., & Gendreau, P. (2009). The prediction of violence in adult offenders: A meta-analytic comparison of instruments and methods of assessment. *Criminal Justice and Behavior, 36*, 567–590. doi:10.1177/0093854809333610

Chu, C. M., Hoo, E., Daffern, M., & Tan, J. (2012). Assessing the risk of imminent aggression in institutionalized youth offenders using the dynamic appraisal of situational aggression. *Journal of Forensic Psychiatry & Psychology, 23*, 168–183. doi:10.1080/14789949.2012.668207

Chu, C. M., Thomas, S. D. M., Daffern, M., & Ogloff, J. R. P. (2012). Should clinicians use average or peak scores on a dynamic risk-assessment measure to most accurately predict inpatient aggression? *International Journal of Mental Health Nursing, 22*, 493–499. doi:10.1111/j.1447-0349.2012.00846.x

Chu, C. M., Thomas, S. D. M., Ogloff, J. R. P., & Daffern, M. (2011). The predictive validity of the Short-Term Assessment of Risk and Treatability (START) in a secure forensic hospital: Risk factors and strengths. *International Journal of Forensic Mental Health, 10*(4), 337–345. doi:10.1080/14999013.2011.629715

Cicchetti, D. V. (2001). The precision of reliability and validity estimates re-visited: Distinguishing between clinical and statistical significance of sample size requirements. *Journal of Clinical and Experimental Neuropsychology, 23*(5), 695–700. doi:10.1076/jcen.23.5.695.1249

Cicchetti, D. V., & Sparrow, S. A. (1981). Developing criteria for establishing interrater reliability of specific items: Applications to assessment of adaptive behavior. *American Journal of Mental Deficiency, 86*, 127–137. Retrieved from http://psycnet.apa.org/psycinfo/1982-00095-001

Clarke, D. E., Brown, A. M., & Griffith, P. (2010). The Brøset Violence Checklist: Clinical utility in a secure psychiatric intensive care setting. *Journal of Psychiatric and Mental Health Nursing, 17*, 614–620. doi:10.1111/j.1365-2850.2010.01558.x

Cook, A. N. (2014). *Risk assessment and management of group-based violence* (Unpublished doctoral dissertation, Simon Fraser University, Burnaby, BC, Canada). Retrieved from http://summit.sfu.ca/item/14289

Cook, A. N., Hart, S. D., & Kropp, P. R. (2013). *Multi-Level Guidelines (MLG) for the assessment and management of group-based violence: User manual*. Burnaby, BC, Canada: Mental Health, Law, and Policy Institute, Simon Fraser University.

Cooke, D. J., & Michie, C. (2010). Limitations of diagnostic precision and predictive utility in the individual case: A challenge for forensic practice. *Law and Human Behavior, 34*, 259–274. doi:10.1007/s10979-009-9176-x

Craig, L. A., Browne, K. D., Beech, A., & Stringer, I. A. N. (2006). Differences in personality and risk characteristics in sex, violent, and general offenders. *Criminal Behaviour and Mental Health, 16*, 183–194. doi:10.1002/cbm.618

Daffern, M., & Howells, K. (2007). The prediction of imminent aggression and self-harm in personality disordered patients of a high security hospital using the HCR-20 Clinical Scale and the Dynamic Appraisal of Situational Aggression. *International Journal of Forensic Mental Health, 6*(2), 137–143. doi:10.1080/14999013.2007.10471258

Daffern, M., Howells, K., Hamilton, L., Mannion, A., Howard, R., & Lilly, M. (2009). The impact of structured risk assessments followed by management recommendations on aggression in patients with personality disorder. *The Journal of Forensic Psychiatry & Psychology, 20*, 661–679. doi:10.1080/14789940903173990

Davis, M. R., & Ogloff, J. R. (2008). Key considerations and problems in assessing risk for violence. In D. V. Canter & R. Zukauskiene (Eds.), *Psychology and law: Bridging the gap* (pp. 191–210). Aldershot, UK: Ashgate.

de Vogel, V., & de Ruiter, C. (2006). Structured professional judgment of violence risk in forensic clinical practice: A prospective study into the predictive validity of the Dutch HCR-20. *Psychology, Crime & Law, 12*, 321–336. doi:10.1080/10683160600569029

de Vogel, V., de Ruiter, C., Bouman, Y., & de Vries Robbé, M. (2012). *SAPROF: Structured Assessment of PROtective Factors for violence risk: Guidelines for the assessment of protective factors for violence risk* (2nd ed.). Utrecht, The Netherlands: Forum Educatief.

de Vogel, V., de Ruiter, C., van Beek, D., & Mead, G. (2004). Predictive validity of the SVR-20 and Static-99 in a Dutch sample of treated sex offenders. *Law and Human Behavior, 28*, 235–251. doi:10.1023/b:lahu.0000029137.41974.eb

de Vries Robbé, M., de Vogel, V. D., & Douglas, K. S. (2013). Risk factors and protective factors: A two-sided dynamic approach to violence risk assessment. *Journal of Forensic Psychiatry & Psychology, 24*, 440–457. doi:10.1080/14789949.2013.818162

de Vries Robbé, M., de Vogel, V., & de Spa, E. (2011). Protective factors for violence risk in forensic psychiatric patients: A retrospective validation study of the SAPROF. *International Journal of Forensic Mental Health, 10*, 178–186. doi:10.1080/14999013.2011.600232

de Vries Robbé, M., de Vogel, V., Douglas, K. S., & Nijman, H. L. I. (2014). Changes in dynamic risk and protective factors for violence during inpatient forensic psychiatric treatment: Predicting reductions in post-discharge community recidivism. *Law and Human Behavior*. Advance online publication. doi:10.1037/lhb0000089

Dempster, R. J. (1998). *Prediction of sexually violent recidivism: A comparison of risk assessment instruments* (Unpublished master's thesis, Simon Fraser University, Burnaby, BC, Canada).

Desmarais, S. L., Nicholls, T. L., Wilson, C. M., & Brink, J. (2012). Using dynamic risk and protective factors to predict inpatient aggression: Reliability and validity of START assessments. *Psychological Assessment, 24*, 685–700. doi:10.1037/a0026668

Douglas, K. S., & Belfrage, H. (2001). Use of the HCR-20 in violence risk management: Implementation and clinical practice. In K. S. Douglas, C. D. Webster, S. D. Hart, D. Eaves, & J. R. P. Ogloff, (Eds.), *HCR-20: Violence risk management companion guide* (pp. 41–58). Burnaby, BC, Canada: Mental Health, Law, and Policy Institute, Simon Fraser University, and Department of Mental Health Law & Policy, University of South Florida.

Douglas, K. S., Cox, D. N., & Webster, C. D. (1999). Violence risk assessment: Science and practice. *Legal and Criminological Psychology, 4*, 149–184. doi:10.1348/135532599167824

Douglas, K. S., Hart, S. D., Groscup, J. L., & Litwack, T. R. (2014). Assessing violence risk. In I. Weiner & R. K. Otto (Eds.), *The handbook of forensic psychology* (4th ed.). Hoboken, NJ: Wiley.

Douglas, K. S., Hart, S. D., Webster, C. D., & Belfrage, H. (2013). *HCR-20^V3: Assessing risk for violence: User guide*. Burnaby, BC, Canada: Mental Health, Law, & Policy Institute, Simon Fraser University.

Douglas, K. S., & Kropp, P. R. (2002). A prevention-based paradigm for violence risk assessment clinical and research applications. *Criminal Justice and Behavior, 29*, 617–658. doi:10.1177/009385402236735

Douglas, K. S., Nicholls, T. L., & Brink, J. (2009). Reducing the risk of violence among persons with mental illness: A critical analysis of treatment approaches. In P. M. Kleespies (Ed.), *Behavioral emergencies: An evidence-based resource for evaluating and managing risk of suicide, violence, and victimization* (pp. 351–376). Washington, DC: American Psychological Association.

Douglas, K. S., Ogloff, J. R., & Hart, S. D. (2003). Evaluation of a model of violence risk assessment among forensic psychiatric patients. *Psychiatric Services, 54*, 1372–1379. doi:10.1176/appi.ps.54.10.1372

Douglas, K. S., & Reeves, K. (2010). The HCR-20 violence risk assessment scheme: Overview and review of the research. In R. Otto & K. S. Douglas (Eds.), *Handbook of violence risk assessment* (pp. 147–185). Oxford, UK: Routledge/Taylor & Francis.

Douglas, K. S., Shaffer, C., Blanchard, A., Guy, L. S., Reeves, K., & Weir, J. (2014). *HCR-20 violence risk assessment scheme: Overview and annotated bibliography*. HCR-20 Violence Risk Assessment White Paper Series, # 1. Mental Health, Law, & Policy Institute, Simon Fraser University, Burnaby, BC, Canada.

Douglas, K., S., & Skeem, J. L. (2005). Violence risk assessment: Getting specific about being dynamic. *Psychology, Public Policy, and Law, 11*, 347–383. doi:10.1037/1076-8971.11.3.347

Douglas, K. S., Strand, S., & Belfrage, H. (2011, June). *Dynamic risk: Evaluating the nature and predictive validity of change on the clinical and risk management scales of* the HCR-20. Paper presented at the annual meeting of the International Association of Forensic Mental Health Services, Barcelona, Spain.

Douglas, K. S., & Webster, C. D. (1999). The HCR-20 violence risk assessment scheme concurrent validity in a sample of incarcerated offenders. *Criminal Justice and Behavior, 26*, 3–19. doi:10.1177/0093854899026001001

Douglas, K. S., Yeomans, M., & Boer, D. P. (2005). Comparative validity analysis of multiple measures of violence risk in a sample of criminal offenders. *Criminal Justice and Behavior, 32*, 479–510. doi:10.1177/0093854805278411

Doyle, M., & Dolan, M. (2002). Violence risk assessment: Combining actuarial and clinical information to structure clinical judgments for the formulation and management of risk. *Journal of Psychiatric and Mental Health Nursing, 9*, 649–657. doi:10.1046/j.1365-2850.2002.00535.x

Dumais, A., Larue, C., Michaud, C., & Goulet, M. H. (2012). Predictive validity and psychiatric nursing staff's perception of the clinical usefulness of the French version of the Dynamic Appraisal of Situational Aggression. *Issues in Mental Health Nursing, 33*, 670–675. doi:10.3109/01612840.2012.697254

Enebrink, P., Långström, N., & Gumpert, C. H. (2006). Predicting aggressive and disruptive behavior in referred 6-to 12-year-old boys: Prospective validation of the EARL-20B Risk/Needs Checklist. *Assessment, 13*, 356–367. doi:10.1177/1073191106290649

Ennis, B. J., & Litwack, T. R. (1974). Psychiatry and the presumption of expertise: Flipping coins in the courtroom. *California Law Review, 62*, 693–752. doi:10.2307/3479746

Fazel, S., Singh, J. P., Doll, H., & Grann, M. (2012). Use of risk assessment instruments to predict violence and antisocial behaviour in 73 samples involving 24,827 people: Systematic review and meta-analysis. *BMJ: British Medical Journal, 345*(7868), 1–12. doi:10.1136/bmj.e4692

Gibas, A. L., Kropp, P. R., Hart, S. D., & Stewart, L. (2008, July). *Validity of the SARA in a Canadian sample of incarcerated adult males*. Paper presented at the annual meeting of the International Association of Forensic Mental Health Services, Vienna, Austria.

Glackman, W. (2004). *Spousal Assault Risk Assessment (SARA) follow-up study: Overall rating and reoffence* (Unpublished report). Victoria, BC, Canada: Ministry of Public Safety and the Solicitor General.

Grann, M., & Wedin, M. (2002). Risk factors for recidivism among spousal assault and spousal homicide offenders. *Psychology, Crime & Law, 8*, 5–23. doi:10683160208401806

Gray, N. S., Benson, R., Craig, R., Davies, H., Fitzgerald, S., Huckle, P., ... Snowden, R. J. (2011). The Short-Term Assessment of Risk and Treatability (START): A prospective study of inpatient behavior. *International Journal of Forensic Mental Health, 10*(4), 305–313. doi:10.1080/14999013.2011.631692

Griffith, J. J., Daffern, M., & Godber, T. (2013). Examination of the predictive validity of the Dynamic Appraisal of Situational Aggression in two mental health units. *International Journal of Mental Health Nursing, 22*, 485–492. doi:10.1111/inm.12011

Grove, W. M., & Meehl, P. E. (1996). Comparative efficiency of informal (subjective, impressionistic) and formal (mechanical, algorithmic) prediction procedures: The clinical-statistical controversy. *Psychology, Public Policy, and Law, 2*, 293–323. doi:10.1037//1076-8971.2.2.293

Grubin, D. (1997). Predictors of risk in serious sex offenders. *British Journal of Psychiatry, 170*, s17–s21. Retrieved from http://psycnet.apa.org/psycinfo/1997-06199-004

Guy, L. S. (2008). *Performance indicators of the structured professional judgment approach for assessing risk for violence to others: A meta-analytic survey* (Unpublished doctoral dissertation, Simon Fraser University, Burnaby, BC, Canada). Retrieved from http://summit.sfu.ca/item/9247

Hájek, A., & Hall, N. (2002) Induction and probability. In P. Machamer & M. Silberstein (Eds.), *The Blackwell Guide to the philosophy of science* (pp. 149–172). Oxford, UK: Blackwell.

Hanson, R. K. (1997). How to know what works with sexual offenders. *Sexual Abuse: A Journal of Research and Treatment, 9*, 129–145. doi:10.1007/bf02674863

Hanson, R. K. (1998). What do we know about sex offender risk assessment? *Psychology, Public Policy, and Law, 4*, 50–72. doi:10.1037//1076-8971.4.1-2.50

Hanson, R. K. (2009). The psychological assessment of risk for crime and violence. *Canadian Psychology/Psychologie Canadienne, 50*, 172–182. doi:10.1037/a0015726

Hanson, R. K., & Morton-Bourgon, K. E. (2009). The accuracy of recidivism risk assessments for sexual offenders: A meta-analysis of 118 prediction studies. *Psychological Assessment, 21*, 1–21. doi:10.1037/a0014421

Hanson, R. K., & Thornton, D. (1999). Static-99: Improving actuarial risk assessments for sex offenders. User Report 99-02. Ottawa, ON, Canada: Department of the Solicitor General of Canada.

Harris, G. T., Rice, M. E., & Quinsey, V. L. (1993). Violent recidivism of mentally disordered offenders the development of a statistical prediction instrument. *Criminal Justice & Behavior, 20*, 315–335. doi:10.1177/0093854893020004001

Hart, S. D. (1998). The role of psychopathy in assessing risk for violence: Conceptual and methodological issues. *Legal and Criminological Psychology, 3*, 121–137. doi:10.1111/j.2044-8333.1998.tb00354.x

Hart, S. D. (2001). Assessing and managing violence risk. In K. S. Douglas, C. D. Webster, S. D. Hart, D. Eaves, & J. R. P. Ogloff (Eds.), *HCR-20 violence risk management companion guide* (pp. 13–25). Burnaby, BC, Canada: Mental Health, Law, & Policy Institute, Simon Fraser University, and Department of Mental Health Law and Policy, Florida Mental Health Institute, University of South Florida.

Hart, S. D. (2003, April). *Assessing risk for sexual violence: The Risk for Sexual Violence Protocol (RSVP)*. Paper presented at the annual meeting of the International Association of Forensic Mental Health Services, Vienna, Austria.

Hart, S. D. (2009). Evidence-based assessment of risk for sexual violence. *Chapman Journal of Criminal Justice, 1*, 143–165. Retrieved from http://heinonline.org/HOL/Page?handle=hein.journals/chapcj1&div=12&g_sent=1&collection=journals

Hart, S. D., & Boer, D. P. (2010). Structured professional judgment guidelines for sexual violence risk assessment: The Sexual Violence Risk-20 (SVR-20) and Risk for Sexual Violence Protocol (RSVP). In R. K. Otto & K. S. Douglas (Eds.), *Handbook of violence risk assessment* (pp. 269–294). New York, NY: Routledge/Taylor & Francis.

Hart, S. D., & Jackson, K. (2008, July). *The predictive validity of the Risk for Sexual Violence Protocol (RSVP)*. Paper presented at the annual meeting of the International Association of Forensic Mental Health Services, Vienna, Austria.

Hart, S. D., Kropp, P. R., Laws, D. R., Klaver, J., Logan, C., & Watt, K. A. (2003). *The Risk for Sexual Violence Protocol (RSVP): Structured professional guidelines for assessing risk of sexual violence*. Burnaby, BC, Canada: Mental Health, Law, and Policy Institute, Simon Fraser University.

Hart, S. D., & Logan, C. (2011). Formulation of violence risk using evidence-based assessments: The structured professional judgment approach. In P. Sturmey & M. McMurran (Eds.), *Forensic case formulation.* (pp. 212–243). Chichester, UK: Wiley-Blackwell.

Hart, S. D., Michie, C., & Cooke, D. J. (2007). Precision of actuarial risk assessment instruments: Evaluating the margins of error of group v. individual predictions of violence. *The British Journal of Psychiatry, 190*, s60–s65. doi:10.1192/bjp.190.5.s60

Hart, S., Sturmey, P., Logan, C., & McMurran, M. (2011). Forensic case formulation. *International Journal of Forensic Mental Health, 10*, 118–126. doi:10.1080/14999013.2011.577137

Heckert, D. A., & Gondolf, E. W. (2004). Battered women's perceptions of risk versus risk factors and instruments in predicting repeat reassault. *Journal of Interpersonal Violence, 19*, 778–800. doi:10.1177/0886260504265619

Heilbrun, K. (1997). Prediction versus management models relevant to risk assessment: The importance of legal decision-making context. *Law and Human Behavior, 21*, 347–359. doi:10.1023/a:1024851017947

Heilbrun, K., Yashuhara, K., & Shah, S. (2010). Violence risk assessment tools. In R. Otto & K. Douglas (Eds.), *Handbook of violence risk assessment* (pp. 1–17). New York, NY: Routledge/Taylor & Francis.

Helmus, L., & Bourgon, G. (2011). Taking stock of 15 years of research on the Spousal Assault Risk Assessment Guide (SARA): A critical review. *International Journal of Forensic Mental Health, 10*, 64–75. doi:10.1080/14999013.2010.551709

Hildebrand, M., De Ruiter, C., & de Vogel, V. (2004). Psychopathy and sexual deviance in treated rapists: Association with sexual and nonsexual recidivism. *Sexual Abuse: A Journal of Research and Treatment, 16*, 1–24. doi:10.1177/107906320401600101

Hill, A., Habermann, N., Klusman, D., Berner, W., & Briken, P. (2008). Criminal recidivism in sexual homicide perpetrators. *International Journal of Offender Therapy and Comparative Criminology, 82*, 5–20. doi:10.1177/0306624x07307450

Hilton, N. Z., Grant, T. H., Rice, M. E., Houghton, R. E., & Eke, A. W. (2008). An in depth actuarial assessment for wife assault recidivism: The Domestic Violence Risk Appraisal Guide. *Law and Human Behavior, 32*, 150–163. doi:10.1007/s10979-007-9088-6

Kansas v. Hendricks, 117 S. Ct. 2072 (1997).

Kemshall, H. (1996). Offender risk and probation practice. In H. Kemshall & J. Pritchard (Eds.), *Good practice in risk assessment* (pp. 133–145). London, UK: Jessica Kingsley.

Kozol, H. L., Boucher, R. J., & Garofalo, R. F. (1972). The diagnosis and treatment of dangerousness. *Crime & Delinquency, 19*, 371–392. doi:10.1177/001112877201800407

Kroner, D. G., Mills, J. F., & Reddon, J. R. (2005). A coffee can, factor analysis, and prediction of antisocial behavior: The structure of criminal risk. *International Journal of Law and Psychiatry, 28*, 360–374. doi:10.1016/j.ijlp.2004.01.011

Kropp, P. R. (2001, April). *The Risk for Sexual Violence Protocol (RSVP).* Paper presented at the first annual meeting of the International Association of Forensic Mental Health Services, Vancouver, BC, Canada.

Kropp, P. R. (2003, April). *Validity of law enforcement officers evaluations of risk.* Paper presented at the annual meeting of the International Association of Forensic Mental Health Services, Miami, Florida.

Kropp, P. R., & Gibas, A. (2010). The Spousal Assault Risk Assessment Guide (SARA). In R. K. Otto & K. S. Douglas (Eds.), *Handbook of violence risk assessment* (pp. 227–250). New York, NY: Routledge/Taylor & Francis.

Kropp, P. R., & Hart, S. D. (2000). The Spousal Assault Risk Assessment (SARA) Guide: Reliability and validity in adult male offenders. *Law and Human Behavior, 24*, 101–118. doi:10.1023/a:1005430904495

Kropp, P. R., Belfrage, H., & Hart, S. D. (2013). *Assessment of risk for honour based violence (PATRIARCH): User manual.* Vancouver, BC, Canada; ProActive ReSolutions.

Kropp, P. R., Hart, S. D., & Belfrage, H. (2005). *Brief Spousal Assault Form for the Evaluation of Risk (B-SAFER): User manual.* Vancouver, BC, Canada: ProActive ReSolutions.

Kropp, P. R., Hart, S. D., & Belfrage, H. (2010). *Brief Spousal Assault Form for the Evaluation of Risk (B-SAFER), Version 2: User manual.* Vancouver, BC, Canada: ProActive ReSolutions.

Kropp, P. R., Hart, S. D., & Lyon, D. R. (2008). *Guidelines for Stalking Assessment and Management (SAM): User manual.* Vancouver, BC, Canada: ProActive ReSolutions.

Kropp, P. R., Hart, S. D., Lyon, D. R., & Storey, J. E. (2011). The development and validation of the guidelines for stalking assessment and management. *Behavioral Sciences & the Law, 29*, 302–316. doi:10.1002/bsl.978

Kropp, P. R., Hart, S. D, Webster, C. D., & Eaves, D. (1994). *Manual for the Spousal Assault Risk Assessment Guide.* Vancouver, BC, Canada: The British Columbia Institute Against Family Violence.

Kropp, P. R., Hart, S. D., Webster, C. D., & Eaves, D. (1995). *Manual for the Spousal Assault Risk Assessment Guide* (2nd ed.). Vancouver, BC, Canada: The British Columbia Institute Against Family Violence.

Kropp, P. R., Hart, S. D., Webster, C. D., & Eaves, D. (1999). *Spousal Assault Risk Assessment: User's guide.* Toronto, ON, Canada: Multi-Health Systems.

Landis, J. R., & Koch, G. G. (1977). The measurement of observer agreement for categorical data. *Biometrics, 33*, 159–174. doi:10.2307/2529310

Lewis, K., Olver, M. E., & Wong, S. C. P. (2013). The Violence Risk Scale: Predictive validity and linking changes in risk with violent recidivism in a sample of high-risk offenders with psychopathic traits. *Assessment, 20*, 150–164. doi:10.1177/1073191112441242

Lidz, C., Mulvey, E., & Gardner, W. (1993). The accuracy of predictions of violence to others. *JAMA, 269*, 1007–1011. doi:10.1001/jama.269.8.1007

Linaker, O. M., & Busch-Iversen, H. (1995). Predictors of imminent violence in psychiatric inpatients. *Acta Psychiatrica Scandinavica, 92*(4), 250–254. doi:10.1111/j.1600-0447.1995.tb09578.x

Litwack, T. R. (1996). "Dangerous" patients: A survey of one forensic facility and review of the issue. *Aggression and Violent Behavior, 1*, 97–122. http://dx.doi.org/10.1016/1359-1789(95)00008-9

Litwack, T. R. (2001). Actuarial versus clinical assessments of dangerousness. *Psychology, Public Policy, and Law, 7*, 409–443. doi:10.1037//1076-8971.7.2.409

Loinaz, I. (2014). Typologies, risk, and recidivism in partner-violent men with the B-SAFER: A pilot study. *Psychology, Crime & Law, 20*, 183–198. doi:10.1080/1068316x.2013.770854

MacKenzie, R., McEwan, T., Pathe, M., James, D., Ogloff, J., & Mullen, P. (2009). *Stalking risk profile: Guidelines for the assessment and management of stalkers.* Melbourne, Australia: StalkInc and the Centre for Forensic Behavioural Science, Monash University.

Maden, T. (2007). *Treating violence: A guide to risk management in mental health*. New York, NY: Oxford University Press.

McDermott, B. E., Quanbeck, C. D., Busse, D., Yastro, K., & Scott, C. L. (2008). The accuracy of risk assessment instruments in the prediction of impulsive versus predatory aggression. *Behavioral Sciences & the Law, 26*, 759–777. doi:10.1002/bsl.842

Meehl, P. E. (1996). *Clinical versus statistical prediction: A theoretical analysis and a review of the literature*. Northvale, NJ: Jason Aronson. (Original work published in 1954.)

Melton, G. B., Petrila, J., Poythress, N., & Slobogin, C. (1997). *Psychological evaluations for the courts: A handbook for mental health professionals and lawyers*. New York, NY: Guilford.

Messing, J., & Thaller, J. (2013). The average predictive validity of intimate partner violence risk assessment instruments. *Journal of Interpersonal Violence, 28*, 1537–1558. doi:10.1177/0886260512468250

Michel, S. F., Riaz, M., Webster, C., Hart, S. D., Levander, S., Müller-Isberner, R.,... Hodgins, S. (2013). Using the HCR-20 to predict aggressive behavior among men with schizophrenia living in the community: Accuracy of prediction, general and forensic settings, and dynamic risk factors. *International Journal of Forensic Mental Health, 12*, 1–13. doi:10.1080/14999013.2012.760182

Monahan, J. (1981). *Predicting violent behavior: An assessment of clinical techniques*. Beverly Hills, CA: Sage.

Monahan, J. (1984). The prediction of violence behavior: Toward a second generation of theory and policy. *American Journal of Psychiatry, 141*, 10–15.

Monahan, J. (2006). A jurisprudence of risk assessment: Forecasting harm among prisoners, predators, and patients. *Virginia Law Review, 92*, 391–435. Retrieved from http://www.jstor.org/stable/4144948

Monahan, J. (2008). Structured risk assessment of violence. In R. Simon & K. Tardiff (Eds.), *Textbook of violence assessment and management* (pp. 17–33). Arlington, VA: American Psychiatric.

Monahan, J., Steadman, H. J., Robbins, P. C., Appelbaum, P., Banks, S., Grisso, T.,... Silver, E. (2005). An actuarial model of violence risk assessment for persons with mental disorders. *Psychiatric Services, 56*, 810–815. doi:10.1176/appi.ps.56.7.810

Monahan, J., Steadman, H. J., Robbins, P. C., Silver, E., Appelbaum, P. S., Grisso, T.,... Roth, L. H. (2007). Developing a clinically useful actuarial tool for assessing violence risk. *The British Journal of Psychiatry, 176*, 312–319. doi:10.1192/bjp.176.4.312

Monahan, J., Steadman, H., Silver, E., Appelbaum, P., Robbins, P., Mulvey, E.,... Banks, S. (2001). *Rethinking risk assessment: The MacArthur Study of mental disorder and violence*. New York, NY: Oxford University Press.

Mowat-Léger, V. (2001). *Risk factors for violence: A comparison of domestic batterers and other violent and non-violent offenders* (Unpublished master's thesis, Carleton University, Ottawa, Canada). Retrieved from ProQuest Dissertations and Theses database. (UMI No. NQ67053)

Neves, A. C., Goncalves, R. A., & Palma-Oliveira, J. M. (2011). Assessing risk for violent and general recidivism: A study of the HCR-20 and the PCL-R with a non-clinical sample of Portuguese offenders. *International Journal of Forensic Mental Health, 10*, 137–149. doi:10.1080/14999013.2011.577290

Nicholls, T. L., Brink, J., Desmarais, S. L., Webster, C. D., & Martin, M. L. (2006). The Short-Term Assessment of Risk and Treatability (START): A prospective validation study in a forensic psychiatric sample. *Assessment, 13*, 313–327. doi:10.1177/1073191106290559

Nicholls, T. L., Petersen, K. L., Brink, J., & Webster, C. (2011). A clinical and risk profile of forensic psychiatric patients: Treatment team STARTs in a Canadian service. *International Journal of Forensic Mental Health, 10*, 187–199. doi:10.1080/14999013.2011.600234

Nonstad, K., Nesset, M. B., Kroppan, E., Pedersen, T. W., Nøttestad, J. A., Almvik, R., & Palmstierna, T. (2010). Predictive validity and other psychometric properties of the Short-Term Assessment of Risk and Treatability (START) in a Norwegian high secure hospital. *International Journal of Forensic Mental Health, 9*(4), 294–299. doi:10.1080/14999013.2010.534958

Ogloff, J. R., & Daffern, M. (2006). The dynamic appraisal of situational aggression: An instrument to assess risk for imminent aggression in psychiatric inpatients. *Behavioral Sciences & the Law, 24*, 799–813. doi:10.1002/bsl.741

Olver, M. E., & Wong, S. C. P. (2011). A comparison of static and dynamic assessment of sexual offender risk and need in a treatment context. *Criminal Justice and Behavior, 38*, 113–126. doi:10.1177/0093854810389534

O'Shea, L. E., & Dickens, G. L. (2014). Short-term assessment of risk and treatability (START): Systematic review and meta-analysis. *Psychological Assessment, 26*, 990–1002. doi:10.1037/a0036794

Quinsey, V. L., Harris, G. T., Rice, M. E., & Cormier, C. A. (1998). *Violent offenders: Appraising and managing risk*. Washington, DC: American Psychological Association.

Quinsey, V. L., Harris, G. T., Rice, M. E., & Cormier, C. A. (2006). *Violent offenders: Appraising and managing risk* (2nd ed.). Washington, DC: American Psychological Association.

Reeves, K. A., Kropp, R., & Cairns, K. (2008, July). *An independent validation study of the SARA*. Paper presented at the annual meeting of the International Association of Forensic Mental Health Services, Vienna, Austria.

Rettenberger, M., & Eher, R. (2007). Predicting reoffense in sexual offender subtypes: A prospective validation study of the German version of the Sexual Offender Risk Appraisal Guide (SORAG). *Sexual Offender Treatment, 2*, 1–12. Retrieved from http://www.sexual-offender-treatment.org/index.php?id=62

Rettenberger, M., Boer, D. P., & Eher, R. (2011). The predictive accuracy of risk factors in the Sexual Violence Risk–20 (SVR-20). *Criminal Justice and Behavior, 38*, 1009–1027. doi:10.1177/0093854811416908

Rettenberger, M., Matthes, A., Boer, D. P., & Eher, R. (2010). Prospective actuarial risk assessment: A comparison of five risk assessment instruments in different sexual offender subtypes. *International Journal of Offender Therapy and Comparative Criminology, 54*, 169–186. doi:10.1177/0306624X08328755

Schmidt, F., Campbell, M. A., & Houlding, C. (2011). Comparative analyses of the YLS/CMI, SAVRY, and PCL:YV in adolescent offenders: A 10-year follow-up into adulthood. *Youth Violence and Juvenile Justice, 9*, 23–42. doi:10.1177/1541204010371793

Singh, J. P., Desmarais, S. L., Hurducas, C., Arbach-Lucioni, K., Condemarin, C., Dean, K.,... Otto, R. K. (2014). International perspectives on the practical application of violence risk assessment: A global survey of 44 countries. *International Journal of Forensic Mental Health, 13*, 193–206. doi:10.1080/14999013.2014.922141

Singh, J. P., & Fazel, S. (2010). Forensic risk assessment: A metareview. *Criminal Justice and Behavior, 37*, 965–988. doi:10.1177/0093854810374274

Singh, J. P., Grann, M., & Fazel, S. (2011). A comparative study of violence risk assessment tools: A systematic review and metaregression analysis of 68 studies involving 25,980 participants. *Clinical Psychology Review, 31*, 499–513. doi:10.1016/j.cpr.2010.11.009

Sjöstedt, G., & Långström, N. (2002). Assessment of risk for criminal recidivism among rapists: A comparison of four different measures. *Psychology, Crime & Law, 8*, 25–40. doi:10.1080/10683160208401807

Skeem, J. L., & Monahan, J. (2011). Current directions in violence risk assessment. *Current Directions in Psychological Science, 20*, 38–42. doi:10.1177/0963721410397271

Sreenivasan, S., Weinberger, L. E., Frances, A., & Cusworth-Walker, S. (2010). Alice in actuarial-land: Through the looking glass of changing Static-99 norms. *Journal of the American Academy of Psychiatry and the Law Online, 38*, 400–406.

Stadtland, C., Hollweg, M., Kleindienst, N., Dietl, J., Reich, U., & Nedopil, N. (2005). Risk assessment and prediction of violent and sexual recidivism in sex offenders: Long-term predictive accuracy of four risk assessment instruments. *Journal of Forensic Psychiatry & Psychology, 16*, 92–108. doi:10.1080/1478994042000270247

Steadman, H. J., & Cocozza, J. (1974). *Careers of the criminally insane*. Lexington, MA: Heath.

Storey, J., Hart, S. D., & Kropp, P. R. (2011). *Elder Abuse Risk Assessment Guide (EARA)*. Vancouver, BC, Canada: Proactive Resolutions.

Storey, J. E., Hart, S. D., Meloy, J. R., & Reavis, J. A. (2009). Psychopathy and stalking. *Law and Human Behavior, 33*, 237–246. doi:10.1007/s10979-008-9149-5

Storey, J. E., Kropp, P. R., Hart, S. D., Belfrage, H., & Strand, S. (2013). Assessment and management of risk for intimate partner violence by police officers using the Brief Spousal Assault Form for the Evaluation of Risk. *Criminal Justice and Behavior, 41*(2), 256–271. doi:10.1177/0093854813503960

Sutherland, A. A., Johnstone, L., Davidson, K. M., Hart, S. D., Cooke, D. J., Kropp, P. R.,... Stocks, R. (2012). Sexual violence risk assessment: An investigation of the interrater reliability of professional judgments made using the risk for sexual violence protocol. *International Journal of Forensic Mental Health, 11*(2), 119–133. doi:10.1080/14999013.2012.690020

Tarasoff v. Regents of the University of California, 17 Cal. 3d 425, 551 P. 2d 334 (1976).

Thomson, L., Davidson, M., Brett, C., Steele, J., & Darjee, R. (2008). Risk assessment in forensic patients with schizophrenia: The predictive validity of actuarial scales and symptom severity for offending and violence over 8–10 years. *International Journal of Forensic Mental Health, 7*, 173–189. doi:10.1080/14999013.2008.9914413

United States v. Salerno, 481 U.S. 739 (1987).

Vaaler, A. E., Iversen, V. C., Morken, G., Fløvig, J. C., Palmstierna, T., & Linaker, O. M. (2011). Short-term prediction of threatening and violent behaviour in an acute psychiatric intensive care unit based on patient and environment characteristics. *BMC Psychiatry, 11*, 44–51. doi:10.1186/1471-244x-11-44

Vaaler, A. E., Morken, G., Fløvig, J. C., Iversen, V. C., & Linaker, O. M. (2006). Effects of a psychiatric intensive care unit in an acute psychiatric department. *Nordic Journal of Psychiatry, 60*, 144–149. doi:10.1080/08039480600583472

Van de Sande, R., Nijman, H. L. I., Noorthoorn, E. O., Wierdsma, A. I., Hellendoorn, E., Van Der Staak, C., & Mulder, C. L. (2011). Aggression and seclusion on acute psychiatric wards: Effect of short-term risk assessment. *The British Journal of Psychiatry, 199*, 473–478. doi:10.1192/bjp.bp.111.095141

Van de Sande, R., Noorthoorn, E., Wierdsma, A., Hellendoorn, E., Staak, C., Mulder, C. L., & Nijman, H. (2013). Association between short-term structured risk assessment outcomes and seclusion. *International Journal of Mental Health Nursing, 22*, 475–484. doi:10.1111/inm.12033

van den Brink, R. H. S., Hooijschuur, A., van Os, T. W. D. P., Savenije, W., & Wiersma, D. (2010). Routine violence risk assessment in community forensic mental healthcare. *Behavioral Sciences & the Law, 28*, 396–410. doi:10.1002/bsl.904

Viljoen, J. L., Cruise, K. R., Nicholls, T. L., Desmarais, S. L., & Webster, C. D. (2012). Taking stock and taking steps: The case for an adolescent version of the Short-Term Assessment of Risk and Treatability. *International Journal of Forensic Mental Health, 11*(3), 135–149. doi:10.1080/14999013.2012.737406

Vincent, G. M., Chapman, J., & Cook, N. (2011). Predictive validity of the SAVRY, racial differences, and the contribution of needs factors. *Criminal Justice and Behavior, 38*, 42–62. doi:10.1177/0093854810386000

Vojt, G., Marshall, L. A., & Thomson, L. D. (2010). The assessment of imminent inpatient aggression: A validation study of the DASA-IV in Scotland. *The Journal of Forensic Psychiatry & Psychology, 21*, 789–800. doi:10.1080/14789949.2010.489952

Watt, K. A., Hart, S. D., Wilson, C., Guy, L., & Douglas, K. S. (2006, March). *An evaluation of the Risk for Sexual Violence Protocol (RSVP) in high risk offenders: Interrater reliability and concurrent validity*. Paper presented at the annual meeting of the American Psychology-Law Society, St. Petersburg, FL.

Watt, K. A., & Jackson, K. (2008, July). *Interrater and structural reliabilities of the Risk for Sexual Violence Protocol (RSVP)*. Paper presented at the annual meeting of the International Association of Forensic Mental Health Services, Vienna, Austria.

Webster, C. D., Douglas, K. S., Eaves, D., & Hart, S. D. (1997). *HCR-20: Assessing risk for violence* (Version 2). Burnaby, BC, Canada: Mental Health, Law, & Policy Institute, Simon Fraser University.

Webster, C. D., Haque, Q., & Hucker, S. J. (2007). *Violence risk assessment and management: Advances through structured professional judgment and sequential redirections* (2nd ed.). West Sussex, UK: Wiley.

Webster, C. D., Martin, M. L., Brink, J., Nicholls, T. L., & Desmarais, S. L. (2009). *Manual for the Short-Term Assessment of Risk and Treatability (START)* (Version 1.1). Port Coquitlam, BC, Canada: Forensic Psychiatric Services Commission.

Webster, C. D., Nicholls, T. L., Martin, M. L., Desmarais, S. L., & Brink, J. (2006). Short-Term Assessment of Risk and Treatability (START): The case for a new structured professional judgment scheme. *Behavioral Sciences & the Law, 24*, 747–766. doi:10.1002/bsl.737

Williams, K. R., & Houghton, A. B. (2004). Assessing the risk of domestic violence reoffending: A validation study. *Law and Human Behavior, 28*, 437–455. doi:10.1023/b:lahu.0000039334.59297.f0

Wilson, C. M., Desmarais, S. L., Nicholls, T. L., & Brink, J. (2010). The role of client strengths in assessments of violence risk using the Short-Term Assessment of Risk and Treatability (START). *International Journal of Forensic Mental Health*, 9, 282–293. doi:10.1080/14999013.2010.534694

Wilson, C. M., Desmarais, S. L., Nicholls, T. L., Hart, S. D., & Brink, J. (2013). Predictive validity of dynamic factors: Assessing violence risk in forensic psychiatric inpatients. *Law and Human Behavior*, 37, 377–388. doi:10.1037/lhb0000025

Wilson, C., & Douglas, K. S. (2009). Assessment of dangerousness. In C. Edwards (Ed.), *Encyclopedia of forensic sciences* (pp. 667–676). Hoboken, NJ: Wiley.

Wollert, R. (2002). The importance of cross-validation in actuarial test construction for correcting inflated recidivism predictions: Shrinkage in the risk estimates for the Minnesota Sex Offender Screening Tool-Revised. *The Journal of Threat Assessment*, 2, 87–102. doi:10.1300/j177v02n01_06

Wong, T., & Hisashima, J. (2008). *Domestic violence exploratory study on the DVSI and SARA, State of Hawaii, 2003–2007* (ICIS Technical Report No. 1). Hawaii State Department of Health, Interagency Council on Intermediate Sanctions. Retrieved from http://icis.hawaii.gov/wp-content/uploads/2013/07/SARA-DVSI-Exploratory-Study-Oct-2008.pdf

Woods, P., & Almvik, R. (2002). The Brøset Violence Checklist (BVC). *Acta Psychiatrica Scandinavica*, 106 (suppl. 412), 103–105. doi:10.1034/j.1600-0447.106.s412.22.x

Woods, P., Ashley, C., Kayto, D., & Heusdens, C. (2008). Piloting violence and incident reporting measures on one acute mental health inpatient unit. *Issues in Mental Health Nursing*, 29(5), 455–469. doi:10.1080/01612840801981207

Yang, M., Wong, S. C. P., & Coid, J. W. (2010). The efficacy of violence prediction: A meta-analytic comparison of nine risk assessment tools. *Psychological Bulletin*, 136, 740–767. doi:10.1037/a0020473

Yoon, D., Spehr, A., & Briken, P. (2011). Structured assessment of protective factors: A German pilot study in sex offenders. *Journal of Forensic Psychiatry and Psychology*, 22, 834–844. doi:10.1080/14789949.2011.617831

Yudofsky, S. C., Silver, J. M., Jackson, W., Endicott, J., & Williams, D. (1986). The Overt Aggression Scale for the objective rating of verbal and physical aggression. *The American Journal of Psychiatry*, 143, 35–39. Retrieved from http://psycnet.apa.org/psycinfo/1986-13476-001

Zanatta, R. G. (2005). *Risk of violent and sexual recidivism: A comparison of dangerous offenders and repetitive sexual offenders* (Unpublished doctoral dissertation, Simon Fraser University, Burnaby, BC, Canada). Retrieved from http://summit.sfu.ca/item/8529

Interventions for Acute Agitation

Stephen M. Strenges *and* Glenn W. Currier

Abstract

Given the considerable and often increasing risks for violence against mental health professionals, the effective evaluation, management, and treatment of patients with acute agitation is of critical importance to ensuring safety. This chapter builds upon several articles of the American Association for Emergency Psychiatry's Project BETA, which proposes guidelines and best practices for the treatment of agitation. We suggest that clinicians use a tiered, progressive approach to treating agitation in which they attempt less-invasive methods such as verbal de-escalation before drug intervention, when medically appropriate. It is argued that treatment should be proportionate to the severity of agitation, and pharmacological intervention should be used as a last resort.

Key Words: acute agitation, BETA, mental health professionals, mental health, violence

On February 12, 2008, David Tarloff, 46, of Manhattan (New York), wearing a heavy coat and pulling a suitcase, entered his psychiatrist's office in East Manhattan to rob his doctor, Kent Shinbach, of $50,000 as part of a plan to "rescue" his mother from a hospital.[1] While waiting for Dr. Shinbach, Tarloff noticed that Shinbach's colleague, psychologist Dr. Kathryn Faughey, had finished seeing her patient. Tarloff entered her office, brutally attacking and killing her with a meat cleaver and mallet he had concealed in his coat. Dr. Shinbach, hearing screams from next door, attempted to restrain Tarloff and was severely injured. In another tragic example of patient violence, a few years prior, Dr. Wayne Fenton, a renowned psychiatrist and associate director of the National Institute of Mental Health, was found dead in his home office after his 19-year-old patient Vitali Davydov beat him to death with his bare hands.[2]

While extreme examples, these cases represent the grave reality of the risks facing mental health professionals. Importantly, these threats do not exist solely in non-medical settings. A 2011 study by the Emergency Nurses Association (ENA), which surveyed more than 7,000 emergency nurses, found that more than half had been victims of physical violence or verbal abuse in the preceding seven days (ENA, 2011).[3] Furthermore, the single most common factor that precipitated violent incidents was "caring for psychiatric patients in the [Emergency Department]" (ENA, 2011, p. 55). Data from the U.S. Bureau of Labor Statistics show that psychiatric aides had an occupational injury and illness rate seven times higher than the national average, while the incidence rate of violence for the occupation was 69 times higher than the national rate (Longton, 2015).

Given these risks, it is understandable that safety is the top priority for medical professionals and their patients. However, the means of balancing the psychiatric, medical, and other dynamics of treatment are not always clear and often involve a multistaged or tiered approach. Clinicians must balance their efforts to de-escalate agitated patients through social and verbal methods, while also weighing the appropriate considerations for drug intervention. Aggressively medicating a patient too early will hinder the efficacy of psychiatric evaluation and assessment. Furthermore, the forcible administration of medication can have a lasting effect on patients that may make them averse to seeking treatment and maintaining their prescribed medication schedules (Currier, 2000). However, a significant delay in medicating a patient can result in increased risks for injury and violence, as well as the potential need for more medication or restraint as their agitation worsens; thereby creating unnecessary and avoidable risks.

This chapter examines interventions for the management and treatment of acute agitation in psychiatric patients. Although research illustrates the importance of drug therapy, this chapter argues that it should be used as a method of last resort. Instead, clinicians should opt for a tiered approach in which various methods are attempted to de-escalate the patient's agitation before escalating to the next appropriate method (or stage). Consequently, the degree of escalation is proportional and will depend in part on the patient's degree of agitation, their condition, medical history, the environment (e.g., acute versus emergency department) and their response to attempts at de-escalation.

Background

Complicating our understanding of the relationship between mental health and violence is the fact that, as others have noted, there are numerous studies that appear to support the varying views of whether or not mental illness results in higher rates of violence (Stuart, 2003). The MacArthur Violence Risk Assessment Study examined more than 1,000 inpatient psychiatric patients in several cities and followed up with them for a year in order to determine whether the prevalence of violence by discharged psychiatric inpatients was higher than in the communities they lived in after their initial treatment (Steadman et al., 1998). The authors found that the prevalence rate of violence among patients without a coexisting substance abuse problem was "statistically indistinguishable" from their control group of community members who also did not have substance abuse problems (Steadman et al., 1998, p. 400). However, the one-year prevalence rate for violence in patients without a substance abuse diagnosis, 17.9%, almost doubled to 31.1% when there was a concurrent substance abuse diagnosis. Importantly, in both groups (patient and community), the existence of a substance abuse disorder increased the prevalence of violence; though they caution readers from making generalizations between these two groups (Steadman et al., 1998). Additionally, they

argue that the assessment and analysis of the overly broad categorization of "discharged mental patients" is problematic, as it does not account for their specific diagnosis or the existence of a co-occurring substance abuse problem, for example (Steadman et al., 1998, p. 400). The initial findings of this study mirrored the conclusions of other, similar studies conducted around the same time (Johns, 1997; Noffsinger & Resnick, 1999; Swanson et al., 1996).

However, other studies have found that a modest increase in violence prevalence remains when comparing psychiatric patients to the general population, even when substance abuse disorders are not present (Hiday, 1995; Mullen, 1997; and see Stuart, 2003). These studies attribute this modest increase to a variety of factors, including the type of illness, the coexistence of substance abuse disorders, as well as social and environmental conditions, for example (see, e.g., Hiday, 1995; Stuart, 2003). That is, mental illness in and of itself is not a sufficient or sole determinant of violence; rather, it is often one of several coexisting conditions or factors that contribute to this increased proclivity to violence. Others have noted that this proclivity is better related to the type of psychotic symptoms than to the broader label of "mental illness" (Link et al., 1992; Marzuk, 1996).

Importantly, as Mullen (1997, p. 9) states

> A more productive response to prejudice is to acknowledge that in some groups of the mentally ill there are increased risks of frightening and violent behaviour, but that this characterises only a minority and when it does occur, the damage, if any, is usually slight and inflicted most often on family members, professionals and fellow sufferers, rather than the general public. **Above all, it is essential to make it clear that violence can be a reflection of a failure of treatment and support, and that, therefore, in principle it is preventable** [*emphasis added*].

As illustrated, the relationship between mental illness and violence is dynamic, complicated, and multifaceted. This discussion illustrates several fundamental points. First, the presence of a concurrent substance abuse disorder greatly increases the risk and potential for violence among those with mental illness (as it also does for the general population). The exacerbation of this is emphasized by Stuart's expression that "those with substance disorders are major contributors to community violence, perhaps accounting for as much as a third of self-reported violent acts, and seven out of every 10 crimes of violence among mentally disordered offenders" (Stuart, 2003, p. 123). Second, the term "mental illness" is vastly encompassing, and the types of illness, their conditions, and other factors are more appropriate for determining the prevalence rate of violence than just broadly categorizing someone in terms of having a mental illness diagnosis. Accounting for these intricacies is important, as some have noted the potential for methodological problems and sampling biases. For example, the MacArthur Study authors noted in another publication that "a diagnosis of schizophrenia was associated with lower rates of violence than was a diagnosis of depression or bipolar disorder" (Monahan et al., 2001; in Torrey et al., 2008, p. 149). However, as Torrey and Stanley argue, patients with schizophrenia who have a "limited awareness of their illness (anosognosia) or paranoid symptoms—or both—are very unlikely to agree" to the follow-up conditions of videotaped interviews and interviewing of their friends or family (Torrey et al., 2008, p. 149). As such, using the broad categorization of "mental illness" overlooks these fundamental characteristics. Third, the potential for violence, although it is difficult to determine and measure precise risks, can be mitigated through appropriate treatment methods, de-escalation, and support. Therefore, the approach to handling agitated patients is critically important to ensuring their successful and long-term treatment beyond their initial assessment. The means and methods for determining the degree of agitation, the best approach for treatment, and the pharmacological options will be discussed in the following sections.

Evaluation and Triage

The fundamental goal of any treatment of a patient with agitation is the safety of the patient and staff, the de-escalation of agitation, and the stabilization of the patient to a point where a psychiatric evaluation can be conducted. In order to select the best approach to treatment, the degree of agitation should first be determined. One article, of a series by the American Association for Emergency Psychiatry's Project BETA[4] (*Best Practices in Evaluation and Treatment of Agitation*), puts forth a set of best practices for medically evaluating and triaging patients with agitation (Nordstrom et al., 2012). The Project BETA series (Nordstrom et al., 2012; Richmond et al., 2012) discusses several available, objective assessments that may be used for determining a patient's degree of agitation: the Overt Agitation Severity Scale, the Overt Aggression Scale, the Scale for the Assessment of Aggressive and Agitated Behaviors, the Staff Observation Aggression Scale, and the Behavioural

Activity Rating Scale (BARS) (Brizer et al., 1987; Kopecky et al., 1998; Palmstierna & Wistedt, 1987; Silver & Yudofsky, 1991; Swift et al., 2002; Yudofsky et al., 1986). Although each of the aforementioned scales is effective, both Nordstrom et al. (2012) and Richmond et al. (2012) make note of BARS as being particularly useful, as it is simple to use and does not require the patient to answer questions, making it particularly effective in non-medical settings.

BARS consists of a seven-point scale, which rates activity from "Difficult or unable to rouse" (1) to "Violent, requires restraint" (7), with "Quiet and awake (normal level of activity)" holding the rank of 4. The report notes that, while patients with a score of 1 should be transferred (if in a non-medical setting) to an emergency department and patients with scores of 2, 3, or 7 should be transferred (if in a non-medical setting) to a medical emergency department or a psychiatric emergency service (PES) with medical capability, the patients exhibiting only mild to moderate agitation (scores of 5 or 6) may be de-escalated using verbal techniques (Nordstrom et al., 2012). Importantly, a patient's BARS score should be determined by their behavior prior to their arrival at a PES or emergency department in order to gather an accurate assessment (Richmond et al., 2012). The initial assessment evaluation and triage stage is also a good opportunity to determine the social history of the patient by interviewing friends, family, bystanders, or other individuals, if available.

As Stowell et al. (2012, p. 11) discuss, when treating patients "in a state of agitation, triage, initial assessment, and de-escalation must occur at the same time the initial assessment is done." Determining a definitive diagnosis is not likely, nor necessary at this initial stage, as the primary focus is to determine a preliminary (or most likely) diagnosis in order to begin a treatment aimed at de-escalating the patient's agitation while simultaneously addressing its likeliest cause. This evaluation should also attempt to diagnose the underlying etiology of agitation to determine if it is due to a general medical condition, substance intoxication/withdrawal, or a psychiatric illness (Nordstrom et al., 2012; Stowell et al., 2012).

Verbal De-escalation of Agitated Patients

Similar to how law enforcement responds to hostile suspects, clinicians should always seek to de-escalate situations, rather than escalate, whenever possible. Similarly, the level of escalation, in terms of their response, should be proportionate and definitive. The response will be determined by the patient's severity of agitation as well as other contextual factors (e.g., medical versus non-medical setting, history of violence, presence of a weapon, preliminary diagnosis, etc.). Historically, patients with severe agitation were often restrained using mechanical restraints, though this has declined in recent years, in part, due to such restraints' potentially "deleterious physical and psychological effects" on both patients and staff (Currier & Trenton, 2002, p. 220; see Fisher, 1994). Additionally, the use of physical restraint tends to reinforce patient beliefs that violence is an appropriate and necessary means to resolve conflict (Richmond et al., 2012). Mechanical restraints and involuntary medication are often traumatic and have been gradually phased out in favor of non-coercive approaches that view the patient as a collaborative partner in their own treatment (Knox & Holloman, 2012). Drug intervention or "chemical tranquilization" should only occur as a last resort if verbal de-escalation does not work, or if the patient's agitation or potential for violence is too high to support only attempts at verbal de-escalation (e.g., a BARS score of 7).

In his outline of the five phases of agitation (calm, psychomotor-agitated, verbal, violent episode, and post-violence), Robert Feinstein (1986) notes that managing patients through the psychomotor and verbal phases of agitation through verbal techniques and other methods (such as offering food if medically appropriate) are often sufficient to de-escalate situations. Furthermore, an avoidance of using mechanical restraints and involuntary medication reduces the potential risks of injury to staff and helps to establish a relationship of trust between the patient and clinician.

The importance of attempting verbal de-escalation, when feasible and appropriate, is emphasized throughout the Project BETA series, but particularly by Richmond et al. (2012) and their proposed three-step approach to de-escalation: verbally engaging the patient; establishing a collaborative relationship with the patient; and verbally de-escalating the patient from their agitated state. As the authors detail, this method is based on four main objectives to working with agitated patients: the safety of the patient, staff, and bystanders; helping the patient manage their emotions and distress and maintain or regain control of their behavior; the avoidance of using restraints (when possible); and the avoidance of coercive interventions that escalate the patient's agitation (Richmond et al., 2012). These are based

on the ten key domains of de-escalation detailed by Avrim Fishkind (2002): Respect the patient's personal space, do not be provocative, establish verbal contact, be concise, identify the patient's wants and feelings, listen closely to what the patient is saying, agree or agree to disagree, lay down the law and set clear limits, offer choices and optimism, and debrief the patient and staff (Richmond et al., 2012). A recurring element in the verbal de-escalation approach is an awareness of one's body language, tone of voice, posture, and other subtle means of communication, which are particularly important for the proper de-escalation of an agitated patient (Feinstein, 1986; Fishkind, 2002; Richmond et al., 2012).

Pharmacological Intervention, Restraint, and Treatment

While verbal de-escalation is oftentimes an effective means of de-escalation, sometimes it is ineffective or not appropriate (e.g., a patient is too violent or aggressive). A subsequent step in this tiered approach to treatment is 'chemical restraint' through the use of medication. Some benefits of this approach include the patient's remaining in their agitated state for a shorter period, the decreased use of restraints, and a generally safer environment for staff during the evaluation process (Currier & Trenton, 2002). However, this approach carries its own risks, as the medication may have potentially negative or harmful side effects, and its administration, particularly if done forcibly, can have a lasting and potentially negative effect on patients even after their initial treatment (Allen, 2000; Currier, 2000). As such, medication should be used as a last resort to stabilize a patient, de-escalate agitation to a level where a psychiatric evaluation can occur, and to ensure the safety of the patient, staff, and bystanders.

The immediate de-escalation and treatment of agitation is a top priority, as agitation can lead to violent incidents (Powell et al., 1994). Since the safety of the patient, staff, and bystanders is of the highest importance, sometimes due to the severity of agitation, the setting, or the rate of escalation, attempting verbal de-escalation may not be appropriate. In such a case, an appropriate psychopharmacological treatment may be necessary in order to de-escalate agitated patients. A 1999 survey of PES directors sponsored by the American Association for Emergency Psychiatry found that 16.2% ± 19.2% of agitated patients required emergency medication (Allen & Currier, 2004; Currier,

2000). Subsequently, clinicians must balance the necessity of using restraints to ensure the safety of the patient and staff, while also ensuring that their methods enable staff to adequately assess, diagnose, and treat the underlying causes of agitation. Overly medicating a patient or beginning a pharmacological approach to treatment too early may hinder the ability of clinicians to appropriately assess and evaluate the underlying cause of their agitation. Conversely, failing to properly medicate the patient puts them and staff at an increased and unnecessary risk of injury.

Importantly, the use of medication does not eliminate the ability to build a collaborative and non-coercive relationship with the patient. While the clinician may have determined that the administration of medication must occur based on their assessment, they can adjust their word choice and presentation of options in such a way that the patients will view themselves as still maintaining a degree of control. For example, as Richmond and colleagues (2012) discuss, when patients have no other options than "fight or flight," the ability of choice acts as a source of empowerment and can help de-escalate situations. This can be something such as offering the patient the choice between oral or parenteral administration, or the ability to choose between two different types of medications based on their potential side-effects. It is important to note that this method does not preclude a degree of assertiveness when addressing aggressive or violent patients, as the offering of alternatives to their threats can serve as a tool for de-escalation (such as, "I don't think that would be a good idea"). These methods allow the clinician to pursue their intended treatment but allow the patient a degree of choice and control in their own treatment. Importantly, the verbal techniques described in the earlier subsection should be used to reestablish the relationship between the patient and clinician as a means of recovery during the post-violence phase (see Richmond et al., 2012). For example, as Feinstein suggests, "It is most helpful to make verbal interventions with therapeutic intent that anticipate the patient's fear of the immediate future" (1986, p. 6PC).

The choice and approach to pharmacological treatment is dynamic and involves an examination and consideration of the potential underlying etiology of agitation, the patient's medical history, and drug choice/administration (e.g., its efficacy, titration schedule, oral versus intramuscular administration).

Approaches to Pharmacological Treatment

This part of the chapter will detail the considerations, guidelines, and methods of using a pharmacological approach to treating agitation. This section builds upon a report on the psychopharmacology of agitation from the American Association for Emergency Psychiatry's Project BETA (see Wilson et al., 2012; see also *Western Journal of Emergency Medicine* 13[1]), which proposes guidelines and best practices for clinicians. The methods of pharmacological treatment are dynamic, and this information is meant to serve as an overview and guide. Careful attention should be paid to the patient's degree of agitation, their medical history, and any potential medical contraindications to suggested treatment plans.

If a pharmacological component of treatment is necessary, such interventions should be implemented with the following principles in mind.

Attempt Treatment of Suspected Etiology

Pharmacological approaches should be based, when possible, on treating the underlying cause of the agitation, as determined by the clinician's preliminary diagnosis. For example, if a psychotic illness is suspected, antipsychotics are preferred to benzodiazepines, as they address the underlying medical cause of a patient's agitation. It is important to remember that, just because a medication decreases a patient's agitation this does not mean it accurately or appropriately addressed the underlying etiology of their agitation. A clinician's preliminary diagnosis will never be 100% accurate 100% of the time, but pharmacological treatment should attempt to treat the underlying cause whenever possible.

Medicate Only to Extent Required

The dosage of medication should only be administered to the extent that it addresses the patient's agitation and, if possible, their underlying medical condition. When attempting to de-escalate agitation, medication should not be given to induce sleep or overly sedate a patient. The underlying goal of pharmacological approaches to treatment should be to de-escalate the patient's degree of agitation to a point where they can be properly evaluated, stabilized, and medically treated. Excessive medication can have adverse consequences (e.g., extrapyramidal symptoms [EPS]), which can make patients disinclined to continue their medication after their initial treatment.

Build a Collaborative Relationship with Medication Selection and Administration

The method of administering medication should be the least invasive and follow patient wishes to the extent that it is medically appropriate. For example, oral medication should be offered before parenteral forms. However, if a patient has a preference for a certain type of medication over another, due to reasons such as a bad experience or personal preference, for example, this should be followed as long as there are no medical contraindications to this substitution. Throughout treatment, including during and after pharmacological intervention, the patient should be viewed as a collaborative partner. An unduly forceful, coercive, or traumatic experience associated with their treatment is likely to hinder their willingness to maintain their prescribed treatment and medication schedules. For instance, treating psychosis is a longer-term process, and a patient's attitude towards treatment may outweigh moderate differences in pharmacological treatment. Additionally, allowing patients to voice their input in the choice of medication choice and method (when medically appropriate) affords them a degree of control that may help de-escalate agitation (Richmond et al., 2012).

Three classes or types of medication are commonly used for treating patients with agitation: first-generation antipsychotics (FGAs, or typical antipsychotics), second-generation antipsychotics (SGAs, or atypical antipsychotics), and benzodiazepines. Each class of medication has its own benefits, risks, and conditions for use. Table 19.1 below provides a brief overview of some recommended medications and their doses.

It is important to note that the following discussion of each drug's efficacy is based on its behavior in clinical trials, which varies from its use and efficacy in emergency situations. Treating patients with severe agitation in an emergency situation is different from treating those in clinical studies. For example, patients in clinical studies must sign an informed consent, and it is unlikely clinicians would propose a clinical trial to a patient who is very aggressive or violent (e.g., has a BARS score of 7). Additionally, patients with coexisting substance abuse disorders are typically screened out of many studies. These are important considerations because the onset and dosing of medication are important when responding to patients with different illnesses and degrees of agitation.

Typical Antipsychotics (First-Generation Antipsychotics, FGAs): Generally, high-potency FGAs (e.g., haloperidol) are considered safer than low-potency versions (e.g., chlorpromazine) and can be administered orally or parenterally (Currier & Trenton, 2002). SGAs are often preferred to FGAs due to their lower risk of EPS. However, in some instances, FGAs are still preferred to SGAs. For example, haloperidol, an FGA, remains the preferred antipsychotic when alcohol intoxication is suspected.

Haloperidol is a commonly used, high-potency FGA used to treat acute agitation. In most settings, it can be administered orally or intramuscularly. The drug has a propensity to lengthen QTc intervals, and cases of *torsades de pointes* (TdP) have been reported in connection with its use (Wilson et al., 2012). Importantly, while still used in some settings, haloperidol is not approved by the US Food and Drug Administration (FDA) for intravenous administration due to the potential risks associated with QT prolongation and TdP (FDA, 2013; Wilson et al., 2012). The use of haloperidol is also associated with a risk of EPS, including akathisia, dystonia, and neuroleptic malignant syndrome (Currier & Trenton, 2002; Van Putten, 1974; Wilson et al., 2012). Haloperidol is often administered with a benzodiazepine to reduce the effects and occurrence of EPS unless there are medical contraindications (Wilson et al., 2012). In one study, the combination of haloperidol and lorazepam was shown to reduce the occurrence of EPS from 20% to 6% (Battaglia et al., 1997; Wilson et al., 2012).

Atypical Antipsychotics (Second-Generation Antipsychotics, SGAs): SGAs are a newer class of drug and are favored due to their reduced risk of EPS (Correll & Schenk, 2008; Dolder & Jeste, 2003; Kane, 2004; Wilson et al., 2012). Some studies place these reported rates of EPS at less than one percent (Correll & Schenk, 2008; Dolder & Jeste, 2003; Kane, 2004), which is significantly lower than those exhibited with haloperidol or the combination of haloperidol and lorazepam (Battaglia et al., 1997; Gillies et al., 2013; Wilson et al., 2012). There is little existing research on the combined use of SGAs with benzodiazepines or on the use of SGAs in alcohol-intoxicated patients. In these instances it is recommended that clinicians opt for an FGA, particularly if they plan to administer benzodiazepines as well (Wilson et al., 2012).

Aripiprazole is a safe and effective SGA for controlling agitation (Currier et al., 2007). It is available

Table 19.1. Medications by Type.

	Initial Dose (mg)	Tmax*	Can Repeat*	Max Dose (per 24 hours; in mg)
Typical Antipsychotics				
Oral				
Haloperidol	5	30–60m	15m	20
Intramuscular				
Haloperidol[#]	5	30–60m	15m	20
Atypical Antipsychotics				
Oral				
Risperidone	2	1h	2h	6
Olanzapine	5–10	6h	2h	20
Intramuscular				
Olanzapine	10	15–45m	20m	30
Ziprasidone	10–20	15m	10mg q 2 h or 20mg q 4 h	40
Benzodiazepines				
Oral				
Lorazepam	2	20–30m	2h	12
Intramuscular				
Lorazepam	2	20–30m	2h	12

Notes: Partially adapted from Wilson et al., 2012, p. 30.

Q 2h = every two hours; q 4h = every four hours.

[#] Higher risk of extrapyramidal side effects.

* m = minutes, h = hours.

in both oral and intramuscular forms. Clinical studies have shown that the drug is as effective as intramuscular haloperidol or lorazepam, while showing significant reductions in the prevalence of EPS (Andrezina et al., 2006; Tran-Johnson et al., 2007; Zimbroff et al., 2007). Aripiprazole is particularly effective when used intramuscularly to control agitation. In their clinical study comparing intramuscular haloperidol to intramuscular aripiprazole, Tran-Johnson and colleagues (2007) found a statistically significant decrease in a patient's agitation as early as 45 minutes after receiving 9.75 mg of intramuscular aripiprazole, compared to 105 minutes for 7.5 mg of haloperidol. However, other studies have challenged aripiprazole's efficacy, finding it slightly lower than that of other SGAs (Citrome, 2007). Given this, aripiprazole is not recommended as a first-line treatment of agitation, as more research is currently needed (Wilson et al., 2012).

Risperidone, is an effective treatment for agitation and is particularly noted for its safety (Wilson et al., 2012). It is available orally as both a liquid and as a tablet. The use of risperidone has proved effective on both positive and negative symptoms of schizophrenia, and it is also associated with low rates of EPS (Currier & Trenton, 2002; Marder, Davis, & Chouinard, 1997; Peuskens, 1995). Additionally, a study by Peuskens (1995) found risperidone had a lower propensity for inducing dystonic symptoms, akathisia, and Parkinsonism than haloperidol.

Olanzapine is available both orally and intramuscularly. It is particularly effective in the treatment of positive, negative, and affective symptoms of schizophrenia, as well as agitation associated with schizophrenia (Beasley et al., 1998; Tollefson et al., 1997; Wright et al., 2001). A study of intramuscular olanzapine by Wright et al. (2001) found its rapid onset particularly effective in reducing agitation when compared to intramuscular haloperidol at the 15-, 30-, and 45-minute intervals following initial injection. Furthermore, they noted its added benefit of significantly lower risks of acute dystonia and QTc prolongation.

Ziprasidone is available intramuscularly and is characterized by its rapid efficacy (Currier & Trenton, 2002; Daniel et al., 2001). In a study by Brook and colleagues (2000), intramuscular ziprasidone was significantly more effective than intramuscular haloperidol in reducing symptoms of acute psychosis by at least double. They also found that it was better tolerated than haloperidol and maintained a "notably lower propensity for inducing movement disorders" (Brook et al., 2000, p. 938).

Benzodiazepines: Benzodiazepines have proven effective for managing agitation through their sedative properties. If psychosis is suspected, antipsychotics should first be attempted before using benzodiazepines, as benzodiazepines will not treat the underlying condition. Using benzodiazepines carries the risk of potential over-sedation and respiratory depression (Wilson et al., 2012). Therefore, the use of benzodiazepines in patients suspected of alcohol intoxication or other central nervous system (CNS) depressants should be avoided. Importantly, the administration of benzodiazepines in conjunction with neuroleptics may also help reduce the dosage of antipsychotics required to achieve sedation (Allen, 2000; Currier & Trenton, 2002).

Lorazepam is the most commonly used benzodiazepine in an emergency setting. It is available for both oral and intramuscular administration and has an onset of effect within 15–30 minutes (Allen, 2000; Currier & Trenton, 2002). In studies comparing lorazepam and haloperidol, while both drugs measured equal in several categories, lorazepam was superior in managing aggression, clinical global improvement, and produced fewer incidents of EPS (Allen, 2000; Foster et al., 1997; Salzman et al., 1991). A study conducted by Battaglia et al. (1997) confirmed lorazepam's utility in managing aggression, finding that it served as a more effective sedative than haloperidol. Their study also found that, for rapid tranquilization, a combination of haloperidol and lorazepam is particularly effective within the first three hours after the initial dose when compared to those who received either haloperidol or lorazepam alone (Battaglia et al., 1997).

Diazepam is considered a lower potency benzodiazepine than lorazepam. When given intramuscularly, diazepam is "absorbed slowly and erratically" (Currier & Trenton, 2002, p. 223). A study by Jimerson et al. (1982) found significant adverse effects associated with high doses of diazepam, including sedation, ataxia, and dysarthria (Currier & Trenton, 2002). Diazepam is not a recommended first-line treatment for agitation.

Summary of Pharmacological Treatment Plans Based on Suspected Cause of Agitation

This section provides an overview of suggested pharmacological treatment plans based on Project BETA guidelines on the psychopharmacology of agitation (Wilson et al., 2012). Each subsection below is organized according to the suspected cause or condition associated with the patient's agitation (e.g., agitation associated with delirium). Each numbered step (or phase) of the suggested pharmacological treatment plan should be followed in order, and advancement to the next consecutive step should only be done if it is medically appropriate and necessary. For example, the suggested pharmacological treatment plan for "agitation associated with delirium: alcohol or benzodiazepine withdrawal not suspected" (the first plan of this section) would involve a clinician's attempting to treat with orally administered SGAs (step one) before escalating to step two, orally administered FGAs (in this example, a low dose of haloperidol).

Agitation Associated with Delirium

Delirium is often associated with an underlying medical condition, which should be identified and treated if possible. An overview of this suggested treatment approach is provided in Figure 19.1.

ALCOHOL OR BENZODIAZEPINE WITHDRAWAL NOT SUSPECTED

If alcohol or benzodiazepine withdrawal is not suspected, the clinician should attempt to identify and treat the underlying cause of the patient's delirium. If pharmacological interventions are required to reduce a patient's agitation, SGAs are preferred (Wilson et al., 2012). It is important to avoid

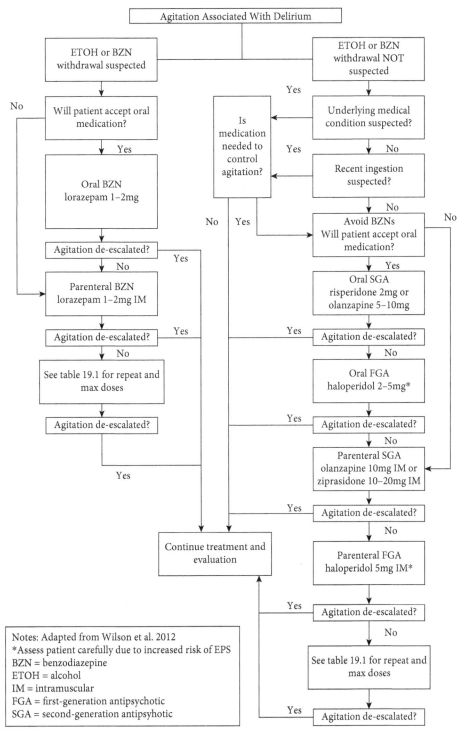

Fig. 19.1 Agitation associated with delirium.

benzodiazepines, as they may exacerbate a patient's delirium and should be avoided (Clegg & Young, 2011; Wilson et al., 2012):

1. Attempt to identify and treat underlying cause
2. If drugs required, SGAs are preferred

3. Avoid benzodiazepines

Note: If the recent ingestion of an unknown substance is the suspected cause of delirium, the delirium will be self-limiting (Wilson et al., 2012). However, if pharmacological control is needed to de-escalate agitation associated with this onset of delirium, follow the same treatment plan for "alcohol or benzodiazepine withdrawal not suspected," presented below.

Suggested pharmacological treatment plan:

Avoid benzodiazepines.
If patient is willing to accept oral medication:

1. Oral SGAs: risperidone (2 mg) or olanzapine (5–10 mg)
2. Oral FGAs: haloperidol (2–5 mg*)

If patient is unwilling to accept oral medication, or the above steps did not successfully de-escalate agitation:

3. Parenteral SGAs: olanzapine (10 mg IM) or ziprasidone (10–20 mg IM)
4. Parenteral FGAs: haloperidol (5 mg IM*)

See Table 19.1 *for additional information on maximum and repeat doses*

Notes: Adapted from Wilson et al., 2012
IM = intramuscular
FGA = first-generation antipsychotic
SGA = second-generation antipsychotic
* Assess patient carefully due to increased risk of EPS

ALCOHOL OR BENZODIAZEPINE WITHDRAWAL SUSPECTED

If alcohol or benzodiazepine *withdrawal* is the suspected cause, clinicians should use a benzodiazepine. It is important to note that if *intoxication* is suspected, benzodiazepines should be avoided.

Suggested pharmacological treatment plan:

If patient is willing to accept oral medication:

1. Oral benzodiazepines: lorazepam (1–2 mg)

If patient is unwilling to accept oral medication, or the above step did not successfully de-escalate agitation:

2. Parenteral benzodiazepines: lorazepam (1–2 mg IM)

See Table 19.1 *for additional information on maximum and repeat doses*

Notes: Adapted from Wilson et al., 2012
IM = intramuscular

WITHDRAWAL FROM A SUBSTANCE OTHER THAN ALCOHOL OR BENZODIAZEPINES

If withdrawal from a substance other than alcohol or benzodiazepines is suspected, clinicians may replace that substance with another that maintains similar pharmacological properties, if this substitution is safe and medically appropriate (such as nicotine for nicotine withdrawal) (Wilson et al., 2012).

Agitation Associated with Intoxication

Treatment of agitation associated with intoxication will depend on whether the substances suspected are CNS stimulants or depressants. An overview of this suggested treatment approach is provided in Figure 19.2.

CNS STIMULANTS SUSPECTED (E.G., AMPHETAMINES)

The approach to treating agitation associated with intoxication from CNS stimulants involves the use of benzodiazepines. It is important to note that, when treating chronic amphetamine users, some may develop psychotic symptoms as a result of their drug use (see Shoptaw et al., 2009). If this occurs, an SGA may complement the administered benzodiazepines (Wilson et al., 2012).

1. Use benzodiazepines.
2. If psychotic symptoms develop, consider adding an SGA.

Suggested pharmacological treatment plan:

If patient is willing to accept oral medication:

1. Oral benzodiazepines: lorazepam (1–2 mg)

If patient is unwilling to accept oral medication, or the above step did not successfully de-escalate agitation:

2. Parenteral benzodiazepines: lorazepam (1–2 mg IM)

See Table 19.1 *for additional information on maximum and repeat doses*

Note: Adapted from Wilson et al., 2012
IM = intramuscular

CNS DEPRESSANTS SUSPECTED (E.G., ALCOHOL)

In general, using medication to treat agitation associated with CNS depressants (such as alcohol

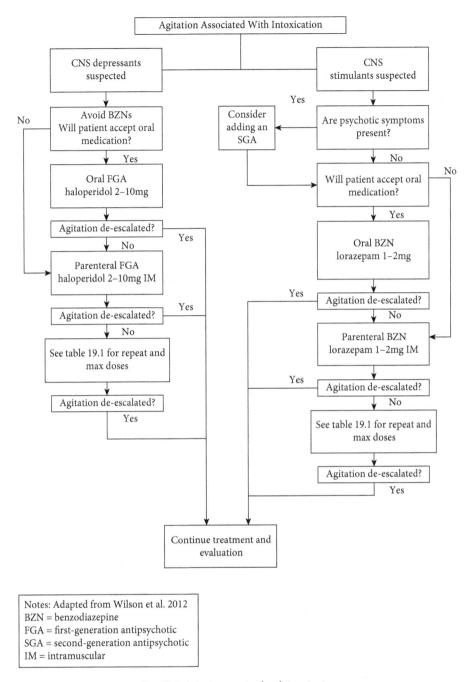

Fig. 19.2 Agitation associated with intoxication.

intoxication) should be avoided. Benzodiazepines should be avoided due to the potential risk of respiratory depression. The use of haloperidol in treating alcohol intoxication has proven particularly effective and is generally recommended. SGAs have not been well studied in this context. It is important to note that the treatment of alcohol

intoxication is significantly different than that of alcohol *withdrawal*.

1. Avoid medication if possible.

2. Avoid benzodiazepines due to risk of respiratory depression.

3. Haloperidol is particularly effective; SGAs not sufficiently studied.

Suggested pharmacological treatment plan:

Avoid benzodiazepines.
If patient is willing to accept oral medication:

1. Oral FGAs: haloperidol (2–10 mg)

If patient is unwilling to accept oral medication, or the above step did not successfully de-escalate agitation:

2. Parenteral FGAs: haloperidol (2–10 mg IM)

See Table 19.1 *for additional information on maximum and repeat doses*

Note: Adapted from Wilson et al., 2012
IM = intramuscular
FGA = first-generation antipsychotic

Agitation Associated with Psychiatric Illnesses

Medication should attempt to treat the underlying cause of psychosis; as such, when psychiatric illness is suspected, antipsychotics are preferred to benzodiazepines. SGAs are preferable to treatment with haloperidol only, or to haloperidol in conjunction with another medication. If initial medication is insufficient, adding a benzodiazepine (e.g., lorazepam) is preferred to using additional doses of the same antipsychotic, or the introduction of another type (Wilson et al., 2012). An overview of this suggested treatment approach is provided in Figure 19.3.

1. Drug selection should attempt to treat underlying psychiatric condition that is causing psychosis.
2. If patient will accept oral medication, risperidone is preferred. If not, intramuscular ziprasidone or olanzapine is preferred for acute control of agitation (Wilson et al., 2012).
3. The addition of a benzodiazepine is preferred if initial antipsychotic dose is insufficient, over the addition of another antipsychotic or additional doses of initial drug.

Suggested pharmacological treatment plan:

If patient is willing to accept oral medication:

1. Oral SGAs: risperidone (2 mg) or olanzapine (5–10 mg)
2. Oral FGAs: haloperidol (2–10 mg) with a benzodiazepine

If patient is unwilling to accept oral medication, or the above steps did not successfully de-escalate agitation:

3. Parenteral SGAs: olanzapine (10 mg IM) or ziprasidone (10–20 mg IM)
4. Parenteral FGAs: haloperidol (2–10 mg IM) with a benzodiazepine

See Table 19.1 *for additional information on maximum and repeat doses*

Notes: Adapted from Wilson et al., 2012
IM = intramuscular

Agitation Associated with Complex or Unknown Presentation

In complex cases whose underlying etiology is unclear, the clinician will have to determine the best approach to treatment. If a patient is displaying psychotic symptoms, then an antipsychotic is preferred. However, in cases where a patient is not displaying psychosis (e.g., hallucinations or paranoia), then benzodiazepines are preferred.

Suggested pharmacological treatment plan:

If patient is displaying psychotic symptoms (same treatment plan as psychiatric illness):
If patient is willing to accept oral medication:

1. Oral SGAs: risperidone (2 mg) or olanzapine (5–10 mg)
2. Oral FGAs: haloperidol (2–10 mg) with a benzodiazepine

If patient is unwilling to accept oral medication, or the above steps did not successfully de-escalate agitation:

3. Parenteral SGAs: olanzapine (10 mg IM) or ziprasidone (10–20 mg IM)
4. Parenteral FGAs: haloperidol (2–10 mg IM) with a benzodiazepine

See Table 19.1 *for additional information on maximum and repeat doses*
If patient is NOT displaying psychotic symptoms (same treatment plan as withdrawal):
If patient is willing to accept oral medication:

1. Oral benzodiazepines: lorazepam (1–2 mg)

If patient is unwilling to accept oral medication, or the above steps did not successfully de-escalate agitation:

2. Parenteral benzodiazepines: lorazepam (1–2 mg IM)

See Table 19.1 *for additional information on maximum and repeat doses*

Notes: Adapted from Wilson et al., 2012
IM = intramuscular
FGA = first-generation antipsychotic
SGA = second-generation antipsychotic

Conclusion

Once thought of as "easy-solution" cases, patients with agitation present a dynamic and challenging case for clinicians. The underlying cause of agitation and the methods by which clinicians de-escalate patients vary significantly, with each requiring different responses and approaches to treatment. Appropriately managing agitation has numerous benefits, including reduced risks for injury to the patient, staff, and bystanders; an increased likelihood of the patients' maintaining their treatment program and schedule; and a faster recovery. However, incorrectly managing agitation through excessive medication or a failure to adequately escalate components of treatment can result in an increased and unnecessary risk of violence and injury. Clinicians should treat agitated patients through a tiered approach that is proportionate to their degree of agitation and aggression. Within this approach, less invasive means of de-escalation such as verbal methods should be attempted before pharmacological intervention, when medically appropriate. Furthermore, patients should be viewed as collaborative partners in their own treatment, and verbal components should be utilized throughout the treatment stages, including when using pharmacological agents.

Throughout our analysis, we have utilized several articles from the American Association for Emergency Psychiatry's Project BETA, which proposes guidelines and best practices for the treatment of agitation, as a framework for our discussion. Underlying all treatments of agitated patients is the necessity of attempting to treat the underlying cause and de-escalation to a point where a patient is stable enough to be evaluated and treated.

Patients with agitation require more attention, as clinicians will need to determine a preliminary diagnosis while also assessing the degree of agitation. As discussed, the BARS is particularly useful and can be done in fast-paced or emergency settings. If a patient is not violent, verbal approaches should be attempted before pharmacological intervention. Verbal de-escalation should be incorporated throughout treatment, even when using pharmacological intervention. For example, asking a patient if they have a preference between two types of medicines allows the patient to feel a degree of control and cooperation, which can promote a degree of de-escalation. Forceful or coercive relationships when initiating treatment plans can make patients averse to seeking help, hostile to medical staff, and can exacerbate their agitation.

Pharmacological intervention should be used as a means of last resort when attempts at verbal de-escalation have failed or when a patient is violent. Importantly, the use of medication should be done so with several considerations: 1) it should attempt to treat the underlying medical condition or etiology of the psychosis; 2) it should only be administered to the extent that it stabilizes the patient and de-escalates the patient to a point where they can be evaluated and treated; and 3) it is done in a manner that builds a collaborative and non-coercive relationship between the patient and clinician. The type of medication and its method of administration are important considerations. The use of medication should also be proportionate. In other words, nonviolent patients who have a lower degree of agitation would not be approached with an intramuscular sedative as a first-line attempt at de-escalating their agitation. In the absence of existing medical contraindications, oral medication is preferred to intramuscular injections, as it is less invasive.

Although mental health clinicians face increased risks, the effective management and treatment of agitation can significantly improve the safety of staff and patients. Benefits to patients and staff extend beyond safety, as successful, collaborative, and non-coercive approaches to treatment can provide a foundation for a patient's successful longer-term treatment. Treatment plans should attempt to build this collaborative relationship at all stages of the tiered approach to de-escalation.

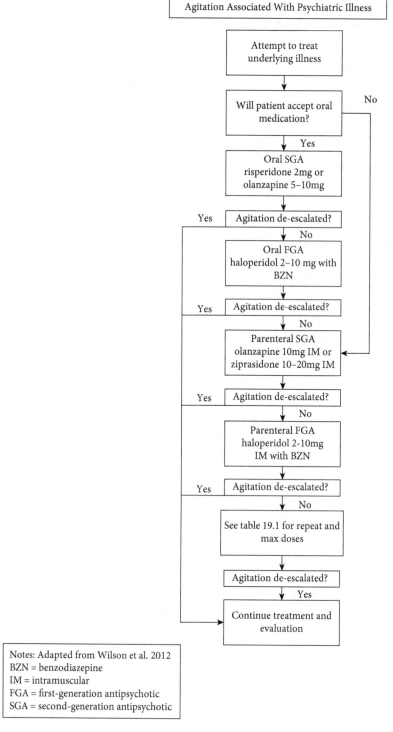

Fig. 19.3 Agitation associated with psychiatric illness.

Notes

1. McKinley, J. C., Jr. (May 2, 2014). "Life Sentence Is Imposed in '08 Killing of Therapist." *The New York Times*. Retrieved from: http://www.nytimes.com/2014/05/03/nyregion/david-tarloff-is-given-life-sentence-for-08-killing-of-psychologist.html?_r=1.

2. Barr, C. W., Londoño, E., & Morse, D. (Sept. 5, 2006). "Patients Admits Killing Psychiatrist, Police Say." *The Washington Post*. Retrieved from: http://www.washingtonpost.com/wp-dyn/content/article/2006/09/04/AR2006090400430.html. Carey, B. (Sept. 19, 2006). "A

Psychiatrist Is Slain, and a Sad Debate Deepens." *The New York Times*. Retrieved from: http://www.nytimes.com/2006/09/19/health/psychology/19slay.html?_r=0.

3. This study uses self-reported survey data and contains the following advisement: "The data are based on replies to a survey that was sent to emergency nurses randomly selected from ENA membership database. Response to the survey was voluntary. ENA does not assume responsibility for the accuracy of the information voluntarily reported by the individuals surveyed."

4. For the complete Project BETA series, see the *Western Journal of Emergency Medicine* 13(1), vi–40.

References

Allen, M. H. (2000). Managing the agitated psychotic patient. *Journal of Clinical Psychiatry*, 61(S14), 11–20.

Allen, M. H., & Currier, G. W. (2004). Use of restraints and pharmacotherapy in academic psychiatric emergency services. *General Hospital Psychiatry*, 26(1), 42–49.

Andrezina, R., Josiassen, R. C., Marcus, R. N., Oren, D. A., Manos, G., Stock, E., . . . Iwamoto, T. (2006). Intramuscular aripiprazole for the treatment of acute agitation in patients with schizophrenia or schizoaffective disorder: a double-blind, placebo-controlled comparison with intramuscular haloperidol. *Psychopharmacology*, 188, 281–292.

Battaglia, J., Moss, S., Rush, J., Kang, J., Mendoza, R., Leedom, L., . . . Goodman, L. (1997). Haloperidol, lorazepam, or both for psychotic agitation? A multicenter, prospective, double-blind, emergency department study. *American Journal of Emergency Medicine*, 15(4), 335–340.

Beasley, C. M., Sayler, M. E., Kiesler, G. M., Potvin, J. H., Sanger, T. M., & Tollefson, G. D. (1998). The influence of pharmacotherapy on self-directed and externally directed aggression in schizophrenia [abstract]. *Schizophrenia Research*, 29, 28.

Brizer, D. A., Convit, A., Krakowski, M., & Volavka, J. (1987). A rating scale for reporting violence on psychiatric wards. *Hospital & Community Psychiatry*, 38(7), 769–770.

Brook, S., Lucey, J. V., & Gunn, K. P. (2000). Intramuscular ziprasidone compared with intramuscular haloperidol in the treatment of acute psychosis. *Journal of Clinical Psychiatry* 61(12), 933–941.

Citrome, L. (2007). Comparison of intramuscular ziprasidone, olanzapine, or aripiprazole for agitation: a quantitative review of efficacy and safety. *Journal of Clinical Psychiatry*, 68(12), 1876–1885.

Clegg, A., & Young, J. B. (2011). Which medications to avoid in people at risk of delirium: a systematic review. *Age and Ageing*, 40, 23–29.

Correll, C. U., & Schenk, E. M. (2008). Tardive dyskinesia and new antipsychotics. *Current Opinion in Psychiatry*, 21, 151–156.

Currier, G. W. (2000). Atypical antipsychotic medications in the psychiatric emergency service. *Journal of Clinical Psychiatry*, 61(S14), 21–26.

Currier, G. W., & Trenton, A. (2002). Pharmacological treatment of psychiatric agitation. *Central Nervous System Drugs*, 16(4), 219–228.

Currier, G. W., Citrome, L. L., Zimbroff, D. L., Oren, D., Manos, G., McQuade, R., . . . Crandall, D. T. (2007). Intramuscular aripiprazole in the control of agitation. *Journal of Psychiatric Practice*, 13(3), 159–169.

Daniel, D. G., Potkin, S. G., Reeves, K. R, Swift, R. H., & Harrigan, E. P. (2001). Intramuscular (IM) ziprasidone 20 mg is effective in reducing acute agitation associated with psychosis: a double-blind, randomized trial. *Psychopharmacology*, 155(2), 128–134.

Dolder, C. R., & Jeste, D. V. (2003). Incidence of tardive dyskinesia with typical versus atypical antipsychotics in very high risk patients. *Biological Psychiatry*, 53, 1142–1145.

Emergency Nurses Association Institute for Emergency Nursing Research. (2011). Emergency Department Violence Study. Available at: https://www.ena.org/practice-research/research/Documents/ENAEDVSReportNovember2011.pdf. Accessed September 8, 2015.

Feinstein, R. E. (1986). Managing violent episodes in the emergency room. *Resident & Staff Physician*, 32, 3PC–6PC.

Fisher, W. A. (1994). Restraint and seclusion: a review of the literature. *American Journal of Psychiatry*, 151(11), 1584–1591.

Fishkind, A. (2002). Calming agitation with words, not drugs: 10 commandments for safety. *Current Psychiatry*, 1(4), 32–39.

Foster, S., Kessel, J., Berman, M. E., & Simpson, G. M. (1997). Efficacy of lorazepam and haloperidol for rapid tranquilization in a psychiatric emergency room setting. *International Clinical Psychopharmacology*, 12, 175–179.

Gillies, D., Beck, A., Sampson, S., & Rathbone, J. (2013). Benzodiazepines for psychosis-induced aggression or agitation. *Cochrane Database of Systematic Reviews*, 4, CD003079.

Hiday, V. A. (1995). The social context of mental illness and violence. *Journal of Health and Social Behavior*, 36(2), 122–137.

Jimerson, D. C., Van Kammen, D. P., Post, R. M., Docherty, J. P., & Bunney, W. E., Jr. (1982). Diazepam in schizophrenia: a preliminary double-blind trial. *American Journal of Psychiatry*, 139(4), 489–491.

Johns, A. (1997). Substance misuse: a primary risk and a major problem of comorbidity. *International Review of Psychiatry*, 9, 233–241.

Kane, J. M. (2004). Tardive dyskinesia rates with atypical antipsychotics in adults: prevalence and incidence. *Journal of Clinical Psychiatry*, 65 (Supp 9), 16–20.

Knox, D. K., & Holloman, G. H. (2012). Use and avoidance of seclusion and restraint: consensus statement of the American Association for Emergency Psychiatry Project BETA Seclusion and Restraint Workgroup. *Western Journal of Emergency Medicine*, 13(1), 35–40.

Kopecky, H. J., Kopecky, C. R., & Yudofsky, S. C. (1998). Reliability and validity of the Overt Agitation Scale in adult psychiatric inpatients. *Psychiatric Quarterly*, 69, 301–323.

Link, B. G., Andrews, H., & Cullen, F. T. (1992). The violent and illegal behavior of mental patients reconsidered. *American Sociological Review*, 57(3), 275–292.

Longton, J. (2015). A look at violence in the workplace against psychiatric aides and psychiatric technicians. *U.S. Bureau of Labor Statistics*. Retrieved from: http://www.bls.gov/opub/mlr/2015/article/a-look-at-violence-in-the-workplace-against-psychiatric-aides-and-psychiatric-technicians.htm. Accessed September 10, 2015.

Marder, S. R., Davis, J. M., & Chouinard G. (1997). The effects of risperidone on the five dimensions of schizophrenia derived by factor analysis: Combined results of the North American Trials. *Journal of Clinical Psychiatry*, 58(12), 538–646.

Marzuk, P. (1996). Violence, crime, and mental illness: how strong a link? *Archives of General Psychiatry*, 53(6), 481–486.

Monahan, J., Steadman, H. J., Silver, E., Applebaum, P. S., Robbins, P. C., Mulvey, E. P., . . . Banks, S. (2001). *Rethinking Risk Assessment: The MacArthur Study of Mental Disorder and Violence*. New York: Oxford University Press.

Mullen, P. E. (1997). A reassessment of the link between mental disorder and violent behaviour, and its implications for clinical practice. *Australian and New Zealand Journal of Psychiatry*, *31*, 3–11.

Noffsinger, S. G., & Resnick, P. J. (1999). Violence and mental illness. *Current Opinion in Psychiatry*, *12*(6), 683–687.

Nordstrom, K., Zun, L. S., Wilson, M. P., Stiebel, V., Ng, A. T., Bregman, B., & Anderson, E. L. (2012). Medical evaluation and triage of the agitated patient: consensus statement of the American Association for Emergency Psychiatry Project BETA Medical Evaluation Workgroup. *Western Journal of Emergency Medicine*, *13*(1), 3–10.

Palmstierna, T., & Wistedt, B. (1987). Staff Observation Aggression Scale, SOAS: presentation and evaluation. *Acta Psychiatrica Scandinavica*, *76*(6), 657–663.

Peuskens, J. (1995). Risperidone in the treatment of patients with chronic schizophrenia: A multi-national, multi-centre, double-blind, parallel-group study versus haloperidol. *British Journal of Psychiatry*, *166*, 712–726.

Powell, G., Caan, W., & Crowe, M. (1994). What events precede violent incidents in psychiatric hospitals? *British Journal of Psychiatry*, *165*, 107–112.

Richmond, J. S., Berlin, J. S., Fishkind, A. B., Holloman, G. H., Zeller, S. L., Wilson, M. P., ... Ng, A. T. (2012). Verbal de-escalation of the agitated patient: consensus statement of the American Association for Emergency Psychiatry Project BETA De-escalation Workgroup. *Western Journal of Emergency Medicine*, *13*(1), 17–25.

Salzman, C., Solomon, D., Miyawaki, E., Glassman, R., Rood, L., Flowers, E., & Thayer, S. (1991). Parenteral lorazepam versus parenteral haloperidol for the control of psychotic disruptive behavior. *Journal of Clinical Psychiatry*, *52*, 177–180.

Shoptaw, S. J., Kao U., & Ling W. (2009). Treatment for amphetamine psychosis. Cochrane *Database of Systematic Reviews*, *1*, CD003026.

Silver, J. M., & Yudofsky, S. C. (1991). The Overt Aggression Scale: overview and guiding principles. *Journal of Neuropsychiatry and Clinical Neurosciences*, *3*, S22–S29.

Steadman, H. J., Mulvey, E. P., Monahan, J., Robbins, P. C., Applebaum, P. S., Grisso, T., ... Silver, E. (1998). Violence by people discharged from acute psychiatric inpatient facilities and by others in the same neighborhoods. *Archives of General Psychiatry*, *55*(5), 393–401.

Stowell, K. R., Florence, P., Harman, H. J., & Glick, Rachel L. (2012). Psychiatric evaluation of the agitated patient: consensus statement of the American Association for Emergency Psychiatry Project BETA Psychiatric Evaluation Workgroup. *Western Journal of Emergency Medicine*, *13*(1), 11–16.

Stuart, H. (2003). Violence and mental illness: an overview. *World Psychiatry*, *2*(2), 121–124.

Swanson, J. W., Borum, R., Swartz, M. S., & Monahan, J. (1996). Psychotic symptoms and disorders and the risk of violent behaviour in the community. *Criminal Behaviour and Mental Health*, *6*, 309–329.

Swift, R. H., Harrigan, E. P., Cappelleri, J. C., Kramer, D., & Chandler, L. P. (2002). Validation of the Behavioural Activity Rating Scale (BARS)TM: a novel measure of activity in agitated patients. *Journal of Psychiatric Research*, *36*, 87–95.

Tollefson, G. D., Beasley, C. M., Tran, P. V., Street, J. S., Krueger, J. A., Tamura, R. N., ... Thieme, M. E. (1997). Olanzapine versus haloperidol in the treatment of schizophrenia and schizoaffective and schizophreniform disorders: results of an international collaborative trial. *American Journal of Psychiatry*, *154*, 457–465.

Torrey, E. F., Stanley, J., Monahan, J., Steadman, H. J., & the MacArthur Study Group. (2008). The MacArthur Violence Risk Assessment Study revisited: Two views ten years after its initial publication. *Psychiatric Services*, *59*(2), 147–152.

Tran-Johnson, T. K., Sack, D. A., Marcus, R. N., Auby, P., McQuade, R. D., & Oren, D. A. (2007). Efficacy and safety of intramuscular aripiprazole in patients with acute agitation: a randomized, double-blind, placebo-controlled trial. *Journal of Clinical Psychiatry*, *68*, 111–119.

U.S. Food and Drug Administration. (2013). Information for healthcare professionals: haloperidol (marketed as haldol, haldol decanoate and haldol lactate). Available at: http://www.fda.gov/Drugs/DrugSafety/PostmarketDrugSafetyInformationforPatientsandProviders/DrugSafetyInformationforHeathcareProfessionals/ucm085203.htm. Accessed September 18, 2015.

Van Putten, T. (1974). Why do schizophrenic patients refuse to take their drugs? *Archives of General Psychiatry*, *31*(1), 67–72.

Wilson, M. P., Pepper, D., Currier, G. W., Holloman, G. H., & Feifel, D. (2012). The psychopharmacology of agitation: consensus statement of the American Association for Emergency Psychiatry Project BETA Psychopharmacology Workgroup. *Western Journal of Emergency Medicine*, *13*(1), 26–34.

Wright, P., Birkett, M., David, S. R., Meehan, K., Ferchland, I., Alaka, K. J., ... Breier, A. (2001). Double-blind, placebo-controlled comparison of intramuscular olanzapine and intramuscular haloperidol in the treatment of acute agitation in schizophrenia. *American Journal of Psychiatry*, *158*, 1149–1151.

Yudofsky, S. C., Silver, J. M., Jackson, W., Endicott, J. & Williams, D. (1986). The Overt Aggression Scale for the objective rating of verbal and physical aggression. *American Journal of Psychiatry*, *143*(1), 35–39.

Zimbroff, D. L., Marcus, R. N., Manos, G., Stock, E., McQuade, R. D., Auby, P., & Oren, D. A. (2007). Management of acute agitation in patients with bipolar disorder: Efficacy and safety of intramuscular aripiprazole. *Journal of Clinical Psychopharmacology*, *27*, 171–176.

The Neurobiology of Suicide and Implications for Treatment and Prevention

Victoria Arango *and* Mark D. Underwood

Abstract

Suicide has a biological component. It is the result not only of the necessary biological vulnerability, but also of multiple factors that must converge to elicit the behavior. These factors are discussed in this chapter and include genetic and epigenetic mechanisms, as well as psychopathologic, environmental, and stressful considerations, such as exposure to early adversity. We present a mathematical model with suicide as the outcome. The equation is based on a conventional stress-diathesis model, but it underscores the complexity of suicide behavior. In addition to discussing the contributors to suicidal behavior, we incorporate in the model protective factors that can reduce the risk of suicide. Because of the anatomical abnormalities in the serotonergic system in the brain of people who have died by suicide, a combination of pharmacotherapy and psychotherapy may be most effective in preventing the behavior.

Key Words: suicide, neurobiology, suicide model, neuroanatomy, review, postmortem, serotonin

This chapter reviews the biological underpinnings associated with suicidal behavior. It discusses these underpinnings in the context of suicide attempts and completed suicides, with the medical damage and emotional instability resulting from suicide attempts constituting an emergency and crisis facing the clinician. Such emergencies and crises are the subject matter of this handbook. The family members most closely related, biologically and physically, to the suicide attempter are of equal importance because genetics and the environment both contribute to suicide. The clinician should be cognizant of the potential for adverse effects as well as for the increased risk for suicide among the family members.

Suicide is a severe (arguably the most extreme) response to stress. Yet many people experience stress, even severe and harsh forms, without turning to suicide as a response. There are multiple contributors to suicide but the underlying causes remain largely not understood. Because of this complexity, suicide for the most part, is not preventable, predictable, or treatable. We propose a modified stress-diathesis model to capture the complexity of the behavior: the amount or intensity of suicidal behavior over a given time interval is equal to an integral of the rate of change of the "stress" (the triggering environmental stressor), plus the integral of the interaction between biological and other trait-dependent factors—for example, psychiatric illness, genetics, or early life adversity (see Figure 20.1).

The model has heuristic value in compartmentalizing the distinct contributors to suicidal behavior. None of the contributors alone is sufficient to result in suicide, but each is important. In addition, the model depicts the importance of the severity of the stress and the time frame over which it occurs or changes.

In this chapter, we emphasize the biological elements of the suicide equation model, but we fully acknowledge that suicide is not the inescapable

Suicide Model

$$\int_0^1 f(\text{suicide})\, dx = f(\text{stress}) + f(\text{biology} * \text{environment}) - \sum_0^n \text{protective factors}$$

Fig. 20.1 Explanatory mathematical model proposed with suicide as an outcome. The equation is based on a conventional stress-diathesis model but modified to capture the complexity of suicide behavior, where the amount or intensity of suicidal behavior over a given time interval is equal to an integral of the rate of change of the "stress" (the triggering environmental stressor), plus the integral of the interaction between biological and other trait-dependent factors (e.g., psychiatric illness, genetics, early life adversity), minus the sum of protective factors (e.g., reasons for living). Note that the model allows for the suicidal behavior to range from ideation to suicide completion and for protective measures to reduce the contribution of stress and trait-dependent components.

result of a neuropathology; psychiatric illness is present in >95% of suicides. Just as suicide does not take place in the absence of an environmental stressor (for example, the loss of a loved one, the diagnosis of a terminal illness, public humiliation, and an absence of reasons for living), biological studies are approaching consensus that completed suicide is associated with neuroanatomical, neurophysiological, and neurochemical differences compared to someone who did not die by suicide, and the findings are arguably interpretable as constituting a neuropathology; suicide is the endpoint of a diseased brain confronted with a severe environmental stressor. The data strongly suggest that brain pathology is present in suicide completers and this partly explains the difficulty in suicide prevention and treatment.

Suicide

Incidence

Suicide claims the lives of nearly 1 million people worldwide each year (World Health Organziation, http://www.who.int/topics/suicide/en/). The rate of suicide varies throughout the world. The highest suicide rates are in Eastern Europe (20–25 per 100,000); the lowest reported rates are in Latin America (5–10 per 100,000). In the United States, the rate is approximately 11 suicides per 100,000 persons (10–15 per 100,000). By contrast, the intentional homicide rate in Eastern Europe is approximately 5.9 per 100,000 and 4.7 per 100,000 in North America (United Nations Office on Drugs and Crime, http://www.unodc.org/gsh/en/data.html).

Causes

Suicide is a complex behavior and is not thought to have a single root cause. Rather, suicidal behavior is heterogeneous in intent and severity, ranging from being highly impulsive to highly planned. Psychiatric illness, diagnosed ante mortem or retrospectively, is present in more than 90% of the cases of completed suicide (Harris & Barraclough, 1997). Major depressive disorder (MDD) is the most common diagnosis, present in approximately 60% of people who have

completed suicides. The other frequent diagnoses for people who have attempted or completed suicide include bipolar disorder, borderline personality disorder, schizophrenia, alcoholism, and substance abuse (Harris & Barraclough, 1997; Gradus et al., 2010). Suicide can take place in the presence or absence of treatment for mental illness, and it is estimated that as many as 66% of people who completed suicide have contact with at least a primary care physician in the month before their terminal act (Luoma, Martin, & Pearson, 2002; Andersen, Andersen, Rosholm, & Gram, 2000).

Triggers can be proximal, either acute or chronic, and more recent studies suggest that triggers for suicide can even be distal. Proximal triggers include a recent tragedy experienced by the person predisposed to suicide. However, only a minority of people experiencing such acute stressors experience the hopelessness that leads to suicide as the inescapable option of choice. Chronic triggers can include (1) medical conditions (chronic pain, cancer, traumatic brain injury, progressive muscular diseases); (2) prognosis of deteriorating quality of life consequent to aging (Conwell, Van Orden, & Caine, 2011); or (3) terminal illness. For example, there was a high rate of suicide associated with HIV in the time of its early recognition as a disease without treatment (Marzuk et al., 1988; Marzuk et al., 1997). More recent studies have found that childhood abuse, particularly sexual physical abuse, is a significant risk factor for suicide in adulthood (Adam et al., 2011; Wingenfeld et al., 2011). Studies of childhood adversity have also indicated the possibility of the stress leading to epigenetic changes that have life-lasting biological effects, including hyper-responsivity to stress and reduced serotonergic neurotransmission (McGowan et al., 2009). This represents at least one means whereby brain alterations can occur, creating a biological risk that can predispose an individual to the proximal trigger.

With the advent of effective pharmacological treatments, mental illnesses are now more like medical conditions insofar as the symptomatology can be reversed or controlled, and data indicate that there are neurochemical and anatomical changes in the brains of individuals with mental illness. Accordingly, different mental illnesses are associated with different neurochemical and or anatomical changes, yet suicide and suicide risk cuts across several psychiatric diagnoses. Without delving into the changes associated with individual mental illnesses or diagnoses, there are a number of changes in the brain that appear to be associated with suicide (as a cause of death) and not with the associated underlying psychiatric diagnosis or diagnoses. Furthermore, medications used and effective for mental illness are not particularly anti-suicidal. SSRIs are effective in reducing the symptoms of MDD, but evidence regarding the extent that SSRIs reduce suicidal behavior or ideation is disputed (Gunnell, Saperia, & Ashby, 2005). Clozapine does appear to reduce suicide in psychotic individuals, but its use as an anti-suicide medication in other mental illnesses is not clear (Meltzer et al., 2003). We believe the evidence of neurochemical changes in suicide, particularly in the serotonergic system in specific brain regions, is what cuts across psychiatric diagnoses. The alterations constitute a neuroanatomical predisposition to suicide by disinhibition of prefrontal cortical brain regions that would otherwise inhibit and prevent self-destructive actions.

Neurobiology

Studies of the cerebral spinal fluid (CSF) were among the first to indicate there is a reduction in the serotonin (5-HT, 5-hydroxytryptamine) system associated with a suicide attempt (Träskman, Åsberg, Bertilsson, & Sjöstrand, 1981; Åsberg, Träskman, & Thorén, 1976). This finding has now been replicated by multiple investigators and is one of the most "stable" findings in biological psychiatry (Lindqvist et al., 2011). Importantly, the results from high performance liquid chromatography (HPLC) analysis of the CSF include other monoamine transmitters and metabolites, including those for dopamine and norepinephrine, and these transmitter systems most commonly are reported not to be associated with suicide, suggesting there is some neurotransmitter specificity for the involvement of 5-HT in suicidal behavior. The literature does support an involvement of neurotransmitters other than 5-HT, however, the weight of evidence suggests that these other changes are in addition to those involving the 5-HT system (see Figure 20.2).

Reduced Serotonergic Neurotransmission

Reduced serotonergic function has been a long-standing theme in the neurobiological etiology of suicide. Data supporting this hypothesis come from diverse studies and methodologies, from cells to

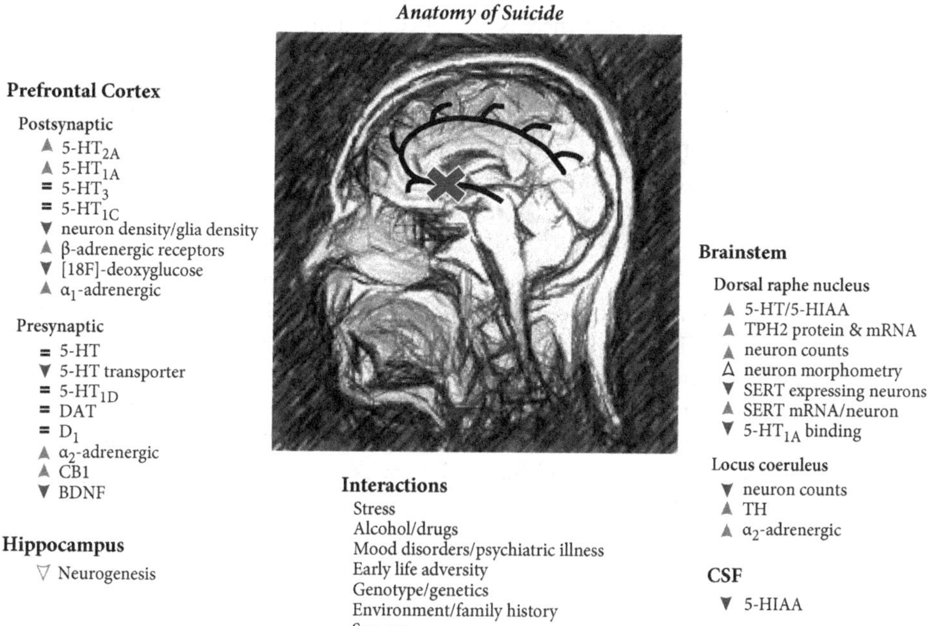

Anatomy of Suicide

Prefrontal Cortex

Postsynaptic
▲ 5-HT$_{2A}$
▲ 5-HT$_{1A}$
= 5-HT$_3$
= 5-HT$_{1C}$
▼ neuron density/glia density
▲ β-adrenergic receptors
▼ [18F]-deoxyglucose
▲ α$_1$-adrenergic

Presynaptic
= 5-HT
▼ 5-HT transporter
= 5-HT$_{1D}$
= DAT
= D$_1$
▲ α$_2$-adrenergic
▲ CB1
▼ BDNF

Hippocampus
▽ Neurogenesis

Interactions
Stress
Alcohol/drugs
Mood disorders/psychiatric illness
Early life adversity
Genotype/genetics
Environment/family history
Sex, age

Brainstem

Dorsal raphe nucleus
▲ 5-HT/5-HIAA
▲ TPH2 protein & mRNA
▲ neuron counts
Δ neuron morphometry
▼ SERT expressing neurons
▲ SERT mRNA/neuron
▼ 5-HT$_{1A}$ binding

Locus coeruleus
▼ neuron counts
▲ TH
▲ α$_2$-adrenergic

CSF
▼ 5-HIAA

Fig. 20.2 Summary of neurobiological findings in suicide. The direction of findings are not absolute and are considered by the authors to be the consensus of the literature. A circuit disconnection is proposed where the findings in the prefrontal cortex are most consistent with reduced function and the changes in the brainstem suggest plasticity and upregulation.

brain regions, from live cases to postmortem brains, from DNA to RNA to neurotransmitter to receptor to second messenger systems. In each case and for each finding there are frequently both positive and negative reports, indicating that the neurochemistry and changes are not requisite or absolute and are likely just one component of the behavior. Likewise, certain changes appear to be epigenetic in origin and may only be present in select subgroups or phenotypes—for example, reduced serotonin transporter (SERT) in association with the short allele of the 5-HTTLPR gene (Lesch et al., 1996; Van Dyck et al., 2004; Wankerl et al., 2014) or reduced SERT binding in MDD, but more so in cases with childhood adversity (Miller et al., 2009).

Direct study of 5-HT in the brain is impossible in living subjects and is complicated even in the postmortem human brain because 5-HT is rapidly degraded postmortem. However, the receptor proteins for 5-HT are more stable, and quantitative autoradiography has allowed the measurement of the amount of neurotransmitter receptors and also the anatomical distribution of the receptors. Several studies, though not all, have found increases in the density of postsynaptic 5-HT_{1A} and 5-HT_{2A} receptors (see Currier & Mann, 2008; Furczyk, Schutová, Michel, Thome, & Büttner, 2013; Mann, 2003) in the prefrontal cortex in depressed individuals who completed suicide compared to normal non-psychiatric controls. An increase in the density of postsynaptic receptors suggests that there is an up-regulation response by cortical neurons as a means of compensation for reduced serotonin release from presynaptic terminals. Consistent with the hypothesis of reduced 5-HT in the prefrontal cortex are reports that there is less SERT binding in the prefrontal cortex in depressed individuals who died by suicide (see Furczyk et al., 2013). The reduction in the density of SERT is reported in the same cortical regions where postsynaptic receptors are increased. A reduction in SERT is also reported in patients with MDD that are treatment naïve (Parsey et al., 2006a), suggesting that the reduction in the amount of SERT may be a trait feature and contribute to the predisposition for either suicide or MDD. The reduction in SERT is reported to be more anatomically restricted in those who completed suicide than in those with MDD (Arango, Underwood, & Mann, 2002).

In vivo brain imaging studies have reported comparable findings to those in postmortem studies, suggesting that these brain changes are present ante mortem and with less than fatal suicidal

behavior. Fluorodeoxyglucose PET studies have found a correlation between the degree of medical injury in a suicide attempt and the cerebral metabolic rate for glucose utilization in the anterior cingulate cortex and the dorsolateral prefrontal cortex (Oquendo et al., 2003). PET studies are also assessing neurotransmitter systems in brain; there is reduced SERT in suicide attempters (Miller et al., 2013; Bah et al., 2008; Cannon et al., 2006), and more 5-HT_{1A} binding in the multiple brain regions of depressed individuals who were medication naïve (Parsey et al., 2006b), findings consistent with postmortem studies.

Anatomical differences in the distribution and concentration of 5-HT receptors in the prefrontal cortex between individuals who have completed suicide and those with MDD are of significance. It suggests that there are functional changes associated with the differences in the concentration of the receptors, and also that the brain functions subserved by those receptors is altered. In the brains of those who have completed suicide, the changes are most different in the orbital and dorsolateral prefrontal cortex, while in those with MDD the changes are more widespread (Arango et al., 2002). The orbital and dorsolateral prefrontal cortex carry out executive-cognitive functions, so a deficit in these areas raises the possibility that those who are suicidal have a compromised ability to cognitively process neural input and may therefore be compromised in inhibiting suicidal ideation, which may thereby allow suicidal acts by disinhibition. Given the widespread symptomatology of MDD, involving mood, cognition, appetite, sleep, and more, it is understandable and expected that the brain regions affected are more diverse.

Cells in the prefrontal cortex

Not only are pre-and postsynaptic neurotransmitter receptors changed in persons who complete suicide, but cells are also changed. We found that there is a lower density of neurons in the prefrontal cortex in depressed people who died by suicide (Arango et al., 2002; Underwood et al., 2012). Rajkowska and colleagues reported not only reductions in neuron density in the dorsolateral prefrontal cortex in MDD, but also reductions in the density of supporting glial cells (Rajkowska, 2000; Rajkowska, Miguel-Hidalgo, Dubey, Stockmeier, & Krishnan, 2005; Rajkowska, 2002). The reduction in neuron density in the PFC in depressed individuals who complete suicide presumably reflects a loss of neurons since a loss of the intervening neuropil without a loss of neurons would result in an increase in the density of neurons and glia. A loss of neurons would, therefore, be expected to adversely contribute to the neuropathology of suicide, especially since there is no neurogenesis in the neocortex. In addition, connections between brain regions would likely be weakened by neuronal loss, thereby decreasing activity in brain circuits that are hypothesized to provide valence to perceived events and contribute to emotional memory. A disconnection hypothesis has been made in MDD based on functional brain maps and diffusion tensor imaging of fiber bundles (Riva-Posse et al., 2014; Choi et al., 2014; Mayberg, 2009); circuit disconnection may also underlie suicidal behavior.

We find 5-HT synthesized in neurons in the raphe groups of cells lying predominantly along the midline of the brainstem. Neurons in the dorsal (DRN) and median raphe nuclei provide nearly all the serotonergic innervation of the forebrain. Studies measuring the amount of 5-HT and 5-HIAA directly in brainstem tissue have found reduced or increased amounts (see Arango & Mann, 1992; Bach et al., 2013 for review) in those with MDD and suicide behavior. Underwood and colleagues hypothesized that the reduction in 5-HT neurotransmission might be due to fewer DRN neurons, but found that the number and density of 5-HT synthesizing neurons was greater in depressed individuals who completed suicide (Underwood et al., 1999). Arango et al. (2001) examined SERT and 5-HT_{1A} autoreceptor binding in the DRN in depressed persons who died by suicide. An index of the total number of 5-HT_{1A} receptors (receptor binding x volume of receptor distribution) was 43% lower in the DRN of suicide deaths, compared with controls. The suicide group also had 54% fewer DRN neurons expressing SERT mRNA compared with controls. In the neurons that expressed the SERT gene, SERT mRNA expression per neuron was greater in suicides. Tryptophan hydroxylase 2 (TPH2) is the rate-limiting biosynthetic enzyme for 5-HT synthesis. Reports of increased tryptophan hydroxylase 2 (TPH2) and TPH2 mRNA in the DRN of depressed suicides (Bach-Mizrachi et al., 2006; Bach-Mizrachi et al., 2008), along with less feedback inhibition of DRN neuron firing via 5-HT_{1A} autoreceptors and enhanced 5-HT action due to less uptake of 5-HT, is consistent with hyperserotonergic function in the serotonergic system in the brainstem as opposed to the evidence suggesting hypofunction in the prefrontal cortex.

Other transmitters and signaling molecules have been investigated in suicide behavior, including dopamine, norepinephrine, cannabinoid receptors, and brain derived neurotrophic factor (BDNF). Differences have variously been reported but a detailed review is beyond the scope of this chapter. Differences are summarized in Figure 20.2.

We hypothesize in suicide that there may be a circuit "disconnect" between the brainstem and the prefrontal cortex; the disconnect results in "upregulatory changes" in both regions with the increase in 5-HT in the brainstem not being communicated, either anatomically and or functionally, to the prefrontal cortex. The end result is reduced 5-HT neurotransmission in PFC regions mediating behavioral inhibition and the outcome is the enabling of suicidal behavior. Moreover, the increase in 5-HT in the brainstem may result in a serotonergic "storm," which is reported to elicit behavioral aggression and impulsivity in animals (Coplan, Gopinath, Abdallah, & Berry, 2014; Isbister & Buckley, 2005). One implication of this disconnection is that treatments bringing about increased 5-HT synthesis may fail because the brainstem neurons synthesizing the 5-HT are not "connected" to the prefrontal cortical areas where the 5-HT is released.

Structural magnetic resonance imaging studies report hyperintensities in several regions of white matter and lower anisotropy in the orbitofrontal cortex region and in the anterior limb of the internal capsule (reviewed in van Heeringen & Mann, 2014). Taken together with functional imaging studies and postmortem findings, the data suggest several anatomical changes in the brain associated with suicide and demonstrate a possible neuropathological underpinning consistent with reduced prefrontal cortex function, due to dysfunctional connections between serotonergic source neurons in the brainstem and target neurons in the prefrontal cortex.

Genetics/Early Adversity

Genes provide the blueprint for an individual's biological constitution, and gene transcription is subject to multiple points of epigenetic modulation. Suicidal behavior is accompanied, or at least preceded, by perceived extreme life stress, and there are hypotheses recently advanced positing that stress and gene regulation intersect with adverse biological outcome contributing to the biological phenotype (Rutter, Moffitt, & Caspi, 2006). Suicide is also heritable and suicide runs in families, however, there is no single suicide gene (Arango, Huang,

Underwood, & Mann, 2003; Clayden, Zaruk, Meyre, Thabane, & Samaan, 2012).

Several genes have been reported to have polymorphisms associated with suicidal behavior including the SERT, the 5-HT$_{2A}$ receptor, 5-HT$_{1A}$ receptor, TPH2, MAOA, BDNF, COMT, dopamine transporter, dopamine D$_2$ receptor, and FKBP5. Despite increasingly large sample sizes, there are few replications.

The SERT gene polymorphism 5-HTTLPR is of particular interest, not only because there is a functionally relevant polymorphism associated with reduced expression and an association with violent suicide and depression reported by some investigators, but also because there is a relationship between the polymorphism and stress. A recent meta-analysis by Karg and colleagues (2011) found strong evidence that the 5-HTTLPR allele is associated with an increased risk of developing depression under stress. Interestingly, childhood abuse is also reported to be associated with less SERT binding in MDD (Miller et al., 2009) and in impulsive aggression (Rylands et al., 2012) later on in adulthood. The interaction of distal as well as recent stressful or adverse life events with gene expression has significance for understanding the vulnerability for suicide. The serotonergic changes in adulthood associated with childhood adversity raise the possibility that the normal development of the serotonergic system can be permanently altered by exposure to stressful events. The interaction of adversity and gene expression with serotonergic neurotransmission deficiency may constitute a biological phenotype for suicide risk. Conversely, childhood adversity without the gene polymorphism and without serotonergic deficiency may be a biological basis for resilience to stressful life events.

Neurogenesis/Plasticity

Neurogenesis in the adult brain means the birth of new neurons and this is prominent in the dentate gyrus of the hippocampus. A role for neurogenesis in the etiology of depression has been made (Jacobs, van Praag, & Gage, 2000) wherein stress inhibits neurogenesis in the dentate gyrus, and antidepressants increase neurogenesis in the same regions and in a serotonin dependent manner. In this hypothesis, reduced 5-HT is a trait factor and stress and/or depression results in decreased neurogenesis; SSRIs increase net 5-HT neurotransmission and increase or restore neurogenesis in the hippocampus. With regard to suicide, however, it is not clear whether or how the hippocampus is involved since most studies do not find hippocampal changes associated with suicide, and SSRIs are not particularly anti-suicide in their effect. The impact of stress is not universally "negative" throughout the brain, as increases in the number, size, and dendritic arbor are observed in serotonin-synthesizing neurons in the dorsal raphe nucleus in depressed individuals who have completed suicide (Underwood et al., 1999). This suggests that there are brain regions such as the hippocampus that are adversely affected by stress, but also that there are other brain regions like the dorsal raphe nucleus that are responsive to stress in a manner consistent with homeostatic changes.

Treatments

Suicide is a complex behavior ranging from non-lethal ideation to fatal suicidal acts, complicated by the level of impulsiveness, the degree of planning, the access to lethal means, and the extent of comorbid psychiatric illness. It is likely that the suicides that are highly impulsive, highly planned, or highly lethal cannot be anticipated or predicted. Alternatively, there are well-recognized risk factors for suicide, and the majority of people who have completed suicide have had contact with a primary care physician within a month of their death (Luoma et al., 2002; Andersen et al., 2000), raising the possibility for prevention and treatment. Treatment for suicide has varying degrees of success and treatments include pharmacotherapy, psychotherapy, and electroconvulsive therapy.

Pharmacotherapy

The most common psychiatric illness in completed and attempted suicide is major depression. This had led to the findings and conclusion that the depression is often untreated and, when treated, it is undertreated (Hirschfeld et al., 1997; Oquendo, Malone, Ellis, Sackeim, & Mann, 1999). There are few studies that find that treating the depressive mood also "treats" the suicide, perhaps because of the low incidence of suicide relative to depression, as well as the difficulty of performing randomized treatment studies of suicide.

Serotonin specific reuptake inhibitors (SSRIs) act by blocking the reuptake of 5-HT after it is released from 5-HT neurons. MDD is associated with reduced 5-HT neurotransmission, and SSRIs are effective in reducing the severity of MDD, but with a time-course of several weeks for efficacy. As noted earlier, there is little evidence that SSRIs have a significant impact on reducing suicide. Furthermore, it has been suggested that the use of SSRIs in adolescents poses a potential risk for suicidal behavior, which is not evident in adults (Nutt, 2003; Gibbons et al., 2007b). It is unclear whether these findings are idiosyncratic. During development, 5-HT undergoes marked change in amount and distribution, and 5-HT is present in greater amounts in childhood and adolescence than in adulthood. SSRIs in adolescence may therefore have the unintended consequence of creating a more hyperserotonergic state, which could lead to anxiety and irritability, which could lead to suicidal thoughts. Meta-analyses have found that suicide rates follow antidepressant prescription rates (Gibbons et al., 2007a). After warnings were placed on SSRI prescriptions, there was a decrease in prescription rates, accompanied by an apparent increase in the rate of suicide (Gibbons et al., 2007a), suggesting the untreated depression raises a greater risk for suicide than the idiosyncratic effects of SSRIs. It has been suggested that the depths of severe depression are sufficient so as to prevent many behaviors, perhaps including suicidal acts, and it is only with improved mood and restoration of cognitive function that the afflicted individual is "enabled" to make a suicide attempt (Gunnell et al., 2005). Interestingly, reduced 5-HT neurotransmission is also hypothesized as being a central component of suicide risk and etiology, though the hypothesized deficit is most pronounced in the orbital and dorsolateral prefrontal cortex. It is therefore unclear why SSRIs would not be effective in reducing suicide behaviors. One possibility is that there is deficient 5-HT for release in persons at risk for suicide; therefore, there is less 5-HT reuptake possible, leaving an unaddressed 5-HT release deficit.

Clozapine is reported to reduce suicide incidence in people with schizophrenia (Meltzer et al., 2003). It is the only medication approved by the FDA for reducing suicide risk in persons with schizophrenia. It is not known whether this effect is related to antidepressant effects of the drug or to antipsychotic actions. Regardless, clozapine has not been found to be anti-suicidal in non-schizophrenic populations. Clozapine is an antagonist at both D_2 and 5-HT_{2A} receptors, and may exert its anti-suicide effects through these receptor systems or alternatively by restoring 5-HT and DA neurotransmission imbalance.

Lithium is reported to reduce suicide risk in bipolar patients (Baldessarini, Tondo, & Hennen, 2003). It is hypothesized that the reduction in suicide risk is due to a reduction in impulsivity and aggression and through facilitation of 5-HT neurotransmission.

On the whole, however, pharmacotherapy for mental illnesses and their predominant symptoms are of limited use in addressing suicide risk. The weight of evidence does suggest that alleviation of symptoms in those conditions reduces suicide risk overall, however, it is unclear as to whether there is a direct connection between the neurochemical changes and the reduction in suicide risk.

Psychotherapy

Psychotherapy can be particularly effective in reducing suicide risk, especially in the acute period immediately following a suicide attempt. This makes psychotherapy an especially valuable adjunct to pharmacotherapy, which can take up to days or weeks to have an effect. Cognitive behavior therapy (CBT) and dialectic behavioral therapy (DBT) are both proven effective at treating and reducing suicide risk in the short term, particularly in borderline personality disorder. The neurobiology of psychotherapy is not well known.

The early studies of the neurobiology of psychotherapy used brain imaging of fluorodeoxyglucose as an index of brain activity. Underactive brain regions including the dorsolateral prefrontal cortex were identified in patients with MDD, and psychotherapy, as well as pharmacotherapy, increased metabolism in these regions (Brody et al., 2001). Mayberg and colleagues have examined brain metabolism in groups of cases and have parsed-out separate brain circuits for MDD patients responding to psychotherapy from those responding to SSRIs (Mayberg et al., 2005; Ressler & Mayberg, 2007). The SSRI-related circuit included the brainstem and BA25 in the prefrontal cortex, while the pharmacotherapy-related circuit involved the dorsomedial cingulate cortex and BA25 (Mayberg, 2003). The identification of two different brain circuits with the anterior cingulate cortex as a region in common has led to hypotheses about "top-down" approaches bringing about cognitive control and "bottom-up" treatments with SSRIs resulting in a similar functional outcome.

The utility of pharmacotherapy takes on additional significance since SSRIs can take weeks to reduce depressive symptoms while cognitive therapy brings more rapid reductions in suicide ideation. There are also a significant number of patients who are pharmacotherapy resistant. This raises the possibility of a need for individualized therapies because the underlying pathological brain circuits affected are different. A multimodal approach may or may not have added benefit in the same way that an SSRI may not be as effective a treatment if the root chemical imbalance is with norepinephrine or dopamine.

Electroconvulsive Therapy

Electroconvulsive therapy (ECT) is an effective treatment for antidepressant resistant depression, and ECT has long been recognized for the added benefit of reducing suicide ideation and suicide attempts (Avery & Winokur, 1978). Expressed suicidal intent is decreased following ECT (Kellner et al., 2005). The mechanisms of action of ECT is not known, but there are numerous effects on brain neurochemistry; 5-HT_{1A} autoreceptors are sensitized, 5-HT_{2A} receptors are decreased, there is an increase in release of glutamate and GABA, and there is decreased autoreceptor function in the noradrenergic and dopaminergic systems with increased release of norepinephrine and dopamine (see Ishihara & Sasa, 1999). Therefore, despite the negative cognitive side effects, ECT remains an effective anti-suicide treatment in antidepressant resistant patients.

Ketamine

Ketamine is a promising potential treatment for suicide, particularly in the emergency setting, since it has a rapid and relatively lasting duration (10 days) of anti-suicide ideation effect (Larkin & Beautrais, 2011). Ketamine in sub-anesthetic doses of 0.5 mg/kg was shown to decrease suicide ideation within 40 minutes of administration which was sustained for hours (Price, Nock, Charney, & Mathew, 2009; Diazgranados et al., 2010; Larkin & Beautrais, 2011). Ketamine is a glutamate N-methyl-D-Aspartate (NMDA) receptor antagonist, with additional effects on muscarinic cholinergic receptors, as well as having possible downstream effects on monoaminergic receptors, which could explain in part the antidepressant impact (Murrough, 2012). Ketamine also has effects on several molecules in the mammalian Target of Rapamycin (mTOR) pathway and it elicits changes in synaptic plasticity and an increase in synaptic spines in the cortex of rats (Li et al., 2010). The antidepressant effects of ketamine were dependent on elevated levels of BDNF (Autry et al., 2011). Responses to ketamine suggest direct effects on neurotransmission and synaptic function at the level of the cerebral cortex which may enhance activity in brain regions deficient in major depression and presumably also in suicidal behavior.

Hypothesis

The primary underlying neuropathology in suicide is an anatomical and functional disconnection between serotonergic/monoaminergic neurons in the brainstem and executive regions in the PFC. Pharmacotherapy is a useful adjunct treatment for the associated psychiatric illness (antidepressants for depression, clozapine for schizophrenia), but it is not particularly effective in treating suicidal behavior because there is insufficient serotonergic neurotransmission in key prefrontal cortical regions (i.e. there is no effect of SSRIs because there is no 5-HT released to block). Psychotherapy has greater success in reducing suicide ideation and intent, particularly in the short term. This is the case because the brain remains plastic, and there is the possibility of establishing alternative "pathways" and cognitive response strategies in cortical brain regions that are (a) critical for the behavioral inhibition of the suicidal impulse and act, and (b) "downstream" of the pathology. The alternative pathways bypass the disconnected brainstem raphe and the orbital and dorsolateral prefrontal cortex, and they enhance connections between the prefrontal cortex and the medial cingulate cortex and amygdala. The alternate circuits provide a short-term means for altering the perception of the triggering adverse life event(s) and reducing the emotional valence of the event while raising the threshold for engaging in suicidal behavior.

Conclusion

Suicide is a complex behavior and can manifest in forms ranging from the unobservable (ideation) to the unpreventable (impulsive or highly planned) lethal act. We propose a model for suicide that one day may be a solvable equation where the risk factors and preventive factors can be quantified and the outcome can help direct a clinician's treatment plan. Biological findings associated with suicide provide the promise for genetic testing, blood testing, or brain imaging to further inform the physician as to the magnitude of the neurobiological risks for suicide behavior. Neuroanatomical findings in the literature indicate that one phenotype for suicide includes an anatomical and physiological "interruption" between serotonin neurons in the brainstem and target neurons in the orbital, ventromedial, and dorsolateral prefrontal cortex. Conventional SSRI treatments for comorbid MDD may not be effective to address this "interruption," and alternative pharmacological treatments are needed with adjunctive psychotherapy in order to utilize other brain circuits to bring about an anti-suicide effect. To this end, the physician should view the suicidal patient as treatable and the family of suicide attempters or completers should know that suicide is a product of an organic brain disease.

References

Adam, E. K., Chyu, L., Hoyt, L. T., Doane, L. D., Boisjoly, J., Duncan, G. J., . . . McDade, T. W. (2011). Adverse adolescent relationship histories and young adult health: Cumulative effects of loneliness, low parental support, relationship instability, intimate partner violence, and loss. *Journal of Adolescent Health, 49,* 278–286.

Andersen, U. A., Andersen, M., Rosholm, J. U., & Gram, L. F. (2000). Contacts to the health care system prior to suicide: A comprehensive analysis using registers for general and psychiatric hospital admissions, contacts to general practitioners, and practising specialists and drug prescriptions. *Acta Psychiatrica Scandinavica, 102,* 126–134.

Arango, V., Huang, Y. Y., Underwood, M. D., & Mann, J. J. (2003). Genetics of the serotonergic system in suicidal behavior. *Journal of Psychiatric Research, 37,* 375–386.

Arango, V., & Mann, J. J. (1992). Relevance of serotonergic postmortem studies to suicidal behavior. *International Review of Psychiatry, 4,* 131–140.

Arango, V., Underwood, M. D., Boldrini, M., Tamir, H., Kassir, S. A., Hsiung, S., . . . Mann, J. J. (2001). Serotonin 1A receptors, serotonin transporter binding and serotonin transporter mRNA expression in the brainstem of depressed suicide victims. *Neuropsychopharmacology, 25,* 892–903.

Arango, V., Underwood, M. D., & Mann, J. J. (2002). Serotonin brain circuits involved in major depression and suicide. *Progress in Brain Research, 136,* 443–453.

Åsberg, M., Träskman, L., & Thorén, P. (1976). 5-HIAA in the cerebrospinal fluid. A biochemical suicide predictor? *Archives of General Psychiatry, 33,* 1193–1197.

Autry, A. E., Adachi, M., Nosyreva, E., Na, E. S., Los, M. F., Cheng, P. F., . . . Monteggia, L. M. (2011). NMDA receptor blockade at rest triggers rapid behavioural antidepressant responses. *Nature, 475,* 91–95.

Avery, D., & Winokur, G. (1978). Suicide, attempted suicide, and relapse rates in depression. *Archives of General Psychiatry, 35,* 749–753.

Bach, H., Huang, Y. Y., Underwood, M. D., Dwork, A. J., Mann, J. J., & Arango, V. (2013). Elevated serotonin and 5-HIAA in the brainstem and lower serotonin turnover in the prefrontal cortex of suicides. *Synapse, 68*(3), 127–130.

Bach-Mizrachi, H., Underwood, M. D., Kassir, S. A., Bakalian, M. J., Sibille, E., Tamir, H., . . . Arango, V. (2006). Neuronal tryptophan hydroxylase mRNA expression in the human dorsal and median raphe nuclei: Major depression and suicide. *Neuropsychopharmacology, 31,* 814–824.

Bach-Mizrachi, H., Underwood, M. D., Tin, A., Ellis, S. P., Mann, J. J., & Arango, V. (2008). Elevated expression of tryptophan hydroxylase-2 mRNA at the neuronal level in the dorsal and median raphe nuclei of depressed suicides. *Molecular Psychiatry, 13,* 507–513.

Bah, J., Lindstrom, M., Westberg, L., Manneras, L., Ryding, E., Henningsson, S., . . . Eriksson, E. (2008). Serotonin transporter gene polymorphisms: Effect on serotonin transporter availability in the brain of suicide attempters. *Psychiatry Research, 162,* 221–229.

Baldessarini, R. J., Tondo, L., & Hennen, J. (2003). Lithium treatment and suicide risk in major affective disorders: Update and new findings. *Journal of Clinical Psychiatry, 64,* 44–52.

Brody, A. L., Saxena, S., Stoessel, P., Gillies, L. A., Fairbanks, L. A., Alborzian, S., . . . Baxter, L. R., Jr. (2001). Regional brain metabolic changes in patients with major depression treated with either paroxetine or interpersonal therapy: Preliminary findings. *Archives of General Psychiatry, 58,* 631–640.

Cannon, D. M., Ichise, M., Fromm, S. J., Nugent, A. C., Rollis, D., Gandhi, S. K., . . . Drevets, W. C. (2006). Serotonin transporter binding in bipolar disorder assessed with [11C]DASB and positron emission tomography. *Biological Psychiatry, 60,* 207–217.

Choi, K. S., Holtzheimer, P. E., Franco, A. R., Kelley, M. E., Dunlop, B. W., Hu, X. P., & Mayberg, H. S. (2014). Reconciling variable findings of white matter integrity in major depressive disorder. *Neuropsychopharmacology, 39,* 1332–1339.

Clayden, R. C., Zaruk, A., Meyre, D., Thabane, L., & Samaan, Z. (2012). The association of attempted suicide with genetic variants in the SLC6A4 and TPH genes depends on the definition of suicidal behavior: A systematic review and meta-analysis. *Translational Psychiatry, 2,* e166.

Conwell, Y., Van Orden, K., & Caine, E. D. (2011). Suicide in older adults. *Psychiatric Clinics of North America, 34,* ix, 451–468.

Coplan, J. D., Gopinath, S., Abdallah, C. G., & Berry, B. R. (2014). A neurobiological hypothesis of treatment-resistant depression—mechanisms for selective serotonin reuptake inhibitor non-efficacy. *Frontiers in Behavioral Neuroscience, 8,* 189.

Currier, D., & Mann, J. J. (2008). Stress, genes and the biology of suicidal behavior. *Psychiatric Clinics of North America, 31,* 247–269.

DiazGranados, N., Ibrahim, L. A., Brutsche, N. E., Ameli, R., Henter, I. D., Luckenbaugh, D. A., . . . Zarate, C. A., Jr. (2010). Rapid resolution of suicidal ideation after a single infusion of an N-methyl-D-aspartate antagonist in patients with treatment-resistant major depressive disorder. *Journal of Clinical Psychiatry, 71,* 1605–1611.

Furczyk, K., Schutová, B., Michel, T. M., Thome, J., & Büttner, A. (2013). The neurobiology of suicide—a review of postmortem studies. *Journal of Molecular Psychiatry, 1,* 2.

Gibbons, R. D., Brown, C. H., Hur, K., Marcus, S. M., Bhaumik, D. K., Erkens, J. A., . . . Mann, J. J. (2007a). Early evidence on the effects of regulators' suicidality warnings on SSRI prescriptions and suicide in children and adolescents. *American Journal of Psychiatry, 164,* 1356–1363.

Gibbons, R. D., Brown, C. H., Hur, K., Marcus, S. M., Bhaumik, D. K., & Mann, J. J. (2007b). Relationship between antidepressants and suicide attempts: An analysis of the Veterans Health Administration data sets. *American Journal of Psychiatry, 164,* 1044–1049.

Gradus, J. L., Qin, P., Lincoln, A. K., Miller, M., Lawler, E., Sorensen, H. T., & Lash, T. L. (2010). Acute stress reaction and completed suicide. *International Journal of Epidemiology, 39,* 1478–1484.

Gunnell, D., Saperia, J., & Ashby, D. (2005). Selective serotonin reuptake inhibitors (SSRIs) and suicide in adults: Meta-analysis of drug company data from placebo controlled, randomised controlled trials submitted to the MHRA's safety review. *British Medical Journal, 330,* 385.

Harris, E. C., & Barraclough, B. (1997). Suicide as an outcome for mental disorders. A meta-analysis. *British Journal of Psychiatry, 170,* 205–228.

Hirschfeld, R. M. A., Keller, M., Panico, S., Arons, B. S., Barlow, D., Davidoff, F., . . . Wyatt, R. J. (1997). The national depressive and manic-depressive association consensus statement on the undertreatment of depression. *Journal of the American Medical Association, 277*, 333–340.

Isbister, G. K., & Buckley, N. A. (2005). The pathophysiology of serotonin toxicity in animals and humans: Implications for diagnosis and treatment. *Clinical Neuropharmacology, 28*, 205–214.

Ishihara, K., & Sasa, M. (1999). Mechanism underlying the therapeutic effects of electroconvulsive therapy (ECT) on depression. *Japanese Journal of Pharmacology, 80*, 185–189.

Jacobs, B. L., van Praag, H., & Gage, F. H. (2000). Depression and the birth and death of brain cells. The turnover of neurons in the hippocampus might help to explain the onset of and recovery from clinical depression. *American Scientist, 88*, 340–345.

Karg, K., Burmeister, M., Shedden, K., & Sen, S. (2011). The serotonin transporter promoter variant (5- HTTLPR), stress, and depression meta-analysis revisited: Evidence of genetic moderation. *Archives of General Psychiatry, 68*, 444–454.

Kellner, C. H., Fink, M., Knapp, R., Petrides, G., Husain, M., Rummans, T., ... Malur, C. (2005). Relief of expressed suicidal intent by ECT: A consortium for research in ECT study. *American Journal of Psychiatry, 162*, 977–982.

Larkin, G. L., & Beautrais, A. L. (2011). A preliminary naturalistic study of low-dose ketamine for depression and suicide ideation in the emergency department. *International Journal of Neuropsychopharmacology, 14*, 1127–1131.

Lesch, K. P., Bengel, D., Heils, A., Sabol, S. Z., Greenberg, B. D., Petri, S., ... Murphy, D. L. (1996). Association of anxiety-related traits with a polymorphism in the serotonin transporter gene regulatory region. *Science, 274*, 1527–1531.

Li, N., Lee, B., Liu, R. J., Banasr, M., Dwyer, J. M., Iwata, M., ... Duman, R. S. (2010). mTOR-dependent synapse formation underlies the rapid antidepressant effects of NMDA antagonists. *Science, 329*, 959–964.

Lindqvist, D., Janelidze, S., Erhardt, S., Traskman-Bendz, L., Engstrom, G., & Brundin, L. (2011). CSF biomarkers in suicide attempters—a principal component analysis. *Acta Psychiatrica Scandinavica, 124*, 52–61.

Luoma, J. B., Martin, C. E., & Pearson, J. L. (2002). Contact with mental health and primary care providers before suicide: A review of the evidence. *Journal of Psychiatry, 159*, 909–916.

Mann, J. J. (2003). Neurobiology of suicidal behaviour. *Nature Reviews Neuroscience, 4*, 819–828.

Marzuk, P. M., Tardiff, K., Leon, A. C., Hirsch, C. S., Hartwell, N., Portera, L., & Iqbal, M. I. (1997). HIV seroprevalence among suicide victims in New York City, 1991–1993. *American Journal of Psychiatry, 154*, 1720–1725.

Marzuk, P. M., Tierney, H., Tardiff, K., Gross, E. M., Morgan, E. B., Hsu, M. A., & Mann, J. J. (1988). Increased risk of suicide in persons with AIDS. *Journal of the American Medical Association, 259*, 1333–1337.

Mayberg, H. S. (2003). Modulating dysfunctional limbic-cortical circuits in depression: Towards development of brain-based algorithms for diagnosis and optimized treatment. *British Medical Bulletin, 65*, 193–207.

Mayberg, H. S. (2009). Targeted electrode-based modulation of neural circuits for depression. *Journal of Clinical Investigation, 119*, 717–725.

Mayberg, H. S., Lozano, A. M., Voon, V., McNeely, H. E., Seminowicz, D., Hamani, C., ... Kennedy, S. H. (2005). Deep brain stimulation for treatment-resistant depression. *Neuron, 45*, 651–660.

McGowan, P. O., Sasaki, A., D'Alessio, A. C., Dymov, S., Labonte, B., Szyf, M., ... Meaney, M. J. (2009). Epigenetic regulation of the glucocorticoid receptor in human brain associates with childhood abuse. *Nature Neuroscience, 12*, 342–348.

Meltzer, H. Y., Alphs, L., Green, A. I., Altamura, A. C., Anand, R., Bertoldi, A., ... Potkin, S. (2003). Clozapine treatment for suicidality in schizophrenia: International Suicide Prevention Trial (InterSePT). *Archives of General Psychiatry, 60*, 82–91.

Miller, J. M., Hesselgrave, N., Ogden, R. T., Sullivan, G. M., Oquendo, M. A., Mann, J. J., & Parsey, R. V. (2013). Positron emission tomography quantification of serotonin transporter in suicide attempters with major depressive disorder. *Biological Psychiatry, 74*, 287–295.

Miller, J. M., Kinnally, E. L., Ogden, R. T., Oquendo, M. A., Mann, J. J., & Parsey, R. V. (2009). Reported childhood abuse is associated with low serotonin transporter binding in vivo in major depressive disorder. *Synapse, 63*, 565–573.

Murrough, J. W. (2012). Ketamine as a novel antidepressant: From synapse to behavior. *Clinical Pharmacology and Therapeutics, 91*, 303–309.

Nutt, D. J. (2003). Death and dependence: Current controversies over the selective serotonin reuptake inhibitors. *Journal of Psychopharmacology, 17*, 355–364.

Oquendo, M. A., Malone, K. M., Ellis, S. P., Sackeim, H. A., & Mann, J. J. (1999). Inadequacy of antidepressant treatment for patients with major depression who are at risk for suicidal behavior. *American Journal of Psychiatry, 156*, 190–194.

Oquendo, M. A., Placidi, G. P., Malone, K. M., Campbell, C., Keilp, J., Brodsky, B., ... Mann, J. J. (2003). Positron emission tomography of regional brain metabolic responses to a serotonergic challenge and lethality of suicide attempts in major depression. *Archives of General Psychiatry, 60*, 14–22.

Parsey, R. V., Hastings, R. S., Oquendo, M. A., Huang, Y. Y., Simpson, N., Arcement, J., ... Mann, J. J. (2006a). Lower serotonin transporter binding potential in the human brain during major depressive episodes. *American Journal of Psychiatry, 163*, 52–58.

Parsey, R. V., Oquendo, M. A., Ogden, R. T., Olvet, D. M., Simpson, N., Huang, Y. Y., ... Mann, J. J. (2006b). Altered serotonin 1A binding in major depression: A [carbonyl-C-11]WAY100635 positron emission tomography study. *Biological Psychiatry, 59*, 106–113.

Price, R. B., Nock, M. K., Charney, D. S., & Mathew, S. J. (2009). Effects of intravenous ketamine on explicit and implicit measures of suicidality in treatment-resistant depression. *Biological Psychiatry, 66*, 522–526.

Rajkowska, G. (2000). Postmortem studies in mood disorders indicate altered numbers of neurons and glial cells [dysfunction in neural circuits involved in the pathophysiology of mood disorders]. *Biological Psychiatry, 48*, 766–777.

Rajkowska, G. (2002). Cell pathology in mood disorders. *Seminars in Clinical Neuropsychiatry, 7*, 281–292.

Rajkowska, G., Miguel-Hidalgo, J. J., Dubey, P., Stockmeier, C. A., & Krishnan, K. R. (2005). Prominent reduction in pyramidal neurons density in the orbitofrontal cortex of elderly depressed patients. *Biological Psychiatry, 58*, 297–306.

Ressler, K. J., & Mayberg, H. S. (2007). Targeting abnormal neural circuits in mood and anxiety disorders: From the laboratory to the clinic. *Nature Neuroscience, 10*, 1116–1124.

Riva-Posse, P., Choi, K. S., Holtzheimer, P. E., McIntyre, C. C., Gross, R. E., Chaturvedi, A., ... Mayberg, H. S. (2014). Defining critical white matter pathways mediating successful subcallosal cingulate deep brain stimulation for treatment-resistant depression. *Biological Psychiatry, 76*(12), 963–969.

Rutter, M., Moffitt, T. E., & Caspi, A. (2006). Gene-environment interplay and psychopathology: Multiple varieties but real effects. *Journal of Child Psychology and Psychiatry, 47*, 226–261.

Rylands, A. J., Hinz, R., Jones, M., Holmes, S. E., Feldmann, M., Brown, G., . . . Talbot, P. S. (2012). Pre- and postsynaptic serotonergic differences in males with extreme levels of impulsive aggression without callous unemotional traits: A positron emission tomography study using (11)C-DASB and (11)C-MDL100907. *Biological Psychiatry, 72*, 1004–1011.

Träskman, L., Åsberg, M., Bertilsson, L., & Sjöstrand, L. (1981). Monoamine metabolites in CSF and suicidal behavior. *Archives of General Psychiatry, 38*, 631–636.

Underwood, M. D., Kassir, S. A., Bakalian, M. J., Galfalvy, H., Mann, J. J., & Arango, V. (2012). Neuron density and serotonin receptor binding in prefrontal cortex in suicide. *International Journal of Neuropsychopharmacology, 15*, 435–447.

Underwood, M. D., Khaibulina, A. A., Ellis, S. P., Moran, A., Rice, P. M., Mann, J. J., & Arango, V. (1999). Morphometry of the dorsal raphe nucleus serotonergic neurons in suicide victims. *Biological Psychiatry, 46*, 473–483.

Van Dyck, C. H., Malison, R. T., Staley, J. K., Jacobsen, L. K., Seibyl, J. P., Laruelle, M., . . . Gelernter, J. (2004). Central serotonin transporter availability measured with [123I]beta-CIT SPECT in relation to serotonin transporter genotype. *American Journal of Psychiatry, 161*, 525–531.

van Heeringen, K., & Mann, J. J. (2014). The neurobiology of suicide. *Lancet Psychiatry, 1*, 63–72.

Wankerl, M., Miller, R., Kirschbaum, C., Hennig, J., Stalder, T., & Alexander, N. (2014). Effects of genetic and early environmental risk factors for depression on serotonin transporter expression and methylation profiles. *Translational Psychiatry, 4*, e402.

Wingenfeld, K., Schaffrath, C., Rullkoetter, N., Mensebach, C., Schlosser, N., Beblo, T., . . . Meyer, B. (2011). Associations of childhood trauma, trauma in adulthood and previous-year stress with psychopathology in patients with major depression and borderline personality disorder. *Child Abuse & Neglect, 35*, 647–654.

Neurobiology of Impulsive Aggression

Jennifer R. Fanning *and* Emil F. Coccaro

Abstract

Aggression is a behavior with evolutionary origins, but in today's society it is often both destructive and maladaptive. The fact that aggression has a strong basis in biological factors has long been apparent from case histories of traumatic brain damage. Research over the past several decades has confirmed the involvement of neurotransmitter function and abnormalities in brain structure and function in aggressive behavior. This research has centered around the "serotonin hypothesis" and on dysfunction in prefrontal brain regions. As this literature continues to grow, guided by preclinical research and aided by the application of increasingly sophisticated neuroimaging methodology, a more complex picture has emerged, implicating diverse neurotransmitter and neuropeptide systems (e.g., glutamate, vasopressin, and oxytocin) and neural circuits. As the current pharmacological and therapeutic interventions are effective but imperfect, it is hoped that new insights into the neurobiology of aggression will reveal novel avenues for treatment of this destructive and costly behavior.

Key Words: aggression, personality disorder, borderline, antisocial, impulsivity, neurobiology, neurotransmitter, neuropeptide, neuroimaging

Behavioral aggression has been studied from a variety of perspectives, including political, social, psychological, and neurobiological. In many natural circumstances, aggression serves an adaptive function: an organism may use aggression to defend itself or its offspring against attack or to secure access to resources that are needed for survival. The evolutionary preservation of aggressive behavior over time and across species reflects its adaptive value in hostile natural and social environments, and this is one indication of the validity of the neurobiological perspective. In humans, however, aggression is often not advantageous. When unchecked or chronic, it is associated with negative consequences both for the individual and for society. There are very limited circumstances today in which outright (e.g., overt) aggression is regarded as acceptable—self-defense being the most obvious.

Researchers often distinguish two forms of aggression: instrumental and impulsive (also called

proactive and reactive; Dodge, 1991). Instrumental aggression is carried out with the primary goal of obtaining some benefit or reward. This type of aggression is most closely associated with psychopathic personality disorder. In contrast, aggression that is carried out impulsively or in anger is termed impulsive or reactive aggression. Impulsive aggression characteristically occurs in response to a provocation (which is often social), a threat, or a frustration. This type of aggression, when it is sufficiently frequent and severe, is exemplified by the diagnosis of intermittent explosive disorder (IED). However, impulsive aggression is also commonly associated with cluster B personality disorders, in particular borderline personality disorder (BPD) and antisocial personality disorder (APD; Berman, Fallon, & Coccaro, 1998; Raine, 1993). In IED, aggression is not due primarily to a neurological lesion or condition, substance intoxication, mood disorder, or psychotic disorder (American Psychiatric Association,

2013). The fact that between 5% and 7% of the general population will meet criteria for IED at some point during their lifetime highlights the importance of understanding and addressing aggressive behavior (Kessler et al., 2006).

The Role of Limbic-Prefrontal Circuits in Emotion and Impulsivity

Research suggests that impulsive aggression arises from dysfunction in brain circuits that mediate normal behavioral aggression, emotion processing, and behavioral control. These circuits include the interconnected structures of the amygdala and orbitofrontal cortex (OFC), as well as associated limbic and prefrontal structures. Recent advances in neuroimaging technologies have allowed researchers to study the brain in living research participants to better understand how structural and functional brain abnormalities give rise to aggressive behavior. The OFC plays a role in a several domains of behavior that are relevant to impulsive aggression, including emotion regulation, social information processing, and impulse control. A growing body of literature points to dysfunction in this region as a key factor contributing to aggression.

The OFC is located on the orbital surface of the frontal lobes, just behind the eyes. The OFC receives sensory information from primary and secondary association cortices (Rolls, 2000) and is interconnected with the amygdala (Ongür & Price, 2000), which processes sensory information to create emotionally-valenced object memories (Cahill, 1995). These memories, or conditioned reinforcers, are then available to influence decision-making processes and behavior. It has been hypothesized that conditioned emotional (e.g., visceral) responses provide information about which options may be advantageous or disadvantageous ("somatic marker hypothesis" [SMH]; Bechara, Damasio, & Damasio, 2000). This notion has been studied using a laboratory-based decision-making task (the Iowa Gambling Task) in which participants choose between decks of cards with varying probabilities and magnitudes of rewards (winning money) and losses (losing money). "Bad decks" yield immediate rewards but greater losses over the course of the task. "Good decks" yield immediate losses but greater rewards over the course of the task (Bechara, Damasio, Damasio, & Anderson, 1994). Over time, healthy participants generate larger skin conductance responses (SCRs) in anticipation of choosing from bad decks compared to good decks, shift their behavior toward choosing from decks that are more advantageous in the long term, and many (though not all) become aware of the contingencies (i.e., the advantageous nature of certain decks over others). Patients with damage to the OFC fail to generate the same visceral responses (e.g., SCRs) to signals of reward and loss as do healthy subjects. These individuals also tend to make decisions based on immediate rewards and punishments rather than making choices that are more advantageous in the long term (Bechara, Tranel, & Damasio, 2000; Tranel, Bechara, & Denburg, 2002). The SMH offers one explanation for how OFC damage may lead to impaired decision-making performance.

Damage to OFC is associated with impairment in decision-making and social functioning, as well as abnormal emotional responding, but it spares general intellectual functioning (including language, learning, memory, and attention functions) and aspects of executive functioning. Early evidence for the role of the OFC in these functions comes from case studies of lesions to this region. The most well-known case is that of Phineas Gage, a railroad foreman in the mid-nineteenth century whose OFC was largely destroyed when an accidental explosion shot a metal tamping rod through the frontal portion of his skull and brain. Gage survived but with dramatic changes to his personality. Whereas before the accident he was a well-respected and responsible member of his crew, after the accident he became profane, impatient, capricious, and generally lacked the social skills that characterized his premorbid functioning (Damasio, Grabowski, Frank, Galaburda, & Damasio, 1994). In fact, the OFC is a frequent site of brain damage following head injury, and a significant literature supports the notion that acquired injury to the frontal lobes is associated with behavior changes that can include impulsive aggression (Brower & Price, 2001; Hesdorffer, Rauch, & Tamminga, 2009). In the Vietnam Head Injury Study, military veterans with damage to the mediofrontal brain region reported more anger and hostility than non–head injured veterans, and those with damage to medial or orbital frontal areas were more aggressive than veterans with lesions in other cortical areas (Grafman et al., 1996). Other studies suggest that lesions to right prefrontal areas such as right OFC and anterior cingulate cortex (ACC) may be more important than left prefrontal areas in emotional processing, decision making, and social behavior (Tranel et al., 2002; Yang & Raine, 2009).

A natural question given these findings is whether individual differences in brain functioning, whether influenced by genetics or more subtle environmental influences, might account for different propensities to aggression across individuals. In the past two decades, neuroimaging methodologies have been used to explore the question of whether aggressive individuals differ from non-aggressive individuals in their brain structure and function. Raine and colleagues (2000) observed reduced prefrontal gray matter, but not white matter, in individuals with APD compared to both healthy subjects and substance abusing individuals. Similarly, Woermann et al. (2000) found reduced gray matter volume in ventrolateral prefrontal cortex of individuals with temporal lobe epilepsy and aggression compared to those without aggression. Other studies have found different abnormalities in prefrontal structure. Antonucci and colleagues (2006) observed a relationship between OFC asymmetry and aggressive behavior in psychiatric patients, with larger right—relative to left—OFC volume being positively linked to aggression history and trait aggressiveness, while Hoptman et al. (2005) found that aggression correlated positively with left OFC gray matter volume and with left and right OFC white matter volumes. Despite some variability across studies, a recent meta-analysis of structural neuroimaging studies in antisocial (including violent) groups found that, on average, antisocial groups showed a small-to-moderate decrement in size and gray matter volume in prefrontal regions (d = −0.36) that trended toward statistical significance (p = 0.085; Yang & Raine, 2009). Diffusion tensor imaging (DTI) has been used to assess white matter integrity. A DTI study by Hoptman et al. (2002) examined white matter integrity in 14 schizophrenic patients with varied histories of aggression. The authors found that aggression correlated with increased *trace*, indicative of greater extracellular space, in an *a priori* region of interest in the ventral medial prefrontal brain region. Given that aggression is hypothesized to arise from impairment in a network involving prefrontal control over limbic activation, more work is needed to explore potential structural connectivity deficits in individuals with problematic aggression.

Aggressive individuals also show abnormalities in brain functioning. This can be measured using imaging methods such as positron emission tomography (PET; assessing cerebral blood flow or glucose metabolism), single-photon emission computed tomography (SPECT; assessing regional blood flow), and functional magnetic resonance imaging (fMRI; assessing changes in blood oxygenation related to neural activity). One of the earliest neuroimaging

studies to report on functional abnormalities in aggressive individuals used PET to compare 22 murderers and 22 control subjects on glucose metabolism during a continuous performance test. Raine and colleagues (1994) found that murderers had reduced prefrontal activity in the prefrontal cortex, including the superior frontal cortex, anterior medial cortex, and OFC (trend level significance), and in the left lateral prefrontal cortex. Differences were not observed in other brain regions such as posterior frontal areas, temporal, or parietal areas. Similar results have also been found in a larger follow-up study and in other independent samples (Raine, Buchsbaum, & LaCasse, 1997). Regional glucose metabolism in the OFC (as well as other frontal regions) has also been shown to correlate negatively with a life history of aggression in personality disordered subjects (r = −0.54; Goyer et al., 1994). In addition, significant metabolic differences between aggressive and non-aggressive individuals have been observed in dorsal prefrontal regions, parietal regions, and temporal regions (including amygdala and hippocampus; Hirono, Mega, Dinov, Mishkin, & Cummings, 2000; Raine et al., 1997; Volkow et al., 1995). Findings generally point to reduced cerebral glucose metabolism, although increased activity has been observed in right amygdala, medial temporal lobe, and visual cortex regions in aggressive individuals (Raine et al., 1997).

One group of researchers used PET imaging to examine regional cerebral blood flow (rCBF) in healthy participants as they visualized (a) an imagined neutral scenario and (b) imagined scenarios involving aggression in response to provocation. Scenarios involving aggression were associated with decreased rCBF in bilateral medial frontal areas. This decrease was most pronounced when subjects imagined engaging in unrestrained aggression. Overall, these findings suggest that prefrontal control mechanisms are part of the "normative" neural circuitry involved in emotion regulation in response to provocation. Furthermore, studies of rCBF and glucose metabolism overall suggest that individuals who are characteristically aggressive show deficient engagement of frontal structures that are involved in emotional and behavioral control.

Studies using fMRI also point to altered frontal and limbic functioning in aggressive individuals. Three processes that rely on intact OFC function, and which, when dysregulated, contribute to impulsive aggression, are emotion processing, social information processing, and impulsivity. These processes all involve accessing of representations. In the case of emotion, these representations are of internal motivational states such as hunger or anger. In social information processing, they are representations of the other's behavior. With impulsivity, they are representations of time-delayed reinforcers and punishments. Evidence from human studies indicates that the role of the medial OFC (and related structures) in processing reward associations is relevant to complex mental representations, including the subjective experience of emotions such as sadness, anger, happiness, and fear (Damasio et al., 2000). In the case of anger, experimentally evoked anger has been found to result in metabolic activation of the medial OFC (Kimbrell et al., 1999). Preliminary evidence points to abnormal OFC function during processing of angry face stimuli in adults with IED (Coccaro, McCloskey, Fitzgerald, & Phan, 2007). Specifically, individuals with IED show enhanced left amygdala activation in response to angry faces compared to healthy subjects. The extent of this activation correlated directly with life history of aggressive behavior. Furthermore, healthy individuals show enhanced functional connectivity (i.e., inversely correlated activity) between prefrontal cortex (OFC) and amygdala, suggesting that the OFC is acting to control or dampen threat-related limbic activity. IED individuals, on the other hand, showed no correlation between OFC and amygdala activity, suggestive of impaired emotion regulation in these individuals. The fMRI studies of realistic simulated aggressive encounters (during which research participants engage in a provocative social interaction) point to the involvement of rostral and dorsal ACC and insula in the decision to aggress against an opponent (Kramer, Jansma, Tempelmann, & Munte, 2007). These areas have previously been implicated in emotion processing (e.g., Dougherty et al., 1999; Phillips, Ladouceur, & Drevets, 2008).

The available evidence suggests that aggressive individuals have abnormalities in brain structure and function. Although a variety of neural structures have been implicated in aggressive behavior across studies, the most reliable differences appear in areas of prefrontal cortex, including OFC and dorsolateral prefrontal cortex (DLPFC). A recent meta-analysis of neuroimaging studies supports this conclusion, finding that antisocial individuals show abnormalities in prefrontal cortical regions both structurally (d = –0.37; small-to-moderate effect) and functionally (d = –0.72; moderate-to-large effect). These deficits are most consistently observed in right OFC (d = –0.48), left DLPFC (d = –0.83),

and right ACC (d = –1.12), while no reliable differences were found in left OFC, right DLPFC, or ventrolateral PFC (VLPFC). These differences are evident in resting and task-based studies, and in response to both emotional and cognitive paradigms. It is worth noting, however, that these results reflect a heterogeneous group of antisocial individuals, and statistical analyses did not reveal differences between violent antisocial and nonviolent antisocial individuals (Yang & Raine, 2009). Given that only a subset of antisocial individuals engage in violent or aggressive behavior, exploration of structural and functional abnormalities that are specifically associated with aggression is an important area for ongoing study.

Neurotransmitter Function

Neurotransmitters are endogenous molecules that transmit signals across synapses to enable communication between neurons.

Serotonin

Serotonin (5-hydroxytryptamine; 5HT), a monoamine, has been the most extensively studied neurotransmitter with respect to aggression. A rich literature points to the involvement of serotonin in suicidal, impulsive, aggressive, and antisocial behavior. Early studies on serotonin focused on the role of serotonin in suicidal behavior (Asberg, 1997; Asberg, Schalling, Traskman-Bendz, & Wagner, 1987; Bourne et al., 1968; Pare, Yeung, Price, & Stacey, 1969). Subsequently, an extensive literature has explored the role of serotonin in aggression and violence. One of the earliest studies to explore this relationship examined cerebrospinal fluid (CSF) 5-hydroxyindoleacetic acid (5-HIAA), a major metabolite of serotonin, in adult military men with aggressive or impulsive behavior (Brown, Goodwin, Ballenger, Goyer, & Major, 1979). CSF 5-HIAA was negatively correlated (r = –0.78) with self-reported life history of aggression. Moreover, a subgroup of the sample diagnosed with impulsive personality disorders had lower 5-HIAA compared to subjects diagnosed with non-impulsive personality disorders (e.g., schizoid, obsessive-compulsive). Those participants with a history of suicide attempt (n = 11) had higher aggression scores and lower 5-HIAA compared to subjects with no such history (Brown et al., 1979). The correlation between CSF 5-HIAA and a life history of aggression was replicated in a subsequent sample of men with borderline personality disorder (BPD; r = –0.53; Brown et al., 1982). Several studies have observed lower levels of CSF 5-HIAA in impulsive violent offenders compared to healthy controls (Lidberg, Tuck, Asberg, Scalia-Tomba, & Bertilsson, 1985; Virkkunen, Nuutila, Goodwin, & Linnoila, 1987), while others have reported correlations between the metabolite and life histories of aggressive behavior (Limson et al., 1991). Not all study results have been positive (e.g., Coccaro, Kavoussi, Cooper, & Hauger, 1997; Hibbeln et al., 2000). Coccaro et al. (1998) found no relation between CSF 5-HIAA and life history of aggression in a sample of various personality disorders (Coccaro, Kavoussi, Hauger, Cooper, Ferris, 1998). Likewise, Simeon and colleagues (1992) found no relation between several indices of 5HT functioning and life history of aggression or impulsivity in a sample of personality disordered individuals with a history of self-harm. Nevertheless, an association between low CSF 5-HIAA and impulsive behaviors has been found in a number of patient groups including those with depression (Asberg, Traskman, & Thoren, 1976; Banki, Arató, Papp, & Kurcz, 1984; Lopez-Ibor, Saiz-Ruiz, & de los Cobos, 1985; Träskman, Asberg, Bertilsson, & Sjöstrand, 1981), substance use (Banki et al., 1984; Limson et al., 1991), and schizophrenia (Banki et al., 1984; Ninan et al., 1984; van Praag, 1983). A more recent study found that when both 5-HIAA and the dopamine metabolite homovanillic acid (HVA) are placed in the same statistical model, CSF 5-HIAA demonstrates a significant, and positive, correlation with aggression (Coccaro & Lee, 2010).

Pharmacochallenge studies also implicate central serotonin functioning in aggressive behavior. A commonly used approach to assessing serotonin function with this method involves acutely administering a serotonergic drug and assessing the downstream hormonal response, a test that provides information about receptor functioning. Coccaro et al. (1989) observed a relationship between prolactin response to the drug d,l-fenfluramine (PRL[d,l-FEN]) and life history of aggression ($r = -0.57$) and self-reported aggressive tendencies ($r = -0.52$) in patients with personality disorder. Trait antisociality (MMPI psychopathic deviance; $r = -0.33$) and trait suspiciousness ($r = -0.03$) did not significantly correlate with PRL[d,l-FEN]. In a subsequent study, Coccaro et al. (1995) found a strong inverse correlation ($r = -0.85$) between the PRL response to d-fenfluramine (d-FEN) challenge and the direct assault scale of the Buss Durkee Hostility Inventory (BDHI) in a mixed sample of personality disorders (e.g., schizoid, passive aggressive), although not with life history of aggressive behavior. However,

a subsequent study did find a relationship between PRL[d-FEN] and life history of aggression in personality disordered (PD) research subjects (Coccaro et al., 1997). Similar inverse associations were observed by New, Trestman, and colleagues (2004) in a large sample of PD patients between PRL[d,l-FEN] and BDHI irritability/assaultiveness in men with PD ($r = -0.21$), which was not accounted for by current depression. Other studies have also found a relationship between blunted hormonal response to serotonergic challenge in BPD patients (Paris et al., 2004), antisocial individuals (Moss, Yao, & Panzak, 1990; O'Keane et al., 1992), and substance abusers (Moeller et al., 1994). Soloff et al. (2005) observed a blunted PRL[d,l-FEN] response in male (but not female) BPD subjects compared to healthy control subjects, which appeared to be accounted for by trait impulsivity, aggression, and antisociality.

While there is considerable support for the notion that 5HT is related to aggressive behavior, it is worth noting that it appears to be particularly important for aggressive behavior that is impulsive as opposed to premeditated. For example, a study by Linnoila et al. (1983) found lower levels of 5-HIAA among murderers and attempted murderers who had committed impulsive crimes compared to those who committed premeditated crimes. Over the years a number of theories have sought to explain the relationship between serotonin and violence. Spoont (1992) proposed that 5HT stabilizes information flow by supporting phase coherence in neural activity, and thereby modulates reactivity to stimuli both internal and external. Thus, high levels of 5HT are associated with behavioral rigidity, while low levels of 5HT are associated with impulsivity and stimulus reactivity (Spoont, 1992). Linnoila and Virkkunen (1992) postulated that a "low serotonin syndrome" characterizes individuals who engage in violent, impulsive, and antisocial behavior. This hypothesis was largely based on studies of 5-HIAA. According to these authors, 5HT serves to constrain behavior, such that a deficit in 5HT is associated with increased impulsivity (Linnoila & Virrkunen, 1992). Another model ("Irritable Aggression Model"; Coccaro, Kavoussi, & Lesser, 1992) suggests that a net hyposerotonergic state is associated with greater irritability, which can be conceptualized as a lower threshold for responding to noxious stimuli. This is consistent with findings of an inverse correlation between self-reported irritability and PRL[d,l-FEN] (Coccaro et al., 1989) and Brown et al.'s (1982) observation that the relationship between a history of suicide attempt and PRL[d,l-FEN] became insignificant when controlling for self-reported impulsivity. Furthermore, research in both animals and humans suggests that noxious, threatening, or provocative stimuli may be necessary to elicit aggressive behavior in a net hyposerotonergic state (Berman, McCloskey, Fanning, Schumacher, & Coccaro, 2009; Marks, Miller, Schulz, Newcorn, & Halperin, 2007).

While early studies on the relationship between serotonin and aggression reported large effect sizes, a recent meta-analysis suggests the relationship may be more modest than previously thought. Duke et al. (2013) analyzed 171 studies on the serotonin-aggression relationship that used (a) 5-HIAA assay; (b) acute tryptophan depletion (ATD); (c) pharmacochallenge; and (d) endocrine challenge methods (Duke, Bègue, Bell, & Eisenlohr-Moul, 2013). The authors found, overall, a small ($r = -0.12$) significant inverse relation between measures of 5HT functioning and aggression. Pharmacochallenge studies yielded the largest effect size ($r = -0.21$) while 5-HIAA yielded the smallest ($r = -0.06$; non-significant). Small significant average effects were found for ATD ($r = -0.10$) and endocrine challenge ($r = -0.14$), while cortisol response was not significantly related to aggression ($r = -0.02$). Notably, characteristics of the samples (e.g., gender, age, psychopathology, and a history of aggression) did not moderate the relationships between indices of 5HT functioning and aggression. Furthermore, the type of drug did not moderate the relationship between pharmacological or endocrine challenge and aggression. These results, as well as null results and conflicting findings in the literature suggest that the relationship between 5HT and behavior is more complex than previously appreciated. It is also worth considering that the 5HT system in the brain is both extensive and complex and comprises at least 14 types of receptors that are distributed both pre- and post-synaptically. Indeed, there is evidence (much of it preclinical) that 5HT receptor subtypes exert unique and perhaps even opposing effects on aggression.

Neuroimaging methodologies have enabled advances in studying neurotransmitter functioning. Imaging methods such as PET offer the opportunity to examine neurotransmitter functioning centrally in living research participants, which may provide a more accurate measure of 5HT system activity and functioning. PET has been used to localize

deficient serotonergic functioning in the brain. In one of the earliest PET studies on aggression, Siever and colleagues (1999) imaged glucose metabolism in six impulsively aggressive patients and five healthy control subjects following administration of a single 60 mg dose of d,l-FEN and placebo in a within-subjects design study. In healthy individuals d,l-FEN was associated with increased glucose metabolism, particularly in left OFC and ACC, while PD patients showed attenuated effects in these areas. Only inferior parietal lobe showed increased metabolism in response to the drug in PD subjects. PRL[d,l-FEN] (placebo-corrected) responses did not differ between patients and healthy controls. PRL[d,l-FEN] correlated $r = 0.58$ and $r = 0.63$ with regions of interest in medial frontal cortex and right middle cingulate, respectively, although these correlations were not significant, which may be due to the small sample size.

A similar finding was obtained in a larger follow-up study. New et al. (2002) studied 13 impulsively aggressive mixed personality disordered patients and 13 healthy subjects using a meta-chlorophenylpiperazine (mCPP) versus placebo challenge. Healthy subjects, but not PD subjects, showed increased glucose metabolism in OFC and anterior cingulate cortex (areas involved in inhibiting aggressive behavior) following mCPP relative to placebo. In addition, a 12-week course of treatment with the selective serotonin reuptake inhibitor (SSRI) fluoxetine has been shown to normalize OFC function in impulsively aggressive BPD patients, supporting the notion that deficits in OFC function are at least partially supported by abnormalities in serotonin function (New, Buchsbaum, et al., 2004).

Other research suggests that impulsively aggressive individuals may have abnormal 5HT synthesis and reuptake. In one study, men with BPD showed lower trapping of a 5HT precursor analog (implicating reduced 5HT synthesis capacity) in medial frontal gyrus, anterior cingulate gyrus (ACG), superior temporal gyrus, and corpus striatum compared to healthy controls, while BPD women had lower trapping in right middle cingulate gyrus and superior temporal gyrus (Leyton et al., 2001). Another study using PET radiotracer for the serotonin transporter (5-HTT) also showed reduced 5-HTT availability in ACG among impulsively aggressive subjects (Frankle et al., 2005). Finally, a study by Koch and colleagues (2007) using SPECT examined the binding of [I-123] ADAM to the serotonin transporter and found increased binding in BPD subjects in both the hypothalamus and brainstem. ADAM binding correlated significantly with impulsivity but not with depression.

In summary, extensive literature supports a role for serotonin in impulsive aggression. Evidence suggests that serotonin modulates activity in areas of the prefrontal cortex, including OFC and ACC. Impulsively aggressive individuals display impaired serotonergic functioning in these brain regions. Over time, a complex picture of the serotonin system has emerged, involving both broad and specific functions, tonic and phasic activity, and multiple receptor subtypes. It is clear that more nuanced models are needed to describe the complex role of 5HT in aggressive behavior.

Dopamine

Dopamine (DA) is a catecholamine neurotransmitter that is involved in a range of functions including learning, memory, and movement. Compared to serotonin, less is known about the relationship between DA functioning and aggression, although research, both preclinical and clinical, suggests some involvement of this neurotransmitter. Pre-clinical studies point to hyperactivity of the DA system in the mesocorticolimbic pathway during and after a provocative aggressive encounter, possibly reflecting motivational aspects of aggressive behavior (Miczek, Fish, De Bold, & De Almeida, 2002). In humans, homovanillic acid (HVA), a major metabolite of dopamine, has been studied as an index of DA turnover. Several studies have examined the relationship between HVA and aggression, but the findings have been mixed. Some studies find no relationship between CSF HVA concentration and aggression or suicide (Brown et al., 1979; Brown et al., 1982; Lidberg et al., 1985; Virkkunen et al., 1987) while other studies show an inverse relationship. Linnoila et al. (1983) observed reduced CSF HVA in antisocial impulsive violent offenders and Virkkunen et al. (1989) reported that recidivist violent offenders had lower CSF HVA concentrations than non-recidivist violent offender controls (Virkkunen, M., De Jong, J., Bartko, J., Goodwin, F. K., & Linnoila, M., 1989). One study observed an inverse correlation between CSF HVA and aggression in alcohol dependent and healthy individuals (Limson et al., 1991), and a similar relationship was reported in a sample of healthy volunteers and personality disorder subjects when CSF 5-HIAA and CSF HVA were placed in the same statistical model (Coccaro & Lee, 2010). There is some evidence of dopaminergic involvement in psychopathy, a personality disorder characterized by callousness and unemotionality (Factor 1 psychopathy) and antisociality (Factor 2 psychopathy). Soderstrom and colleagues (2001) observed a positive correlation between CSF HVA (r = .41; marginally significant) and Factor 1 psychopathy and Factor 2 psychopathy (r = .65) in 22 violent offenders (Soderstrom, Blennow, Manhem, & Forsman, 2001). CSF 5-HIAA and HVA intercorrelate significantly; therefore, it is possible that these effects may be partly attributable to serotonergic function. The interaction between serotonin and dopamine may also have implications for aggressive behavior, with dopamine playing a facilitating role in aggression and serotonin a constraining role (Seo, Patrick, & Kennealy, 2008). In line with this notion, Soderstrom, Blennow Sjodin, and Forsman (2003) observed a relationship between the ratio of 5-HIAA to DA (HVA:5-HIAA) and Factor 1 (r = 0.53) and Factor 2 (r = 0.52) psychopathy. The relationship between HVA and HVA:5-HIAA was replicated for Factor 2 psychopathy in a follow-up study of violent offenders (Soderstrom et al., 2003). Finally, evidence for the involvement of DA in aggression comes from research showing that drugs targeting DA receptors (albeit non-specifically) are effective in reducing aggression in humans (see Comai, Tau, Pavlovic, & Gobbi, 2012 for a review).

Norepinephrine

Norepinephrine (NE) is involved in modulating an organism's responses to stimuli. The central NE system originates in the locus coeruleus and surrounding brain structures and comprises both tonic and phasic activity. NE activity appears to vary with degrees of wakefulness and arousal; it is implicated in orienting to novel stimuli, focusing attention, and enacting behavioral responses (Berridge & Waterhouse, 2003), and is involved in the stress response as part of hypothalamic-pituitary-adrenal (HPA) axis (Dunn & Swiergiel, 2009). A role of norepinephrine in behavioral domains such as affective instability and aggression has been suggested (Siever & Davis, 1991); however, empirical support for these hypotheses has so far been both limited and mixed (Oquendo & Mann, 2000).

Pre-clinical studies suggest that NE plays a "permissive" role in aggression by facilitating "fight or flight" responses to threat (Miczek & Fish, 2005). Findings in humans have been inconsistent. 3-methyoxy-4-hydroxyphenylglycol (MHPG), a metabolite of norepinephrine, has been studied as a marker of NE activity. One early study reported a positive correlation between MHPG in CSF (r = 0.64; Brown et al., 1979). However, other studies have reported no relation between MHPG and aggression/antisociality (Brown et al., 1982; Lidberg et al., 1985; Virrkunen et al., 1989; Virrkunen et al., 1994), and some have found an inverse relationship between plasma MHPG and aggression (Coccaro, Lee, & McCloskey, 2003). Virrkunen et al. (1987) observed a positive correlation between criminal behavior (but not violent crime) and MHPG in arsonists, but also higher concentrations of NE in healthy participants compared to violent criminals and arsonists. Coccaro, Lawrence, Klar, and Siever (1991) used clonidine, an α2-NE receptor agonist, to assess the sensitivity of α2-NE receptors in patients with personality disorder, remitted mood disorder (MD), and healthy subjects via growth hormone (GH) response in plasma. The authors found that GH response differed only between MD and the other two groups. PD and healthy subjects showed greater GH response to clonidine and a positive correlation between GH response and irritability, but not assaultiveness. This finding, however, was not replicated in a separate study in a larger group of subjects (Coccaro & Kavoussi, 2010). Another study found that, among siblings of heroin abusers, those with antisocial personality traits showed blunted GH response to clonidine challenge (indicative of subsensitive α2-NE receptors) and β-endorphin response to clonidine challenge (indicative of subsenstive α1-NE receptors) compared to healthy siblings of heroin abusers and healthy control subjects (Gerra et al., 1994). Differences in these reports may be due to the high correlation between irritability and depression in this sample of heroin abusing subjects.

There is considerable evidence that HPA axis functioning is disturbed in individuals with disorders such as BPD and posttraumatic stress disorder (PTSD), both of which are associated with irritability and aggressive behavior. However, the nature of this disturbance is complex and poorly understood, as empirical studies have yielded both conflicting and null results. Basal NE function has generally not been distinguishable between BPD and non-BPD individuals. One study found no difference between BPD and healthy subjects in urine NE (Simeon, Knutelska, Smith, Baker, & Hollander, 2007), while another found no difference in urine NE or MHPG between bulimic women with borderline personality features and healthy women (Vaz-Leal, Rodríguez-Santos, García-Herráiz, & Ramos-Fuentes, 2011). One other study found that BPD patients showed no difference from healthy subjects in plasma NE response to a stress challenge

paradigm (the Trier Social Stress Test; Nater et al., 2010). Studies have also used pharmacochallenge methods to assess NE functioning in BPD. Paris (2004) found no difference between BPD patients and healthy subjects in growth hormone response to clonidine GH[CLON] (Paris et al., 2004). Later time to peak GH[CLON] response was positively associated with self-reported assaultiveness (r = 0.47) but the GH response was unrelated to mood symptoms and impulsivity (Paris et al., 2004). Cortisol is a product of HPA axis reactivity in response to stress. Abnormalities in basal and acute cortisol levels have been associated with various psychiatric disorders, and are likely to reflect long term changes in HPA axis functioning, perhaps in combination with predisposing individual variation. However, understanding of this complex system and its links to disorders and symptoms remains incomplete. Zimmerman and Choi-Kain (2009) reviewed more than a dozen studies of HPA axis functioning in BPD, including studies that examined basal cortisol levels, cortisol response to dexamethasone challenge (an index of negative feedback inhibition of HPA axis activity), and cortisol response to psychosocial stress challenge. Results of these studies were mixed with respect to both basal cortisol and cortisol response to challenge, with some studies showing no difference between BPD patients and controls, and others showing conflicting findings. History of childhood trauma and comorbid depression and PTSD are likely to significantly affect cortisol functioning.

Glutamate

Glutamate is the primary excitatory neurotransmitter in the central nervous system and is involved in neurodevelopment, learning, and memory. In general it is thought that glutamate plays a facilitory role in aggressive behavior. Studies in cats and rodents show that stimulation of the hypothalamus (in a region labeled the "hypothalamic attack area") induces defensive aggressive behavior, and that aggression is induced by glutamate and inhibited by GABA and serotonin in this region (Haller, 2013). While limited data are available in humans, glutamate concentrations assessed in CSF have been shown to correlate with both aggression and impulsivity in subjects with PD and healthy subjects, although glutamate levels did not differ between healthy subjects and those with PD. Glutamate concentration also did not differ as a function of personality disorder cluster (A, B, or C; Coccaro, Lee, & Vezina, 2013). Higher levels of glutamic acid have been observed in CSF of pathological gamblers compared to healthy research participants (Nordin, Gupta, & Sjödin, 2007). Furthermore, there is preclinical evidence that interfering with glutamate via administration of NMDA receptor antagonists or by inhibiting glutamate synthesis can reduce aggression in mice. In humans, treatment with memantine (an NMDA receptor antagonist) has been shown to reduce agitation and aggression in individuals with Alzheimer's disease (Wilcock, Ballard, Cooper, & Loft, 2011). In sum, there is evidence that glutamate regulates aggression and that abnormal glutamate activity may contribute to the pathophysiology of aggressive behavior. It is very likely that over the next several years attention to the role of this neurotransmitter in psychopathology will continue to increase.

GABA

While glutamate is the primary excitatory neurotransmitter in the central nervous system, GABA (Υ-aminobutyric acid) is the primary *inhibitory* neurotransmitter. GABA receptors are expressed heavily in areas of frontal and limbic cortex and are found at both inhibitory-inhibitory and inhibitory-excitatory synapses. Studies of the relationship between GABA and impulsivity and aggression have been mixed. Preclinical studies have shown that aggressive animals show reduced brain levels of GABA and glutamic acid decarboxylase (GAD), an enzyme that catalyzes glutamate into GABA. In humans, GABA levels in plasma have been shown to correlate negatively with trait aggressiveness in psychiatrically healthy individuals. Lee, Petty, and Coccaro (2009) found an inverse relationship between trait impulsivity (but not aggression) and CSF GABA levels in individuals with personality disorder and healthy control subjects. However, GABA levels were also found to be higher in individuals with a history of suicide attempt. Drugs that enhance GABAergic effects (including the antipsychotic drug clozapine, anticonvulsants toprimate and valproate, and the mood stabilizer lithium) have been shown to reduce aggression (Comai, Tau, & Gobbi, 2012), suicidal behavior (lithium; Baldessarini, Tondo, & Hennen, 2003), and behavioral dysregulation (carbamazepine; Cowdry & Gardner, 1988). Valproate has been shown to reduce aggression in individuals with BPD (Hollander, Swann, Coccaro, Jiang, & Smith, 2005). These studies suggest that GABA functions in an inhibitory manner in relation to aggression. Other studies, however, suggest a more complex relationship. Certain allosteric modulators of GABA$_A$

receptors show a biphasic, bidirectional relationship with aggression. Specifically, these substances, which include some benzodiazapines, barbiturates, and alcohol, enhance aggression at low doses and reduce aggression at high doses. This "paradoxical" effect is likely to be influenced by the particular subunit composition of the benzodiazepine receptor at GABA$_A$ receptor sites, which may explain why some benzodiazepines show no such aggression heightening effect. In the case of alcohol, alcohol-heightened aggressive behavior in mice is enhanced by repeated earlier exposure to alcohol (Miczek & Fish, 2005). Individuals with BPD may be particularly prone to paradoxical reactions to benzodiazepines. Cowdry and Gardner (1988) observed that BPD patients engaged in more severe acts of aggression and self-aggression while taking alprazolam compared to a placebo in a six-week double-blind crossover trial.

Neuropeptides

Neuropeptides are signaling molecules that share many characteristics of classical neurotransmitters. Neuropeptide molecules are characteristically larger than traditional neurotransmitters. They are released from distinct large dense-core vesicles located in various parts of the neuron and not recycled back into the cell following secretion. As such, their effects are often more diffuse than those of typical neurotransmitters and can take place over longer distances and time spans. Arginine-vasopressin (AVP) and oxytocin (OXT) are neuropeptides that play a key role in the regulation of social cognition and the stress response.

Vasopressin

Aggressive behavior is characterized by abnormalities in perceiving and responding to threat. However, the function of AVP in human social cognition is just beginning to be understood. For example, intranasal AVP has been shown to reduce recognition of negative facial expressions in men (Uzefovsky, Shalev, Israel, Knafo, & Ebstein, 2012), but also to enhance recognition of both happy and angry faces (Guastella, Kenyon, Alvares, Carson, & Hickie, 2010).

Stress activates the HPA axis, setting into motion a hormonal cascade that includes the secretion of corticotrophin-releasing hormone (CRH), adrenocorticotropic hormone (ACTH), and cortisol. AVP is involved in this system, interacting with CRF to increase the release of ACTH from the anterior pituitary. AVP is anxiogenic, and may play a role in mediating the development of depression and anxiety following stress (Beurel & Nemeroff, 2014). Preclinical research suggests that vasopressin plays a facilitory role in aggressive behavior. AVP microinjections into the hypothalamus of hamsters increase offensive aggression (Ferris et al., 1997), while vasopressin V1a receptor antagonists injected in anterior hypothalamus in hamsters inhibit inter-male aggressive behavior (Ferris et al., 2006; Ferris & Potegal, 1988). Serotonin has been shown to block AVP-facilitated aggression (Delville, Mansour, & Ferris, 1996). An early study on basal AVP levels in humans found no difference between clinical groups (APD, intermittent explosive disorder, and alcohol dependent) and healthy individuals in CSF AVP concentrations (Virrkunen et al., 1994). However, CSF AVP has been found to correlate (r = 0.41) with life history of aggressive behavior. AVP has also been found to inversely correlate with PRL[d-FEN] response, and emerged as an independent predictor of aggressive behavior in a hierarchical regression analysis (Coccaro et al., 1998). In the latter study, AVP did not correlate with a measure of trait impulsivity, state depression, or state anxiety, and AVP levels did not vary as a function of any subtype of personality disorder.

Research suggests that AVP modulates an organism's response to stress, but possibly in a sex-specific manner (Taylor et al., 2000). Thompson, Gupta, Miller, Mills, and Orr (2004) found that AVP (but not placebo) led male participants to display similarly aggressive facial responses (corrugator electromyogram; EMG) to angry faces as to neutral faces. In women, AVP was associated with decreased aggressive facial responses to same-sex happy and angry faces and increased affiliative facial responses to neutral and happy faces (Thompson, George, Walton, Orr, & Benson, 2006). Using fMRI, studies show that vasopressin activates neural structures involved in fear regulation and mentalizing (Zink et al., 2011; Zink, Stein, Kempf, Hakimi, & Meyer-Lindenberg, 2010). In one fMRI study designed to assess the role of AVP in cooperative versus antagonistic behavior, male participants engaged in a prisoner's dilemma game with a confederate. Participants who received intranasal AVP showed increased cooperative behavior, and cooperation was associated with increased activation in stria terminalis and lateral septum, which are part of vasopressinergic circuitry (Rilling et al., 2012). In another study (Brunnlieb, Münte, Krämer, Tempelmann, & Heldmann, 2013), male participants engaged in a laboratory aggression paradigm with a research confederate during which the pair set noise blasts of varying intensity for each other. Intranasal AVP administration showed no effects on aggressive behavior, however, was associated with activation in the amygdala when participants were deciding the level of noise to set for the other person, an effect that was not observed in the placebo condition. Given its role in social cognitive and emotional processes and the stress response, AVP dysregulation may contribute to the behavioral and emotional disturbances seen in many psychiatric disorders. Accordingly, a rapidly growing body of research is investigating the role of AVP in this area.

Oxytocin

Like vasopressin, OXT plays a role in regulating social behavior, although these neuropeptides often display opposing effects. With regard to aggression, while CSF vasopressin levels correlate positively with aggression, CSF OXT correlates inversely with aggression (Lee et al., 2009). Intranasal oxytocin administration has been linked to improved emotional recognition, empathy, and attachment (Buchheim et al., 2009; Hurlemann et al., 2010), and it has also been shown to enhance positive communication between couples during a disagreement and to decrease cortisol response during the interaction (Ditzen et al., 2013). Oxytocin may also increase trust (Kosfeld, Heinrichs, Zak, Fischbacher, & Fehr, 2005), and it has been shown to reduce laboratory-assessed aggressive behavior among women with high state anxiety, suggestive of anxiolytic effects (Campbell & Hausmann, 2013). However, the effects of oxytocin on mood and behavior may not all be positive. Oxytocin (compared to a placebo) has been shown to increase negative emotions such as envy and schadenfreude (Shamay-Tsoory et al., 2009) and to increase noncooperation toward members of out-groups (see De Dreu, 2012, for a review). Like vasopressin, oxytocin is involved in the stress response; however, oxytocin has anxiolytic properties and is thought to play a role in buffering stress (Neumann & Landgraf, 2012).

Given the prominence of impulsive aggression in BPD, it is of interest whether dysregulation of oxytocin may contribute to BPD symptoms and whether enhancing oxytocin function may lead to a reduction in symptoms (Stanley & Siever, 2010). Women with BPD have been reported to have reduced OXT concentrations in plasma (Bertsch, Schmidinger, Neumann, & Herpertz, 2013). Furthermore, trauma exposure early in life (which is common among individuals with BPD and IED) has been found to inversely predict CSF oxytocin levels in women

(Bertsch, Schmidinger, et al., 2013; Heim et al., 2009). The largest effects have been found for emotional abuse and neglect. CSF OXT also showed a strong negative correlation with state anxiety. The results suggest that adverse experiences early in life may negatively affect oxytocin functioning and that decreased OXT functioning is associated with mood disturbance. However, it is not clear that higher levels of endogenous OXT are necessarily predictive of better functioning. Another study found that higher levels of oxytocin in plasma correlated inversely with relationship quality in women (Taylor et al., 2006).

Studies employing oxytocin challenge have similarly yielded mixed results. In individuals with BPD, augmenting oxytocin through intranasal administration has been shown to reduce both dysphoria and plasma cortisol levels following a stress challenge (Simeon et al., 2011). In contrast, in a modified Prisoner's Dilemma task, BPD participants who received intranasal OXT were less trusting of their partner and were less likely to cooperate even when they anticipated cooperation on the part of their partner (Bartz et al., 2011). Whether oxytocin enhanced or decreased cooperation (relative to placebo) was moderated by attachment style. Oxytocin had no effect on cooperation among low-anxiety participants, while OXT decreased cooperation among highly anxious and avoidant participants, and *increased* cooperation among highly anxious non-avoidant participants. These results would suggest that OXT is acting to enhance predispositions to approach or avoid cooperation among highly anxious individuals. In another study, women with BPD showed enhanced amygdala activation when viewing angry and fearful faces, but OXT reduced the effect of angry faces on amygdala activation, suggesting it may reduce sensitivity to threat in women in BPD (Bertsch, Gamer, et al., 2013).

In sum, research on OXT in BPD is both preliminary and mixed. There is some evidence that OXT may be anxiolytic in patients with BPD; however it may also exacerbate preexisting behavioral tendencies. Further research is needed to better understand whether and how oxytocin may be involved in the role of oxytocin in impulsive aggression.

Other Neurochemical Systems

Besides the major neurotransmitter and neuropeptide systems reviewed here, the role of other neurotransmitter and neuropeptide systems have been investigated as to their roles in aggressive behavior. Although a thorough review of this research is beyond the scope of this chapter, these systems include testosterone (aggression, psychopathy; Carré, McCormick, & Hariri, 2011; Yildirim & Derksen, 2012); neuropeptide Y (Coccaro, Lee, Liu, & Mathe, 2012); substance P (Coccaro, Lee, Owens, Kinead, & Nemeroff, 2012), and inflammatory cytokines (Coccaro, Lee, & Coussons-Read, 2014a, 2014b; Serafini et al., 2013). In addition, it has become increasingly apparent that aggressive behavior is subserved by complex interactions between neurotransmitter systems, and there have been some preliminary investigations into how NT systems interact to influence behavior. Some hypotheses speculate on interactions between serotonin and dopamine (Seo et al., 2008), and more recently between testosterone and cortisol (Terburg, Morgan, & van Honk, 2009). Our understanding of these relationships will no doubt continue to grow over the coming years.

Conclusion

The development of enhanced neuroimaging methodologies over the past couple of decades has permitted a more mechanistic understanding of the neurobiology of impulsive aggression. The predominant hypothesis regarding the neurobiology of impulsive aggression involves altered structure and function of fronto-limbic emotional and social information processing circuits, as well as altered neurotransmitter function subserving these systems. In response to provocation, impulsively aggressive individuals are less able to regulate their emotional reaction and behavioral responses due to abnormal prefrontal (particularly orbitofrontal) functioning. This hypothesis requires further testing, particularly to understand how aggressive behavior diverges from other forms of non-aggressive antisocial behavior. It is likely that over the next several years, continued work in neuroimaging and experimental pharmacological research will enhance our understanding of the neurobiological mechanisms underlying aggressive behavior.

References

Antonucci, A. S., Gansler, D. A., Tan, S., Bhadelia, R., Patz, S., & Fulwiler, C. (2006). Orbitofrontal correlates of aggression and impulsivity in psychiatric patients. *Psychiatry Research*, 147, 213–220.

Asberg, M. (1997). Neurotransmitters and suicidal behavior: The evidence from cerebrospinal fluid studies. *Annals of the New York Academy of Sciences*, 836, 158–181.

Asberg, M., Schalling, D., Traskman-Bendz, L., & Wagner, A. (1987). Psychobiology of suicide, impulsivity, and related phenomena. In H. Y. Metzer (ed.), *Psychopharmacology: The third generation of progress* (pp. 665–668). New York, NY: Raven Press.

Asberg, M., Traskman, L., & Thoren, P. (1976). 5-HIAA in the cerebrospinal fluid: A biochemical suicide predictor? *Archives of General Psychiatry, 33,* 1193–1197.

American Psychiatric Association (2013). *Diagnostic and Statistical Manual of Mental Disorders-5.* Arlington, VA: American Psychiatric Association.

Baldessarini, R. J., Tondo, L., & Hennen, J. (2003). Lithium treatment and suicide risk in major affective disorders: Update and new findings. *Journal of Clinical Psychiatry, 64* (Suppl 5), 44–52.

Banki, C. M., Arató, M., Papp, Z., & Kurcz, M. (1984). Biochemical markers in suicidal patients: Investigations with cerebrospinal fluid amine metabolites and neuroendocrine tests. *Journal of Affective Disorders, 6,* 341–350.

Bartz, J., Simeon, D., Hamilton, H., Kim, S., Crystal, S., Braun, A., . . . Hollander, E. (2011). Oxytocin can hinder trust and cooperation in borderline personality disorder. *Social Cognitive and Affective Neuroscience, 6,* 556–563.

Bechara, A., Damasio, A. R., Damasio, H., & Anderson, S. W. (1994). Insensitivity to future consequences following damage to human prefrontal cortex. *Cognition, 50,* 7–15.

Bechara, A., Damasio, H., & Damasio, A. R. (2000). Emotion, decision making, and the orbitofrontal cortex. *Cerebral Cortex, 10,* 295–307.

Bechara, A., Tranel, D., & Damasio, H. (2000). Characterization of the decision-making deficit of patients with ventromedial prefrontal cortex lesions. *Brain, 123,* 2189–2202.

Berman, M. E., Fallon, A. E., & Coccaro, E. F. (1998). The relationship between personality psychopathology and aggressive behavior in research volunteers. *Journal of Abnormal Psychology, 107,* 651–658.

Berman, M. E., McCloskey, M. S., Fanning, J. R., Schumacher, J. A., & Coccaro, E. F. (2009). Serotonin augmentation reduces response to attack in aggressive individuals. *Psychological Science, 20,* 714–720.

Berridge, C. W., & Waterhouse, B. D. (2003). The locus coeruleus-noradrenergic system: Modulation of behavioral state and state-dependent cognitive processes. *Brain Research Reviews, 42,* 33–84.

Bertsch, K., Gamer, M., Schmidt, B., Schmidinger, I., Walther, S., Kästel, T.,. . . Herpertz, S. C. (2013). Oxytocin and reduction of social threat hypersensitivity in women with borderline personality disorder. *American Journal of Psychiatry, 170,* 1169–1177.

Bertsch, K., Schmidinger, I., Neumann, I. D., & Herpertz, S. C. (2013). Reduced plasma oxytocin levels in female patients with borderline personality disorder. *Hormones and Behavior, 63,* 424–429.

Beurel, E., & Nemeroff, C. B. (2014). Interaction of stress, corticotropin-releasing factor, arginine vasopressin and behaviour. *Current Topics in Behavioral Neuroscience, 18,* 1–14.

Bourne, H. R., Bunney, W. E., Colburn, R. W., Davis, J. M., Davis, J. N., Shaw, D. M., . . . Coppen, A. J. (1968). Noradrenaline, 5-hydroxytryptamine, and 5-hydroxyindoleacetic acid hindbrains of suicidal patients. *Lancet, 292,* 805–808.

Brower, M. C., & Price, B. H. (2001). Neuropsychiatry of frontal lobe dysfunction in violent and criminal behaviour: A critical review. *Journal of Neurology, Neurosurgery, and Psychiatry, 71,* 720–726.

Brown, G. L., Goodwin, F. K., Ballenger, J. C., Goyer, P. F., & Major, L. F. (1979). Aggression in humans correlates fluid amine metabolites with cerebrospinal. *Psychiatry Research, 1,* 131–139.

Brown, L., Ebert, H., Goyer, F., Jimerson, D. C., Klein, J., Bunney, W., & Goodwin, F. K. (1982). Aggression, suicide, and serotonin: Relationships to CSF amine metabolites. *American Journal of Psychiatry, 139,* 741–746.

Brunnlieb, C., Münte, T. F., Krämer, U., Tempelmann, C., & Heldmann, M. (2013). Vasopressin modulates neural responses during human reactive aggression. *Social Neuroscience, 8,* 148–164.

Buchheim, A., Heinrichs, M., George, C., Pokorny, D., Koops, E., Henningsen, P., ... Gündel, H. (2009). Oxytocin enhances the experience of attachment security. *Psychoneuroendocrinology, 34,* 1417–1422.

Cahill, L. (1995). The amygdala and emotional memory. *Nature, 377,* 295–296.

Campbell, A., & Hausmann, M. (2013). Effects of oxytocin on women's aggression depend on state anxiety. *Aggressive Behavior, 39,* 316–322.

Carré, J. M., McCormick, C. M., & Hariri, A. R. (2011). The social neuroendocrinology of human aggression. *Psychoneuroendocrinology, 36,* 935–944.

Coccaro, E., Kavoussi, R., & Hauger, R. (1995). Physiological responses to d-fenfluramine and ipsapirone challenge correlate with indices of aggression in males with personality disorder. *International Clinical Psychopharmacology, 10,* 177–179.

Coccaro, E., Lee, R., Liu, T., & Mathe, A. (2012). Cerebrospinal fluid neuropeptide Y-like immunoreactivity correlates with impulsive aggression in human subjects. *Biological Psychiatry, 72,* 997–1003.

Coccaro, E., Lee, R., & McCloskey, M. S. (2003). Norepinephrine function in personality disorder: Plasma free MHPG correlates inversely with life history of aggression. *CNS Spectrums, 8,* 731–736.

Coccaro, E., Lee, R., Owens, M. J., Kinead, B., & Nemeroff, C. B. (2012). Cerebrospinal fluid substance P-like immunoreactivity correlates with aggression in personality disordered subjects. *Biological Psychiatry, 72,* 238–243.

Coccaro, E. F., & Kavoussi, R. J. (2010). GH response to intravenous clonidine challenge: Absence of relationship with behavioral irritability, aggression, or impulsivity in human subjects. *Psychiatry Research, 178,* 443–445.

Coccaro, E. F., Kavoussi, R. J., Cooper, T. B., & Hauger, R. L. (1997). Central serotonin activity and aggression: Inverse relationship with prolactin response to d-fenfluramine, but not CSF 5-HIAA concentration, in human subjects. *American Journal of Psychiatry, 154,* 1430–1435.

Coccaro, E. F., Kavoussi, R. J., Hauger, R. L., Cooper, T. B., & Ferris, C. F. (1998). Cerebrospinal fluid vasopressin levels: Correlates with aggression and serotonin function in personality-disordered subjects. *Archives of General Psychiatry, 55,* 708–714.

Coccaro, E. F., Kavoussi, R. J., & Lesser, J. C. (1992). Self- and other-directed human aggression: The role of the central serotonergic system. *International Clinical Psychopharmacology, 6,* 70–83.

Coccaro, E. F., Lawrence, T., Klar, H. M., & Siever, L. J. (1991). Growth hormone responses to intravenous clonidine challenge correlate with behavioral irritability in psychiatric patients and healthy volunteers. *Psychiatric Research, 39,* 129–139.

Coccaro, E. F., & Lee, R. (2010). Cerebrospinal fluid 5-hydroxyindolacetic acid and homovanillic acid: Reciprocal relationships with impulsive aggression in human subjects. *Journal of Neural Transmission, 117,* 241–248.

Coccaro, E. F., Lee, R., & Coussons-Read, M. (2014a). Cerebrospinal fluid and plasma C-reactive protein and aggression in personality-disordered subjects: A pilot study. *Journal of Neural Transmission, 122*, 1–6.

Coccaro, E. F., Lee, R., & Coussons-Read, M. (2014b). Elevated plasma inflammatory markers in individuals with Intermittent Explosive Disorder and correlation with aggression in humans. *JAMA Psychiatry, 71*, 158–165.

Coccaro, E. F., Lee, R., & Vezina, P. (2013). Cerebrospinal fluid glutamate concentration correlates with impulsive aggression in human subjects. *Journal of Psychiatric Research, 47*, 1247–1253.

Coccaro, E. F., McCloskey, M. S., Fitzgerald, D. A., & Phan, K. L. (2007). Amygdala and orbitofrontal reactivity to social threat in individuals with impulsive aggression. *Biological Psychiatry, 62*, 168–178.

Coccaro, E. F., Siever, L. J., Klar, H. M., Maurer, G., Cochrane, K., Cooper, T. B., ... David, K. L. (1989). Serotonergic studies in patients with affective and personality disorders. *Archives of General Psychiatry, 46*, 587–599.

Comai, S., Tau, M., & Gobbi, G. (2012). The psychopharmacology of aggressive behavior: A translational approach: Part 1: Neurobiology. *Journal of Clinical Psychopharmacology, 32*, 83–94.

Comai, S., Tau, M., Pavlovic, Z., & Gobbi, G. (2012). The psychopharmacology of aggressive behavior: A translational approach: Part 2: Clinical studies using atypical antipsychotics, anticonvulsants, and lithium. *Journal of Clinical Psychopharmacology, 32*, 237–260.

Cowdry, R. W., & Gardner, D. L. (1988). Pharmacotherapy of borderline personality disorder. *Archives of General Psychiatry, 45*, 111–119.

Damasio, A. R., Grabowski, T. J., Bechara, A., Damasio, H., Ponto, L. L., Parvizi, J., ... Hichwa, R. D. (2000). Subcortical and cortical brain activity during the feeling of self-generated emotions. *Nature Neuroscience, 3*, 1049–1056.

Damasio, H., Grabowski, T., Frank, R., Galaburda, A. M., & Damasio, A. R. (1994). The return of Phineas Gage: Clues about the brain from the skull of a famous patient. *Science, 264*, 1102–1105.

De Dreu, C. K. (2012). Oxytocin modulates cooperation within and competition between groups: An integrative review and research agenda. *Hormones and Behavior, 61*, 419–428.

Delville, Y., Mansour, K. M., & Ferris, C. F. (1996). Serotonin blocks vasopressin-facilitated offensive aggression: Interactions within the ventrolateral hypothalamus of golden hamsters. *Physiology & Behavior, 59*, 813–816.

Ditzen, B., Nater, U. M., Schaer, M., La Marca, R., Bodenmann, G., Ehlert, U., & Heinrichs, M. (2013). Sex-specific effects of intranasal oxytocin on autonomic nervous system and emotional responses to couple conflict. *Social Cognitive and Affective Neuroscience, 8*, 897–902.

Dodge, K. (1991). *The structure and function of reactive and proactive aggression.* The development and treatment of childhood aggression (pp. 201–218). Hillsdale, NJ: Lawrence Erlbaum Associates, Inc.

Dougherty, D. D., Shin, L. M., Alpert, N. M., Pitman, R. K., Orr, S. P., Lasko, M., ... Rauch, S. L. (1999). Anger in healthy men: a PET study using script-driven imagery. *Biological Psychiatry, 46*, 466–472.

Duke, A. A., Bègue, L., Bell, R., & Eisenlohr-Moul, T. (2013). Revisiting the serotonin-aggression relation in humans: A meta-analysis. *Psychological Bulletin, 139*, 1148–1172.

Dunn, A. J., & Swiergiel, A. H. (2009). The role of corticotropin-releasing factor and noradrenaline in stress-related responses, and the inter-relationships between the two systems. *European Journal of Pharmacology, 583*, 186–193.

Ferris, C. F., Lu, S.-F., Messenger, T., Guillon, C. D., Heindel, N., Miller, M., ... Simon, N. G. (2006). Orally active vasopressin V1a receptor antagonist, SRX251, selectively blocks aggressive behavior. *Pharmacology, Biochemistry, and Behavior, 83*, 169–174.

Ferris, C. F., Melloni, R. H., Koppel, G., Perry, K. W., Fuller, R. W., & Delville, Y. (1997). Vasopressin/serotonin interactions in the anterior hypothalamus control aggressive behavior in golden hamsters. *The Journal of Neuroscience 17*, 4331–4340.

Ferris, C. F., & Potegal, M. (1988). Vasopressin receptor blockade in the anterior hypothalamus suppresses aggression in hamsters. *Physiology & Behavior, 44*, 235–239.

Frankle, W. G., Lombardo, I., New, A. S., Goodman, M., Talbot, P. S., Huang, Y., ... Siever, L. J. (2005). Brain serotonin transporter distribution in subjects with impulsive aggressivity: A positron emission study with [11 C] McN 5652. *American Journal of Psychiatry, 162*, 915–923.

Gerra, G., Caccavari, R., Marcato, A., Zaimovic, A., Avanzini, P., Monica, C., ... Brambilla, F. (1994). Alpha-1–and 2-adrenoceptor subsensitivity in siblings of opioid addicts with personality disorders and depression. *Acta Psychiatrica Scandinavica, 90*, 269–273.

Goyer, P. F., Andreason, P. J., Semple, W. E., Clayton, A. H., King, A. C., Compton-Toth, B. A., ... Cohen, R. M. (1994). Positron-emission tomography and personality disorders. *Neuropsychopharmacology, 10*, 21–28.

Grafman, J., Schwab, K., Warden, D., Pridgen, A., Brown, H. R., & Salazar, A. M. (1996). Frontal lobe injuries, violence, and aggression: A report of the Vietnam Head Injury Study. *Neurology, 46*, 1231–1238.

Guastella, A. J., Kenyon, A. R., Alvares, G. A., Carson, D. S., & Hickie, I. B. (2010). Intranasal arginine vasopressin enhances the encoding of happy and angry faces in humans. *Biological Psychiatry, 67*, 1220–1222.

Haller, J. (2013). The neurobiology of abnormal manifestations of aggression: A review of hypothalamic mechanisms in cats, rodents, and humans. *Brain Research Bulletin, 93*, 97–109.

Heim, C., Young, L. J., Newport, D. J., Mletzko, T., Miller, A. H., & Nemeroff, C. B. (2009). Lower CSF oxytocin concentrations in women with a history of childhood abuse. *Molecular Psychiatry, 14*, 954–958.

Hesdorffer, D. C., Rauch, S. L., & Tamminga, C. A. (2009). Long-term psychiatric outcomes following traumatic brain injury: A review of the literature. *The Journal of Head Trauma Rehabilitation, 24*, 452–459.

Hibbeln, J. R., Umhau, J. C., George, D. T., Shoaf, S. E., Linnoila, M., & Salem, N. (2000). Plasma total cholesterol concentrations do not predict cerebrospinal fluid neurotransmitter metabolites: Implications for the biophysical role of highly unsaturated fatty acids. *American Journal of Clinical Nutrition, 71*, 331S–338S.

Hirono, N., Mega, M. S., Dinov, I. D., Mishkin, F., & Cummings, J. L. (2000). Left frontotemporal hypoperfusion is associated with aggression in patients with dementia. *Archives of Neurology, 57*, 861–866.

Hollander, E., Swann, A. C., Coccaro, E. F., Jiang, P., & Smith, T. B. (2005). Impact of trait impulsivity and state aggression on divalproex versus placebo response in borderline personality disorder. *American Journal of Psychiatry, 162*, 621–624.

Hoptman, M. J., Volavka, J., Johnson, G., Weiss, E., Bilder, R. M., & Lim, K. O. (2002). Impulsivity in men with schizophrenia: A preliminary study. *Biological Psychiatry*, 52, 9–14.

Hoptman, M. J., Volavka, J., Weiss, E. M., Czobor, P., Szeszko, P. R., Gerig, G., ... Bilder, R. M. (2005). Quantitative MRI measures of orbitofrontal cortex in patients with chronic schizophrenia or schizoaffective disorder. *Psychiatry Research*, 140, 133–145.

Hurlemann, R., Patin, A., Onur, O. A., Cohen, M. X., Baumgartner, T., Metzler, S., ... Kendrick, K. M. (2010). Oxytocin enhances amygdala-dependent, socially reinforced learning and emotional empathy in humans. *Journal of Neuroscience*, 30, 4999–5007.

Kessler, R. C., Coccaro, E. F., Fava, M., Jaeger, S., Jin, R., & Walters, E. (2006). The prevalence and correlates of DSM-IV intermittent explosive disorder in the National Comorbidity Survey Replication. *Archives of General Psychiatry*, 63, 669–678.

Kimbrell, T. A., George, M. S., Parekh, P. I., Ketter, T. A., Podell, D. M., Danielson, A. L., ... Post, R. M. (1999). Regional brain activity during transient self-induced anxiety and anger in healthy adults. *Biological Psychiatry*, 46, 454–465.

Koch, W., Schaaff, N., Pöpperl, G., Mulert, C., Juckel, G., Reicherzer, M., ... Pogarell. O. (2007). [I-123] ADAM and SPECT in patients with borderline personality disorder and healthy control subjects. *Journal of Psychiatry & Neuroscience*, 32, 234–240.

Kosfeld, M., Heinrichs, M., Zak, P. J., Fischbacher, U., & Fehr, E. (2005). Oxytocin increases trust in humans. *Nature*, 435, 673–676.

Kramer, U. M., Jansma, H., Tempelmann, C., & Munte, T. F. (2007). Tit-for-tat: The neural basis of reactive aggression. *Neuroimage*, 38, 203–211.

Lee, R., Petty, F., & Coccaro, E. F. (2009). Cerebrospinal fluid GABA concentration: Relationship with impulsivity and history of suicidal behavior, but not aggression, in human subjects. *Journal of Psychiatric Research*, 43, 353–359.

Leyton, M., Okazawa, H., Diksic, M., Paris, J., Rosa, P., Mzengeza, S., ... Benkelfat, C. (2001). Brain regional alpha-[11c]methyl-L-tryptophan trapping in impulsive subjects with borderline personality disorder. *American Journal of Psychiatry*, 158, 775–782.

Lidberg, L., Tuck, J. R., Asberg, M., Scalia-Tomba, G. P., & Bertilsson, L. (1985). Homicide, suicide, and CSF 5-HIAA. *Acta Psychiatrica Scandinavica*, 71, 230–236.

Limson, R., Goldman, D., Roy, A., Lamparski, D., Ravitz, B., Adinoff, B., & Linnoila, M. (1991). Personality and cerebrospinal fluid monoamine metabolites in alcoholics and controls. *Archives of General Psychiatry*, 48, 437–441.

Linnoila, M., Virkkunen, M., Scheinin, M., Nuutila, A., Rimon, R., & Goodwin, F. (1983). Low cerebrospinal fluid 5-hydroxyindoleacetic acid concentration differentiates impulsive from nonimpulsive violent behavior. *Life Sciences*, 33, 2609–2614.

Linnoila, V. M., & Virrkunen, M. (1992). Aggression, suicidality, and serotonin. *Journal of Clinical Psychiatry*, 53, 46–51.

Lopez-Ibor, J. J., Saiz-Ruiz, J., & de los Cobos, J. C. P. (1985). Biological correlations of suicide and aggressivity in major depression (with melancholia): 5-hydroxyindoleacetic acid and cortisol in cerebral spinal fluid, dexamethasone suppression test and therapeutic response to 5-hydroxytroptophan. *Neuropsychobiology*, 14, 67–74.

Marks, D. J., Miller, S. R., Schulz, K. P., Newcorn, J. H., & Halperin, J. M. (2007). The interaction of psychosocial adversity and biological risk in childhood aggression. *Psychiatry Research*, 151, 221–230.

Miczek, K. A., & Fish, E. W. (2005). *Monoamines, GABA, glutamate, and aggression*. Biology of Aggression (pp. 114–150). New York, NY: Oxford University Press.

Miczek, K. A., Fish, E. W., De Bold, J. F., & De Almeida, R. M. M. (2002). Social and neural determinants of aggressive behavior: Pharmacotherapeutic targets at serotonin, dopamine, and gamma-aminobutyric acid systems. *Psychopharmacology*, 163, 434–458.

Moeller, F. G., Steinberg, J. L., Petty, F., Fulton, M., Cherek, D. R., Kramer, G., & Garver, D. L. (1994). Serotonin and impulsive/aggressive behavior in cocaine dependent subjects. *Progress in Neuro-Psychopharmacology & Biological Psychiatry*, 18, 1027–1035.

Moss, H. B., Yao, J. K., & Panzak, G. L. (1990). Serotonergic responsivity and behavioral dimensions in antisocial personality disorder with substance abuse. *Biological Psychiatry*, 28, 235–238.

Nater, U. M., Bohus, M., Abbruzzese, E., Ditzen, B., Gaab, J., Kleindienst, N., ... Ehlert, U. (2010). Increased psychological and attenuated cortisol and alpha-amylase responses to acute psychosocial stress in female patients with borderline personality disorder. *Psychoneuroendocrinology*, 35, 1565–1572.

Neumann, I. D., & Landgraf, R. (2012). Balance of brain oxytocin and vasopressin: Implications for anxiety, depression, and social behaviors. *Trends in Neurosciences*, 35, 649–659.

New, A. S., Buchsbaum, M. S., Hazlett, E. A., Goodman, M., Koenigsberg, H. W., Lo, J., ... Siever, L. J. (2004). Fluoxetine increases relative metabolic rate in prefrontal cortex in impulsive aggression. *Psychopharmacology*, 176, 451–458.

New, A. S., Hazlett, E. A., Buchsbaum, M. S., Goodman, M., Reynolds, D., Mitropoulou, V. S., ... Siever, L. J. (2002). Blunted prefrontal cortical 18 fluorodeoxyglucose positron emission tomography response to meta-chlorophenylpiperazine in impulsive aggression. *Archives of General Psychiatry*, 59, 621–629.

New, A. S., Trestman, R. F., Mitropoulou, V., Goodman, M., Koenigsberg, H. H., Silverman, J., ... Siever, L. J. (2004). Low prolactin response to fenfluramine in impulsive aggression. *Journal of Psychiatric Research*, 38, 223–230.

Ninan, T., van Kammen, D. P. V., Scheinin, M., Linnoila, M., Bunney, W., & Goodwin, K. (1984). CSF 5-hydroxyindoleacetic acid levels in suicidal schizophrenic patients. *American Journal of Psychiatry*, 141, 566–569.

Nordin, C., Gupta, R. C., & Sjödin, I. (2007). Cerebrospinal fluid amino acids in pathological gamblers and healthy controls. *Neuropsychobiology*, 56, 152–158.

O'Keane, V., Moloney, E., O'Neill, H., O'Connor, A., Smith, C., & Dinan, T. G. (1992). Blunted prolactin responses to d-fenfluramine in sociopathy: Evidence for subsensitivity of central serotonergic function. *British Journal of Psychiatry*, 160, 643–646.

Ongür, D., & Price, J. L. (2000). The organization of networks within the orbital and medial prefrontal cortex of rats, monkeys and humans. *Cerebral Cortex*, 10, 206–219.

Oquendo, M. A., & Mann, J. J. (2000). The biology of impulsivity and suicidality. *Psychiatric Clinics of North America*, 23, 11–25.

Pare, C. M. B., Yeung, D. P. H., Price, K., & Stacey, R. S. (1969). 5-hydroxytryptamine, noradrenaline, and dopamine in brainstem, hypothalamus, and caudate nucleus of controls and of patients committing suicide by coal-gas poisoning. *Lancet*, 2, 133–135.

Paris, J., Zweig-Frank, H., Ng Ying Kin, N. M. K., Schwartz, G., Steiger, H., & Nair, N. P. V. (2004). Neurobiological correlates of diagnosis and underlying traits in patients with borderline personality disorder compared with normal controls. *Psychiatry Research, 121*, 239–252.

Phillips, M. L., Ladouceur, C. D., & Drevets, W. C. (2008). A neural model of voluntary and automatic emotion regulation: Implications for understanding the pathophysiology and nuerodevelopment of bipolar disorder. *Molecular Psychiatry, 13*, 833–857.

Raine, A. (1993). Features of borderline personality and violence. *Journal of Clinical Psychology, 49*, 277–281.

Raine, A., Buchsbaum, M., & LaCasse, L. (1997). Brain abnormalities in murderers indicated by positron emission tomography. *Biological Psychiatry, 42*, 495–508.

Raine, A., Buchsbaum, M. S., Stanley, J., Lottenberg, S., Abel, L., & Stoddard, J. (1994). Selective reductions in prefrontal glucose metabolism in murderers. *Biological Psychiatry, 36*, 365–373.

Raine, A., Lencz, T., Bihrle, S., LaCasse, L., & Colletti, P. (2000). Reduced prefrontal gray matter volume and reduced autonomic activity in antisocial personality disorder. *Archives of General Psychiatry, 57*, 119–127.

Rilling, J. K., DeMarco, A. C., Hackett, P. D., Thompson, R., Ditzen, B., Patel, R., & Pagnoni, G. (2012). Effects of intranasal oxytocin and vasopressin on cooperative behavior and associated brain activity in men. *Psychoneuroendocrinology, 37*, 447–461.

Rolls, E. T. (2000). The orbitofrontal cortex and reward. *Cerebral Cortex, 10*, 284–294.

Seo, D., Patrick, C. J., & Kennealy, P. J. (2008). Role of serotonin and dopamine system interactions in the neurobiology of impulsive aggression and its comorbidity with other clinical disorders. *Aggression and Violent Behavior, 13*, 383–395.

Serafini, G., Pompili, M., Seretti, M. E., Stefani, H., Palermo, M., Coryell, W., & Girardi, P. (2013). The role of inflammatory cytokines in suicidal behavior: A systematic review. *European Neuropsychopharmacology, 23*, 1672–1686.

Shamay-Tsoory, S. G., Fischer, M., Dvash, J., Harari, H., Perach-Bloom, N., & Levkovitz, Y. (2009). Intranasal administration of oxytocin increases envy and schadenfreude (gloating). *Biological Psychiatry, 66*, 864–870.

Siever, L. J., Buchsbaum, M. S., New, A. S., Spiegel-Cohen, J., Wei, T., Hazlett, E. A., ... Mitropoulou, V. (1999). d,l-fenfluramine response in impulsive personality disorder assessed with [18F]fluorodeoxyglucose positron emission tomography. *Neuropsychopharmacology, 20*, 413–423.

Siever, L. J., & Davis, K. L. (1991). A psychobiological perspective on the personality disorders. *American Journal of Psychiatry, 148*, 1647–1658.

Simeon, D., Bartz, J., Hamilton, H., Crystal, S., Braun, A., Ketay, S., & Hollander, E. (2011). Oxytocin administration attenuates stress reactivity in borderline personality disorder: A pilot study. *Psychoneuroendocrinology, 36*, 1418–1421.

Simeon, D., Knutelska, M., Smith, L., Baker, B. R., & Hollander, E. (2007). A preliminary study of cortisol and norepinephrine reactivity to psychosocial stress in borderline personality disorder with high and low dissociation. *Psychiatry Research, 149*, 177–184.

Simeon, D., Stanley, B., Frances, A., Mann, J., Winchel, R., & Stanley, M. (1992). Self-mutilation in personality disorders: Psychological and biological correlates. *American Journal of Psychiatry, 149*, 221–226.

Soderstrom, H., Blennow, K., Manhem, A., & Forsman, A. (2001). CSF studies in violent offenders: I. 5-HIAA as a negative and HVA as a positive predictor of psychopathy. *Journal of Neural Transmission, 108*, 869–878.

Soderstrom, H., Blennow, K., Sjodin, A. K., & Forsman, A. (2003). New evidence for an association between the CSF HVA:5-HIAA ratio and psychopathic traits. *Journal of Neurology, Neurosurgery, and Psychiatry, 74*, 918–921.

Soloff, P. H., Meltzer, C. C., Becker, C., Greer, P. J., & Constantine, D. (2005). Gender differences in a fenfluramine-activated FDG PET study of borderline personality disorder. *Psychiatry Research: Neuroimaging, 138*, 183–195.

Spoont, M. R. (1992). Modulatory role of serotonin in neural information processing: Implications for human psychopathology. *Psychological Bulletin, 112*, 330–350.

Stanley, B., & Siever, L. (2010). The interpersonal dimension of borderline personality disorder: Toward a neuropeptide model. *American Journal of Psychiatry, 167*, 24–39.

Taylor, S. E., Gonzaga, G. C., Klein, L. C., Hu, P., Greendale, G. A., & Seeman, T. E. (2006). Relation of oxytocin to psychological stress responses and hypothalamic-pituitary-adrenocortical axis activity in older women. *Psychosomatic Medicine, 68*, 238–245.

Taylor, S. E., Klein, L. C., Lewis, B. P., Gruenewald, T. L., Gurung, R. A. R., & Updegraff, J. A. (2000). Biobehavioral responses to stress in females: Tend-and-befriend, not fight-or-flight. *Psychological Review, 107*, 411–429.

Terburg, D., Morgan, B., & van Honk, J. (2009). The testosterone-cortisol ratio: A hormonal marker for proneness to social aggression. *International Journal of Law and Psychiatry, 32*, 216–223.

Thompson, R., Gupta, S., Miller, K., Mills, S., & Orr, S. (2004). The effects of vasopressin on human facial responses related to social communication. *Psychoneuroendocrinology, 29*, 35–48.

Thompson, R. R., George, K., Walton, J. C., Orr, S. P., & Benson, J. (2006). Sex-specific influences of vasopressin on human social communication. *Proceedings of the National Academy of Sciences, 16*, 7889–7894.

Tranel, D., Bechara, A., & Denburg, N. L. (2002). Asymmetric functional roles of right and left ventromedial prefrontal cortices in social conduct, decision-making, and emotional processing. *Cortex, 38*, 589–612.

Träskman, L., Asberg, M., Bertilsson, L., & Sjöstrand, L. (1981). Monoamine metabolites in CSF and suicidal behavior. *Archives of General Psychiatry, 38*, 631–636.

Uzefovsky, F., Shalev, I., Israel, S., Knafo, A., & Ebstein, R. P. (2012). Vasopressin selectively impairs emotion recognition in men. *Psychoneuroendocrinology, 37*, 576–580.

van Praag, H. M. (1983). CSF 5-HIAA and suicide in non-depressed schizophrenics. *Lancet, 2*, 977–978.

Vaz-Leal, F. J., Rodríguez-Santos, L., García-Herráiz, M. A., & Ramos-Fuentes, M. I. (2011). Neurobiological and psychopathological variables related to emotional instability: A study of their capability to discriminate patients with bulimia nervosa from healthy controls. *Neuropsychobiology, 63*, 242–251.

Virkkunen, M., De Jong, J., Bartko, J., Goodwin, F. K., & Linnoila, M. (1989). Relationship of psychobiological variables to recidivism in violent offenders and impulsive fire setters. A follow-up study. *Archives of General Psychiatry, 46*, 600–603.

Virkkunen, M., Nuutila, A., Goodwin, F. K., & Linnoila, M. (1987). Cerebrospinal fluid monoamine metabolite levels in male arsonists. *Archives of General Psychiatry*, 44, 241–247.

Virkkunen, M., Rawlings, R., Tokola, R., Poland, R. E., Guidotti, A., Nemeroff, C., . . . Linnoila, M. (1994). CSF biochemistries, glucose metabolism, and diurnal activity rhythms in alcoholic, violent offenders, fire setters, and healthy volunteers. *Archives of General Psychiatry*, 51, 20–27.

Volkow, N. D., Tancredi, L. R., Grant, C., Gillespie, H., Valentine, A., Mullani, N., . . . Hollister, L. (1995). Brain glucose metabolism in violent psychiatric patients: A preliminary study. *Psychiatry Research*, 61, 243–253.

Wilcock, G. K., Ballard, C. G., Cooper, J. A., & Loft, H. (2011). Memantine for agitation/aggression and psychosis in moderately severe to severe Alzheimer's disease: A pooled analysis of 3 studies, *Journal of Clinical Psychiatry*, 69, 341–348.

Woermann, F. G., Elst, L. T. V., Koepp, M. J., Free, S. L., Thompson, P. J., Trimble, M. R., & Duncan, J. (2000). Reduction of frontal neocortical grey matter associated with affective aggression in patients with temporal lobe epilepsy: An objective voxel by voxel analysis of automatically segmented MRI. *Journal of Neurology, Neurosurgery, and Psychiatry*, 68, 162–169.

Yang, Y., & Raine, A. (2009). Prefrontal structural and functional brain imaging findings in antisocial, violent, and psychopathic individuals: A meta-analysis. *Psychiatry Research*, 174, 81–88.

Yildirim, B. O., & Derksen, J. J. (2012). A review on the relationship between testosterone and the interpersonal/affective facet of psychopathy. *Psychiatry Research*, 197, 181–198.

Zimmerman, D. J., & Choi-Kain, L. W. (2009). The hypothalamic-pituitary-adrenal axis in borderline personality disorder: A review. *Harvard Review of Psychiatry*, 17, 167–183.

Zink, C. F., Kempf, L., Hakimi, S., Rainey, C. A., Stein, J. L., & Meyer-Lindenberg, A. (2011). Vasopressin modulates social recognition-related activity in the left temporoparietal junction in humans. *Translational Psychiatry*, 1, 1–5.

Zink, C. F., Stein, J. L., Kempf, L., Hakimi, S., & Meyer-Lindenberg, A. (2010). Vasopressin modulates medial prefrontal cortex-amygdala circuitry during emotion processing in humans. *Journal of Neuroscience*, 30, 7017–7022.

Behavioral Emergencies with the Elderly

Working Sensitively and Effectively to Reduce Suicide Risk Among Older Adults: A Humanistic Approach

Marnin J. Heisel *and* Paul R. Duberstein

Abstract

Suicide is a uniquely human phenomenon, necessitating a human response. Suicide disproportionately claims the lives of older adults, and men in particular. Effective clinical practice with at-risk older adults requires sensitivity to contributing developmental, intrapersonal, social, and existential factors. Whereas the presence of suicide thoughts and behavior may be conceptualized as potential signs of an incipient mental health emergency, demanding quick and decisive action, working clinically with at-risk older adults nevertheless extends temporally beyond moments of behavioral crisis and conceptually beyond risk assessment and management. The field of later-life suicide prevention is in its relative infancy; however, progress is being made in investigating associated risk and resiliency factors and in developing, testing, and disseminating approaches to assessment and intervention. We provide an overview of the literature and call for a more sensitive, compassionate, and effective approach to suicide prevention among older adults, drawing on individually tailored and humanistic-existential approaches to care.

Key Words: suicide prevention, suicide ideation, suicide behavior, risk factors, resiliency, meaning in life, assessment, intervention, humanistic-existential therapy, knowledge translation

The Problem of Suicide in Later Life

Suicide is a human tragedy and a cause of unnecessary pain and preventable loss of human life. Suicide is one of the most extreme forms of mental health crisis faced by psychologists and other mental healthcare providers, necessitating understanding of sensitive and effective approaches to risk reduction. This chapter is intended for the mental healthcare practitioner. In it, we provide a brief introduction to the topic of suicide and its prevention among "older adults," a term we will use to refer to individuals 65 years of age or older, and provide a basic overview of the epidemiology, risk and resiliency factors, and assessment and treatment approaches with which providers should be familiar.

Whereas Durkheim acknowledged the high rates of suicide among older adults in the 1890s,

the field of older adult suicide prevention is yet in its relative infancy. With one notable exception (Miller, 1978), retrospective studies of older adults who died by suicide were only initially published in the 1990s (e.g., Conwell, Olsen, Caine, & Flannery, 1991; Henriksson et al., 1995), and assessment tools and intervention trials specifically focusing on at-risk older adults have only begun in earnest within the past two decades (Heisel & Duberstein, 2005). Recent years have witnessed a significant advancement in theory, research, and knowledge translation regarding later-life suicide and its prevention. However, we still lack answers to basic questions, necessitating additional research and efforts to enhance clinical practice with at-risk older adults. In this chapter we explicitly posit that sensitive, individualized clinical care, influenced

Case Example: "Roland." *Roland, a divorced 63-year-old man of Eastern European birth, was referred to a psychologist by his family physician for treatment of "cognitive concerns and depression with passive thoughts of death." On initial presentation for care, Roland wearily explained that he is a full professor and former chair in the Department of Physics at the local university, with a long and distinguished career as an eminent researcher and lecturer. Over the past few years, and increasingly within the past six months, he has been finding himself forgetting the dates of key citations in his field, becoming easily irritated during faculty meetings with his colleagues, whom he finds "trite and unimaginative," and struggling to find interest in writing up his research findings, at times wondering "Why bother?" He is worried that these "lapses," typified by poor focus and attention and increasing apathy, are symptomatic of "Alzheimer's," noting that a beloved former mentor "succumbed to that horrifying disease after a long and piteous illness." Roland has a somewhat superficial relationship with his two children, now in their early-to-mid-30s, and infrequently sees them or his grandchildren. Extremely dedicated to his career, Roland spent little time with his children when they were growing up, a situation exacerbated by his divorce from their mother, to whom he granted uncontested custody when they were pre-adolescents. Roland's father died of heart disease 10 years ago, and his frail mother, who struggles with emphysema and recurrent bouts of depression, lives in an assisted-living facility in Europe. He has two younger siblings, both of whom also live in Europe, and with whom he speaks rarely and generally only when they wish to update him on their mother's health. Roland lives alone in an apartment, which he describes as a "small but neatly kept bachelor pad, about a 20-minute bike ride from campus." He is in generally good health, aside from slight hypertension and elevated cholesterol, both of which are well controlled by medication. Although he previously only consulted his physician for routine biannual physicals and annual occupational health visits required by his university, he has been making increasingly regular medical visits since his sixtieth birthday, complaining of aches, pains, fatigue, sleeping difficulties, occasional memory lapses, and a palpable sense of dread, which is no longer assuaged by a "good stiff drink." Following a lengthy battery of medical tests, all of which were negative, Roland admitted to his physician that he frequently feels "weepy" and empty, increasingly feels useless, and contemplates "taking the man's way out," noting that in parts of Europe he could request a prescription in order to end his life. Roland expressed the concern that he will be pushed to retire within the next few years, as "office space is limited" in his department and in order to make way for young physicists with "new ways of thinking," but notes that he has few extracurricular interests, little savings, and has made no plans for his life after retirement.*

by humanistic-existential psychology and psychotherapy, may substantially advance clinical efforts to enhance mental health and well-being, and ultimately help prevent suicide in later life. We begin with a fictional case example for illustrative purposes, integrating elements from the literature base together with clinical experience with at-risk older adults.

Roland's case reflects a constellation of biological, psychological, social, and existential characteristics commonly encountered by mental healthcare providers working with older adults potentially at risk for suicide. Older adults, and men in particular, have among the highest suicide rates in the U.S. (see Figure 22.1) and worldwide (WHO, 2014). Suicide risk is higher among those who are divorced or widowed, live alone, and are socially isolated; have rigid personality traits, and mood or other mental disorders; misuse substances; and struggle in the face of challenging

life transitions (Duberstein, Heisel, & Conwell, 2011). However, in addition to these socio-demographic and clinical risk indicators, Roland's case exemplifies some of the profounder existential issues associated with mental healthcare provision with at-risk older adults, including a shifting sense of self and identity that can accompany aging, questions of one's worth in the context of retirement and our society's negative attitude towards older adulthood, and issues of responsibility, intergenerational relationships, generativity, and questions about one's meaning in life.

In this chapter, we treat a client's endorsement of suicide ideation or engagement in suicide behavior as a sign of potential mental health crisis, and articulate methods for incorporating an evidence-supported humanistic-existential approach into sensitive clinical care aimed to reduce the risk for suicide in later life. We will return periodically to Roland's story, focusing on considerations to be

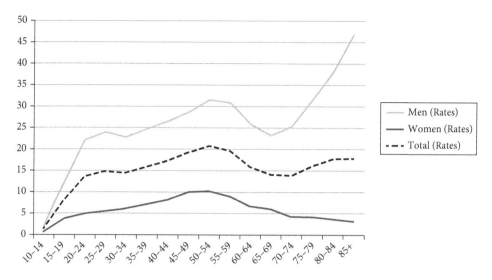

Fig. 22.1 U.S. suicide rates over the life course for men, women, and both sexes for 2012.

Note: Data comprise crude rates of suicide, expressed as the raw number who died by suicide in the U.S. in 2012 per 100,000 population members, for men, women, and both sexes across the life course. Data were derived from the WISQARS database.

borne in mind by clinicians when working with older adults.

The Epidemiology of Suicide in Later Life

Suicide is a significant cause of preventable morbidity and mortality, claiming over 800,000 lives every year, exceeding the number of lives lost to war and homicide combined, and accounting for approximately 1.4% of all deaths worldwide (WHO, 2014). The distribution of deaths by suicide among older adults varies by sex, age, and ethno-cultural background. In the United States, 40,600 people died by suicide in 2012, 6,652 of whom were 65 years or older, more than seven times the 883 older adults lost to homicide (Web-Based Injury Statistics Query and Reporting System [WISQARS] database; Centers for Disease Control and Prevention). Older Americans had a suicide rate (15.42/100,000) nearly 20% higher than the national average (12.94/100,000; WISQARS) in 2012. The "gender paradox of suicide" holds that whereas women are far more likely than men to engage in self-injury, men are far more likely to die by suicide (Canetto, 1992; Canetto & Lester, 1998). This is partly due to the fact that men use more lethal means of suicide. In 2012, 79% (4,393/5,556) of older men and 37% (406/1,096) of older women who died by suicide in the United States did so by way of a firearm, necessitating clinician vigilance and sensitivity to individual, State, and cultural beliefs and practices

towards firearm ownership and access. Whereas specific reasons for sex differences in suicide behavior remain elusive, theory suggests a culturally mediated effect of sex role socialization regarding perceptions of power and control, and comfort in seeking help for emotional difficulties (Canetto, 1992; Kaplan, Huguet, McFarland, & Mandle, 2011). Euro-American/White men accounted for 76% (5,095/6,652) of the deaths by suicide among Americans 65 years and older in 2012 (see Figure 22.2). These findings suggest that the experience of aging among White men may involve a declining sense of personhood and social value, and increasing feelings of worthlessness, uselessness, hopelessness, and meaninglessness that may culminate in suicide. The high lethality of suicide behavior in later life necessitates early and aggressive intervention and enhanced attention to sensitive means of suicide risk detection.

The high rate of suicide among older adults is especially daunting given the rapid expansion of the older adult population in North America and much of the Western world (Cohen, 2003; Ortman, Velkoff, & Hogan, 2014; Statistics Canada, 2005; WHO, 2001). This shift in population demographics creates a significant challenge to healthcare systems and practices, partly because Western culture places a high value on youth, often to the exclusion of respectful consideration and care for older individuals. The prevalence of anti-aging products and services, combined with zestful marketing of youth-oriented

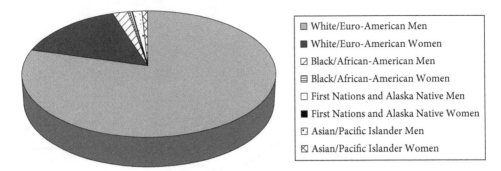

Fig. 22.2 Distribution of deaths by suicide for men and women 65 years and older in the U.S. in 2012.

Note: Data comprise the raw number of deaths by suicide across demographic groups. Data were derived from the WISQARS database for individuals who died by suicide in 2012, from age 65 through Unknown age. The vast majority of those who died by suicide were considered to be "Non-Hispanic" (6,410/6,652 or 96.4%). A majority of "Hispanic" older adults who died by suicide (219/6,652 or 3.3%) comprised "White/Euro-American Men" (180) and "Women" (37). Ethnicity was not provided for 23 older adults who died by suicide.

clothing, technology, and pastimes, sends a clear message that ours is not a society that honors being or growing old. As the size of the older adult population increases, it is possible that prevalent negativistic attitudes towards aging may begin to wane. If not, mental healthcare systems will need to prepare for a population of older individuals who feel deprived of meaningful roles and devalued in modern society.

An estimated 25% of North Americans will be 65 years or older by 2031 (Ortman et al., 2014; Statistics Canada, 2005), coincident with the aging of the vast Baby Boom cohort, whose members began reaching age 65 in 2011. The "boomers" compose a demographic with historically high rates of suicide (Blazer, Bachar, & Manton, 1986; Bongar,

1992; Mościcki, 1996). U.S. mortality data indicate increasing suicide rates among baby boomers over the past decade (see Figure 22.3), reversing an earlier decline in numbers of deaths by suicide in later life.

The experience of aging is ever changing. The baby boomers were born into an optimistic postwar period, and share formative cultural experiences that influence their approaches and perspectives to wellness, health, and healthcare. They witnessed tremendous cultural, social, and technological change over the course of their lives, including the birth of rock and roll, the race for space, war, a boom in postwar consumerism, the 1960s drug culture, increasing distrust of government, scientific innovation and advancement, the nuclear arms race,

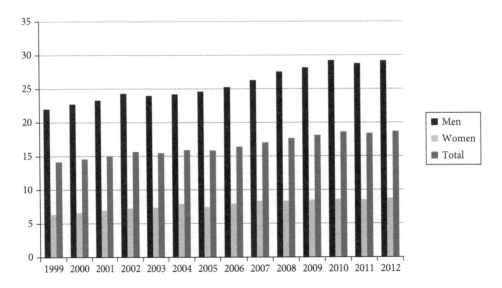

Fig. 22.3 U.S. suicide rates for baby-boomers, men, women, and totals, for 1999–2012.

Note: Suicide rates are expressed as the number who died by suicide divided by 100,000 population members. Figures were computed using WISQARS data for individuals born between 1946 and 1964.

and shifting trends in art, literature, music, cuisine, health, fitness, and sexuality, advocacy for greater sexual, racial, and cultural equality, and increased longevity. These shifts in cultural mores and practices may leave some feeling disconnected from the world around them or at a loss for role models to help them make a smooth and healthy transition into their later years, potentially conferring risk for what Durkheim (1966) termed *anomic suicide*. The boomers may be less deferential toward healthcare providers than older cohorts, more highly educated about mental health issues and interventions, and less likely to unquestioningly endorse a strictly biomedical approach rather than personally relevant and individually tailored approaches to care. The nature of interactions between the boomers and healthcare providers may be increasingly important for suicide prevention in coming decades, as people are living longer, have more chronic diseases, and are assuming a greater role in their own healthcare. Humanistic-existential approaches to care may be increasingly attractive to new generations of older adults, as a result of their having grown up in an era of social conscience and of personal and spiritual exploration. Shifting population demographics might thus not simply portend changing patterns of risk for suicide among older adults, but may also necessitate shifting approaches to its prevention.

Roland's Story (continued). *As a sexagenarian of Eastern European descent, Roland belongs to a demographic at elevated risk for suicide. Roland's healthcare providers should bear in mind that his sex, age, marital status, and cultural background can raise his overall risk, and seek to understand how his unique personal, social, demographic, and clinical risk indices work together to confer risk for suicide. They should ascertain whether he owns or has access to a firearm or other potentially lethal implements, and whether, how, and under what circumstances he might use them to harm or kill himself. Efforts are additionally needed to explore factors that contribute to his sense of meaning and enjoyment in life, to seek to enhance his social relations in a manner that is acceptable to him, and to help him find ways of transitioning to a fulfilling retirement.*

As a boomer who was raised in post–Second World War Eastern Europe, Roland witnessed the impact of war and the effects of totalitarian regimes, hatred, hunger for power, expansionism, and the corporatization of evil on society. He managed to emigrate to the United States, looking to share in the spirit of

optimism that pervaded American culture in the immediate postwar period; yet, he quickly found himself exposed to the counterculture of the Vietnam War while a graduate student. He became increasingly disenchanted with life in the United States, yet the thought of returning to his family of origin in Eastern Europe presented logistical difficulties and appeared to him to be an admission of failure. As he grows older, Roland finds himself yearning for some of the cultural touchstones of his youth in his birthplace, but the notion of leaving the United States, and his children and grandchildren, is anathema to him. And now, frightened by the potential impact of retirement on his day-to-day activities; not having cultivated interests, pursuits, and relationships outside of work; fearing a loss of authority, autonomy, and personal control, elements central to his identity; and having witnessed the sad decline of his once-vibrant mentor and the dismissive manner in which that "great man" was treated by others, Roland sees death as a potentially preferable alternative to growing older.

Assessment of Suicide Risk in Later Life: Can We Predict the Unpredictable?

The sensitive detection of suicide risk is critically important in decreasing the likelihood of death by suicide in mental healthcare services (Jacobs et al., 2003) and when striving to work effectively with at-risk older adults (Heisel, 2006). Clinicians seeking to detect the presence of older adult suicide risk, to assess its severity, and to monitor its progress over time are thus advised to bear a number of considerations in mind.

1) *Suicide risk is a theoretical construct, and no tool or approach has yet been shown to effectively, or with sufficient sensitivity and specificity, quantify risk for killing oneself.* Clinicians are thus advised to never attempt to quantify a percentage likelihood that an individual will kill one's self. Rather, they are advised to learn to identify unique factors and situations that might increase a specific individual's risk for suicide, and to devise individually tailored strategies for risk reduction consistent with that person's needs and values.

2) *Suicide risk may be associated with but is conceptually distinct from suicide ideation, suicide intent, lethality, and suicide behavior (Silverman & Berman, 2014).* Clinicians are advised to strive for precision when discussing a client's suicide risk, clearly articulating what they mean by specific

terms (O'Carroll et al., 1996; Silverman et al., 2010a, 2010b) and in the context of a specific client. They must not assume that an individual who endorses suicide ideation on a risk-assessment scale or communicates thoughts of suicide in clinical practice is necessarily at imminent, extreme, chronic, or constant risk for suicide, or that one who denies thoughts of suicide may not ultimately be at risk, as expression of the wish to end one's life can wax and wane over time (Szanto, Mulsant, Houck, Dew, & Reynolds, 2003; Szanto et al., 2007) and may have different meanings (Nissim, Gagliese, & Rodin, 2009). Far more people contemplate suicide than act on those thoughts, and far more people engage in suicide behavior than die by suicide; suicide ideation is thus at best an imperfect proxy measure for risk for death by suicide (Links, Heisel, & Quastel, 2005). Indeed, a client's expression of thoughts of suicide to a clinician may be immediately relieving, afford an opportunity for empathic engagement and the experience of support, and ultimately help lessen one's risk for suicide (Duberstein, 2001; Duberstein et al., 2000). For some, thinking about suicide affords them a psychological release from the stresses that otherwise threaten to overwhelm them; clinicians are thus advised to cautiously explore the meaning of suicide ideation to the unique client, and to seek to understand the underlying purpose behind contemplations of suicide.

3) *Current cohorts of older adults tend to downplay or deny the existence of psychological symptoms, including depressive symptoms and suicide ideation (Duberstein et al., 1999).* Clinicians are thus advised to be proactive and persistent in inquiring into an older adult's thoughts of suicide, not to relax their vigilance in the face of a client's denial of thoughts of suicide, and to sensitively reassess risk for suicide on an ongoing basis in a fashion that is respectful of their client's style of communication (Canadian Coalition for Seniors' Mental Health [CCSMH], 2006; Shea, 1999). Clinicians are further advised to develop skill, in accordance with the limits of their professional competencies, in effectively selecting, administering, scoring, and interpreting age-appropriate tools and approaches when seeking to investigate someone's suicide thoughts, plans, and behavior (Heisel & Flett, 2006), and to strive to engage an older person's family members and/or other collateral informants when assessing suicide risk (Heisel, Conwell, Pisani, & Duberstein, 2011).

4) *Although it may be possible to gauge the general severity of suicide-related thoughts and/or behavior,* *death by suicide is considered statistically unpredictable (Pokorny, 1993).* Clinicians are thus advised to focus on determining the presence and severity of suicide ideation and associated signs and symptoms empirically associated with the likelihood of dying by suicide, but to bear in mind that, despite these efforts, an individual might still kill himself or herself.

5) *No assessment instrument can do anything on its own.* As with any tool, a sufficiently skilled operator is required in order to effectively utilize suicide risk detection tools and approaches, and to do so in a manner that enhances sensitive and effective suicide risk assessment and intervention (CCSMH, 2006). Clinicians are thus advised to seek appropriate training, supervision, and/or consultation in selecting, administering, scoring, and interpreting suicide risk-assessment measures and to provide appropriate training and supervision to less experienced clinicians and healthcare providers wishing to do the same. This includes developing skill in building client trust and engendering genuine therapeutic rapport.

Approaches to Suicide Risk Identification

As with any complex health-related condition, early detection of suicide risk can serve as an effective risk reduction strategy, provided that it is accurate and leads to appropriate intervention. Focused approaches are thus encouraged in order to identify older adults potentially at risk for suicide. Common approaches used by clinicians to detect and/or assess the severity of suicide risk include:

1) Assessing factors that are positively associated with death by suicide (so-called risk factors) and those that are negatively associated with the likelihood of dying by suicide (so-called resiliency or protective factors);

2) Using screening or assessment tools and clinical interviews designed to assess suicide ideation or other risk indices; and

3) Assessing suicide warning signs (Rudd, Berman, et al., 2006; Rudd, Mandrusiak, et al., 2006).

These approaches are briefly considered next.

ASSESSMENT OF SUICIDE RISK AND RESILIENCY FACTORS

Suicide is not a specific disorder but rather a complex sociocultural phenomenon with multiple determinants and multidimensional contributing biological, psychological, social, and existential factors. Identification of variables that have been empirically associated with heightened risk of dying by suicide may aid in the detection of those at risk, and may thus inform clinical intervention. Efforts to predict individual deaths by suicide utilizing such approaches have not been successful (e.g., Modai, Ritsner, Kurs, Mendel, & Ponizovsky, 2002), probably due both to the low base rate and to the myriad unique combinations of risk factors and personal life contexts among at-risk individuals (e.g., Kjølseth, Ekeberg, & Steihaug, 2009).

Research findings derived largely from "psychological autopsy studies," referring to controlled retrospective studies investigating death by suicide, identified a set of common variables significantly linked with elevated suicide risk among older adults (see Duberstein, Heisel, & Conwell, 2011, for a review of this literature). Expression of the wish to die or to kill oneself is common among older adults who die by suicide (Kjølseth & Ekeberg, 2012). Older adults who die by suicide are significantly more likely than controls to endorse suicide ideation, death ideation, a wish to die, or the intention to harm or kill themselves (Chiu et al., 2004; Conwell, Duberstein, & Caine, 2002; De Leo, Draper, Snowdon, & Kõlves, 2013; Hawton, Zahl, & Weatherall, 2003; Kim et al., 2012; Rubenowitz, Waern, Wilhelmson, & Allebeck, 2001; Waern, Beskow, Runeson, & Skoog, 1999). Late-life suicide risk has also been associated with having a recent or more remote history of mental health treatment and one or more mental disorders, whether diagnosed or undiagnosed, potentially including mood, anxiety, psychotic, and/or substance-misuse disorders (Beautrais, 2002; Chiu et al., 2004; Conwell et al., 1996, 2000, 2002; Harwood, Hawton, Hope, & Jacoby, 2001; Suominen et al., 2003; Waern, Runeson, et al., 2002). Personality disorders have been associated with risk for suicide in later life (Harwood et al., 2001; Henriksson et al., 1995), as have specific personality traits that might impede the ability to cope flexibly with life's challenges and vicissitudes (Duberstein, 2001; Heisel, Duberstein, et al., 2006; Heisel, Links, Conn, van Reekum, & Flett, 2007; Segal, Marty, Meyer, & Coolidge, 2012; Tsoh et al., 2005).

Psychosocial challenges and stressors are commonly present among individuals at risk for suicide (Kjølseth, Ekeberg, & Steihaug, 2010b), and they provide key points of entry for clinical discussion of factors underlying thoughts of suicide in later life (Fässberg et al., 2012). Examples of these include concern about health, finances, place of residence, and interpersonal difficulties and challenges. The experience of social conflict, loss, isolation, concerns about burdening others, a perceived futility in ever having satisfying interpersonal connections, and negative events and life transitions, can individually or collectively contribute to the advent or exacerbation of distress, despair, hopelessness, difficulty coping or problem-solving, and may eventuate in a suicidal crisis (Conwell et al., 2002; Duberstein, Conwell, Conner, Eberly, Evinger, et al., 2004; Rubenowitz et al., 2001; Turvey et al., 2002; Van Orden et al., 2010). Psychosocial challenges often interact with underlying health problems to increase risk for suicide. The older adult in dire financial straits may thus be at elevated risk for suicide when experiencing or anticipating significant health decline; this may be especially true for those whose financial difficulties act as a barrier to receipt of effective healthcare services. However, even great wealth does not protect against suicide risk in later life (see, e.g., Conwell & Heisel, 2012).

Pain and physical health problems, including neurological disorders, chronic breathing problems such as chronic obstructive pulmonary disease (COPD) and emphysema, and certain forms of cancer, are also associated with risk for suicide (Duberstein, Conwell, Conner, Eberly, & Caine, 2004; Fässberg et al., 2016; Juurlink, Herrmann, Szalai, Kopp, & Redelmeier, 2004; Quan, Arboleda-Flórez, Fick, Stuart, & Love, 2002; Turvey et al., 2002; Waern, Rubenowitz, et al., 2002). Some evidence additionally supports an association between suicide thoughts, behavior, or deaths, and current or anticipated impairment in cognitive, sensory, and physical functioning (De Leo, Hickey, Meneghel, & Cantor, 1999; Harwood et al., 2001; Heisel, Flett, & Besser, 2002; Rubio et al., 2001; Waern, Rubenowitz, et al., 2002); however, more research is needed to identify whether and in what contexts cognitive decline might contribute to suicide risk.

Although physical illness, pain, and functional decline are all associated with suicide risk in later life, empirical findings and clinical experience both indicate that most suicidal older adults are not terminally ill, and most terminally ill older adults are not suicidal. A retrospective U.S. study of older adults who died by suicide reported that whereas 30–40% were medically ill at the time of death, only 2–3% had a terminal illness (Kleespies, Hughes, & Gallacher, 2000). Suicide among older adults does not typically occur in the context of terminal illness, but rather in the context of psychological pain. Mental health clinicians are thus encouraged to carefully assess suicide intent among individuals expressing a wish to hasten death in an end-of-life context (King, Heisel, & Lyness, 2005) and to remain vigilant to expressions of an extreme need for perceived autonomy and be wary of high-risk periods, including following communication of a severe/frightening diagnosis or a terminal prognosis, and to take the time to sensitively and compassionately inquire into each client's unique reception, understanding, thoughts, and feelings about that information. News that may be of a routine nature to a clinician might easily be disconcerting to a client, and could induce despair or even trigger existential terror, potentially eliciting a suicidal crisis. Mental health clinicians can thus also intervene with medical specialists (e.g., oncologists, neurologists, intensivists) who routinely communicate bad news to patients. Specifically, mental health clinicians can design and implement interventions to help specialty medical providers communicate diagnostic or prognostic information, especially regarding potentially life-threatening and degenerative conditions. Psychologically informed communication interventions targeting medical specialists could plausibly decrease suicide risk in very ill patients (Hoerger et al., 2013; Tulsky et al., 2011).

The study of psychological resiliency factors has historically received far less attention than has that of risk factors in the field of later-life suicide prevention, necessitating focused investigation of this topic (CCSMH, 2006; Heisel & Flett, 2008, 2014). Theory and research suggest that recognition of meaning in life (MIL), perception of purpose in life (PIL), reasons for living (RFL), and associated existential factors enables one to weather life's challenges even in the context of extreme physical and mental pain as well as other risk factors for morbidity and mortality (Heisel & Flett, 2006, 2008, 2014; Heisel, Neufeld, & Flett, 2016; Moore, 1997; Orbach, Mikulincer, Gilboa-Schechtman, & Sirota, 2003). Clinicians can benefit from an enhanced conceptual understanding of processes that either increase or decrease an individual's risk for suicide, so as to influence outreach, risk identification, and intervention (Heisel & Flett, 2014). Suicide risk assessment necessitates a sensitive and dynamic consideration of a constellation of risk and resiliency factors, together with a focused consideration of the intrapersonal, interpersonal, and environmental contexts of the individual's life (CCSMH, 2006). Clinicians may find it helpful to augment their clinical approaches to suicide risk assessment with the use of standardized screening and risk-assessment measures to better understand the psychological factors that potentially contribute to suicide risk, and to investigate psychological resiliency factors potentially protective against suicide.

USE OF ASSESSMENT TOOLS AND SYMPTOM RATING SCALES

Controversy exists over the practice of screening for suicide risk in clinics and communities; given its statistical rarity, screening tools tend to overestimate the presence of risk for death by suicide, leading healthcare administrators and policy-makers to question its cost–benefit ratio (O'Connor, Gaynes, Burda, Soh, & Whitlock, 2013). Research findings have nevertheless indicated that use of rating scales assessing the presence and severity of symptoms of depression, hopelessness, and suicide ideation can help identify at-risk individuals (Edelstein et al., 2008; Heisel, Duberstein, Lyness, & Feldman, 2010). Providers are encouraged to employ assessment tools developed or standardized with older adults (American Psychological Association, 2004), as non-standardized measures are of limited use and might even hamper risk detection.

Measures designed to assess aspects of suicide risk among older adults include Draper and colleagues' (2002; Draper, Brodaty, Low, & Richards, 2003) Harmful Behaviors Scale (HBS) and Edelstein and colleagues' (2009) Reasons for Living scale–Older Adults version (see Heisel et al., 2016). Perhaps the most widely used measure of suicide ideation in research with older adults is the Geriatric Suicide Ideation Scale (GSIS; Heisel & Flett, 2006), a 31-item 5-point Likert-scored measure, designed to meet the need for a suicide ideation assessment tool specific to the experiences and reporting styles of at-risk older adults (see Heisel & Flett, 2016, for a recent review of this scale). GSIS items were written in the first person in order to reflect the phenomenological experiences of a suicidal older adult, incorporating items assessing both frank and subtler thoughts of suicide, and were based on a review of existing theory, research, and clinical experience with at-risk individuals. The GSIS component subscales assess Suicide Ideation (10 items; e.g., "I want to end my life"), referring to thoughts, plans, desire, or intent to end one's life; Death Ideation (5 items; e.g., "I welcome the thought of drifting off to sleep and never waking up"), a variable sometimes termed "passive suicide ideation," reflecting a wish to die although not necessarily at one's own hand; Loss of Personal and Social Worth (7 items; e.g., "I generally feel pretty worthless"), reflecting a diminished sense of self and negative self-evaluation based on research demonstrating associations between suicide risk and perceptions of social disconnection, of burden, and of worthlessness (Joiner, 2005; Purcell et al., 2012; Rowe, Conwell, Schulberg, & Bruce, 2006); and Perceived Meaning in Life (8 items; e.g., "I am certain that I have something to live for"), reflecting theory (e.g., Frankl, 1985) and research suggesting that the perception of MIL and other positive psychological factors, including a sense of value, dignity, and enjoyment of life, enhance psychological resiliency and reduce suicide risk (Breitbart et al., 2010; Heisel & Flett, 2004, 2008, 2014, 2016, in press; Moore, 1997). The GSIS also contains an item assessing a respondent's history of suicide behavior, given the strong association of this variable with death by suicide (Kim et al., 2012).

Research findings have demonstrated strong psychometric properties for the GSIS in clinical and community samples, including internal consistency, test-retest reliability, criterion and construct validity (Heisel & Flett, 2006, 2007, 2008; Heisel & the Meaning-Centered Men's Group Project Team, 2016; Heisel & Flett, 2016; Jahn, Cukrowicz, Litton, & Prabhu, 2011; Marty et al., 2010; Neufeld & O'Rourke, 2009), and sensitivity to clinical change (Heisel, Talbot, King, Tu, & Duberstein, 2015). A greater focus is needed on testing the measurement characteristics of the GSIS and other suicide ideation measures with culturally and socioeconomically diverse samples of older adults and investigating their effective and sensitive integration into clinical practice. Although the GSIS can be administered effectively in self-report or interview format by a clinician or trained research assistant in less than five minutes, use of a 31-item assessment tool is less feasible in busy medical settings or at community health fairs, prompting the development and initial validation of 5- and 10-item versions (Heisel & Flett, 2012).

REMAINING VIGILANT FOR SUICIDE WARNING SIGNS

An expert panel from the American Association of Suicidology (AAS) identified a need for vigilance for suicide warning signs, referring to indicators that an individual may be at acute or imminent risk for suicide (Rudd, Berman, et al., 2006). They reviewed the literature for variables significantly associated with risk for death by suicide, and arranged them as the acronym "IS PATH WARM," suggesting that an individual with one or more of these warning signs might be on the path towards suicide: Ideation (thoughts of death or of suicide, suicide plans and/or preparations); Substance (misuse of alcohol, drugs, medications, or vitamins/supplements); Purposelessness (lacking in reasons for living or perceived meaning in life); Anxiety (or agitation); Trapped (feeling like there is no way out); Hopelessness (pessimism about the future); Withdrawal (from friends, family, and/or care-providers); Anger (rage, frustration, irritability, or wish for revenge); Recklessness (risk-taking or behavioral impulsivity); and Mood (mood swings or emotional dysregulation or lability). These warning signs may be readily recalled without iatrogenic effect (Rudd, Mandrusiak, et al., 2006). This mnemonic has been incorporated into late-life suicide-prevention knowledge translation tools (CCSMH, 2008; Perlman, Neufeld, Martin, Goy, & Hirdes, 2011); research is needed that evaluates the use of these warning signs in clinical outreach and mental health service delivery with at-risk older adults. Clinicians meanwhile are encouraged to remain vigilant for the presence of these potential warning signs in their older clients, to sensitively assess for suicide risk among individuals endorsing one or more of them, and to attempt to understand their onset, course, and contribution to an individual's overall mental state and potential risk for suicide.

Putting It All Together: A Process for Sensitively Detecting Older Adult Suicide Risk

A challenge to the assessment of suicide risk in clinical services stems from the erroneous belief, held by many clinicians, that if a client is suicidal, then (s)he will either independently raise the issue for discussion or the clinician will somehow sense it. Clinicians who do not typically work with older adults might further believe suicide risk to be minimal in the absence of a history of prior suicide behavior or current severe suicide ideation, neglecting a host of other clinical and demographic risk indices (Heisel & Duberstein, 2005). Others may minimize the presence of depressive symptoms and/or expression of thoughts about or wishes to die or for suicide, believing them to be age-appropriate and ubiquitous, and fail to recognize that endorsement of death ideation and/or suicide ideation may be reflective of a clinical emergency, necessitating responsive action. Identification of suicide risk can be further hampered by response characteristics; current cohorts of older adults tend to minimize their distress during assessments, and under-report symptoms of depression and suicide risk (Duberstein et al., 1999; Gallo, Rabins, & Anthony, 1999; Kjølseth, Ekeberg, & Steihaug, 2010a; Lyness et al., 1995). Risk identification can further be impeded by a lack of clinician expertise or confidence in discussing mental health issues with older adults and in referring them for appropriate mental health care (Adamek & Kaplan, 1996; Alvidrez & Areán, 2002; Feldman et al., 2007; Kaplan, Adamek, & Calderon, 1999; Samuels & Katz, 1995).

Assessment of suicide risk is best done in the context of a sensitive and trusting professional relationship (CCSMH, 2006). Approaches to detecting suicide risk in clinical services are predicated on first establishing therapeutic rapport in order to enhance the client's trust in the mental health provider, to increase the likelihood that an individual will share his or her innermost thoughts regarding death and suicide (Grek, 2007), and to enable the clinician to better appreciate why a particular individual might feel so overwhelmed, disconsolate, or hopeless at this moment in time as to consider ending one's life (Pompili, 2015). Even in the face of therapeutic rapport, clients might be apprehensive about sharing their intimate thoughts with a provider, and may have reasons for not openly doing so, including shame and stigma, and fear of being hospitalized or of being prevented from being able to end their life, should they ultimately choose to do so. Inquiring into an older person's intimate thoughts, including hope for life and contemplation of death, must be done with respect and an appreciation of that person's dignity.

Risk detection may be enhanced by the appropriate use of assessment and interview techniques designed to assess depression, hopelessness, death ideation, suicide ideation, self-harm history, presence of a suicide plan, and the degree of intent to die (Heisel & Flett, 2006; Joiner, Walker, Rudd, & Jobes, 1999; Shea, 1999), and to motivate patients to report thoughts of self-harm to a clinician (Shah et al., 2014). Busch, Fawcett, and Jacobs (2003) reported that, among a sample of current or recently discharged mental health patients who died by suicide, 78% had denied suicide ideation as a final communication before death; some did so as little as five to ten minutes prior to killing themselves. Some might interpret this statistic as reflecting a paucity of effective suicide risk-assessment tools or a high level of dishonesty among suicidal mental health clients. An alternative interpretation of this finding is that mental healthcare services may be largely ineffective at reducing suicide risk when they focus more on providing services in a rote or routine manner, ticking off "to-do" lists, rather than in a more person-centered or individualized manner, focusing on cultivating an unfolding helping relationship. To that end, clinicians are advised to attend not only to a client's spoken words, but to the unspoken, including the client's history of suicide ideation and behavior; behavioral signs and symptoms of distress, hopelessness, anger, apathy, or of giving up; and to their own instinct, clinical judgement, and experience. Clinicians are advised to only use suicide

risk-detection instruments or approaches that fall within their sphere of professional competence, to work collaboratively with providers with appropriate training in assessing suicide risk among older adults, and to avoid placing undue emphasis on the results of any specific assessment tool or approach, especially when these fail to identify someone as contemplating suicide (CCSMH, 2006). Clumsy or indiscreet efforts at assessing late-life suicide ideation or intent are of questionable value, as is the use of rating scales by people without appropriate psychometric training. A blunt, rushed, impersonal, or superficial assessment of suicide risk may ultimately prove futile, potentially inducing silence or antipathy (Ganzini et al., 2013). These approaches are further discouraged as they stand in the way of good clinical rapport and could yield false negative findings that incorrectly alleviate clinician concerns about a client's potential risk for suicide (Heisel & Duberstein, 2005). From a humanistic perspective, these practices are not in keeping with the sensitive interactions necessary to reengage a suffering person in the process of living and to help that individual metaphorically step away from the precipice.

Clinicians should strive to assess risk for suicide in a respectful and humanistic fashion, develop sensitivity to cultural diversity and to the unique life circumstances and values of those seeking their care, and communicate an empathic acceptance of the client to encourage honest reporting of symptoms and life circumstances. Any indication, during the assessment process, that suicide or self-harm is viewed as morally wrong, pathological, upsetting, or otherwise likely to induce negative clinician judgement or of being sent to or detained in a hospital might encourage deception. Suggestions for incorporating suicide risk assessment into clinical practice involve making a concerted effort to get to know the client, in order to better understand ones developmental history, life experiences, worldview, and contexts that potentially underlie risk for suicide. Clinicians are encouraged to begin the assessment with potentially less threatening questions, such as about a client's current circumstances, social network, activities of daily living, sleep, appetite, and other physical health symptoms, before gradually moving into questions assessing mental health difficulties. Given the tendency of some older adults to under-endorse or deny suicide thoughts and plans that are present (Duberstein et al., 1999), providers are encouraged to initially note that it is not uncommon for individuals who are facing difficult circumstances to feel tense or stressed about those circumstances or even to acknowledge feeling over-whelmed or unable to endure them anymore. The clinician might then gently ask the client how often (s)he feels that way. The clinician can then progress further, in a similar fashion, asking about interpersonal and financial issues, mood symptoms, misuse of alcohol and of prescription medications, hopelessness, feeling tired of living, thinking of death, wanting to die, thinking of risky or dangerous behavior, contemplating ways of killing one's self, and so on, up to recurrent or persistent thoughts of suicide and/or clear plans and preparations for taking one's life (Cooper-Patrick, Crum, & Ford, 1994; Grek, 2007; Shea, 1999). Clinicians are also encouraged to assess risk for violence towards others, including risk for murder-suicide (e.g., Malphurs & Cohen, 2005) and for elder abuse, and anticipated losses and transitions. Older clients are more likely to admit to having these thoughts and experiences if asked in a fashion that is sensitive, understanding, and inviting of their disclosure. Clinicians are encouraged to ask "how often" a client finds himself or herself having those thoughts and feelings, rather than asking "whether" (s)he does so. Asking "how often" may be seen as more permissive or welcoming of the disclosure and subtly suggests that these experiences are commonplace, and even expected. An individual can still deny thinking of suicide when asked "how often" by answering "never"; however, this approach tends to facilitate endorsement of suicide ideation. Moreover, unlike the closed question "Have you thought of ending your life?" which enables a negative response potentially shutting-down discourse, asking "how often" encourages a more open discussion.

Clinicians should strive to assess and work to enhance clients' psychological resiliency over the course of clinical care with at-risk older adults, as risk assessment requires considering factors that prevent the onset of suicide thoughts and behavior. Research consistently demonstrates significant negative associations between suicide ideation and the recognition of MIL and RFL in older adults (Heisel et al., 2016); clinicians are strongly encouraged to enter into the experiential world of their at-risk clients, to better understand how their life history, expectations, and experiences might elicit frank risk for suicide, and to conceptualize individually tailored approaches to risk reduction. Frankl (1971) advised following a client's denial of suicide ideation by asking what makes their life meaningful, and to ask why, given the client's challenging life circumstances, (s)he is not considering suicide, and then listening carefully

both for the potential sources of meaning that confer resilience to thoughts of suicide and to subtle signs that a client might be dissembling. At a pragmatic level, providers might consider adopting the conservative practice of presuming the presence of suicide risk until proven otherwise. Research findings suggest that older adults' family members and close interpersonal others can detect the presence of depression (Duberstein et al., 2011) and suicide ideation (Heisel et al., 2011), supporting the clinical practice of also seeking collateral information from members of an older client's social network (CCSMH, 2006), including family, friends, other healthcare providers, the police or other authorities, and journals, diaries, letters, or other written or electronic materials that might provide insight into a client's subjective world.

Clinicians should bear in mind that asking about suicide will not plant the idea in one's mind; studies have shown that assessing for the presence and severity of suicide ideation does not induce it (Eynan et al., 2014; Reynolds, Lindenboim, Comtois, Murray, & Linehan, 2006). Clinicians are additionally advised not to use a "no suicide contract," even if they had once been taught to do so. The literature is now clear that such an approach is not only unlikely to reduce a client's risk for suicide, but can potentially erode clinical rapport, and might even encourage client deception (Kroll, 2000; Lewis, 2007). Clients are better encouraged to develop trust in the honest and straightforward clinician who listens carefully, offers empathic support and assistance, and acts in such a fashion as to uphold a client's dignity, even if one's risk for suicide necessitates hospitalization. When done well, a sensitive suicide risk assessment can be therapeutic, helping a client feel listened to and understood, and can even begin to decrease risk for suicide.

Roland's Story (continued). *Having worked closely with Roland for years, his physician has developed a warm rapport with him, and has grown to know him well. Having attended to Roland's description of worries about his health, well-being, anticipated retirement, increasing despondency regarding his current life experiences, and admission of hopelessness and occasional suicide ideation, the doctor has grown concerned about Roland's risk for suicide. He thus initially prescribed Roland an antidepressant and referred him for psychological services to an on-site psychologist who works as an integrated* *member of the healthcare team, citing the empirical evidence supporting psychotherapy for amelioration of anxiety, depression, hopelessness, and suicide ideation among middle-age and older adults. He then walked Roland down the hall and introduced him to the clinic psychologist, waiting until the two made an appointment to meet for an initial session the following week.*

Older Adult Suicide Prevention: A Mental Health and Public Health Priority

Once considered a moral or religious issue, suicide and its prevention have long been viewed through a mental health lens. Studies have indicated that a majority of people who died by suicide would have met criteria for a mental disorder at the time of death, that a history of suicide behavior is associated with longer duration of illness, a poorer course of treatment for mood disorders, and is a predictor of subsequent suicide behavior and death by suicide (Claassen et al., 2007; Duberstein, Heisel, & Conwell, 2011; Kim et al., 2011). Bertolote, Fleischmann, De Leo, and Wasserman (2004) reviewed 31 articles on death by suicide published between 1959 and 2001 and identified mood disorders (30.2%), substance-misuse disorders (17.6%), schizophrenia and associated disorders (14.1%), and personality disorders (13.0%) as the most common mental disorders associated with death by suicide across the life course. Considerable attention has been paid to the detection, assessment, diagnosis, and treatment of psychopathology as a means for decreasing suicide risk, but the persistently high suicide rates among at-risk individuals suggest that existing approaches to mental health service provision are insufficient.

The prevention of suicide necessitates enhancements in mental healthcare services and systems, incorporating early detection of suicide risk and effective intervention; however, although highly prevalent, not everyone who dies by suicide has a mental disorder or uses mental health services (Duberstein & Wittink, 2015; Ernst et al., 2004; Juurlink et al., 2004; Kjølseth, Ekeberg, & Steihaug, 2010a). In recent years, the largely clinical focus of suicide prevention efforts, also known as "indicated interventions" for those at risk for suicide, has expanded to include a public health perspective incorporating greater consideration of societal factors that contribute to suicide risk, and social policy interventions that might

help alleviate it (Conner et al., 2014; Erlangsen et al., 2011; Kaplan, McFarland, & Huguet, 2009; Knox, Conwell, & Caine, 2004; Potter, Powell, & Kachur, 1995). These "universal interventions" have included the development and dissemination of evidence-informed suicide prevention strategies and treatment guidelines (American Psychiatric Association, 2010; CCSMH, 2006), guidelines for safe media reporting on suicide (Etzersdorfer & Sonneck, 1998; Niederkrotenthaler et al., 2010), and legislation to restrict access to firearms and other lethal means, including creating physical barriers to suicide on bridges and restricting pack sizes of medications potentially lethal on overdose (Beautrais, 2007; Hawton, 2007; Hawton et al., 2009; Pirkis et al., 2013; Yip et al., 2012). Others have focused on community-level suicide prevention efforts targeting potentially at-risk groups. These "selective interventions" include such efforts at engaging at-risk older adults as telephone distress and outreach services (De Leo, Dello Buono, & Dwyer, 2002) and multimodal community interventions incorporating public outreach, lectures, screenings, and counseling for late-life depression (Oyama, Koida, Sakashita, & Kudo, 2004; Oyama et al., 2005, 2008). These interventions have been found to be primarily effective in reducing suicide risk among women (Duberstein & Heisel, 2014); more recent data suggest the potential efficacy of community interventions in reducing the likelihood of suicide behavior and death among men (Ono et al., 2013).

The empirical literature base supports a multi-layered approach for reducing suicide risk. Mann and colleagues (2005) conducted a systematic review of the suicide prevention literature for a period extending from 1966–2005, aiming to synthesize available empirical findings on suicide prevention across the life-span and incorporating multiple levels and modalities. Yet, of the 93 articles that met the inclusion criteria for their review, only one explicitly referenced an intervention with older adults, and it did not focus on prevention of death by suicide. Clinical research efforts to test multimodal interventions have been found effective in helping to reduce risk for suicide behavior (Hegerl, Althaus, Schmidtke, & Niklewski, 2006; Hegerl et al., 2009), but likewise have not focused primarily on at-risk older adults. Efforts are needed to enhance the meager clinical evidence base focusing on the prevention of suicide among older adults.

Suicide Prevention in Later Life: A Summary of the Clinical Evidence Base

The current focus on evidence-based healthcare places a high value on empirically validated clinical interventions. However, precious few clinical intervention trials have been conducted with the specific aim of reducing suicide ideation or behavior in later life (Duberstein & Heisel, 2014; Lapierre et al., 2011; Links et al., 2005). For years, individuals with suicide ideation and behavior had been commonly excluded from randomized controlled clinical intervention trials (Pearson, Stanley, King, & Fisher, 2001); only recently has this trend changed, given an increase in federal efforts to prevent suicide (National Action Alliance for Suicide Prevention, 2014; U.S. Department of Health and Human Services, 2012). Interventions effective in reducing risk for suicide among middle-age adults may work with older individuals; however, focused attention is recommended to age-specific factors that contribute to the onset or maintenance of suicide risk, and to the development and evaluation of focused interventions with promise in alleviating risk and potentially enhancing mental health and well-being in later life.

Empirical findings support the effectiveness of programs designed to improve the assessment and treatment of late-life depression in primary care by integrating evidence-based mental healthcare into primary care services (Alexopoulos et al., 2009; Bartels et al., 2004; Bruce et al., 2004; Unützer et al., 2006). However, the field has been slow to translate these promising research findings into efficient, effective, and pragmatic clinical services, and these trials have not shown a significant reduction in deaths by suicide. U.S. federal government investment in alternative models of treatment delivery notwithstanding, concerns have been raised about the "real-world" applicability of collaborative care models incorporating multi-component and inter-professional intervention (e.g., Lebowitz, 2004); these notes of caution have become increasingly relevant in the current era of reduced healthcare expenditure. In addition to pragmatic concerns about the cost and effort required for effective collaborative care is the fear that simply adding providers to clinical services may not serve to address a suicidal older adult's need for empathy, support, compassion, and connection, or ensure well-integrated delivery of care or sensitive and personalized approaches to suicide prevention (Duberstein & Wittink, 2015). A systematic review identified few new suicide prevention programs among older adults, in which suicide ideation, suicide behavior, or rates

of suicide were the outcomes of interest (Lapierre et al., 2011). One exception was our small trial of Interpersonal Psychotherapy (IPT) adapted for older adults at risk for suicide (Heisel, Duberstein, Talbot, King, & Tu, 2009; Heisel et al., 2015).

Arguing, in part, that previous trials focused on testing models of care with depressed older adults, whereas individualized clinical interventions are needed for suicidal older adults being seen in mental healthcare services, we conducted a trial of 16-session, once weekly, individual IPT adapted for older adults with current suicide ideation and/or recent self-harm (Heisel et al., 2015). All participants were receiving active treatment for a mood disorder at the time of study referral, and yet all retained sufficient risk for suicide to be referred to our study. Following humanistic psychological practice, we sought to individually tailor treatment to participants' emotional and existential concerns, helping them attend to sources of MIL, and emphasizing enhancing, rebuilding, or cultivating supportive relationships, aiming to enhance psychological well-being. We additionally sought to seal gaps in the mental health system for our study participants, by updating their psychiatrists or other mental healthcare clinicians on their progress; assisting clients in accessing additional healthcare services as needed; accompanying clients to the emergency department if they were judged to be at imminent risk; scheduling weekly appointments with study participants and contacting them immediately in the event of a missed or cancelled session; engaging in ongoing discussions regarding their life circumstances, relationships, and any symptoms of depression, anxiety, and/or suicide ideation; and providing them with information on accessing mental health and/or crisis services around the clock, including a list of community resources, a telephone distress line, and the therapist's cell-phone number. Participants reported finding these system-level improvements effective and felt supported by them. They experienced a significant reduction in the presence or severity of suicide ideation, the wish to die, perceptions of having lost personal and social worth, and improvement in perceptions of meaning in life and in psychological well-being, gains that were maintained or increased further over a six-month period of follow-up (Heisel et al., 2015). Limitations of this study included its small sample size, lack of a control group and of blinding, necessitating larger controlled trials, investigation of treatment moderators, and efforts to facilitate dissemination and uptake of promising research findings into frontline practice. The findings of this study suggest

Roland's Story (continued). *During their initial session, Roland's psychologist balanced the hour focusing on three primary aims:*

1) Developing initial rapport with Roland, in order to lay a foundation of mutual respect and trust, and to encourage Roland's confiding in him and being more open to receiving his feedback and support;

2) Assessing the immediate and underlying reasons for Roland's seeking out mental healthcare at this moment in time, and initially ascertaining Roland's risk for self-harm in the imminent future;

3) Getting to know Roland better, as a unique human being, including forming an initial impression of his personality, coping style, developmental history, factors that motivate him, and those that potentially enhance his mental health and well-being and that might be called upon to reduce his risk for suicide.

that there is value in focusing on working to promote psychological resiliency while working to decrease risk for suicide among older adults, and further support our call for more individually tailored humanistic-existential approaches to care.

By the end of the initial session, he had an initial impression that Roland is a very serious-minded and exacting individual with relatively few outlets, aside from his work. He learned of Roland's personal history, including his upbringing in Eastern Europe following the Second World War, the relative privation that his family and their community experienced, and how Roland's intelligence and zeal helped him emerge from these circumstances. He asked specifically about Roland's interpersonal life in the United States in order to learn some rudimentary facts about his former marriage and his relationships with his children and now grandchildren. He noted that Roland's age (60-plus), sex (male), region of origin (Eastern Europe), marital status (divorced), symptoms of depression, presence of occasional suicide ideation and death ideation, fears regarding cognitive decline, relative social isolation, and the prospect of facing a difficult life transition together conferred risk for eventual death by suicide. However, he also identified a number of potential resiliency features that tempered his risk, including Roland's love for his children and grandchildren and his wish to not hurt them, presence of family in Europe whom he loves and respects and

who look up to him, extensive problem-solving skills, and a strong wish to overcome his current challenges. He also recognized Roland's optimism, idealism, and drive, which prompted him to leave Europe and move to the United States as a young man in order to pursue his education and a new way of life. He noted that Roland has considerable determination: examples include his having developed a successful career in a competitive field, and his refusal to give in to self-doubt and return to Europe, yet he also recognized that extreme determination could increase the likelihood of engaging in fatal self-harm, should Roland's thoughts of suicide not resolve. He saw that Roland's fear of cognitive deterioration, of losing the respect and admiration of his peers, and of being able to continue making a meaningful contribution to his field, all figure prominently in his current mental state. He noted that Roland denied having access to a firearm, did not have an active plan for suicide, and had never engaged in self-harm behavior. He further noted that Roland enjoys a healthy lifestyle, takes the time to cook healthy meals, and bicycles to work on a routine basis. However, Roland rarely socializes with others outside of work, does not belong to any clubs or organizations, and only sees or speaks to his children or grandchildren on a sporadic basis. For his part, Roland found his psychologist earnest and sincere, interested in him, and genuinely committed to helping him overcome his current challenges and improve his life, and yet he felt somewhat skeptical about the ability of someone else to truly understand him in all of his complexity, and to help solve his problems. He also wondered whether clinical intervention could ever effectively resolve his fears for the future, hopelessness, and wish to die.

Suicide Prevention in Later Life: A Call for Sensitive Clinical Care

Clinical work with individuals at risk for suicide is challenging and demanding, and it necessitates empathy, concern, compassion, skill in clinical risk assessment and intervention, and the ability to engage a client on a human level and to tolerate a client's and one's own fear, anger, and other intense emotions. In a now-classic treatise on "necessary and sufficient conditions" for psychotherapeutic change, Rogers (1957) articulated that the effective therapist shows empathy, genuineness, and unconditional positive regard for her/his clients. At a deeper level, Roger's gentle philosophy is elevating of human beings, arguing that within us lies the potential for growth and self-improvement, and that the job of the therapist, in large part, is to clear away the emotional debris that is impeding growth. Rogers termed this debris "conditions of worth," noting that when an individual's early years are typified by the belief that one is only acceptable or lovable if one meets particular contingencies (e.g., "little boys mustn't cry" or "little girls mustn't express anger"), this can lead to a distancing from oneself and the advent of mental health problems. In a similar fashion, when therapists convey the message to a client that certain thoughts, expressions, or actions are acceptable or unacceptable, iatrogenic damage can ensue. Use of the term "problems of living" instead of "psychopathology" can help normalize the act of seeking therapy to help someone struggling with emotional difficulties. The humanistic therapist gently enables the client to share his/her story, reflecting empathically on the deeper emotional and experiential content of the client's report, and showing a profound acceptance of the client's individuality and right to be. The process of effective therapy along these lines leads to an unfolding and deepening of a client's experience, and to the client's experience of being increasingly understood by another human being in all of her/his uniqueness. Engaging in guided emotional exploration and empathic understanding is intended to help clear away the conditions of worth that might bind the individual, enable a natural, growth-oriented "actualizing tendency" to flourish, and engender greater self-acceptance. Frankl's (1985) meaning-centered approach to psychotherapy also supports the uniqueness of the individual, and inspires a response to meaningful challenges in the world, rather than a myopic focus on one's expectations of oneself or those of others. Researchers are finding success in interpersonal (Heisel et al., 2015) and humanistic-existential approaches to psychological care with older adults, including reminiscence or life review (Bohlmeijer, Roemer, Cuijpers, & Smit, 2007; Korte, Westerhof, & Bohlmeijer, 2012) and enhancing recognition of MIL for individuals struggling with life transitions, end-of-life issues, and contemplations of suicide (e.g., Breitbart et al., 2010; Heisel & the Meaning-Centered Men's Group Project Team, in press; Lapierre, Dubé, Bouffard, & Alain, 2007).

The threat of a client's death by suicide is one of the most daunting considerations that a mental healthcare clinician can face. Unlike other causes of a client's death, in which a provider and client might naturally assume a common stance against a condition, disease, or disorder, suicide is somewhat unique in that it is largely self-determined, creating a situation in which some providers find themselves at odds with a client, rather than against the underlying conditions that contribute to that individual's risk for suicide. Some providers struggle with feelings of frustration, disheartenment, and even anger towards suicidal clients (Maltsberger & Buie, 1974; Singer & Erreger, 2015). Clients receiving mental healthcare are often extremely sensitive to interpersonal subtleties and the emotional expression of others and routinely recognize negative attitudes when present in providers (Strike, Rhodes, Bergmans, & Links, 2006). It is not uncommon for an individual who has been to the emergency department in suicidal crisis to note that, whereas providers can see and sympathetically treat the wounds of those with physical maladies, they are unable to see the very real emotional wounds of those struggling with psychological concerns. This need not be the case. Clinicians are encouraged to recognize that it can be better to appropriately acknowledge difficult feelings that they experience when working with clients at risk for suicide, in the spirit of Rogerian "congruence" or genuineness, both to model honest communication with one's clients and to endeavor to overcome such challenges, than to outright deny difficult feelings that they themselves might be having. Clinicians are additionally encouraged to recognize that at-risk clients often struggle with intense emotions and may have long and challenging histories of interpersonal conflict (e.g., Zweig & Hinrichsen, 1993), including with healthcare providers and systems, and so can benefit from more open and supportive interactions. It can be helpful for clinicians to endeavor to side with their clients, albeit against their problematic constitution, upbringing, traumatic life experiences, self-derision, and challenging circumstances. Providers are encouraged to support and attempt to elevate the individual. They may also endeavor to differentiate between the individual and her/his emotional problems, just as one might do with a client suffering from cancer or other physical illness. Doing so might help clients distance themselves from their mental health symptoms or syndromes (Lukas, 1984), and to rekindle hope in their ability to face and perhaps even overcome challenges and live a fulfilling existence (Kjølseth et al., 2010b). Some providers convey subtler messages of discomfort in working with at-risk clients, including adopting a highly businesslike "clinical" tone; avoiding eye contact with those expressing emotional pain; not taking the time to thoroughly ask about suicide thoughts, feelings, and intentions; and not following up suggestive comments, such as that one might "not be around much longer." Every provider who works with potentially at-risk older adults is encouraged to thoroughly consider and review her/his thoughts, feelings, beliefs, and attitudes about working clinically with suicidal individuals, and to strive to resolve negative or otherwise problematic thoughts and feelings, in order to be fully present, supportive, and compassionate (Maltsberger & Buie, 1974). Those who cannot do this should refer at-risk clients to those who can.

Clinicians are strongly encouraged to seek out focused training, supervision, and consultation with providers more experienced in working effectively with individuals at risk for suicide, both to assist in managing some of the difficulties that can be engendered by this work, and to enhance their clinical skill-development and care. They are also encouraged to check in with their at-risk clients, to find out how the clients respond to them, and to gauge the strength of the working alliance. Clinicians are advised to be cognizant of their own health and well-being, to strive for effective self-care, and to ideally work collaboratively with other providers in communities of practice (CCSMH, 2006). It is not uncommon, when working with individuals at risk for suicide, to occasionally question one's skills and competence, especially when a client is struggling in spite of a clinician's best efforts, and to experience anxiety about the client's potential risk for suicide. And yet mental healthcare providers who feel excessively uncomfortable working with individuals at risk for suicide, or who, conversely, have no qualms or concerns about losing a client to suicide, might consider moving into areas of the field in which direct patient contact is not required. Otherwise, it is critical for providers to develop the skills and attitudes requisite for sensitive, empathic, compassionate, and effective care with individuals contemplating suicide.

A retrospective study of 36 therapists who lost a client to suicide while in therapy identified a set of common problems in psychotherapy with suicidal individuals (Hendin, Haas, Maltsberger, Koestner, & Szanto, 2006). Findings of this study suggest a need for thoroughness in investigating the life circumstances, experiences, and symptoms of an at-risk client, and open and effective communication with the client and with his/her close interpersonal others and healthcare providers. Clinicians are further advised to fully and appropriately intervene to alleviate psychopathology and suicide risk, integrating care with other providers as needed. Leenaars (2006) identified a number of common factors in effective psychotherapy with suicidal individuals, including the need to know one's client, to form rapport and develop a strong "I–Thou" relationship (Buber, 1984), to mutually set goals and collaborate to reach them, and to be open to multimodal approaches to care, given the complexities involved in the

experiences of at-risk individuals. We have thus summarized a set of factors and considerations that can help ensure effective humanistic mental healthcare with at-risk older adults. These include the need for:

1) *Engagement, rapport, and human contact.* Suicide risk may be initiated, and is typically increased, by perceptions of loneliness, isolation, and/or interpersonal alienation (Durkheim, 1966; Joiner, 2005). Actively engaging an at-risk individual and helping him/her feel wanted, socially included, and valued can go a long way towards decreasing risk (Heisel et al., 2009, 2015).

2) *Interdisciplinary care.* Risk for suicide often arises out of a constellation of biological, psychological, social, and existential factors. Alleviating the myriad associated contributory factors requires teamwork (CCSMH, 2006). A care network is additionally required in order to seal the numerous gaps extant in the healthcare system, and can help ensure that appropriate supports are in place for providers working with at-risk individuals.

3) *Information.* As noted in the section on assessment, it is critical for providers working with at-risk older adults to assess suicide risk thoroughly, to seek to know their clients on an individual basis, and to understand what factors might increase or decrease their risk for suicide. When working actively with an at-risk client, providers additionally require ongoing information about the client's life circumstances, successes, and drawbacks, and must follow up immediately when something seems awry. When working with at-risk clients, "no news" is often not "good news." Input and feedback from others involved in a client's life can help identify moments of increased risk, enabling timely and effective intervention (Heisel et al., 2011).

4) *Access to care when needed.* Healthcare providers are strongly encouraged to provide an at-risk client with around-the-clock access to mental healthcare service, recognizing both that clients may desperately need help outside of business hours, and that suicide risk can increase at any moment in time. Lives are sometimes lost because a client is unable to access support and care at the precise moment when the call to suicide is at its loudest. As such, providers are encouraged to think creatively about ways to be present, even if only in a virtual fashion, during those key moments of risk. With currently available technological options, including cell phones, email, social media, and electronic applications, the ability to provide that sort of protective service is much greater

than it once was (see, e.g., Mishara & Kerkhof, 2013). Of course, prior to implementing these approaches, providers must first investigate the legal, professional, and local regulations and guidelines for client–provider confidentiality and potential privacy risks associated with use of technology.

5) *Remaining up-to-date on the empirical literature.* Compared with the study and prevention of suicide among the young and middle-aged, the empirical literature on later-life suicide risk assessment and intervention lags behind (Heisel, 2006). And, yet, an evidence base is growing slowly for promising approaches to enhancing older adult suicide risk detection and intervention. Providers are encouraged to remain up-to-date on this growing literature base, and to strive for compassion and sensitivity to older clients' values, individuality, and dignity. Those contributing to the clinical literature are encouraged to be cognizant of the need for knowledge translation across multiple avenues, including newsletters, listserves, social media, papers, presentations, workshops, and individualized instruction and mentorship of providers.

6) *Developing approaches to care that are relevant to the experiences and responsive to the needs of at-risk populations.* Empirical findings demonstrate risk for post-retirement morbidity and mortality, including by suicide, and thereby suggest the potential benefit of preventive interventions for vulnerable individuals facing retirement (Bamia, Trichopoulou, & Trichopoulos, 2008; Brockman, Müller, & Helmert, 2009; Qin, Agerbo, & Mortensen, 2003; Schneider et al., 2011). A study is currently underway that has been designed to develop, implement, test, and initially disseminate Meaning-Centered Men's Groups (MCMG; Heisel & the Meaning-Centered Men's Group Project Team, in press) for men struggling to transition to retirement. The aim of this study is to develop a sense of camaraderie among men facing retirement and to enhance their psychological resiliency and well-being, including meaning in life (MIL), social connectedness, and satisfaction with retirement, and to prevent the onset of suicide risk. This intervention thus responds to the need for focused interventions targeting men at risk for suicide (Wålinder & Rutz, 2001), draws on theory (e.g., Frankl, 1985) and research (e.g., Heisel & Flett, 2008, 2014, 2016) demonstrating that recognition of MIL is negatively associated with depression, hopelessness, and suicide ideation, and is consistent with our findings of increasing MIL among older adults who experienced a significant

Roland's Story (continued). *Roland continued meeting with his psychologist, on roughly a weekly basis, for a number of months. After initially becoming acquainted and developing a rudimentary level of mutual respect and trust, Roland's psychologist helped him gradually articulate his inner experience of dread regarding growing older and his fears of losing his sense of vitality, usefulness, and importance. Roland indicated that his position as an eminent physicist and university professor makes him feel valued and worthwhile, something that, as a frightened little boy in postwar Europe, he never dreamed he might achieve. Roland additionally admitted to often wondering whether "it was all worth it," noting that he missed a lot of close experiences with his family over the years by living halfway around the world from some and alienating those nearby with his constant over-working. Roland acknowledged and expressed emotional pain he had experienced as a young man when he pursued the opportunity of studying abroad, leaving behind a childhood girlfriend, whom he described as the "love of his life." Discussing his failed marriage, Roland mourned the lost opportunity of living a quieter, happy life, with someone who loved and accepted him in a profound manner, for someone who never made him feel the way that his first love had. As he reviewed and shared these deep emotional wounds, Roland experienced a growing sense of internal peace, and a deeper appreciation and regard for his therapist. His therapist, in turn, gently guided Roland through these discussions, helping him acknowledge both the real pain in his memories, and yet a deeper meaning in his sacrifices, noting that the world might have lost a brilliant physicist had he remained in Europe with his true love. He further articulated the possibility that Roland might have grown to resent the relationship that kept him from pursuing his dream and of fulfilling the promise of his talents. He highlighted the kindness Roland had shown to others, both his family in Europe, to whom he routinely sent money, and in the United States, having chosen not to contest his ex-wife's request for custody of the children, recognizing that they needed their mother and to spare them the animosity of a contentious divorce. And he helped Roland contemplate the next steps in a life well-lived, noting that as a still-vibrant, intelligent, and successful individual, he still has a lot he can offer to others, including mentees, members of his community, his family, and possibly a significant other. Roland began seeing the possibilities in* *this next phase of life, and became more settled in his contemplation of retirement. With an attendant reduction in his experience of stress and self-doubt, he noted an improvement in his memory functioning and was less disturbed by occasional memory lapses, accepting them as age-appropriate "senior moments."*

reduction in suicide ideation with psychotherapeutic care (Heisel et al., 2015). The initial findings of this ongoing study are promising.

Knowledge Translation (KT): Moving Promising Empirical Findings into Practice

Given the typical lengthy delay in translating promising research findings into clinical services (Agency for Health Research and Quality, 2001; Graham, Tetroe, & the KT Theories Research Group, 2007), research is now needed that investigates the translation and integration of focused interventions targeting at-risk older adults into sensitive, frontline mental healthcare. When older adults at risk for suicide successfully access mental health services, they rarely receive recommended care, due in part to a lack of available interdisciplinary services and to a paucity of provider knowledge and sensitivity regarding suicide risk detection and intervention (Heisel & Duberstein, 2005). This issue stems, at least in part, from a lack of strong focus on suicide in healthcare training programs and, until recently, a near-absence of clear guidelines for provider training in suicide risk assessment and intervention (Ellis & Dickey, 1998; Kleespies & Berman, 2004; Kleespies et al., 2005; Kleespies, Penk, & Forsyth, 1993; Snowdon, 1997). Perceptions that suicidal older adults are noncompliant with treatment (Kaplan et al., 1999), the anticipation of lengthy sessions, and fears of losing a client to suicide might further discourage practicing clinicians from gaining experience with at-risk individuals. At a fundamental level, providers may object to the effort needed to extend life for those who appear to not wish to live, when others actively seek out care to extend life. Providers may also feel that they lack the necessary skills to help.

Focused education and training can effectively enhance provider knowledge and attitudes concerning working with suicidal individuals (Huh et al., 2012; Schmall & Pratt, 1993), and help reduce depressive symptom severity and the likelihood of self-harm (Almeida et al., 2012). Stand-alone educational programs have been developed for frontline providers and other "gatekeepers" to broadly identify individuals potentially at risk for suicide;

however, with a few exceptions, these programs have not been well evaluated, or have been shown to be lacking (Pisani, Cross, & Gould, 2011; Sareen et al., 2013; Wyman et al., 2008). A decade ago, the Public Health Agency of Canada commissioned the Canadian Coalition for Seniors' Mental Health (CCSMH), a collaborative of mental healthcare professionals dedicated to facilitating older adult mental health, to develop a series of national guidelines in four priority areas: suicide, depression, delirium, and long-term care (Conn et al., 2006). The objective of the suicide risk-assessment and prevention guideline was to provide practical advice for clinicians and frontline providers who work with at-risk older adults regarding assessment, intervention, and population-level prevention, and to influence policy-makers (CCSMH, 2006; Heisel et al., 2006). Additional late-life suicide-prevention knowledge translation (KT) tools have since been developed, including a clinician quick-reference pocket card, an interactive training DVD, a guide for family members of at-risk older adults, and a facilitator's guide for healthcare educators. These tools were developed by providers and researchers sensitive to a humanistic and individualized approach to mental health service delivery with at-risk older adults. An evaluation of half-day training workshops for frontline providers in late-life suicide risk assessment and intervention incorporating the CCSMH training tools suggested a subsequent improvement in provider knowledge and attitudes toward working with at-risk older adults (Heisel, Bowman, Moore, & Wilson, 2012). Provider toolkits for suicide risk assessment and/or intervention in later life have also been developed by American groups (Holkup, 2002; SAMHSA, 2011). Additional work is needed in translating empirical findings regarding older-adult suicide prevention into practical tools and sensitive approaches for use by frontline providers, and in disseminating and rigorously evaluating those tools with respect to clinical outcomes.

Conclusion: Where Do We Go Next?

The challenges facing those wishing to prevent suicide among older adults are many and varied, and include limitations associated with a relatively small mental healthcare workforce trained to work with at-risk older adults, a relative paucity of approaches to the effective assessment and intervention with at-risk individuals, and, at a basic level, challenges to accessing existing services. Access to sensitive and effective mental healthcare remains an ongoing concern among older adults in North

America, and varies by geographic region and across sociodemographic gradients (Administration on Aging, 2001). Although this issue flows in large part from the growing size of older cohorts, it also reflects continuing challenges with mental health service delivery, stemming, in part, from a general paucity of high-quality mental healthcare services for at-risk older adults, especially in rural, remote, and under-serviced regions (Institute of Medicine, 2008, 2012). Challenges abound in well-serviced urban settings as well, largely assuming the form of lengthy wait-times to see specialists, and poor integration between and across healthcare services and systems. Services that might be available to those with employer-provided healthcare benefits may be inaccessible to retirees or those without post-employment healthcare benefits. In difficult economic times, employers often expend resources on benefits for current employees at the cost of reducing benefits and services for retirees. Mental healthcare that is available on a fee-for-service basis may be nearly impossible to access for many older adults, especially for those in lower socioeconomic strata. In addition to these policy and access-related issues are pragmatic considerations: depressed and suicidal older adults have historically sought treatment in primary care settings and not in specialty mental health settings (Bartels et al., 2004). Although baby boomers may be more comfortable than prior birth cohorts in accessing mental health services directly, changes in healthcare policy and their attendant funding and administrative requirements are necessary in order to ensure that current and future generations of older adults can quickly access competent personalized mental health services.

Mental healthcare providers are advised to familiarize themselves with epidemiological trends in the issue of suicide among older adults, in order to remain cognizant of demographics at elevated risk, and to attend both to aggregate risk and potential resiliency factors and to individual-level conditions, factors, and experiences of unique clients. Providers are further encouraged to incorporate a humanistic-existential sensibility when assessing and intervening to reduce risk for suicide, remaining sensitive to the uniqueness of a given client and to factors that lend that individual a reason for living, despite challenging circumstances. By combining a sensitive, humanistic, clinical approach with solid knowledge of evidence-supported practices, providers may become increasingly effective at engaging with at-risk clients, helping restore dignity and meaning to their lives, and ultimately reducing their risk for suicide.

> **Roland's Story (conclusion).** *Six months after terminating therapy at a mutually agreed upon time, Roland emailed his psychologist an update. He reported a deepening sense of calm and acceptance, with occasional anxiety, during his transition to semi-retirement. He noted finding meaning in enjoyable pastimes, and now takes violin lessons, something he had wished to do as a child but that his family could not afford. He reached out to his children, expressing a heartfelt wish to spend more time with them and his grandchildren. After a few get-togethers over dinner, he gradually began doing so on a routine basis. Having joined an adult education class, he met a divorced woman whom he found "sophisticated, intriguing, stimulating, and fun" and began seeing her regularly. Roland expressed warm thanks to his therapist for believing in him, showing him that he has a lot of living left to do, and a lot to offer others. He added "I don't think about suicide anymore, and can't believe that I ever did."*

Suicide Prevention Resources
Websites

- American Association of Suicidology: www.suicidology.org
- American Foundation for Suicide Prevention: www.afsp.org
- Canadian Coalition for Seniors' Mental Health: www.ccsmh.ca/en/projects/suicide.cfm
- Centre for Suicide Prevention: www.suicideinfo.ca
- International Association for Suicide Prevention: www.iasp.info/
- Suicide Prevention Resource Center: www.sprc.org
- U.S. Department of Veterans Affairs: http://www.mentalhealth.va.gov/suicide_prevention/

References

Adamek, M. E., & Kaplan, M. S. (1996). Managing elder suicide: A profile of American and Canadian crisis prevention centers. *Suicide and Life-Threatening Behavior, 26*(2), 122–131.

Administration on Aging. (2001). *Older Adults and Mental Health: Issues and Opportunities.* Washington, DC: U.S. Department of Health and Human Services.

Agency for Health Research and Quality. (2001). *Translating Research into Practice (TRIP)-II.* Washington, DC: Agency for Health Research and Quality. Available at: http://www.ahrq.gov/research/trip2fac.htm. Accessed February 16, 2012.

Alexopoulos, G. S., Reynolds, C. F. III, Bruce, M. L., ... PROSPECT Group. (2009). Reducing suicidal ideation and depression in older primary care patients: 24-month outcomes of the PROSPECT study. *American Journal of Psychiatry, 166,* 882–890.

Almeida, O. P., Pirkis, J., Kerse, N., Sim, M., Flicker, L., Snowdon, J., . . . Pfaff, J. J. (2012). A randomized trial to reduce the prevalence of depression and self-harm behavior in older primary care patients. *Annals of Family Medicine, 10,* 347–356.

Alvidrez, J., & Areán, P. A. (2002). *Physician willingness to* refer older depressed patients for psychotherapy. *The International Journal of Psychiatry in Medicine, 32*(1), 21–35.

American Psychiatric Association. (2010). *Practice guideline for the assessment and treatment of patients with suicidal behaviors.* Available from http://psychiatryonline.org/pb/assets/raw/sitewide/practice_guidelines/guidelines/suicide.pdf. Accessed March 3, 2016.

American Psychological Association. (2004). Guidelines for psychological practice with older adults. *American Psychologist, 59,* 236–260.

Bamia, C., Trichopoulou, A., & Trichopoulos, D. (2008). Age at retirement and mortality in a general population sample: The Greek EPIC Study. *American Journal of Epidemiology, 167,* 561–569.

Bartels, S. J., Coakley, E. H., Zubritsky, C., Ware, J. H., Miles, K. M., Areán, P. A., . . . Levkoff, S. E., & PRISM-E investigators (2004). Improving access to geriatric mental health services: A randomized trial comparing treatment engagement with integrated versus enhanced referral care for depression, anxiety, and at-risk alcohol use. *American Journal of Psychiatry, 161,* 1455–1462.

Beautrais, A. L. (2002). A case control study of suicide and attempted suicide in older adults. *Suicide and Life-Threatening Behavior, 32,* 1–9.

Beautrais, A. (2007). Suicide by jumping: A review of research and prevention strategies. *Crisis, 28*(S1), 58–63.

Bertolote, J. M., Fleischmann, A., De Leo, D., & Wasserman, D. (2004). Psychiatric diagnoses and suicide: Revisiting the evidence. *Crisis, 25,* 147–155.

Blazer, D. G., Bachar, J. R., & Manton, K. G. (1986). Suicide in late life: Review and commentary. *Journal of the American Geriatrics Society, 34,* 519–525.

Bohlmeijer, E., Roemer, M., Cuijpers, P., & Smit, F. (2007). The effects of reminiscence on psychological well-being in older adults: A meta-analysis. *Aging & Mental Health, 11,* 291–300.

Bongar, B. (Ed., 1992). *Suicide: Guidelines for assessment, management, and treatment.* New York: Oxford University Press.

Breitbart, W., Rosenfeld, B., Gibson, C., Pessin, H., Poppito, S., Nelson, C., . . . Olden, M. (2010). Meaning-centered group psychotherapy for patients with advanced cancer: A pilot randomized controlled trial. *Psychooncology, 19,* 21–28.

Brockman, H., Müller, R., & Helmert, U. (2009). Time to retire—time to die? A prospective cohort study of the effects of early retirement on long-term survival. *Social Science & Medicine, 69,* 160–164.

Bruce, M. L., Ten Have, T. R., Reynolds, C. F. III, Katz, I. I., Schulberg, H. C., Mulsant, B. H., . . . Alexopoulos, G. S. (2004). Reducing suicidal ideation and depressive symptoms in depressed older primary care patients. A randomized controlled trial. *Journal of the American Medical Association, 291,* 1081–1091.

Buber, M. (1984). *I and thou.* New York: Scribner.

Busch, K. A., Fawcett, J., & Jacobs, D. G. (2003). Clinical correlates of inpatient suicide. *Journal of Clinical Psychiatry, 64,* 14–19.

Canadian Coalition for Seniors' Mental Health. (2006). *National guidelines for seniors' mental health: The assessment of suicide risk and prevention of suicide.* Toronto: Author.

Canadian Coalition for Seniors' Mental Health. (2008). *Suicide Assessment & Prevention for Older Adults. Based on: Canadian Coalition for Seniors' Mental Health (CCSMH) National Guidelines: The Assessment of Suicide Risk and Prevention of Suicide.* Toronto: Author.

Canetto, S. S. (1992). Gender and suicide in the elderly. *Suicide and Life-Threatening Behavior, 22,* 80–97.

Canetto, S. S., & Lester, D. (1998). Gender, culture, and suicidal behavior. *Transcultural Psychiatry, 35,* 163–190.

Centers for Disease Control and Prevention, National Center for Injury Prevention and Control. (2005). *WISQARS (Web-Based Injury Statistics Query and Reporting System) Fatal Injury Reports National and Regional, 1999–2013.* Data file. Retrieved January, 2015 from http://webappa.cdc.gov/sasweb/ncipc/mortrate10_us.html.

Chiu, H. F. K., Yip, P. S. F., Chi, I., Chan, S., Tsoh, J., Kwan, C. W., . . . Caine, E. (2004). Elderly suicide in Hong Kong: A case-controlled psychological autopsy study. *Acta Psychiatrica Scandinavica, 109,* 299–305.

Claassen, C. A., Trivedi, M. H., Rush, A. J., Husain, M. M., Zisook, S., Young, E., . . . Alpert, J. (2007). Clinical differences among depressed patients with and without a history of suicide attempts: Findings from the STAR*D trial. *Journal of Affective Disorders, 97,* 77–84.

Cohen, J. E. (2003). Human population: The next half century. *Science, 302,* 1172–1175.

Conn, D. K., Malach, F. M., Wilson, K. J., Buchanan, D., Gibson, M. C., Grek, A., . . . Tourigny-Rivard, M.-F. (2006). National Guidelines for Seniors' Mental Health: Introduction and project background. *The Canadian Journal of Geriatrics, 9*(Suppl. 2), S36–S41.

Conner, K. R., Huguet, N., Caetano, R., Giesbrecht, N., McFarland, B. H., Nolte, K. B., & Kaplan, M. S. (2014). Acute use of alcohol and methods of suicide in a US national sample. *American Journal of Public Health, 104,* 171–178.

Conwell, Y., Duberstein, P. R., & Caine, E. D. (2002). Risk factors for suicide in later life. *Biological Psychiatry, 52,* 193–204.

Conwell, Y., Duberstein, P. R., Cox, C., Herrmann, J. H., Forbes, N. T., & Caine, E. D. (1996). Relationships of age and Axis I diagnoses in victims of completed suicide: A psychological autopsy study. *The American Journal of Psychiatry, 153,* 1001–1008.

Conwell, Y., & Heisel, M. J. (2012). The elderly. In R. I. Simon & R. E. Hales (Eds.), *The American Psychiatric Publishing Textbook of Suicide Assessment and Management* (Second Edition), pp. 367–388. Arlington, VA: Author.

Conwell, Y., Lyness, J. M., Duberstein, P., Cox, C., Seidlitz, L., DiGiorgio, A., & Caine, E. D. (2000). Completed suicide among older patients in primary care practices: A controlled study. *Journal of the American Geriatrics Society, 48,* 23–29.

Conwell, Y., Olsen, K., Caine, E. D., & Flannery, C. (1991). Suicide in later life: Psychological autopsy findings. *International Psychogeriatrics, 3,* 59–66.

Cooper-Patrick, L., Crum, R. M., & Ford, D. E. (1994). Identifying suicidal ideation in general medical patients. *Journal of the American Medical Association, 272,* 1757–1762.

De Leo, D., Dello Buono, M., & Dwyer, J. (2002). Suicide among the elderly: The long-term impact of a telephone support and assessment intervention in northern Italy. *British Journal of Psychiatry, 181,* 226–229.

De Leo, D., Draper, B. M., Snowdon, J., & Kõlves, K. (2013). Suicides in older adults: A case-control psychological autopsy study in Australia. *Journal of Psychiatric Research, 47,* 980–988.

De Leo, D., Hickey, P. A., Meneghel, G., & Cantor, C. H. (1999). Blindness, fear of sight loss, and suicide. *Psychosomatics, 40*, 339–344.

Draper, B., Brodaty, H., Low, L.-F., & Richards, V. (2003). Prediction of mortality in nursing home residents: Impact of passive self-harm behaviors. *International Psychogeriatrics, 15*, 187–196.

Draper, B., Brodaty, H., Low, L.-F., Richards, V., Paton, H., & Lie, D. (2002). Self-destructive behaviors in nursing home residents. *Journal of the American Geriatrics Society, 50*, 354–358.

Duberstein, P. R. (2001). Are closed-minded people more open to the idea of killing themselves? Suicide and Life-Threatening Behavior, 31, 9–14.

Duberstein, P. R., Conwell, Y., Conner, K. R., Eberly, S., & Caine, E. D. (2004). Suicide at 50 years of age and older: Perceived physical illness, family discord and financial strain. *Psychological Medicine, 34*, 137–146.

Duberstein, P. R., Conwell, Y., Conner, K. R., Eberly, S., Evinger, J. S., & Caine, E. D. (2004). Poor social integration and suicide: Fact or artifact? *Psychological Medicine, 34, 1331-1337.*

Duberstein, P. R., Conwell, Y., Seidlitz, L., Denning, D. G., Cox, C., & Caine, E. D. (2000). Personality traits and suicidal behavior and ideation in depressed inpatients 50 years of age and older. *Journal of Gerontology, 55B*(1), P18–P26.

Duberstein, P. R., Conwell, Y., Seidlitz, L., Lyness, J. M., Cox, C., & Caine, E. D. (1999). Age and suicidal ideation in older depressed inpatients. *The American Journal of Geriatric Psychiatry, 7*, 289–296.

Duberstein, P. R., & Heisel, M. J. (2014). Suicidal behavior among older adults: A call for prevention. In M. K. Nock (Ed.), *Oxford Handbook of Suicide and Self-Injury* (pp. 113–132). Oxford University Press.

Duberstein, P. R., Heisel, M. J., & Conwell, Y. (2011). Suicide in older adults. In M. E. Agronin & G. Maletta (Eds.), *Principles and Practice of Geriatric Psychiatry* (2nd ed.). Philadelphia, PA: Lippincott Williams & Wilkins.

Duberstein, P. R., & Wittink, M. N. (2015). Person-centered suicide prevention. In B. Bensadon (Ed.), *Psychology and Geriatrics* (Chapter 8, pp. 153–181). New York: Elsevier.

Durkheim, E. (1966). *Suicide: A study in sociology.* New York: Free Press.

Edelstein, B. A., Heisel, M. J., McKee, D. R., Martin, R. R., Koven, L. P., Duberstein, P. R., & Britton, P. C. (2009). Development and psychometric evaluation of the reasons for living-older adults scale: A suicide risk assessment inventory. *The Gerontologist, 49*, 736–745.

Edelstein, B. A., Woodhead, E. L., Segal, D. L., Heisel, M. J., Bower, E. H., Lowery, A. J., & Stoner, S. A. (2008). Older adult psychological assessment: Current instrument status and related considerations. *Clinical Gerontologist, 31*, 1–35.

Ellis, T. E., & Dickey, T. O. (1998). Procedures surrounding the suicide of a trainee's patient: A national survey of psychology internships and psychiatry residency programs. *Professional Psychology: Research and Practice, 29*, 492–497.

Erlangsen, A., Nordentoft, M., Conwell, Y., Waern, M., De Leo, D., Lindner, R., . . . International Research Group on Suicide Among the Elderly. (2011). Key considerations for preventing suicide in older adults: Consensus opinions of an expert panel. *Crisis, 32*, 106–109.

Ernst, C., Lalovic, A., Lesage, A., Seguin, M., Tousignant, M., & Turecki, G. (2004). Suicide and no Axis I psychopathology. *BMC Psychiatry, 4*, 7.

Etzersdorfer, E., & Sonneck, G. (1998). Preventing suicide by influencing mass-media reporting. The Viennese experience 1980–1996. *Archives of Suicide Research, 4*, 67–74.

Eynan, R., Bergmans, Y., Antony, J., Cutcliffe, J. R., Harder, H. G., Ambreen, M., ... Links, P. S. (2014). The effects of suicide ideation assessments on urges to self-harm and suicide. *Crisis, 35*, 123–131.

Fässberg, M. M., Cheung, C., Canetto, S. Erlangsen, A., Lapierre, S., Lindner, R., . . . Waern, M. (2016). A systematic review of physical illness, functional disability and suicidal behaviour among older adults. *Aging and Mental Health, 20*, 166–194.

Fässberg, M. M., van Orden, K. A., Duberstein, P., Erlangsen, A., Lapierre, S., Bodner, E., . . . Waern, M. (2012). A systematic review of social factors and suicidal behavior in older adulthood. *International Journal of Environmental Research and Public Health, 9*, 722–745.

Feldman, M. D., Franks, P., Duberstein, P. R., Vannoy, S., Epstein, R., & Kravitz, R. L. (2007). Let's not talk about it: suicide inquiry in primary care. *Annals of Family Medicine, 5*, 412–418.

Frankl, V. E. (1971). *The doctor and the soul: From psychotherapy to logotherapy* (R. and C. Winston, Trans.). New York: Bantam.

Frankl, V. E. (1985). *Man's search for meaning.* New York: Simon & Schuster.

Gallo, J. J., Rabins, P. V., & Anthony, J. C. (1999). Sadness in older persons: A 13-year follow-up of a community sample in Baltimore, Maryland. *Psychological Medicine, 29*, 341–350.

Ganzini, L., Denneson, L. M., Press, N., Bair, M. J., Helmer, D. A., Poat, J., & Dobscha, S. K. (2013). Trust is the basis for effective suicide risk screening and assessment in veterans. *Journal of General Internal Medicine, 28*, 1215–1221.

Graham, I. D., Tetroe, J., & the KT Theories Research Group. (2007). Some theoretical underpinnings of knowledge translation. *Academic Emergency Medicine, 14*, 936–941.

Grek, A. (2007). Clinical management of suicidality in the elderly: An opportunity for involvement in the lives of older patients. *Canadian Journal of Psychiatry, 52*(6 Suppl. 1), 47S–57S.

Harwood, D., Hawton, K., Hope, T., & Jacoby, R. (2001). Psychiatric disorder and personality factors associated with suicide in older people: A descriptive and case-control study. *International Journal of Geriatric Psychiatry, 16*, 155–165.

Hawton, K. (2007). Restricting access to methods of suicide: Rationale and evaluation of this approach to suicide prevention. *Crisis: The Journal of Crisis Intervention and Suicide Prevention, 28*(S1), 4.

Hawton, K., Bergen, H., Simkin, S., Wells, C., Kapur, N., & Gunnell, D. (2009). Effect of withdrawal of co-proxamol on prescribing and deaths from drug poisoning in England and Wales: time series analysis. *British Medical Journal, 338.*

Hawton, K., Zahl, D., & Weatherall, R. (2003). Suicide following deliberate self-harm: Long-term follow-up of patients who presented to a general hospital. *British Journal of Psychiatry, 182*, 537–542.

Hegerl, U., Althaus, D., Schmidtke, A., & Niklewski, G. (2006). The alliance against depression: 2-year evaluation of a community-based intervention to reduce suicidality. *Psychological Medicine, 36*, 1225–1233.

Hegerl, U., Wittenburg, L., Arensman, E., Van Audenhove, C., Coyne, J. C., McDaid, D., . . . Bramesfeld, A. (2009). Optimizing suicide prevention programs and their implementation in Europe (OSPI Europe): An evidence-based multi-level approach. *BMC Public Health, 9,* 428.

Heisel, M. J. (2006). Suicide and its prevention among older adults. *Canadian Journal of Psychiatry, 51,* 143–154.

Heisel, M. J., Bowman, J. C., Moore, S. L., & Wilson, K. (2012). Late-life suicide prevention knowledge translation update. *Newslink: A Publication of the American Association of Suicidology,* February 2012 issue.

Heisel, M. J., Conwell, Y., Pisani, A. R., & Duberstein, P. R. (2011). Concordance of self- and proxy-reported suicide ideation in depressed adults 50 years of age or older. *The Canadian Journal of Psychiatry, 56,* 219–226.

Heisel, M. J., & Duberstein, P. R. (2005). Suicide prevention in older adults. *Clinical Psychology: Science and Practice, 12,* 242–259.

Heisel, M. J., Duberstein, P. R., Conner, K. R., Franus, N., Beckman, A., & Conwell, Y. (2006). Personality and reports of suicide ideation among depressed adults 50 years of age or older. *Journal of Affective Disorders, 90,* 175–180.

Heisel, M. J., Duberstein, P. R., Lyness, J. M., & Feldman, M. D. (2010). Screening for suicide ideation among older primary care patients. *The Journal of the American Board of Family Medicine, 23,* 260–269.

Heisel, M. J., Duberstein, P. R., Talbot, N. L., King, D. A., & Tu, X. M. (2009). Adapting interpersonal psychotherapy for older adults at risk for suicide: Preliminary findings. *Professional Psychology: Research and Practice, 40,* 156–164.

Heisel, M. J., & Flett, G. L. (2016). Does recognition of meaning in life confer resiliency to suicide ideation among community-residing older adults?: A longitudinal investigation. *The American Journal of Geriatric Psychiatry, 24,* 455–466.

Heisel, M. J., & Flett, G. L., (2004). Purpose in life, satisfaction with life and suicide ideation in a clinical sample. *Journal of Psychopathology and Behavioral Assessment, 26,* 127–135.

Heisel, M. J., & Flett, G. L. (2006). The development and initial validation of the Geriatric Suicide Ideation Scale. *The American Journal of Geriatric Psychiatry, 14,* 742–751.

Heisel, M. J., & Flett, G. L. (2007). Meaning in life and resilience to suicidal thoughts among older adults. In P. T. P. Wong, L. C. J. Wong, M. McDonald, & D. Klaassen (Eds.), *The Positive Psychology of Meaning and Spirituality* (pp. 183–196). Abbotsford, BC: INPM Press.

Heisel, M. J., & Flett, G. L. (2008). Psychological resilience to suicide ideation among older adults. *Clinical Gerontologist, 31,* 51–70.

Heisel, M. J., & Flett, G. L. (2012). Screening for suicide ideation among older adults: The development and initial validation of abbreviated versions of the Geriatric Suicide Ideation Scale. *Canadian Psychology, 53*(2a, abridged), 228.

Heisel, M. J., & Flett, G. L. (2014). Do meaning in life and purpose in life protect against suicide ideation among community-residing older adults? In A. Batthyany & P. Russo-Netzer (Eds.), *Meaning in positive and existential psychology* (pp. 303–324). New York: Springer.

Heisel, M. J., & Flett, G. L. (2016). Investigating the psychometric properties of the Geriatric Suicide Ideation Scale (GSIS) among community-residing older adults. *Aging and Mental Health, 20,* 208-221.

Heisel, M. J., Flett, G. L., & Besser, A. (2002). Cognitive functioning and geriatric suicide ideation: Testing a mediational model. *The American Journal of Geriatric Psychiatry, 10,* 428–436.

Heisel, M. J., Grek, A., Moore, S. L., Jackson, F., Vincent, G., Malach, F. M., & Mokry, J. (2006). National Guidelines for Seniors' Mental Health: The assessment of suicide risk and prevention of suicide. *The Canadian Journal of Geriatrics, 9*(Supplement 2), S65–S70.

Heisel, M. J., Links, P. S., Conn, D., van Reekum, R., & Flett, G. L. (2007). Narcissistic personality and vulnerability to late-life suicidality. *American Journal of Geriatric Psychiatry, 15,* 734–741.

Heisel, M. J., Neufeld, E., & Flett, G. L. (2016). Reasons for living, meaning in life, and suicide ideation: Investigating the roles of key positive psychological factors in reducing suicide risk in community-residing older adults. *Aging and Mental Health, 20,* 195-207.

Heisel, M. J., Talbot, N. L., King, D. A., Tu, X. M., & Duberstein, P. R. (2015). Adapting interpersonal psychotherapy for older adults at risk for suicide. *The American Journal of Geriatric Psychiatry, 23,* 87–98.

Heisel, M. J., & the Meaning-Centered Men's Group Project Team. (2016). Enhancing psychological resiliency in older men facing retirement with Meaning-Centered Men's Groups. *The Annual Review of Logotherapy and Existential Analysis* (pp. 165–173). Switzerland: Springer International.

Hendin, H., Haas, A. P., Maltsberger, J. T., Koestner, B., & Szanto, K. (2006). Problems in psychotherapy with suicidal patients. *The American Journal of Psychiatry, 163,* 67–72.

Henriksson, M. M., Marttunen, M. J., Isometsä, E. T., Heikkinen, M. E., Aro, H. M., Kuoppasalmi, K. I., & Lönnqvist, J. K. (1995). Mental disorders in elderly suicide. *International Psychogeriatrics, 7,* 275–286.

Hoerger, M., Epstein, R. M., Winters, P. C., Fiscella, K., Duberstein, P. R., Gramling, R., . . . Kravitz, R. L. (2013). *Values and Options in Cancer Care (VOICE): Study design and rationale for a patient-centered communication and decision-making intervention for physicians, patients with advanced cancer, and their caregivers. BMC Cancer, 13,* 188. Epub April 9, 2013. PMCID: PMC3637237

Holkup, P. (June 2002). Evidence-based protocol. Elderly suicide: Secondary prevention. University of Iowa Gerontological Nursing Interventions Research Center, Research Dissemination Core.

Huh, J. T., Weaver, C. M., Martin, J. L., Caskey, N. H., O'Riley, A., & Kramer, B. J. (2012). Effects of a late-life suicide risk–assessment training on multidisciplinary healthcare providers. *Journal of the American Geriatrics Society, 60,* 775–780.

Institute of Medicine of the National Academies. (2008). *Retooling for an aging America: Building the health care workforce.* Retrieved January, 2015 from: www.iom.edu/agingamerica.

Institute of Medicine. (2012). *The Mental Health and Substance Use Workforce for Older Adults: In Whose Hands?* Retrieved January, 2015 from: http://www.iom.edu/Reports/2012/The-Mental-Health-and-Substance-Use-Workforce-for-Older-Adults.aspx.

Jacobs, D. G., Baldessarini, R. J., Conwell, Y., Fawcett, J. A., Horton, L., Meltzer, H., . . . Simon, I. (2003). *American Psychiatric Association Practice Guidelines: Practice guidelines for the assessment and treatment of patients with suicidal behaviors.* Arlington, VA: American Psychiatric Association.

Jahn, D. R., Cukrowicz, K. C., Litton, K., & Prabhu, F. (2011). The mediating effect of perceived burdensomeness on the relation between depressive symptoms and suicide ideation in a community sample of older adults. *Aging & Mental Health, 15,* 214–220.

Joiner, T. E. (2005). *Why people die by suicide.* Cambridge, MA: Harvard University Press.

Joiner, T. E., Walker, R. L., Rudd, M. D., & Jobes, D. A. (1999). Scientizing and routinizing the assessment of suicidality in outpatient practice. *Professional Psychology: Research and Practice, 30*, 447–453.

Juurlink, D. N., Herrmann, N., Szalai, J. P., Kopp, A., & Redelmeier, D. A. (2004). Medical illness and the risk of suicide in the elderly. *Archives of Internal Medicine, 164*, 1179–1184.

Kaplan, M. S., Adamek, M. E., & Calderon, A. (1999). Managing depressed and suicidal geriatric patients: Differences among primary care physicians. *The Gerontologist, 39*, 417–425.

Kaplan, M. S., Huguet, N., McFarland, B. H., & Mandle, J. A. (2011). Factors associated with suicide by firearm among U.S. older adult men. *Psychology of Men & Masculinity, 13*, 65–74.

Kaplan, M. S., McFarland, B. H., & Huguet, N. (2009). Firearm suicide among veterans in the general population: Findings from the National Violent Death Reporting System. *Journal of Trauma-Injury Infection & Critical Care, 67*, 503–507.

Kim, H. M., Smith, E. G., Ganoczy, D., Walters, H., Stano, C. M., Ilgen, M. A., . . . Valenstein, M. (2012). Predictors of suicide in patient charts among patients with depression in the Veterans Health Administration health system: Importance of prescription drug and alcohol abuse. *Journal of Clinical Psychiatry, 73*, e1269–e1275.

Kim, S.-W., Stewart, R., Kim, J.-M., Shin, I.-S., Yoon, J.-S., Jung, S.-W., . . . Jun, T.-Y. (2011). Relationship between a history of a suicide attempt and treatment outcomes in patients with depression. *Journal of Clinical Psychopharmacology, 31*, 449–456.

King, D. A., Heisel, M. J., & Lyness, J. M. (2005). Assessment and psychological treatment of depression in terminally ill older adults. *Clinical Psychology: Science and Practice, 12*, 339–353.

Kjølseth, I., & Ekeberg, Ø. (2012). When elderly people give warning of suicide. *International Psychogeriatrics, 24*, 1393–1401.

Kjølseth, I., Ekeberg, Ø., & Steihaug, S. (2009). "Why do they become vulnerable when faced with the challenges of old age?" Elderly people who committed suicide, described by those who knew them. *International Psychogeriatrics, 21*, 903–912.

Kjølseth, I., Ekeberg, Ø., & Steihaug, S. (2010a). Elderly people who committed suicide—their contact with the health service. What did they expect, and what did they get? *Aging & Mental Health, 14*, 938–946.

Kjølseth, I., Ekeberg, Ø., & Steihaug, S. (2010b). Why suicide? Elderly people who committed suicide and their experience of life in the period before their death. *International Psychogeriatrics, 22*, 209–218.

Kleespies, P. M., & Berman, A. L. (2004). The pre-doctoral internship: A prime site for training in behavioral emergencies. *APPIC Newsletter, March 2004, 5*, 15–16.

Kleespies, P. M., Berman, A. L., Ellis, T. E., McKeon, R., McNiel, D. E., Nock, M., . . . Yufit, R. I. (2005). *Report on education and training in behavioral emergencies: Abridged version, by the Task Force on Education and Training of the Section on Clinical Emergencies and Crises (Section VII), Society of Clinical Psychology (Division 12), American Psychological Association.* Washington, DC: American Psychological Association.

Kleespies, P., Hughes, D., & Gallacher, F. (2000). Suicide in the medically and terminally ill: Psychological and ethical considerations. *Journal of Clinical Psychology, 56*, 1153–1171.

Kleespies, P. M., Penk, W. E., & Forsyth, J. P. (1993). The stress of patient suicidal behavior during clinical training: Incidence, impact, and recovery. *Professional Psychology: Research and Practice, 24*, 293–303.

Knox, K. L., Conwell, Y., & Caine, E. D. (2004). If suicide is a public health problem, what are we doing to prevent it? *Public Health Matters, 94*, 37–45.

Korte, J., Westerhof, G. J., & Bohlmeijer, E. T. (2012). Mediating processes in an effective life-review intervention. *Psychology and Aging, 27*, 1172–1181.

Kroll, J. (2000). Use of no-suicide contracts by psychiatrists in Minnesota. *The American Journal of Psychiatry, 157*, 1684–1686.

Lapierre, S., Dubé, M., Bouffard, L., & Alain, M. (2007). Addressing suicidal ideations through the realization of meaningful personal goals. *Crisis, 28*, 16–25.

Lapierre, S., Erlangsen, A., Waern, M., De Leo, D., Oyama, H., Scocco, P., . . . Quinnett, P., and the International Research Group for Suicide among the Elderly. (2011). A systematic review of elderly suicide prevention programs. *Crisis, 32*, 88–98.

Lebowitz, B. D. (2004). Clinical trials in late life: New science in old paradigms. *The Gerontologist, 44*, 452–458.

Leenaars, A. (2006). Psychotherapy with suicidal people: The commonalities. *Archives of Suicide Research, 10*, 305–322.

Lewis, L. M. (2007). No-harm contracts: A review of what we know. *Suicide and Life-Threatening Behavior, 37*, 50–57.

Links, P. S., Heisel, M. J., & Quastel, A. (2005). Is suicide ideation a surrogate endpoint for geriatric suicide? *Suicide and Life-Threatening Behavior, 35*, 193–205.

Lukas, E. S. (1984). *Meaningful living: A logotherapy book.* Cambridge, MA: Institute of Logotherapy Press.

Lyness, J. M., Cox, C., Curry, J., Conwell, Y., King, D. A., & Caine, E. D. (1995). Older age and the underreporting of depressive symptoms. *Journal of the American Geriatrics Society, 43*, 216–221.

Malphurs, J. E., & Cohen, D. (2005). A statewide case–control study of spousal homicide-suicide in older persons. *The American Journal of Geriatric Psychiatry, 13*, 211–217.

Maltsberger, J. T., & Buie, D. H. (1974). Countertransference hate in the treatment of suicidal patients. *Archives of General Psychiatry, 30*, 625–633.

Mann, J. J., Apter, A., Bertolote, J., Beautrais, A., Currier, D., Hass, A., . . . Hendin, H. (2005). Suicide prevention strategies: A systematic review. *Journal of the American Medical Association, 294*, 2064–2074.

Marty, M. A., Segal, D. L., & Coolidge, F. L. (2010). Relationships among dispositional coping strategies, suicidal ideation, and protective factors against suicide in older adults. *Aging & Mental Health, 14*, 1015–1023.

Miller, M. (1978). Geriatric suicide: The Arizona study. *The Gerontologist, 18*, 488–495.

Mishara, B. L., & Kerkhof, A. J. F. M. (2013). *Suicide prevention and new technologies: Evidence based practice.* New York: Palgrave Macmillan.

Modai, I., Ritsner, M., Kurs, R., Mendel, S., & Ponizovsky, A. (2002). Validation of a computerized suicide risk scale: A backpropagation neural network instrument (CSRS-BP). *European Psychiatry, 17*, 75–81.

Moore, S. L. (1997). A phenomenological study of meaning in life in suicidal older adults. *Archives of Psychiatric Nursing, 11*, 29–36.

Mościcki, E. K. (1996). Epidemiology of suicide. In J. L. Pearson & Y. Conwell (Eds.), *Suicide and aging: International perspectives* (pp. 3–14). New York: Springer.

National Action Alliance for Suicide Prevention: Research Prioritization Task Force. (2014). *A prioritized research agenda for suicide prevention: An action plan to save lives.* Rockville, MD: National Institute of Mental Health and the Research Prioritization Task Force.

Neufeld, E., & O'Rourke, N. (2009). Impulsivity and hopelessness as predictors of suicide-related ideation among older adults. *Canadian Journal of Psychiatry, 54,* 49–57.

Niederkrotenthaler, T., Voracek, M., Herberth, A., Till, B., Strauss, M., Etzersdorfer, E., . . . Sonneck, G. (2010). Role of media reports in completed and prevented suicide: Werther v. Papageno effects. *The British Journal of Psychiatry, 197,* 234–243.

Nissim, R., Gagliese, L., & Rodin, G. (2009). The desire for hastened death in individuals with advanced cancer: A longitudinal qualitative study. *Social Science and Medicine, 69,* 165–171.

O'Carroll, P. W., Berman, A. L., Maris, R. W., Moscicki, E. K., Tanney, B. L., & Silverman, M. M. (1996). Beyond the Tower of Babel: A nomenclature for suicidology. *Suicide and Life-Threatening Behavior, 26,* 237–252.

O'Connor, E., Gaynes, B. N., Burda, B. U., Soh, C., & Whitlock, E. P. (2013). Screening for and treatment of suicide risk relevant to primary care: a systematic review for the US Preventive Services Task Force. *Annals of Internal Medicine, 158,* 741–754.

Ono, Y., Sakai, A., Otsuka, K., Uda, H., Oyama, H., Ishizuka, N., . . . Yonemoto, N. (2013). Effectiveness of a multimodal community intervention program to prevent suicide and suicide attempts: A quasi-experimental study. *PLoS ONE, 8,* e74902.

Orbach, I., Mikulincer, M., Gilboa-Schechtman, E., & Sirota, P. (2003). Mental pain and its relationship to suicidality and life meaning. *Suicide and Life-Threatening Behavior, 33,* 231–241.

Ortman, J. M., Velkoff, V. A., & Hogan, H. (2014). *An aging nation: The older population in the United States. Population estimates and projections.* U.S. Census Bureau. https://www.census.gov/prod/2014pubs/p25%971140.pdf. Accessed January 2015.

Oyama, H., Koida, J., Sakashita, T., & Kudo, K. (2004). Community-based prevention for suicide in elderly by depression screening and follow-up. *Community Mental Health Journal, 40,* 249–263.

Oyama, H., Sakashita, T., Ono, Y., Goto, M., Fujita, M., & Koida, J. (2008). Effect of community-based intervention using depression screening on elderly suicide risk: A meta-analysis of the evidence from Japan. *Community Mental Health Journal, 44,* 311–320.

Oyama, H., Watanabe, N., Ono, Y., Sakashita, T., Takenoshita, Y., Taguchi, M., . . . Kumagai, K. (2005). Community-based suicide prevention through group activity for the elderly successfully reduced the high suicide rate for females. *Psychiatry and Clinical Neurosciences, 59,* 337–344.

Pearson, J.L., Stanley, B., King, C.A., & Fisher, C.B. (2001). Intervention research with persons at high risk for suicidality: Safety and ethical considerations. *Journal of Clinical Psychiatry, 62*(Supplement 25), 17-26.

Perlman, C. M., Neufeld, E., Martin, L., Goy, M., & Hirdes, J. P. (2011). *Suicide risk assessment inventory: A resource guide for Canadian health care organizations.* Toronto, ON: Ontario Hospital Association and Canadian Patient Safety Institute.

Pirkis, J., Spittal, M. J., Cox, G., Robinson, J., Cheung, Y. T. D., & Studdert, D. (2013). The effectiveness of structural interventions at suicide hotspots: a meta-analysis. *International Journal of Epidemiology, 42,* 541–548.

Pisani, A. R., Cross, W. F., & Gould, M. S. (2011). The assessment and management of suicide risk: State of workshop education. *Suicide and Life-Threatening Behavior, 41,* 255–276.

Pokorny, A. D. (1993). Suicide prediction revisited. *Suicide and Life-Threatening Behavior, 23,* 1–10.

Pompili, M. (2015). Our empathic brain and suicidal individuals. *Crisis: The Journal of Crisis Intervention and Suicide Prevention, 36,* 227–230.

Potter, L. B., Powell, K. E., & Kachur, S. P. (1995). Suicide prevention from a public health perspective. *Suicide & Life-Threatening Behavior, 25,* 82–91.

Purcell, B., Heisel, M. J., Speice, J., Franus, N., Conwell, Y., & Duberstein, P. R. (2012). Family connectedness moderates the association between living alone and suicide ideation in a clinical sample of adults 50 years and older. *The American Journal of Geriatric Psychiatry, 20,* 717–723.

Qin, P., Agerbo, E., & Mortensen, P. B. (2003). Suicide risk in relation to socioeconomic, demographic, psychiatric, and familial factors: A National Register–based study of all suicides in Denmark, 1981–1997. *The American Journal of Psychiatry, 160,* 765–772.

Quan, H., Arboleda-Flórez, J., Fick, G. H., Stuart, H. L., & Love, E. J. (2002). Association between physical illness and suicide among the elderly. *Social Psychiatry and Psychiatric Epidemiology, 37,* 190–197.

Reynolds, S. K., Lindenboim, N., Comtois, K. A., Murray, A., & Linehan, M. M. (2006). Risky assessments: Participant suicidality and distress associated with research assessments in a treatment study of suicidal behavior. *Suicide and Life-Threatening Behavior, 36,* 19–34.

Rogers, C. R. (1957). The necessary and sufficient conditions of therapeutic personality change. *Journal of Consulting Psychology, 21* (95–203). This article was reprinted in 1992, under the same title, in *Journal of Consulting and Clinical Psychology, 60,* 827–832.

Rowe, J. L., Conwell, Y., Schulberg, H. C., & Bruce, M. L. (2006). Social support and suicidal ideation in older adults using home healthcare services. *The American Journal of Geriatric Psychiatry, 14,* 758–766.

Rubenowitz, E., Waern, M., Wilhelmson, K., & Allebeck, P. (2001). Life events and psychosocial factors in elderly suicides: A case-control study. *Psychological Medicine, 31,* 1193–1202.

Rubio, A., Vestner, A. L., Stewart, J. M., Forbes, N. T., Conwell, Y., & Cox, C. (2001). Suicide and Alzheimer's pathology in the elderly: A case-control study. *Biological Psychiatry, 49,* 137–145.

Rudd, M. D., Berman, A. L., Joiner, T. E., Nock, M. K., Silverman, M. M., Mandrusiak, M., . . . Witte, T. (2006). Warning signs for suicide: Theory, research, and clinical applications. *Suicide and Life-Threatening Behavior, 36,* 255–262.

Rudd, M. D., Mandrusiak, M., Joiner, T. E., Berman, A. L., Van Orden, K. A., & Hollar, D. (2006). The emotional impact and ease of recall of warning signs for suicide: A controlled study. *Suicide and Life-Threatening Behavior, 36,* 288–295.

Samuels, S. C., & Katz, I. R. (1995). Depression in the nursing home. *Psychiatric Annals, 25,* 418–424.

Sareen, J., Isaak, C., Bolton, S.-L., Enns, M. W., Elias, B., Deane, F., . . . Katz, L. Y. (2013). Gatekeeper training for suicide prevention in First Nations community members: A randomized controlled trial. *Depression and Anxiety, 30,* 1021–1029.

Schmall, V. L., & Pratt, C. C. (1993). Community education on mental health in later life: Findings from an evaluation of a series of three model programs. *The Journal of Mental Health Administration, 20*, 190–200.

Schneider, B., Grebner, K., Schnabel, A., Hampel, H., Georgi, K., & Seidler, A. (2011). Impact of employment status and work-related factors on risk of completed suicide: A case-control psychological autopsy study. *Psychiatry Research, 190*, 265–270.

Segal, D. L., Marty, M. A., Meyer, W. J., & Coolidge, F. L. (2012). Personality, suicidal ideation, and reasons for living among older adults. *The Journals of Gerontology, Series B: Psychological Sciences and Social Sciences, 67*, 159–166.

Shah, R., Franks, P., Jerant, A., Feldman, M., Duberstein, P., Fernandez y Garcia, E., . . . Kravitz, R. L. (2014). The effect of targeted and tailored patient depression engagement interventions on clinician inquiry about suicidal thoughts: a randomized control trial. *Journal of General Internal Medicine, 29*, 1148–1154.

Shea, S. C. (1999). *The practical art of suicide assessment: A guide for mental health professionals and substance abuse counselors.* New York: Wiley.

Silverman, M. M., & Berman, A. L. (2014). Suicide risk assessment and risk formulation part I: A focus on suicide ideation in assessing suicide risk. *Suicide and Life-Threatening Behavior, 44*, 420–431.

Silverman, M. M., Berman, A. L., Sanddal, N. D., O'Carroll, P. W., & Joiner, T. E. (2010a). Rebuilding the Tower of Babel: A revised nomenclature for the study of suicide and suicidal behaviors, part 1: Background, rationale, and methodology. *Suicide and Life-Threatening Behavior, 37*, 248–263.

Silverman, M. M., Berman, A. L., Sanddal, N. D., O'Carroll, P. W., & Joiner, T. E. (2010b). Rebuilding the Tower of Babel: A revised nomenclature for the study of suicide and suicidal behaviors, part 2: Suicide-related ideations, communications, and behaviors. *Suicide and Life-Threatening Behavior, 37*, 264–277.

Singer, J., & Erreger, S. (2015). Let's talk about suicide: #LanguageMatters. *New Social Worker.* http://www.socialworker.com/feature-articles/practice/lets-talk-about-suicide-languagematters/

Snowdon, J. (1997). Suicide rates and methods in different age groups: Australian data and perceptions. *International Journal of Geriatric Psychiatry, 12*, 253–258.

Statistics Canada. (2005). *Population Projections for Canada, Provinces, and Territories: 2005–2031.* Retrieved January 2015 from: http://www.statcan.gc.ca/pub/91%97520-x/00105/4095095-eng.htm.

Strike, C., Rhodes, A. E., Bergmans, Y., & Links, P. (2006). Fragmented pathways to care: the experiences of suicidal men. *Crisis, 27*, 31–38.

Substance Abuse and Mental Health Services Administration. (2011). *Promoting Emotional Health and Preventing Suicide: A Toolkit for Senior Living Communities.* HHS Publication No. SMA 4515, CMHS-NSPL-0197. Rockville, MD: Center for Mental Health Services, Substance Abuse and Mental Health Services Administration.

Suominen, K., Henriksson, M., Isometsä, E., Conwell, Y., Heilä, H., & Lönnqvist, J. (2003). Nursing home suicides: A psychological autopsy study. *International Journal of Geriatric Psychiatry, 18*, 1095–1101.

Szanto, K., Mulsant, B. H., Houck, P. R., Dew, M. A., Dombrovski, A., Pollock, B. G., & Reynolds, C. F. (2007).

Emergence, persistence, and resolution of suicidal ideation during treatment of depression in old age. *Journal of Affective Disorders, 98*, 153–161.

Szanto, K., Mulsant, B. H., Houck, P., Dew, M. A., & Reynolds, C. F. III (2003). Occurrence and course of suicidality during short-term treatment of late-life depression. *Archives of General Psychiatry, 60*, 610–617.

Tsoh, J., Chiu, H. F. K., Duberstein, P. R., Chan, S. M., Chi, I., Yip, P. S. F., & Conwell, Y. (2005). Attempted suicide in elderly Chinese persons: A multi-group, controlled study. *The American Journal of Geriatric Psychiatry, 13*, 562–571.

Tulsky, J. A., Arnold, R. M., Alexander, S. C., Olsen, M. K., Jeffreys, A. S., Rodriguez, K. L., . . . Pollak, K. I. (2011). Enhancing communication between oncologists and patients with a computer-based training program: a randomized trial. *Annals of Internal Medicine, 155*, 593–601.

Turvey, C. L., Conwell, Y., Jones, M. P., Phillips, C., Simonsick, E., Pearson, J. L., & Wallace, R. (2002). Risk factors for late-life suicide: A prospective, community-based study. *The American Journal of Geriatric Psychiatry, 10*, 398–406.

United States Department of Health and Human Services. (2012). *National Strategy for Suicide Prevention: goals and objectives for action. A Report of the U.S. Surgeon General and of the National Action Alliance for Suicide Prevention.* Washington, DC: Author.

Unützer, J., Tang, L., Oishi, S., Katon, W., Williams, J. W., Hunkeler, E., . . . Langston, C., for the IMPACT Investigators. (2006). Reducing suicidal ideation in depressed older primary care patients. *Journal of the American Geriatrics Society, 54*, 1550–1556.

Van Orden, K. A., Witte, T. K., Cukrowicz, K. C., Braithwaite, S. R., Selby, E. A., & Joiner, T. E. (2010). The interpersonal theory of suicide. *Psychological Review, 117*, 575–600.

Waern, M., Beskow, J., Runeson, B., & Skoog, I. (1999). Suicidal feelings in the last year of life in elderly people who commit suicide. *The Lancet, 354*, 917–918.

Waern, M., Rubenowitz, E. Runeson, B., Skoog, I., Wilhelmson, K., & Allebeck, P. (2002). Burden of illness and suicide in elderly people: Case-control study. *British Medical Journal, 324*, 1355.

Waern, M., Runeson, B. S., Allebeck, P., Beskow, J., Rubenowitz, E., Skoog, I., & Wilhelmson, K. (2002). Mental disorder in elderly suicides: A case-control study. *The American Journal of Psychiatry, 159*, 450–455.

Wälinder, J., & Rutz, W. (2001). Male depression and suicide. *International Clinical Psychopharmacology, 16*, S21–S24.

World Health Organization. (2001). *World population ageing: 1950–2050.* New York: Author.

World Health Organization. (2014). *Preventing suicide: A global imperative.* Geneva, Author.

Wyman, P. A., Brown, C. H., Inman, J., Cross, W., Schmeelk-Cone, K., Guo, J., & Pena, J. B. (2008). Randomized trial of a gatekeeper program for suicide prevention: 1-year impact on secondary school staff. *Journal of Consulting and Clinical Psychology, 76*, 104–115.

Yip, P. S., Caine, E., Yousuf, S., Chang, S. S., Wu, K. C. C., & Chen, Y. Y. (2012). Means restriction for suicide prevention. *The Lancet, 379*(9834), 2393–2399.

Zweig, R. A., & Hinrichsen, G. A. (1993). Factors associated with suicide attempts by depressed older adults: A prospective study. *American Journal of Psychiatry, 150*, 1687–1692.

Aggression and Violence in the Elderly

Reva B. Klein

Abstract

Aggression and violence are often overlooked in the aging population. Changes in personality, behavior, and mood are well known in psychiatric disorders, but they are also seen in neurologic conditions, often where there is alteration in brain chemistry, as in metabolic disorders; or alteration in brain structure, as in degenerative disorders, strokes, subdural hematomas, and tumors; or with alteration in brain function, as in epileptic and nonconvulsive status. This chapter provides an overview of specific behaviors, the underlying neurochemistry and pathophysiology behind specific disorders, and some treatment approaches. The consequences of unrecognized and untreated behavioral changes in the elderly can have dire consequences on quality of life—for example, leading to early institutionalization. Regular follow-up that includes questions about behavior would allow for early work-up and treatment to prevent out-of-control escalation. Family education, support, caregiver relief, and prevention of complications can go a long way in improving the quality of life for patients and their families.

Key Words: aggression, violence, behavioral changes, neurochemistry, psychopharmacology, dementia, elderly

Aggression and violence are often overlooked phenomena in the aging population and can take friends, family members, and caregivers by surprise. Personality and behavioral changes are seen in many psychiatric disorders and are often brought to the attention of primary care providers and psychiatrists. However changes in personality, behavior, and mood are also seen in a plethora of neurologic conditions, most often where there is alteration of brain chemistry, as in metabolic disorders; or alteration of brain structure, as in the degenerative disorders, strokes, subdural hematomas, and tumors; or with alterations of brain function, as in epileptic and nonconvulsive status, to name a few. Education and understanding the pathophysiology of these changes are essential for accurate diagnosis, appropriate treatment, and assuring the safety and quality of life for patients, families, and caregivers. One of the more common reasons for an elderly individual's admission to a nursing home is the presence

of personality, behavioral, and mood changes that remain unmanageable in a community setting. In this chapter I will provide an overview of the specific behaviors, their underlying neurochemistry, and the pathophysiology of specific disorders, and I will outline some treatment approaches. Elder abuse, self-inflicted harm, and the effect of comorbid substance abuse are covered elsewhere in this volume (see chapters 23, 25, and 30). The bulk of my discussion will center on the various dementias.

The prevalence of behavioral and psychiatric symptoms in the community is very difficult to quantify because of the large number of precipitating factors that exist with few standardized measures and an absence of good longitudinal data (Chan, Kasper, Black, & Rabins, 2003). The prevalence of these symptoms in institutionalized elders is also difficult to quantify because of the under-recognition and underreporting that stem from an employee's fear of blame, cultural differences between patients and hired caregivers, or the cumulative effect of staff burnout under the growing pressure to provide high-level care in the face of personal risk (Scott, Ryan, James, & Mitchell, 2011). In addition, the prevalence will vary depending on the neuropathology of the dementia, the stage of the disease, and a plethora of comorbid factors. As more studies are conducted, it seems likely we will find that most, if not all, patients with dementia experience neuropsychiatric symptoms at one point or another in the course of their disease. Given that current estimates of patients with dementia severe enough to impact daily life are about 6.5% in those over age 65, this is not an insignificant problem. Although the focus often tends to be on cognitive impairment, the behavioral aspects of neurologic disorders cannot be overlooked (Ford, 2014). As personality, behavioral, and mood changes are better understood and better recognized as an integral part of the pathophysiology of brain disease, treatment will hopefully become more effective and lead to a better quality of life for the patient as well as the family and paid caregivers.

The first step would be to recognize what these personality, behavioral, and mood changes look like. The most important factor in this recognition process is knowing the baseline of the patient. This would require an accurate report from an outside observer, usually a close family member or friend who would recognize a change from baseline function. A corroborating history is essential, as the first-hand experience of a patient with brain dysfunction is unreliable. Under-recognition of these symptoms can lead to inadequate treatment with significant consequences, such as diminished quality of life of the patient and caregiver, increased caregiver stress and burnout, early institutionalization and its inherent complications, more frequent hospitalizations, and more rapid cognitive and functional decline. Symptoms can be thought of in categories of psychotic symptoms, mood/affective symptoms, apathy, and agitation/aggression (Ford, 2014). This discussion will focus on the latter.

Pathophysiology

As the pathophysiology of aggressive behavior is better understood, more effective targeted treatments can be developed. Neurotransmitters are produced in and have their effect on specific anatomic areas of the brain. Levels of various neurotransmitters and their ratios to each other create the brain chemistry that allows neuropsychiatric function. Changes in brain chemistry can be correlated with changes in brain function. For example,

it is well known that deficits in dopamine from degeneration of the substantia nigra lead to clinical Parkinson's disease. It is also well known that decreased serotonin can result in clinical depression. Likewise, changes in brain chemistry can result in behavioral changes. One group of neurotransmitters, derived chemically from monoamines has been looked at in particular. Studies aiming to identify brain region-specific monoaminergic neurotransmitters looked at correlating dopamine, serotonin, 3-methoxy-4-hydroxyphenylglycol (MHPG), and norepinephrine and its metabolites dihydroxyphenylacetic acid (DOPAC), homovanillic acid, and 5-hydroxyindoleacetic acid (5-HIAA) with cognitive function on the Mini-Mental Status Exam (MMSE). Dementia severity as measured by the MMSE correlated with hippocampal 5-HIAA levels and 5-hydroxytryptamine (5-HT) levels of the superior temporal gyrus as well as the cerebellar cortex. Also found was an inverse relationship between hippocampal 5-HIAA levels with agitation. Thalamic MHPG levels were correlated with hallucinations. Cerebellar DOPAC/dopamine ratios indicating dopamine turnover correlated with physical agitation, and MHPG levels correlated with affective disorders (Vermeiren, Van Dam, Aerts, Engelborghs, & DeDeyn, 2014). A complete and comprehensive discussion of brain chemistry and its effects is beyond the scope of this discussion, but the point remains that understanding this chemistry can lead to better interventions and forms the basis of the pharmacologic interventions discussed in more detail in what follows.

About 20% of strokes are hemorrhagic with about half of these being secondary to subarachnoid bleeding from aneurysm leakage or rupture. Most often aneurysms are seen in the anterior circulation where rupture impacts frontal lobe function. In addition to focal deficits, agitation can be a serious complication, often interfering with treatment of the underlying aneurysm and blood pressure control. Similarly, agitation can occur in traumatic brain injury, with frontal contusions and interventricular blood also impacting the frontal lobes, causing aggression. In addition, secondary vasospasm can further complicate the picture with hypoxia exacerbating agitation. Treatment consists of treating the underlying cause, preventing/treating vasospasm, and undertaking prompt aggressive pharmacologic treatment with agents such as beta blockers, while avoiding benzodiazepines that can paradoxically increase agitation. Antipsychotics, which can cause neuroleptic malignant syndrome and tardive dyskinesia, should be avoided (Ibrahim & Viswanathan, 2012). Ischemic stroke can also cause agitation from decreased perfusion and hypoxia disrupting normal neurotransmitter function. Subdural bleeding can trigger subacute onset of agitation secondary to mass effect on the frontal lobe as venous blood slowly accumulates and compresses normal brain.

Specific Disorders
Dementias

Dementia affects about 6.5% of the population over 65, increasing in prevalence with increasing age. Cognitive impairment is central to the diagnosis of dementia and most patients present with memory complaints. Changes in personality, behavior, and mood, however, are considered inevitable, but they are rarely volunteered in a history without direct questioning and they are often a source of embarrassment and/or confusion for family members. These changes frequently have adverse outcomes resulting in earlier institutionalization and higher mortality. Underlying neurologic factors were previously discussed, but these also include patient, caregiver, and environmental factors (Ford, 2014).

Two questions often arise: what difference does it make in diagnosing which dementia is present, and why go through the time and cost involved to reach an accurate diagnosis? The various dementias can look very similar early on and they end at the same point down the line, but arriving at a diagnosis that is as accurate as possible can go a long way in managing what happens in the middle. The prominent symptomatology, the course of each dementia, and the personality, behavioral, and mood changes can be quite different depending on which part of the brain and which neurotransmitters are affected. Although treatment is largely symptomatic, knowing what to expect and what is unusual can be helpful in preventing early and/or unnecessary institutionalization, which can have an enormous financial, emotional, and personal impact on quality of life, not just for the patient but for the family and caregivers as well. A full discussion of each type of the many dementias is beyond the scope of this discussion, but in the following we will touch on characterizing the major types of dementia, with particular attention to changes in comportment. Treatment begins with identifying the behavior and its triggers. Pharmacologic management should be the last resort, and it will be discussed in the context of each dementia, with other treatment options to follow.

Alzheimer's disease. The most commonly diagnosed dementia is Alzheimer's disease (AD). It is a clinical diagnosis based on a progressive decline of memory, usually resulting in episodic memory interfering with new learning, in combination with impairment in other domains, which can include executive systems, language, and visuospatial. These findings are consistent with the pathologically confirmed neuronal cell loss in the medial temporal lobes and MRI quantitative measures of the temporal lobes (Albert, 2011).

Pathologically Alzheimer's is characterized by abnormal depositions of extracellular amyloid plaques, predominantly composed of amyloid beta peptide. The amyloid beta is normally degraded by enzymatic breakdown or cleared by low-density lipoprotein receptors. It can, however, also change configuration causing a greater propensity to self-aggregate and form fibrils, and this can cause other proteins to do the same, fueling the process. This course is somehow influenced by apolipoprotein E. One form is ApoE4, which is the major genetic risk factor for the development of late onset AD. The underlying mechanism of interactions involving the apolipoproteins remains unknown (Hauser & Ryan, 2013). The hallmark pathology of Alzheimer's includes amyloid deposits and neurofibrillary tangles composed of hyperphosphorylated tau protein, which can be measured in CSF. Shifting the focus from pathology to neurochemistry, researchers found rebalancing cholinergic input improved cognition by either inhibiting acetylcholine esterase or blocking the N-methyl-D-aspartate (NMDA) receptor by memantine. Enhancing the effects of acetylcholine was thought to have therapeutic benefit in ameliorating symptoms of Alzheimer's disease (Allgaier & Allgaier, 2014). Blocking its breakdown with acetylcholinesterase inhibitors has become the mainstay of therapy since the introduction in 1997 of the acetylcholinesterase inhibitors. Studies have found little difference in efficacy between the three available agents; donepezil, galantamine, and rivastigmine. These agents are widely used as first line agents, approved for mild to moderate Alzheimer's disease (Birks, 2006). More recent investigation into these agents, as well as the newer memantine, question whether the small clinical effects seen with them are worth the high cost of these drugs, and some formularies have begun to restrict their use. Repeat studies have demonstrated that they are effective in stabilizing or slowing decline in cognition, function, behavior, and global change when used at therapeutic doses, although they lack dramatic improvement in function (Tan et al., 2014).

In addition to cognitive decline, about 80% of Alzheimer's patients have behavioral and psychological symptoms as well. These changes are one of the most common reasons for early institutionalization, so understanding these symptoms and designing appropriate treatment strategies are critical for maintaining quality of life and minimizing financial stress. Agitation and aggression are particularly common, along with anxiety and phobias, but because of the risk of self-harm or harming a caregiver, these behaviors are linked more often with institutionalization and a poorer overall prognosis. All the medications for Alzheimer's that were just mentioned were looked at for efficacy in the treatment of behavioral symptoms; memantine and rivastigmine seemed to be most effective, with galantamine the least (Cumbo & Liqori, 2014). Rivastigmine was also shown to be particularly efficacious in treating symptoms of depression associated with Alzheimer's disease by restoring function to the hippocampal serotoninergic system (Islam, Moriguchi, Tagashira, & Fukunaga, 2014). Depression and psychosis in Alzheimer's have been associated with worsening cognitive decline. Psychosis was correlated with increased caregiver dependence, and rates of increased agitation and aggression were correlated with both cognitive decline and increased caregiver dependence. Therefore, for this reason as well, appropriate diagnosis and treatment for changes in behavior and mood have a direct effect on prognosis (Zahodne, Omstein, Cosetino, Devanand, & Stem, 2013).

Antipsychotics, once the mainstay of treatment for behavioral changes in Alzheimer's and most dementias, are no longer recommended, except as a last resort when the safety and well-being of the patient and/or caregiver are threatened, and then only under careful monitoring. Some data link their use to increased mortality, concluding the risk of antipsychotic use outweighs the benefits, although other factors influencing mortality cannot be ignored, such as age, stage of disease, and comorbid complications (Gardette et al., 2012).

Other agents for the treatment of agitation are being investigated that have a better safety record and remain well tolerated. Citalopram was looked at, and there is some evidence that adding this to the anti-cholinesterase inhibitors can significantly decrease agitation, relieving caregiver stress. The use of citalopram, however, is limited by cognitive and cardiac adverse effects at the 30

mg daily recommended dose (Porsteinsson et al., 2014). Sertraline was also studied for treatment of agitation and psychosis, and it was found to decrease agitation compared to the placebo, as did trazodone, and both were well tolerated (Sietz et al., 2011). Trazodone was also found to be effective in aiding sleep, reducing anxiety, and decreasing symptoms of depression (Osvath, 2013). Anti-epileptic medications, often used for mood stabilization, were investigated as well. Valproate was not effective in managing agitation and was also not well tolerated in the aging population (Herrmann, Lanctot, Rothenburg, & Eryavec, 2007). There is some evidence that topiramate and/or levetiracetam may not only reduce problem behaviors but also reduce amyloid plaques and increase amyloid clearance (Shi et al., 2013). Clinically significant decreases in aggression were also demonstrated with low-dose gabapentin without adverse effects (Cooney, Murphy, Tessema, & Freyne, 2013). Benzodiazepines are not recommended in dementia and have been found to cause worsening gait impairment, paradoxical agitation, and dependence (Borson & Raskind, 1997). If all other strategies have been exhausted, weighing the risk–benefit ratio, atypical antipsychotics in small doses can effectively control psychotic features of delusions and hallucinations, as well as agitation and aggression, and can be used if needed (Daiello, 2007).

Treating aggressive behavior as well as other changes in behavior and mood in Alzheimer's patients is an important but time-consuming process that may take multiple medication trials to obtain adequate control, which is necessary to assure patient and caregiver safety.

Vascular dementias. The second most common dementia found in about a third of cases is vascular (Sonnen et al., 2007), a heterogeneous group encompassing a large number of different entities including diffuse ischemic vascular changes in the subcortical white matter, small vessel disease, large artery territorial infarcts, subarachnoid hemorrhages, and subdural hematomas, as well as Cerebral Amyloid Angiopathy (CAA), and genetic disorders such as Cerebral Autosomal Dominant Arteriopathy with Subcortical Infarcts and Leukoencephalopathy (CADASIL). Small artery lacunar infarcts most likely associated with dementia involve lesions of the basal ganglia, caudate, thalamus, internal capsule, cerebellum, and brainstem, which are common in the setting of hypertension and diabetes (Smith, Schneider, Wardlaw, & Greenberg, 2012). Vascular dementia patients often present with cognitive impairment other than memory deficits, which appear later rather than as the presenting factor (as in Alzheimer's disease) leading to the term Vascular Cognitive Impairment (O'Brien et al., 2003). Many of the risk factors overlap with those of cardiac and cerebrovascular disease but are not as well characterized. Neuropsychological testing that shows deficits in executive system function in patients with metabolic syndrome suggests this could be a prodromal phase (Segura et al., 2009). There seems to be an increasing incidence of vascular dementia, possibly related to improved survival rates or increased prevalence of risk factors (Ukraintseva, Sloan, Arbeev, & Yashin, 2006).

To further complicate the picture, Alzheimer's disease and vascular dementia often present as a mixed pattern that proves difficult to untangle and may also involve the ApoE genotype (Langa, Foster, & Larson, 2004). The clinical presentations can be categorized into cortical and subcortical patterns according to the dominant features. Cortical syndromes are directly related to the anatomic localization of the infarct. Medial frontal infarcts result in executive system dysfunction, abulia, and, if bilateral, akinetic mutism. Dominant left parietal lesions cause aphasia, apraxia, or agnosia, while nondominant right parietal lesions cause neglect syndromes, such as anosognosia, confusion, agitation, and visuospatial and constructional difficulties. Medial temporal lesions cause anterograde amnesia. Subcortical infarcts effect the deep gray nuclei and white matter paths that connect distant areas and can cause focal motor signs, gait disturbance, falls, urinary symptoms, pseudobulbar palsy, abulia, apathy, depression, psychomotor slowing, mild memory impairment, and executive system dysfunction (Staekenborg et al., 2008). The course can be gradual or a stepwise decline.

Neuropsychiatric manifestations of vascular dementia depend on the underlying pathology and localization of the infarcts. Treatment is targeted more specifically at the particular behavior. Treatment of the underlying dementia includes preventing further vascular lesions. Aggression and psychotic features can occur as in Alzheimer's disease, but use of the atypical antipsychotics appears to be safer, without a significant increase in mortality, at least with quetiapine, risperidone, or olanzapine (Sultana et al., 2014). Unlike other dementias, depression is the most common neuropsychiatric manifestation in vascular dementia,

unrelated to subtype or severity. Symptoms include mostly apathy but also psychomotor slowing, abulia, and poor motivation (Gupta et al., 2014). There is some evidence that small vessel subcortical infarcts result in more apathy and symptoms of depression while larger vessel strokes lead to more prominent agitation and aggression (Staekenborg et al., 2010). Treatment also centers around first finding triggers and using nonpharmacologic approaches. The medication choice is symptom-driven, limited by comorbid entities such as hypertension, diabetes, obesity, heart disease, and physical impairment.

Dementia with Lewy bodies/Parkinson's disease dementia. The prevalence of dementia with Lewy bodies (DLB) is rapidly increasing, in part because of greater recognition by practitioners, and some consider it the second most common degenerative dementia. The primary clinical features include progressive dementia with fluctuating cognitive function, visual hallucinations, and parkinsonian features often associated with REM sleep disorder and severe neuroleptic sensitivity. As in the other dementias, behavioral changes are common and include aggression, irritability, and disinhibition, including inappropriate sexual behavior related to frontal lobe involvement. Most often these changes occur late in the disease process. There is some evidence that the inappropriate sexual behavior responds to quetiapine (Prakash, Pathak, Munda, & Bagati, 2009). The most common neuropsychiatric feature was depression with a higher prevalence than in any of the other dementias and more often associated with other psychiatric symptoms, although few patients are on antidepressants (Sakai, Yamane, Yamamoto, & Maeda, 2013).

Hallucinations and delusions were also much more common in the synucleinopathies, including both dementia with Lewy bodies and Parkinson's disease dementia (PDD). Symptoms are thought to result from disruption of cholinergic and serotonergic neurotransmission. Cholinesterase inhibitors appear to be helpful for hallucinations, particularly in PDD, while antipsychotics are again not recommended, especially given their dopamine-blocking properties, known to increase parkinsonian symptoms (Ballard, Aarsland, Francis, & Corbett, 2013). Potentially the most troubling feature is the very common visual hallucinations, which can be treated if they are disturbing to the patient. Atypical antipsychotics are very effective, but these patients are extremely sensitive to neuroleptics and often do not tolerate their use. Neuroleptics have also been linked to increased mortality in the elderly with dementia. Sometimes anticholinesterase inhibitors can help mild hallucinations. If hallucinations are severe and unresponsive to other agents, quetiapine or clozapine can be used under close scrutiny. Cholinesterase inhibitors were not efficacious for cognitive decline; however rivastigmine was found to reduce neuropsychiatric symptoms with less apathy, anxiety, delusions, and hallucinations. Donepezil was also helpful for these symptoms and, contrary to other studies, also helpful for global cognitive function (Hanagasi, Bilgic, & Emre, 2013).

The course of dementia with Lewy bodies consists of cognitive decline, persistent psychotic features, especially visual hallucination, and worsening parkinsonism. Parkinson's disease shares many clinical features with DLB, however, the clinical features of dementia associated with Parkinson's disease are preceded by parkinsonism by more than a year, and they are rapidly responsive to dopaminergic agents. Both diseases have significant cortical deficits of acetylcholine, and while the cholinesterase inhibitors are helpful for dementia in Parkinson's disease, they are not as helpful in Lewy body disease (Rolinski, Fox, Maidmet, & McShane, 2012). Memantine was also found to be ineffective in dementia with Lewy bodies with no clinically significant effect on motor function, cognition, or behavioral symptoms (Matsunagai, Kishi, & Iwata, 2013). Treatment should consist of eliminating medications with anticholinergic effects. Dopamine can help motor symptoms in about half the patients. Other Parkinson's disease medications are rarely effective. Low-dose clonazepam can help the REM sleep disorder. Melatonin can also be beneficial, with or without the clonazepam. Stimulants can be helpful if excess daytime somnolence is prominent (Rolinski, Fox, Maidmet, & McShane, 2012).

Frontotemporal dementia. The most prominent features of frontotemporal dementia (FTD) are the neuropsychiatric symptoms that occur as a direct result of cell loss. This is a neurodegenerative disorder with focal degeneration in the frontal lobes giving rise to a progressive decline in behavior, commonly associated with psychotic features. There may be some evidence for genetic links and overlap with schizophrenia (Shinagawa et al., 2014). Frontotemporal dementia is considered a clinical spectrum of disorders of unknown etiology that are heterogeneous in symptoms, pathology, and genetics, but all cause an early onset degenerative dementia. Most patients with frontotemporal dementia present around 45–64 years of age with a set of characteristic behavior changes, executive dysfunction, and language impairment. There are three main types identified as *the behavioral variant* (frontal lobe atrophy, decline in behavior, executive system dysfunction), *semantic dementia* (loss of word meaning, anomia, anterior temporal lobe atrophy), and *progressive nonfluent aphasia* (left perisylvian atrophy). There is also overlap between these syndromes with ALS, atypical parkinsonian syndromes, progressive supranuclear palsy (PSP), and corticobasal degeneration (CBD). Others have classified these disorders based on the presence of microtubule-associated tau protein, DNA-binding protein, or sarcolemma protein. About 40% have a family history of frontotemporal dementia, and at least six genetic mutations have been described.

No disease modifying agents exist, but trials are looking at the role of neurotransmitter control to treat the behavioral, motor, and cognitive features, including SSRI's, atypical antipsychotics, acetylcholinesterase inhibitors, and glutamate NMDA receptor antagonists. As with the other dementias, behavioral, environmental, and other non-pharmacologic treatments are also maximized (Seltman & Matthews, 2012). The behavioral changes prominent in frontotemporal dementia make this a devastating disease with severely impaired social and emotional behavior in the context of difficulty recognizing emotions (Oliver, Virani, Finger, & Mitchell, 2014). Pharmacologic treatments of the core behavioral changes are rarely effective, making these patients particularly difficult to manage, resulting in early institutionalization and sedation to keep them and caregivers safe. The disruption of the frontal and anterior temporal lobes can alter the concept of self, impair social cognition, disrupt empathy, and cause loss of limbic-mediated emotion, disrupting the features that define the person. These disorders are not infrequently misdiagnosed as purely psychiatric disorders and not degenerative brain disease, delaying effective treatments (Miller, 2014).

Subcortical dementia. The subcortical dementias are also a heterogeneous group of disorders identified by their anatomic localization and not based on pathological changes or neurotransmitter deficits. This would include the diffuse white matter disruption between the frontal and thalamic tracts seen in ischemic vascular disease described earlier, causing slow speed of processing (Duering et al., 2014). Parkinson's disease dementia and the so-called Parkinson's-plus syndromes of progressive supranuclear palsy (PSP), multisystem atrophy (MSA), and corticobasal degeneration (CBD) are included in this group. They all can have an associated subcortical dementia with similar features and associated behavioral or mood changes, but they are not generally characterized by aggression or agitation, with the exception of complications of treatment for Parkinson's disease.

Parkinson's disease is a neurodegenerative disorder of the substantia nigra causing the dopamine cells to deteriorate. Motor signs are usually the presenting feature with later onset subcortical dementia characterized by slow speed of processing or bradyphrenia, abulia, apathy, and poor motivation. Other behavioral and mood changes can develop either as a result of the dopamine depletion or because of the treatment aimed to increase the dopamine. Hallucinations are common as discussed earlier, REM sleep disorders can be seen, deep brain stimulation can unmask depression or anxiety (Castrioto, Lhommee, Moro, & Krack, 2014), and impulse control disorders precipitated by dopamine agonists, such as compulsive gambling, can be a serious problem (Yip & Potenza, 2014). In addition, there have been reports of extreme aggression after adjustment to an implanted deep brain stimulator in the bilateral subthalamic nuclei to treat extrapyramidal motor symptoms, requiring immediate readjustment of the parameters (Rose, Mostrenko, McMaster, & Honey, 2011).

Alcoholic dementia. Chronic excessive alcohol use affects the nervous system at almost every level, including peripheral nerves, the spinal cord, and the brain, through both direct and indirect mechanisms. Brain degeneration and atrophy can occur more focally in the cerebellum, mammillary bodies, hippocampal temporal lobes, and frontal lobes, leading to cognitive impairment in executive function, episodic memory, and visuospatial dysfunction. Disinhibited behavior from frontal lobe degeneration can lead to aggression and poor judgment (Bernardin, Maheur-Bosser, & Paille, 2014). Indirect effects of alcohol on the liver can cause hyperammonemia and metabolic encephalopathy with more generalized confusion. Thiamine deficiencies can lead to severe and sometimes permanent cognitive impairments like Wernicke or Korsakoff's dementia, with severe amnesia and prominent executive systems dysfunction (Van Oort & Kessels, 2009). Obtaining an individual's drinking history is important in diagnosing the cause of aggressive behavior. Aggression in alcoholics may predate the onset of cognitive impairment and be independent of the dementia. There seems to also be some evidence that recovered alcoholics, abstinent for at least three years, can exhibit higher levels of aggression than nonalcoholics, even in the absence of psychiatric comorbidities or personality disorders. If there is also a later degenerative dementia, the aggression can seem out of proportion to what is typically expected (Ziherl, Cebasek Travnik, Kores Plesnicar, Tomori, & Zalar, 2007).

Other Neurologic Disorders

Metabolic encephalopathy. Metabolic encephalopathy or delirium presents with mental status changes characterized by a prominent attentional disorder, but it can often include changes in personality, behavior, and mood. The main clinical feature is a disturbance in the level of consciousness, with impairment in the ability to focus, sustain, or shift attention. The classic presentation includes attentional impairment, impairment in multiple other cognitive domains, and changes in motor behavior, perception, sleep, and thinking. Delirium is very common in the elderly who are often also agitated and combative and may require chemical restraint for their safety. There can be underlying delusions, hallucinations, anxiety, or pain. Unlike dementia with its slow progression, encephalopathic mental status fluctuates day to day or even moment to moment, but it can still sometimes be difficult to differentiate from dementia. Most often, metabolic encephalopathy is caused by medications, intoxication, infections, or chemical abnormalities. Life threatening causes include hypoxia, hypoglycemia, and hypotension. Multiple neurotransmitter systems are affected (Burns, Jacoby, & Levy, 1990). Workup includes an exam and careful search for underlying causes. Brain imaging and EEG may also be indicated (Harrington & Vardi, 2014). An intensive care unit is a common setting for the acute or subacute onset of an encephalopathy. The causes can be divided into environmental or medical— for example, sleep disruption, sensory deprivation or overload, severe depression, anxiety, posttraumatic stress disorder, cognitive impairment, or patients can become encephalopathic after anesthesia for surgery. Immobility can make the generalized confusion and inattention worse (Tonkovic et al., 2012). The biochemical etiology of delirium seems to be multifactorial with global neurotransmitter effects as well as focal brainstem effects impacting the reticular activating system. Acetylcholine, in particular, has been well documented to be a common etiology for confusional states. Many medications have anticholinergic effects and any patient with delirium needs a careful pharmacologic survey to eliminate underlying causes (Campbell et al., 2009).

Treatment is aimed at correcting the underlying cause and maximizing non-pharmacologic treatment, paying attention to the environmental light, noise, and temperature while minimizing changes, with frequent reorientation, reassurance, touch, and the presence of familiar people.

Interim pharmacologic treatment may be necessary to keep the patient and caregivers safe. Currently there are no FDA-approved medications for delirium-related agitation, aggression, or psychosis. The general guidelines are not opposed to the use of short-term antipsychotics, making them the treatment of choice (Vardi & Harrington, 2014). The newer agents have gained favor with fewer side effects, including quetiapine, risperidone, ziprasidone, and olanzapine, but they can still result in sedation and extrapyramidal side effects (Rea, Battistone, Fong, & Devin, 2007). Benzodiazepines have a more rapid onset of action but can worsen sedation and confusion, exacerbating the delirium. They are effective, however, in the setting of alcohol withdrawal (Drach, 2014) or seizures. As previously noted, acetylcholine was thought to be a prominent factor in delirium, so rivastigmine, one of the anticholinesterase inhibitors, was looked at for efficacy in treating delirium, however, it was found to be related to a higher mortality and is not recommended in this setting (Van Eijik et al., 2010).

Traumatic brain injury. Traumatic brain injury is a diagnosis that includes a wide range of neuropathology. Many behavioral changes can be seen, the most striking of which is the severe agitation that commonly surfaces in the setting of a severe brain injury. Diffuse axonal injury, frontal subdural, intracerebral hemorrhage, or anoxia can contribute to agitation that is mostly refractory to behavioral intervention, particularly during the early stages when there is more profound amnesia and limited carryover. Most psychotropic medications result in over-sedation, which can affect recovery and the ability to participate in rehabilitation. Patients can also pose a threat to themselves and to caregivers, so the risk–benefit ratio has to be considered and medications chosen accordingly. In dangerous situations, benzodiazepines and neuroleptics can be used temporarily, but they can lead to significant adverse effects. Antiepileptics have also proven effective as mood stabilizers (Bascunana, Villarreal, Alfonso, Bernabeu, & Terre, 2000). Amitriptyline was found to be an effective treatment option without significant negative impact on cognition, although there can be associated anticholinergic effects and it should only be used as long as needed (Jackson, Corrigan, & Arnett, 1985). Alternative options include carbamazepine, other antidepressants, and beta blockers like propranolol (Bascunana, Villarreal, Alfonso, Terre, & Bernabeu, 2000) or pindolol.

Anoxic encephalopathy, with or without brain trauma, may also result in agitation and aggression, which can be even more difficult to treat, especially with associated cognitive deficits. Amitriptyline also seems to be a viable option after anoxia and was better tolerated than the more commonly used neuroleptics (Szlabowicz & Stewart, 1990). Other options include estrogens, antiandrogens, antidepressants, anti-parkinsonian medications, antipsychotics, antiepileptic, lithium, buspirone, and psychostimulants (Levy et al., 2005). Comparing beta blockers (Inderal, pindolol), Parkinson's medications (amantadine), and psychostimulants (methylphenidate), the best management of aggression was found with the beta blockers (Fleminger, Greenwood, & Oliver, 2006). Other studies favored carbamazepine and SSRI antidepressants (Richard, Perrouin-Verbe, Rome, Bernat, & Mathe, 2003). It may take a trial and error period involving multiple agents before the most efficacious agent with the lowest side effect profile can be found.

Spells. Various spells can present with agitation, combativeness, and aggression. These would include unrecognized seizures, complex partial seizures, postictal states, non-epileptic spells, status epilepticus, and the often underappreciated nonconvulsive status epilepticus. An EEG can be helpful in the evaluation of the aggressive older patient. New onset seizures can occur in up to 25% of patients over the age of 65 (Ramsey, Rowan, & Pryor, 2004). The incidence is even higher in the presence of dementia and particularly associated with Alzheimer's disease (Sherzai, Losey, Vega, & Sherzai, 2014). Seizures in the elderly are more often partial onset and can be associated with an underlying brain disease, such as dementia, strokes, or tumors. Complex partial seizures are the most common type in the elderly and, unlike temporal lobe origins in younger patients, they arise more commonly from the frontal lobe with behavioral phenomena, including hallucinations, delusions, confusion, fear, and laughter (Kasper, Kasper, Pauli, & Stefan, 2010). Postictal states can result in generalized confusion associated with agitation and aggression and they can be prolonged in the elderly (Sanya, 2010). Non-epileptic spells are somatoform disorders that present clinically looking like seizures, but they do not have any EEG electrophysiological correlate. Once true seizures are ruled out, treatment becomes psychiatric, and antiepileptic medications are not indicated (Yates, 2014). Both status epilepticus and nonconvulsive status can present as acute confusional states including agitation, aggression, or unresponsiveness. Continuous EEG monitoring is needed to diagnose nonconvulsive status by demonstrating evidence of electrophysiological seizures, which are not evident by any outward clinical manifestations other than changes in mental status (Naeije, Gaspard, Depondt, Pepersack, & Legros, 2012). Aggressive urgent treatment with continuous monitoring in a critical care setting is needed.

Antiepileptic medications are the treatment for seizures, complex partial seizures, status epilepticus and nonconvulsive status. The choice of agent, as well as the dosing, has to be very cautious in the elderly because of drug interactions, sensitivity to medications, comorbidities, and side effect profiles (Jankovic & Dostic, 2012). Specific recommendations for treating each seizure type are beyond the scope of this discussion.

Sleep disorders. REM sleep behavioral disorder was only recently characterized in 1986 when it was incorporated into the first edition of the International Classification of Sleep Disorders. The hallmark finding is a polysomnogram that documents intermittent or sustained loss of the usual muscle paralysis resulting in a lack of normal atonia in skeletal muscle during REM sleep—a mandatory finding to meet the diagnostic criteria (Tachibana, 2009). REM sleep behavior disorder can occur in isolation, but it is frequently associated with Parkinson's disease and considered a diagnostic feature of dementia with Lewy bodies. In this disorder, when the usual muscle paralysis does not occur during REM sleep, patients are able to act out their dreams (Peever, Luppi, & Montplaisir, 2014). This commonly can include aggression, resulting in harm to the patient about one-third of the time and/or to a bed partner about two-thirds of the time. Workup includes an evaluation looking for underlying degenerative disorders known

as synucleinopathies, which include idiopathic Parkinson's disease, dementia with Lewy bodies, multisystem atrophy, as well as brainstem lesions, psychiatric disorders, and drug withdrawal. There is a large male preponderance in these disorders with the mean age of onset at 64.4 years. Clonazepam can be useful for treatment, as well as measures that ensure environmental safety (Olson, Boeve, & Siliberm, 2000), such as moving bedside tables, locking windows, and removing sharp objects. For those who do not tolerate clonazepam or who do not respond, melatonin can be an effective adjunctive or alternative treatment (Boeve, Silber, & Ferman, 2003).

Circadian rhythm disorders are common among the elderly and even more common among those with dementia. The combination of altered circadian rhythm, environmental factors, social aspects, and impaired cognition can cause agitation, confusion, anxiety, and aggression, often in the late afternoon, evening, or nighttime. The postulated mechanism of these disorders involves degeneration of the suprachiasmatic nucleus of the hypothalamus, which regulates circadian rhythms through secretion of melatonin. This phenomenon is more commonly referred to as *sundowning* and can lead to early institutionalization. Treatment options include bright light therapy, melatonin, acetylcholinesterase inhibitors, NMDA antagonists, antipsychotics, and behavioral modifications (Khachiyants, Trinkle, Son, & Kim, 2011).

There can also be more generalized disturbances in elderly sleep–wake cycles, especially for those who are hospitalized or institutionalized, because of disrupted nighttime sleep triggered by light, noise, pain, anxiety, frequent voiding, nighttime dosing of medications, caffeine, and medication side effects that can also lead to daytime agitation and aggression. The treatment involves an investigation into precipitating factors that can be ameliorated, sleep aids such as melatonin, and bright-light pulsed therapy in the evening (Satlin, Volicer, Ross, Herz, & Campbell, 1992).

There are many other sleep disorders commonly found in the elderly including all the insomnias and obstructive sleep apnea, as well as the less common narcolepsy. These tend to lead to excess daytime somnolence, which can impact arousal, attention, cognition, pain tolerance, and mood, but they do not necessarily result in aggressive agitated behavior. Attention to sleep hygiene is important, such as going to sleep and waking at regular times, manipulating the bedroom environment, avoiding liquids after dinner, avoiding food too close to sleep, avoiding TV and other distractions when trying to sleep, treating pain adequately, eliminating stimulating medications, eliminating all caffeine, even early in the day, and exercising regularly earlier in the day.

Specific Behaviors and Treatment Approaches

Many types of behaviors have been reported by family members and caregivers that are seldom witnessed by medical personnel. Family members and caregivers are encouraged to be as accurate as possible in their descriptions, which can affect treatment options. Sometimes behaviors can be videotaped to show providers, offering enormous insight, which can guide treatment. These descriptions should always be in the context of changes from baseline behaviors. Symptoms can be thought of in the following categories: psychotic symptoms, mood/affective symptoms, apathy, and agitation/aggression. The majority of dementia patients experience neuropsychiatric symptoms at some point during the course of their disease, with widely variable prevalence depending on the underlying pathology, stage of disease, comorbid factors, and their environment. The most common symptoms include apathy, depression, anxiety, and agitation. Because behavioral changes often depend on the underlying type of dementia, making an accurate diagnosis is essential in choosing treatment and educating family and caregivers (Ford, 2014). Psychotic features can include visual or auditory hallucinations, paranoia, and delusions. There can be obsessive compulsive disorders, hoarding, shadowing, severe perseveration, and changes in eating habits. Apathy can include severe abulia with failure to thrive. The other end of this spectrum would include impulsivity, disinhibition, inappropriate sexual behaviors, and overeating. There can also be wandering, compulsive pacing, restlessness, intermittent screaming or shouting, oppositional behavior, resistance to care, inappropriate language and other antisocial behaviors, anxiety, and fear of abandonment. Aggression can occur as a sort of final common pathway with any of these behaviors, or with attempts to redirect from these behaviors, and they can be verbal or physical. It is helpful, therefore, to gather as much behavioral information as possible when choosing a treatment approach.

Triggers can include pain, infection, metabolic changes, a new neurologic event (stroke, SDH, and so on), seizures, medication changes, sleep disruption, and physical discomfort that cannot be expressed such as hunger, constipation, urinary retention, or boredom. The most common triggers are less obvious and relate to fluctuations in the environment, including changes in food, caregiver, schedule, ambient light or noise level, ambient temperature, roommate, caregiver shift, or they can be brought on by a sudden memory that cannot be articulated. Triggers can revolve around care, including feeding, dressing, showering/bathing, or getting into a car or van. They can result from transitions and changing activities such as getting up or going to sleep, or the sun setting in the afternoon (Department of Psychiatry, Mount Sinai School of Medicine, Neugroschi, 2002). Psychotic symptoms and, in particular, delusions can be a trigger leading to aggression as well. These are less obvious and may be harder to unravel during the investigation for triggers (Deutsch et al., 1991).

Ideally, non-pharmacologic treatment should always precede pharmacologic management. Accurately identifying the behaviors and the triggers can go a long way in preventing aggression. Educating family and caregivers to identify behaviors and their triggers is essential to successful treatment. Education and support is also important to let them know how common behavioral changes are, to limit embarrassment, to prevent social isolation, and to ameliorate caregiver burnout. Other tactics include providing redirection, reassurance, and social interaction, as well as calming techniques such as personalized music, recordings of family members reading, family videotapes, aromatherapy, providing familiar items to see and touch, or dimming the lights (Ballard et al., 2009). Preventing caregiver burnout can also indirectly help the patient: teaching effective strategies and interventions to caregivers to manage patients will potentially keep them socially connected and in their own familiar environment a little longer. Day programs and periods of respite can be invaluable for the caregiver, as well as counseling and support groups.

Correcting any underlying precipitating disorders should always be considered first as this can ameliorate the need for more long-term symptomatic treatments. This would mean a workup including B/P, pulse oximetry, glucose, electrolytes, renal function, liver function including ammonia, calcium, white count, thyroid functions, toxicology screens, and possibly CSF studies, EEG, and neuroimaging studies, among other things. If correcting underlying precipitating factors and non-pharmacologic approaches have been exhausted, and the health, safety, and well-being of the patient, family, and/or caregiver are threatened, pharmacologic management can be considered.

Again, treatment should target the specific behavior. Depressive features respond to antidepressants, psychotic features to antipsychotics, anxiety to anxiolytics, apathy to activating agents, and so forth. Some behaviors do not have any specific treatment and require generalized sedation for safety, such as wandering, and disinhibited and inappropriate behavior. Sexual aggression can sometimes respond to estrogen, although the risk–benefit ratio needs to be seriously considered, as in all treatments. Sleep disorders can be targeted as a way to eliminate a trigger. Many medications target more than one behavior. For example, trazodone has been found to be effective in helping with sleep as well as in reducing anxiety, depression, and agitation (Osvath, 2013).

Underlying pain should always be considered in a dementia patient with behavioral changes. This is a difficult area to target because of the difficulty in assessing a patient who cannot accurately communicate symptoms. Observing pain behaviors becomes crucial in identifying pain as a source of agitation, such as grimacing, vocalizations, guarding, poor sleep, irritability, and aggression. About 50% of patients with dementia experience pain on a regular basis. A lower threshold for pain perception was postulated as a mechanism for high incidences of pain in this population. A stepwise symptomatic approach is helpful along with educated caregivers. White matter disconnections can lead to central neuropathic pain in vascular dementia. Prefrontal atrophy in frontotemporal dementias can result in decreased affective components of pain (Achterberg et al., 2013).

Concluding Remarks

The consequences of unrecognized and untreated behavioral changes in the elderly can have dire consequences on quality of life. Aggression and violence can injure a family member and/or a caregiver. The patients can injure themselves, either intentionally or unintentionally. Access to cars, alcohol, drugs (including their medications), knives, power tools, and/or weapons should be carefully monitored and limited as needed. Inappropriate behavior can lead to legal and financial problems, and unmanageable behavior can prompt early institutionalization. Regular follow-up visits that include questions about behavior will allow for an early workup and treatment to prevent out-of-control escalation. Family education, support, caregiver relief, and prevention of complications can go a long way in improving the quality of life for the patient and the family.

References

Achterberg, W. P., Pieper, M. J., van Dalen-Kok A. H., de Waal, M. W., Husebo, B. S., Lautenbacher, S., . . . Corbett, A. (2013). Pain management in patients with dementia. *Clinical Interventions in Aging, 8*, 1471–1482.

Albert, M. S. (2011). Changes in cognition. *Neurobiology of Aging, 32* (Suppl 1), S58–S63.

Allgaier, M., & Allgaier, A. (2014). An update on drug treatment options of Alzheimer's disease. *Frontiers of Bioscience, 19*, 1345–1354.

Ballard, C., Aarsland, D., Francis, P., & Corbett, A. (2013). Neuropsychiatric symptoms in patients with dementias associated with cortical Lewy bodies: Pathophysiology, clinical features, and pharmacological management. *Drugs and Aging, 30*(8), 603–611.

Ballard, C., Brown, R., Fossey, J., Douglas, S., Bradley, P., Hancock, J., . . . Howard, R. (2009). Brief psychosocial therapy for the treatment of agitation in Alzheimer disease (the CALM-AD trial). *American Journal of Geriatric Psychiatry. 17*(9), 726–733.

Bascunana, H., Villarreal, I., Alfonso, S., Bernabeu, M., & Terre, R. (2000). Agitation in head injury. I. Definition and treatment with anxiolytic neuroleptics and antiepileptic drugs. *Review of Neurology, 30*(9), 850–854.

Bascunana, H., Villarreal, I., Alfonso, S., Terre, R., & Bernabeu, M. (2000). Agitation in head injury. II. Treatment with antidepressant, sympathomimetic, beta blocker, dopaminergic, and other drugs. *Review Neurology, 30*(11), 1044–1047.

Bernardin, F., Maheur-Bosser, A., & Paille, F. (2014). Cognitive impairment of alcohol-dependent subject. *Review Practicum, 64*(4), 462–465.

Birks, J. (2006). Cholinesterase inhibitors for Alzheimer's disease. *Cochrane Database Systematic Reviews, 25*(1).

Boeve, B. F., Silber, M. H., & Ferman, T. J. (2003). Melatonin for treatment of REM sleep behavior disorder in neurologic disorders: Results in 14 patients. *Sleep Medicine, 4*(4), 281–284.

Borson, S., & Raskind, M. A. (1997). Clinical features and pharmacologic treatment of behavioral symptoms of Alzheimer's disease. *Neurology, 48*(5 Suppl 6), S17–S24.

Burns, A., Jacoby, R., & Levy, R. (1990). Psychiatric phenomena in Alzheimer's disease. IV: Disorders of behavior. *British Journal of Psychiatry, 157*, 86–94.

Campbell, N., Boustani, M., Limbil, T., Ott, C., Fox, C., Maidment, I.,... Gulati, R. (2009). The cognitive impact of anticholinergics: A clinical review. *Clinical Interventions in Aging, 4*, 225–233.

Castrioto, A., Lhommee, E., Moro, E., & Krack, P. (2014). Mood and behavioral effects of subthalamic stimulation in Parkinson's disease. *Lancet Neurology, 13*(3), 287–305.

Chan, D. C., Kasper, J. D., Black, B. S., & Rabins, P. V. (2003). Prevalence and correlates of behavioral and psychiatric symptoms in community-dwelling elders with dementia or mild cognitive impairment: The Memory and Medical Care Study. *International Journal of Geriatric Psychiatry, 18*(2), 174–182.

Cooney, C., Murphy, S., Tessema, H., Freyne, A. (2013). Use of low-dose gabapentin for aggressive behavior in vascular and mixed vascular/Alzheimer dementia. *Journal of Neuropsychiatry in Clinical Neuroscience, 25*(2), 120–125.

Cumbo, E., & Liqori, L. D. (2014). Differential effects of current specific treatments on behavioral and psychological symptoms in patients with Alzheimer's disease: A 12-month, randomized, open-label trial. *Journal of Alzheimer's Disease, 39*(3), 477–485.

Daiello, L. A. (2007). Atypical antipsychotics for the treatment of dementia-related behaviors: An update. *Medical Health Rhode Island, 90*(6), 191–194.

Deutsch, L. H., Bylsma, F. W., Rovner, B. W., Steele, C., & Folstein, M. F. (1991). Psychosis and physical aggression in probable Alzheimer's disease. *American Journal of Psychiatry, 148*, 1159–1163.

Drach, L. M. (2014). Psychopharmacological treatment of delirium in the elderly [Abstract]. *Medizinische Monatsschrift fur Pharmazeuten, 37*(4), 124–131.

Duering, M., Gesierich, B., Seiler, S., Pirpamer, L., Gonik, M., Hofer, E., . . . Dichgans, M. (2014). Strategic white matter tracts for processing speed deficits in age-related small vessel disease. *Neurology, 82*(22), 1946–1950.

Fleminger, S., Greenwood, R. J., & Oliver, D. L. (2006). Pharmacological management for agitation and aggression in people with acquired brain injury. *Cochrane Database Systematic Reviews, 18*(4), CD003299.

Ford, A. H. (2014). Neuropsychiatric aspects of dementia. *Maturitas, 79*(2), 209–215.

Gardette, V., Lapeyre-Mestre, M., Coley, N., Cantet, C., Montastruc, J. L., Vellas, B., & Andrieu, S. (2012). Antipsychotic use and mortality risk in community-dwelling Alzheimer's disease patients: Evidence for a role of dementia severity. *Current Alzheimer Research, 9*(9), 1106–1116.

Gupta, M., Dasgupta, A., Khwaja, G. A., Chowdhury, D., Patidar, Y., & Batra, A. (2014). Behavioural and psychological symptoms in poststroke vascular cognitive impairment. *Behavioural Neurology. 2014*(2014): 430128. doi:10.1155/430128. Advanced online publication.

Hanagasi, H. A., Bilgic, B., & Emre, M. (2013). Neuroimaging, biomarkers, and management of dementia with Lewy bodies. *Frontiers of Neurology, 4*, 151.

Harrington, C. J., & Vardi, K. (2014). Delirium: Presentation, epidemiology, and diagnostic evaluation (Part 1). *Rhode Island Medical Journal, 97*(6), 18–23.

Hauser, P. S., & Ryan, R. O. (2013). Impact of apolipoprotein E on Alzheimer's disease. *Current Alzheimer Research, 10*(8), 809–817.

Herrmann, N., Lanctot, K. L., Rothenburg, L. S., & Eryavec, G. (2007). A placebo-controlled trial of valproate for agitation and aggression in Alzheimer's disease. *Dementia, Geriatrics, and Cognitive Disorders, 23*(2), 116–119.

Ibrahim, F., & Viswanathan, R. (2012). Management of agitation following aneurysmal subarachnoid hemorrhage: Is there a role for beta-blockers? *Case Reports in Psychiatry, 2012*.

Islam, M. R., Moriguchi, S., Tagashira, H., & Fukunaga, K. (2014). Rivastigmine improves hippocampal neurogenesis and depression-like behaviors via 5-HT1A receptor stimulation in olfactory bulbectomized mice. *Neuroscience, 272,* 116–130.

Jackson, R. D., Corrigan, J. D., & Arnett, J. A. (1985). Amitriptyline for agitation in head injury. *Archives of Physical Medicine and Rehabilitation, 66*(3), 180–181.

Jankovic, S. M., & Dostic, M. (2012). Choice of antiepileptic drugs for the elderly: Possible drug interactions and adverse effects. *Expert Opinion on Drug Metabolic Toxicology, 8*(1), 81–91.

Kasper, B. S., Kasper, E. M., Pauli, E., & Stefan, H. (2010). Phenomenology of hallucinations, illusions, and delusions as part of seizure semiology. *Epilepsy and Behavior, 18*(1–2), 13–23.

Khachiyants, N., Trinkle, D., Son, S. J., & Kim, K. Y. (2011). Sundown syndrome in persons with dementia: An update. *Psychiatry Investigation, 8*(4), 275–287.

Langa, K. M., Foster, N. L., & Larson, E. B. (2004). Mixed dementia: Emerging concepts and therapeutic implications. *Journal of the American Medical Association, 292*, 2901.

Levy, M., Berson, A., Cook, T., Bollegala, N., Seto, E., Tursnski, S., . . . Bhalerao, S. (2005). Treatment of agitation following traumatic brain injury: A review of the literature. *Neurologic Rehabilitation, 20*(4), 279–306.

Matsunagai, S., Kishi, T., & Iwata, N. (2013). Memantine for Lewy body disorders: Systematic review and meta-analysis. *American Journal of Geriatric Psychiatry.* doi:10.10.1016/j.japg.2013.11.007. Advanced online publication.

Miller, B. L. (2014). Frontotemporal dementia. Book review by Edward D. Huey, MD. *American Journal of Psychiatry, 171*, 695–696.

Naeije, G., Gaspard, N., Depondt, C., Pepersack, T., & Legros, B. (2012). Acute confusional state of unknown cause in the elderly: A study with continuous EEG monitoring. *Epilepsy and Behavior, 23*(3), 330–334.

Neugroschi, J. (2002). Agitation. How to manage behavior disturbances in the older patient with dementia. *Geriatrics, 57*(4), 33–37.

O'Brien, J. T., Erkinjuntti, T., Reisberg, B., Roman, G., Sawada, T., Pantoni, L., . . . Dekosky, S. T. (2003). Vascular cognitive impairment. *Lancet Neurology, 2*(2), 89–98.

Oliver, L. D., Virani, K., Finger, E. C., & Mitchell, D. G. (2014). Is the emotion recognition deficit associated with frontotemporal dementia caused by selective inattention to diagnostic facial features? *Neuropsychologia.* Advanced online publication.

Olson, E. J., Boeve, B. F., & Siliberm, M. H. (2000). Rapid eye movement sleep behavior disorder: Demographic, clinical, and laboratory findings in 93 cases. *Brain, 123*(pt2), 331–339.

Osvath, P. (2013). Current treatment of depression and agitation in the elderly-clinical use of trazodone [Abstract]. *Neuropsychopharmacology of Hungary, 15*(3), 147–155.

Peever, J., Luppi, P. H., & Montplaisir, J. (2014). Breakdown in REM sleep circuitry underlies REM sleep behavior disorder. *Trends in Neuroscience, 37*(5), 279–288.

Porsteinsson, A. P., Drye, L. T., Pollock, B. G., Devanand, D. P., Frangakis, C., Ismail, Z., . . . Lyketsos, C. G. (2014). CitAD Research Group. Effect of citalopram on agitation in Alzheimer's disease: The CitAD randomized clinical trial. *Journal of the American Medical Association, 311*(7), 682–691.

Prakash, R., Pathak, A., Munda, S., & Bagati, D. (2009). Quetiapine effective in treatment of inappropriate sexual behavior of Lewy body disease with predominant frontal lobe signs. *American Journal of Alzheimer's Disease and Other Dementias, 24*(2), 136.

Ramsey, R. E., Rowan, A. J., & Pryor, F. M. (2004). Special considerations in treating the elderly patient with epilepsy. *Neurology, 62*(5 Suppl 2), S24–S29.

Rea, R. S., Battistone, S., Fong, J. J., & Devin, J. W. (2007). Atypical antipsychotics versus haloperidol for treatment of delirium in acutely ill patients. *Pharmacotherapy, 27*(4), 588–594.

Richard, I., Perrouin-Verbe, B., Rome, J., Bernat, C., & Mathe, J. F. (2003). Pharmacological treatment of post-traumatic behavioral disorders. *Annales de Readaptation et de Medecine Physique, 46*(1), 49–57.

Rolinski, M., Fox, C., Maidmet, I., & McShane, R. (2012). Cholinesterase inhibitors for dementia with Lewy bodies, Parkinson's disease dementia, and cognitive impairment in Parkinson's disease. *Cochrane Database Systematic Reviews, 14*, 3.

Rose, N. G., Mostrenko, M., McMaster, J., & Honey, C. R. (2011). Severe agitation following deep brain stimulation for parkinsonism. *Canadian Journal of Emergency Medicine, 13*(4), 279–283.

Sakai, K., Yamane, Y., Yamamoto, Y., & Maeda, K. (2013). Depression in dementia with Lewy bodies [Abstract]. *Seishin Shinkeigaku Zasshi, 115*(11), 1127–1134.

Sanya, E. O. (2010). Peculiarity of epilepsy in elderly people: A review. *West African Journal of Medicine, 29*(6), 365–372.

Satlin, A., Volicer, L., Ross, V., Herz, L., & Campbell, S. (1992). Bright light treatment of behavioral and sleep disturbances in patients with Alzheimer's disease. *American Journal of Psychiatry, 149*(8), 1028–1032.

Scott, A., Ryan, A., James, I., & Mitchell, E. A. (2011). Perceptions and implications of violence from care home residents with dementia: A review and commentary. *International Journal of Older People Nursing, 6*(2), 110–122.

Segura, B., Jurado, M. A., Freixenet, N., Albuin, C., Muniesa, J., & Junque C. (2009). Mental slowness and executive dysfunctions in patients with metabolic syndrome. *Neuroscience Letter, 462*, 49.

Seltman R. E., & Matthews B. R. (2012). Frontotemporal lobar degeneration: Epidemiology, pathology, diagnosis, and management. *Central Nervous System Drugs, 26*(10), 841–870.

Sherzai, D., Losey, T., Vega, S., & Sherzai, A. (2014). Seizures and dementia in the elderly: Nationwide Inpatient Sample 1999–2008. *Epilepsy and Behavior, 36*, 53–56.

Shi, J. Q., Wang, B.R., Tian, Y. Y., Xu, J., Gao, L., Zhao, S. L., ... Zhang, Y. D. (2013). Antiepileptics topiramate and levetiracetam alleviate behavioral deficits and reduce neuropathology in APPswe/PS1dE9 transgenic mice. *Central Nervous System Neuroscience Therapeutics, 19*(11), 871–881.

Shinagawa, S., Nakajima, S., Pittman, E., Graff-Guerrero, A., Mimura, M., Nakayama, K., & Miller, B. L. (2014). Psychosis in frontotemporal dementia. *Journal of Alzheimers Disease.* doi:10.3233/JAD-140312 Advanced online publication.

Sietz, D. P., Adunuri, N., Gill, S. S., Gruneir, A., Herrmann, N., & Rochon, P. (2011). Antidepressants for agitation and psychosis in dementia. *Cochrane Database Systematic Reviews, 6*(2), 1.

Smith, E. E., Schneider, J. A., Wardlaw, J. M., & Greenberg, S. M. (2012). Cerebral microinfarcts: The invisible lesions. *Lancet Neurology, 11*(3), 272–282.

Sonnen, J. A., Larson, E. B., Crane, P. K., Haneuse, S., Li, G., Schellenberg, G. D., ... Montine, T. J. (2007). Pathological correlates of dementia in a longitudinal, population-based sample of aging. *Annals of Neurology, 62*(4), 406–413.

Staekenborg, S. S., Su, T., van Straaten, E C., Lane, R., Scheltens, P., Barkhof, F., & van der Flier, W. M. (2010). Behavioral and psychological symptoms in vascular dementia: Differences between small- and large-vessel disease. *Journal of Neurology, Neurosurgery, and Psychiatry, 81*(5), 547–551.

Staekenborg, S. S., van der Flier, W. M., van Straaten, E. C., Lane, R., Barkhof, F., & Scheltens, P. (2008). Neurological signs in relation to type of cerebrovascular disease in vascular dementia. *Stroke, 39*(2), 317–322.

Sultana, J., Chang, C. K., Hayes, R. D., Broadbent, M., Stewart, R., Corbett, A., & Ballard, C. (2014). Associations between risk of mortality and atypical antipsychotic use in vascular dementia: A clinical cohort study. *International Journal of Geriatric Psychiatry.* doi:10.1002/gps.4101. Advanced online publication.

Szlabowicz, J. W., & Stewart, J. T. (1990). Amitriptyline treatment of agitation associated with anoxic encephalopathy. *Archives of Physical Medicine and Rehabilitation, 71*(8), 612–613.

Tachibana, N. (2009). Historical overview of REM sleep behavior disorder in relation to its pathophysiology [Abstract]. *Brain and Nerve, 61*(5), 558–568.

Tan, C. C., Yu, J. T., Wang, H. F., Tan, M. S., Meng, X. F., Wang, C.,... Tan, L. (2014). Efficacy and safety of donepezil, galantamine, rivastigmine, and memantine for the treatment of Alzheimer's disease: A systemic review and meta-analysis. *Journal of Alzheimers Disease.* doi:10.3233/JAD-132690Advanced online publication.

Tonkovic, D., Adam, V. N., Kovacevic, M., Bogovic, T. Z., Drvar, Z., & Baronica, R. (2012). Perioperative disorders of mental functions [Abstract]. *Acta Medica Croatica, 66*(1), 73–79.

Ukraintseva, S., Sloan, F., Arbeev, K., & Yashin, A. (2006). Increasing rates of dementia at time of declining mortality from stroke. *Stroke, 37*, 1155–1159.

Van Eijik, M. M., Roes, K. C., Honing, M. L., Kuiper, M.A., Karakus, A., van der Jagt, M.,. . . Slooter, A. J. (2010). Effect of rivastigmine as an adjunct to usual care with haloperidol on duration of delirium and mortality in critically ill patients: A multicenter, double-blind, placebo-controlled randomized trial. *Lancet, 376*, 1829–1837.

Van Oort, R., & Kessels, R. P. (2009). Executive dysfunction in Korsakoff's syndrome: Time to revise the DSM criteria for alcohol-induced persisting amnestic disorder? *International Journal of Psychiatry in Clinical Practice, 13*(1), 78–81.

Vardi, K., & Harrington, C. J. (2014). Delirium: Treatment and prevention (Part 2). *Rhode Island Medical Journal, 97*(6), 24–28.

Vermeiren, Y., Van Dam, D., Aerts, T., Engelborghs, S., & DeDeyn, P. P. (2014). Brain region-specific monoaminergic correlates of neuropsychiatric symptoms in Alzheimer's Disease. *Journal of Alzheimer's Disease, 41*(3), 819–833.

Yates, E. (2014). Psychogenic non-epileptic seizures in the older adult. *Journal of Psychosocial Nursing and Mental Health Services, 52*(5), 17–20.

Yip, S. W., & Potenza, M. N. (2014). Treatment of gambling disorders. Current treatment options. *Psychiatry, 1*(2), 189–203.

Zahodne, L. B., Omstein, K., Cosetino, S., Devanand, D. P., & Stem, Y. (2013). Longitudinal relationships between Alzheimer disease progression and psychosis, depressed mood, and agitation/aggression. *American Journal of Geriatric Psychiatry, 23*(2), 130–140. Advanced online publication.

Ziherl, S., Cebasek Travnik, Z., Kores Plesnicar, B, Tomori, M., & Zalar, B. (2007). Trait aggression and hostility in recovered alcoholics. *European Addiction Research, 13*(2), 89–93.

Elder Abuse: Prevention and Reporting

Joah L. Williams, Melba A. Hernandez-Tejada, *and* Ron Acierno

Abstract

Elder abuse and neglect are serious problems affecting tens of thousands of older adults each year. In this chapter, we discuss elder abuse in its various forms (including emotional, physical, and sexual abuse, financial maltreatment, and neglect) and provide recommendations for screening and prevention relevant to health-care providers working with geriatric populations. We further highlight clinical and contextual issues pertinent to screening for elder abuse and to its prevention, followed by a review of information regarding emergency management and care in cases of suspected or confirmed elder abuse. We conclude with a discussion about mandated reporting laws and community-based intervention strategies. We hope that this chapter will improve providers' knowledge of the prevalence and consequences of elder abuse and strengthen the willingness to screen for and intervene in situations where an older adult may be the victim of elder abuse or neglect.

Key Words: elder abuse, neglect, financial exploitation, caregivers, cognitive impairment, mandated reporting

By 2030, nearly one in five Americans will be an "older adult," that is, above age 60 (He, Sengupta, Velkoff, & DeBarros, 2005). Fully 10% of these who are relatively independent and community-residing older adults will experience some form of elder mistreatment *each* year (Acierno et al., 2010). Because older adults are frequent consumers of health-care resources, health-care providers are among the professionals most likely to be in contact with victims of elder abuse and are thus in a potentially key position to identify abuse and intervene. Such intervention will typically take the form of a referral to services (e.g., for emotional abuse where the abuser and the victim want to remain together) or reports to authorities (e.g., where mandated and for physical or sexual abuse), as it is unrealistic to expect health-care providers to deliver violence reduction or prevention types of interventions unless they have had specific training to do so. Rather, providers are well placed to facilitate access to other specialty services or to protective authorities.

Indeed, recognizing the potentially central role of health-care providers in opening these doors, the US Preventive Services Task Force (Moyer, 2013), recommends violence assessment (and subsequent action where indicated) for adult women. The American Medical Association recommends screening more broadly (AMA, 2008).

Prevalence and Characteristics of Elder Abuse

Data from two recent epidemiological surveys assessing the prevalence of elder abuse in the United States—the National Social Life, Health, and Aging Project (NSHAP; Laumann, Leitsch, & Waite, 2008) and the National Elder Mistreatment Study (NEMS; Acierno et al., 2010)—suggest that as many as one in 10 community-residing older adults experience some form of elder abuse each year, with the majority of these cases comprising relatively severe emotional abuse. In addition to emotional/psychological mistreatment, common categories of elder abuse assessed in prevalence studies and reported by Adult Protective Services agencies generally include physical abuse, sexual abuse, financial exploitation, and elder neglect. There is some debate regarding classification of elder mistreatment as "abuse" insofar as historically an abuse designation required the mistreatment acts to take place in the context of a "trust relationship" (National Research Council [NRC], 2003). However, from the perspective of the victim, and from the perspective of the health-care provider, being hit, threatened, or sexually assaulted are acts of violence demanding remedy, irrespective of the perpetrator relationship to the victim. Moreover, as both the outcomes (e.g., injury, depression, isolation) and the remedies (e.g., reporting to authorities, referral for services) are similar, independent of a trust relationship, such debate is not terribly relevant to the question of what a provider should do when violence is identified. Moreover, such debate and artificial distinction among elder mistreatment distracts policymakers, researchers, and clinicians from the core problem at hand: elders are being mistreated quite a bit more frequently than previously thought. Thus, for the purpose of this review, and consistent with the National Elder Mistreatment Study, we will reference *elder abuse* as violence against those over age 60, and then subsequently advise distinction among perpetrator classes, with respect to trust relationships, as mistreatment perpetrated by strangers, intimate partners, children, other family members, and known acquaintances. Caretaker/dependency status is also a relevant categorization metric. The terms *abuse* and *mistreatment* will be used interchangeably. We will now discuss the prevalence and characteristics of each category of elder abuse, providing definitions of the type of mistreatment as used in the National Elder Mistreatment Study.

Emotional Abuse

Emotional or psychological abuse of elders can include verbally attacking or yelling at an individual in such a way that he or she feels repeatedly afraid or threatened. Additionally, emotional mistreatment may involve actively ignoring an older adult for days at a time. Acierno and colleagues (2010) also included verbally humiliating older adults (e.g., calling them "stupid") or harassing them in their definition of emotional abuse. Emotional abuse is perhaps the most common form of elder abuse, with between 5% and 9% of older adults reporting at least one severe episode in the past year (Acierno et al., 2010; Laumann et al., 2008). For example, in

the NSHAP, 9% of older adults between the ages of 57 and 85 reported being "insulted" or "put down" in the past year. Data from the NSHAP also suggest that women are twice as likely as men to experience emotionally abusive verbal mistreatment, while data from the NEMS also suggest that lower age (that is, being younger than 70) and poor social support are associated with increased risk for emotional abuse.

Physical Abuse

Physical mistreatment of elders includes hitting an older adult with a hand or other object or physically restraining an older adult (e.g., tying a person down or locking someone in a room). Such actions as hitting or restraining often result in visible, physical injuries like cuts or bruises. Nearly 1.6% of older adults experience physical abuse each year, and lower age, limited social support, and isolation appear to convey greater risk for physical abuse (Acierno et al., 2010). Alcohol abuse and social isolation on the part of perpetrators also appear to increase the risk for physical abuse (Reay & Browne, 2001) and thus may be important factors to consider when assessing whether an older adult is at risk for future victimization.

Sexual Abuse

As with emotional and physical mistreatment, sexual abuse can take many forms and includes a range of sexually exploitative behaviors. These behaviors include forced intercourse, molestation (being forced to touch someone else's breasts or genitals or having someone forcefully touch one's own breasts or genitals), and being forced to undress. Some definitions also include being undressed and photographed against one's will. Sexual abuse appears to be somewhat less common than other forms of abuse, with 0.6% of older adults reporting some form of sexual abuse in the past year (Acierno et al., 2010). However, sexual abuse shares similar risk factors as emotional and physical abuse in that poor social support is associated with greater risk for sexual abuse (Acierno et al., 2010.). It is also very likely that this highly stigmatizing event is underreported.

Financial Exploitation

Older adults frequently have family members or other parties help them manage their finances and other assets, and it is in this context that financial exploitation typically occurs. Financial exploitation is particularly difficult to identify because it may occur on a continuum. While stealing money from grandmother's wallet is clearly financial abuse, keeping the two dollars and change from money given by grandmother for grocery shopping to pay for gas is less obviously so. Alternatively, while forging a signature on a check to steal Social Security benefits is a criminal act, less clear is making a risky investment in good faith that in retrospect was quite foolish. The range of acts that may qualify as financial abuse is extremely wide. For example, financial exploitation can vary from spending an older adult's money or selling their property without obtaining their permission to blatantly stealing money or property from an older adult to theft of, or restrictive use of, their property. Financial exploitation can also involve deception on the part of a family member or other trusted person who helps with finances. For example, forging signatures in order to sell property or get access to an older adult's financial accounts clearly constitutes exploitation, as does using deception to trick an older adult into signing a document that grants someone else access to their accounts or assets. Estimates from the NSHAP and NEMS suggest that financial exploitation is sadly commonplace, with between 3.5% and 5.2% of older adults experiencing some form of exploitation. Rates of financial exploitation also appear to differ somewhat across racial and ethnic groups. For instance, in the NSHAP, African American elders reported higher rates of financial exploitation relative to Caucasian elders, while being Latino appears to be protective in that Latino elders endorsed lower rates of financial exploitation compared to Caucasian elders.

Elder Neglect

The key issue in understanding elder neglect is that the older adult (1) has unmet needs for daily living, and (2) there is an identified responsible individual who frequently refuses to address these needs. These needs might include adequate transportation to the grocery store or medical appointments, a supportive person who can ensure that the elder has sufficient food and medicine, or someone who can assist with daily activities like cooking and cleaning. Note that neglect can be broken down into (a) situations where a core need exists, but is unmet (potential neglect), or (b) a core need exists, is unmet, and an individual has been identified as responsible for that need (neglect). Among older adults in the NEMS, 5.1% reported situations suggestive of potential neglect, and non-White racial minorities, and individuals with significant health conditions appeared to be most at risk for neglect,

even after controlling for factors such as socioeconomic status. A third type of neglect, distinct from aforementioned instances of neglect by others, is self-neglect, which refers to situations where an older adult refuses to meet his or her own health, nutritional, or hygienic needs. This form of neglect is typically not included in the category of neglect as elder abuse (Abrams, Lachs, McAvay, Keohane, & Bruce, 2002).

Characteristics of Elder Abuse Perpetrators

Although the NEMS did not find that elderly women were more likely to be mistreated than elderly men (Amstadter, Cisler, et al., 2010; note: this was in contrast to earlier research—see Biggs, Manthorpe, Tinker, Doyle, & Erens, 2009; Pillemer & Finkelhor, 1988; Yaffe, Weiss, Wolfson, & Lithwick, 2007), the NEMS did find key gender differences in terms of perpetrator characteristics across mistreatment types. For example, women were more likely than men to be abused by a relative (63% vs. 52%). Men who were victims of emotional mistreatment were more likely than female victims to be dependent on the perpetrator (29% vs. 10%). Moreover, perpetrators of physical mistreatment against men were more likely to be unemployed and to have had a history of legal problems compared to perpetrators of physical mistreatment against women. Female victims of physical mistreatment were more likely to live with the perpetrator, and the perpetrator was more likely to be a relative. The low prevalence of sexual abuse in existing elder mistreatment samples precluded analyses by perpetrators for this abuse type, however, earlier research suggests that perpetrators of elder sexual abuse are more likely to have engaged in prior criminal behavior (Jeary, 2005). In the NEMS, about one-third of the perpetrators had a prior legal history. Interestingly, a majority of sexual mistreatment perpetrators were not related to the victim and did not live with them.

Health Impact of Elder Abuse

Although national epidemiological research is lacking, existing smaller scale studies indicate that elder abuse is associated with myriad physical and mental health problems. Of course, causality cannot be determined in these cross-sectional studies. Beyond the obvious physical injuries like bruises that can result from physical mistreatment, other medical problems are also found in increased frequency alongside mistreatment, including fractures, dementia, malnutrition, and death (Dong, 2005; Dong et al., 2009). Older adults with a history of elder abuse also experience higher rates of emotional problems, such as depression and anxiety, relative to those without a history of abuse (e.g., Dong, Beck, & Simon, 2010; Dyer, Pavlik, Murphy, & Hyman, 2000), and evidence suggests that elder abuse is independently associated with emotional distress over and above other known risk factors including physical health, social support, and prior trauma history (Cisler, Begle, Amstadter, & Acierno, 2012). Indeed, more severe emotional distress in the context of elder abuse may exacerbate other health problems (Amstadter, Begle, et al., 2010) and mortality risk (Dong et al., 2011). Because of the significant physical and psychological burden of elder abuse among older adults, health-care providers can play a vital role in screening for and preventing elder abuse, especially among those adults seeking health care for problems associated with abuse.

Screening and Prevention Issues for Health-Care Providers

Problem recognition is an obvious first step in any successful prevention or intervention effort, and brief screening tools are available for clinicians working with older adults. However, clinicians and other health-care providers must consider several contextual and clinical issues when screening for elder abuse, especially in emergent situations. In this section, we discuss these issues with special attention to environmental and patient-specific factors that may affect an older person's willingness and ability to disclose abuse. We also provide specific recommendations regarding screening tools and strategies that may be useful to practicing clinicians.

Abuse in Community versus Long-Term Care Settings

Older adult victims of elder abuse in domestic or community settings may be reluctant to discuss abuse with clinicians for a variety of reasons. For example, in the case of an adult child abusing an older parent, elders may feel a sense of personal responsibility for the abuse, blaming their own parenting style for their child's behavior, or perhaps their own history of abusive interactions (Acierno, 2003; Acierno et al., 2010). For those elders in domestic violence relationships, stigma may inhibit reports. Moreover, feelings of embarrassment or powerlessness may lessen an older adult's willingness to disclose abuse perpetrated by a family member. Alternatively, the abusive family member may also meet essential

transportation, health-care, or other needs that allow the older individual to remain in their home, and disclosure might end this arrangement.

In long-term care settings, however, older adults are likely to face different barriers to reporting than those in domestic settings. Long-term care settings include nursing homes and assisted care facilities, and evidence suggests that rates of abuse and neglect in long-term care facilities are far higher than those reported in samples of community-residing older adults (Lachs, Bachman, Wiliams, & O'Leary, 2007; Rosen, Pillemer, & Lachs, 2008). However, the perpetrators appear to be other residents, not staff. Resident on resident aggression, particularly among those with dementia, is a problem of housing design and staffing level. However, staff perpetrated abuse, albeit less frequent than resident on resident abuse, may also be prevalent, particularly with respect to neglect. For example, in a study of nursing home residents in the greater Atlanta, Georgia, area, 44% of residents reported experiencing some form of elder abuse, and approximately 38% reported seeing another resident being abused (Broyles, 2000). Broyles also reported that a staggering 95% of nursing home residents in the same study reported experiencing or witnessing others being neglected (for example, a resident with limited mobility is not cleaned in a timely manner after having a bowel movement).

Despite the widespread prevalence of apparent elder abuse in long-term care settings, older adult residents may be hesitant to report abuse for a number of reasons. For one, older adult residents of long-term care facilities are more likely than community-residing older adults to have physical and cognitive limitations that make them more dependent on others for care, and, thus, they may be fearful that reporting abuse will result in retaliation or other negative consequences (Hawes, 2003). Another reason is that older adults with cognitive impairments such as Alzheimers or other dementia may be unable to report or may be unaware of avenues for reporting. In the following section we discuss clinical issues relevant to screening for elder abuse among older adults with physical and cognitive impairments.

Screening in the Context of Physical and Cognitive Impairments

Approximately one in three adults over age 65 in the United States has a disability (National Center on Elder Abuse [NCEA], 2012). Such disabilities can make screening for and identifying elder abuse challenging for health-care providers, even more so than the same disability in younger adults, given decrements in hearing, reduced inability to sit for long periods, and other physical realities of aging. In the case of physical disabilities, for instance, the older adult victim of elder abuse may be confined to home or residence and not be provided with regular access to health care by caregivers, limiting their opportunity to report potential abuse. In both domestic and long-term care settings, identifying potential cases of elder abuse may be most challenging among older adults with cognitive limitations. Older adults with dementia may lack awareness of whether potentially abusive behavior is, in fact, abusive, and they are likely to be unaware of strategies for reporting unwanted, abusive behavior. Older adults with dementia may also have memory impairments and, therefore, not remember episodes of abuse, or may not be able to understand the abuse (e.g., financial), further complicating the assessment of mistreatment in this vulnerable population (Hansberry, Chen, & Gorbien, 2005).

Health-care providers working with these individuals should draw upon multiple levels of information to identify potential cases of abuse, especially considering that dementia and cognitive impairment place older adults at increased risk for future abuse. In one recent study involving a sample of community-residing, older adults with dementia and their caregivers, nearly half of older adults with dementia (47.3%) experienced elder abuse in the form of emotional abuse, physical abuse, or neglect (Wiglesworth et al., 2010). Ironically, researchers noted that one potential reason for these high rates of abuse is that adults with dementia may be more psychologically and physically aggressive toward caregivers. Because of such increased aggression, even well-intentioned caregivers may be more likely to employ strategies such as using restraints or handling an older adult more forcefully than is appropriate in an attempt to prevent themselves, the older adult, or others from being hurt. Thus, an important part of screening for elder abuse among older adults with dementia or other cognitive impairments is being sure to empathically and nonjudgmentally talk with the older adult's family and/or immediate caregivers about strategies used to care for the elderly person, as well as assessment of aggression by the elder.

In addition to talking with caregivers, clinicians may obtain useful information relevant to screening for elder abuse by reviewing the patient's medical history. In older adults with dementia, behavioral changes such as refusal of medications, social withdrawal, and changes in sleep and/or appetite may all be signs of possible mistreatment, and a review of medical records may reveal that these individuals have a history of multiple hospitalizations with irregular medical follow-up (Hansberry et al., 2005). In some cases, older adults with dementia may present to acute care settings, such as emergency rooms, for health problems directly related to episodes of elder abuse, and the most common injuries seen among physically abused elders presenting to emergency departments include bruises, lacerations, fractures, and head injuries (Clarke & Pierson, 1999; Jones, Dougherty, Schelble, & Cunningham, 1988). Clinicians must be mindful, though, that these injuries may also occur in the context of other medical conditions wholly unrelated to elder abuse, and noting the location and type of injury may help clinicians distinguish abusive from nonabusive injuries. Fall-related injuries among older adults with cognitive impairment, for instance, might include breast contusions and internal injuries such as upper limb dislocation (Ziminski, Phillips, & Woods, 2012). In contrast, older adults with injuries resulting from physical abuse may be more likely to present with head and neck injuries due to being choked, punched, or grabbed (Ziminski, Wiglesworth, Austin, Phillips, & Mosqueda, 2013). Unexplained sexually transmitted diseases are a clear red flag indicating elder sexual abuse, particularly when an older adult lacks the apparent mental and physical capacity to consent to sexual activity (Bond & Butler, 2013), and malnutrition, dehydration, and poor hygiene may also be part of the clinical presentation for older adult victims of serious neglect (Dyer, Connolly, & McFeeley, 2003). In sum, the detection of elder abuse among adults with physical and cognitive impairments is complicated by multiple factors, including the adult's level of access to clinical care and functional ability to actually report abuse, but skilled clinicians may still be able to identify and prevent potential episodes of abuse by drawing on multiple sources of information, including caregiver reports and medical history.

Caregiver versus Elder Self-Report

In the previous section, we discussed the importance of obtaining collateral information from caregivers when a cognitively impaired older adult is unable to report possible abuse, but obtaining such collateral information may be useful even when a victim of elder abuse is not cognitively impaired, with their permission of course. Indeed, albeit counterintuitive, several studies demonstrate that family and professional caregivers are in many cases willing to report their own abusive behaviors when directly asked about such behaviors. In fact, Pillemer and Suitor (1992) found that, when interviewed, approximately 6% of family members of dementia patients reported violence toward the patient. In a more recent study of staff working at Israeli long-term care facilities for older adults, over 50% of staff reported engaging in abusive acts over the past year, with the majority of staff admitting to elder neglect (Ben Natan, Matthews, & Lowenstein, 2010).

However, this is not to say that one should rely solely on family or professional caregivers for information about possible elder abuse. In long-term care facilities, for instance, professional caregivers may face immediate consequences, such as job loss and criminal prosecution, upon disclosing their own abusive behavior (Acierno, 2003) and thus be less likely to actually admit to abuse. For more than a decade (e.g., Acierno, Resnick, & Kilpatrick, 1997), clinicians have been encouraged to ask youth and younger adults themselves about potential abuse, and this recommendation extends to older adults as well. Providers should err on the side of inclusion when considering cognitive status in deciding whether or not to query. Moreover, adult women who experienced domestic abuse even tend to favor routine, patient-centered screening for interpersonal violence (e.g., Gielen et al., 2000; Titus, 1996), and, because elder abuse closely parallels intimate partner domestic abuse, one can conclude that older adult victims of elder abuse would generally be comfortable with direct screening questions. In the next section, we discuss some commonly used screening measures that can be easily adapted to multiple clinical settings to assist clinicians and health-care providers in the identification of elder abuse.

Assessment Tools

Several screening measures exist for use with both caregivers and older adults themselves and can serve as part of a comprehensive, multidimensional assessment of elder abuse. One brief measure designed to identify potentially abusive caregivers is the Caregiver Abuse Screen (CASE; Reis & Nahmiash, 1995)—an eight-item measure designed to be completed by caregivers. Evidence suggests that abusers

tend to score higher on the CASE than nonabusers, supporting its clinical utility in detecting probable cases of elder abuse. The Hwalek-Sengstock Elder Abuse Screening Test (H-S/EAST; Nelson, Nygren, McInerney, & Klein, 2004) is a 15-item measure designed to be completed by the older adult and includes questions that assess aspects of abuse including physical abuse, exploitation, and neglect. However, one potential drawback of the H-S/EAST is that some of the questions are not specific to abuse per se (e.g., feeling no one wants you around) and, as with any screening instrument, clinicians should follow up with more in-depth questioning if the screen is suggestive of probable abuse. Another more recent screening measure designed specifically for older adult respondents is the Elder Abuse Suspicion Index (EASI; Yaffe, Wolfson, Lithwick, & Weiss, 2008). Like the H-S/EAST, the EASI has been validated for use in community-residing older adults and minimizes respondent burden in that it consists of five items assessing each of the major categories of elder abuse (i.e., physical, emotional, and sexual abuse, financial exploitation, and neglect). The EASI also includes a sixth item completed by providers documenting any observable physical signs of abuse such as bruises, lacerations, and poor hygiene. Along different lines, epidemiological surveys, such as our National Elder Mistreatment Survey (Acierno et al., 2010), are specifically designed to elicit focused responses regarding the occurrence/non-occurrence of abusive events and have also been modified to assess abuse in clinical settings. An advantage of most epidemiological surveys is that the questions use specific behavior descriptions of abusive events that may help minimize differences in reporting across patients due to willingness to disclose, intellect, or cultural differences in definitions of abuse (Acierno, Resnick, Kilpatrick, & Stark-Riemer, 2003; Acierno et al., 2010).

Interventions and Reporting

Once clinicians or other health-care providers reasonably suspect that an older adult is a victim of mistreatment, responding with appropriate interventions requires sensitivity to the adult's immediate needs as well as consideration of broader social and environmental factors relevant to their independence, legal rights to self-determination, and long-term safety and care. Here, we discuss several acute interventions relevant to responding to elder abuse, drawing on lessons from the child abuse literature, and perhaps more relevant, domestic violence literature, to inform clinical intervention strategies.

Emergency Management and Care

An obvious first step in responding to an identified case of elder abuse is ensuring that an older adult receives appropriate medical care for any injuries sustained in the context of abuse. In the context of emergency departments, physicians or other providers will obviously conduct a full physical examination to look for possible signs of abusive injuries that require medical attention. Less obvious is the potential need for medical forensic photography of any suspicious injuries (such as lacerations, lesions, or bedsores) to be included in the patient's medical records or for potential police reports (Clarke & Pierson, 1999). If an older adult is presenting for medical care in the context of sexual abuse, as in cases of completed rape, a full forensic rape examination may be needed. This information is likely to be helpful in any law enforcement or social services investigations that may follow acute medical care. It is absolutely critical, though, that physicians and other health-care providers conducting physical and/or forensic examinations be sensitive and mindful of an older adult's rights to refusal (i.e., assuming capacity) before and throughout such an examination. One of the ultimate goals of intervening is to help foster older adults' sense of dignity and autonomy and, most importantly, their sense of control, which may have been taken from them by the perpetrator, and should not be taken again by providers.

Though physical injuries secondary to most elder mistreatment (i.e., emotional abuse) are rare, some outcomes of abuse will require hospital admission. Clarke and Pierson (1999) note that this may have secondary advantages in that admitting patients presenting with serious abuse-related medical problems also gives the health-care team time to mobilize social support resources who can help care for the older adult post-hospitalization while temporarily separating the older adult from the abuser or abusers. One final point noted by Clarke and Pierson is that hospital admission on the basis of a specific medical problem secondary to the abuse or neglect, such as dehydration, may make the inpatient stay more acceptable to patients and their families than admission on the basis of abuse.

Mandated Reporting

Once an older adult's physical needs are met in the form of proper medical care, providers must consider the issue of mandated reporting. All states and the District of Columbia have laws governing the reporting of suspected or confirmed elder abuse, and clinicians should be familiar with the laws governing mandated reporting in the jurisdiction in which they practice. Mandated reporters across jurisdictions typically include physicians, mental health professionals, home health providers, and others in the helping professions. Mandated reporting laws are derived from child abuse models of intervention in that, as previously discussed, some impaired older adults, like young children, lack the capacity to protect themselves from ongoing abuse. This is, of course, a minority of older adults and a smaller minority of community-residing older adults. Therefore, a key factor in many jurisdictions regarding mandated reporting is whether or not the older adult victim of elder abuse is "vulnerable" in the sense of having physical or cognitive impairments that may limit his or her ability to ensure that personal needs, including safety, are met. In other words, in many states, "age per se" is not sufficient to define "vulnerability," but rather decision-making capacity and physical status must be considered. Adults who lack ambulation, who have severe hearing or vision impairment, or who live in long-term care facilities are generally considered vulnerable by virtue of requiring more intensive, long-term support. Making determinations regarding an older adult's decision-making capacity, on the other hand, can be more difficult than determining vulnerability on the basis of physical impairments. Moreover, considerations regarding capacity will be made more conservatively when the decision at hand has significant consequences, such as that involving wills, legal residence, and health, compared with a decision that concerns selling a car or painting one's kitchen.

Part of the difficulty in determining an older adult's decision-making capacity is that such capacity relies on several cognitive and procedural abilities, depending on the capacity domain in question (Moye, Gurrera, Karel, Edelstein, & O'Connell, 2006; Moye & Marson, 2007). Sexual consent capacity, for example, is thought to involve primarily cognitive abilities, including knowledge of the sexual activities taking place and relevant information regarding the risks and benefits of such activities, an understanding of the options related to sexual activities, and voluntariness (American Bar Association & American Psychological Association, 2008). In contrast, financial management capacity involves both cognitive and procedural abilities. These abilities include declarative knowledge about financial concepts and events related to personal financial data, procedural knowledge about tasks such as counting money, and judgment about whether a given financial decision is in one's best interest (Moye & Marson, 2007). In the absence of such cognitive and/or procedural abilities, clinicians may determine that an older adult lacks the decision-making capacity to, say, engage in sexual activity or give financial control of his or her money to a relative or family member, making the adult vulnerable to harm or undue influence.

If an older adult is not vulnerable in the sense of having physical or cognitive impairments that limit his or her capacity for self-care, and if the perpetrator of abuse is an adult family member, then the adult-family-on-adult-family crime should be considered a form of domestic violence. Clinicians should discuss the possibility of involving community-based services to help reduce the risk of future violence but must also respect the older adult's wishes if they do not want the abuse reported to an outside agency. For example, a healthy, cognitively intact 66-year-old woman presenting with bruises inflicted by her physically violent 68-year-old husband may tell her provider that she does not want the abuse reported and she does not expect it to happen again, and, in such a case, reporting may, in fact, not be appropriate (depending on state law). Nevertheless, clinicians are strongly encouraged to consult with Adult Protective Services or other state or local agencies responsible for assisting adult victims of abuse if they are unsure whether or not a specific case is reportable. State specific resources for reporting abuse can be found on the NCEA website (http://www.ncea.aoa.gov/Stop_Abuse/Get_Help/State/index.aspx). When in doubt about reporting requirements and documentation requirements, ask.

Mandated reporting laws do not necessarily translate into higher rates of health-care provider reporting and, unfortunately, many cases of elder abuse are never reported. Researchers have offered several potential barriers to reporting elder abuse, which include unfamiliarity with mandated reporting laws, fear of offending patients or their families, or of hurting the provider–patient relationship (Kleinschmidt, 1997). Similarly, Rodriguez, Wallace, Woolf, and Mangione (2006) reported that many physicians were concerned that reporting abuse would adversely impact rapport with their patients or adversely affect the patient's quality of life by having the patient moved into an unwanted care environment. Thus, efforts to increase compliance with mandated reporting laws might include educating health-care professionals about how to talk with patients and their families about such laws

and even engaging patients and/or family members in the reporting process in order to maintain trust and rapport.

Involving Community-Based Services

Regardless of whether a confirmed case of elder abuse falls under the umbrella of the mandated reporting laws, providers and older adult victims of abuse can work together to decide whether the adult may benefit from involvement with community-based agencies that can help address any immediate and long-term needs. Because the great majority of elder mistreatment is perpetrated by family members (Acierno et al., 2010), the first step in deciding how to intervene with an elder abuse case is to determine if one should follow a domestic violence model (violence by an independent adult family member against an independent adult family member), or a child abuse model (violence by an independent adult family member against a dependent person) (see Figure 24.1) (Wolfe, 2003).

When a case involves an impaired older adult who is incapable of making an informed decision about his or her immediate care, mandated reporting laws generally stipulate that health-care providers report the abuse to Adult Protective Services. Consistent with child abuse models where abused children are removed from the custody of an abusive parent, Adult Protective Services may attempt to obtain judicial approval to place cognitively impaired older adults in emergency protective placements for up to 24 or 72 hours until a suitable, long-term living environment is obtained for the adult (NRC, 2003). Typically, though, such intensive interventions are considered a last resort, and Adult Protective Services also provides a number of other services when responding to elder abuse. One service increasingly used by Adult Protective Services modeled on Child Protective Services interventions is to place elder abusers on state registries that can be used by families and care facilities in an effort to keep potential abusers out of positions where they may hold power over a vulnerable older adult. Providers who are involved with Adult Protective Services in cases of elder abuse should speak with staff about whether such registries exist in their state.

Adult Protective Services may also assist with prosecuting abusers, even in cases where the older adult victim of abuse is not physically or cognitively impaired but consents to help with legal services. Law enforcement victim advocates may serve a similar function, helping older adults navigate the

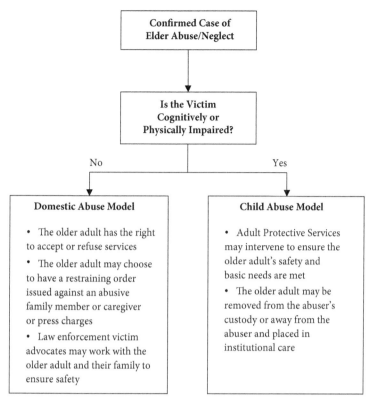

Fig. 24.1 Elder abuse in relation to domestic and child abuse models.

legal system. Strategies for providing legal recourse for older adult victims of elder abuse who are not "vulnerable" in the sense of having a serious physical or cognitive impairment tend to mirror domestic violence models for younger adults. For example, Adult Protective Services staff, victim advocates, or other senior legal service providers may help victims of elder abuse obtain restraining orders against abusers, complete the paperwork necessary to have property or money returned to a victim, and even file an order for removal of an abuser from the older adult's property (NCEA, 2006).

By contrast, in a majority of cases, the perpetrator and victim are independent, community-residing adults, and a domestic violence model of intervention should be adopted. In this case, empowerment of the victim in the form of mutual decision making with the provider will be key. As with abuse of vulnerable older adults described earlier, the primary intervention on the part of the provider will be information and referral, not violence intervention or prevention strategies. Consistent with domestic violence approaches, the first step is to identify immediate safety and the potential for additional mistreatment. If providers expect that the perpetrator will again engage in physically assaultive behavior,

they are mandated to report this to authorities in virtually all municipalities. If no explicit threat of harm is apparent, domestic violence referral options should be reviewed (e.g., shelter, counseling) and information regarding the likelihood of future violence (e.g., "the cycle of violence") should be offered to the patient. There is an extensive literature outlining health-care provider response to domestic violence for which Liebschutz and Rothman (2012) provide an excellent summary.

Summary

The US Preventive Services Task Force (2013) and the American Medical Association (2008) outline the benefits associated with screening for intimate partner violence and domestic violence by health-care providers, and they make specific recommendations that this screening take place in health-care settings. These recommendations should be extended to elders as well, given that elder mistreatment, also referred to as elder abuse, elder maltreatment, and elder domestic violence, affects approximately 10% of the US population over age 60 *each year*. Forms of abuse include emotional, physical, sexual, and financial abuse, and neglect. Emotional and psychological abuse are the most common types of elder mistreatment, although the extent of financial abuse and exploitation is somewhat difficult to gauge, and may be as frequent as emotional abuse. Often, perpetrators of abuse are relatives of the victim, usually an intimate partner, and hence the domestic violence model of abuse, as opposed to the child abuse model, is typically most appropriate for considering *community*-based elder mistreatment.

Screening and identification of elder mistreatment by health-care providers is very feasible, despite the shortened span of contemporary visits. Several standardized screening tools exist, from questionnaires that identify symptoms of abuse to assessments of explicit signs of physical mistreatment. Relatedly, several states have mandated protocols of reporting if abuse is detected, although there is by no means a nationwide standard with respect to this issue.

Overall, the central point of this chapter involves realization that the health-care provider is in a prime position to assess and intervene in cases of elder mistreatment, with intervention taking the form of providing information and referral. This chapter offers several suggestions regarding how these suggestions can be put into practice, starting with regular assessment of elder abuse events by health-care providers. Indeed, each health-care contact represents an opportunity to reach the elder abuse victims. However, the allocation of resources and time to make use of this opportunity is very likely contingent on the willingness of policymakers and clinic directors to accept the finding that older people are more frequently abused than we originally thought.

References

Abrams, R. C., Lachs, M., McAvay, G., Keohane, D. J., & Bruce, M. L. (2002). Predictors of self-neglect in community-dwelling elders. *American Journal of Psychiatry*, *159*, 1724–1730.

Acierno, R. (2003). Elder mistreatment: Epidemiological assessment methodology. In R. J. Bonnie & R. B. Wallace (Eds.), *Elder mistreatment: Abuse, neglect, and exploitation in an aging America* (pp. 261–302). Washington, DC: National Academies Press.

Acierno, R., Hernandez, M. A., Amstadter, A. B., Resnick, H. S., Steve, K., Muzzy, W., & Kilpatrick, D. G. (2010). Prevalence and correlates of emotional, physical, sexual, and financial abuse and potential neglect in the United States: The National Elder Mistreatment Study. *American Journal of Public Health*, *100*, 292–297.

Acierno, R., Resnick, H. S., & Kilpatrick, D. G. (1997). Health impact of interpersonal violence 1: Prevalence rates, case identification, and risk factors for sexual assault, physical assault, and domestic violence in men and women. *Behavioral Medicine*, *23*, 53–64.

Acierno, R., Resnick, H., Kilpatrick, D., & Stark-Reimer, W. (2003). Assessing elder victimization: Demonstration of a methodology. *Social Psychiatry and Psychiatric Epidemiology*, *38*, 644–653.

American Bar Association & American Psychological Association Assessment of Capacity in Older Adults Project Working Group. (2008). *Assessment of older adults with diminished capacity: A handbook for psychologists.* Retrieved from http://www.apa.org/pi/aging/programs/assessment/capacity-psychologist-handbook.pdf

American Medical Association (AMA). (2008). *Code of medical ethics: Opinion 2.02. Physicians' obligations in preventing, identifying, and treating violence and abuse.* Retrieved from http://www.ama-assn.org/ama/pub/physician-resources/medical-ethics/code-medical-ethics/opinion202.page?

Amstadter, A. B., Begle, A. M., Cisler, J. M., Hernandez, M. A., Muzzy, W., & Acierno, R. (2010). Prevalence and correlates of poor self-rated health in the United States: The National Elder Mistreatment Study. *American Journal of Geriatric Psychiatry*, *18*, 615–623.

Amstadter, A. B., Cisler, J. M., McCauley, J., Hernandez, M. A., Muzzy, W., & Acierno, R. (2010). Do incident and perpetrator characteristics of elder mistreatment differ by gender of the victim? Results from the National Elder Mistreatment Study. *Journal of Elder Abuse and Neglect*, *23*, 43–57.

Ben Natan, M., Matthews, P., & Lowenstein, A. (2010). Study of factors that affect abuse of older people in nursing homes. *Nursing Management*, *17*(8), 20–24.

Biggs, S., Manthorpe, J., Tinker, A., Doyle, M., & Erens, B. (2009). Mistreatment of older people in the United Kingdom: Findings from the first national prevalence study. *Journal of Elder Abuse and Neglect*, *21*, 1–14.

Bond, M. C., & Butler, K. H. (2013). Elder abuse and neglect: Definitions, epidemiology, and approaches to emergency department screening. *Clinics in Geriatric Medicine*, *29*, 257–273.

Broyles, K. (2000). *The silenced voice speaks out: A study of abuse and neglect of nursing home residents.* A report from the Atlanta Long Term Care Ombudsman Program and Atlanta Legal Aid Society to the National Citizens Coalition for Nursing Home Reform. Atlanta, GA: Author.

Cisler, J. M., Begle, A. M., Amstadter, A. B., & Acierno, R. (2012). Mistreatment and self-reported emotional symptoms: Results from the National Elder Mistreatment Study. *Journal of Elder Abuse & Neglect*, *24*, 216–230.

Clarke, M. E., & Pierson, W. (1999). Management of elder abuse in the emergency department. *Emergency Medicine Clinics of North America*, *17*, 631–644.

Dong, X. (2005). Medical implications of elder abuse and neglect. *Clinics in Geriatric Medicine*, *21*, 293–313.

Dong, X. Q., Beck, T., & Simon, M. (2010). The associations of gender, depression, and elder mistreatment in a community-dwelling Chinese population: The modifying effect of social support. *Archives of Gerontology and Geriatrics*, *50*, 202–208.

Dong, X. Q., Simon, M., Beck, T. T., Farran, C., McCann, J. J., Mendes de Leon, C.,... Evans, D. A. (2011). Elder abuse and mortality: The role of psychological and social wellbeing. *Gerontology*, *57*, 549–558.

Dong, X. Q., Simon, M., Mendes de Leon, C., Fulmer, T., Beck, T., Hebert, L.,... Evans, D. (2009). Elder self-neglect and abuse and mortality risk in a community-dwelling population. *Journal of the American Medical Association*, *302*(5), 517–526.

Dyer, C. B., Connolly, M. T., & McFeeley, P. (2003). The clinical and medical forensics of elder abuse and neglect. In R. J.

Bonnie & R. B. Wallace (Eds.), *Elder mistreatment: Abuse, neglect, and exploitation in an aging America* (pp. 339–381). Washington, DC: National Academies Press.

Dyer, C. B., Pavlik, V. N., Murphy, K. P., & Hyman, D. J. (2000). The high prevalence of depression and dementia in elder abuse or neglect. *Journal of the American Geriatrics Society, 48*, 205–208.

Gielen, A. C., O'Campo, P. J., Campbell, J. C., Schollenberger, J., Woods, A. B., Jones, A. S.,... Wynne, E. C. (2000). Women's opinions about domestic violence screening and mandatory reporting. *American Journal of Preventive Medicine, 19*, 279–285.

Hansberry, M. R., Chen, E., & Gorbien, M. J. (2005). Dementia and elder abuse. *Clinics in Geriatric Medicine, 21*, 315–332.

Hawes, C. (2003). Elder abuse in residential long-term care settings: What is known and what information is needed? In R. J. Bonnie & R. B. Wallace (Eds.), *Elder mistreatment: Abuse, neglect, and exploitation in an aging America* (pp. 446–500). Washington, DC: National Academies Press.

He, W., Sengupta, M., Velkoff, V. A., & DeBarros, K. A. (2005, December). *U.S. Census Bureau Current Population Reports: 65+ in the United States: 2005* (P23–209). Washington, DC: US Government Printing Office.

Jeary, K. (2005). Sexual abuse and sexual offending against elderly people: A focus on perpetrators and victims. *Journal of Forensic Psychiatry & Psychology, 16*, 328–343.

Jones, J., Dougherty, J., Schelble, D., & Cunningham, W. (1988). Emergency department protocol for the diagnosis and evaluation of geriatric abuse. *Annals of Emergency Medicine, 17*, 1006–1015.

Kleinschmidt, K. C. (1997). Elder abuse: A review. *Annals of Emergency Medicine, 30*, 463–472.

Lachs, M., Bachman, R., Williams, C., & O'Leary, M. (2007). Resident to resident elder mistreatment and police contact in nursing homes: Findings from a population-based cohort. *Journal of the American Geriatrics Society, 55*, 840–845.

Laumann, E. O., Leitsch, S. A., & Waite, L. J. (2008). Elder mistreatment in the United States: Prevalence estimates from a nationally representative study. *Journals of Gerontology: Series B, 63*, S248–S254.

Liebschutz, J., & Rothman, E. (2012). Intimate-partner violence: What physicians can do. *New England Journal of Medicine, 367*, 2071–2073.

Moye, J., Gurrera, R. J., Karel, M. J., Edelstein, B., & O'Connell, C. (2006). Empirical advances in the assessment of the capacity to consent to medical treatment: Clinical implications and research needs. *Clinical Psychology Review, 26*, 1054–1077.

Moye, J., & Marson, D. C. (2007). Assessment of decision-making capacity in older adults: An emerging area of practice and research. *Journal of Gerontology: Psychological Sciences, 62B*, 3–11.

Moyer, V. (2013). Screening for intimate partner violence and abuse of elderly and vulnerable adults: U.S. Preventive Services Task Force recommendation statement. *Annals of Internal Medicine, 158*, 478–486.

National Center on Elder Abuse (NCEA). (2006, March). *Domestic violence in later life: A guide to the aging network for domestic violence and victim service programs* (Issue Brief). Washington, DC: Author.

National Center on Elder Abuse (NCEA). (2012). *Abuse of adults with a disability* (Research Brief). Washington, DC: Author.

National Research Council (NRC). (2003). Evaluating interventions. In R. J. Bonnie & R. B. Wallace (Eds.), *Elder mistreatment: Abuse, neglect, and exploitation in an aging America* (pp. 121–139). Washington, DC: National Academies Press.

Nelson, H. D., Nygren, P., McInerney, Y., & Klein, J. (2004). Screening women and elderly adults for family and intimate partner violence: A review of the evidence for the U.S. Preventive Services Task Force. *Annals of Internal Medicine, 140*, 387–396.

Pillemer, K., & Finkelhor, D. (1988). The prevalence of elder abuse: A random sample survey. *Gerontologist, 28*, 51–57.

Pillemer, K., & Suitor, J. J. (1992). Violence and violent feelings: What causes them among family caregivers? *Journal of Gerontology, 47*, S165–S172.

Reay, A. M., & Browne, K. D. (2001). Risk factors for caregivers who physically abuse or neglect their elderly dependents. *Aging and Mental Health, 5*, 56–62.

Reis, M., & Nahmiash, D. (1995). Validation of the caregiver abuse screen (CASE). *Canadian Journal on Aging, 14*, 45–60.

Rodriguez, M. A., Wallace, S. P., Woolf, N. H., & Mangione, C. M. (2006). Mandatory reporting of elder abuse: Between a rock and a hard place. *Annals of Family Medicine, 4*, 403–409.

Rosen, T., Pillemer, K., & Lachs, M. (2008). Resident to resident aggression in long-term care facilities: An understudied problem. *Aggression and Violent Behavior, 13*, 77–87.

Titus, K. (1996). When physicians ask, women tell about domestic abuse and violence. *Journal of the American Medical Association, 275*, 1863–1865.

US Preventive Services Task Force. (2013). Final Recommendation Statement. *Intimate Partner Violence and Abuse of Elderly and Vulnerable Adults: Screening*. Retrieved from http://www.uspreventiveservicestaskforce.org/Page/Document/RecommendationStatementFinal/intimate-partner-violence-and-abuse-of-elderly-and-vulnerable-adults-screening#consider

Wiglesworth, A., Mosqueda, L., Mulnard, R., Liao, S., Gibbs, L., & Fitzgerald, W. (2010). Screening for abuse and neglect of people with dementia. *Journal of the American Geriatrics Society, 58*, 493–500.

Wolfe, D. A. (2003). Elder abuse intervention: Lessons from child abuse and domestic violence initiatives. In R. J. Bonnie & R. B. Wallace (Eds.), *Elder mistreatment: Abuse, neglect, and exploitation in an aging America* (pp. 501–525). Washington, DC: National Academies Press.

Yaffe, M. J., Weiss, D., Wolfson, D., & Lithwick, M. (2007). Detection and prevalence of abuse of older males: Perspectives from family practice. *Journal of Elderly Abuse and Neglect, 19*, 47–60.

Yaffe, M. J., Wolfson, C., Lithwick, M., & Weiss, D. (2008). Development and validation of a tool to improve physician identification of elder abuse: The Elder Abuse Suspicion Index (EASI). *Journal of Elder Abuse & Neglect, 20*, 276–300.

Ziminski, C. E., Phillips, L. R., & Woods, D. L. (2012). Raising the index of suspicion for elder abuse: Cognitive impairment, falls, and injury patterns in the emergency department. *Geriatric Nursing, 33*, 105–112.

Ziminski, C. E., Wiglesworth, A., Austin, R., Phillips, L. R., & Mosqueda, L. (2013). Injury patterns and causal mechanisms of bruising in physical elder abuse. *Journal of Forensic Nursing, 9*, 84–91.

Medical Illness, Suicide, and Assisted Death

Phillip M. Kleespies

Abstract

Because of their focus on psychopathology, mental health clinicians may overlook the potential significance of medical illness as a risk factor for suicide. In this chapter, the author presents evidence that physical illness, particularly certain physical illnesses, can be independent risk factors for suicide. In a number of these illnesses, depression is clearly a confounding risk factor, while in others the illness itself or its consequent functional impairments may lead to increased risk. When an individual has multiple physical illnesses, as often happens with the elderly, the cumulative burden can become overwhelming and heighten the risk of suicide. When physical illness becomes terminal, the competent patient has the right to refuse life-sustaining treatment. Whether that individual can receive assistance in dying has been more controversial. The chapter concludes with a presentation of data from a state where assisted suicide, also known as assisted death, has been legalized.

Key Words: suicide, suicide risk, suicide in medical illness, suicide in physical illness, suicide in terminal illness, burden of illness, assisted suicide, assisted death

It is practically axiomatic to state that there is a strong correlation between mental illness and the risk of suicide. Less attention, however, has been given to the fact that there may be an independent association between physical illness, particularly certain physical illnesses, and the risk of suicide (Druss & Pincus, 2000; Goodwin, Marusic, & Hoven, 2003; Harwood, Hawton, Hope, Harriss, & Jacoby, 2006; Ruzicka, Choi, & Sadkowsky, 2005).

In this chapter, I examine the existing data suggesting that medical or physical illness, and/or its effects, might be considered significant risk factors for suicide, independent of mental illness. I then discuss depression as a confounding risk factor for suicide in the medically ill. Next, I review particular medical illnesses and conditions from meta-analytic reviews and/or large register linkage studies that have been found to be associated with suicide. Finally, I discuss findings on the prevalence of suicide among individuals who are terminally ill, as well as data on assisted death (referred to by some as assisted

suicide) in states such as Oregon, Washington, and Vermont, where it has been legalized.

Mental Illness and Medical Illness as Risk Factors for Suicide

Psychological autopsy studies (or retrospective studies of those who have committed suicide) have consistently found that approximately 90% or more of suicide victims (as per the official reports of coroners) have had a mental or emotional disorder (see, for example, Bertolote & Fleischmann, 2002; Beskow, 1979; Chynoweth, Tonge, & Armstrong, 1980; Rich, Young, & Fowler, 1986). On the other hand, Whitlock (1986) and Mackenzie and Popkin (1990) cumulatively reviewed more than 25 psychological autopsy studies, most of which had included 100 suicides or more, and found, respectively, that 34% and 43% of the suicides had a medical illness at the time of death. Moreover, in a psychological autopsy study undertaken in five counties in England, looking at 100 suicides within an elderly population (60 years of age or greater), Harwood, Hawton, Hope, Harriss, and Jacoby (2006) found that physical health problems were present in 82% of the sample, and they were thought to be contributory to suicide in 62% of the cases.

Although it seems clear that mental illness is more prevalent than physical illness among suicides, there is nonetheless evidence that physical illness may be a risk factor for suicidal behavior and suicide. Druss and Pincus (2000), in a large probability survey with an adolescent and young adult population (ages 17–39), collected information about lifetime suicidal ideation and suicide attempts as well as data on general medical conditions, depression, and alcohol use. They found that medical and mental illness each contributed independently to risk of suicidality. Greater risk of suicidal ideation, and particularly of suicide attempts, was conferred when an individual had more than one medical illness.

Using data from a national comorbidity study of late adolescents and adults (ages 15–54), Goodwin, Marusic, and Hoven (2003) examined associations between a self-report checklist of medical illnesses and responses to a question about lifetime suicide attempts. They found significantly increased odds of a suicide attempt with physical illness, even after controlling for demographic characteristics and mental disorders. They also found a linear, dose-response association between the total number of physical illnesses and the likelihood of a suicide attempt. In addition, Ruzicka, Choi, and Sadkowsky (2005), following the introduction of multiple-cause-of-death coding in Australia, reviewed all completed suicides over 5 years (1997–2001) and compared them with deaths by accident during that same period. Their findings confirmed the significant relationship of suicide with mental health problems, but they also found that certain physical diseases (most notably HIV and cancer) were significantly associated with suicide. In general, mental disorders were more prevalent than physical illnesses among suicide victims under age 60, while physical illnesses were more prevalent than mental disorders among suicide victims age 60 and over.

Further, Waern et al. (2002) and Conwell et al. (2010) did case-control studies to examine the association of suicide with medical and psychiatric illness. In both studies, the authors examined samples of individuals who had committed suicide (n = 85 and n = 86, respectively) with matched living community samples. In the study by Waern et al. (2002), the data for the suicide group were gathered from

interviews with next-of-kin and by record review, while the data for the community sample were gathered directly by interview with control group participants. In the study by Conwell et al. (2010), the data for both groups were gathered from interviews with next-of-kin and by record review. The results in both studies supported previous findings of an association between psychiatric illness and suicide, and they both also found that physical illness was a significant, independent risk factor for suicide in the elderly. In the study by Conwell et al., it was also determined that the perception of deteriorating health and functional impairment were significant risk factors, with functional impairment being the more robust predictor of suicide.

Finally, Qin, Webb, Kapur, and Sorensen (2013) utilized a nested case-control design to study the association of hospitalization for physical illness, inpatient and outpatient treatment of psychiatric illness, and socioeconomic status in relation to suicide. They were able to use Danish national registers to detect 27,262 suicide cases during the period 1981–2006, and to select 468,007 live population controls from the national population of Denmark during that same time frame. Using conditional logistic regression to analyze the data, the investigators found that a history of physical illness significantly increased the risk of suicide and the effect was greater among women than men. They also noted a progressively increased risk of suicide associated with both the frequency of previous medical hospitalizations and the recency of the last hospitalization—the greater the number of hospitalizations or the more recent the last hospitalization, the higher the risk of suicide. When the data were adjusted for history of psychiatric illness, the associated risks were reduced to a certain extent, but the risk associated with physical illness remained highly elevated. They concluded that their robust findings supported a strong link between physical illness and risk of suicide in the general population. They also asserted that the progressive increase in suicide risk associated with frequency of hospitalization and multiple comorbidities indicated that the severity of physical illness was an important factor in the risk of subsequent suicide.

As Ruzicka et al. (2005) noted, the suicide risk associated with certain physical illnesses could well be mediated by secondary mood or affective symptoms; or, as suggested by Conwell et al. (2010), perceived health status or functional impairment might also mediate risk. In this regard, Kaplan, McFarland, Huguet, and Newsom (2007) reported on a study in which they examined physical illness and functional limitations as risk factors for suicide. They used data collected from a 1986 to 1994 National Health Interview Survey of 594,267 non-institutionalized people from 50 states and the District of Columbia and linked the data to the National Death Index. A Cox proportional hazard model showed that the respondents with functional limitations were at a higher risk for suicide relative to those without a functional limitation (HR = 2.78, 95% confidence interval [CI] = 1.42–5.43). The authors concluded that functional limitation appeared to be a much more powerful risk factor for suicide than physical illness. The findings suggest that clinicians should regard the burden of certain physical illnesses, or an accumulation of physical illnesses (possibly mediated by depression and/or functional limitation), as risk factors for suicide.

Depression as a Confounding Risk Factor for Suicide in People with Medical Illness

As noted earlier, many medical illnesses that have a heightened risk of suicide also have an associated heightened rate of depression. Webb et al. (2012) used the United Kingdom's General Practice Research Database (GRPD; which includes virtually every resident of the UK) to investigate how the risk of suicide varies among different types of physical illness and to what degree depression explains the elevated risk. The GRPD was linked to the national mortality registration systems. For a case control study, the investigators drew 873 adult suicide cases and 17,460 living controls from approximately 4.7 million patient records during the period from January 1, 2001 to December 31, 2008. The 11 major conditions that they examined were cancer, coronary heart disease, hypertension, stroke, diabetes, asthma, chronic obstructive pulmonary disease, osteoarthritis, osteoporosis, back pain, and epilepsy. They found that, for women, there was an elevated risk of suicide for cancer and coronary heart disease that was independent of depression while, for men, there was an elevated risk of suicide for osteoporosis that was independent of depression. The risk for suicide in the other diseases and conditions was confounded by or attributable to depression.

We see in this study by Webb et al. that there are some physical illnesses that seem to have an independent association with suicide, while there may be many others in which associated depression accounts for the suicide risk. There is a large body of evidence that demonstrates that depression is highly comorbid with specific medical illnesses (Cassem,

1995; Harrington, 2002; Iosifescu, 2007). As Harrington (2002) has noted, depression is second only to hypertension as the most common diagnosis in primary care populations. Depression and medical comorbidity have been associated with high utilization of medical services, unexplained symptoms, increased functional disability, diminished quality of life, and increased morbidity and mortality (Harrington, 2002; Iosifescu, 2007).

As I mentioned at the beginning of this chapter, the great majority of completed suicides suffer from a major psychiatric disorder (Clark & Fawcett, 1992). Moreover, depression is the mental disorder most frequently associated with suicide. Thus, an estimated 50% of suicides suffer from depression at the time of death (Pokorny, 1983; Rich, Young, & Fowler, 1986). If serious medical illness is frequently associated with depression, it seems highly probable that there is a heightened risk of suicide among those with comorbid depression and physical illness.

Medical staff, however, often fail to detect depression in the medically ill, or they view it as *appropriate* to the patient's condition (Berman & Pompili, 2011; Cassem, 1995; Harrington, 2002). Therefore, depression, an important risk factor for suicide, is frequently under-diagnosed and under-treated in the medically ill. Part of the problem may be that the diagnosis of depression in the medically ill is made difficult by the fact that the vegetative symptoms of depression (e.g., loss of appetite, decreased energy, loss of weight) may also be caused by the physical disease itself rather than by depression. Moreover, there is difficulty in distinguishing depression and demoralization (or the so-called *giving up* syndrome) in those with serious medical illness.

Just as the symptoms of depression can overlap with the symptoms of a particular medical disease, so too demoralization and depression can overlap, making the diagnosis of depression still more difficult. Nonetheless. given the current state of under-diagnosis and under-treatment of depression, Harrington (2002) has recommended having a relatively low threshold, or erring on the side of over-inclusion in the diagnosis and treatment of depression in the medically ill. His point is underscored when one considers the elevated risk of suicide in this population.

Specific Medical Illnesses Associated with Risk of Suicide

There are many medical illnesses and conditions. Most of them, as single diseases or injuries, appear to have little known risk of suicide (Berman & Pompili, 2011; Harris & Barraclough, 1994). As noted in Kleespies, Hough, and Romeo (2009), however, there are a few for which there is evidence of an associated risk of suicide. A number of these illnesses and conditions are considered neurological disorders (Arciniegas & Anderson, 2002).

Neurological Disorders

Many factors are thought to contribute to an increased risk of suicide in certain neurological disorders—associated depression, anxiety, cognitive impairment, pain, loss or decrease in function. In this section, I present the neurological disorders for which there is empirical evidence of a heightened risk of suicide. (For further information on neurobiological factors in suicide, see chapter 20 by Victoria Arango and Mark Underwood of this volume.)

Epilepsy. It has long been recognized that there is a high incidence of depression among epileptic patients (Baker, 2006; Schmitz, 2005), and clinical observation has suggested that there is an elevated risk of suicide. Blumer, Wakhlu, Davies, and Hermann (1998), for example, warned that severe interictal dysphoric disorders may be associated with sudden suicide attempts during episodes of intense depressive mood.

A meta-analytic review of 29 studies involving over 50,000 patients with epilepsy seems to have confirmed that the risk of suicide is indeed heightened (Pompili, Girardi, Ruberto, & Tatarelli, 2005; Pompili, Girardi, & Tatarelli, 2006). In this review, most of the 29 cohorts indicated that suicide in patients with epilepsy was more frequent (and in some studies many times more frequent) than suicide in the general population. Only three of the cohorts had lower suicide rates than the general population.

In a case control study by Nilsson, Ahlbom, Farahmand, Asberg, and Tomson (2002), onset of epilepsy at an early age was found to be strongly associated with an increased risk of suicide. The relative risk was 16 times greater for onset at age 18 or younger compared to onset after age 29, and early onset of epilepsy has been associated with depression and perceived stigma.

In a seemingly paradoxical finding, a meta-analytic review of 11 studies of suicide after surgical treatment (to reduce seizure frequency) revealed that suicide in surgically treated epileptic patients was more frequent than suicide in the general population (Pompili, Girardi, Tatarelli, Angeletti, & Tatarelli, 2006). In a study by Blumer et al. (2002), which looked at over 10,000 patients treated at an epilepsy center in Memphis, five suicides were found, and all of them had a history of early onset (mean age 9.5 years) of long-standing complex partial seizures with very high seizure frequency. All of them committed suicide within a range of 3 months to 3 years after they had obtained full control of seizures for the first time either by temporal lobectomy (n = 3), by medication (n = 1), or by vagus nerve stimulation (n = 1). All of them also had a history of interictal dysphoria or depression. Antidepressant medications have been found to be very effective in treating the depression of chronic epilepsy and their use has been recommended in conjunction with the surgical treatment of epilepsy (Blumer et al., 1998).

Traumatic brain injury. Studies have found a heightened risk of psychiatric disorders (e.g., major depression, panic disorder, obsessive-compulsive disorder, substance abuse), as well as an increased risk of suicidal ideation and suicide attempts, following a traumatic brain injury (Silver, Kramer, Greenwald, & Weissman, 2001; Simpson & Tate, 2005; Simpson & Tate, 2002). Although there were occasional patients in these samples who had a pre-injury suicide attempt, the vast majority of suicide attempts occurred post-injury. Moreover, in the study by Silver et al. (2001), the risk of suicide attempt remained elevated after adjusting for demographics and alcohol abuse.

Surprisingly, there has not been a great deal of research on completed suicide and traumatic brain injury (TBI), but there has been an excellent large register linkage study on this topic in Denmark. Teasdale and Engberg (2001b) selected patients on a national register of hospital admissions between 1979 and 1993 for three types of TBI: concussion (n = 126,114), cranial fracture (n = 7,560), and cerebral contusion or traumatic intracranial hemorrhage (n = 11,766). They then screened these patients in a national register of deaths for the same period. Standardized mortality ratios [SMR], stratified by sex and age, showed that the incidence of completed suicide was increased for all three groups relative to the general population (SMR = 3.0, 2.7, and 4.1, respectively). Further, regression analyses for proportional hazards showed a significantly greater risk of suicide among those with more serious brain injury, such as cerebral contusions or intracranial hemorrhages, relative to those with concussions or cranial fractures. Interestingly, there was also an increased rate of suicide among patients with only a concussion or with a cranial fracture with no known cerebral lesion.

The authors suggested that the greater suicide risk among the more serious cases might be attributed to concomitant risk factors, such as the development of psychiatric conditions or the physical, psychological, and social consequences of the injuries. The presence of a co-diagnosis of substance abuse was associated with increased suicide rates in all three diagnostic groups. Interestingly, the mortality rates were greater for females than for males, although the reverse is true in the general population.

Stroke. Studies in Denmark and Finland have suggested that there is an elevated risk of suicide in patients who suffer a stroke. Stenager, Madsen, Stenager, and Boldsen (1998) did a linkage study with stroke patients in a single county of Denmark. They found that SMRs were markedly increased for suicide, particularly among relatively younger patients (<60 years of age), and among women. Likewise, Bronnum-Hansen, Davidsen, and Thorvalsen (2001) studied causes of death after a first stroke in Copenhagen County during the years 1982–1991. Although the major cause of death was cardiovascular disease, there were other causes of death with elevated risk including suicide.

Teasdale and Engberg (2001a) attempted to replicate the findings of Stenager et al. (1998) using a full national cohort of stroke patients in Denmark. Their sample consisted of 114,098 patients identified in the computerized National Bureau of Health's Register of Hospitalization during the years 1979–1993. The overall annual incidence rate of suicide in the cohort was 83 out of 100,000 compared to an expected annual figure of 45 out of 100,000. Across all age groups, the SMR was 1.88 for men and 1.78 for women. SMRs were greatest (2.85) for patients under 50 years of age, and least (1.30) for patients 80 or older. Survival analysis suggested that suicide risk was greatest during the first 5 years after a stroke.

In a study by Forsstrom, Hakko, Nordstrom, Rasanen, and Mainio (2010) in the province of Oulu in northern Finland, researchers examined all suicides (N = 2283) that occurred during the years 1988–2007. They based the determination of death by suicide on death certificates from forensic medical-legal investigations. The diagnoses of the suicide victims were obtained from the Finnish Hospital Discharge Register. The investigators reported that 3.4% of the suicide victims (n = 75) had suffered from a stroke in their lifetime. Since depression is the most common psychiatric complication after a stroke, they also investigated whether the stroke victims in their sample had suffered from pre-stroke depression, post-stroke depression, or neither. They found that about 70% of the stroke victims with pre-stroke depression had committed suicide within a 2-year period after the stroke, while only 30% with no depression or post-stroke depression had done so within the same 2-year time frame. They concluded that a history of pre-stroke depression increased the risk of accelerated suicide among stroke victims, and they suggested that suicide risk be closely monitored with those exhibiting pre-stroke depression during the first 2 years following a stroke.

As Teasdale and Engberg (2001a) and Williams (2005) have pointed out, post-stroke depression is widely recognized. Forsstrom et al. (2010) caution clinicians to also attend to suicide risk when there is a history of pre-stroke depression. As with epilepsy and TBI, depression and other neuropsychiatric sequelae of stroke may be contributing to the heightened risk of suicide.

Multiple sclerosis. According to meta-analytic studies done 20 years ago (Harris & Barraclough, 1994; Stenager & Stenager, 1992), patients with multiple sclerosis (MS) appeared to have a suicide rate that was twice that of the general population. In a more recent systematic review of suicide risk in MS individuals, Pompili et al. (2012) found six studies that confirmed an increased risk of suicide in MS patients and one that did not. Evidence from this review suggested that the suicide risk in MS patients was greater in males and that male patients with onset of MS before age 30 were at the highest risk. They also reported evidence that the risk was particularly high in the first year following diagnosis.

Large record linkage studies in Denmark and Sweden have been consistent with the preceding findings. Bronnum-Hansen, Stenager, Stenager, and Koch-Henriksen (2005) linked the Danish Multiple Sclerosis Registry, consisting of more than 10,000 patients, with the Cause of Death Registry for the period from 1953 to 1996. They found the standardized mortality ratio for suicide indicated the risk for patients with MS was more than twice that for the general population (SMR = 2.12). The increased risk was particularly high in the first year after diagnosis (SMR = 3.15), and the risk remained elevated (relative to the general population) more than 20 years after diagnosis.

In a study by Fredrikson, Cheng, Jiang, and Wasserman (2003), the 12,284 cases of MS in the Swedish Hospital Inpatient Register during the period 1969–1996 were linked with the Swedish Cause of Death Register. Suicide risk for patients with MS was again found to be more than twice that of the general population (SMR = 2.3). As in the Danish study, risk was particularly high in the first year after diagnosis. In this study, however, a gender difference was noted—the elevation in risk seemed greatest in young males but, for females, the risk was greatest in middle age (ages 30–59).

Studies have repeatedly found high rates of depression in patients with MS with the lifetime prevalence estimated in the range of 40%–60% (Caine & Schwid, 2002; Goldman Consensus Group, 2005; Siegert & Abernathy, 2005; Wallin, Wilken, Turner, Williams, & Kane, 2006; Williams et al., 2005). A number of factors may be involved in the increased incidence of depression—for example, the negative psychosocial effects of MS disability, the direct effect of lesions on brain structures that regulate mood, and the immune system dysfunction found in MS. It has also been suspected that depression and suicidality might be a side effect of some of the disease-modifying treatments (e.g., interferon-B) that have been used in the past decade to delay the progression of MS. Studies to date, however, have not provided clear evidence to support such a conclusion (Feinstein, 2000; Goeb et al., 2006; Patten & Metz, 2002).

Depression is the mental and emotional disorder with the highest associated rate of suicide, and it frequently goes undetected in patients with MS (Caine & Schwid, 2002; Goldman Consensus Group, 2005). Practitioners need to be alert to depression and potential suicide risk in patients with MS, and they need to treat it adequately. It should also be noted, however, that not all suicides among individuals with MS occur in the context of a depressive episode or disorder. Other factors, such as decreased quality of life, decreased ability to participate in meaningful activity, and loss of self-determination and control, have also been implicated (Williams et al., 2005).

Huntington's disease. Huntington's disease (HD) is a disorder involving degeneration of nerve cells in the brain. There is progressive loss of mental function, including personality change, loss of cognitive ability, such as speech and judgment, and the development of neuropsychiatric symptoms (Paulsen, Ready, Hamilton, Mega, & Cummings, 2001). Abnormal facial and body movements are experienced, including rapid jerking movements. There is no known cure. As early as 1872, there was recognition of an association between mental illness

and an increased risk for suicide with a diagnosis of HD (Huntington, 1872).

More recently, suicidal ideation was investigated in 4,171 individuals in the Huntington Study Group database (Paulsen, Hoth, Nehl, & Stierman, 2005). Similar to previous research, the findings highlighted elevated rates of depressive symptoms in individuals with Huntington's disease. More than 40% of patients endorsed having current depressive symptoms and more than 10% had made a suicide attempt. These findings by Paulsen et al. (2005) and others (Robins Wahlin et al., 2000; Larsson, Luszcz, Bui, & Robins Wahlin, 2006) support the notion that there are two critical periods for increased risk of suicidal behavior in HD. The first critical period is just before receiving a formal diagnosis, and the second is in stage 2 of the disease, when independent functioning diminishes. Results showed that 19.8% of at-risk persons with soft neurological signs (i.e., non-specific motor abnormalities) had suicidal ideation while 23.5% of persons with possible HD (i.e., motor abnormalities that may be signs of HD but are not sufficient for a final diagnosis) had suicidal ideation. In persons who had been formally diagnosed with HD, 16.7% had suicidal ideation in stage 1, and 21.6% had suicidal ideation in stage 2 (Paulsen et al., 2005). The proportion of individuals with suicidal ideation diminished in stages 3, 4, and 5.

The occurrence of completed suicide in HD has been estimated to be four to five times that of the rate of the general population (Farrer, 1986). Di Maio et al. (1993) studied suicide risk in the families of 2,793 individuals who were registered with the National Huntington's Disease Roster. Suicide rates were much higher than in the general population, based on 205 (7.3%) identified suicide events. Sorensen and Fenger (1992) reviewed the etiology of death among 395 Danish people with HD and among 282 of their unaffected siblings. They compared the findings with the suicide rate in the general Danish population. Suicide accounted for 5.6% of deaths among the individuals with HD, and 5.3% of deaths among their unaffected siblings. Both occurrences of suicide were significantly higher than the general Danish population rate of 2.7%. Not only is HD potentially demoralizing in itself, but the frequent co-occurrence of depression and other symptoms of mental disorder seem to heighten the risk of suicidal behavior and suicide.

A few studies have identified factors associated with increased risk of suicide in HD. A retrospective case-controlled study of instances of suicide in

HD revealed that among a variety of clinical and social variables, the most important risk factor was having no children, with an odds ratio of 13.6 (Lipe, Schultz, & Bird, 1993). In a study by Almqvist, Bloch, Brinkman, Craufurd, and Hayden (1999), both employment status and psychiatric history within the 5 years leading up to testing were significantly related to the frequency of an adverse event following predictive testing for HD; and age, gender, and marital status did not influence the likelihood of an event. Further, in a recent prospective study of patients with prodromal HD, Fiedorowicz, Mills, Ruggle, Langbehn, and Paulsen (2011) found that a history of suicide attempts and the presence of depression were strongly predictive of suicidal behavior in these patients as compared with a control group.

Spinal cord injury/disorder. People with spinal cord injury/disorder (SCI/D) are more vulnerable to certain life-threatening illnesses such as pneumonia, septicemia, cutaneous and bladder cancer, pulmonary emboli, and stroke. According to mortality studies of people with SCI in Japan and Australia (Imai, Kadowaki, & Aizawa, 2004; Soden et al., 2000), over the past two decades there has been a reduction in deaths due to these life-threatening illnesses. The result has apparently been an increased life expectancy that approaches 70% of normal for those with complete quadriplegia and 86% of normal for those with complete paraplegia.

There are some differences in the literature, however, in regard to the death rate by suicide among patients with SCI. In the relatively small Australian study by Soden et al. (2000), researchers found an SMR of 2.5 for suicide before 1980 and an SMR of 8.7 since then. This led to the suggestion that as the overall duration of survival had increased for SCI patients, the likelihood of suicide had also increased. Yet, in a larger study in the United States, Cao, Massaro, Krause, Chen, and Devivo (2014) linked the National Spinal Cord Injury Statistical Center database across three time periods (1973–1979, 1980–1989, and 1990–1999) to the National Death Index and the Social Security Death Index. Within the 31,339 SCI participants, 5,167 were found to be deceased at the end of the follow-up period and 198 of those had died by suicide. After controlling for age, sex, and race, they compared the SCI suicide rate to the suicide rate in the US general population and found the SMR for suicide to be 5.24 for the 1973–1979 SCI cohort, 3.65 for the 1980–1989 group, and 2.98 for 1990–1999. They interpreted these findings as indicating that there was a declining rate of suicide among individuals with SCI across this nearly 30-year period in the United States. Despite this decline, the authors pointed out that, in comparison to the general US population, all three SCI cohorts had higher rates of mortality due to suicide. They also identified three risk factors for suicide among individuals with SCI: (1) being non-Hispanic white; (2) being in the first 6 years of having an SCI; and (3) having thoracic 1 (T1) to sacral 3 (S3) injury levels with American Spinal Injury Association Impairment Scale ratings of A, B, or C.

Harris and Barraclough (1994) and Stenager and Stenager (1992) have pointed out that a heightened rate of mood disorders and substance abuse disorders in the SCI population may, in part, account for the heightened risk of suicide. Thus, alcohol or drug intoxication is often involved in the accidents that result in spinal cord injuries, and suicide attempts by those who are depressed and/or abusing substances are, at times, the cause of SCI. Estimates of the proportion of spinal cord injuries that result from suicide attempts have been modest—in the range of 1.5%–6.8% (Harris, Barraclough, Grundy, Bamford, & Inskip, 1996; Kennedy, Rogers, Speer, & Frankel, 1999; Pickett, Simpson, Walker, & Brison, 2003; Stanford, Soden, Bartrop, Mikk, & Taylor, 2007)—while Charlifue and Gerhart (1991) found that approximately 7% of patients with SCI who actually committed suicide had sustained their SCI in a prior suicide attempt.

Findings about a relationship between functional levels of impairment (e.g., complete quadriplegia, incomplete quadriplegia, complete paraplegia, and so on) and suicide risk have been inconsistent (see e.g., Hagen, Lie, Rekand, Gilhus, & Gronning, 2010; Hartkopp, Bronnum-Hansen, Seidenschnur, & Biering-Sorensen, 1998; Lidal et al., 2007; Soden et al., 2000). Suicide risk among SCI patients in general, however, appears to be greatest in the first 4–6 years after the injury (Cao et al., 2014; Charlifue & Gerhart, 1991; DeVivo, Black, Richards, & Sover, 1991). Thus, in a study of 5,200 individuals with SCI covering a 30-year period, Charlifue and Gerhart found that, of those who died by suicide, 50% did so within 3 years of onset of SCI and 76% within 4 years. These investigators also found several factors that distinguished individuals with SCI who committed suicide from matched non-suicidal people with SCI; these included (1) post-injury despondency, (2) experiences of shame, apathy, and helplessness, and (3) pre-injury family fragmentation.

Cancer

Large cohort studies that linked national cancer and death registries (totaling nearly 0.5 million to more than one million patients) have examined suicide risk in cancer patients. These studies, performed in Norway (Hem, Loge, Haldorsen, & Ekeberg, 2004), Sweden (Björkenstam, Edberg, Ayoubi, & Rosén, 2005), and Denmark (Yousaf, Christensen, Engholm, & Storm, 2005), found an elevated risk of suicide, similar to that reported by Harris and Barraclough (1994)—from 1.55 to 2.5 times greater than expected for males and from 1.35 to 2.9 for females. A multiple decade cohort study of one Japanese hospital also found similar results, despite a smaller sample size, with an overall increased suicide risk that was 1.8 times greater than expected at 5 years after cancer diagnosis (Tanaka et al., 1999).

In one of the first, if not the first, large cohort study in the United States comparing suicide rates of patients with cancer to the suicide rate of the general population, it was found that the incidence of suicide among more than 3.5 million patients diagnosed with cancer between 1973 and 2002 was nearly twice that of the general population (SMR = 1.88) (Misono, Weiss, Fann, Redman, & Yueh, 2008). As with the gender differences in the general population, the frequency of completed suicides for these female cancer patients was one-fifth that of the males, with a hazard ratio of 6.2 for male suicide relative to female suicide (Kendal, 2007).

Research has also pointed to an association between cancer-related suicide and age at diagnosis. In a case-control study of suicide risk associated with medical illness among New Jersey residents age 65 and older, cancer was the only medical condition that remained associated with suicide in adjusted analyses that accounted for psychiatric illness and the risk of dying within a year (Miller, Mogun, Azrael, Hempstead, & Solomon, 2008). In addition, Misono et al. (2008) documented higher rates of suicide with increasing age at cancer diagnosis among men. An examination of suicide rates by age at cancer diagnosis revealed that the highest SMR of 2.51 occurred for male and female patients in the uppermost age bracket of 85 years and older.

Three of the studies mentioned earlier reported that the increased risk of suicide was greatest within the first year of cancer diagnosis. Hem et al. (2004) noted an SMR of 3.09 for males and 2.18 for females within 5 months of diagnosis. The rate then dropped to 2.4 and 1.68, respectively,

at 11 months post-diagnosis. Yousaf et al. (2005) found the increased risk for males was greatest within 3 months of diagnosis while for females it was at 3–12 months. Tanaka et al. (1999) found the greatest risk of suicide at 3–5 months following diagnosis. In the United States, Misono et al. (2008) reported the risk of suicide among patients with cancer greatest in the first 5 years after diagnosis. Although the risk declined after this, Misono and colleagues cautioned that it remained elevated compared with the general population for 15 years after diagnosis.

A number of studies have suggested that there is an elevated suicide risk associated with particular cancer sites, but these findings have been inconsistent. Harris and Barraclough (1994), for example, reported that suicides in individuals with head and neck cancers were nine times higher than expected in the general population and about four times higher than that of persons with other cancer diagnoses. More recent studies, however, have not offered strong confirmation of that finding, but have determined other sites to have an elevated risk of suicide. Hem et al. (2004) reported that the male relative risk of suicide was highest in cancer of the respiratory organs defined as the bronchus, trachea, and lung, with an SMR of 4.08, while Björkenstam et al. (2005) found the greatest rates in pancreatic cancer, followed by cancer of the esophagus, cancer of the lung, and cancer of the biliary passages and liver.

A more fruitful approach seems to be one in which there is an investigation of a possible association between suicide risk and prognosis and/or cancer stage at diagnosis. In a study by Dormer, McCaul, and Kristjanson (2008), specific types of cancer were grouped according to prognosis (5-year relative survival rates), and a very high SMR of 12.07 occurred for the poor prognosis group in the first 3 months after diagnosis. Similarly, Robinson, Renshaw, Okello, Moller, and Davies (2009) found that cancers with high fatality carried a higher risk of suicide in both men (SMR = 2.67) and women (SMR = 2.17) compared to those with low fatality. Several studies found suicide risk related to cancer stage at diagnosis. Rates of suicide have been noted to be higher for patients in the United States with advanced disease at diagnosis (Misono et al., 2008). For example, data indicate that risk of suicide is elevated for metastatic disease at diagnosis (Kendal, 2007), particularly for prostate cancer (Fang et al., 2010). Kendal (2007) also found that cancer-directed surgery that could not be carried out (for head and neck cancers), high-grade tumors, and treatment contraindications all were associated with elevated suicide risk. Examining suicide rates across various types of cancer, Robinson et al. (2009) reported a strong effect of advanced stage of disease in women.

These findings suggest that varying rates of suicide across cancer sites may be explained, at least in part, by variation in associated survival rates. It is notable that even when the likelihood of survival is high, cancer is still associated with increased suicide risk relative to the general population (Christensen, Yousaf, Engholm, & Storm, 2006).

HIV/AIDS

When the HIV/AIDS epidemic was at its peak and there was no effective treatment, a diagnosis of HIV/AIDS was clearly associated with a heightened risk of suicide. In the often cited review of studies from 1966–1992, Harris and Barraclough (1994) estimated that the relative risk of suicide for men with HIV was seven times higher than the rate for men in the general population. By 1996, however, improved treatments, such as the highly active antiretroviral therapy (HAART) were introduced, raising the question of whether a more hopeful outlook for survival would lead to a decrease in the suicide rate among those with HIV/AIDS.

At least two studies initially suggested otherwise. In a study by Krentz, Kliewer, and Gill (2005) in southern Alberta, Canada, that linked patients with HIV/AIDS to cause-of-death data for the 20-year period of 1984–2003, deaths from AIDS-related causes decreased significantly, but deaths from non-AIDS-related causes, including suicide and drug overdose, increased across this time span. In a similar fashion, Lu et al. (2006) linked national HIV/AIDS registry data in Taiwan with cause of death and health insurance claims data for the period from 1994 to 2002. They also found that deaths from AIDS-related causes had decreased, but deaths from suicide had increased threefold during that time. Their conclusion was that as the duration of survival for patients with HIV/AIDS increased, the likelihood of suicide also increased. It was hypothesized that the prospect of lifelong HAART treatment with its discomforting side effects (including mood disorder) might lead patients to feel that longer life did not necessarily lead to better quality of life.

Recent studies, however, have been more consistent with the hypothesis that, with the introduction of HAART and increased life expectancy, the suicide rate has decreased for HIV/AIDS patients. Keiser et al. (2010) studied time trends and predictors of suicide in the pre-HAART era (1988–1995) and in the HAART era (1996–2008) in Switzerland. They linked patients from a national HIV cohort study of 15,275 individuals to a national mortality database and then calculated standardized mortality ratios that compare suicide in HIV-infected patients with suicide in the general population. In men, SMRs declined from 13.7 (95% CI = 11.0–17.0) in the pre-HAART era to 3.5 (95% CI = 2.5–4.8) in the HAART era; there was a similar decline with women, from 11.6 (95% CI = 6.4–20.9) to 5.7 (95% CI = 3.2–10.3).

Further, Rice, Smith, and Delpech (2010) investigated suicide among adults diagnosed with HIV in England, Wales, and Northern Ireland, from the beginning of the HAART era (1997) until well into it (2008). They examined causes of death as reported directly to the national HIV and AIDS new-diagnosis database, as well as in the annual census of people accessing HIV-related care. In addition to suicidal deaths, they included possible suicides (e.g., drug overdoses, carbon monoxide poisoning). As a result, they cautioned that their estimates of possible suicides may overestimate true suicides. Nonetheless, they found that the rate of possible suicides among adults accessing HIV-related services had decreased from 137.7 per 100,000 persons in 1997 to 31.6 per 100,000 in 2008, a seemingly clear decrease in suicides across the HAART era of treatment.

In a US study, Rockett, Wang, Lian, and Stack (2007) utilized the national Multiple Cause of Death files that contained information on both mental and physical health problems among those who had died by suicide in the years 1999–2003. The investigators had a comparison group of decedents whose underlying cause of death was unintentional injury. Unconditional logistic regression analyses revealed that three categories of comorbid psychopathology and one category of physical disease showed excess likelihood of being recorded on death certificates for suicides relative to death certificates for unintentional injuries. They were depression/mood disorders, schizophrenia, a residual nonorganic mental health category, and cancer. Given that, as mentioned earlier, HIV/AIDS had been found in the meta-analytic review by Harris and Barraclough (1994) to be clearly associated with an elevated rate of suicide, the authors commented on how it no longer seemed to have such an association. They felt that a plausible explanation of the difference was that, in the intervening years, the effective use of HAART had altered the mindset of those who tested positive for HIV.

Despite the fact that the studies cited in this section suggest that suicide risk, since the introduction of HAART, has decreased for patients with HIV/AIDS, Carrico (2010) has reminded us that the suicide rate among HIV positive persons remains significantly elevated relative to the general population. Clinicians need to continue to be cautious about the risk of suicide in this population.

End-Stage Renal Disease

According to Fabrazzo and De Santo (2006), depression is the most frequent psychiatric problem in patients with chronic renal disease. They link depression in end-stage renal disease (ESRD) patients to the many stressors that accompany the disease and its treatment. With renal dialysis, patients become dependent on the dialysis machine and the dialysis staff for life-sustaining treatment. They can become fearful of dying. The need to be dialyzed several times a week can lead to time constraints and functional limitations which, in turn, can lead to loss of employment, loss of income, and possibly a diminished role in the family. Sexual dysfunction in dialysis patients is not uncommon. The routine of being dialyzed may become tedious. Continuous ambulatory peritoneal dialysis, which can be performed at home, may reduce feelings of dependency, but it is not necessarily easy. The patient must observe a scrupulous antiseptic technique to avoid infections. Regardless of the dialysis technique, the patient needs to adhere to a low-phosphate, low-potassium, low-sodium, and restricted fluid intake diet. As noted by Levy (2000), these stressors can make the patient vulnerable to demoralization and/or depression. Such conditions can also be a breeding ground for suicidal thoughts and behavior.

In the past, ESRD patients were thought to have a very elevated rate of suicide. Bostwick and Cohen (2009), however, have contended that, by present-day standards, the past estimates of the suicide rate for ESRD patients may have been somewhat inflated. They base their argument on the fact that ethical thought about the rights of patients to refuse life-sustaining medical treatment (LSMT) has shifted markedly in the past 35–40 years in the direction of respecting the autonomous choices of the patient. They point out that in the past, the US health-care system was more paternalistic and likely to view an ESRD patient's refusal of, or request to discontinue, renal dialysis as a suicidal act. Current medical ethics (e.g., Beauchamp and Childress, 2008), however, views the competent patient as having the right to refuse any LSMT, renal dialysis included, should they find it invasive and not in keeping with their wish to have personal control of what happens with their body. Death under these circumstances is not considered suicide.

Nonetheless, there appears to be a moderately elevated rate of suicide among ESRD patients in the United States. In a large register linkage study (Kurella, Kimmel, Young, & Chertow, 2005), 465,563 patients who initiated dialysis between 1995 and 2000 and who were registered in the United States Renal Data System (USRDS) were linked to the ESRD Death Notification Form register. The ESRD Death Notification Form makes a distinction between those who decide to withdraw from dialysis before death and those who commit suicide. Having made this distinction, the investigators nonetheless found a suicide incidence ratio of 1.84, indicating that the ESRD patients had a suicide rate that was 84% higher than the rate for the general population, even after accounting for demographic differences.

The rates of suicide among renal dialysis patients in the study by Kurella et al. (2005) tended to increase with age, with those 60 and over having the highest rates. There appears to be a somewhat different picture, however, with renal disease patients who received a kidney transplant. Ojo et al. (2000) took a sample of 86,502 kidney transplant patients who were registered with the United Network for Organ Sharing or with USRDS between 1988 and 1997 and linked them with cause-of-death information from a transplant recipient follow-up form and the ESRD Death Notification Form. They found an elevated rate of suicide for transplant patients (15.7 per 100,000 persons a year) relative to the general population rate (9 per 100,000 persons a year). Interestingly, 35% of the suicides occurred in the first 12 months after the transplant, and 16 months was the median time from transplantation to suicide. The mean age of the sample was 39 years, suggesting a higher risk of suicide at a younger age for transplant patients relative to the dialysis patients in the Kurella et al. study. The reasons for this apparent age difference are as yet undetermined.

Suicide and Assisted Death in Terminal Illness

Among medical illnesses, one might think that those illnesses that are in a terminal phase would be most likely to engender despair and hopelessness and, therefore, lead frequently to suicide. To the contrary, major psychological autopsy studies have suggested that a rather small percentage of suicide victims (approximately 2%–3%) had a terminal illness at the time of death (Clark & Horton-Deutsch, 1992). Some would argue that this estimate is low given that suicides among the terminally ill may be reported to the coroner as deaths caused by their physical illness (Quill, 1991). Jamison (1996), in fact, reported that he did an investigation of assisted suicides and found that the great majority of them (125 of 140) were recorded as deaths due to natural causes. Be this as it may, it seems unlikely that a large percentage of suicides have a terminal illness. As Joiner, Van Orden, Witte, & Rudd (2009) have noted, there is a basic instinct for self-preservation, and we naturally fight against annihilation, often even when hopelessly ill and clearly dying. That is partly why suicide is a low base rate event and often accompanied by great ambivalence.

As discussed in the previous section on end-stage renal disease, present-day medical ethics in the United States supports the right of the competent terminally ill patient to refuse life-sustaining treatment, opt for comfort care only, and let the disease run its course. More controversial, however, is the practice of assisted suicide or assisted death in which a physician assists a competent, terminally ill patient in dying (if requested voluntarily) by providing a prescription for medication to be used with the primary intention of ending his or her own life.[1] A patient is considered terminally ill if he or she has an incurable condition with unacceptable suffering, and his or her condition is expected to cause death in the next 6 months. Physician-assisted death is currently legal in four states—Oregon, Washington, and Vermont through legislation, and in Montana by a court decision. It is also legal in one county of New Mexico through a court decision.

Perhaps the most reliable information on assisted death or assisted suicide with the terminally ill can be found in the data kept by the state of Oregon, the first state to approve physician-assisted death.[2] The Oregon Death with Dignity Act (ODDA) has been in effect since 1998 (Oregon Health Authority—Public Health Division, 2014). There were 752 individuals who used the law to hasten death through 2013. Of those, 97.3% were white, 1.1% were Asian American, 0.7% were Hispanic American, and 0.1% were African American. A few more men (52.7%) than women (47.3%) used the Act. The median age was 71 with an age range of 25–96. Fifty-six percent were in the age range of 65–84. Of those who used the ODDA, 46.2% were married, 22.6% divorced, 22.8% widowed, and 8.4% never married. Those who exercised their right under the law tended to be more highly educated (45.6% had baccalaureate degrees or higher).

Participants have been most likely to have cancer (78.9%), and cancer of the lung and of the bronchus were the most frequent locations (18.6% of those with cancer). Another 7.6% of the cancer patients had breast cancer and 6.5% pancreatic cancer. Amyotrophic lateral sclerosis (ALS) was the diagnosis in 7.2% of participants, 4.5% had chronic lower respiratory disease, 1.9% had heart disease, and 1.2% HIV/AIDS. Ninety-five percent of the patients died at home with 90.1% of them enrolled in hospice. Only 1.7% did not have health insurance. The median duration of their patient-physician relationship was 12 weeks.

The most frequently mentioned end-of-life concerns were loss of autonomy (91.4%), decreasing ability to participate in activities that made life enjoyable (88.9%), loss of dignity (80.9%), and loss of the control of bodily functions (50.3%). Only 23.7% mentioned inadequate pain control or concern about that. Under the ODDA, if the patient's judgment is considered impaired by a psychiatric or psychological disorder, the patient must be referred for a psychological examination. Only 5.9% of patients were referred for a psychiatric or psychological evaluation.

The report of the Oregon Department of Human Services on the ODDA has not been without its critics. Foley and Hendin (1999) contended that since the ODDA does not require a psychiatric evaluation for all those who requested assisted death, the report could not have accurate information about the degree to which depression might have impaired the judgment of those making requests. They also argued that the report is based solely on information obtained from physicians and provided no data on how thoroughly physicians assessed the reasons for patients' requests.

The arguments for and against assisted death for the competent, terminally ill patient who requests it have been discussed at length by Kleespies (2004), by Rosenfeld (2004), and by Werth and Wineberg (2005) among others. It is beyond the scope of this chapter to repeat them here. One concern of the opponents to assisted death, however, has not been supported by the Oregon data. It has been argued that the legitimization of assisted death will put us on a *slippery slope* where it will be too easy for the less scrupulous to coerce vulnerable people who are lacking in resources to accept it. The Oregon data suggest that those who have sought assisted death have not been particularly vulnerable, but have actually been people who are relatively well educated and who have had health insurance and hospice services.

Concluding Remarks

In assessing for suicide risk, the mental health clinician must take into account, among many other factors, the presence of mental illness, particularly depression, bipolar disorder, schizophrenia, and alcohol use disorder. There is increasing evidence, however, that certain physical illnesses, the functional impairments that they engender, and/or the prospect of deteriorating physical health are also risk factors for suicide that the clinician is well advised to consider in arriving at an estimate of risk. Untreatable illnesses such as HIV/AIDS (before the introduction of HAART) and incurable conditions like Huntington's Disease have been known to entail great suffering with little hope of survival. Such circumstances can easily lead to despair and suicidality. Especially in the elderly, coping with multiple physical illnesses and conditions can affect the quality of life and become a burden that is hard to bear.

It is of interest that the most frequent end-of-life concerns of the terminally ill who made use of the ODDA were loss of autonomy, a decreasing ability to participate in activities that made life enjoyable, loss of dignity, and loss of the control of bodily functions. I suspect that many of these concerns are shared by those who have diseases such as multiple sclerosis and end-stage renal disease who become suicidal. A focus on finding ways to diminish these concerns may go a long way toward increasing meaning, instilling hope, improving quality of life, and decreasing the risk of suicide in those for whom physical illness is a risk factor.

Notes

1. In general, those who are opposed to physician assistance in hastening death in the terminally ill refer to this type of death as "assisted suicide," while those who support it do not consider it suicide and use the term "assisted death."
2. Data on those who have used the Washington Death with Dignity Act can be obtained at http://www.doh.wa.gov/DataandStatisticalReports/VitalStatisticsData/DeathwithDignityData and information about the recently enacted Vermont Death with Dignity Act can be found at http://www.deathwithdignity.org/in-vermont.

References

Almqvist, E. W., Bloch, M., Brinkman, R., Craufurd, D., & Hayden, M. R. (1999). A worldwide assessment of the frequency of suicide, suicide attempts, or psychiatric hospitalization after predictive testing for Huntington disease. *American Journal of Human Genetics, 64,* 1293–1304.

Arciniegas, D., & Anderson, C. (2002). Suicide in neurologic illness. *Current Treatment Options in Neurology, 4,* 457–468.

Baker, G. (2006). Depression and suicide in adolescents with epilepsy. *Neurology, 66* (Suppl 3), S5–S12.

Beauchamp, T., & Childress, J. (2008). *Principles of biomedical ethics (6th ed.).* New York, NY: Oxford University Press.

Berman, A., & Pompili, M. (2011). Introduction. In A. Berman & M. Pompili (Eds.), *Medical conditions associated with suicide risk.* Washington, DC: American Association of Suicidology.

Bertolote, J., & Fleischmann, A. (2002). Suicide and psychiatric diagnosis: A worldwide perspective. *World Psychiatry, 1,* 181–185.

Beskow, J. (1979). Suicide and mental disorder in Swedish men. *Acta Psychiatrica Scandinavica, 277* (Suppl.), 1–138.

Björkenstam, C., Edberg, A., Ayoubi, S., & Rosén, M. (2005). Are cancer patients at higher suicide risk than the general population? *Scandanavian Journal of Public Health, 33,* 208–214.

Blumer, D., Montouris, G., Davies, K., Wyler, A., Phillips, B., & Hermann, B. (2002). Suicide in epilepsy: Psychopathology, pathogenesis, and prevention. *Epilepsy and Behavior, 3,* 232–241.

Blumer, D., Wakhlu, S., Davies, K., & Hermann, B. (1998). Psychiatric outcome of temporal lobectomy for epilepsy: Incidence and treatment of psychiatric complications. *Epilepsia, 39,* 478–486.

Bostwick, J., & Cohen, L. (2009). Differentiating suicide from life-ending acts and end-of-life decisions: A model based on chronic kidney disease and dialysis. *Psychosomatics, 50,* 1–7.

Bronnum-Hansen, H., Davidsen, M., & Thorvaldsen, P. (2001). Long-term survival and causes of death after stroke. *Stroke, 32,* 2131–2136.

Bronnum-Hansen, H., Stenager, E., Stenager, E. N., & Koch-Henriksen, N. (2005). Suicide among Danes with multiple sclerosis. *Journal of Neurology, Neurosurgery, and Psychiatry, 76,* 1457–1459.

Caine, E., & Schwid, S. (2002). Multiple sclerosis, depression, and the risk of suicide. *Neurology, 59,* 662–663.

Cao, Y., Massaro, J., Krause, J., Chen, Y., & Devivo, M. (2014). Suicide mortality after spinal cord injury in the United States: Injury cohorts analysis. *Archives of Physical Medicine and Rehabilitation, 95,* 230–235.

Carrico, A. (2010). Elevated suicide rate among HIV-positive persons despite benefits of antiretroviral therapy: Implications for a stress and coping model of suicide. *American Journal of Psychiatry, 167,* 117–119.

Cassem, E. (1995). Depressive disorders in the medically ill: An overview. *Psychosomatics. 36,* S2–S10.

Charlifue, S., & Gerhart, K. (1991). Behavioral and demographic predictors of suicide after traumatic spinal cord injury. *Archives of Physical Medicine and Rehabilitation, 72,* 488–492.

Christensen, M.-L. M., Yousaf, U., Engholm, G., & Storm, H. H. (2006). Increased suicide risk among Danish women with non-melanoma skin cancer, 1971–1999. *European Journal of Cancer Prevention, 15,* 266–268.

Chynoweth, R., Tonge, J., & Armstrong, J. (1980). Suicide in Brisbane: A retrospective psychosocial study. *Australia and New Zealand Journal of Psychiatry, 14,* 37–45.

Clark, D., & Fawcett, J. (1992). Review of empirical risk factors for evaluation of the suicidal patient. In B. Bongar (Ed.),

Suicide: Guidelines for assessment, management, and treatment (pp. 16–48). New York, NY: Oxford University Press.

Clark, D., & Horton-Deutsch, S. (1992). Assessment in absentia: The value of the psychological autopsy method for studying antecedents of suicide and predicting future suicide. In R. Maris, A. Berman, J. Maltsberger, and R. Yufit (Eds.), *Assessment and prediction of suicide* (pp. 144–182). New York, NY: Guilford.

Conwell, Y., Duberstein, P., Hirsch, J., Conner, K., Eberly, S., & Caine, E. (2010). Health status and suicide in the second half of life. *International Journal of Geriatric Psychiatry, 25*, 371–379.

DeVivo, M., Black, K., Richards, J. S., & Stover, S. (1991). Suicide following spinal cord injury. *Paraplegia, 29*, 620–627.

Di Maio, L., Squitieri F., Napolitano G., Campanella, G., Trofatter, J. A., & Conneally, P. M. (1993). Suicide risk in Huntington's disease. *Journal of Medical Genetics, 30*, 293–295.

Dormer, N. R. C., McCaul, K. A., & Kristjanson, L. J. (2008). Risk of suicide in cancer patients in Western Australia, 1981–2002. *Medical Journal of Australia, 188*, 140–143.

Druss, B., & Pincus, H. (2000). Suicidal ideation and suicide attempts in general medical illnesses. *Archives of Internal Medicine, 160*, 1522–1526.

Fabrazzo, M., & De Santo, R. M. (2006). Depression in chronic kidney disease. *Seminars in Nephrology, 26*, 56–60.

Fang, F., Keating, N., Mucci, L., Adami, H., Stampfer, M., Valdimarsdottir, U., & Fall, K. (2010). Immediate risk of suicide and cardiovascular death after a prostate cancer diagnosis: Cohort study in the United States. *Journal of the National Cancer Institute, 102*, 307–314.

Farrer, L. A. (1986). Suicide and attempted suicide in Huntington disease: Implications for preclinical testing of persons at risks. *American Journal of Medical Genetics, 24*, 305–311.

Fiedorowicz, J., Mills, J., Ruggle, A., Langbehn, D., & Paulsen, J. (2011). Suicidal behavior in prodromal Huntington Disease. *Neurodegenerative Disease, 8*, 483–490.

Feinstein, A. (2000). Multiple sclerosis, disease modifying treatments and depression: A critical methodological review. *Multiple sclerosis, 6*, 343–348.

Foley, K., & Hendin, H. (1999). The Oregon report: Don't ask, don't tell. *Hastings Center Report, 29*, 37–42.

Forsstrom, E., Hakko, H., Nordstrom, T., Rasanen, P., & Mainio, A. (2010). Suicide in patients with stroke: A population-based study of suicide victims during the years 1988–2007 in northern Finland. *The Journal of Neuropsychiatry and Clinical Neurosciences, 22*, 182–187.

Fredrikson, S., Cheng, Q., Jiang, G., & Wasserman, D. (2003). Elevated suicide risk among patients with Multiple Sclerosis in Sweden. *Neuroepidemiology, 22*, 146–152.

Goeb, J., Even, C., Nicolas, G., Gohier, B., Dubas, F., & Garre, J. (2006). Psychiatric side effects of interferon-B in multiple sclerosis. *Psychiatry, 21*, 186–193.

Goldman Consensus Group. (2005). The Goldman Consensus statement on depression in multiple sclerosis. *Multiple Sclerosis, 11*, 328–337.

Goodwin, R., Marusic, A., & Hoven, C. (2003). Suicide attempts in the United States: The role of physical illness. *Social Science and Medicine, 56*, 1783–1788.

Hagen, E. M., Lie, S. A., Rekand, T., Gilhus, N. E., & Gronning, M. (2010). Mortality after traumatic spinal cord injury: 50 years of follow-up. *Journal of Neurology, Neurosurgery, and Psychiatry, 81*, 368–373.

Harrington, C. (2002). Depression in the medically ill. *Medicine and Health/Rhode Island, 85*, 273–277.

Harris, E., & Barraclough, B. (1994). Suicide as an outcome for medical disorders. *Medicine Baltimore, 73*, 281–296.

Harris, E., Barraclough, B., Grundy, D., Bamford, E., & Inskip, H. (1996). Attempted suicide and completed suicide in traumatic spinal cord injury: Case reports. *Spinal Cord, 34*, 752–753.

Hartkopp, A., Bronnum-Hansen, H., Seideschnur, A., & Biering-Sorensen, F. (1998). Suicide in a spinal cord injured population: Its relation to functional status. *Archives of Physical Medicine and Rehabilitation, 79*, 1356–1361.

Harwood, D., Hawton, K., Hope, T., Harriss, L., & Jacoby, R. (2006). Life problems and physical illness as risk factors for suicide in older people: A descriptive and case-control study. *Psychological Medicine, 36*, 1265–1274.

Hem, E., Loge, J., Haldorsen, T., & Ekeberg, O. (2004). Suicide risk in cancer patients from 1960 to 1999. *Journal of Clinical Oncology, 22*, 4209–4216.

Huntington, G. (1872). On chorea. *Medical Surgical Reporter, 26*, 317–321.

Imai, K., Kadowaki, T., & Aizawa, Y. (2004). Standardized indices of mortality among persons with spinal cord injury: Accelerated aging process. *Industrial Health, 42*, 213–218.

Iosifescu, D. (2007). Treating depression in the medically ill. *Psychiatric Clinics of North America, 30*, 77–90.

Jamison, S. (1996). When drugs fail: Assisted deaths and not-so-lethal drugs. *Journal of Pharmaceutical Care and Pain and Symptom Control, 4*, 223–243.

Joiner, T., Jr., Van Orden, K., Witte, T., & Rudd, M. D. (2009). *The interpersonal theory of suicide: Guidance for working with suicidal clients.* Washington, DC: APA Books.

Kaplan, M., McFarland, B., Huguet, N., & Newsom, J. (2007). Physical illness, functional limitations, and suicide risk: A population-based study. *American Journal of Orthopsychiatry, 77*, 56–60.

Keiser, O., Spoerri, A., Brinkhof, M. W., Hasse, B., Gayet-Ageron, A., Tissot, F.,... Egger, M. (2010). Suicide in HIV-infected individuals and the general population in Switzerland, 1988–2008. *American Journal of Psychiatry, 167*(2), 1–8.

Kendal, W. S. (2007). Suicide and cancer: A gender-comparative study. *Annals of Oncology, 18*, 381–387.

Kennedy, P., Rogers, B., Speer, S., & Frankel, H. (1999). Spinal cord injuries and attempted suicide: A retrospective review. *Spinal Cord, 37*, 847–852.

Kleespies, P. (2004). *Life and death decisions: Psychological and ethical considerations in end-of-life care.* Washington, DC: APA Books.

Kleespies, P., Hough, S., & Romeo, A. (2009). Suicide risk in people with medical and terminal illness. In P. Kleespies (Ed.), *Behavioral emergencies: An evidence—based resource for evaluating and managing risk of suicide, violence, and victimization* (pp. 3–121). Washington, DC: APA Books.

Krentz, H., Kliewer, G., & Gill, M. (2005). Changing mortality rates and causes of death for HIV-infected individuals living in Southern Alberta, Canada from 1984 to 2003. *HIV Medicine, 6*, 99–106.

Kurella, M., Kimmel, P., Young, B., & Chertow, G. (2005). Suicide in the United States End-Stage Renal Disease Program. *Journal of the American Society of Nephrology, 16*, 774–781.

Larsson, M. U., Luszcz, M. A., Bui, T.-H., & Robins Wahlin, T.-B. (2006). Depression and suicidal ideation after predictive testing for Huntington's disease: A two-year follow-up study. *Journal of Genetic Counseling, 15*, 361–374.

Levy, N. (2000). Psychiatric considerations in the primary medical care of the patient with renal failure. *Advances in Renal Replacement Therapy, 7*, 231–238.

Lidal, I., Snekkevik, H., Aamodt, G., Hjeltnes, N., Stanghelle, J., & Biering-Sorenson, F. (2007). Mortality after spinal cord injury in Norway. *Journal of Rehabilitation Medicine, 39*, 145–151.

Lipe, H., Schultz, A., & Bird, T. D. (1993). Risk factors for suicide in Huntington's disease: A retrospective case-controlled study. *American Journal of Medical Genetics, 48*, 231–233.

Lu, T., Chang, H., Chen, L., Chu, M., Ou, N., & Jen, I. (2006). Changes in causes of death and associated conditions among persons with HIV/AIDS after the introduction of highly active antiretroviral therapy in Taiwan. *Journal of the Formosan Medical Association, 105*, 604–609.

Mackenzie, T., & Popkin, M. (1990). Medical illness and suicide. In S. Blumenthal & D. Kupfer (Eds.), *Suicide over the life cycle: Risk factors, assessment, and treatment of suicidal patients* (pp. 205–232). Washington, DC: American Psychiatric Press.

Miller, M., Mogun, H., Azrael, D., Hempstead, K., & Solomon, D. H. (2008). Cancer and the risk of suicide in older Americans. *Journal of Clinical Oncology, 26*, 4720–4724.

Misono, S., Weiss, N. S., Fann, J. R., Redman, M., & Yueh, B. (2008). Incidence of suicide in persons with cancer. *Journal of Clinical Oncology, 26*, 4731–4738.

Nilsson, L., Ahlbom, A., Farahmand, B., Asberg, M., & Tomson, T. (2002). Risk factors for suicide in epilepsy: A case control study. *Epilepsia, 43*, 644–651.

Ojo, A., Hanson, J., Wolfe, R., Leichtman, A., Agodoa, L., & Port, F. (2000). Long-term survival in renal transplant recipients with graft function. *Kidney International, 57*, 307–313.

Oregon Health Authority—Public Health Division. (2014). *Oregon Death with Dignity Act Annual Reports.* Retrieved from http://public.health.oregon.gov/ProviderPartnerResources/EvaluationResearch/DeathwithDignityAct/Pages/index.aspx

Patten, S., & Metz, L. (2002). Interferon B1a and depression in secondary progressive MS: Data from the SECTRIMS Trial. *Neurology, 59*, 744–746.

Paulsen, J. S., Hoth, K. F., Nehl, C., & Stierman, L. (2005). Critical periods of suicide risk in Huntington's Disease. *American Journal of Psychiatry, 162*, 725–731.

Paulsen, J. S., Ready, R., Hamilton, J., Mega, M., & Cummings, J. (2001). Neuropsychiatric aspects of Huntington's disease. *Journal of Neurology, Neurosurgery, and Psychiatry, 71*, 310–314.

Pickett, W., Simpson, K., Walker, J., & Brison, R. (2003). Traumatic spinal cord injury in Ontario, Canada. *The Journal of Trauma, Injury, Infection, and Critical Care, 55*, 1070–1076.

Pokorny, A. (1983). Prediction of suicide in psychiatric patients, *Archives of General Psychiatry, 40*, 249–259.

Pompili, M., Forte, A., Palermo, M., Stefani, H., Lamis, D., Serafini, G.,. . . Girardi, P. (2012). Suicide risk in multiple sclerosis: A systematic review of current literature. *Journal of Psychosomatic Research, 73*, 411–417.

Pompili, M., Girardi, P., Ruberto, A., & Tatarelli, R. (2005). Suicide in the epilepsies: A meta-analytic investigation of 29 cohorts. *Epilepsy and Behavior, 7*, 305–310.

Pompili, M., Girardi, P., & Tatarelli, R. (2006). Death from suicide versus mortality from epilepsy in the epilepsies: A meta-analysis. *Epilepsy and Behavior, 9*, 641–648.

Pompili, M., Girardi, P., Tatarelli, G., Angeletti, G., & Tatarelli, R. (2006). Suicide after surgical treatment in patients with epilepsy: A meta-analytic investigation. *Psychological Reports, 98*, 323–338.

Qin, P., Webb, R., Kapur, N., & Sorensen, H. T. (2013). Hospitalization for physical illness and risk of subsequent suicide: A population study. *Journal of Internal Medicine, 273*, 48–58.

Quill, T. (1991). Death and dignity: A case of individualized decision making. *New England Journal of Medicine, 324*, 691–694.

Rice, B., Smith, R., & Delpech, V. (2010). HIV infection and suicide in the era of HAART in England, Wales, and Northern Ireland. *AIDS, 24*, 1795–1797.

Rich, C., Young, D., & Fowler, R. (1986). San Diego suicide study: I: Young vs. old subjects. *Archives of General Psychiatry, 43*, 577–582.

Robinson, D., Renshaw, C., Okello, C., Møller, H., & Davies, E. A. (2009). Suicide in cancer patients in South East England from 1996 to 2005: A population-based study. *British Journal of Cancer, 101*, 198–201.

Robins Wahlin, T.-B., Bäckman, L., Lundin, A., Haegermark, A., Winblad, B., & Anvret, M. (2000). High suicidal ideation in persons testing for Huntington's disease. *Acta Neurologica Scandinavica, 102*, 150–161.

Rockett, I., Wang, S., Lian, Y., & Stack, S. (2007). Suicide-associated comorbidity among U. S. males and females: A multiple cause-of-death analysis. *Injury Prevention, 13*, 311–315.

Rosenfeld, B. (2004). *Assisted suicide and the right to die: The interface of social science, public policy, and medical ethics.* Washington, DC: APA Books.

Ruzicka, L., Choi, C., & Sadkowsky, K. (2005). Medical disorders of suicides in Australia: Analysis using multiple-cause-of-death approach. *Social Science and Medicine, 61*, 333–341.

Schmitz, B. (2005). Depression and mania in patients with epilepsy. *Epilepsia, 46* (Suppl 4), 45–49.

Siegert, R., & Abernathy, D. (2005). Depression in multiple sclerosis: A review. *Journal of Neurology, Neurosurgery, and Psychiatry, 76*, 469–475.

Silver, J., Kramer, R., Greenwald, S., and Weissman, M. (2001). The association between head injuries and psychiatric disorders: The findings from the New Haven NIMH Epidemiologic Catchment Area Study. *Brain Injury, 15*, 935–945.

Simpson, G., & Tate, R. (2005). Clinical features of suicide attempts after traumatic brain injury. *The Journal of Nervous and Mental Disease, 193*, 680–685.

Simpson, G., & Tate, R. (2002). Suicidality after traumatic brain injury: Demographic, injury and clinical correlates. *Psychological Medicine, 32*, 687–697.

Soden, R., Walsh, J., Middleton, J., Craven, M., Rutkowski, S., & Yeo, J. (2000). Causes of death after spinal cord injury. *Spinal Cord, 38*, 604–610.

Sorensen, S.A., & Fenger, K. (1992). Causes of death in patients with Huntington's disease and in unaffected first degree relatives. *Journal of Medical Genetics, 29*, 911–914.

Stanford, R., Soden, R., Bartrop, R., Mikk, M., & Taylor, T. (2007). Spinal cord and related injuries after attempted suicide: Psychiatric diagnosis and long-term follow-up. *Spinal Cord, 45*, 437–443.

Stenager, E. N., & Stenager, E. (1992). Suicide and patients with neurologic diseases. *Archives of Neurology, 49*, 1296–1303.

Stenager, E. N., Madsen, C., Stenager, E., & Boldsen, J. (1998). Suicide in patients with stroke: Epidemiological study. *British Medical Journal, 316*, 1206.

Tanaka, H., Tsukuma, H., Masaoka, T., Ajiki, W., Koyama, T., Knioshita, N.,. . . Oshima, A. (1999). Suicide risk among cancer patients: Experience at one medical center in Japan, 1978–1994. *Japanese Journal of Cancer Research, 90*, 812–817.

Teasdale, T., & Engberg, A. (2001a). Suicide after a stroke: A population study. *Journal of Epidemiology and Community Health, 55*, 863–866.

Teasdale, T., & Engberg, A. (2001b). Suicide after traumatic brain injury: A population study. *Journal of Neurology, Neurosurgery, and Psychiatry, 71,* 436–440.

Waern, M., Rubenowitz, E., Runeson, B., Skoog, I., Wilhelmson, K., & Allebeck, P. (2002). Burden of illness and suicide in elderly people: Case-control study. *British Medical Journal, 324,* 1355–1358.

Wallin, M., Wilken, J., Turner, A., Williams, R., and Kane, R. (2006). Depression and multiple sclerosis: Review of a lethal combination. *Journal of Rehabilitation Research & Development, 43,* 45–62.

Webb, R., Kontopantellis, E., Doran, T., Qin, P., Creed, F., & Kapur, N. (2012). Suicide risk in primary care patients with major physical diseases: A case-control study. *Archives of General Psychiatry, 69,* 256–264.

Werth, J., Jr., & Wineberg, H. (2005). A critical analysis of criticisms of the Oregon Death with Dignity Act. *Death Studies, 29,* 1–27.

Whitlock, F. (1986). Suicide and physical illness. In A. Roy (Ed.), *Suicide.* Baltimore, MD: Williams and Wilkins.

Williams, L. (2005). Depression and stroke: Cause or consequence? *Seminars in Neurology, 25,* 396–409.

Williams, R., Turner, A., Hatzakis, M., Jr., Bowen, J., Rodriquez, A., & Haselkorn, J. (2005). Prevalence and correlates of depression among veterans with multiple sclerosis. *Neurology, 64,* 75–80.

Yousaf, U., Christensen, M., Engholm, G., & Storm, H. (2005). Suicides among Danish cancer patients 1971–1999. *British Journal of Cancer, 92,* 995–1000.

Crises and Conditions Associated with Behavioral Emergencies

Nonsuicidal Self-Injury and Its Relation to Suicidal Behavior

Joseph Chad Franklin *and* Matthew K. Nock

Abstract

Nonsuicidal self-injury (NSSI) is the direct and intentional destruction of one's own body tissue in the absence of suicidal intent. Although NSSI itself is explicitly nonsuicidal, nearly half of individuals who engage in NSSI also engage in suicidal behavior, and nearly all individuals who engage in suicidal behavior also engage in NSSI. Moreover, recent studies suggest that NSSI is one of the strongest known predictors of future suicide attempts, even exceeding the predictive power of prior suicide attempts in some instances. In this chapter we review the basic features and correlates of NSSI, evaluate the evidence for traditional models of NSSI, and discuss how an emerging model of NSSI may provide insight into the strong association between NSSI and suicidal behavior. We conclude by recommending how to evaluate when NSSI is a behavioral emergency and by noting the most crucial future directions for research on this topic.

Key Words: nonsuicidal self-injury, NSSI, suicide, Behavioral emergency, Predictors, NSSI models

Nonsuicidal Self-Injury

Avoiding injury is vital to survival. Without the instinct to avoid injury, pain, and stimuli associated with potential injury, our lives would be significantly curtailed and our species would soon die out. People born with an extremely rare condition known as congenital insensitivity to pain provide an unfortunate illustration of this point. Due to their insensitivity to pain, their short lives are marred by constant infections, unnoticed injuries, and self-mutilation such as chewing of the tongue, lips, and fingertips. Many suffer injury-related deaths as infants, few live beyond childhood, and almost none live beyond age 25 (Protheroe, 1991; Daneshjou, Jafarieh, & Raaeskarami, 2012). Given the evolutionary imperative to avoid injury, how is it possible that each year millions of people (without congenital insensitivity to pain) intentionally injure themselves in the absence of suicidal intent?

This phenomenon is known as nonsuicidal self-injury (NSSI) and most commonly involves behaviors such as self-cutting or self-burning. There are multiple accepted definitions of NSSI (e.g., Nock & Favazza, 2009; American Psychiatric Association, 2013), but nearly all include six main criteria. First, the behavior must be performed without any suicidal intent. Second, it must be intentional rather than accidental. Third, it must be direct, meaning that there must be no intervening steps between the act and the injury (i.e., this excludes indirect injury such as the long-term effects of alcohol on the liver). Fourth, NSSI does not include socially sanctioned behaviors such as piercings and tattoos (see Favazza, 2009, for a cross-cultural discussion of this point). Fifth, the behavior must lead to a moderate degree of injury. Studies sometimes include minor behaviors such as skin-picking and lip-biting as NSSI, but these behaviors are qualitatively different from moderate behaviors such as self-cutting and self-burning. Specifically, compared to minor behaviors, moderate behaviors are associated with greater psychopathology, psychiatric hospitalizations, suicide ideation, and suicide attempts (Lloyd-Richardson, Perrine, Dierker, & Kelley, 2007; Klonsky & Olino, 2008; Whitlock, Muehlenkamp, & Eckenrode, 2008; Tang, Ma, et al., 2013). Sixth, NSSI is distinguished from the highly repetitive minor self-injury (e.g., constant head-banging) associated with some developmental disorders and the major self-injury (e.g., self-amputations) associated with some psychotic disorders (Nock & Favazza, 2009).

Many researchers and clinicians are familiar with NSSI through its association with borderline personality disorder. Indeed, some form of NSSI or NSSI-like behavior has been listed as a symptom of borderline personality disorder since the first official classification of personality disorders in the *Diagnostic and Statistical Manual of Mental Disorders* (third ed.; American Psychiatric Association, 1980). This historical association has contributed to the misconception that NSSI is *only* indicative of borderline personality disorder and to the dominance of NSSI theories (e.g., emotion dysregulation and regulation) and treatments (e.g., dialectical behavior therapy [DBT]) originally designed for borderline personality disorder. Recent research has begun to change this perception, however, with several studies demonstrating that NSSI is associated with a wide range of psychopathologies and can occur in the absence of a psychiatric diagnosis (e.g., Nock, Joiner, Gordon, Lloyd-Richardson, & Prinstein, 2006; Selby, Bender, Gordon, Nock, & Joiner, 2012; Glenn & Klonsky, 2013). This emerging perception of NSSI as a distinct entity is reflected in the inclusion of NSSI in the Conditions for Further Study section of the *Diagnostic and Statistical Manual of Mental Disorders* (fifth ed.; American Psychiatric Association, 2013).

This is also reflected in evidence that NSSI prevalence rates greatly exceed the prevalence rates of borderline personality disorder and other disorders. Studies indicate that NSSI rates are very high in many inpatient populations, usually exceeding 30% and often exceeding 75% (e.g., DiClemente, Ponton, & Hartley, 1991; Penn, Esposito, Schaeffer, Fritz, & Spirito, 2003; Nock & Prinstein, 2004). Rates in non-clinical samples also are surprisingly high. A recent meta-analysis found that NSSI rates approach 17% among adolescents, 13% among young adults, and 5% among adults (Swannell, Martin, Page, Hasking, & St. John, 2014). Rates in children and young adolescents (i.e., 3rd to 9th grade) are similarly high, with Barrocas et al. (2012) obtaining an overall rate near

8%. It is important to note, however, that rates vary greatly depending on the types of behaviors categorized as NSSI (i.e., rates are much higher when minor behaviors are included) and the method of NSSI assessment (Swannell et al., 2014). For example, rates of unambiguously moderate NSSI behaviors such as self-cutting or self-burning tend to be about half that of overall reported rates (e.g., Klonsky, 2011; Barrocas, Hankin, Young, & Abela, 2012). In terms of demographics, NSSI rates do not appear to vary significantly by gender (Klonsky, 2011; Swannell et al., 2014), country (Plener, Libal, Keller, Fegert, & Muehlenkamp, 2009; Giletta, Scholte, Engels, Ciairano, & Prinstein, 2012; Swannell et al., 2014), or ethnicity (Klonsky, 2011; though see Kuentzel, Arble, Boutros, Chugani, & Barnett, 2012; Chesin, Moster, & Jeglic, 2013). However, several studies have found that NSSI rates are much higher among individuals with non-heterosexual orientations, especially bisexual orientations (e.g., Whitlock et al., 2011, 2013; Wilcox et al., 2012; Sornberger, Smith, Toste, & Heath, 2013).

Researchers and clinicians have devoted considerable effort toward treating these highly prevalent and dangerous behaviors, with most interventions being based on an emotion dysregulation/regulation model of NSSI. The most commonly advocated treatments include DBT or DBT-like therapies (Linehan, 1993; Lynch & Cozza, 2009; Bentley, Nock, & Barlow, 2014), cognitive behavior therapy (Newman, 2009; Andover, 2012), and pharmacotherapy (Sandman, 2009; Cullen, Westlund, LaRiviere, & Klimes-Dougan, 2013). Despite these efforts, several recent reviews have concluded that no intervention has been shown to consistently reduce NSSI in controlled studies (Nock, 2010; Brausch & Girresch, 2012; Washburn et al., 2012; Gonzales & Bergstrom, 2013).

These null findings include DBT, which many assume is an effective treatment for NSSI. This perception may be due in part to the findings of several single-group DBT studies showing a reduction in NSSI (Stanley, Brodsky, Nelson, & Dulit, 2007; Taylor, Winmill, & Alfoadari, 2008; Plener, Sukale, Ludolph, & Stegemann, 2010; Fleischhaker et al., 2011; James, Winmill, Anderson, & Alfoadari, 2011; Geddes, Dziurawiec, & Lee, 2013; Fischer & Peterson, 2014). Although this single-group evidence appears promising, these reductions are likely due to passage of time and regression to the mean effects rather than treatment effects. This is because nearly all longitudinal NSSI studies—including nontreatment studies—find large reductions in

NSSI during the course of the study (e.g., over 50% reductions in nontreatment studies; Guerry & Prinstein, 2009; Prinstein et al., 2010; Glenn & Klonsky, 2011; You, Lin, Fu, & Leung, 2013; Franklin, Puzia, et al., 2014; Tuisku et al., 2014). Consistent with these findings, controlled DBT treatment studies find that all groups show substantial reductions in NSSI and similar behaviors and that these reductions are similar across treatment conditions (Katz, Cox, Gunasekara, & Miller, 2004; Linehan et al., 2006; Pistorello, Fruzzetti, MacLane, Gallop, & Iverson, 2012). This lack of intervention success indicates that there is much room to improve on traditional models of NSSI that focus on emotion dysregulation and regulation. The following sections provide a brief overview of the evidence for and against this emotion regulation model, describe new research that points the way toward a new model of NSSI and novel treatment targets, and discuss how this new model may provide insight into the link between NSSI and suicidal behaviors.

NSSI and Emotion Dysregulation and Regulation

Owing to its historical association with borderline personality disorder, many NSSI models can be described as emotion regulation models. There are several variants of this model (Linehan, 1993; Chapman, Gratz, & Brown, 2006; Selby & Joiner, 2009), but each shares the following core features: (a) people who engage in NSSI display high levels of emotion dysregulation; (b) this results in extreme negative affect, which directly precedes and motivates NSSI; and (c) NSSI reduces negative affect, which negatively reinforces the behavior. Some aspects of this model have received empirical support, but others have not. These limitations may help to explain why treatments based on this model (e.g., DBT) are not effective interventions for NSSI. In the following we briefly outline the evidence for and against this popular model.

Emotion Dysregulation

Retrospective self-report evidence is highly consistent with the emotion regulation model tenet that people who engage in NSSI have high levels of emotion dysregulation. This effect is large and has been demonstrated across several populations (e.g., Nock et al., 2008; Glenn, Blumenthal, Klonsky, & Hajcak, 2011; Franklin, Lee, Hanna, & Prinstein, 2013). Supporting these self-report findings, evidence also indicates that NSSI is associated with more intense physiological

arousal during a frustrating task (Nock & Mendes, 2008). These findings contribute to the traditional conceptualization of NSSI as a behavior that people engage in when they experience powerful and prolonged negative emotion, possess few healthy emotion regulation skills, and desperately need to feel better.

Interestingly, however, the vast majority of daily diary, experimental, longitudinal, and physiological studies do not support this view. Daily diary studies have found that NSSI is associated with higher overall levels of negative emotion (Bresin, 2014; Victor & Klonsky, 2014) but normative negative emotion in response to stressful events and normative returns to prestressor emotion levels (Bresin, 2014). Moreover, this generalized increase in negative affect may be better described as a specific increase in self-dissatisfaction (Victor & Klonsky, 2014). In line with these findings, recent experimental studies have shown that NSSI is associated with high baseline negative emotion but not emotion dysregulation (i.e., no evidence of abnormally increased or prolonged negative affect during laboratory stressors; Franklin et al., 2010; Kaess et al., 2012; Weinberg & Klonsky, 2012; Bresin & Gordon, 2013). Of note, these experimental emotional responses were normative even though the NSSI groups in these studies scored significantly higher than comparison groups on self-report inventories of emotion reactivity and dysregulation. Echoing these findings, most physiological studies have failed to find evidence of emotion dysregulation in NSSI groups. Specifically, NSSI is associated with normative startle eyeblink reactivity, heart rate, and cortisol in the context of a stressful speech task (Franklin et al., 2010; Kaess et al., 2012) and normative startle eyeblink reactivity in the context of unpleasant images (Glenn et al., 2011). Once again, these physiological responses were normative despite the fact that these same NSSI groups scored significantly higher than control groups on self-report inventories of emotion dysregulation. Additionally, longitudinal studies tend to find that scores on these emotion dysregulation inventories and related measures are weak or nonsignificant predictors of NSSI (Glenn & Klonsky, 2011; Franklin, Puzia, et al., 2014; Tuisku et al., 2014).

Ecological momentary assessment studies provide partial support for the emotion regulation model tenet that increased negative affect precedes NSSI episodes (Muehlenkamp et al., 2009; Nock, Prinstein, & Sterba, 2009; Armey, Crowther, & Miller, 2011). Specifically, these studies suggest that there are slight increases in negative affect before NSSI but not the extreme increases that one might expect based on the emotion regulation model (cf. experimental results noted previously: Franklin et al., 2010; Kaess et al., 2012; Weinberg & Klonsky, 2012; Bresin & Gordon, 2013). Consistent with daily diary studies (Bresin, 2014; Victor & Klonsky, 2014), it is likely that these pre-NSSI elevations in negative affect reflect slight increases in self-dissatisfaction or self-criticism rather than emotion dysregulation.

Taken together, these findings show that retrospective self-reported emotion dysregulation is a strong correlate of NSSI but a weak risk factor for NSSI. Even more inconsistent with the emotion regulation model, nearly all daily diary, experimental, and physiological studies suggest that emotion dysregulation is not associated with NSSI. This casts considerable doubt on traditional conceptualizations of NSSI and helps to explain why treatments such as DBT are not effective NSSI interventions: they target a factor (i.e., emotion dysregulation) that does not appear to play a direct role in NSSI.

Emotion Regulation

In contrast to the weak evidence for the emotion dysregulation aspects of this model, there are multiple lines of evidence that strongly support the emotion regulation tenet. In addition to retrospective self-report evidence (see Klonsky, 2007), this is supported by ecological momentary assessment (Muehlenkamp et al., 2009; Nock et al., 2009; Armey et al., 2011), experimental (Weinberg & Klonsky, 2012; Bresin & Gordon, 2013), and physiological studies (Franklin et al., 2010; Franklin, Puzia, et al., 2013). This work indicates that a phenomenon called *pain offset relief* is one of the primary mechanisms that generates emotion regulation during NSSI. Specifically, compared to a pre-pain baseline, the removal (or even slight reduction) of a painful stimulus causes reduced negative emotion, increased positive emotion, and reduced physiological arousal (Franklin, Lee, et al., 2013). Interestingly, this phenomenon is not specific to people who engage in NSSI; it has been observed in healthy controls, rats, and even fruit flies (for reviews see Gerber et al., 2014; Bastian, Jetten, Hornsey, & Leknes, 2014). This work suggests that individuals who engage in NSSI tap into a natural relief mechanism and that this mechanism can occur in the absence of trait and state emotion dysregulation.

Summary

The emotion regulation model of NSSI has generated many empirical studies that have greatly advanced knowledge about NSSI. In particular, this work has shown that emotion dysregulation may not play a direct role in NSSI but that emotion regulation plays a central role in NSSI. More generally, this evidence is consistent with the four-function model of NSSI (Nock & Prinstein, 2004; Bentley et al., 2014), which proposes that NSSI serves both emotional (positive and negative reinforcement) and social (positive and negative social reinforcement) functions. This information is valuable, but the evidence against the emotion dysregulation tenet of this model creates important theoretical gaps. For example, if not emotion dysregulation, what motivates NSSI? What leads someone to select NSSI over other regulating behaviors that do not require injury? Why do some people engage in NSSI episodically and others engage in NSSI regularly? Which factors best predict NSSI, and what are the best NSSI treatment targets? And why is NSSI so strongly associated with suicidal behaviors? In the following we describe an emerging model of NSSI that both accounts for the functions of NSSI (Bentley et al., 2014) and proposes empirically based answers to these questions.

The Barriers and Benefits Model of NSSI

This emerging model is called the barriers and benefits model of NSSI (Franklin & Hooley, 2014; Franklin, Puzia, et al., 2013; Franklin, Lee, Puzia, & Prinstein, 2014), and it has two central tenets. First, NSSI carries many benefits, and all of these are natural and normal. These proposed benefits include improved affect (e.g., Franklin, Puzia, et al., 2013), fulfillment of self-punishment motives (Schoenleber, Berenbaum, & Motl, 2014), affiliation with a desired peer group (Prinstein, Guerry, Browne, & Rancourt, 2009), and powerful communication of distress or strength (Nock, 2008). This model proposes that all members of the population have access to these benefits and that the experience of these benefits does not differentiate between individuals who do and do not engage in NSSI. For example, both healthy individuals and individuals with a history of NSSI experience a similar level of improved affect after the removal of a painful stimulus (Russ et al., 1992; Franklin et al., 2010; Franklin, Puzia, et al., 2013; Bresin & Gordon, 2013). Accordingly, these benefits play an important role in NSSI, but they are nonspecific, difficult (if not impossible) to change or prevent, and poor treatment targets. In other words, these benefits play an important role in NSSI but do not provide much help in answering the questions posed at the end of the preceding section.

Second, there are many barriers to NSSI that dissuade most people from engaging in these behaviors. For NSSI to occur, an individual has to overcome each of these barriers, which include a positive association with the self, physical pain, and aversion to NSSI-related stimuli, among others (see Franklin & Hooley, 2014). Reductions in these barriers are abnormal, meaning that—unlike NSSI benefits—most of these factors should differentiate between NSSI and non-NSSI groups at baseline, longitudinally predict NSSI, and serve as important NSSI treatment targets. Next we describe three of these barriers in greater detail.

Positive Association With the Self

It is normal to have a positive association with the self (Koole, Dijksterhuis, & van Knippenberg, 2001). This helps to explain why objects associated with the self (e.g., receiving a postcard during a study) quickly gain a positive valence (e.g., Gawronski & LeBel, 2008). This positive association acts as a barrier because it is difficult to inflict pain and injury on someone that you like (i.e., yourself). It follows that this barrier should be eroded among people who engage in NSSI. Supporting this hypothesis, several recent studies have shown that, relative to controls, individuals with a history of NSSI score higher on factors indicative of a negative association with the self, including self-criticism, self-blame, self-dissatisfaction, shame, and a negative self-view (e.g., Hooley, Ho, Slater, & Lockshin, 2010; Weismoore & Esposito-Smythers, 2010; Swannell et al., 2012; Schoenleber et al., 2014; Victor & Klonsky, 2014). In addition to reducing a barrier to NSSI, a negative association with the self instantiates the belief that one deserves pain, injury, and punishment (Hooley et al., 2010; St. Germain & Hooley, 2012). These beliefs may play a key role in motivating the selection of NSSI over other behaviors that carry similar emotional and social benefits (e.g., alcohol consumption). Consistent with this possibility, self-anger and similar factors are among the most commonly endorsed reasons for initially engaging in NSSI (Muehlenkamp, Brausch, Quigley, & Whitlock, 2013), and self-criticism is one of the few factors that differentiates between direct (e.g., NSSI) and indirect (e.g., substance abuse) self-injury (St. Germain & Hooley, 2012).

There are at least two major mechanisms that contribute to the development of a negative association with the self. First, distal factors such as family, peer, and relationship problems—especially maltreatment and criticism—may generate a trait-like negative association with the self (Glassman, Weierich, Hooley, Deliberto, & Nock, 2007; Swannell et al., 2012; Baetens et al., 2013). Second, it may be natural for failure, criticism, and disappointment to generate a temporary negative association with the self in most people. For example, Chatard and Selimbegovic (2011) found that failure- and disappointment-related primes increased the accessibility to suicide-related thoughts in healthy individuals. Similarly, Tang, Wu, and Miao (2013) found that these primes caused increased implicit identification with death/suicide in healthy controls. These findings help to explain why NSSI often occurs after acute stressors and why high levels of trait and state emotion dysregulation do not appear to play a central role in NSSI. Specifically, a negative association with the self is indicative of negative affect but not necessarily extreme or prolonged negative affect (cf. Bresin, 2014; Victor & Klonsky, 2014). These two pathways toward a negative association with the self may also help to explain why some people engage in NSSI regularly and others engage in NSSI episodically (see Klonsky & Olino, 2008; Whitlock et al., 2008): individuals with a trait-like negative association with the self may be regularly motivated to punish themselves whereas other individuals may be motivated only for short periods of time after rare events. Consistent with this possibility, a negative association with the self is strongly correlated with both past (Schoenleber et al., 2014) and future NSSI (Franklin, Fox, Harris, Hooley, & Nock, 2014).

Given that a negative association with the self appears to be a key motivating factor for NSSI, it is an important treatment target. Recent experimental evidence demonstrates that traditional therapies can be modified to target this factor (Hooley & St. Germain, 2014). It may also be possible to employ evaluative conditioning, a technique most commonly studied in social psychology, for this purpose. For example, Dijksterhuis (2004) asked participants to pair personal pronouns (e.g., "I") with positive adjectives and found that this increased self-esteem and resistance to negative feedback. Preliminary results from our laboratory suggest that a modified version of this technique may substantially reduce NSSI compared to a control intervention (Franklin, Fox, Puzia, et al., 2014).

Physical Pain

Few things motivate escape and avoidance as powerfully as pain and stimuli associated with pain. Contrary to this evolutionarily conserved instinct, NSSI requires that individuals intentionally seek out and self-administer pain. Whereas physical pain serves as a significant barrier to NSSI for most people, this does not appear to be a deterrent for people who engage in NSSI. Several laboratory studies support this view, finding that NSSI is associated with increased pain endurance across a wide range of painful stimuli (e.g., Russ et al., 1992; Hooley et al., 2010; Franklin, Aaron, Arthur, Shorkey, & Prinstein, 2012; St. Germain & Hooley, 2012). These findings have prompted a perplexing question: *why* is NSSI associated with abnormal pain perception?

One popular hypothesis has been that people who engage in NSSI possess biological abnormalities that alter central and peripheral pain perception (e.g., Schmahl et al., 2006; Sher & Stanley, 2009; Ballard and Bosk, 2010). Unfortunately, we are not aware of any studies that have directly tested this hypothesis, and one indirect test is inconsistent with this explanation. Pavony and Lenzenweger (2013) found that a borderline personality disorder sample (many of whom had a history of NSSI) did not show generalized exteroceptive or proprioceptive abnormalities even though they displayed increased pain endurance. This argues against a general sensory deficit among people who engage in NSSI and suggests that a pain-specific psychological mechanism may play a large role in this effect.

One such psychological mechanism appears to be a negative association with the self. During the course of their study on NSSI and pain, Hooley et al. (2010) noted that many participants spontaneously mentioned that they believed that they deserved pain and punishment. This led to the hypothesis that people who engage in NSSI endure pain longer to satisfy these beliefs. Results supported this possibility as self-critical beliefs were strongly associated with pain endurance. To more stringently test this hypothesis, Hooley and St. Germain (2014) examined the effects of a brief self-criticism intervention on pain endurance in a sample of people with a history of NSSI. Strikingly, this intervention normalized pain endurance among participants with a history of NSSI; control interventions did not have this effect. These findings provide strong evidence in favor of the view that a negative association with the self plays a causal role in increased pain endurance among people who engage in NSSI.

The foregoing work shows that whereas physical pain may be a deterrent for most people, it may actually attract others to NSSI because it may serve to satisfy self-punishment motivations. Correspondingly, heightened pain endurance appears to be secondary to a negative association with the self. This underscores the importance of assessing and treating a negative association with the self and suggests that pain endurance itself is not a fruitful treatment target.

Aversion to NSSI Stimuli

As with physical pain, humans have an instinctive aversion to NSSI-related stimuli such as blood, wounds, and knives. Several studies have shown that, in healthy individuals, such stimuli evoke more aversion than general unpleasant stimuli such as spiders, snakes, and guns (e.g., Bradley, Codispoti, Sabatinelli, & Lang, 2001; Schupp et al., 2004; Franklin, Fox, Puzia, et al., 2014). This aversion motivates most people to avoid NSSI as a behavioral option. Overcoming this barrier, however, individuals with a history of NSSI display diminished aversion to NSSI stimuli across explicit, implicit, and physiological measures (e.g., Haines, Williams, Brain, & Wilson, 1995; Glenn & Klonsky, 2010; Plener, Bubalo, Fladung, Ludolph, & Lulé, 2012; Franklin, Lee, et al., 2014). Suggesting that this diminished aversion may play a direct role in NSSI and influence NSSI trajectory, it is strongly correlated with both lifetime frequency of NSSI (Franklin, Lee, et al., 2014) and the frequency of future NSSI (Franklin, Puzia, Lee, & Prinstein, 2014).

To advance the understanding of how to best prevent and treat NSSI, it is critical to understand how this diminished aversion develops. Unfortunately, there are few published studies on this topic; nevertheless, preliminary work suggests at least two potential mechanisms. First, the mere exposure effect (Zajonc, 2001) may play a minor role in reducing aversion to NSSI stimuli. Across exposures to these stimuli via the media, the Internet, peers, or one's own NSSI, individuals may habituate to these stimuli. Initial experimental evidence supports this possibility, showing that aversion to NSSI stimuli decreases across over 100 exposures during a single laboratory session (Franklin, Fox, Puzia, et al., 2014). Second, a phenomenon known as pain offset relief conditioning may also play a role. As described earlier, pain offset generates a powerful state of relief. Several basic studies have shown that stimuli presented during this state of relief become associated with relief and accordingly gain a more positive valence (see Bastian et al., 2014; Gerber et al., 2014). Several instances of relief may occur within a single episode of NSSI (Franklin, Puzia, et al., 2013), meaning that stimuli present during an NSSI episode—such as blood, wounds, and knives—become associated with relief. Gradually, this conditioning may shift the association with NSSI stimuli toward a more neutral or even positive valence (Franklin, Lee, et al., 2014). Preliminary experimental evidence is consistent with this mechanism (Franklin, Fox, Puzia, et al., 2014), but more studies are needed to investigate this possibility.

This barrier represents a novel treatment target that interventions may benefit from considering. Early experimental evidence from our laboratory suggests that aversive conditioning (i.e., pairing NSSI stimuli with the onset of shocks; Franklin, Fox, Puzia, et al., 2014) and evaluative conditioning (i.e., pairing NSSI stimuli with unpleasant words and pictures; Franklin, Fox, Puzia, et al., 2014) may rebuild this barrier and reduce NSSI.

Summary

The barriers and benefits model accounts for the supported elements of traditional models (e.g., emotional and social benefits) and recent findings that are inconsistent with these models. This emerging model places an emphasis on the barriers to NSSI—particularly a negative association with the self and aversion to NSSI stimuli—as factors that are crucial for distinguishing between NSSI and non-NSSI groups, longitudinally predicting NSSI, and designing new NSSI interventions. As described in the following sections, these factors may also help to explain the strong link between NSSI and suicidal behaviors and ultimately may provide insight into how to more effectively predict and treat suicidal behaviors.

The Association Between NSSI and Suicidal Behaviors

Some researchers have argued that there is little to be gained from distinguishing between NSSI and suicidal behaviors (e.g., Kapur, Cooper, O'Connor, & Hawton, 2013). However, others have pointed out that these two behaviors differ in several important ways that warrant their separate classifications (Andover, Morris, Wren, & Bruzzese, 2012; Butler & Malone, 2013). First, these behaviors tend to take different forms, with NSSI most often taking less lethal forms such as self-cutting and self-burning, and suicidal behaviors most often taking more lethal forms such as gunshots and hangings.

Second, their functions and motivations differ, as NSSI is most often motivated by self-punishment or a desire to feel better whereas suicidal behaviors are most often motivated by a desire to die. Third, NSSI is a high-frequency behavior (exceeding thousands of episodes in some cases) whereas suicidal behavior tends be have a much lower frequency. Fourth, whereas suicidal behavior often elicits care and compassion from the environment, NSSI typically elicits disgust and blame. Although there is a clear distinction between these two behaviors, recent research has demonstrated that there is an important association between NSSI and suicidal behaviors. Joiner (2005) eloquently described this link when discussing his father's suicide:

> Despite my dad's substantial history of injury and definite stoicism and fearlessness, when it came to producing his own death, he seemingly needed to work up to the act. He died by piercing his own heart, but first, he worked up to that by cutting other areas of his body. This fact about my dad's suicide—still painful to write about after many years—is, I think, important. In one way or another, everyone who dies by suicide has to work up to the act, certainly over the long-term (through getting used to pain) and sometimes over the short-term, by trying out means of death in a milder, non-lethal way. (p. 13)

Although it is currently unclear if all or even most suicide attempts are preceded by other self-injurious behaviors, a growing literature strongly suggests that NSSI may greatly increase risk for future suicidal behavior. For example, Andover and Gibb (2010) found that NSSI frequency and suicide attempt frequency were moderately correlated ($r = .41$). Nearly all studies of this association have found that a substantial proportion of individuals with a history of NSSI also report a history of suicide attempt. Lower estimates of this overlap range from 9.8% to 27.8% (Brausch & Gutierrez, 2010; Cloutier, Martin, Kennedy, Nixon, & Muehlenkamp, 2010; Tang et al., 2011; Jenkins, Singer, Conner, Calhoun, & Diamond, 2014), and higher estimates range from 46.1% to 70% (Nock et al., 2006; Ferrara, Terrinoni, & Williams, 2012; Cheung et al., 2013). Such findings indicate that a large proportion of people who engage in NSSI also report at least one suicide attempt, but this pales in comparison to the reverse overlap. Specifically, the proportion of people with a history of suicide attempt who also report a history of NSSI (vs. the proportion with a history of NSSI who also report a suicide attempt) is close to 100% in most studies (e.g., Brausch & Gutierrez, 2010; Cloutier et al., 2010; Tang, Ma, et al., 2013). In other words, many people who engage in NSSI also have a history of suicide attempt, but nearly everyone with a history of suicide attempt reports a history of NSSI.

Many recent studies have shown that, compared to people with a history of either NSSI or suicide attempt, people with a history of both behaviors display particularly severe levels of psychopathology and suicidality. These latter individuals score higher on measures of depressive symptoms, borderline personality disorder symptoms, and hopelessness, among many others (Dougherty et al., 2009; Andover & Gibb, 2010; Boxer, 2010; Brausch & Gutierrez, 2010; Cloutier et al., 2010; Wolff et al., 2013; Zetterqvist, Lundh, & Svedin, 2013). Additionally, a history of both behaviors is associated with a greater severity of suicide attempts (Andover & Gibb, 2010). These findings are consistent with latent class analyses of NSSI samples, which show that a sizable subset of people who engage in NSSI report severe and wide-ranging psychopathology, high-frequency NSSI, high levels of suicide ideation, and a history of suicide attempts (Klonsky & Olino, 2008; Whitlock et al., 2008; Hamza & Willoughby, 2013).

There is clear evidence that NSSI has a strong cross-sectional association with suicide attempts (Hamza, Stewart, & Willoughby, 2012; Klonsky, May & Glenn, 2013; Victor & Klonsky, 2014), but in recent years several studies have demonstrated a robust longitudinal association as well (Asarnow et al., 2011; Wilkinson, Kelvin, Roberts, Dubicka, & Goodyer, 2011; Cox et al., 2012; Goldstein et al., 2012; Guan, Fox, & Prinstein, 2012; Whitlock et al., 2013). Furthermore, studies that directly compare the predictive power of prior suicide attempts and NSSI have found that NSSI is comparable (Goldstein et al., 2012; Guan et al., 2012) or even superior to prior attempts (Asarnow et al., 2011; Cox et al., 2012; Wilkinson et al., 2011). This appears to be a dose-response relationship, where more frequent NSSI translates into higher suicide attempt risk (Whitlock et al., 2013; cf. cross-sectional results of Andover & Gibb, 2010). Indeed, a recent meta-analysis suggests that NSSI—particularly high-frequency NSSI—is the strongest overall predictor of future suicide attempts (prior suicide attempts are a close second; Franklin, Glenn, & Nock, 2014). It should be noted, however, that no published studies have investigated the ability of NSSI to predict death by suicide. In sum, NSSI appears to be a robust and powerful risk factor for suicide attempts.

Explaining the NSSI–Suicide Association

The foregoing evidence clearly shows that NSSI has a strong cross-sectional and longitudinal association with suicidal behavior, but *why* does this association exist? Advancing knowledge about this link would improve the identification of which people who engage in NSSI are likely to go on to make a suicide attempt, further the understanding of the mechanisms involved in suicidal behavior, and establish novel treatment targets for suicidal behavior. In this section, we evaluate several proposed mechanisms and relate these mechanisms to the barriers and benefits model of NSSI described previously.

Psychopathology as a Third Variable

Some estimates suggest that up to 90% of individuals who engage in NSSI (Nock et al., 2006) and suicidal behavior (Cavanagh, Carson, Sharpe, & Lawrie, 2003) may have a diagnosable psychiatric disorder. This raises the possibility that the NSSI–suicide link may be explained by a common association with psychopathology or related factors such as psychological distress, difficult life circumstances, and genetics. Consistent with this view, Caspi et al. (2014) argue that a single factor undergirds most (if not all) psychopathology and that specific symptoms are largely shaped by specific environmental circumstances. From this perspective, one might hypothesize that both NSSI and suicidal behavior are indicative of severe psychopathology (i.e., high loadings on this factor), with individuals who engage in one behavior possessing a high vulnerability to the other behavior and environmental circumstances determining which behavior is selected.

Although this explanation seems reasonable, recent studies do not support it. A recent meta-analysis of all longitudinal studies of self-injurious thoughts and behaviors (Franklin, Glenn, et al., 2014) found that internalizing, externalizing, psychotic, and personality disorder symptoms are generally insignificant or weak (i.e., weighted odds ratios ~1.0) predictors of both NSSI and suicide attempts. By comparison, NSSI is a strong predictor of future suicide attempts (i.e., weighted odds ratio ~ 5.0). It is unlikely that the strong predictive power of NSSI is subsumed by the weak predictive power of psychopathology. More directly, several studies have shown that the NSSI–suicide association remains strong after controlling for a wide range of psychopathological symptoms (e.g., Whitlock et al., 2008; Andover & Gibb, 2010; Asarnow et al., 2011; Tang et al., 2011; Wilkinson et al., 2011). For example, across four samples, Klonsky et al. (2013)

found that there was a strong association between NSSI and suicidal behavior and that this remained after controlling for depression, anxiety, impulsivity, and borderline personality disorder symptoms. Consistent with the barriers and benefits model, these studies indicate that factors such as psychopathology and emotion dysregulation are correlated with self-injurious behavior but do not play a central role in these behaviors.

NSSI as a Gateway to Suicidal Behavior

Some researchers have proposed that NSSI may act as a gateway to suicidal behavior (for a review, see Hamza et al., 2012). The strong form of this hypothesis is that NSSI is a necessary first step toward suicidal behavior. Supporting this hypothesis, the average age of onset is around 13 for NSSI and around 16 for suicide attempts (Nock, Wedig, Holmberg, & Hooley, 2008; Darke, Torke, Kaye, & Ross, 2010; Ougrin et al., 2012), NSSI is a strong longitudinal predictor of suicidal behavior (see earlier discussion), and suicide attempts are weaker longitudinal predictors of NSSI than the converse (Asarnow et al., 2011; Wilkinson et al., 2011). Inconsistent with this hypothesis, however, many (and perhaps most; see earlier discussion) people who engage in NSSI never go on to make a suicide attempt. Likewise, NSSI is a strong predictor of future suicide attempts *relative* to other factors whose predictive ability have been tested, but the *absolute* magnitude of this association (i.e., weighted odds ratio ~ 5) indicates that NSSI is far from a prerequisite for suicidal behavior. Taken together, these findings are more consistent with a weaker form of this hypothesis: NSSI may directly increase the risk for NSSI but does not always lead to suicidal behavior and is not necessary for suicidal behavior to occur.

Greater Relief Across NSSI Episodes

Based on the interpersonal theory of suicide (Joiner, 2005; Van Orden et al., 2010; Joiner, Ribeiro, & Silva, 2012), the NSSI–suicide association may be partially explained by increasing relief across NSSI episodes (and, more generally, across exposures to any painful or provocative events). This is based in part on the opponent process theory of acquired motivation (Solomon, 1980), which proposes that all stimuli provoke a primary process and an opponent process. Across repeated exposures to a given stimulus, the primary process becomes weaker while the opponent process becomes stronger. For NSSI, the primary process would be pain

and the opponent process would be relief, meaning that, across episodes, NSSI would become less painful and more relieving. Consequently, across episodes, it should become easier (less painful) and more rewarding (greater relief) to engage in NSSI. This effect may then generalize, leading an individual who engages in NSSI to view any type of self-injury—including suicidal self-injury—as potentially rewarding (Joiner, 2005; Van Orden et al., 2010). This hypothesis is indirectly supported by the strong association between NSSI frequency and suicide attempts (e.g., Andover & Gibb, 2010; Whitlock et al., 2013). Few studies have directly tested this hypothesis, but preliminary work does not support this explanation. Franklin, Puzia, et al. (2013) found that physiological indices of pain offset relief were not correlated with NSSI frequency. In fact, pain offset relief intensity did not differentiate between individuals with no history of NSSI and individuals who reported thousands of NSSI episodes. Similarly, Franklin, Fox, Harris, et al. (2014) found that pain offset relief was not correlated with self-reported measures of painful and provocative events or capability for suicide. Based on this evidence, the opponent process of NSSI (i.e., relief) does not appear to be malleable; accordingly, it is unlikely that increasing relief across self-injury episodes plays a role in the association between NSSI and suicidal behavior. This interpretation is consistent with the barriers and benefits theory as it indicates that emotional benefits of self-injury are natural and difficult to alter and that the barriers to self-injury may provide more insight into who is at risk for these behaviors.

Diminished Pain Perception Across NSSI Episodes

A related hypothesis based on the interpersonal theory of suicide is that repeated exposures to painful and provocative events such as NSSI gradually cause habituation to pain, thereby increasing the capability to engage in suicidal behavior (Joiner, 2005; Van Orden et al., 2010; Joiner et al., 2012). Consistent with this possibility, cross-sectional studies show that painful and provocative events in general (Bender, Gordon, Bresin, & Joiner, 2011; Franklin, Hessel, & Prinstein, 2011) and NSSI in particular (e.g., Hooley et al., 2010; Franklin et al., 2012) are associated with increased pain endurance and self-reported capability for suicide. Additionally, suicidal behavior is associated with increased pain endurance (e.g., Orbach, Mikulincer, King, Cohen, & Stein, 1997). Although these findings are promising, three issues cast doubt on this hypothesis.

First, NSSI frequency appears to be, at best, weakly correlated with pain endurance (Hooley et al., 2010; St. Germain & Hooley, 2013). As with pain offset relief described previously, this suggests that experience with NSSI does not play a direct causal role in altering pain tolerance. Second, we are unaware of any studies that have attempted to employ pain endurance to longitudinally predict NSSI. Such studies are necessary to stringently test this hypothesis; however, given the weak cross-sectional association between pain endurance and NSSI frequency, it is likely that the longitudinal association between these two variables is also weak. Third, as noted before, cross-sectional (Hooley et al., 2010) and experimental evidence (Hooley & St. Germain, 2014) strongly suggest that the NSSI-pain association is largely mediated by a negative association with the self. If repeated NSSI episodes diminished pain perception via opponent processes or some similar mechanism, one might expect that a brief intervention targeting self-criticism should have no effect on pain endurance levels. Nevertheless, as demonstrated by Hooley and St. Germain (2014), this brief intervention normalizes pain tolerance among people who engage in NSSI.

Consistent with the barriers and benefits model of NSSI, this evidence suggests that pain endurance abnormalities among self-injurers are secondary to a negative association with the self. Indeed, this latter factor is associated with both NSSI and suicidal behavior (St. Germain & Hooley, 2012) and is one of the few factors that distinguishes between direct and indirect self-injury. Taking all of these findings together, one of the primary reasons for the link between NSSI and suicidal behavior may be that both behaviors are rooted in a negative association with the self. This removes an important barrier to all forms of self-harm, increases pain endurance, and instantiates the desire to self-inflict pain and punishment.

Diminished Aversion to Injury- and Death-Related Stimuli Across NSSI Episodes

As with the instinctive aversion to NSSI stimuli, all organisms have a powerful instinct to avoid death and stimuli associated with death. According to the interpersonal theory of suicide (Joiner, 2005; Van Orden et al., 2010; Joiner et al., 2012), people who overcome the instinctive aversion to death/suicide are at an increased risk for suicidal behavior. Supporting this hypothesis, a history of suicidal

behavior is associated with higher scores on a self-report measure of suicide capability—particularly the fearlessness about death component of suicide capability (Ribeiro et al., 2014). Similarly, our laboratory recently found that explicit and implicit responses to death- and suicide-themed pictures is strongly associated with self-reported suicide capability, ideation, plans, and attempts (Franklin, Fox, Harris, et al., 2014). Preliminary evidence indicates that responses to these images also prospectively predicts suicide ideation, plans, and attempts (Franklin, Fox, Harris, et al., 2014).

These findings demonstrate that diminished aversion to death/suicide stimuli play an important role in suicidal behavior, but how might NSSI influence this factor? Unfortunately, no empirical studies have directly investigated this question, but at least two NSSI-related explanations have been proposed. First, the interpersonal theory of suicide posits that opponent processes may play a role. Specifically, engaging in NSSI may reduce the instinctive aversion associated with any kind of self-injury (i.e., primary process) and increase behavioral approach toward stimuli related to self-injury (i.e., opponent process). However, as noted earlier, initial laboratory studies are inconsistent with an opponent process explanation. Second, a related but distinct potential mechanism is pain offset relief conditioning. During NSSI, specific injury-related stimuli (e.g., blood, knives, wounds) may become paired with relief. Across time, this relief–injury association may gradually generalize to a wider and wider array of injury-related phenomena, eventually culminating in diminished aversion to death/suicide stimuli. Although intriguing, there are many questions left to be answered about this potential mechanism (e.g., how exactly does this generalization process work?), and many other mechanisms may contribute to the diminished aversion to death/suicide stimuli.

Summary

A full explanation for the robust association between NSSI and suicidal behavior continues to elude researchers, but knowledge has advanced substantially on this front over the last few years. At least four plausible potential explanations have been ruled out: (a) a common association with psychopathology, (b) the strong form of the gateway hypothesis, (c) greater relief across NSSI episodes, and (d) diminished pain tolerance across NSSI episodes. At the same time, two other explanations have shown some initial promise: (a) a common association with a negative self-view and (b) diminished aversion to death/suicide stimuli across NSSI episodes. These two explanations are consistent with the barriers and benefits model of NSSI and suggest that some of the most important factors that give rise to NSSI also contribute to suicidal self-injury. Nonetheless, few empirical studies have directly investigated these explanations, and it is likely that several additional mechanisms play a role in the association between NSSI and suicidal behaviors.

In addition to furthering knowledge about the basic connection between NSSI and suicidal behaviors, future studies should also endeavor to address other pressing questions about this association. For example, how often does NSSI directly precede suicidal behavior (e.g., as in Joiner's [2005] description of his father's suicidal behavior)? Given the high degree of overlap between these two behaviors, this may be a common phenomenon. Such information would be helpful for assessing suicide risk in emergency settings. Similarly, is the onset of NSSI or a sudden increase in NSSI a warning sign for suicidal behavior (see Rudd et al., 2006), or does NSSI primarily indicate a general elevation in suicidal capability? Additionally, how might researchers and clinicians reliably distinguish between (a) individuals who frequently engage in NSSI but report no suicidality and (b) individuals who frequently engage in NSSI and report high suicidality (see latent class analyses of Hamza & Willoughby, 2013)? In other words, under what conditions is high-frequency NSSI a marker for suicidality?

Recommendations for Emergency Situations

It is important to recognize that NSSI itself is rarely a medical emergency. Even moderate NSSI behaviors such as self-cutting and self-burning tend to have very low levels of lethality. Occasionally, such behaviors may result in the accidental severing of a major artery or vein, but by definition NSSI wounds are moderate and accordingly do not typically represent medical emergencies. It is also important to distinguish between nonsuicidal and suicidal self-injury. Often friends, family members, and even clinicians may find NSSI alarming and incorrectly assume that behaviors such as self-cutting are suicide attempts. On the other hand, it is also imperative that mental health care providers not assume that a given behavior (e.g., self-cutting) is *non*suicidal. Indeed, cutting/piercing accounts for nearly 2% of all suicide deaths (McIntosh & Drapeau, 2012). As such, we strongly recommend that mental health care providers administer short but thorough semistructured assessment instruments such as the Self-Injurious Thoughts and Behaviors Interview (Nock, Joiner, Gordon, Lloyd-Richardson, & Prinstein, 2006) to ascertain the nature, history, and potential future of a patient's self-injury.

As noted previously, NSSI is most concerning due to its association with suicidal behavior. Although NSSI may be among the most powerful predictors of future suicide attempts, this risk should be viewed in absolute terms. In other words, NSSI is associated with a nearly five-fold increase in risk for suicide attempts, but suicide attempts have an extremely low base rate. Accordingly, at any given time, people who engage at NSSI have an extremely low absolute risk of engaging in suicidal behavior, and many people who engage in NSSI never engage in suicidal behavior. However, it is just as important not to dismiss NSSI simply because the behavior itself is nonsuicidal. On balance, we recommend that mental health care providers view NSSI as a major long-term risk factor for suicidal behavior and view the acute escalation of NSSI as a potential warning sign for more imminent suicidal behavior. In the context of traditional warning signs (e.g., agitation, dramatic changes in mood, feeling trapped), this latter factor may be particularly concerning, but in the absence of these warnings signs, NSSI may carry much less risk for suicidal behavior. Studies are needed to evaluate these possibilities in order to advance the understanding of when NSSI is a behavioral emergency and to provide a more firm empirical basis for best practices.

References

American Psychiatric Association. (1980). *Diagnostic and statistical manual of mental disorders* (3rd ed.). Washington, DC: Author.

American Psychiatric Association. (2013). *Diagnostic and statistical manual of mental disorders* (5th ed.). Washington, DC: Author.

Andover, M. S. (2012). A cognitive-behavioral approach to case formulations for nonsuicidal self-injury. *Journal of Cognitive Psychotherapy*, 26(4), 318–330.

Andover, M. S., & Gibb, B. E. (2010). Non-suicidal self-injury, attempted suicide, and suicidal intent among psychiatric inpatients. *Psychiatry Research*, 178(1), 101–105.

Andover, M. S., Morris, B. W., Wren, A., & Bruzzese, M. E. (2012). The co-occurrence of non-suicidal self-injury and attempted suicide among adolescents: Distinguishing risk factors and psychosocial correlates. *Child and Adolescent Psychiatry and Mental Health*, 6(11), 1–7.

Armey, M. F., Crowther, J. H., & Miller, I. W. (2011). Changes in ecological momentary assessment reported affect associated with episodes of nonsuicidal self-injury. *Behavior Therapy*, 42(4), 579–588.

Asarnow, J. R., Porta, G., Spirito, A., Emslie, G., Clarke, G., Wagner, K. D., … Brent, D. A. (2011). Suicide attempts and nonsuicidal self-injury in the treatment of resistant depression in adolescents: Findings from the TORDIA study. *Journal of the American Academy of Child & Adolescent Psychiatry*, 50(8), 772–781.

Baetens, I., Claes, L., Hasking, P., Smits, D., Grietens, H., Onghena, P., & Graham, M. (2013). The relationship between parental expressed emotions and NSSI: The mediating roles of self-criticism and depression. *Journal of Child and Family Studies.* Advance online publication. doi: 10.1007/s10826-013-9861-8

Barrocas, A. L., Hankin, B. L., Young, J. F., & Abela, J. R. (2012). Rates of nonsuicidal self-injury in youth: Age, sex, and behavioral methods in a community sample. *Pediatrics*, 130(1), 39–45.

Ballard, E., & Bosk, A. (2010). Invited commentary: Understanding brain mechanisms of pain processing in adolescents' non-suicidal self-injury. *Journal of Youth and Adolescence*, 39(4), 327–334.

Bastian, B., Jetten, J., Hornsey, M. J., & Leknes, S. (2014). The positive consequences of pain: A biopsychosocial approach. *Journal of Personality and Social Psychology.*

Bender, T. W., Gordon, K. H., Bresin, K., & Joiner, T. E. Jr. (2011). Impulsivity and suicidality: The mediating role of painful and provocative experiences. *Journal of Affective Disorders*, 129(1), 301–307.

Bentley, K. H., Nock, M. K., & Barlow, D. H. (2014). The four-function model of nonsuicidal self-injury: Key directions for future research. *Clinical Psychological Science.* Advance online publication: doi: 10.1177/2167702613514563

Boxer, P. (2010). Variations in risk and treatment factors among adolescents engaging in different types of deliberate self-harm in an inpatient sample. *Journal of Clinical Child and Adolescent Psychology*, 39(4), 470–480.

Bradley, M. M., Codispoti, M., Sabatinelli, D., & Lang, P. J. (2001). Emotion and motivation II: Sex differences in picture processing. *Emotion*, 1(3), 300–319.

Brausch, A. M., & Gutierrez, P. M. (2010). Differences in nonsuicidal self-injury and suicide attempts in adolescents. *Journal of Youth and Adolescence*, 39(3), 233–242.

Brausch, A. M., & Girresch, S. K. (2012). A review of empirical treatment studies for adolescent nonsuicidal self-injury. *Journal of Cognitive Psychotherapy*, 26(1), 3–18.

Bresin, K. (2014). Five indices of emotion regulation in participants with a history of nonsuicidal self-injury: A daily diary study. *Behavior Therapy*, 45(1), 56–66.

Bresin, K., & Gordon, K. H. (2013). Changes in negative affect following pain (vs. nonpainful) stimulation in individuals with and without a history of nonsuicidal self-injury. *Personality Disorders*, 4(1), 62–66.

Butler, A. M., & Malone, K. (2013). Attempted suicide v. nonsuicidal self-injury: Behaviour, syndrome or diagnosis? *British Journal of Psychiatry*, 202(5), 324–325.

Caspi, A., Houts, R. M., Belsky, D. W., Goldman-Mellor, S. J., Harrington, H., Israel, S., … Moffitt, T. E. (2014). The p factor: One general psychopathology factor in the structure of psychiatric disorders? *Clinical Psychological Science*, 2(2), 119–137.

Cavanagh, J. T., Carson, A. J., Sharpe, M., & Lawrie, S. M. (2003). Psychological autopsy studies of suicide: A systematic review. *Psychological Medicine*, 33(3), 395–405.

Chapman, A. L., Gratz, K. L., & Brown, M. Z. (2006). Solving the puzzle of deliberate self-harm: The experiential avoidance model. *Behaviour Research and Therapy*, 44(3), 371–394.

Chatard, A., & Selimbegović, L. (2011). When self-destructive thoughts flash through the mind: Failure to meet standards affects the accessibility of suicide-related thoughts. *Journal of Personality and Social Psychology*, 100(4), 587–605.

Chesin, M. S., Moster, A. N., & Jeglic, E. L. (2013). Nonsuicidal self-injury among ethnically and racially diverse emerging adults: Do factors unique to the minority experience matter? *Current Psychology*, 32(4), 318–328.

Cheung, Y. T. D., Wong, P. W. C., Lee, A. M., Lam, T. H., Fan, Y. S. S., & Yip, P. S. F. (2013). Non-suicidal self-injury and suicidal behavior: prevalence, co-occurrence, and correlates of suicide among adolescents in Hong Kong. *Social Psychiatry and Psychiatric Epidemiology*, 48(7), 1133–1144.

Cloutier, P., Martin, J., Kennedy, A., Nixon, M. K., & Muehlenkamp, J. J. (2010). Characteristics and co-occurrence of adolescent non-suicidal self-injury and suicidal behaviours in pediatric emergency crisis services. *Journal of Youth and Adolescence*, 39(3), 259–269.

Cox, L. J., Stanley, B. H., Melhem, N. M., Oquendo, M. A., Birmaher, B., Burke, A., … Brent, D. A. (2012). A longitudinal study of nonsuicidal self-injury in offspring at high risk for mood disorder. *Journal of Clinical Psychiatry*, 73(6), 821–828.

Cullen, K. R., Westlund, M. K., LaRiviere, L. L., & Klimes-Dougan, B. (2013). An adolescent with nonsuicidal self-injury: A case and discussion of neurobiological research on emotion regulation. *American Journal of Psychiatry*, 170(8), 828–831.

Darke, S., Torok, M., Kaye, S., & Ross, J. (2010). Attempted suicide, self-harm, and violent victimization among regular illicit drug users. *Suicide and Life-Threatening Behavior*, 40(6), 587–596.

Daneshjou, K., Jafarieh, H., & Raaeskarami, S. R. (2012). Congenital insensitivity to pain and anhydrosis (CIPA) syndrome: A report of 4 cases. *Iranian Journal of Pediatrics*, 22(3), 412–416.

DiClemente, R. J., Ponton, L. E., & Hartley, D. (1991). Prevalence and correlates of cutting behavior: Risk for HIV transmission. *Journal of the American Academy of Child & Adolescent Psychiatry*, 30(5), 735–739.

Dijksterhuis, A. (2004). I like myself but I don't know why: Enhancing implicit self-esteem by subliminal evaluative conditioning. *Journal of Personality and Social Psychology*, 86(2), 345–355.

Dougherty, D. M., Mathias, C. W., Marsh-Richard, D. M., Prevette, K. N., Dawes, M. A., Hatzis, E. S., & Nouvion, S. O. (2009). Impulsivity and clinical symptoms among adolescents with non-suicidal self-injury with or without attempted suicide. *Psychiatry Research*, 169(1), 22–27.

Favazza, A. R. (2009). A cultural understanding of nonsuicidal self-injury. In M. K. Nock (Ed.), *Understanding nonsuicidal self-injury: Origins, assessment, and treatment* (pp. 19–36). Washington, DC: American Psychological Association.

Ferrara, M., Terrinoni, A., & Williams, R. (2012). Non-suicidal self-injury (NSSI) in adolescent inpatients: Assessing personality features and attitude toward death. *Child and Adolescent Psychiatry and Mental Health*, 6(1), 1–8.

Fischer, S., & Peterson, C. (2014). Dialectical behavior therapy for adolescent binge eating, purging, suicidal behavior, and non-suicidal self-injury: A pilot study. *Psychotherapy.* Advance online publication: doi: 10.1037/a0036065

Fleischhaker, C., Böhme, R., Sixt, B., Brück, C., Schneider, C., & Schulz, E. (2011). Dialectical Behavioral Therapy for Adolescents (DBT-A): A clinical trial for patients with suicidal and self-injurious behavior and borderline symptoms with a one-year follow-up. *Child and Adolescent Psychiatry and Mental Health*, 5(1), 3.

Franklin, J. C., Hessel, E. T., Aaron, R. V., Arthur, M. S., Heilbron, N., & Prinstein, M. J. (2010). The functions of nonsuicidal self-injury: Support for cognitive-affective regulation and opponent processes from a novel psychophysiological paradigm. *Journal of Abnormal Psychology*, 119(4), 850–862.

Franklin, J. C., Hessel, E. T., & Prinstein, M. J. (2011). Clarifying the role of pain tolerance in suicidal capability. *Psychiatry Research*, 189(3), 362–367.

Franklin, J. C., Aaron, R. V., Arthur, M. S., Shorkey, S. P., & Prinstein, M. J. (2012). Nonsuicidal self-injury and diminished pain perception: The role of emotion dysregulation. *Comprehensive Psychiatry*, 53(6), 691–700.

Franklin, J. C., Lee, K. M., Hanna, E. K., & Prinstein, M. J. (2013). Feeling worse to feel better: Pain-offset relief simultaneously stimulates positive affect and reduces negative affect. *Psychological Science*, 24(4), 521–529.

Franklin, J. C., Puzia, M. E., Lee, K. M., Lee, G. E., Hanna, E. K., Spring, V. L., & Prinstein, M. J. (2013). The nature of pain offset relief in nonsuicidal self-injury: A laboratory study. *Clinical Psychological Science*, 1(2), 110–119.

Franklin, J. C., Fox, K. R., Harris, J., Hooley, J. M., & Nock, M. K. (2014, November). Self-criticism and diminished aversion to death/suicide stimuli predicts future suicidal behavior. In M. Prinstein (Chair), *Measuring and predicting suicidal behavior: New directions and innovative methods*. Prepared for the annual meeting of the Association for Behavioral and Cognitive Therapies, Philadelphia, PA.

Franklin, J. C., Fox, K. R., Puzia, M. E., Lee, K. M., Hooley, J. M., Prinstein, M. J., & Nock, M. K. (2014, November). Reestablishing the instinctive barriers to nonsuicidal and suicidal self-injury: Preliminary evidence for a new approach to treatment. In K. Bentley (Chair), *Utilizing technology to advance treatment for the range of direct and indirect self-injurious behaviors: Results for substance abuse, eating disorders, NSSI, and suicidality*. Prepared for the annual meeting of the Association for Behavioral and Cognitive Therapies, Philadelphia, PA.

Franklin, J. C., Glenn, C. R., & Nock, M. K. (2014, May). Meta-analysis of risk factors for suicidal behavior. In I. Galynker (Chair), *Frontiers in suicide risk assessment*. Presented at the annual meeting of the American Psychiatric Association, New York.

Franklin, J. C., Lee, K. M., Puzia, M. E., & Prinstein, M. J. (2014). Recent and frequent nonsuicidal self-injury is associated with diminished implicit and explicit aversion toward self-cutting stimuli. *Clinical Psychological Science*, 2, 306–318.

Franklin, J. C., Puzia, M. E., Lee, K. M., & Prinstein, M. J. (2014). Low implicit and explicit aversion toward self-cutting stimuli longitudinally predict nonsuicidal self-injury. *Journal of Abnormal Psychology*, 123(2), 463–469.

Franklin, J.C., & Hooley, J.M. (2014). *Why do people hurt themselves? A new conceptual model of nonsuicidal self-injury*. Manuscript submitted for publication.

Gawronski, B., & LeBel, E. P. (2008). Understanding patterns of attitude change: When implicit measures show change, but explicit measures do not. *Journal of Experimental Social Psychology*, 44(5), 1355–1361.

Geddes, K., Dziurawiec, S., & Lee, C. W. (2013). Dialectical behaviour therapy for the treatment of emotion dysregulation and trauma symptoms in self-injurious and suicidal adolescent females: A pilot programme within a community-based child and adolescent mental health service. *Psychiatry Journal*, 4, 1–10.

Gerber, B., Yarali, A., Diegelmann, S., Wotjak, C. T., Pauli, P., & Fendt, M. (2014). Pain-relief learning in flies, rats, and man: Basic research and applied perspectives. *Learning & Memory*, 21, 232–252.

Giletta, M., Scholte, R. H., Engels, R. C., Ciairano, S., & Prinstein, M. J. (2012). Adolescent non-suicidal self-injury: A cross-national study of community samples from Italy, the Netherlands and the United States. *Psychiatry Research*, 197(1), 66–72.

Glassman, L. H., Weierich, M. R., Hooley, J. M., Deliberto, T. L., & Nock, M. K. (2007). Child maltreatment, non-suicidal self-injury, and the mediating role of self-criticism. *Behaviour Research and Therapy*, 45(10), 2483–2490.

Glenn, C. R., Blumenthal, T. D., Klonsky, E. D., & Hajcak, G. (2011). Emotional reactivity in nonsuicidal self-injury: Divergence between self-report and startle measures. *International Journal of Psychophysiology*, 80(2), 166–170.

Glenn, C. R., & Klonsky, E. D. (2010). The role of seeing blood in non-suicidal self-injury. *Journal of Clinical Psychology*, 66(4), 466–473.

Glenn, C. R., & Klonsky, E. D. (2011). Prospective prediction of nonsuicidal self-injury: A 1-year longitudinal study in young adults. *Behavior Therapy*, 42(4), 751–762.

Glenn, C. R., & Klonsky, E. D. (2013). Nonsuicidal self-injury disorder: An empirical investigation in adolescent psychiatric patients. *Journal of Clinical Child and Adolescent Psychology*, 42(4), 496–507.

Goldstein, T. R., Ha, W., Axelson, D. A., Goldstein, B. I., Liao, F., Gill, M. K., . . . Birmaher, B. (2012). Predictors of prospectively examined suicide attempts among youth with bipolar disorder. *Archives of General Psychiatry*, 69(11), 1113–1122.

Gonzales, A. H., & Bergstrom, L. (2013). Adolescent non-suicidal self-injury (NSSI) interventions. *Journal of Child and Adolescent Psychiatric Nursing*, 26(2), 124–130.

Guan, K., Fox, K. R., & Prinstein, M. J. (2012). Nonsuicidal self-injury as a time-invariant predictor of adolescent suicide ideation and attempts in a diverse community sample. *Journal of Consulting and Clinical Psychology*, 80(5), 842–849.

Guerry, J. D., & Prinstein, M. J. (2009). Longitudinal prediction of adolescent nonsuicidal self-injury: Examination of a cognitive vulnerability-stress model. *Journal of Clinical Child and Adolescent Psychology*, 39(1), 77–89.

Haines, J., Williams, C. L., Brain, K. L., & Wilson, G. V. (1995). The psychophysiology of self-mutilation. *Journal of Abnormal Psychology*, 104(3), 471–489.

Hamza, C. A., Stewart, S. L., & Willoughby, T. (2012). Examining the link between nonsuicidal self-injury and suicidal behavior: A review of the literature and an integrated model. *Clinical Psychology Review*, 32(6), 482–495.

Hamza, C. A., & Willoughby, T. (2013). Nonsuicidal self-injury and suicidal behavior: A latent class analysis among young adults. *PLoS One*, 8(3), e59955.

Hooley, J. M., & Germain, S. A. S. (2014). Nonsuicidal self-injury, pain, and self-criticism: Does changing self-worth change pain endurance in people who engage in self-injury? *Clinical Psychological Science*, 2(3), 297–305.

Hooley, J. M., Ho, D. T., Slater, J., & Lockshin, A. (2010). Pain perception and nonsuicidal self-injury. *Personality Disorders: Theory, Research, and Treatment*, 1(3), 170–179.

James, A. C., Taylor, A., Winmill, L., & Alfoadari, K. (2008). A preliminary community study of dialectical behavior therapy with adolescent females demonstrating persistent, deliberate self-harm. *Child and Adolescent Mental Health*, 13, 148–152.

James, A. C., Winmill, L., Anderson, C., & Alfoadari, K. (2011). A preliminary study of an extension of community dialectical behavior therapy (DBT) program to adolescents in the looked after care system. *Child and Adolescent Mental Health*, 16, 9–13.

Jenkins, A. L., Singer, J., Conner, B. T., Calhoun, S., & Diamond, G. (2014). Risk for suicidal ideation and attempt among a primary care sample of adolescents engaging in nonsuicidal self-injury. *Suicide and Life-Threatening Behavior*. Advance online publication. doi: 10.1111/sltb.12094

Joiner, T. (2009). *Why people die by suicide*. Cambridge, MA: Harvard University Press.

Joiner, T. E., Ribeiro, J. D., & Silva, C. (2012). Nonsuicidal self-injury, suicidal behavior, and their co-occurrence as viewed through the lens of the interpersonal theory of suicide. *Current Directions in Psychological Science*, 21(5), 342–347.

Kaess, M., Hille, M., Parzer, P., Maser-Gluth, C., Resch, F., & Brunner, R. (2012). Alterations in the neuroendocrinological stress response to acute psychosocial stress in adolescents engaging in nonsuicidal self-injury. *Psychoneuroendocrinology*, 37(1), 157–161.

Kapur, N., Cooper, J., O'Connor, R. C., & Hawton, K. (2013). Non-suicidal self-injury v. attempted suicide: New diagnosis or false dichotomy? *British Journal of Psychiatry*, 202(5), 326–328.

Katz, L. Y., Cox, B. J., Gunasekara, S., & Miller, A. L. (2004). Feasibility of dialectical behavior therapy for suicidal adolescent inpatients. *Journal of the American Academy of Child & Adolescent Psychiatry*, 43(3), 276–282.

Klonsky, E. D. (2011). Non-suicidal self-injury in United States adults: Prevalence, sociodemographics, topography and functions. *Psychological Medicine*, 41(9), 1981–1986.

Klonsky, E. D.Klonsky, E. D. (2007). The functions of deliberate self-injury: A review of the evidence. *Clinical Psychology Review*, 27(2), 226–239.

Klonsky, E. D., May, A. M., & Glenn, C. R. (2013). The relationship between nonsuicidal self-injury and attempted suicide: Converging evidence from four samples. *Journal of Abnormal Psychology*, 122(1), 231.

Klonsky, E. D., & Olino, T. M. (2008). Identifying clinically distinct subgroups of self-injurers among young adults: A latent class analysis. *Journal of Consulting and Clinical Psychology*, 76(1), 22–27.

Koole, S. L., Dijksterhuis, A., & van Knippenberg, A. (2001). What's in a name: Implicit self-esteem and the automatic self. *Journal of Personality and Social Psychology*, 80(4), 669–685.

Kuentzel, J. G., Arble, E., Boutros, N., Chugani, D., & Barnett, D. (2012). Nonsuicidal self-injury in an ethnically diverse college sample. *American Journal of Orthopsychiatry*, 82(3), 291.

Linehan, M. (1993). *Cognitive-behavioral treatment of borderline personality disorder*. New York: Guilford Press.

Linehan, M. M., Comtois, K. A., Murray, A. M., Brown, M. Z., Gallop, R. J., Heard, H. L., . . . Lindenboim, N. (2006). Two-year randomized controlled trial and follow-up of dialectical behavior therapy vs therapy by experts for suicidal behaviors and borderline personality disorder. *Archives of General Psychiatry*, 63(7), 757–766.

Lloyd-Richardson, E. E., Perrine, N., Dierker, L., & Kelley, M. L. (2007). Characteristics and functions of non-suicidal self-injury in a community sample of adolescents. *Psychological Medicine*, 37(8), 1183–1192.

Lynch, T. R., & Cozza, C. (2009). Behavior therapy for nonsuicidal self-injury. In M. K. Nock (Ed.), *Understanding nonsuicidal self-injury: Origins, assessment, and treatment* (pp. 222–250). Washington, DC: American Psychological Association.

McIntosh, J. L., & Drapeau, C. W. (2012). USA suicide: 2010 official data. Washington, DC: American Association for Suicidology.

Muehlenkamp, J., Brausch, A., Quigley, K., & Whitlock, J. (2013). Interpersonal features and functions of nonsuicidal self-injury. *Suicide and Life-Threatening Behavior*, 43(1), 67–80.

Muehlenkamp, J. J., Engel, S. G., Wadeson, A., Crosby, R. D., Wonderlich, S. A., Simonich, H., & Mitchell, J. E. (2009). Emotional states preceding and following acts of nonsuicidal self-injury in bulimia nervosa patients. *Behaviour Research and Therapy*, 47(1), 83–87.

Newman, C. F. (2009). Cognitive therapy for nonsuicidal self-injury. In M. K. Nock (Ed.), *Understanding nonsuicidal self-injury: Origins, assessment, and treatment* (pp. 201-219). Washington, DC: American Psychological Association.

Nock, M. K. (2008). Actions speak louder than words: An elaborated theoretical model of the social functions of self-injury and other harmful behaviors. *Applied and Preventive Psychology*, 12(4), 159–168.

Nock, M. K. (2010). Self-injury. *Annual Review of Clinical Psychology*, 6, 339–363.

Nock, M. K., Borges, G., Bromet, E. J., Cha, C. B., Kessler, R. C., & Lee, S. (2008). Suicide and suicidal behavior. *Epidemiologic Reviews*, 30(1), 133–154.

Nock, M. K., & Favazza, A. R. (2009). Nonsuicidal self-injury: Definition and classification. In M.K. Nock (Ed.), *Understanding nonsuicidal self-injury: Origins, Assessment, and Treatment* (pp. 9–18). Washington, DC: American Psychological Association.

Nock, M. K., Holmberg, E. B., Photos, V. I., & Michel, B. D. (2007). Self-Injurious Thoughts and Behaviors Interview: Development, reliability, and validity in an adolescent sample. *Psychological Assessment*, 19(3), 309–317.

Nock, M. K., Joiner, T. E. Jr., Gordon, K. H., Lloyd-Richardson, E., & Prinstein, M. J. (2006). Non-suicidal self-injury among adolescents: Diagnostic correlates and relation to suicide attempts. *Psychiatry Research*, 144(1), 65–72.

Nock, M. K., & Mendes, W. B. (2008). Physiological arousal, distress tolerance, and social problem-solving deficits among adolescent self-injurers. *Journal of Consulting and Clinical Psychology*, 76(1), 28.

Nock, M. K., & Prinstein, M. J. (2004). A functional approach to the assessment of self-mutilative behavior. *Journal of Consulting and Clinical Psychology*, 72(5), 885–890.

Nock, M. K., Prinstein, M. J., & Sterba, S. K. (2009). Revealing the form and function of self-injurious thoughts and behaviors: A real-time ecological assessment study among adolescents and young adults. *Journal of Abnormal Psychology*, 118(4), 816–827.

Nock, M. K., Wedig, M. M., Holmberg, E. B., & Hooley, J. M. (2008). The emotion reactivity scale: Development, evaluation, and relation to self-injurious thoughts and behaviors. *Behavior Therapy*, 39(2), 107–116.

Orbach, I., Mikulincer, M., King, R., Cohen, D., & Stein, D. (1997). Thresholds and tolerance of physical pain in suicidal and nonsuicidal adolescents. *Journal of Consulting and Clinical Psychology*, 65(4), 646–652.

Ougrin, D., Zundel, T., Kyriakopoulos, M., Banarsee, R., Stahl, D., & Taylor, E. (2012). Adolescents with suicidal and nonsuicidal self-harm: Clinical characteristics and response to therapeutic assessment. *Psychological Assessment*, 24(1), 11–20.

Pavony, M. T., & Lenzenweger, M. F. (2013). Somatosensory processing and borderline personality disorder features: A signal detection analysis of proprioception and exteroceptive sensitivity. *Journal of Personality Disorders*, 27(2), 208–221.

Penn, J. V., Esposito, C. L., Schaeffer, L. E., Fritz, G. K., & Spirito, A. (2003). Suicide attempts and self-mutilative behavior in a juvenile correctional facility. *Journal of the American Academy of Child & Adolescent Psychiatry*, 42(7), 762–769.

Pistorello, J., Fruzzetti, A. E., MacLane, C., Gallop, R., & Iverson, K. M. (2012). Dialectical behavior therapy (DBT) applied to college students: A randomized clinical trial. *Journal of Consulting and Clinical Psychology*, 80(6), 982.

Plener, P. L., Bubalo, N., Fladung, A. K., Ludolph, A. G., & Lulé, D. (2012). Prone to excitement: Adolescent females with non-suicidal self-injury (NSSI) show altered cortical pattern to emotional and NSS-related material. *Psychiatry Research: Neuroimaging*, 203(2), 146–152.

Plener, P. L., Libal, G., Keller, F., Fegert, J. M., & Muehlenkamp, J. J. (2009). An international comparison of adolescent non-suicidal self-injury (NSSI) and suicide attempts: Germany and the USA. *Psychological Medicine*, 39(9), 1549–1558.

Plener, P. L., Sukale, T., Ludolph, A. G., & Stegemann, T. (2010). "Stop cutting—rock!" A pilot study of a music therapeutic program for self-injuring adolescents. *Music and Medicine*, 2(1), 59–65.

Prinstein, M. J., Guerry, J. D., Browne, C. B., & Rancourt, D. (2009). Interpersonal models of nonsuicidal self-injury. In M. K. Nock (Ed.), *Understanding nonsuicidal self-injury: Origins, assessment, and treatment* (pp. 79–98). Washington, DC: American Psychological Association.

Prinstein, M. J., Heilbron, N., Guerry, J. D., Franklin, J. C., Rancourt, D., Simon, V., & Spirito, A. (2010). Peer influence and nonsuicidal self injury: Longitudinal results in community and clinically referred adolescent samples. *Journal of Abnormal Child Psychology*, 38(5), 669–682.

Protheroe, S. M. (1991). Congenital insensitivity to pain. *Journal of the Royal Society of Medicine*, 84(9), 558–559.

Ribeiro, J. D., Witte, T. K., Van Orden, K. A., Selby, E. A., Gordon, K. H., Bender, T. W., & Joiner, T. E. Jr. (2014). Fearlessness about death: the psychometric properties and construct validity of the revision to the Acquired Capability for Suicide Scale. *Psychological Assessment*, 26(1), 115–126.

Rudd, M. D., Berman, A. L., Joiner, T. E., Nock, M. K., Silverman, M. M., Mandrusiak, M., . . . Witte, T. (2006). Warning signs for suicide: Theory, research, and clinical applications. *Suicide and Life-Threatening Behavior*, 36(3), 255–262.

Russ, M. J., Roth, S. D., Lerman, A., Kakuma, T., Harrison, K., Shindledecker, R. D., . . . Mattis, S. (1992). Pain perception in self-injurious patients with borderline personality disorder. *Biological Psychiatry*, 32(6), 501–511.

Sandman, C. A. (2009). Psychopharmacologic treatment of nonsuicidal self-injury. In M. K. Nock (Ed.), *Understanding nonsuicidal self-injury: Origins, assessment, and treatment* (pp. 291–323). Washington, DC: American Psychological Association.

Schmahl, C., Bohus, M., Esposito, F., Treede, R. D., Di Salle, F., Greffrath, W., . . . Seifritz, E. (2006). Neural correlates of antinociception in borderline personality disorder. *Archives of General Psychiatry*, 63(6), 659–666.

Schoenleber, M., Berenbaum, H., & Motl, R. (2014). Shame-related functions of and motivations for self-injurious behavior. *Personality Disorders*, 5(2), 204–211.

Schupp, H., Cuthbert, B., Bradley, M., Hillman, C., Hamm, A., & Lang, P. (2004). Brain processes in emotional perception: Motivated attention. *Cognition and Emotion*, 18(5), 593–611.

Sher, L., & Stanley, B. (2009). Biological models of nonsuicidal self-injury. In M. K. Nock (Ed.), *Understanding nonsuicidal self-injury: Origins, assessment, and treatment* (pp. 99–117). Washington, DC: American Psychological Association.

Selby, E. A., Bender, T. W., Gordon, K. H., Nock, M. K., & Joiner, T. E. Jr. (2012). Non-suicidal self-injury (NSSI) disorder: A preliminary study. *Personality Disorders: Theory, Research, and Treatment*, 3(2), 167.

Selby, E. A., & Joiner, T. E. Jr. (2009). Cascades of emotion: The emergence of borderline personality disorder from emotional and behavioral dysregulation. *Review of General Psychology*, 13(3), 219.

Solomon, R. L. (1980). The opponent-process theory of acquired motivation: The costs of pleasure and the benefits of pain. *American Psychologist*, 35(8), 691–712.

Sornberger, M. J., Smith, N. G., Toste, J. R., & Heath, N. L. (2013). Nonsuicidal self-injury, coping strategies, and sexual orientation. *Journal of Clinical Psychology*, 69(6), 571–583.

St. Germain, S. A., & Hooley, J. M. (2012). Direct and indirect forms of non-suicidal self-injury: Evidence for a distinction. *Psychiatry Research*, 197(1), 78–84.

St. Germain, S. A., & Hooley, J. M. (2013). Aberrant pain perception in direct and indirect non-suicidal self-injury: An empirical test of Joiner's interpersonal theory. *Comprehensive Psychiatry*, 54(6), 694–701.

Stanley, B., Brodsky, B., Nelson, J. D., & Dulit, R. (2007). Brief dialectical behavior therapy (DBT-B) for suicidal behavior and non-suicidal self injury. *Archives of Suicide Research*, 11(4), 337–341.

Swannell, S., Martin, G., Page, A., Hasking, P., Hazell, P., Taylor, A., & Protani, M. (2012). Child maltreatment, subsequent non-suicidal self-injury and the mediating roles of dissociation, alexithymia and self-blame. *Child Abuse & Neglect*, 36(7), 572–584.

Swannell, S. V., Martin, G. E., Page, A., Hasking, P., & St. John, N. J. (2014). Prevalence of nonsuicidal self-injury in nonclinical samples: Systematic review, meta-analysis and meta-regression. *Suicide and Life-Threatening Behavior*, 44(3), 273–303.

Tang, J., Ma, Y., Guo, Y., Ahmed, N. I., Yu, Y., & Wang, J. (2013). Association of aggression and non-suicidal self injury: A school-based sample of adolescents. *PloS One*, 8(10), e78149.

Tang, J., Wu, S., & Miao, D. (2013). Experimental test of escape theory: Accessibility to implicit suicidal mind. *Suicide and Life-Threatening Behavior*, 43(4), 347–355.

Tang, J., Yu, Y., Wu, Y., Du, Y., Ma, Y., Zhu, H., & Liu, Z. (2011). Association between non-suicidal self-injuries and suicide attempts in Chinese adolescents and college students: A cross-section study. *PloS One*, 6(4), e17977.

Tuisku, V., Kiviruusu, O., Pelkonen, M., Karlsson, L., Strandholm, T., & Marttunen, M. (2014). Depressed adolescents as young adults: Predictors of suicide attempt and non-suicidal self-injury during an 8-year follow-up. *Journal of Affective Disorders*, 152, 313–319.

Van Orden, K. A., Witte, T. K., Cukrowicz, K. C., Braithwaite, S., Selby, E. A., & Joiner, T. E. Jr. (2010). The interpersonal theory of suicide. *Psychological Review*, 117(2), 575–600.

Victor, S. E., & Klonsky, E. D. (2014). Daily emotion in non-suicidal self-injury. *Journal of Clinical Psychology*, 70(4), 364–375.

Washburn, J. J., Richardt, S. L., Styer, D. M., Gebhardt, M., Juzwin, K. R., Yourek, A., & Aldridge, D. (2012). Psychotherapeutic approaches to non-suicidal self-injury in adolescents. *Child and Adolescent Psychiatry and Mental Health*, 6(1), 1–8.

Weinberg, A., & Klonsky, E. D. (2012). The effects of self-injury on acute negative arousal: A laboratory simulation. *Motivation and Emotion*, 36(2), 242–254.

Weismoore, J. T., & Esposito-Smythers, C. (2010). The role of cognitive distortion in the relationship between abuse, assault, and non-suicidal self-injury. *Journal of Youth and Adolescence*, 39(3), 281–290.

Whitlock, J., Muehlenkamp, J., & Eckenrode, J. (2008). Variation in nonsuicidal self-injury: Identification and features of latent classes in a college population of emerging adults. *Journal of Clinical Child and Adolescent Psychology*, 37(4), 725–735.

Whitlock, J., Muehlenkamp, J., Eckenrode, J., Purington, A., Baral Abrams, G., Barreira, P., & Kress, V. (2013). Nonsuicidal self-injury as a gateway to suicide in young adults. *Journal of Adolescent Health*, 52(4), 486–492.

Whitlock, J., Muehlenkamp, J., Purington, A., Eckenrode, J., Barreira, P., Baral Abrams, G., . . . Knox, K. (2011). Nonsuicidal self-injury in a college population: General trends and sex differences. *Journal of American College Health*, 59(8), 691–698.

Wilcox, H. C., Arria, A. M., Caldeira, K. M., Vincent, K. B., Pinchevsky, G. M., & O'Grady, K. E. (2012). Longitudinal predictors of past-year non-suicidal self-injury and motives among college students. *Psychological Medicine*, 42(4), 717–726.

Wilkinson, P., Kelvin, R., Roberts, C., Dubicka, B., & Goodyer, I. (2011). Clinical and psychosocial predictors of suicide attempts and nonsuicidal self-injury in the Adolescent Depression Antidepressants and Psychotherapy Trial (ADAPT). *American Journal of Psychiatry*, 168(5), 495–501.

Wolff, J., Frazier, E. A., Esposito-Smythers, C., Burke, T., Sloan, E., & Spirito, A. (2013). Cognitive and social factors associated with NSSI and suicide attempts in psychiatrically hospitalized adolescents. *Journal of Abnormal Child Psychology*, 41(6), 1005–1013.

You, J., Lin, M. P., Fu, K., & Leung, F. (2013). The best friend and friendship group influence on adolescent nonsuicidal self-injury. *Journal of Abnormal Child Psychology*, 41(6), 993–1004.

Zajonc, R. B. (2001). Mere exposure: A gateway to the subliminal. *Current Directions in Psychological Science*, 10(6), 224–228.

Zetterqvist, M., Lundh, L. G., & Svedin, C. G. (2013). A comparison of adolescents engaging in self-injurious behaviors with and without suicidal intent: Self-reported experiences of adverse life events and trauma symptoms. *Journal of Youth and Adolescence*, 42(8), 1257–1272.

Neurological Disorders and Symptoms Associated with Psychological/Behavioral Problems

Maxine H. Krengel *and* Roberta F. White

Abstract

Several neurological syndromes and neurocognitive disorders can result in behavioral and affective symptoms that may be present in an emergent situation or are present in the medical context. Clinicians who see patients with new or unusual behavioral symptoms are often faced with the challenge of determining when patients are in need of follow-up diagnostic evaluation. The purpose of this chapter is to discuss the expression of behavioral changes in neurological disease that we have encountered in our own extensive clinical experience. We do not provide an exhaustive review of all disorders or neurocognitive symptoms, but rather focus on common conditions that present frequently in the context of behavioral emergencies. This discussion is aimed at sensitizing clinicians to the possibility of neurologic disease in patients with prominent behavioral symptomatology.

Key Words: neurocognitive, neuropsychological, neurologic, dementia, cerebrovascular disease, movement disorders

The purpose of this chapter is to provide an overview of the neurological diagnoses and neuropsychological or behavioral symptoms that may present in either an emergent situation or in a medical clinic and that require further evaluation. Because neurological symptoms and behavioral syndromes often coexist and causative factors are difficult to distinguish, it is essential for clinicians to be able to identify neurologic symptoms that require follow-up care. Historically, there was a distinct differentiation between what was *neurologic* and what was *psychiatric*. This differentiation is no longer applicable as disorders documented in the Diagnostic and Statistical Manual (DSM; American Psychiatric Association, 2013) are known to have neurobiological bases. In addition, many times individuals with neurologic disease will first present to a mental health practitioner with acute or gradual onset of depression, anxiety, or other symptoms that are due to a primary progressive neurologic disease or traumatic brain injury.

In this chapter we provide symptom clarification for appropriate diagnosis. Common symptoms of neurologic conditions are discussed, including hallucinations, delusions, paranoia, apathy, restlessness, agitation, depression, anxiety, denial, and regression. We also discuss common disorders, including primary progressive dementias such as Alzheimer's disease and frontotemporal lobe dementias; movement disorders such as Parkinson's disease and Huntington's disease; cerebrovascular disease; traumatic brain injury, and epilepsy. This is not an exhaustive list, but includes common conditions that present frequently in the context of behavioral emergencies.

We provide an overview of recent literature on these syndromes and behavioral symptoms. Our discussion largely emanates, however, from our own extensive clinical experience as clinical psychologists with a subspecialty in neuropsychology. We focus our discussion on the systematic expression of behavioral changes in neurological disease that go beyond the traditional cognitive deficits assessed in neuropsychology.

Interview Guidelines

There are several important interview topics to consider when reviewing considerations for neurologic disease. Developmental and educational history can offer information pertaining to prenatal and perinatal exposure to toxicants, educational disabilities, and traumatic experiences. Social and occupational history are also relevant in the documentation of exposures, recent decline in social and behavioral comportment, and insight into current behaviors. Of course medical history, including prior diagnosis of seizure disorder, heart disease, diabetes, substance abuse, and brain injury, should be adequately documented, in addition to the time course, which may aid in appropriate diagnostic considerations. Lastly, current physical symptoms, especially recent changes in physical health, may improve diagnostic accuracy. What follows are more thorough descriptions of the above interview topics. Of course it should be noted that often it is necessary for family members or caregivers to be interviewed because the patient with a neurological illness may not be able to provide adequate documentation of symptoms.

Developmental and Educational History

The need to document prenatal and perinatal complications arises because patients who have experienced exposure to neurotoxicants in utero, birth trauma, early head injuries, or encephalitis/meningitis are at greater risk of neurological disorders later in life, including epilepsy. In addition, multiple risk factors for neurologic illness will need to be documented because they may increase the amount and alter the types of symptoms. This is especially true of multiple concussive injury, when a "minor bump to the head" may result in more profound deficits than expected. Individuals may present in emergent situations with symptoms of "blanking out" or daydreaming episodes at school or at home, in addition to emotional dyscontrol symptoms consistent with epilepsy.

School history should include information pertaining to trouble paying attention, restlessness, hyperactivity, or an inability to complete tasks—behavioral symptoms seen in individuals with attention-deficit hyperactivity disorder (ADHD). Impulse control disorders and an inability to inhibit, such as with ADHD, may lead the patient to make inappropriate choices, resulting in emergent

psychiatric crises. These same kinds of problems may be seen in patients with below average general intelligence, childhood or adolescent onset of a neurogenetic disorder (such as Huntington's disease), or childhood exposure to neurotoxicants, such as lead or mercury, at unsafe levels. These issues will likely result in varying treatment methodologies, depending on the cause of the behavioral dysfunction.

Social and Occupational History

In a number of patients with primary neurological disorder, initial manifestation of the illness can be seen in the patient's social or occupational life. Undiagnosed brain tumors, strokes, primary progressive dementias, neurotoxicant exposures, or multiple sclerosis can result in deterioration in social relationships and an inability to retain a job. In some occupational histories, the patient's job status may decline as an undiagnosed illness progresses. When these patients are questioned closely, it often becomes apparent that the change in occupational status is due to an inability to carry out job demands prior to diagnosis. In other cases, the patient may have insufficient insight into the reasons for job status changes. Other patients present as behavioral emergencies because of a social change noted in behavioral control. The patient may have suddenly or gradually become irritable and aggressive, paranoid, sexually disinhibited, unable to follow rules or obey the law or normal codes of behavior, apathetic, or consistently confused. These kinds of changes can be seen in patients with primary progressive dementias but can also occur in patients with slow-growing lesions such as brain tumors.

Medical History

A number of medical conditions predispose patients to the development of neurological disease, which can then present as behavioral emergencies. Chronic heart failure, hypertension, and diabetes are all associated with increased risk of cerebrovascular disease or sudden changes in behavioral control. Any patient with a history of stroke or transient ischemic attacks should be considered at risk for behavioral or cognitive changes attributable to the vascular condition.

Physical Symptoms

Physical symptoms that can be seen in many neurological disorders include incontinence, fatigue, dizziness, weakness, and headaches. Visual disturbances (e.g., double vision, blindness) are common in multiple sclerosis and may wax and wane or even disappear for years. Sensitivity to heat and cold are often seen in multiple sclerosis, at which time symptoms seem to worsen. Gait disturbance and tremors or abnormal movements may be seen in patients with Parkinson's disease or Huntington's disease or other disorders involving the brain's motor system (including strokes in motor areas and, in particular, nutritionally related alcoholic neuropathies and exposure to neurotoxicants, including inhalant abuse). Weight loss in the year prior to diagnosis is commonly reported in patients who develop primary progressive dementias. These patients may also develop sensitivity to cold. Parasthesias (numbness or tingly feelings in the skin) may also be seen with peripheral nervous system involvement (e.g., in alcoholic and toxicant induced disorders).

Psychological and Behavioral Symptoms in Neurological Disorders

In this section we discuss a number of neurological disorders. We begin with a general description of the medical features of a disorder. Next, we summarize the types of psychological symptoms that may herald the onset of a disorder or be prominently featured in a patient with a disease who presents with a behavioral emergency.

Alzheimer's Disease

Alzheimer's disease (AD), the most common neurodegenerative disorder, causes progressive cognitive decline, especially a striking memory impairment, in addition to behavioral changes early in the process. The dementia associated with AD has an insidious onset, beginning typically with loss of memory for new information, and there is a progressive decline in almost all areas of cognitive functioning. AD is characterized by accumulation of fibrillary amyloid-B protein in placques and vessels, neurofibullary tangles, and synaptic and neuronal loss. It is diagnosed presumptively and confirmed by autopsy or biopsy.

In addition to the deterioration in cognitive functioning that defines the dementia associated with AD (i.e., impairments in memory, attention, executive functioning, language, and visualspatial abilities identified on neuropsychological testing), profound psychological sequelae and personality changes are characteristic of the disease process. In the early stages of the disease, patients often show a loss of interest, apathy, lowered energy levels, and depressed mood. Changes in functional capacities early on in the disease process can also result in depression and in some cases an increased risk for suicide.

Apathy ranges in frequency from 25% to 50% in patients with AD (Starkstein, Jorge, Mizrahi, & Robinson, 2006). Apathy is far more frequent in mild AD than are delusions, irritability, agitation, and hallucinations, which tend to occur in later states (Meguro et al., 2004). Several studies have demonstrated a significant association between apathy and both reduced metabolic activity in prefrontal regions and more severe motor findings such as Parkinsonism, suggesting that neuropathological changes in specific brain areas may underlie the high frequency of apathy in AD. However, severity of cognitive deficits is not directly correlated with level of apathy.

Depression associated with AD is experienced as diminished interest in previously pleasurable activities. This change can be best described as reflecting apathy and passivity rather than feelings of sadness, worthlessness, or the anhedonia seen in clinical depression.

In DSM-5, diagnostic criteria for dementia now include the subspecifier of *with behavioral disturbance* or *without behavioral disturbance*. Behavioral alterations include psychotic symptoms, mood disturbance, agitation, or apathy. As individuals begin to lose cognitive abilities, they might underestimate or not be aware of diminished capabilities and engage in risky behavior, including driving or using equipment that requires intense attention. These risky behaviors may also result in injury, requiring emergency room visits.

As the disease progresses, common behavioral symptoms may also include anxiety, agitation, extreme restlessness, and irritability. It is not uncommon for AD patients in later stages to present with delusions or hallucinations, which may occur in as many as 40% to 60% of patients (Eror, Lopez, Dekosky, & Sweet, 2005). The hallucinations are most often visual or auditory, but can be olfactory or tactile. Common delusions include the belief that people are stealing from the patient and that there are unwanted people living in their home, or that the house they are living in is not their real home. Wandering, coupled with severe memory impairments, may lead to patients becoming lost and being brought to the emergency department after being found by the police. The delusions tend to dissipate as the dementia becomes more severe. Clinically, psychosis in AD has been associated with more rapid cognitive decline and increased risk of agitated and aggressive behavior.

Although mania is rare in patients with AD, it may be seen in patients who have disturbances in their sleep-wake cycle. These patients may present with symptoms such as irritability, agitation, poor judgment, and insomnia.

Word-finding difficulty and impaired confrontation naming evidenced on neuropsychological tests are the hallmarks of the language disturbance in AD. These language disturbances are markedly different from the language disturbance seen in schizophrenia and its related disorders. Qualitatively, the language and speech problems observed in patients with AD often include circumlocutions that are reflective of the inability to identify the correct word. The loosening of associations and the speech disorder that is indicative of a thought disorder are not present. In the later stages of AD, however, speech may become neologistic and incomprehensible.

Frontal Lobe Dementias

A few primary progressive dementing disorders affect the frontal lobes most extensively, known as frontal lobe dementias (FLD). Although these conditions, such as Pick's disease, primary progressive aphasia, and frontotemporal dementia, are relatively rare, the initial presentations are frequently behavioral, and patients are often evaluated first in the emergency setting. The cardinal features of the change evident in FLD are best summarized as a loss of behavioral control or monitoring. The patient may become irritable, aggressive and unable to exercise self-control or monitor behavior. These patients are unable to inhibit aggressive acts that were previously inhibited, and they have diminished social comportment. Similarly, behavior may become sexually disinhibited, with the patient approaching inappropriate people, exhibiting an increased sexual drive, or talking inappropriately about sexual behavior. Occasionally, patients with no history of criminal behavior begin to break the law, stealing objects or money or breaking into buildings. Faulty behavioral monitoring can be seen as a lack of insight into behavioral changes, in which the patient does not notice the inappropriateness of behaviors or even that he or she is acting differently than in the past. Finally, we see patients diagnosed with this type of dementia who appear to have lost the capacity for guilt, failing to ascribe any fault for change in behaviors.

Cerebrovascular Disease

Cerebrovascular disease (CVD) is a term referring to the constellation of lesions that occur because of vascular pathology in the brain. It encompasses entities known as multi-infarct dementia, leukoariosis, and Binswanger's disease. CVD is thought to occur rather commonly, perhaps accounting for 57% of dementia diagnoses. Patients with vascular disease may have experienced large clinical strokes, often with other small lesions identifiable by brain imaging, or may have no clinically identified strokes despite showing evidence of lesions on imaging and exhibiting cognitive, behavioral, and neurological signs of such lesions. By the time of diagnosis, patients may have a variety of lesions that can involve the cortex, connections between cortical regions or subcortical white matter, basal ganglia, cerebellum, brain stem, or combinations of these areas. Patients with multiple lesions may show behavioral changes that are attributable to lesions occurring in specified brain regions or systems, and they may also show secondary or cumulative effects of having multiple lesion sites. The latter generally show up in group studies of these patients as *frontal system* dysfunction, observable on neuropsychological tests of attention and executive functioning. Focal deficits are harder to establish in group studies of patients with CVD, presumably because the sites of these lesions vary among patients. Patients with diffuse lesions, however, may show evidence of behavioral changes attributable to frontal dysfunction, similar to those seen in frontal dementias.

From the perspective of behavioral emergencies, CVD is an important disorder because behavioral (especially affective) changes are often the first symptoms that bring a patient in for diagnosis; recent research has shown increased psychiatric symptomatology with increased severity of white matter changes in the brain.

In our experience, CVD is a diagnostic category that is also common among geriatric patients receiving inpatient psychiatric evaluation and care (especially when it is the first psychiatric admission they have experienced). We frequently find that a history of strokes, abnormal imaging, and evidence of multifocal vascular disease are ignored etiologically in an evaluation of the patient's behavioral status.

Symptomatic changes that are behavioral in nature and that occur across the many types of presentation of multiple lesions in patients with CVD are often seen as a new presentation of agitation or agitated depression. The patient is frequently at a loss to explain any precipitants for periods or episodes of agitation or a sense of anxiety and may be quite debilitated because of it. The agitation may also be accompanied by tearfulness or irritability. In lesions involving the frontal lobes, aggression, major depression, and generalized anxiety are not uncommon. Many patients with CVD are apathetic or amotivational when presented with cognitive tasks or life circumstances. When patients are apathetic or lethargic, their behavioral changes may be interpreted by others as reflecting a depression, although diagnosis and treatment for clinical depression would be inappropriate.

Patients with severe bilateral CVD may exhibit a chronic or episodic confusional state. This state can be accompanied by a number of symptoms, including paranoid delusions. These delusions are often fixed in terms of their central theme. However, details of the patient's report about incidents that recently occurred in relation to the delusion are often highly variable from one report to another, and the patient may completely forget having reported specific information related to the delusion. For example, one afternoon the patient may report that family members or strangers are spying with a television camera and another day say the spying occurred with a tape recorder. In addition to delusions, illusions or interpretations of sensory distortions caused by damage to the parietal or occipital lobes are seen. For example, one patient thought that a big black raven was sitting on his shoulder. This illusion was also vague and changeable, with the patient sometimes reporting that the bird was always there (other times it was not) and with the bird switching between the right and left shoulders.

A similar phenomenon known as reduplicative paramnesia can occur, in which the patient multiplies objects or people in the environment. Common manifestations include the patient's belief that he or she has two or more hospital rooms or homes. The belief can extend to the patient's body, so that the patient believes that he or she has many arms or legs. In the most dramatic case of this phenomenon we have seen, the patient believed that he had a double of himself who followed him around. Another behavioral anomaly that may be seen in patients with posterior cortical damage is that of anosagnosia, in which the patient expresses a form of denial about medical status or physical functioning. In such cases, he or she may refuse to acknowledge hemiparesis, even when it is quite severe. This phenomenon does not seem to represent classic psychoanalytical denial but rather reflects the patient's altered perception of somatic functioning as a result of brain damage.

In addition to the changes just noted, patients may exhibit a wide variety of behavioral symptoms related to focal or lateralized brain damage. Patients with left hemisphere strokes may develop depressive symptoms that are not entirely reactive in nature, and patients with right hemisphere strokes may show an unawareness of deficit or an indifference or lack of emotional comprehension. Similarly, a patient may lose the ability to read the emotional states other people reveal in facial expressions or body posture and may be surprised by statements others make about their feelings. Patients with a right frontal lesion may develop paranoid delusions. Those with left temporal lesions may report auditory hallucinations, whereas other patients with temporal lesions may become extremely religious. Occipital lesions may be associated with visual hallucinations (often of lights, colors, or spots), and gustatory or olfactory hallucinations are seen in some patients with temporal lesions. Finally, changes in sexual behaviors, including hypersexuality, are sometimes seen in these individuals.

Multiple Sclerosis

Multiple Sclerosis (MS) is a neurological disorder in which the myelin sheaths of nerve fibers are damaged, producing lesions called demyelinating plaques. These lesions may occur throughout the central nervous system and, therefore, there is wide variability in symptom presentation. Symptoms are transient in the early stages of the illness. There is often motor weakness, visual disturbance, numbness, vertigo, seizures, unformed auditory hallucinations, fatigue, and mood changes. Additionally, apathy, irritability, and hypersexuality are not uncommon. The course of the illness may be rapidly progressive, but the disease often persists for many years.

MS is sometimes confused with hysteria or somatoform disorder. This is because of the fleeting, evanescent nature of the physical symptoms, the preoccupation with physical functioning that occurs in some MS patients, and the tendency of MS patients to show profiles similar to those seen in patients with hysteria or somatoform disorders on personality tests such as the MMPI2.

Affective disorders are commonly seen in MS and may occur as commonly as in the general population. The neurovegetative symptoms of depression may overlap with MS symptoms. MS patients may also present with suicidal ideation and, in some cases, depression and suicidal ideation may occur prior to physical symptoms. Patients may also present to the emergency department with emotional lability, fatigue, irritability, and recent mood changes.

A smaller group of patients with MS present with delusions and hallucinations. Patients may have fixed persecutory delusions. They may also have symptoms consistent with frontal and temporal dysfunction, including hyperreligiosity (White et al., 1992b).

Parkinson's Disease

Idiopathic Parkinson's disease (PD) is characterized by motor symptoms such as tremor, rigidity, fatigue, slowness of movements, and an inability to initiate movement. Gait disturbance, slurred speech, and small and tremulous writing are also cardinal features of the disease. It is a progressive illness, with patients in the early stages showing mild motor signs (from unilateral to bilateral involvement), and patients later in the disease process showing more severe motor impairment. Cognitive deficits can be seen at various stages, including visuospatial processing deficits, impaired retrieval of information, and attentional variability. Mood changes are commonly seen in patients with PD. In addition, psychiatric symptoms such as hallucinations and paranoia are seen in patients with PD, even early in the disease process.

Depression is fairly common in patients with untreated PD. There is controversy over whether mood changes are a result of neurochemical processes or a reaction to having the illness. It is fairly well documented that the mood changes do not correlate reliably with motor signs, age of onset, or duration of the motor symptoms. There is some indication that patients who are young at disease onset are more likely to have depressive symptoms predating the motor symptoms. When motor symptoms are treated, the depression may initially improve slightly. This change in mood, however, does not appear to hold over time, even with continued improvement in motor symptoms.

Patients with early PD may present with visual hallucinations. These most often involve fuzzy animals, hooded people, or indistinct people (White et al., 1992a). Later in the course of the illness, patients may present with confusion and psychosis. The hallucinations may involve both auditory and visual modalities and are seen during confusional states. Paranoid beliefs or delusions are seen to a lesser extent; however, when they occur they are associated with anxiety and fear. It is unclear which, if any, of these symptoms are related to medication side effects, although some patients complain of visual hallucinations even before they begin medications.

There is also some indication that medication treatment for PD may cause vivid and disturbing dreams, visual hallucinations, and paranoid delusions. Other treatment effects include confusional states with disorientation as to time and place, anxiety, or mania. This is especially true for older patients. Visual hallucinations are the most common side effect of medication and the frequency of hallucinations ranges from 6% to 38% of patients treated with dopaminergic medication. Fully formed images of humans or animals are common. They are most often experienced at night and are recurrent nearly every night. Most patients report that these are nonthreatening hallucinations. Other patients who are taking anticholinergic drugs and are on medications longer are most likely to have visual hallucinations.

Delusions are rare in untreated PD. However, they are found in conjunction with a variety of medication treatments and may represent emerging toxicity. Delusions from anti-Parkinsonian treatment tend to be persecutory in nature, involving fears of being harmed.

Mood elevation, which varies from euphoria to full-blown manic episodes, has been reported in patients on anti-Parkinsonian medications. Again, these episodes are related to amount of drug use and they diminish with decreased drug use. Less common symptoms that have been found to relate to the amount of drug use include increased anxiety, irritability, and insomnia.

Delirious states with fluctuating arousal, impaired attention, and incoherent verbal output have been observed in up to 25% of treated PD patients, most often later in the disease process after years of medication treatment. Overall, PD patients who are older, with dementia, on higher doses of medication, and with a history of psychiatric illness predating the PD motor signs are described as more likely to suffer from frank psychiatric symptoms.

Huntington's Disease

Although Huntington's disease (HD) is relatively rare, the presenting symptoms are often behavioral and psychological in nature. HD is an autosomal dominant genetic disease with complete penetrance, meaning that the offspring of an affected individual has a 50% chance of being affected. It is characterized by a combination of symptoms that are described as uncontrollable involuntary movements, psychiatric disturbances, and progressive dementia. After the initial appearance of the symptoms, there is a progressive decline in cognitive and motor functioning.

Patients with HD show considerable variability in the onset of motor symptoms and in emotional and cognitive disturbances. The characteristics of the behavioral and personality changes observed in HD share features with other disorders of subcortical structures in the brain. For example, depression and apathy are commonly seen in PD as well as HD. These mood state or affective changes are not typically a reaction to having a debilitating degenerative disease. Investigators have found evidence of behavioral and mood changes occurring several years before the onset of the motor impairments. The finding that HD patients experience manic episodes in addition to depression also constitutes evidence suggesting the organic nature of the changes since neither bipolar disorder nor mania is an expected functional reaction to living with this debilitating disease.

Presently, affective disorders (including depression, mania, and bipolar disorder) are reported as the most common psychiatric syndrome in HD. In one study, up to 40% of the HD patients sampled reported major affective illness. Irritability is also relatively common, sometimes even severe enough to warrant the diagnosis of intermittent explosive disorder. Patients with HD may have difficulty inhibiting impulsive behavior. There is a great deal of evidence of antisocial behavior associated with HD, ranging from criminal assaults and minor crimes to child abuse and neglect. However, the relationship between the development of these symptoms and the social effects of living in an HD family and the neuropathology of the disease are controversial.

There is a significant level of alcohol and substance abuse in affected individuals and their families. The majority of alcohol use is during earlier stages of the disease and tends to drop as the disease progresses.

Disorders characteristic of schizophrenia have also been reported to occur in 5% to 10% of HD patients, with hallucinations and paranoid delusions frequently reported by HD patients. White and colleagues (1992c) documented that there are significant changes in mood state that do not reach the level of diagnosable affective disorders, including vegetative, biological signs of depression; psychomotor retardation; and insomnia, often resulting from chorea and restlessness and anorexia. Patients tend to lose more weight than would be expected from calories required to accommodate the increase in movement due to chorea alone.

The extraordinarily high suicide rate in this population was noted in the seminal paper by Huntington. After statistically adjusting for age and sex, the suicide rate in an HD group has been found to be more than eight times the rate for individuals aged 50 to 69 years (Halpin, 2012). Further, it has been concluded that a preponderance of successful suicides were committed by individuals who have not yet been diagnosed. White et al. (1992c), described patients who experienced command hallucinations regarding suicide, some who reported a compulsive urge to kill themselves, and some for whom suicidal ideation is secondary to their depression and demoralization related to the disease. (For further discussion of suicide risk in particular neurological disorders, see chapter 26 of this volume.)

Traumatic Brain Injury

Recently the popular media has raised the issue of multiple concussive events and mood disorders. Traumatic brain injury (TBI) can result when a person is moving and strikes an obstacle (i.e., the brain accelerates and quickly decelerates) or when a person is struck by an object (i.e., creating pressure gradients from the skull distortion). Contusions and tissue shearing seen with more severe closed head injury can cause loss of consciousness. The duration of loss of consciousness and the duration of posttraumatic amnesia correlate with the severity of the head injury in terms of mortality and cognitive and emotional functioning. In addition to blunt trauma, the impact of pressure waves from blast injury has been noted especially in military personnel as potentially causing lasting cognitive and emotional distress.

Patients who experience psychological and personality disturbances are remarkable in that they frequently appear to be physically healthy and normal. Often, no physical or neurologic consequences of the TBI remain, yet the behavior and personality changes that result from the injury cause significant difficulty. Lezak, Howieson, & Loring (2004) reported that for some patients, behavioral and emotional disturbances are more debilitating than residual cognitive and physical disabilities. Although it is likely that individuals with more mild TBIs return to baseline within 3 months, a minority of individuals may continue to experience symptoms even years after the event, including depression, sleep disorder, and visual disturbances.

The exact nature of the behavioral and cognitive disturbances associated with head injuries is directly dependent on the locations of the primary and secondary injuries. In addition to behavioral consequences related to the specific site of injury, diffuse damage (i.e., small lesions and lacerations throughout the brain) can accompany the injury. Even patients with mild injuries who were never admitted to the hospital, who may not have gone to an emergency department at the time of the injury, and whose laboratory findings conclude brain imaging as normal may experience emotional symptoms that later require emergent care. In addition, multiple TBIs may result in significant behavioral disturbance, even in the absence of frank symptoms immediately following any of the events.

Lezak et al. (2004) depicted the kinds of alterations in a brain-injured patient's character that can cause the most distress and adjustment problems for patients' families and loved ones. These include impaired social perceptiveness and an inability to reflect and monitor behavior. Patients may lose insight and empathy, so that their understandings of and feelings for others are diminished. In addition, brain-injured patients often become impulsive, restless, impatient; this may lead to legal problems resulting from the commission of criminal acts. There is often a lack of drive and an impaired capacity for social learning; although a patient's ability to learn new information may be intact, he or she fails to learn from experience. In addition to impulsivity and heightened emotional experiences, some TBI patients may experience mania and paranoia or suicidal thoughts that may lead them to seek psychiatric care.

Temporal Lobe Epilepsy

Seizures are a common symptom of a wide range of neurological disorders and the hallmark symptom of epilepsy. A seizure results when an overactive group of neurons (i.e., the seizure focus) is released from its usual physiological control, resulting in abnormal electrical rhythms in the brain. This transient disturbance is caused by an excessive discharge of cortical neurons. The excitation can spread and excite adjacent regions. Depending on the number of neurons affected, the excitation can lead to widespread electrical dysrhythmias. These generalized seizures are characterized by loss of consciousness and stereotyped motor activity, including convulsions.

Seizures can result from infections, head injuries, vascular malformation, strokes, tumors, toxicants, high fevers, and other neurologic disorders. Seizures of unknown etiology are referred to as idiopathic. Idiopathic temporal lobe epilepsy (ITLE) has been of particular interest to neuropsychologists, as psychiatric and psychological problems are common. Patients with ITLE often experience affective and behavioral disturbances, hallucination, psychosis and personality changes.

During the seizure itself (i.e., ictus) patients can experience a wide range of sensory, motor, and emotional phenomena, including autonomic sensations (e.g., butterflies in the stomach, blushing), cognitive disturbances (e.g., feelings of déjà vu, hallucinations), alterations in mood (e.g., fear, panic, depression, elation), illusions (e.g., misperceptions of real external stimuli), and automatisms (e.g., lip smacking, grimacing, automatic behavior).

ITLE is thought to be the type of epilepsy most frequently associated with the psychiatric changes known as the interictal behavioral syndrome (IBS). However, there is considerable controversy in the field of neuropsychology regarding the specificity of this association. The personality disturbances commonly described as part of the IBS include changes in sexual behavior (mostly hyposexuality), viscosity (i.e., social clinging), religiosity, hypergraphia, and increased intensity of emotions.

ITLE patients can also show considerable changes in the manner of their interactions and conversations. Their speech is often circumstantial, weighted down with numerous unnecessary details, overly serious, and perhaps pedantic. An important difference between this type of circumstantial speech and the tangential speech of schizophrenia is that patients with ITLE, if given enough time, will eventually reach their point; however, patients with a thought disorder are pulled away from the point and are not able to return to it.

Patients with ITLE often have trouble controlling their anger. Irritable and impulsive behavior in the form of angry outbursts is common, and on rare occasions behavior may be violent or abusive. Often, a specific quality of moral indignation or feeling that an injustice has occurred accompanies the anger or aggressive outburst. For some patients, the IBS can be more debilitating than the seizure disorder itself.

Psychological and psychiatric attention is often required for patients who are experiencing not only anger and aggression more intensely but fear and depression as well. The depression of some patients is so severe that they are at risk for suicide. Interictal psychosis is less frequently seen than personality and affective changes. In the latter stages of ITLE, a paranoid psychosis can develop that resembles schizophrenia.

Concluding Remarks

In this chapter we provide an update on the behavioral and psychological symptoms often seen in patients who have neurological conditions. We included examples of psychological emergencies during which affected patients may come to the attention of mental health-care workers. We illustrate that thinking of disorders as either psychiatric or neurological imposes a false dichotomy. In the context of what may appear to be a behavioral emergency, it can be beneficial to consider the patient's neurological and medical status. It is of the utmost importance to understand the need for follow-up care when these issues emerge. When an individual provides a history of cardiovascular risk factors, toxicant exposures, TBI, or movement disorder, the clinician would be wise to refer him or her for a more extensive medical or neurological evaluation to rule out medical causes of behavioral limitations. In addition, a family history of neurologic illness may raise concerns about potential causes for behavioral changes and should also be further evaluated. (For a discussion of neurobiological factors in suicide and violence, see chapters 21 and 22 of this volume respectively.)

References

American Psychiatric Association. (2013). *Diagnostic and statistical manual of mental disorders* (5th ed.). Arlington, VA: American Psychiatric Association.

Eror, E. A., Lopez, O. L., Dekosky, S. T., & Sweet, R. A. (2005). Alzheimer disease subjects with psychosis have increased schizotypal symptoms before dementia onset. *Biological Psychiatry, 58*, 325–330.

Halpin, M. (2012). Accounts of suicidality in the Huntington Disease community. *Omega, 65*, 317–334.

Lezak, M. D., Howieson, D. B., & Loring, D. W. (2004). *Neuropsychological assessment* (4th ed.). New York, NY: Oxford University Press.

Meguro, K., Meguro, M., Tanaka, Y., Akanuma, K., Yamaguchi, K., & Itoh, I. (2004). Risperidone is effective for wandering and disturbed sleep/wake patterns in Alzheimer's Disease. *Journal of Geriatric Psychiatry and Neurology, 17*, 61–67.

Starkstein, S. E., Jorge, R., Mizrahi, R., & Robinson, R. G. (2006). A prospective longitudinal study of apathy in Alzheimer's disease. *Journal or Neurology, Neurosurgery, and Psychiatry, 77*, 8–11.

White, R. F., Au, R., Durson, R., & Moss, M. B. (1992a). Neuropsychological function in Parkinson's disease. In R. F. White (Ed.), *Clinical syndromes in adult neuropsychology: The practitioner's handbook* (pp. 213–251). Amsterdam, the Netherlands: Elsevier.

White, R. F., Nyenhuis, D. S., & Sax, D. S. (1992b). Multiple sclerosis. In R. F. White (Ed.), *Clinical syndromes in adult neuropsychology: The practitioner's handbook* (pp. 177–212). Amsterdam, the Netherlands: Elsevier.

White, R. F., Vasterling, J. J., Koroshetz, W., & Myers, R. (1992c). Neuropsychological function in Huntington's disease. In R. F. White (Ed.), *Clinical syndromes in adult neuropsychology: The practitioner's handbook* (pp. 213–251). Amsterdam, the Netherlands: Elsevier.

Endocrine Disorders Associated with Psychological/Behavioral Problems

Tara L. Lauriat *and* Jacqueline A. Samson

Abstract

Common endocrine disorders often present with psychiatric symptoms and may be mistaken for primary psychiatric disorders. Dysregulation of the following endocrine systems commonly affects behavior: the adrenocorticoid system, the thyroid system, the parathyroid system, the pancreas and regulation of glucose, and the reproductive system. Symptoms of depression and anxiety are common across the spectrum of endocrine disorders and more severe cases may include psychotic features. Clinicians are often faced with the challenge of identifying an underlying endocrine etiology for behavioral changes based on relatively nonspecific symptoms. A general understanding of the signs and symptoms associated with elevated or decreased hormone levels can assist in the differential diagnosis and ultimately increase the likelihood that a patient receives appropriate treatment. Accurate diagnosis can be especially critical in acute behavioral emergencies.

Key Words: endocrine, thyroid, parathyroid, reproductive system, hormone, depression

Rapid and accurate assessment of the underlying cause of a behavioral emergency is essential for the selection of the most effective intervention. Among the most difficult distinctions are the differential diagnoses of primary mental disorders versus imbalances or dysfunctions in underlying endocrine systems. As the underlying signs and symptoms that are secondary to endocrine dysfunction are somewhat nonspecific, it is important to be aware of all possibilities and rule out alternative diagnoses by using additional laboratory tests and clinical knowledge. In this chapter we review the major endocrine dysfunctions associated with emergent behavioral problems with an eye to assisting clinicians in achieving an accurate diagnosis.

The endocrine system is one of the most important mechanisms the body uses to regulate emotions, cognitive functioning, and behavioral response. Stability in levels of arousal, quality and speed of motor activity, circadian rhythms, temperature regulation, mood, cognitive processing, and response to stressors all depend upon proper functioning in

the endocrine system (see Table 28.1). Endocrine functioning can be disrupted by endogenous gland pathology or environmental toxins. When the endocrine system pathology results in abnormal elevations or decreases in levels of any hormones, mood changes can occur, cognitive processing can become cloudy or even psychotic, behavior can become impulsive and racy or sluggish, and medications may not produce desired effects (see Table 28.2). Most endocrine disorders are associated with specific findings on physical examinations as well as changes in appetite, sleep, and body temperature. There is a general progression from symptoms specific to a particular diagnostic category to very general features in later stages that can be not only difficult to interpret from an etiological standpoint, but also life-threatening. These generalized symptoms typically progress from cognitive difficulties to psychotic features and, eventually, to coma or even death. This pattern may be observed in endocrine disorders as well as prolonged states of sleep deprivation or malnutrition.

Table 28.1. Functions of Primary Endocrine Hormones.

Hormone	Gland or Organ	Function
Thyroxine (T4)	Thyroid	Regulates metabolism: precursor to T3
Triiodothyronine (T3)	Thyroid	Regulates metabolism: active hormone
Thyroid stimulating hormone (TSH)	Pituitary	Stimulates production of T4 and in turn T3
Thyroid releasing hormone (TRH)	Hypothalamus	Stimulates production of TSH by pituitary
Parathyroid hormone	Parathyroid	Increases calcium level in the blood
Calcitonin	Parathyroid	Decreases calcium levels in the blood
Cortisol	Adrenal glands	Increases blood sugar and regulates numerous physiological functions
Adrenocorticotropic hormone (ACTH)	Pituitary	Stimulates secretion of glucocorticoids
Corticotropin releasing hormone (CRH)	Hypothalamus	Stimulates production of ACTH
Estrogens	Ovaries, Placenta, Adipose tissue, Brain, Bone	Female reproductive hormones (include Estrone, Estradiol, Estriol)
Progesterone	Ovaries, Placenta Adrenal glands	Regulates menstrual cycle and pregnancy, neurosteroid
Testosterone	Testes	Male reproductive hormone
Follicle-stimulating hormone (FH)	Pituitary	Stimulates follicle growth in the ovaries
Luteinizing hormone (LH)	Pituitary	Stimulates release of egg or sperm and thickening of endometrium
Gonadotropin releasing hormone (GnRH)	Hypothalamus	Stimulates production of FSH and LH
Dehydroepiandrosterone (DHEA)	Brain, Adrenal glands, Gonads	Precursor to sex steroids, neurosteroid

The most common behavioral emergencies that may require immediate management by a mental health clinician include acute suicidal behavior, sudden mood shifts, panic attacks, unprovoked rage, and acute psychotic episodes (Samson, Levin, & Richardson, 1998; Tsatourian & Samson, 2009). The five endocrine systems that interface with these psychiatric symptoms are the adrenocorticoid system, the thyroid system, parathyroid system, glucose regulation by the pancreas, and the reproductive systems. Suicidal behavior may be associated with alterations in thyroid, cortisol, or glucose levels. Mood symptoms are most commonly related to disturbances in thyroid hormone or changes in estrogen and progesterone levels. Sudden panic may be related to thyroid levels or low blood glucose. Unprovoked rage can be associated with steroid hormones, most commonly exogenous androgens. Finally, symptoms of acute psychosis may occur with any endocrine disturbance when it reaches an extreme level. In some cases, failure to identify an endocrine basis for the behavioral state can result in inappropriate treatment choices. In other cases, the acute crisis can be managed with standard psychotropic medications but identification and treatment of the underlying cause may be a critical factor in preventing future episodes.

In this chapter, we provide an overview of the signs and symptoms associated with diseases and the altered function of each of these systems. Throughout the chapter, we include brief vignettes taken from

Table 28.2. Prevalence Rates of Endocrine Disorders.

Cushing's Syndrome	0.0001%–0.0015%
Addison's Disease	0.011%–0.015%
Hyperthyroidism	1%
Hypothyroidism	4.6%
Hyperparathyroidism	0.3% (1%–3% postmenopausal women)
Hypoparathyroidism	Rare
Diabetes	9.3%

cases reported in the literature to illustrate the diagnostic challenges that clinicians may encounter.

Adrenal Gland Disorders and Behavior

The adrenal glands consist of the adrenal medulla, which secretes catecholamines (epinephrine and norepinephrine), and the adrenal cortex, which secretes glucocorticoids (cortisol), mineralocorticoids (aldosterone), and adrenal androgens (dehydroepiandrosterone [DHEA] and DHEA sulfate [DHEAS], androstenedione). Cortisol regulates metabolism and levels increase during periods of stress. Both elevated and decreased cortisol levels are associated with behavioral changes. Cortisol levels are affected both by primary adrenal disorders, such as Cushing's disease and Addison's disease, as well as steroid medications used for conditions, such as asthma and autoimmune diseases.

Overview of the Adrenocorticoid System

The action of the adrenocorticoid system is most observable in an acute stress response (sometimes called the fight-flight-freeze response). On exposure to perceived extreme threat, the amygdala sends an alarm signal to the hypothalamus. The hypothalamus then activates two systems, one directly through the nervous system in the periphery and another via hormonal factors in the central nervous system. The peripheral sympathetic nervous system, in addition to activating glands and smooth muscles, acts directly on the adrenal medulla to increase the release of norepinephrine, and epinephrine into the bloodstream. The resulting behavioral changes are helpful in quick reactions, such as heightened arousal, hypervigilance to threatening stimuli, increased heart rate, increased respiration, increased motor activity,

---

increased availability of glucose and fat, and decreased gastrointestinal motility. These actions serve to ensure the body's ability for quick action. In the central nervous system, the hypothalamus initiates increased production of corticotropin releasing hormone, which then acts to send a signal to the pituitary gland to secrete ACTH, which then acts on the adrenal cortex in the periphery to initiate the release of multiple hormones into the bloodstream, including cortisol. These hormones add to the effects of the stress response listed earlier, but in excess they also decrease the immune response. The drop in cortisol levels signals the parasympathetic nervous system to slow the sympathetic response down. Cortisol levels normally rise and fall throughout the day in a circadian rhythm. Prolonged exposure to stress can lead to abnormally high levels of circulating cortisol and impair the circadian rhythms of cortisol secretion, resulting in decreased immunity and increasing risk of cardiovascular disease and cancer.

Hypercortisolism

Excess amounts of circulating cortisol, known as hypercortisolism, are most often exogenous in people who use corticosteroids for treatment of medical conditions, including rheumatoid arthritis, asthma, some forms of cancer, and other autoimmune and inflammatory conditions. In addition, cortisol levels can be elevated due to prolonged exposure to stress, major depressive disorder, anxiety disorders, chronic alcoholism, obesity, anorexia nervosa, or medical illness. Less commonly, hypercortisolism is associated with Cushing's disease or with the presence of a benign or malignant tumor in the pituitary or adrenal glands. Cushing's syndrome is a general term used to refer to the signs and symptoms associated with elevated cortisol, whereas Cushing's disease refers specifically to the state where a pituitary adenoma secretes large amounts of ACTH. Often, determining whether elevated cortisol is the result of a primary psychiatric diagnosis or if the depressive symptoms are caused by a primary endocrine disorder can be challenging.

Physical signs and symptoms associated with hypercortisolism include elevated blood sugar, elevated blood pressure, fatigue, proximal muscle weakness, poor sleep, increased abdominal fat with thin arms and legs, build-up of fatty tissue around the neck between the shoulder blades, round face, lowered immune functioning, decreased bone density with low impact fractures, chronic pain, backaches, hair loss, and acne. If untreated, the chronic elevation in blood sugar may lead to diabetes in a subset of patients. In women, there may be excess hair growth on the face, chest, or thighs. The skin may become fragile, easily bruised, slow to heal, and may have purple stretch marks.

Behavioral symptoms may include irritability, impulsivity, hyperactivity, pressured speech, decreased libido, and increased aggression. Some people also experience cognitive deficits related to hypervigilance and memory impairments. Cognitive and behavioral changes may be accompanied by anxiety or depressed mood. On the other hand, mania and hypomania are more commonly observed with use of exogenous steroid medications (Pope & Katz, 1994). In acute or medically uncontrolled situations, paranoia, hallucinations, and depersonalization have been described (Nussey & Whitehead, 2001). Although the presentation in Cushing's disease may resemble that of major depressive disorder, Cushing's disease tends to involve greater mood lability and neurovegetative symptoms that are associated with atypical depression, such as hypersomnia and hyperphagia (Wolkowitz, Burke, Epel, & Reus, 2009).

Another rare but important diagnostic challenge occurs when a patient presents with both Cushing's syndrome and an eating disorder. The multiple parallel symptoms —elevated cortisol, osteoporosis, weakness, depression, and amenorrhea—make the diagnosis of Cushing's syndrome particularly challenging in this population.

Case: Cushing's Syndrome Coupled with Eating Disorder. A young woman with a history of anorexia nervosa and treatment-resistant depression was admitted to a medical floor with a diagnosis of Cushing's syndrome. An adrenal tumor was identified through a CT (computerized tomography) scan and elevated cortisol was established using a dexamethasone suppression test and corticotropin-releasing hormone stimulation test. Following surgery, symptoms of both depression and the eating disorder improved markedly (Sawicka, Gryczynska, Sowinski, Tamborska-Zedlewska, & Ruchala, 2013).

Adrenal Insufficiency

Adrenal insufficiency may occur secondary to damage to the adrenal cortex from autoimmune disorders such as Addison's disease, infection, amyloidosis,

hemochromatosis, or decreased function of the pituitary or adrenal glands due to tumor growth. Low cortisol levels can also be seen in individuals withdrawing from treatment with glucocorticoids. In addition, most studies have found that patients with a diagnosis of posttraumatic stress disorder (PTSD) have low cortisol levels (Morris, Compas, & Garber, 2012). Thus, the response of the adrenal system in individuals with PTSD as well as those who experienced childhood maltreatment is the opposite of depression, where cortisol levels are typically elevated. Childhood maltreatment can have lasting effects on the adrenal system that can affect cortisol secretion in adulthood.

Physical signs and symptoms of adrenal insufficiency include darkening of skin pigmentation, craving for salt, nausea or vomiting, lowered blood pressure, lowered blood glucose levels, weight loss, loss of body hair, irregular menses, decreased immune functioning, anorexia, muscle pain, and fatigue.

Behaviorally, individuals may exhibit social withdrawal, apathy, and decreased stamina. Cognitive changes include prolonged response latency, thought distortions, memory problems, limited attention span, and impaired concentration. The overall mood presentation tends to be irritable, depressed, or apathetic. In acute conditions, psychotic symptoms and delirium may occur. Thus, depressed mood characterizes altered cortisol levels in both directions.

It is important to note that Addison's disease may be mistaken for anorexia nervosa in young women due to the many common symptoms including weight loss and decreased appetite. However, individuals with Addison's disease do not endorse the body image disturbance and preoccupation with weight loss that are characteristic of anorexia nervosa (Blaustein, Golden, & Shenker, 1998). Moreover, cortisol is typically elevated in individuals with anorexia nervosa.

Pheochromocytoma

A pheochromocytoma is a rare, usually benign, adrenal tumor that secretes catecholamines. The classic presentation includes brief spells with headache, profuse sweating, and palpitations, together with severe hypertension. Such episodes may be infrequent or as often as several times per day. In addition, patients sometimes experience anxiety or a sense of doom during these spells. These episodes of anxiety may be mistaken for panic attacks. Other signs and symptoms may include tremor, weakness, nausea, constipation, and weight loss. The tumors most commonly secrete norepinephrine and epinephrine, resulting in a presentation consistent with elevated levels of these catecholamines. Although most pheochromocytomas are sporadic, some tumors are associated with genetic mutations and may be cancerous. If a person who is experiencing anxiety attacks has a diagnosis or family history of neurofibromatosis, multiple endocrine neoplasia type 2, or von Hippel-Lindau syndrome, the signs and symptoms just listed may be indicative of a possible pheochromocytoma.

DIAGNOSIS

Laboratory testing of the morning ACTH (adrenocorticotropic hormone) and cortisol levels together with electrolytes can be used as a screening test. An ACTH stimulation test is used for diagnosis of adrenal insufficiency, whereas a dexamethasone suppression test is the usual workup when endogenous Cushing's syndrome is suspected. Measuring blood or salivary cortisol levels multiple times throughout the day is useful in determining whether diurnal variation is altered from the typical pattern.

EFFECT OF CORTICOSTEROID MEDICATIONS ON BEHAVIORAL SYMPTOMS

Corticosteroid medications have been associated with multiple psychiatric presentations as well as cognitive deficits. Side effects can include mood symptoms ranging from depression to mania, anxiety, panic, delirium, suicidal ideation, aggression, insomnia, and agitation. These medications can also impair cognitive function, with effects on attention, concentration, and memory. Elderly patients taking corticosteroids may experience a form of dementia that is often misdiagnosed as early Alzheimer's disease (Kenna, Poon, de los Angeles, & Koran, 2011). Psychiatric side effects have a rapid onset, often within 1 to 2 weeks of starting the medication. There are no clear predictors of which patients are likely to experience behavioral side effects from these medications. These psychiatric symptoms can be treated by gradually reducing the steroid dose if possible or by adding appropriate psychotropic medications, such as an antidepressant or mood stabilizer.

Thyroid Disorders and Behavior

Altered thyroid hormone levels can occur as a result of autoimmune disease processes that destroy thyroid tissue (Hashimoto's thyroiditis), surgery, medications (amiodarone, lithium), or be secondary to pituitary disease. Thyrotoxicosis is the result of immune processes that result in overproduction of thyroid hormones (Graves' disease), the presence of thyroid nodules, treatment with the antiarrhythmic medication amiodarone, or may be transient in thyroid inflammation. More commonly, disturbances occur following exposure to corrective treatment for thyroid problems, radiation therapy, or from damage or a tumor in the pituitary. Alternatively, thyroid levels may be off as a result of dietary changes or deficiencies (insufficient iodine or selenium intake), although such deficiencies are uncommon in the United States. Moreover, thyroid dysregulation can occur as a consequence of disturbances in other associated hormone systems, such as with changes in gonadal hormone production postpartum or in menopause.

The relationship between abnormal thyroid function and psychiatric symptoms can be particularly complex in patients with bipolar disorder who are treated with lithium. Lithium inhibits thyroid hormone release by inhibiting TSH (thyroid stimulating hormone) and it is commonly associated with hypothyroidism. Older female patients taking lithium are at higher risk of developing hypothyroidism (Lazarus, 2009). However, long-term use of lithium has been associated with hyperthyroidism in rare cases as well. Although the mechanism for decreased thyroid hormone levels with lithium treatment has not been fully elucidated, it is thought to be related to damage to the thyroid gland that occurs over time. The thyroid disruption induced by lithium can result in further mood symptoms that can include mania, complicating treatment.

Overview of the Thyroid System

The primary function of the hypothalamic-pituitary-thyroid (HPT) system is to regulate metabolism or the conversion of oxygen and calories to energy. The HPT system also helps control body temperature, influences heart rate, and helps regulate production of proteins. These functions are accomplished by a complex system that centers on the thyroid gland. Thyroid cells uniquely absorb iodine and combine it with tyrosine to produce triiodothyronine (T3) and thyroxine (T4). T3 and T4 then circulate throughout the body and bind to receptors in cells or indirectly stimulate centers in the central nervous system that regulate metabolic activity. The system regulates itself through a hypothalamic-pituitary feedback loop. When levels of circulating T3 and T4 become too low, the hypothalamus increases release of thyroid releasing hormone (TRH), which then tells the pituitary to produce more TSH. When the pituitary produces more TSH, it stimulates the thyroid to produce more T3 and T4 into circulation, which then communicates back to the hypothalamus to produce less TRH and slows TSH production.

Hyperthyroidism

Medical signs and symptoms characteristic of hyperthyroidism include palpable enlargement of the thyroid gland, heat sensitivity, warm moist skin, weight loss despite normal eating habits, change in menstrual cycles, erectile dysfunction or reduced libido, fine tremor in the hands or fingers, heart palpitations, increased frequency of bowel movements, fine brittle hair, and red or thickened skin on the shins or tops of the feet. In Graves' disease, increased fluid in the retroorbital space results in a characteristic proptosis or a bulging appearance to the eyes and can be associated with vision changes and light sensitivity. Such ophthalmologic signs together with behavioral changes may be a clue to the clinician that a patient has an overactive thyroid gland. However, proptosis is present only in approximately half the patients with Graves' disease and is absent in individuals with "toxic" nodular goiters.

Behavioral signs include fidgeting, fatigue, increased appetite, trouble sleeping, exaggerated startle response, poorly controlled motor responses, decreased ability to tolerate stressors such as crowds or noise, restlessness, and hyperactivity. In the elderly, symptoms may appear as mostly cognitive, with a decline in short-term memory, decreased attention, and problems with multitasking activities. Mood swings are common, along with anxiety, irritability, and nervousness. Appetite can be suppressed with weight loss that mimics a malignancy, sometimes referred to as "apathetic hyperthyroidism" of the elderly.

Thyroid Storm

Thyroid storm is a rare and potentially fatal condition with a challenging differential diagnosis. Patients may experience life-threatening cardiac events, hyperthermia, vomiting and diarrhea, cognitive disturbances, and seizures. The psychiatric presentation can range from mild agitation to delirium and psychosis. The Burch and Wartofsky

scoring system can aid in the differential diagnosis of thyroid storm (Burch & Wartofsky, 1993). This condition can develop in patients with untreated hyperthyroidism but can also occur in patients with no history of thyroid problems following a precipitating event such as trauma or infection.

Case: Manic and Psychotic Symptoms Associated with Hypothyroidism. A middle-aged woman presented to the emergency department with symptoms of acute mania and psychotic features. She had also experienced weight gain, cold intolerance, dry skin, abnormal menstrual cycles, and tiredness. Laboratory testing showed a low free T4, elevated TSH, and positive tests for anti-thyroglobulin and anti-thyroperoxidase (TPO) antibodies, leading to a diagnosis of hypothyroidism related to Hashimoto's thyroiditis. After the initial acute episode was controlled with thyroid medication together with a mood stabilizer and antipsychotic, the patient was discharged on maintenance thyroid medication but no psychotropic medication. Following appropriate treatment, the patient remained euthyroid and free of psychiatric symptoms (Lin, Yang, & Shiah, 2013).

Hypothyroidism

Medical signs and symptoms of hypothyroidism include lethargy, weight gain, intolerance to cold, constipation, dry hair and skin, hair loss, slow movements, periorbital puffiness, impaired hearing, diminished sweating, hoarseness, and irregular menstrual cycles. The pituitary increases production of thyroid stimulating hormone (TSH) in response to low thyroid hormone levels and may result in an enlarged gland or goiter.

Behavioral symptoms include those commonly seen in depression, including fatigue, decreased libido, and irritability. Cognitive deficits including memory deficits and reduced attention span may also be observed. Patients may occasionally present with psychotic symptoms. Subclinical hypothyroidism (mild elevation in TSH, usually 5–10 mcU/mL with normal free T4) is associated with increased risk of depression. However, although the common mood disturbance associated with hypothyroidism is depression, multiple cases of acute mania have been reported (Khemka, Ali, & Koch, 2011). Hashimoto's thyroiditis is an autoimmune attack on the thyroid gland that leads to inflammation and lymphocyte accumulation in the thyroid. The condition is the main cause of hypothyroidism in women, but mild cases are not always associated with hypothyroidism.

Thyroid Disease during Pregnancy and the Postpartum Period

Pregnancy has a substantial effect on thyroid function with increases in thyroid hormones and iodine requirements (Stagnaro-Green et al., 2011). Overt hypothyroidism during pregnancy can have an adverse effect on the fetus as well as the mother and should be treated (De Groot et al., 2012).

Postpartum thyroiditis (PPT) is an autoimmune thyroid condition that presents in the first year after giving birth. Approximately half the women who have antibodies to thyroid peroxidase during the first trimester develop PPT. The typical presentation of PPT includes elevated T3 and T4 levels in the first two postpartum months, followed by a decrease in T3 and T4, as well as an increase in TSH during the third through fifth postpartum months (Okano, 1998). Women typically return to a euthyroid state during the sixth through twelfth months. The relationship between PPT and postpartum depression remains unclear.

Case: Postpartum Psychosis Associated with Graves' Disease. A young woman with Graves' disease developed postpartum psychosis shortly after delivery with a clinical presentation that included delirium, catatonia, and prominent auditory hallucinations. The patient's interaction with her newborn was also impaired. Her symptoms improved significantly after appropriate medications were initiated and titrated to a therapeutic dose (Dahale et al., 2014).

DIAGNOSIS

Levels of thyroid hormones can be easily measured with routine blood tests, although interpretation of the results is not straightforward in all cases. A typical individual with primary hypothyroidism has a low T4 and elevated TSH level. However, if the underlying cause is a failure of the pituitary to secrete adequate TSH, both levels will be low. In this case, the thyroid is not releasing T4 because it is not receiving the proper signal from the pituitary and is considered secondary hypothyroidism. It is useful to test for anti-thyroid antibodies to determine whether the condition is the result of autoimmune thyroiditis. Anti-TG

antibodies target thyroglobulin protein and anti-TPO antibodies target TPO, an enzyme involved in converting T4 to T3.

EFFECT OF THYROID MEDICATION ON BEHAVIORAL SYMPTOMS

Treatment of hypothyroidism with synthetic T4 is often effective in alleviating behavioral symptoms, provided that the dose is optimized. If the dose is too high, the patient may begin to experience symptoms that are characteristic of hyperthyroidism, such as nervousness and insomnia. Most patients require medication indefinitely, although some cases caused by excessive iodine or medications and may be reversible. Despite the improvements in mood observed when hypothyroid patients are treated with thyroid hormone, evidence that thyroid hormone improves antidepressant efficacy of selective serotonin reuptake inhibitors in euthyroid individuals with depression remains equivocal (Connolly & Thase, 2011).

Parathyroid Disorders and Behavior

The primary role of the parathyroid is to regulate calcium levels. Because of the important role that calcium plays in ensuring proper neurotransmission, it follows logically that altered levels of parathyroid hormone affect behavior at least subtly if not overtly.

Overview of the Parathyroid System

The parathyroid consists of four small glands in the neck, each about the size of a grain of rice. The primary role of the parathyroid glands is regulation of calcium levels, which in turn regulates electrical conductivity in the nervous system and muscle contraction. Parathyroid hormone is secreted in response to decreased serum calcium levels. Calcium is then removed from the bones and secreted into the bloodstream. In addition, parathyroid hormone increases the ability of the gut to absorb calcium from food and allows the kidneys to hold onto calcium that would otherwise be lost in the urine.

Hyperparathyroidism

Primary hyperparathyroidism results from enlargement of one or more of the parathyroid glands. The majority of cases involve a benign adenoma in a single gland, although some cases involve two or more glands. In contrast, secondary hyperparathyroidism is caused by medical conditions that lower calcium or raise phosphorus, such as kidney disease or deficiencies in calcium or vitamin D. Tertiary hyperparathyroidism is seen in longstanding end-stage renal disease. Parathyroid cancer is a rare cause of elevated parathyroid hormone. Primary hyperparathyroidism is most commonly seen in postmenopausal women. Familial cases typically involve a characterized genetic mutation, although most cases are sporadic. Patients who take lithium are at increased risk of developing parathyroid disease as are individuals who have had radiation therapy to the head, neck, or chest. In mild cases of hypercalcemia, patients may be asymptomatic. In other cases, depression, fatigue, mood swings, irritability, apathy, difficulty sleeping, or cognitive impairments may be present. However, although depression is the typical mood presentation, some patients may experience manic symptoms, which may lead clinicians astray in the differential diagnosis. Common cognitive complaints include short attention span, poor concentration, and impaired memory. Slower processing of information, decreased motivation, and decreased ability to plan activities may also be observed. Often the patient does not identify symptoms as problematic but may acknowledge an improvement in how he or she feels following treatment. If elevated calcium is present in combination with low magnesium, the clinical presentation may include auditory or visual hallucinations. In severe cases, patients may experience delirium or even coma. At very high calcium levels, confusion is likely to be the predominant feature as opposed to mood symptoms.

Medical signs and symptoms result from poor muscle tone, loss of calcium from the bones and damage to organs from excessive serum calcium. Demineralization of the bones can lead to osteoporosis, putting a person at risk of spontaneous fractures. Patients may experience bone pain and weakness. Excessive serum calcium can lead to kidney stones, increased thirst, skin itch, and gritty eyes. Patients frequently experience gastrointestinal symptoms including constipation, intractable acid reflux, loss of appetite, abdominal pain, and nausea. When bone pain and gastrointestinal complaints are present together with psychiatric symptoms, primary hyperparathyroidism should be considered as a possible explanation. Some individuals may also have hypertension or cardiac abnormalities.

Hypoparathyroidism

Hypoparathyroidism leads to severe hypocalcemia. It is relatively rare but can also present with psychiatric and cognitive symptoms. Some families have a genetic predisposition and in these cases

symptoms may begin early in life. The condition can also occur following surgical removal of all parathyroid glands. The clinical presentation typically includes severe muscle cramps, tingling sensations in the fingers and toes and around the mouth. Hoarseness and wheezing may also occur due to the effect of low calcium levels on muscle contraction, including muscles in the larynx. Other signs may include dry skin, brittle nails, and hair loss, as well as problems with the teeth. Some people may also experience pain, difficulty walking, and headaches.

Behavioral symptoms may include irritability, mood swings, anxiety, altered mental status, loss of memory, fatigue, and psychosis. Patients are at risk of seizures due to electrolyte disturbances when calcium levels are very low. Notably, one cause of hypoparathyroidism is 22q11.2 deletion syndrome (also known as velocardiofacial syndrome or DiGeorge syndrome), which is associated with psychiatric disorders. Children with this genetic mutation are frequently diagnosed with autism spectrum disorder or attention deficit hyperactivity disorder, and adults are at increased risk of developing schizophrenia and other mental health conditions.

DIAGNOSIS

Elevated levels of parathyroid hormone and calcium are indicative of primary hyperparathyroidism. High parathyroid hormone levels with normal or low calcium are seen in vitamin D deficiency, renal failure, and hypophosphatemic syndromes. Additional tests such as metabolic panels, bone density scans, and kidney function tests can provide information about the degree of damage to the bones and kidneys that has occurred. Localization of a parathyroid adenoma is done by a sestamibi parathyroid scan or by an ultrasound of the neck.

EFFECT OF TREATMENT
ON BEHAVIORAL SYMPTOMS

Surgical removal of a parathyroid adenoma is a minimally invasive, low-risk procedure that is usually performed as outpatient surgery. The vast majority of patients report improvements in symptoms following treatment, related to normalization of calcium levels. Patients may notice an improvement in energy levels, mood, or cognitive function, or a reduction in pain despite having considered themselves asymptomatic. Depressive symptoms have been shown to improve following parathyroidectomy (Weber et al., 2007). Neuropsychological performance on memory and other tests also improves in at least a subset of patients following surgery (Benge et al., 2009). Studies examining the effect of parathyroid surgery on sleep disturbances have had mixed results. The improvement in symptoms that may have been regarded as normal is likely to result in better quality of life.

Case: Hyperparathyroidism with Manic Symptoms. A woman with hyperparathyroidism and hypercalcemia presented with mania as the predominant mood feature. An adrenal mass consistent with an adenoma was identified with a sestamibi parathyroid scan. The patient was agitated with an irritable mood, tangential thought processes, hypersexuality, and paranoia. She also reported worsening abdominal pain and nausea. The differential diagnosis included bipolar disorder and mania secondary to hyperparathyroidism, but there was no history to support a primary diagnosis of bipolar disorder. The patient's inability to recognize the severity of her medical issues due to her mania further complicated her treatment (Brown, Vyas, & Spiegel, 2007).

Behavioral Aspects of Diabetes and Altered Glucose Regulation

Diabetes is a condition that results from either lack of insulin due to an autoimmune condition (type 1) or loss of insulin sensitivity (type 2). Diabetes affects multiple organ systems and can lead to severe medical complications. Mental health issues are common and require careful management both by physicians and behavioral clinicians.

Glucose and Insulin Regulation by the Pancreas

Regulation of blood glucose is accomplished by the two important hormones. Insulin facilitates entry of glucose into cells and conversion of glucose to glycogen and fatty acids. Glucagon triggers conversion of glycogen to glucose when blood sugar levels are low.

Diabetes is a condition where the body is unable to use glucose for energy due to either lack of production of insulin by the pancreas or inability to use insulin properly. Consequently, glucose does not enter cells, resulting in hyperglycemia. Type 1 diabetes is an autoimmune condition where the beta cells of the pancreas are destroyed, with complete lack of insulin production. Such individuals require daily insulin injections to regulate their blood sugar. Type 2 diabetes usually involves insulin resistance, where the pancreas is no longer able to keep up with an increased demand for insulin in response to a rise in blood sugar. Treatment is focused on management of insulin resistance with diet and exercise as well as medication or gastric bypass surgery. Many obese patients start on oral medications but will often need insulin to keep blood sugars under control later on, some 10 to 15 years following diagnosis. Gestational diabetes occurs when a woman develops insulin resistance and high blood sugar during pregnancy. It is believed to occur as a result of placental hormones interfering with insulin action. The extra glucose can cross the placenta to the baby, causing the baby to produce more insulin. High insulin acts as a growth factor and leads to "big babies," defined as greater than 9 pounds at birth.

Classic symptoms of diabetes are excessive thirst, frequent urination, blurred vision, weight loss despite adequate food intake, fatigue, and tingling or numbness. Approximately half the people with diabetes have some form of nerve damage, known as diabetic neuropathy. The eyes, feet, kidneys, and heart are commonly affected. Some conditions, such as diabetic ketoacidosis, constitute a medical emergency and can result in death. Ketoacidosis is a condition that results from burning fat for energy when glucose is unavailable. Fruity smelling breath together with nausea and confusion is often a clue that a person is experiencing ketoacidosis.

Hyperglycemia

Many of the classic signs and symptoms of diabetes are associated with elevated blood sugar or hyperglycemia. Chronic hyperglycemia leads to cognitive declines in both type 1 and type 2 diabetes. Attention and executive function are frequently impaired, whereas deficits in learning and memory are more characteristic of type 2 diabetes (McCrimmon, Ryan, & Frier, 2012). The cognitive deficits and perceptual changes are often associated with neuropathies and other physical limitations.

Hypoglycemia

If a person with diabetes is not careful with insulin dosing and diet, hypoglycemia or low blood sugar can occur. Initially, signs may include shakiness, sweating, rapid heart rate, hunger, and weakness. These signs may be accompanied by behavioral symptoms including anxiety or nervousness and irritability, and thus may be interpreted as an anxiety disorder. Hypoglycemia impairs multiple aspects of neuropsychological functioning such as associative learning, attention, and mental flexibility (Hutto, 1998). In severe cases, hypoglycemia can lead to delirium, seizures, and coma. Mild cases of hypoglycemia can be treated by consuming simple carbohydrates, but more severe cases may require glucagon administration or emergency treatment. In some cases, people who experience frequent hypoglycemic episodes may not recognize when they are experiencing low glucose and may attribute their symptoms to anxiety or other factors. This phenomenon is referred to as hypoglycemia unawareness.

Case: Agitation Associated with Hypoglycemia. A middle-aged male with a history of schizoaffective disorder was brought to the emergency room by the police due to agitation and combative behavior at the community residence where he lived. On the psychiatric unit, the patient presented with extreme agitation and incoherent speech that did not respond to medication. Laboratory and neuroimaging tests were all normal except for a blood glucose level of 10 mg/dL. The patient was given intravenous glucose and his condition improved markedly. No obvious endocrine explanation for the hypoglycemia could be identified, leading the physicians to question the possibility of a medication error at the facility where the patient lived (Padder, Jaghab, & Gorman, 2006).

Psychological Concerns Associated with Diabetes

Diabetes distress is a term used to describe feelings such as worry, guilt, and a sense of being overwhelmed that result from the burdensome self-management tasks that are required on a daily basis to control blood glucose levels (Ducat, Philipson, & Anderson, 2014). These tasks include monitoring blood glucose levels and paying careful attention to diet and exercise. Some individuals with diabetes may spend a lot of time worrying about possible medical complications, such as blindness. Notably, some evidence suggests that diabetes-specific emotional distress is more closely associated with poor glycemic control than depression and anxiety

(Strandberg, Graue, Wentzel-Larsen, Peyrot, & Rokne, 2014). The persistent stress of ongoing self-management tasks together with reduced stress tolerance that may result from hormonal and metabolic changes can lead to more severe behavioral or psychiatric symptoms, such as irritability, poor motivation, and altered sleep patterns.

Psychiatric Diagnoses Associated with Diabetes

Mental health issues associated with diabetes include depression, anxiety disorders, eating disorders, psychosis, and dementia. The prevalence rate of depression is three times higher among individuals with type 1 diabetes and two times higher among those with type 2 diabetes compared with the general population (Roy & Lloyd, 2012). Conversely, the incidence of diabetes among people with depressive symptoms is also increased (Rotella & Mannucci, 2013). When diabetes is accompanied by depression, patients are less likely to adhere to treatment regimens, placing them at increased risk of complications, poor glucose control, and impaired quality of life. Longitudinal data indicate that the combination of diabetes and depression is associated with increased cardiovascular and all-cause mortality compared with either one individually (Pan et al., 2011). Increased risk of diabetes among individuals with depression is believed to result from a combination of health-risk behaviors, such as lack of exercise, and biological factors, such as increased cortisol and inflammatory factors (Park & Reynolds, 2015). Conversely, depression interferes with diabetes self-management by affecting cognition, energy levels, and executive function. The metabolic changes associated with diabetes likely lead to changes in brain structure and function that result in increased vulnerability to depression (Jacobson, Samson, Weinger, & Ryan, 2002). Alternatively, there may be a common factor that predisposes certain individuals to both diabetes and depression. One plausible mechanism is developmental trauma.

Anxiety disorders are common in patients with diabetes, either with or without a comorbid mood disorder. Anxiety can be particularly problematic for individuals with diabetes, because symptoms can be difficult to differentiate from hypoglycemia that requires treatment. Fear of severe hypoglycemia is a concern for many patients and it sometimes leads patients to maintain a blood glucose level above the recommended range.

Women with type 1 diabetes are at increased risk of developing eating disorders and subthreshold disordered eating. These women may engage in episodes of binge eating followed by purging through insulin restriction. Some professionals use the term "diabulimia" to describe the practice of intentionally restricting insulin in an effort to lose weight (Ruth-Sahd, Schneider, & Haagen, 2009). The strict attention to diet that is required to maintain glycemic control in diabetes parallels the rigid thinking about diet that characterizes eating disorders. The combination of diabetes and an eating disorder can lead to serious medical risks, such as diabetic ketoacidosis and retinopathy, which exceed the risks of either illness alone.

The relationship between diabetes and psychiatric disorders is bidirectional. Atypical antipsychotics are known to put patients at risk for developing metabolic syndrome, a precursor to type 2 diabetes. Some evidence suggests that medical emergencies associated with diabetes, such as diabetic ketoacidosis, may be more common in people with schizophrenia than in the general population (Henderson et al., 2007). However, the increased prevalence of diabetes among people with severe mental illness cannot be attributed only to medications, as elevated rates of diabetes in this population were noted even before the introduction of second generation antipsychotics. Lifestyle factors such as poor diet and lack of exercise that are common among the severely mentally ill contribute to the increased risk of diabetes in this population. Moreover, the majority of individuals with schizophrenia are smokers, which can worsen vascular and other complications of diabetes. On the other hand, individuals with poorly controlled diabetes may present with psychotic features, making the differential diagnosis challenging.

In older patients with diabetes, poor glycemic control may increase the risk of dementia (Biessels, Staekenborg, Brunner, Brayne, & Scheltens, 2006). Long-term hyperglycemia may lead to microvascular changes in the brain that result in cognitive impairment (Strachan, Reynolds, Frier, Mitchell, & Price, 2009). Although the exact biological mechanism accounting for this relationship remains uncertain, hyperglycemia, insulin resistance, and altered HPA axis function have been implicated.

DIAGNOSIS

The hemoglobin A1c test, fasting plasma glucose test, and oral glucose tolerance test can be used to diagnose diabetes. If the results are elevated but not high enough to diagnose diabetes, the patient may be diagnosed with pre-diabetes. Acute unexplained episodes of hypoglycemia such as that described in the case vignette can be identified easily with a plasma glucose test.

EFFECT OF TREATMENT ON BEHAVIORAL SYMPTOMS

The effects of medications commonly prescribed for diabetes on mental health remain unclear. Some evidence suggests that metformin may improve cognitive function, but findings have been mixed (Moore et al., 2013; Ying et al., 2014). There is evidence to support the use of metformin to manage diabetes in patients with schizophrenia and diabetes but the primary goal is management of metabolic issues rather than psychiatric symptoms.

Behavioral Aspects of Reproductive System Changes

The primary hormones that regulate the female reproductive system are estrogens and progesterone. Changes in estrogen levels associated with the menstrual cycle, pregnancy, and menopause have effects on mood and behavior that can range from mild symptoms to behavioral emergencies. Estrogen and progesterone affect the major neurotransmitter systems that influence behavior, including serotonin and GABA (gamma-aminobutyric acid). These gonadal steroid hormones are believed to play a role in mood disorders associated with reproductive system function, but the specific role of hormones in triggering mood symptoms and the factors that make some women more vulnerable to the effects of hormonal shifts remain unclear.

The Female Reproductive System

Fluctuations in female reproductive hormones are associated with psychiatric symptoms that can emerge across the menstrual cycle, during pregnancy and the postpartum period, and during menopause. The estrogens are a group of chemically similar hormones that regulate reproduction and secondary sex characteristics in females. Estrogens enhance the activity of neurotransmitters involved in mood regulation, and brain regions that regulate mood have a large number of estrogen receptors (Wharton, Gleason, Olson, Carlsson, & Asthana, 2012). Thus, women tend to feel better when estrogen levels are higher. Specifically, estrogens are believed to enhance serotonergic function and inhibit dopamine receptors. Notably, in addition to estrogen produced in the ovaries in the form of estradiol, estrogens are produced in other tissues including adipose tissue, bone, breasts, and brain (Simpson et al., 2000). The primary estrogen produced in these tissues is estrone. When circulating estrogen levels from the ovaries decline during menopause, there is an increased reliance on locally acting estrogen from these other tissues. In fact, adipose tissue is the main source of estrogen in postmenopausal females and thus older women with little body fat are more vulnerable to the deleterious effects of low estrogen. Estriol is produced by the placenta and thus is only present at significant levels during pregnancy. Estradiol is produced from cholesterol, which is converted to androstenedione and then testosterone. Aromatase converts testosterone to estradiol, linking the primary male and female reproductive hormones.

Progesterone is the other important female steroid hormone that regulates reproduction. This hormone is produced by the ovaries in the corpus luteum after ovulation and prepares the lining of the uterus to receive an egg in the event that it is fertilized. If the fertilized egg is not implanted, the progesterone level drops and menstruation occurs. Progesterone is also produced by the placenta during pregnancy.

Psychiatric Disorders Affected by the Menstrual Cycle

Many women report physical, psychological, or behavioral symptoms during the late luteal phase of the menstrual cycle when estrogen and progesterone levels are low. In contrast to premenstrual syndrome where symptoms are not clinically significant, premenstrual dysphoric disorder (PMDD) is characterized by symptoms that markedly interfere with daily functioning and are not an exacerbation of another psychiatric disorder (Yonkers, O'Brien, & Eriksson, 2008). Symptoms of PMDD typically worsen about 6 days before and peak 2 days before the onset of menses. The most severe behavioral symptoms are often anger and irritability. Other symptoms are similar to those that characterize mood and anxiety disorders. The main difference between PMDD and premenstrual worsening of a mood or anxiety disorder is that women with PMDD have an asymptomatic period around days 6 through 10 of the menstrual cycle (Biggs & Demuth, 2011). When a patient's presentation

seems to be consistent with PMDD, it is valuable to have her chart mood symptoms over at least two menstrual cycles. Serotonergic antidepressants are often effective and the improvement in symptoms is frequently faster than the typical time course of antidepressant action for this class of medications.

A large study of patients with bipolar disorder found that women who experienced premenstrual exacerbation of their symptoms tended to have more severe symptoms, a shorter time to relapse, and a worse course of illness than female patients whose symptoms did not worsen in the premenstrual phase (Dias et al., 2011). Although antidepressants are generally effective for managing depressive symptoms in PMDD, they may trigger a switch to mania in some patients whose depression is actually part of a bipolar diagnosis.

Symptoms of schizophrenia and psychosis also fluctuate across the menstrual cycle. Estrogens are believed to have a protective effect against psychotic symptoms (Markham, 2012). This function is likely due at least in part to the inhibitory effect of estrogen on dopamine receptors. Although findings vary, studies generally report improvement in symptoms during the phase of the menstrual cycle when estrogen and progesterone levels are higher (Seeman, 2012).

Notably, psychotropic medications may have different efficacy during different phases of the menstrual cycle due to the synergistic or antagonistic effect of hormonal shifts. Some patients may benefit from having medication doses titrated across the menstrual cycle.

Psychiatric Disorders Associated with Pregnancy and the Postpartum Period

Many women experience mood changes shortly after childbirth, ranging from mild postpartum blues to severe postpartum psychosis that can endanger both a new mother and her infant. Across the spectrum of mood disorders, women with a preexisting mood disorder have a high likelihood of experiencing a mood episode in the perinatal period (Di Florio et al., 2013). Women with bipolar I disorder or recurrent major depression are at particularly high risk. Psychosocial factors such as conflict with the partner, limited social support, or ongoing stress further increase risk of perinatal mood disorders.

Baby blues is the term used to describe the mild mood changes that affect many women shortly after childbirth. The blues are thought to be caused by hormonal changes that occur upon giving birth, but the underlying mechanism is not fully understood. This condition is characterized by mild depressive symptoms and mood reactivity that begin in the days immediately after delivery and resolve within two weeks. Other symptoms include irritability, difficulty sleeping, changes in appetite, and difficulty concentrating. This phenomenon is thought to have a distinct etiology and not simply represent a milder form of depression.

Postpartum depression (PPD) is a clinically significant affective disorder occurring in the postpartum period. This condition occurs in approximately 15% of new mothers, with a peak rate around 12 weeks after giving birth (Gaynes et al., 2005). The rapid decline in estrogen and progesterone is believed to contribute to the development of symptoms in women who are susceptible because of a combination of personal or family history and psychosocial factors (Doucet, Dennis, Letourneau, & Blackmore, 2009). Changes in thyroid hormone levels can also contribute to mood disturbances in new mothers. Some women who experience PPD, particularly those who do not respond to antidepressant treatment, will ultimately be diagnosed with bipolar disorder (Sharma & Khan, 2010). This distinction is important because an incorrect diagnosis is likely to lead to inappropriate treatment strategies.

The most severe and dangerous psychiatric disorder associated with the postpartum period is postpartum psychosis. Most cases of postpartum psychosis are actually a variant of bipolar disorder triggered by childbirth (Doucet et al., 2009). The core feature is a disturbance in mood that is often manic but may be predominantly depressed. Some patients exhibit significant mood lability as well as delusions, hallucinations, confusion, and perplexity. The rapid shift in mood and sudden onset of symptoms makes the disorder particularly challenging and dangerous. Postpartum psychosis typically requires hospitalization and treatment with antipsychotics or mood stabilizers to ensure the safety of the mother and her infant.

Postpartum obsessive compulsive disorder (OCD) receives less attention than mood disorders and often goes undiagnosed. Both postpartum onset and worsening of existing OCD during pregnancy or the postpartum period are relatively common. A woman may develop intrusive thoughts of harming her infant coupled with a fear of acting on the obsessive thoughts. Some women also report an exacerbation or onset of compulsions related to contamination or checking. The peak period of onset is 2 to 4 weeks postpartum (Brandes, Soares, & Cohen, 2004). A key distinction between the delusions of postpartum psychosis and the obsessions about harming the infant in postpartum OCD is that the new mother is frightened by the impulses in OCD. As a result, she may avoid activities associated with harming the child, such as bathing the infant or using knives. In contrast, a woman with postpartum psychosis usually does not experience distress from her thoughts, and thus is at much higher risk of actually harming her child or herself. A new mother may be reluctant to share these obsessions out of shame or fear of having her child taken away.

Psychiatric Symptoms Associated with Menopause

The transition to menopause is characterized by the depletion of ovarian follicles, cessation of the production of ovarian estrogens and progesterone, and secondary changes in the hypothalamic-pituitary-gonadal axis that ultimately result in cessation of menstruation. However, hormonal changes may occur earlier in the perimenopausal period. During the transition to menopause, women often experience psychological symptoms such as anxiety, irritability, and poor concentration; somatic symptoms such as fatigue and pain; and other symptoms such as disturbed sleep (Clayton & Ninan, 2010). Consequently, women are at increased risk of experiencing a major depressive episode during this period. Although women with a history of depression are five times more likely to experience an episode during the perimenopausal period than those with no prior history of depression, women who have not previously experienced depressive episodes may also develop depression at this point in their lives (Freeman, Sammel, Lin, & Nelson, 2006). Women with greater hormonal fluctuations may have an elevated risk. Psychosocial factors such as stressful life events or a negative attitude toward aging and menopause also increase the likelihood of experiencing depression (Clayton & Ninan, 2010). Women who report a history of premenstrual or perinatal mood disorders are also more vulnerable to the effects of the hormonal changes that occur in the menopausal transition. Among women with no history of depression, those who enter perimenopause at an earlier age are also at greater risk of experiencing an initial episode during perimenopause (Cohen, Soares, Vitonis, Otto, & Harlow, 2006). Treatment with estrogens may have an antidepressant effect during perimenopause (Schmidt, 2005).

Male Reproductive System and Behavior

Testosterone affects behavior, and behavior in turn also influences testosterone levels. In particular, sexual behavior, exercise, diet, and alcohol can affect androgen levels. Studies have reported a relationship between testosterone levels and aggression (Christiansen, 2001). There is evidence that violent prisoners have higher testosterone levels than nonviolent offenders. Testosterone may interact with serotonin to influence aggressive behavior. High testosterone and low serotonin levels may act synergistically to trigger aggression and violence.

Fewer reports have focused on the role of gonadal steroids in affective and psychotic disorders in men. Data on mood disorders in relation to endogenous testosterone levels are inconclusive; some studies have found a relationship between low testosterone and depression whereas others have not found any correlation (Johnson, Nachtigall, & Stern, 2013). Placebo-controlled trials of testosterone as an augmentation strategy in depressed men have also yielded inconsistent results. Although the data are equivocal, some men with low testosterone levels experience mood disorders and other behavioral symptoms.

In addition, some studies have found evidence for an inverse relationship between testosterone levels and negative symptoms in men with schizophrenia (Ko et al., 2007; Markham, 2012). Decreased levels of biologically active testosterone have been demonstrated in newly diagnosed patients, suggesting that the results are related to the illness and not exposure to antipsychotic medications.

The Male Reproductive System

Testosterone is a hormone produced in the testes that regulates sex drive, sperm production, bone density, fat distribution, male hair distribution, and muscle mass. Testosterone is produced from cholesterol through a series of enzymatic conversions. Synthesis is regulated by luteinizing hormone from the pituitary. The vast majority of circulating testosterone is secreted by the testes, although weak androgen precursors can be converted to testosterone in other tissues and organs. After secretion, most testosterone is converted to inactive metabolites and excreted. Testosterone levels are highest in adolescence and young adulthood and decline slightly as men age. This decrease in androgen

levels is much more gradual than the abrupt decrease in estrogen levels that females experience during menopause. When the decline is more pronounced than normal, a man may experience a variety of symptoms that may be misinterpreted as part of the aging process. Men who are obese or have a chronic illness may have low testosterone levels at a younger age than healthy men.

Anabolic Steroid Effects on Behavior

Abuse of anabolic steroids by men and boys to enhance athletic performance is frequently associated with behavioral changes. Anabolic steroids trigger clinically significant psychiatric symptoms in a subset of individuals that include mania and occasionally psychotic features (Kanayama, Hudson, & Pope, 2010). Men often experience major depressive episodes when withdrawing from anabolic steroids due to the suppression of the hypothalamic-pituitary-gonadal axis induced by these hormones. Many individuals use steroids without prominent behavioral changes and it is unclear why certain men are vulnerable to psychiatric symptoms.

Use of anabolic steroids also leads to aggression and violence in some men that is often inconsistent with their baseline personality. There have been numerous reports of violent crimes, including murders, committed by anabolic steroid users. Although it is difficult to demonstrate a causal relationship between steroid use and violence, some steroid users experience a decrease in aggression when they are not using steroids.

Other Hormones and Nutritional Factors Affecting the Endocrine System and Behavior
Dehydroepiandrosterone

Dehydroepiandrosterone (DHEA) and DHEA sulfate (DHEAS) are weaker androgen hormones that are secreted by the adrenal glands as well as the brain. They are classified as neurosteroids and have diverse functions in the brain including neuroprotection and regulation of neurotransmitter synthesis and release (Maninger, Wolkowitz, Reus, Epel, & Mellon, 2009). Studies examining the relationship between levels of these hormones and psychiatric disorders or symptoms have yielded mixed results. There is some evidence that treatment with DHEA may be beneficial for individuals with psychiatric disorders including depression, although further studies are warranted. Data from observational studies and clinical trials suggest that clinicians should be attentive to the role of these and other neuroactive steroids as potential contributing factors to observed symptoms. Notably, multiple cases have been reported linking the use of DHEA supplements to hypomania even in the absence of a prior psychiatric history.

Case: Mania Associated with DHEA Supplements. A man in his 60s with no previous psychiatric history was hospitalized with manic symptoms. The patient reported using DHEA supplements in an effort to increase his energy level and sex drive. He presented with pressured speech, tangential thinking, and grandiosity including plans to start a business. Although a conclusive relationship between the DHEA and manic presentation could not be made, the patient believed that the two were linked upon regaining insight. This and similar cases highlight the need for clinicians to inquire about dietary and herbal supplements and their effects on behavior (Markowitz, Carson, & Jackson, 1999).

Endocrine Disrupting Chemicals

Endocrine disrupting chemicals (EDCs) are substances found in the environment that act by mimicking or altering endogenous steroid hormones (Frye et al., 2012). Human exposure can occur through eating contaminated meat and fish, occupational exposure, or through use of certain household products. Dietary components such as phytoestrogens, certain pharmaceutical compounds, pesticides, and plastic contaminants are among the sources of EDCs. EDCs affect reproductive hormones and the thyroid, and thus have an impact on the systems described in this chapter.

Behavioral symptoms in adults that are linked to EDCs may be difficult to identify as they may actually reflect the lasting effects of exposure during prenatal development or early childhood. EDCs affect the sexually dimorphic development of the brain. It has been hypothesized that disruption of sexually dimorphic neurodevelopmental processes may contribute to the increased prevalence of certain childhood-onset disorders including autism spectrum disorders and attention deficit hyperactivity disorder. Prenatal and early childhood exposure to EDCs appears to have adverse effects on stress response and emotional reactivity (Frye et al., 2012). Bisphenol A

(BPA), a chemical that until recently was found in many plastic food containers and other plastics, has been linked to altered development of the reproductive system, altered sexual behavior, increased body weight, and effects on the immune system (Richter et al., 2007). There have been reports of altered internalizing and externalizing behaviors in children with high prenatal or childhood urinary levels of the EDC BPA (Harley et al., 2013). Multiple cohort studies have provided evidence of an association between exposure to endocrine disruptors such as BPA and behavioral problems in children. There are some limitations to these findings, however, and thus they are still inconclusive.

Iron Deficiency and Excess

Iron deficiency is the most common micronutrient deficiency, disproportionately affecting infants and toddlers, adolescents, and women of childbearing age (Georgieff, 2011). The deficiency state is not an endocrine dysfunction per se but is tied indirectly to the endocrine system. For example, iron deficiency anemia is common in menstruating women due to loss of iron during monthly cycling. Iron deficiency affects cognitive performance, emotions, and behavior. Symptoms of anemia may be mistaken for hypothyroidism, as cold intolerance, fatigue, pallor, and hair loss are common to both conditions. Low levels of iron or ferritin, a measure of iron stores, have been associated with increased depressive symptoms, particularly among oral contraceptive users (Murray-Kolb, 2011). Iron supplementation has been associated with improvement in depressive symptoms among women of reproductive age. Iron supplementation has also been associated with improvements in cognitive function in women, including measures of learning, memory, attention, and reasoning (Lomagno et al., 2014). Notably, iron deficiency early in life can have effects on brain circuitry, cognitive function, and behavior that persist even after the deficiency has been corrected (Georgieff, 2011; Lozoff, 2000). Children and adolescents who experienced iron deficiency in infancy or early childhood exhibit increased anxiety and depression, attentional deficits, and difficulty with inhibitory control (Georgieff, 2011). Thus, a behavioral emergency could be associated with iron deficiency despite normal levels of iron and ferritin.

Hemochromatosis or iron overload is associated with both endocrine issues and symptoms that may be interpreted as depression. Epidemiological evidence suggests that excess iron is associated with an increased risk of type 2 diabetes (Rajpathak et al., 2009; Simcox & McClain, 2013). Multiple studies have identified a relationship between high iron levels in the body and insulin resistance, although a direct causal relationship has not been established. Fatigue, loss of libido, and unexplained weight loss may be mistaken for depression. Notably, individuals with hemochromatosis may have an abnormal bronze skin tone. The condition runs in families due to a polymorphism in the *HFE* gene, which affects iron absorption. Hemochromatosis should be considered when individuals with a family history exhibit signs and symptoms consistent with iron overload.

Vitamin D Deficiency

The prevalence rate of vitamin D deficiency in the United States is 41% overall and 82% in the Black population (Forrest & Stuhldreher, 2011). Vitamin D deficiency is not an endocrine disorder itself but has an indirect effect on the endocrine system by stimulating the parathyroid glands, resulting in secondary hyperparathyroidism and bone loss (Holick, 2007). A serum level of 25-hydroxyvitamin D below 20 ng/mL is generally regarded as a deficiency state, although there is no clear consensus on optimal levels. Levels above 32 ng/mL are necessary to suppress parathyroid hormone and avoid bone loss and are recommended by most endocrinologists. An inverse relationship exists between serum vitamin D and other endocrine disorders including diabetes and polycystic ovary syndrome, although it is not clear that supplementation is associated with reduced risk (Muscogiuri et al., 2014).

Individuals with depression have lower serum vitamin D levels than controls, although it remains unclear whether there is a causal relationship underlying the correlation (Anglin, Samaan, Walter, & McDonald, 2013; Ju, Lee, & Jeong, 2013). At this time, the evidence supporting vitamin D supplementation for depression is inconclusive (Li et al., 2014). Vitamin D is associated with increased dopamine levels and also plays a role in multiple aspects of brain development (Eyles, Burne, & McGrath, 2013). Consequently, some investigators have begun to examine a possible relationship between vitamin D and neuropsychiatric disorders with a developmental basis such as schizophrenia and autism.

Sunlight is a major natural source of vitamin D, making deficiency more likely in individuals with limited exposure to sunlight, such as people living in northern latitudes and people who are indoors most of the day. People with dark skin and people who keep their skin covered are at increased risk of deficiency.

The ozone layer and sunscreen also block production of vitamin D. The role of sunlight also confounds studies of vitamin D and depression as individuals who are depressed may spend less time outdoors, resulting in reverse causality. Fortified milk, cereal, and other foods are dietary sources although diet alone does not usually provide an adequate supply. Individuals who are deficient or at risk for deficiency can either take daily supplements or high-dose prescription supplements on a weekly or monthly basis.

Hormonal Influence on Behavior in Cancer

Cancer patients frequently experience depression, anxiety, fatigue, and sleep disturbances due to the major effects of a cancer diagnosis on a person's life, as well as because of the agents used to treat the cancer. In addition to the psychological factors that contribute to depression and anxiety in this population, the hormonal treatments used for reproductive cancers may be an additional contributing factor. Tamoxifen is an antiestrogen that has been associated with impaired performance on tests of verbal memory and executive functioning (Schilder et al., 2010). Men with prostate cancer receiving antiandrogen hormone therapy had higher rates of depression and anxiety than those who were not being treated with hormones (Sharpley, Christie, & Bitsika, 2014). Furthermore, altered patterns of cortisol secretion have been demonstrated in patients and survivors of breast and other cancers (Miller, Ancoli-Israel, Bower, Capuron, & Irwin, 2008). These changes in the HPA axis appear to trigger an inflammatory response that may be associated with the behavioral symptoms.

Strategies for Making a Differential Diagnosis

The following steps can help clinicians in distinguishing between endocrine disorders with psychiatric symptoms and primary psychiatric diagnoses.

1. Ask for detailed information about the first occurrence of the symptoms.

2. Check for comorbidity if the person suffers from a chronic endocrine disorder and confirm that all medications are being taken as directed.

3. If symptoms suggest a possible endocrine disorder, ask for additional tests. When symptoms appear with sudden onset and no clear precipitants, be especially vigilant for endocrine involvement.

4. Be especially vigilant during periods of hormonal change, including puberty and the perimenopausal period.

Conclusion

This chapter highlights the diagnostic challenges that clinicians face in differentiating between endocrine disorders with behavioral symptoms and primary psychiatric disorders. Rapid resolution of a behavioral emergency depends on selection of an appropriate treatment based on etiology. Therefore, it is important that psychologists and other clinicians have a basic understanding of common endocrine disorders.

Acknowledgment

We thank Mihaela Blendea, MD, for her critical review of the manuscript.

Online Resources for Clinicians and Patients

http://www.endocrine.niddk.nih.gov
The National Endocrine and Metabolic Diseases Information Service from the National Institute of Diabetes and Digestive and Kidney Diseases provides fact sheets and other resources for both clinicians and patients.

http://www.endocrine.org
The Endocrine Society is the primary professional society for clinicians and researchers in the field of endocrinology. The society publishes practice guidelines, scholarly journals, books, and other resource materials for professionals.

http://www.aace.com
The American Association of Clinical Endocrinologists publishes clinical practice guidelines, position statements, and other resource materials.

http://www.hormone.org
The Hormone Health Network is an educational resource produced by the Endocrine Society for patients and the public that includes fact sheets and patient guides.

http://www.diabetes.org
The American Diabetes Association provides extensive information for patients, including advice for living with diabetes, on a site designed for the public. The organization also maintains a professional website with clinical practice guidelines and other resources for professionals.

http://www.nadf.us
The National Adrenal Diseases Foundation provides useful tools for managing an adrenal crisis as well as general information about Addison's disease, Cushing's disease, and other conditions related to adrenal hormones. The site provides information for medical professionals as well as for patients.

http://www.thyroid.org
The American Thyroid Association provides information for physicians and patients about thyroid disease. The organization publishes *Clinical Thyroidology for the Public* to help patients and others understand the information published in the organization's professional journal.

References

Anglin, R. E., Samaan, Z., Walter, S. D., & McDonald, S. D. (2013). Vitamin D deficiency and depression in adults: Systematic review and meta-analysis. *The British Journal of Psychiatry: The Journal of Mental Science*, 202, 100–107. doi:10.1192/bjp.bp.111.106666

Benge, J. F., Perrier, N. D., Massman, P. J., Meyers, C. A., Kayl, A. E., & Wefel, J. S. (2009). Cognitive and affective sequelae of primary hyperparathyroidism and early response to parathyroidectomy. *Journal of the International Neuropsychological Society: JINS*, 15(6), 1002–1011. doi:10.1017/S1355617709990695

Biessels, G. J., Staekenborg, S., Brunner, E., Brayne, C., & Scheltens, P. (2006). Risk of dementia in diabetes mellitus: A systematic review. *The Lancet Neurology*, 5(1), 64–74. doi:S1474–4422(05)70284–2

Biggs, W. S., & Demuth, R. H. (2011). Premenstrual syndrome and premenstrual dysphoric disorder. *American Family Physician*, 84(8), 918–924.

Blaustein, S. A., Golden, N. H., & Shenker, I. R. (1998). Addison's disease mimicking anorexia nervosa. *Clinical Pediatrics*, 37(10), 631–632.

Brandes, M., Soares, C. N., & Cohen, L. S. (2004). Postpartum onset obsessive-compulsive disorder: Diagnosis and management. *Archives of Women's Mental Health*, 7(2), 99–110. doi:10.1007/s00737-003-0035-3

Brown, S. W., Vyas, B. V., & Spiegel, D. R. (2007). Mania in a case of hyperparathyroidism. *Psychosomatics*, 48(3), 265–268. doi:10.1176/appi.psy.48.3.265

Burch, H. B., & Wartofsky, L. (1993). Life-threatening thyrotoxicosis. Thyroid storm. *Endocrinology and Metabolism Clinics of North America*, 22(2), 263–277.

Christiansen, K. (2001). Behavioural effects of androgen in men and women. *The Journal of Endocrinology*, 170(1), 39–48. doi:10.1677/joe.0.1700039

Clayton, A. H., & Ninan, P. T. (2010). Depression or menopause? Presentation and management of major depressive disorder in perimenopausal and postmenopausal women. *Primary Care Companion to the Journal of Clinical Psychiatry*, 12(1), PCC.08r00747. doi:10.4088/PCC.08r00747blu

Cohen, L. S., Soares, C. N., Vitonis, A. F., Otto, M. W., & Harlow, B. L. (2006). Risk for new onset of depression during the menopausal transition: The Harvard study of moods and cycles. *Archives of General Psychiatry*, 63(4), 385–390. doi:10.1001/archpsyc.63.4.385

Connolly, K. R., & Thase, M. E. (2011). If at first you don't succeed: A review of the evidence for antidepressant augmentation, combination and switching strategies. *Drugs*, 71(1), 43–64. doi:10.2165/11587620-000000000-00000

Dahale, A. B., Chandra, P. S., Sherine, L., Thippeswamy, H., Desai, G., & Reddy, D. (2014). Postpartum psychosis in a woman with Graves' disease: A case report. *General Hospital Psychiatry*, 36(6), 761.e7–761.e8. doi:10.1016/j.genhosppsych.2014.07.003

De Groot, L., Abalovich, M., Alexander, E. K., Amino, N., Barbour, L., Cobin, R. H., ... Sullivan, S. (2012). Management of thyroid dysfunction during pregnancy and postpartum: An Endocrine Society clinical practice guideline. *The Journal of Clinical Endocrinology and Metabolism*, 97(8), 2543–2565. doi:10.1210/jc.2011-2803

Di Florio, A., Forty, L., Gordon-Smith, K., Heron, J., Jones, L., Craddock, N., & Jones, I. (2013). Perinatal episodes across the mood disorder spectrum. *JAMA Psychiatry*, 70(2), 168–175. doi:10.1001/jamapsychiatry.2013.279

Dias, R. S., Lafer, B., Russo, C., Del Debbio, A., Nierenberg, A. A., Sachs, G. S., & Joffe, H. (2011). Longitudinal follow-up of bipolar disorder in women with premenstrual exacerbation: Findings from STEP-BD. *The American Journal of Psychiatry*, 168(4), 386–394. doi:10.1176/appi.ajp.2010.09121816

Doucet, S., Dennis, C. L., Letourneau, N., & Blackmore, E. R. (2009). Differentiation and clinical implications of postpartum depression and postpartum psychosis. *Journal of Obstetric, Gynecologic, and Neonatal Nursing: JOGNN/NAACOG, 38*(3), 269–279. doi:10.1111/j.1552-6909.2009.01019.x

Ducat, L., Philipson, L. H., & Anderson, B. J. (2014). The mental health comorbidities of diabetes. *JAMA, 312*(7), 691–692. doi:10.1001/jama.2014.8040

Eyles, D. W., Burne, T. H. J., & McGrath, J. J. (2013). Vitamin D, effects on brain development, adult brain function, and the links between low levels of vitamin D and neuropsychiatric disease. *Frontiers in Neuroendocrinology, 34*(1), 47–64. doi:10.1016/j.yfrne.2012.07.001

Forrest, K. Y., & Stuhldreher, W. L. (2011). Prevalence and correlates of vitamin D deficiency in US adults. *Nutrition Research, 31*(1), 48–54. doi:10.1016/j.nutres.2010.12.001

Freeman, E. W., Sammel, M. D., Lin, H., & Nelson, D. B. (2006). Associations of hormones and menopausal status with depressed mood in women with no history of depression. *Archives of General Psychiatry, 63*(4), 375–382. doi: 10.1001/archpsyc.63.4.375

Frye, C. A., Bo, E., Calamandrei, G., Calza, L., Dessi-Fulgheri, F., Fernandez, M., ... Panzica, G. C. (2012). Endocrine disrupters: A review of some sources, effects, and mechanisms of actions on behaviour and neuroendocrine systems. *Journal of Neuroendocrinology, 24*(1), 144–159. doi:10.1111/j.1365-2826.2011.02229.x

Gaynes, B. N., Gavin, N., Meltzer-Brody, S., Lohr, K. N., Swinson, T., Gartlehner, G., ... Miller, W. C. (2005). Perinatal depression: Prevalence, screening accuracy, and screening outcomes. In *AHRQ Evidence Report Summaries* (*119*; pp. 1–8). Rockville, Md.: Agency for Healthcare Research and Quality.

Georgieff, M. K. (2011). Long-term brain and behavioral consequences of early iron deficiency. *Nutrition Reviews, 69* (Suppl 1), S43–S48. doi:10.1111/j.1753-4887.2011.00432.x

Harley, K. G., Gunier, R. B., Kogut, K., Johnson, C., Bradman, A., Calafat, A. M., & Eskenazi, B. (2013). Prenatal and early childhood bisphenol A concentrations and behavior in school-aged children. *Environmental Research, 126*, 43–50. doi:10.1016/j.envres.2013.06.004

Henderson, D. C., Cagliero, E., Copeland, P. M., Louie, P. M., Borba, C. P., Fan, X., ... Goff, D. C. (2007). Elevated hemoglobin A1c as a possible indicator of diabetes mellitus and diabetic ketoacidosis in schizophrenia patients receiving atypical antipsychotics. *The Journal of Clinical Psychiatry, 68*(4), 533–541.

Holick, M. F. (2007). Vitamin D deficiency. *The New England Journal of Medicine, 357*(3), 266–281. doi:357/3/266

Hutto, B. (1998). Subtle psychiatric presentations of endocrine diseases. *The Psychiatric Clinics of North America, 21*(4), viii, 905–916.

Jacobson, A. M., Samson, J. A., Weinger, K., & Ryan, C. M. (2002). Diabetes, the brain, and behavior: Is there a biological mechanism underlying the association between diabetes and depression? *International Review of Neurobiology, 51*, 455–479.

Johnson, J. M., Nachtigall, L. B., & Stern, T. A. (2013). The effect of testosterone levels on mood in men: A review. *Psychosomatics, 54*(6), 509–514. doi:10.1016/j.psym.2013.06.018

Ju, S. Y., Lee, Y. J., & Jeong, S. N. (2013). Serum 25-hydroxyvitamin D levels and the risk of depression: A systematic review and meta-analysis. *The Journal of Nutrition, Health & Aging, 17*(5), 447–455. doi:10.1007/s12603-012-0418-0

Kanayama, G., Hudson, J. I., & Pope, H. G. Jr. (2010). Illicit anabolic-androgenic steroid use. *Hormones and Behavior, 58*(1), 111–121. doi:10.1016/j.yhbeh.2009.09.006

Kenna, H. A., Poon, A. W., de los Angeles, C. P., & Koran, L. M. (2011). Psychiatric complications of treatment with corticosteroids: Review with case report. *Psychiatry and Clinical Neurosciences, 65*(6), 549–560. doi:10.1111/j.1440-1819.2011.02260.x

Khemka, D., Ali, J. A., & Koch, C. A. (2011). Primary hypothyroidism associated with acute mania: Case series and literature review. *Experimental and Clinical Endocrinology & Diabetes: Official Journal, German Society of Endocrinology [and] German Diabetes Association, 119*(8), 513–517. doi:10.1055/s-0031-1277137

Ko, Y. H., Jung, S. W., Joe, S. H., Lee, C. H., Jung, H. G., Jung, I. K., ... Lee, M. S. (2007). Association between serum testosterone levels and the severity of negative symptoms in male patients with chronic schizophrenia. *Psychoneuroendocrinology, 32*(4), 385–391. doi:S0306-4530(07)00034-0

Lazarus, J. H. (2009). Lithium and thyroid. *Best Practice & Research. Clinical Endocrinology & Metabolism, 23*(6), 723–733. doi:10.1016/j.beem.2009.06.002

Li, G., Mbuagbaw, L., Samaan, Z., Falavigna, M., Zhang, S., Adachi, J. D., ... Thabane, L. (2014). Efficacy of vitamin D supplementation in depression in adults: A systematic review. *The Journal of Clinical Endocrinology and Metabolism, 99*(3), 757–767. doi:10.1210/jc.2013-3450

Lin, C., Yang, S., & Shiah, I. (2013). Acute mania in a patient with hypothyroidism resulting from Hashimoto's thyroiditis. *General Hospital Psychiatry, 35*(6), 683.e1–683.e2. doi:10.1016/j.genhosppsych.2013.06.013

Lomagno, K. A., Hu, F., Riddell, L. J., Booth, A. O., Szymlek-Gay, E. A., Nowson, C. A., & Byrne, L. K. (2014). Increasing iron and zinc in pre-menopausal women and its effects on mood and cognition: A systematic review. *Nutrients, 6*(11), 5117–5141. doi:10.3390/nu6115117

Lozoff, B. (2000). Perinatal iron deficiency and the developing brain. *Pediatric Research, 48*(2), 137–139. doi:10.1203/00006450-200008000-00003

Maninger, N., Wolkowitz, O. M., Reus, V. I., Epel, E. S., & Mellon, S. H. (2009). Neurobiological and neuropsychiatric effects of dehydroepiandrosterone (DHEA) and DHEA sulfate (DHEAS). *Frontiers in Neuroendocrinology, 30*(1), 65–91. doi:10.1016/j.yfrne.2008.11.002

Markham, J. A. (2012). Sex steroids and schizophrenia. *Reviews in Endocrine & Metabolic Disorders, 13*(3), 187–207. doi:10.1007/s11154-011-9184-2

Markowitz, J. S., Carson, W. H., & Jackson, C. W. (1999). Possible dihydroepiandrosterone-induced mania. *Biological Psychiatry, 45*(2), 241–242. doi:10.1016/S0006-3223(98)00091-2

McCrimmon, R. J., Ryan, C. M., & Frier, B. M. (2012). Diabetes and cognitive dysfunction. *Lancet, 379*(9833), 2291–2299. doi:10.1016/S0140-6736(12)60360-2

Miller, A. H., Ancoli-Israel, S., Bower, J. E., Capuron, L., & Irwin, M. R. (2008). Neuroendocrine-immune mechanisms of behavioral comorbidities in patients with cancer. *Journal of Clinical Oncology: Official Journal of the American Society of Clinical Oncology, 26*(6), 971–982. doi:10.1200/JCO.2007.10.7805

Moore, E. M., Mander, A. G., Ames, D., Kotowicz, M. A., Carne, R. P., Brodaty, H., ... AIBL Investigators. (2013). Increased risk of cognitive impairment in patients with diabetes is associated with metformin. *Diabetes Care, 36*(10), 2981–2987. doi:10.2337/dc13-0229

Morris, M. C., Compas, B. E., & Garber, J. (2012). Relations among posttraumatic stress disorder, comorbid major depression, and HPA function: A systematic review and meta-analysis. *Clinical Psychology Review, 32*(4), 301–315. doi:10.1016/j.cpr.2012.02.002

Murray-Kolb, L. E. (2011). Iron status and neuropsychological consequences in women of reproductive age: What do we know and where are we headed? *The Journal of Nutrition, 141*(4), 747S–755S. doi:10.3945/jn.110.130658

Muscogiuri, G., Mitri, J., Mathieu, C., Badenhoop, K., Tamer, G., Orio, F., . . . Pittas, A. (2014). Mechanisms in endocrinology: Vitamin D as a potential contributor in endocrine health and disease. *European Journal of Endocrinology/European Federation of Endocrine Societies, 171*(3), R101–110. doi:10.1530/EJE-14-0158

Nussey, S., & Whitehead, S. (2001). *Endocrinology: An integrated approach.* Oxford: BIOS Scientific Publishers. doi:NBK22

Okano, T. (1998). Thyroid function and postpartum psychiatric disorders. *Archives of Women's Mental Health, 1*(4), 157.

Padder, T., Jaghab, K., & Gorman, J. M. (2006). A 56-year-old male presenting with acute psychosis and acute change in mental status. *Journal of Psychiatric Practice, 12*(6), 411–414. doi:00131746-200611000-00011

Pan, A., Lucas, M., Sun, Q., van Dam, R. M., Franco, O. H., Willett, W. C., . . . Hu, F. B. (2011). Increased mortality risk in women with depression and diabetes mellitus. *Archives of General Psychiatry, 68*(1), 42–50. doi:10.1001/archgenpsychiatry.2010.176

Park, M., & Reynolds, C. F., 3rd. (2015). Depression among older adults with diabetes mellitus. *Clinics in Geriatric Medicine, 31*(1), 117–137. doi:S0749-0690(14)00092-5

Pope, H. G., Jr., & Katz, D. L. (1994). Psychiatric and medical effects of anabolic-androgenic steroid use. A controlled study of 160 athletes. *Archives of General Psychiatry, 51*(5), 375–382.

Rajpathak, S. N., Crandall, J. P., Wylie-Rosett, J., Kabat, G. C., Rohan, T. E., & Hu, F. B. (2009). The role of iron in type 2 diabetes in humans. *Biochimica Et Biophysica Acta, 1790*(7), 671–681. doi:10.1016/j.bbagen.2008.04.005

Richter, C. A., Birnbaum, L. S., Farabollini, F., Newbold, R. R., Rubin, B. S., Talsness, C. E., . . . vom Saal, F. S. (2007). In vivo effects of bisphenol A in laboratory rodent studies. *Reproductive Toxicology, 24*(2), 199–224. doi:10.1016/j.reprotox.2007.06.004

Rotella, F., & Mannucci, E. (2013). Depression as a risk factor for diabetes: A meta-analysis of longitudinal studies. *The Journal of Clinical Psychiatry, 74*(1), 31–37. doi:10.4088/JCP.12r07922

Roy, T., & Lloyd, C. E. (2012). Epidemiology of depression and diabetes: A systematic review. *Journal of Affective Disorders, 142*(Suppl), S8–S21. doi:10.1016/S0165-0327(12)70004-6

Ruth-Sahd, L. A., Schneider, M., & Haagen, B. (2009). Diabulimia: What it is and how to recognize it in critical care. *Dimensions of Critical Care Nursing: DCCN, 28*(4), 147–153; quiz 154–155. doi:10.1097/DCC.0b013e3181a473fe

Samson, J. A., Levin, R., & Richardson, G. (1998). Psychological symptoms in endocrine disorders. In P. M. Kleepsies (Ed.), *Emergencies in mental health practice.* (pp. 332–353). New York, NY: Guilford Press.

Sawicka, N., Gryczynska, M., Sowinski, J., Tamborska-Zedlewska, M., & Ruchala, M. (2013). Two diagnoses become one? Rare case report of anorexia nervosa and Cushing's syndrome. *Neuropsychiatric Disease and Treatment, 9*, 431–435. doi:10.2147/NDT.S40398

Schilder, C. M., Seynaeve, C., Beex, L. V., Boogerd, W., Linn, S. C., Gundy, C. M., . . . Schagen, S. B. (2010). Effects of tamoxifen and exemestane on cognitive functioning of postmenopausal patients with breast cancer: Results from the neuropsychological side study of the tamoxifen and exemestane adjuvant multinational trial. *Journal of Clinical Oncology: Official Journal of the American Society of Clinical Oncology, 28*(8), 1294–1300. doi:10.1200/JCO.2008.21.3553

Schmidt, P. J. (2005). Mood, depression, and reproductive hormones in the menopausal transition. *The American Journal of Medicine, 118* (12), 54–58. doi:S0002-9343(05)00889-2

Seeman, M. V. (2012). Menstrual exacerbation of schizophrenia symptoms. *Acta Psychiatrica Scandinavica, 125*(5), 363–371. doi:10.1111/j.1600-0447.2011.01822.x

Sharma, V., & Khan, M. (2010). Identification of bipolar disorder in women with postpartum depression. *Bipolar Disorders, 12*(3), 335–340. doi:10.1111/j.1399-5618.2010.00809.x

Sharpley, C. F., Christie, D. R., & Bitsika, V. (2014). Do hormone treatments for prostate cancer cause anxiety and depression? *International Journal of Clinical Oncology, 19*(3), 523–530. doi:10.1007/s10147-013-0569-y

Simcox, J. A., & McClain, D. A. (2013). Iron and diabetes risk. *Cell Metabolism, 17*(3), 329–341. doi:10.1016/j.cmet.2013.02.007

Simpson, E., Rubin, G., Clyne, C., Robertson, K., O'Donnell, L., Jones, M., & Davis, S. (2000). The role of local estrogen biosynthesis in males and females. *Trends in Endocrinology and Metabolism: TEM, 11*(5), 184–188. doi:S1043-2760(00)00254-X

Stagnaro-Green, A., Abalovich, M., Alexander, E., Azizi, F., Mestman, J., Negro, R., . . . American Thyroid Association Taskforce on Thyroid Disease During Pregnancy and Postpartum. (2011). Guidelines of the American Thyroid Association for the diagnosis and management of thyroid disease during pregnancy and postpartum. *Thyroid: Official Journal of the American Thyroid Association, 21*(10), 1081–1125. doi:10.1089/thy.2011.0087

Strachan, M. W., Reynolds, R. M., Frier, B. M., Mitchell, R. J., & Price, J. F. (2009). The role of metabolic derangements and glucocorticoid excess in the aetiology of cognitive impairment in type 2 diabetes. Implications for future therapeutic strategies. *Diabetes, Obesity & Metabolism, 11*(5), 407–414. doi:10.1111/j.1463-1326.2008.00963.x

Strandberg, R. B., Graue, M., Wentzel-Larsen, T., Peyrot, M., & Rokne, B. (2014). Relationships of diabetes-specific emotional distress, depression, anxiety, and overall well-being with HbA1c in adult persons with type 1 diabetes. *Journal of Psychosomatic Research, 77*(3), 174–179. doi:10.1016/j.jpsychores.2014.06.015

Tsatourian, K., & Samson, J. (2009). Psychological and behavioral symptoms in endocrine disorders. In P. M. Kleepsies (Ed.), *Behavioral emergencies: An evidence-based resource for evaluating and managing risk of suicide, violence, and victimization* (pp. 311–335). Washington, DC: American Psychological Association.

Weber, T., Keller, M., Hense, I., Pietsch, A., Hinz, U., Schilling, T., . . . Buchler, M. W. (2007). Effect of parathyroidectomy on quality of life and neuropsychological symptoms in primary hyperparathyroidism. *World Journal of Surgery, 31*(6), 1202–1209. doi:10.1007/s00268-007-9006-6

Wharton, W., Gleason, C. E., Olson, S. R., Carlsson, C. M., & Asthana, S. (2012). Neurobiological underpinnings of the estrogen–mood relationship. *Current Psychiatry Reviews, 8*(3), 247–256. doi:10.2174/157340012800792957

Wolkowitz, O. M., Burke, H., Epel, E. S., & Reus, V. I. (2009). Glucocorticoids: Mood, memory, and mechanisms. *Annals of the New York Academy of Sciences, 1179*, 19–40. doi:10.1111/j.1749-6632.2009.04980.x

Ying, M. A., Maruschak, N., Mansur, R. R., Carvalho, A. F., Cha, D. S., & McIntyre, R. S. (2014). Metformin: Repurposing opportunities for cognitive and mood dysfunction. *CNS & Neurological Disorders Drug Targets, 13* (10), 1836–1845. doi:CNSNDDT-EPUB-63701

Yonkers, K. A., O'Brien, P. M., & Eriksson, E. (2008). Premenstrual syndrome. *Lancet, 371*(9619), 1200–1210. doi:10.1016/S0140-6736(08)60527-9

The Treatment of Patients with Recurrent or Ongoing Risk

The Psychopharmacological Treatment of Individuals at Risk of Recurrent Suicidal Behavior

John C. Bradley

Abstract

Mental illness is the primary risk factor for suicidal ideation, attempts, and completion. Effective treatment of the psychiatric condition is the foundational strategy to reduce the risk of suicide associated with these conditions, but few medications can be demonstrated to independently reduce the risk of suicide. This chapter will describe how psychopharmacological treatment can be included as a component of bio-psycho-social treatments within the context of a recovery model for suicide prevention. The evidence for medication therapies will be reviewed both for specific behavioral health conditions and for any reduced suicide risk independent of general therapeutic effects to treat underlying conditions. A framework strategy will be described for the integration of evidence-based clinical decision making to provide the most effective treatment that also specifically targets suicide risk for patients.

Key Words: suicide, psychopharmacotherapy, antidepressants, mood stabilizers, antipsychotics, lithium, clozapine, ketamine

Suicide is a major public health problem across the globe. While suicide rates among different cultures vary considerably, the greatest burden is seen within industrialized and developing countries. Many nations are creating public health policies targeting primary and secondary prevention. At the core of these prevention efforts is the need to understand the risk factors associated with suicidal behavior and the reasons behind demographic differences between cultures, races, religions, genders, and ages over time. While these risk factors are important from an epidemiological perspective, they are less useful in the clinical setting where the more important question is to identify which factors are predictive of a suicide attempt. Until we improve our predictive power to understand who is at risk for a suicide attempt in the near future, our clinical efforts will lack targeted efficacy, and the same treatments will be recommended without regard for the

level of suicide risk and the relative impact on risk reduction.

Psychopharmacologic treatments play an important role in the treatment of individuals at risk for suicide. Many retrospective studies report that up to 90% of people who have died by suicide met the criteria to be diagnosed with a mental illness at the time of their death (Mann et al., 2005). Mood disorders; substance use disorders; anxiety, psychotic, and personality disorders are all significantly associated with suicide, with comorbidity being the rule (Hawton & van Heeringen, 2009). Unfortunately, many of these individuals either had not been diagnosed at the time of their suicide, or were not in treatment for their psychiatric condition. It is imperative to minimize the burden of mental illness as a risk factor for suicide through early identification, effective treatment, and relapse prevention. Public education and stigma reduction play an important role in this effort to be sure, but more needs to be done to demonstrate the efficacy of clinical interventions to both treat the underlying illness and to reduce the risk of suicide attempt and death.

This chapter will describe the role of psychopharmacological treatment to reduce the risk of death by suicide. First, it must be said that there is no evidence whatsoever to support the use of psychopharmacotherapies to reduce the risk of suicide for any person who does not have a psychiatric illness contributing to the risk of suicide. The evidence that does exist must be viewed in the context of specific psychiatric conditions. Furthermore, while effective treatment of the underlying mental illness is imperative, there is only limited evidence that effective treatment of the underlying condition alone is sufficient to lower the risk of suicide associated with that mental illness. The existing evidence for specific suicide risk-reduction pharmacotherapies will be presented so that clinicians may make informed recommendations to their patients at risk for a suicide attempt.

Background and Scope

Suicide is responsible for one million deaths a year globally, or 14.5 deaths per 100,000 people (WHO, 2002). This global burden places suicide as the 10th leading cause of death worldwide (Hawton & van Heeringen, 2009). In the United States in 2014, suicide ranked as the 10th leading cause of death overall, accounting for 42,773 total deaths, or 13.4 suicide deaths per 100,000 people per year. In adolescents and young adults aged 15–34, however, suicide is the second leading cause of death, only behind accidents (Crosby, Ortega, Stevens, & Centers for Disease Control [CDC], 2011). In the United Kingdom in 2012, suicide was a leading cause of death, accounting for 5,981 total deaths, or 11.6 deaths per 100,000 people. Suicide was the leading cause of death for both men and women aged 20–34 (Office for National Statistics, 2014). The rates of suicide vary widely across countries and regions within countries. A general trend is that suicide rates are higher in more northern latitudes, but many other factors contribute to suicide, such as socioeconomic factors and rates of substance use disorders. Värnik (2012) reports that Lithuania, Sri Lanka, South Korea, and Russia all have annual suicide rates above 30 per 100,000, while countries in the Middle East report annual rates below 0.1 in 100,000. Ethnicity also plays an important role within a particular country, as evidenced by lower rates of suicide among Hispanic and African American people in the United States compared with Whites (McKenzie, Serfaty, & Crawford, 2003).

There is no single cause for suicidal behavior. Suicide can be thought of as the confluence of four factors: *traits* that may be heritable or behavioral; *states* that result from experience or the occurrence of illness; *precipitating factors* or overwhelming stressors; and the *availability of lethal means*. Mann (2003) described the "stress-diathesis model" in which the predisposition toward suicide is activated by acute stressors to precipitate suicidal behavior. The predisposing state is defined by a negative worldview that feels hopeless, compounded by feelings of anger or poor impulse control. Onto this canvas is painted an acute or chronic psychiatric disorder and then an acute psychosocial crisis that overwhelms all coping strategies. The symptom burden and psychological distress become unbearable, and suicide appears to be the only solution to end the seemingly interminable suffering.

Joiner (2005), in the interpersonal theory of suicide, describes three interrelated factors that create the conditions necessary for suicide attempt (Figure 29.1). A sense of "thwarted belongingness" to social groups and "perceived burdensomeness" to others combine to create a desire for suicide (suicidal ideation). An additional condition must be present to enable the "capability for suicide." He postulates that there must be some habituation to the fear of death through exposure or rehearsal that enables the suffering person to act on the suicidal impulse. In Joiner's model, the suicidal person believes "I am alone, I am a burden, and I am not afraid to die."

Fig. 29.1 An interpersonal model of suicidal behavior. (adapted with permission from Joiner, 2005).

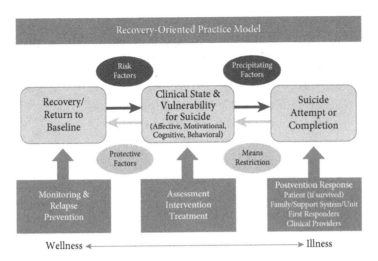

Fig. 29.2 A recovery-oriented practice model for the management of suicidal behavior. (by author and adapted from Department of Veterans Affairs/Department of Defense, 2013).

In the Department of Veterans Affairs/Department of Defense's (2013) Clinical Practice Guideline for the Assessment and Management of Patients at Risk for Suicide, the authors describe a recovery model (Figure 29.2) where chronic risk factors that are modifiable (state) and non-modifiable (trait) increase the general level of risk of suicidal behavior. Acute risk factors such as stressors and precipitating events cause a tipping point toward suicidal acts. There are also many protective factors that disincline the potential for suicide, and opportunities for means restriction that place obstacles in the path of suicidal self-directed violence. This model acknowledges that suicide risk is fluid and multifactorial. It encourages the identification of acute stressors and modifiable risk factors as targets for clinical intervention. It also cautions the clinician to be aware of the risk of relapse after recovery from the acute episode.

Risk factors are important targets for intervention when treating a suicidal patient. Acute precipitating factors must be addressed immediately while more chronic and underlying factors begin to be treated. It may be useful to organize the acute, chronic, and non-modifiable risk factors into a bio-psycho-social construct (Table 29.1) in order to align treatment efforts most effectively. From the psychopharmacological perspective, treatment of underlying mental illness and the management of acute, destabilizing symptomatology, such as insomnia, agitation, and panic, are particularly important, while suicide-focused psychotherapeutic and psychosocial interventions are initiated.

Clinical Relevance

Suicide is an enormous burden not only on individual sufferers, but also on the loved ones and clinicians supporting, managing, and treating the person at risk. The suicidal crisis often includes a component of conflict about autonomy and control. In its most dangerous form, the suicidal person seeks to conceal his or her distress and intent from caregivers either to follow through with a formulated plan or to resolve the crisis without telling anyone. Often there exists a component of shame that the individual fears will be compounded as more people become aware. This creates a paradox that with increasing distress there is the potential for increasing secrecy and isolation. Add to the shame a fear of loss of autonomy through hospitalization or involuntary commitment, and a real power struggle obscures the ability for an empathic, collaborative, therapeutic partnership as advocated by Jobes (2006) in his model for a Collaborative Assessment for the Management of Suicide.

As mental illness is the most significant risk factor for a suicide attempt (Hawton & van Heeringen, 2009), the psychiatric practitioner can ally with the suicidal patient around the treatment of the acute symptoms of illness and its distress to create a therapeutic partnership that restores some control to the patient. Again, the bio-psycho-social approach can serve as a nonjudgmental focus for the collaborative framework for the treatment.

Most mental disorders are associated with an increased risk of suicide (Harris & Barraclough, 1997). As the most serious symptom of a mental illness, suicide risk should be a primary focus of assessment

Table 29.1. Bio-Psycho-Social Risk Factors for Suicidal Behavior.

	Biological	Psychological	Social
Acute (More highly predictive of suicide attempt)	Agitation Insomnia Intoxication/withdrawal Pain Functional limitation Medication-induced New major illness Start/stop/change Antidepressant (~90 days)	Impulsivity Self-loathing Perceived burdensomeness Hopelessness Anxiety (panic) Dysphoria Suicide bereavement	*Stressful Life Events:* Loss of status/respect/rank (Public humiliation, being bullied or abused, failure work/task) Loss of relationship (divorce, separation) Loss of loved one (grief) Recent change in level of care (d/c from inpatient psychiatry) Other adverse events (e.g., fired, arrested, evicted, assaulted)
Chronic	Chronic pain Function limitation History of Traumatic Brain Injury (TBI) Terminal disease HIV/AIDS Worsening of chronic illness	Affective disorder Psychotic disorder Trauma-related disorder Anxiety disorder Substance use disorder Personality disorder	*Financial Problems:* Unemployment, Underemployment Unstable housing, homeless Excessive debt, poor finances *Legal Problems:* DUI/DWI Lawsuit Criminal offense and incarceration *Social Support:* Poor relationships Geographic isolation Barriers to MH care
Non-Modifiable (Less predictive of attempt)	Gender (Male) Age (<29 or >45) Race (Caucasian) Family history of suicide/mental disorder	Prior suicide attempt Prior psychiatric hospitalization for SI Hx of child maltreatment Sexual assault	Marital status (separate, widowed) Lower education level Same sex orientation (LGBT)

and treatment. Mood disorders pose the greatest risk of both suicide attempts and suicide death. Bipolar disorder is associated with a 10%–15% risk of death by suicide (Goodwin & Jamison, 2007) and the risk of suicide attempts is manifold higher. Major depression confers a 4% risk of death by suicide with the highest risk associated with severity of the illness, and episodes requiring hospitalization (Hawton & van Heeringen, 2009). Schizophrenia, particularly in its early stages, results in suicide death in 5%–6% of patients (Palmer, Pankratz, & Bostwick, 2005). This risk may be more closely related to depressive symptoms rather than hallucinations or delusions. Substance use disorders, particularly those involving alcohol or opioids, are significantly associated with suicidal behavior and death. The exact incidence of suicide in these conditions is difficult to discern because many of the behaviors associated with these disorders are inherently dangerous, leaving open the question of accidental versus intentional death on psychological autopsy (Harris & Barraclough, 1997).

Untreated mental illness is a serious problem as there is little hope for spontaneous remission of psychiatric conditions. Without resolution of the suicidal patient's underlying mental disorder, the risk of a suicide attempt remains elevated. In an analysis of National Comorbidity Survey data, Kessler and colleagues (2001) estimate that only 40% of people with serious mental illness receive stable treatment. Many factors may be responsible for this significant under-treatment problem, which include lack of access to care, lack of acceptance that the person has an illness that requires treatment, and lack of belief in treatment efficacy. The most significant reason reported by respondents to this survey was a desire to solve the problem on their own.

Scope of Chapter

This chapter will focus on the evidence for psychopharmacological treatment of mental illnesses and associated conditions that have been shown to reduce the risk of suicidal behavior or completion. Every attempt will be made to distinguish between the positive effect of treating the underlying condition and any medication effect that specifically impacts the risk of suicide. As the author served as co-chair of the Department of Veterans Affairs/Department of Defense's Clinical Practice Guideline for Assessment and Management of Patients at Risk for Suicide (2013), the literature review performed by this group will serve as a foundation for the recommendations presented here. Additional studies will be included that may not have met the rigorous inclusion criteria for the Guideline, but they may offer some additional insights for consideration. This chapter will be limited to psychopharmacological agents, and we will not discuss naturopathic, complementary, alternative, or non-medication treatments such as electroconvulsive therapy, transcranial magnetic stimulation, or vagus nerve stimulation.

Definitions

One of the significant challenges in reviewing the literature about treatment to reduce the risk of suicide is lack of a consistent nomenclature. Imprecise language about specific outcomes creates confusion about treatment effects. Many monographs refer to "suicidality" as a symptom of illness or a side effect of treatment. This term does not adequately distinguish between suicidal ideation, suicidal behavior, or death. Many groups have advocated the adoption of standard definitions to describe the spectrum of suicidal thoughts and behaviors. The Centers for Disease Control and Prevention published recommendations for uniform definitions and data elements to address this problem.

Self-directed violence (analogous to self-injurious behavior). Behavior that is self-directed and deliberately results in injury or the potential for injury to oneself. The intent of this behavior may be suicidal or non-suicidal. The National Institute for Clinical Excellence (2004) recommended the term "deliberate self-harm" to describe this phenomenon.

Non-suicidal self-directed violence. Behavior that is self-directed and deliberately results in injury or the potential for injury to oneself. There is no evidence, however, whether the behavior is implicit or explicit of suicidal intent. The CDC and most suicidologists recommend against using the term "suicide gesture" for this behavior, as this term is generally considered pejorative and serves to irresponsibly minimize the risk of a future suicide attempt or completion.

Suicidal self-directed violence. Behavior that is self-directed and deliberately results in injury or the potential for injury to oneself. In this case, there is evidence whether the behavior is implicit or explicit of suicidal intent. The individual intends to die as a result, whether or not the attempt involves a lethal method.

Suicide. Death caused by self-directed injurious behavior with any evidence of intent to die as a result. This determination is not always straightforward, as in the case of single-vehicle motor accidents, firearm "accidents," and asphyxiations. A "psychological autopsy" can often shed light on the deceased's frame of mind by considering collateral evidence of a wish to be dead, such as a suicide note and survivor statements.

Suicide attempt. A nonfatal self-directed potentially injurious behavior with any evidence of intent to die as a result of the behavior. A suicide attempt may or may not result in injury or death.

The Department of Veterans Affairs/Department of Defense's Clinical Practice Guideline for Assessment and Management of Patients at Risk for Suicide (2013) adopted these definitions for use and added the following recommendations for use by clinicians.

Suicidal ideation. Thoughts of engaging in suicide-related behavior. This includes all degrees of frequency, intensity, and duration, such as passive or fleeting suicidal thoughts.

Suicidal intent. There is past or present evidence from the history or from collateral sources that an individual wishes to die, means to kill himself or herself, and understands the probable consequences of his or her actions or potential actions. Suicidal intent can be determined retrospectively or inferred in the absence of suicidal behavior.

Preparatory behavior. Acts or preparation toward engaging in self-directed violence, up to the point before the potential for injury has begun. This can include any behavior beyond a verbalization or thought, such as researching a method, assembling a method (e.g., buying a firearm, collecting pills), or preparing for one's death by suicide (e.g., writing a suicide note, preparing a will, or giving possessions away).

Rehearsal behavior. A form of preparatory behavior that involves acts of habituation toward engaging in self-directed violence. This can include such activities as reviewing the sequential details of a suicidal plan, handling a firearm, preparing a location, or visiting a location.

Re-Attempters

Previous history of a suicide attempt is the most predictive risk factor for a re-attempt or completed suicide (Hawton & van Heeringen, 2009). A retrospective review reveals that 40% of suicides have had a history of a previous suicide attempt (Cavanagh, Carson, Sharpe, & Lawrie, 2003). Conversely, 60% of individuals who have completed suicides have had no identifiable history of suicide attempt and were successful on their first try. This fact underscores that as much as a history of a suicide attempt is a positive predictor for a future attempt, the absence of a prior suicide attempt cannot be interpreted as an indicator of low risk. As much of the literature about medication efficacy relates to preventing re-attempt, we can only infer that the same treatments may be useful in preventing a first, potentially fatal attempt.

Psychopharmacology of Suicide

There is only limited evidence for the efficacy of medications to reduce the risk of a suicide attempt. There are many problems that limit the ability to study the direct anti-suicidal effects of medications in drug trials. In most of the available literature, suicidal subjects are excluded from randomization. There are only a few available clinical trials that specifically include subjects with a history of a suicide attempt. Additionally, as suicide is a rare event, few studies are sufficiently powered to demonstrate significant effect. Most of the available literature consists of naturalistic studies that report on suicide events and, as such, caution must be exercised in concluding that any difference in the suicide attempt rate is directly related to a medication effect rather than attributable to treatment of the illness. This leaves the field wanting in many respects, but there are a few meta-analyses from which solid recommendations can be drawn. As all the available evidence exists in the context of treating an underlying mental illness, there is no evidence for the use of any pharmacotherapy to reduce the risk of suicide in the absence of a diagnosed psychiatric condition.

General Principles in Psychopharmacology

Medication therapy should be considered as part of the treatment plan for any mental illness when the patient is at risk for suicide. Effective treatment is imperative to the recovery of the condition that elevates the risk of suicide. As the evidence for a direct anti-suicide effect of medications is extremely limited, with only a few exceptions, it is best to conceptualize that psychopharmacological treatment of mental illness may be a "necessary, but not sufficient" component of treatment to reduce the risk of suicide. There is no evidence for any medication to reduce the acute risk of a suicide attempt. In cases where an anti-suicide effect is seen, this usually becomes evident for antidepressants and antipsychotics after months, or after years in the case of lithium. Medication therapy should be considered only one component of a bio-psycho-social treatment plan that focuses specifically on the acute and chronic suicide risk.

When assessing and managing a patient at risk for suicide from a psychopharmacological perspective, a review of current psychiatric and non-psychiatric medications and recreational drugs should be performed to identify any agents that may be associated with suicidal thoughts or behavior (Micromedex, 2015) (Table 29.2). A thorough medication review and reconciliation should be performed for patients at risk for suicide to assure safe and effective treatment and to minimize the risk of adverse drug interactions. The choice of treatment should take into account the toxicity of prescribed drugs in overdose, consider strategies to limit the quantity dispensed, or identify another person to be responsible for limiting access to lethal quantities of prescribed medications.

TREATING UNDERLYING MENTAL ILLNESS

Effective treatment of any underlying mental illness is absolutely critical to reduce the risk of suicide associated with these conditions. Many clinical practice guidelines and treatment algorithms exist to inform the most effective course of treatment for your patient. Evidence-based treatment begins with a comprehensive structured clinical evaluation to establish the correct diagnosis. Increasingly, our

Table 29.2. Medications Associated with Suicide Risk (Micromedex, *Accessed 2015*).

Medications Associated with Suicide Risk

Alemtuzumab	Mianserin
Amitriptyline Hydrochloride	Mirtazapine
Amoxapine	Moclobemide
Apremilast	Nefazodone Hydrochloride
Aripiprazole	Nortriptyline Hydrochloride
Belimumab	Olanzapine/Fluoxetine Hydrochloride
BupropionCertolizumab Pegol	Paroxetine Hydrochloride
Chlordiazepoxide/Amitriptyline Hydrochloride	Paroxetine Mesylate
Citalopram Hydrobromide	Peginterferon Alfa-2a
Ciprofloxacin	Peginterferon Alfa-2b
Clomipramine Hydrochloride	Phenelzine Sulfate
Desipramine Hydrochloride	Phentermine
Doxepin Hydrochloride	Propoxyphene
Efavirenz	Protriptyline Hydrochloride
Elvitegravir	Ribavirin
Ethinyl Estradiol	Rilpivirine Hydrochloride
Escitalopram Oxalate	Rivastigmine
Fluoxetine Hydrochloride	Rufinamide
Fluvoxamine Maleate	Sertraline Hydrochloride
Imipramine Hydrochloride	Sibutramine
Imipramine Pamoate	Sodium Oxybate
Isotretinoin	Sofosbuvir
Lacosamide	Suvorexant
Levetiracetam	Thalidomide
LevomilnacipranHydrochloride	Topiramate
Levonorgestrel	Tranylcypromine Sulfate
Levorphanol Tartrate	Trazodone Hydrochloride
Maprotiline Hydrochloride	Varenicline
Mefloquine Hydrochloride	Venlafaxine Hydrochloride
Methsuximide	Vilazodone
Methylphenidate	Zaleplon

treatment strategies are being refined for the sub-types of conditions. Ensuring diagnostic rigor will be the most effective pathway to effective treatment, reduction in symptoms, instillation of hope and re-covery, and resolution of suicidality. It is hopeless to presumptively treat a patient's symptoms with-out a clear formulation of the diagnosis as it per-tains to the presenting syndrome. For example, the treatment for bipolar depression is much different than for unipolar depression. In considering how best to manage a patient at high risk, first initiate the most effective evidence-based treatment for the condition. When equally efficacious options exist, consider the option that also has evidence for re-ducing the risk of a suicide attempt. If symptoms are not adequately treated, or suicide risk persists, then consider more strongly an effective treatment with evidence for suicide risk reduction. As most of the evidence that exists for anti-suicide benefit is only realized with longer-term treatment, medica-tions cannot be expected to reduce suicide risk in the short term. Patients must be monitored closely, especially early in the course of treatment, for wors-ening suicidality.

Psychotic Disorders. Patients with psychotic disorders are especially vulnerable to suicide. Approximately 20% of patients with schizophrenia and schizoaffective disorder attempt suicide, and 5%–6% die by suicide (Palmer, 2005). In a large meta-review, schizophrenia patients had a standard-ized mortality ratio of 12.9 (90% CI 0.7–174.3) (Chesney, Goodwin, & Fazel, 2014). The risk of suicide is highest early in the course of the illness and during depressive episodes, which are common in these conditions. Additional high-risk periods are after a psychotic episode or hospitalization. Co-occurring substance use disorders significantly increase risk.

Mood Disorders. The vast majority of all suicides occur in the context of a mood disorder. Bipolar disorder accounts for approximately one-quarter of all suicides, and this condition increases the risk of suicide attempts 15-fold compared with the general population. The depressive phase of this illness and the early recovery phase are especially high-risk periods (Marangell et al., 2006). In this population, suicide risk is most highly correlated with the number of days in a depressive phase over the past year as well as with the past history of a suicide attempt (American Psychiatric Association, 2013).

The International Society for Bipolar Disorders Task Force on Suicide conducted a meta-analysis of correlates of suicide in bipolar disorder. They showed that the variables significantly associated with suicide attempts were female gender, younger age at illness onset, depressive polarity of first or most recent illness episode, comorbid anxiety disorder, any comorbid substance use disorder, borderline personality disorder, and first-degree family history of suicide. Suicide deaths, however, were significantly associated with male gender and a first-degree family history of suicide. Importantly, this meta-analysis found that bipolar type (I or II) was not variably associated with suicidal attempts, and co-occurring substance use disorder or psychosis was not associated with suicide deaths (Schaffer et al., 2014).

Unipolar depression is significantly associated with suicide attempts, with most completed suicides occurring in the context of a major depressive episode. Depressive disorders confer a standardized mortality ratio of 19.7 (95% CI 12.2–32.0), the highest among the major "Axis I" conditions in Chesney, Goodwin, and Fazel's (2014) meta-review. Among patients with a major depressive episode, the strongest predictor of a suicide attempt is a previous attempt (Oquendo, Currier, & Mann, 2006). Factors associated with completed suicide are male gender, living alone, and feeling hopeless. Co-occurring conditions such as anxiety disorders, substance use disorders, or personality disorders such as borderline personality disorder elevate the risk further (American Psychiatric Association, 2013).

Anxiety Disorders. Anxiety disorders, such as a panic disorder and generalized anxiety disorder, are well-known risk factors for suicide. Data from the National Epidemiological Survey on Alcohol and Related Conditions show that 70% of subjects who reported a lifetime history of a suicide attempt also met the criteria for at least one anxiety disorder. In this study, the presence of any anxiety disorder conferred an increased risk of a suicide attempt when correcting for the presence of a mood, psychotic, substance use, or personality disorder (AOR = 1.70; 1.40–2.08; p < 0.01). Almost one-third (29.8%) of panic disorder subjects reported a history of suicide attempt (AOR = 1.44; 1.16–1.79; p < 0.01), with a similar proportion (31.1%) of subjects with generalized anxiety also reporting a suicide attempt (AOR = 1.26; 1.04–1.52; p < 0.05) (Nepon, Belik, Bolton, & Sareen, 2010).

Traumatic Stress Disorders. Trauma associated with childhood physical or sexual abuse increases a person's suicide risk (Afifi et al., 2008). In the National Epidemiological Survey on Alcohol and Related Conditions mentioned earlier, posttraumatic stress disorder (PTSD), then considered under the anxiety disorders, was the most highly correlated with a history of suicide. Thirty percent (30.4%) of the subjects with PTSD reported a history of suicide attempt (AOR = 1.89; 1.51–2.36; p < 0.01) (Nepon et al., 2010). PTSD was also confirmed to be a risk factor for suicide ideation (AOR = 2.79; 2.02–3.84; p < 0.01) and attempts (AOR = 2.67; 1.82–3.91; p < 0.01) in a post-hoc analysis of data from the National Comorbidity Study (Sareen, Houlahan, Cox, & Asmundson, 2005). The adjusted odds ratio was higher in this study as this analysis did not correct for the presence of comorbid conditions.

Traumatic Brain Injury. The prevalence of suicidal behavior in patients with traumatic brain injury (TBI) has not been well understood. Attempts to correlate the risk of suicidality with injury severity have been inconclusive. A recent Swedish population study reviewed the cause of death in 218,300 subjects with TBI. The risk of mortality from suicide was elevated (AOR = 3.3; 95% CI 2.9–3.7) compared with matched controls. Previous or co-occurring psychiatric illness (depression especially) and substance use disorders (alcohol especially) significantly increased the risk of suicide attempts in this population (Fazel, Wolf, Pillas, Lichtenstein, & Långström, 2014). In a recent prospective study of patients with mild to severe TBI, 25% of subjects reported suicidal ideation within the first year after injury. In this study, the strongest predictor of suicidal ideation was the initial, post-injury depression screening score (Mackelprang et al., 2014). Suicide is also associated with the chronic pain, mood dysregulation, impulsivity, and executive dysfunction related to moderate to severe TBI.

Substance Use Disorders. Substance use disorders (SUDs) are associated with an increased risk for suicide both independently and because of the associated co-occurrence of substance-induced and primary psychiatric conditions (Aharonovich, Liu, Nunes, & Hasin, 2002). SUDs have high rates of comorbidity with primary mood and anxiety disorders, as well as their associated secondary substance-induced mood disorders. The co-occurrence of SUD and mood disorder places the individual at serious risk of suicidal behavior, with data from the National Epidemiological Survey on Alcohol and Related Conditions revealing that the presence of a co-occurring condition approximately doubles the risk of suicide over that associated with the psychiatric condition alone (Nepon et al., 2010). Alcohol use disorder is associated with suicide risk during periods of severe intoxication due to the mood destabilizing and disinhibiting effects of the substance. Opioid use disorders are also associated with a high suicide risk. Like alcohol, opioids are linked with severe primary and secondary mood disorders, with depressive episodes representing an especially high-risk situation. Data on suicide rates are difficult to ascertain, because it is often difficult to determine whether an opioid overdose death is accidental or intentional.

The Role of Medication in Suicide Risk Reduction

As stated earlier, the most effective, evidence-based treatment for a particular mental illness should be recommended as the treatment of choice for patients at risk for suicide. The focus should always remain on the effective treatment of the underlying illness. Medications should be titrated aggressively to ensure adequate treatment with therapeutic monitoring. Undertreatment irresponsibly exposes the patient to all the risks with none of the therapeutic benefits of medication.

For patients at high risk for suicide, those with warning signs of acute risk such as expressing suicidal ideation or a wish to die, and those with a significant burden of risk factors and/or a lack of protective factors, clinicians should consider medications that have preferential evidence of an anti-suicide effect. All other factors being equal, a suicide-reducing medication should be chosen over an agent with a lack of evidence for reducing the risk of suicide. When a given agent is demonstrating a partial effect against suicidality, augmentation strategies that derive from evidence-based treatment algorithms should be recommended, with preference given wherever an agent with suicide-reducing evidence is available.

Antidepressants. The evidence for antidepressant use to reduce the risk of suicide attempts is inconclusive. While this class of medication is shown to be effective in the treatment of depressive illness—a major risk factor for a suicide attempt—there is little evidence that antidepressants have a direct effect to reduce suicidal ideation or behavior. However, there are numerous observational studies that have shown a reduction in suicide rate in parallel with increasing rates of antidepressant use (Isacsson, Rich, Jureidini, & Raven, 2010). This association has continued to be demonstrated after the introduction of serotonin reuptake inhibitors. This may be related to the improved tolerability and adherence of this class of medication, and also to a safety profile that increases the comfort of clinicians to prescribe at effective therapeutic dosages.

A Cochrane review examined the efficacy of antidepressant therapy to reduce the risk of deliberate self-harm (DSH) behaviors in repeat attempters (Hawton et al., 1999). The authors concluded that there was little evidence that antidepressants were effective in preventing repetitions of DSH. One exception was revealed in the subgroup analysis of a paroxetine trial that showed a reduction in repeat DSH behaviors for patients with a history of four or fewer suicide attempts.

There are several case reports that have linked antidepressant therapy to an increase in suicidal behavior. In 2003, the UK Department of Health warned against prescribing any selective serotonin reuptake inhibitor (SSRI), except fluoxetine, to children and adolescents due to the lack of efficacy in depression (fluoxetine excepted), and the increased risk of suicidal thoughts and behaviors for all SSRIs. Pediatric data presented to the US Food and Drug Administration had demonstrated a significant two-fold relative risk of suicidal ideation and behavior. This led the FDA to institute a boxed warning in 2004 to caution practitioners about the increased risk of suicidal behaviors in children and adolescents prescribed antidepressants. This warning was expanded in 2007 to include young adults up to age 24.

To explore this relationship further, the American College of Neuropsychopharmacology (ACNP) appointed a task force to examine two questions: the efficacy of antidepressant therapy in children; and the relative risk of antidepressant therapy versus no antidepressants in suicidal youth (Mann et al., 2006). The ACNP meta-analysis concluded that depression in youth is a serious public health problem with a significant risk of suicide, ranking as the third leading cause of death in 15–24 year olds. The data revealed that only fluoxetine and citalopram were more effective than a placebo for the treatment of depression in this age group. The task force concluded that, in youth, suicidal ideation and attempts were not common; no suicides occurred; and SSRIs as a class were associated with a twofold (4% vs. 2%) risk of suicidal ideation or attempt.

A meta-analysis by Stone and colleagues (2009) pooled the FDA databases and reviewed 327 double-blind, randomized, placebo-controlled clinical trials, with a total of 99,231 adult subjects. Overall, antidepressant therapy was not associated with an increase in suicidal ideation or behavior, including preparatory acts, suicide attempts, or completed suicides. When age stratification was performed, a twofold risk (OR = 2.30, 95% CI 1.04–5.09, p = 0.04) of suicidal behavior was identified in patients younger than 25 years of age, identified in 32 out of 4,780 subjects compared with eight out of 2,621 controls. Subjects over 25 years of age showed a slight decrease in suicidal ideation, but there was no significant change in risk of suicidal behavior compared with the placebo groups. Subjects aged 65 and older demonstrated a significant reduction in suicidal ideation and behavior over the controls.

Barbui, Esposito, and Cipriani (2009) performed a systematic review of observational studies to examine the association between SSRI exposure and the risk of suicide attempts or completion. They reviewed eight clinical studies with over 200,000 subjects of all age groups. They confirmed the age-related effect that patients aged 6–18 years experienced a twofold (OR = 1.92, 95% CI 1.51–2.44, I2 = 0.0%) increased risk of suicidal behavior.

Gibbons et al. (2007) further examined the relationship between SSRI treatment and suicidal behavior. They analyzed the medical records of 226,866 veteran subjects with depression who were treated with SSRIs, non-SSRI antidepressants, or no medication. This retrospective study showed that antidepressant treatment significantly reduced the risk of suicide attempts in all adult age groups compared with those patients not treated with an antidepressant. SSRIs (OR = 0.37, 95% CI 0.29–.47, p < 0.0001) and tricyclic antidepressants (TCAs; OR = 0.29, 95% CI 0.11–0.78, p = 0.006) demonstrated significantly greater benefit than other non-SSRI, second-generation antidepressants (OR = 0.83, 95% CI 0.64–1.08, p = 0.16). All classes of antidepressants demonstrated significant 50% reductions in suicide attempts when comparing pre- and post-treatment phases, but this could not be shown to be independent of the antidepressant effect.

In comparisons of the individual antidepressants, several studies are informative. Schneeweiss and colleagues (2010) conducted a nine-year cohort study of 287,543 subjects treated with SSRIs, SNRIs (serotonin-norepinephrine reuptake inhibitors), MAOIs (monoamine oxidase inhibitors), TCAs, and newer atypical antidepressants. They found no clinically significant change in the risk of suicide attempts between the classes or between agents within a class. They did, however, identify a trend that most of the suicide events occurred within the first six months of treatment.

A meta-analysis of 41 clinical trials comparing fluoxetine or venlafaxine to a placebo involving 9,185 subjects of all ages confirmed a linear reduction in suicidal thoughts and behavior for all age groups except youths (Gibbons et al., 2012). This reduction in suicidal ideation and attempts was directly related to relief of depressive symptom burden.

Treatment with paroxetine was compared to bupropion in a small, head-to-head comparison to examine the effect on suicidal behavior, ideation, and mood in patients with major depressive disorder and a prior suicide attempt or current suicidal ideation (Grunebaum et al., 2012). While the paroxetine arm showed a trend toward more rapid reduction in suicide ideation, this was not significant. There was no difference in the rate of suicidal behavior.

The FDA's boxed warning was subsequently amended to include language emphasizing that depression is a serious illness that increases the risk for suicidal behavior, and that it should be treated effectively.

Changes in antidepressant therapy have been shown to transiently increase the risk of suicide in adults (Valenstein et al., 2009). Whether this is due to a drug effect as appears to be the case in children, or related to other factors, such as indication bias, remains unclear. This retrospective study of 887,859 veterans revealed a transient elevation of suicide risk for the initial 12-week period after antidepressants are started, stopped, adjusted, or switched. This effect was greatest in the 61–80 years age group.

Extreme caution should be exercised in the use of antidepressants to treat bipolar affective disorders. Antidepressants are used in the treatment of bipolar patients in 35%–55% of cases according the NIMH STEP-BD study (Yerevanian & Choi, 2013). SSRIs are well known to increase the risk of mood destabilization, rapid cycling, and mixed states in bipolar patients. Their impact on rates of suicidal behavior was examined in a retrospective review of 405 adults with bipolar disorder followed longitudinally for three years (Yerevanian, Koek, & Mintz, 2007a, 2007b; Yerevanian, Koek, Mintz, & Akiskal, 2007). A clear relationship was demonstrated between antidepressant therapy and severe suicidal behavior, with antidepressant monotherapy faring worst (RR = 6.72), and the combination therapy with mood stabilizer demonstrating intermediate risk (RR = 2.44) when compared to mood stabilizer monotherapy. In several comparative studies, venlafaxine was associated with the highest risk of suicidal behavior, and fluoxetine demonstrated the lowest risk when compared to the placebo (Hammad, Laughren, & Racoosin, 2006; Tiihonen et al., 2006).

In summary, patients with unipolar depressive disorders should be treated with an antidepressant with the understanding that the evidence is limited for any direct anti-suicide effect. No antidepressant has clearly been shown to be superior in targeting suicidal behavior. There is, however, limited evidence that fluoxetine, citalopram, and paroxetine may afford a slight advantage against suicidal ideation. Children, adolescents, their parents and guardians, and young adults should be informed about the risk of medication-related suicidal behavior when an antidepressant is recommended. All patients should be monitored closely for at least 12-weeks whenever antidepressants are started, stopped, adjusted, or switched. Antidepressants should be avoided in patients with bipolar spectrum disorders at high risk for suicide.

Mood Stabilizers. Lithium is the only mood stabilizer convincingly demonstrating a reduction in suicide attempts and completed suicides in patients with bipolar illness. It is unclear whether lithium exerts a direct anti-suicide effect, whether the benefits are realized because of a reduction in aggression or impulsivity through a serotonin-mediated pathway, or perhaps the reduction is because of the indirect benefit of long-term intensive clinical monitoring. Tondo, Hennen, and Baldessarini (2001) conducted a meta-analysis involving 5,647 subjects that demonstrated an 82% reduction in suicide deaths for patients treated with lithium compared to no treatment. Baldessarini, Tondo, and Hennen (2003) conducted a review of 34 studies involving 16,201 subjects and concluded that bipolar patients treated with lithium experienced a 95% reduction in suicidal behavior and an 82% reduction in suicides over patients who were untreated or treated with medications other than lithium. The most robust anti-suicide effect is seen in patients receiving long-term lithium therapy (Oquendo, Chaudhury, & Mann, 2005). In their review of all major affective disorders and drug treatments, Baldessarini et al.

(2006) again confirmed a robust protective effect of lithium, demonstrating an 80% reduction in the risk of a suicide attempt (RR = 4.91; 3.82–6.31; p < 0.0001) over any other agent for patients treated for at least 18 months. As no risk reduction has been seen in the first year of treatment by any clinical study, lithium cannot be considered efficacious for acute suicidality.

Lithium has been shown in a large observational study to outperform valproate and carbamazepine in reducing the risk of suicide in patients with bipolar disorder (Goodwin et al., 2003). Additional studies of these other two mood stabilizing antiepileptic drugs have not demonstrated any benefit in reducing suicidal ideation, behavior, or death in this population (Ernst & Goldberg, 2004). This would appear to address the question of whether lithium's efficacy is due to an indirect effect of close clinical monitoring.

Lithium has also been shown to reduce the risk of suicide in patients with unipolar depression (Cipriani et al., 2006), although the quality of the evidence is not as strong as that for bipolar disorder. Guzzetta, Tondo, Centorrino, and Baldessarini (2007) reviewed seven studies of major depressive disorder encompassing 2,434 person-years of treatment. Those treated with lithium in addition to any other drug treatments demonstrated a highly significant 88.5% reduction in the risk of suicide and suicide attempts (IRR = 8.71; 2.10–77.2; p = 0.0005).

In their systematic review, Cipriani, Hawton, Stockton, and Geddes (2013) again confirmed lithium's effectiveness over a placebo. They revalidated its superiority over all other agents in bipolar patients and unipolar depression, and its superiority over all antiepileptic drugs for deliberate self-harm. Lithium should be recommended as the first-line augmentation strategy for partially responding depressed patients at high risk for suicide.

In addition to the bipolar literature, there is limited evidence for lithium preventing suicide death in patients with schizoaffective depression, dysthymia, and rapid cycling (Cipriani, Pretty, Hawton, & Geddes, 2005). In their review of seven studies, lithium patients were less likely to die by suicide (OR = 0.26; 0.09–0.77) than those treated with other agents.

There is little evidence to support the use of antiepileptic drugs (AEDs) to specifically reduce the risk of suicide in patients with mood disorders. However, AEDs have been shown to reduce suicide attempts when compared to no treatment

(Gibbons, Hur, Brown, & Mann, 2009). There has been some evidence about the risk of worsening suicidality with AEDs in patients with epilepsy, with a 2008 FDA meta-analysis indicating a twofold increase in suicidal ideation and behavior compared to the placebo. Patorno and colleagues (2010) conducted a meta-analysis of 297,620 subjects treated for any indication with any AED. They evaluated all suicidal acts and violent deaths. This study revealed that gabapentin (HR 1.42), valproate (HR 1.65), lamotrigine (HR 1.84), oxcarbazepine (HR 2.07), and tiagabine (HR 2.41) were associated with the highest risk of suicidal acts or violent deaths of all the AEDs. Redden and colleagues (2011) examined the risk of suicide in a trans-diagnostic group of patients treated with valproate. This study showed no increased risk of suicide attempt or completion.

A retrospective review of patients treated with AED monotherapy was conducted to examine the relationship of the drugs and diagnosis to suicide-related behaviors. This review concluded that the strongest predictor of suicidal behavior was the presence of an affective disorder prior to the start of AED therapy (VanCott et al., 2010). They saw no specific drug effect. Furthermore, several large observational studies found that AEDs were not associated with an increased risk of suicide attempts in patients with psychiatric illness (Arana, Wentworth, Ayuso-Mateos, & Arellano, 2010) or bipolar disorder specifically (Leon et al., 2012). A recent expert consensus concluded that AEDs can be associated with psychiatric conditions that may lead to suicidal behavior, but the actual risk of suicide attempts attributable to these medications was low (Yerevanian & Choi, 2013).

In summary, lithium should be strongly considered as a first-line treatment for patients with bipolar disorder and bipolar depression at high risk for suicide, both for its mood stabilizing and long-term anti-suicide effects. Lithium augmentation should also be considered for patients with unipolar depression who are not responding fully to antidepressant therapy, and it may be beneficial for antidepressant responders who remain at risk for suicide. Antiepileptic drugs are superior to no treatment for patients with a mood or impulse control disorder.

Antipsychotics. Antipsychotic medications are used to treat a variety of conditions from psychotic illnesses to mood, anxiety, and trauma-related disorders. Atypical antipsychotics carry indications for a first-line therapy for bipolar disorder, and as augmentation therapy with antidepressants for depressive illness. Several studies report slight increases in suicidal ideation (Goldberg et al., 2005) or suicide attempt (Calabrese et al., 2005) when used to treat non-psychotic illness. In bipolar disorder, patients treated with antipsychotic monotherapy demonstrated a 10-fold relative risk (32.8 vs. 3.48 events/100 patient-years) of a suicide attempt compared with mood stabilizer monotherapy (Yerevanian, Koek, & Mintz, 2007a). While atypical antipsychotics are effective for the treatment of bipolar-spectrum illness, mood stabilizers are preferred for patients at high risk for suicide, with lithium being most preferred. Patients with mood or anxiety disorders should be monitored closely and informed of the risk of suicidal ideation or behavior when using an atypical antipsychotic.

In a large Finnish study of schizophrenic patients, the effect of antipsychotic medication on suicidal behavior was examined. Current treatment with an antipsychotic medication was associated with decreased mortality due to suicide (HR = 0.52; 0.34–0.81; p = 0.004) (Haukka, Tiihonen, Härkänen, & Lönnqvist, 2008). Tiihonen et al. (2006) showed a 37-fold increased risk of suicidal behavior for patients not receiving antipsychotic therapy. Clearly, effective treatment of schizophrenia is a primary strategy for reducing the risk of suicide.

Clozapine is the first agent of any class to receive an FDA indication specifically for reduction in risk of recurrent suicidal behavior in patients with schizophrenia and schizoaffective disorder. Additionally, there are some data to suggest that clozapine may reduce the risk of suicide attempts in other conditions, such as bipolar disorder (Nielsen, Kane, & Correll, 2012).

The International Suicide Prevention Trial (InterSePT) examined the role of antipsychotic medications to reduce the risk of suicide in patients with schizophrenia and schizoaffective disorder who were at high risk because of a prior suicide attempt. In this 2-year prospective study, Meltzer and colleagues (2003) showed that clozapine patients had significantly fewer suicide behaviors compared to olanzapine (HR = 0.76; 0.58–0.97; p = 0.03). In a subsequent analysis to determine if concomitant psychotropic medications prescribed to many of these patients was a confounding factor, the clozapine group was shown to have received significantly lower dosage equivalents of mood stabilizers, antidepressants, and anxiolytics. It was concluded that the anti-suicide benefits were due to the clozapine itself, and not the adjunctive medications (Glick et al., 2004).

Modestin, Dal Pian, and Agarwalla (2005) conducted a retrospective review of patients with schizophrenia before, during, and after a period of treatment with clozapine. The mean duration of each phase of treatment was 15 months. They found a significant reduction (OR = 11.6; 95% CI = 3.4–39.9) in suicidal behavior requiring medical attention associated with the period of treatment. The protective effect appeared to diminish after discontinuation, with the rate of suicidal behavior being 28% in the pre-treatment phase, 3% in the clozapine phase, and 18% in the post-clozapine phase.

Hennen and Baldessarini's meta-analysis (2005) of six studies again demonstrated clozapine's superiority over other antipsychotic medications in reducing the risk threefold for suicidal behaviors (RR = 3.3; 1.7–6.3; p < 0.0001) and for completed suicide (RR = 2.9; 1.5–5.7; p = 0.002).

In a Finnish population-based cohort study of mortality in patients with schizophrenia, Tiihonen and colleagues (2009) confirmed clozapine's superiority in reducing risk of death by suicide and also for all-cause mortality. The comparators included typical and atypical antipsychotics, with clozapine demonstrating the lowest rate of suicide of any of the antipsychotic medications (HR = 0.34; 0.20–0.57) compared to perphenazine (HR = 1) and to all others combined (HR = 1.55; 1.07–2.25).

Anxiolytics. As anxiety is a significant risk factor for a suicide attempt, targeting this symptom with an anxiolytic would seem intuitive to reduce the risk of suicide, particularly short-term use in patients with acute anxiety, agitation, or panic. Unfortunately, these agents have not been studied in any systematic way, so no evidence is available to understand their potential role in suicide risk reduction. As benzodiazepines have the potential to be disinhibiting and they are also lethal in overdose, they should be prescribed with caution with due consideration for the risk–benefit ratio.

Sedative-Hypnotics. While insomnia is an independent risk factor for suicide, caution must be exercised when choosing a treatment for this condition. In an analysis of the National Comorbidity Survey Replication data, Brower et al. (2011) found that patients prescribed zolpidem or zaleplon were 3.4 times more likely to attempt suicide than controls.

Ketamine. Ketamine is an exciting new agent for the treatment of severe depression with an emerging body of literature supporting its use in suicide risk reduction. This N-methyl-D-aspartate (NMDA) receptor antagonist has a novel mechanism of action and demonstrates acute but short-term resolution

of depressive symptoms. Ketamine is administered in sub-anaesthetic doses (0.5mg/kg) via intravenous infusion over 40 minutes. Dramatic antidepressant effect is seen within the first hours and lasts for several days. Little is known about the safety or efficacy of ketamine for maintenance therapy. Several feasibility trials of intramuscular and intranasal ketamine are ongoing.

A recent systematic review of the literature evaluated ketamine's efficacy in patients with major depressive disorder, bipolar depression, and treatment-resistant depression. Nine randomized clinical trials were included in this review. These studies include drug-free subjects as well as non-washout subjects reflecting the clinical population. Overall, this meta-analysis demonstrated that ketamine was effective in reducing depressive symptoms over controls (Standardized Mean Difference [SMD] = –0.99; 95% CI = –1.23 to –0.75; p < 0.01) (Fond et al., 2014).

Subgroup analysis showed ketamine's efficacy both in patients with major depressive disorder (SMD = –0.91; 95% CI = –1.19 to –0.64; p < 0.01) and in bipolar disorder (SMD = –1.34; 95% CI = –1.94 to –0.75; p < 0.01). Drug-free subjects and non–drug-free subjects each demonstrated significant improvement in this analysis. Subjects with treatment-resistant depression in both the major depressive disorder and the bipolar disorder groups demonstrated robust responses to ketamine. In the included studies with placebo controls, ketamine's effectiveness was confirmed to be robust (SMD = –0.99; 95% CI = –1.33 to –0.64; p < 0.01) (Fond et al., 2014).

Fond and colleagues (2014) also reviewed clinical trials of ECT patients comparing ketamine against other anaesthetic agents (thiopental or propofol). Of the subjects in the available trials, depression scores were significantly improved in the ketamine arms (SMD = –0.56; 95% CI = –1.10 to –0.02; p < 0.04).

The question of a direct anti-suicide effect of ketamine was also evaluated in the meta-analysis by Fond and colleagues (2014). The data were mixed and limited by the availability of suicide measures on depression screens. Price and colleagues (2014) attempted to answer this question in their randomized control trial of treatment-resistant, unipolar depression subjects. In this study, subjects were randomized to a ketamine arm (N = 36) or to midazolam (N = 21) used as a psychoactive placebo. The subjects' suicidal ideation was assessed using the Beck Scale for Suicidal Ideation (BSS), the suicide item of the Montgomery-Asberg Rating Scale, and the Implicit Association Test (IAT). At 24 hours, 53% of ketamine patients scored zero on all three measures compared with 24% of the controls (χ^2 = 4.6; p = 0.03).

As with all treatments, the question of whether ketamine's anti-suicide effect is independent of the antidepressant effect is important. In a study of 133 unipolar and bipolar subjects with moderate to severe major depressive episodes, ketamine was administered and outcomes were assessed using the Scale for Suicidal Ideation (SSI), the Beck Depression Inventory (BDI), Hamilton Rating Scales for Depression (HAM-D), and Anxiety (HAM-A). Ketamine was associated with reductions in suicidal ideation that were both related to, and independent of, depression and anxiety scores. Importantly, ketamine had a significant impact on two cognitive components of suicidality that are predictive of a future suicide attempt. The "wish to live" was increased, and the "wish to die" was decreased with ketamine administration, with peak effects seen at 40 minutes post-infusion and lasting for 72 hours in this study (Ballard et al., 2014).

Risk Management Issues

The risk of overdose is a significant concern whenever medications are prescribed for individuals at risk for suicide. This risk must be addressed as part of the treatment planning and informed consent process. The toxicity of prescribed drugs should be understood and considered when treatment begins and any time suicide risk is increased. When a choice exists between drugs of equivalent efficacy, it is wise to recommend the medication with the more benign toxicity profile. When a potentially toxic medication is the most efficacious agent to treat a psychiatric condition, one need not avoid its use, but care should be exercised to limit the dispensed quantity or to identify another person to manage the availability of the medication during the high-risk period (Department of Veterans Affairs/Department of Defense, 2013). The concern about drug toxicity, however, should not cause the clinician to undertreat the illness with inadequate dosing. This strategy imposes all the risks of drug therapy with none of the benefits and should be avoided.

Conclusion

Mental illness is the primary risk factor for suicidal ideation, attempt, and completion. All behavioral health patients should receive a comprehensive diagnostic evaluation that includes a thorough suicide risk assessment. Diagnostic accuracy is imperative as all subsequent treatment recommendations follow the evidence associated with a particular diagnosis. The initial assessment should include a review of current medications, over-the-counter medications, and substances of abuse to identify any agent that may be contributing to a mood disorder or suicidality. Effective treatment of the psychiatric condition is the foundational strategy to reduce the risk of suicide associated with these conditions, but few medications can be demonstrated to independently reduce the risk of suicide.

Psychopharmacological treatment should be considered an integral component of the bio-psycho-social treatments within the context of recovery model for suicide prevention. When there is a choice between evidence-based treatments, and there is evidence of a direct suicide risk-reducing benefit of a particular medication, that agent should be preferred to optimize treatment of both the underlying condition as well as the risk of suicide. As many medications have narrow therapeutic windows, or are lethal in overdose, the clinician should be mindful of toxicity, prescribe sublethal quantities, enlist caregivers to monitor supplies, and provide close follow-up to maximize treatment adherence. Clinicians should not avoid maximizing adequate dosing because of a fear of overdose, but use collaborative strategies to limit access to lethal quantities.

Effective treatment of mood disorders represents the greatest opportunity to reduce suicide risk. Antidepressant treatment should be optimized to treat unipolar depressive disorders but cannot be relied upon to independently reduce the risk of suicide. As suicidal ideation and behavior is associated with antidepressant use, particularly for children, adolescents, and young adults, these patients and their parents or guardians should be educated about the risks of suicide as part of the informed consent process. All patients receiving antidepressant therapy should be monitored closely for the emergence of suicidal ideation and behavior whenever an antidepressant is started, dosage changed, medication switched or discontinued for a period of at least twelve weeks.

Lithium demonstrates compelling effectiveness to reduce the risk of suicide in patients with bipolar disorder and unipolar depression. Lithium's effect, however, is not seen in the acute phase of treatment, but only after years of treatment and, therefore, it is not efficacious to reduce the acute risk of suicide. Patients at risk for suicide with bipolar spectrum illness should be offered lithium as the most evidence-based treatment to target long-term suicide risk. Other mood stabilizing agents demonstrate some evidence of protective effect over the placebo or non-treatment and should be recommended if lithium is contraindicated or an AED demonstrates more favorable efficacy for the condition.

Antipsychotic medications significantly reduce the risk of suicide in patients with schizophrenia and schizoaffective disorder through a nonspecific effect of treating these high-risk conditions. The only antipsychotic that appears to demonstrate a specific benefit to reduce the risk of suicide attempt is clozapine. Clinical algorithms should be used to optimize treatment and clozapine should be offered at the earliest opportunity for patients with a history of suicide attempt, at high risk for suicide, or who demonstrate suboptimal treatment response after adequate trials of other antipsychotics. These patients should be closely monitored early in the course of illness, watching also for depressive symptoms, as this time represents a particularly high-risk phase of the illness.

Anxiolytics and sedative-hypnotics should only be used with caution in patients at high risk for suicide. A careful risk–benefit analysis should be done when their short-term use is indicated for anxiety or insomnia. As these agents can be highly lethal, especially in combination with other sedating agents such as alcohol, clinicians should be mindful of the quantity prescribed at any given time, and monitor these patients closely.

Ketamine is the most promising new agent that appears to provide rapid resolution of depressive symptomatology *and* reduce suicidal ideation and behavior. Ketamine is not yet approved by the FDA for use as an antidepressant, and the safety, tolerability, and administration is not well understood. No studies have been published describing recommendation for repetitive dosing, duration of treatment, and long-term effects. As most of the studies have used intravenous administration, it is not known if an intramuscular, nasal, or oral route of administration would be effective.

Future Directions

Much is yet to be done to understand the pathophysiology of suicide. The complex interplay of mood disorder, impulsivity, and hopelessness as mediated by noradrenergic and serotonergic pathways is beginning to inform the pharmacotherapy of suicide prevention. The roles of GABA-ergic

and glutamatergic modulators may prove useful and should be studied to shed light on the role of anxiety and agitation as risk factors and to inform future treatment of these states. The most exciting new development is the role of NMDA-antagonism in mood disorders in general and suicide specifically. Ketamine represents great promise for the rapid treatment of acute depressive and suicidal symptoms. It remains to be seen whether it can be safely used for maintenance therapy or as an early phase intervention in a stepped-care model while other maintenance therapies are initiated. We have advanced the treatment of suicide risk far beyond the limitations of simply treating the underlying psychiatric condition. Much more needs to be done to study suicidal ideation and behavior with prospective randomized clinical trials to discover more effective strategies to reduce this profound public health problem.

References

Afifi, T. O., Enns, M. W., Cox, B. J., Asmundson, G. J., Stein, M. B., & Sareen, J. (2008). Population attributable fractions of psychiatric disorders and suicide ideation and attempts associated with adverse childhood experiences. *American Journal of Public Health, 98*(5), 946–952.

Aharonovich, E., Liu, X., Nunes, E., & Hasin, D. S. (2002). Suicide attempts in substance abusers: Effects of major depression in relation to substance use disorders. *American Journal of Psychiatry, 159*(9), 1600–1602.

American Psychiatric Association. (2013). *Diagnostic and statistical manual of mental disorders* (5th ed.). Arlington, VA: Author.

Arana, A., Wentworth, C. E., Ayuso-Mateos, J. L., & Arellano, F. M. (2010). Suicide-related events in patients treated with antiepileptic drugs. *New England Journal of Medicine, 363*(6), 542–551.

Baldessarini, R. J., Tondo, L., Davis, P., Pompili, M., Goodwin, F. K., & Hennen, J. (2006). Decreased risk of suicides and attempts during long-term lithium treatment: A meta-analytic review. *Bipolar Disorders, 8*(5 Pt 2), 625–639.

Baldessarini, R. J., Tondo, L., & Hennen, J. (2003). Lithium treatment and suicide risk in major affective disorders: Update and new findings. *Journal of Clinical Psychiatry, 64* (Suppl 5), 44–52.

Ballard, E. D., Ionescu, D. F., Vande Voort, J. L., Niciu, M. J., Richards, E. M., Luckenbaugh, D. A.,... Zarate, C. A. (2014). Improvement in suicidal ideation after ketamine infusion: Relationship to reductions in depression and anxiety. *Journal of Psychiatric Research, 58*, 161–166.

Barbui, C., Esposito, E., & Cipriani, A. (2009). Selective serotonin reuptake inhibitors and risk of suicide: A systematic review of observational studies. *Canadian Medical Association Journal, 180*(3), 291–297.

Brower, K. J., McCammon, R. J., Wojnar, M., Ilgen, M. A., Wojnar, J., & Valenstein, M. (2011). Prescription sleeping pills, insomnia, and suicidality in the National Comorbidity Survey Replication. *Journal of Clinical Psychiatry, 72*(4), 515–521.

Calabrese, J. R., Shelton, M. D., Rapport, D. J., Youngstrom, E. A., Jackson, K., Bilali, S.,... Findling, R. L. (2005). A 20-month, double-blind, maintenance trial of lithium versus divalproex in rapid-cycling bipolar disorder. *American Journal of Psychiatry, 162*(11), 2152–2161.

Cavanagh, J. T., Carson, A. J., Sharpe, M., & Lawrie, S. M. (2003). Psychological autopsy studies of suicide: A systematic review. *Psychological Medicine, 33*(3), 395–405.

Chesney, E., Goodwin, G. M., & Fazel, S. (2014). Risks of all-cause and suicide mortality in mental disorders: A meta-review. *World Psychiatry, 13*(2), 153–160.

Cipriani, A., Hawton, K., Stockton, S., & Geddes, J. R. (2013). Lithium in the prevention of suicide in mood disorders: Updated systematic review and meta-analysis. *British Medical Journal, 346*, f3646.

Cipriani, A., Pretty, H., Hawton, K., & Geddes, J. R. (2005). Lithium in the prevention of suicidal behavior and all-cause mortality in patients with mood disorders: A systematic review of randomized trials. *American Journal of Psychiatry, 162*(10), 1805–1819.

Cipriani, A., Smith, K., Burgess, S., Carney, S., Goodwin, G., & Geddes, J. (2006). Lithium versus antidepressants in the long-term treatment of unipolar affective disorder. *Cochrane Database Systematic Review, 18*(4), CD003492.

Crosby, A. E., Ortega, L., Stevens, M. R., & Centers for Disease Control and Prevention. (2011). Suicides—United States, 1999–2007. *MMWR Surveillance Summary, 60 Suppl*, 56–59.

Department of Veterans Affairs/Department of Defense, Committee on Suicide Prevention. Bradley, J., Katz, I., Kemp, J., & Schneider, B. (Eds.). (2013). *VA/DoD Clinical practice guideline for the assessment and management of patients at risk for suicide.* Washington, DC: Authors.

Ernst, C. L., & Goldberg, J. F. (2004). Antisuicide properties of psychotropic drugs: A critical review. *Harvard Review of Psychiatry, 12*(1), 14–41.

Fazel, S., Wolf, A., Pillas, D., Lichtenstein, P., & Långström, N. (2014). Suicide, fatal injuries, and other causes of premature mortality in patients with traumatic brain injury: A 41-year Swedish population study. *Journal of the American Medical Association Psychiatry, 71*(3), 326–333.

Fond, G., Loundou, A., Rabu, C., Macgregor, A., Lançon, C., Brittner, M.,... Boyer, L. (2014). Ketamine administration in depressive disorders: A systematic review and meta-analysis. *Psychopharmacology (Berl), 231*(18), 3663–3676.

Gibbons, R. D., Brown, C. H., Hur, K., Davis, J., & Mann, J. J. (2012). Suicidal thoughts and behavior with antidepressant treatment: Reanalysis of the randomized placebo-controlled studies of fluoxetine and venlafaxine. *Archives of General Psychiatry, 69*(6), 580–587.

Gibbons, R. D., Brown, C. H., Hur, K., Marcus, S. M., Bhaumik, D. K., & Mann, J. J. (2007). Relationship between antidepressants and suicide attempts: An analysis of the Veterans Health Administration data sets. *American Journal of Psychiatry, 164*(7), 1044–1049.

Gibbons, R. D., Hur, K., Brown, C. H., & Mann, J. J. (2009). Relationship between antiepileptic drugs and suicide attempts in patients with bipolar disorder. *Archives of General Psychiatry, 66*(12), 1354–1360.

Glick, I. D., Zaninelli, R., Hsu, C., Young, F. K., Weiss, L., Gunay, I., & Kumar, V. (2004). Patterns of concomitant psychotropic medication use during a 2-year study comparing clozapine and olanzapine for the prevention of suicidal behavior. *Journal of Clinical Psychiatry, 65*(5), 679–685.

Goldberg, J. F., Allen, M. H., Miklowitz, D. A., Bowden, C. L., Endick, C. J., Chessick, C. A.,... Sachs, G. S. (2005).

Suicidal ideation and pharmacotherapy among STEP-BD patients. *Psychiatric Services, 56*(12), 1534–1540.

Goodwin, F. K., Fireman, B., Simon, G. E., Hunkeler, E. M., Lee, J., & Revicki, D. (2003). Suicide risk in bipolar disorder during treatment with lithium and divalproex. *Journal of the American Medical Association, 290*(11), 1467–1473.

Goodwin, F. K., & Jamison, K. R. (2007). *Manic-depressive illness: Bipolar disorders and recurrent depression* (2nd ed.). New York, NY: Oxford University Press.

Grunebaum, M. F., Ellis, S. P., Duan, N., Burke, A. K., Oquendo, M. A., & Mann, J. J. (2012). Pilot randomized clinical trial of an SSRI vs bupropion: Effects on suicidal behavior, ideation, and mood in major depression. *Neuropsychopharmacology, 37*(3), 697–706.

Guzzetta, F., Tondo, L., Centorrino, F., & Baldessarini, R. J. (2007). Lithium treatment reduces suicide risk in recurrent major depressive disorder. *Journal of Clinical Psychiatry, 68*(3), 380–383.

Hammad, T. A., Laughren, T., & Racoosin, J. (2006). Suicidality in pediatric patients treated with antidepressant drugs. *Archives of General Psychiatry, 63*(3), 332–339.

Harris, E. C., & Barraclough, B. (1997). Suicide as an outcome for mental disorders. A meta-analysis. *British Journal of Psychiatry, 170*, 205–228.

Haukka, J., Tiihonen, J., Härkänen, T., & Lönnqvist, J. (2008). Association between medication and risk of suicide, attempted suicide, and death in nationwide cohort of suicidal patients with schizophrenia. *Pharmacoepidemiological Drug Safety, 17*(7), 686–696.

Hawton, K. K. E., Townsend, E., Arensman, E., Gunnell, D., Hazell, P., House, A., & van Heeringen, K. (1999). *Psychosocial and pharmacological treatments for deliberate self harm* [Review]: Wiley.

Hawton, K., & van Heeringen, K. (2009). Suicide. *Lancet, 373*(9672), 1372–1381.

Hennen, J., & Baldessarini, R. J. (2005). Suicidal risk during treatment with clozapine: A meta-analysis. *Schizophrenia Research, 73*(2–3), 139–145.

Isacsson, G., Rich, C. L., Jureidini, J., & Raven, M. (2010). The increased use of antidepressants has contributed to the worldwide reduction in suicide rates. *British Journal of Psychiatry, 196*(6), 429–433.

Jobes, D. A. (2006). *Managing suicidal risk: A collaborative approach.* New York, NY: Guilford Press.

Joiner, T. E. (2005). *Why people die by suicide.* Cambridge, MA: Harvard University Press.

Kessler, R. C., Berglund, P. A., Bruce, M. L., Koch, J. R., Laska, E. M., Leaf, P. J.,... Wang, P. S. (2001). The prevalence and correlates of untreated serious mental illness. *Health Services Research, 36*(6 Pt 1), 987–1007.

Leon, A. C., Solomon, D. A., Li, C., Fiedorowicz, J. G., Coryell, W. H., Endicott, J., & Keller, M. B. (2012). Antiepileptic drugs for bipolar disorder and the risk of suicidal behavior: A 30-year observational study. *American Journal of Psychiatry, 169*(3), 285–291.

Mackelprang, J. L., Bombardier, C. H., Fann, J. R., Temkin, N. R., Barber, J. K., & Dikmen, S. S. (2014). Rates and predictors of suicidal ideation during the first year after traumatic brain injury. *American Journal of Public Health, 104*(7), e100–e107.

Mann, J. J. (2003). Neurobiology of suicidal behaviour. *Nature Review Neuroscience, 4*(10), 819–828.

Mann, J. J., Apter, A., Bertolote, J., Beautrais, A., Currier, D., Haas, A.,... Hendin, H. (2005). Suicide prevention strategies: A systematic review. *Journal of the American Medical Association, 294*(16), 2064–2074.

Mann, J. J., Emslie, G., Baldessarini, R. J., Beardslee, W., Fawcett, J. A., Goodwin, F. K.,... Wagner, K. D. (2006). ACNP Task Force report on SSRIs and suicidal behavior in youth. *Neuropsychopharmacology, 31*(3), 473–492.

Marangell, L. B., Bauer, M. S., Dennehy, E. B., Wisniewski, S. R., Allen, M. H., Miklowitz, D. J.,... Thase, M. E. (2006). Prospective predictors of suicide and suicide attempts in 1,556 patients with bipolar disorders followed for up to 2 years. *Bipolar Disorders, 8*(5 Pt 2), 566–575.

McKenzie, K., Serfaty, M., & Crawford, M. (2003). Suicide in ethnic minority groups. *British Journal of Psychiatry, 183*, 100–101.

Medications associated with suicide risk. (2015). Micromedex Solutions. *Truven Health Analytics*. Retrieved March 5, 2015, from http://www.micromedexsolutions.com.

Meltzer, H. Y., Alphs, L., Green, A. I., Altamura, A. C., Anand, R., Bertoldi, A.,... International Suicide Prevention Trial Study Group. (2003). Clozapine treatment for suicidality in schizophrenia: International Suicide Prevention Trial (InterSePT). *Archives of General Psychiatry, 60*(1), 82–91.

Modestin, J., Dal Pian, D., & Agarwalla, P. (2005). Clozapine diminishes suicidal behavior: A retrospective evaluation of clinical records. *Journal of Clinical Psychiatry, 66*(4), 534–538.

National Institute for Clinical Excellence. (2004). *Self-harm: The short-term physical and psychological management and secondary prevention of self-harm in primary and secondary care: Quick reference guide*. London, UK: National Institute for Clinical Excellence.

Nepon, J., Belik, S. L., Bolton, J., & Sareen, J. (2010). The relationship between anxiety disorders and suicide attempts: Findings from the National Epidemiologic Survey on Alcohol and Related Conditions. *Depression and Anxiety, 27*(9), 791–798.

Nielsen, J., Kane, J. M., & Correll, C. U. (2012). Real-world effectiveness of clozapine in patients with bipolar disorder: Results from a 2-year mirror-image study. *Bipolar Disorders, 14*(8), 863–869.

Office for National Statistics. (2014). *Suicides in the United Kingdom, 2012 registrations*. London, UK: National Records of Scotland/Northern Ireland Statistics and Research Agency/Office for National Statistics.

Oquendo, M. A., Chaudhury, S. R., & Mann, J. J. (2005). Pharmacotherapy of suicidal behavior in bipolar disorder. *Archives of Suicide Research, 9*(3), 237–250.

Oquendo, M. A., Currier, D., & Mann, J. J. (2006). Prospective studies of suicidal behavior in major depressive and bipolar disorders: What is the evidence for predictive risk factors? *Acta Psychiatrica Scandinavica, 114*(3), 151–158.

Palmer, B. A., Pankratz, V. S., & Bostwick, J. M. (2005). The lifetime risk of suicide in schizophrenia: A reexamination. *Archives of General Psychiatry, 62*(3), 247–253.

Patorno, E., Bohn, R. L., Wahl, P. M., Avorn, J., Patrick, A. R., Liu, J., & Schneeweiss, S. (2010). Anticonvulsant medications and the risk of suicide, attempted suicide, or violent death. *Journal of the American Medical Association, 303*(14), 1401–1409.

Price, R. B., Iosifescu, D. V., Murrough, J. W., Chang, L. C., Al Jurdi, R. K., Iqbal, S. Z.,... Mathew, S. J. (2014). Effects of ketamine on explicit and implicit suicidal cognition: A randomized controlled trial in treatment-resistant depression. *Depression and Anxiety, 31*(4), 335–343.

Redden, L., Pritchett, Y., Robieson, W., Kovacs, X., Garofalo, M., Tracy, K., & Saltarelli, M. (2011). Suicidality and divalproex sodium: Analysis of controlled studies in multiple indications. *Annals of General Psychiatry, 10*(1), 1.

Sareen, J., Houlahan, T., Cox, B. J., & Asmundson, G. J. (2005). Anxiety disorders associated with suicidal ideation and suicide attempts in the National Comorbidity Survey. *Journal of Nervous and Mental Disease, 193*(7), 450–454.

Schaffer, A., Isometsä, E. T., Tondo, L., Moreno, D. H., Turecki, G., Reis, C.,... Yatham, L. N. (2014). International Society for Bipolar Disorders Task Force on Suicide: Meta-analyses and meta-regression of correlates of suicide attempts and suicide deaths in bipolar disorder. *Bipolar Disorders, 17*(1), 1–16.

Schneeweiss, S., Patrick, A. R., Solomon, D. H., Mehta, J., Dormuth, C., Miller, M.,... Wang, P. S. (2010). Variation in the risk of suicide attempts and completed suicides by antidepressant agent in adults: A propensity score-adjusted analysis of 9 years' data. *Archives of General Psychiatry, 67*(5), 497–506.

Stone, M., Laughren, T., Jones, M. L., Levenson, M., Holland, P. C., Hughes, A.,... Rochester, G. (2009). Risk of suicidality in clinical trials of antidepressants in adults: Analysis of proprietary data submitted to US Food and Drug Administration. *British Medical Journal, 339*, b2880.

Tiihonen, J., Lönnqvist, J., Wahlbeck, K., Klaukka, T., Niskanen, L., Tanskanen, A., & Haukka, J. (2009). 11-year follow-up of mortality in patients with schizophrenia: A population-based cohort study (FIN11 study). *Lancet, 374*(9690), 620–627.

Tiihonen, J., Lönnqvist, J., Wahlbeck, K., Klaukka, T., Tanskanen, A., & Haukka, J. (2006). Antidepressants and the risk of suicide, attempted suicide, and overall mortality in a nationwide cohort. *Archives of General Psychiatry, 63*(12), 1358–1367.

Tondo, L., Hennen, J., & Baldessarini, R. J. (2001). Lower suicide risk with long-term lithium treatment in major affective illness: A meta-analysis. *Acta Psychiatrica Scandinavica, 104*(3), 163–172.

Valenstein, M., Kim, H. M., Ganoczy, D., McCarthy, J. F., Zivin, K., Austin, K. L.,... Olfson, M. (2009). Higher-risk periods for suicide among VA patients receiving depression treatment: Prioritizing suicide prevention efforts. *Journal of Affective Disorders, 112*(1–3), 50–58.

VanCott, A. C., Cramer, J. A., Copeland, L. A., Zeber, J. E., Steinman, M. A., Dersh, J. J.,... Pugh, M. J. (2010). Suicide-related behaviors in older patients with new antiepileptic drug use: Data from the VA hospital system. *BMC Medicine, 8*, 4.

Värnik, P. (2012). Suicide in the world. *International Journal of Environmental Research and Public Health, 9*(3), 760–771.

WHO report on violence and health. (2002). *Public Health Report, 117*(5), 479–480.

Yerevanian, B. I., & Choi, Y. M. (2013). Impact of psychotropic drugs on suicide and suicidal behaviors. *Bipolar Disorders, 15*(5), 594–621.

Yerevanian, B. I., Koek, R. J., & Mintz, J. (2007a). Bipolar pharmacotherapy and suicidal behavior. Part 1: Lithium, divalproex, and carbamazepine. *Journal of Affective Disorders, 103*(1–3), 5–11.

Yerevanian, B. I., Koek, R. J., & Mintz, J. (2007b). Bipolar pharmacotherapy and suicidal behavior. Part 3: Impact of antipsychotics. *Journal of Affective Disorders, 103*(1–3), 23–28.

Yerevanian, B. I., Koek, R. J., Mintz, J., & Akiskal, H. S. (2007). Bipolar pharmacotherapy and suicidal behavior. Part 2: The impact of antidepressants. *Journal of Affective Disorders, 103*(1–3), 13–21.

Interventions for the Reduction of Violence by Persons with Serious Mental Illnesses

Kevin S. Douglas, Tonia L. Nicholls, *and* Johann Brink

Abstract

Violence perpetrated by persons with serious mental illness (SMI), although certainly not the norm among this group, is of clinical and legal import in numerous settings. Among these are civil commitment, forensic psychiatry (insanity acquittees), and the criminal justice system. In this chapter, we provide a critical review of interventions and their empirical support that are used to reduce violence among persons with SMI. Promising findings support the use of cognitive behavioral, social learning, and cognitive skills approaches that are consistent with the Risk-Need-Responsivity (RNR) approach to crime and violence prevention. Anger management remains a promising, focused intervention with reasonable support in the literature. Dialectical behavioral therapy (DBT) has substantial general support. Community-based mandatory service programs such as outpatient commitment and mental health courts appear effective. Finally, the evidence base for the violence-reducing effect of certain psychotropic medication, particularly clozapine, is promising yet inconsistent.

Key Words: SMI, RNR, DBT, Dialectical Behavioral Therapy, serious mental illness, Risk-Need-Responsivity, violence, service, anger management

Although the association between serious mental illness (SMI) and violence remains controversial and incompletely understood, the bulk of contemporary scholarship would support that a link does exist, even though most persons with mental illness are not violent (Guy & Douglas, 2014). The link is not simple; it probably is driven by specific, active features of mental illness (i.e., positive symptoms of psychosis; manic states) as well as by associated features of mental illness (i.e., lack of interpersonal support; substance use). In addition, research is clear that risk factors that have been identified among people without mental illness (i.e., antisocial peers; antisocial attitudes; psychopathy) are also risk factors for people with mental illness (Bonta, Blais, & Wilson, 2014; Guy & Douglas, 2014). As such, as we wrote some years ago, treatments that focus solely on mental illness typically will not be optimally effective in terms of reducing risk for violence among persons with mental illness (Douglas, Nicholls, & Brink, 2009).

The use of treatment and other intervention efforts to reduce violence among persons with mental illness is relevant in numerous legal and clinical contexts. For instance, in most jurisdictions, persons with SMI can be civilly committed if they pose a risk of violence to others (or themselves). Planning for discharge from hospitalization includes anticipating risk for violence in the community, and how to reduce that risk (Douglas, Hart, Groscup, & Litwack, 2014). Similarly, persons with SMI who have been found not criminally responsible of committing crimes will usually be held within forensic institutions until their risk for violence is diminished to levels that are deemed not to pose undue risks to society if they were to be discharged. Offenders who have been found guilty of offences, despite having an SMI, similarly must be deemed not to pose an undue risk in order to receive parole into the community (in those jurisdictions that have parole). And, of course, risk of violence within these institutions must also be managed.

Therefore, treatment to reduce violence among persons with SMI is of high legal and clinical relevance in numerous settings. The stakes are high. Despite this, there remains a paucity of research directly on point. There are many (hundreds if not thousands) studies of crime-reduction programs and treatment programs to reduce general recidivism among non–mentally disordered offenders (Andrews, 2012). There are many fewer that focus on persons (offenders or otherwise) with SMI, and fewer still among those that focus on violence (as opposed to general criminality) as the outcome of interest.

In this chapter, we will review the evidence for treatment and other intervention programs for the reduction of violence among persons with SMI. We will need to address the broader literature as well, given the smaller number of studies of people with SMI. However, we will focus our investigation on whether this general literature can be generalized to people with SMI. We will also review psychopharmacological interventions, which of course apply specifically to people with SMI.

Cognitive and Behavioral Approaches

The majority of treatment programs to reduce violence find their roots in a cognitive behavioral approach. As such, they include both behavioral (e.g., reinforcement contingencies; token economies; shaping; modeling) and cognitive techniques (i.e., problem-solving skills; social skills acquisition). Most crime and violence reduction studies have been conducted within offender and juvenile justice samples, with general criminal recidivism as the outcome of interest. We will briefly describe this body of work, and then evaluate the extent to which it can be generalized to violence reduction among persons with SMI. To do so, we will first discuss the concept of RNR (Andrews, 2012; Andrews & Bonta, 2003). There is firm evidence, detailed in meta-analyses, that interventions that subscribe to the RNR model are more likely to reduce crime and violence than those that do not (Andrews, 2012).

Risk-Need-Responsivity

Developed in an offender crime-reduction paradigm, the principles of *risk, need,* and *responsivity* are meant to guide the construction and implementation of recidivism-reduction programs. As Andrews (2012) discussed, the risk principle indicates that higher risk people should receive more intensive intervention than moderate or low-risk people. The need principle specifies that the targets of intervention should be empirically supported

dynamic (changeable) risk factors, often called *criminogenic needs*. Focusing on factors that neither change nor are linked to crime and violence will fail. The responsivity principle holds that intervention should be delivered in a manner that is responsive to the learning styles and capacities of those receiving it. Usually, structured, concrete approaches (e.g., cognitive behavioral therapy [CBT]; psychosocial interventions) will be more successful than, say, insight-oriented psychodynamic approaches, which tend to be more amorphous and less strongly linked to empirically supported risk factors.

Treatments that are consistent with the RNR approach systematically outperform other treatments in terms of recidivism reduction. In a summary of meta-analyses, Andrews (2012) reported that when programs were aligned with each principle, recidivism reduction often came close to 50%, which is a very strong effect. RNR-consistent interventions tend to be based on CBT principles, in order to be consistent with the responsivity principle. For instance, programs tend to adopt cognitive skills training (identifying and challenging cognitions that support or condone crime), problem solving (learning and practicing prosocial ways to deal with conflict and other challenges), anger management (identifying anger cues and developing strategies to cope with anger), behavior modification (application of reinforcement contingencies that reward prosocial behavior), and other behavioral techniques (modeling; shaping; role rehearsal). Decades ago, these principles were collectively referred to as the "principles of effective correctional treatment" (Gendreau & Goggin, 1996). The primary questions, however, are to what extent is there support for these approaches for the reduction of violence (as opposed to general crime) specifically, and to what extent for the reduction of violence among those with SMI?

Do the Principles of Effective Correctional Treatment Apply to Violence?

As mentioned above, most RNR research focuses on general offending. An early meta-analysis showed that such principles were applicable to violence as an outcome as well (Dowden & Andrews, 2000). Across 35 samples, a small effect size of $r = .07$ was observed. More nuanced analyses, however, showed a larger effect size of .20 when each of the RNR principles was observed (equivalent to a 20% reduction in violent recidivism). Andrews (2012) described an updated meta-analytic summary based on 42 studies, and reported, again, that the effect size for treatment programs that were in adherence with all three RNR principles was .20, compared to .15 (two principles), .07 (one principle) and –.01 (no principles).

Do the Principles of Effective Correctional Treatment Apply Among People with SMI?

There have now been many attempts to answer this question. Braham, Jones, and Hollins (2008) conducted a small pilot study of 13 patients within a high-security (forensic) hospital in the United Kingdom. The program comprised 280 hours of group treatment plus individualized weekly treatment to address specific risk factors. The CBT-based program content drew from relapse prevention, cognitive skills, emotion regulation, and social problem solving. Early phases focused on facilitation of the awareness of problems and taking responsibility for change, as well as buy-in to the program. Later phases shifted to skill acquisition. Outcomes were indirect, but promising. First, 10 of 13 patients completed the program, which is a reasonable completion rate. Second, reductions were observed post-treatment on measures of violence risk, procriminal ideation, anger, and impulsivity. Long-term effects on violence recidivism were not addressed in this study, and there was no control group, both of which are limitations to the research.

Yates et al. (2005) evaluated a CBT/cognitive skills program for patients in state psychiatric facilities. It included a behavioral reward system, psychiatric management, and substance use treatment. After discharge, patients were followed in the community with case management and standard psychiatric aftercare. Program modules included problem solving, creative thinking, social skills, critical reasoning, and management of emotions. Only half the patients completed the program and were then discharged. Kunz et al. (2004) followed 85 of the discharged patients. Of these, 33 (39%) remained in the community (up to four years) without further hospitalizations or arrests. Thirty-five (42%) patients were rehospitalized, and 17 (20%) were arrested, although only five of these arrests were for violent offences.

In a subsequent follow-up study of this program, Yates, Kunz, Khan, Volavka, and Rabinowitz (2010) followed 145 male and female patient program-completers for up to five years. Of these patients, 21% remained stable in the community, 46% were rehospitalized, and 32% were rearrested and/or rehospitalized. Few (14%) of the arrests included violence. There were fewer arrests and hospitalizations compared to the pre-program phase. The strongest predictor of remaining stable was medication compliance, a topic we address in some detail later in the chapter.

Ashford, Wong, and Sternbach (2008) evaluated whether a "generic" correctional program could reduce general and violent recidivism among offenders with SMI released from California prisons. They compared 24 offenders who were enrolled in a cognitive intervention that addressed procriminal attitudes and hostile attributions (offenders were also engaged in other services, such as Forensic Assertive Community Treatment, mental health court intervention, psychiatric treatment, and housing services) to a group of offenders with SMI who received treatment as usual within prison. Those who completed the program committed fewer general and violent offences in the 12 months post-release compared to the treatment-as-usual group. They also showed improvements in criminal attitudes and attributional biases in pre-post tests. These results are promising in terms of offenders with SMI being able to benefit from programs designed for offenders without SMI, although the non-random assignment must temper confidence in results.

Haddock et al. (2009) used a single-blind randomized clinical trial to test CBT for psychosis and anger against social activity therapy in terms of its potential to reduce violence. Both groups also received treatment as usual. Participants ($n = 77$) were receiving inpatient or outpatient services and had a history of violence. Findings were promising during the treatment stage, as those in the CBT group were less likely to be violent. However, during a 12-month follow-up, there was no difference between groups. These findings suggest that CBT for psychosis specifically may also require a post-treatment maintenance phase.

Another CBT-based approach called *aggression control therapy* (ACT) was described by Hornsveld, Nijman, Hollin, and Kraaimaat (2008). Modeled after aggression-replacement therapy derived in correctional settings, its components include anger management training, social skills training, self-regulation skills, and moral reasoning. Hornsveld et al. (2008) summarized its use in the Dutch forensic psychiatric system as leading to reductions of aggression, but more so for less psychopathic patients. Importantly, in the Dutch forensic system, many patients have primary diagnoses of personality disorder and not SMI; hence, the extension of this approach to SMI populations is in need of clarification.

In another CBT-based residential program (case management; anger management; cognitive skills; life skills; stress management; symptom recognition; relapse prevention) with 448 offenders with SMI, Lovell et al. (2001) used a pre-post design with a subgroup of 140 offenders with at least 18 months pre- and post-program. Staff assaults significantly decreased in the post-program period. As with much research in this area, the study lacked a control group.

Another group of studies is grounded more solidly within a *social learning approach*. This approach posits that behavioral principles (reinforcement and modeling) will decrease violence. In an early example, Donnelly and Scott (1999) evaluated a social learning program originally used with offenders, called the *Reasoning and Rehabilitation* (R&R) cognitive skills model (Ross & Fabiano, 1985), within a sample of psychiatric patients with histories of crime or violence. The program addressed self-control, thinking style, emotion management, critical reasoning, and cognitive skills. There were 54 group sessions across five months. A pilot test enrolled 24 patients (12 in the intervention group, 12 in a comparison group), all with past violence, and most with diagnoses of schizophrenia. The program led to relatively greater improvements in problem-solving abilities and the social adjustment in the treatment group (violence was not measured).

In the first randomized controlled trial of a cognitive skills program for the reduction of post-release violence among mentally disordered offenders in forensic hospitals, Cullen et al. (2012) investigated the R&R program (using 36 group sessions rather than 54) among 84 male patients randomly selected from six medium secure forensic facilities in the United Kingdom. They followed the patients for 12 months post-discharge. Notably, roughly half the participants did not complete the program. This is an important finding in and of itself. Regardless, those in the experimental group showed lower verbal aggression and leave-violations during treatment, and the effect on verbal aggression was maintained at 12 months. The effect on physical violence was not significant at follow-up. However, among those who completed the program, both physical and verbal aggression were lower after controlling for psychopathy. Within this rigorous methodology, findings promisingly suggest that cognitive skills training can reduce antisocial outcomes and appear particularly important for those who actually complete the program. This latter finding suggests that sufficient effort must go into program retention.

In this same sample, Cullen, Soria, Clarke, Dean, and Fahy (2011) investigated predictors of dropout. Not surprisingly, they found that antisocial personality disorder, psychopathy, and recent violence predicted dropout. The implications of such findings are that it is necessary to find strategies to engage higher risk, psychopathic patients.

Given concerns about potential attrition with youth and mentally disordered offenders, the R&R program was modified for these groups (Young & Ross, 2007). The number of sessions was reduced from 36 to 16, but supplemented with individual sessions and the use of a mentor. Evaluating this program in a non-RCT study of UK mentally disordered offenders (Young, Chick, & Gudjonsson, 2010), the attrition rate was somewhat better, at 35%. However, of the patients initially invited to participate, 22% refused. Therefore, it should be expected that some meaningful proportion of patients will also refuse to start treatment, and an additional meaningful proportion (35–50%) will not complete what they started. In Young et al. (2010), those completing the program showed reductions in nurse-rated disruptive behavior, and improved attitudes.

Another evaluation of the revised model from the United Kingdom included 59 male patients with SMI who were in a high-security setting (Yip et al., 2013), 30 of whom were assigned to the treatment group, and 29, to the treatment-as-usual group. Promisingly, 24 of 30 (80%) participants completed the program (defined as completing at least 12 of 16 sessions). At post-treatment evaluation, the treatment group showed improvements on a variety of psychological indices, including violent attitudes and problem solving, and less disruptive behavior than the comparison group. In another UK study of the modified R&R program among 121 male forensic patients drawn from six medium and four low secure settings, Rees-Jones, Gudjonsson, and Young (2012) observed a similar 78% completion rate. As with Yip et al. (2013), those completing the treatment, compared to those in treatment as usual, showed significant improvement in violent attitudes, problem solving, and anger cognition. Unfortunately, disruptive behavior was not reduced. At a three-month follow-up, the reduction in violent attitudes persisted.

In these studies on R&R, recruitment occurred within hospitals. What happens when recruitment occurs within the community? That is, once patients have already been discharged, will they volunteer to engage in this program? In a surprisingly disappointing study, it appears that the answer is a solid "no" (Hodgins, Carlin, Moorhouse, Legge, & Khalid, 2011). Although all patients completed a lengthy introductory research interview, and one-third to one-half completed follow-up interviews in the community (all of which were financially compensated); 25 of 28 participants did not complete a single session in the program. Reasons provided to the researchers included being too busy, being afraid, and not having permission to leave the ward (for those currently living in the hospital). These findings suggest some sort of leverage might be required to enhance community participation rates (i.e., that their living in the community is contingent upon their agreeing to attend treatment). We will return to this concept of mandated community treatment later in the chapter.

Perhaps the most rigorous and comprehensive evaluation of a social learning program was one of the original studies on point—conducted by Paul and Lentz (1977). The authors randomly assigned chronic psychiatric inpatients to a social learning program (versus milieu therapy or traditional care) that included a token economy, skills training, and behavioral methods (shaping, modeling). There was a repeated-measures element as well, with measurements taking place every six months for four and a half years in the hospital and one and a half in the community, for a total of 6 years and 12 measurements. The 24 patients per group were replaced as necessary in cases of attrition. In addition to using principles of reinforcement, the authors also used seclusion (up to 48 hours) to punish (in strictly behavioral terms—the application of a noxious or unwanted stimulus in response to a behavior) patients for assaultive behavior.

Generally, assaultive behavior was reduced (and prosocial behavior enhanced) in both treatment conditions, but more so in the social learning group, compared to treatment as usual. The social learning group demonstrated a drastic reduction in assaults—from roughly 30 per week at baseline to 10 per week after two years. Interestingly, because of a state-mandated reduction in seclusion times to two hours, the authors were presented with an opportunity to evaluate the dosage of "punishment." Assaults increased substantially within two years of the reduction—from 10 to 75 per week in the social learning group. In the milieu group they were even higher, at more than 300 per week. The hospital lobbied the state to increase seclusion times, and were allowed to increase them somewhat (to 5:30 a.m. the following day). Assaults again decreased

in the final six months of the study. The merits of seclusion can be left to other outlets; however, these findings simply underscore that, along with reinforcing wanted (prosocial) behaviors, the application of consequences for unwanted (violent) behaviors (technically termed "punishment" in behavioral parlance) appears to be an important part of a comprehensive social approach.

No study to date has truly replicated Paul and Lentz's (1977) work. However, a smaller scale study using an AB design reported consistent findings (Beck, Menditto, Baldwin, Angelone, and Maddox, 1991). Other studies of skills-based programs (cognitive, social, or life) have tended to suffer from weak designs (i.e., no comparison group; no control of covariates; small number of participants) or outcome measures not directly relevant to violence (i.e., ratings of hostility; reduction of anxiety) (Derks, 1996; Fleck, Thompson, & Narroway, 2001; Hodel & West, 2003; Hornsveld, 2005; Liberman, Mueser, & Wallace, 1986; McMurran, Egan, Richardson, & Ahmadi, 1999; Timmerman & Emmelkamp, 2005). Many of these studies have reported positive findings, although others have not. Given their limitations and indirect relevance to violence, we will not consider them further.

Anger Management
What Is Anger and Is It Relevant to the Treatment of Individuals with Serious Mental Illness?

Anger has been defined by Novaco (2010) as "an eruptive and turbulent emotion" (p. 465). However, anger is considered a common human experience that can be either adaptive or maladaptive (Nicoll, Beail, & Saxon, 2013; Saini, 2009). Although anger may share certain properties with aggression, it is important to acknowledge that the two constructs are distinct. Experts (e.g., Novaco, 1994; Spielberger, Reheiser, & Sydeman, 1995, cited in Nicoll et al., 2013) recommend conceptualizing anger as a subjective emotional state that is a reflection of hostile cognitions and physiological arousal, which can be considered a causal determinant of aggression, the resulting behavior. Anger is "neither necessary nor sufficient for violence; individuals can be angry and not behave violently, or can be violent without being angry" (Joyce, Dillane, & Vasquez, 2013, p. 248; also see Howells, 2004; Novaco, 1994); however, empirical research demonstrates links between anger and aggressive behaviors (e.g., Novaco, 1998). Furthermore, mood, anxiety, and substance use disorders have been associated with anger severity (e.g., Barrett, Mills, & Teesson, 2013). Therefore, anger is an important consideration in the treatment of seriously mentally ill individuals at risk of violence.

Anger can activate violent behavior among psychiatric patients, before, during, and after hospitalization, and occurs concurrently with a diverse array of psychiatric illnesses (e.g., impulse-control dysfunctions, mood disorders, many personality disorders, and schizophrenia) (Novaco, 2010). Anger is also well recognized as a common clinical feature found among individuals presenting with brain damage, dissociative disorders, trauma, and particularly among patients with posttraumatic stress disorder (Novaco, 2010). Anger is also found among persons with mental state disturbances produced by general medical conditions, such as dementia, substance abuse disorders, and neurological dysfunctions resulting from perinatal difficulties (Novaco, 2010). Novaco (2010) concluded that there is an expansive research base on anger in psychopathology. As such, anger is an important variable to consider as an indicator of risk for violence and a treatment target when caring for individuals living with serious mental illnesses. As recently as 2011, however, Novaco asserted that anger has not been given sufficient priority in forensic mental health (also see Saini, 2009).

HOW IS ANGER RELEVANT TO RISK OF VIOLENCE AMONG MENTALLY ILL INDIVIDUALS?

Most individuals living with severe mental illness are never violent; however, experts generally agree that there is a modest but significant association between mental illness, particularly schizophrenia and other psychotic disorders, and violence (Douglas, Guy, & Hart, 2009; Fazel, Gulati, Linsell, Geddes, & Grann, 2009). The relevance of anger to the association between mental illness and violence remains a neglected aspect of research, despite an acknowledgment that anger is considered an important risk factor for violence among individuals with mental illness, given its prevalence among individuals with a wide variety of psychiatric disorders (Novaco, 2000), and the evidence that it is a malleable or dynamic risk factor (Beck & Fernandez, 1998; Hanson & Harris, 2000). For instance, meta-analytic reviews demonstrate that anger declines in response to treatment (Beck & Fernandez, 1998; Edmondson & Conger, 1996). Anger can thus be considered a transdiagnostic (Novaco, 2010; Novaco & Whittington, 2013) dynamic risk factor

(Hanson & Harris, 2000; Howells, Watt, Hall & Baldwin, 1997). Anger has consistently been demonstrated to be associated with violence in both the general population and psychiatric populations (Reagu et al., 2013). Delusions and hallucinations are major conduits for anger activation among individuals with serious mental illness (Novaco & Whittington, 2013). That being said, authorities (e.g., Jones & Hollin, 2004; Joyce et al., 2013) assert that the link between anger and violence remains insufficiently understood.

Unfortunately, most studies that have evaluated the utility of anger-management treatment have not included individuals with serious mental illness; in particular, patients with psychosis and persons with histories of violent behavior. To demonstrate, a recent systematic review and meta-analysis by Reagu, Jones, Kumari, and Taylor (2013) examined the relationship between anger and violence in the context of psychotic illness. Just five studies were included in the meta-analysis, which examined adults with schizophrenia (and associated psychosis) and employed systematic measures of anger and violence to examine whether people with psychosis who exhibit violence show excessive anger and/or poor anger regulation. In total, 11 studies fit the criteria, but data could only be extracted from five ($n = 510$), and the findings from the other six studies ($n = 610$) were provided in a narrative synthesis.

All of the studies revealed significantly higher anger scores for the individuals who had committed a violent act, compared to those who had not. The findings further demonstrated a consistent relationship between anger and violence in psychotic individuals; however, several limitations were acknowledged (Reagu et al., 2013). The authors noted that there has been little consistency in measures used to assess both anger and violence. In addition, the temporal relationship between anger and violence varied between the studies. Importantly, the studies included both self-directed and other-directed violence. Reagu and colleagues (2013) concluded that both groups of studies lend considerable support to the relevance of anger to violence in the context of psychotic illness, and the fact that the findings were consistent across diverse methods, settings, and populations is evidence that the findings are robust. In closing, the authors suggested that there are several pathways that may lead from anger to aggression (e.g., see Anderson & Bushman, 2002), although causality has not been established (Reagu et al., 2013).

Despite limitations in the extant literature, given considerable evidence that anger is associated with various forms of aggression and offending (e.g., impulsive and premeditated violence alike), anger-management programs have been implemented widely (Chemtob, Novaco, Hamada, & Gross, 1997) among adults with diverse characteristics. For instance, research suggests that the treatment of anger is relevant to patients with PTSD (Chemtob et al., 1997), individuals with intellectual disabilities (Nicoll, Beail, & Saxon, 2013; Travis & Sturmey, 2013), people with psychosis (Reagu et al., 2013), and diverse offender (Hollenhorst, 1998) and mental health populations (Bradbury & Clarke, 2007; Wilson, Barton, & Maguire, 2011).

WHAT IS ANGER MANAGEMENT?

Anger management theory posits that cognitive restructuring can modify irrational or skewed thoughts and perceptions that can lead to anger and/or violence. Novaco (1975) adapted Meichenbaum's Stress Inoculation Training for Anxiety to apply it to anger. Stress inoculation enhances coping skills and is based on three primary elements: cognitive preparation, skill acquisition, and application training (Beck & Fernandez, 1998). These are used to challenge attitudes, perceptions, and self-statements that can lead to violence. A varying range of techniques, including relaxation and skills training, are taught in order to manage and improve one's regulation of anger through exposure to provoking circumstances (Wright, Day, & Howells, 2009). The enhancement of cognitive skills in relation to thoughts of anger and aggression has proven to be a meaningful skill for self-regulation of anger and distress tolerance (Wright et al., 2009).

HOW EFFECTIVE IS ANGER MANAGEMENT GENERALLY?

In one of the first meta-analyses of anger management treatment available, Beck and Fernandez's (1998) inclusion criteria resulted in an examination of 50 studies. Based on a total combined sample size of 1,640 patients, including adults and children (inmates, college students, abusive parents, adolescent delinquents in residential facilities, children with aggressive behavior in the classroom), Beck and Fernandez concluded that the average recipient of the treatment was better off than 76% of the untreated patients. Given the heterogeneity of the samples examined and statistically significant findings across studies, the authors concluded

their meta-analysis provided robust support for the efficacy of CBT for reducing anger (Beck & Fernandez, 1998). Novaco and Whittington (2013) recently concluded that there are now nine meta-analyses examining cognitive behavioral anger treatment that have generally demonstrated medium to large effect sizes (Beck & Fernandez, 1998; Del Vecchio & O'Leary, 2004; DiGiuseppe & Tafrate, 2003; Edmondson & Conger, 1996; Gansle, 2005; Ho, Carter, & Stephenson, 2010; Saini, 2009; Sukhodolsky, Kassinove, & Gorman, 2004; Tafrate, 1995).

Saini (2009) examined nine different forms of treatment (e.g., cognitive, CBT, psychodynamic, psychoeducational, relaxation-based, skills-based) from 96 studies (139 effect sizes) and concluded there is strong evidence that psychological interventions are moderately effective for reducing anger problems. The dependent variables considered included general anger, anger expressions, and anger control, among others. Saini reported an overall effect size (Cohen's *d*) across all categories of outcomes of 0.76, demonstrating that the treatment participants had substantially lower anger scores after participating in the various anger-treatment modalities than the comparison groups. However, there was considerable heterogeneity across interventions, and moderators need to be considered (e.g., sample/setting, sample size, published/unpublished, number of treatment sessions). Overall, the author concluded that the findings were consistent with prior meta-analytic reviews and asserted that there is strong evidence that psychological treatment for anger-related problems is moderately effective with diverse populations and dependent variables (Saini, 2009).

With regard to implications, Saini (2009) proposed that psychological interventions should follow a consideration of the extent to which pharmacological interventions are called for, and should be integrated with the psychological treatment. The author further recommended a minimum of eight treatment sessions, adherence to manuals, and fidelity checks, as well as verifying the extent to which the client is satisfied with the approach (for a related discussion on cost-effective strategies, also see Beck & Fernandez, 1998). Limitations of the meta-analysis include the fact that the majority of the studies were from the United States, and one-third sampled undergraduate students (Saini, 2009). The study also had many strengths, in particular a large number of studies (4,000 screened down to 96) using a comprehensive screening, and the inclusion of unpublished studies. For our present purposes, however, it is particularly important to note that the criteria for inclusion in the Saini meta-analysis did not include a discernible psychiatric disorder; thus, the relevance to mentally ill individuals must be considered cautiously.

HOW EFFECTIVE IS ANGER MANAGEMENT TREATMENT FOR THE PREVENTION OF VIOLENCE AMONG SERIOUSLY MENTALLY ILL PERSONS?

Few studies have investigated the effectiveness of anger management directly for the reduction of violence among persons with SMI, and although meta-analytic reviews (e.g., Beck & Fernandez, 1998; DiGiuseppe & Tafrate, 2003) suggest that cognitive-behavioral approaches are effective for anger reduction, their relevance to psychiatric populations and violence remains in a black box. It cannot be assumed that the findings from undergraduate, general population, and offender samples, can be generalized to clinical samples or vice versa (e.g., Reagu et al., 2013), nor that reducing anger will be an effective means of reducing violence.

A growing number of studies has examined the efficacy of anger treatment with forensic and correctional samples. An early study compared 20 forensic psychiatric patients (as a control group) to 20 patients in anger-control treatment (Stermac, 1986). Although the treatment group evidenced lower levels of anger and better coping strategies compared to the control group, violence *per se* was not measured. Becker, Love, and Hunter (1997) conducted four *n* = 1 analyses of persistently violent patients. Use of anger management treatment substantially reduced their subsequent violence.

Another small study assigned nine forensic inpatients with intellectual disabilities to a CBT-based anger management treatment group, and 10 patients to a wait-list control (who later received the treatment) (Taylor, Novaco, Gillmer, & Thorne, 2002). Although patients receiving the experimental treatment had lower self-reported anger reaction scores post-treatment than the wait-list control did pre-treatment, staff ratings of anger largely did not vary across groups. Verbal and physical acts of aggression were rare in the post-treatment period for both groups; hence, meaningful comparisons could not be made. Finally, Renwick, Black, Ramm, and Novaco (2011) found that the application of anger control treatment procedures to severely disordered

psychiatric patients resulted in modest but significant treatment gains.

In their 2004 study reviewing the development and implementation of anger management programs specifically designed for mentally disordered offenders in a high-security setting, Jones and Hollin reported positive preliminary results through the implementation of a CBT-based treatment program. Their study included the assessment of eight male patients who exhibited aggressive behavior within the hospital and had significant anger problems. They subsequently participated in the 36-week treatment program. Patients were assessed in relation to the frequency and intensity of anger incidents and on a number of psychological variables. Repeated assessments showed positive changes on these measures, both during the program and at follow-up. It was found that enhancing intrinsic motivation through dialogue and group-based activities could be positively associated with longer lasting change in patients. Moreover, there was a significant reduction in both the frequency and the intensity of anger incidents during treatment, which was maintained at a four-week follow-up, and the successful insurance of a low dropout rate could be contributed to the integration of a program with components of typical anger treatment, alongside a motivational approach. In all cases, which are described in helpful detail, violence was substantially decreased.

Another recent meta-analysis examining CBT in adults with intellectual disabilities with encouraging findings also was published recently (Nicoll et al., 2013). Of the 20 studies originally identified, after the removal of duplicated studies, 12 eligible studies (10 from the UK and two from Australia) were considered in the quality appraisal, and nine were evaluated in the meta-analysis. Nicoll et al. (2013) conducted an appraisal of methodological rigor and concluded that, out of a possible score of 32, the mean quality score across all 12 studies was 23.75 (standard deviation [SD] = 5.39). The studies included in the meta-analysis had a higher overall quality rating (85%) compared to the complete sample (75%). The average effect size across these studies (k = 9) was 0.88. As the authors noted, the number of publications available on this unique subpopulation remained small (n = 20), and there was considerable overlap, requiring the review and meta-analysis to be limited to 12 and nine studies, respectively. However, Nicoll and colleagues concluded this emerging literature base is increasingly employing reliable and valid measures of anger and there is a "good level of methodological rigour"

(p. 60). That being said, Nicoll et al. (2013) recommended that larger sample sizes and agreement on one type of control group would allow commentators to make stronger assertions about the effectiveness of anger treatment. Despite its limitations, the study revealed large effect sizes for CBT anger interventions with adults with intellectual disabilities.

CONCLUSION

The strength of this literature is in the growing body of meta-analyses yielding consistently positive findings. Limitations include predominantly U.S. samples and a concentration of work on college students. Additionally, anger is considered by some to be a multidimensional construct and thus various studies may be measuring different aspects of anger (Reagu et al., 2013). Furthermore, there is little evidence of consistency in the outcomes measured across studies. Few studies specifically evaluate *violence* (as opposed to a measure of anger) as the outcome of interest. Although the evidence base for anger management is promising, certainly more research is needed among persons with SMI. Further, anger management likely will not be effective for people whose violence is not related to anger (Watt & Howells, 1999).

Dialectical Behavior Therapy

Dialectical behavior therapy (DBT) originally was developed by Marsha Linehan to treat women with borderline personality disorder (BPD), and associated self-harming and suicidal behaviors, a challenging and difficult-to-treat population for whom no prior effective interventions had been available (Berzins & Trestman, 2004; Linehan, 2013; Wix, 2003). An adaptation of CBT, DBT is a comprehensive behavioral treatment predicated on Linehan's work addressing the etiology and maintenance of BPD and its associated behavioral patterns (Linehan, 1987, 1993). The treatment combines basic strategies of behavior therapy, validation, and acceptance-based interventions (Linehan, 2000); cognitive therapy techniques (Robins & Chapman, 2004); and Eastern mindfulness/Zen practices (Berzins & Trestman, 2004; Linehan, 1993). The core strategies integrate a balance and synthesis of validation (acceptance) and problem solving (change) (Robins & Chapman, 2004; Scheel, 2000) that reduce maladaptive behaviors by teaching participants self-management skills, including emotion regulation, interpersonal effectiveness, mindfulness, and distress tolerance (Linehan, 1993; Scheel, 2000). Standard DBT treatment is provided

in outpatient contexts and is characterized by four core components: weekly individual psychotherapy, weekly skills training, weekly therapist consultation (to prevent therapist burnout), and the availability of around-the-clock coaching by a skills group leader or therapist (Frazier & Vela, 2014).

General Empirical Evidence for the Efficacy of DBT

As recently as 2000, Linehan (2000; also see Scheel, 2000) herself noted that, although empirical evaluation of DBT thus far was promising, it was nonetheless quite limited. The validation literature on DBT has since grown substantially, and it now has been the subject of more than 40 randomized trials (Linehan, 2013). The therapy has been shown to be effective with diverse populations, including individuals with substance misuse and dependence, eating disorders, anxiety, and depression (Linehan, 2013; Sakdalan & Gupta, 2014).

RATIONALE FOR CONSIDERING DBT AS A TREATMENT FOR VIOLENCE

Although DBT originally was developed to treat BPD, it has also become widely recognized as a means to reduce violence risk (Berzins & Trestman, 2004; Frazier & Vela, 2014; McCann, Ball, & Ivanoff, 2000). For instance, in their examination of the relevance of DBT to correctional and forensic populations, Berzins and Trestman (2004) pointed to the high rates personality disorder in these settings and the high prevalence of comorbidity between Axis I and Axis II disorders (McCann et al., 2000). Proponents of expanding DBT to forensic settings also refer to the many similarities between individuals with BPD and persons at risk of harming others, including dysfunctional thinking patterns, poor affect-regulation, anger, hopelessness, hostility, deficits in interpersonal relationship stability, disrupted attachment, poor problem-solving capacities, and childhood upbringings that are invalidating and often marred by serious familial dysfunction, victimization, and trauma (Galietta & Rosenfeld, 2012; Sakdalan & Gupta, 2014; Shingler, 2004). DBT is a comprehensive form of CBT (Frazier & Vela, 2014) with highly structured behavioral components (Berzins & Trestman, 2004; McCann et al., 2000). The structured problem-reduction approach to emotional dysregulation (McCann et al., 2000) and evidence of empirical support with other challenging populations and problems (Lynch, Chapman, Rosenthal, Kuo, & Linehan, 2006), including evidence of application and efficacy in prison and forensic settings

(Frazier & Vela, 2014; Sakdalan & Gupta, 2014; Van den Bosch, Hysaj, & Jacobs, 2012), has resulted in widespread interest in the application of this effective intervention beyond persons with BPD. Specifically, DBT is considered a promising treatment for individuals involved with the criminal justice system (Berzins & Trestman, 2004; Shelton, Sampl, Kesten, Zhang, & Trestman, 2009) and persons at risk of both general physical aggression (Frazier & Vela, 2014) and sexual offending (Sakdalan & Gupta, 2014; Shingler, 2004). In recent years, DBT (often with modifications) has been tested with several populations at risk of committing violence, including intimate-partner violence offenders (Fruzzetti & Levensky, 2000), stalkers (Rosenfeld et al., 2007), forensic psychiatric inpatients (McCann et al., 2000), difficult-to-manage prison inmates (Shelton et al., 2009), and individuals with psychopathy (Galietta & Rosenfeld, 2012).

An early review by Berzins and Trestman (2004) revealed that DBT was being employed in approximately 12 forensic psychiatric settings and eight criminal justice settings across North America, the United Kingdom, and Australia; the authors concluded that the application of DBT to forensic samples was in its infancy. A decade later, considerably broader application of DBT to forensic populations exists, and much more evidence has been accumulated regarding the efficacy of the treatment to reduce anger and aggression. However, research remains rigidly focused on individuals with personality disorders (i.e., to the neglect of individuals with Axis I disorders), and outcomes tend to focus on anger, and to a lesser extent, aggression (i.e., with limited relevance to serious violence risk).

Frazier and Vela (2014) completed a systematic review of all 21 peer-reviewed articles published between 1998 and 2013 reporting on the extent to which DBT is an appropriate treatment for reducing anger, aggression, and violence. Importantly, although many studies sampled individuals with BPD, as well as other personality disorders, the review's intention was not to study traditional symptoms and behavioral problems associated with BPD, but rather to focus on outcomes associated with anger and aggression. In total, nine studies examined the capacity of DBT to resolve anger/aggression among individuals with a variety of diagnoses, and 12 studies focused on anger/aggression within samples of individuals with BPD. Eight of the nine studies examining diverse populations saw significantly reduced scores on measures of anger and aggression after a DBT intervention (Frazier &

Vela, 2014). Of the nine published articles, many of the studies involved modified programs or adaptations to DBT, and although a handful of the studies compared the intervention group with a control group (Koons et al., 2001; Lynch et al., 2007; McMain et al., 2009; Neacsiu, Rizvi, & Linehan, 2010), Frazier and Vela noted (2014) that the majority of the research to date has employed pre-post designs (Gutteling, Montagne, Nijs, & van den Bosch, 2012; Koons et al., 2006; Long, Fulton, Dolley, & Hollin, 2011; Nelson-Gray et al., 2006). The weight of the evidence in both the studies of individuals with BPD (10 of 12) and the studies employing more diverse samples (8 of 9) showed significant reductions on measures of anger/aggression (Frazier & Vela, 2014).

As Frazier and Vela's (2014) review demonstrated, several studies have concluded that DBT is effective for reducing violence among persons with disorders other than BPD, and notably, these reductions have often been demonstrated in reasonably high-risk populations (e.g., inmates with a history of violent offending). For instance, in a pre-post study of 44 patients (70% with personality disorder [PD]) in a medium-secure hospital, Long et al. (2011) reported reduced aggressive behaviors at a three-month follow-up to an adapted DBT program (individual therapy plus skills group). Weekly 90-minute group sessions covered topics ranging from distress tolerance to emotional vulnerability and regulation, along with individual sessions designed to address issues relating to skills practice. Upon completion of the intervention, assessors used the Overt Aggression Scale (Yudofsky, Silver, Jackson, Endicott, & Williams, 1986) to compare rates of physical aggression against self and others, and verbal aggression between completers (i.e., those who attended 12 or more intervention sessions) and non-completers (i.e., those who had attended fewer than 12 sessions). There was a significant reduction in risk behaviors following treatment for completers, with a significant reduction in physical assaults.

In another high-risk sample, Shelton and colleagues (2009) examined DBT with a mixed-ethnic sample of inmates in a correctional facility, many of whom had a history of violent crimes. This team reported on a 16-week (twice-weekly) DBT–Corrections modified program with impulsive and difficult-to-manage male ($n = 45$ adults and youths) and female ($n = 18$) inmates in Connecticut. When the DBT coaching group was compared to a treatment-as-usual (TAU) group (case management), the findings were quite mixed.

The authors reported trends toward improved affect, and decreased impulsivity, psychopathology, and aggression for both groups, but evidence of greater improvement in the DBT group, particularly for the males (Shelton et al., 2009). With regard to aggression, a significant reduction in the number of disciplinary tickets (a system-wide measure of behavior) from baseline ($M = .27$) to the 16-week follow up was found ($M = .14$).

Evershed et al. (2003) conducted a study of the efficacy of DBT in a small sample of patients diagnosed with personality disorders in a high-security hospital; none of the patients was experiencing symptoms of mental illness (DBT group = 8 males; TAU group = 9). Although the frequency of incidents remained comparable, patients who were treated with DBT showed a 53% reduction in the seriousness of violent behaviors compared to the control group (22% reduction). When compared to the control group, DBT patients were also found to be more effective at managing externalizing aggressive behaviors, and showed reduced cognitive, covert, and dispositional aspects of hostility and anger. It is also worth noting that a handful of studies have been completed with adolescents and have similarly reported that DBT skills training can result in improvements by reducing aggressive behaviors among incarcerated (Shelton, Kesten, Zhang, & Trestman, 2011; Trupin, Stewart, Beach, & Boesky, 2002) and outpatient adolescents (Nelson-Gray et al., 2006; Woodbury & Popenoe, 2008).

EMPIRICAL EVIDENCE FOR DBT
AS A TREATMENT FOR AGGRESSION
AND VIOLENCE IN PEOPLE WITH SMI

In contrast to the reasonably well-established body of work on DBT generally, there remains a paucity of studies that have evaluated the efficacy of DBT for treating seriously mentally ill individuals at risk of committing violence. In particular, there is an absence of research on persons with psychosis and other serious mental disorders, and there remains a need for studies that explicitly examine violence as opposed to anger or aggression. Van den Bosch et al. (2012) compared two groups treated with DBT: 29 forensic patients with BPD (10 males, 19 females) referred to a forensic outpatient clinic because of criminal behavior, and 58 female patients with DBT voluntarily participating in a DBT study. The authors concluded that a DBT program could be successfully implemented with forensic patients; however, the study was unable to speak to the extent to which DBT results in changes in criminal behavior.

Our review of the literature through to the end of 2014 indicates that, even using highly inclusive criteria, there are just four studies that have tested DBT as a treatment for reducing aggression/violence in samples of seriously mentally ill individuals. The first was a study of 35 outpatients over the age of 55 who met criteria for depression and at least one personality disorder (Lynch et al., 2007). Lynch and colleagues (2007) reported that following either 24 weeks of TAU (medication management alone) or 24 weeks of DBT plus medication management led to non-significant though superior reductions in depression in the DBT group (71% met remission in DBT vs. 50% in TAU), nine clients in the DBT arm and seven clients in the TAU no longer met criteria for personality disorders, and substantial decreases in interpersonal aggression were also found. The extent to which the findings from this sample are relevant to younger adults is questionable, and the dependent variables have limited application to many of the contexts that are relevant to violence prevention.

In another sample of individuals with Axis I disorders, Koons et al. (2006) examined adults in outpatient vocational rehabilitation that tested an adapted DBT program (weekly DBT for 6 months) in a small sample of adults with a mean of three psychiatric diagnoses ($n = 11$ women; 1 man; 4 patients dropped out). Diagnoses were most commonly personality disorders (83%, including 58% BPD) and major depression (50%). Substance abuse disorders (42%), psychotic disorders (33%), and anxiety disorders (25%) were also present, with the mean number of diagnoses being three per participant; only one participant had a single diagnosis. The authors concluded that even in a complex and difficult-to-treat sample, an adapted DBT program showed promise for reducing anger on the State-Trait Anger Inventory (Koons et al., 2006). Again, the generalizability and relevance of the study is limited by the small sample size, the lack of replication, and the absence of violence as an outcome measure.

To our knowledge, two published studies have tested DBT interventions with persons with intellectual and/or developmental disabilities. Sakdalan, Shaw, and Collier (2010) conducted the first study of DBT in a small sample of adults with intellectual disabilities ($n = 9$). Six participants completed 80% of sessions. The patients were found to show improvements on three of four outcomes: decreased risk and increased strength ratings and improved overall functioning, but coping skills improvements were non-significant.

Brown, Brown, and Dibiasio (2013) reported similarly promising findings from their sample of 40 adults with developmental disabilities (most also had intellectual disabilities and aggression was highly common [88%] in the patients' histories). The authors reported significant improvements in all three categories of challenging behavior—red flags (e.g., yelling), dangerous situations (e.g., verbal threats), and lapses (e.g., aggression, self-injury) following one hour of individual DBT and one hour of group skills system training, as well as an additional hour of group therapy for individuals with a history of sexual offending behaviors. Despite a considerable amount of missing data, benefits of the intervention were also evident in the dramatically reduced proportion of patients admitted to jails and forensic hospitals—28 (70%) of the total 40 patients at baseline versus two patients at the two-year follow-up—as well as a reduced number of days in custody (228 days/annum vs. ~20 days/annum). Interestingly, the largest therapeutic gains found by Brown and colleagues were noted to take place in the first year of follow-up, but for the most severe behaviors (i.e., lapses), the improvements occurred more slowly over the four-year follow-up.

The utility of DBT for reducing severe emotional and behavioral regulation problems is well established. Although there is a very promising and rapidly expanding evidence base to support the relevance of DBT for the treatment of anger, aggression, and violence among forensic populations with a range of diagnostic presentations and behavioral challenges, there are several limitations in the literature to date. First, the starting point of these evaluations is with the application of a replicable intervention. As such, we concur with Koerner and Dimeff (2000) that researchers and clinicians should attempt to integrate DBT with considerable fidelity (i.e., with fidelity scales to evaluate the rigor of the implementations), and modifications to the treatment need to be extensively documented to allow replication. The focus of DBT treatment evaluations needs to be extended to include outcomes more specific to aggression and violence, as well as a reduction in recidivism, in addition to traditional maladaptive coping common to BPD (e.g., suicide, self-harm, psychopathology). Moreover, samples need to be expanded to include males and ethnic minorities and individuals with diagnoses beyond BPD.

Furthermore, there is a lack of replication in the literature, inhibiting generalizability of the research to date. Specifically, based on the extant literature,

it is difficult to draw firm conclusions, given the diversity of the samples across studies (adolescents and adults; diverse diagnostic groups; correctional and forensic settings). In addition, researchers are employing variable outcomes, many of which have relatively limited relevance to "violence." Also, operational definitions and measures vary across projects. Moreover, several studies have employed very short follow-up periods, and missing data have been a challenge for researchers employing lengthier follow-up periods. Finally, the proportion of samples composed of females remains high, and researchers will want to examine the extent to which gender moderates the relationship between the intervention and improved outcomes.

Nonetheless, there is sufficiently strong conceptual and empirical evidence to suggest that DBT is worthy of clinical consideration for the prevention of violence (also see Frazier & Vela, 2014; McCann et al., 2000; Sakdalan & Gupta, 2014; Wix, 2003). In particular, several commentators have noted that there are many similarities in the clinical and behavioral presentation of patients in general and forensic mental health settings (e.g., Seto, Crocker, Nicholls, & Côté, 2014; Petersen et al., 2015; Van den Bosch et al., 2012). In addition, the skills needed to manage angry, aggressive and impulsive behaviors share considerable commonalities with the affective regulation and other skills developed through DBT (McCann et al., 2000).

Mandated Community Service Approaches

Some treatments or service approaches designed to operate primarily within the community may require the cooperation and involvement of legal players (e.g., mental health courts), or unfold within the context of legal supervision and leverage (e.g., outpatient commitment). The common core to these approaches is that patients can choose to enroll, but they must be compliant to remain in the community. Examples include intensive case management, assertive community treatment, outpatient commitment, and mental health courts. As with most programs, there is evidence both for and against these approaches. However, the bulk of the evidence would suggest that, if services are intensive enough, they can reduce community crime and violence (Gilbert et al., 2010; Swartz, Swanson, Steadman, Robbins, & Monahan, 2009) and reduce costs (Swanson et al., 2013).

For example, Phelan et al. (2010) compared matched groups (assisted outpatient commitment vs. treatment as usual) in New York for one year.

Serious violence was lower in the outpatient commitment group, a finding consistent with that of earlier high-quality research (Swanson et al., 2000). In Swanson et al.'s work, which used a randomized controlled trial design, those receiving outpatient commitment for at least six months were less likely to be violent than those in the treatment-as-usual group (27% vs. 42%). Several factors contributed to the effectiveness of outpatient commitment, including regular outpatient psychiatric services, medication compliance, and no misuse of substances. Hough and O'Brien (2005) also observed decreased violence (from 18% to 7%) for outpatient commitment in an A-B-A design study of 553 Australian patients.

Mohamed (2013), in a large sample of 3,422 veterans with dual diagnoses of SMI and substance abuse, reported a decrease in violence after six months of intensive case management. This approach holds that services that are delivered at higher doses ought to result in improved functioning and lower adverse outcomes such as violence. Although some other studies have also supported intensive case management for the reduction of violence (Ventura, Cassel, Jacoby, & Huang, 1998), some have not (Solomon, Draine, & Meyerson, 1994; Walsh et al., 2001). One reason for this could be a lack of attention to criminogenic needs in such services, which tend to focus primarily on psychiatric services. A related approach—assertive community treatment—involves actively helping patients achieve basic needs such as housing, employment, and treatment. Such programs do tend to improve general clinical outcomes, but evidence for their effect on violence is again less consistent (Bond, Drake, Mueser, & Latimer, 2001; Calsyn et al., 2005; Killaspy et al., 2006) or fails to differentiate between violent and nonviolent outcome measures (Ford et al., 2001; McCoy, Roberts, Hanrahan, Clay, & Luchins, 2004; Wilson, Tien, & Eaves, 1995).

Finally, *mental health courts* (MHCs) have become commonplace. In an evaluation of the first MHC in the United States, Christy et al. (2005) reported violence- and arrest-related outcomes. Although there were few differences in terms of criminal justice outcomes, there were fewer arrests in the MHC group, and fewer self-reported serious violent incidents (3% vs. 11%) than in the matched sample. Cosden, Ellens, Schnell, Yamini-Diouf, and Wolfe (2003) reported reduced recidivism in patients randomly assigned to MHC vs. treatment as usual, although this was not specifically *violent* recidivism. In a recent study that compared (matched)

patients supervised by an MHC with those receiving treatment as usual, McNiel, Sadeh, Delucchi, and Binder (2015) reported a substantial reduction of subsequent community violence (25% vs. 42%).

Although the evidence is somewhat mixed, as it is in most areas of violence treatment, on average there appears to be support for the use of mandated community services such as outpatient commitment and mental health courts. Importantly, the services that are delivered within these programs must target dynamic risk factors for violence, or risk improving only general clinical functioning and not violence.

The Role of Psychotropic Medication

Although research on medications and violence is growing, it remains plagued by important challenges. For instance, researchers have identified the lack of universally agreed-upon definitions of violence, aggression, or hostility as a barrier to greater integration of research regarding the efficacy of psychiatric medications in the management of violence (Topiwala & Fazel, 2011). This gap introduces difficulties when one is reviewing the literature on the efficacy of pharmacological approaches to violence in persons with psychosis. The identified studies examined by Topiwala and Fazel (2011) all reported on heterogeneous populations, with some including only individuals with schizophrenia, while other studies allowed a broader range of psychotic diagnoses and treatment settings. The researchers identified only one randomized controlled trial (RCT) that selected patients on the basis of previous violence, which may limit the degree of legitimate generalization of findings and conclusions. Other variables across studies included treatment length, dose-regime differences, and selection of outcome measures, which ranged from hostility to serious physical violence (Topiwala & Fazel, 2011). Many investigations included a follow-up period of just a few weeks, which is unlikely to reveal a change in the frequency or severity of assaults. The exclusion of patients with substance misuse in some trials introduced a further source of variance, as this is a risk factor for violent behavior (Topiwala & Fazel, 2011). Furthermore, some studies did not control for concurrent prescribing or medication adherence (Fazel et al., 2009; Milton et al., 2001).

Nonadherence and Violence

Evolving evidence indicates that noncompliance with psychopharmacological treatment is associated with elevated violence rates in schizophrenia. Research findings indicate that the majority of persons who are prescribed psychotropic medication do not adhere to it as prescribed, with reported rates of non-adherence ranging from 20–89%, and a mean rate of about 50% (Chan et al., 2014; Dolder, Lacro, Dunn, & Jeste, 2002; Fenton, Blyler, & Heinssen, 1997). Moreover, 74% of 1,432 subjects in the National Institute of Mental Health (NIMH) Clinical Antipsychotic Trials of Intervention Effectiveness (CATIE) trial discontinued medication before conclusion of the 18-month study period (Stroup et al., 2009).

In a study of 1,908 persons with major mental illness, Ascher-Svanum and colleagues (2006) examined nonadherence to medication in a three-year multisite study. Nonadherence was associated with poorer functional outcomes, including greater risks of psychiatric hospitalizations, use of emergency psychiatric services, arrests, violence, victimizations, poorer mental functioning, poorer life satisfaction, greater substance use, and more alcohol-related problems (all $p < .001$). Adherence was relatively stable, with 77.3% of patients maintaining the same adherence status from the first year to the second year. Nonadherence in the first year predicted significantly poorer outcomes in the following two years (Ascher-Svanum et al., 2006).

In keeping with the findings from the Ascher-Svanum et al. (2006) study, Lindenmayer and colleagues (2009) reported results that suggest an interaction between nonadherence and hostility. In a post hoc analysis of a randomized, double-blind study comparing olanzapine in patients with schizophrenia or schizoaffective disorder and suboptimal response to current treatment, greater hostility as measured by the Positive and Negative Syndrome Scale item was demonstrated as a possible risk factor for nonadherence (hazard ratio [HR]: 1.1; 95% confidence interval [CI]: 1.0–1.3) (Lindenmayer et al., 2009).

In their review of the adherence literature, Higashi and colleagues (2013) examined 37 papers since 2001 on antipsychotic medication nonadherence and identified the key drivers of nonadherence as lack of insight, medication beliefs, and substance abuse. Key consequences of nonadherence included greater risk of relapse, hospitalization, and self-directed violence. Of note to clinicians is that factors positively related to adherence were a good therapeutic relationship with the physician and perception of benefits of medication (Higashi et al., 2013).

Antipsychotic Medication

Antipsychotic medications and mood stabilizers are standard pharmacological interventions for a range of psychiatric disorders, including schizophrenia and related psychotic disorders, bipolar

disorder, depression, and other diagnoses. In their seminal paper from 1993, Volavka, Zito, Vitrai, and Czobor (1993), and in a subsequent review Citrome and Volavka (2000), concluded that there was encouraging evidence to support clozapine as an anti-aggressive medication in the management of violence. Citrome and Volavka (2000) also proposed beta blockers as potentially helpful adjuncts to antipsychotic treatment, but commented on the paucity of methodologically robust research studies in the area. In a more recent review, Volavka and Citrome (2008) cited two RCTs as providing further support for clozapine's anti-aggression properties. As in 2000, the authors reported equivocal evidence for the use of other antipsychotic medications in aggression management (Volavka & Citrome, 2008).

In a meta-analysis, Aleman and Kahn (2001) reported on seven controlled trials investigating the effect of risperidone on aggression in schizophrenia. In five methodologically rigorous sub-analyses, risperidone was reported as significantly better than typical antipsychotics (Aleman & Kahn, 2001).

Recent systematic reviews demonstrate that antipsychotic medications and mood stabilizers assist in reducing relapse and readmission rates in schizophrenia (Leucht et al., 2012); bipolar disorder (Beynon, Soares-Weiser, Woolacott, Duffy, & Geddes, 2009; Geddes, Burgess, Hawton, Jamison, & Goodwin, 2004); treatment-resistant depression (Nelson & Papakostas, 2009); and BPD (Mercer, Douglass, & Links (2009). Despite these advances, evidence about the effects of pharmacotherapy on other important outcomes, including violent behavior, is scarce (Topiwala & Fazel, 2011).

According to reviews, including the Cochrane Database of Systematic Reviews and clinical guidelines, the existing evidence for pharmacological interventions in the mitigation of violence risk is inconclusive and not robust (Barnes & the Schizophrenia Consensus Group of the British Association for Psychopharmacology, 2011; Fazel et al., 2009; Huband, Ferriter, Nathan, & Jones, 2010; Leucht, Werner, McGrath, & White, 2007). Furthermore, reviews of research data over the past decade or so suggest that, although depot injection of antipsychotics (e.g., zuclopenthixol decanoate) seems to reduce relapse rates compared with orally administered antipsychotics (Arango, Bombín, González-Salvador, García-Cabeza, & Bobes, 2006; Leucht et al., 2011), it remains unclear if these benefits extend to mitigation of violence risk (Fazel, Zetterqvist, Larsson, Långström, & Lichtenstein, 2014). Nonetheless, there is evidence to suggest the efficacy of some atypical antipsychotics, such as clozapine, in reducing a multitude of different outcomes.

Clozapine is proven to enhance overall functioning in treatment-resistant schizophrenia, reduce aggression, and also decrease suicidal behavior in persons with schizophrenia (Hennen & Baldessarini, 2005). Similarly, Krakowski, Czobor, Citrome, Bark, and Cooper (2006) from a RCT reported the beneficial effects of clozapine in schizophrenia, as did Volavka and colleagues (2004). Swanson et al. (2008) reporting on the results of the CATIE project, found no advantage of atypical over typical antipsychotics in symptom reduction; however, this study did not initially include clozapine.

Citrome and Volavka (2000) reported data from the first RCT in support of clozapine, findings that were subsequently confirmed in a review by Volavka and colleagues in 2004. The study design randomized inpatients with severe schizophrenia and who had been violent to double-blind trials of clozapine, olanzapine, risperidone, or haloperidol for 14 weeks. Clozapine was found to be superior to haloperidol in reducing the incidence and severity of violent incidents (Volavka et al., 2004).

A study by Krakowski and colleagues (2006) provided further evidence in support of clozapine in a population with a recent history of violent behavior. In a randomized, double-blind trial, patients with schizophrenia or schizoaffective disorder (n = 110) received clozapine, olanzapine, or haloperidol over a 12-week period. Inclusion criteria included an episode of physical assault directed against another person during the current hospitalization, and persistence of aggression (Krakowski et al., 2006). The clozapine group had the lowest total scores, and the lowest physical and verbal aggression scores. Clozapine was superior to haloperidol, but not to olanzapine, in reducing aggression against property. However, olanzapine was superior to haloperidol in reducing both physical and verbal aggression scores. These effects could not be explained by a reduction in psychopathology or an increase in sedation (Krakowski et al., 2006).

In a recent review of the literature on clozapine, Frogley, Taylor, Dickens, and Picchioni (2012) identified six animal studies, four RCTs, 12 prospective non-controlled studies, and 22 retrospective studies. The authors reported considerable evidence in support of clozapine's ability to reduce violent and aggressive behavior. Clozapine's anti-aggressive effect was most commonly explored in patients with schizophrenia (Frogley et al., 2012).

Given the increasing "off-label" use of clozapine for non-psychotic disorders, the available research indicates less evidence for other psychiatric disorders, including BPD, autistic spectrum disorders, post-traumatic stress disorder, bipolar disorder, and learning disability. There was mixed evidence to address the question of whether or not clozapine was any more effective than other antipsychotics. In the case of schizophrenia, there was evidence to suggest that clozapine's anti-aggressive effect was more marked, particularly in those with treatment-resistant illness (Frogley et al., 2012).

Thus, although RCTs testing the anti-aggressive effect of clozapine are relatively scarce, the evidence based on existing studies supports its efficacy (Volavka, Swanson, & Citrome, 2012). The evidence also supports the inclusion of clozapine in expert consensus guidelines (Kane, Leucht, Carpenter, & Docherty, 2003), and in support for clozapine, there is general agreement on the superiority of its anti-aggressive effect in schizophrenia, as reflected, for example, in standard textbooks (Volavka et al., 2012) and in published expert-consensus guidelines (Kane et al., 2003, p. 38).

Swanson and colleagues (2008) compared the relative anti-aggression effect of atypical antipsychotic medications on a subsample (n = 653) of participants in the CATIE study. In the CATIE study, a large multisite RCT in the United States involving 1,493 inpatients and community patients with schizophrenia, 231 patients dropped out of the intention-to-treat cohort because of lack of efficacy of the treatments. The remaining participants were randomized to perphenazine, risperidone, olanzapine, ziprasidone, or quetiapine (Swanson et al., 2008). In a sequential design, those who had dropped out of the study because of their limited response to the original medication were randomized to a second antipsychotic preparation. The study demonstrated no specific benefit of any antipsychotic medication over another in reducing violence risk (Swanson et al., 2008), but this finding appears to be in contrast with other published trials (Topiwala & Fazel, 2011). Methodological challenges, such as the inclusion or not of clozapine, variable follow-up times, baseline patient-symptom severity, and different outcomes provide candidate explanations for these discrepancies. For example, variation in the maximum dose of antipsychotic medication used, and differences in prescription protocols may have resulted in non-alignment of results, like the findings that the maximum doses of antipsychotics used were not equivalent and protocols regarding the continuation of previously prescribed mood stabilizers varied (see Topiwala & Fazel, 2011).

Other published controlled studies have reported the superiority of atypical agents (including clozapine) over typical antipsychotics in violence reduction. Swanson, Swartz, and Elbogen (2004) compared the effectiveness of atypical antipsychotic medications to that of conventional neuroleptics in reducing violent behavior among patients with schizophrenia under "usual care" conditions in the community over a two-year period. Participants (n = 229) were adults with schizophrenia spectrum disorders receiving inpatient or outpatient services. Atypical antipsychotic medications (clozapine, risperidone, or olanzapine) were found to have a significant effect in violence reduction, but treatment with conventional neuroleptics did not have this same beneficial effect. A cumulative effect on reduced violence was attributable to consistent compliance with atypical antipsychotic medications over a two-year period (Swanson et al., 2004).

In a three-year prospective European study, Bitter, Czobor, Dossenbach, and Volavka (2005) reported the efficacy of olanzapine and risperidone over haloperidol and, surprisingly, also over clozapine. Other studies have demonstrated the superiority of other atypical antipsychotics, such as quetiapine (Arango & Bernardo, 2005) and ziprasidone (Citrome et al., 2006), in reducing violent behavior.

Mood Stabilizers

The scientific evidence is uneven as to whether mood stabilizers reduce aggressive or violent behavior (Fazel et al., 2014; Huband et al., 2010; Jones et al., 2011). Fazel and colleagues (2014) explored the anti-aggression benefits of antipsychotic or mood stabilizing medications in a Swedish cohort of over 80,000 persons prescribed psychiatric medication. The researchers reported a 64% reduction in the violent crime rate for any antipsychotic or mood stabilizer (HR 0·36, 95% CI 0·34–0·39). People with bipolar disorder who were prescribed mood stabilizers had a similarly reduced risk of committing violent crime, but these potential effects of mood stabilizers did not generalize to those with schizophrenia or related psychoses (Fazel et al., 2014). Furthermore, the addition of antipsychotics to mood stabilizers in a person with schizophrenia was more effective than was treatment with a mood stabilizer alone, but the addition of a mood stabilizer to an antipsychotic did not have any effect. In short, for a patient with schizophrenia, the addition of a mood

stabilizer to reduce violence risk is not supported by the research data (Falkai et al., 2005; Fazel et al., 2014). As the researchers correctly emphasize, this is an important finding because, despite available evidence (Schwarz, Volz, Li, & Leucht, 2008), the administration of antipsychotics and mood stabilizers in combination remains a not-uncommon practice in psychiatry (Jones et al., 2011; see also Hodgins, 2014).

There is some evidence for the use of mood stabilizers in non-psychotic violent populations (Lindenmayer & Kotsaftis, 2000; Cade, 1949; Prado-Lima, Knijnik, Juruena, & Padilla, 2001; Sheard, 1971; Sheard, Marini, Bridges, & Wagner, 1976; Tupin et al., 1973; Van Putten & Sanders, 1975). For instance, Gobbi, Gaudreau, and Leblanc (2006) demonstrated that topiramate shows promise as a treatment option. In this study, violent male patients with schizophrenia in a maximum security facility received topiramate plus an antipsychotic agent, valproate plus an antipsychotic, or topiramate plus valproate plus an antipsychotic. Valproate was superior at decreasing verbal aggression and agitation. Furthermore, treatment with topiramate, valproate, or both in combination decreased physical aggression against others (Gobbi et al., 2006).

A recent systematic review of the evidence for mood stabilizers in the management of aggression and associated impulsivity in non–mentally ill populations by Huband et al. (2010) summarized results from 14 placebo-controlled, prospective trials. Results indicated the superior efficacy of sodium valproate and divalproex over placebo for men with impulsive aggression, for impulsive aggression in persons with disruptive personality disorders, and for conduct-disordered youths (Huband et al., 2010).

The same review appraised the evidence for the use of antiseizure medication in reducing violence (Huband et al., 2010). Carbamazepine was superior to placebo in reducing acts of self-directed aggression in women with borderline personality disorder. Verbal aggression and aggression against objects in adults with intermittent explosive disorder responded better to oxcarbazepine as compared to placebo. Additionally, phenytoin was superior to placebo in reducing aggression in male prisoners, outpatients, and men with personality disorder (Huband et al., 2010). Despite these findings, Huband and colleagues (2010) concluded that results from other studies with equivocal findings precluded firm recommendations regarding the use of mood stabilizers in the management of aggression and violence in non-psychotic populations (for detailed discussion, see Fazel et al., 2014).

Beta Blockers

Beta blockers have been used in the management of violence as an adjunct to antipsychotics. Some studies (Allan et al., 1996; Alpert et al., 1990) support the efficacy of the lipophilic agent propranolol and the more hydrophilic nadolol, at least in the short term, with improvement in symptom scores and aggressive behavior. However, intolerance of side effects poses a challenge for longer term adherence (Allan et al., 1996; Alpert et al., 1990; Ratey et al., 1992).

Other Medications

Various other medications such as omega-3 fatty acids, methylphenidate, anti-androgens, buspirone, clonidine, and some serotonergic antidepressants have been used in the management of psychosis-related violence. Some single studies have provided evidence of their efficacy, but there is no RCT evidence of these preparations reducing violence rates in patients with schizophrenia (Fazel et al., 2014).

Rapid Tranquilization (RT) Protocols for Psychosis-Induced Agitation and Acute Violence Risk

Several rapid tranquilization (RT) protocols are available and widely used in the management of acutely agitated and violent patients with psychosis or mania. While the use of single pharmacological agents, such as lorazepam, on their own or in combination with typical or atypical antipsychotics is common, rigorous reviews of their efficacy prove findings to be equivocal. In a detailed review of the literature, Gillies, Sampson, Beck, and Rathbone (2013) examined 21 trials with a total of 1,968 participants. For the single trial that compared benzodiazepines with placebo, there was no significant difference for most outcomes, although there was a higher risk of no improvement with the use of placebo alone in the medium term (one to 48 hours) (n = 102, 1 RCT, Rate Ratio [RR] 0.62, 95% CI 0.40 to 0.97) (Gillies et al., 2013). No difference was found in the number of patients who evidenced no improvement in the medium term when benzodiazepines were compared with antipsychotics (n = 308, 5 RCTs, RR 1.10, 95% CI 0.85 to 1.42). As anticipated, fewer extrapyramidal side effects were reported in those receiving benzodiazepines alone, as opposed to those who received an antipsychotic agent as well (n = 536, 8 RCTs, RR 0.15, 95% CI 0.06 to 0.39). Data comparing combined

benzodiazepines and antipsychotics versus benzodiazepines alone did not yield any significant results (Gillies et al., 2013).

When comparing combined benzodiazepines/antipsychotics (all studies compared haloperidol) with the same antipsychotics alone (haloperidol), Gillies and colleagues (2013) found no difference between groups in improvement in the medium term, but combination therapy was more likely to result in sedation. Of note is the finding that combined benzodiazepine and haloperidol evidenced lower efficacy in the medium term when compared to participants receiving olanzapine or ziprasidone; however, these findings were low in terms of quality of evidence. When haloperidol and midazolam were compared with olanzapine, there was some evidence that the combination was superior in terms of symptom improvement, sedation, and behavior (Gillies et al., 2013). Other researchers have reviewed the evidence for existing, as well as emerging, single and/or combination medication protocols, such as haloperidol (Khushu, Powney, & Adams, 2012; Powney, Adams, & Jones, 2011), loxapine inhaler (Vangala, Ahmed, & Ahmed, 2012), risperidone (Ahmed, Rehman, Jones, and Adams (2011), aripiprazole (Pagadala, Jayaram, & Mitra, 2009), and quetiapine (Wilkie & Fenton, 2012).

In summary, while psychopharmacological intervention has robust research support for symptom severity attenuation in persons with major mental illness, the efficacy of antipsychotics, mood stabilizers, and antiseizure medications in the management of violence in such persons is less well established. With the exception of clozapine, for which the beneficial effect in violence reduction is well established, more methodologically robust RCTs targeting larger populations are needed to determine the relative efficacy of single or medication combination protocols in the reduction of violence in those with severe mental illness.

Conclusion and Future Directions

Despite the various approaches covered in this chapter, we must remain somewhat cautious in our conclusions. The perfect study has not been done. There are very few RCTs on point. All studies in the field have flaws. Yet there is a convergence of evidence from diverse sources, methods, and approaches that certain intervention approaches to reducing violence among those with SMI will, on balance, do so. In our view, there is sufficient evidence that CBT and social learning approaches that are consistent with the RNR approach, if implemented with integrity, are likely to reduce violence among persons with SMI. Anger management remains a promising focused intervention with reasonable support in the literature. We would advise, however, that it not be used as a panacea—people whose violence is not caused by anger do not need anger management.

DBT has substantial general support, and its support base is slowly but surely making its way into the violence and mental disorder fields. Yet much more should be done with this promising approach, which remains in its infancy with respect to violence among people with SMI. Community-based mandatory service programs such as outpatient commitment and mental health courts appear effective, particularly if delivered in sufficient dosage and if targeting dynamic risk factors. Finally, the evidence base for the violence-reducing effect of psychotropic medication is promising yet inconsistent. An exception to this inconsistency is the effect of clozapine.

The issue of violence treatment among persons with SMI remains in desperate need of more high-quality research. We know a good deal, but stand to learn more. We do know that it is incredibly hard to conduct research in this area, and we both commend and encourage those who have done so. We also call for an enhanced focus on gender and ethnicity in this research field. These topics are essentially absent from existing research, and we welcome the next generation of research that incorporates these issues.

References

Ahmed, U., Rehman, F., Jones, H., & Adams, C. E. (2011). Risperidone for psychosis-induced aggression or agitation. *Cochrane Database of Systematic Reviews 2011, 11.* Art. No.: CD009412. doi:10.1002/14651858.CD009412

Aleman, A., & Kahn, R. (2001). Effects of the atypical antipsychotic risperidone on hostility and aggression in schizophrenia: A meta-analysis of controlled trials. *European Neuropsychopharmacology, 11*(4), 289–293.

Allan, E. R., Alpert, M., Sison, C. E., Citrome, L., Laury, G., & Berman, I. (1996). Adjunctive nadolol in the treatment of acutely aggressive schizophrenic patients. *Journal of Clinical Psychiatry, 57*(10), 455–459.

Alpert, M., Allan, E. R., Citrome, L., Laury, G., Sison, C., & Sudilovsky, A. (1990). A double-blind, placebo-controlled study of adjunctive nadolol in the management of violent psychiatric patients. *Psychopharmacology Bulletin, 26*(3), 367–371.

Anderson, C. A., & Bushman, B. J. (2002). Human aggression. *Annual Review of Psychology, 53,* 27–51. doi:10.1146/annurev.psych.53.100901.135231

Andrews, D. A. (2012). The risk-need-responsivity (RNR) model of correctional assessment and treatment. In J. A. Dvoskin, J. L. Skeem, R. W. Novaco, & K. S. Douglas (Eds.), *Using social science to reduce violent offending* (pp. 127–156). New York, NY: Oxford University Press.

Andrews, D. A., & Bonta, J. (2003). *The psychology of criminal conduct* (3rd ed.). Cincinnati, OH: Anderson.

Arango, C., & Bernardo, M. (2005). The effect of quetiapine on aggression and hostility in patients with schizophrenia. *Human Psychopharmacology, 20*(4), 237–241.

Arango, C., Bombín, I., González-Salvador, T., García-Cabeza, I., & Bobes, J. (2006). Randomised clinical trial comparing oral versus depot formulations of zuclopenthixol in patients with schizophrenia and previous violence. *European Psychiatry, 21,* 34–40.

Ascher-Svanum, H., Faries, D. E., Zhu, B., Ernst, F. R., Swartz, M. S., & Swanson, J. W. (2006). Medication adherence and long-term functional outcomes in the treatment of schizophrenia in usual care. *Journal of Clinical Psychiatry, 76,* 453–460.

Ashford, J. B., Wong, K. W., & Sternbach, K. O. (2008). Generic correctional programming for mentally ill offenders: A pilot study. *Criminal Justice and Behavior, 35,* 457–473.

Barnes, T. R. E., & the Schizophrenia Consensus Group of the British Association for Psychopharmacology. (2011). Evidence-based guidelines for the pharmacological treatment of schizophrenia: Recommendations from the British Association for Psychopharmacology. *Journal of Psychopharmacology, 25,* 567–620.

Barrett, E. L., Mills, K. L., & Teesson, M. (2013). Mental health correlates of anger in the general population: Findings from the 2007 National Survey of Mental Health and Wellbeing. *Australian and New Zealand Journal of Psychiatry, 4,* 470–476. doi:10.1177/0004867413476752

Beck, N. C., Menditto, A. A., Baldwin, L., Angelone, E., & Maddox, M. (1991). Reduced frequency of aggressive behavior in forensic patients in a social learning program. *Hospital and Community Psychiatry, 42,* 750–752.

Beck, R., & Fernandez, E. (1998). Cognitive-behavioral therapy in the treatment of anger: A meta-analysis. *Cognitive Therapy and Research, 22,* 63–74. doi:10.1023/A:1018763902991

Becker, M., Love, C. C., & Hunter, M. E. (1997). Intractability is relative: Behaviour therapy in the elimination of violence in psychotic forensic patients. *Legal and Criminological Psychology, 2* (Part 1), 89–101. doi:10.1111/j.2044-8333.1997.tb00335.x

Berzins, L. G., & Trestman, R. L. (2004). The development and implementation of dialectical behavior therapy in forensic settings. *International Journal of Forensic Mental Health, 3*(1), 93–103.

Beynon, S., Soares-Weiser, K., Woolacott, N., Duffy, S., & Geddes, J. (2009). Pharmacological interventions for the prevention of relapse in bipolar disorder: A systematic review of controlled trials. *Journal of Psychopharmacology, 23,* 574–591.

Bitter, I., Czobor, P., Dossenbach, M., & Volavka, J. (2005). Effectiveness of clozapine, olanzapine, quetiapine, risperidone, and haloperidol monotherapy in reducing hostile and aggressive behavior in outpatients treated for schizophrenia: A prospective naturalistic study (IC-SOHO). *European Psychiatry, 20*(5–6), 403–408.

Bond, G. R., Drake, R. E., Mueser, K. T., & Latimer, E. (2001). Assertive community treatment for people with severe mental illness. *Disease Management and Health Outcomes, 9,* 141–159.

Bonta, J., Blais, J., & Wilson, H. A. (2014). A theoretically informed meta-analysis of the risk for general and violent recidivism for mentally disordered offenders. *Aggression and Violent Behavior, 19,* 278–287.

Bradbury, K. E., & Clarke, I. (2007). Cognitive behavioural therapy for anger management: Effectiveness in adult mental health services. *Behavioural and Cognitive Psychotherapy, 35,* 201–208. doi:10.1017/S135246580600333X

Braham, L., Jones, D., & Hollin, C. R. (2008). The violent offender treatment program (VOTP): Development of a treatment program for violent patients in a high security psychiatric hospital. *International Journal of Forensic Mental Health, 7*, 157–172. doi:10.1080/14999013.2008.9914412

Brown, J. F., Brown, M. Z., & Dibiasio, P. (2013). Treating individuals with intellectual disabilities and challenging behaviors with adapted dialectical behavior therapy. *Journal of Mental Health Research in Intellectual Disabilities, 6*(4), 280–303. doi:10.1080/19315864.2012.700684

Cade, J. (1949). Lithium salts in the treatment of psychotic excitement. *Medical Journal of Australia, 2*(10), 349–352.

Calsyn, R. J., Yonker, R. D., Lemming, M. R., Morse, G. A., & Klinkenberg, W. D. (2005). Impact of assertive community treatment and client characteristics on criminal justice outcomes in dual disorder homeless individuals. *Criminal Behaviour and Mental Health, 15*, 236–248.

Chan, K., Hui, L., Wong, H., Lee, H., Chang, W., & Chen, Y. (2014). Medication adherence, knowledge about psychosis, and insight among patients with a schizophrenia-spectrum disorder. *Journal of Nervous and Mental Disease, 202*(1), 25–29.

Chemtob, C. M., Novaco, R. W., Hamada, R. S., & Gross, D. M. (1997). Cognitive-behavioral treatment for severe anger in posttraumatic stress disorder. *Journal of Consulting and Clinical Psychology, 65*, 184–189. doi:10.1037/0022-006X.65.1.184

Christy, A., Poythress, N. G., Boothroyd, R. A., Petrila, J., & Shabnam, M. (2005). Evaluating the efficiency and community safety goals of the Broward County Mental Health Court. *Behavioral Sciences and the Law, 23*, 227–243.

Citrome, L., & Volavka, J. (2000). Management of violence in schizophrenia. *Psychiatric Annals, 30*(1), 41–52.

Citrome, L., Volavka, J., Czobor, P., Brook, S., Loebel, A., & Mandel, F. (2006). Efficacy of ziprasidone against hostility in schizophrenia: *Post hoc* analysis of randomized, open-label study data. *Journal of Clinical Psychiatry, 67*(4), 638–642.

Cosden, M., Ellens, J. K., Schnell, J. L., Yamini-Diouf, Y., & Wolfe, M. M. (2003). Evaluation of a mental health treatment court with assertive community treatment. *Behavioral Sciences and the Law, 21*, 415–427.

Cullen, A. E., Clarke, A. Y., Kuipers, E., Hodgins, S., Dean, K., & Fahy, T. (2012). A multisite randomized trial of a cognitive skills program for male mentally disordered offenders: Violence and antisocial behavior outcomes. *Journal of Consulting and Clinical Psychology, 80*, 1114–1120.

Cullen, A. E., Soria, C., Clarke, A. Y., Dean, K., & Fahy, T. (2011). Factors predicting dropout from the Reasoning and Rehabilitation program with mentally disordered offenders. *Criminal Justice and Behavior, 38*, 217–230.

Del Vecchio, T. & O'Leary, K. D. (2004). Effectiveness of anger treatments for specific anger problems: A meta-analytic review. *Clinical Psychology Review, 24*, 15–34.

Derks, F. C. H. (1996). A forensic day treatment program for personality-disordered criminal offenders. *International Journal of Offender Therapy and Comparative Criminology, 40*, 123–134.

DiGiuseppe, R., & Tafrate, R. C. (2003). Anger treatment for adults: A meta-analytic review. *Clinical Psychology: Science and Practice, 10*, 70–84. doi:10.1093/clipsy/10.1.70

Dolder, C. R., Lacro, J., Dunn, L. B., & Jeste, D. V. (2002). Antipsychotic medication adherence: Is there a difference between typical and atypical agents? *American Journal of Psychiatry, 159*(1), 103–108.

Donnelly, J. P., & Scott, M. F. (1999). Evaluation of an offending behaviour programme with a mentally disordered offender population. *British Journal of Forensic Practice, 1*, 25–32.

Douglas, K. S., Guy, L. S., & Hart, S. D. (2009). Psychosis as a risk factor for violence to others: A meta-analysis. *Psychological Bulletin, 135*, 679–706.

Douglas, K. S., Hart, S. D., Groscup, J. L., & Litwack, T. R. (2014). Assessing violence risk. In I. Weiner & R. K. Otto (Eds.), *The handbook of forensic psychology* (4th edition). Hoboken, NJ: JoJ.J.hn Wiley & Sons.

Douglas, K. S., Nicholls, T. L., & Brink, J. (2009). Reducing the risk of violence among persons with mental illness: A critical analysis of treatment approaches (pp. 351–376). In P. M. Kleespies (Ed.), *Behavioral emergencies: An evidence-based resource for evaluating and managing risk of suicide, violence, and victimization*. Washington, DC: American Psychological Association.

Dowden, C., & Andrews, D. A. (2000). Effective correctional treatment and violent reoffending: A meta-analysis. *Canadian Journal of Criminology, 42*, 449–467.

Edmondson, C. B., & Conger, J. C. (1996). A review of treatment efficacy for individuals with anger problems: Conceptual, assessment, and methodological issues. *Clinical Psychology Review, 16*, 251–275.

Evershed, S., Tennant, A., Boomer, D., Rees, A., Barkham, M., & Watson, A. (2003). Practice-based outcomes of dialectical behaviour therapy (DBT) targeting anger and violence, with male forensic patients: A pragmatic and non-contemporaneous comparison. *Criminal Behaviour and Mental Health, 13*(3), 198–213.

Falkai, P., Wobrock, T., Lieberman, J., Glenthoj, B., Wagner, F., Gattaz, H. J. M., & WFSBP Task Force on Treatment Guidelines for Schizophrenia. (2005). World Federation of Societies of Biological Psychiatry (WFSBP) guidelines for biological treatment of schizophrenia, Part 1: Acute treatment of schizophrenia. *World Journal of Biological Psychiatry, 6*(3), 132–191.

Fazel, S., Gulati, G., Linsell, L., Geddes, J. R., & Grann, M. (2009). Schizophrenia and violence: Systematic review and meta-analysis. *PLoS Medicine, 6*(8), e1000120. doi:10.1371/journal.pmed.1000120

Fazel, S., Zetterqvist, J., Larsson, H., Långström, N., & Lichtenstein, P. (2014). Antipsychotics, mood stabilisers, and risk of violent crime. *The Lancet, 384*(9949), 1206–1214.

Fenton, W. S., Blyler, C. R., & Heinssen, R. K. (1997). Determinants of medication compliance in schizophrenia: Empirical and clinical findings. *Schizophrenia Bulletin, 23*, 637–651.

Fleck, D., Thompson, C. L., & Narroway, L. (2001). Implementation of the Problem Solving Skills Training Programme in a medium secure unit. *Criminal Behaviour and Mental Health, 11*, 262–272.

Ford, R., Barnes, A., Davies, R., Chalmers, C., Hardy, P., & Muijen, M. (2001). Maintaining contact with people with severe mental illness: 5-year follow-up of assertive outreach. *Social Psychiatry and Psychiatric Epidemiology, 36*, 444–447.

Frazier, S. N., & Vela, J. (2014). Dialectical behavior therapy for the treatment of anger and aggressive behavior: A review. *Aggression and Violent Behavior, 19*(2), 156–163.

Frogley, C., Taylor, D., Dickens, G., & Picchioni, M. (2012). A systematic review of the evidence of clozapine's anti-aggressive effects. *International Journal of Neuropsychopharmacology, 15*(9), 1–21.

Fruzzetti, A. E., & Levensky, E. R. (2000). Dialectical behavior therapy for domestic violence: *Cognitive and Behavioral Practice, 7*, 435–447.

Galietta, M., & Rosenfeld, B. (2012). Adapting dialectical behavior therapy (DBT) for the treatment of psychopathy. *The International Journal of Forensic Mental Health*, *11*(4), 325–335. doi:10.1080/14999013.2012.746762

Gansle, K. A. (2005). The effectiveness of school-based anger interventions and programs: A meta-analysis. *Journal of School Psychology*, *43*, 321–341.

Geddes, J. R., Burgess, S., Hawton, K., Jamison, K., & Goodwin, G. M. (2004). Long-term lithium therapy for bipolar disorder: Systematic review and meta-analysis of randomized controlled trials. *American Journal of Psychiatry*, *161*, 217–222.

Gendreau, P., & Goggin, C. (1996). Principles of effective programming with offenders. *Forum on Corrections Research*, *8*, 38–40.

Gilbert, A. R., Moser, L. L., Van Dorn, R. A., Swanson, J. W., Wilder, C. M., Robbins, P. C., ... Swartz, M. S. (2010). Reductions in arrest under assisted outpatient treatment in New York. *Psychiatric Services*, *61*, 996–999.

Gillies, D., Sampson, S., Beck, A., & Rathbone, J. (2013). Benzodiazepines for psychosis-induced aggression or agitation. *Cochrane Database of Systematic Reviews*, *4*, CD003079.

Gobbi, G., Gaudreau, P., & Leblanc, N. (2006). Efficacy of topiramate, valproate, and their combination on aggression/agitation behavior in patients with psychosis. *Journal of Clinical Psychopharmacology*, *26*(5), 467–473.

Gutteling, B. M., Montagne, B., Nijs, M., & van den Bosch, L. M. (2012). Dialectical behavior therapy: Is outpatient group psychotherapy an effective alternative to individual psychotherapy?: Preliminary conclusions. *Comprehensive Psychiatry*, *53*(8), 1161–1168. doi:10.1016/j.comppsych.2012.03.017

Guy, L. S., & Douglas, K. S. (2014). Major mental disorder and violence. In C. A. Pietz & C. A. Mattson (Eds.), *Violent offenders: Understanding and assessment* (p. 77–98). New York, NY: Oxford.

Haddock, G., Barrowclough, Shaw, J. J., Dunn, G., Novaco, R. W., & Tarrier, N. (2009). Cognitive-behavioural therapy v. social activity therapy for people with psychosis and a history of violence: Randomised controlled trial. *British Journal of Psychiatry*, *194*, 152–157.

Hanson, R. K., & Harris, A. J. R. (2000). Where should we intervene? Dynamic predictors of sexual offense recidivism. *Criminal Justice and Behavior*, *27*, 6–35.

Hennen, J., & Baldessarini, R. (2005). Suicidal risk during treatment with clozapine: A meta-analysis. *Schizophrenia Research*, *73*(2), 139–145.

Higashi, K., Medic, G., Littlewood, K. J., Diez, T. Granström, O., & De Hert, M. (2013). Medication adherence in schizophrenia: Factors influencing adherence and consequences of nonadherence, a systematic literature review. *Therapeutic Advances in Psychopharmacology*, *3*(4), 200–218.

Ho, B. V., Carter, M., & Stephenson, J. (2010). Anger management using a cognitive-behavioural approach for children with special education needs: A literature review and meta-analysis. *International Journal of Disability, Development and Education*, *57*, 245–265. doi:10.1080/1034912X.2010.501169

Hodel, B., & West, A. (2003). A cognitive training for mentally ill offenders with treatment-resistant schizophrenia. *Journal of Forensic Psychiatry and Psychology*, *14*, 554–568.

Hodgins, S. (2014). Antipsychotics, mood stabilisers, and reductions in violence. *The Lancet*, *384*(9949), 1167–1168.

Hodgins, S., Carlin, P., Moorhouse, R., Legge, K., & Khalid, F. (2011). Letter to the editor: Reducing antisocial behaviour among patients with severe mental illness living in the community: A feasibility study of the Reasoning and Rehabilitation programme. *Criminal Behaviour and Mental Health*, *21*, 75–76.

Hollenhorst, P. S. (1998). What do we know about anger management programs in corrections? *Federal Probation*, *62*, 52–64.

Hornsveld, R. H. J. (2005). Evaluation of aggression control therapy for violent forensic psychiatric patients. *Psychology, Crime and Law*, *11*, 403–410.

Hornsveld, R. H. J., Nijman, H. L. I., Hollin, C. R., & Kraaimaat, F. W. (2008). Aggression control therapy for violent forensic psychiatric patients: Method and clinical practice. *International Journal of Offender Therapy and Comparative Criminology*, *52*, 222–233.

Hough, W. G., & O'Brien, K. P. (2005). The effect of community treatment orders on offending rates. *Psychiatry, Psychology and the Law*, *12*, 411–423.

Howells, K. (2004). Anger and its links to violent offending. *Psychiatry, Psychology and Law*, *11*, 189–196. doi:10.1375/1321871042707278

Howells, K., Watt, B., Hall, G., & Baldwin, S. (1997). Developing programs for violent offenders. *Legal and Criminological Psychology*, *2*, 117–128.

Huband, N., Ferriter, M., Nathan, R., & Jones, H. (2010). Antiepileptic drugs for treating recurrent aggression and associated impulsivity. *Cochrane Database of Systematic Reviews*, *2*, CD003499.

Jones, D., & Hollin, C. R. (2004). Managing problematic anger: The development of a treatment program for personality disordered patients in high security. *The International Journal of Forensic Mental Health*, *3*, 197–210. doi:10.1080/14999013.2004.10471207

Jones, R. M., Arlidge, J., Gillham, R., Reagu, S., van den Bree, M., & Taylor, P. J. (2011). Efficacy of mood stabilisers in the treatment of impulsive or repetitive aggression: Systematic review and meta-analysis. *British Journal of Psychiatry*, *198*, 93–98.

Joyce, C. J., Dillane, J., & Vasquez, E. A. (2013). The role of anger in offending: A grounded theory analysis of mentally disordered patients. *Journal of Forensic Psychiatry and Psychology*, *24*, 247–268. doi:10.1080/14789949.2013.773454

Kane, J. M., Leucht, S., Carpenter, D., & Docherty, J. P. (2003). The expert consensus guideline series: Optimizing pharmacologic treatment of psychotic disorders. *Journal of Clinical Psychiatry*, *64*(Suppl. 12), 1–100.

Khushu, A., Powney, M. J. & Adams, C. E. (2012). Haloperidol for long-term aggression in psychosis (Protocol). *Cochrane Database of Systematic Reviews*, *5*, CD009830.

Killaspy, H., Bebbington, P., Blizard, R., Johnson, S., Nolan, F., Pilling, S., & King, M. (2006). The REACT study: Randomised evaluation of assertive community treatment in north London. *British Medical Journal*, *332*, 815–820.

Koerner, K. & Dimeff, L. A. (2000). Further data on dialectical behavior therapy. *Clinical Psychology: Science and Practice*, *7*(1), 104–112. doi:10.1093/clipsy/7.1.104

Koons, C. R., Chapman, A. L., Betts, B. B., O'Rourke, B., Morse, N., & Robins, C. J. (2006). Dialectical behavior therapy adapted for the vocational rehabilitation of significantly disabled mentally ill adults. *Cognitive and Behavioral Practice*, *13*(2), 146–156. doi:10.1016/j.cbpra.2005.04.003

Koons, C. R., Robins, C. J., Tweed, J. L., Lynch, T. R., Gonzalez, A. M., Morse, J. Q., ... Bastian, L. A. (2001). Efficacy of dialectical behavior therapy in women veterans with borderline personality disorder. *Behavior Therapy*, *32*(2), 371–390. doi:10.1016/S0005-7894(01)80009-5

Krakowski, M. I., Czobor, P., Citrome, L., Bark, N., & Cooper, T. (2006). Atypical antipsychotic agents in the treatment of violent patients with schizophrenia and schizoaffective disorder. *Archives of General Psychiatry, 63*(6), 622–629.

Kunz, M., Yates, K. F., Czobor, P., Rabinowitz, S., Lindenmayer, J-P, & Volavka, J. (2004). Course of patients with histories of aggression and crime after discharge from a cognitive-behavioral program. *Psychiatric Services, 55,* 654–659.

Leucht, C., Heres, S., Kane, J. M., Kissling, W., Davis, J. M., &Leucht, S. (2011). Oral versus depot antipsychotic drugs for schizophrenia—A critical systematic review and meta-analysis of randomised long-term trials. *Schizophrenia Research, 127,* 83–92.

Leucht, S., Tardy, M., Komossa, K., Heres, S., Kissling, W., Salanti, G., & Davis, J. M. (2012). Antipsychotic drugs versus placebo for relapse prevention in schizophrenia: A systematic review and meta-analysis. *The Lancet, 379*(9831), 2063–2071.

Leucht, S., Werner, K., McGrath, J., & White, P. (2007). Carbamazepine for schizophrenia. *Cochrane Database of Systematic Reviews, 3,* CD001258.

Liberman, R. P., Mueser, K. T., & Wallace, C. J. (1986). Social skills training for schizophrenic individuals at risk for relapse. *American Journal of Psychiatry, 143,* 523–526.

Lindenmayer, J. P., & Kotsaftis, A. (2000). Use of sodium valproate in violent and aggressive behaviors: A critical review. *Journal of Clinical Psychiatry, 61,* 123–128.

Lindenmayer, J., Liu-Seifert, H., Kulkarni, P. M., Kinon, B. J., Stauffer, V., Edwards, S. E., . . . Volavka, J. (2009). Medication nonadherence and treatment outcome in patients with schizophrenia or schizoaffective disorder with suboptimal prior response. *Journal of Clinical Psychiatry, 70*(7), 990–996.

Linehan, M. M. (1987). Dialectical behavioral therapy: A cognitive behavioral approach to parasuicide. *Journal of Personality Disorders, 1,* 328–333.

Linehan, M. M. (1993). *Cognitive-behavioral treatment of borderline personality disorder.* New York, NY: Guilford.

Linehan, M. M. (2000). The empirical basis of dialectical behavior therapy: Development of new treatments versus evaluation of existing treatments. *Clinical Psychology: Science and Practice, 7*(1), 113–119. doi:10.1093/clipsy/7.1.113

Linehan, M. M. (2013). What psychiatrists should know about dialectical behavior therapy. *Psychiatric Annals, 43*(4), 148. doi:10.3928/00485713-20130403-02

Long, C. C., Fulton, B., Dolley, O., & Hollin, C. R. (2011). Dealing with feelings: The effectiveness of cognitive behavioural group treatment for women in secure settings. *Behavioural and Cognitive Psychotherapy, 39*(2), 243–247.

Lovell, D., Allen, D., Johnson, C., & Jemelka, R. (2001). Evaluating the effectiveness of residential treatment for prisoners with mental illness. *Criminal Justice and Behavior, 28,* 83–104.

Lynch, T. R., Chapman, A. L., Rosenthal, M. Z., Kuo, J. R., & Linehan, M. M. (2006). Mechanisms of change in dialectical behavior therapy: Theoretical and empirical observations. *Journal of Clinical Psychology, 62*(4), 459–480.

Lynch, T. R., Cheavens, J. S., Cukrowicz, K. C., Thorp, S. R., Bronner, L., & Beyer, J. (2007). Treatment of older adults with co-morbid personality disorder and depression: A dialectical behavior therapy approach. *International Journal of Geriatric Psychiatry, 22*(2), 131–143. doi:10.1002/gps.1703

McCann, R. A., Ball, E. M., & Ivanoff, A. (2000). DBT with an inpatient forensic population: The CMHIP forensic model. *Cognitive and Behavioral Practice, 7*(4), 447–456. doi:10.1016/S1077-7229(00)80056-5

McCoy, M. L., Roberts, D. L., Hanrahan, P., Clay, R., & Luchins, D. J. (2004). Jail linkage assertive community treatment services for individuals with mental illnesses. *Psychiatric Rehabilitation Journal, 27,* 243–250.

McMain, S. F., Links, P. S., Gnam, W. H., Guimond, T., Cardish, R. J., Korman, L., & Streiner, D. L. (2009). A randomized trial of dialectical behavior therapy versus general psychiatric management for borderline personality disorder. *The American Journal of Psychiatry, 166*(12), 1365–1374. doi:10.1176/appi.ajp.2009.09010039

McMurran, M., Egan, V., Richardson, C., & Ahmadi, S. (1999). Social problem solving in mentally disordered offenders: A brief report. *Criminal Behaviour and Mental Health, 9,* 315–322.

McNiel, D. E., Sadeh, N., Delucchi, K. L., & Binder, R. L. (2015). Prospective study of violence risk reduction by a mental health court. *Psychiatric Services, 66,* 598–603.

Meichenbaum, D. (1985). *Stress inoculation training.* New York, NY: Plenum Press.

Mercer, D., Douglass, A. B., & Links, P. S. (2009). Meta-analyses of mood stabilizers, antidepressants and antipsychotics in the treatment of borderline personality disorder: Effectiveness for depression and anger symptoms. *Journal of Personality Disorders, 23,* 156–174.

Milton, J., Amin, S., Harrison, G., Jones, P., Croudace, P., Medley, I., & Brewen, J. (2001). Aggressive incidents in first-episode psychosis. *British Journal of Psychiatry, 178,* 433–440.

Mohamed, S. (2013). Dual diagnosis among intensive case management participants in the Veterans Health Administration: Correlates and outcomes. *Journal of Dual Diagnosis, 9,* 311–321.

Neacsiu, A. D., Rizvi, S. L., & Linehan, M. M. (2010). Dialectical behavior therapy skills use as a mediator and outcome of treatment for borderline personality disorder. *Behaviour Research and Therapy, 48*(9), 832–839. doi:10.1016/j.brat.2010.05.017

Nelson, J., & Papakostas, G. (2009). Atypical antipsychotic augmentation in major depressive disorder: A meta-analysis of placebo-controlled randomized trials. *American Journal of Psychiatry, 166,* 980–981.

Nelson-Gray, R. O., Keane, S. P., Hurst, R. M. Mitchell, J. T., Warbuton, J. B., Chok, J. T., & Cobb, A. R. (2006). A modified DBT skills training program for oppositional defiant adolescents: Promising preliminary findings. *Behaviour Research and Therapy, 44*(12), 1811–1820.

Nicoll, M., Beail, N., & Saxon, D. (2013). Cognitive behavioural treatment for anger in adults with intellectual disabilities: A systematic review and meta-analysis. *Journal of Applied Research in Intellectual Disabilities, 26,* 47–62. doi:10.1111/jar.12013

Novaco R. W. (1994). Anger as a risk factor for violence among the mentally disordered. In J. Monahan & H. Steadman (Eds.), *Violence and mental disorder: Developments in risk assessment* (pp. 232–259). University of Chicago Press, Chicago, IL.

Novaco, R. W. (1975). *Anger control: The development and evaluation of an experimental treatment.* Lexington, MA: Health.

Novaco, R. W. (1998). Anger as a risk factor for violence among the mentally disordered. In J. Monahan & H. Steadman (Eds.), *Violence and mental disorder: Developments in risk assessment* (pp. 21–59). Chicago, IL: University of Chicago Press.

Novaco, R. W. (2000). Anger. In A. Kazdin (Ed.), *Encyclopedia of psychology* (pp. 170–174). New York, NY: Oxford University Press.

Novaco, R. W. (2010). Anger and psychopathology. In M. Potegal, G. Stemmler, & C. Spielberger (Eds.), *International handbook of anger: Constituent and concomitant biological, psychological, and social processes* (pp. 465–497). New York, NY: Springer.

Novaco, R. W., & Whittington, R. (2013). Anger regulation for psychotic patients. In E. Fernandez (Ed.), *Treatments for anger in specific populations: Theory, application, and outcome* (pp. 114–137). New York, NY: Oxford University Press.

Pagadala, B., Jayaram, M. B., & Mitra, L. (2009). Aripiprazole for psychosis-induced aggression or agitation (Protocol). *Cochrane Database of Systematic Reviews, 4,* CD008074.

Paul, G. L., & Lentz, R. J. (1977). *Psychosocial treatment of chronic mental patients: Milieu versus social-learning programs.* Cambridge, MA: Harvard University Press.

Petersen, K., Nicholls, T., Brink, J., Douglas, K., Gagnon, N., Schmitz, N., Leech, N., & Lesage, A. (2015). Forensic and tertiary civil psychiatric inpatients: Comparing psychosocial, clinical, and risk profiles, and the prevalence of negative outcomes. Manuscript under review.

Phelan, J. C., Sinkewicz, M., Castille, D. M., Huz, S., & Link, B. G. (2010). Effectiveness and outcomes of assisted outpatient treatment in New York State. *Psychiatric Services, 61,* 137–143.

Powney, M. J., Adams, C. E., & Jones, H. (2011). Haloperidol (rapid tranquilisation) for psychosis induced aggression or agitation. *Cochrane Database of Systematic Reviews, 10,* CD009377.

Prado-Lima, P., Knijnik, L., Juruena, M., & Padilla, A. (2001). Lithium reduces maternal child abuse behaviour: A preliminary report. *Journal of Clinical Pharmacy and Therapeutics, 26* (4), 279–282.

Ratey, J. J.J.J., Sorgi, P., O'Driscoll, G. A., Sands, S., Daehler, M. L., Fletcher, J. R., . . . Lindem, K. J. (1992). Nadolol to treat aggression and psychiatric symptomatology in chronic psychiatric inpatients: A double-blind, placebo-controlled study. *Journal of Clinical Psychiatry, 53*(2), 41–46.

Reagu, S., Jones, R., Kumari, V., & Taylor, P. J. (2013). Angry affect and violence in the context of a psychotic illness: A systematic review and meta-analysis of the literature. *Schizophrenia Research, 146,* 46–52. doi:10.1016/j.schres.2013.01.024

Rees-Jones, A., Gudjonsson, G., Young, S. (2012). A multi-site controlled trial of a cognitive skills program for mentally disordered offenders. *BMC Psychiatry, 12,* 44.

Renwick, S., Black, L., Ramm, M., & Novaco, R. W. (2011). Anger treatment with forensic hospital patients. *Legal and Criminological Psychology, 2,* 103–116.

Robins, C. J. & Chapman, A. L. (2004). Dialectical behavior therapy: Current status, recent developments, and future directions. *Journal of Personality Disorders 18,* 73–89. doi:10.1521/pedi.18.1.73.32771

Rosenfeld, B., Galietta, M., Ivanoff, A., Garcia-Mansilla, A., Martinez, R., Fava, J., . . . Green, D. (2007). Dialectical behavior therapy for the treatment of stalking offenders. *The International Journal of Forensic Mental Health, 6*(2), 95–103. doi:10.1080/14999013.2007.10471254

Ross, R. R., & Fabiano, E. A. (1985). *Time to think: A cognitive model of delinquency prevention and offender rehabilitation.* Johnson City, TN: Institute of Social Science and Arts.

Saini, M. (2009). A meta-analysis of the psychological treatment of anger: Developing guidelines for evidence-based practice. *Journal of The American Academy of Psychiatry and the Law, 37,* 473–488.

Sakdalan, J. A., & Gupta, R. (2014). Wise mind—risky mind: A reconceptualisation of dialectical behaviour therapy concepts and its application to sexual offender treatment. *Journal of Sexual Aggression, 20*(1), 110–120. doi:10.1080/13552600.2012.724457

Sakdalan, J. A., Shaw, J., & Collier, V. (2010). Staying in the here-and-now: A pilot study on the use of dialectical behaviour therapy group skills training for forensic clients with intellectual disability. *Journal of Intellectual Disability Research, 54*(6), 568–572. doi:10.1111/j.1365-2788.2010.01274.x

Scheel, K. R. (2000). The empirical basis of dialectical behavior therapy: Summary, critique, and implications. *Clinical Psychology: Science and Practice, 7*(1), 68–86. doi:10.1093/clipsy/7.1.68

Schwarz, C., Volz, A., Li, C., & Leucht, S. (2008). Valproate for schizophrenia. *Cochrane Database of Systematic Reviews, 3,* CD004028.

Seto, M. C., Crocker, A. G., Nicholls, T. L., Côté, G. (2014). Towards a national agenda on mental health and criminal justice. *Psynopsis, 36*(1), 12–13.

Sheard, M. (1971). Effect of lithium on human aggression. *Nature, 230* (12), 113–114.

Sheard, M., Marini, J., Bridges, C., & Wagner, E. (1976). The effect of lithium on impulsive aggressive behavior in man. *American Journal of Psychiatry, 133,* 1409–1413.

Shelton, D., Kesten, K., Zhang, W., & Trestman, R. (2011). Impact of a dialectic behavior therapy—Corrections modified (DBT-CM) upon behaviorally challenged incarcerated male adolescents. *Journal of Child and Adolescent Psychiatric Nursing, 24*(2), 105–113. doi:10.1111/j.1744-6171.2011.00275.x

Shelton, D., Sampl, S., Kesten, K. L., Zhang, W., & Trestman, R. L. (2009). Treatment of impulsive aggression in correctional settings. *Behavioral Sciences and the Law, 27*(5), 787–800.

Shingler, J. (2004). A process of cross-fertilization: What sex offender treatment can learn from dialectical behaviour therapy. *Journal of Sexual Aggression, 10*(2), 171–180. doi:10.1080/13552600412331289050

Solomon, P., Draine, J., & Meyerson, A. (1994). Jail recidivism and receipt of community mental health services. *Hospital and Community Psychiatry, 45,* 793–797.

Spielberger C. D., Reheiser E. C. & Sydeman S. J. (1995). Measuring the experience, expression, and control of anger. In H. Kassinove (Ed.), *Anger disorders: Definitions, diagnosis, and treatment* (pp. 49–67). Washington, DC: Taylor & Francis.

Stermac, L. E. (1986). Anger control treatment for forensic patients. *Journal of Interpersonal Violence, 1,* 446–457.

Stroup, T., Lieberman, J. A., McEvoy, J. P., Davis, S. M., Swartz, M. S., Keefe, R. E., . . . Hsiao, J. K. (2009). Results of phase 3 of the CATIE schizophrenia trial. *Schizophrenia Research, 107*(1), 1–12.

Sukhodolsky, D. G., Kassinove, H., & Gorman, B. S. (2004). Cognitive-behavioral therapy for anger in children and adolescents: A meta-analysis. *Aggression and Violent Behavior, 9,* 247–269.

Swanson, J. W., Swartz, M. S., Borum, R., Hiday, V. A., Wagner, H. R., & Burns, B. J. (2000). Involuntary out-patient commitment and reduction of violent behaviour in persons with severe mental illness. *British Journal of Psychiatry, 176,* 324–331.

Swanson, J. W., Swartz, M. S., Elbogen, E. B., & Van Dorn, R. A. (2004). Reducing violence risk in persons with schizophrenia: Olanzapine versus risperidone. *Journal of Clinical Psychiatry, 65,* 1666–1673.

Swanson, J. W., Van Dorn, R. A., Swartz, M. S., Robbins, P. C., Steadman, H. J., McGuire, T. G., & Monahan, J. (2013). The cost of assisted outpatient treatment: Can it save states money? *American Journal of Psychiatry, 170*, 1423–1432.

Swanson, J., Swartz, M., & Elbogen, E. (2004). Effectiveness of atypical antipsychotic medications in reducing violent behavior among persons with schizophrenia in community-based treatment. *Schizophrenia Bulletin, 30*(1), 3–20.

Swanson, J., Swartz, M., Van Dorn, R., Volavka, J., Monahan, J., Stroup, T., ... Lieerman, J. A. (2008). Comparison of antipsychotic medication effects on reducing violence in people with schizophrenia. *British Journal of Psychiatry, 193*(1), 37–43.

Swartz, M. S., Swanson, J. W., Steadman, H., Robbins, P., & Monahan, J. (2009). *New York State assisted outpatient treatment program evaluation.* Durham, NC: Duke University School of Medicine.

Tafrate, R. C. (1995). Evaluation of treatment strategies for adult anger disorders. In H. Kassinove (Ed.), *Anger disorders: Definition, diagnosis, and treatment* (pp. 109–129). Washington, DC: Taylor & Francis.

Taylor, J. L., Novaco, R. W., Gillmer, B., & Thorne, I. (2002). Cognitive-behavioural treatment of anger intensity among offenders with intellectual disabilities. *Journal of Applied Research in Intellectual Disabilities, 15*, 151–165.

Timmerman, I. G. H., & Emmelkamp, P. M. G. (2005). The effects of cognitive-behavioral treatment for forensic in-patients. *International Journal of Offender Therapy and Comparative Criminology, 49*, 590–606.

Topiwala, A., & Fazel, S. (2011). The pharmacological management of violence in schizophrenia: A structured review. *Expert Review of Neurotherapeutics, 11*(1), 53–63.

Travis, R. W., & Sturmey, P. (2013). Using behavioural skills training to treat aggression in adults with mild intellectual disability in a forensic setting. *Journal of Applied Research in Intellectual Disabilities, 26*, 481–488. doi:10.1111/jar.12033

Trupin, E. W., Stewart, D. G., Beach, B., & Boesky, L. (2002). Effectiveness of a dialectical behaviour therapy program for incarcerated female juvenile offenders. *Child and Adolescent Mental Health, 7*(3), 121–127.

Tupin, J., Smith, D., Clanon, T., Kim, L., Nugent, A., & Group, A. (1973). The long-term use of lithium in aggressive prisoners. *Comprehensive Psychiatry, 14*(4), 311–317.

Van den Bosch, L. M. C., Hysaj, M., & Jacobs, P. (2012). DBT in an outpatient forensic setting. *International Journal of Law and Psychiatry, 35*, 311–316.

Van Putten, T., & Sanders, D. (1975). Lithium in treatment failures. *Journal of Nervous and Mental Disease, 161*(4), 255–264.

Vangala, R., Ahmed, U. & Ahmed, R. (2012). Loxapine inhaler for psychosis-induced aggression or agitation (Protocol). *Cochrane Database of Systematic Reviews, 11*, CD010190.

Ventura, L. A., Cassel, C. A., Jacoby, J. E., & Huang, B. (1998). Case management and recidivism of mentally ill persons released from jail. *Psychiatric Services, 49*, 1330–1337.

Volavka, J., & Citrome, L. (2008). Heterogeneity of violence in schizophrenia and implications for long-term treatment. *International Journal of Clinical Practice, 62*(8), 1237–1245.

Volavka, J., Czobor, P., Nolan, K., Sheitman, B., Lindenmayer, J. P., Citrome, L., ... Lieberman, J. A. (2004). Overt aggression and psychotic symptoms in patients with schizophrenia treated with clozapine, olanzapine, risperidone, or haloperidol. *Journal of Clinical Psychopharmacology, 24*(2), 225–228.

Volavka, J., Swanson, J. W., Citrome, L. L. (2012). Understanding and managing violence in schizophrenia. In J. A. Lieberman & R. M. Murray (Eds.), *Comprehensive care of schizophrenia: A textbook of clinical management* (pp. 262–290). New York, NY: Oxford University Press.

Volavka, J., Zito, J., Vitrai, J., & Czobor, P. (1993). Clozapine effects on hostility and aggression in schizophrenia. *Journal of Clinical Psychiatry, 13*(4), 287–289.

Walsh, E., Gilvarry, C., Samele, C., Harvey, K., Manley, C., Tyrer, P., ... Fahy, T. (2001). Reducing violence in severe mental illness: Randomised controlled trial of intensive case management compared with standard care. *British Medical Journal, 323*, 1–5.

Watt, B. D., & Howells, K. (1999). Skills training for aggression control: Evaluation of an anger management programme for violent offenders. *Legal and Criminological Psychology, 4*(Part 2), 285–300. doi:10.1348/135532599167914

Wilkie, F. & Fenton, M. (2012). Quetiapine for psychosis-induced aggression or agitation (Protocol). *Cochrane Database of Systematic Reviews, 4*, CD009801.

Wilson, D., Tien, G., & Eaves, D. (1995). Increasing the community tenure of mentally disordered offenders: An assertive case management program. *International Journal of Law and Psychiatry, 18*, 61–69.

Wilson, H., Barton, L., & Maguire, T. (2011). Implementation of anger management interventions in a psychiatric intensive care unit. *Journal of Psychiatric Intensive Care, 7*, 35–39. doi:10.1017/S1742646410000208

Wix, S. (2003). Dialectical behaviour therapy observed. *The British Journal of Forensic Practice, 5*(2), 3–8. doi:10.1108/14636646200300008

Woodbury, K. A., & Popenoe, E. J. (2008). Implementing dialectical behaviour therapy with adolescents and their families in a community outpatient clinic. *Cognitive and Behavioral Practice, 15*(3), 277–286.

Wright, S., Day, A., & Howells, K. (2009). Mindfulness and the treatment of anger problems. *Aggression and Violent Behavior, 14*(5), 396–401. doi:10.1016/j.avb.2009.06.008

Yates, K. F., Kunz, M., Khan, A., Volavka, J., & Rabinowitz, S. (2010). Psychiatric patients with a history of aggression and crime five years after discharge from a cognitive-behavioral program. *The Journal of Forensic Psychiatry and Psychology, 21*, 167–188.

Yates, K., Kunz, M., Czobor, P., Rabinowitz, S., Lindenmayer, J-P, & Volavka, J. (2005). A cognitive, behaviorally based program for patients with persistent mental illness and a history of aggression, crime, or both: Structure and correlates of completers of the program. *Journal of the American Academy of Psychiatry and the Law, 33*, 214–222.

Yip, V. C.-Y., Gudjonsson, G. H., Perkins, D., Doidge, A., Hopkin, G., & Young, S. (2013). A non-randomised controlled trial of the R&R2MHP cognitive skills program in high risk male offenders with severe mental illness. *BMC Psychiatry, 13*, 267. doi:10.1186/1471-244X-13-267

Young, S., Chick, K., & Gudjonsson, G. (2010). A preliminary evaluation of reasoning and rehabilitation 2 in mentally disordered offenders (R&R2M) across two secure forensic settings in the United Kingdom. *The Journal of Forensic Psychiatry and Psychology, 21*, 336–349.

Young, S. J., & Ross, R. R. (2007). *R&R2 for youths and adults with mental health problems: A prosocial competence training program.* Ottawa, ON: Cognitive Centre of Canada.

Yudofsky, S. C., Silver, J. M., Jackson, W., Endicott, J., & Williams, D. (1986). The Overt Aggression Scale for the objective rating of verbal and physical aggression. *American Journal of Psychiatry, 143*, 35–39.

The Psychological Treatment of Victims of Interpersonal Violence

Monica M. Fitzgerald *and* Nyla Nasser

Abstract

This chapter provides a brief overview of empirically supported psychosocial treatments for adults who have developed serious clinical psychiatric disorders, such as posttraumatic stress disorder (PTSD), and other psychosocial and behavioral problems as a result of exposure to interpersonal victimization and violence. In this chapter, we will describe important aspects of creating a safe and therapeutic environment for victims of interpersonal violence and the evidence-based core treatment components and strategies for use with adult victims of interpersonal violence with PTSD. Finally, we will introduce three empirically supported treatment programs incorporating some or all of the core treatment components discussed. We will also discuss emerging and novel interventions for the treatment of PTSD in adults that have varying levels of theoretical and empirical evidence.

Key Words: interpersonal violence, victim, intervention, evidence-based treatment, violent victimization, adult exposure therapy, cognitive-behavioral intervention

As defined by the World Health Organization, interpersonal violence is the "intentional use of physical force or power, threatened or actual, against another person that either results in or has a high likelihood of resulting in injury, death, psychological harm, maldevelopment, or deprivation" (World Health Organization [WHO], 2014). Interpersonal violence refers to violence between individuals, and it can be subdivided into the two categories: *family and intimate partner violence* and *community violence*. Family and intimate partner violence includes instances of child maltreatment (e.g., sexual, physical, and psychological), intimate partner violence, and elder abuse. Community violence includes youth violence, assault by strangers, violence related to property crimes, and violence in the workplace and other institutions (WHO, 2014).

Interpersonal violence is an enormous public health problem and one of the leading causes of death in adolescents and young adults in the United States and around the world. Estimates from the WHO's global burden of disease indicate that approximately 486,493 people died in 2011 as a result of interpersonal violence (Mercy et al., 2014). Fatal injuries, however, represent only a small fraction of the burden of interpersonal violence (Mercy, Krug, Dahlberg, & Zwi, 2003). The health and social consequences of nonfatal interpersonal violence are much broader than the risk of death and injury, often increasing lifelong vulnerability to a broad range of emotional, behavioral, and physical health problems for the victim, while also compromising national and local economics (Mercy et al., 2014).

In this chapter, we will address the treatment of adults who have developed serious clinical psychiatric disorders, such as posttraumatic stress disorder (PTSD), and other psychosocial and behavioral problems as a result of their exposure to interpersonal victimization and violence. These victims are seeking recovery to healthy levels of functioning and require help beyond the immediate management of a behavioral emergency or crisis situation. (For more information on the immediate management of a behavioral emergency or crisis situation with an adult, please refer to chapters in section III of this volume.) This chapter will discuss a number of psychosocial interventions currently available to reduce PTSD symptoms in adult victims when at least 1 month has passed since the victim's index event. We will begin by describing the potential mental, behavioral, physical, and social impacts that interpersonal violence can have on its victims. Next, we will discuss important aspects of creating a safe and therapeutic environment for victims of interpersonal violence to engage in treatment, as well as the evidence-based core treatment components and strategies for adult victims of interpersonal violence with PTSD. Finally, we will introduce three empirically supported treatment programs incorporating some or all of the core treatment components discussed. We will also address several emerging and novel interventions for the treatment of PTSD in adults that have varying levels of theoretical and empirical evidence.

The Prevalence and Impact of Interpersonal Violence

A large number of epidemiological studies with nationally representative samples of youth in the United States document high rates of victimization and violence exposure in childhood and adolescence, with approximately 60% of youth reporting exposure to violence within the past year, and one in 10 experiencing five or more different types of victimization (Finkelhor, Turner, Ormrod, Hamby, & Kracke, 2009). Ongoing studies tracking large groups of people throughout their lives to assess the prevalence and impact of violence exposure and childhood stressors on health find similar rates of exposure. For example, the Adverse Childhood Experiences Study tracked over 17,000 health maintenance organization participants and found that 63% had experienced at least one category of childhood trauma in their lifetime. Over 20% have experienced three or more categories of *adverse childhood experiences* (ACE), including but not limited to physical abuse, sexual abuse, physical neglect, violence within the home, and household alcohol and/or drug use (Felitti et al., 1998; Brown et al., 2009). These two large studies, as well as other research, confirm that children are not only frequently exposed to violence, but many are experiencing multiple forms of violence beginning at an early age (Abram et al., 2013; Chapman, Dube, & Anda, 2007; Ford, Grasso, Hawke, & Chapman, 2013; Walsh, Gonsalves, Scalora, King, & Hardyman, 2012).

Fortunately, many youth and adult victims react to their exposure to violence with remarkable resilience, showing a decrease in psychological symptoms within a few days or weeks of the traumatic event (Bonnano, 2004; Bonnano, Westphal, & Mancini, 2011). However, a significant portion of youth experiencing interpersonal violence will suffer from high levels of anxiety, stress, depression, uncontrollable anger, and impaired interpersonal and vocational functioning (Finkelhor et al., 2009; Hillis et al., 2004). Although it is estimated that only 5%–10% of victims will go on to develop serious psychiatric disorders, such as PTSD, major depression, and substance use disorders (Ozer, Best, Lipsey, & Weiss, 2003), victims of abuse and violence experience much higher rates of mental health problems relative to peers who have had no exposure to these experiences (e.g., Godbout, Briere, Sabourin, & Lussier, 2014; Briere & Elliott, 2003; Finkelhor, Turner, Hamby, & Ormrod, 2011). In fact, exposure to interpersonal violence accounts for 25.9%–32% of later onset disorders in adolescents and adults (Green et al., 2010). (For a more detailed description of the prevalence of violent victimization and the acute and chronic medical and psychological problems commonly experienced by victims of crime, please refer to chapter 11 in this volume.)

The development of PTSD is the most commonly reported negative psychological outcome in adult victims *of interpersonal violence,* with a lifetime prevalence of nearly 8% among individuals who have reported exposure to at least one traumatic event in their lives (McLaughlin et al., 2013). PTSD is characterized by recurrent reexperiencing of the traumatic event, avoidance of reminders of the event, emotional numbing and withdrawal, and hyperarousal. Criteria for PTSD in the Diagnostic and Statistical Manual of Mental Disorders (5th ed., DSM-5; American Psychiatric Association [APA], 2013) is met by the following characteristics, each of which must have occurred for a period of more than 1 month following the index event: (a) reliving the traumatic event or frightening elements of it; (b) persistent avoidance of thoughts, memories, people, and places associated with the event; (c) negative alterations in cognitions and mood, and emotional numbing; and (d) symptoms of elevated arousal and reactivity beginning or worsening after the traumatic event(s) occurred (APA, 2013). It is important to note that PTSD is more often associated with other co-occurring disorders than as a sole diagnosis. National epidemiological research has shown that 61%–80% of individuals with lifetime PTSD also suffer from lifetime depression, anxiety disorders, chemical abuse/dependence, or suicidal attempts (Foa, Keane, & Friedman, 2000; Pietrzak, Goldstein, Southwick, & Grant, 2011). Comorbidity with PTSD may involve the individual developing a primary psychiatric disorder first, which then predisposes him or her to experiencing trauma and associated PTSD. Consistent with this view, a significant proportion of individuals with PTSD and a comorbid disorder develop PTSD after prior onset of another disorder (e.g., Breslau, 2009; Cottler, Compton, & Mager, 1992). There is additional research showing that the onset of PTSD can lead to simultaneous or subsequent vulnerability to developing other clinical disorders (Breslau, 2009). A PTSD diagnosis following exposure to interpersonal violence is also said to increase vulnerability to adverse physical health outcomes including cardiovascular, neurological, and gastrointestinal health, such as ischemic heart disease, cancer, chronic lung disease, skeletal fracture, and liver disease (Pacella, Hruska, & Delahanty, 2013; Felitti et al., 1998). Further, if left untreated, PTSD tends to follow a chronic, unremitting course. (Please see chapter 11 in this volume to gain additional information about vulnerability to PTSD and its comorbid psychiatric counterparts.

Finally, exposure to interpersonal violence and traumatic and stressful childhood events also increase a victim's likelihood to engage in countless risk behaviors, delinquency, violent offenses and revictimization (Whitfield, Anda, Dube, & Felitti, 2003), suicidal attempts (Brodsky et al., 2001), and development of health problems, such as regular smoking (Adams et al., 2013), drinking alcohol and using illicit drugs in early and mid-adolescence (Dube et al., 2006), early age of first intercourse and development of sexually transmitted diseases (Hillis, Anda, Felitti, Nordenberg, & Marchbanks, 2000), and adolescent pregnancy (Anda et al., 2002; Hillis et al., 2004). (For a more comprehensive review of the impact of early life trauma on health and disease, see Lanius, Vermetten, & Pain [2010], and refer to chapter 11 of this volume to learn more about the links between violent victimization, offending, and mental health.)

It is important for a clinician working with victims of interpersonal violence to be aware of the different factors specific to the victim and the victim's experience of trauma that influence the impact on that particular individual. Abuse variables that have been associated with long-term psychological and social difficulties include (a) age at onset of maltreatment, (b) whether the abuse was intrafamilial or extra familial, (c) the frequency and/or duration of the abusive incidents, and (d) the invasiveness of the act (e.g., penetration during sexual abuse, injury resulting from physical abuse, and so on) (Briere & Jordan, 2009). In addition, gender, race, lower socioeconomic status, previous psychological dysfunction or disorder, less functional coping styles, family dysfunction, and a history of psychopathology and genetic disposition have also been identified as determinants for negative psychological outcomes (Briere & Jordan, 2009; Breslau, 2009). Nationally representative surveys (e.g., Forbes et al., 2014) and meta-analytic studies (e.g., Chen et al., 2010) emphasize the increased risk for PTSD among individuals with prior trauma history, with evidence of a dose-response relationship between the number of prior traumatic experiences and subsequent PTSD symptom severity (Cougle, Resnick, & Kilpatrick, 2013; Finkelhor et al., 2011; Norman et al., 2012). Finally, individuals with the capacity to react to a traumatic event with optimism, cognitive flexibility, and active coping skills are more likely to be resilient to serious negative psychological impact than individuals who interpret a traumatic experience as intensely negative (Bradley et al., 2011; Iacoviello & Charney, 2014). This type of information is useful for clinicians learning about the unique experiences and reactions of individuals seeking mental health treatment who have experienced violence and trauma. Clinicians are encouraged to emphasize the strengths of these individuals in their recovery.

Initiating Treatment with Victims: Assessment, Safety, and the Therapeutic Alliance
Initial and Ongoing Assessment

Mental health providers treating victims of interpersonal violence should be ready to consider the full range of potential victimization effects on an individual when preparing to initiate treatment. With such complexity, there is a need for flexible intervention strategies that are customized the experience of a victim, address a larger portion of the victim's symptoms and are multimodal in approach. Relevant interventions for any given victim may range from treatment for victimization-related symptoms (e.g., exposure therapy, cognitive therapy, and/or pharmacotherapy), interventions for maladaptive or risky behaviors (e.g., substance abuse treatment, safe-sex education, parenting training), and advocacy with social service agencies for basic life necessities (e.g., referral to a shelter, financial aid, food stamps). For example, the treatment of a woman with a history of physical abuse as a child and interpersonal violence in previous relationships, who was recently held at gunpoint during a home burglary, may include interventions that (a) provide a safety plan and improve home safety measures (e.g., alarm system, new locks) to minimize fear in her home; (b) address cognitive distortions, such as all men are dangerous and out to hurt her, she is cursed, and/or she will never trust again; (c) provide in-vivo exposure and stress management techniques to decrease anxiety and establish feelings of safety in her home; (d) advocate for her with law enforcement and other supportive social agencies regarding the perpetrator's jail release and whereabouts, her legal rights, and her safety plan; and (e) help her gain stronger interpersonal skills.

There is a need for clinicians to intervene with each victim based on their specific clinical and social situation as opposed to making assumptions that certain symptoms or problems are present and, therefore, a specific treatment is indicated. Thus, clinicians must be knowledgeable and familiar with the empirical literature on victimization prevalence and trauma impact, yet they should also meet each client as a complete individual and strive to learn about the specific makeup of, and personal meaning created from, the victimization experience for him or her.

Initial and ongoing assessments are two very crucial components in identifying and successfully treating an individual's treatment targets. Initial assessment involves gathering detailed information about safety level, victimization history, mental health status, functional impairment, current substance abuse, and how these factors are affecting the individual's day-to-day experience at the start of treatment. The purpose of the initial screening is for the clinician to make a decision regarding the most appropriate intervention strategy for that particular client. Ongoing assessment is also important and should be considered a standard practice throughout the course of treatment. Clinicians should orient individuals to the importance of ongoing assessment and help them observe the progress they are making throughout treatment. This approach allows the individual to learn how their symptoms and concerns are changing over the course of therapy.

When conducting initial and ongoing assessments, it is important for the clinician to use validated measures. (For more information on the

assessment of PTSD, as well as a number of validated measures for use with adults with PTSD, please visit the US Department of Veterans Affairs National Center for PTSD website [http://www. ptsd.va.gov].)

Based on what a practitioner learns from the assessment, he or she selects an appropriate intervention. Fortunately, a number of highly effective trauma-focused, cognitive-behavioral interventions are available. Some are implemented soon after the traumatic event (i.e., within 4 weeks) to accelerate recovery and prevent long-term mental health problems such as the development of PTSD (e.g., Forbes et al., 2012). There are promising findings regarding the positive impact of modified evidence-based interventions, such as three sessions of prolonged exposure therapy delivered within hours of the trauma in the emergency department, in decreasing posttraumatic stress reactions and depression, compared with assessment alone (Rothbaum et al., 2012). A safe, therapeutic environment is critical for adult victims of interpersonal violence to effectively engage in both assessment and treatment.

The Importance of Safety

An important aspect of successfully initiating treatment in victims of interpersonal violence is to ensure that PTSD and trauma-specific therapy is begun only after a victim has been safely removed from any presenting crisis situations. Prior to beginning treatment, the clinician should first assess any medical problems or concerns that require immediate attention. Next, the likelihood of physical danger within an individual's environment should be assessed (Briere & Scott, 2006). Another immediate safety concern to address prior to beginning formal treatment is whether the individual is suicidal or a potential danger to others. These behaviors require immediate stabilization and often the clinician will need to make external referrals to emergency medical or psychiatric services, law enforcement, or social services. The presence of suicidal or homicidal ideation, self-destructive and impulsive behaviors, as well as any severe psychosis should continue to be routinely assessed throughout treatment. Finally, if an individual is in need of substance abuse detoxification, it is also important to address this problem before treatment begins (Foa et al., 2000). Individuals who actively use substances to relieve stress or avoid unpleasant emotions may not be able to tolerate the additional distress that can be activated by certain aspects of trauma-specific therapy approaches (Briere & Scott, 2006; Resick & Schnicke, 1992). However, there are promising integrative interventions (see McCauley, Killeen, Gros, Brady, & Back, 2012) gaining support that combine trauma-focused cognitive behavioral treatment with risk reduction treatment strategies for simultaneously addressing trauma-related psychopathology (e.g., PTSD and depression) and risk behaviors (substance use/abuse, risky sexual behavior, non-suicidal self-injury) (Danielson, 2007; Najavits, 2002).

The Therapeutic Alliance

Establishing a working relationship that is genuinely collaborative is essential for supporting effective psychological assessment and treatment with victims of violence (Foa & Rothbaum, 1998). A strong therapeutic alliance established in treatment has proven to be associated with positive therapeutic outcomes and considered an active ingredient in the remediation of PTSD in victims of interpersonal violence (e.g., Cloitre, Chase Stovall-McClough, Miranda, & Chemtob, 2004). The willingness of a client to open up and share his or her concerns, fears, anger, sadness, shame, regret, and other reactions related to traumatic experiences is likely to be increased by a positive, collaborative, warm relationship, and decreased by an evaluative, hierarchical, overly pragmatic, and/or coercive relationship. A clinician's sensitivity to developing a therapeutic alliance is critical given that some victims of interpersonal violence may have difficulty entering into and sustaining a working relationship with a clinician because of their issues with trusting others, especially authoritative figures (Briere & Scott, 2006). Consistently showing a warm, connected, empathic response to a client and collaboratively setting up predictable routines with treatment delivery will enhance a victims' feelings of safety and alliance. Many effective intervention techniques for the treatment of victims of interpersonal violence are based on some level of exposure to feared stimuli, cognitions, and painful memories associated with the individual's victimization experience. Clinicians must pay attention, therefore, to setting up a context or creating a space to help clients face their fears and gain mastery over painful trauma-related memories. A strong therapeutic bond established in an early phase of treatment has proven to predict how well individuals are able to make use of emotional regulation skills under the conditions of exposure, which in turn predicts the amelioration of PTSD symptoms (Cloitre et al.,

2004). The importance of working to develop and maintain a strong therapeutic alliance cannot be overemphasized to enhance engagement in treatment, collaborative goal-setting, clear communication if safety is disrupted, and taking steps toward achieving goals.

Evidence-Based Interventions for PTSD and Trauma Symptoms

There are several core treatment components, or intervention techniques, shared among trauma-focused interventions that are effective in improving long-term outcomes for victims of interpersonal violence with PTSD and other psychological sequelae (Chard, Ricksecker, Healy, Karlin, & Resick, 2012; Foa, Gillihan, & Bryant, 2013; Resick, Williams, Suvak, Monson, & Gradus, 2012; Foa et al., 2000; Rothbaum, Meadows, Resick, & Foy, 2000; Riggs, Cahill, & Foa, 2006). Treatments for victims of violence are often described as "trauma-focused," which means they deal directly with the trauma and its consequences. Most trauma-focused treatments are cognitive-behavioral interventions with two main characteristics: (a) helping clients confront safe trauma reminders through direct discussions about the trauma or through approaching trauma-related situations or images; and (b) aiming to refute clients' dysfunctional, damaging beliefs and perceptions related to their victimization or trauma experience (Foa et al., 2013). The core components of trauma-focused treatments in the field include (1) psychoeducation, (2) anxiety management training, (3) exposure therapy, and (4) cognitive therapy. These four techniques, rarely used in isolation, are commonly employed in combination in the context of various different interventions. The components may be conceptualized as the "active ingredients" of empirically supported or evidence-based treatments (EBTs), or "treatments that work." EBTs are those with written protocols that have been tested in well-controlled clinical trials, which generate better outcomes than passage of time, usual care, or alternative interventions. (For a discussion of EBTs, see Borkovec & Costonguay, 1998.) EBTs are structured, behavioral and goal-oriented. They involve working with individuals to identify target problems, set goals, measure progress toward those goals, build specific coping skills through practice, and give specific behavioral assignments.

EBTs involve manualized treatment protocols, which are sometimes criticized as being too rigid and less useful in real-world applications for clinicians treating individuals with complex presentations. However, most interventions are component-based and teach many generalizable skills, and there is a growing body of research showing that these treatments work with extremely diverse and complex trauma populations in the United States and internationally (Foa et al., 2013). Treatment protocols can be powerful tools to achieve optimal mental health outcomes for victims when they are tailored to meet the specific characteristics and concerns of the individual while maintaining adequate fidelity to evidence-based components within the protocol.

Core Intervention Techniques

Psychoeducation. Psychoeducation involves providing individuals with accurate information about the nature and prevalence of different forms of interpersonal violence and the common reactions people have after experiencing traumatic events. Victims experience a range of cognitive and emotional reactions including anxiety, shock, anger, confusion, and self-blame. Victims of violence may have misinformation that is fueling their cognitive and emotional responses. Psychoeducation can help validate clients' experiences, normalize their reactions, and dispel myths and faulty beliefs, all of which are associated with posttraumatic functioning. In simpler terms, psychoeducation helps clients learn (a) *they are not alone* (i.e., they are not the only ones to experience trauma), which can reduce feelings of stigma and isolation; (b) *they are not crazy or strange for feeling the way they do*, which can normalize and validate their trauma reactions; (c) *they are not to blame* or responsible for the victimization/abuse experience; and (d) *they can get better*, which instills hope and motivation for recovery. Psychoeducation is presented at the very beginning of treatment, sometimes starting with the initial phone call to engage clients in treatment. Psychoeducation should also be provided on an ongoing, as needed, basis whenever victims may benefit from additional information or to evince cognitive distortions about the trauma. Psychoeducation can be provided verbally, but printed materials that provide accurate information about trauma and its impact can also be helpful tools for educating victims, and they are easily accessible on the internet (e.g., http://www.ptsd.va.gov/public/understanding_ptsd/booklet.pdf). When presenting psychoeducation, it is helpful to fully engage the clients and explore their knowledge of trauma in an interactive, unbiased

manner, and to avoid didactic or passive reviews of the material. (For examples on how to present psychoeducation to victims, see Foa, Hembree, & Rothbaum, 2007; Resick & Schnicke, 1996; [http://www.musc.edu/cpt].)

Anxiety management training. Psychoeducation is often followed by some form of relaxation training or anxiety management training (AMT), in which individuals are taught strategies to reduce their overall levels of anxiety and cope with trauma-related distress using skills such as breathing retraining and progressive muscle relaxation (PMR) (Briere & Scott, 2006; Foa et al., 2007). These techniques are helpful when victims experience destabilizing, overwhelming emotions, physical agitation, and hypertension connected to the trauma, which might emerge throughout treatment. AMT techniques aim to build victims' emotion regulation skills to help them handle negative feelings and overwhelming distress so they can be successful in their lives, manage daily tasks (household chores, child care, work tasks), and not be derailed by intrusive trauma reminders, emotionally laden memories, and chronic levels of anxiety, dysphoria, and posttraumatic arousal.

AMT techniques are also referred to as *distress reduction* and *affect regulation skills training* (Cloitre, Koenen, Cohen, & Han, 2002). These strategies are intended to reduce acute destabilizing emotions and symptoms during therapy and to help clients increase their more general capacity to regulate emotional states (i.e., decrease negative emotional states and increase positive ones). AMT techniques are customized to the client and then practiced and rehearsed so the individual gains mastery of these skills in daily life to help deal with the trauma symptoms that often interfere with focusing at work, caring for children, managing a household, and being in social and public situations.

The most basic form of arousal reduction during treatment is learned relaxation, which includes breath training to teach the client how to optimally breathe and reduce hyperventilation and inappropriate ventilation, which victims often experience when anxious and distressed. PMR is often used to distinguish between feelings of tension and relaxation through a series of guided techniques of clenching and releasing muscles sequentially. Mindfulness-based breath training, guided visualization, yoga, meditation, and grounding techniques are often taught throughout treatment as well so that victims have a variety of approaches to manage their anxiety and inner experience. There are many resources, such as clinical workbooks and Web courses that describe how to implement the different AMT techniques in a step-by-step, detailed process, often with accompanying scripts (e.g., Rothbaum, Foa, & Hembree, 2007; Foa & Rothbaum, 2001; Cloitre et al., 2002; Levitt & Cloitre, 2006). Regardless of the label, anxiety management approaches all focus on increasing the client's capacity to tolerate painful emotional states related to trauma and to gain mastery in regulating these emotions in order to be present and thrive in life. When victims achieve a level of mastery of the use of AMT, exposure therapy techniques can then be introduced.

Exposure therapy. Exposure therapies for PTSD are considered first-line, gold standard treatment. With overwhelming scientific evidence proving they are efficacious in many randomized clinical trials, exposure therapies reliably reduce PTSD symptoms and other trauma-related symptoms in a wide range of populations, including female rape survivors and other assault victims, male and female veterans, and refugees (see Cahill, Rothbaum, Resick, & Follette, 2009). Exposure therapy is a cognitive-behavioral intervention technique that involves direct exposure, either in vivo or imaginal to the feared stimuli associated with the traumatic event. These feared stimuli (trauma cues) can include objects, people, places, situations, and information that remind the individual of the traumatic event. Exposure therapies include *imaginal exposure*, which consists of repeated revisiting of the traumatic memory, as well as in vivo *exposure*, which involves confronting feared situations that are objectively safe. Exposure therapy should occur in the context of a safe and supportive therapeutic environment and, during exposure exercises, individuals are only exposed to stimuli that are objectively harmless (e.g., do not conduct in-vivo exposure exercises in dangerous locations).

The imaginal forms of exposure are often described as "reliving the trauma." This procedure involves the use of careful, repeated, and detailed imagining of the traumatic event(s) in a safe, controlled context to help victims face and gain control of the fear and distress that was overwhelming during the actual event(s). To use conditioning terminology, participants in exposure-based treatments are taught to expose themselves to the conditioned trauma cues until the conditioned anxiety response is extinguished. More specifically, during imaginal exposure, the patient is instructed to describe the traumatic event in as much detail as possible, focusing on the cognitions and emotions that

they experience during the trauma. Repeated imaginal exposure is thought to facilitate extinction, which refers to the gradual reduction in anxiety over time. This process of deliberately confronting a feared memory in a supportive therapeutic setting may also foster feelings of mastery and courage, and it helps clients realize that the trauma memory is not dangerous. Exposure exercises may also involve writing about the traumatic events and reading these writings to the clinician (Cloitre et al., 2002; Foa & Rothbaum, 1998; Resick & Schnicke, 1996).

During in vivo *exposure*, individuals are taught to expose themselves to trauma-related stimuli that cause them distress and perpetuate avoidance in their daily lives. Victims typically create a hierarchy of real-life cues, such as people, places, or situations that have been paired with the trauma, and they practice exposing themselves to those cues in a graduated fashion. It is critical for victims to only expose themselves to situations that are actually safe. Therefore, the clinician should evaluate the safety of each situation and only safe situations should be included on the hierarchy list (Foa & Rothbaum, 1998). For example, if a rape victim avoids walking in the vicinity where she was previously assaulted, and the actual danger level of this neighborhood is relatively high during the day and night, she should not be encouraged to expose herself to this situation. If the victim avoids going to restaurants because she was assaulted in the parking lot of one in the past, it is safe to do in vivo exposures to help her feel comfortable going out to eat again, particularly if that used to be an enjoyable activity in her life. However, the exposure would only be indicated for restaurants in neighborhoods that are considered safe, and precautions are typically warranted and encouraged in dark parking lots to enhance safety.

Treatment programs that include both kinds of exposure, such as prolonged exposure (Foa et al., 2007), tend to produce better outcomes compared with intervention protocols that include only one of the components (see Bryant et al., 2008). However, in vivo exposure techniques are unnecessary when the client is not avoiding real-life cues but instead is experiencing most distress by internal trauma cues, such as intrusive painful memories and thoughts.

When engaging victims in any type of exposure therapy, clinicians should routinely measure the victim's distress level before, during, and after each exercise. Rating scales, or "anxiety thermometers" such as Wolpe's (1958) Subjective Units of

Discomfort scale (0–100) are extremely helpful in monitoring individual's discomfort level and progress during exposures inside and outside of session. Exposure exercises should be graduated and/or titrated based on the intensity of fear the different situations or recalled material provoke (see Rothbaum et al., 2007).

Cognitive therapy. Cognitive interventions aim to reduce trauma-related anxiety and distress by teaching individuals to become more aware of the maladaptive thoughts and beliefs associated with their traumatic experience (e.g., guilt, responsibility, self-blame). Individuals in cognitive therapy are taught to analyze and modify their negative cognitions using restructuring techniques. Various combinations of these components have been used in comprehensive, evidence-based treatment approaches designed for victims of trauma, including interpersonal violence (Follette & Ruzek, 2006). These components are grounded in distinct, but overlapping, theoretical frameworks and have only recently been isolated and explored in efficacy research. For example, Aderka and colleagues (2013) found that pure exposure intervention (i.e., prolonged exposure; see section that follows) affected posttraumatic symptoms, which in turn affected depressive symptoms, but exposure combined with cognitive therapy (i.e., prolonged exposure plus cognitive restructuring) had a more reciprocal relationship between posttraumatic and depressive symptoms (Aderka, Gillihan, McLean, & Foa, 2013). Further research is needed in order to determine the definite empirical status of each of these components individually.

Empirically Supported Treatments for Posttraumatic Stress Disorder

Next, we briefly describe three gold standard empirically supported treatment programs for adults diagnosed with PTSD that incorporate some or all of the four core treatment components just described into a single intervention package: exposure therapy, cognitive therapy, and eye movement desensitization and reprocessing (EMDR). (This is not an exhaustive list of the trauma interventions for adults; for more information about these treatments, please refer to Foa et al.'s [2013] review of PTSD treatments and the Substance Abuse and Mental Health Services Administration's online registry of mental health interventions called the National Registry of Evidence-based Programs and Practices [http://www.nrepp.samhsa.gov].)

Exposure Therapy

Exposure-based therapies were among the first interventions to demonstrate efficacy in PTSD treatment research. To date, exposure remains an integral component in most trauma-focused treatment interventions, specifically when treating PTSD (see description in previous section). Exposure methods share the common feature of helping individuals to confront fear-evoking stimuli, with the aim of reducing irrational fear or anxiety (Follette & Ruzek, 2006; Rothbaum & Foa, 1999). While most trauma-focused treatment programs do not consist solely of exposure techniques, the use of exposure is typically central to the treatment plan and occupies a significant amount of the time spent in therapy. Other accompanying treatment components are often presented as preliminary ways of preparing an individual for exposure (Follette & Ruzek, 2006).

There are several theories about the use of exposure therapy and why it works. First, repeated reliving of the traumatic memory is thought to promote habituation to the memory, and thus reduce anxiety previously associated with the event and correct the maladaptive belief that avoidance is the only way to reduce persisting anxiety. Second, repeated reliving of the traumatic memory in a supportive therapeutic environment incorporates feelings of support and safety into the memory, thereby helping the individual to realize that remembering the traumatic event is not dangerous. Third, focusing on the traumatic memory for a prolonged period of time helps the individual to categorize the traumatic event as a distinct occurrence and, thus, correct the generalization that the traumatic event is a lifetime representation of a dangerous world and an incompetent self. Finally, the skill of revisiting the traumatic memory with a stable attitude and without distress helps the individual to develop feelings of mastery and courage over their traumatic experience (Rothbaum & Foa, 1999).

Prolonged exposure therapy. Prolonged exposure (PE; Foa & Rothbaum, 1998) is an exposure-based therapy that has been shown to effectively treat both PTSD-specific distress, as well as more general trauma-related symptoms such as depression, anxiety, guilt, and anger (see Cahill et al., 2009; Foa et al., 2005; Resick, Nishith, Weaver, Astin, & Feuer, 2002). Versions of PE have been especially helpful in preventing the development of chronic PTSD following rape (Foa, Molnar, & Cashman, 1995) and in treating PTSD in abused children (Deblinger, McLeer, & Henry, 1990), as well as with victims with traumatic brain injury, active duty military service members, and war veterans (Schnurr & Friedman, 2008). Research shows that the benefits of PE are rapid, dramatic, and enduring (e.g., Powers, Halpern, Ferenschak, Gillihan, & Foa, 2010). There have been major efforts to widely disseminate and implement PE in the field to increase its availability (Foa et al., 2013; McLean & Foa, 2013).

PE involves attending 9–12 therapy sessions, each lasting an average of 60–120 minutes (Foa & Rothbaum, 1998). The first sessions of PE involve the introduction and use of psychoeducation and AMT, which are then continually provided in various stages throughout the intervention. The focus of the treatment model, however, is imaginal and/or in vivo exposure. During imaginal exposure, the individual is instructed to describe the traumatic event in vivid detail using the first person present tense, while focusing on the cognitions and emotions experienced during the traumatic event, attending to cues in all five senses. The therapist encourages the individual to focus on the areas that elicit the most emotion in the traumatic memory. Alternately, imaginal exposure in PE can involve the individual writing about the traumatic event(s) and reading the account to the clinician. During in vivo exposure, individuals are instructed to expose themselves to trauma-related stimuli that cause distress and avoidance in their daily lives. The individual and therapist construct a hierarchy of fearful real-life cues and, in a gradual fashion, the individual practices exposing himself or herself to the cues (Foa & Rothbaum, 1998). During this portion of treatment, the individual provides the clinician with periodic ratings of the "subjective units of distress" (described earlier in the chapter) so that the therapist can monitor the discomfort level and progress during exposure both inside and outside of sessions. Once a significant decrease in distress has been achieved, a "cool down" phase begins that prepares the individual for leaving therapy after each exposure session.

Innovative delivery systems have been developed and tested for disseminating and implementing PE in the field (McLean & Foa, 2013; Foa et al., 2013). Examples include the "PE Coach" Smartphone Application (Reger et al., 2013), PE via videoconferencing, virtual reality tools (Opris et al., 2012; Rizzo et al., 2011), and tele-health approaches (Gros, Yoder, Tuerk, Lozano, & Acierno, 2011; Tuerk, Yoder, Ruggiero, Gros, & Acierno, 2010). These systems attempt to make the intervention interactive and convenient to engage in and, ultimately, to improve implementation, fidelity, and homework adherence.

Treatment considerations. It is important to recognize that many individuals seeking treatment may be wary of activities that involve intentionally reliving the trauma and confronting feared situations. Numerous misconceptions regarding exposure-based interventions exist (e.g., it elevates symptoms, results in a high dropout rate compared to other interventions, is not well tolerated), some of which also have limited empirical backing. Many rigorous scientific investigations refute the notion that exposure intensifies patient distress of PTSD symptoms over time (e.g., Foa, Feske, Murdock, Kozak, & McCarthy, 1991; Foa et al., 1999; Foa et al., 2005; Foa, Zoellner, Feeny, Hembree, & Alvarez-Conrad, 2002). In fact, the average PE-treated patient fares better than 86% of patients in control conditions (Powers et al., 2010). Moreover, the initial increase in distress in early sessions of PE is actually associated with superior post-treatment outcomes (Foa et al., 2002), and many clients with PE continue to improve even after treatment termination (Powers et al., 2010; Foa et al., 1991). While this method of intervention may seem counterintuitive and unsafe to the individual, it is important to educate clients about the benefits. Thus, before engaging in exposure exercises, it is critical for the clinician to provide a strong rationale for the use of exposure, providing individuals with several neutral examples and analogies of how exposure and extinction work so that they can understand that exposure to anxiety-producing situations will result in decreased anxiety. It is also important for clinicians to discuss individuals' concerns and/or any misinformation they may have about engaging in this process. Explaining the gradual and systematic nature of exposure therapy and the collaborative process of creating a hierarchy may reduce anxiety levels related to the process. (For helpful suggestions and scripts for teaching exposure, see Foa & Rothbaum, 1998; Rothbaum et al., 2007.)

Cognitive-Based Therapy

For many patients, the combination of psychoeducation, AMT, and exposure in PE is sufficient to yield a reduction in PTSD symptoms. Others, however, may continue to experience dysfunctional thoughts about their traumatic event (Brewin, Andrews, & Valentine, 2000). For these individuals, cognitive restructuring techniques may be needed to help modify a victim's negative emotions and cognitive distortions.

Cognitive therapy techniques aim to alter maladaptive thought patterns correlated with an individual's appraisals of the world, other people, and themselves (Beck, 1976). Trauma-focused cognitive therapy aims to reduce trauma-related anxiety and distress by teaching patients to become more aware of the maladaptive beliefs and cognitions associated with their trauma experience (e.g., self-blame, responsibility, worth, justice, sexuality), and to modify these beliefs using cognitive restructuring techniques. For example, the aforementioned client that was the afraid to go to restaurants following her assault believed that nighttime was an unsafe time to go out and that all parking lots were dangerous and to be avoided after dusk. Her generalized fear response (darkness, restaurants, parking lots) and overestimation of danger at nighttime caused distress and significantly impaired her social life. Thus, her perceptions of danger needed to be examined using cognitive restructuring techniques. Trauma-focused cognitive interventions encourage individuals to explore how their prior experiences and beliefs were affected by the traumatic event they experienced (e.g., believing the world is an unsafe place, others are not trustworthy, they are incompetent, they have no hope, and so on) (Resick & Schnicke, 1992).

Cognitive processing therapy. Cognitive processing therapy (CPT; Resick & Schnicke, 1992; http://www.musc.edu/ctp) is a predominantly cognitive behavioral treatment for PTSD. CPT was originally developed to treat PTSD in rape victims, although randomized control trials have indicated CPT's applicability for treatment with survivors of a range of different traumatic events (e.g., military trauma, assault, accidents, child abuse) (Resick, Monson, Gutner, & Maslej, 2014; Chard, 2005), who are experiencing PTSD and/or related symptoms (e.g., depression, guilt, dissociation, anger, and cognitive distortions) (Chard et al., 2012). CPT elicits memories of the traumatic event and then directly confronts maladaptive beliefs about it, which some believe may be even more effective than prolonged exposure alone—activating the memory structure while also working to correct and reintegrate the traumatic memory (Resick & Schnicke, 1992).

CPT is typically a 12–15 session treatment process that can be delivered in a group, individualized, or in a combined group and individual format.

There are four main parts of CPT: (1) Learning about PTSD symptoms and treatment, (2) Becoming aware of thoughts and feelings, (3) Learning skills to question or challenge thoughts related to traumatic event(s), and (4) Understanding changes in beliefs.

In the first segment of this treatment, therapists provide psychoeducation on basic emotions, common PTSD responses, and the theory behind CPT. Clients are invited to write an Impact Statement on why they believe the traumatic event occurred and how the event has shaped their attitudes about the world, others, and themselves. Individuals are also encouraged to comment on any changes that they have experienced regarding their beliefs about safety, trust, power, competence, esteem, and intimacy. Over the next few sessions, clients are taught the connection between events, thoughts, and feelings using the A-B-C sheet (Activating events, Beliefs, and Consequences) to become more aware of the connection between thoughts, feelings, and behavior, and to begin to identify places where they have become "stuck" related to interpretations of their trauma (e.g., "It was my fault the trauma occurred," or "I cannot trust anyone"). Stuck points reflect conflicting beliefs or frightening thoughts that interfere with acceptance of the traumatic event. Additional sessions focus on creation of the trauma narrative. Individuals write a detailed account of their most traumatic experience(s), including information on the sensations, thoughts, and feelings that were present at the time of the event. They then read their narrative aloud in session and the trauma-writing assignment is repeated to facilitate exposure. During the remaining sessions, patients learn how to confront common faulty thinking patterns (e.g., overgeneralization, mind reading, emotional reasoning). Cognitive restructuring techniques are used to address any remaining thinking patterns related to these thought distortions and the five main themes of safety, trust, power, esteem, and intimacy. Clients use tools such as the Challenging Questions Worksheet (CQW), the Patterns of Problematic Thinking sheet, and the Challenging Beliefs Worksheet (CBW) to examine their beliefs from different angles. Near the end of therapy, the client rewrites the Impact Statement to compare it with the version written at the beginning of therapy. This gives the individual the opportunity to see the changes they have made in their thoughts, feelings, and behaviors throughout therapy. In the final session, the therapist also makes time to look to the future, identifying any potential problems that may arise for the individual, and discussing ways in which the client might be able to manage these issues using CPT techniques (Chard et al., 2012). (For more detailed information regarding implementation of this treatment, clinicians can complete the free CPT Web-based training course [http://www.musc.edu/ctp].)

CPT is an appropriate treatment specifically for victims of interpersonal violence, as this treatment has been shown to result in significant decreases in both primary PTSD symptoms and secondary symptoms of co-occurring depression, anxiety, guilt, and anger in several well-controlled trials with this population (Chard, 2005; Resick et al., 2002; Resick et al., 2008). CTP has been found to help victims gain more accurate perceptions of life situations, increased safety behaviors, a sense of self-efficacy, increased hope, and interpersonal relationship functioning (Iverson, Gradus, Resick, Suvak, & Smith, 2011). Women who experienced reductions in PTSD and depressive symptoms over the course of CPT treatment also reported less occurrence of intimate partner violence (IPV) at a 6-month follow-up in Iverson and colleagues' 2011 study.

Treatment considerations. Several international and clinical practice guidelines for PTSD have concluded that CBTs are efficacious and recommended as first-line treatments (Cahill et al., 2009; Institute of Medicine, 2008; VA/DoD Guideline Working Group, 2010). The specific CBT protocols of CPT have been demonstrated to be efficacious in ameliorating PTSD (Foa, Keane, Friedman, & Cohen, 2008; Forbes et al., 2010) and related symptoms, particularly comorbid depression (Chard, 2005; Resick et al., 2008; Resick et al., 2002; Resick & Schnicke, 1992). Because of the strong emphasis on increasing cognitive connections and decreasing the amount of exposure necessary, it is believed CPT is more palatable to individuals with PTSD than other treatment models (Cukor, Olden, Lee, & Difede, 2010).

Although CPT can be implemented with a wide range of patients, there remain a few conditions in which CPT is still not an appropriate treatment choice. These include patients who are actively psychotic, patients with unmedicated bipolar mania, patients with active suicidal or homicidal intent, and patients who are substance dependent (Chard et al., 2012). When deciding whether or not CPT is the right treatment choice, mental health professionals should consider that individuals who are illiterate, have cognitive limitations, or suffer from mental dementia are also not very appropriate candidates for this treatment, given the emphasis on completing homework assignments throughout treatment (Chard et al., 2012).

Several lingering questions about the efficacy of CBT have recently been answered. Prior to 2012, follow-up assessments in CBT had ranged from a short period of only 3–6 months, and any studies following participants for 1 year or more had methodological limitations (e.g., Foa et al., 2005). A study by Resick and colleagues (2012) on the long-term impact of CBT confirmed that maintenance of long-term CBT treatment gains is in fact possible through a follow-up period of 6 years. Another defining area that has recently been explored is the interrelationship of changes in both PTSD and co-occurring depression during the course of CPT treatment. Given that many therapeutic techniques in CPT stem from Beck's (1976) original cognitive therapy for depression, it was not surprising to find that in CPT, both PTSD and depression improve concurrently (Liverant, Suvak, Pineles, & Resick, 2012). Liverant and colleagues revealed that CPT and its treatment components act on a common mechanism of change affecting both disorders simultaneously, indicating how integral each different component of this treatment model is in addressing the comorbid needs of many victims of interpersonal violence (Liverant et al., 2012).

Eye Movement Desensitization and Reprocessing

Another psychotherapy model that has received considerable attention in research literature is eye movement desensitization and reprocessing (EMDR; Shapiro, 1995). EMDR is an eight-phase therapy that involves a sequentially ordered set of interventions among which the key components are (a) the identification of a target trauma and its associated negative cognition, and the development of a more positive cognition to replace the negative cognition; (b) the use of bilateral stimulation on the individual while holding in mind the traumatic image; (c) the installation of the newly established positive cognition; and (d) a body scan to identify any residual disturbing body sensations or affect connected to the traumatic memory.

The eight phases of EMDR treatment may be completed in a few sessions, or over a period of months, depending upon the needs of the individual and/or the seriousness of the pathology. The first of the eight phases of EMDR is *history taking*. This phase is comprised of a thorough screening to identify the past events that have laid the groundwork for the individual's pathology, the current triggers, and future needs. Phase two, *preparation*, involves building rapport, providing psychoeducation about the individual's symptom picture, and instilling a sense of stabilization and personal control in order to begin the EMDR processing of targets. During the third phase, *assessment,* the individual and therapist jointly identify a target memory and its associated mental images, beliefs, emotions, and the physical sensations closely associated with the traumatic event (usually identifying the most representative mental image of traumatic event to be used first). Baseline measures of these responses are taken. The clinician helps the individual become aware of the cognitive distortions experienced in relation to this memory, and introduces information that contradicts this distortion, correcting it with a more positive belief. Post measures are then taken. The next three phases of EMDR involve the use of bilateral stimulation in conjunction with procedural elements designed to facilitate information processing. Phase four is called *desensitization,* and it involves asking the individual to focus on a memory target, letting "whatever happens, happen," while eye movements (or other forms of bilateral stimulation) are initiated. *Installation* then focuses on incorporating and increasing the strength of the positive cognition to replace the original negative cognition in the memory network. During the *body scan* phase, the individual is asked to access both the targeted event and the new identified positive cognition, and by doing so, gives the clinician the opportunity to measure the current level of physiological and/or affective disturbance associated with the new connection. The individual identifies any residual tension being experienced in the form of body sensations and any such persisting somatic responses are noted for further processing. The seventh phase, *closure,* is used to ensure client stability at the completion of each EMDR session and between sessions. Finally, the *reassessment* phase evaluates the treatment effects and fosters integration of the therapy into the individual's larger social system (Shapiro, 2014).

Some have argued that the primary component of the EMDR memory-processing procedure is exposure. However, as previously indicated, EMDR does not entail the extended exposures used in other CBT models. Research suggests that the long exposures that characterize CBT cause extinction in the memory network, while the short exposure sequences in EMDR cause reconsolidation (Suzuki et al., 2004). As described by Craske, Herman, and Vansteenwegen (2006), extinction does not eliminate the previous associations, but rather results in new learning that competes with the old memory. On the other hand, the reconsolidation implicated in EMDR therapy is believed to cause the original memory to be changed and stored in a completely

altered form following treatment. As indicated by the Adaptive Information Processing model (Shapiro, 2001, 2007, 2014) guiding this form of therapy, EMDR conceptualizes the unprocessed memory as encoded with the emotions, perspectives, and physical sensations that occurred at the time of the traumatic event. The episodic memory becomes integrated and stored within existing semantic networks without the previous dysfunctional beliefs, emotions, and physical sensations (Shapiro, 2001), and the original unprocessed memory is no longer stored in the brain. A new meta-analysis of eye movement research has confirmed that this component does in fact also contribute to positive treatment effects and the processing of emotional memories in EMDR therapy (Lee & Cuijpers, 2013). Research-supported explanations for the effects of the eye-movements are that they (a) tax working memory, (b) elicit an orienting response, and (c) link into the same processes that occur during rapid eye movement (REM) sleep (Kuiken, Chudleigh, & Racher, 2010; Lee & Cuijpers 2013). Shapiro asserts that each of these three mechanisms come into play at different times during the therapy process to create the positive outcomes (Shapiro, 2014).

Treatment considerations. EMDR therapy has been established as an empirically validated treatment for PTSD by a wide range of organizations both nationally and internationally (e.g., VA/DoD, 2010; WHO, 2013). Recent practice guidelines by the WHO (2013) discuss the effectiveness of EMDR therapy as whole, its divergence from other forms of trauma treatment, and why some favorable clinical outcomes have been achieved with EMDR that have not been achieved with other therapy models.

While CBT exposure therapies entail detailed descriptions of the disturbing event and extended concentration on the trauma both during treatment sessions and in homework, EMDR therapy involves intermittent attention to disturbing information and an associative process that is stimulated during the sets of eye movements in the presence of the therapist. Since detailed descriptions of the event are unnecessary, EMDR therapy is particularly amenable to trauma populations suffering from shame or guilt, such as sexual abuse victims. In addition, EMDR therapy does not require individuals to complete homework outside of the treatment sessions and, therefore, can be used by clinicians to treat victims on a consecutive-day or single extended session basis. In EMDR, it is expected that single-trauma victims can be efficiently treated after a mean of 5.4 hours with a 100% remission rate (Marcus, Marquis, & Sakai, 2004).

Comparing Treatment Approaches

It is clear that several highly effective trauma-focused treatments exist in the field, and the research is growing to support their positive, long-term effects with diverse populations and their innovative ways of delivery (tele-health, Web-based, virtual reality, group, individual). The main challenge is that evidence-based trauma treatments are underutilized in community-based "usual practice" settings. As one notices from the earlier descriptions, when comparing treatment approaches, clinicians find overlapping or complementary components of exposure, stress management, and cognitive processing. We now have three decades of support for the use of exposure-based therapy (e.g., Powers et al., 2010), decades of research on the effectiveness of cognitive therapies (Chard, 2005), and growing research showing that the hybrid psychotherapy, EMDR, is highly effective for treating PTSD and other trauma impact (Spates, Koch, Pagoto, Cusack, & Waller, 2008; Nathan & Gorman, 2007; Ponniah & Hollon, 2009). Even though a growing number of meta-analyses also support the use of EMDR (e.g., Bisson, et al., 2007; Seidler & Wagner, 2006), there is still some controversy noted in the field regarding this treatment being selected over others. The Institute of Medicine's report (2008) reviewed the body of evidence for PTSD treatments and concluded that only approaches that include an exposure component currently have sufficient evidence to be considered efficacious (Bomyea & Lang 2012). Nonetheless, research on adult trauma treatment continues to grow and there is much to be learned about the powerful mechanisms or "active ingredients" of effective treatment for victims of interpersonal violence that will guide our decision making and increase the treatment response rate.

Emerging and Novel Interventions for the Treatment of Posttraumatic Stress Disorder

The current availability of evidence-based treatments for individuals suffering from PTSD is vast, painting a picture of promise and hope for recovery in many. Nonetheless, a significant portion of PTSD-diagnosed individuals remain symptomatic after completing treatment, or they drop out of treatment or never access empirically supported treatments for their mental health condition (Schottenbauer, Glass, Arnkoff, Tendick, & Gray, 2008). Despite existing efficacious treatment approaches, it is evident that outcomes for PTSD interventions leave room for improvement, with approximately 20%–50% of treatment completers retaining a PTSD diagnosis after treatment (Resick et al., 2002; Schnurr et al., 2007). So far, no single intervention approach for PTSD has been universally effective and/or acceptable for all victims suffering from this disorder (Bradley, Greene, Russ, Dutra, & Westen, 2005; Schottenbauer et al., 2008). Knowledge on the matching of treatment protocols to symptom profiles will translate into a better understanding of not only what works, but also what works for whom, and under what specific circumstances (Bomyea & Lang, 2012). Continued research on improving PTSD interventions and delivery models is certainly warranted (Bomyea & Lang, 2012).

The treatment of PTSD populations would benefit from several methodological and practical advances, and emerging interventions have started to incorporate these (Bomyea & Lang, 2012). For example, researchers have begun to examine dosage, psychotherapy components (singly and in combination), strategic enhancements to existing protocols, accessibility and acceptability of treatment for specific populations, and the testing of alternative models. In order to develop innovative treatment models that explicitly address the difficulties among victims of violence and PTSD-diagnosed adults, research calls for (a) adaptations to target specific trauma populations; (b) interventions that have different conceptual bases for treating PTSD, changes in therapeutic approaches such as integrated treatment, and the use of phase-based or sequential approaches; (c) cognitive process modification programs that provide an option for individuals who are unwilling or unable to participate in traditional psychosocial interventions (e.g., those with high levels of avoidance behavior); and (d) third-wave approaches. Future work is needed to evaluate the efficacy for many of these recently developed interventions given their many existing methodological limitations (Bomyea & Lang, 2012).

Examples of emerging and novel hybrid interventions for the treatment of PTSD in adults include treatments for survivors of child abuse who suffer from debilitating and chronic PTSD symptoms, emotion regulation problems, and interpersonal difficulties, such as the phase-based Skills Training in Affect and Interpersonal Regulation modified PE (STAIR-mPE; Cloitre et al., 2002). (For more information, see the free, Web-based clinical skills training on STAIR offered through the National Center for PTSD [http://www.ptsd.va.gov/professional/continuing_ed/STAIR_online_training.asp].) Other emerging phase-based treatments are designed for victims of complex PTSD who have experienced repeated, chronic abuse of an interpersonal nature and who struggle with emotional, social, cognitive, and/or psychological competencies that either failed to develop properly or that have deteriorated due to their prolonged exposure to complex trauma. (For more information, see the American Psychological Association and International Society for the Study of Trauma and Dissociation's guidelines for complex PTSD in adults [Cloitre et al., 2012].)

Treatments also exist that focus on populations such as battered women with PTSD who have experienced repeated, prolonged trauma in many different forms (e.g., threats, stalking, sexual abuse), as well as a history of exposure to interpersonal violence, such as childhood physical and/or sexual abuse (Kubany & Watson, 2002). Cognitive trauma therapy for battered women with PTSD (CTT-BW; Kubany et al., 2004) is an example of a comprehensive treatment model including several treatment elements adapted from existing cognitive–behavioral treatments for PTSD, including (a) psychoeducation, (b) AMT, and (c) exposure work.

Finally, a number of treatment models and protocols for the combined treatment of PTSD and substance use disorder (SUD) have been developed and implemented in clinical practice and are receiving more empirical support (Torchalla, Nosen, Rostam, & Allen, 2012). Individuals with PTSD-SUD tend to present with a more complicated clinical picture, experiencing more severe symptoms (Driessen et al., 2008), higher rates of additional psychiatric disorders (Brady, Killeen, Saladin, Dansky, & Becker, 1994), and poorer physical health (Tate, Norman, McQuaid, & Brown, 2007). Currently the *Seeking Safety* cognitive behavioral therapy model (Najavits, 2002) has the most extensive empirical backing as an integrated treatment for this population (Najavits, 2007). (For more information on this treatment, see Najavits, 2009, or visit the Seeking Safety website at http://www.treatment-innovations.org/seeking-safety.html. For further details on emerging PTSD and SUD treatments, see van Dam and colleagues' systematic review [van Dam, Vedel, Ehring, & Emmelkamp, 2012].)

Third-wave treatment approaches have also gained positive attention in the last decade, becoming widely accepted methods for relieving symptoms related to many psychological issues across different populations, including victims of interpersonal violence (Hofmann, Sawyer, Witt, & Oh, 2010). Third-wave interventions that have been made applicable to the treatment of PTSD in adults include acceptance and commitment therapy (ACT; see Ost, 2008), dialectical behavior therapy (DBT; Linehan, 1993a; see National Alliance on Mental Illness, 2013), and mindfulness-based therapy (MBT). Third-wave approaches for the treatment of PTSD in adults include integrating techniques such as mindfulness for tolerating uncomfortable feelings and images, developing emotional regulation skills in individuals, and helping to increase awareness and flexibility in responding to emotional experiences (Baer, Smith, Hopkins, Krietemeyer, & Toney, 2006; Hofmann et al., 2010; Linehan, 1993b; Ramel, Goldin, Carmona, & McQuaid, 2004). Mindfulness has also been shown to improve the effectiveness of exposure treatments, and to increase an individual's ability to recall painful memories, thoughts, and feelings without engaging in avoidance strategies (Follette, Palm, & Pearson, 2006).

Conclusion

While the prevalence of violence and victimization exposure in childhood and adulthood has remained somewhat stable over the past decade, we have made major strides in developing long-lasting, effective treatments that reduce the debilitating impact of trauma and help adults thrive in their lives. The field is struggling to increase the availability and access of high quality interventions for victims. Part of this effort involves educating consumers about what works and providing the training and resources to clinicians in the field delivering services. There are promising new Web-based tools and tele-health options that are improving our ability to widely disseminate PTSD treatments. There are also increasing efforts to encourage policymakers and the public health community locally and globally to highlight the needs of victims of interpersonal violence and demand best practices in mental health treatment delivery.

References

Abram, K. M., Teplin, L. A., King, D. C., Longworth, S. L., Emanuel, K. M., Romero, E. G.... Olson, N. D. (2013). PTSD, trauma, and comorbid psychiatric disorders in detained youth. *Juvenile Justice Bulletin*. Retrieved from http://www.iacpyouth.org/Portals/0/Resources/Comorbid_Psychiatric_Disorders.pdf

Adams, Z. W., McCart, M. R., Zajac, K., Danielson, C. K., Sawyer, G. K., Saunders, B. E.,... Kilpatrick, G. E. (2013).

Psychiatric problems and trauma exposure in nondetained delinquent and nondelinquent adolescents. *Journal of Clinical Child and Adolescent Psychology, 42*(3), 323–331. doi:10.1080/15374416.2012.749786

Aderka, I. M., Gillihan, S. J., McLean, C. P., & Foa, E. B. (2013). The relationship between posttraumatic and depressive symptoms during prolonged exposure with and without cognitive restructuring for the treatment of posttraumatic stress disorder. *Journal of Consulting and Clinical Psychology, 81*(3), 375–382. doi:10.1037/a0031523

American Psychiatric Association. (2013). *Diagnostic and statistical manual of mental health disorders* (5th ed.). Arlington, VA: American Psychiatric Publishing.

Anda, R. F., Chapman, D. P., Felitti, V. J., Edwards, V., Williamson, D., Croft, J. B., & Giles, W. H. (2002). Adverse childhood experiences and risk of paternity in teen pregnancy. *Obstetrics and Gynecology, 100*(1), 37–45.

Baer, R. A., Smith, G. T., Hopkins, J., Krietemeyer, J., & Toney, L. (2006). Using self-report assessment methods to explore facets of mindfulness. *Assessment, 13*, 27–44. doi:10.1177/1073191105283504

Beck, A. T. (1976). *Cognitive therapy and the emotional disorders.* Madison, CT: International Universities Press.

Bisson, J. I., Ehlers, A., Matthews, R., Pilling, S., Richards, D., & Turner, S. (2007). Psychological treatments for chronic post-traumatic stress disorder: Systematic review and meta-analysis. *The British Journal of Psychology, 190*, 97–104. doi:10.1192/bjp.bp. 106.021402

Bomyea, J., & Lang, A. J. (2012). Emerging interventions for PTSD: Future directions for clinical care and research. *Neuropharmacology, 62*(2012), 607–616. doi:10.1016/j.neuropharm.2011.05.028

Bonnano, G. A. (2004). Loss, trauma, and human resilience: Have we underestimates the human capacity to thrive after extremely aversive events? *American Psychologist, 59*(1), 20–28. doi:10.1037/0003-066X.59.1.20

Bonnano, G. A., Westphal, M., & Mancini, A. D. (2011). Resilience to loss and potential trauma. *Annual Review of Clinical Psychology, 7*, 511–535. doi:10.1146/annurev-clinpsy-032210-104526

Borkovec, T. D., & Costonguay, L. G. (1998). What is the scientific meaning of empirically supported therapy? *Journal of Consulting and Clinical Psychology, 66*(1), 136–142. doi:10.1037/0022-006X.66.1.136

Brady, K. T., Killeen, T., Saladin, M. E., Dansky, B., & Becker, S. (1994). Comorbid substance abuse and posttraumatic stress disorder. *The American Journal on Additions, 3*(2), 160–164.

Bradley, B., DeFife, J. A., Guarnaccia, C., Phifer, J., Fani, N., Ressler, K. J., & Westen, D. (2011). Emotion dysregulation and negative affect: Association with psychiatric symptoms. *Journal of Clinical Psychiatry, 72*(5), 685–691. doi:10.4088/JCP.10m06409blu

Bradley, R., Greene, J., Russ, E., Dutra, L., & Westen, D. (2005). A multidimensional meta-analysis of psychotherapy for PTSD. *American Journal of Psychiatry, 162*(2), 214–227. doi:10.1176/appi.ajp.162.2.214

Breslau, N. (2009). The epidemiology of trauma, PTSD, and other posttrauma disorders. *Trauma, Violence & Abuse, 10*(3), 198–210. doi:10.1177/1524838009334448

Brewin, C. R., Andrews, B., & Valentine, J. D. (2000). Meta-analysis of risk factors for posttraumatic stress disorder in trauma-exposed adults. *Journal of Consulting and Clinical Psychology, 68*(5), 748–766. doi:10.1037/0022-006X.68.5.748

Briere, J., & Elliott, D. M. (2003). Prevalence and psychological sequelae of self-reported childhood physical and sexual abuse in a general population sample of men and women. *Child Abuse & Neglect, 27*(2003), 1205–1222. doi:10.1016/j.chiabu.2003.09.008

Briere, J., & Jordan, C. E. (2009). Childhood maltreatment, intervening variables, and adult psychological difficulties in women. *Trauma, Violence & Abuse, 10*(4), 375–388. doi:10.1177/1524838009339757

Briere, J., & Scott, C. (2006). *Principles of trauma therapy. A guide to symptoms, evaluation, and treatment.* Thousand Oaks, CA: Sage.

Brodsky, B. S., Oquendo, M., Ellis, S. P., Haas, G. L., Malone, K. M., & Mann, J. J. (2001). The relationship of childhood abuse to impulsivity and suicidal behavior in adults with major depression. *American Journal of Psychiatry, 158*(11), 1871–1877.

Brown, D. W., Anda, R. F., Henning, T., Tiemeier, H., Felitti, V. J., Edwards, V. J.,... Giles, W. H. (2009). Adverse childhood experiences and the risk of premature mortality. *American Journal of Preventative Medicine, 37*(5), 389–396. doi:10.1016/j.amepre.2009.06.021

Bryant, R. A., Moulds, M. L., Guthrie, R. M., Dang, S. T., Mastrodomenico, J., Nixon, R. D.,... Creamer, M. (2008). A randomized controlled trial of exposure therapy and cognitive restructuring for posttraumatic stress disorder. *Journal of Consulting and Clinical Psychology, 76*(4), 695–703. doi:10.1037/a0012616

Cahill, S. P., Rothbaum, B., Resick, P. A., & Follette, V. M. (2009). Cognitive-behavioral therapy for adults. In E. B. Foa, T. M. Keane, M. J., Friedman, & J. A. Cohen (Eds.), *Effective treatments for PTSD: Practice guidelines from the International Society for Traumatic Stress Studies* (2nd ed., pp. 139–222). New York, NY: Guilford Press.

Chapman, D. P., Dube, S. R., & Anda, R. F. (2007). Adverse childhood events as risk factors for negative mental health outcomes. *Psychiatric Annals, 37*(5), 359–364.

Chard, K. M. (2005). An evaluation of cognitive processing therapy for the treatment of posttraumatic stress disorder related to childhood sexual abuse. *Journal of Consulting and Clinical Psychology, 73*(5), 965–971.

Chard, K. M., Ricksecker, E. G., Healy, E. T., Karlin, B. E., & Resick, P. A. (2012). Dissemination and experience with cognitive processing therapy. *Journal of Rehabilitation Research & Development, 49*(5), 667–678. doi:10.1682/JRRD.2011.10.0198

Chen, L. P., Murad, H. M., Paras, M. L., Colbenson, K. M., Sattler, A. L., Goranson, E. N.,... Zirakzadeh, A. (2010). Sexual abuse and lifetime diagnosis of psychiatric disorders: Systematic review and meta-analysis. *Mayo Clinic Proceedings, 85*(7), 618629. doi:10.4065/mcp.2009.0583

Cloitre, M., Chase Stovall-McClough, K., Miranda, R., & Chemtob, C. M. (2004). Therapeutic alliance, negative mood regulation, and treatment outcome in child abuse-related posttraumatic stress disorder. *Journal of Consulting and Clinical Psychology, 72*(3), 411–416. doi:10.1037/0022-006X.72.3.411

Cloitre, M., Courtois, C. A., Ford, J. D., Green, B. L., Alexander, B., Briere, J.,... Van der Hart, O. (2012). The ISTSS expert consensus treatment guidelines for complex PTSD in adults. Retrieved from http://www.istss.org/AM/Template.cfm?Section=ISTSS_Complex_PTSD_Treatment_Guidelines&Template=%2FCM%2FContentDisplay.cfm&ContentID=5185

Cloitre, M., Koenen, K. C., Cohen, L. R., & Han, H. (2002). Skills training in affective and interpersonal regulation followed by exposure: A phase-based treatment for PTSD related to childhood abuse. *Journal of Consulting and Clinical Psychology, 70*(5), 1067–1074. doi:10.1037/0022-006X.70.5.1067

Cottler, L. B., Compton, W. M., III& Mager, D. (1992). Posttraumatic stress disorder among substance users from the general population. *The American Journal of Psychiatry, 149*(5), 664–670. doi:10.1176/ajp.149.5.664

Cougle, J. R., Resnick, H., & Kilpatrick, D. G. (2013). Factors associated with chronicity in posttraumatic stress disorder: A prospective analysis of a national sample of women. *Psychological Trauma: Theory, Research, Practice, and Policy, 5*(1), 43–49. doi:10.1037/a0025954

Craske, M., Herman, D., & Vansteenwegen, D. (Eds.) (2006). *Fear and learning: From basic processes to clinical implications.* Washington, DC: APA Press.

Cukor, J., Olden, M., Lee, F., & Difede, J. (2010). Evidence-based treatments for PTSD, new directions, and special challenges. *Annals of the New York Academy of Sciences, 1208*(2010), 82–89. doi:10.1111/j.1749-6632.2010.05793.x

Danielson, C. K. (2007). *Risk Reduction through Family Therapy (RRFT) treatment manual.* Charleston: Medical University of South Carolina, National Crime Victims Research & Treatment Center.

Deblinger, E., McLeer, S. V., & Henry, D. (1990). Cognitive behavioral therapy for sexually abused children suffering post-traumatic stress: Preliminary findings. *Journal of the American Academy of Child & Adolescent Psychiatry, 19*(5), 747–752.

Driessen, M., Schulte, S., Luedecke, C., Schaefer, I., Sutmann, F., Ohlmeier, M.,... Havemann-Reinicke, U. (2008). Trauma and PTSD in patients with alcohol, drug, or dual dependence: A multi-center study. *Alcoholism, Clinical and Experimental Research, 32*(3), 481–488. doi:10.1111/j.1530-0277.2007.00591.x

Dube, S. R., Miller, J. W., Brown, D. W., Giles, W. H., Felitti, V. J., Dong, M.,... Anda, R. F. (2006). Adverse childhood experiences and the association with ever using alcohol and initiating alcohol use during adolescence. *Journal of Adolescent Health, 38*(4), 444.e1–444.e10. doi:10.1016/j.jadohealth.2005.06.006

Felitti, V. J., Anda, R. F., Nordenberg, D., Williamson, D. F., Spitz, A. M., Edwards, V.,... Marks, J. S. (1998). Relationship of childhood abuse and household dysfunction to many of the leading causes of death in adults. *American Journal of Preventive Medicine, 14*(4), 245–258.

Finkelhor, D., Turner, H., Hamby, S., & Ormrod, R. (2011). Polyvictimization: Children's exposure to multiple types of violence, crime, and abuse. *Juvenile Justice Bulletin.* US Department of Justice, Office of Justice Programs. Retrieved from https://www.ncjrs.gov/pdffiles1/ojjdp/235504.pdf

Finkelhor, D., Turner, H., Ormrod, R., Hamby, S., & Kracke, K. (2009). *Children's Exposure to violence: A comprehensive national survey.* Washington, DC: Office of Juvenile Justice and Delinquency Prevention.

Foa, E. B., Dancu, C. V., Hembree, E. A., Jaycox, L. H., Meadows, E. A., & Street, G. P. (1999). A comparison of exposure therapy, stress inoculation training, and their combination for reducing posttraumatic stress disorder in female assault victims. *Journal of Consulting and Clinical Psychology, 67*(2), 194–200.

Foa, E. B., Feske, U., Murdock, T. B., Kozak, M. J., & McCarthy, P. R. (1991). Processing of threat-related information in rape victims. *Journal of Abnormal Psychology, 100*(2), 156–162.

Foa, E. B., Gillihan, S. J., & Bryant, R. A. (2013). Challenges and successes in dissemination of evidence-based treatments for posttraumatic stress: Lessons learned from prolonged exposure therapy for PTSD. *Psychological Science in the Public Interest, 14*(2), 65–111. doi:10.1177/1529100612468841

Foa, E. B., Hembree, E. A., Cahill, S. P., Rauch, S. A., Riggs, D. S., & Feeny, N. C. (2005). Randomized trial of prolonged exposure for posttraumatic stress disorder with and without cognitive restructuring: Outcome at academic and community clinics. *Journal of Consulting and Clinical Psychology, 73*(5), 953–964. doi:10.1037/0022-006X.73.5.953

Foa, E. B., Hembree, E. A., & Rothbaum, B. O. (2007). *Prolonged exposure therapy for PTSD: Emotional procession of traumatic experiences: Therapist guide.* New York, NY: Guilford Press.

Foa, E. B., Keane, T. M., & Friedman, M. J. (2000). Guidelines for treatment of PTSD. *Journal of Traumatic Stress, 13*(4), 539–588.

Foa, E. B., Keane, T. M., Friedman, M. J., & Cohen, J. A. (Eds.). (2008). *Effective treatments for PTSD: Practice guidelines from the international society for traumatic stress studies* (2nd ed.). New York, NY: Guilford Press.

Foa, E. B., Molnar, C., & Cashman, L. (1995). Change in rape narratives during exposure therapy for posttraumatic stress disorder. *Journal of Traumatic Stress, 8*(4), 675–690.

Foa, E. B., & Rothbaum, B. O. (1998). *Treating the trauma of rape: A cognitive-behavioral therapy for PTSD.* New York, NY: Guilford Press.

Foa, E. B., & Rothbaum, B. O. (2001). *Treating the trauma of rape: Cognitive-behavioral therapy for PTSD.* New York, NY: Guilford Press.

Foa, E. B., Zoellner, L. A., Feeny, N. C., Hembree, E. A., & Alvarez-Conrad, J. (2002). Does imaginal exposure exacerbate PTSD symptoms? *Journal of Consulting and Clinical Psychology, 70*(4), 1022–1028. doi:10.1037//0022-006X.70.4.1022

Follette, V. M., Palm, K. M., & Pearson, A. N. (2006). Mindfulness and trauma: Implications for treatment. *Journal of Rational-Emotive and Cognitive-Behavior Therapy, 24*(1), 45–61. doi:10.1007/s10942-006-0025-2

Follette, V. M., & Ruzek, J. I. (2006). *Cognitive behavioral therapies for trauma.* New York, NY: Guilford Press.

Forbes, D., Creamer, M., Bisson, J. I., Cohen, J. A., Crow, B. E., Foa, E. B.,... Ursano, R. J. (2010). A guide to guidelines for the treatment of PTSD and related conditions. *Journal of Traumatic Stress, 23*(5), 537–552. doi:10.1002/jts.20565

Forbes, D., Fletcher, S., Parslow, R., Phelps, A., O'Donnell, M., Bryant, R. A.,... Creamer, M. (2012). Trauma at the hands of another: Longitudinal study of differences in posttraumatic stress disorder symptom profile following interpersonal compared with noninterpersonal trauma. *Journal of Clinical Psychiatry, 73*(3), 372–376. doi:10.4088/JCP.10m06640

Forbes, D., Lockwood, E., Phelps, A., Wade, D., Creamer, M., Bryant, R. A.,... O'Donnell, M. (2014). Trauma at the hands of another: Distinguishing PTSD patterns following intimate and nonintimate interpersonal and noninterpersonal trauma in a nationally representative sample. *The Journal of Clinical Psychiatry, 75*(2), 147–153. doi:10.4088/JCP.13m08374

Ford, J. D., Grasso, D. J., Hawke, J., & Chapman, J. F. (2013). Poly-victimization among juvenile justice-involved youths. *Child Abuse & Neglect, 37*(10), 788–800. doi:10.1016/j.ciabu.2013.01.005

Godbout, N., Briere, J., Sabourin, S., & Lussier, Y. (2014). Child sexual abuse and subsequent relational and personal functioning: The role of parental support. *Child Abuse & Neglect, 38*(2014), 317–325. doi:10.1016/j.chiabu.2013.10.001

Green, J. G., McLaughlin, K. A., Berglund, P. A., Gruber, M. J., Sampson, N. A., Zaslavsky, A. M.,... Kessler, R. C. (2010). Childhood adversities and adult psychiatric disorders in the national comorbidity survey replication I. *Arch General Psychiatry*, *67*(2), 113–123. doi:10.1001/archgenpsychiatry.2009.186

Gros, D. F., Yoder, M., Tuerk, P. W., Lozano, B. E., & Acierno, R. (2011). Exposure therapy for PTSD delivered to veterans via telehealth: Predictors of treatment completion and outcome and comparison to treatment delivered in person. *Behavior Therapy*, *42*(2), 276–283. doi:10.1016/j.beth.2010.07.005

Hillis, S. D., Anda, R. F., Dube, S. R., Felitti, V. J., Marchbanks, P. A., & Marks, J. S. (2004). The association between adverse childhood experiences and adolescent pregnancy, long-term psychosocial consequences, and fetal death. *Pediatrics*, *113*(2), 320–328. doi:10.1542/peds.113.2.320

Hillis, S. D., Anda, R. F., Felitti, V. J., Nordenberg, D., & Marchbanks, P. A. (2000). Adverse childhood experiences and sexually transmitted diseases in men and women: A retrospective study. *Pediatrics*, *106*(1), 1–6.

Hofmann, S. G., Sawyer, A. T., Witt, A. A., & Oh, D. (2010). The effect of mindfulness-based therapy on anxiety and depression: A meta-analytic review. *Journal of Consulting and Clinical Psychology*, *78*(2), 169–183. doi:10/1037/a0018555

Iacoviello, B. M., & Charney, D. S. (2014). Psychosocial facets of resilience: Implications for preventing posttrauma psychopathology, treating trauma survivors, and enhancing community resilience. *European Journal of Psychotraumatology*, *5*. doi:10.3402/ejpt.v5.23970

Institute of Medicine. (2008). *Treatment of PTSD: An assessment of the evidence*. Washington, DC: National Academies Press.

Iverson, K. M., Gradus, J. L., Resick, P. A., Suvak, M. K., & Smith, K. F. (2011). Cognitive-behavioral therapy for PTSD and depression symptoms reduces risk for future intimate partner violence among interpersonal trauma survivors. *Journal of Consulting and Clinical Psychology*, *79*(2), 193–202. doi:10.1037/a0022512

Kubany, E. S., Hill, E. E., Owens, J. A., Iannce-Spencer, C., McCaig, M. A., & Tremayne, K. J. (2004). Cognitive trauma therapy for battered women with PTSD (CTT-BW). *Journal of Consulting and Clinical Psychology*, *72*(1), 3–18. doi:10.1037/0022-006X.72.1.3

Kubany, E. S., & Watson, S. B. (2002). Cognitive trauma therapy for formerly battered women with PTSD: Conceptual bases and treatment outlines. *Cognitive and Behavioral Practice*, *9*(2), 111–127. doi:10.1016/S1077-7229(02)80005-0

Kuiken, D., Chudleigh, M., & Racher, D. (2010). Bilateral eye movements, attention flexibility, and metaphor comprehension: The substrate of REM dreaming? *Dreaming*, *20*(4), 227–247. doi:10.1037/a0020841

Lanius, R. A., Vermetten, E., & Pain, C. (2010). *The impact of early life trauma on health and disease: The hidden epidemic*. Cambridge, UK: Cambridge University Press.

Lee, C. W., & Cuijpers, P. (2013). A meta-analysis of the contribution of eye movements in processing emotional memories. *Journal of Behavior Therapy and Experimental Psychiatry*, *44*(2), 231–239. doi:10.1016/j.jbtep.2012.11.001

Levitt, J. T., & Cloitre, M. (2006). A clinician's guide to STAIR/MPE: Treatment for PTSD related to childhood abuse. *Cognitive and Behavioral Practice*, *12*(1), 40–52. doi:10.1016/S1077-7229(05)80038-0

Linehan, M. M. (1993a). *Cognitive-behavioral treatment of borderline personality disorder*. New York, NY: Guilford Press.

Linehan, M. M. (1993b). *Skills training manual for treating borderline personality disorder. Diagnosis and treatment of mental disorders*. New York, NY: Guilford Press.

Liverant, G. I., Suvak, M. K., Pineles, S. L., & Resick, P. A. (2012). Changes in posttraumatic stress disorder and depressive symptoms during cognitive processing therapy: Evidence for concurrent change. *Journal of Consulting and Clinical Psychology*, *80*(6), 957–967. doi:10.1037/a0030485

Marcus, S., Marquis, P., & Sakai, C. (2004). Three-and 6-month follow-up of EMDR treatment of PTSD in an HMO setting. *International Journal of Stress Management*, *11*(3), 195–208. doi:10.037/1072-5245.11.3.195

McCauley, J. L., Killeen, T., Gros, D. F., Brady, K. T., & Back, S. E. (2012). Posttraumatic stress disorder and co-occurring substance use disorders: Advances in assessment and treatment. *Clinical Psychology: Science and Practice*, *19*(3), 283–304. doi:10.1111/cpsp.12006

McLaughlin, K. S., Koenen, K. C., Hill, E. D., Petukhova, M., Sampson, N. A., Zaslavsky, A. M.,... Kessler, R. C. (2013). Trauma exposure and posttraumatic stress disorder in a national sample of adolescents. *Journal of the American Academy of Child and Adolescent Psychiatry*, *52*(8), 815–830. doi:10.1016/j.jaac.2013.05.011

McLean, C. P., & Foa, E. B. (2013). Dissemination and implementation of prolonged exposure therapy for posttraumatic stress disorder. *Journal of Anxiety Disorders*, *27*(8), 788–792. doi:10.1016/j.janxdis.2013.03.004

Mercy, J. A., Hillis, S. D., Butchart, A., Bellis, M. A., Ward, C. L., Fang, X.,... Rosenberg, M. L. (2014). *Chapter 7. Interpersonal violence: Global impact and paths to prevention*. Retrieved from http://www.dcp-3.org/sites/default/files/chapters/V7%20C7%20Mercy_for%20web%201-27-14.pdf

Mercy, J. A., Krug, E. G., Dahlberg, L. L., & Zwi, A. B. (2003). Violence and health: The United States in a global perspective. *American Journal of Public Health*, *93*(2), 256–261.

Najavits, L. M. (2002). *Seeking Safety: A treatment manual for PTSD and substance abuse*. New York, NY: Guildford Press.

Najavits, L. M. (2007). Seeking safety protocol for men and women. *Psychiatric Services*, *58*(10), 1376.

Najavits, L. M. (2009). Psychotherapies for trauma and substance abuse in women: Review and policy implications. *Trauma, Violence & Abuse*, *10*(290), 290–298. doi:10.1177/1524838009334455

Nathan, P. E., & Gorman, J. M. (Eds.). (2007). *A guide to treatments that work* (3rd ed.). New York, NY: Oxford Press.

National Alliance on Mental Illness. (2013). Dialectical behavior therapy fact sheet. Retrieved from http://www.nami.org/Content/NavigationMenu/Inform_Yourself/About_Mental_Illness/About_Treatments_and_Supports/Dialectical_Behavior_Therapy_%28DBT%29.htm

Norman, R. E., Byambaa, M., De, R., Butchart, A., Scott, J., & Vos, T. (2012). The long-term health consequences of child physical abuse and neglect: A systematic review and meta-analysis. *PLoS Medicine*, *9*(11), e1001349. doi:10.1371/journal.pmed.1001349

Opris, D., Pintea, S., Garcia-Palacios, A., Botella, C., Szamoskozi, S., & David, D. (2012). Virtual reality exposure therapy in anxiety disorders: A qualitative meta-analysis. *Depression and Anxiety*, *29*, 85–93. doi:10.1002/da.20910

Ost, L. G. (2008). Efficacy of third wave behavioral therapies: A systematic review and meta-analysis. *Behaviour Research and Therapy*, *46*(3), 296–321. doi:10.1016/j.brat.2007.12.005

Ozer, E. J., Best, S. R., Lipsey, T. L., & Weiss, D. S. (2003). Predictors of posttraumatic stress disorder and symptoms in adults: A meta-analysis. *Psychological Bulletin, 129*(1), 52–73.

Pacella, M. L., Hruska, B., & Delahanty, D. L. (2013). The physical health consequences of PTSD and PTSD symptoms: A meta-analytic review. *Journal of Anxiety Disorder, 27*(1), 33–46. doi:10.1016/j.janxdis.2012.08.004

Pietrzak, R. H., Goldstein, R. B., Southwick, S. M., & Grant, B. F. (2011). Prevalence of axis I comorbidity of full and partial posttraumatic stress disorder in the United States: Results from wave 2 of the national epidemiologic survey on alcohol and related conditions. *Journal of Anxiety Disorders, 25*(3), 456–465. doi:10.1016/j.anxdis.2010.11.010

Ponniah, K., & Hollon, S. D. (2009). Empirically supported psychological treatments for adult acute stress disorder and posttraumatic stress disorder: A review. *Depression and Anxiety, 26*(12), 1086–1109. doi:10.1002/da.20635

Powers, M. B., Halpern, J. M., Ferenschak, M. P., Gillihan, S. J., & Foa, E. B. (2010). A meta-analytic review of prolonged exposure for posttraumatic stress disorder. *Clinical Psychology Review, 30*(6), 635–641. doi:10.1016/j.cpr.2010.04.007

Ramel, W., Goldin, P. R., Carmona, P. E., & McQuaid, J. R. (2004). The effects of mindfulness meditation on cognitive processes and affect in patients with past depression. *Cognitive Therapy and Research, 28*(4), 433–455. doi:0147-5916/04/0800-0433/0

Reger, G. M., Hoffman, J., Riggs, D., Rothbaum, B. O., Ruzek, J., & Holloway, K. M. (2013). The "PE coach" smartphone application: An innovative approach to improving implementation, fidelity, and homework adherence during prolonged exposure. *Psychological Services, 10*(3), 342–349. doi:10.1037/a0032774

Resick, P. A., Galovski, T. E., Uhlmansiek, M. O., Scher, C. D., Clum, G. A., & Young-Xu, Y. (2008). A randomized clinical trial to dismantle components of cognitive processing therapy for posttraumatic stress disorder in female victims of interpersonal violence. *Journal of Consulting and Clinical Psychology, 76*(2), 243–258. doi:10.1037/0022-006X.76.2.243

Resick, P. A., Monson, C. M., Gutner, C. A., & Maslej, M. M. (2014). Psychosocial treatments for adults with PTSD. In M. J. Friedman, T. M. Keane, & P. A. Resick (Eds.), *Handbook of PTSD: Science and practice* (2nd ed., pp. 419–436). New York, NY: Guilford Press.

Resick, P. A., Nishith, P., Weaver, T. L., Astin, M. C., & Feuer, C. A. (2002). A comparison of cognitive-processing therapy with prolonged exposure and a waiting condition for the treatment of chronic posttraumatic stress disorder in female rape victims. *Journal of Consulting and Clinical Psychology, 70*(4), 867–879.

Resick, P. A., & Schnicke, M. K. (1992). Cognitive processing therapy for sexual assault victims. *Journal of Consulting and Clinical Psychology, 60*(5), 748–756.

Resick, P. A., & Schnicke, M. (1996). *Cognitive processing therapy for rape victims: A treatment manual.* Newbury Park, CA: Sage.

Resick, P. A., Williams, L. F., Suvak, M. K., Monson, C. M., & Gradus, J. L. (2012). Long-term outcomes of cognitive-behavioral treatments for posttraumatic stress disorder among female rape survivors. *Journal of Consulting and Clinical Psychology, 80*(2), 201–210. doi:10.1037/a0026602

Riggs, D. S., Cahill, S. P., & Foa, E. B. (2006). Prolonged exposure treatment of posttraumatic stress disorder. In V. M. Follette & J. I. Ruzek (Eds.), *Cognitive behavioral therapies for trauma* (pp. 65–95). New York, NY: Guilford Press.

Rothbaum, B. O., & Foa, E. B. (1999). *Reclaiming your life after rape: Cognitive behavioral therapy for posttraumatic stress disorder.* New York, NY: Oxford University Press.

Rothbaum, B. O., Foa, E. B., & Hembree E. A. (2007). *Reclaiming your life from a traumatic experience.* New York, NY: Oxford University Press.

Rothbaum, B. O., Kearns, M. C., Price, M., Malcoun, E., Davis, M., Ressler, K. J.,... Houry, D. (2012). Early intervention may present the development of posttraumatic stress disorder: A randomized pilot civilian study with modified prolonged exposure. *Biological Psychiatry, 72*(11), 957–963. doi:10.1016/j.biopsych.2012.06.002

Rothbaum, B. O., Meadows, E. A., Resick, P., & Foy, D. W. (2000). Cognitive-behavioral therapy. In E. B., Foa, T. M., Keane, & M. J. Friedman (Eds.), *Effective treatments for PTSD: Practice guidelines from the International Society for Traumatic Stress Studies* (pp. 320–325). New York, NY: Guilford Press.

Rizzo, A., Parsons, T. D., Lange, B., Kenny, P., Buckwalter, J. G., Rothbaum, B.,... Reger, G. (2011). Virtual reality goes to war: A brief review of the future of military behavioral healthcare. *Journal of Clinical Psychology in Medical Settings, 2011*(18), 176–187. doi:10.1007/s10880-011-9247-2

Schnurr, P. P., & Friedman, M. J. (2008). Treatment for PTSD: Understanding the evidence. *PTSD Research Quarterly, 19*(3), 2–11.

Schnurr, P. P., Friedman, M. J., Engel, C. C., Foa, E. B., Shea, T. M., Chow, B. K.,... Bernardy, N. (2007). Cognitive behavioral therapy for posttraumatic stress disorder in women: A randomized controlled trial. *JAMA, 297*(8), 820–830. doi:10.1001/jama.297.8.820

Schottenbauer, M. A., Glass, C. R., Arnkoff, D. B., Tendick, V., & Gray, S. H. (2008). Nonresponse and dropout rates in outcome studies on PTSD: Review and methodological considerations. *Psychiatry: Interpersonal and Biological Processes, 71*(2), 134–168. doi:10.1521/psyc.2008.71.2.134

Seidler, G. H., & Wagner, F. E. (2006). Comparing the efficacy of EMDR and trauma-focused cognitive-behavioral therapy in the treatment of PTSD: A meta-analytic study. *Psychological Medicine, 36*(11), 1515–1522. doi:10.1017/S0033291706007963

Shapiro, F. (1995). *Eye movement desensitization and reprocessing: Basic principles, protocols, and procedures.* New York, NY: Guilford Press.

Shapiro, F. (2001). *Eye movement desensitization and reprocessing: Basic principles, protocols, and procedures* (2nd ed.). New York, NY: Guilford Press.

Shapiro, F. (2007). EMDR, adaptive information procession, and case conceptualization. *Journal of EMDR Practice and Research, 1*(2), 68–87. doi:10.1891/1933-3196.1.2.68

Shapiro, F. (2014, Spring). EMDR therapy: A brief overview of trauma research, clinical practice, and proposed neurobiological mechanisms. *Division 56, Trauma Psychology, American Psychology Association Newsletter*, 5–8. Retrieved from http://www.apatraumadivision.org/newsletter/newsletter_2014_spring.pdf

Spates, C. R., Koch, E., Pagoto, S., Cusack K., & Waller, S. (2008). Eye movement desensitization and reprocessing for adults, children, and adolescents. In E. Foa, T. Keane, M. Friedman, & J. Cohen (Eds.), *Effective treatments for PTSD* (p. 279). New York, NY: Guilford Press.

Suzuki, A., Josselyn, S. A., Frankland, P. W., Masushige, S., Silva, A. J., & Kida, S. (2004). Memory reconsolidation and extinction have distinct temporal and biochemical signatures. *Journal of Neuroscience, 24,* 4787–4795.

Tate, S. R., Norman, S. B., McQuaid, J. R., & Brown, S. A. (2007). Health problems of substance-dependent veterans with and those without trauma history. *Journal of Substance Abuse Treatment, 33*(1), 25–32. doi:10.1016/j.sat.2006.11.006

Torchalla, I., Nosen, L., Rostam, H., & Allen, P. (2012). Integrated treatment programs for individual with concurrent substance use disorders and trauma experiences: A systematic review and meta-analysis. *Journal of Substance Abuse, 42*(2012), 65–77. doi:10.1016/j.jsat.2011.09.001

Tuerk, P. W., Yoder, M., Ruggiero, J., Gros, D. F., & Acierno, R. (2010). A pilot study of prolonged exposure for posttraumatic stress disorder delivered via telehealth technology. *Journal of Traumatic Stress, 23*(1), 116–123. doi:10.1002/jts.20494

VA/DoD Guideline Working Group. (2010). VA/DoD clinical practice guideline for management of post-traumatic stress. Retrieved from http://www.healthquality.va.gov/ptsd/ptsdsum_2010a.pdf

van Dam, D., Vedel, E., Ehring, T., & Emmelkamp, P. M. G. (2012). Psychological treatments for concurrent posttraumatic stress disorder and substance use disorder: A systematic review. *Clinical Psychology Review, 32*(2012), 202–214. doi:10.1016/j.cpr.2012.01.004

Walsh, K., Gonsalves, V. M., Scalora, M. J., King, S., & Hardyman, P. L. (2012). Child maltreatment histories among female inmates reporting inmate on inmate sexual victimization in prison: The mediating role of emotion dysregulation. *Journal of Interpersonal Violence, 27*(3), 492–512. doi:10.1177/0886260511421670

Whitfield, C. L., Anda, R. F., Dube, S. R., & Felitti, V. J. (2003). Violent childhood experiences and the risk of intimate partner violence in adults: Assessment in a large health maintenance organization. *Journal of Interpersonal Violence, 18*(2), 166–185. doi:10.1177/0886260502238733

Wolpe, J. (1958). Psychotherapy by reciprocal inhibition. *Conditional Reflex: A Pavlovian Journal of Research & Therapy, 3*(4), 234–240.

World Health Organization. (2013). *Guidelines for the management of conditions specifically related to stress.* Geneva, Switzerland: Author.

World Health Organization. (2014). *Definition and typology of violence.* Retrieved from http://www.who.int/violenceprevention/approach/definition/en/

Legal, Ethical, and Psychological Risk Management

Legal and Ethical Risk Management with Behavioral Emergencies

Dana Lockwood, Houri Parsi, Wendy Packman, *and* Bruce Bongar

Abstract

Working with patients presenting with serious harm to themselves or others is an experience many mental health professionals will have during their careers. The possibility of working with this population might cause some apprehension for treatment providers because of the patient and professional risks involved. In this chapter we review the applicable legal theories of professional negligence and focus on the potential legal and professional ramifications that occur when mental health professionals do not rise to the applicable standard of care when working with suicidal or aggressive patients. Additionally, this chapter provides an outline of the legally imposed duties that treatment providers have to their patients so as to promote effective and ethical treatment of those presenting with the possibility of serious harm to themselves and others.

Key Words: risk management, professional negligence, standard of care, suicide, aggression

At various points over the course of their careers, mental health practitioners are likely to treat patients who present with a risk of self-harm or aggression toward others. In discussions on this topic, patients' suicidal or violent acts have been termed "behavioral emergencies," which is the focus of this chapter. Many practitioners feel understandably apprehensive about treating patients who present with a high risk of self-harm or violence. The obvious concern is potential harm to a patient or to a violent patient's victims, but practitioners treating such individuals are also often troubled by the professional consequences that may directly affect themselves.[1] Indeed, when a mental health practitioner's conduct falls below the legal standard of care, there can be consequences to his or her practice, as well as legal ramifications. Complaints can also be filed with state licensing boards and/or the APA Ethics Committee, entities that require psychologists be competent (American Psychological Association, 2010; Ethical Standards 2.01, 2.03) and that their work be based on established scientific and professional knowledge

(2.04). Such complaints could result in expulsion from the association or even suspension or revocation of the practitioner's license. Although serious, these results often remain somewhat less foreign or unpredictable and, therefore, less anxiety-provoking than the legal consequences that may arise from treating patients with behavioral emergencies. With regard to the latter, the primary mechanism would be a lawsuit against a mental health practitioner for malpractice. The following chapter will explore this legal concept with specific application to practitioners who work with dangerous or harmful clients.

Mental Health Malpractice, Generally

Often mental health practitioners question whether they can be sued in a particular instance, or a specific set of circumstances. The general rule of thumb is yes—a practitioner can be sued in any circumstance or situation. There is little practitioners can do to inoculate themselves from the general litigiousness in society, particularly when facing disturbed or grieving patients and families who are eager to find fault or blame as a means of explaining a personal tragedy. However, the more applicable question should not be whether a lawsuit can be filed, but whether a lawsuit against one's practice would be successful. Fortunately, practitioners can make generally educated guesses about the likely outcome of a suit against themselves. While there are no guarantees in a court of law, the likelihood of whether a practitioner will not be held liable in a lawsuit, in other words, the likelihood that he or she will "win" the case, will depend on the facts of the specific case. For this reason, although those who work in high-risk contexts will, to some extent, always remain vulnerable to litigation, they can take important steps to modify their professional conduct to prevent or reduce lawsuits and to increase the likelihood of successfully defending against any that do arise. To this end, we believe that properly applied knowledge of common legal issues (and the responsibilities they bring with them) constitutes the best legal defense. In this chapter, we first provide an instructional summary of the legal criteria of medical malpractice aimed at a clinical audience. Next, we use case examples to discuss and illustrate some of the most common types of professional liability that can occur when providing treatment for suicidal and violent patients.

Negligence Law: Purpose and Context

Most commonly, a legal case that follows a mental health patient having inflicted harm, either on another person or on self, will take the form of the patient or victim (or the patient or victim's family members) bringing a medical malpractice lawsuit against an individual or group of mental health practitioners (or the facility in question) (Andalibian et al., 2006). The term *malpractice* refers simply to a particular type of negligence that occurs in the context of a particular professional standard. Therefore, the negligence will nearly always be the main issue or legal theory[2] in cases involving a practitioner's treatment of a suicidal or violent patient. The following overview of this legal area will shed light on how each of the elements or legal criteria of negligence is applied in these particular types of cases (Andalibian et al., 2006).

Negligence is "the failure to exercise the standard of care that a reasonably prudent person would have exercised in a similar situation" (Black, 1996, p. 1405). The area of negligence law falls under the broader category of torts, which refer to a civil wrong [allegedly] committed by one individual (the defendant) that has caused some injury to another

(the plaintiff) (Packman & Harris, 1998). Torts, generally, are then distinguished between intentional torts (e.g., battery, assault, fraud, trespass, and the like) and negligence. Unlike the former group, negligence does not require the plaintiff to prove that the defendant *intended* to cause the harm that occurred. One easily imagined example is the tort of battery, an intentional tort which is defined as "the use of force against another resulting in harmful or offensive contact" (Black, 1996). For a defendant to be held liable for battery, he or she must have intended to harm the victim. This requirement seems common sense for lawyers and laymen alike—that hitting someone when you did not intend to does not a battery make. On the other hand, in a negligence case the defendant may bear no intentions of harm whatsoever but may be held liable nonetheless. Here, a nonlawyer may wonder why the legal system makes room for a person to be liable for something they never meant to do. Indeed, we propose that a better understanding of the fundamental value of negligence law is essential to being on the winning side of it. What negligence law provides is essentially some compensation to a person who becomes hurt by someone else who either did something he or she should not have done (an act of commission) or failed to do something he or she should have (act of omission) (Simon, 1988). Put more plainly, negligence is how we as a society compensate victims when they have been hurt by accidents or mistakes that could have been avoided if the players had been sufficiently careful. Negligence law says that if we have the potential to hurt people with our conduct, we owe it to them to exercise a basic level of attention. Still, mistakes do happen. And appreciating the lack of a requirement of intent in these lawsuits is crucial; it is what leaves health-care practitioners vulnerable to liability even when they have the best intentions (Andalibian et al., 2006).

The preceding is a general discussion of how negligence is applied. More specifically, the tort has four specific criteria. This means that to recover on a claim of negligence, the person bringing the lawsuit—the plaintiff—must prove that the facts of the case meet the definitions in each legal *element* that makes up the claim. A plaintiff must allege and then prove all the elements in a claim to win the suit. Therefore, if a defendant can prove that the facts of the case do not meet the definition of just one of the necessary elements, the defendant would escape liability (Andalibian et al., 2006). Indeed, attempting to refute one or more of the four elements in negligence is the primary tactic in preventing liability.[3] Specifically, those four elements are damages, causation, duty, and breach of duty (Prosser, 1971).[4] In explaining each in detail, we shall begin with the most basic—damages—and end with the existence and breach of duty.

Understanding Damages

The element of *damages* provides a requirement that the plaintiff must have suffered some harm in order to be compensated (Packman, Pennuto, Bongar, & Orthwein, 2004). Simply put, a defendant may have made an avoidable error or not acted as he or she should have, but he or she would not be required to compensate a plaintiff unless there was actually some injury resulting from the error or substandard conduct. For example, if a practitioner's negligence leads to a patient's unsuccessful suicide attempt that fortunately results in no psychological or physical harm, then the practitioner would not be liable. How much harm or injury must have occurred? The law does not say. Therefore, while insignificant or minor injuries may make it unlikely that a plaintiff would find it worthwhile to file a suit, the law itself requires only that some injury—no matter how slight—occur for this element to be met. For the purposes of our discussion on behavioral emergencies, loss of life and psychological and/or physical damages that result from either a completed suicide or even an attempt would easily satisfy the damages requirement. Violent patients whose behavior results in harm to themselves or others would also satisfy this element, regardless of the degree of injury. Thus, in cases such as these, an argument of whether there were any damages is waived. Instead, the more salient issue in court becomes determining the *extent* of damages that resulted from the negligence (Andalibian et al., 2006) and characterizing it by some appropriate amount of monetary compensation. The amount of compensation is determined by the court (either the jury or the judge) and is both fact-specific to each case, as well as widely varied and unpredictable between jurisdictions. Thus, in a field that is, by definition, composed of illness and injury, it can be futile for a practitioner to either avoid the occurrence of damages, or to try to predict the correct compensatory amount when they are sustained. For this reason, the professional defending against malpractice would likely be more successful attacking a different element of negligence and showing that his or her conduct was not the *cause* of the damage.

Understanding Causation: Cause in Fact and Proximate Cause

The element of causation actually refers to two distinct legal analyses that are often viewed as separate elements in and of themselves: *cause in fact* and *proximate cause* (foreseeability). A defendant's conduct or failure to act must satisfy both types of causation in a successful negligence claim. The former requires a simple and concrete evaluation of the sequence of facts in time to identify what in layman's terms is often called a "cause-and-effect relationship." Proximate cause, on the other hand, is analyzed entirely in the abstract. All hypothetical causes have hypothetical potential effects, and some effects are more likely than others. A proximate cause analysis requires that hypothetical outcomes have to have been contemplated in advance by the defendant, and the attempt to avoid unwanted outcomes is what should have governed the behavior or conduct. Because of this, the determination of what hypothetical conduct would be the proximate cause of certain injuries is also used in the determination of the legal standard of care, which is the next element in our negligence analysis. We will discuss these each in turn, with case examples used to illustrate how the elements are determined in mental health cases.

Cause in fact: Explained. Cause in fact is also known as *actual causation*—a well-fitting term insofar as it refers to the aspect of causation that most closely fits a lay definition. Namely, the rule provides that to evoke liability, a plaintiff's damages must have resulted from the defendant's negligence (Packman et al., 2004). One determines this to be the case when "the resulting harm would not have occurred without the party's conduct" (Black, 1996, p. 81). The latter definition is commonly known as the "but for" test and posits the question, "but for (without) the defendant's conduct, would the damages have still occurred?" If not, then there is cause in fact, or actual causation.

If it appears as though actual causation casts a wide net, that is because it does. The purpose of this element is simply to exclude from liability any actions that are wholly unlinked to the set of consequences before the court. Therefore, as with damages, this element is commonly satisfied in negligence lawsuits. The exponential character of any chain of events helps explain why. For example, assume that Dr. Ash is a manager at a high-risk clinic and he hires Dr. Brown, a clinical psychologist (without prescription privileges). During an intake, Dr. Brown misdiagnoses a patient who then goes to see Dr. Cerulean—a psychiatrist. Dr. Cerulean then writes a prescription for a medicine that is ordinarily indicated by the disease documented in the chart by Dr. Brown. The patient thereupon takes the medication and suffers unpleasant side effects. Who would be responsible for the physical suffering that the patient endured?

A review of the facts would lead most to conclude that Dr. Cerulean caused the suffering (he indisputably caused it; whether he was understandably excused for doing so is a different matter). And given how significant Dr. Brown's misdiagnosis was to the prescription, it would also easily seem that he, too, caused the patient's eventual distress. But what about the manager, Dr. Ash? Can the court find that the ultimate consequence—in this case, the side effects, were *caused* not only by the doctors who misdiagnosed the patient and prescribed the medicine, but by the *original* doctor who hired one of those doctors as well? When reviewing causation under this first tier of analysis, the answer would be yes. Using the "but for" test, one can work backwards and plainly deduce that if Dr. Ash hadn't hired Dr. Brown, then Dr. Brown wouldn't have been there to misdiagnose the patient, thereby not indicating the medication. Thus, the patient would never have experienced its side effects. This analysis connects all actions to every subsequent consequence that follows it—whether as a direct result, or indirectly along a chain of events.

Fortunately for all of us, however, actual causation is only half of the equation. If we could legally be determined to have caused everything that follows in time from our every move, the potential for lawsuits would be infinite! How we decide what actions in a chain of events caused the others and which are too far removed is legally dubbed, "proximate cause." It is this sub-element that seeks to curtail the otherwise broad scope of liability that simple cause in fact (or actual cause) would create. Where actual causation asks simply, "Is the consequence connected to the action by any link in a sequential chain?" proximate cause asks, "Is the consequence connected to the action closely enough that it would be reasonable to link them?"

Proximate cause: Explained. Officially, proximate cause prescribes that a defendant is only responsible for damages or injuries if the resulting harm was a "reasonably foreseeable consequence" of the conduct. Taking the case of our doctors from the preceding example, recall that Dr. Brown's hiring decision was a cause-in-fact, or actual cause of the

side effects a patient later experienced. But to find Dr. Brown to have proximately caused these side effects, the court would have to conclude that, at the time, Dr. Brown should have known that a wrong choice for a new clinic psychologist makes it likely that a patient would eventually be given incorrect medicine by another provider and suffer unnecessary side effects. Most likely, however, the court would find this conclusion to be too much of a stretch—particularly given that the role Dr. Brown was seeking to fill did not include writing prescriptions. So an injury that resulted from prescriptions given by another party would be too far removed from the last thing that Dr. Brown did. One may posit that Dr. Brown nevertheless *should* carry some responsibility even if he did not prescribe the medication. For example, it may be argued that if it was common practice at this particular clinic to have psychologists refer patients to psychiatrists on site and pass along medical chart to them, then the diagnosing psychologist *would* have had certain prescribing powers by virtue of his *professional influence* in the prescription decisions. If both arguments hold sway in your mind, then you are beginning to understand why the issues in malpractice lawsuits often go on for years.

Next, to illustrate the power of the proximate cause analysis to assign responsibility (not just limit it), we shall present the same facts with a slight change: Assume now that Dr. Ash, in his hurried schedule to locate a much-needed clinician, failed to read Dr. Brown's graduate transcripts, which would have revealed that he had taken and failed his courses in psychodiagnosis twice before finally passing them with Cs. And assume that due to scheduling constraints, Dr. Ash failed to check any references or even so much as question Dr. Brown about diagnostic matters during the employment interview. After adding in these factors, the proximate cause analysis would easily turn the other way. Here is the crux of the analysis: the misdiagnosis by the hiree, and a subsequent mistreatment by the psychiatrist to whom he referred his patient, represents precisely the type of injury that one would expect to occur from hurried and incomplete hiring practices in clinical settings. And that is the essence of proximate cause. To evaluate whether the causal link is sufficient to be reasonably foreseeable, ask yourself why the action should have been avoided in the first place? What is the purpose of requiring that a person in charge of hiring doctors *not* make such decisions until after he has completed a careful review of the applicant's qualifications? We can all plainly agree that it is because a clinician who cannot make a correct clinical determination is likely to cause a patient at some point to be mistreated or harmed—either directly or by misinforming another clinician about the case. It is for this very reason, or at least inclusive of it, that those in charge of the employment selection process at a clinic must conduct the process in a way that reduces this possibility. This connection between a substandard action (or omission) and the *reason* we have deemed it substandard[5] is what characterizes proximate cause. From this perspective, revising the formal definition should make the concept clearer. A sloppily arrived at hiring decision proximately causes subsequent incorrect treatment because it is *reasonably foreseeable* that if the person in charge of hiring doctors does so without careful review of their qualifications, at some point a patient would be mistreated. Put simply, proximate cause acts like a "you should've known better" or a "you got what you asked for" type of test. It is a legal articulation of a common analysis that every parent or disciplinarian has likely become all too familiar with after having had to allocate responsibility or fault. Yet in more complex or serious circumstances, such a determination can become a foggy and unpredictable judicial proceeding.

For clinicians whose patients harm or attack themselves or others, determining whether their treatment (or lack thereof) was the cause is seldom black and white. With regard to behavioral emergencies, whether the tragic act of suicide or violence was foreseeable often becomes a heated issue in court upon which the outcome of the case can entirely hinge. If proximate cause is met, it can be damning to a defendant's case. If a court decides that a suicide or violent attack was foreseeable, then liability is often likely (after all, he should have known this would happen!). Reciprocally, however, if a court determines that the harmful event was *not* a reasonably foreseeable consequence of a practitioner acting substandardly, then the practitioner would most likely not be held liable (because, after all, how could he have known?) (Andalibian et al., 2006).

Proximate cause in mental health cases. A few legal case examples illustrate situations where a particular injury *was* foreseeable (and should, therefore, have been guarded against more carefully), as well as cases that identify the bottom boundary of the analysis—situations that did *not* warrant treatment or actions designed to have prevented a behavioral emergency. The case of *Stallman v. Robinson* (1953) was one of the first to address the issue of proximate cause in the context of behavioral emergencies, and it is illustrative of situations where a particular injury was determined to be foreseeable enough to have warranted protection against its occurrence. In *Stallman*, the decedent's husband sued for the death of his wife who committed suicide while she was an inpatient at a private hospital. During her 4-day stay, the patient tore strips of fabric from her nightgowns and successfully committed suicide by hanging herself. In finding the hospital liable, the court reasoned that "the most important single factor in determining whether a hospital was negligent in failing to prevent suicide of a patient is whether hospital authorities under the circumstances could have reasonably anticipated that the patient might harm himself" (p. 746). The court added that, "whether these determinative factors are present depends on the detailed facts and circumstances of the particular case" (p. 746). The patient in *Stallman* was preliminarily diagnosed prior to her death as either manic-depressive or schizophrenic with paranoid ideas. In addition, the patient had a history of four previous suicide attempts. In the court's view, a suicide was foreseeable given the patient's history and specific risk factors.

The basic tenet of rule in *Stallman* has stayed intact since its decision. More recently, in *Dodd v. Sparks Regional Medical Center* (2005), the decedent's husband brought a wrongful death action against a mental health clinic and its staff following the patient's suicide during her inpatient treatment. Specifically, the patient hung herself with a sheet tied to a doorstop at the top of a door. Following a similar analysis as that in *Stallman*, the court found the clinic was not the cause of the suicide, because there was no evidence to suggest that removing the doorstop would have ultimately prevented the decedent from committing suicide (actual cause). And conversely, the existence of the doorstop did not make the suicide any more foreseeable (proximate cause).

In addition to the circumstances of the case, patient risk factors will also indicate the foreseeability of harm, or lack thereof, if a threshold is not met. For example, the case of *Lawlor v. Orlando* (2001) explains that a patient's depression diagnosis alone is not enough to create a foreseeable danger of self-harm, especially when a risk assessment has been completed and found to be unremarkable. The ruling in *Lawlor* seems to indicate that even if the patient's self-harm would not have occurred but for certain precautions from the treatment team, because there was insufficient evidence to support any reasonable likelihood of self-harm, the failure to take those precautions was not the proximate cause of the harm; the treatment was in line with the risk factors that were identifiable to the treatment staff. In that case, it was only a diagnosis of depression, and that is not enough.

Understanding When a Duty of Care Is Owed

The elements of *duty* and *breach of duty* are the fundamental bases of negligence law since they establish the standard of care which, when not met, renders a defendant negligent (Packman et al., 2004). When considering the element of duty, the courts primarily consider whether the defendant owed the plaintiff a duty. A particular relationship established between the two parties can create the duty to exercise reasonable care. As this pertains to our discussion, any health practitioner will owe a duty to his or her patient simply by taking on the role of health practitioner.

In the 1953 case of *Stallman* that we referred to previously, the court noted that "the doctors in the case were specialists in mental health treatment and care. By accepting the patient in the hospital operated by these doctors, they owed the patient a specific duty (*Stallman*, 1953)." However, in contrast, the court in *Paddock v. Chacko* (1988), did not find liability in an action filed against a psychiatrist following a patient's unsuccessful suicide attempt. In that case, the psychiatrist initially conversed with the patient and her father and recommended either hospitalization or an increase in the patient's medication dosage. The patient refused both options. Thereafter, she surrendered herself to her father's custody, but in a period during which she was left unsupervised, she cut her wrists and set her shirt on fire. The court found the psychiatrist did not owe a duty to the patient because she had not surrendered herself to his care but rather to her father, who had refused to hospitalize her.

Paddock is an excellent example of how the element of duty is relative to the damage or injury that is being reviewed. As the facts of the case state that the psychiatrist was making medication recommendations to the woman, deciding whether *any* clinical duty existed on the part of the psychiatrist would be easily found in the affirmative.

After all, he has a duty to make such recommendations according to competent standards. However, the court was not evaluating anything specifically identified as relating to the medication, but rather the woman's suicide attempt. In evaluating whether a psychiatrist owes a duty of care with regard to supervision and/or prevention of a suicide attempt of an outpatient who was under another person's care, the court simply found that he did not. We emphasize here that lack of liability for breach of a duty to prevent one injury does not imply that *no* duty exists. Simply put, a mental health practitioner will almost always owe a duty to his or her patient. What the specific duty actually requires is what often becomes the issue to be argued, and it is what practitioners should take care to determine as clearly as possible in the early stages of treatment, and ongoing (Andalibian et al., 2006).

Breach of the Standard of Care: Understanding What the Duty Requires

In any negligence case, after the initial determination of whether any duty is owed, the court will need to identify what, specifically, the duty required of the defendant. This is called the *standard of care*, and refers to the actions that a defendant practitioner must undertake or avoid with regard to the patient (or to whomever the duty is owed). When the practitioner fails to operate at this abstract level, it is the breach of duty that essentially defines negligence. It is also the single element of negligence over which the health practitioner actually has control after accepting the patient. While it's true that the other elements can be debated and refuted by the parties' legal counsel after a case has been filed, the practitioner has no say in determining what the duty requires as he or she treats patients, whether a behavioral emergency should be foreseeable (regardless of whether he or she actually foresaw it), or whether damages occur. However, the practitioner is solely in control of the actions that constitute the standard of care at which he or she operates. And therefore this is the most important element for practitioners who are seeking to protect themselves from litigation (Andalibian et al., 2006). In order to both provide patients with proper care and minimize their own liability, practitioners must understand and examine what clearly constitutes their duty (i.e., practicing within the standard of care).

The Standard of Care in Behavioral Emergencies: Examples of Legally Recognized Duties

It is against the legal background of negligence law that we provide examples of common duties triggered by the circumstances and relationships present in a clinical setting with high potential for behavioral emergencies. The following list is not exhaustive, and new duties are often held to be required as the law continues to better understand and govern therapeutic relationships with high-risk populations. Practitioners are encouraged to use the following summaries as illustrative, or as a starting point for further research to become better informed of the most current and applicable standards in their own geographic and theoretical areas of practice.

Duty to Properly Diagnose Risk

Mental health practitioners are expected to reach the proper diagnosis and not misdiagnosis patients. That is, if the clinician had exercised ordinary and accepted care in reaching a diagnosis, the clinician would have ascertained that the patient was suicidal (*Dillmann v. Hellman*, 1973). Misdiagnosis refers to a negligent failure to both recognize the nature of the patient's condition and then to implement proper measures before harm occurs (Packman et al., 1994). In a well-known treatise, Gutheil and Appelbaum (1982) commented that misdiagnosis of psychiatric conditions "is a ripe area for future litigation and for consciousness raising" (p. 151) in the mental health profession.

Liability under this theory may also be misleading as it is often referred to as a "failure to predict," indicating that the clinician should have been able to predict the patient's suicidal tendencies had adequate steps and procedures been employed (Packman et al., 2004). It is because of this misnomer that the standard of care may become discolored by the previously discussed concept of foreseeable consequences in the abstract (proximate cause). Although the foreseeability of the injuries is a powerful indicator in determining whether a practitioner was negligent in a particular case, it is nevertheless important to distinguish foreseeability from predictability, and this is particularly true with regard to suicides. Foreseeable consequences are any that are likely or probable results of certain treatments, actions, or failures. There can be multiple, various consequences that could probably result from a single action or treatment decision; all of them should be guarded against. To predict that a consequence will occur, however, implies a degree of certainty that is much higher than finding that it is simply likely or probable. It logically follows that a greater certainty of a particular consequence would impose a greater responsibility to prevent it. Thus, by erroneously interpreting proximate cause as a determination that the defendant could have predicted the consequence at issue, one would inadvertently be placing a heightened, and often impossible, standard of responsibility on the defendant.

Indeed, research on this issue maintains that mental health practitioners cannot predict suicidal behavior reliably and validly; attempting to do so invariably results in a high degree of false-positives (Berman & Jobes, 1991). Thus, while negligence law requires that practitioners take steps to prevent harm that is reasonably foreseeable, this requirement can only go so far as to mandate comprehensive and reasonable assessment risks, and then to treat accordingly. It cannot require the prediction and prevention of the worst-case scenario. Nevertheless, once in court, a skilled litigator can purposefully blur the lines between foreseeability and predictability to impose upon a practitioner this impossible task. Schultz (2000) described how looking backward from a tragedy to determine whether it was foreseeable can be a biased cognitive exercise: "When a suicide is viewed through the lens of hindsight, it can take on a quality of apparent predictability." The same reasoning may apply to other salient incidents, such as attacks by violent patients. Because of this tendency to overestimate the obviousness of something significant after it has occurred, plaintiffs hold a psychological advantage in malpractice cases. This is one reason why we recommend that practitioners practice within and even above the applicable standard of care (Packman et al., 2004) when reviewing a patient's history and risk factors.

In *O'Sullivan v. Presbyterian Hospital in City of New York at Columbia Presbyterian Medical Center* (1995), the court found a psychiatrist failed to properly diagnose the extent of depression suffered by a man who committed suicide. Specifically, the survivor's expert illustrated that the psychiatrist failed to diagnose major depression, formulate a treatment plan, detect the severity and acuteness of the patient's problem, order a physical examination, consult the patient's treating physician about the patient's weight loss, assign the patient a therapist, or refer him for psychotropic medication. Given this evidence of deficient diagnosis and treatment, the court held there was no basis to conclude that the psychiatrist conducted a competent evaluation (Packman et al., 2004).

More recently, in *Perez v. United States* (2012), a psychiatrist was found liable for negligent care that was determined to have ultimately caused a patient's suicide. Despite the psychiatrist assessing for—and the patient denying—any suicidal ideation, the court identified a breach of duty because the psychiatrist did not make a proper diagnosis. Specifically, he failed to gather an accurate history during intake, to review medical records, to conduct regular check-ins regarding the patient's mental status, or to disclose pertinent information regarding the patient's condition to the patient. Thus, although the psychiatrist's treatment may have complied with the standard of care that his assessment called for, the psychiatrist conducted a substandard assessment that failed to identify key risk factors in the patient's history. Therefore, he breached the standard of care, because the standard was not governed by only the risk factors he had identified, but rather by the actual risk factors present, or at least those that would have been discerned by a competent assessment.

Duty to Take Adequate Protective Measures against Self-Harm or Violence

Mental health clinicians owe their patients a duty to take adequate protective measures to ensure their safety and well-being. This may refer to a variety of techniques, procedures, or methods. Liability under this legal theory may include the failure to observe or supervise and assess, the failure to medicate, the failure to control, and the failure to restrain (Packman et al., 2004). A general rule is that the clinician must take adequate precautions against patient suicide, consistent with accepted psychotherapeutic practices and based on his or her knowledge and thorough assessment of the patient (see *Dimitrijevic v. Chicago Wesley Memorial Hospital*, 1968; *Topel v. Long Island Jewish Medical Center*, 1981). VandeCreek and Knapp (1989) cite the case of *Dinnerstein v. United States* (1973), which held that clinicians are liable when a treatment plan overlooks or neglects the patient's suicidal tendencies. VandeCreek and Knapp (1989) also note that courts will generally not find a psychotherapist liable when the patient's suicide attempt was not foreseeable. This is in line with the analysis of negligence mentioned earlier, which explained that the harms or consequences that are foreseeable in the abstract are what dictate the specific duties in the standard of care. This is because the standard of care will always include doing what is reasonably possible to prevent those injuries you can foresee as likely or probable.

A primary protective measure that is required is supervision and assessment. In fact, VandeCreek and colleagues discovered that hospitals and clinicians are not typically found liable if reasonable steps were taken to supervise and assess the patient (VandeCreek, Knapp, & Herzog, 1987). In situations where the hospital did know or should have known about a patient's suicidal tendencies but was negligent by allowing the patient to be in a high-risk situation, adequate supervision and/or assessment has not been met. Liability has been frequently imposed in these situations (Packman et al., 2004). The legal lesson is that a reasonably prudent practitioner would not allow a known suicidal patient (or any patient that the practitioner should have known was suicidal) to be in a high-risk situation. Doing so would be a breach of duty; the following are examples of such breaches.

In *Meier v. Ross General Hospital* (1968), a physician in charge of the psychiatric wing of a hospital was held liable for the death of a patient because he had assigned him to a psychiatric wing on the second floor after the patient had attempted to commit suicide by slashing his wrists. Following the assignment, the patient jumped head first through an open window in his room. The court reasoned that the facts of the case supported a duty on the part of the practitioner to protect the decedent from his own actions, voluntary or involuntary. The practitioner was held liable based on his failure to do so.

Failure to properly supervise was also the legal theory that led to liability in *Fatuck v. Hillside Hospital* (1974). Here, an action was brought claiming that the hospital was negligent in failing to prevent a patient from escaping the grounds approximately 2–3 hours before the patient committed suicide by jumping from the roof of a building. Evidence included a 14-year history of mental health problems and recently expressed suicidal threats. During the patient's 9-day hospital stay, there were notations made in his record stating that he was not to be permitted to wander off. The patient was also placed on 15-minute checks for 2 days after admission; however, there was no notation that the checks were ever conducted. The court held that the evidence established negligence on the part of the hospital, which had failed to meet the duty of adequate supervision (Packman et al., 2004).

Duty to Disclose

The duty to warn a patient or patient's family of a risk of suicide differs from the duty to warn of a risk of danger to another (see discussion regarding violent patients, in what follows). In some cases, the courts have found liability for the failure of a physician or psychiatrist to warn family members of a patient's condition or to disclose pertinent information regarding the patient's condition to the patient (Packman et al., 2004). In *Wozniak v. Lipoff* (1988), the court found fault on the part of an internist for a patient's suicide. The internist had diagnosed and treated the patient for Grave's disease, a thyroid condition. However, he did not tell her or her family that those suffering from Grave's disease become anxious and irritable, engage in inappropriate behavior, or might develop serious psychiatric problems, including deep depression. The court held that this omission on the part of the internist constituted a breach of the duty to disclose or warn.

In contrast, in *Bellah v. Greenson* (1978), liability was not established for failing to warn particular people of a patient's condition. Specifically, the parents of Tammy Bellah, who died from an intentional overdose of pills, brought an action against their daughter's outpatient therapist. The court agreed with the family's argument that a psychiatrist–patient relationship existed and that the psychiatrist knew of the patient's suicidal propensity. However, the court ultimately reasoned that imposing a duty on a psychiatrist to disclose to others vague or even specific manifestations of suicidal tendencies on the part of the patient who is being treated in an outpatient setting could inhibit psychiatric treatment. The court also added that the therapeutic relationship between psychotherapists and their patients is highly complex, with intimate privacy being a virtual necessity for successful treatment. Although the *Bellah* court did not impose a *Tarasoff*-type duty to warn relatives of potential suicide risk, it remains an option that clinicians should consider seriously when a patient presents as a risk for suicide (Bongar, 2002; Fremouw, de Perczel, & Ellis, 1990). Additionally, in the previously mentioned *Lawlor* case, a duty to warn was not imposed on the treating psychotherapist following the patient's suicide. The patient had a depression diagnosis but never mentioned or threatened suicide and a recent suicide screener was not significant. The court explained that the patient's diagnosis of depression was not enough to create a foreseeable zone of danger and, as such, no duty to warn was triggered.

Duty to Commit or Confine and Prevent Negligent Release of Patients

Along the same lines as the duty to take protective measures that we just discussed, clinicians can be found liable for failing to commit or confine a client at high-risk for suicide. This includes negligently allowing a patient to leave a confined environment to go on a pass or releasing a patient prematurely. The issue, as with the other duty scenarios, is whether the mental health practitioner operated below the standard of care or made a valid professional judgment (Andalibian et al., 2006). In *Tabor v. Doctors Memorial Hospital* (1990), an emergency room physician failed to admit a suicidal patient because his parents could not pay the hospital's deposit. The patient was depressed and had taken a dangerous amount of sleeping pills. The court held that the doctor's decision not to admit the patient in an emergency because of his inability to pay the $400 deposit constituted a failure to follow the appropriate standard of care.

In a related vein, hospitals have also been found negligent in releasing a suicidal patient. In *Bell v. New York City Health and Hospital Corporation* (1982), a physician recommended the release of a psychiatric patient despite the presence of the patient's potentially harmful delusions. The physician failed to investigate the previous psychiatric history of the patient, the patient's delusions, or an incident that occurred the evening before the patient's release during which the patient had to be restrained. The court held the hospital negligent in releasing the patient and found the negligent acts to be the cause of his suicide following his release.

As noted, a clinician may be found liable for the early release of a patient if the release is negligent and not a valid exercise of professional judgment (Robertson, 1988). On the other hand, Fremouw et al. (1990) pointed out that when a clinician makes a reasonable assessment of danger and believes a risk no longer exists, he or she is not held liable for the death of a patient after discharge. Note how in *Lawlor* the psychotherapist completed a clinical risk assessment despite the patient's denial of suicidal thinking. It was the psychotherapist's reasonableness that ultimately protected him from liability. Similarly, in *Johnson v. United States* (1981), the court did not find a psychiatrist responsible for the post-discharge suicide of a patient because the psychiatrist had assessed the patient and reasonably concluded that the benefits of release outweighed the potential risks of danger. Furthermore, the court observed that "accurate prediction of dangerous behavior, and particularly of suicide and homicide, are almost never possible" (Fremouw et al., 1990, p. 8). This holding again highlights the importance of reasonableness in all negligence cases. Practitioners who use caution and document their reasoning when making decisions regarding the confinement, supervision, and release of their patients have the best protection against liability.

Duty to Obtain and Maintain Adequate History and Records

Clinicians must obtain an adequate history of each patient and continue to maintain up-to-date documentation. History gathering is properly completed upon intake of the patient and must include information involving past suicide attempts, prior incidents of self-harm, past suicidal ideation or impulses, as well as information about attempted and completed suicides in the patient's family (Baerger, 2001). Obtaining a complete history should also entail gathering past records and risk assessment data (Packman & Harris, 1998). Maintaining appropriate records is simply an exercise in accurate documentation and, ultimately, a form of risk management. In *Abille v. United States* (1980), the status of a psychiatric inpatient was changed, allowing him to leave the unit unattended. The treating clinician failed to record a written order changing the patient's status, nor did he prepare documentation explaining the reasoning behind the lowered precautions. The patient committed suicide while away from the unit. In evaluating the clinician's behavior, the court found him negligent, stating that the "failure to maintain contemporaneous notes, orders, or other records adequately recording and explaining his action in reclassifying [the patient] fell below the applicable standard of care" (*Abille*, p. 709). This case illustrates how the success or failure of a lawsuit can hinge on the documentation and reasoning behind the practitioner's behavior. The requirement of maintaining adequate records cannot be overstated, but documentation can be a double-edged sword, because treatment must conform to what the documented notes require or indicate. This is seen in *Klein v. Solomon* (1998), where a university psychologist failed to refer a suicidal student to proper services despite writing in notes that the patient had suicidal ideation.

Concluding Remarks

Working with a patient presenting with serious harm to self or others can be worrisome for an uninformed clinician. It is important for mental health professionals to be aware of the ever-evolving changes in professional negligence law in order to develop an understanding of applicable and necessary standards of care. This can be accomplished through discussions with legal counsel in addition to meeting continued education requirements. Specifically, it is important for mental health professionals to have an understanding of their legally imposed duties so as to shape their professional behavior. As discussed, these include duties to properly diagnose risk, disclose dangerousness, take adequate protective measures against self-harm or violence, confine and prevent negligent release, and obtain and maintain adequate patient history and records. Through gaining an understanding of these duties and, if necessary, modifying professional behaviors to be in line with legal requirements, mental health professionals will have increased opportunities to provide effective services to patients.

Notes

1. Throughout this article, the terms "mental health practitioner" or "clinician" are intended to refer specifically to both psychologists and psychiatrists and may be applied where appropriate to other licensed mental or behavioral health practitioners, such as licensed therapists and social workers. Note that different titles, degrees, and licenses often impose different standards of care. As a general rule, higher education and more stringent licensure requirements will impose a greater responsibility on the practitioner. The theories of liability, case law, and risk management guidelines are sufficiently similar for these professions to warrant addressing them together.

2. In litigation, a legal theory, the issue upon which a lawsuit rests, is called a *cause of action*. Most lawsuits that are filed contain multiple causes of action that are related to one another. Other causes of action that may arise in a clinical context may include such torts as intentional infliction of emotional distress or false imprisonment or fraud, among others. These torts are outside the scope of this chapter but clinicians are encouraged to educate themselves about these and any other potential allegations applicable to their practice.

3. The other form of defense that is used is legally referred to as an *affirmative defense*. Affirmative defenses are legal claims that the defendant can make to excuse his or her conduct when all the elements of the tort are otherwise met (Black, 1996). Essentially, this means that the court can find that a tort (e.g., negligence) has been committed, but the wrongdoer (the defendant) will not be responsible for any damages because he or she had a legally viable reason for what he or she did. Affirmative defenses against negligence do exist; however, they rarely prevent full liability and serve mainly to mitigate, or reduce, the amount of damages the defendant must pay (Andalibian et al., 2006). These defenses for negligence include *assumption of the risk* and *comparative liability*. The former relates to the theory that the plaintiff knowingly accepted some or all of the risk going into the situation that led to the harm and, as such,

the defendant should not be held liable (Black, 1996). Comparative liability is more commonly used and refers to the idea that the plaintiff's own actions were also at fault, and thus the defendant shouldn't be 100% liable—instead it should be proportionally lessened (Black, 1996). A full and detailed discussion of the legal theories of assumption of risk and comparative liability are outside the scope of this chapter. Practitioners wanting a more thorough understanding should consult other legal sources.

4. In legal references, the customary order of the elements of negligence is (1) duty, (2) breach of duty, (3) causation, (4) damages. In other words, first the court would determine whether there was a duty; if there is no duty on the part of the defendant then there can be no negligence. For the purpose of the discussion of this paper, the elements were addressed in a different order. This is because damages and causation are generally easily met in malpractice suits and were, therefore, explained first. But the crux of the malpractice issue hinges on whether there was a duty on the part of the clinician and if it was breached. The authors discuss these more complex and nuanced elements secondly, at greater length.

5. "Substandard" conduct refers to the standard of care in professions—a topic explained in greater detail further along in this chapter.

References

Abille v. United States, 482 F. Supp. 703 (N.D. Cal. 1980).

American Psychological Association. (2010). *Ethical principles of psychologists and code of conduct*. Retrieved from http://www.apa.org/ethics/code/index.aspx

Andalibian, H., Howe, L., Milner, M., Eudy, K, Bongar, B., & Packman, W. (2006). Medical-Legal aspects of treating suicidal schizophrenic patients. In R. Tatarelli, M. Pompili, & P. Girardi (Eds.), *Suicide in Schizophrenia* (pp. 1–16). Hauppauge, NY: Nova.

Baerger, D. R. (2001). Risk management with the suicidal patient: Lessons from case law. *Professional Psychology: Research and Practice, 32* (4), 359–366.

Bell v. New York City Health and Hospitals Corporation, 90 A.D.2d 270, 456 N.Y.S.2d 787 (1982).

Bellah v. Greenson, 81 Cal. App. 3d 614, 146 Cal. Rptr. 535 (1978).

Berman, A. L., & Jobes, D. A. (1991). *Adolescent suicide: Assessment and intervention*. Washington, DC: American Psychological Association.

Black, H. C. (1996). *Black's law dictionary*. St. Paul, MN: West.

Bongar, B. (2002). *The suicidal patient: Clinical and legal standards of care* (2nd ed.). Washington, DC: American Psychological Association.

Dillmann v. Hellman, 283 So.2d 388 (Fla. Dist. Ct. App. 1973).

Dimitrijevic v. Chicago Wesley Memorial Hospital, 92 Ill. App.2d 251, 236 N.E.2d 309 (Ill.App. 1 Dist. 1968).

Dinnerstein v. United States, 486 F.2d 34 (2d Cir. 1973).

Dodd v. Sparks Regional Medical Center, 90 Ark. App. 191 (Ark.App. div. IV 2005).

Fatuck v. Hillside Hospital, 45 A.D.2d 708, 356 N.Y.S.2d 105 (New York, 1974).

Fremouw, W. J., de Perczel, M., & Ellis, T. E. (1990). *Suicide risk: Assessment and response guidelines*. New York, NY: Pergamon Press.

Gutheil, T. G., & Appelbaum, P. S. (1982). *Clinical handbook of psychiatry and the law*. New York, NY: McGraw-Hill.

Johnson v. United States, 409 F. Supp. 1283 (M.D. Fl. 1981).

Klein v. Solomon, 513 N.W.2d 75 (N.D. 1998).

Lawlor v. Orlando, 795 So.2d 147 (Fla. Dist. App. 1st 2001).

Meier v. Ross General Hospital, 69 Cal.2d 420, 445 P.2d 519, 71 Cal.Rptr. 903 (Cal. 1968).

O'Sullivan v. Presbyterian Hosp. in City of New York at Columbia Presbyterian, 217 A.D.2d 98, 634 N.Y.S.2d 101 (1995).

Packman, W. L., Cabot, M. G., & Bongar, B. (1994). Malpractice arising from negligent psychotherapy: Ethical, legal, and clinical implications of Osheroff v. Chestnut Lodge. *Ethics and Behavior, 4* (3), 175–197.

Packman, W. L., & Harris, E. A. (1998). Legal issues and risk management in suicidal patients. In B. Bongar, A. L. Berman, R. W. Maris, M. M. Silverman, E. A. Harris, & W. L. Packman (Eds.), *Risk management with suicidal patients* (pp. 150–186). New York, NY: Guilford Press.

Packman, W. L., Pennuto, T. O., Bongar, B., & Orthwein, J. (2004). Legal issues of professional negligence in suicide cases. *Behavioral Science and the Law, 22* (5), 697–713.

Paddock v. Chacko, 522 So.2d 410 (Fla. Dist. App. 5th 1988).

Perez v. United States, 883 F.Supp.2d 1257 (S.D. Fl. 2012).

Prosser, W. L. (1971). *Handbook of the law of torts* (4th ed.). St. Paul, MN: West.

Restatement Second of Torts §314(A) & §315 (1965).

Robertson, J. D. (1988). *Psychiatric malpractice: Liability of mental health professionals*. New York, NY: Wiley.

Schultz, D. (2000). Defending the psychiatric malpractice suicide. *Health Care Law* (August), 13–26.

Simon, R. I. (1988). *Concise guide to clinical psychiatry and the law*. Washington, DC: American Psychiatric Press.

Stallman v. Robinson, 364 Mo. 275, 260 S.W.2d743. (1953).

Tabor v. Doctors Memorial Hospital, 563 So.2d 233 (La. 1990).

Tarasoff v. Regents of the University of California, 13 Cal. 3d 177(1974).

Tarasoff v. Regents of the University of California, 17 Cal.3d 425 (1976).

Topel v. Long Island Jewish Medical Center, 431 N.E.2d 293 (1981).

VandeCreek, L., & Knapp, S. (1989). *Tarasoff and beyond: Legal and clinical considerations in the treatment of life-endangering patients*. Sarasota, FL: Professional Resource Exchange.

VandeCreek, L., Knapp, S., & Herzog, C. (1987). Malpractice risks in the treatment of dangerous patients. *Psychotherapy: Theory, Research and Practice, 24*, 145–153.

Wozniak v. Lipoff, 242 Kan. 583, 750 P.2d 971 (Kan. 1988).

The Duty to Protect

James L. Werth, Jr.

Abstract

The purpose of this chapter is to provide the reader with an introduction to the issue of the *duty to protect* as it applies to situations involving clients who may pose a potential harm to others or possible harm to themselves. Two famous court cases are used to introduce the material. In addition to reviewing basic legal, regulatory, and ethical principles, the chapter contains information on standard and atypical kinds of duty to protect situations, identifies assessment and intervention considerations, and provides resources for more information. After reading the chapter, professionals should have a clearer picture of what to do when faced with clients who may harm themselves or others.

Key Words: duty to protect, suicide, homicide, *Tarasoff*, standards of care

The purpose of this chapter is to provide the reader with an introduction to the issue of the *duty to protect* as it applies to situations involving clients who may pose a potential harm to others or possible harm to themselves. Two cases will help illustrate the material covered. In addition to reviewing basic legal, regulatory, and ethical principles, the chapter contains information on standard and atypical kinds of duty to protect situations, identifies assessment and intervention considerations, and provides resources for more information.

I have decided to use first person language and to infuse the chapter with lessons I have learned while presenting continuing education workshops on the duty to protect across the country to a variety of mental health professionals and in a number of different settings. My experience in leading these workshops mirrors the literature (Pabian, Welfel, & Beebe, 2009) in that audience members often believe they know the information I review in this chapter, but their responses to questions I pose on the material before presenting it are typically, at best, incomplete and often completely incorrect.

Basic Legal, Regulatory, and Ethical Principles

There are some basic principles that must be reviewed before moving on to the specifics related to the duty to protect itself. In this section I review the concept of a "duty" and discuss the issue of negligence.

Concept of a "Duty"

Duties may be created in a number of ways. First, state or federal statutes can lead to obligations for clinicians. A clear example of this at the federal level is the Health Insurance Portability and Accountability Act (HIPAA), which has requirements for professionals regarding the handling of clients' health information. State laws also may create obligations, such as abuse and neglect reporting laws, which establish a duty to report suspected abuse or neglect of vulnerable individuals (e.g., children, older adults, individuals with developmental disabilities; see, e.g., Kalichman, 1999). Proven violations of federal or state laws can lead to fines or other civil or criminal sanctions.

State laws that create and empower professional licensure boards have implications for therapists because the relevant boards develop regulations that direct clinicians around issues such as continuing education requirements and standards of professional practice. Notably, these standards of practice may or may not incorporate professional codes of ethics. If they do not, there is the possibility of state standards being more, or less, stringent than ethics codes around issues such as multiple relationships and informed consent. Regulations can vary significantly across professions within a state as well as across states. Therefore, therapists who work with colleagues who hold different licenses will want to be familiar with their requirements. Further, if a therapist is licensed in another state, she or he will need to read the regulations in all states where licensed. The primary issue is that if a state board determines that a professional has violated the regulations, and if the violation is severe enough, the professional can lose the license to practice. Even if the license is not suspended or revoked, a determination of a violation can impact the professional's malpractice insurance, as well as the therapist's standing on insurance panels and the general ability to attract and retain clients. Determination of a violation can lead to additional consequences, such as civil lawsuits or criminal charges.

Another way that duties can be created on either a national or state-by-state basis is through case law. Court decisions on a variety of topics can have implications for professionals, such as who is considered eligible to testify as an expert witness and the scope of practice of various professions. Of most relevance to the present chapter are court decisions that create and/or define requirements regarding professional actions in various situations, such as when clients may be a potential danger to themselves or others.

Finally, ethics codes create duties for members of professions. As noted in the preceding, codes may be incorporated into state-level regulations, in which case they (in essence) have the force of law. If not, they create duties directly because members of associations agree to abide by the codes, or they create them indirectly because they influence the *standard of care*. Standard of care is typically understood to be the type of response to a given situation that is expected of a professional based on what a substantial minority (at least) of other similarly trained and reasonably prudent professionals would do. Ethics codes provide direction for professionals in areas such as competence, confidentiality, and relationships with clients and other professionals. These codes typically begin with an "aspirational" section that reviews overarching principles that underlie the standards section. These ideals often mirror, or are modifications of, the principles of biomedical ethics detailed by Beauchamp and Childress (1979/2012; i.e., autonomy, beneficence, nonmaleficence, and justice) and brought into mental health by Kitchener (1984; i.e., the original four, plus fidelity). For the present purposes, the more important part of the ethics codes is the section detailing the enforceable standards, because a determination that the clinician has violated one or more of these standards can lead to a sanction of up to and including expulsion from the organization as well as additional consequences, such as loss of license, civil or criminal suits, and loss of insurance or credentialing with payers.

Concept of Negligence

If something bad happens, then there may be some consideration by those who were injured (e.g., either personally injured or who had a loved one who was injured or killed) about whether the injury was the result of negligence on the part of another. We will focus on the potential negligence of a mental health professional. If there is an allegation of negligence, the plaintiff needs to prove that the defendant had a *duty*, was *derelict* in performing the tasks resulting from that duty, that the dereliction was the *direct* cause of the injury, and that the injury/death resulted in *damages* (see Rachlin, 1984).

Assuming for the present purposes that an injury or death occurred, the issue then becomes whether the therapist had a duty to try to prevent these damages. If an individual agrees to become a client of the practitioner and the professional agrees to accept the person as a client, this leads to obligations (i.e., duties) by the therapist, as noted earlier. Thus, the first issue that needs to be proved is whether the person is a current client, was never a client, or was a client but termination occurred. Documentation will be important, such as signed informed consent forms, the presence of case notes, and whether there is evidence of formal termination. Termination ends the duty of the therapist, so it must be as clear as possible when the therapeutic relationship is officially over. Thus, the record should show not just an indication that the client stopped coming but that the case notes provide information about the termination process. This may involve (a) a planned, mutual termination; (b) documentation that the client unilaterally terminated (e.g., the client said he or she was moving and would not be back even though the treatment plan was not completed); (c) therapy was terminated by the therapist (e.g., because the client or a significant other threatened the professional or a staff member); or (d) the presence of a letter sent to the patient indicating that the file would be closed if the client did not reestablish contact with the therapist by a certain date and, if this contact did not occur, the presence of a note placed in the file that the case was closed, as per the letter that was sent.

The next issue is whether the professional was derelict in attempting to meet this duty. This is one place where the standards of care mentioned earlier come into play. Because the event already took place, all that is available for review are the written records. This should make it obvious why documentation is so important and why the old adage that "if it isn't written down, it didn't happen" is said in one way or another in virtually any presentation or chapter/article related to ethical and legal issues or risk management. The expert witness for the plaintiff and the expert for the defendant will look through the patient's file for evidence that the defendant did or did not do a competent, appropriate assessment and then perform competent, appropriate interventions consistent with the assessment. One way to increase the likelihood that the assessment and subsequent interventions were competent and appropriate is to consult with another competent, or expert, practitioner and then document that the consultant concurred with the direction planned (and then implemented by the defendant) or that the approach planned (and then implemented) was modified to be consistent with the consultant's feedback.

The fourth piece is whether the action or inaction of the professional could be seen as the direct cause of the damages. Notable here is that time is not an overriding factor in determining direct causation, which is one reason why documenting termination is important. The bad event could occur an extended period of time after the last contact between the provider and the client, but the plaintiff will argue that if the professional had done something different (e.g., called to follow up on a no-show), the bad outcome would not have occurred.

The determination of each of these pieces is context-dependent, because a minor change in the facts, or in how the facts are presented or interpreted, could alter the outcome. For the purpose of the present chapter, we will focus on situations where the potential "damage" is that the client may harm someone else or the client may harm himself or herself. In such instances, the next issue becomes whether there is a "duty" and, if so, what it is. Assuming such a duty exists, professionals need to know what to do to attempt to meet the standard of care, which will allow for a response to both the "dereliction" and "direct" causation components of the assertion that the professional acted negligently. The next several sections speak to these issues.

Duty Situations
Potential Harm to Others

The best known and perhaps most misunderstood case related to the duty to protect is *Tarasoff v. Regents of the University of California* (*Tarasoff*, 1976). The case has been the subject of numerous books, chapters, and articles, and it has been mentioned in countless other sources, but these summaries often contain misinformation that contributes to confusion over its true meaning and impact. In this section, I summarize the facts of the case and the two rulings by the California Supreme Court and then review the implications. The case summary is drawn from the published court decision (*Tarasoff*, 1976).

Dr. Thomas Moore was a psychologist at the University of California Berkeley counseling center who was seeing a client named Prosenjit Poddar. Over the course of their work together, Moore learned that Poddar liked a girl named Tatiana Tarasoff but she apparently had spurned his affections and he was upset with her about this. During one of the sessions, Poddar expressed a desire to hurt an unnamed woman. Moore determined that Poddar was talking about Tarasoff and spoke with his supervisor. Subsequently, Moore sent a letter to the campus police expressing concern about Poddar. The police picked up and questioned Poddar but released him after he assured them that he would not hurt anyone. Poddar did not return to counseling. The director of the counseling center wanted the letter to the police returned and directed that no more action be taken. Tarasoff was out of the country while these events unfolded. When she returned, Poddar went to her house and stabbed her multiple times before calling the police and admitting what he had done.

The case eventually rose to the level of the California Supreme Court. In 1974, the court ruled that professionals had a "duty to warn" if they believed a client had the potential to hurt someone else. This ruling led to significant concern by mental health professionals in California, who flooded the court with official documents expressing a desire for the court to rehear the case. In an unusual move, the court decided to rehear the case and in 1976 issued a slightly revised ruling. In the 1976 case, the court changed the language to state that professionals had a "duty to protect" potential victims.

Some of the most important implications of this case that are often misunderstood include the following:

(1) The final decision in the more recent *Tarasoff* case (i.e., the one decided in 1976), which is the controlling one, was that professionals have a *duty to protect* NOT a *duty to warn* in situations where a client may be a potential harm to others.

(2) The court stated that it would not dictate how this protection was to occur, instead leaving it up to the professionals themselves (through the standard of care) or up to the state (through the legislative process) to determine acceptable approaches; the court made it clear, however, that warning was not the only way of protecting third parties and that it was not necessarily the best method.

(3) The *Tarasoff* ruling only applies to harm to others, not harm to oneself (more on this in the section on harm to self that follows).

(4) The court stated that the duty to protect applies when the treating professional knows of the threat because the client expressed it or should have known of the potential for harm if she or he had done an adequate assessment.

(5) The duty to protect applies if the potential victim is identified by the patient or is identifiable by the treatment provider.

(6) The case was heard by the California Supreme Court and therefore was binding only in California. However, it set a precedent that led to other state courts and legislatures across the United States either accepting the reasoning in the case or rejecting it and developing their own specified courses of action through state laws or state court rulings.

(7) All that the court decided was that the case could move forward against the counseling center mental health professionals involved. It did not determine that they did anything wrong. In fact, the case ended up being settled out of court, so the mental health professionals were never able to defend themselves in court (Burris, 2001). We, therefore, do not know whether their actions would have been deemed sufficient.

(8) The case is no longer binding because California has had several subsequent cases and passed state laws.

I next turn to situations involving potential harm to self before discussing the issues of assessment and intervention. For more information on *Tarasoff* (1976), I advocate reading the actual case, which is available online, or reading an article by a former president of the American Psychological Association who holds both a psychology degree and a law degree (Bersoff, 2014).

Potential Harm to Self

Just as the crucial case on the duty to protect others came from California, so, too, did one of the foundational cases in situations involving the duty to protect in cases involving potential harm to oneself. In *Bellah v. Greenson* (1978), a lower court in California decided a case involving the parents of an adult woman who died by suicide, suing their daughter's treating psychiatrist. The girl had been in therapy with the psychiatrist for some time and his case notes documented that he knew she was suicidal and decided to continue to treat her on an outpatient basis and not to alert anyone else to the seriousness of her suicidality. Eventually, she did end up killing herself and the parents sued the psychiatrist, claiming that, under *Tarasoff* (1976), the psychiatrist had a duty to warn them of their daughter's potential harm to herself. The case did not reach the California Supreme Court but did rise to an appellate level so the case itself was precedent-setting.

The judge in the case made sure to clarify the holding and implications of the *Tarasoff* case before rendering his own decision. He reiterated that the final holding in the 1976 *Tarasoff* case was that professionals had a duty to protect, not a duty to warn. He also said that *Tarasoff* involved only harm to others, not harm to self, and that the court did not specify what therapists had to do to meet the expectation of protection. However, he then went on to say that outpatient therapists had a duty to protect in *harm to self* situations. Yet, consistent with the *Tarasoff* court, he did not specify what the therapist had to do to meet the duty to protect in these situations.

The *Bellah* case, therefore, stated that a duty applies in situations of both harm to self and harm to others for outpatient therapists; it maintained a focus on protection instead of just warning; and it left the determination of what interventions were appropriate to the mental health community or legislature as opposed to stating what practitioners must do to satisfy the duty. The *Bellah* case focused specifically on suicide while the *Tarasoff* case focused on the use of violence against another person. Since these cases were decided, however, other types of situations have been discussed in the duty to protect literature. The next section highlights a few examples of ways that the duty to protect has been extended to cases that do not involve explicit or even implicit threats of homicide or suicide.

Additional Types of Duty to Protect Situations

Once the duty to protect was established in paradigmatic cases of possible suicide or homicide, it was predictable that cases would come to light that led to an expansion of the duty to include additional situations of potential harm to oneself or others. At this point, many duty to protect (or duty to warn) statutes are not restricted to the possibility that a client may *kill* someone else for the duty to apply; they also include the threat of "serious bodily injury or death" (VA statute § 54.1-2400.1) or "serious physical harm or death" (ID statute 6-1902). Similarly, suicide or homicide are not the only types of harm covered in involuntary hospitalization/civil commitment statutes, with the language often being broad enough to include a risk of "serious physical harm to himself [or herself] or others" as well as some variation of grave disability, which may be described as "lack of capacity to protect himself from harm or to provide for his basic human needs" (VA statute § 37.2-808).

Other examples of potential harm to others that have been discussed in the literature are driving or operating equipment while impaired (Knapp & VandeCreek, 2009), threatening intimate partner violence (Rosenbaum & Dowd, 2009), and spreading communicable diseases (Kooyman & Barret, 2009). Different states have varying requirements in these types of situations, with some requiring documentation if something is reported but not obligating the professional to take additional action. Other states have an explicit prohibition on breaking confidentiality unless one is a medical professional or empowered to do so by the state. Public officials have received a special focus as well because there are specific requirements to break confidentiality in the event of threats to such individuals (Randazzo & Keeney, 2009).

Regarding potential harm to oneself, the literature attempts to distinguish the potential for suicide as it is traditionally defined from self-harm that does not involve suicidal thought or intent (Walsh, 2009). A different type of self-harming activity that has received attention is anorexia nervosa, with some attempting to make the case that at a certain point the condition may be severe enough to lead to duty to protect considerations (Werth, Wright, Archambault, & Bardash, 2003). Although the controversy has settled down in recent years, previously there was debate over the role of a mental health professional when a terminally ill client was considering a decision that could hasten her or his death (Kleespies, 2004). Currently, it appears as if the major issue centers on whether the person has a condition that may affect the ability to make decisions (e.g., severe major depression) and, if so, whether that condition actually is impairing the person's capacity to use higher level reasoning to choose among options and explain the decision (Werth & Richmond, 2009). States that explicitly allow physicians to provide medication to terminally ill people so that they can have control over the timing and manner of death often include some mention of assessment for impaired judgment (Werth, 2015).

Regardless of the variation, the underlying issues are the same: the clinician must (a) determine there is a potential risk, so that the duty to protect applies; (b) conduct an assessment to determine the next steps; and (c) intervene and follow up appropriately, based on the results of the assessment. Knowledge of state and federal laws, cases, professional ethics codes, and standards of care is necessary for all these steps. This section has dealt with determining that the duty applies. The next section reviews what to do once the therapist decides that the duty to protect may be present.

Assessment and Intervention

A fundamental issue in duty to protect situations is determining whether there is risk of harm. Not asking a client about the possibility of harm, or merely asking if he or she is thinking of harming someone else and, if the answer is no, moving on without revisiting the issue or exploring it further, probably would not be considered sufficient assessment, depending on the circumstances. If something bad happens, the client's records will be reviewed and one or more expert witnesses will evaluate the record to determine whether the provider did an adequate job of assessing for risk and of intervening if risk was found to be present. Inadequate or inappropriate assessment or intervention could lead to a finding by a licensing board, ethics committee, or a judge or jury that the professional was negligent and that sanctions are warranted.

However, giving a psychological battery to every client who has anger issues or expresses a desire to act out is not realistic. A more reasonable approach is required. Entire treatises have been written about threat assessment (e.g., Meloy & Hoffman, 2013) and suicide assessment (Shea, 1999), and chapters in this text also include additional information (see chapters 4, 10, 14, 19, and 20). One resource, the Iterative Classification Tree, developed by a team of experts (Monahan et al., 2000) is readily available (i.e., free online). The tree uses patient characteristics to walk the professional through a decision-making process to determine the likelihood of a particular patient acting out, based on statistical analyses of people who have engaged in violence. Similarly, Scott and Resnick (2006) did a review of the literature and identified issues to explore with patients, while Otto (2000) offered some areas to delve into and questions to ask if there is concern about the risk of violence.

Once it is determined that a client is a potential threat to others, the issue becomes whether warning the potential victim or law enforcement (or both) is the only class of intervention options open (i.e., there is a *duty to warn*) or whether the professional could (or must) consider other alternatives (i.e., there is a *duty to protect*). In theory, one possibility could be to do nothing, but that entails risk to the provider's professional career as well as to her or his conscience should something bad happen. The options available to providers, or required of them, will vary as a result of the state laws or court cases that apply where the patient is being seen. To demonstrate how laws can differ, I provide statutes from Idaho (a duty to warn state; see Table 33.1) and Virginia (a duty to protect state; see Table 33.2). Because of limited space, I excerpted only the statutory language regarding the available/required interventions and when they apply, but not other important parts of the statute(s), such as the protections

available to the professional who acts in good faith in accordance with the statute(s).

The Idaho statutes clearly demonstrate that there is a duty to warn in that state and that professionals who do not do so are at risk of breaking the law. However, in the Virginia statute, the directive to warn is only included in two of the five options—meaning that the provider in Virginia has several other options available. Both statutes specify that the client has to have both the "intent" and "ability" to harm someone else, and both indicate that special rules apply if the person at risk is a minor. Of special note in the Virginia statute is the clause at the beginning of part C (see Table 33.2) that states that the professional should take "one or more of the following actions." Thus, professionals in Virginia should consider all five of the interventions and indicate why they selected or rejected each of them.

Beyond specific duty to protect/duty to warn statues, the other area where professionals will often find mention of the potential to harm oneself or others is in involuntary hospitalization/civil commitment statutes (Benjamin, Kent, & Sirikantraporn, 2009; see Werth, 2001 for a focus on suicide). For example, Table 33.3 contains two Virginia statutes (§ 37.2-808 and § 37.2-809) that show how the duty to protect is embedded into other types of laws. The language in these statutes is quite broad and written permissively. In other words, these statutes *can* be used if the professional has concern about potential harm to self or others, but the therapist is not obligated to use them in these circumstances. Historically, this has been

Table 33.1. Idaho Duty to Warn Statutes.

Idaho
LIMITATION OF A MENTAL HEALTH PROFESSIONAL'S DUTY TO WARN
6-1902. A MENTAL HEALTH PROFESSIONAL'S DUTY TO WARN. A mental health professional has a duty to warn a victim if a patient has communicated to the mental health professional an explicit threat of imminent serious physical harm or death to a clearly identified or identifiable victim or victims, and the patient has the apparent intent and ability to carry out such a threat.
6-1903. DISCHARGE OF A MENTAL HEALTH PROFESSIONAL'S DUTY TO WARN. (1) The duty to warn arises only under the limited circumstances specified in section 6-1902, Idaho Code. The duty to warn a clearly identifiable victim shall be discharged when the mental health professional has made a reasonable effort to communicate, in a reasonable timely manner, the threat to the victim and has notified the law enforcement agency closest to the patient's or victim's residence of the threat of violence, and has supplied a requesting law enforcement agency with any information he has concerning the threat of violence. If the victim is a minor, in addition to notifying the appropriate law enforcement agency as required in this subsection, the mental health professional shall make a reasonable effort to communicate the threat to the victim's custodial parent, noncustodial parent, or legal guardian.

Table 33.2. Virginia Duty to Protect Statute.

Virginia

---

§ 54.1-2400.1. MENTAL HEALTH SERVICE PROVIDERS; DUTY TO PROTECT THIRD PARTIES; IMMUNITY.

B. A mental health service provider has a duty to take precautions to protect third parties from violent behavior or other serious harm only when the client has orally, in writing, or via sign language, communicated to the provider a specific and immediate threat to cause serious bodily injury or death to an identified or readily identifiable person or persons, if the provider reasonably believes, or should believe according to the standards of his profession, that the client has the intent and ability to carry out that threat immediately or imminently. If the third party is a child, in addition to taking precautions to protect the child from the behaviors in the above types of threats, the provider also has a duty to take precautions to protect the child if the client threatens to engage in behaviors that would constitute physical abuse or sexual abuse as defined in §18.2-67.10. The duty to protect does not attach unless the threat has been communicated to the provider by the threatening client while the provider is engaged in his professional duties.

C. The duty set forth in subsection B is discharged by a mental health service provider who takes one or more of the following actions:

---

1. Seeks involuntary admission of the client under Article 16 (§16.1-335 et seq.) of Chapter 11 of Title 16.1 or Chapter 8 (§37.2-800 et seq.) of Title 37.2.

---

2. Makes reasonable attempts to warn the potential victims or the parent or guardian of the potential victim if the potential victim is under the age of 18.

---

3. Makes reasonable efforts to notify a law-enforcement official having jurisdiction in the client's or potential victim's place of residence or place of work, or place of work of the parent or guardian if the potential victim is under age 18, or both.

---

4. Takes steps reasonably available to the provider to prevent the client from using physical violence or other means of harm to others until the appropriate law-enforcement agency can be summoned and takes custody of the client.

---

5. Provides therapy or counseling to the client or patient in the session in which the threat has been communicated until the mental health service provider reasonably believes that the client no longer has the intent or the ability to carry out the threat.

---

the case for most states, but with instances of mass violence occurring, states are changing their laws. Practitioners need to review applicable laws on a regular basis, and state/provincial mental health associations need to do so as well, sending out alerts to members when necessary.

Once a patient is in the custody of law enforcement or has been hospitalized, the therapist should be documenting the decision-making process up to that point and making plans for what will happen once the person is no longer the responsibility of other entities. State law may specify if something is to happen post-release from jail or hospitalization, such as mandating that the local community mental health center attempt to coordinate care, or it may remain silent on the topic, in which case the professional may once again be considered the responsible provider. Depending on the last contact with the professional, the therapist may or may not be able to get the person back into treatment. Given that

suicide remains a risk in the time immediately post-discharge (Qin & Nordentoft, 2005), some sort of follow-up seems appropriate.

There is evidence that harm to others and harm to oneself can coincide (see chapter 1 of this volume; Joiner, 2014), so professionals should consider assessing for both types of potential harm, especially in cases involving older men with depression and/or substance use issues who are serving as caregivers (Eliason, 2009). Interventions in these types of situations will differ depending on what is driving the ideation, but the professional should take into account both components and demonstrate how the plan is intended to reduce risk of suicide and risk of homicide (for further information on homicide-suicide, see chapter 16 of this volume).

Conclusion

The duty to protect has been misunderstood since the California Supreme Court changed its language

Table 33.3. Examples of Virginia Statutes that Involve Potential Harm to Self.

§ 37.2-808. EMERGENCY CUSTODY; ISSUANCE AND EXECUTION OF ORDER.

A. Any magistrate shall issue, upon the sworn petition of any responsible person, treating physician, or upon his own motion, an emergency custody order when he has probable cause to believe that any person (i) has a mental illness and that there exists a substantial likelihood that, as a result of mental illness, the person will, in the near future, (a) cause serious physical harm to himself or others as evidenced by recent behavior causing, attempting, or threatening harm and other relevant information, if any, or (b) suffer serious harm due to his lack of capacity to protect himself from harm or to provide for his basic human needs, (ii) is in need of hospitalization or treatment, and (iii) is unwilling to volunteer or incapable of volunteering for hospitalization or treatment. Any emergency custody order entered pursuant to this section shall provide for the disclosure of medical records pursuant to § 37.2-804.2. This subsection shall not preclude any other disclosures as required or permitted by law.

When considering whether there is probable cause to issue an emergency custody order, the magistrate may, in addition to the petition, consider (1) the recommendations of any treating or examining physician or psychologist licensed in Virginia, if available, (2) any past actions of the person, (3) any past mental health treatment of the person, (4) any relevant hearsay evidence, (5) any medical records available, (6) any affidavits submitted, if the witness is unavailable and it so states in the affidavit, and (7) any other information available that the magistrate considers relevant to the determination of whether probable cause exists to issue an emergency custody order.

. . . .

§ 37.2-809. INVOLUNTARY TEMPORARY DETENTION; ISSUANCE AND EXECUTION OF ORDER.

. . . .

B. A magistrate shall issue, upon the sworn petition of any responsible person, treating physician, or upon his own motion and only after an evaluation conducted in-person or by means of a two-way electronic video and audio communication system as authorized in § 37.2-804.1 by an employee or a designee of the local community services board to determine whether the person meets the criteria for temporary detention, a temporary detention order if it appears from all evidence readily available, including any recommendation from a physician or clinical psychologist treating the person, that the person (i) has a mental illness and that there exists a substantial likelihood that, as a result of mental illness, the person will, in the near future, (a) cause serious physical harm to himself or others as evidenced by recent behavior causing, attempting, or threatening harm and other relevant information, if any, or (b) suffer serious harm due to his lack of capacity to protect himself from harm or to provide for his basic human needs, (ii) is in need of hospitalization or treatment, and (iii) is unwilling to volunteer or incapable of volunteering for hospitalization or treatment. The magistrate shall also consider the recommendations of any treating or examining physician licensed in Virginia if available either verbally or in writing prior to rendering a decision. Any temporary detention order entered pursuant to this section shall provide for the disclosure of medical records pursuant to §37.2-804.2. This subsection shall not preclude any other disclosures as required or permitted by law.

C. When considering whether there is probable cause to issue a temporary detention order, the magistrate may, in addition to the petition, consider (i) the recommendations of any treating or examining physician or psychologist licensed in Virginia, if available, (ii) any past actions of the person, (iii) any past mental health treatment of the person, (iv) any relevant hearsay evidence, (v) any medical records available, (vi) any affidavits submitted, if the witness is unavailable and it so states in the affidavit, and (vii) any other information available that the magistrate considers relevant to the determination of whether probable cause exists to issue a temporary detention order.

. . . .

in the *Tarasoff* (1976) case from the original wording describing the duty mental health professionals have from the narrow obligation to "warn" to the broader requirement to "protect." The majority of states require that therapists who are concerned that a client may harm someone else or self implement an intervention to protect the client or others, and statutes often specify the options available to professionals. Given the wide variation across jurisdictions, it is imperative that professionals know what the statutes specify in every state where they hold a license and that they keep updated on changes after well-publicized events. When working with patients who may harm themselves or other people, therapists are advised to consult with others and to thoroughly document their assessment and intervention decisions.

References

Beauchamp, T. L., & Childress, J. F. (2012) *Principles of biomedical ethics* (7th ed.). New York, NY: Oxford University Press. [1st edition published in 1979]

Bellah v. Greenson, 146 Cal. Rptr. 535, 81 Cal.App.3d 614 (1978).

Benjamin, G. A. H., Kent, L., & Sirikantraporn, S. (2009). A review of duty-to-protect statutes, cases, and procedures for positive practice. In J. L. Werth Jr., E. R. Welfel, & G. A. H. Benjamin (Eds.), *The duty to protect: Ethical, legal, and professional considerations for mental health professionals* (pp. 9–28). Washington, DC: American Psychological Association.

Bersoff, D. N. (2014). Protecting victims of violent patients while protecting confidentiality. *American Psychologist, 69*, 461–467.

Burris, S. (2001). Clinical decision-making in the shadow of the law. In J. Anderson & B. Barret (Eds.), *Ethics in HIV-related psychotherapy: Clinical decision-making in complex cases* (pp. 99–129). Washington, DC: American Psychological Association.

Eliason, S. (2009). Murder-suicide: A review of the recent literature. *Journal of the American Academy of Psychiatry & Law, 37*, 371–376.

Joiner, T. (2014). *The perversion of virtue: Understanding murder-suicide.* New York, NY: Oxford University Press.

Kalichman, S. C. (1999). *Mandated reporting of suspected child abuse: Ethics, law, and policy* (2nd ed.). Washington, DC: American Psychological Association.

Kitchener, K. S. (1984). Intuition, critical evaluations, and ethical principles: The foundation for ethical decisions in counseling psychology. *The Counseling Psychologist, 12*(3), 43–55. Retrieved from http://dx.doi.org/10.1177/0011000084123005

Kleespies, P. M. (2004). *Life and death decisions: Psychological and ethical considerations in end-of-life care.* Washington, DC: American Psychological Association.

Knapp, S., & VandeCreek, L. (2009). Driving and operating other equipment: Legal and ethical issues. In J. L. Werth Jr., E. R. Welfel, & G. A. H. Benjamin (Eds.), *The duty to protect: Ethical, legal, and professional considerations for mental health professionals* (pp. 127–140). Washington, DC: American Psychological Association.

Kooyman, L., & Barret, B. (2009). The duty to protect: Mental health practitioners and communicable diseases. In J. L. Werth Jr., E. R. Welfel, & G. A. H. Benjamin (Eds.), *The duty to protect: Ethical, legal, and professional considerations for mental health professionals* (pp. 141–159). Washington, DC: American Psychological Association.

Meloy, J. R., & Hoffman, J. (Eds.). (2013). *International handbook of threat assessment.* New York, NY: Oxford University Press.

Monahan, J., Steadman, H., Appelbaum, P., Robbins, P., Mulvey, E., Silver, E.,. . . Grisso, T. (2000). Developing a clinically useful actuarial tool for assessing violence risk. *British Journal of Psychiatry, 176*, 312–319. Retrieved from http://bjp.rcpsych.org/cgi/reprint/176/4/312

Otto, R. K. (2000). Assessing and managing violence risk in outpatient settings. *Journal of Clinical Psychology, 56*, 1239–1262.

Pabian, Y., Welfel, E. R., & Beebe, R. S. (2009). Psychologists' knowledge of their states' laws pertaining to Tarasoff-type situations. *Professional Psychology: Research and Practice, 40*, 8–14. Retrieved from http://dx.doi.org/10.1037/a0014784

Qin, P., & Nordentoft, M. (2005). Suicide risk in relation to psychiatric hospitalization: Evidence based on longitudinal registers. *Archives of General Psychiatry, 62*, 427–432.

Rachlin, S. (1984). Double jeopardy: Suicide and malpractice. *General Hospital Psychiatry, 6*, 302–307.

Randazzo, M. R., & Keeney, M. (2009). Threats against public officials: Considerations for risk assessment, reporting, and intervention. In J. L. Werth Jr., E. R. Welfel, & G. A. H. Benjamin (Eds.), *The duty to protect: Ethical, legal, and professional considerations for mental health professionals* (pp. 111–125). Washington, DC: American Psychological Association.

Rosenbaum, A., & Dowd, L. S. (2009). Risk assessment and the duty to protect in cases involving intimate partner violence. In J. L. Werth Jr., E. R. Welfel, & G. A. H. Benjamin (Eds.), *The duty to protect: Ethical, legal, and professional considerations for mental health professionals* (pp. 79–94). Washington, DC: American Psychological Association.

Scott, C. L., & Resnick, P. J. (2006). Violence risk assessment in persons with mental illness. *Aggression and Violent Behavior, 11*, 598–611.

Shea, S. (1999). *The practical art of suicide assessment.* New York, NY: Wiley.

Tarasoff v. Regents of University of California. 551 P.2d 334 (1976).

Walsh, B. (2009). Strategies for responding to self-injury: When does the duty to protect apply? In J. L. Werth Jr., E. R. Welfel, & G. A. H. Benjamin (Eds.), *The duty to protect: Ethical, legal, and professional considerations for mental health professionals* (pp. 181–193). Washington, DC: American Psychological Association.

Werth, J. L., Jr. (2001). U.S. involuntary mental health commitment statutes: Requirements for persons perceived to be a potential harm to self. *Suicide and Life-Threatening Behavior, 31*, 348–357.

Werth, J. L., Jr. (2015). Legal issues in end-of-life decision-making. In J. M. Stillion & T. Attig (Eds.), *Death, dying, and bereavement: Contemporary perspectives, institutions, and practices* (pp. 59–73). New York, NY: Springer.

Werth, J. L., Jr., & Richmond, J. M. (2009). End-of-life decisions and the duty to protect. In J. L. Werth Jr., E. R. Welfel, & G. A. H. Benjamin (Eds.), *The duty to protect: Ethical, legal, and professional considerations for mental health professionals* (pp. 195–208). Washington, DC: American Psychological Association.

Werth, J. L., Jr., Wright, K. S., Archambault, R. J., & Bardash, R. J. (2003). When does the "duty to protect" apply with a client who has anorexia nervosa? *The Counseling Psychologist, 31*, 427–450.

When Negative Events Happen: Dealing with the Stress

Phillip M. Kleespies, Basak Efe, *and* Rebecca M. Ametrano

Abstract

It is difficult to be reminded that all our efforts to deal with behavioral emergencies are not necessarily brought to a positive conclusion. Given that mental health providers are very limited in their ability to detect patients who are at imminent risk of harm to self or others, there are times when there are negative outcomes, and patients who are in treatment nonetheless commit suicide or become violent toward others or even toward the provider. In this chapter, we examine the incidence of such events in clinical practice and the psychological and emotional impact on the clinician or clinicians involved. We also review how clinicians might be better prepared for and cope with the stress induced by such tragic events.

Key Words: stress, behavioral emergencies, health providers, violence, suicide

You have been seeing a young married couple in weekly therapy for about two months. They came to therapy because the young woman, Martha, had become suspicious that her male partner, John, had been cheating on her. He had been coming home late and said that he had been out socializing with friends from work, something that he felt was important in terms of improving his work relationships and his chances for advancement. The couple had argued about this issue on a number of occasions, and some of the arguments had become physical with Martha slapping and scratching John, and John restraining her. These fights usually occurred when Martha had been drinking and became somewhat angry and paranoid. You had worked with her around the negative effects that her alcohol use had on her mood, and she had been able to cut back on her drinking.

Upon getting into John's car to come to therapy this week, Martha found a woman's scarf in the car and confronted John. He said that he had given a woman from work a ride home and she must have dropped it in the car. Martha was unconvinced and

they got into a heated argument in which Martha accused John of being unfaithful. They were still very tense when they started the therapy session and Martha erupted into an accusatory outburst in which she threatened to find the other woman and shoot her. John said that that was the last straw. He claimed that he hadn't been cheating, but he wanted out of the marriage if Martha was going to make threats like that. Martha became even more agitated and angry with John's remarks. You were able, however, to have them take a time-out to calm down.

You then questioned Martha about her threat and about whether she owned a gun. Having calmed down, she said that she didn't think that she could shoot anyone. She acknowledged owning a small handgun that she sometimes carried for protection if she was going someplace where she felt unsafe. John also said that he owned two handguns and that he enjoyed engaging in target practice at a local shooting range. You counseled the couple on the dangers to themselves and to others when there are guns in the home, especially during times of emotional turmoil. Neither of them wanted to get rid of their guns, but they agreed to keep them unloaded and locked in a gun closet. John again denied any infidelity and Martha seemed inclined to believe him. She said that she gets lonely when he is out at night and she asked that he be more attentive to her needs in that regard. You suggested that they be careful about jumping to conclusions about each other.

The crisis seemed to be over. You made a safety plan with them indicating things that they might do or people whom they might call (yourself included) in the event that another such heated argument occurs. You scheduled their next appointment.

Early in the next week, you were called out of a therapy session by your administrative assistant to take a call from a local hospital. The doctor on the phone said that he understood that you had been the psychologist treating John and Martha. He then said that John was in their intensive care unit with a gunshot wound and that he was asking to see you. He was expected to survive. He had informed them that when he came home, Martha had been drinking and said that a woman had called asking for him. The woman seemed surprised to learn that he had a wife and refused to leave a message. Martha had taken this as further evidence that he was having an affair. She had retrieved her gun and in a rage she shot John in the chest and then fatally shot herself in the head. A neighbor heard the gunshots and called the police.[1]

If such an event happened in your therapy practice, how might you feel? Would you feel sad about such a tragic event? Would you wonder if you had missed how volatile and impulsive Martha could be when under stress and drinking? Would you think about whether you should have had her hospitalized when she made a threat in your last session? Would you blame yourself, or be concerned that you would be blamed for not foreseeing that this sort of thing could happen? Events like this one are typically in the news. Would you be concerned that it would affect your professional reputation? Would you worry that you might be sued?

Dealing with such negative outcomes can be very stressful for therapists. In this chapter, we discuss the incidence of patient suicide, patient violence toward clinicians, and events in which patients are the victims of violence. We discuss the potential impact of such events on the treating clinician, and we discuss how clinicians might cope with the emotional aftermath of such tragic events.

The Incidence of Negative Events in Clinical Practice

In an era in which positive psychology seems to be the *zeitgeist*, it is difficult to be reminded that mental health or behavioral emergencies are not always brought to a positive resolution. In fact, negative outcomes may occur in the practice of mental health clinicians more than is typically realized. In this section, we discuss the incidence of adverse outcomes with the three major behavioral emergencies—patient suicide, patient violence toward others, and instances in which patients are the victims of interpersonal violence.

Patient Suicide and Suicidal Behavior

Some years ago, Chemtob, Bauer, Hamada, Pelowski, and Muraoka (1989) referred to patient suicide as an "occupational hazard" for mental health clinicians. Unfortunately, that term remains applicable to the present day. According to the latest suicide statistics in the United States (Drapeau & McIntosh, 2015), there has been a slow but steady increase in the suicide rate from 2005 (11.0 per 100,000) through 2014 (13.4 per 100,000). As of this writing, the year 2013 is the latest year for which there are available statistics and, in that year, the number of suicides in the United States exceeded 41,000.

It has been estimated that a third of suicide completers had contact with mental health services within a year of their death, and one in five had contact within the last month of their life (Luoma, Martin, & Pearson, 2002). These estimates suggest that there may be a significant number of mental health clinicians who might be affected by a patient suicide, particularly given that many patients or clients have more than one mental health provider. In addition, there are many nonfatal patient suicide attempts that can also be very stressful for treatment providers (Jacobson, Ting, Sanders, & Harrington, 2004; Kleespies, Penk, & Forsyth, 1993). There is now evidence that the risk of having a patient suicide cuts across mental health disciplines in the United States. Some 25 years ago, Chemtob, Hamada, Bauer, Kinney, and Torigoe (1988) studied a national sample of psychiatrists and found that 51% of their sample had a patient who committed suicide at some point in their careers. A similar percentage was found in a study by Ruskin, Sakinofsky, Bagby, Dickens, and Sousa (2004), in which they reported that 50% of a sample of 239 psychiatrists and psychiatry residents had experienced at least one patient suicide. In a national survey of psychologists, Pope and Tabachnick (1993) found that

28.8% of their sample had experienced a patient suicide; while Chemtob, Hamada, Bauer, Torigoe, and Kinney (1988), in another national sample, reported that 22% of psychologists stated having had a patient who committed suicide. Clinical social workers and mental health counselors have also not been able to avoid such incidents. Nearly a third of a large national random sample of social workers who were engaged in mental health services were found to have had a client who committed suicide (Jacobson et al., 2004). In addition, McAdams and Foster (2000), in a study of mental health counselors, reported that 23% of their sample had had a client suicide.

Mental health clinicians in training have not been immune or protected from such negative outcomes. Ruskin et al. (2004) noted that a third of the psychiatry respondents in their study were in training status at the time that they had a patient suicide, while Kleespies et al. (1993) found that 11.3% of the nearly 300 psychology participants in their sample had experienced a patient suicide during their predoctoral training years, and another 29% had a patient who made a suicide attempt. Moreover, nearly a fourth of the mental health counselors who had had a client suicide in the study by McAdams and Foster (2000) reported that the client suicide occurred during their training years.

There is now evidence that patent suicide is also an issue in countries other than the United States. A study conducted with 107 Flemish psychiatrists (Rothes, Scheerder, Van Audenhove, & Henriques, 2013) indicated that 92% reported having had at least one patient who died of suicide and 94% reported having had at least one patient attempt suicide during their career. Thomyangkoon and Leenaars (2008) also conducted a survey with 167 psychiatrists from Thailand and found that 56.3% of their sample had at least one patient die by suicide. Wurst et al. (2013) investigated the prevalence of patient suicide among therapists in Germany. They found that 73% of the 226 therapists in their sample had lost at least one patient to suicide within 5 years of the study. The rates were similar in Switzerland where 70% of a sample of 448 physicians and mental health care providers lost at least one patient to suicide within 5 years of the study (Gulfi, Dransart, Heeb, & Gutjahr, 2010). Among the professionals who participated in the study, 32% reported having one patient who committed suicide, 44% reported having two to four such patients, and 24% reported having five or more patients who died of suicide.

To better understand the occurrence of suicide among the patients of mental health providers, there have been some efforts to identify clinician or practice variables associated with this outcome. Clinicians who work in inpatient, emergency, or outpatient mental health agency settings appear to be at higher risk (Chemtob et al., 1989; Ruskin et al., 2004), as do those who work with patients who abuse substances and have organic, affective, or psychotic disorders. Additionally, psychiatrists who are more oriented toward pharmacotherapy and/or electroconvulsive therapy have been found to have substantially higher risk of patient suicide (Ruskin et al., 2004). It is hypothesized that these practitioners are more likely to see patients who have severe mental disorders and who have a higher incidence of suicidal ideation with intent. Additionally, these clinicians have a higher volume of patients and may be more likely to prescribe medication that can be used in a suicide by overdose.

Patient Violence toward Mental Health Clinicians

As with patient suicide, patient violence toward others has also been referred to as an "occupational hazard" for mental health providers (Anderson & West, 2011; Flannery, LeVitre, Rego, & Walker, 2011; Rueve & Welton, 2008). The risk of violence toward third parties in various populations has been addressed in several of the chapters in sections II, III, and IV of this volume. In the present section of this chapter, we will address the more specific issue of the incidence of patient violence that is directed at mental health professionals themselves.

In discussing this topic, it is important to emphasize that although we are presenting evidence related to the risk of violence as perpetrated by individuals with a mental disorder, we are not implying that the mentally ill are responsible for a significant amount of the violence in the general population. Serious mental illness (e.g., schizophrenia, bipolar disorder, major depressive disorder) is not a common occurrence and, therefore, does not contribute to any great degree to the overall rate of violence in the United States (Friedman, 2006; Walsh & Fahy, 2002). It has been estimated that the contribution of the mentally ill to the country's rate of violence is approximately 3% to 5% (Swanson et al., 2002; Swanson, Holzer, Ganju, & Jono, 1990). Moreover, it can be said that the majority of individuals with serious mental illness do not become violent.

Mental health providers need to know, however, that although the seriously mentally ill (SMI) cannot be "scapegoated" as responsible for the high rate of violence nationally, they nonetheless have a moderately elevated risk of violence relative to the general population (Swanson et al., 1990). Flannery and colleagues have kept data on assaults by psychiatric patients on staff in the Massachusetts Department of Mental Health for better than 20 years (Flannery, Farley, et al., 2006; Flannery et al., 2011). In a recent review, Flannery, Wyshak, Tecce, and Flannery (2014) reported that from 2000 to 2012, there were close to 11,000 assaults by psychiatric patients in the United States. Of these patients, 51% were diagnosed with schizophrenia, 15% with affective disorders, and 17% with other disorders. Additionally, they were characterized by histories of violence toward others (84%), past personal victimization (55%), and histories of substance abuse (65%). Overall, the findings indicate that patients diagnosed with schizophrenia are at the highest risk for being the perpetrators of assaults as well as individuals with previous histories of violence toward others, those who were victims of violence themselves, and those with substance abuse histories.

In a study of what appeared to be an increase in violent incidents directed at mental health staff, the Department of Psychiatry at the University of Rochester Medical Center designed a survey instrument to study the prevalence of staff endangerment as well as threats and assaults on staff in both inpatient and outpatient settings (Privitera, Weisman, Cerulli, Tu, & Groman, 2005). They also studied trends in the incidence of violent events over time. The survey was sent to 742 department employees and there was a 51% response rate. The investigators divided the respondents into those who were clinicians (i.e., nurses, doctors, social workers) and those who were non-clinicians (i.e., billing clerks, secretaries, medical record clerks, and so forth).

Fifty-five percent of the clinicians, but only 14% of non-clinicians reported that they had been threatened with physical harm. Thirty-four percent of clinicians but only 8% of non-clinicians stated that they had experienced physical assault. Among clinical staff, nurses, physicians (predominantly psychiatrists), and advanced practice nurses reported the highest prevalence of assaults. Additionally, threats and assaults significantly increased over time.

In a mail survey of mental health providers in Georgia (including clinical social workers, licensed counselors, psychiatrists, and psychologists), Arthur, Brende, and Quiroz (2003) reported that 61% of the respondents had been victims of violent acts of a psychological (e.g., stalking, harassment) and/or

physical nature. Moreover, 29% of the sample said that they had feared for their lives at some point while they worked with clients or patients.

In terms of the incidence of violence directed specifically at practicing psychologists, Tryon (1986) reported on a survey of 500 members of the division of Psychologists in Independent Practice, Division 42, of the American Psychological Association (APA). She had a 60% response rate and found that 12% of therapists in private practice and 24% in hospitals and clinics had been victims of patient violence at some point in their careers. Moreover, 81% of those surveyed reported having had experienced some form of verbal abuse or threat.

In a second survey, a randomized sample of 750 psychologists was drawn from members of the APA division of Psychotherapy (Division 29) and the APA division of Psychologists in Independent Practice (Guy, Brown, & Poelstra, 1990). There was a response rate of 48.5%. The investigators reported that 49% of this sample of psychologists had been threatened with physical attack by a patient and 39.9% indicated that they had actually been attacked. The greatest number of attacks occurred in public psychiatric units (40.5%) followed by private psychiatric hospitals or units (21.9%), but there was a substantive number of attacks that also occurred in private practice (13.6%) and in outpatient clinic and counseling centers (11.3%). The data from these studies suggest that 20%–40% of APA-affiliated psychologists who practice in psychiatric hospitals or units and 12%–13% of APA-affiliated psychologists in private practice may be at risk of being assaulted by a patient at some time during their graduate school and professional careers.

Although any clinician can become a victim, there are some findings that suggest that the risk is greater for newer and, perhaps, less experienced clinicians. Thus, Jayaratne, Croxton, and Mattison, (2004) reported that being young and male placed social workers at greater risk, while Privitera et al. (2005) found that length of clinical experience was correlated with fewer episodes of patient violence. Guy et al. (1990) noted that 46% of all attacks on psychologists involved graduate students or trainees, and another 33% occurred in the first 5 years after completing the doctoral degree. These data suggest that nearly 80% of patient assaults on psychologists may occur in their first 8–10 years in the field. Guy and Brady (1998) have hypothesized that there may be a number of reasons for this phenomenon. Newer therapists may be less alert to cues of violence. They may set fewer limits and allow aggressive behavior to escalate. They may be more likely to work in inpatient settings, and there has been a practice in these settings of assigning more severely impaired patients to clinicians in training with senior staff in a supervisory role.

While there have been instances in which a patient assault resulted in serious injury or death to the clinician, most patient attacks seem to result in minor injury or no injury at all (Arthur et al., 2003). In their national survey, Guy et al. (1990) reported that only 30% of those assaulted suffered any physical injury, while only 10% reported moderate injury. Usually, the emotional distress was far more disturbing than any physical injury. Aside from years of clinical experience, there is little in the literature that would suggest a set of characteristics attributable to a typical therapist victim (Guy & Brady, 1998).

Patient Victims of Violence

As previously noted, the seriously mentally ill have a moderately elevated risk of being violent to others. There is evidence, however, that the greater risk for the mentally ill is that they will become the victims of interpersonal violence. Desmarais et al. (2014) pooled the baseline data from five studies of adults with mental illness (n = 4480) to examine the 6-month prevalence and nature of community violence perpetration and victimization. Overall, 23.9% of this sample reported perpetrating violence, but 30.9% reported being the victims of violence. They also found that there was a strong association between perpetration and victimization, such that the occurrence of one was associated with an 11-fold increase in risk for the other.

Teplin, McClelland, Abram, and Weiner (2005) compared rates of violence against adults with SMI to those reported in the National Crime Victimization Survey and found that violent crime against this vulnerable group was almost 12 times higher than in the general population. More than 25% of participants with SMI reported victimization in the year preceding the interviews. Assault and personal theft were among the more common forms of violence they experienced. Lifetime history of victimization among persons with SMI reaches to nearly 88%, with 46% reporting lifetime incidence of PTSD (McFarlane, Schrader, Bookless, & Browne, 2006). Although the effects of victimization can have a significant impact on prognosis, it is important to note that comorbid PTSD is frequently underdiagnosed in this population (McFarlane et al., 2006).

Of course, it is known that not all individuals who experience trauma have negative outcomes; it has been well established, however, that many victims are at risk of psychological difficulties. Among other problems, both major depression and, as mentioned earlier, posttraumatic stress disorder (PTSD) are related to interpersonal violence (Nixon, Resick, & Nishith, 2004), as are alcohol and drug use (Kaslow et al., 2002). Moreover, Stark and Flitcraft (1996) found that 35%–40% of female victims of interpersonal violence reported a history of multiple suicide attempts.

The sequelae of interpersonal violence have the potential to lead victims to treatment where therapists are confronted with the need to address the impact of the victimization. In some sense, therapists bear witness to the violence, pain, and suffering that has been inflicted on their patients who have been victimized. They may hear graphically of child sexual or physical abuse, of intimate partner violence, of sexual assault or rape, of the trauma of war, and given the value that they place on empathy, they are typically not unmoved.

The Impact of Negative Events in Clinical Practice

Kleespies and Dettmer (2000) have pointed out that the sensitivity that allows mental health clinicians to understand their patients' mental and emotional pain and suffering may also make them vulnerable to the emotional distress that can follow negative clinical events such as a patient suicide or patient violence.

Impact of Patient Suicide and Suicidal Behavior

Norman Farberow (2005), considered by many to be one of the founders of the modern study of suicidal behavior and a strong advocate of suicide prevention, has written with extraordinary candor about the suicide of a member of a suicide survivor group which he co-led. She was a woman who was described as depressed, in deep mourning over the recent suicide of her adolescent daughter, and preoccupied with ending her own life. Dr. Farberow and his co-leaders had discussed at length whether she was too depressed and too suicidal to be in the group. They voiced their concerns with the patient, and she said that it might be helpful to see how others were handling their feelings of grief over the loss of their loved ones to suicide. In her first two group sessions, the patient apparently seemed to be relating well to the other group members and vice versa. She, however, spoke of her perceived failure as a mother. The group members assured her that she had done all that she could with respect to her daughter.

On a follow-up call to the patient after the second group session, however, Dr. Farberow and his co-leaders learned that she had been found dead of an apparent massive overdose of antidepressant medication. Upon learning of her death, Dr. Farberow described his first reactions as shock and disbelief. He questioned why she hadn't called him or his co-leaders or the Suicide Prevention Center. He began to feel guilty and as though he and his fellow clinicians must have missed something. He also began to feel shame and anger. He felt angry at her for killing herself when he was responsible for her. He had a sense of betrayal. In retrospect, accepting her into the group seemed like an obvious mistake. He thought that his colleagues would be questioning his judgment.

Dr. Farberow's feelings and reactions are very similar to those reported in studies on the impact of patient suicide on clinicians more generally. In fact, there has been accumulating, albeit retrospective, evidence that when confronted with a patient's suicide, clinicians from virtually all of the mental health disciplines (e.g., psychology, psychiatry, social work) often report feelings of shock, disbelief, failure, self-blame, guilt, shame, helplessness, anxiety, and depression (Brown, 1987; Chemtob, Hamada, Bauer, Kinney, et al., 1988; Chemtob, Hamada, Bauer, Torigoe, et al., 1988; Grad, Zavasnik, & Groleger, 1997; Hendin, Haas, Maltsberger, Szanto, & Rabinowicz, 2004; Jacobson et al., 2004; Kleespies et al., 1993; Kleespies, Smith, & Becker, 1990; Ruskin et al., 2004; Sanders, Jacobson, & Ting, 2005; Ting, Sanders, Jacobson, & Power, 2006). A number of studies have found elevations on the *intrusion* and *avoidance* scales of the Impact of Event Scale (Horowitz, Wilner, & Alvarez, 1979), suggesting that those clinicians who have a patient suicide frequently struggle with intrusive thoughts of the event and/or make efforts to avoid reminders of it (Chemtob, Hamada, Bauer, Kinney, et al., 1988; Chemtob, Hamada, Bauer, Torigoe, et al., 1988; Jacobson et al., 2004; Kleespies et al., 1993; Kleespies et al., 1990; Ruskin et al., 2004).

Similar to studies conducted in the United States, researchers in other countries (i.e., Belgium, Thailand, and Germany) have also found that patient suicide has a strong impact on mental health clinicians. Investigators in these countries have found that therapists often report severe distress and psychological symptoms following a patient's suicide, including sadness, hopelessness, helplessness, depression, guilt, despair, pain, and powerlessness (Rothes et al., 2013; Thomyangkoon & Leenaars, 2008; Wurst et al., 2013). Therapist characteristics that were associated with more severe distress included being female, being younger (Gulfi et al., 2010; Wurst et al., 2013), and not being supported by the institutions in which they worked (Wurst et al., 2013). Researchers from Switzerland also found that clinicians' reactions were stronger when the suicide occurred in the institution rather than in the community (Gulfi et al., 2010). A study conducted in Belgium found that psychiatrists reported making changes in their clinical practice following a patient's suicide. The most commonly pronounced changes were (a) increased vigilance toward suicidal ideation, (b) incorporation of formal assessment methods to risk assessment, (c) improving communication among the teams and team members, and (d) establishing greater empathy toward patients in distressing situations (Rothes et al., 2013).

Among mental health social workers in the United States, Jacobson et al. (2004), found that female therapists were more likely to have elevations on intrusive thoughts while male therapists were more likely to have elevations on avoidance. Brown (1987) and Kleespies et al. (1993) found that these intense emotional reactions usually diminish substantially over a period of weeks or months, but some emotional effects (particularly anxiety when evaluating suicidal patients) can remain for years.

Some have suggested that clinicians in training who have a patient suicide may be protected from negative emotional effects because they are under supervision and do not bear ultimate ethical or legal responsibility (Brown, 1987). Others, however, have suggested the opposite—that trainees are more likely to assume responsibility for "fixing the client" (Rodolfa, Kraft, & Reilley, 1988, p. 47) and thus have stronger feelings of inadequacy when treatment interventions are unsuccessful. There is now some evidence that those in training tend to be even more distressed by patient suicide than those at the professional level (Ruskin et al., 2004). In addition, Kleespies et al. (1993) reported a negative relationship between intrusive thoughts and images and the year in training in which a patient suicide was experienced (i.e., the earlier in training that the suicide occurred, the greater the perceived impact). It is hypothesized that trainees who are less experienced may feel less prepared, less secure in their roles, and/or more surprised or shocked by patient suicidal behavior than more experienced trainees and professionals.

Many clinicians who have a patient suicide worry about how they will be perceived by the patient's family and friends, and how they will be received if they make contact with them. They also worry, of course, about whether the family will bring a lawsuit. Peterson, Luoma, and Dunne (2002) have collected some interesting data relative to these issues. These investigators distributed a survey at several survivors of suicide national conventions, and a total of 71 complete surveys were returned. All respondents were relatives or friends of an individual who had committed suicide and who was in treatment at the time of the suicide. Ninety-four percent of the respondents reported that they knew that their loved one was in treatment, and 74% said that they knew who the treatment provider was. Only 39% of respondents reported that the clinician had made contact with the family on his or her own. Seventy-four percent of those who were not contacted by the clinician tried to make contact. Overall, 78% of respondents reported that they and/or other family members had some type of contact with the clinician after the suicide.

Of those who had contact with the clinician, nearly half (48%) felt that the clinician was withholding information, and 40% said that they believed that clinicians held back information that might be damaging to themselves. Sixty-four percent felt that the clinician had not done all that he or she could have done to save their loved one's life. Seventy-two percent thought that the clinician made mistakes in his or her treatment of the patient. The most commonly reported perceived mistake involved prescribing the wrong medication or the wrong dosage of medication. The next most common perceived mistake was not involving the family in the patient's treatment. When asked what they felt would have been helpful in the clinician's behavior after the suicide, the two most frequent responses were immediate contact with the clinician and disclosure of the medical records. Seventy percent of the total sample believed that the clinician should not be bound by confidentiality after the death.

Fifty-six percent of respondents believed that the clinician grieved the loss of their loved one. Twenty-two percent invited the clinician to the funeral or memorial service, and in cases where the clinician did not attend, 44% said that they would have wanted him or her to do so. A third of the respondents (34%) considered bringing a malpractice

lawsuit against the clinician and, of these, 57% consulted a lawyer while 23% actually brought a lawsuit.

The investigators concluded that most survivors wanted to speak to their loved one's clinician after the suicide given that 74% of those who were not contacted attempted to make contact. They noted that clinicians who were seen as grieving the loss of the patient and who openly answered questions and concerns about the patient's treatment were less likely to be considered for a lawsuit. The authors emphasized that, in the aftermath of a patient suicide, clinicians must manage both their own grief and the grief of the surviving family and friends while meeting their ethical and legal obligations (e.g., in terms of confidentiality) to the deceased patient.

Impact of Patient Violent Behavior

In January 2015, the chief psychologist at the El Paso VA Healthcare Clinic, Dr. Timothy Fjordbak, was shot and killed by an Iraq War veteran who subsequently took his own life. The shooter, Jerry Serrato, had worked at the clinic as a clerk in 2013 (Thompson, 2015). His motive(s) in shooting Dr. Fjordbak is not known (and may never be known), but it has been reported that he was upset about having his service-connected claim for PTSD denied. It is known that Mr. Serrato had previously made a threatening remark to Dr. Fjordbak in October 2013, when he approached the psychologist in a grocery store and, in so many words, said "I know what you did, and I will take care of it." At the time, Dr. Fjordbak reported the threat to the local police.

Dr. Fjordbak has been described by colleagues as a kind, compassionate, dedicated, and brilliant clinician, who provided excellent service to veterans. Those who knew him at the VA clinic in El Paso have struggled to make sense of his violent death. It has clearly been a great loss to his family, his friends, his colleagues, and to veterans in the El Paso area.

Despite the enormous attention that the media devotes to homicide–suicides such as this one, they are statistically rare events (see chapter 15 of this volume). This lethal level of violence directed toward clinicians is also very infrequent. Sadly, however, events such as those in El Paso serve to remind us that there is a risk of violence in the work that we do as mental health treatment providers.

The impact of patient violence on mental health staff was of sufficient magnitude in a public mental health-care system in Massachusetts that Flannery and colleagues (Flannery, Stone, Rego, & Walker, 2001) initiated a program called the Assaulted Staff Action Program (ASAP)—a voluntary, system-wide, peer-help, crisis intervention program to help staff cope with the psychological sequelae of patient violence. Those involved with the ASAP program have noted that a significant number of staff victims report psychological sequelae such as a disruption in a sense of mastery of their work, a disruption of their caring attachments, and distress about the meaning of the event.

These findings of Flannery et al. seem consistent with earlier findings reported by Guy, Brown, and Poelstra (1991). In a national survey of the consequences of patient violence directed at psychotherapists, these investigators found that 40% of clinicians who reported one or more instances of patient violence experienced a dramatically increased sense of vulnerability in the aftermath. The greater the extent of any physical injury, the greater the sense of fear and vulnerability that followed. Some clinician victims reported a decrease in overall emotional well-being and of professional competency. As many of the victims of patient attacks are students or those early in their postdoctoral years (as previously noted), it is easy to see how a sense of self-doubt and incompetence can be heightened even though the actual ability to predict patient violence is limited.

Most clinicians in the survey by Guy et al. (1990) did not reduce their workload after a patient attack, but many engaged in protective measures. The most common protective measure was to refuse to accept patients whom they perceived as having a potential for violence. This more cautious approach was especially true of those clinicians who believed that they could have predicted and/or prevented the previous episode of violence. Their tendency was to refer such patients to other clinicians. Therapist victims also reported being more active about setting limits on patient behavior and about formulating contingency plans for obtaining assistance in the event of another such incident in the future. Some were reported to have relocated to a safer building or office and/or to have their home phone number unlisted. Others avoided working alone in the office, hired a secretary, or had a security alarm system installed.

In more recent research outside the United States, Wildgoose, Briscoe, and Lloyd (2003) conducted a study with all clinical staff (76% nurses and 24% doctors and other professional staff; n = 156) on the acute psychiatric wards in Exeter in the United Kingdom. They obtained an 81.4% response rate. Following actual or threatened violence by a patient

toward a staff member, they assessed for minor psychiatric pathology (as measured by the General Health Questionnaire–12 [GHQ–12]; Goldberg and Williams, 1988) and for PTSD symptoms (using the Impact of Event Scale [IES]; Horowitz et al., 1979). They found that the majority of the clinical staff (72%) reported having had at least one incident of actual or threatened violence from a patient in the previous year. The staff members that experienced actual or threatened violence were more likely to indicate psychiatric pathology on the GHQ–12 compared with staff who didn't experience such violence. PTSD symptoms were assessed only among clinical staff that had experienced actual or threatened violence. Among those staff members, 15.5% reported PTSD symptoms that were in the low range, and 37% reported PTSD symptoms that were in the high range, as measured on the IES. The duration of these symptoms was not assessed.

Richter and Berger (2006) conducted a prospective study of patient assaults on staff members in nine state mental health institutions in Germany over a 6-month period. There was a total of 46 staff members who were assaulted who agreed to participate in the study. They were interviewed and assessed for PTSD (using the Impact of Event Scale–Revised [Weiss & Marmar, 1996], and the Posttraumatic Stress Disorder Checklist–Civilian [Weathers, Litz, Huska, & Keane, 1994]) after the incident and at 2-month and 6-month follow-up intervals. Although the participants were predominantly nurses (70%), there were other professions (such as physicians and social workers) also represented. At 2-month and 6-month intervals, it was found that three (9%) and four (11%) staff members met criteria for PTSD. The investigators concluded that a small number of assaulted staff members can suffer from PTSD after a patient assault.

Treating Victims of Violence: Is There a Negative Impact on the Clinician?

It has been suggested that clinicians who work with patients who have been traumatized may themselves become indirectly traumatized through empathic engagement with their patients' emotion-laden descriptions of traumatic events. There have been several theories that attempt to account for this type of phenomenon. The two most prominent ones have been known as *vicarious traumatization* (VT; McCann & Pearlman, 1990) and *secondary traumatic stress* (STS; Figley, 1995).

Vicarious traumatization is a concept developed within a constructivist self-development theory for assessing and treating victims of violence. It hypothesizes that psychotherapists who work with traumatized individuals are at risk of being so affected by the fear, pain, abuse, and suffering of their patients that their own inner experience is transformed in negative ways. More specifically, the clinician's beliefs or assumptions about such issues as safety, power, independence, esteem, and intimacy are eroded through the cumulative exposure to events in which patients have been victimized. Cognitive changes are the defining characteristic of VT, but it is assumed that PTSD-like symptoms will also develop.

Secondary traumatic stress, on the other hand, refers to the development of PTSD-like symptoms in individuals who play a significant role in a traumatized person's life and come to know his or her trauma and suffering. STS is said to occur quickly in reaction to learning the details of one or more traumatic events. Cognitive shifts in beliefs and assumptions are hypothesized to be symptoms of the secondary traumatization. It is said that STS does not affect clinicians exclusively, but can affect family members, friends, and confidants of the traumatized individual.[2]

VT and STS are distinguished from the notion of *burnout*. Burnout refers to the emotional exhaustion that occurs with job strain or stress and a reduced sense of accomplishment at work. It is a gradual process and can occur with any type of work. VT and STS, however, are specific to work with trauma survivors.

There have been at least two excellent and extensive reviews and a meta-analysis of the evidence base for the proposed phenomena of VT and STS. In the first review, Sabin-Farrell and Turpin (2003) primarily examined the quantitative and qualitative evidence for vicarious traumatization. At that time, although much had been written about the effects of VT, the number of empirical studies investigating it were few.

The two most cited studies were by Schauben and Frazier (1995) and Pearlman and MacIan (1995). Schauben and Frazier studied the percentage of sexual violence survivors in counselors' caseloads and found significant correlations between higher percentages of survivors in the caseload and symptoms of PTSD and disruptions in the belief in the goodness of other people. However, the correlations were weak (between 0.16 and 0.27), and the checklist used to determine PTSD symptoms was not standardized and had limited internal consistency. In their study, Pearlman and MacIan

investigated the effects of working with trauma in self-identified trauma therapists. They administered the Traumatic Stress Institute (TSI) Belief Scale (Pearlman, MacIan, Johnson, & Mas, 1992) and found that only one subscale, that of *self-trust*, was significantly correlated with the percentage of trauma survivors in therapists' caseloads; but the correlation was negative suggesting that the higher the percentage of trauma survivors in the caseload, the greater the therapist's self-trust.

Other quantitative studies reviewed by Sabin-Farrell and Turpin were also found to have mixed results. Brady, Guy, Poelstra, and Brokaw (1999), for example, found that mental health workers with more cumulative exposure to sexual abuse clients had more PTSD symptoms as measured by the Impact of Event Scale. This finding suggested that there may be secondary trauma effects from work with traumatized clients. In this same study, however, scores on the TSI Belief Scale were not associated with greater exposure. The study therefore was not found to provide any evidence for the cognitive aspects of VT.

Sabin-Farrell and Turpin also reviewed a number of qualitative studies of VT in which the subjective reports of therapists provided some support for VT-related negative effects of work with traumatized patients or clients. They concluded, however, that "the evidence to support the concepts of VT and secondary trauma is meager and inconsistent, relying on small and variable correlations between symptomatic distress and trauma exposure. The relationship between exposure and altered cognitions and beliefs is even less robust" (Sabin-Farrell & Turpin, 2003, p. 467).

Between 2003 (when Sabin-Farrell & Turpin published their review) and 2010, Elwood, Mott, Lohr, and Galovski (2011) identified over 300 articles in peer-reviewed journals on VT and STS. In their review, they chose to focus on the terms *secondary trauma* or *secondary traumatization*, but they also reviewed for cognitive shifts such as those that are said to occur in VT. They further reviewed for the validity of the STS construct, claims about its unique relations with trauma therapy, and the level of distress and impairment associated with its symptoms.

In studies comparing treatment providers who saw, for example, survivors of sexual violence versus cancer patients versus general practice clients, there were no significant differences between groups in regard to secondary trauma on any measure including changes in trauma-related cognitions, PTSD symptoms, or symptoms of burnout. While there were some studies that supported unique responses by trauma clinicians, overall, Elwood et al. were of the opinion that findings using mental health comparison groups suggest that trauma clinicians generally experience emotional responses that are similar to the responses of other mental health groups working with difficult patient populations.

Although there were some studies in the review by Elwood, et al. that supported an association between the number of trauma clients in a clinician's caseload and the development of secondary trauma symptoms, other studies frequently failed to find such an association. The findings led Elwood and her colleagues to conclude that evidence in regard to a relationship between exposure to traumatic material and STS are inconsistent.

Some have proposed that clinicians with a personal trauma history are particularly vulnerable to developing STS or VT (Pearlman & Saakvitne, 1995). Elwood et al., however, again found mixed results with a slightly greater number of studies reporting no significant relationship between a personal history of trauma and the development of STS. They also raised the question of whether what is referred to as STS in clinicians with a personal trauma history might not be better conceptualized as an exacerbation of preexisting PTSD symptoms (from personal trauma) in reaction to exposure to the trauma of patients or clients.

Elwood et al. (2011) concluded their review by stating the following.

> Despite the significant attention given to secondary trauma symptoms since Sabin-Farrell and Turpin's previous review (2003), consideration of current research lead the present authors to reiterate the previous conclusion that findings are neither clear nor consistent and warrant additional research." (p. 34)

Since there is little data on impairment from STS (if present), they also noted that the extant research does not seem to warrant the systematic and large-scale implementation of prevention and treatment recommendations.

The meta-analysis of risk factors for STS was conducted by Hensel, Ruiz, Finney, and Dewa (2015). In a computer-generated search, these investigators identified nearly 2000 references to STS. They selected 140 full-text articles for review based on four criteria: (a) the participants had a work role that involved developing a relationship with traumatized clients resulting in indirect exposure to trauma; (b) validated outcome measures were used

in the study; (c) the study described and measured risk factors; and (d) the study provided an analysis of the relationship between a risk factor and the outcome. After independent review by two raters, 38 studies were included in the analysis and 17 risk factors for STS among professionals were examined.

It was found that demographic factors had very little influence on risk of STS. Small significant mean effect sizes were found, however, for occupational exposure (i.e., caseload) and personal trauma history ($r = 0.12$ and 0.19, respectively). Considering caseload to be a complex factor, the investigators further examined three measures of caseload—caseload frequency (or the monthly or weekly frequency of contact with traumatized clients), caseload volume (or the number of traumatized clients encountered), and caseload ratio (the estimated proportion of time spent with traumatized clients in the clinician's caseload). The strongest effect size among these three was for caseload ratio ($r = 0.19$). Hensel et al. stated that this finding suggested that the proportion of time spent with trauma survivors may matter more than the actual number or the frequency of contacts with them.

The findings highlighted in the two critical reviews and the meta-analysis of risk factors for STS provide evidence for small but significant effects. This suggests that there are some clinicians who experience secondary traumatic stress. The authors agree with Sabin-Farrell and Turpin; Elwood et al.; and Hensel et al. that further research is needed not only to validate the phenomenon of STS more definitively, but also to attempt to identify what contributes to making what seems to be a subgroup of clinicians vulnerable to developing STS.

Dealing with the Stress of Negative Events in Clinical Practice

In the preceding sections of this chapter, we have seen that patient suicide, patient violence toward the clinician, and, in some instances, exposure to the pain and suffering of patient victims of violence can be very distressing for mental health treatment providers. Patient suicide and/or patient violence can induce feelings of self-doubt and self-blame in clinicians. These events can leave the clinician feeling helpless or ineffective, and, although not an entirely negative development, they can modify so-called rescue fantasies.

Coping with Patient Suicide

As Kleespies and Ponce (2009) have pointed out, efforts to cope with the impact of patient suicide or suicidal behavior can be complicated by the nature of the clinician's relationship with the patient. Both Farberow (1993) and Jones (1987) suggested long ago that patient suicidal behavior can bring about both a personal crisis and a professional crisis for the clinician. On a personal level, the clinician often comes to know the person and his or her most intimate feelings and, so, may have intense reactions to the patient's self-destructiveness. On the professional level, however, the clinician may have concerns about responsibility, malpractice suits, censure from colleagues, damage to reputation, and so forth. The professional concerns can thus complicate and inhibit the clinician's personal reactions. They can cause the therapist to withdraw from colleagues and to become isolated from potential sources of support.

Several investigators (Chemtob, Hamada, Bauer, Kinney, et al., 1988; Chemtob, Hamada, Bauer, Torigoe, et al., 1988; Kleespies, 1998; Kleespies et al., 1993; Menninger, 1991) have suggested that an initial step in coping with an event like patient suicide is anticipating that it can and does occur and preparing those in training for such a possibility.

Recently, there have been at least two efforts to develop a curriculum on coping with patient suicide. The curriculum by Lerner, Brooks, McNiel, Cramer, and Haller (2012) includes two distinct components: (1) a biennial half-day workshop on medical-legal issues and coping skills; and (2) an as-needed module for individual clinicians should they have a patient suicide. These investigators had 39 psychiatry residents and three psychiatry faculty participate in the half-day workshop. There was a pre-test and a post-test on perceived competence in responding to patient suicide. The participants also read a fictional case vignette about a patient who committed suicide. One case vignette was presented with the pre-test and one with the post-test in counterbalanced order. They were asked to answer a series of open-ended questions about the vignettes that assessed their knowledge of relevant emotional and medical-legal issues. Their responses were independently rated by two psychiatrists who were blind to whether the responses were to the pre-test or the post-test.

The participants showed large and significant increases in their ratings of how knowledgeable they felt about documentation needs following a patient suicide, how comfortable they felt supporting a colleague who had a patient suicide, and how capable they felt about participating in a discussion with involved clinicians after a patient suicide. Participation in the workshop was also associated with a statistically significant increase in knowledge about coping with a patient suicide. The investigators noted a number of limitations to their study including small sample size, lack of a comparison group, and lack of validation for outcome measures. They called for further research on these issues and on the extent to which the positive findings might be maintained longitudinally.

A second curriculum has been developed and described by Prabhakar et al. (2013) and Prabhakar et al. (2014). It is contained in a DVD entitled *Collateral Damages* and consists of four components: (1) a video program that includes five brief vignettes from clinicians on their patients who killed themselves and the clinicians' immediate emotions, thoughts, and behaviors; (2) a PowerPoint presentation emphasizing epidemiological facts about suicide, emotional reactions to patient suicide, and an overview of resources for grieving individuals; (3) a patient-based learning exercise covering Accreditation Council for Graduate Medical Education competencies for suicide risk evaluation and management; and (4) pre- and post-test questionnaires.

The curriculum was given a pilot test at eight residency training programs and 167 of a possible 240 psychiatric residents (69.6%) completed it. The investigators found improvements in self-perceived knowledge of issues related to suicide, in awareness of what steps to take in the event of a patient suicide, in awareness of support systems, and in risk management and documentation after a patient suicide. They concluded that this interactive curriculum appeared to be a viable strategy to help psychiatric residents enhance their knowledge of patient suicide. They noted that this pilot study did not provide information on whether actual clinical behavior was altered or whether increased knowledge of patient suicide translated into improved coping skills with any future patient suicides.

These efforts to aid mental health trainees in preparing to cope with a patient suicide are clearly still in development. It is hoped that they will undergo further testing aimed at demonstrating their validity.

There have been a number of single case reports of what proved helpful to clinicians in coping with the aftermath of a patient suicide (e.g., Alexander, 1991; Berman, 1995; Spiegelman & Werth, 2005). Other investigators have attempted to gather data from larger samples on this topic. Thus, Kleespies et al. (1990, 1993) found that former psychology interns reported coping with patient suicide primarily by the use of support systems and case reviews. The greatest percentage turned to their case supervisors for emotional support, followed by seeking out peers, other staff members, and, less frequently, their own family or significant others. They also found discussions of the case with their supervisor very beneficial.

Talking with a colleague who knew the patient or who had a similar experience with a patient has been reported as beneficial in reducing isolation and providing support (Alexander, 1991; Berman, 1995; Spiegelman & Werth, 2005). At times, this sort of discussion has happened in a group format. Thus, Kolodny, Binder, Bronstein, and Friend (1979) reported how meaningful it was for four therapists to meet over the course of a year to discuss their reactions to patient suicides that each had recently experienced. In addition, Jones (1987) has described a successful self-help support group for therapist-survivors. The group provides a nonjudgmental atmosphere in which therapists can share their feelings and issues related to patient suicide.

Finally, the study by Hendin et al. (2004) is noteworthy in a discussion of coping. These investigators conducted in-depth personal interviews with 34 therapists who had had a patient suicide. They found that one-third of them reported severe distress in the aftermath. The therapists who were less distressed as compared to those who were severely distressed appeared to have a greater capacity to view the situation as a learning opportunity rather than as an occasion for self-reproach. One interpretation of this finding is that if a clinician can adopt the position that he or she will derive something positive (for his or her clinical work in the future) from such a negative outcome, coping may be improved.

Coping with Patient Violence

Coping with the after-effects of patient violence toward clinicians is, of course, important for clinicians themselves, but it is also important because it has been suggested that it can also indirectly affect quality of patient care. Arnetz and Arnetz (2001) conducted a study in which questionnaires on the work environment were completed by staff at a large 850-bed general hospital in Sweden. In the questionnaires, staff were asked if they had been a victim of violence or of the threat of violence. They were also asked about the frequency of violence, the perpetrator of the violence, and the nature of the incident. At the same time, both inpatients and outpatients at the hospital were asked to complete a quality-of-care questionnaire.

The staff had response rates of 76% (n = 3500) in 1994, 61% (n = 2617) in 1995, and 71% (n = 2414) in 1997. Patient questionnaires were anonymous with response rates of 50% (n = 1834) in 1994, 57% (n = 2466) in 1995, and 71% (n = 3593) in 1997. Regression analysis was used to see which combination of work environment and quality-of-care variables would best predict a positive overall grade for quality of care from the patient perspective. Violence entered consistently as an important predictor in each of the three best regression equations for 1994, 1995, and 1997, respectively. The investigators concluded that the results of their analysis suggested that the violence experienced by health-care staff is associated with lower patient ratings of quality of care. They further noted that patient–staff violence may not be merely an occupational hazard, but may have significant implications for the quality of care provided to patients.

Many of the suggestions for coping with the aftermath of a patient's suicidal behavior also apply to coping with the aftermath of a patient's violent behavior. Some clinicians seem to go through a natural recovery process and prefer to cope on their own. Others may wish to do as suggested by Guy and Brady (1998) and find a trusted colleague with whom to discuss the issues and sort through feelings of guilt or responsibility for the patient's behavior. As reported by Guy et al. (1991), it is not unusual for some clinicians who were attacked by patients to enter or re-enter personal psychotherapy following the incident. Psychological issues regarding personal vulnerability and safety can be activated by a physical assault. A therapist can assist the clinician-victim in dealing with the concerns that can arise and in reducing the possibility that these concerns interfere with the individual's professional work.

As noted earlier in this chapter, Flannery and his colleagues (1991) have developed a voluntary program in a state mental health system called the Assaulted Staff Action Program (ASAP). Initially, this program included *critical-incident stress debriefing* as one of its services to staff victims (Flannery, Fulton, Tausch, & DeLoffi, 1991). However, given the controversy in recent years over whether such intense debriefings shortly after a traumatizing event are helpful or harmful (Tuckey, 2007), the program now emphasizes an approach that is more consistent with a supportive or so-called *psychological first aid* approach (Flannery, Juliano, Cronin, & Walker, 2006). When a patient assault occurs, an ASAP team member responds to the individual staff member to offer support and see if any needed medical care is being provided. The team member discusses whether the victim feels able to manage his or her feelings and continue to work. The staff victim might be referred to a weekly support group for assaulted staff members. The team member offers to call back in 3 days and at 10 days to see how the victim is doing.

The model proposed by Flannery and his colleagues seems to offer guidance in regard to dealing with patient violence toward staff. It suggests assessing whether the individual has the resources to cope on his or her own. If some supportive care might help, it is offered. If there proves to be greater impairment, the person can be referred for a group or individual therapeutic intervention. It does not assume that everyone will develop PTSD and need treatment.

Coping with Patient Victimization

As mentioned earlier in this chapter, there appear to be studies in which small but significant effects provide evidence in support of the fact that some clinicians who work with traumatized patients develop secondary traumatic stress. Given that, it is important to consider whether there are ways in which these individuals might cope more effectively and reduce their risk of STS.

Schauben and Frazier (1995) surveyed female psychologists and counselors who worked with victims of sexual violence in regard to how they coped emotionally with the impact of hearing about such events. Some, usually those with greater levels of distress, reported disengaging from the patient, but most reported using active strategies such as working hard to solve problems with the patient and seeking out their own support systems. In discussing work with self-injuring trauma survivors, Deiter, Nicholls, and Pearlman (2000) as well as Trippany, White Kress, and Wilcoxin (2004) have emphasized the need to attend to professional needs like continuing education, ongoing supervision, and consultation from trauma-sensitive colleagues. They recommended balancing this type of work with other work and with play and rest. In discussing the stress of hearing about the trauma experienced by combat veterans, Munroe (1990) also suggested that therapists may need to learn to use supervision and consultation to address potential secondary traumatization. He felt that the review of therapist responses to trauma material should be a regular function of supervision and consultation. He also recommended that trauma therapists do their work as part of a clinical team in which team members have an awareness of the stress of this work and can be supportive of each other.

Although trauma therapists tend to believe that these coping strategies will be helpful, Bober and Regehr (2006) did not find an association between traumatic stress scores and time devoted to leisure, self-care, or supervision. They recommend a focus on structural changes to protect therapists, a suggestion also put forth by Bell, Kulkarni, and Dalton (2003). A significant change, for example, might include distributing workloads in a manner that puts some limits on the exposure to traumatized patients.

Concluding Remarks

Psychologists and other mental health practitioners frequently work with patients or clients who are at risk of suicidal behavior, of violence, or of becoming the victims of violence. This work can be stressful in itself, but when there is a negative outcome (e.g., the patient commits suicide or becomes violent toward the clinician), the impact on the treatment provider can be considerable. We have noted ways that clinicians have found to cope with such events on an individual basis. Efforts to cope, however, can be supported or made difficult by the environment or system within which one works. As Kleespies and Dettmer (2000) have noted, clinical sites and training programs need to be sensitive to clinicians who undertake the often stressful task of treating patients or clients who are at high risk, or clinicians who have a case in which there is a negative outcome. Thus, clinics and hospitals can try to foster a health-promotive environment (Stokols, 1992) in which clinicians and clinicians-in-training feel supported and protected in their efforts to work with and discuss such difficult cases, or they can be primarily focused on defending institutional interests narrowly defined. It is our contention that those who take the former approach will ultimately reap the benefit of having clinicians who are less stressed and better able to function to their fullest capacities.

Notes

1. This case scenario is based on actual events, but changes have been made in the description of the couple and of the circumstances to protect the identity of those involved.
2. Figley (1995) has used the term *compassion fatigue* as interchangeable with STS. The one difference is that compassion fatigue refers almost exclusively to clinicians or others in the helping professions.

References

Alexander, V. (1991). *Words I never thought to speak: Stories of life in the wake of suicide*. New York, NY: Lexington Books.

Anderson, A., & West, S. (2011). Violence against mental health professionals: When the treater becomes the victim. *Innovations in Clinical Neuroscience, 8,* 34–39.

Arnetz, J., & Arnetz, B. (2001). Violence toward healthcare staff and possible effects on the quality of patient care. *Social Science and Medicine, 52,* 417–427.

Arthur, G., Brende, J., & Quiroz, S. (2003). Violence: Incidence and frequency of physical and psychological assaults affecting mental health providers in Georgia. *The Journal of General Psychology, 130,* 22–45.

Bell, H., Kulkarni, S., & Dalton, L. (2003). Organizational prevention of vicarious trauma. *Families in Society: The Journal of Contemporary Human Services, 84,* 463–470.

Berman, A. (1995). "To engrave herself on all our memories; to force her body into our lives": The impact of suicide on psychotherapists. In B. Mishara (Ed.), *The impact of suicide* (pp. 85–99). New York, NY: Springer.

Bober, T., & Regehr, C. (2006). Strategies for reducing secondary or vicarious trauma: Do they work? *Brief Treatment and Crisis Intervention, 6,* 1–9.

Brady, J., Guy, J., Poelstra, P., & Brokaw, B. (1999). Vicarious traumatization, spirituality, and the treatment of sexual abuse survivors: A national survey of women psychotherapists. *Professional Psychology: Research and Practice, 30,* 386–393.

Brown, H. (1987). Patient suicide during residency training: Incidence, implications, and program response. *Journal of Psychiatric Education, 11,* 201–216.

Chemtob, C., Bauer, G., Hamada, R., Pelowski, S., & Muraoka, M. (1989). Patient suicide: Occupational hazard for psychologists and psychiatrists. *Professional Psychology: Research and Practice, 20,* 294–300.

Chemtob, C., Hamada, R., Bauer, G., Kinney, B., & Torigoe, R. (1988). Patients' suicides: Frequency and impact on psychiatrists. *American Journal of Psychiatry, 145,* 224–228.

Chemtob, C., Hamada, R., Bauer, G., Torigoe, R., & Kinney, B. (1988). Patient suicide: Frequency and impact on psychologists. *Professional Psychology: Research and Practice, 19,* 416–420.

Deiter, P., Nicholls, S., & Pearlman, L. (2000). Self-injury and self-capacities: Assisting an individual in crisis. *Journal of Clinical Psychology, 56,* 1173–1191.

Desmarais, S., Van Dorn, R., Johnson, K., Grimm, K., Douglas, K., & Swartz, M. (2014). Community violence perpetration and victimization among adults with mental illness. *American Journal of Public Health, 104,* 2342–2349.

Drapeau, C., & McIntosh, J. (For the American Association of Suicidology) (2015). *U.S.A. suicide 2014: Official final data.* Washington, DC: American Association of Suicidology, dated December 22, 2015, downloaded from http://www.suicidology.org.

Elwood, L., Mott, J., Lohr, J., & Galovski, T. (2011). Secondary trauma symptoms in clinicians: A critical review of the construct, specificity, and implications for trauma-focused treatment. *Clinical Psychology Review, 31,* 25–36.

Farberow, N. (1993). Bereavement after suicide. In A. Leenaars, A. Berman, P. Cantor, R. Litman, & R. Maris (Eds.), *Suicidology: Essays in honor of Edwin Shneidman* (pp. 337–345). Northvale, NJ: Jason Aronson.

Farberow, N. (2005). The mental health practitioner as suicide survivor. *Clinical Neuropsychiatry, 2,* 13–20.

Figley, C. (1995). Compassion fatigue as secondary traumatic stress disorder: An overview. In C. R. Figley (Ed.), *Compassion fatigue: Coping with secondary traumatic stress disorder in those who treat the traumatized* (pp. 1–20). New York, NY: Brunner/Mazel.

Flannery, R., Jr., Farley, E., Rego, S., & Walker, A. (2006). Characteristics of staff victims of psychiatric patient assaults: 15-year analysis of the Assaulted Staff Action Program (ASAP). *Psychiatric Quarterly, 78,* 25–37.

Flannery, R., Fulton, P., Tausch, J., & DeLoffi, A. (1991). A program to help staff cope with psychological sequelae of assaults by patients. *Hospital and Community Psychiatry, 42,* 935–938.

Flannery, R., Juliano, J., Cronin, S., & Walker, A. (2006). Characteristics of assaultive psychiatric patients: Fifteen-year analysis of the Assaulted Staff Action Program (ASAP). *Psychiatric Quarterly, 77,* 239–249.

Flannery, R., Jr., LeVitre, V., Rego, S., & Walker, A. (2011). Characteristics of staff victims of psychiatric patient assaults: 20-year analysis of the Assaulted Staff Action Program. *Psychiatric Quarterly, 82,* 11–21.

Flannery, R., Stone, P., Rego, S., & Walker, A. (2001). Characteristics of staff victims of patient assault: Ten year analysis of the Assaulted Staff Action program (ASAP). *Psychiatric Quarterly, 72,* 237–248.

Flannery, R., Jr., Wyshak, G., Tecce, J., & Flannery, G. (2014). Characteristics of American assaultive psychiatric patients: Review of published findings, 2000–2012. *Psychiatric Quarterly, 85,* 319–328.

Friedman, R. (2006). Violence and mental illness—How strong is the link? *New England Journal of Medicine, 355,* 2064–2066.

Goldberg, D., & Williams, P. (1988). *A user's guide to the General Health Questionnaire.* Windsor, UK: NFER-Nelson.

Grad, O., Zavasnik, A., & Groleger, U. (1997). Suicide of a patient: Gender differences in bereavement reactions of therapists. *Suicide and Life-Threatening Behavior, 27,* 379–386.

Gulfi, A., Dransart, D. A. C., Heeb, J-L., & Gutjahr, E. (2010). The impact of patient suicide on the professional reactions and practices of mental health caregivers and social workers. *Crisis, 31,* 202–210.

Guy, J., & Brady, J. L. (1998). The stress of violent behavior for the clinician. In P. Kleespies (Ed.), *Emergencies in mental health practice: Evaluation and management.* New York, NY: Guilford Press.

Guy, J., Brown, C., & Poelstra, P. (1991). Living with the aftermath: A national survey of the consequences of patient violence directed at psychotherapists. *Psychotherapy in Private Practice, 9,* 35–44.

Guy, J., Brown, C., & Poelstra, P. (1990). Who gets attacked? A national survey of patient violence directed at psychologists in clinical practice. *Professional Psychology: Research and Practice, 21,* 493–495.

Hendin, H., Haas, A., Maltsberger, J., Szanto, K., & Rabinowicz, H. (2004). Factors contributing to therapists' distress after the suicide of a patient. *American Journal of Psychiatry, 161,* 1442–1446.

Hensel, J., Ruiz, C., Finney, C., & Dewa, C. (2015). Meta-analysis of risk factors for secondary traumatic stress in therapeutic work with trauma victims. *Journal of Traumatic Stress, 28,* 83–91.

Horowitz, M., Wilner, N., & Alvarez, W. (1979). Impact of Event Scale: A measure of subjective stress. *Psychosomatic Medicine, 41,* 209–218.

Jacobson, J., Ting, L., Sanders, S., & Harrington, D. (2004). Prevalence and reactions to fatal and nonfatal client suicidal behavior: A national study of mental health social workers. *Omega, 49*, 237–248.

Jayaratne, S., Croxton, T., & Mattison, D. (2004). A national survey of violence in the practice of social work. *Families in Society: The Journal of Contemporary Social Services, 85*, 445–453.

Jones, F., Jr. (1987). Therapists as survivors of client suicide. In E. Dunne, J. McIntosch, & K. Dunne-Maxim (Eds.), *Suicide and its aftermath: Understanding and counseling the survivors* (pp. 126–141). New York, NY: W. W. Norton.

Kaslow, N. J., Thompson, M. P., Okun, A., Price, A., Young, S., Bender, M., . . . Parker, R. (2002). Risk and protective factors for suicidal behavior in abused African American women. *Journal of Consulting and Clinical Psychology, 70*, 311–319.

Kleespies, P. (1998). Introduction. In P. Kleespies (Ed.), *Emergencies in mental health practice: Evaluation and management* (pp. 1–6). New York, NY: Guilford Press.

Kleespies, P., & Dettmer, E. (2000). The stress of patient emergencies for the clinician: Incidence, impact, and means of coping. *Journal of Clinical Psychology, 56*, 1353–1369.

Kleespies, P., & Ponce, A. (2009). The stress and emotional impact of clinical work with the patient at risk. In P. Kleespies (Ed.), *Behavioral emergencies: An evidence-based resource for evaluating and managing risk of suicide, violence, and victimization* (pp. 431–448). Washington, DC: APA Books.

Kleespies, P., Penk, W., & Forsyth J. (1993). The stress of patient suicidal behavior during clinical training: Incidence, impact, and recovery. *Professional Psychology: Research and Practice, 24*, 293–303.

Kleespies, P., Smith, M., & Becker, B. (1990). Psychology interns as patient suicide survivors: Incidence, impact, and recovery. *Professional Psychology: Research and Practice, 21*, 257–263.

Kolodny, S., Binder, R., Bronstein, A., & Friend, R. (1979). The working through of patients' suicides by four therapists. *Suicide and Life-Threatening Behavior, 9*, 33–46.

Lerner, U., Brooks, K., McNiel, D., Cramer, R., & Haller, E. (2012). Coping with a patient's suicide: A curriculum for psychiatry residency training programs. *Academic Psychiatry, 36*, 29–33.

Luoma, J. B., Martin, C. E., & Pearson, J. L. (2002). Contact with mental health and primary care providers before suicide: A review of the evidence. *American Journal of Psychiatry, 159*, 909–916.

McAdams, C., & Foster, V. (2000). Client suicide: Its frequency and impact on counselors. *Journal of Mental Health Counseling, 22*, 107–121.

McCann, L., & Pearlman, L. (1990). Vicarious traumatization: A framework for understanding the psychological effects of working with victims. *Journal of Traumatic Stress, 3*, 131–149.

McFarlane, A., Schrader, G., Bookless, C., & Browne, D. (2006). Prevalence of victimization, posttraumatic stress disorder, and violent behaviour in the seriously mentally ill. *Australian and New Zealand Journal of Psychiatry, 40*, 1010–1015.

Menninger, W. (1991). Patient suicide and its impact on the psychotherapist. *Bulletin of the Menninger Clinic, 55*, 216–227.

Munroe, J. (1990). Therapist traumatization from exposure to clients with combat-related post-traumatic stress disorder: Implications for administration and supervision. (Unpublished doctoral dissertation.) Northeastern University, Boston, MA.

Nixon, R. D., Resick, P. A., & Nishith, P. (2004). An exploration of comorbid depression among female victims of intimate partner violence with posttraumatic stress disorder. *Journal of Affective Disorders, 82*, 315–320.

Pearlman, L., & MacIan, P. (1995) Vicarious traumatization: An empirical study the effects of trauma work on trauma therapists. *Professional Psychology: Research and Practice, 26*, 558–565.

Pearlman, L., & Saakvitne, K. (1995). Treating therapists with vicarious traumatization and secondary traumatic stress disorders. In C. R. Figley (Ed.), *Compassion fatigue: Coping with secondary traumatic stress disorder in those who treat the traumatized* (pp. 150–177). New York, NY: Brunner/Mazel.

Pearlman, L., MacIan, P., Johnson, G., & Mas, K. (1992). *Understanding cognitive schemas across groups: Empirical findings and their implications.* Paper presented at the Eighth Annual Meeting of the International Society for Traumatic Stress Studies, Los Angeles, CA.

Peterson, E., Luoma, J., & Dunne, E. (2002). Suicide survivors' perceptions of the treating clinician. *Suicide and Life-Threatening Behavior, 32*, 158–166.

Pope, K., & Tabachnick, B. (1993). Therapists' anger, hate, fear, and sexual feelings: National survey of therapist responses, client characteristics, critical events, formal complaints, and training. *Professional Psychology: Research and Practice, 24*, 142–152.

Prabhakar, D., Anzia, J. M., Balon, R., Gabbard, G., Gray, E., Hatzis, N., . . . Zisook, S. (2013). "Collateral damages": Preparing residents for coping with patient suicide. *Academic Psychiatry, 37*, 429–430.

Prabhakar, D., Balon, R., Anzia, J. M., Gabbard, G., Lomax, J., Bandstra, B. S., . . . Zisook, S. (2014). Helping psychiatry residents cope with patient suicide. *Academic Psychiatry, 38*, 593–597.

Privitera, M., Weisman, R., Cerulli, C., Tu, X., & Groman, A. (2005). Violence toward mental health staff and safety in the work environment. *Occupational Medicine, 55*, 480–486.

Richter, D., & Berger, K. (2006). Post-traumatic stress disorder following patient assaults among staff members of mental health hospitals: A prospective longitudinal study. *BMC Psychiatry, 6*, 15–19.

Rodolfa, E., Kraft, W., & Reilley, R. (1988). Stressors of professionals and trainees at APA-approved counseling and VA medical center internship sites. *Professional Psychology: Research and Practice, 19*, 43–49.

Rothes, I. A., Scheerder, G., Van Audenhove, C., & Henriques, M. R. (2013). Patient suicide: The experience of Flemish psychiatrists. *Suicide and Life-Threatening Behavior, 43*, 379–394.

Rueve, M., & Welton, R. (2008). Violence and mental illness. *Psychiatry, 5*, 34–48.

Ruskin, R., Sakinofsky, I., Bagby, R., Dickens, S., & Sousa, G. (2004). Impact of patient suicide on psychiatrists and psychiatry trainees. *Academic Psychiatry, 28*, 104–110.

Sabin-Farrell, R., & Turpin, G. (2003). Vicarious traumatization: Implications for the mental health of health workers? *Clinical Psychology Review, 23*, 449–480.

Sanders, S., Jacobson, J., & Ting, L. (2005). Reactions of mental health social workers following a client suicide completion: A qualitative investigation. *Omega, 51*, 197–216.

Schauben, L., & Frazier, P. (1995). Vicarious trauma: The effects on female counselors of working with sexual violence victims. *Psychology of Women Quarterly, 19*, 49–64.

Spiegelman, J., & Werth, J., Jr. (2005). Don't forget about me: The experiences of therapists-in-training after a client has attempted or died by suicide. In K. Weiner (Ed.), *Therapeutic and legal issues for therapists who have survived a* client suicide: *Breaking the silence* (pp. 35–37). Binghamton, NY: Hawthorn Press.

Stark, E., & Flitcraft, A. (1996). *Women at risk, domestic violence and women's health.* Thousand Oaks: CA: Sage Publications.

Stokols, D. (1992). Establishing and maintaining healthy environments: Towards a social ecology of health promotion. *American Psychologist, 47,* 6–22.

Swanson, J., Holzer, C., Ganju, V., & Jono, R. (1990). Violence and psychiatric disorder in the community: Evidence from the epidemiologic catchment area surveys. *Hospital and Community Psychiatry, 41,* 761–770.

Swanson, J., Swartz, M., Essock, S., Osher, F., Wagner, H. R., Goodman, L., . . . Meador, K. (2002). The social-environmental context of violent behavior in persons treated for severe mental illness. *American Journal of Public Health, 92,* 1523–1531.

Teplin, L. A., McClelland, G. M., Abram, K. M., & Weiner, D. A. (2005). Crime victimization in adults with severe mental illness: Comparison with the National Crime Victimization Survey. *Archives of General Psychiatry, 62,* 911–921.

Thompson, M. (2015, January 9). Killed in action, far from the battlefield: VA psychologist gunned down by Iraq War vet. *Time.* Retrieved from http://time.com/3661300/veterans-mental-health-ptsd-suicide/

Thomyangkoon, P., & Leenaars, A. (2008). Impact of death by suicide of patients on Thai psychiatrists. *Suicide and Life-Threatening Behavior, 38,* 728–740.

Ting, L., Sanders, S., Jacobson, J., & Power, J. (2006). Dealing with the aftermath: A qualitative analysis of mental health social workers' reactions after a client suicide. *Social Work, 51,* 329–341.

Trippany, R. L., White Kress, V. E., & Wilcoxin, S. A. (2004). Preventing vicarious trauma: What counselors should know when working with trauma survivors. *Journal of Counseling & Development, 82,* 31–37.

Tryon, G. (1986). Abuse of therapist by patient: A national survey. *Professional Psychology: Research and Practice, 17,* 357–363.

Tuckey, M. (2007). Issues in the debriefing debate for emergency services: Moving research outcomes forward. *Clinical Psychology: Science and Practice, 14,* 106–116.

Walsh, E., & Fahy, T. (2002). Violence in society: Contribution of mental illness is low. *British Medical Journal, 325,* 507–508.

Weathers, F., Litz, B., Huska, J., & Keane, T. (1994). *The PTSD Checklist-Civilian Version.* Boston, MA: National Center for PTSD.

Weiss, D., & Marmar, C. (1996). The Impact of Event Scale–Revised. In J. Wilson & T. Keane (Eds.), *Assessing psychological trauma and PTSD* (pp. 399–411). New York, NY: Guilford Press.

Wildgoose, J., Briscoe, M., & Lloyd, K. (2003). Psychological and emotional problems in staff following assaults by patients. *Psychiatric Bulletin, 27,* 295–297.

Wurst, K. M., Kunz, I., Skipper, G., Wolfersdorf, M., Beine, K., Vogel, R., . . . Thon, N. (2013). How therapists react to patient's suicide: Findings and consequences for health care professionals' wellbeing. *General Hospital Psychiatry, 35,* 565–570.

Conclusion

Future Directions and Conclusion

Phillip M. Kleespies

Abstract

In this concluding chapter, further emphasis is given to the critical need for education and training for psychologists and other mental health providers in the evaluation and management of behavioral emergencies. It is noted that the need for such training has been cited by several national and international organizations concerned with health care. Next, there is a discussion of some aspects of behavioral emergencies that are in need of future research and some promising directions for the prevention of suicide and interpersonal violence (e.g., means restriction and means restriction counseling). Finally, the importance of remaining evidence-based in clinical work is discussed, as well as what "evidence-based" might mean in a dynamic area of practice such as behavioral emergencies.

Key Words: Behavioral emergencies, training for behavioral emergencies, research in behavioral emergencies, suicide prevention, violence prevention, means restriction

In *The Oxford Handbook of Clinical Psychology*, the editor, David Barlow (2011), placed the chapter "Behavioral Emergencies and Crises" (Kleespies & Hill, 2011) in the part of the book titled "Specialty Areas and Trends in Practice." While I had no quarrel with that categorization, it seems remarkable in some respects that behavioral emergencies should be considered a specialty area or a trend in professional psychology at this point in the field's development. But so it has been.

I say this because, although mental health clinicians need to develop particular knowledge and skill to deal with behavioral emergencies, my opinion is that doing so should constitute developing a competency that is part of developing overall competence as a clinician. I don't think that learning to deal with behavioral emergencies should only be for those who specialize in this particular area of practice (Kleespies, 2014; see Chapter 3 of this volume). Moreover, I still occasionally find it hard to believe that, at this stage in the development of professional psychology, we consider work with behavioral

emergencies a "trend." Behavioral emergencies are some of the most difficult and trying situations that clinicians face. If they are mismanaged, there can be a fatal outcome for the patient and/or others, and serious consequences for family members of the patient, for the clinician or clinicians, for the clinic or medical center, and for the patient's community. Yet, training in behavioral emergencies is considered a "trend" in clinical psychology rather than the norm.

In this final chapter, I will discuss issues and problems (such as that noted in the paragraphs above) that I think require future attention. First is the need for more universal and systematic education and training in behavioral emergencies for psychologists and other mental health providers. Next, I will note some areas related to behavioral emergencies that I think are particularly in need of further research. Then, I will mention means restriction as an approach to suicide and violence prevention that I think holds promise for reducing the suicide rate and the homicide rate in the United States. Finally, I will offer a few concluding remarks.

The Need for Education and Training in Behavioral Emergencies

As far back as the 1970s, several leaders in the field of clinical psychology attempted to draw the attention of the field to the benefits and importance of training psychologists in emergency services (Barlow, 1974; Pederson & Weiner, 1970; Zimet & Weissberg, 1979). Subsequent to these efforts, several investigators conducted surveys demonstrating the prevalence of patient suicidal and violent behavior in clinical practice, as well as its impact on clinicians. These surveys have been discussed in the chapter preceding this one, titled "When Negative Events Happen: Dealing with the Stress." Virtually all of the investigators cited in that chapter called for improved training for psychologists in the evaluation and management of suicidal and potentially violent patients.

Beyond the efforts of individuals, and particularly in the area of suicide prevention, national and international organizations have called for improved training for mental health professionals in the assessment and management of suicide risk. These organizations have included the Institute of Medicine (2002), which referred to reducing suicide as a "national imperative"; the Joint Commission (2010), which declared suicide a "sentinel event"; the U.S. Department of Health and Human Services (2001), which issued a national strategy for suicide prevention; and the World Health Organization (1996), which issued guidelines for the formulation and implementation of national strategies for preventing suicide. In addition, the Surgeon General of the United States in 1999, Dr. David Satcher, issued *The Surgeon General's Call to Action to Prevent Suicide*. In this document, he offered a comprehensive national suicide prevention strategy that included training mental health professionals to competence in the assessment and management of suicide risk (U.S. Public Health Service, 1999).

As Schmitz et al. (2012) have pointed out, the original *National Strategy for Suicide Prevention* by the U.S. Department of Health and Human Services (2001) listed as one of its objectives to increase, by 2005, the proportion of clinical social work, counseling, and psychology graduate programs that include training in assessment and management of suicide risk. Schmitz and his colleagues further noted that this national strategic objective has apparently been almost entirely ignored. The Suicide Prevention Resource Center (SPRC) and the Suicide Prevention Action Network (SPAN) (2010) presented their *2010 Progress Review of the National Strategy*. They reviewed the training standards for 11 different mental health professional groups (the American Psychological Association included) and found that only the Council for the Accreditation of Counseling and Related Educational Programs had increased its emphasis on training in suicide risk assessment and management in its latest (2009) standards compared to its earlier standards.

A more recent U.S. Surgeon General (2009–2013), Dr. Regina M. Benjamin, in conjunction with the National Action Alliance for Suicide Prevention, published the *2012 National Strategy for Suicide Prevention: Goals and Objectives for Action* (U.S. Department of Health and Human Services [HHS], 2012). In this document, the Surgeon General has stated that an objective is to "develop and promote the adoption of core education and training guidelines on the prevention of suicide and related behaviors by all health professions, including graduate and continuing education" (p. 77). She has also stated that another objective is to "develop and promote the adoption of core education and training guidelines on the prevention of suicide and related behaviors by credentialing and accreditation bodies" (p. 77). Whether or not Dr. Benjamin's national strategy will have proved more effective than Dr. Satcher's call to action remains an empirical question.

As noted in the preceding chapter in this volume, the suicide rate in the United States has been rising for approximately the past decade. It was 11/100,000 in 2005, and by 2014 it had gradually increased to 13.4/100,000 (with a total of 42,773 actual suicides in 2014; Drapeau & McIntosh, 2015). In the most recent year for which we have data for both suicides and homicides (i.e., 2013), there were 41,149 deaths by suicide, and, despite the great public concern recently about mass shootings, there were far fewer homicides in the United States (i.e., 16,121 homicides in 2013; Centers for Disease Control & Prevention, 2015). It has been estimated that 90% of suicides have a mental disorder. Roughly a third of those in the United States who completed suicide had had contact with mental health services within a year of their death, and about 20% had had such contact within the last month of their life (Luoma, Martin, & Pearson, 2002). Those who commit suicide are our patients, or people who might have been our patients. Yet, as a mental health discipline, we seem to do precious little to formally educate and train psychologists to assess and manage suicide risk.

There clearly is a knowledge base for educating mental health providers about behavioral emergencies. (Hopefully, this book, among others, in some measure, provides it.) It is also known that training in assessing and managing behavioral emergencies can improve clinical skill (see Chapter 3 of this volume). Yet, as Schmitz and colleagues have said, there seems to be a serious gap in U.S. mental health training. Their focus was on education and training in the assessment and management of suicide risk, but the gap exists for all of the behavioral emergencies.

Schmitz and colleagues (2012) had several recommendations for closing this gap, at least in regard to training in evaluating and managing suicide risk:

Recommendation #1: Accrediting organizations must include suicide-specific education and skill acquisition as part of their requirements for post-baccalaureate degree program accreditation (p. 298).

Recommendation #2: State licensing boards must require suicide-specific continuing education as a requirement for the renewal of every mental health professional's license (p. 299).

Recommendation #3: State and federal legislation should be enacted requiring health care systems and facilities receiving state or federal funds to show evidence that mental health professionals in their systems have had explicit training in suicide risk detection, assessment, management, treatment, and prevention (p. 299).

Recommendation #4: Accreditation and certification bodies for hospital and emergency department settings must verify that staff members have the requisite training in assessment and management of suicidal patients (p. 300).

The tone of these recommendations seems legislative, but Schmitz et al. have taken this approach because of the failure of the mental health field to implement changes in training that have been recommended by national and international healthcare organizations for 15 years or more. They also seemed to feel that such an approach is needed to protect the safety of a vulnerable population, the seriously mentally ill.

In regard to Recommendation #2, Washington, in 2012, became the first state in the nation to require mental health professionals to receive training in suicide risk assessment and management. With the passage of the Matt Adler Suicide Assessment, Treatment, and Management Act of 2012 (ESHB 2366), mental health clinicians in Washington (psychologists included) are required to receive six hours of training every six years as part of their continuing education requirement for licensure. Kentucky,

with the passage of Senate Bill 72 in the 2013 Regular Session, became the second state to enact such legislation. Kentucky law now requires mental health providers to attend a two-hour training program on suicide prevention every six years.

These legislative efforts seem to be a good start, and it is hoped that other states will follow suit. What the laws in Washington and Kentucky require, however, seems far from an organized curriculum and program of training in suicide risk assessment and management, not to speak of education and training for other behavioral emergencies, such as violence risk assessment and management and assessment and care for victims of interpersonal violence. Clearly, a future direction is to continue to advocate for improved training in the behavioral emergencies in graduate and postgraduate mental health training programs where more systematic approaches to education and training are possible.

Directions for Future Research

Concurrent with advocating for improved training in the evaluation and management of behavioral emergencies, there is also a need to further investigate several issues as discussed in chapters 2 and 3 of this volume; i.e., the interrelatedness of the behavioral emergencies, the management of stress during behavioral emergencies, the process of arriving at good decisions in behavioral emergencies, the criteria for competence in this area of practice, and the development of models for assessing competence.

In Chapter 2, in terms of the interrelatedness of the behavioral emergencies, I have presented evidence showing that violent or sexual victimization in childhood or adolescence is associated with violent and/or suicidal behavior in adolescence and young adulthood. Similarly, I described studies showing evidence that violent behavior is associated with suicidal behavior, and vice versa. Only a few of these studies, however, were longitudinal, prospective studies (e.g., Brown, Cohen, Johnson, & Smailes, 1999; Ehrensaft et al., 2003). This type of prospective study is difficult to do and takes years to complete, but it is sorely needed to confirm and extend the findings of the few existing studies that have been done. In addition, while there is evidence that interpersonal victimization is associated with subsequent violent and/or suicidal behavior, it is not clear why some individuals who are maltreated become violent, while some become suicidal, and others become both. Further research is needed to determine if there are factors that may move an individual down a pathway to one outcome or the other.

In Chapter 3, I have described studies demonstrating the potential impact of stress on decision making as well as a model for stress training; i.e., stress exposure training or SET (Johnston & Cannon-Bowers, 1996). The SET model has been described as having three objectives. The first is to convey knowledge or inform the trainee of the stressful task and environment. The second is to have the individual develop the cognitive and behavioral skills needed to perform the task. The third is to have the individual build confidence in his or her ability to perform under stress. Although this model seems to make sense intuitively for training in behavioral emergencies, its effectiveness has not been tested empirically. Future research is needed to demonstrate that the SET model can assist the individual to acquire knowledge and skill in dealing with actual behavioral emergency situations.

I have described, in Chapter 3, several naturalistic decision-making models that seem appropriate to the conditions that can occur in emergency services; particularly the *recognition-primed* decision model and the *recognition/metacognition* decision model. These models have been proposed as a better fit for the decision-making task that can occur in dynamic and fast-paced emergency conditions, and they are contrasted with the rational and deliberative decision model of the researcher or scientist. They arose when it was seen that the rational decision-making model for research was inadequate or even detrimental if employed in situations where fast-paced decision making was necessary. They also arose as it was learned that some individuals who worked under emergency conditions could become very good at what they did despite working with incomplete information and under time pressure. Again, further research is needed to see if working within this naturalistic decision-making framework aids the clinician who must deal with a behavioral emergency.

Again, in Chapter 3, I have discussed training for competence in evaluating and managing behavioral emergencies at some length. As noted in that chapter, "competence" would include both knowledge and clinical skill. In regard to assessing the skill component, McNeil and his colleagues (McNiel, Hung, Cramer, Hall, & Binder, 2011; Hung et al., 2012) have been forerunners in formulating and testing their Competency Assessment Instrument for Violence (CAI-V) and their Competency Assessment Instrument for Suicide Risk (CAI-S) for use in a case-based format. In developing these

instruments, they have set forth some potential criteria by which to assess competence. These criteria include skill in interviewing and data collection, and ability at case formulation and presentation, treatment planning, and documentation, to name a few. Their case-based method is consistent with the recommendations of the APA Task Force on the Assessment of Competence in Professional Psychology (American Psychological Association, 2006) in that they not only emphasize validity and feasibility, but also fidelity, or the degree to which the assessment reflects the actual behaviors that the clinician must perform in practice.

McNeil and his colleagues had junior psychiatry residents and psychology interns interview simulated (or standardized) patients who followed a script. A faculty member was present during the interview and used the CAI-V or CAI-S to subsequently rate the resident's or intern's performance. While the use of a simulated patient enables an assessment that is near the experience of assessing an actual patient, it has been criticized in that a simulated patient may not show the range of problems and affects that are comparable to an actual patient. An alternative involving assessment during actual practice would be to have the assessment of competence (by a faculty member) take place in an ER or urgent care clinic with an actual patient who is potentially violent or suicidal. Of course, with this approach, there can be no standardization of the patient or comparison with how examinees perform with the same patient relative to their peers. Future research comparing and contrasting these methods (and possibly others) is needed.

Future Directions for Suicide and Violence Prevention

It has been noted that instrumentality can affect the rates of suicide and homicide as well as intent (Miller, Azrael, & Hemenway, 2002a; Miller, Azrael, & Hemenway, 2002b). The United States has the highest rate of gun ownership and the highest homicide rate of any developed nation (Hemenway & Miller, 2000). Metzl and MacLeish (2015) have reported that two-thirds of homicides and over 50% of suicides in the United States are by firearm.

Miller et al. (2002a) used publicly available survey data on household firearm ownership to study its association with deaths from suicide, firearm suicide, and non-firearm suicide over a 10-year period (1988–1997) for nine regions and 50 states in the United States. They found that in both regional and state-level analyses, for the U.S. population as a whole, for both males and females, and for virtually every age group, there was a strong association between levels of household firearm ownership and suicide rates. States with high levels of gun ownership had higher rates of firearm suicide. Both firearm suicides and total suicides were associated with regional and state gun ownership levels, but non-firearm suicides were not. The association between gun ownership levels and firearm suicides remained strong despite controlling for alcohol, poverty, urbanization, divorce, unemployment, and education.

In a study to test if underlying suicidal ideation and plans might account for the relationship between gun ownership and suicide noted in the study above (Miller et al., 2002a), Betz, Barber, and Miller (2011) examined data from a Centers for Disease Control and Prevention (CDC) cross-sectional, random-digit-dial, telephone survey of households in all 50 states from 2001 to 2003. Similar proportions of those with or without a home firearm reported suicidal thoughts, plans, and attempts. Among those with suicidal plans, those with firearms at home (compared to those with no firearms at home) were seven times as likely to report a plan involving a firearm. Betz et al. concluded that their results suggest that individuals with firearms at home may not be more likely to be suicidal, but, when suicidal, may be more likely to develop a plan for suicide using a very lethal method (i.e., a firearm).

To further investigate the question of whether underlying suicidality accounts for the relationship between gun ownership and suicide, Miller, Barber, White, and Azrael (2013) obtained state-level measures of past-year suicide attempts from the 2008 National Survey on Drug Use and Health. Suicide mortality data for each state was obtained from the CDC for 2008–2009, and state-level data on household gun prevalence was obtained from the Behavioral Risk Factor Surveillance System, which is sponsored by the CDC. Higher rates of firearm ownership were again found to be strongly associated with higher rates of overall suicide and with firearm suicide, but not with non-firearm suicide. Suicide attempt rates were not significantly associated with suicide mortality rates, or with rates of household gun ownership. The investigators concluded that their findings support the hypothesis that prevalence of household gun ownership largely determines suicide mortality across the 50 states independent of underlying rates of suicidal behavior (i.e., prior suicide attempts).

In a parallel study, this same group of investigators (Miller et al., 2002b) studied the association between rates of household firearm ownership and homicide rates. They used pooled cross-sectional time-series data (1988–1997) to estimate the association between rates of household firearm ownership and rates of overall homicide, gun-related homicide, and non-gun-related homicide. At the state level, they found a significant relationship between rates of household gun ownership and homicide victimization for the entire population, and for every age group aged five and older. The results were attributed to elevated gun-related homicide rates in states with higher rates of firearm ownership. Results remained constant even after controlling for poverty, urbanization, unemployment, alcohol consumption, and nonlethal violent crime. In this study, corresponding non-gun-related homicide rates were also somewhat elevated for states with higher rates of household gun ownership, although not as highly elevated as the gun-related homicide rates.

Findings similar to those of Miller et al. (2002b) have been reported by Miller, Azrael, and Hemenway (2007). Using survey data on rates of household gun ownership from 2001–2003, it was again found that states with higher rates of household gun ownership had higher rates of firearm homicide and overall homicide. A robust relationship held for both genders and all age groups after controlling for rates of aggravated assault, robbery, unemployment, urbanization, alcohol consumption, and poverty. In this study, however, there was no significant association between gun prevalence and non-firearm homicide.

The findings reported above emphasize the importance of reducing access to firearms for individuals who are suicidal or potentially violent. The Consortium for Risk-Based Firearm Policy (2013) has taken a federal policy and public health approach to this issue. Being mindful of the recent national dialogue around mental illness and gun violence, and not wanting to scapegoat the mentally ill for the violence in the United States, this group has focused on evidence-based risk factors for violence rather than on mental illness. They recommend prohibitions on the purchase and possession of firearms for (1) individuals convicted of a violent misdemeanor; (2) individuals subject to a temporary domestic-violence restraining order; (3) individuals convicted of two or more DWI (driving while intoxicated) or DUI (driving under the influence) offenses in a period of five years; and (4) individuals convicted of two or more misdemeanor crimes involving a controlled substance in a period of five years.

The Consortium has pointed out that current federal law prohibits individuals who have been involuntarily committed to inpatient psychiatric care, individuals found incompetent to stand trial or acquitted because of serious mental illness, and persons placed under conservatorship because of serious mental illness from having a gun. They recommend maintaining that law and increasing its use, but they also recommend adding that involuntary outpatient commitment would also disqualify individuals from purchasing or possessing firearms if there is a court finding of substantial likelihood of future danger to self or others. They further recommend the development of consistent and effective processes for the restoration of gun possession that protects judicial due process. As they have noted, the success of their recommendations would depend on all firearm transfers requiring a background check under federal law.

On an individual level, Bryan, Stone, and Rudd (2011) have advocated for means-restriction counseling with patients at risk of suicide. The effectiveness of means restriction as a suicide prevention strategy has been documented in a number of studies (see Mann et al., 2005). Bryan et al. suggest collaborating with the patient and taking the perspective that the suicidal individual doesn't necessarily want to die, but rather wishes to alleviate their mental and emotional suffering. Means restriction can then be presented as a method to maximize safety while working on this shared goal of alleviating the individual's pain. The patient can be educated about the heightened risk when there is easy access to lethal means in the home. If the individual has access to lethal means, they can be presented with a menu of options for restricting access until they are no longer suicidal. The options can include complete removal from the house by disposing of the weapon, complete removal by giving it to a supportive friend until the suicidal crisis has passed, or locking the weapon in a safe or secure box with the combination or key held by a supportive friend until the individual is in a more stable condition and no longer suicidal.

Bryan and colleagues further suggest developing, with the patient's agreement, a "crisis support plan" that involves educating the supportive friend about the patient's current risk level and his or her risk management plan. It also includes identifying supportive actions that the supportive other can take to help the patient, as well as emergency procedures in the event of imminent risk. Although heavily weighted toward restriction of access to firearms,

the authors indicate that the same approach can be taken with other methods of suicide (e.g., the stockpiling of medication). I might add that a similar approach could be applied in cases in which the patient is at risk of violence to others.

Concluding Remarks

All of the mental health disciplines (psychology, psychiatry, clinical social work, counseling, and others) work with some patients or clients who are at high risk of harm to self and/or others. Those of us who engage in mental health practice do so, first and foremost, for the good of our patients, and the good of our patients would seem to require that we be prepared to assist them in their most trying moments; i.e., when, as a result of their mental disorder, they are at risk of suicide or violence to others. That is why it is difficult to understand why the mental health disciplines generally (and psychology in particular) have apparently failed to respond to the calls of national and international organizations (as noted earlier) for improved training in such behavioral emergencies as risk of suicide and the risk of violence.

The good of our patients would also seem to imply that, to the best of our ability, we try to base our assessment, management, and treatment decisions on the best available evidence. According to the American Psychological Association Presidential Task Force on Evidence-Based Practice (American Psychological Association, 2005), "Evidence-based practice in psychology (EBPP) is the integration of the best available research with clinical expertise in the context of patient characteristics, culture, and preferences" (p. 5). The best available research is said to include multiple research designs, starting with clinical observation and, to name a few, progressing to qualitative research, single case studies, cohort studies, case-control studies, register linkage studies, randomized clinical trials (RCT), and meta-analysis of multiple studies. Randomized clinical trials are, of course, considered to be the standard for arriving at causal inferences about a variable or variables. At times, it seems that evidence-based practice has been taken to mean basing treatment interventions exclusively, or nearly exclusively, on RCT studies.

The authors in this book have been encouraged to be "evidence-based" in presenting their chapters. If that term is taken to mean utilizing evidence derived exclusively from RCTs, it would not seem possible to attain such a goal in an area of practice like behavioral emergencies. It is difficult to do randomized controlled trials with participants who may become suicidal or violent during the course of the study. When such risk becomes known to the investigator, the participant is typically screened out or removed from the study and treated lest he or she commit suicide or seriously hurt or kill someone else. So, often, it is not possible to study those at the greatest immediate risk. This makes it exceedingly hard to study what characteristics or conditions move particular individuals from ideation to fatal action. In this regard, this book has attempted to be consistent with the APA Presidential Task Force perspective on being evidence-based and has attempted to cite the best available evidence after examining studies with multiple research designs.

References

American Psychological Association. (2005). *Report of the 2005 Presidential Task Force on Evidence-Based Practice.* Washington, DC: American Psychological Association.

American Psychological Association. (2006). *APA Task Force on the Assessment of Competence in Professional Psychology: Final Report.* Washington, DC: American Psychological Association.

Barlow, D. (1974). Psychologists in the emergency room. *Professional Psychology, 5,* 251–256.

Barlow, D. (Ed.) (2011). *The Oxford handbook of clinical psychology.* New York: Oxford University Press.

Betz, M., Barber, C., & Miller, M. (2011). Suicidal behavior and firearm access: Results from the Second Injury Control and Risk Survey. *Suicide and Life-Threatening Behavior, 41,* 384–391.

Brown, J., Cohen, P., Johnson, J., & Smailes, E. (1999). Childhood abuse and neglect: Specificity of effects on adolescent and young adult depression and suicidality. *Journal of the American Academy of Child and Adolescent Psychiatry, 38,* 1490–1496.

Bryan, C., Stone, S., & Rudd, M. D. (2011). A practical, evidence-based approach for means-restriction counseling with suicidal patients. *Professional Psychology: Research and Practice, 42,* 339–346.

Centers for Disease Control and Prevention. (2015). *FastStats—Homicide.* Retrieved on July 8, 2015, from www.cdc.gov/nchs/faststats/homicide.htm

Consortium for Risk-Based Firearm Policy. (2013). *Guns, public health, and mental illness: An evidence-based approach for federal policy.* Retrieved on August 25, 2015, from http://www.jhsph.edu/research/centers-and-institutes/johns-hopkins-center-for-gun-policy-and-research/publications/GPHMI-Federal.pdf

Drapeau, C., & McIntosh, J. (for the American Association of Suicidology). (2015). *U.S.A. Suicide 2014: Official final data.* Washington, DC: American Association of Suicidology, dated December 22, 2015, downloaded from http://www.suicidology.org.

Ehrensaft, M., Cohen, P., Brown, J., Smailes, E., Chen, H., & Johnson, J. (2003). Intergenerational transmission of partner violence: A 20-year prospective study. *Journal of Consulting and Clinical Psychology, 71,* 741–753.

Hemenway, D., & Miller, M. (2000). Firearm availability and homicide rates across 26 high income countries. *The Journal of Trauma, Injury, Infection, and Critical Care, 49,* 985–988.

Hung, E., Binder, R., Fordwood, S., Hall, S., Cramer, R., & McNiel, D. (2012). A method for evaluating competency in assessment and management of suicide risk. *Academic Psychiatry, 36,* 23–28.

Institute of Medicine. (2002). *Reducing suicide: A national imperative.* Washington, DC: National Academies Press.

Johnston, J., & Cannon-Bowers, J. (1996). Training for stress exposure. In J. Driskell & E. Salas (Eds.), *Stress and human performance* (pp. 223–256). Mahwah, NJ: Erlbaum.

Joint Commission. (2010). *Sentinel event alert: A follow-up report on preventing suicide. Focus on medical/surgical units and the emergency department.* Retrieved on July 3, 2015, from http://www.jointcommission.org/assets/1/18/SEA_46.pdf

Kleespies, P. (2014). *Decision making in behavioral emergencies: Acquiring skill in evaluating and managing high-risk patients.* Washington, DC: APA Books.

Kleespies, P., & Hill, J. (2011). Behavioral emergencies and crises. In D. Barlow (Ed.), *The Oxford handbook of clinical psychology* (pp. 739–761). New York: Oxford University Press.

Luoma, J. B., Martin, C. E., & Pearson, J. L. (2002). Contact with mental health and primary care providers before suicide: A review of the evidence. *American Journal of Psychiatry, 159,* 909–916.

Mann, J., Apter, A., Bertolote, J., Beautrais, A., Currier, D., Haas, A., ... Hendin, H. (2005). Suicide prevention strategies: A systematic review. *Journal of the American Medical Association, 294,* 2064–2074.

McNiel, D., Hung, E., Cramer, R., Hall, S., & Binder, R. (2011). An approach to evaluating competence in assessing and managing violence risk. *Psychiatric Services, 62,* 90–92.

Metzl, J., & MacLeish, K. (2015). Mental illness, mass shootings, and the politics of American firearms. *American Journal of Public Health, 105,* 240–249.

Miller, M., Azrael, D., & Hemenway, D. (2002a). Household firearm ownership and suicide rates in the United States. *Epidemiology, 13,* 517–524.

Miller, M., Azrael, D., & Hemenway, D. (2002b). Rates of household firearm ownership and homicide across US regions and states, 1988–1997. *American Journal of Public Health, 92,* 1988–1993.

Miller, M., Azrael, D., & Hemenway, D. (2007). State-level homicide victimization rates in the U.S. in relation to survey measures of household firearm ownership, 2001–2003. *Social Science and Medicine, 64,* 656–664.

Miller, M., Barber, C., White, R., & Azrael, D. (2013). Firearms and suicide in the United States: Is risk independent of underlying suicidal behavior? *American Journal of Epidemiology, 178,* 946–955.

Pederson, A., & Weiner, I. (1970). Psychology training in emergency services. *American Psychologist, 25,* 474–476.

Schmitz, W., Jr., Allen, M., Feldman, B., Gutin, N., Jahn, D., Kleespies, P., ... Simpson, S. (2012). Preventing suicide through improved training in suicide risk assessment and care: An American Association of Suicidology task force report addressing serious gaps in U.S. mental health training. *Suicide and Life-Threatening Behavior, 42,* 292–304.

The Suicide Prevention Resource Center (SPRC) and the Suicide Prevention Action Network (SPAN). (2010). *Charting the future of suicide prevention: A 2010 progress review of the national strategy and recommendations for the decade ahead.* Retrieved July 5, 2015, from http://www.sprc.org/library/ChartingTheFuture_Fullbook.pdf

U.S. Department of Health and Human Services. (2001). *National strategy for suicide prevention: Goals and objectives for action*. Retrieved July 3, 2015, from http://www.ncbi.nlm.nih.gov/books/NBK44281/pdf/TOC.pdf

U.S. Department of Health and Human Services (HHS) Office of the Surgeon General and National Action Alliance for Suicide Prevention. (2012). *2012 National strategy for suicide prevention: Goals and objectives for action.* Washington, DC: HHS.

U.S. Public Health Service. (1999). The Surgeon General's call to action to prevent suicide. Retrieved July 3, 2015, from http://www.surgeongeneral.gov/library/calltoaction/calltoaction.pdf

World Health Organization. (1996). *Prevention of suicide: Guidelines for the formulation and implementation of national strategies (ST/ESA/245).* Geneva, Switzerland: Author.

Zimet, C., & Weissberg, M. (1979). The emergency service: A setting for internship training. *Psychotherapy: Theory, Research, and Practice, 16,* 336.

INDEX

Note: Tables, figures, and notes are indicated by *t*, *f*, and *n*.

emotional numbing, 148, 189
emotional regulation/dysregulation
    NSSI and, 402, 403–4
    veteran violence and, 187
empathy, 536
    adult suicide and, 118
    bullying and, 86
    elderly suicide and, 348
    FTD and, 365
    homicide-suicide and, 219
    OXT and, 325
    RULER for, 95
    STR for, 93
    youth violence and, 63
empirically supported risk factors
    for adult violence, 133–35
    for targeted violence in schools, 97
employment
    adult suicide and, 116
    disability abuse and, 254
    homicide-suicide and, 216
    sexual assault and, 238
    veterans and
        suicide and, 168, 170, 171
        violence and, 187, 190
    youth violence and, 66
ENA. *See* Emergency Nurses Association
enactment, in SIP, 204
endocrine disorders. *See also* diabetes
    of adrenal gland, 428–30
    cancer and, 441
    differential diagnosis for, 441
    of female reproductive system, 436–38
    of male reproductive system, 439
    mental illness and, 426–42
    of parathyroid gland, 432–34
    prevalence of, 428*t*
    of thyroid gland, 430–32
endocrine disrupting chemicals
    (EDCs), 440
endocrine hormones, 427*t*
end-stage renal disease (ESRD), suicide
    and, 393
engagement, for adult violence, 140
environment barriers, disability abuse
    from, 253–54
epilepsy, 386, 387, 424
epinephrine, pheochromocytoma and, 431
ESRD. *See* end-stage renal disease
estranged wives, homicide of, 17
estrogens, 427*t*, 436–37, 438
evidence-based practice in psychology
    (EBPP), 554
evidence-based treatments (EBTs)
    for PTSD, 493–502
    for victimization of violence, 493–96
Ewing v. Goldstein, 128
executive function
    adult suicide and, 116
    cancer and, 441
exposure therapy, for victimization of
    violence, 158, 495–96
extended suicide, 217

extrafamilial homicide-suicide, 218
eye movement desensitization and
    reprocessing (EMDR), 496,
    499–500

failure to supervise, in legal and ethical
    framework, 518
familicide-suicide, 218
family
    adult suicide and, 116, 120
    disability abuse and, 254–55
    elder abuse and, 373–82
    HS and, 218
    interventions with, for child
        maltreatment, 77–81
    rape and, 235
    youth suicide and, 48
        bullying and, 96–97
Fatuck v. Hillside Hospital, 518
fear avoidance theory, 222
feasibility, in competence assessment, 33
feature matching, 23
females. *See also* rape; sexual assault
    adults and
        victims of violence by, 147
        violence by, 132
    bullies and, 87
    disability abuse toward, 248–49, 250,
        252–53, 255, 259
    IPV against, 198
    peer aggression against, 87
    relational aggression with, 87–88
    reproductive system of, endocrine
        disorders of, 436–38
    veteran suicide and, 171, 174
    youth violence in, 63–64
femicide-suicide, 217
feminist theory, for IPV, 200–201
FGAs. *See* first-generation antipsychotics
FH. *See* follicle-stimulating hormone
fidelity
    adult violence and, 129
    in competence assessment, 33
filicide-suicide, 217
financial abuse
    in disability abuse, 250, 251
    in elder abuse, 374–75
firearms
    adult suicide by, 120–21
    Consortium for Risk-Based Firearm
        Policy for, 553–54
    HS by, 216
    veteran suicide by, 178
    youth suicide by, 49–50, 51
first-generation antipsychotics
    (FGAs), 294
flashbacks, veteran violence and, 189
FLD. *See* frontal lobe dementias
fluoxetine, 321
    for depression, 458
    suicide and, 457–58
fMRI. *See* functional magnetic
    resonance imaging

follicle-stimulating hormone
    (FH), 427*t*
forensic psychology, for adult
    violence, 130
fractures
    from adult victimization by
        violence, 148
    from child maltreatment, 73
    from IPV, 198
frontal lobe dementias (FLD), 420
frontotemporal dementia (FTD), 365
functional magnetic resonance imaging
    (fMRI), 318–19
    AVP and, 325

GABA. *See* ϒ-aminobutyric acid
gabapentin, 460
    for AD, 363
GAD. *See* glutamic acid decarboxylase
galantamine, for AD, 362, 363
gay. *See* lesbian/gay/bisexual/transgender
gender. *See also* females; males
    adult violence and, 132
    bullies and, 87
    depression and, 45
    NSSI and, 402
    youth and
        attempted suicide and, 40
        suicide and, 40–41
generalized anxiety disorder
    bullying and, 86
    youth suicide and, 47
General Personality and Social
    Psychological Model of Criminal
    Conduct, 66
    for antisocial behavior, 68
General Practice Research Database
    (GRPD), 386
Geriatric Suicide Ideation Scale
    (GSIS), 241–42
GH. *See* growth hormone
giving-up syndrome, 386
glucagon, 434
glucose
    diabetes and, 434–36
    in OFC, 318, 321
    pancreas and, 434
glutamate, impulsive aggression
    and, 323–24
glutamate N-methyl-D-Aspartate
    (NMDA)
    AD and, 362
    receptor antagonists, 312, 323, 365
glutamic acid decarboxylase
    (GAD), 324
gonadotropin releasing hormone
    (GnRH), 427*t*
Graves' disease, 431, 432
growth hormone (GH), 323
GRPD. *See* General Practice Research
    Database
GSIS. *See* Geriatric Suicide
    Ideation Scale